Life-Span Development

TENTH EDITION

John W. Santrock

University of Texas at Dallas

McGraw Hill

Boston   Burr Ridge, IL   Dubuque, IA   Madison, WI   New York
San Francisco   St. Louis   Bangkok   Bogotá   Caracas   Kuala Lumpur
Lisbon   London   Madrid   Mexico City   Milan   Montreal   New Delhi
Santiago   Seoul   Singapore   Sydney   Taipei   Toronto

Life-Span Development

With special appreciation to my parents,
Ruth and John Santrock

About the Author

John W. Santrock

John Santrock received his Ph.D. from the University of Minnesota in 1973. He taught at the University of Charleston and the University of Georgia before joining the Program in Psychology and Human Development at the University of Texas at Dallas, where he currently teaches a number of undergraduate courses. In 1982, John created the life-span development course at UT–Dallas and has taught it every year since then.

John has been a member of the editorial boards of *Child Development* and *Developmental Psychology*. His research on father custody is widely cited and used in expert witness testimony to promote flexibility and alternative considerations in custody disputes. John also has authored these exceptional McGraw-Hill texts: *Psychology* (7th edition), *Child Development* (10th edition), *Children* (8th edition), *Adolescence* (10th edition), and *Educational Psychology* (2nd edition).

For many years, John was involved in tennis as a player, teaching professional, and coach of professional tennis players. He has been married for more than 35 years to his wife, Mary Jo, who is a realtor. He has two daughters—Tracy, who is a technology specialist at Nortel in Raleigh, North Carolina, and Jennifer, who is a medical sales specialist at Medtronic. He has one granddaughter, Jordan, age 13, and one grandson, Alex, age 1. Tracy recently completed the New York Marathon, and Jennifer was in the top 100 ranked players on the Women's Professional Tennis Tour. In the last decade, John also has spent time painting expressionist art.

John Santrock, teaching in his undergraduate course in life-span development.

Brief Contents

Contents

S E C T I O N 2 Beginnings

SECTION 3 Infancy

S E C T I O N   4 Early Childhood

CHAPTER 8

Physical and Cognitive Development in Early Childhood 224

CHAPTER 9

Socioemotional Development in Early Childhood 254

SECTION 5 Middle and Late Childhood

S E C T I O N   6 Adolescence

SECTION 7 Early Adulthood

SECTION 8 Middle Adulthood

SECTION 9 Late Adulthood

SECTION 10 Endings

Preface

Preparing a new edition of *Life-Span Development* is both a joy and a challenge. I enjoy revising this text because I continue to learn more about the human life span and the journey of life each of us takes. It also is gratifying to revise the text because the feedback from students and instructors has been consistently enthusiastic. The challenge of revising a successful text is always to continue meeting readers' needs and expectations, while keeping the material fresh and up to date. For the tenth edition of *Life-Span Development*, I have expanded coverage in a number of key areas, incorporated the latest research and applications, and fine-tuned the aspects of the book that make learning easier and more engaging.

RESEARCH AND APPLICATIONS

Above all, a text on life-span development must include a solid research foundation.

Recent Research

This edition of *Life-Span Development* presents the latest, most contemporary research on each period of the human life span and includes more than 2,100 citations from the twenty-first century. The new research material includes:

- Paul Baltes' (2003; Baltes & Smith, 2003) most recent ideas about aging with important new material on the very different characteristics of the young old and oldest old (chapter 1).
- The new field of evolutionary developmental psychology (Bjorklund & Pellegrini, 2002) and the epigenetic view of heredity and environment (Gottlieb, 2004) (chapter 3).
- A new section on the biological foundations and environmental experiences involved in infant emotion, including early development of the brain and its link to emotion (Lewis & Steiben, 2004; Thompson, Easterbrooks, & Walker, 2003) (chapter 7).
- Gender differences in prosocial behavior (Eisenberg & Morris, 2004) (chapter 11).
- New section on development of the brain in adolescence (Keating, 2003, 2004) (chapter 13).
- New section on falling out of love (chapter 15).
- New section on stress and disease (chapter 16).
- New coverage of the increasingly discussed mitochondrial theory of aging (chapter 18).

- New section on source memory in older adults (Hasher, 2003) (chapter 19).
- New section on diversity in older adults' lifestyles, including new subsections on divorce and remarriage, older parents and their adult children, great-grandparenting, sibling relationships, and never-married older adults (chapter 20).
- New coverage of meaning-making coping (Folkman & Moskowitz, 2004; Hayslip & Hansson, 2003) (chapter 21).

Shortly, I will list the main chapter-by-chapter content changes in more detail.

Research in Life-Span Development Interludes

Research in Life-Span Development interludes are new to this edition. Appearing once in each chapter, they provide a more in-depth look at research related to a topic in the chapter. I call them interludes rather than boxes because they follow directly in the text after they have been introduced. In most instances they consist of a description of a research study, including the identity of the participants, the methods used to obtain data, and the main results. In most cases they are research studies that have been conducted in the twenty-first century. Because students often have more difficulty reading about research studies than other text material, I wrote these with an eye toward student understanding. Here are some examples of the new Research in Life-Span Development interludes:

- Memory in the A.M. and P.M. and Memory for Meaningful Information (Hasher & others, 2001; Hess & others, 2003).
- Studying the Newborn's Perception (Bendersky & Sullivan, 2002).
- Young Children's Gender Schemas of Occupations (Levy, Sadovsky, & Torseth, 2000).
- Evaluation of a Family Program Designed to Reduce Drinking and Smoking in Young Adolescents (Bauman & others, 2002).
- Adolescents' Self-Images (Bacchini & Magliulo, 2003).
- Personal Growth Following a Romantic Relationship Breakup (Tashiro & Frazier, 2003).
- The Stress of Caring for an Alzheimer Patient at Home (Kiecolt-Glaser & others, 2003).
- The Women's Health Initiative Study of Widowhood and Health (Wilcox & others, 2003).

Expert Research Consultants

Life-span development has become an enormous, complex field and no single author, or even several authors, can possibly be an expert in many different areas of life-span development. To solve this problem, I have sought the input of leading experts in many different research areas of life-span development. The experts will provide me with detailed evaluations and recommendations for a chapter(s) in their area(s) of expertise. The expert research consultants for *Life-Span Development* (10th edition) were:

Pamela Balls Organista, *University of San Francisco*
Diversity throughout the book

Elizabeth Vera, *Loyola University*   Diversity throughout the book

David Moore, *Claremont Graduate School*   Chapter 3: Biological Beginnings

Linda Mayes, *Yale University*   Chapter 4: Prenatal Development and Birth

Jean Berko Gleason, *Boston University*   Chapter 6: Cognitive Development in Infancy; Chapter 8: Physical and Cognitive Development in Early Childhood; and Chapter 10: Physical and Cognitive Development in Middle and Late Childhood

Karen Adolph, *New York University*   Chapter 6: Cognitive Development in Infancy

Joseph Campos, *University of California–Berkeley*   Chapter 7: Socioemotional Development in Infancy

Ross Parke, *University of California–Riverside*   Chapters 9 and 11: Socioemotional Development in Early Childhood, and in Middle and Late Childhood

Elizabeth Susman, *Pennsylvania State University*   Chapter 12: Physical and Cognitive Development in Adolescence

James Garbarino, *Boston College*   Chapter 13: Socioemotional Development in Adolescence

James Birren, *UCLA*   Chapter 16: Physical and Cognitive Development in Middle Adulthood; Chapter 18: Physical Development in Late Adulthood

William Hoyer, *Syracuse University*   Chapter 14: Physical and Cognitive Development in Early Adulthood; Chapter 16: Physical and Cognitive Development in Middle Adulthood; Chapter 18: Physical Development in Late Adulthood

Toni Antonucci, *University of Michigan*   Chapter 20: Socioemotional Development in Late Adulthood

Robert Kastenbaum, *Arizona State University*   Chapter 21: Death and Grieving

Applications

It is important to not only present the scientific foundations of life-span development to students, but also to provide applied examples of concepts and to give students a sense that the field of life-span development has personal meaning for them. Among the new applications are:

- Recent ideas on family policy (Hawkins & Hiteman, 2004; Kalil & DeLeire, 2004) (chapter 1).
- A new section on being a wise consumer of information about life-span development (chapter 2).

- Expanded coverage of post-partum depression (Bonari & others, 2004; Clay & Seehusen, 2004) (chapter 4).
- Child care strategies for parents (McCartney, 2003) (chapter 7).
- Emotion-coaching and emotion-dismissing parents (chapter 9).
- Television and adolescent sexual behavior (Ward, 2003) (chapter 12).
- Evaluation of low-carb diets and effective strategies for losing weight, as well as a new section on alcoholism (Noakes & Clifton, 2004; Stern & others, 2004) (chapter 14).
- Women in happy and unhappy marriages (Gallo & others, 2003) (chapter 15).
- A new section on substance use in older adults (chapter 18).
- Meaning-making coping and spirituality in helping individuals cope with a death (Folkman & Lazarus, 2004; Hayslip & Hansson, 2003) (chapter 21).

In addition to giving special attention throughout the text to health and well-being, parenting, and educational applications, the tenth edition of *Life-Span Development* also includes *Careers in Life-Span Development* inserts in every chapter. They profile an individual whose career relates to the chapter's content. Most of these inserts have a photograph of the person at work. A number of new individuals are featured in the Careers in Life-Span Development in this edition. In addition, a Careers in Life-Span Development appendix follows Chapter 1 and describes a number of careers in education/research, clinical/counseling, medical/nursing/physical, and family/relationships categories. Numerous Web links provide students with opportunities to read about these careers in greater depth.

ADULT DEVELOPMENT, AGING, AND DIVERSITY

Two very important aspects of a text on life-span development are strong coverage of adult development and aging, as well as diversity.

Adult Development and Aging

Instructors have repeatedly told me that most life-span texts don't give adequate attention to adult development and aging. In the tenth edition, I have substantially modified, expanded, and updated the adult development and aging content, continuing a process I began a number of editions ago. Examples of new coverage include:

- Recent research on exercise and brain tissue loss in older adults (Colcombe & others, 2003).
- How the health care system too often fails older adults (Wenger & others, 2003).
- Recent research that documents variability in emerging adulthood (Cohen & others, 2003).
- New coverage of perimenopause and updated research on hormonal replacement therapy (Landgren & others, 2004; National Institutes of Health, 2004).

- Expanded coverage of stress in midlife, including recent research on daily hassles as well as an updated discussion of midlife crisis (Almeida & Horn, 2004; Lachman, 2004).
- Recent research on the Mankato Nuns (Mortimer & others, 2004; Snowdon, 2003).
- New section on aging and the immune system (Hawkley & Cacioppo, 2004).
- Information about mild cognitive impairment (MCI) and its possible link as a risk factor for Alzheimer disease (Grundman & others, 2004; Jungworth & others, 2004).
- New coverage of gender differences in emotional support experienced by older adults (Gurung, Taylor, & Seeman, 2003; Nacumey & Newsom, 2004).
- Discussion of recent study on cognitive factors involved in the severity of grief (Boelen, van den Bout, & van den Hout, 2003).

Diversity

Diversity is another key aspect of life-span development. I made every effort to explore diversity issues in a sensitive manner in each chapter. In addition to weaving diversity into discussions of life-span topics, I've included *Diversity in Life-Span Development* interludes in each chapter. Coverage of diversity includes these new Diversity interludes:

- Culture and Child Rearing (chapter 2)
- The Increased Diversity of Adopted Children and Adoptive Parents (chapter 3)
- Prenatal Care in the United States and Around the World (chapter 4)
- Bilingual Education (chapter 10)

The discussion of diversity also includes extensive new material in the Diversity in Life-Span Development interlude in chapter 1—Women's Struggle for Equality: An International Journey (UNICEF, 2004), the transition to parenting for African American and Latino couples (Florsheim & others, 2003), updated and expanded coverage of illness and health in children around the world (UNICEF, 2003) (chapter 8), developmental pathways to gay and lesbian identity (Savin-Williams & Diamond, 2004) (chapter 12), a new section on global traditions and changes in adolescence (Larson & Wilson, 2004) (chapter 13), updated and expanded coverage of ethnic identity with a special focus on immigration and generational change (Phinney, 2003; Umana-Taylor, 2004) (chapter 13), updated and expanded discussion of gay and lesbian couples (Peplau & Beals, 2004) (chapter 15), and recent research comparing Mexican American widows and widowers (Angel, Douglas, & Angel, 2003) (chapter 21).

ACCESSIBILITY AND INTEREST

The new edition of this text should be accessible to students because of the extensive rewriting, organization, and learning system.

Writing and Organization

Every sentence, paragraph, section, and chapter of this book was carefully examined and, when appropriate, revised and rewritten. The result is a much clearer, better-organized presentation of material in this new edition.

The Learning System

I strongly believe that students should not only be challenged to study hard and think more deeply and productively about life-span development, but should also be provided with an effective learning system. Instructors and students have commented about how student-friendly this book has become in recent editions.

Now more than ever, students struggle to find the main ideas in their courses, especially in courses like life-span development, which include so much material. The learning system centers on learning goals that, together with the main text headings, keep the key ideas in front of the reader from the beginning to the end of the chapter. Each chapter has no more than five main headings and corresponding learning goals, which are presented side-by-side in the chapter-opening spread. At the end of each main section of a chapter, the learning goal is repeated in a featured called "Review and Reflect," which prompts students to review the key topics in the section and poses a question to encourage them to think critically about what they have read. At the end of the chapter, under the heading, "Reach Your Learning Goals," the learning goals guide students through the bulleted chapter review.

In addition to the verbal tools just described, maps that link up with the learning goals are presented at the beginning of each major section in the chapter. At the end of each chapter, the section maps are assembled into a complete map of the chapter that provides a visual review guide. The complete learning system, including many additional features not mentioned here, is presented later in a section titled Visual Tour for Students.

CHAPTER-BY-CHAPTER CHANGES

All 21 chapters of *Life-Span Development,* tenth edition, feature substantial changes. The highlights of these changes follow.

CHAPTER 1
Introduction

- New discussion of recent research on exercise and brain tissue loss in older adults.
- New coverage of a recent study on how the health care system often fails older adults.
- New discussion of Baltes & Smith's view on differences between the young old and oldest old.
- New section on socioeconomic status (SES) and coverage of Jeanne Brooks-Gunn and her colleagues' research on children living in poverty.

- New coverage of recent research comparing six risk factors in lives of children growing up in poor and middle-income circumstances.
- Discussion of recent ideas on family policy.
- New material on a worldwide study of how a lower percentage of girls than boys receive no education at all, including new figure 1.4.
- New Research in Life-Span Development interlude: Memory in the A.M. and P.M. and Memory for Meaningful Information, including new research figure 1.7.

CHAPTER 2
The Science of Life-Span Development

- New section on Physiological Measures.
- New Research in Life-Span Development interlude: Research Journals.
- New section on Being a Wise Consumer of Information about Life-Span Development.
- New Diversity in Life-Span Development interlude: Culture and Child Rearing.

CHAPTER 3
Biological Beginnings

- Extensive rewriting and reorganization of chapter; inclusion of several new introductions to topics and transitions between topics for improved clarity and understanding.
- New section on evolutionary developmental psychology.
- Much-expanded coverage of adoption, including new Diversity in Life-Span Development interlude: The Increased Diversity of Adopted Children and Adoptive Parents.
- New Research in Life-Span Development interlude: Genetics and Life Expectancy.
- New research on the recent reduction in multiple births by IVF mothers.
- Deletion of section on heredity, environment, and intelligence with movement of that material to chapter 10, where intelligence is discussed.
- New section, The Epigenetic View (Gottlieb, 2004).

CHAPTER 4
Prenatal Development and Birth

- Expanded discussion of alcohol effects on the fetus, including recent research linking moderate drinking to preterm risk and birth size.
- Updated coverage of cocaine use by pregnant women, including increasing evidence of its negative effects.
- New discussion of risks to the fetus and child when a pregnant woman eats certain fish.

- New Diversity in Life-Span Development interlude: Prenatal Care in the United States and Around the World, including new figure 4.6 on the use of timely prenatal care by women from different ethnic groups in the United States.
- Updated research on low birth weight infants, including new figure 4.8.
- New section on kangaroo care, including recent research of its positive effects on preterm infants.
- New Research in Life-Span Development interlude: Tiffany Field's Research on Massage Therapy.
- Much-expanded coverage of postpartum depression, including new figure 4.11.

CHAPTER 5
Physical Development in Infancy

- New coverage of shaken baby syndrome.
- Discussion of recent study indicating that the cephalocaudal pattern does not always hold.
- New coverage of a national research study documenting that many U.S. babies are being fed too few fruits and vegetables and too much junk food.
- Research updating of breast feeding, including recent data on the increase in breast feeding by U.S. mothers.
- Research updating of SIDS, including coverage of the role of arousal.
- Research updating of toilet training.
- Discussion of dynamic systems theory is moved to the beginning of the motor development section for better student comprehension, and updated and revised.
- New discussion of Karen Adolph's research, including new figure from her research.
- Coverage of recent research study by Amy Needham and her colleagues, revealing that "sticky mittens" benefit infants' exploration of objects, including new figure 5.14 of the "sticky mittens" research.
- Improved discussion of the ecological theory of perception for better student understanding.
- New Research in Life-Span Development interlude: Studying the Newborn's Perception, with coverage of the visual preference method, habituation and dishabituation, tracking, and equipment.
- New coverage of binocular vision and its emergence at 3 to 4 months of age, providing a powerful cue to depth.
- Expanded coverage of hearing in infancy to include changes in the perception of loudness, pitch, and localization.

CHAPTER 6
Cognitive Development in Infancy

- New section on cognitive processes in Piaget's theory with new coverage of schemes, organization, equilibrium, and equilibration.

- New Research in Life-Span Development interlude, including the violated-expectations method and new figure related to it.
- New summary figure 6.1 of the six substages of sensorimotor development.
- New coverage of attention, including recent research on distractibility in infants and links between attention and memory in infancy.
- Updated discussion of infant memory.
- New section on language rules with new summary figure 6.7.
- Extensive rewriting and reorganization of language section with the development of language now preceding the section on biological and environmental influences.

CHAPTER 7
Socioemotional Development in Infancy

- Extensive rewriting of material on emotional development based on Joseph Campos' work.
- New discussion of the roles of biological foundations and environmental experience in emotion.
- New section on early developmental change in emotion, including new figures 7.1 and 7.2.
- New section on temperament in the biological foundations of temperament.
- New section on the significance of attachment.
- Change of section title and discussion from day care to child care.
- Coverage of recent research on the transition to parenting for African American and Latino couples.
- Extensively updated coverage of the National Institute of Child Health and Development's longitudinal study of child care in a new Research in Life-Span Development interlude.
- Coverage of recent commentary by experts on child care and child care expert Kathleen McCartney's child care strategies for parents.

CHAPTER 8
Physical and Cognitive Development in Early Childhood

- New coverage of growth hormone deficiency in young children.
- New coverage of eating inadequate amounts of quality meats and dark green vegetables in low-income families, which is linked to iron deficiency anemia.
- New discussion of the contexts of safety and accident prevention, based on Bronfenbrenner's theory, including new figure.
- Significantly updated discussion of the state of illness and health in the world's children.
- Added example of the zone of proximal development; clarified discussion of language and thought in Vygotsky's theory.

- New Research in Life-Span Development interlude: How Parents Can Subtly Suggest False Events to Their Children.
- New discussion of recent research on the transformation of the relatively stimulus-driven toddler to the more flexible, goal-directed, problem-solving young child.
- New section on the Reggio Emilia approach to early childhood education.
- New section on curriculum controversy in early childhood education.
- New section on what constitutes school readiness.

CHAPTER 9
Socioemotional Development in Early Childhood

- New discussion of gender differences in shame.
- New section on emotion-coaching and emotion-dismissing parents.
- Much-expanded, updated discussion of the evolutionary theory of gender.
- New discussion of recent research on links between individual hostility and marital hostility and the use of physical punishment with children.
- Expanded, updated discussion of gender and peer relations, including new figure on developmental changes.
- Expanded coverage of authoritative parenting and Ruth Chao's research on parenting styles in Asian American families.
- Much-expanded and updated coverage of different types of child abuse.
- New Research in Life-Span Development interlude: Young Children's Gender Schemas of Occupations, including new research figure.
- Added discussion of recent research on sex-assignment surgery and the adjustment of genetic males raised as girls.

CHAPTER 10
Physical and Cognitive Development in Middle and Late Childhood

- New Images of Life-Span opening story: Zhang Liyin, which focuses on the pressures of achievement placed on children in sports.
- Updated coverage of obesity and exercise in children, including recent research.
- Updated, expanded discussion of learning disabilities.
- Updated coverage of ADHD.
- New discussion of imagery and elaboration as memory strategies children can use, including new research figure.
- Updated new section on the roles of heredity and environment in intelligence, previously covered in chapter 3, with

new coverage of stereotype threat and Robert Serpell's work on culture and intelligence.

- New Research in Life-Span Development interlude: The Abecedarian Project, and updated coverage of early intervention.
- New Diversity in Life-Span Development interlude: Bilingual Education.

CHAPTER 11
Socioemotional Development in Middle and Late Childhood

- Much-expanded and updated coverage of links between self-esteem and performance, initiative, and happiness.
- New discussion of Kohlberg's interest in a seventh stage of moral development and expanded discussion of criticisms of his theory, including assessment issues.
- New Research in Life-Span Development interlude: The Consistency and Development of Prosocial Behavior.
- New coverage of gender differences in prosocial behavior.
- New discussion of William Pollack's ideas about real boys.
- Expanded and updated coverage of self-care/latchkey children.
- Updated coverage of peer relations, including coverage of average children, longitudinal research on peer statuses in childhood and problem behaviors in adulthood, and bullying.
- New section on contemporary approaches to student learning and assessment, with subsections on direct instruction, constructivist approach, and accountability.

CHAPTER 12
Physical and Cognitive Development in Adolescence

- New discussion of television and adolescent sexual behavior.
- New coverage of developmental pathways to gay or lesbian identity in adolescence.
- New material on the roles of self-regulation, parental monitoring, and parent-adolescent communication in adolescent sexual risk-taking.
- New figure 12.6 on cross-cultural comparisons of adolescent pregnancy rates.
- New section on changes in the brain during adolescence.
- Updated coverage of adolescent drug use.
- Recent research on factors involved in becoming a regular smoker in adolescence.
- New Research in Life-Span Development interlude: Evaluation of a Family Program Designed to Reduce Drinking and Smoking in Young Adolescents, including two research figures (fig. 12.8 and fig. 12.9).
- New coverage of changes in sleep during adolescence.

CHAPTER 13
Socioemotional Development in Adolescence

- New Research in Life-Span Development interlude: Adolescents' Self-Images.
- Updated and expanded coverage of ethnic identity with a special focus on immigration and generational change.
- New section, Emotional Development, including recent research and views, and new figure 13.3 on extremes of emotion in adolescents and their mothers and fathers.
- Expanded evaluation of links between adolescent-parent attachments and adolescent outcomes.
- New section, Global Traditions and Changes in Adolescence, with contemporary coverage of cross-cultural comparisons involving adolescent health, gender, families, peers, and schools.
- New section on how adolescents around the world spend their time, including new figure 13.7.

CHAPTER 14
Physical and Cognitive Development in Early Adulthood

- Expanded discussion of emerging adulthood, including personal and social aspects, and recent longitudinal research.
- Updated coverage of obesity, including strategies for losing weight, and new material on possible health risks of low-carbohydrate diets.
- New section on alcoholism, including recent research on links with heredity and environment, and strategies for reducing alcohol use.
- Change of labeling from sexually transmitted disease (STD) to sexually transmitted infection (STI) in keeping with current acceptance.
- Updated and expanded coverage of date or acquaintance rape, including strategies for reducing its incidence and new Research in Life-Span Development interlude on a major study of campus sexual assault.
- Expanded, updated coverage of positive and negative aspects of working during college.

CHAPTER 15
Socioemotional Development in Early Adulthood

- New Images of Life-Span Development—Gwenna & Greg: Her Pursuit and His Lack of Commitment.
- Expanded coverage of adult attachment and links between infant attachment and adult attachment.
- New section, Falling Out of Love.

- New Research in Life-Span Development interlude: Personal Growth Following a Romantic Relationship Breakup, including new figure 15.4, Examples of Positive Changes in the Aftermath of a Romantic Breakup.
- Updated coverage of marital trends, including new figure 15.7, Percent of Men and Women Never Married in the United States: 1970 and 2000.
- Inclusion of recent research on the health of women in happy and unhappy marriages.
- Updated coverage of cohabitation, including recent trends.
- New figure 15.10, Percent of Divorced Women and Men in the U.S.
- Updated discussion of gay and lesbian parents, including new figure 15.12.

CHAPTER 16
Physical and Cognitive Development in Middle Adulthood

- New discussion of baby boomers' views on health, disease, and interest in plastic surgery and Botox.
- New Research in Life-Span Development interlude on the first large-scale observational study to examine fitness in relation to risk factors for heart disease in middle age.
- Major new section on stress and disease, including the immune system, cardiovascular disease, and cancer.
- New introduction to work in midlife, emphasizing its diversity and change.
- Updated coverage of menopause and hormone replacement therapy, and new discussion of perimenopause.
- Updated, expanded discussion of erectile dysfunction, including new alternatives to Viagra.
- New comparison of causes of death in middle age and old age.
- Added concept of *sarcopenia*, an age-related loss of muscle mass and strength.

CHAPTER 17
Socioemotional Development in Middle Adulthood

- Expanded discussion of stress in midlife including recent research on daily hassles and education level.
- New discussion of George Vaillant's three longitudinal studies showing links between midlife characteristics and health and well-being at ages 75 and 80.
- Updated, expanded discussion of midlife crisis.
- New section on stress and midlife, including recent research on how middle-aged adults experience stress and on gender differences in types of stressors in middle age.
- New introduction and overview of the importance of middle-aged adults in the lives of the young and old.
- New section on grandparenting, previously in Late Adulthood section, added to this chapter based on adopter and

reviewer feedback; includes a new subsection on gender and grandparenting.
- New Research in Life-Span Development interlude: "We Had a Nice Little Chat": Mothers' and Daughters' Descriptions of Their Enjoyable Visits.
- Very recent research from the Midlife in the United States (MIDUS) survey.

CHAPTER 18
Physical Development in Late Adulthood

- Expanded, updated coverage of centenarians.
- New discussion of Baltes' view on problems and issues faced by the oldest old.
- New coverage of the mitochondrial theory of aging.
- Expansion of hormonal stress theory to include a decline in immune system functioning, and new section on immune system functioning in older adults.
- Revised, updated, expanded discussion of aging and the brain, including recent research on neurotransmitters and aging.
- New Research in Life-Span Development interlude on the Mankato Nuns.
- Much-expanded discussion of vision and aging, including new subsections on color vision, depth perception, and diseases of the eye.
- New section on substance use in older adults.
- New Careers in Life-Span Development insert: Sarah Kagan, Geriatric Nurse.
- Updated coverage of calorie restriction in older adults, including new figure 18.13 on calorie restriction in monkeys.
- Inclusion of recent longitudinal study on cardiovascular disease.
- Description of recent research on a link between Vitamin C blood levels and mortality in late adulthood.
- Expanded discussion of movement in older adults.
- New discussion of undernutrition without adequate vitamins and minerals, especially in women, in late adulthood.
- New coverage of recent research on a link between Vitamin E consumption and early death.

CHAPTER 19
Cognitive Development in Late Adulthood

- Expanded coverage of selective attention in late adulthood, including a recent observational study of selective attention and driving.
- Description of recent study by Baltes and others on cognitive mechanics/pragmatics distinction in older adults 70 to 100 years old.
- New section on source memory in older adults, including recent research.

- New coverage of research on optimistic and pessimistic accounts of memory in older adults.
- Recent research on the role of physical fitness in older adults' cognitive functioning.
- Discussion of recent research on lower depressive symptoms in older adults.
- New discussion of mild cognitive impairment (MCI) as a possible risk factor for Alzheimer disease.
- Change of terminology from Alzheimer's disease to Alzheimer disease and Parkinson's disease to Parkinson disease in keeping with current terminology in this field of research and care; expanded coverage of Alzheimer disease, including links with cardiovascular disease.
- New Research in Life-Span Development interlude that focuses on a longitudinal study by Janet Kiecolt-Glaser and her colleagues showing elevated stress and lower immune chemical levels in the caregivers of Alzheimer patients compared to a control group of non-caregivers; includes two graphs of data.
- Description of recent research on the role of religion in the lives of White and African American older adults.

CHAPTER 20
Socioemotional Development in Late Adulthood

- Coverage of recent longitudinal study on links between activities and happiness, functioning, and mortality in older adults.
- New Research in Life-Span Development interlude: Changes in Emotion across the Adulthood Years.
- Description of recent study on a decrease in negative interactions in close relationships as adults become older in both the United States and Japan.
- New section on lifestyle diversity in older adults.
- New section on divorced and remarried older adults.
- New section on older adult parents and their adult children.
- New section on great-grandparenting.
- New section on older adults' sibling relationships.
- New section on never married older adults, including an increase in cohabiting.
- New section on romance and sexuality in older adults' relationships.
- Discussion of recent study on gender differences in emotional support experienced by older adults.

CHAPTER 21
Death and Grieving

- New Images of Life-Span Development opening story: Paige Farley-Hackel & Ruth McCourt, who died in the terrorist attacks on 9/11/2001.

- Recent research on meaning and purpose in life, as well as spirituality, in helping dying individuals cope.
- New Research in Life-Span Development interlude: The Women's Health Initiative Study of Widowhood and Health.
- Coverage of recent study on cognitive factors involved in the severity of grief.
- Discussion of recent study on the effects of euthanasia on the grief of bereaved family members and friends.
- Much-expanded coverage of developmental aspects of death, including the impact of a parent's or sibling's death on children and adolescents, causes of death in early adulthood, and the impact of a young child's death on parents.
- Coverage of recent study comparing Mexican-American widows and widowers.
- New Careers in Life-Span Development insert: Kathy McLaughlin, Home Hospice Nurse.

ACKNOWLEGMENTS

I very much appreciate the support and guidance provided to me by many people at McGraw-Hill. Steve Rutter, Publisher, and Mike Sugarman, Executive Editor, have brought a wealth of publishing knowledge and vision to bear on improving my texts. Elsa Peterson, Senior Developmental Editor, has done a superb job of organizing and monitoring the many tasks necessary to move this book through the editorial and production process. Kate Russillo, Editorial Coordinator, has once again worked wonders in obtaining reviewers and handling many editorial chores. Laura Edwards also performed excellent work in her capacity as freelance developmental editor. Melissa Caughlin, Marketing Manager, has contributed in numerous positive ways, and Susan Trentacosti very competently managed the production of the book. Laurie Entringer, Manager of Design, created a beautiful design, and Bea Sussman once again did a stellar job in copyediting the book.

REVIEWERS

I owe a special gratitude to the reviewers who provided detailed feedback about the book.

Expert Consultants

I already listed the expert consultants earlier in the preface. Their photographs and biographies appear later on pages xxx–xxxiii. Life-span development has become an enormous, complex field and no single author can possibly be an expert in all areas of the field. To solve this problem, beginning with the sixth edition, I have sought the input of leading experts in many different areas of life-span development. This tradition continues in the tenth edition. The experts have provided me with detailed recommendations of new research to include in every period of the life span. The panel of experts is literally a who's who in the field of life-span development.

General Text Reviewers

I also owe a great debt of thanks to the instructors teaching the life-span course who have provided feedback about the book. Many of the changes in *Life-Span Development*, tenth edition, are based on their input. In this regard, I thank these individuals:

Pre-Revison Reviewers

Kristy Allen, *Ozark Technical College*
Leslie Ault, *Hostos Community College–CUNY*
Julia Braungart-Rieke, *University of Notre Dame*
Kathy Brown, *California State University at Fullerton*
Dominique Charlotteaux, *Broward Community College*
Bill Cheney, *Crichton College*
Saundra Ciccarelli, *Florida Gulf University*
Bailey Drechsler, *Cuesta College*
Tasha Howe, *Humboldt State University*
Kathy Lein, *Community College of Denver*
James Messina, *University of Phoenix*
Jessica Miller, *Mesa State College*

Tenth Edition Reviewers

Jackie Adamson, *South Dakota School of Mines & Technology*
Pamela Adelmann, *Saint Paul Technical College*
Yiwei Chen, *Bowling Green State University*
Lena Eriksen, *Western Washington University*
John Hotz, *Saint Cloud State University*
Terry Isbell, *Northwestern State University of Louisiana*
Nadene L'Amoreaux, *Indiana University of Pennsylvania*
Jennifer Parker, *University of South Carolina*
Mary Ann Wisniewski, *Carroll College*

EXPERT CONSULTANTS FOR PREVIOUS EDITIONS

Toni C. Antonucci, *University of Michigan–Ann Arbor;* **Paul Baltes,** *Max Planck Institute for Human Development;* **Diana Baumrind,** *University of California–Berkeley;* **Carol Beal,** *University of Massachusetts at Amherst;* **James Birren,** *University of California–Los Angeles;* **Marc H. Bornstein,** *National Institute of Child Health & Development;* **Sue Bredekamp,** *National Association for the Education of Young Children;* **Urie Bronfenbrenner,** *Cornell University;* **Rosalind Charlesworth,** *Weber State University;* **Florence Denmark,** *Pace University;* **Joseph Durlack,** *Loyola University;* **Glen Elder,** *University of North Carolina–Chapel Hill;* **Tiffany Field,** *University of Miami;* **Alan Fogel,** *University of Utah;* **Jean Berko Gleason,** *Boston University;* **Gilbert Gottlieb,** *University of North Carolina;* **Julia Graber,** *Columbia University;* **Sandra Graham,** *University of California–Los Angeles;* **Jane Halonen,** *Alverno College;* **Yvette R. Harris,** *Miami University–Ohio;* **Algea O. Harrison-Hale,** *Oakland University;* **Craig Hart,** *Brigham Young University;* **Bert Hayslip,** *University of North Texas;* **Ravenna Helson,** *University of California–Berkeley;*

Cigdem Kagitcibasi, *Koc University (Turkey);* **Robert Kastenbaum,** *Arizona State University;* **Gisela Labouvie-Vief,** *Wayne State University;* **Barry M. Lester,** *Women and Infants' Hospital;* **Jean M. Mandler,** *University of California–San Diego;* **James Marcia,** *Simon Fraser University;* **Scott Miller,** *University of Florida;* **Phyllis Moen,** *Cornell University;* **Ross D. Parke,** *University of California–Riverside;* **James Reid,** *Washington University;* **Carolyn Saarni,** *Sonoma State University;* **Barba Patton,** *University of Houston–Victoria;* **K. Warner Schaie,** *Pennsylvania State University;* **Jan Sinnott,** *Towson State University;* **Margaret Beale Spencer,** *University of Pennsylvania;* **Ross A. Thompson,** *University of Nebraska–Lincoln;* **Marian Underwood,** *University of Texas at Dallas;* **Susan Whitbourne,** *University of Massachusetts–Amherst.*

GENERAL TEXT REVIEWERS FOR PREVIOUS EDITIONS

Patrick K. Ackles, *Michigan State University;* **Berkeley Adams,** *Jamestown Community College;* **Joanne M. Alegre,** *Yavapai College;* **Gary L. Allen,** *University of South Carolina;* **Lilia Allen,** *Charles County Community College;* **Susan E. Allen,** *Baylor University;* **Doreen Arcus,** *University of Massachusetts–Lowell;* **Frank. R. Ashbur,** *Valdosta State College;* **Leslie Ault,** *Hostos Community College–CUNY;* **Renee L. Babcock,** *Central Michigan University;* **Daniel R. Bellack,** *Trident Technical College;* **Helen E. Benedict,** *Baylor University;* **Alice D. Beyrent,** *Hesser College;* **John Biondo,** *Community College of Allegheny County–Boyce Campus;* **James A. Blackburn,** *University of Wisconsin–Madison;* **Stephanie Blecharczyk,** *Keene State College;* **Belinda Blevin-Knabe,** *University of Arkansas–Little Rock;* **Karyn Mitchell Boutlin,** *Massasoit Community College;* **Donald Bowers,** *Community College of Philadelphia;* **Saundra Y. Boyd,** *Houston Community College;* **Michelle Boyer-Pennington,** *Middle Tennessee State University;* **Ann Brandt-Williams,** *Glendale Community College;* **Jack Busky,** *Harrisburg Area Community College;* **Joan B. Cannon,** *University of Lowel;* **Jeri Carter,** *Glendale Community College;* **Vincent Castranovo,** *Community College of Philadelphia;* **Ginny Chappeleau,** *Muskingum Area Technical College;* **M. A. Christenberry,** *Augusta College;* **Andrea Clements,** *East Tennessee State University;* **Meredith Cohen,** *University of Pittsburgh;* **Diane Cook,** *Gainesville College;* **Ava Craig,** *Sacramento City College;* **Kathleen Crowley-Long,** *College of Saint Rose;* **Cynthia Crown,** *Xavier University;* **Dana Davidson,** *University of Hawaii at Manoa;* **Diane Davis,** *Bowie State University;* **Tom L. Day,** *Weber State University;* **Doreen DeSantio,** *West Chester University;* **Jill De Villiers,** *Smith College;* **Darryl M. Dietrich,** *College of St. Scholastica;* **Mary B. Eberly,** *Oakland University;* **Margaret Sutton Edmonds,** *University of Massachusetts–Boston;* **Martha M. Ellis,** *Collin County Community College;* **Richard Ewy,** *Pennsylvania State University;* **Dan Fawaz,** *Georgia Perimeter College;* **Shirley Feldman,** *Stanford University;* **Roberta Ferra,** *University of Kentucky;* **Linda E. Flickinger,** *St. Claire Community College;* **Lynne Andreozzi Fontaine,** *Community College of Rhode Island;* **Tom Frangicetto,** *Northhampton Community*

College; **Kathleen Corrigan Fuhs,** *J. Sargeant Reynolds Community College;* **J. Steven Fulks,** *Utah State University;* **Cathy Furlong,** *Tulsa Junior College;* **Duwayne Furman,** *Western Illinois University;* **John Gat,** *Humboldt State University;* **Marvin Gelman,** *Montgomery County College;* **Rebecca J. Glare,** *Weber State College;* **Jean Berko Gleason,** *Boston University;* **David Goldstein,** *Temple University;* **Judy Goodell,** *National University;* **Mary Ann Goodwyn,** *Northeast Louisiana University;* **Caroline Gould,** *Eastern Michigan University;* **Peter C. Gram,** *Pensacola Junior College;* **Dan Grangaard,** *Austin Community College;* **Tom Gray,** *Laredo Community College;* **Michele Gregoire,** *University of Florida at Gainesville;* **Michael Green,** *University of North Carolina;* **Rea Gubler,** *Southern Utah University;* **Gary Gute,** *University of Northern Iowa;* **Laura Hanish,** *Arizona State University;* **Ester Hanson,** *Prince George's Community College;* **Marian S. Harris,** *University of Illinois at Chicago;* **Amanda W. Harrist,** *Oklahoma State University;* **Robert Heavilin,** *Greater Hartford Community College;* **Donna Henderson,** *Wake Forest University;* **Debra Hollister,** *Valencia Community College;* **Heather Holmes-Lonergan,** *Metropolitan State College of Denver;* **Ramona O. Hopkins,** *Brigham Young University;* **Donna Horbury,** *Appalachian State University;* **Susan Horton,** *Mesa Community College;* **Sharon C. Hott,** *Allegany College of Maryland;* **Kimberley Howe-Norris,** *Cape Fear Community College;* **Stephen Hoyer,** *Pittsburgh State University;* **Kathleen Day Hulbert,** *University of Massachusetts–Lowell;* **Derek Isaacowitz,** *Brandeis University;* **Kathryn French Iroz,** *Utah Valley State College;* **Erwin Janek,** *Henderson State University;* **James Jasper-Jacobsen,** *Indiana University–Purdue;* **Christina Jose-Kampfner,** *Eastern Michigan University;* **Ursula Joyce,** *St. Thomas Aquinas College;* **Seth Kalichman,** *Loyola University;* **Barbara Kane,** *Indiana State University;* **Kevin Keating,** *Broward Community College;* **James L. Keeney,** *Middle Georgia College;* **Elinor Kinarthy,** *Rio Hondo College;* **Karen Kirkendall,** *Sangamon State University;* **A. Klingner,** *Northwest Community College;* **Steven J. Kohn,** *Nazareth College;* **Amanda Kowal,** *University of Missouri;* **Jane Krump,** *North Dakota State College of Science;* **Joseph C. LaVoie,** *University of Nebraska at Omaha;* **Jean Hill Macht,** *Montgomery County Community College;* **Salvador Macias,** *University of South Carolina–Sumter;* **Karen Macrae,** *University of South Carolina;* **Christine Malecki,** *Northern Illinois University;* **Kahty Manuel,** *Bossier Parish Community College;* **Myra Marcus,** *Florida Gulf Coast University;* **Allan Mayotte,** *Riverland Community College;* **Susan McClure,** *Westmoreland Community College;* **Dorothy H. McDonald,** *Sandhills Community College;* **Robert C. McGinnis,** *Ancilla College;* **Clara McKinney,** *Barstow College;* **Robert McLaren,** *California State University at Fullerton;* **Sharon McNeeley,** *Northeastern Illinois University;* **Heather E. Metcalfe,** *University of Windsor;* **Karla Miley,** *Black Hawk College;* **Jessica Miller,** *Mesa State College;* **Teri M. Miller-Schwartz,** *Milwaukee Area Technical College;* **David B. Mitchell,** *Loyola University;* **Joann Montepare,** *Emerson College;* **Martin D. Murphy,** *University of Akron;* **Malinda Muzi,** *Community College of Philadelphia;* **Gordon K. Nelson,** *Pennsylvania State University;* **Michael Newton,** *Sam Houston State University;* **Beatrice Norrie,** *Mount Royal College;* **Jean O'Neil,** *Boston College;* **Laura Overstreet,** *Tarrant County College–Northeast;* **Pete Peterson,** *Johnson County Community College;* **Richard Pierce,** *Pennsylvania State University–Altoona;* **David Pipes,** *Caldwell Community College;* **Leslee Pollina,** *Southeast Missouri State University;* **Robert Poresky,** *Kansas State University;* **Christopher Quarto,** *Middle Tennessee State University;* **Bob Rainey,** *Florida Community College;* **Nancy Rankin,** *University of New England;* **H. Ratner,** *Wayne State University;* **Cynthia Reed,** *Tarrant County College–Northeast;* **Russell Riley,** *Lord Fairfax Community College;* **Mark P. Rittman,** *Cuyahoga Community College;* **Clarence Romeno,** *Riversity Community College;* **Paul Roodin,** *SUNY–Oswego;* **Ron Rossac,** *University of North Florida;* **Julia Rux,** *Georgia Perimeter College;* **Gayla Sanders,** *Community College of Baltimore County–Essex;* **Toru Sato,** *Shippensburg University;* **Nancy Sauerman,** *Kirkwood Community College;* **Cynthia Scheibe,** *Ithaca College;* **Robert Schell,** *SUNY–Oswego;* **Edythe Schwartz,** *California State University at Sacramento;* **Lisa Scott,** *University of Minnesota–Twin Cities;* **Owen Sharkey,** *University of Prince Edward Island;* **Elisabeth Shaw,** *Texarkana College;* **Susan Nakayama Siaw,** *California State Polytechnic University;* **Vicki Simmons,** *University of Victoria;* **Gregory Smith,** *University of Maryland;* **Jon Snodgrass,** *California State University–Los Angeles;* **Donald Stanley,** *North Dallas Community College;* **Jean A. Steitz,** *University of Memphis;* **Collier Summers,** *Florida Community College at Jacksonville;* **Barbara Thomas,** *National University;* **Stacy D. Thompson,** *Oklahoma State University;* **Debbie Tindell,** *Wilkes University;* **Stephen Truhon,** *Winston-Salem State University;* **James Turcott,** *Kalamazoo Valley Community College;* **Gaby Vandergiessen,** *Fairmount State College;* **Stephen Werba,** *Community College of Baltimore County–Catonsville;* **B. D. Whetstone,** *Birmingham Southern College;* **Nancy C. White,** *Reynolds Community College;* **Lyn W. Wickelgren,** *Metropolitan State College;* **Ann M. Williams,** *Luzerne County Community College;* **Myron D. Williams,** *Great Lakes Bible College;* **Linda B. Wilson,** *Quincy College.*

SUPPLEMENTS

The tenth edition of *Life-Span Development* is accompanied by a comprehensive and fully integrated array of supplemental materials, both print and electronic, written specifically for instructors and students of life-span development. In addition, a variety of generic supplements are available to further aid in the teaching and learning of life-span development.

For the Instructor

Once again, based on comprehensive and extensive feedback from instructors, we spent considerable time and effort in expanding and improving the ancillary materials.

Instructor's Manual *Gail Edmunds* This comprehensive manual provides a variety of useful tools for both seasoned instructors and those new to the life-span development course. The Instructor's Manual provides the following tools.

- Enhanced list of Learning Goals provides detailed components to support each of the chapter's Learning Goals listed in the text.
- Fully integrated chapter outlines to help instructors better use the many resources for the course. Most of the supplementary materials offered in conjunction with *Life-Span Development*, tenth edition, are represented in this outline and have been correlated to the main concepts in each chapter.
- Lecture suggestions, classroom activities, and research project ideas. As appropriate, these include critical thinking multiple-choice and essay exercises, all of which provide answers where appropriate.
- Classroom activities include logistics for required materials, such as accompanying handouts, varying group sizes, and time needed for completion.
- Personal Application projects guide students in applying life-span development topics to their own lives.
- Media resources for each chapter: Video segments (found on the LifeMap student CD) are listed; as well as Feature Film Suggestions, which provide a synopsis of movies pertaining to chapter topics; as well as updated URLs for useful Internet sites.

Computerized Test Bank on Instructor's Resource CD-ROM

Kristina D. Allen, Ozark Technical Community College; Shirley Cassara, Bunker Hill Community College This comprehensive Test Bank has once again been extensively revised to include over 2,400 multiple-choice and short answer/brief essay questions for the text's 21 chapters. Each multiple-choice item is classified as factual, conceptual, or applied, as defined by Benjamin Bloom's taxonomy of educational objectives. New to this edition, each test question is now keyed to a chapter Learning Goal, and the Test Bank notes which learning goal each item addresses. In response to customer feedback, this Test Bank also provides page references that indicate where in the text the answer to each item can be found.

Available on the Instructor's Resource CD-ROM, the Test Bank is compatible with both Windows and Macintosh platforms. The CD-ROM provides an editing feature that enables instructors to integrate their own questions, scramble items, and modify questions.

PowerPoint Slide Presentations

Linda Ann Butzin, Owens Community College The chapter-by-chapter PowerPoint lectures for this edition integrate the text's learning goals and provide key text material and illustrations. These presentations are designed to be useful in both small- and large-lecture settings, and are easily tailored to suit an individual instructor's lectures.

The McGraw-Hill Developmental Psychology Image Bank

This set of 200 full-color images was developed using the best selection of our human development art and tables, and is available online for instructors on the text's Online Learning Center.

Online Learning Center

The extensive website designed especially to accompany Santrock, *Life-Span Development*, tenth edition, offers an array of resources for both instructor and student. For instructors, the website includes a full set of PowerPoint Presentations, and hotlinks for the text's topical Web links that appear in the margins and for the Taking It to the Net exercises that appear at the end of each chapter. These resources and more can be found by logging on to the website at **www.mhhe. com/santrockld10**.

Annual Editions—Developmental Psychology

Published by Dushkin/McGraw-Hill, this is a collection of articles on topics related to the latest research and thinking in human development. These editions are updated annually and contain helpful features including a topic guide, an annotated table of contents, unit overviews, and a topical index. An Instructor's Guide containing testing materials is also available.

Sources: Notable Selections in Human Development

This volume presents a collection of more than 40 articles, book excerpts, and research studies that have shaped the study of human development and our contemporary understanding of it. The selections are organized topically around major areas of study within human development. Each selection is preceded by a headnote that establishes the relevance of the article or study and provides biographical information about the author.

Taking Sides

This debate-style reader is designed to introduce students to controversial viewpoints on the field's most crucial issues. Each issue is carefully framed for the student, and the pro and con essays represent the arguments of leading scholars and commentators in their fields. An Instructor's Guide containing testing material is available.

For the Student

Student Study Guide

Tasha R. Howe, Humboldt State University The revised Study Guide provides a complete introduction for students on how best to use each of the various study aids plus invaluable strategies on setting goals, benefiting from class, reading for learning, taking tests, and memory techniques in the section "Being an Excellent Student." Each study guide chapter begins with a list of Learning Goals from the text and an outline of the chapter. The self-test sections contain short-answer Checking Your Understanding questions, multiple-choice and true-false questions, and comprehensive essays with suggested answers. The Study Guide also includes out-of-class research projects, personal application projects, Internet projects, and Web links that complement the revised student research projects and allow for more effective student learning.

LifeMap Interactive CD-ROM for Students

The LifeMap CD is especially designed to accompany Santrock, *Life-Span Development*, tenth edition. Each of the book's 21 chapters features one or more video segments, accompanied by pretest and posttest questions and Web links to further explore issues raised in the video. In addition, each chapter features a multiple-choice quiz with feedback to encourage active learning. The LifeMap CD also features an interactive time line covering the stages of development through the life span.

Online Learning Center www.mhhe.com/santrockld10
The extensive website designed especially to accompany Santrock, *Life-Span Development,* tenth edition, offers an array of resources for instructors and students. For students, the website offers interactive quizzing with feedback, flashcards, and matching exercises. It also offers hotlinks for the text's topical Web links that appear in the margins and for the *Taking It to the Net* exercises that appear at the end of each chapter. Self-assessments related to chapter topics encourage students to examine their personal feelings and experiences in relation to life-span development. These resources and more can be found on the Online Learning Center at www.mhhe.com/santrockld10.

Guide to Life-Span Development for Future Educators and Guide to Life-Span Development for Future Nurses
These course supplements help students apply the concepts of human development to careers in education and nursing respectively. They contain information, exercises, and sample tests designed to help students prepare for certification and understand human development from a professional perspective.

Resources for Improving Human Development This useful booklet provides descriptions and contact information for organizations and agencies that can provide helpful information, advice, and support related to particular problems or issues in life-span development. Organized in chronological order by periods of the life span, the booklet also describes recommended books and journals.

Expert Consultants

Pamela Balls Organista

Dr. Organista is a leading expert on culture and ethnicity and is Professor of Psychology at the University of San Francisco. She completed her bachelor's degree in Psychology and Black Studies at Washington University in St. Louis, Doctorate in Clinical Psychology at Arizona State University, and Clinical Psychology post-doctorate in the Department of Psychiatry at the University of California–San Francisco. Her research interests include prevention interventions and ethnic minority health issues. Dr. Organista's publications include *Readings in Ethnic Psychology: African Americans, American Indians, Asian Americans, and Hispanics/Latinos,* and *Acculturation,* which she co-edited with Kevin Chun and Gerardo Marin. She has published several articles on migrant laborers and AIDS and on stress and coping in primary care patients. Dr. Organista is the founding and present faculty coordinator of the Ethnic Studies Program at the University of San Francisco and from 1998–2000 served as the Director of Academic Advising in the College of Arts and Sciences at the University of San Francisco.

Elizabeth Vera

Dr. Vera is a leading expert on culture and ethnicity and is an Associate Professor in the School of Education at Loyola University Chicago. She received her Ph.D. in Counseling Psychology from Ohio State University. Dr. Vera teaches classes in human development, adolescence, prevention, and supervision. She conducts research on urban adolescents and families in the Chicago area and has written extensively about multiculturalism and social justice.

David S. Moore

Dr. Moore is a leading expert on the early biological, cognitive, and environmental determinants of development. He is currently a professor of psychology at Pitzer College and Claremont Graduate University in Claremont, California. Dr. Moore's research examines perception and cognition in human infants, and has focused recently on the categorization of infant-directed speech. Articles reporting this work have appeared in *Developmental Psychology, Developmental Psychobiology,* and *The Journal of Experimental Child Psychology,* among others. His highly acclaimed, accessible book, *The Dependent Gene: The Fallacy of Nature vs. Nurture,* examines how development contributes to the appearance of our traits.

Linda Mayes

Dr. Mayes is a leading expert on prenatal development. She is the Arnold Gesell Professor of Child Psychiatry, Pediatrics, and Psychology in the Yale Child Study Center and has been a Yale University School of Medicine faculty member since 1985. Dr. Mayes coordinates the early childhood programs in the Center and is the principal investigator on a National Institute of Health (NIH) funded longitudinal study of attention and arousal capacities in high risk children. Dr. Mayes oversees a behavioral and psychophysiology laboratory at the Child Study Center. She is also a member of the directorial team of the Anna Freud Centre in London. Trained as both a child and adult psychoanalyst and as a pediatrician, neonatologist, and child developmentalist, Dr. Mayes integrates perspectives from developmental psychology, neuroscience, and child psychiatry in her work. Her scientific papers and chapters are published in the child psychiatric, developmental psychology, pediatric, and psychoanalytic literature. Her book for parents (written with Dr. Donald Cohen), *The Yale Child Study Center Guide to Understanding Your Child's Development* seeks to help parents learn more about their children's development and to reflect on their own development as parents.

Jean Berko Gleason

Dr. Gleason is one of the world's leading experts on language development. She is a professor in the Department of Psychology at Boston University and is also a faculty member and former director of Boston University's Graduate Program in Applied Linguistics. She has been a visiting scholar at Stanford University, Harvard, and the Linguistics Institute of the Hungarian Academy of Sciences in Budapest. She received her undergraduate and graduate degrees from Harvard/Radcliffe.

Dr. Gleason has been president of the International Association for the Study of Child Language, and is the author and editor of leading textbooks on language development and psycholinguistics. Since writing her doctoral dissertation on how children learn to make plurals and past tenses in English, she has published over one hundred articles on aphasia, language attrition, language development in children, gender differences in parents' speech, and cross-cultural differences. Her work is frequently cited in the professional literature, and has been featured in the popular press and on television.

Karen Adolph

Dr. Adolph is one of the world's leading experts on infant learning and motor skill acquisition. She is Associate Professor in the Department of Psychology and the Center for Neuroscience at New York University. She received her B.A. from Sarah Lawrence College and her M.A. and Ph.D. from Emory University. Dr. Adolph was Assistant Professor at Carnegie Mellon University's Department of Psychology. She

has received a James McKeen Cattell Sabbatical Award, the Robert L. Fantz Memorial Award from the American Psychological Foundation, the Boyd McCandless Award from the American Psychological Association, and the Young Investigator Award from the International Society for Infant Studies. Her research examines learning and development in the context of infant motor skill acquisition. Dr. Adolph is author of SRCD monograph *Learning in the Development of Infant Locomotion*, and is on the editorial boards of *Infancy* and *Ecological Psychology*.

Joseph Campos

Dr. Campos is one of the world's leading experts on socioemotional development in infancy. He is Professor of Psychology at the University of California, Berkeley. He currently is President of the International Society for Infant Studies, and previously, was the first Executive Officer of the International Society for Research on Emotions. He has authored

Development in Infancy, with Michael Lamb, and has co-edited one of the volumes of the *Handbook of Child Psychology* (fifth edition), as well as the 2003 book, *Emotions Inside Out: 130 Years After Darwin's* The Expression of the Emotions in Man and Animals. He holds Distinguished Teaching Awards from the University of Denver and the University of Illinois at Urbana-Champaign, and also is Distinguished Guest Professor at Beijing Normal University.

Ross D. Parke

Dr. Parke is one of the leading pioneers in the field of socioemotional development. He is Distinguished Professor of Psychology and Director of the Center for Family Studies at the University of California, Riverside. Dr. Parke was educated at the Universities of Toronto and Waterloo and previously was affiliated with the Universities of Wisconsin and Illinois and the Fels Research Institute. He has been President

of Division 7, the Developmental Psychology Division of the American Psychological Association, and President of the Society for Research in Child Development. His interests include the relation between families and peers, ethnic variation in families, and the impact of new reproductive technologies on families. He has been editor of *Developmental Psychology*, an associate editor of *Child Development*, and editor of the *Journal of Family Psychology*. Dr. Parke is the author of *Fathers, Fatherhood*, and coauthor of *Child Psychology* and *Throwaway Dads*.

Elizabeth Susman

Dr. Susman is one of the world's leading experts on puberty and adolescent development. She is the Jean Phillips Shibley Professor of Biobehavioral Health in the Department of Biobehavioral Health, Pennsylvania State University. Her research program combines biology, behavioral endocrinology, and developmental psychology, focusing on the

important issue of how changes in emotions and antisocial behavior parallel hormonal changes in puberty. This research has been funded by the National Institute of Child Health and Human Development, National Institute of Mental Health, John D. and Catherine T. MacArthur Foundation, National Institute of Justice, and the William T. Grant Foundation. She has been co-editor of the *Journal of Research on Adolescence* and is the President of the Society for Research on Adolescence.

James Garbarino

Dr. Garbarino is one of the world's leading experts on children's and adolescents' socioemotional development. He is currently Elizabeth Lee Vincent Professor of Human Development at Cornell University. Previously, he served as President of the Erikson Institute for Advanced Study in Child Development (1985–1994). He earned his B.A. from St. Lawrence University and his Ph.D. from Cornell University. Dr. Garbarino is a Fellow of the American Psychological Association. Books he has authored or edited include: *And Words Can Hurt Forever, Parents Under Siege, Lost Boys, Raising Children in a Socially Toxic Environment, Let's Talk About Living in a World with Violence, Children in Danger,* and many others. He serves as a consultant to television, magazine, and newspaper reports on children and families. The National Conference on Child Abuse and Neglect honored Dr. Garbarino in 1985 with its first C. Henry Kempe Award, in recognition of his efforts on behalf of abused and neglected children. Dr. Garbarino has received the American Psychological Association's Division on Child, Youth and Family Services' Nicholas Hobbs Award, and the President's Celebrating Success Award from the National Association of School Psychologists. In 2003, he received the Outstanding Service to Children Award from the Chicago Association for the Education of Young Children.

James E. Birren

Dr. Birren is one of the leading pioneers in the field of life-span development and an expert on the biological dimensions of aging. He currently is Associate Director of the UCLA Center on Aging, and also is Professor Emeritus of Gerontology and Psychology at the University of Southern California. He received his M.A. and Ph.D. from Northwestern University. Dr. Birren's career includes serving as founding Executive Director and Dean of the Ethel Percy Andrus Gerontology Center at the University of Southern California; and past president of the Gerontological Society of America, the Western Gerontological Society, and the Division on Adult Development and Aging of the American Psychological Association. In addition, he has served as Chief of the Section on Aging of the National Institute of Mental Health. His awards include the Brookdale Foundation Award for Gerontological Research; Honorary Doctorates from the University of Gothenberg, Sweden, Northwestern University, and St. Thomas University, Canada; the Gerontological Society Award for Meritorious Research; the 1989 Sandoz Prize for Gerontological Research; and the Canadian Association of Gerontology, 1990, Award for Outstanding Contribution to Gerontology. Dr. Birren has published extensively in the area of aging. He is Series Editor of the internationally recognized *Handbooks on Aging* and has over 250 publications in academic journals and books.

William J. Hoyer

Dr. Hoyer is one of the world's leading experts on cognitive development in adults, is currently Professor of Psychology at Syracuse University. He received his B.S. degree from Rutgers College, and his M.S. and Ph.D. in experimental psychology from West Virginia University. Dr. Hoyer has contributed over 100 articles, books, and book chapters to the professional literature. Currently, he is Principal Investigator of a five-year research grant on cognitive aging from the National Institute on Aging. He is a Fellow of the American Psychological Association, the American Psychological Society, and the Gerontological Society of America, and he has served on the editorial boards for a number of professional journals including *Journal of Gerontology: Psychological Sciences* and *Psychology and Aging*. The major focus of Dr. Hoyer's current research is to specify the mechanisms that account for age-related differences in learning, visual selective attention, and skilled performance.

Toni Antonucci

Dr. Antonucci is one of the world's leading experts on socioemotional development in adult development and aging. She is the Elizabeth M. Douvan Collegiate Professor of Psychology and Program Director of the Life Course Development Program of the Institute for Social Research at the University of Michigan. Her research focuses on social relationships across the life span, including multigenerational studies of the family and comparative studies of social relationships across the life span in the United States, Europe, and Japan. She is Past President of Division 20 (Adult Developmental and Aging) of the American Psychological Association (APA). In 2001, Dr. Antonucci received the Master Mentor Award from this APA division. She also is Past President of the Gerontological Society of America.

Robert Kastenbaum

Dr. Kastenbaum is one of the world's leading experts on death and grieving. He has been active as therapist, researcher, program director, and educator since receiving his doctorate at the University of Southern California. Dr. Kastenbaum's books include *The Psychology of Death; Death, Society, and Human Experience;* and *On Our Way: The Final Passage Through Life and Death* (2004). He has served as director of a geriatric hospital and is co-founder of the National Black Caucus on Aging. Dr. Kastenbaum has been editor of the *International Journal of Aging and Human Development* and *Omega: A Journal of Death and Dying.* He also explores themes of love and death in theater pieces such as the opera *Closing Time* and the musical play *Parlor Games.*

A Visual Tour for Students

This book provides you with important study tools to help you more effectively learn about life-span development. Especially important is the learning goals system that is integrated throughout each chapter. In the visual walkthrough of features, pay special attention to how the learning goals system works.

THE LEARNING GOALS SYSTEM

Using the learning goals system will help you to learn more material more easily. Key aspects of the learning goals system are the learning goals, chapter maps, Review and Reflect, and Reach Your Learning Goals sections, which are all linked together.

At the beginning of each chapter, you will see a page that includes both a chapter outline and three to six learning goals that preview the chapter's main themes and underscore the most important ideas in the chapter. Then, at the beginning of each major section of a chapter, you will see a mini-chapter map that provides you with a visual organization of the key topics you are about to read in the section.

At the end of each section is Review and Reflect, in which the learning goal for the section is restated, a series of review questions related to the mini-chapter map are asked, and a question that encourages you to think critically about a topic related to the section appears. At the end of the chapter, you will come to a section titled Reach Your Learning Goals. This includes an overall chapter map that visually organizes all of the main headings, a restatement of the chapter's learning goals, and a summary of the chapter's content that is directly linked to the chapter outline at the beginning of the chapter and the questions asked in the Review part of Review and Reflect within the chapter. The summary essentially answers the questions asked in the within-chapter Review sections.

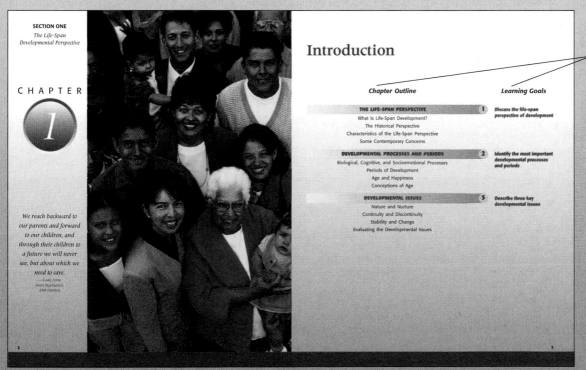

Chapter Opening Outline and Learning Goals

The outline shows the organization of topics by headings. Primary topic headings are printed in capital letters. The Learning Goals highlight the main ideas in the chapter by section.

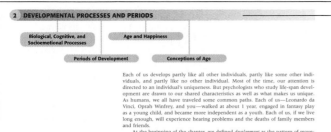

Mini-Chapter Map

This visual preview displays the main headings and subheadings for each section of the chapter.

Reach Your Learning Goals

This section includes a complete chapter map and a summary restating the Learning Goals and answering the bulleted review questions from the chapter. Use it as a guide to help you organize your study of the chapter—*not* as a substitute for reading the chapter.

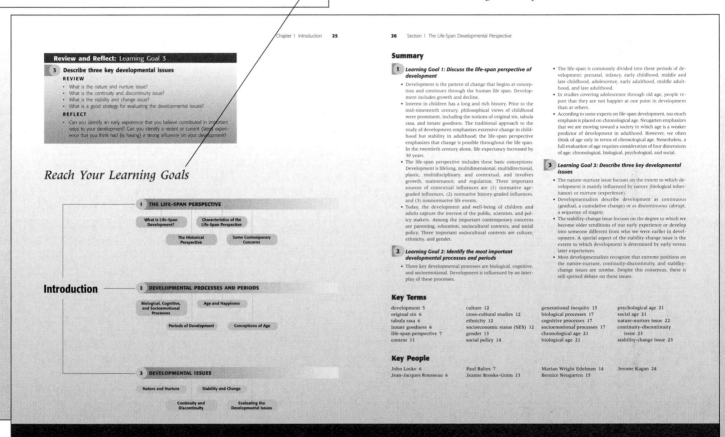

Review and Reflect

Review questions enable you to quiz yourself on the key ideas and find out whether you've met the learning goals for one section of a chapter before continuing to the next main topic. The question for reflection helps you to think about what you've just read and apply it. Answering these questions will help you to remember key points and concepts.

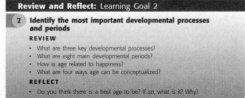

OTHER LEARNING SYSTEM FEATURES

Images of Life-Span Development
How Did Ted Kaczynski Become Ted Kaczynski and Alice Walker Become Alice Walker?

The intellectual Ted Kaczynski sprinted through high school, not bothering with his junior year and making only passing efforts at social contact. Off to Harvard at age 16, Kaczynski was a loner during his college years. One of his roommates at Harvard said that he avoided people by quickly shuffling by them and slamming the door behind him. After obtaining his Ph.D. in mathematics at the University of Michigan, Kaczynski became a professor at the University of California at Berkeley.

His colleagues there remember him as hiding from social circumstances—no friends, no allies, no networking. After several years at Berkeley, Kaczynski resigned and moved to a rural area of Montana where he lived as a hermit in a crude shack for 25 years. Town residents described him as a bearded eccentric. Kaczynski traced his own difficulties to growing up as a genius in a kid's body and sticking out like a sore thumb in his surroundings as a child. In 1996, he was arrested and charged as the notorious Unabomber, America's most wanted killer who sent 16 mail bombs in 17 years that left 23 people wounded or maimed, and 3 people dead. In 1998, he pleaded guilty to the offenses and was sentenced to life in prison.

Ted Kaczynski, the convicted Unabomber, traced his difficulties to growing up as a genius in a kid's body and not fitting in when he was a child.

A decade before Kaczynski allegedly mailed his first bomb, Alice Walker, who would later win a Pulitzer Prize for her book *The Color Purple*, spent her days battling racism in Mississippi. She had recently won her first writing fellowship, but rather than use the money to follow her dream of moving to Senegal, Africa, she put herself into the heart and heat of the civil rights movement. Walker grew up knowing the brutal effects of poverty and racism. Born in 1944, she was the eighth child of Georgia sharecroppers who earned $300 a year. When Walker was 8, her brother accidentally shot her in the left eye with a BB gun. By the time her parents got her to the hospital a week later (they had no car), she was blind in that eye and it had developed a disfiguring layer of scar tissue. Despite the counts against her, Walker went on to become an essayist, a poet, an award-winning novelist, a short-story writer, and a social activist who, like her characters (especially the women), has overcome pain and anger.

Alice Walker won the Pulitzer Prize for her book *The Color Purple*. Like the characters in her book, Walker overcame pain and anger to triumph and celebrate the human spirit.

What leads one individual, so full of promise, to commit brutal acts of violence and another to turn poverty and trauma into a rich literary harvest? If you have ever wondered why people turn out the way they do, you have asked yourself the

4

Images of Life-Span Development

Each chapter opens with a high-interest story that is linked to the chapter's content.

---

neighborhoods with high levels of violence, and unsafe play areas. Thus, intervention may need to continue beyond the early child years into the elementary school years and even adolescent years to improve the lives of children living in poverty. Other researchers are seeking ways to help families living in poverty improve their well-being (Blumenfeld & others, 2004; Clampet-Lundquist & others, 2004; Evans, 2004; McLoyd, 2005; Perry-Jenkins, 2004).

Whereas sex refers to the biological dimension of being female or male, **gender** involves the psychological and sociocultural dimensions of being female or male. Few aspects of our development are more central to our identity and social relationships than gender (Hyde, 2004; Lippa, 2005; Maracek & others, 2003; Matlin, 2004; Poelmans, 2005). Our society's attitudes about gender are changing. But how much? The gender-related topics we will discuss include these:

- The mother's role and the father's role
- Parental and peer roles in gender development
- Gender similarities and differences
- Femininity, masculinity, and androgyny
- Carol Gilligan's care perspective
- Gender communication patterns
- Family work
- Gender and aging

We will discuss sociocultural contexts and diversity in each chapter. In addition, a Diversity in Life-Span Development interlude appears in every chapter. The first one about women's international struggle for equality appears next.

gender The psychological and sociocultural dimensions of being female or male.

Diversity in Life-Span Development

Life-Span Development gives special attention to diversity issues including culture, ethnicity, and gender. Most chapters have an interlude that highlights a dimension of life-span development pertaining to diversity.

Diversity in Life-Span Development
Women's Struggle for Equality: An International Journey

The educational and psychological conditions of women around the world are a serious concern (Lakes & Carter, 2004; Malley-Morrison, 2004; Maracek & others, 2003; UNICEF, 2004). Inadequate educational opportunities, violence, and lack of political access are just some of the problems they face.

A recent analysis found that a higher percentage of girls than boys around the world have never had any education (UNICEF, 2004) (see figure 1.4). The countries with the fewest females being educated are in Africa, where in some areas girls and women are receiving no education at all. Canada, the United States, and Russia have the highest percentages of educated women. In developing countries, 67 percent of women over the age of 25 (compared with 50 percent of men) have never been to school. At the beginning of the twenty-first century, 80 million more boys than girls were in primary and secondary educational settings around the world (United Nations, 2002).

FIGURE 1.4 Percentage of Children 7 to Years of Age Around the World Who Have Never Been to School of Any Kind

---

Chapter 1 Introduction **19**

adulthood period. For example, Paul Baltes and Jacqui Smith (2003) argue that a major change takes place in older adults' lives on average at about 85 years of age (as they become the oldest old). They concluded that considerable plasticity and adaptability characterize older adults from their sixties until their mid-eighties, but that the oldest old are at the limits of their functional capacity, which makes interventions to improve their lives difficult. Here are some comparisons of the young old (which was classified as 65 through 84 in this analysis) and oldest old in terms of their functioning (Baltes & Smith, 2003):

- **The Young Old (65 to 84)**
  Increase their life expectancy with more older adults living longer
  Have considerable potential for improved physical and cognitive fitness
  Retain much of their cognitive capacity
  Can develop strategies to cope with the gains and losses of aging
- **The Oldest Old (85 and older)**
  Show considerable loss in cognitive skills
  Experience an increase in chronic stress
  Alzheimer disease more common and individuals more frail
  Dying with dignity less likely

Thus, in Baltes and Smith's analysis, the process of optimizing life is inherently more difficult for the oldest old than for the young old. Nonetheless, as we will see in chapter 18, "Physical Development in Late Adulthood," and chapter 19, "Cognitive Development in Late Adulthood," considerable variation exists in how much the oldest old, including those 100 years and older, retain their capabilities or show considerable decline. And as you will see next in the Research in Life-Span Development interlude, the contexts in which older adults are tested play an important role in how well they perform.

Research in Life-Span Development
Memory in the A.M. and P.M. and Memory for Something Meaningful

Laura Helmuth (2003) recently described how researchers are finding that certain testing conditions have exaggerated age-related declines in performance in older adults. To determine how age is related to behavior, thought, and feeling, researchers try to carefully compare participants of different ages. Participants come to the same research setting and take the same tests, for example. However, optimum testing conditions are not the same for young adults as they are for older adults. Most researchers conduct their studies in the afternoon, a convenient time for researchers and undergraduate participants. Traditional-aged college students in their late teens and early twenties are often more alert and function more optimally in the afternoon, but about 75 percent of older adults are "morning people," performing at their best early in the day (Helmuth, 2003).

Lynn Hasher and her colleagues (2001) tested the memory of college students 18 to 32 years of age and community volunteers 58 to 78 years of age in the late afternoon (about 4 to 5 P.M.) and in the morning (about 8 to 9 A.M.). Regardless of the time of day, the younger college students performed better than the older adults on the memory tests, which involved recognizing sentences from a story and memorizing a list of words. However, when the participants took the memory tests in the morning rather than in the late afternoon, the age difference in performance decreased considerably (see figure 1.7).

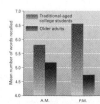

FIGURE 1.7 Memory, Age, and Time of Day Tested (A.M. or P.M.)

The traditional-aged college students performed better than older adults both in the A.M. and the P.M. However, note that the memory of the older adults was better when they were tested in the morning than in the afternoon, whereas the memory of the traditional-aged college students was not as good in the morning as it was in the afternoon.

Research in Life-Span Development

Highlighting important and recent research topics, a Research in Life-Span Development interlude appears in most chapters.

34 Section 1 The Life-Span Developmental Perspective

nursing care or other arrangements. As with other doctors, they may work in private practice, in a medical clinic, in a hospital, or in a medical school. They also may primarily treat the diseases and health problems of older adults, but geriatric physicians in medical school settings also may teach future physicians and conduct research.

Neonatal Nurse

A neonatal nurse is involved in the delivery of care to the newborn infant. The neonatal nurse may work to improve the health and well-being of infants born under normal circumstances or be involved in the delivery of care to premature and critically ill neonates. A minimum of an undergraduate degree in nursing with a specialization in the newborn is required. This training involves coursework in nursing and the biological sciences, as well as supervisory clinical experiences.

Nurse-Midwife

A nurse-midwife formulates and provides comprehensive care to selected maternity patients, cares for the expectant mother as she prepares to give birth and guides her through the birth process, and cares for the postpartum patient. The nurse-midwife also may provide care to the newborn, counsel parents on the infant's development and parenting, and provide guidance about health practices. Becoming a nurse-midwife generally requires an undergraduate degree from a school of nursing. A nurse-midwife most often works in a hospital setting.

Pediatric Nurse

Pediatric nurses have a degree in nursing that takes two to five years to complete. Some also may go on to obtain a master's or doctoral degree in pediatric nursing. Pediatric nurses take courses in biological sciences, nursing care, and pediatrics, usually in a school of nursing. They also undergo supervised clinical experiences in medical settings.

They monitor infants' and children's health, work to prevent disease or injury, and help children attain optimal health. They may work in hospitals, schools of nursing, or with pediatricians in private practice or at a medical clinic.

Geriatric Nurse

Geriatric nurses seek to prevent or intervene in the chronic or acute health problems of older adults. They take courses in a school of nursing and obtain a degree in nursing. This takes anywhere from two to five years. As in the case of a pediatric nurse, a geriatric nurse also may obtain a master's or doctoral degree in his or her specialty.

Geriatric nurses take courses in biological sciences, nursing care, and mental health. They also experience supervised clinical training in geriatric settings. They may work in hospitals, nursing homes, schools of nursing, or with geriatric medical specialists or psychiatrists in a medical clinic or in private practice.

Physical Therapist

Physical therapists usually have an undergraduate degree in physical therapy and are licensed by a state. They take courses and experience supervised training in physical therapy. Many physical therapists work with people of all ages, although some specialize in working with a specific age group, such as children or older adults. They work directly with these individuals who have a physical problem either due to disease or injury to help them function as competently as possible. They may consult with other professionals and coordinate services for the individual.

8 Section 1 The Life-Span Developmental Perspective

Careers in Life-Span Development

K. Warner Schaie, Professor of Human Development

K. Warner Schaie is a professor of human development and psychology at Pennsylvania State University, where he teaches and conducts research on adult development and aging. He also directs the Gerontology Center there. He is one of the pioneering psychologists who helped to create the life-span perspective. He is the author or editor of more than 25 books and more than 250 journal articles and book chapters on adult development and aging. Dr. Schaie conducted the Seattle Longitudinal Study of intellectual development, a major research investigation which revealed that many intellectual skills are maintained or even increase in middle age.

Life-span developmentalist K. Warner Schaie *(right)* with two older adults who are actively using their cognitive skills.

www.mhhe.com/santrockldt10

Exploring Aging Issues
National Aging Information Center
Global Resources on Aging
Adult Development and Aging
The Gerontological Society of America
Geropsychology Resources

there are many components, such as abstract intelligence, nonverbal intelligence, and social intelligence. You can read about K. Warner Schaie, a leading theorist and researcher who has studied intellectual development in the adulthood years, in the Careers in Life-Span Development insert.

Development Is Multidirectional Throughout life, some dimensions or components of a dimension expand and others shrink. In language development, when one language (such as English) is acquired early in development, the capacity for acquiring second and third languages (such as French and Spanish) decreases later in development, especially after early childhood (Levelt, 1989). In socioemotional development, individuals begin to have more contact with opposite-sex peers during adolescence. As they establish emotional or sexual relationships, their relationships with friends might decrease. In cognitive development, older adults might become wiser by being able to call on experience to guide their intellectual decision making (Baltes & Kunzmann, 2003). However, they perform more poorly on tasks that require speed in processing information (Li & others, 2004; Madden, 2001; Salthouse, 2000).

Development Is Plastic A key developmental research agenda is the search for plasticity and its constraints (Kagan & Herschkowitz, 2005; Maurer, 2001; Prickaerts & others, 2004). *Plasticity* means the capacity for change. For example, can intellectual skills still be improved through education for individuals in their seventies or eighties? Or might these intellectual skills be fixed by the time people are in their thirties so that further improvement is impossible? In one research study, the reasoning abilities of older adults were improved through retraining (Willis & Schaie, 1994). However, developmentalists debate how much plasticity people have at different points in their development; possibly we possess less capacity for change when we become old (Baltes, 2003; Baltes & Smith, 2003; Singer, Lindenberger, & Baltes, 2003). Later in the chapter we will discuss the issue of stability and change in development, which has close ties with the concept of plasticity.

Development Is Multidisciplinary Psychologists, sociologists, anthropologists, neuroscientists, and medical researchers all study human development and share an interest in unlocking the mysteries of development through the life span. Research questions that cut across disciplines include:

- What constraints on intelligence are set by the individual's heredity and health status?
- How universal are cognitive and socioemotional changes?
- How do environmental contexts influence intellectual development?

Development Is Contextual The individual continually responds to and acts on contexts, which include a person's biological makeup, physical environment, cognitive processes, historical contexts, social contexts, and cultural contexts. The contextual

Careers in Life-Span Development

Every chapter has one or more Careers in Life-Span Development inserts, which feature a person working in a life-span field related to the chapter's content.

A Careers in Life-Span Development Appendix that describes a number of careers appears between chapter 1 and chapter 2.

Chapter 1 Introduction 23

that a genetic blueprint produces commonalities in growth and development. We walk before we talk, speak one word before two words, grow rapidly in infancy and less so in early childhood, experience a rush of sexual hormones in puberty, reach the peak of our physical strength in late adolescence and early adulthood, and then physically decline. The nature proponents acknowledge that extreme environments—those that are psychologically barren or hostile—can depress development. However, they believe that basic growth tendencies are genetically wired into humans.

By contrast, other psychologists emphasize the importance of nurture, or environmental experiences, in development. Experiences run the gamut from the individual's biological environment (nutrition, medical care, drugs, and physical accidents) to the social environment (family, peers, schools, community, media, and culture) (Garbarino, Bradshaw, & Kostelny, 2005; Gottlieb, 2004).

Continuity and Discontinuity

Think about your own development for a moment. Did you become the person you are gradually, like the seedling that slowly, cumulatively grows into a giant oak? Or did you experience sudden, distinct changes in your growth, like the caterpillar that changes into a butterfly (see figure 1.11)? For the most part, developmentalists who emphasize nurture usually describe development as a gradual, continuous process. Those who emphasize nature often describe development as a series of distinct stages.

The **continuity-discontinuity issue** focuses on the extent to which development involves gradual, cumulative change (continuity) or distinct stages (discontinuity). In terms of continuity, as the oak grows from seedling to giant oak, it becomes a larger version of what it was—its development is continuous. Similarly, a child's first word, though seemingly an abrupt, discontinuous event, is actually the result of weeks and months of growth and practice. Puberty, another seemingly abrupt, discontinuous occurrence, is actually a gradual process occurring over several years.

In terms of discontinuity, each person is described as passing through a sequence of stages in which change is qualitatively rather than quantitatively different. As the caterpillar changes to a butterfly, it is not just a larger caterpillar, it is a *different kind* of organism—its development is discontinuous. Similarly, at some point a child moves from not being able to think abstractly about the world to being able to. This is a qualitative, discontinuous change in development, not a quantitative, continuous change.

Stability and Change

Another important developmental topic is the **stability-change issue,** which addresses whether development is best described by stability or change. The stability-change issue involves the degree to which we become older renditions of our early experience (stability) or whether we develop into someone different from who we were at an earlier point in development (change). Will the shy child who hides behind the sofa when visitors arrive be a wallflower at college dances, or will the child become a sociable, talkative individual? Will the fun-loving, carefree adolescent have difficulty holding down a 9-to-5 job as an adult or become a straitlaced, serious conformist?

The stability-change issue is linked with Paul Baltes' (1987, 2003) view, which we discussed earlier, that plasticity or change is an important life-span issue. Recall that in the life-span perspective, plasticity or change is possible throughout the life span, although experts such as Baltes argue that older adults often show less capacity for change than younger adults (Singer, Lindenberger, & Baltes, 2003).

One of the reasons why adult development was ignored by researchers until fairly recently was the predominant belief for many years that nothing much changes in adulthood. The major changes were believed to take place in childhood, especially during the first five years of life. Today, most developmentalists conclude that some change is possible throughout the human life span, although they disagree, sometimes vehemently, about just how much change can take place, and how much stability there is.

The video titled "Intelligence: The Nature and Nurture of Twins" considers these biological and environmental experience issues as they relate to the development of identical twins Cory and Eric.

FIGURE 1.11 Continuity and Discontinuity in Development
Is our development like that of a seedling gradually growing into a giant oak? Or is it more like that of a caterpillar suddenly becoming a butterfly?

continuity-discontinuity issue Focuses on the extent to which development involves gradual, cumulative change (continuity) or distinct stages (discontinuity).

stability-change issue Involves the degree to which we become older renditions of our early experience (stability) or whether we develop into someone different from who we were at an earlier point in development (change).

Key Terms and Glossary

Key terms appear in boldface. Their definitions appear in the margin near where they are introduced.

Key Terms

development 5	culture 12	generational inequity 15	psychological age 21
original sin 6	cross-cultural studies 12	biological processes 17	social age 21
tabula rasa 6	ethnicity 12	cognitive processes 17	nature-nurture issue 22
innate goodness 6	socioeconomic status (SES) 12	socioemotional processes 17	continuity-discontinuity
life-span perspective 7	gender 13	chronological age 21	issue 23
context 11	social policy 14	biological age 21	stability-change issue 23

Key People

John Locke 6	Paul Baltes 7	Marian Wright Edelman 14	Jerome Kagan 24
Jean-Jacques Rousseau 6	Jeanne Brooks-Gunn 13	Bernice Neugarten 15	

Key terms also are listed and page-referenced at the end of each chapter.

Key terms are alphabetically listed, defined, and page-referenced in a Glossary at the end of the book.

G–2 Glossary

constructive play Play that combines sensorimotor and repetitive activity with symbolic representation of ideas. Constructive play occurs when children engage in self-regulated creation or construction of a product or a problem solution. 283

contemporary life-events approach Emphasizes that how a life event influences the individual's development depends not only on the life event, but also on mediating factors, the individual's adaptation to the life event, the life-stage context, and the sociohistorical context. 283

context The setting in which development occurs, which is influenced by historical, economic, social, and cultural factors. 11

continuity-discontinuity issue Focuses on the extent to which development involves gradual, cumulative change (continuity) or distinct stages (discontinuity). 23

controversial children Children who are frequently nominated both as someone's best friend and as being disliked. 347

conventional reasoning The second, or intermediate, level in Kohlberg's theory of moral development. At this level, individuals abide by certain standards but they are the standards of others such as parents or the laws of society. 334

convergent thinking Thinking that produces one correct answer and is characteristic of the kind of thinking tested by standardized intelligence tests. 306

cooperative play Play that involves social interaction in a group with a sense of group identity and organized activity. 282

coordination of secondary circular reactions Piaget's fourth sensorimotor substage, which develops between 8 and 12 months of age. In this substage, several significant changes take place involving the coordination of schemes and intentionality. 176

correlational research The goal is to describe the strength of the relationship between two or more events or [char]acteristics. 59

[cre]ative thinking The ability to think in [no]vel and unusual ways and to come up [wi]th unique solutions to problems. 306

[cri]sis Marcia's term for a period of identity [de]velopment during which the adolescent is [cho]osing among meaningful alternatives. 399

[cri]tical thinking Thinking reflectively and [pro]ductively, as well as evaluating the [evi]dence. 55

[cr]oss-cultural studies Comparisons of one [cul]ture with one or more other cultures. [The]se provide information about the degree

to which development is similar, or universal, across cultures, and to the degree to which it is culture-specific. 12

cross-sectional approach A research strategy in which individuals of different ages are compared at one time. 60

crowd A larger group structure than a clique, a crowd is usually formed based on reputation and members may or may not spend much time together. 409

crystallized intelligence Accumulated information and verbal skills, which increase with age, according to Horn. 513

cultural-familial retardation Retardation that is characterized by no evidence of organic brain damage, but the individual's IQ is between 50 and 70. 318

culture The behavior patterns, beliefs, and all other products of a group that are passed on from generation to generation. 12

culture-fair tests Tests of intelligence that are designed to be free of cultural bias. 316

Date or acquaintance rape Coercive sexual activity directed at someone with whom the perpetrator is at least casually acquainted. 450

dating scripts The cognitive models that individuals use to guide and evaluate dating interactions. 411

deferred imitation Imitation that occurs after a time delay of hours or days. 181

dementia A global term for any neurological disorder in which the primary symptoms involve a deterioration of mental functioning. 596

denial and isolation Kübler-Ross' first stage of dying, in which the dying person denies that she or he is really going to die. 643

depression Kübler-Ross' fourth stage of dying, in which the dying person comes to accept the certainty of her or his death. A period of depression or preparatory grief may appear. 644

descriptive research Has the purpose of observing and recording behavior. 55

development The pattern of change that begins at conception and continues through the life span. Most development involves growth, although it also includes decline brought on by aging and dying. 5

developmental quotient (DQ) An overall developmental score that combines subscores in motor, language, adaptive, and personal/social domains in the Gesell assessment of infants. 183

developmentally appropriate practice Education that focuses on the typical developmental patterns of children (age-appropriateness) and the uniqueness of each child (individual-appropriateness). 247

differentiation versus role preoccupation One of the three developmental tasks of aging described by Peck, in which older adults must redefine their worth in terms of something other than work roles. 609

difficult child A child who tends to react negatively and cry frequently, who engages in irregular daily routines, and who is slow to accept new experiences. 205

direct instruction approach A teacher-centered approach characterized by teacher direction and control, mastery of academic skills, high expectations for students, and maximum time spent on learning tasks. 350

disease model of addiction The view that addictions are biologically based, lifelong diseases that involve a loss of control over behavior and require medical and/or spiritual treatment for recovery. 444

disengagement theory The theory that to cope effectively, older adults should gradually withdraw from society. 611

dishabituation Recovery of an habituated response after a change in stimulation. 159

divergent thinking Thinking that produces many answers to the same question and is characteristic of creativity. 306

divided attention Concentrating on more than one activity at the same time. 584

DNA A complex molecule that contains genetic information. 80

doula A caregiver who provides continuous physical, emotional, and educational support for the mother before, during, and after childbirth. 120

Down syndrome A chromosomally transmitted form of mental retardation, caused by the presence of an extra copy of chromosome 21. 85

dynamic systems theory The perspective on motor development that seeks to explain how motor behaviors are assembled for perceiving and acting. 150

dyslexia A category of learning disabilities involving a severe impairment in the ability to read and spell. 298

Easy child A child who is generally in a positive mood, who quickly establishes regular routines in infancy, and who adapts easily to new experiences. 205

Chapter 1 Introduction **11**

- The best way to parent
- Support systems for families
- Marital relationships
- Intergenerational relations
- Aging parents

Research on Family and Peer Relations One issue that interests researchers who study families and parents focuses on links between family and peer functioning. In one recent study of maltreated children (children who have been abused) and nonmaltreated children, the maltreated children were more likely to be repeatedly rejected by their peers across the childhood and adolescent years (Bolger & Patterson, 2001). The main reason for the rejection was the high rate of aggressive behavior shown by the children who had been abused by their parents. Why do you think the abuse by parents resulted in more aggression toward their peers by the children? We will have more to say about maltreated children in chapter 9, "Socioemotional Development in Early Childhood."

Education In the past 10 to 15 years, the American educational system has been sharply criticized (Marzano, Pickering, & Pollock, 2005; Pintrich & Maehler, 2004; Sadker & Sadker, 2005; Schunk, 2005). A national committee appointed by the Office of Education concluded that children are being poorly prepared for the increasingly complex future they will face. The educational topics we will explore include these:

- Variations in early childhood education
- Ethnicity, poverty, and schools
- Programs to improve children's critical thinking
- School and family coordination
- Bilingual education
- The best schools for adolescents

Research on Mentoring Mentoring programs are increasingly being advocated as a strategy for improving the achievement of children and adolescents who are at risk for academic failure (Hamilton & Hamilton, 2004). One study focused on 959 adolescents who had applied to the Big Brothers/Big Sisters program (Rhodes, Grossman, & Resch, 2000). Half of the adolescents were mentored through extensive discussions about school, careers, and life, as well as participation in leisure activities with other adolescents. The other half were not mentored. Mentoring led to reduced unexcused absences from school, improvements in classroom performance, and better relationships with parents.

Sociocultural Contexts and Diversity The tapestry of American culture has changed dramatically in recent years. Nowhere is the change more dramatic than in the increasing diversity of America's citizens. The diversity occurs in terms of ethnicity, gender, sexual orientation, ability/disability, national origin, and religion. This changing demographic tapestry promises not only the richness that diversity produces, but also difficult challenges in extending the American dream to all individuals (Books, 2004; Fuligni & others, 2005; Poelmans, 2005).

Sociocultural contexts include five important concepts: context, culture, ethnicity, socioeconomic status (SES), and gender. A **context** is the setting in which development occurs. This setting is influenced by historical, economic, social, and cultural factors. Contexts include families, schools, peer groups, churches, cities, neighborhoods, university laboratories, countries, and many others. Each of these settings has meaningful historical, economic, social, and cultural legacies (Leyendecker & others, 2005; Matsumoto, 2004; Triandis, 2003; Yang, 2005).

Children learn to love when they are loved

www.mhhe.com/santrockld10

Health Links
Educator's Reference Desk
Diversity
Social Policy
Trends in the Well-Being of
Children and Youth

context The setting in which development occurs, which is influenced by historical, economic, social, and cultural factors.

Web Links

Web icons appear a number of times in each chapter. They signal you to go to the book's website where you will find connecting links that provide additional information on the topic discussed in the text.

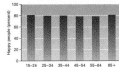

Chapter 1 Introduction **21**

adulthood years were found (Inglehart, 1990) (see figure 1.9). About the same percentage of people in each age group—slightly less than 20 percent—reported that they were "very happy."

Why might older people report as much happiness and life satisfaction as younger people? Every period of the life span has its stresses, pluses and minuses, hills and valleys. Although adolescents must cope with developing an identity, feelings of insecurity, mood swings, and peer pressure, the majority of adolescents develop positive perceptions of themselves, feelings of competence about their skills, positive relationships with friends and family, and an optimistic view of their future. And while older adults face a life of reduced income, less energy, decreasing physical skills, and concerns about death, they are also less pressured to achieve and succeed, have more time for leisurely pursuits, and have accumulated many years of experience that help them adapt to their circumstances with a wisdom they may not have had in their younger years. Because growing older is a certain outcome of living, we can derive considerable pleasure from knowing that we are likely to be just as happy as older adults as when we were younger.

FIGURE 1.9 Age and Happiness
Analysis of surveys of nearly 170,000 people in 16 countries found no age differences in happiness from adolescence into the late adulthood years.

Conceptions of Age

In our description of the periods of the life span, we associated an approximate age range with each. However, life-span expert Bernice Neugarten (1988) emphasizes that we are rapidly becoming an age-irrelevant society. She says we are already familiar with the 28-year-old mayor, the 35-year-old grandmother, the 65-year-old father of a preschooler, the 55-year-old widow who starts a business, and the 70-year-old student. Neugarten stresses that choices and dilemmas do not spring forth at 10-year intervals. Decisions are not made and then left behind as if they were merely beads on a chain. Neugarten argues that most adulthood themes appear and reappear throughout the human life span. The issues of intimacy and freedom can haunt couples throughout their relationship. Feeling the pressure of time, reformulating goals, and coping with success and failure are not the exclusive property of adults of a particular age.

Neugarten's ideas raise questions about how age should be conceptualized. Some of the ways in which age has been conceptualized are as chronological age, biological age, psychological age, and social age (Hoyer & Roodin, 2003):

- **Chronological age** is the number of years that have elapsed since birth. Many people consider chronological age to be synonymous with the concept of age. However, some developmentalists argue that chronological age is not very relevant to understanding a person's psychological development (Botwinick, 1978). Time is a crude index of many events and experiences, and it does not cause anything.
- **Biological age** is a person's age in terms of biological health. Determining biological age involves knowing the functional capacities of a person's vital organs. One person's vital capacities may be better or worse than those of others of comparable age. The younger the person's biological age, the longer the person is expected to live, regardless of chronological age.
- **Psychological age** is an individual's adaptive capacities compared with those of other individuals of the same chronological age. Thus, older adults who continue to learn are flexible, are motivated, control their emotions, and think clearly who are engaging in more adaptive behaviors than their chronological age-mates who do not continue to learn, are rigid, are unmotivated, do not control their emotions, and do not think clearly.
- **Social age** refers to social roles and expectations related to a person's age. Consider the role of "mother" and the behaviors that accompany the role

How old would you be if you didn't know how old you were?
—SATCHEL PAIGE
American Baseball Pitcher, 20th Century

chronological age The number of years that have elapsed since birth.

biological age A person's age in terms of biological health.

psychological age An individual's adaptive capacities compared with those of other individuals of the same chronological age.

social age Social roles and expectations related to a person's age.

Quotations

These appear at the beginning of the chapter and occasionally in the margins to stimulate further thought about a topic.

---

12 Section 1 The Life-Span Developmental Perspective

Two Korean-born children on the day they became United States citizens. Asian American and Latino children are the fastest-growing immigrant groups in the United States. *How diverse are the students in this class on life-span development that you now are taking? How are their experiences in growing up likely similar to or different from yours?*

Culture encompasses the behavior patterns, beliefs, and all other products of a particular group of people that are passed on from generation to generation. Culture results from the interaction of people over many years. A cultural group can be as large as the United States or as small as an African hunter-gatherer group. Whatever its size, the group's culture influences the behavior of its members (Saraswathi & Mistry, 2003). **Cross-cultural studies** involve a comparison of a culture with one or more other cultures. The comparison provides information about the degree to which development is similar, or universal, across cultures, or is instead culture-specific. For example, the United States is an achievement-oriented culture with a strong work ethic. However, cross-cultural studies of American and Japanese children showed that Japanese children are better at math, spend more time working on math at school, and do more math homework than American children (Stevenson, 1995, 2000). The topics on culture that we will discuss include:

- Child-care policy around the world
- Vygotsky's sociocultural cognitive theory
- Gender roles in Egypt and China
- Cross-cultural comparisons of secondary schools
- Marriage around the world
- Death and dying in different cultures

Ethnicity (the word *ethnic* comes from the Greek word for "nation") is rooted in cultural heritage, nationality characteristics, race, religion, and language. Not only does ethnic diversity exist with a culture such as found in the United States, diversity also exists within each ethnic group. These groups include African Americans, Latinos, Asian Americans, Native Americans, Polish Americans, Italian Americans, and so on. Not all African Americans live in low-income circumstances. Not all Latinos are Catholics. Not all Asian Americans are high school math whizzes. It is easy to fall into the trap of stereotyping an ethnic group by thinking that all of its members are alike. A more accurate ethnic group portrayal is diversity (Jenkins & others, 2003; Koppelman & Goodhart, 2005; Powell & Caseau, 2004; Sheets, 2005).

Among the ethnicity topics we will examine in later chapters are:

- Similarities, differences, and diversity
- Immigration
- Support systems for ethnic minority individuals
- Ethnicity and schooling
- Value conflicts
- Being old, female, and ethnic

culture The behavior patterns, beliefs, and all other products of a group that are passed on from generation to generation.

cross-cultural studies Comparisons of one culture with one or more other cultures. These provide information about the degree to which development is similar, or universal, across cultures, and to the degree to which it is culture-specific.

ethnicity A characteristic based on cultural heritage, nationality characteristics, race, religion, and language.

socioeconomic status (SES) Refers to the grouping of people with similar occupational, educational, and economic characteristics.

Race and ethnicity are sometimes misrepresented. *Race* is a controversial classification of people according to real or imagined biological characteristics such as skin color and blood group membership (Corsini, 1999). An individual's ethnicity can include his or her race but also many other characteristics. Thus, an individual might be White (a racial category) and a fifth-generation Texan who is a Catholic and speaks English and Spanish fluently.

Socioeconomic status (SES) refers to the grouping of people with similar occupational, educational, and economic characteristics. Socioeconomic status implies certain inequalities. Generally, members of a society have (1) occupations that vary in prestige, and some individuals have more access than others to higher-status occupations; (2) different levels of educational attainment, and some individuals have more access than others to better education; (3) different economic resources; and (4) different levels of power to influence a community's institutions. These differences in the ability to control resources and to participate in society's rewards produce unequal opportunities for children.

Critical Thinking and Content Questions in Photograph Captions

Most photographs have a caption that ends with a critical thinking or knowledge question in italics to stimulate further thought about a topic.

Summary

1 *Learning Goal 1: Discuss the life-span perspective of development*

- Development is the pattern of change that begins at conception and continues through the human life span. Development includes growth and decline.
- Interest in children has a long and rich history. Prior to the mid-nineteenth century, philosophical views of childhood were prominent, including the notions of original sin, tabula rasa, and innate goodness. The traditional approach to the study of development emphasizes extensive change in childhood but stability in adulthood; the life-span perspective emphasizes that change is possible throughout the life span. In the twentieth century alone, life expectancy increased by 30 years.
- The life-span perspective includes these basic conceptions: Development is lifelong, multidimensional, multidirectional, plastic, multidisciplinary, and contextual, and involves growth, maintenance, and regulation. Three important sources of contextual influences are (1) normative age-graded influences, (2) normative history-graded influences, and (3) nonnormative life events.
- Today, the development and well-being of children and adults capture the interest of the public, scientists, and policy makers. Among the important contemporary concerns are parenting, education, sociocultural contexts, and social policy. Three important sociocultural contexts are culture, ethnicity, and gender.

2 *Learning Goal 2: Identify the most important developmental processes and periods*

- Three key developmental processes are biological, cognitive, and socioemotional. Development is influenced by an interplay of these processes.

- The life-span is commonly divided into these periods of development: prenatal, infancy, early childhood, middle and late childhood, adolescence, early adulthood, middle adulthood, and late adulthood.
- In studies covering adolescence through old age, people report that they are not happier at one point in development than at others.
- According to some experts on life-span development, too much emphasis is placed on chronological age. Neugarten emphasizes that we are moving toward a society in which age is a weaker predictor of development in adulthood. However, we often think of age only in terms of chronological age. Nonetheless, a full evaluation of age requires consideration of four dimensions of age: chronological, biological, psychological, and social.

3 *Learning Goal 3: Describe three key developmental issues*

- The nature-nurture issue focuses on the extent to which development is mainly influenced by nature (biological inheritance) or nurture (experience).
- Developmentalists describe development as continuous (gradual, a cumulative change) or as discontinuous (abrupt, a sequence of stages).
- The stability-change issue focuses on the degree to which we become older renditions of our early experience or develop into someone different from who we were earlier in development. A special aspect of the stability-change issue is the extent to which development is determined by early versus later experiences.
- Most developmentalists recognize that extreme positions on the nature-nurture, continuity-discontinuity, and stability-change issues are unwise. Despite this consensus, there is still spirited debate on these issues.

Key Terms

development 5	culture 12	generational inequity 15	psychological age 21
original sin 6	cross-cultural studies 12	biological processes 17	social age 21
tabula rasa 6	ethnicity 12	cognitive processes 17	nature-nurture issue 22
innate goodness 6	socioeconomic status (SES) 12	socioemotional processes 17	continuity-discontinuity
life-span perspective 7	gender 13	chronological age 21	issue 23
context 11	social policy 14	biological age 21	stability-change issue 23

Key People

John Locke 6	Paul Baltes 7	Marian Wright Edelman 14	Jerome Kagan 24
Jean-Jacques Rousseau 6	Jeanne Brooks-Gunn 13	Bernice Neugarten 15	

Key People

The most important theorists and researchers in a chapter are listed and page-referenced at the end of each chapter.

---

that a genetic blueprint produces commonalities in growth and development. We walk before we talk, speak one word before two words, grow rapidly in infancy and less so in early childhood, experience a rush of sexual hormones in puberty, reach the peak of our physical strength in late adolescence and early adulthood, and then physically decline. The nature proponents acknowledge that extreme environments—those that are psychologically barren or hostile—can depress development. However, they believe that basic growth tendencies are genetically wired into humans.

By contrast, other psychologists emphasize the importance of nurture, or environmental experiences, in development. Experiences run the gamut from the individual's biological environment (nutrition, medical care, drugs, and physical accidents) to the social environment (family, peers, schools, community, media, and culture) (Garbarino, Bradshaw, & Kostelny, 2005; Gottlieb, 2004).

Continuity and Discontinuity

Think about your own development for a moment. Did you become the person you are gradually, like the seedling that slowly, cumulatively grows into a giant oak? Or did you experience sudden, distinct changes in your growth, like the caterpillar that changes into a butterfly (see figure 1.11)? For the most part, developmentalists who emphasize nurture usually describe development as a gradual, continuous process. Those who emphasize nature often describe development as a series of distinct stages.

The **continuity-discontinuity issue** focuses on the extent to which development involves gradual, cumulative change (continuity) or distinct stages (discontinuity). In terms of continuity, as the oak grows from seedling to giant oak, it becomes a larger version of what it was—its development is continuous. Similarly, a child's first word, though seemingly an abrupt, discontinuous event, is actually the result of weeks and months of growth and practice. Puberty, another seemingly abrupt, discontinuous occurrence, is actually a gradual process occurring over several years.

In terms of discontinuity, each person is described as passing through a sequence of stages in which change is qualitatively rather than quantitatively different. As the caterpillar changes to a butterfly, it is not just a larger caterpillar, it is a *different kind of* organism—its development is discontinuous. Similarly, at some point a child moves from not being able to think abstractly about the world to being able to. This is a qualitative, discontinuous change in development, not a quantitative, continuous change.

Stability and Change

Another important developmental topic is the **stability-change issue,** which addresses whether development is best described by stability or change. The stability-change issue involves the degree to which we become older renditions of our early experience (stability) or whether we develop into someone different from who we were at an earlier point in development (change). Will the shy child who hides behind the sofa when visitors arrive be a wallflower at college dances, or will the child become a sociable, talkative individual? Will the fun-loving, carefree adolescent have difficulty holding down a 9-to-5 job as an adult or become a straitlaced, serious conformist?

The stability-change issue is linked with Paul Baltes' (1987, 200_) we discussed earlier, that plasticity or change is an important life-sp_ that in the life-span perspective, plasticity or change is possible thro_ span, although experts such as Baltes argue that older adults often s_ ity for change than younger adults (Singer, Lindenberger, & Baltes,_

One of the reasons why adult development was ignored by resear_ recently was the predominant belief for many years that nothing m_ adulthood. The major changes were believed to take place in childhood_ ing the first five years of life. Today, most developmentalists conclude t_ is possible throughout the human life span, although they disagree, _ mently, about just how much change can take place, and how much_

The video titled "Intelligence: The Nature and Nurture of Twins" considers these biological and environmental experience issues as they relate to the development of identical twins Cory and Eric.

Continuity,

Discontinuity

FIGURE 1.11 Continuity and Discontinuity in Development
Is our development like that of a seedling gradually growing into a giant oak? Or is it more like that of a caterpillar suddenly becoming a butterfly?

Video

In the margins are icons directing you to the LifeMap CD-ROM that accompanies the book. There you'll find one or more videos for each chapter.

E-LEARNING TOOLS

Online Learning Center

At the end of each chapter you are guided to exercises in Self-Assessment; Taking It to the Net; and Health and Well-Being, Parenting, and Education. These resources and more are found on the Online Learning Center for Santrock, *Life-Span Development,* tenth edition, at www.mhhe.com/santrockld10.

E-Learning Tools

To help you master the material in this chapter, you'll find a number of valuable study tools on the LifeMap CD-ROM that accompanies this book and on the Online Learning Center for *Life-Span Development,* tenth edition, at www.mhhe.com/santrockld10.

Video Clips

In the margins of this book there are icons directing you to the LifeMap CD-ROM that accompanies the book. In chapter 1 you'll find a video called "Intelligence: The Nature and Nurture of Twins." This segment examines the nature-nurture connection by tracing the development of identical twins Cory and Eric.

Self-Assessment

Connect to www.mhhe.com/santrockld10 to learn more about your career options by completing the self-assessment, *Evaluating My Interest in a Career in Life-Span Development.*

Taking It to the Net

Connect to www.mhhe.com/santrockld10 to research the answers to these questions.

1. Janice plans to join a small family practice group upon completion of her medical school pediatrician residency. Why should Janice, as a pediatrician, be involved in detecting and helping to prevent violence in the lives of her young patients?
2. Derrick has heard about a recent book that has stirred up a lot of controversy about the role of parents and peers in development. What is the book, what is its premise, and why has it generated so many strong feelings?
3. Carmen is completing her Ph.D. in clinical psychology. She is interested in geropsychology. What are some of the areas in which geropsychologists might conduct research and practice?

Health and Well-Being, Parenting, and Education Exercises

Build your decision-making skills by trying your hand at the health and well-being, parenting, and education exercises.

Connect to www.mhhe.com/santrockld10 **to research the answers and complete the exercises.**

Life-Span Development

CHAPTER

We reach backward to our parents and forward to our children, and through their children to a future we will never see, but about which we need to care.

—CARL JUNG
Swiss Psychiatrist, 20th Century

Introduction

Chapter Outline	*Learning Goals*

THE LIFE-SPAN PERSPECTIVE

> 1   Discuss the life-span perspective of development

What Is Life-Span Development?

The Historical Perspective

Characteristics of the Life-Span Perspective

Some Contemporary Concerns

DEVELOPMENTAL PROCESSES AND PERIODS

> 2   Identify the most important developmental processes and periods

Biological, Cognitive, and Socioemotional Processes

Periods of Development

Age and Happiness

Conceptions of Age

DEVELOPMENTAL ISSUES

> 3   Describe three key developmental issues

Nature and Nurture

Continuity and Discontinuity

Stability and Change

Evaluating the Developmental Issues

Images of Life-Span Development
How Did Ted Kaczynski Become Ted Kaczynski and Alice Walker Become Alice Walker?

Ted Kaczynski, the convicted Unabomber, traced his difficulties to growing up as a genius in a kid's body and not fitting in when he was a child.

Alice Walker won the Pulitzer Prize for her book *The Color Purple*. Like the characters in her book, Walker overcame pain and anger to triumph and celebrate the human spirit.

The intellectual Ted Kaczynski sprinted through high school, not bothering with his junior year and making only passing efforts at social contact. Off to Harvard at age 16, Kaczynski was a loner during his college years. One of his roommates at Harvard said that he avoided people by quickly shuffling by them and slamming the door behind him. After obtaining his Ph.D. in mathematics at the University of Michigan, Kaczynski became a professor at the University of California at Berkeley.

His colleagues there remember him as hiding from social circumstances—no friends, no allies, no networking. After several years at Berkeley, Kaczynski resigned and moved to a rural area of Montana where he lived as a hermit in a crude shack for 25 years. Town residents described him as a bearded eccentric. Kaczynski traced his own difficulties to growing up as a genius in a kid's body and sticking out like a sore thumb in his surroundings as a child. In 1996, he was arrested and charged as the notorious Unabomber, America's most wanted killer who sent 16 mail bombs in 17 years that left 23 people wounded or maimed, and 3 people dead. In 1998, he pleaded guilty to the offenses and was sentenced to life in prison.

A decade before Kaczynski allegedly mailed his first bomb, Alice Walker, who would later win a Pulitzer Prize for her book *The Color Purple*, spent her days battling racism in Mississippi. She had recently won her first writing fellowship, but rather than use the money to follow her dream of moving to Senegal, Africa, she put herself into the heart and heat of the civil rights movement. Walker grew up knowing the brutal effects of poverty and racism. Born in 1944, she was the eighth child of Georgia sharecroppers who earned $300 a year. When Walker was 8, her brother accidentally shot her in the left eye with a BB gun. By the time her parents got her to the hospital a week later (they had no car), she was blind in that eye and it had developed a disfiguring layer of scar tissue. Despite the counts against her, Walker went on to become an essayist, a poet, an award-winning novelist, a short-story writer, and a social activist who, like her characters (especially the women), has overcome pain and anger.

What leads one individual, so full of promise, to commit brutal acts of violence and another to turn poverty and trauma into a rich literary harvest? If you have ever wondered why people turn out the way they do, you have asked yourself the central question we will explore in this book.

PREVIEW

This chapter previews the themes and issues that we will consider throughout our study of life-span development. First, we will familiarize ourselves with the life-span perspective, then we will explore the processes and periods that characterize human development. Finally, we will examine the primary issues that developmentalists debate, issues that will come up repeatedly in this text.

1 **THE LIFE-SPAN PERSPECTIVE**

What Is Life-Span Development?

Characteristics of the Life-Span Perspective

The Historical Perspective

Some Contemporary Concerns

Why study life-span development? Perhaps you are or will be a parent or teacher, and responsibility for children is or will be a part of your everyday life. The more you learn about children, the better you can guide them. Perhaps you hope to gain an understanding of your own history—as an infant, a child, an adolescent, or a young adult. Perhaps you want to know what your life will be like as you grow into middle age or old age. Whatever your reasons, you will discover that the study of life-span development is provocative, intriguing, and informative. The life-span perspective offers insights into who we are, how we came to be this way, and where our future will take us.

What Is Life-Span Development?

Development is the pattern of change that begins at conception and continues throughout the human life span. Most development involves growth, although it also includes decline brought on by aging and dying. Thus, we will explore development from the point in time when life begins until the time when it ends. You will see yourself as an infant, as a child, and as an adolescent, and be stimulated to think about how those years influenced the kind of individual you are today. And you will see yourself as a young adult, as a middle-aged adult, and as an adult in old age, and be stimulated to think about how your experiences today will influence your development through the remainder of your adult years.

Life-span development is linked with many different areas of psychology. Neuroscience, cognitive psychology, abnormal psychology, social psychology, and virtually all other areas of psychology explore how people develop in these areas. For example, how memory works is a key aspect of cognitive psychology. In this book you will read about how memory develops from infancy through old age.

The Historical Perspective

Interest in the development of children has a long and rich history, but interest in adults began to develop seriously only in the latter half of the twentieth century. Prior to that time, the number of people living into their sixties and seventies was small compared with the rest of the population, and development was considered

development The pattern of change that begins at conception and continues through the life span. Most development involves growth, although it also includes decline brought on by aging and dying.

PEANUTS reprinted by permission of United Features Syndicate, Inc.

to be something that happened only during childhood. Although child development is important, a complete view of development now requires that we also consider developmental changes in the adult years. In this section, we will look briefly at how the prevailing view of children and adults has changed.

Child Development Ideas about childhood have varied. Throughout history, philosophers have speculated about the nature of children and how they should be reared. In the West, three influential philosophical views are based on the ideas of original sin, tabula rasa, and innate goodness:

- According to the Christian doctrine of **original sin,** children are born into the world corrupted, with an inclination toward evil. The goal of child rearing is to save children from sin.
- Toward the end of the seventeenth century, English philosopher John Locke proposed that at birth each child is a **tabula rasa**—a "blank tablet." Locke proposed that people acquire their characteristics through experience and that childhood experiences are important in determining adult characteristics. He advised parents to spend time with their children and help them become contributing members of society.
- In the eighteenth century, the concept of **innate goodness** was presented by Swiss-born French philosopher Jean-Jacques Rousseau. He stressed that children are inherently good. As a result, Rousseau said that they should be permitted to grow naturally with little parental monitoring or constraint.

These conflicting views formed the historical backdrop for the study of childhood and for child-rearing practices. Today, we conceive of childhood as a highly eventful and unique period of life that lays an important foundation for the adult years and is highly differentiated from them (Pittman & Diversi, 2003). Most approaches to childhood identify distinct periods in which special skills are mastered and new life tasks are confronted. We now value childhood as a special time of growth and change, and we invest great resources in caring for and educating our children (Parke & Clarke-Stewart, 2003). That investment includes creating government provisions for helping them when ordinary family support systems fail or when families seriously endanger the child's well-being (Crouter & Booth, 2004).

Life-Span Development The *traditional approach* to the study of development emphasizes extensive change from birth to adolescence (especially during infancy), little or no change in adulthood, and decline in old age. In contrast, the *life-span approach* emphasizes developmental change throughout adulthood as well as childhood (Birren & Schaie, 2001; Nussbaum & Coupland, 2004; Overton, 2003).

Recent changes in human life expectancy have changed the way life-span development is viewed. Although it took 5,000 years to extend human life expectancy from 18 to 41 years of age, in the twentieth century alone, life expectancy increased by 30 years, thanks to improvements in sanitation, nutrition, and medicine (see figure 1.1). Today, for most individuals in developed countries, childhood and adolescence represent only about one-fourth of the life span (Schaie & Willis, 2002).

How much has the older adult population grown in the United States? Figure 1.2 reveals a dramatic increase in the over-65 age group since 1900 and projects continued increases through 2040. A significant increase also will occur in the number of individuals in the 85-and-over and in the 100-and-over age categories. In 2000, there were 77,000 American centenarians (persons 100 years of age or older), and this number is projected to increase to more than 800,000 in 2050. A baby girl born in the United States today has a 1-in-3 chance of living to be 100 years of age!

www.mhhe.com/santrockld10

History of Childhood
Children's Issues
Children's Rights
UNICEF

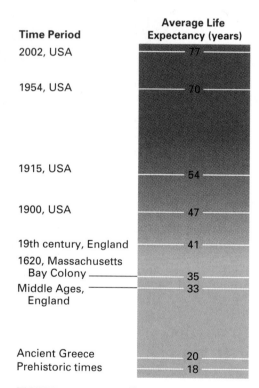

Time Period	Average Life Expectancy (years)
2002, USA	77
1954, USA	70
1915, USA	54
1900, USA	47
19th century, England	41
1620, Massachusetts Bay Colony	35
Middle Ages, England	33
Ancient Greece	20
Prehistoric times	18

FIGURE 1.1 Human Life Expectancy at Birth from Prehistoric to Contemporary Times

original sin The view that children were basically bad and born into the world as evil beings.

tabula rasa The idea, proposed by John Locke, that children are like a "blank tablet."

innate goodness The idea, presented by Swiss-born philosopher Jean-Jacques Rousseau, that children are inherently good.

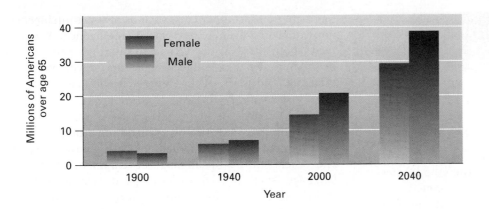

FIGURE 1.2 The Aging of America
Millions of Americans over age 65 from 1900 to the present and projected to the year 2040.

Although we are living longer, on the average, than we did in the past, the maximum life span of humans has not changed since the beginning of recorded history. The upper boundary of the life span (based on the oldest age documented) is 122 years, and as indicated in figure 1.3, our only competition from other species for the maximum recorded life span is the Galápagos turtle.

For too long we believed that development was something that happened only to children. To be sure, growth and development are dramatic in the first two decades of life, but a great deal of change goes on in the next five or six (or seven or eight) decades of life, too. Consider these descriptions of adult development:

> The next five or six decades are every bit as important, not only to those adults who are passing through them but to their children, who must live with and understand parents and grandparents. The changes in body, personality, and abilities through these later decades are great. Developmental tasks are imposed by marriage and parenthood, by the waxing and waning of physical prowess and of some intellectual capacities, by the children's flight from the nest, by the achievement of an occupational plateau, and by retirement and the prospect of final extinction. (Sears & Feldman, 1973, pp. v–vi)

As the older population continues to increase in the twenty-first century, the increasing number of older adults who will be without either a spouse or children (traditionally the main sources of support for older adults) has become a cause for concern (Bennett, 2004; Berado, 2003; Bonanno, Wortman, & Nesse, 2004). In recent decades, American adults are less likely to be married, more likely to be childless, and more likely to be living alone than earlier in the twentieth century. As these individuals become older, they will have even greater need for social relationships, networks, and supports.

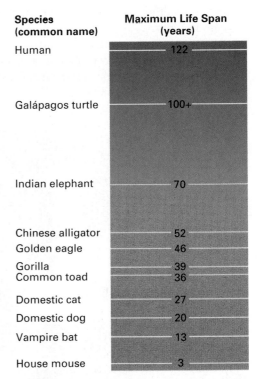

Species (common name)	Maximum Life Span (years)
Human	122
Galápagos turtle	100+
Indian elephant	70
Chinese alligator	52
Golden eagle	46
Gorilla	39
Common toad	36
Domestic cat	27
Domestic dog	20
Vampire bat	13
House mouse	3

FIGURE 1.3 Maximum Recorded Life Span for Different Species

Characteristics of the Life-Span Perspective

The belief that development occurs throughout life is central to the life-span perspective, but according to life-span development expert Paul Baltes (1987, 2000, 2003), the **life-span perspective** should be thought of as lifelong, multidimensional, multidirectional, plastic, multidisciplinary, and contextual, and involves growth, maintenance, and regulation. Let's look at each of these concepts.

Development Is Lifelong   In the life-span perspective, early adulthood is not the endpoint of development; rather, no age period dominates development. Researchers increasingly study the experiences and psychological orientations of adults at different points in their lives. Later in this chapter we will describe the age periods of development and their characteristics.

Development Is Multidimensional   Development consists of biological, cognitive, and socioemotional dimensions. Even within a dimension, such as intelligence,

life-span perspective The perspective that development is lifelong, multidimensional, multidirectional, plastic, multidisciplinary, and contextual, and involves growth, maintenance, and regulation.

Careers in Life-Span Development

K. Warner Schaie, Professor of Human Development

K. Warner Schaie is a professor of human development and psychology at Pennsylvania State University, where he teaches and conducts research on adult development and aging. He also directs the Gerontology Center there. He is one of the pioneering psychologists who helped to create the life-span perspective. He is the author or editor of more than 25 books and more than 250 journal articles and book chapters on adult development and aging. Dr. Schaie conducted the Seattle Longitudinal Study of intellectual development, a major research investigation which revealed that many intellectual skills are maintained or even increase in middle age.

Life-span developmentalist K. Warner Schaie *(right)* with two older adults who are actively using their cognitive skills.

Exploring Aging Issues
National Aging Information Center
Global Resources on Aging
Adult Development and Aging
The Gerontological Society of America
Geropsychology Resources

there are many components, such as abstract intelligence, nonverbal intelligence, and social intelligence. You can read about K. Warner Schaie, a leading theorist and researcher who has studied intellectual development in the adulthood years, in the Careers in Life-Span Development insert.

Development Is Multidirectional Throughout life, some dimensions or components of a dimension expand and others shrink. In language development, when one language (such as English) is acquired early in development, the capacity for acquiring second and third languages (such as French and Spanish) decreases later in development, especially after early childhood (Levelt, 1989). In socioemotional development, individuals begin to have more contact with opposite-sex peers during adolescence. As they establish emotional or sexual relationships, their relationships with friends might decrease. In cognitive development, older adults might become wiser by being able to call on experience to guide their intellectual decision making (Baltes & Kunzmann, 2003). However, they perform more poorly on tasks that require speed in processing information (Li & others, 2004; Madden, 2001; Salthouse, 2000).

Development Is Plastic A key developmental research agenda is the search for plasticity and its constraints (Kagan & Herschkowitz, 2005; Maurer, 2001; Prickaerts & others, 2004). *Plasticity* means the capacity for change. For example, can intellectual skills still be improved through education for individuals in their seventies or eighties? Or might these intellectual skills be fixed by the time people are in their thirties so that further improvement is impossible? In one research study, the reasoning abilities of older adults were improved through retraining (Willis & Schaie, 1994). However, developmentalists debate how much plasticity people have at different points in their development; possibly we possess less capacity for change when we become old (Baltes, 2003; Baltes & Smith, 2003; Singer, Lindenberger, & Baltes, 2003). Later in the chapter we will discuss the issue of stability and change in development, which has close ties with the concept of plasticity.

Development Is Multidisciplinary Psychologists, sociologists, anthropologists, neuroscientists, and medical researchers all study human development and share an interest in unlocking the mysteries of development through the life span. Research questions that cut across disciplines include:

* What constraints on intelligence are set by the individual's heredity and health status?
* How universal are cognitive and socioemotional changes?
* How do environmental contexts influence intellectual development?

Development Is Contextual The individual continually responds to and acts on contexts, which include a person's biological makeup, physical environment, cognitive processes, historical contexts, social contexts, and cultural contexts. The contextual view regards individuals as changing beings in a changing world. Baltes and other life-span developmentalists (Baltes, 2000; Schaie & Willis, 2002) argue that three important sources of contextual influences are (1) normative age-graded influences, (2) normative history-graded influences, and (3) nonnormative life events.

Normative age-graded influences are biological and environmental influences that are similar for individuals in a particular age group. These influences include biological processes such as puberty and menopause. They also include sociocultural, environmental processes such as entry into formal education (usually at about age 6 in most cultures) and retirement (which takes place in the fifties and sixties in most Western countries).

Normative history-graded influences are common to people of a particular generation because of the historical circumstances they experience. Examples include economic impacts (such as the Great Depression in the 1930s), war (such as World War II in the 1940s and the Vietnam war in the 1960s and 1970s), the changing role of women, the current technology revolution, and political upheaval and change (such as the decrease in hard-line communism in the 1990s and into the twenty-first century) (Modell & Elder, 2002).

Paul Baltes, 65, conversing with one of the longtime research participants (now 93 years old) in the Berlin Aging Study. She joined the study 14 years ago. Since, she has participated six times in extensive physical, medical, psychological, and social assessments. In her professional life, she was a practicing MD.

Nonnormative life events are unusual occurrences that have a major impact on the individual's life and usually are not applicable to many people. Such events might include the death of a parent when a child is young, pregnancy in early adolescence, a disaster (such as a fire that destroys a home), or an accident. Nonnormative life events also can include positive events (such as winning the lottery or getting an unexpected career opportunity with special privileges).

Development Involves Growth, Maintenance, and Regulation Baltes and his colleagues (Baltes, 2003; Baltes, Staudinger, & Lindenberger, 1999; Krampe & Baltes, 2003) assert that the mastery of life often involves conflicts and competition among three goals of human development: growth, maintenance, and regulation. As individuals age into middle and late adulthood, the maintenance and regulation of their capacities takes center stage away from growth. Thus, for many individuals, the goal is not to seek growth in intellectual capacities (such as memory) or physical capacities (such as physical strength), but to maintain those skills or minimize their deterioration. In section 9, "Late Adulthood," we will discuss these ideas about maintenance and regulation in greater depth.

Some Contemporary Concerns

Earlier in the chapter, we examined life-span development from a historical perspective. The life-span perspective also addresses a number of contemporary concerns from infancy through old age. Consider some of the topics you read about every day in newspapers and magazines: gene research, child abuse, mental retardation, parenting, intelligence, career changes, divorce, addiction and recovery, the increasing ethnic minority population, gender issues, homosexuality, midlife crises, stress and health, retirement, and aging. What life-span experts are discovering in each of these areas influences our understanding of children and adults and informs our decisions as a society about how they should be treated.

The roles that health and well-being, parenting, education, and sociocultural contexts play in life-span development, as well as their importance in social policy, are a particular focus of this textbook. Here we will preview these themes and highlight a research study pertaining to each one.

Careers in Life-Span Development

Luis Vargas, Child Clinical Psychologist

Luis Vargas is Director of the Clinical Child Psychology Internship Program and a professor in the Department of Psychiatry at the University of New Mexico Health Sciences Center. He also is Director of Psychology at the University of New Mexico Children's Psychiatric Hospital.

Luis obtained an undergraduate degree in psychology from St. Edwards University in Texas, a master's degree in psychology from Trinity University in Texas, and a Ph.D. in clinical psychology from the University of Nebraska–Lincoln.

Luis' main interests are cultural issues and the assessment and treatment of children, adolescents, and families. He is motivated to find better ways to provide culturally responsive mental health services. One of his special interests is the treatment of Latino youth for delinquency and substance abuse.

Luis Vargas *(left)* conducting a child therapy session.

Health and Well-Being Health and well-being have been important goals for just about everyone for most of human history. Asian physicians in 2600 B.C. and Greek physicians in 500 B.C. recognized that good habits are essential for good health. They did not blame the gods for illness or think that magic would cure it—they realized that people have some control over their health and well-being. A physician's role became that of a guide, assisting patients to restore a natural physical and emotional balance.

In the twenty-first century, we once again recognize the power of lifestyles and psychological states in health and well-being (Blonna, 2005; Corbin & others, 2004; Robbins, Powers, & Burgess, 2005). In every chapter of this book, issues of health and well-being are integrated into our discussion of life-span development. They also are highlighted through the Internet connections that appear with World Wide Web icons throughout the book.

The topics on health and well-being we will discuss include:

- Drug and alcohol use during pregnancy
- Early intervention
- At-risk adolescents
- Women's health issues
- Addiction and recovery
- Loneliness
- Adaptive physical skills in aging adults
- Coping with death

Clinical psychologists are among the health professionals who help people improve their well-being. Luis Vargas is a child clinical psychologist who has a deep concern about helping adolescents who have become juvenile delinquents and/or substance abusers get their lives on track. You can read about Luis Vargas and his work in the Careers in Life-Span Development insert.

Research on Exercise and Brain Tissue Loss in Older Adults One recent study examined the link between aerobic fitness and brain tissue density (determined by magnetic resonance image brain scans) in 55 older adults (Colcombe & others, 2003). Consistent with previous findings on aging and brain density, the density of brain tissue declined with age in older adults. However, the losses were substantially reduced in the older adults who exercised regularly and were aerobically fit. We will further discuss the role of exercise in older adults in chapter 18, "Physical Development in Late Adulthood."

Parenting We hear a lot about pressures on the contemporary family (Luster & Okaghi, 2005; Maccoby, 2002; Parke, 2004; Segrin & Flora, 2005; Zaslow, 2004). In later chapters, we will evaluate issues related to family functioning and parenting. Some of the topics we will consider are:

- Child care
- Children and adults in divorced families

- The best way to parent
- Support systems for families
- Marital relationships
- Intergenerational relations
- Aging parents

Research on Family and Peer Relations One issue that interests researchers who study families and parents focuses on links between family and peer functioning. In one recent study of maltreated children (children who have been abused) and nonmaltreated children, the maltreated children were more likely to be repeatedly rejected by their peers across the childhood and adolescent years (Bolger & Patterson, 2001). The main reason for the rejection was the high rate of aggressive behavior shown by the children who had been abused by their parents. Why do you think the abuse by parents resulted in more aggression toward their peers by the children? We will have more to say about maltreated children in chapter 9, "Socioemotional Development in Early Childhood."

Education In the past 10 to 15 years, the American educational system has been sharply criticized (Marzano, Pickering, & Pollock, 2005; Pintrich & Maehr, 2004; Sadker & Sadker, 2005; Schank, 2004). A national committee appointed by the Office of Education concluded that children are being poorly prepared for the increasingly complex future they will face. The educational topics we will explore include these:

- Variations in early childhood education
- Ethnicity, poverty, and schools
- Programs to improve children's critical thinking
- School and family coordination
- Bilingual education
- The best schools for adolescents

Children learn to love when they are loved

Research on Mentoring Mentoring programs are increasingly being advocated as a strategy for improving the achievement of children and adolescents who are at risk for academic failure (Hamilton & Hamilton, 2004). One study focused on 959 adolescents who had applied to the Big Brothers/Big Sisters program (Rhodes, Grossman, & Resch, 2000). Half of the adolescents were mentored through extensive discussions about school, careers, and life, as well as participation in leisure activities with other adolescents. The other half were not mentored. Mentoring led to reduced unexcused absences from school, improvements in classroom performance, and better relationships with parents.

www.mhhe.com/santrockld10

Health Links
Educator's Reference Desk
Diversity
Social Policy
Trends in the Well-Being of
Children and Youth

Sociocultural Contexts and Diversity The tapestry of American culture has changed dramatically in recent years. Nowhere is the change more dramatic than in the increasing diversity of America's citizens. The diversity occurs in terms of ethnicity, gender, sexual orientation, ability/disability, national origin, and religion. This changing demographic tapestry promises not only the richness that diversity produces, but also difficult challenges in extending the American dream to all individuals (Books, 2004; Fuligni & others, 2005; Poelmans, 2005).

Sociocultural contexts include five important concepts: context, culture, ethnicity, socioeconomic status (SES), and gender. A **context** is the setting in which development occurs. This setting is influenced by historical, economic, social, and cultural factors. Contexts include families, schools, peer groups, churches, cities, neighborhoods, university laboratories, countries, and many others. Each of these settings has meaningful historical, economic, social, and cultural legacies (Leyendecker & others, 2005; Matsumoto, 2004; Triandis, 2001; Yang, 2005).

context The setting in which development occurs, which is influenced by historical, economic, social, and cultural factors.

Two Korean-born children on the day they became United States citizens. Asian American and Latino children are the fastest-growing immigrant groups in the United States. *How diverse are the students in this class on life-span development that you now are taking? How are their experiences in growing up likely similar to or different from yours?*

Culture encompasses the behavior patterns, beliefs, and all other products of a particular group of people that are passed on from generation to generation. Culture results from the interaction of people over many years. A cultural group can be as large as the United States or as small as an African hunter-gatherer group. Whatever its size, the group's culture influences the behavior of its members (Saraswathi & Mistry, 2003). **Cross-cultural studies** involve a comparison of a culture with one or more other cultures. The comparison provides information about the degree to which development is similar, or universal, across cultures, or is instead culture-specific. For example, the United States is an achievement-oriented culture with a strong work ethic. However, cross-cultural studies of American and Japanese children showed that Japanese children are better at math, spend more time working on math at school, and do more math homework than American children (Stevenson, 1995, 2000). The topics on culture that we will discuss include:

- Child-care policy around the world
- Vygotsky's sociocultural cognitive theory
- Gender roles in Egypt and China
- Cross-cultural comparisons of secondary schools
- Marriage around the world
- Death and dying in different cultures

Ethnicity (the word *ethnic* comes from the Greek word for "nation") is rooted in cultural heritage, nationality characteristics, race, religion, and language. Not only does ethnic diversity exist with a culture such as found in the United States, diversity also exists within each ethnic group. These groups include African Americans, Latinos, Asian Americans, Native Americans, Polish Americans, Italian Americans, and so on. Not all African Americans live in low-income circumstances. Not all Latinos are Catholics. Not all Asian Americans are high school math whizzes. It is easy to fall into the trap of stereotyping an ethnic group by thinking that all of its members are alike. A more accurate ethnic group portrayal is diversity (Jenkins & others, 2003; Koppelman & Goodhart, 2005; Powell & Caseau, 2004; Sheets, 2005).

Among the ethnicity topics we will examine in later chapters are:

- Similarities, differences, and diversity
- Immigration
- Support systems for ethnic minority individuals
- Ethnicity and schooling
- Value conflicts
- Being old, female, and ethnic

Race and ethnicity are sometimes misrepresented. *Race* is a controversial classification of people according to real or imagined biological characteristics such as skin color and blood group membership (Corsini, 1999). An individual's ethnicity can include his or her race but also many other characteristics. Thus, an individual might be White (a racial category) and a fifth-generation Texan who is a Catholic and speaks English and Spanish fluently.

Socioeconomic status (SES) refers to the grouping of people with similar occupational, educational, and economic characteristics. Socioeconomic status implies certain inequalities. Generally, members of a society have (1) occupations that vary in prestige, and some individuals have more access than others to higher-status occupations; (2) different levels of educational attainment, and some individuals have more access than others to better education; (3) different economic resources; and (4) different levels of power to influence a community's institutions. These differences in the ability to control resources and to participate in society's rewards produce unequal opportunities for children.

culture The behavior patterns, beliefs, and all other products of a group that are passed on from generation to generation.

cross-cultural studies Comparisons of one culture with one or more other cultures. These provide information about the degree to which development is similar, or universal, across cultures, and to the degree to which it is culture-specific.

ethnicity A characteristic based on cultural heritage, nationality characteristics, race, religion, and language.

socioeconomic status (SES) Refers to the grouping of people with similar occupational, educational, and economic characteristics.

Children who grow up in poverty represent a special concern (Bernstein, 2004; Books, 2004; Evans, 2004; Linver & others, 2004). In a review of research, Jeanne Brooks-Gunn and her colleagues (2003) concluded that poverty in the first few years of life is a better predictor of school completion and achievement at 18 than poverty in the adolescent years. However, she also revealed that early intervention for two or three years doesn't permanently reduce socioeconomic disparities in children's achievement because poor children are likely to continue facing obstacles to success, such as schools that are not conducive to learning, neighborhoods with high levels of violence, and unsafe play areas. Thus, intervention may need to continue beyond the early child years into the elementary school years and even adolescent years to improve the lives of children living in poverty. Other researchers are seeking ways to help families living in poverty improve their well-being (Blumenfeld & others, 2005; Clampet-Lundquist & others, 2004; Evans, 2004; McLoyd, 2005; Perry-Jenkins, 2004).

Whereas sex refers to the biological dimension of being female or male, **gender** involves the psychological and sociocultural dimensions of being female or male. Few aspects of our development are more central to our identity and social relationships than gender (Hyde, 2004; Lippa, 2005; Maracek & others, 2003; Matlin, 2004; Poelmans, 2005). Our society's attitudes about gender are changing. But how much? The gender-related topics we will discuss include these:

- The mother's role and the father's role
- Parental and peer roles in gender development
- Gender similarities and differences
- Femininity, masculinity, and androgyny
- Carol Gilligan's care perspective
- Gender communication patterns
- Family work
- Gender and aging

We will discuss sociocultural contexts and diversity in each chapter. In addition, a Diversity in Life-Span Development interlude appears in every chapter. The first one about women's international struggle for equality appears next.

gender The psychological and sociocultural dimensions of being female or male.

Diversity in Life-Span Development
Women's Struggle for Equality: An International Journey

The educational and psychological conditions of women around the world are a serious concern (Lakes & Carter, 2004; Malley-Morrison, 2004; Maracek & others, 2003; UNICEF, 2004). Inadequate educational opportunities, violence, and lack of political access are just some of the problems they face.

A recent analysis found that a higher percentage of girls than boys around the world have never had any education (UNICEF, 2004) (see figure 1.4). The countries with the fewest females being educated are in Africa, where in some areas girls and women are receiving no education at all. Canada, the United States, and Russia have the highest percentages of educated women. In developing countries, 67 percent of women over the age of 25 (compared with 50 percent of men) have never been to school. At the beginning of the twenty-first century, 80 million more boys than girls were in primary and secondary educational settings around the world (United Nations, 2002).

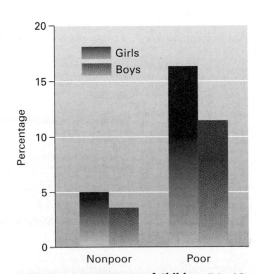

FIGURE 1.4 Percentage of Children 7 to 18 Years of Age Around the World Who Have Never Been to School of Any Kind

Around the world women too often are treated as burdens rather than assets in the political process. *What can be done to strengthen women's roles in the political process?*

Women in every country experience violence, often from someone close to them (Arai, 2004; Malley-Morrison, 2004). Partner abuse occurs in one of every six households in the United States, with the vast majority of the abuse being directed at women by men (Walker, 2001). In a survey, "The New Woman Ethics Report," wife abuse was listed as number one among fifteen of the most pressing concerns facing society (Johnson, 1990). Although most countries around the world now have battered women's shelters, beating women continues to be accepted and expected behavior in some countries (Ashy, 2004; Sheridan & Ghorayeb, 2004).

Women's struggles don't go on merely in impoverished lands. In a study of depression in high-income countries, women were twice as likely as men to be diagnosed as depressed (Nolen-Hoeksema, 1990). In the United States, from adolescence through adulthood, females are more likely than males to be depressed (Davison & Neale, 2004; Hammen, 2003). Many sociocultural inequities and experiences (such as income disparity and unequal employment opportunities) have contributed to the greater incidence of depression in females than males (Whiffen, 2001). Also, possibly more women are diagnosed with depression than actually have depression (Nolen-Hoeksema, 2004). Some argue that the issues of women are only likely to be addressed when women share equal power with men (Carter, 2004; Parker, 2004).

Research on Poverty in Children's Lives   One recent study explored multiple risks of children from poverty and middle-income backgrounds (Evans & English, 2002). Six multiple risk factors were examined in 287 eight- to ten-year-old non-Latino White children living in rural areas of upstate New York: family turmoil, child separation (a close member often being away from home), exposure to violence, crowding, noise level, and housing quality. As shown in figure 1.5, a higher percentage of children in poor families were exposed to each of the six risk factors.

Social Policy   **Social policy** is a national government's course of action designed to promote the welfare of its citizens. The shape and scope of social policy is strongly tied to the political system. Our country's policy agenda and the welfare of the nation's citizens are influenced by the values held by individual lawmakers, by the nation's economic strengths and weaknesses, and by partisan politics.

Out of concern that policy makers are doing too little to protect the well-being of children and older adults, life-span researchers increasingly are undertaking studies that they hope will lead to effective social policy (Bernstein, 2004; Bogenschneider, 2002; Bornstein & Bradley, 2003). When more than 15 percent of all children and almost half of all ethnic minority children are being raised in poverty, when 40 to 50 percent of all children can expect to spend at least five years in a single-parent home, when children and young adolescents are becoming parents, when the use and abuse of drugs is widespread, when the specter of AIDS is present, and when the provision of health care for older adults is inadequate, our nation needs revised social policy. Marian Wright Edelman, president of the Children's Defense Fund, has been a tireless advocate of children's rights (Children's Defense Fund, 2004). Especially troublesome to Edelman (1997) are the indicators of social neglect that place the United States at or near the lowest rank for industrialized nations in the treatment of children.

Edelman says that parenting and nurturing the next generation of children is our society's most important function and that we need to take it more seriously than we

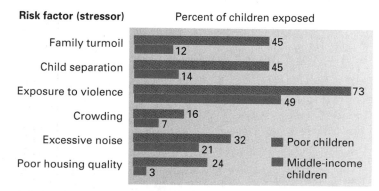

FIGURE 1.5 Percentage of Poor and Middle-Income Children Exposed to Each of Six Stressors

social policy A national government's course of action designed to promote the welfare of its citizens.

Marian Wright Edelman, president of the Children's Defense Fund (shown here interacting with young children), has been a tireless advocate of children's rights and has been instrumental in calling attention to the needs of children. *What are some of these needs?*

have in the past. She points out that we hear a lot from politicians about "family values," but that when we examine our nation's policies for families, they don't reflect the politicians' words.

The family policies of the United States are overwhelmingly treatment-oriented: Only those families and individuals who already have problems are eligible. Few preventive programs are available on any widespread basis. For example, families in which the children are on the verge of being placed in foster care are eligible, and often required, to receive counseling; families in which problems are brewing but are not yet full-blown usually cannot qualify for public services. Most experts on family policy believe that more attention should be given to preventing family problems (Hawkins & Whiteman, 2004; Kalil & DeLeire, 2004).

At the other end of the life span, our aging society and older persons' status in this society raise policy issues about the well-being of older adults (Thompson, Robinson, & Beisecker, 2004). Special concerns are escalating health-care costs and the access of older adults to adequate health care (Hill & others, 2002). One recent study found that the health-care system fails older adults in many areas (Wenger & others, 2003). For example, older adults received the recommended care for general medical conditions such as heart disease only 52 percent of the time. Appropriate care related to Alzheimer disease and undernutrition in older adults occurred only 31 percent of the time.

The need for social welfare resources far exceeds what policy makers have seen fit to provide. Then who should get the bulk of government dollars for improved well-being? Children? Their parents? Older adults? **Generational inequity,** a social policy concern in which an aging society is being unfair to its younger members, occurs because older adults receive a disproportionately large allocation of resources in the form of entitlement programs such as Social Security and Medicare. Generational inequity raises questions about whether the young should have to pay to care for the old and whether an "advantaged" older population is using up resources that should go to disadvantaged children. The argument is that older adults are advantaged because they have publicly financed pensions, health care, food stamps, housing subsidies, tax breaks, and other benefits that younger groups do not have. While the trend of greater services for older adults has been occurring, the percentage of children in poverty has been rising.

Bernice Neugarten (1988) says the problem should be viewed not as one of generational inequity, but rather as a major shortcoming of our broader economic and social policies. She suggests developing a spirit of support for improving the range of options for all people in our society. Also, it is important to keep in mind that children will one day become older adults and will in turn be supported by the efforts of younger people (Williams & Nussbaum, 2001). If there were no Social

Maggie Kuhn, founder of the Gray Panthers, an international advocacy group that began in 1970 with five older women committed to improving the social conditions of older adults.

generational inequity A social policy concern in which an aging society is being unfair to its younger members.

Security system, many adult children would have to bear the burden of supporting their aging parents and spend less of their resources on educating children.

Research on How Children Come to Endorse Democracy   For a democracy like the United States to remain secure and stable, each new generation of citizens must believe in the system and trust that it works for people like them. Research by Constance Flanagan and her colleagues (Flanagan, 2002, 2004; Flanagan & Faison, 2001; Flanagan, Gill, & Galley, 1998) with different ethnic groups of American youth points to the pivotal role of teaching in this regard. They have found that the extent to which teachers ensure that all students are treated equally and listen to and respect each other is related to the students' endorsement of democracy.

Review and Reflect: Learning Goal 1

1   **Discuss the life-span perspective of development**

REVIEW

- What is meant by the term *life-span development?*
- What is the historical background of life-span development?
- What are seven main characteristics of the life-span perspective? What are three sources of contextual influences?
- What are some contemporary concerns in life-span development?

REFLECT

- Imagine what your development would have been like in a culture that offered fewer or distinctly different choices than your own. How might your development have been different if your family had been significantly richer or poorer than it was?

---

2   DEVELOPMENTAL PROCESSES AND PERIODS

Biological, Cognitive, and Socioemotional Processes

Age and Happiness

Periods of Development

Conceptions of Age

Each of us develops partly like all other individuals, partly like some other individuals, and partly like no other individual. Most of the time, our attention is directed to an individual's uniqueness. But psychologists who study life-span development are drawn to our shared characteristics as well as what makes us unique. As humans, we all have traveled some common paths. Each of us—Leonardo da Vinci, Oprah Winfrey, and you—walked at about 1 year, engaged in fantasy play as a young child, and became more independent as a youth. Each of us, if we live long enough, will experience hearing problems and the deaths of family members and friends.

At the beginning of the chapter, we defined *development* as the pattern of movement or change that begins at conception and continues through the life span. The pattern of movement is complex because it is the product of biological, cognitive, and socioemotional processes.

Biological, Cognitive, and Socioemotional Processes

Biological processes produce changes in an individual's physical nature. Genes inherited from parents, the development of the brain, height and weight gains, changes in motor skills, the hormonal changes of puberty, and cardiovascular decline all reflect the role of biological processes in development.

One area of biological research with immense importance for development seeks to slow the aging process and extend the human life span. Although researchers have not yet succeeded, they are making significant strides in understanding the cellular processes that might enable people to live longer (Dynek & Smith, 2004; Hamet & Tremblay, 2003). We will have more to say about the biological processes involved in aging in chapter 18, "Physical Development in Late Adulthood."

Cognitive processes refer to changes in the individual's thought, intelligence, and language. Watching a colorful mobile swinging above the crib, putting together a two-word sentence, memorizing a poem, imagining what it would be like to be a movie star, and solving a crossword puzzle all involve cognitive processes.

Researchers have found that the responsiveness of caregivers provides important support for children's advances in cognitive development (Michael, 2004). In one recent study, the mother's responsiveness was linked with a number of language milestones in children's development (Tamis-LeMonda, Bornstein, & Baumwell, 2001). Children with responsive mothers (such as mothers who respond to a child's bids for attention and to a child's play) spoke their first words earlier and combined parts of speech earlier than children whose mothers responded to them infrequently. We will have much more to say about language development, including how to talk with babies and toddlers, in chapter 6, "Cognitive Development in Infancy."

Socioemotional processes involve changes in the individual's relationships with other people, changes in emotions, and changes in personality. An infant's smile in response to her mother's touch, a young boy's aggressive attack on a playmate, a girl's development of assertiveness, an adolescent's joy at the senior prom, and the affection of an elderly couple all reflect the role of the socioemotional processes in development.

One socioemotional process that interests researchers is marital relations. In a number of research studies, John Gottman and his colleagues (Gottman, 1994; Gottman & others, 2002) found that an important factor in whether wives or husbands felt satisfied with the sex, romance, and passion in their marriage was the quality of the couple's friendship. We will have more to say about marital relations and Gottman's research in chapter 15, "Socioemotional Development in Early Adulthood."

Biological, cognitive, and socioemotional processes are inextricably intertwined. For example, consider a baby smiling in response to its mother's touch. This response depends on biological processes (the physical nature of touch and responsiveness to it), cognitive processes (the ability to understand intentional acts), and socioemotional processes (the act of smiling often reflects a positive emotional feeling and smiling helps to connect us in positive ways with other human beings).

In many instances biological, cognitive, and socioemotional processes are bidirectional. For example, biological processes can influence cognitive processes and vice versa. In section 9, "Late Adulthood," you will read about how poor health (a biological process) is linked to lower intellectual functioning (a cognitive process). You also will read about how positive thinking about the ability to control one's environment (a cognitive process) can have a powerful effect on an individual's health (a biological process). Thus, although usually we will study the different processes (biological, cognitive, and socioemotional) in separate locations, keep in mind that we are talking about the development of an integrated individual with a mind and body that are interdependent (see figure 1.6).

biological processes Changes in an individual's physical nature.

cognitive processes Changes in an individual's thought, intelligence, and language.

socioemotional processes Changes in an individual's relationships with other people, emotions, and personality.

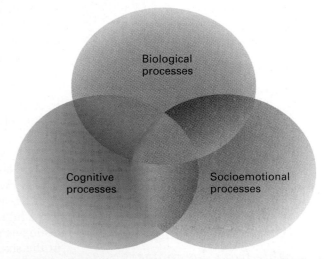

FIGURE 1.6 Developmental Changes Are the Result of Biological, Cognitive, and Socioemotional Processes
These processes interact as individuals develop.

Periods of Development

The concept of *developmental period* refers to a time frame in a person's life that is characterized by certain features. For the purposes of organization and understanding, we commonly describe development in terms of these periods. The most widely used classification of developmental periods involves this sequence: prenatal period, infancy, early childhood, middle and late childhood, adolescence, early adulthood, middle adulthood, and late adulthood. Approximate age ranges are listed here for the periods to provide a general idea of when a period begins and ends.

The *prenatal period* is the time from conception to birth. It involves tremendous growth—from a single cell to an organism complete with brain and behavioral capabilities, produced in approximately a nine-month period.

Infancy is the developmental period from birth to 18 or 24 months. Infancy is a time of extreme dependence upon adults. Many psychological activities are just beginning—language, symbolic thought, sensorimotor coordination, and social learning, for example.

Early childhood is the developmental period from the end of infancy to about 5 or 6 years. This period is sometimes called the "preschool years." During this time, young children learn to become more self-sufficient and to care for themselves, develop school readiness skills (following instructions, identifying letters), and spend many hours in play with peers. First grade typically marks the end of early childhood.

Middle and late childhood is the developmental period from about 6 to 11 years of age, approximately corresponding to the elementary school years. This period is sometimes called the "elementary school years." The fundamental skills of reading, writing, and arithmetic are mastered. The child is formally exposed to the larger world and its culture. Achievement becomes a more central theme of the child's world, and self-control increases.

Adolescence is the developmental period of transition from childhood to early adulthood, entered at approximately 10 to 12 years of age and ending at 18 to 22 years of age. Adolescence begins with rapid physical changes—dramatic gains in height and weight, changes in body contour, and the development of sexual characteristics such as enlargement of the breasts, development of pubic and facial hair, and deepening of the voice. At this point in development, the pursuit of independence and an identity are prominent. Thought is more logical, abstract, and idealistic. More time is spent outside the family.

Early adulthood is the developmental period that begins in the late teens or early twenties and lasts through the thirties. It is a time of establishing personal and economic independence, career development, and, for many, selecting a mate, learning to live with someone in an intimate way, starting a family, and rearing children.

Middle adulthood is the developmental period from approximately 40 years of age to about 60. It is a time of expanding personal and social involvement and responsibility; of assisting the next generation in becoming competent, mature individuals; and of reaching and maintaining satisfaction in a career.

Late adulthood is the developmental period that begins in the sixties or seventies and lasts until death. It is a time of adjustment to decreasing strength and health, life review, retirement, and adjustment to new social roles.

Life-span developmentalists increasingly distinguish between two age groups in late adulthood: the *young old*, or *old age*, and the *old old*, or *late old age*. Still others distinguish the *oldest old* (85 years and older) from younger older adults. Beginning in the sixties and extending to more than 100 years of age, late adulthood has the longest span of any period of development.

Combining this lengthy span with the dramatic increase in the number of adults living to older ages, we will see increased attention given to differentiating the late

*O*ne's children's children's children. Look back to us as we look to you; we are related by our imaginations. If we are able to touch, it is because we have imagined each other's existence, our dreams running back and forth along a cable from age to age.

—ROGER ROSENBLATT
American Writer, 20th Century

adulthood period. For example, Paul Baltes and Jacqui Smith (2003) argue that a major change takes place in older adults' lives on average at about 85 years of age (as they become the oldest old). They concluded that considerable plasticity and adaptability characterize older adults from their sixties until their mid-eighties, but that the oldest old are at the limits of their functional capacity, which makes interventions to improve their lives difficult. Here are some comparisons of the young old (which was classified as 65 through 84 in this analysis) and oldest old in terms of their functioning (Baltes & Smith, 2003):

- **The Young Old (65 to 84)**
  Increase their life expectancy with more older adults living longer
  Have considerable potential for improved physical and cognitive fitness
  Retain much of their cognitive capacity
  Can develop strategies to cope with the gains and losses of aging
- **The Oldest Old (85 and older)**
  Show considerable loss in cognitive skills
  Experience an increase in chronic stress
  Alzheimer disease more common and individuals more frail
  Dying with dignity less likely

Thus, in Baltes and Smith's analysis, the process of optimizing life is inherently more difficult for the oldest old than for the young old. Nonetheless, as we will see in chapter 18, "Physical Development in Late Adulthood," and chapter 19, "Cognitive Development in Late Adulthood," considerable variation exists in how much the oldest old, including those 100 years and older, retain their capabilities or show considerable decline. And as you will see next in the Research in Life-Span Development interlude, the contexts in which older adults are tested play an important role in how well they perform.

Research in Life-Span Development

Memory in the A.M. *and* P.M. *and Memory for Something Meaningful*

Laura Helmuth (2003) recently described how researchers are finding that certain testing conditions have exaggerated age-related declines in performance in older adults. To determine how age is related to behavior, thought, and feeling, researchers try to carefully compare participants of different ages. Participants come to the same research setting and take the same tests, for example. However, optimum testing conditions are not the same for young adults as they are for older adults. Most researchers conduct their studies in the afternoon, a convenient time for researchers and undergraduate participants. Traditional-aged college students in their late teens and early twenties are often more alert and function more optimally in the afternoon, but about 75 percent of older adults are "morning people," performing at their best early in the day (Helmuth, 2003).

Lynn Hasher and her colleagues (2001) tested the memory of college students 18 to 32 years of age and community volunteers 58 to 78 years of age in the late afternoon (about 4 to 5 P.M.) and in the morning (about 8 to 9 A.M.). Regardless of the time of day, the younger college students performed better than the older adults on the memory tests, which involved recognizing sentences from a story and memorizing a list of words. However, when the participants took the memory tests in the morning rather than in the late afternoon, the age difference in performance decreased considerably (see figure 1.7).

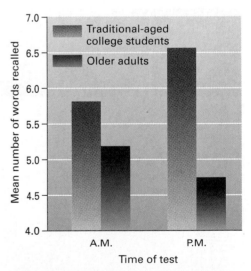

FIGURE 1.7 Memory, Age, and Time of Day Tested (A.M. or P.M.)
The traditional-aged college students performed better than older adults both in the A.M. and the P.M. However, note that the memory of the older adults was better when they were tested in the morning than in the afternoon, whereas the memory of the traditional-aged college students was not as good in the morning as it was in the afternoon.

The relevance of information also affects an older adult's memory performance. Thomas Hess and his colleagues (2003) asked younger adults (18 to 30 years of age) and older adults (62 to 84 years of age) to listen to a drawn-out description that was identified as either someone's experiences on a first job or their experiences while searching for a retirement home. The younger adults remembered the details of both circumstances. However, the older adults showed a keen memory for the retirement-home search but not for the first job experience. Researchers have found that age differences in memory are robust when they ask for information that doesn't matter much, but when older adults are asked about information that is relevant to their lives, differences in the memory of younger and older adults often decline considerably (Hasher, 2003).

The periods of the human life span are shown in figure 1.8, along with the processes of development—biological, cognitive, and socioemotional. The interplay of these processes produces the periods of the human life span.

Age and Happiness

When individuals report how happy they are and how satisfied they are with their lives, no particular age group says they are happier or more satisfied than any other age group (Diener, 2004; Diener, Lucas, & Oishi, 2002). When nearly 170,000 people in 16 countries were surveyed, no differences in their happiness from adolescence into the late

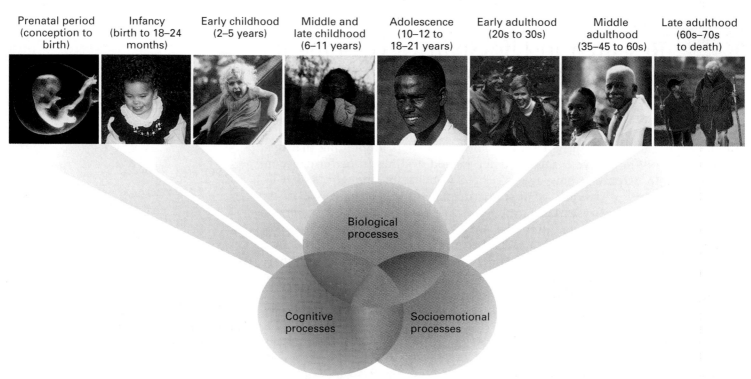

FIGURE 1.8 Processes and Periods of Development
The unfolding of life's periods of development is influenced by the interaction of biological, cognitive, and socioemotional processes.

adulthood years were found (Inglehart, 1990) (see figure 1.9). About the same percentage of people in each age group—slightly less than 20 percent—reported that they were "very happy."

Why might older people report as much happiness and life satisfaction as younger people? Every period of the life span has its stresses, pluses and minuses, hills and valleys. Although adolescents must cope with developing an identity, feelings of insecurity, mood swings, and peer pressure, the majority of adolescents develop positive perceptions of themselves, feelings of competence about their skills, positive relationships with friends and family, and an optimistic view of their future. And while older adults face a life of reduced income, less energy, decreasing physical skills, and concerns about death, they are also less pressured to achieve and succeed, have more time for leisurely pursuits, and have accumulated many years of experience that help them adapt to their circumstances with a wisdom they may not have had in their younger years. Because growing older is a certain outcome of living, we can derive considerable pleasure from knowing that we are likely to be just as happy as older adults as when we were younger.

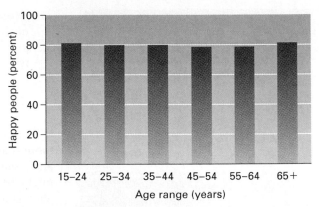

FIGURE 1.9 Age and Happiness
Analysis of surveys of nearly 170,000 people in 16 countries found no age differences in happiness from adolescence into the late adulthood years.

Conceptions of Age

In our description of the periods of the life span, we associated an approximate age range with each. However, life-span expert Bernice Neugarten (1988) emphasizes that we are rapidly becoming an age-irrelevant society. She says we are already familiar with the 28-year-old mayor, the 35-year-old grandmother, the 65-year-old father of a preschooler, the 55-year-old widow who starts a business, and the 70-year-old student. Neugarten stresses that choices and dilemmas do not spring forth at 10-year intervals. Decisions are not made and then left behind as if they were merely beads on a chain. Neugarten argues that most adulthood themes appear and reappear throughout the human life span. The issues of intimacy and freedom can haunt couples throughout their relationship. Feeling the pressure of time, reformulating goals, and coping with success and failure are not the exclusive property of adults of a particular age.

Neugarten's ideas raise questions about how age should be conceptualized. Some of the ways in which age has been conceptualized are as chronological age, biological age, psychological age, and social age (Hoyer & Roodin, 2003):

How old would you be if you didn't know how old you were?
—Satchel Paige
American Baseball Pitcher, 20th Century

- **Chronological age** is the number of years that have elapsed since birth. Many people consider chronological age to be synonymous with the concept of age. However, some developmentalists argue that chronological age is not very relevant to understanding a person's psychological development (Botwinick, 1978). Time is a crude index of many events and experiences, and it does not cause anything.
- **Biological age** is a person's age in terms of biological health. Determining biological age involves knowing the functional capacities of a person's vital organs. One person's vital capacities may be better or worse than those of others of comparable age. The younger the person's biological age, the longer the person is expected to live, regardless of chronological age.
- **Psychological age** is an individual's adaptive capacities compared with those of other individuals of the same chronological age. Thus, older adults who continue to learn are flexible, are motivated, control their emotions, and think clearly are engaging in more adaptive behaviors than their chronological age-mates who do not continue to learn, are rigid, are unmotivated, do not control their emotions, and do not think clearly.
- **Social age** refers to social roles and expectations related to a person's age. Consider the role of "mother" and the behaviors that accompany the role

chronological age The number of years that have elapsed since birth.

biological age A person's age in terms of biological health.

psychological age An individual's adaptive capacities compared with those of other individuals of the same chronological age.

social age Social roles and expectations related to a person's age.

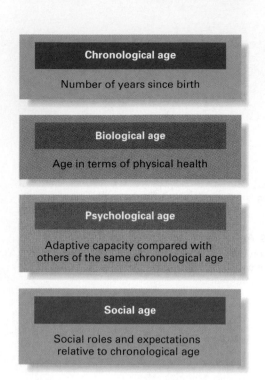

FIGURE 1.10 Conceptions of Age

(Huyck & Hoyer, 1982). In predicting an adult woman's behavior, it may be more important to know that she is the mother of a 3-year-old child than to know whether she is 20 or 30 years old. We still have some expectations for when certain life events—such as getting married, having children, becoming a grandparent, and retiring—should occur. However, as Neugarten concluded, chronological age has become a less accurate predictor of these life events in our society.

From a life-span perspective, an overall age profile of an individual involves more than just chronological age. It also consists of biological age, psychological age, and social age (see figure 1.10). For example, a 70-year-old man (chronological age) might be in good physical health (biological age), be experiencing memory problems and not be coping well with the demands placed on him by his wife's recent hospitalization (psychological age), and have a number of friends with whom he regularly golfs (social age).

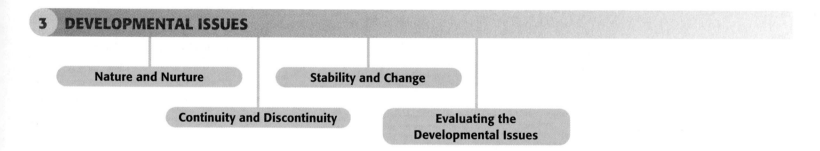

Review and Reflect: Learning Goal 2

2 Identify the most important developmental processes and periods

REVIEW

- What are three key developmental processes?
- What are eight main developmental periods?
- How is age related to happiness?
- What are four ways age can be conceptualized?

REFLECT

- Do you think there is a best age to be? If so, what is it? Why?

---

3 DEVELOPMENTAL ISSUES

Nature and Nurture   **Stability and Change**

Continuity and Discontinuity   **Evaluating the Developmental Issues**

The most important issues in the study of development include nature and nurture, continuity and discontinuity, and stability and change.

Nature and Nurture

nature-nurture issue Refers to the debate about whether development is primarily influenced by nature or nurture. Nature refers to an organism's biological inheritance, nurture to its environmental experiences. The "nature proponents" claim biological inheritance is the most important influence on development; the "nurture proponents" claim that environmental experiences are the most important.

The **nature-nurture issue** involves the debate about whether development is primarily influenced by nature or by nurture. *Nature* refers to an organism's biological inheritance, *nurture* to its environmental experiences. "Nature proponents" claim that the most important influence on development is biological inheritance. "Nurture proponents" claim that environmental experiences are the most important influence.

According to the nature advocates, just as a sunflower grows in an orderly way—unless defeated by an unfriendly environment—so does the human grow in an orderly way. The range of environments can be vast, but the nature approach argues that a genetic blueprint produces commonalities in growth and development. We walk before we talk, speak one word before two words, grow rapidly in infancy and less so in early childhood, experience a rush of sexual hormones in puberty, reach the peak of our physical strength in late adolescence and early adulthood, and then physically decline. The nature proponents acknowledge that extreme environments—those that are psychologically barren or hostile—can depress development. However, they believe that basic growth tendencies are genetically wired into humans.

By contrast, other psychologists emphasize the importance of nurture, or environmental experiences, in development. Experiences run the gamut from the individual's biological environment (nutrition, medical care, drugs, and physical accidents) to the social environment (family, peers, schools, community, media, and culture) (Garbarino, Bradshaw, & Kostelny, 2005; Gottlieb, 2004).

Continuity and Discontinuity

Think about your own development for a moment. Did you become the person you are gradually, like the seedling that slowly, cumulatively grows into a giant oak? Or did you experience sudden, distinct changes in your growth, like the caterpillar that changes into a butterfly (see figure 1.11)? For the most part, developmentalists who emphasize nurture usually describe development as a gradual, continuous process. Those who emphasize nature often describe development as a series of distinct stages.

The **continuity-discontinuity issue** focuses on the extent to which development involves gradual, cumulative change (continuity) or distinct stages (discontinuity). In terms of continuity, as the oak grows from seedling to giant oak, it becomes a larger version of what it was—its development is continuous. Similarly, a child's first word, though seemingly an abrupt, discontinuous event, is actually the result of weeks and months of growth and practice. Puberty, another seemingly abrupt, discontinuous occurrence, is actually a gradual process occurring over several years.

In terms of discontinuity, each person is described as passing through a sequence of stages in which change is qualitatively rather than quantitatively different. As the caterpillar changes to a butterfly, it is not just a larger caterpillar, it is a *different kind* of organism—its development is discontinuous. Similarly, at some point a child moves from not being able to think abstractly about the world to being able to. This is a qualitative, discontinuous change in development, not a quantitative, continuous change.

Stability and Change

Another important developmental topic is the **stability-change issue,** which addresses whether development is best described by stability or change. The stability-change issue involves the degree to which we become older renditions of our early experience (stability) or whether we develop into someone different from who we were at an earlier point in development (change). Will the shy child who hides behind the sofa when visitors arrive be a wallflower at college dances, or will the child become a sociable, talkative individual? Will the fun-loving, carefree adolescent have difficulty holding down a 9-to-5 job as an adult or become a straitlaced, serious conformist?

The stability-change issue is linked with Paul Baltes' (1987, 2003) view, which we discussed earlier, that plasticity or change is an important life-span issue. Recall that in the life-span perspective, plasticity or change is possible throughout the life span, although experts such as Baltes argue that older adults often show less capacity for change than younger adults (Singer, Lindenberger, & Baltes, 2003).

One of the reasons why adult development was ignored by researchers until fairly recently was the predominant belief for many years that nothing much changes in adulthood. The major changes were believed to take place in childhood, especially during the first five years of life. Today, most developmentalists conclude that some change is possible throughout the human life span, although they disagree, sometimes vehemently, about just how much change can take place, and how much stability there is.

 The video titled "Intelligence: The Nature and Nurture of Twins" considers these biological and environmental experience issues as they relate to the development of identical twins Cory and Eric.

Continuity

Discontinuity

FIGURE 1.11 Continuity and Discontinuity in Development
Is our development like that of a seedling gradually growing into a giant oak? Or is it more like that of a caterpillar suddenly becoming a butterfly?

continuity-discontinuity issue Focuses on the extent to which development involves gradual, cumulative change (continuity) or distinct stages (discontinuity).

stability-change issue Involves the degree to which we become older renditions of our early experience (stability) or whether we develop into someone different from who we were at an earlier point in development (change).

What is the nature of the early- and later-experience issue in development?

An important dimension of the stability-change issue is the extent to which early experiences (especially in infancy) or later experiences determine a person's development. That is, if infants experience negative, stressful circumstances in their lives, can the effects of those experiences be counteracted by later, more positive experiences? Or are the early experiences so critical, possibly because they are the infant's first, prototypical experiences, that they cannot be overridden by an enriched environment later in development?

The early-later experience issue has a long history and continues to be hotly debated among developmentalists (Gottlieb, 2002, 2004). Plato was sure that infants who were rocked frequently became better athletes. Nineteenth-century New England ministers told parents in Sunday sermons that the way they handled their infants would determine their children's future character. More recently, some researchers have stressed that unless infants experience warm, nurturant caregiving in the first year or so of life, their development will not likely be optimal (Waters & others, 2000).

The early-experience doctrine contrasts with the later-experience view that development, like a river, ebbs and flows continuously. The later-experience advocates argue that children are malleable throughout development and that later sensitive caregiving is just as important as earlier sensitive caregiving. A number of life-span developmentalists stress that too little attention has been given to later experiences in development (Baltes & Smith, 2003; Birren & Schaie, 2001). They argue that early experiences are important contributors to development, but no more important than later experiences.

Jerome Kagan (2000) points out that even children who show the qualities of an inhibited temperament, which is linked to heredity, have the capacity to change their behavior. In his research, almost one-third of a group of children who had an inhibited temperament at 2 years of age were not unusually shy or fearful when they were 4 years of age.

People in Western cultures, especially those steeped in the Freudian view that the key experiences in development are children's relationships with their parents in the first five years of life, have tended to support the idea that early experiences are more important than later experiences. But the majority of people in the world do not share this belief. For example, people in many Asian countries believe that experiences occurring after about 6 to 7 years of age are more important to development than earlier experiences. This stance stems from the long-standing belief in Eastern cultures that children's reasoning skills begin to develop in important ways in the middle childhood years.

Evaluating the Developmental Issues

Most life-span developmentalists do not take extreme positions on the three developmental issues. They acknowledge that nature *and* nurture, continuity *and* discontinuity, and stability *and* change characterize development throughout the human life span (Lerner, 2002; Tomasello & Slobin, 2005; Overton, 2004). Rather than either factor alone, the key to development is their interaction.

Despite this level of general agreement, spirited debate continues regarding how strongly development is influenced by each of these factors (Spencer & Harpalani, 2004; Waters, 2001). Are girls less likely to do well in math because of their "feminine" nature, or because of society's masculine bias? How extensively can the elderly be trained to reason more effectively? How much, if at all, does our memory decline in old age? Can techniques be used to prevent or reduce the decline? Can enriched experiences in adolescence remove "deficits" resulting from childhood experiences of poverty, neglect by parents, and poor schooling?

The answers given by developmentalists to such questions depend on their stances regarding the issues of nature and nurture, continuity and discontinuity, and stability and change. Answers to these questions also bear on public policy decisions about children, adolescents, and adults, and consequently, on each of our lives.

Review and Reflect: Learning Goal 3

3 **Describe three key developmental issues**

REVIEW

- What is the nature and nurture issue?
- What is the continuity and discontinuity issue?
- What is the stability and change issue?
- What is a good strategy for evaluating the developmental issues?

REFLECT

- Can you identify an early experience that you believe contributed in important ways to your development? Can you identify a recent or current (later) experience that you think had (is having) a strong influence on your development?

Reach Your Learning Goals

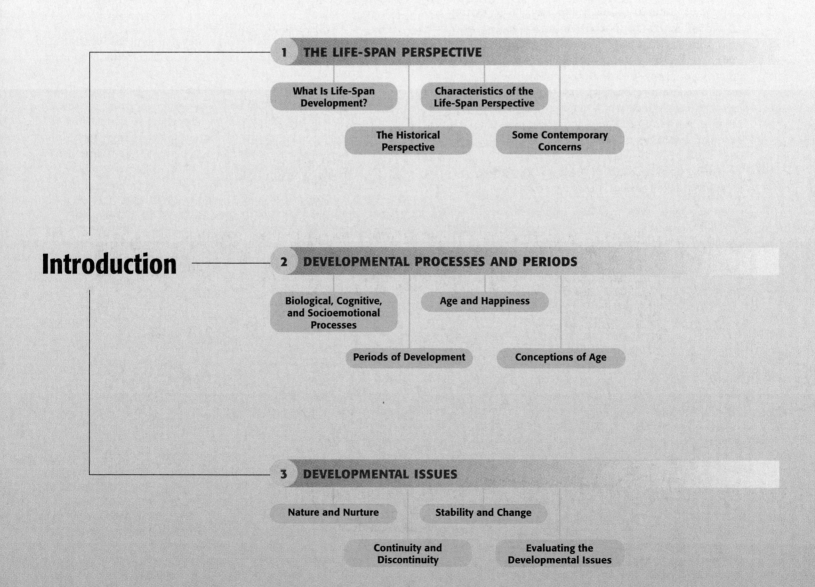

Introduction

1 THE LIFE-SPAN PERSPECTIVE

What Is Life-Span Development?

Characteristics of the Life-Span Perspective

The Historical Perspective

Some Contemporary Concerns

2 DEVELOPMENTAL PROCESSES AND PERIODS

Biological, Cognitive, and Socioemotional Processes

Age and Happiness

Periods of Development

Conceptions of Age

3 DEVELOPMENTAL ISSUES

Nature and Nurture

Stability and Change

Continuity and Discontinuity

Evaluating the Developmental Issues

Summary

 Learning Goal 1: Discuss the life-span perspective of development

- Development is the pattern of change that begins at conception and continues through the human life span. Development includes growth and decline.
- Interest in children has a long and rich history. Prior to the mid-nineteenth century, philosophical views of childhood were prominent, including the notions of original sin, tabula rasa, and innate goodness. The traditional approach to the study of development emphasizes extensive change in childhood but stability in adulthood; the life-span perspective emphasizes that change is possible throughout the life span. In the twentieth century alone, life expectancy increased by 30 years.
- The life-span perspective includes these basic conceptions: Development is lifelong, multidimensional, multidirectional, plastic, multidisciplinary, and contextual, and involves growth, maintenance, and regulation. Three important sources of contextual influences are (1) normative age-graded influences, (2) normative history-graded influences, and (3) nonnormative life events.
- Today, the development and well-being of children and adults capture the interest of the public, scientists, and policy makers. Among the important contemporary concerns are parenting, education, sociocultural contexts, and social policy. Three important sociocultural contexts are culture, ethnicity, and gender.

 Learning Goal 2: Identify the most important developmental processes and periods

- Three key developmental processes are biological, cognitive, and socioemotional. Development is influenced by an interplay of these processes.

- The life-span is commonly divided into these periods of development: prenatal, infancy, early childhood, middle and late childhood, adolescence, early adulthood, middle adulthood, and late adulthood.
- In studies covering adolescence through old age, people report that they are not happier at one point in development than at others.
- According to some experts on life-span development, too much emphasis is placed on chronological age. Neugarten emphasizes that we are moving toward a society in which age is a weaker predictor of development in adulthood. However, we often think of age only in terms of chronological age. Nonetheless, a full evaluation of age requires consideration of four dimensions of age: chronological, biological, psychological, and social.

 Learning Goal 3: Describe three key developmental issues

- The nature-nurture issue focuses on the extent to which development is mainly influenced by nature (biological inheritance) or nurture (experience).
- Developmentalists describe development as continuous (gradual, a cumulative change) or as discontinuous (abrupt, a sequence of stages).
- The stability-change issue focuses on the degree to which we become older renditions of our early experience or develop into someone different from who we were earlier in development. A special aspect of the stability-change issue is the extent to which development is determined by early versus later experiences.
- Most developmentalists recognize that extreme positions on the nature-nurture, continuity-discontinuity, and stability-change issues are unwise. Despite this consensus, there is still spirited debate on these issues.

Key Terms

development 5	culture 12	generational inequity 15	psychological age 21
original sin 6	cross-cultural studies 12	biological processes 17	social age 21
tabula rasa 6	ethnicity 12	cognitive processes 17	nature-nurture issue 22
innate goodness 6	socioeconomic status (SES) 12	socioemotional processes 17	continuity-discontinuity
life-span perspective 7	gender 13	chronological age 21	issue 23
context 11	social policy 14	biological age 21	stability-change issue 23

Key People

John Locke 6	Paul Baltes 7	Marian Wright Edelman 14	Jerome Kagan 24
Jean-Jacques Rousseau 6	Jeanne Brooks-Gunn 13	Bernice Neugarten 15	

 **E-Learning Tools**

To help you master the material in this chapter, you'll find a number of valuable study tools on the LifeMap CD-ROM that accompanies this book and on the Online Learning Center for *Life-Span Development*, tenth edition, at www.mhhe.com/santrockld10.

Video Clips

In the margins of this book there are icons directing you to the LifeMap CD-ROM that accompanies the book. In chapter 1 you'll find a video called "Intelligence: The Nature and Nurture of Twins." This segment examines the nature-nurture connection by tracing the development of identical twins Cory and Eric.

Self-Assessment

Connect to www.mhhe.com/santrockld10 to learn more about your career options by completing the self-assessment, *Evaluating My Interest in a Career in Life-Span Development.*

Taking It to the Net

Connect to www.mhhe.com/santrockld10 to research the answers to these questions.

1. Janice plans to join a small family practice group upon completion of her medical school pediatrician residency. Why should Janice, as a pediatrician, be involved in detecting and helping to prevent violence in the lives of her young patients?
2. Derrick has heard about a recent book that has stirred up a lot of controversy about the role of parents and peers in development. What is the book, what is its premise, and why has it generated so many strong feelings?
3. Carmen is completing her Ph.D. in clinical psychology. She is interested in geropsychology. What are some of the areas in which geropsychologists might conduct research and practice?

Health and Well-Being, Parenting, and Education Exercises

Build your decision-making skills by trying your hand at the health and well-being, parenting, and education exercises.

Connect to www.mhhe.com/santrockld10 to research the answers and complete the exercises.

Appendix *Careers in Life-Span Development*

Some of you may be quite sure about what you plan to make your life's work. Others of you might not have decided on a major yet and might be uncertain about which career path you want to follow. Each of us wants to find a rewarding career and enjoy the work we do. The field of life-span development offers an amazing breadth of career options that can provide extremely satisfying work.

If you decide to pursue a career in life-span development, what career options are available to you? College and university professors teach courses in many different areas of life-span development, education, family development, nursing, and medicine. Teachers impart knowledge, understanding, and skills to children and adolescents.

Counselors, clinical psychologists, nurses, and physicians help people of different ages to cope more effectively with their lives and improve their well-being. Various professionals work with families to improve the quality of family functioning. Although an advanced degree is not absolutely necessary in some areas of life-span development, you usually can considerably expand your opportunities (and income) by obtaining a graduate degree. Many careers in life-span development pay reasonably well. For example, psychologists earn well above the median salary in the United States. Also, by working in the field of life-span development, you can guide people in improving their lives, understand yourself and others better, possibly advance the state of knowledge in the field, and have an enjoyable time while you are doing these things.

If you are considering a career in life-span development, would you prefer to work with infants? children? adolescents? older adults? As you go through this term, try to spend some time with people of different ages. Observe their behavior. Talk with them about their lives. Think about whether you would like to work with people of this age in your life's work.

Another important aspect of exploring careers is to talk with people who work in various jobs. For example, if you have some interest in becoming a school counselor, call a school, ask to speak with a counselor, and set up an appointment to discuss the counselor's career and work. If you have an interest in becoming a nurse, think about whether you would rather work with babies, children, adolescents, or older adults. Call the nursing department at a hospital and set up an appointment to speak with the nursing coordinator about a nursing career.

Something else that should benefit you is to work in one or more jobs related to your career interests while you are in college. Many colleges and universities have internships or work experiences for students who major in such fields as life-span development. Some of these opportunities are for course credit or pay; others are strictly on a volunteer basis. Take advantage of these opportunities. They can provide you with valuable experiences to help you decide if this is the right career area for you, and they can help you get into graduate school, if you decide you want to go.

In the upcoming sections, we will profile a number of careers in four areas: education/research; clinical/counseling; medical/nursing/physical development; and families/relationships. These are not the only career options in life-span development, but they should provide you with an idea of the range of opportunities available and information about some of the main career avenues you might pursue. In profiling these careers, we will address the amount of education required, the nature of the training, and a description of the work.

By going to the website for this book, you can obtain more detailed career information about the various careers in life-span development described in this appendix.

EDUCATION/RESEARCH

There are numerous career opportunities in life-span development that involve education and/or research. These range from being a college professor to day-care director to school psychologist.

College/University Professor

Courses in life-span development are taught in many different programs and schools in colleges and universities, including psychology, education, nursing, child and family studies, social work, and medicine. A Ph.D. or master's degree almost always is required to teach in some area of life-span development in a college or university.

Obtaining a doctoral degree usually takes four to six years of graduate work. A master's degree requires approximately two years of graduate work. The professional job might be at a research university with one or more master's or Ph.D. programs in life-span development, at a four-year college with no graduate programs, or at a community college.

The training involves taking graduate courses, learning to conduct research, and attending and presenting papers at professional meetings. Many graduate students work as teaching or research assistants for professors in an apprenticeship relationship that helps them to become competent teachers and researchers. The work that college professors do includes teaching courses either at the undergraduate or graduate level (or both), conducting research in a specific area, advising students and/or directing their research, and serving on college or university committees.

Some college instructors do not conduct research as part of their job but instead focus mainly on teaching. However, research is part of the job description at most universities with master's and Ph.D. programs.

If you are interested in becoming a college or university professor, you might want to make an appointment with your instructor in this class on life-span development to learn more about their profession and what their work is like.

Researcher

Some individuals in the field of life-span development work in research positions. Most have either a master's or a Ph.D. in some area of life-span development. They might work at a university, in some cases in a university professor's research program, in government at such agencies as the National Institute of Mental Health, or in private industry. Individuals who have full-time research positions in life-span development generate innovative research ideas, plan studies, and carry out the research by collecting data, analyzing the data, and then interpreting it. Then, they will usually attempt to publish the research in a scientific journal. A researcher often works in a collaborative manner with other researchers on a project and may present the research at scientific meetings, where she or he also learns about other research. One researcher might spend much of his or her time in a laboratory; another researcher might work out in the field, such as in schools, hospitals, and so on.

Elementary or Secondary School Teacher

Becoming an elementary or secondary school teacher requires a minimum of an undergraduate degree. The training involves taking a wide range of courses with a major or concentration in education as well as completing a supervised practice teaching internship. The work of an elementary or secondary school teacher involves teaching in one or more subject areas, preparing the curriculum, giving tests, assigning grades, monitoring students' progress, conducting parent-teacher conferences, and attending in-service workshops.

Exceptional Children (Special Education) Teacher

Becoming a teacher of exceptional children requires a minimum of an undergraduate degree. The training consists of taking a wide range of courses in education and a concentration of courses in educating children with disabilities or children who are gifted.

The work of a teacher of exceptional children involves spending concentrated time with individual children who have a disability or are gifted. Among the children a teacher of exceptional children might work with are children with learning disabilities, ADHD, mental retardation, or a physical disability such as cerebral palsy.

Some of this work will usually be done outside of the student's regular classroom; some of it will be carried out when the student is in the regular classroom. The exceptional children teacher works closely with the student's regular classroom teacher and parents to create the best educational program for the student. Teachers of exceptional children often continue their education after obtaining their undergraduate degree and attain a master's degree.

Early Childhood Educator

Early childhood educators work on college faculties and have a minimum of a master's degree in their field. In graduate school, they take courses in early childhood education and receive supervisory training in day-care or early childhood programs. Early childhood educators usually teach in community colleges that award an associate degree in early childhood education.

Preschool/Kindergarten Teacher

Preschool teachers teach mainly 4-year-old children, and kindergarten teachers primarily teach 5-year-old children. They usually have an undergraduate degree in education, specializing in early childhood education. State certification to become a preschool or kindergarten teacher usually is required. These teachers direct the educational activities of young children.

Family and Consumer Science Educator

Family and consumer science educators may specialize in early childhood education or instruct middle and high school students about such matters as nutrition, interpersonal relationships, human sexuality, parenting, and human development. Hundreds of colleges and universities throughout the United States offer two- and four-year degree programs in family and consumer science. These programs usually include an internship requirement. Additional education courses may be needed to obtain a teaching certificate. Some family and consumer educators go on to graduate school for further training, which provides a background for possible jobs in college teaching or research.

Educational Psychologist

An educational psychologist most often teaches in a college or university and conducts research in such areas of educational psychology as learning, motivation, classroom management, and assessment. Most educational psychologists have a doctorate in education, which takes four to six years of graduate work. They help train students who will take various positions in education, including educational psychology, school psychology, and teaching.

School Psychologist

School psychologists focus on improving the psychological and intellectual well-being of elementary, middle/junior, and high school students. They usually have a master's or doctoral degree in school psychology. In graduate school, they take courses in counseling, assessment, learning, and other areas of education and psychology. School psychologists may work in a centralized office in a school district or in one or more schools. They give psychological tests, interview students and their parents, consult with teachers, and may provide counseling to students and their families.

Gerontologist

Gerontologists usually work in research in some branch of the federal or state government. They specialize in the study of aging with a particular focus on government programs for older adults, social policy, and delivery of services to older adults. In their research, gerontologists define problems to be studied, collect data, interpret the results, and make recommendations for social policy. Most gerontologists have a master's or doctoral degree and have taken a concentration of course work in adult development and aging.

CLINICAL/COUNSELING

There are a wide variety of clinical and counseling jobs that are linked with life-span development. These range from child clinical psychologist to adolescent drug counselor to geriatric psychiatrist.

Clinical Psychologist

Clinical psychologists seek to help people with psychological problems. They work in a variety of settings, including colleges and universities, clinics, medical schools, and private practice. Clinical psychologists have either a Ph.D. (which involves clinical and research training) or a Psy.D. degree (which only involves clinical training). This graduate training usually takes five to seven years and includes courses in clinical psychology and a one-year supervised internship in an accredited setting toward the end of the training.

In most cases, they must pass a test to become licensed in a state and to call themselves a clinical psychologist. Some clinical psychologists only conduct psychotherapy, others do psychological assessment and psychotherapy, and some also do research.

In regard to life-span development, clinical psychologists might specialize in a particular age group, such as children (child clinical psychologist) or older adults (often referred to as a geropsychologist). Many geropsychologists pursue a year or two of postdoctoral training.

Psychiatrist

Psychiatrists obtain a medical degree and then do a residency in psychiatry. Medical school takes approximately four years, and the psychiatry residency another three to four years. Unlike most psychologists (who do not go to medical school), psychiatrists can administer drugs to clients (recently, several states, such as New Mexico, gave clinical psychologists the right to prescribe drugs).

Like clinical psychologists, psychiatrists might specialize in working with children (child psychiatry) or with older adults (geriatric psychiatry). Psychiatrists might work in medical schools in teaching and research roles, in a medical clinic or hospital, or in private practice. In addition to administering drugs to help improve the lives of people with psychological problems, psychiatrists also may conduct psychotherapy.

Counseling Psychologist

Counseling psychologists go through much of the same training as clinical psychologists, although in a graduate program in counseling rather than clinical psychology. Counseling psychologists have either a master's degree or a doctoral degree. They also must go through a licensing procedure. One type of master's degree in counseling leads to the designation of licensed professional counselor. They work in the same settings as clinical psychologists, and may do psychotherapy, teach, or conduct research. Many counseling psychologists do not do therapy with individuals who have more severe mental disorders, such as schizophrenia.

School Counselor

School counselors help identify students' abilities and interests, guide students in developing academic plans, and explore career options with students. They may help students cope with adjustment problems. They may work with students individually, in small groups, or even in a classroom. They often consult with parents, teachers, and school administrators when trying to help students with their problems. School counselors usually have a master's degree in counseling.

High school counselors advise students on choosing a major, admissions requirements for college, taking entrance exams, applying for financial aid, and on appropriate vocational and technical training. Elementary school counselors are mainly involved in counseling students about social and personal problems. They may observe children in the classroom and at play as part of their work.

Career Counselor

Career counselors help individuals to identify what the best career options are for them and guide them in applying for jobs. They may work in private industry or at a college or university. They usually interview individuals and give them vocational and/or psychological tests to help provide students with information about appropriate careers that fit their interests and abilities. Sometimes they help individuals to create professional resumes or conduct mock interviews to help them feel comfortable in a job interview. They might create and promote job fairs or other recruiting events to help individuals obtain jobs.

Rehabilitation Counselor

Rehabilitation counselors work with individuals to identify career options, develop adjustment and coping skills to maximize independence, and resolve problems related to jobs, abilities, and the impact that disabilities may have on other aspects of their lives. A master's degree in rehabilitation counseling, counseling or guidance, or counseling psychology is generally considered the minimum educational requirement.

Social Worker

Many social workers are involved in helping people with social or economic problems. They may investigate, evaluate, and attempt to rectify reported cases of abuse, neglect, endangerment, or domestic disputes. They can intervene in families if necessary and provide counseling and referral services to individuals and families. They have a minimum of an undergraduate degree from a school of social work that includes course work in various areas of sociology and psychology. Some social workers also have a master's or doctoral degree. They often work for publicly funded agencies at the city, state, or national level, although increasingly they work in the private sector in areas such as drug rehabilitation and family counseling.

In some cases, social workers specialize in a certain area, as is true of a medical social worker, who has a master's degree in social work (M.S.W.). This involves graduate coursework and supervised clinical experiences in medical settings. A medical social worker might coordinate a variety of support services to people with a severe or long-term disability. Family-care social workers often work with families with children or an older adult who needs support services.

Drug Counselor

Drug counselors provide counseling to individuals with drug-abuse problems. They may work on an individual basis with a substance abuser or conduct group therapy sessions. At a minimum, drug counselors go through an associate's or certificate program. Many have an undergraduate degree in substance-abuse counseling, and some have master's and doctoral degrees. They may work in private practice, with a state or federal government agency, with a company, or in a hospital setting. Some drug counselors specialize in working with adolescents or older adults. Most states provide a certification procedure for obtaining a license to practice drug counseling.

MEDICAL/NURSING/PHYSICAL DEVELOPMENT

This third main area of careers in life-span development includes a wide range of careers in the medical and nursing areas, as well as jobs pertaining to improving some aspect of the person's physical development.

Obstetrician/Gynecologist

An obstetrician/gynecologist prescribes prenatal and postnatal care and performs deliveries in maternity cases. The individual also treats diseases and injuries of the female reproductive system. Becoming an obstetrician/gynecologist requires a medical degree plus three to five years of residency in obstetrics/gynecology. Obstetricians may work in private practice, in a medical clinic, a hospital, or in a medical school.

Pediatrician

A pediatrician monitors infants' and children's health, works to prevent disease or injury, helps children attain optimal health, and treats children with health problems. Pediatricians have attained a medical degree and then do a three- to five-year residency in pediatrics.

Pediatricians may work in private practice, in a medical clinic, in a hospital, or in a medical school. As a medical doctor, they can administer drugs to children and may counsel parents and children on ways to improve the children's health. Many pediatricians on the faculty of medical schools also teach and conduct research on children's health and diseases.

Geriatric Physician

A geriatric physician has a medical degree and has specialized in geriatric medicine by doing a three- to five-year residency. Geriatric physicians diagnose medical problems of older adults, evaluate treatment options, and make recommendations for nursing care or other arrangements. As with other doctors, they may work in private practice, in a medical clinic, in a hospital, or in a medical school. They also may primarily treat the diseases and health problems of older adults, but geriatric physicians in medical school settings also may teach future physicians and conduct research.

Neonatal Nurse

A neonatal nurse is involved in the delivery of care to the newborn infant. The neonatal nurse may work to improve the health and well-being of infants born under normal circumstances or be involved in the delivery of care to premature and critically ill neonates. A minimum of an undergraduate degree in nursing with a specialization in the newborn is required. This training involves coursework in nursing and the biological sciences, as well as supervisory clinical experiences.

Nurse-Midwife

A nurse-midwife formulates and provides comprehensive care to selected maternity patients, cares for the expectant mother as she prepares to give birth and guides her through the birth process, and cares for the postpartum patient. The nurse-midwife also may provide care to the newborn, counsel parents on the infant's development and parenting, and provide guidance about health practices. Becoming a nurse-midwife generally requires an undergraduate degree from a school of nursing. A nurse-midwife most often works in a hospital setting.

Pediatric Nurse

Pediatric nurses have a degree in nursing that takes two to five years to complete. Some also may go on to obtain a master's or doctoral degree in pediatric nursing. Pediatric nurses take courses in biological sciences, nursing care, and pediatrics, usually in a school of nursing. They also undergo supervised clinical experiences in medical settings.

They monitor infants' and children's health, work to prevent disease or injury, and help children attain optimal health. They may work in hospitals, schools of nursing, or with pediatricians in private practice or at a medical clinic.

Geriatric Nurse

Geriatric nurses seek to prevent or intervene in the chronic or acute health problems of older adults. They take courses in a school of nursing and obtain a degree in nursing. This takes anywhere from two to five years. As in the case of a pediatric nurse, a geriatric nurse also may obtain a master's or doctoral degree in his or her specialty.

Geriatric nurses take courses in biological sciences, nursing care, and mental health. They also experience supervised clinical training in geriatric settings. They may work in hospitals, nursing homes, schools of nursing, or with geriatric medical specialists or psychiatrists in a medical clinic or in private practice.

Physical Therapist

Physical therapists usually have an undergraduate degree in physical therapy and are licensed by a state. They take courses and experience supervised training in physical therapy. Many physical therapists work with people of all ages, although some specialize in working with a specific age group, such as children or older adults. They work directly with these individuals who have a physical problem either due to disease or injury to help them function as competently as possible. They may consult with other professionals and coordinate services for the individual.

Occupational Therapist

Occupational therapists may have an associate, bachelor's, master's, and/or doctoral degree with education ranging from two to six years. Training includes occupational therapy courses in a specialized program. National certification is required and licensing/registration is required in some states. Occupational therapy is a health and rehabilitation profession that helps people regain, develop, and build skills that are important for independent functioning, health, well-being, security, and happiness. The occupational therapist (OTR) initiates the evaluation of clients and manages the treatment process for clients with various impairments.

Therapeutic/Recreation Therapist

Therapeutic/recreation therapists maintain or improve the quality of life for people with special needs through intervention, leisure education, and recreation participation. They work in hospitals, rehabilitation centers, local government agencies, at-risk youth programs, as well as other settings. Becoming a therapeutic/recreation therapist requires an undergraduate degree with coursework in leisure studies and a concentration in therapeutic recreation. National certification is usually required. Coursework in anatomy, special education, and psychology are beneficial.

Audiologist

An audiologist has a minimum of an undergraduate degree in hearing science. This includes courses and supervisory training. Audiologists assess and identify the presence and severity of hearing loss, as well as problems in balance. Some audiologists also go on to obtain a master's or doctoral degree. They may work in a medical clinic, with a physician in private practice, in a hospital, or in a medical school.

Speech Therapist

Speech therapists are health-care professionals who are trained to identify, assess, and treat speech and language problems. They may work with physicians, psychologists, social workers, and other health-care professionals in a team approach to helping individuals with physical or psychological problems in which speech and language are involved in the problem. Speech pathologists have a minimum of an undergraduate degree in speech and hearing science or communications disorders area. They may work in private practice, in hospitals and medical schools, and in government agencies with individuals of any age. Some may specialize in working with children, others with the elderly, or in a particular type of speech disorder.

Genetic Counselor

Genetic counselors are health professionals with specialized graduate degrees and experience in the areas of medical genetics and counseling. Most enter the field after majoring in undergraduate school in such disciplines as biology, genetics, psychology, nursing, public health, and social work.

Genetic counselors work as members of a health-care team, providing information and support to families who have members with birth defects or genetic disorders and to families who may be at risk for a variety of inherited conditions. They identify families at risk and provide supportive counseling. They serve as educators and resource people for other health-care professionals and the public. Almost one-half work in university medical centers, and another one-fourth work in private hospital settings.

FAMILIES/RELATIONSHIPS

A number of careers and jobs are available for working with families and relationship problems across the life span. These range from being a home health aide to working as a marriage and family therapist.

Home Health Aide

No higher education is required for this position. There is brief training by an agency. A home health aide provides direct services to older adults in the older adults' homes, providing assistance in basic self-care tasks.

Child Welfare Worker

A child welfare worker is employed by the Child Protective Services unit of each state. The child welfare worker protects the child's rights, evaluates any maltreatment of the child, and may have the child removed from the home if necessary. A child social worker has a minimum of an undergraduate degree in social work.

Child Life Specialist

Child life specialists work with children and their families when the child needs to be hospitalized. They monitor the child's activities, seek to reduce the child's stress, help the child cope effectively, and assist the child in enjoying the hospital experience as much as possible. Child life specialists may provide parent education and develop individualized treatment plans based on an assessment of the child's development, temperament, medical plan, and available social supports. Child life specialists have an undergraduate degree, and they take courses in child development and education, as well as usually taking additional courses in a child life program.

Marriage and Family Therapist

Marriage and family therapists work on the principle that many individuals who have psychological problems benefit when psychotherapy is provided in the context of a marital or family relationship. Marriage and family therapists may provide marital therapy, couple therapy to individuals in a relationship who are not married, and family therapy to two or more members of a family.

Marriage and family therapists have a master's or doctoral degree. They go through a training program in graduate school similar to a clinical psychologist but with the focus on marital and family relationships. In most states, it is necessary to go through a licensing procedure to practice marital and family therapy.

WEBSITE CONNECTIONS FOR CAREERS IN LIFE-SPAN DEVELOPMENT

By going to the website for this book, you can obtain more detailed career information about the various careers in life-span development described in this appendix. Go to the Web connections in the Career Appendix section, where you will read a description of the websites. Then click on the title, and you will be able to go directly to the website described. Here are the website connections:

Education/Research

Careers in Psychology
Elementary and Secondary School Teaching

Exceptional Children Teachers
Early Childhood Education
Family and Consumer Science Education
Educational Psychology
School Psychology
Gerontology

Clinical Counseling

Clinical Psychology
Psychiatry
Counseling Psychology
School Counseling
Rehabilitation Counseling
Social Work
Drug Counseling

Medical/Nursing/Physical Development

Obstetrics and Gynecology
Pediatrics
Nurse-Midwife
Neonatal Nursing
Pediatric Nursing
Gerontological Nursing
Physical Therapy
Occupational Therapy
Therapeutic/Recreation Therapy
Audiology and Speech Pathology
Genetic Counseling

Families/Relationships

Child Welfare Worker
Child Life Specialist
Marriage and Family Therapist

There is nothing quite so practical as a good theory.
—KURT LEWIN
American Social Psychologist,
20th Century

The Science of Life-Span Development

Images of Life-Span Development
The Childhoods of Erikson and Piaget

Imagine that you have developed a major theory of development. What would influence you to construct this theory? A person interested in developing such a theory usually goes through a long university training program that culminates in a doctoral degree. As part of the training, the future theorist is exposed to many ideas about a particular area of life-span development, such as biological, cognitive, or socioemotional development. Another factor that could explain why someone develops a particular theory is that person's life experiences. Two important developmental theorists, whose views will be described later in the chapter, are Erik Erikson and Jean Piaget. Let's examine a portion of their lives as they were growing up to discover how their experiences might have contributed to the theories they developed.

Erik Homberger Erikson (1902–1994) was born near Frankfurt, Germany, to Danish parents. Before Erik was born, his parents separated, and his mother left Denmark to live in Germany. At age 3, Erik became ill, and his mother took him to see a pediatrician named Homberger. Young Erik's mother fell in love with the pediatrician, married him, and named Erik after his new stepfather.

Erik attended primary school from the age of 6 to 10 and then the gymnasium (high school) from 11 to 18. He studied art and a number of languages. Erik did not like the atmosphere of formal schooling, and this attitude was reflected in his grades. Rather than going to college at age 18, the adolescent Erikson wandered around Europe, keeping a diary about his experiences. After a year of travel through Europe, he returned to Germany and enrolled in art school, became dissatisfied, and enrolled in another. Later he traveled to Florence, Italy. Psychiatrist Robert Coles described Erikson at this time:

> To the Italians he was the young, tall, thin Nordic expatriate with long blond hair. He wore a corduroy suit and was seen by his family and friends as not odd or "sick" but as a wandering artist who was trying to come to grips with himself, a not unnatural or unusual struggle. (Coles, 1970, p. 15)

Contrast Erikson's experiences with those of Jean Piaget. Piaget (1896–1980) was born in Neuchâtel, Switzerland. Jean's father was an intellectual who taught young Jean to think systematically. Jean's mother was also very bright. His father had an air of detachment from his mother, whom Piaget described as prone to frequent outbursts of neurotic behavior.

In his autobiography, Piaget detailed why he chose to study cognitive development rather than social or abnormal development:

> I started to forego playing for serious work very early. Indeed, I have always detested any departure from reality, an attitude which I relate to . . . my mother's poor health. It was this disturbing factor which at the beginning of my studies in psychology made me keenly interested in psychoanalytic and pathological psychology. Though this interest helped me to achieve independence and widen my cultural background, I have never since felt any desire to involve myself deeper in that particular direction, always much preferring the study of normalcy and of the workings of the intellect to that of the tricks of the unconscious. (Piaget, 1952, p. 238)

These snapshots of Erikson and Piaget illustrate how personal experiences might influence the direction in which a particular theorist goes. Erikson's wanderings and search for self contributed to his theory of identity development, and Piaget's intellectual experiences with his parents and schooling contributed to his emphasis on cognitive development.

PREVIEW

Theories are part of the science of life-span development. Some individuals have difficulty thinking of life-span development as a science like physics, chemistry, and biology. Can a discipline that studies how parents nurture children, whether watching TV long hours is linked with being overweight, and the factors involved in life satisfaction among older adults be equated with disciplines that study the molecular structure of a compound and how gravity works? The answer is yes. Science is defined not by *what* it investigates, but by *how* it investigates. Whether you're studying photosynthesis, butterflies, Saturn's moons, or human development, it is the way you study that makes the approach scientific or not.

This chapter introduces the theories and methods that are the foundation of the science of life-span development. At the end of the chapter, we will explore some of the ethical challenges and biases that researchers must guard against to protect the integrity of their results and respect the rights of the participants in their studies.

1 THEORIES OF DEVELOPMENT

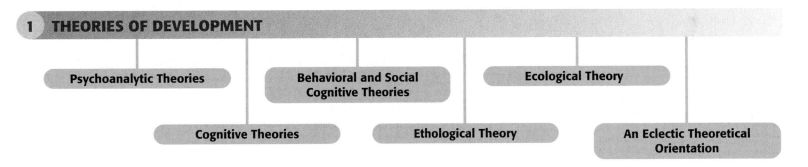

All scientific knowledge stems from a rigorous, systematic method of investigation (Rosnow & Rosenthal, 2005; Wozniak, 2004). The *scientific method* is essentially a four-step process:

1. Conceptualize a process or problem to be studied.
2. Collect research information (data).
3. Analyze data.
4. Draw conclusions.

In step 1, when researchers are formulating a problem to study, they often draw on *theories* and develop *hypotheses*. A **theory** is an interrelated, coherent set of ideas that helps to explain and make predictions. **Hypotheses** are specific assumptions and predictions that can be tested to determine their accuracy. For example, a theory on mentoring might attempt to explain and predict why sustained support, guidance, and concrete experience make a difference in the lives of children from impoverished backgrounds. A hypothesis might state that individual attention from an adult will improve an adolescent's performance at school.

The diversity of theories makes understanding life-span development a challenging undertaking. Just when you think one theory has the correct explanation of life-span development, another theory crops up and makes you rethink your earlier conclusion. To keep from getting frustrated, remember that life-span development is a complex, multifaceted topic. No single theory has been able to account for all aspects of it. Each theory contributes an important piece to the life-span development puzzle. Although the theories sometimes disagree about certain aspects of life-span development, much of their information is complementary rather than

theory An interrelated, coherent set of ideas that helps to explain and make predictions.

hypotheses Specific assumptions and predictions that can be tested to determine their accuracy.

Sigmund Freud, the pioneering architect of psychoanalytic theory. *How did Freud believe each individual's personality is organized?*

contradictory. Together they let us see the total landscape of life-span development in all its richness.

Psychoanalytic Theories

Psychoanalytic theory describes development as primarily unconscious (beyond awareness) and heavily colored by emotion. Psychoanalytic theorists emphasize that behavior is merely a surface characteristic and that a true understanding of development requires analyzing the symbolic meanings of behavior and the deep inner workings of the mind. Psychoanalytic theorists also stress that early experiences with parents extensively shape development. These characteristics are highlighted in the main psychoanalytic theory, that of Sigmund Freud.

Freud's Psychosexual Theory   Freud (1856–1939) developed his ideas about psychoanalytic theory while working with mental patients. A medical doctor who specialized in neurology, he spent most of his years in Vienna, though he moved to London near the end of his career because of Nazi anti-Semitism. Freud (1917) proposed that personality has three structures: the id, the ego, and the superego. The *id*, he said, consists of instincts, which are an individual's reservoir of psychic energy. In Freud's view, the id is totally unconscious; it has no contact with reality. As children experience the demands and constraints of reality, a new part of personality emerges—the *ego*, the Freudian personality structure that deals with the demands of reality. The ego is called the executive branch of personality because it uses reasoning to make decisions. The id and the ego have no morality. They do not take into account whether something is right or wrong. The *superego* is the Freudian structure of personality that is the moral branch of personality. The superego decides whether something is right or wrong. Think of the superego as what we often refer to as our "conscience." You probably are beginning to sense that both the id and the superego make life rough for the ego. Your ego might say, "I will have sex only occasionally and be sure to take the proper precautions because I don't want the intrusion of a child in the development of my career." However, your id is saying, "I want to be satisfied; sex is pleasurable." Your superego is at work, too: "I feel guilty about having sex."

   As Freud listened to, probed, and analyzed his patients, he became convinced that their problems were the result of experiences early in life. Freud argued that we go through five stages of psychosexual development, and that at each stage of development we experience pleasure in one part of the body more than in others. Freud maintained that our adult personality is determined by the way we resolve conflicts between these early sources of pleasure—the mouth, the anus, and then the genitals—and the demands of reality. When these conflicts are not resolved, the individual may become fixated at a particular stage of development. Fixation occurs when the individual remains locked in an earlier developmental stage because needs are under- or overgratified. For example, a parent might wean a child too early, be too strict in toilet training the child, punish the child for masturbation, or "smother" the child with too much attention. Figure 2.1 illustrates the five Freudian stages.

psychoanalytic theory Describes development as primarily unconscious and heavily colored by emotion. Behavior is merely a surface characteristic, and the symbolic workings of the mind have to be analyzed to understand behavior. Early experiences with parents are emphasized.

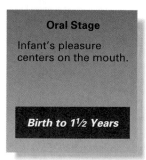

Oral Stage

Infant's pleasure centers on the mouth.

Birth to 1½ Years

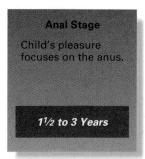

Anal Stage

Child's pleasure focuses on the anus.

1½ to 3 Years

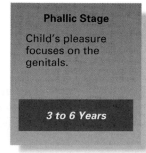

Phallic Stage

Child's pleasure focuses on the genitals.

3 to 6 Years

Latency Stage

Child represses sexual interest and develops social and intellectual skills.

6 Years to Puberty

Genital Stage

A time of sexual reawakening; source of sexual pleasure becomes someone outside the family.

Puberty Onward

FIGURE 2.1 Freudian Stages

The *oral stage* is the first Freudian stage of development, occurring during the first 18 months of life, in which the infant's pleasure centers around the mouth. Chewing, sucking, and biting are the chief sources of pleasure. These actions reduce tension in the infant.

The *anal stage* is the second Freudian stage of development, occurring between $1\frac{1}{2}$ and 3 years of age, in which the child's greatest pleasure involves the anus or the eliminative functions associated with it. In Freud's view, the exercise of anal muscles reduces tension.

The *phallic stage* is the third Freudian stage of development. The phallic stage occurs between the ages of 3 and 6; its name comes from the Latin word *phallus,* which means "penis." During the phallic stage, pleasure focuses on the genitals as both boys and girls discover that self-manipulation is enjoyable.

In Freud's view, the phallic stage has a special importance in personality development because it is during this period that the Oedipus complex appears. This name comes from Greek mythology, in which Oedipus, the son of the King of Thebes, unwittingly kills his father and marries his mother. The *Oedipus complex* according to Freudian theory, is the young child's development of an intense desire to replace the same-sex parent and enjoy the affections of the opposite-sex parent.

How is the Oedipus complex resolved? At about 5 to 6 years of age, children recognize that their same-sex parent might punish them for their incestuous wishes. To reduce this conflict, the child identifies with the same-sex parent, striving to be like him or her. If the conflict is not resolved, though, the individual may become fixated at the phallic stage.

The *latency stage* is the fourth Freudian stage of development, which occurs between approximately 6 years of age and puberty. During this period, the child represses all interest in sexuality and develops social and intellectual skills. This activity channels much of the child's energy into emotionally safe areas and helps the child forget the highly stressful conflicts of the phallic stage.

The *genital stage* is the fifth and final Freudian stage of development, occurring from puberty onward. The genital stage is a time of sexual reawakening; the source of sexual pleasure now becomes someone outside of the family. Freud believed that unresolved conflicts with parents reemerge during adolescence. When these conflicts have been resolved, the individual is capable of developing a mature love relationship and functioning independently as an adult.

Freud's theory has undergone significant revisions by a number of psychoanalytic theorists (Eagle, 2000). Many contemporary psychoanalytic theorists place less emphasis on sexual instincts and more emphasis on cultural experiences as determinants of an individual's development. Unconscious thought remains a central theme, but most contemporary psychoanalysts stress that conscious thought makes up more of the mind than Freud envisioned. Next, we will explore the ideas of an important revisionist of Freud's ideas—Erik Erikson.

Erikson's Psychosocial Theory   Erik Erikson recognized Freud's contributions but believed that Freud misjudged some important dimensions of human development. For one thing, Erikson (1950, 1968) said we develop in *psychosocial* stages, rather than in *psychosexual* stages, as Freud maintained. For Freud, the primary motivation for human behavior was sexual in nature, for Erikson it was social and reflected a desire to affiliate with other people. Erikson emphasized developmental change throughout the human life span, whereas Freud argued that our basic personality is shaped in the first five years of life. In **Erikson's theory,** eight stages of development unfold as we go through the life span (see figure 2.2). Each stage consists of a unique developmental task that confronts individuals with a crisis that must be resolved. According to Erikson, this crisis is not a catastrophe but a turning point of increased vulnerability and enhanced potential. The more successfully an individual resolves the crises, the healthier development will be (Hopkins, 2000).

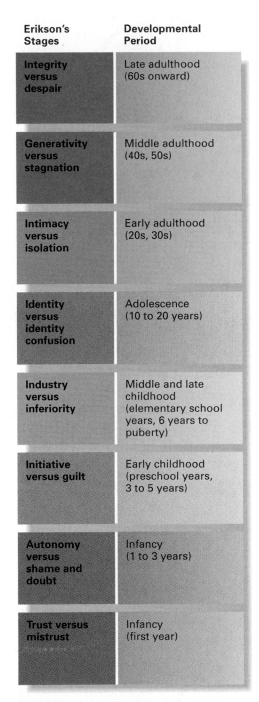

Erikson's Stages	Developmental Period
Integrity versus despair	Late adulthood (60s onward)
Generativity versus stagnation	Middle adulthood (40s, 50s)
Intimacy versus isolation	Early adulthood (20s, 30s)
Identity versus identity confusion	Adolescence (10 to 20 years)
Industry versus inferiority	Middle and late childhood (elementary school years, 6 years to puberty)
Initiative versus guilt	Early childhood (preschool years, 3 to 5 years)
Autonomy versus shame and doubt	Infancy (1 to 3 years)
Trust versus mistrust	Infancy (first year)

FIGURE 2.2 Erikson's Eight Life-Span Stages

Erikson's theory Includes eight stages of human development. Each stage consists of a unique developmental task that confronts individuals with a crisis that must be resolved.

Freud's Theory
Erikson's Theory

Erik Erikson with his wife, Joan, an artist. Erikson generated one of the most important developmental theories of the twentieth century. *Which stage of Erikson's theory are you in? Does Erikson's description of this stage characterize you?*

Trust versus mistrust is Erikson's first psychosocial stage, which is experienced in the first year of life. A sense of trust requires a feeling of physical comfort and a minimal amount of fear and apprehension about the future. Trust in infancy sets the stage for a lifelong expectation that the world will be a good and pleasant place to live.

Autonomy versus shame and doubt is Erikson's second stage of development. This stage occurs in late infancy and toddlerhood (1 to 3 years). After gaining trust in their caregivers, infants begin to discover that their behavior is their own. They start to assert their sense of independence, or autonomy. They realize their *will*. If infants are restrained too much or punished too harshly, they are likely to develop a sense of shame and doubt.

Initiative versus guilt, Erikson's third stage of development, occurs during the preschool years. As preschool children encounter a widening social world, they are challenged more than when they were infants. Active, purposeful behavior is needed to cope with these challenges. Children are asked to assume responsibility for their bodies, their behavior, their toys, and their pets. Developing a sense of responsibility increases initiative. Uncomfortable guilt feelings may arise, though, if the child is irresponsible and is made to feel too anxious. Erikson has a positive outlook on this stage. He believes that most guilt is quickly compensated for by a sense of accomplishment.

Industry versus inferiority is Erikson's fourth developmental stage, occurring approximately in the elementary school years. Children's initiative brings them in contact with a wealth of new experiences. As they move into middle and late childhood, they direct their energy toward mastering knowledge and intellectual skills. At no other time is the child more enthusiastic about learning than at the end of early childhood's period of expansive imagination. The danger in the elementary school years is that the child can develop a sense of inferiority—feeling incompetent and unproductive. Erikson believed that teachers have a special responsibility for children's development of industry. Teachers should "mildly but firmly coerce children into the adventure of finding out that one can learn to accomplish things which one would never have thought of by oneself" (Erikson, 1968, p. 127).

Identity versus identity confusion is Erikson's fifth developmental stage, which individuals experience during the adolescent years. At this time, individuals are faced with finding out who they are, what they are all about, and where they are going in life. Adolescents are confronted with many new roles and adult statuses—vocational and romantic, for example. Parents need to allow adolescents to explore many different roles and different paths within a particular role. If the adolescent explores such roles in a healthy manner and arrives at a positive path to follow in life, then a positive identity will be achieved. If an identity is pushed on the adolescent by parents, if the adolescent does not adequately explore many roles, and if a positive future path is not defined, then identity confusion reigns.

Intimacy versus isolation is Erikson's sixth developmental stage, which individuals experience during the early adulthood years. At this time, individuals face the developmental task of forming intimate relationships with others. Erikson describes intimacy as finding oneself yet losing oneself in another. If the young adult forms healthy friendships and an intimate relationship with another individual, intimacy will be achieved; if not, isolation will result.

Generativity versus stagnation is Erikson's seventh developmental stage, which individuals experience during middle adulthood. A chief concern is to assist the younger generation in developing and leading useful lives—this is what Erikson means by generativity. The feeling of having done nothing to help the next generation is stagnation.

Integrity versus despair is Erikson's eighth and final stage of development, which individuals experience in late adulthood. During this stage, a person reflects on the past and either pieces together a positive review or concludes that life has not been spent well. Through many different routes, the older person may have developed a positive outlook in most or all of the previous stages of development. If so, the retrospective glances will reveal a picture of a life well spent, and the person will feel a sense of satisfaction—integrity will be achieved. If the older adult resolved many of the earlier stages negatively, the retrospective glances likely will yield doubt or gloom—the despair Erikson described.

Erikson did not believe that the proper solution to a stage crisis is always completely positive. Some exposure or commitment to the negative side of the person's conflict is sometimes inevitable—for example, learning to trust is an important outcome of Erikson's first stage, but you cannot trust all people under all circumstances and survive. Nonetheless, in the healthy solution to a stage crisis, the positive resolution dominates. We will discuss Erikson's theory again on a number of occasions in the chapters on socioemotional development in this book.

Evaluating the Psychoanalytic Theories The contributions of psychoanalytic theories include these factors:

- Early experiences play an important part in development.
- Family relationships are a central aspect of development.
- Personality can be better understood if it is examined developmentally.
- The mind is not all conscious; unconscious aspects of the mind need to be considered.
- Changes take place in adulthood as well as in childhood (Erikson).

These are some criticisms of psychoanalytic theories:

- The main concepts of psychoanalytic theories have been difficult to test scientifically.
- Much of the data used to support psychoanalytic theories come from individuals' reconstruction of the past, often the distant past, and are of unknown accuracy.
- The sexual underpinnings of development are given too much importance (especially in Freud's theory).
- The unconscious mind is given too much credit for influencing development.
- Psychoanalytic theories present an image of humans that is too negative (especially in Freud's theory).
- Psychoanalytic theories are culture- and gender-biased (especially in Freud's theory).

Cognitive Theories

Whereas psychoanalytic theories stress the importance of unconscious thoughts, cognitive theories emphasize conscious thoughts. Three important cognitive theories are Piaget's cognitive developmental theory, Vygotsky's sociocultural cognitive theory, and the information-processing theory.

Piaget's theory will be covered in detail later in this book, when we discuss cognitive development in infancy, early childhood, middle and late childhood, and adolescence. Here we briefly present the main ideas of his theory.

Piaget's Cognitive Developmental Theory **Piaget's theory** states that children actively construct their understanding of the world and go through four stages of cognitive development. Two processes underlie this cognitive construction of the world: organization and adaptation. To make sense of our world, we organize our experiences. For example, we separate important ideas from less important ideas. We connect one idea to another. In addition to organizing our observations and experiences, we *adapt* our thinking to include new ideas because additional information furthers understanding.

Piaget (1954) believed that we adapt in two ways: assimilation and accommodation. **Assimilation** occurs when individuals incorporate new information into

Jean Piaget, the famous Swiss developmental psychologist, changed the way we think about the development of children's minds. *What are some key ideas in Piaget's theory?*

Piaget's theory States that children actively construct their understanding of the world and go through four stages of cognitive development.

assimilation Occurs when individuals incorporate new information into their existing knowledge.

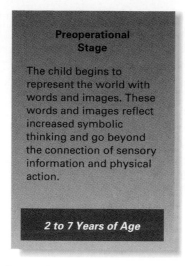
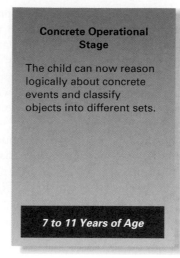
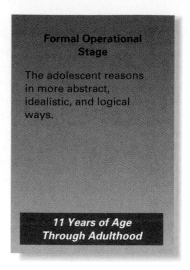

FIGURE 2.3 Piaget's Four Stages of Cognitive Development

their existing knowledge. **Accommodation** occurs when individuals adjust to new information. Consider a circumstance in which a 9-year-old girl is given a hammer and nails to hang a picture on the wall. She has never used a hammer, but from observation and vicarious experience she realizes that a hammer is an object to be held, that it is swung by the handle to hit the nail, and that it is usually swung a number of times. Recognizing each of these things, she fits her behavior into the information she already has (assimilation). However, the hammer is heavy, so she holds it near the top. She swings too hard and the nail bends, so she adjusts the pressure of her strikes. These adjustments reveal her ability to alter slightly her conception of the world (accommodation).

Piaget also believed that we go through four stages in understanding the world (see figure 2.3). Each of the stages is age-related and consists of distinct ways of thinking. In the Piagetian view, the *different* way of understanding the world makes one stage more advanced than another, not simply knowing *more* information. This is what Piaget meant when he said the child's cognition is *qualitatively* different in one stage compared with another (Vidal, 2000). What are Piaget's four stages of cognitive development like?

The *sensorimotor stage,* which lasts from birth to about 2 years of age, is the first Piagetian stage. In this stage, infants construct an understanding of the world by coordinating sensory experiences (such as seeing and hearing) with physical, motoric actions—hence the term *sensorimotor.* At the beginning of this stage, newborns have little more than reflexive patterns with which to work. At the end of the stage, 2-year-olds have complex sensorimotor patterns and are beginning to operate with primitive symbols.

The *preoperational stage,* which lasts from approximately 2 to 7 years of age, is the second Piagetian stage. In this stage, children begin to represent the world with words, images, and drawings. Symbolic thought goes beyond simple connections of sensory information and physical action. However, although preschool children can symbolically represent the world, according to Piaget, they still lack the ability to perform *operations,* the Piagetian term for internalized mental actions that allow children to do mentally what they previously did physically.

The *concrete operational stage,* which lasts from approximately 7 to 11 years of age, is the third Piagetian stage. In this stage, children can perform operations, and logical reasoning replaces intuitive thought as long as reasoning can be applied to specific or concrete examples. For instance, concrete operational thinkers cannot imagine the steps necessary to complete an algebraic equation, which is too abstract for thinking at this stage of development.

accommodation Occurs when individuals adjust to new information.

The *formal operational stage,* which appears between the ages of 11 and 15 and continues through adulthood, is the fourth and final Piagetian stage. In this stage, individuals move beyond concrete experiences and think in abstract and more logical terms. As part of thinking more abstractly, adolescents develop images of ideal circumstances. They might think about what an ideal parent is like and compare their parents to this ideal standard. They begin to entertain possibilities for the future and are fascinated with what they can be. In solving problems, formal operational thinkers are more systematic, developing hypotheses about why something is happening the way it is, then testing these hypotheses in a deductive manner. We will examine Piaget's cognitive developmental theory further in chapters 6, 8, 10, 12, and 14.

Piaget's Theory
Vygotsky's Theory

Vygotsky's Sociocultural Cognitive Theory   Like Piaget, the Russian developmentalist Lev Vygotsky (1896–1934) also believed that children actively construct their knowledge. However, Vygotsky gave social interaction and culture far more important roles in cognitive development than Piaget did. **Vygotsky's theory** is a sociocultural cognitive theory that emphasizes how culture and social interaction guide cognitive development. Vygotsky was born the same year as Piaget, but he died much earlier, at the age of 37. Both Piaget's and Vygotsky's ideas remained virtually unknown to American scholars until the 1960s. In the past several decades, American psychologists and educators have shown increased interest in Vygotsky's (1962) views.

Vygotsky portrayed the child's development as inseparable from social and cultural activities. He believed that the development of memory, attention, and reasoning involves learning to use the inventions of society, such as language, mathematical systems, and memory strategies. In one culture, this might consist of learning to count with the help of a computer. In another, it might consist of counting on one's fingers or using beads.

Vygotsky's theory has stimulated considerable interest in the view that knowledge is *situated* and *collaborative* (John-Steiner & Mahn, 2003; Rogoff, 2003; Tudge, 2004). In this view, knowledge is not generated from within the individual but rather is constructed through interaction with other people and objects in the culture, such as books. This suggests that knowledge can best be advanced through interaction with others in cooperative activities.

Vygotsky argued that children's social interaction with more-skilled adults and peers is indispensable in advancing cognitive development. Through this interaction, less-skilled members of the culture learn to use the tools that will help them adapt and be successful in the culture. For example, when a skilled reader regularly helps a child learn how to read, this not only advances a child's reading skills but also communicates to the child that reading is an important activity in the culture.

Lev Vygotsky. There is considerable interest today in Vygotsky's sociocultural cognitive theory of child development. *What are some characteristics of Vygotsky's theory?*

The Information-Processing Theory   Machines may be the best candidate for the title of "founding father" of information-processing theory. Although a number of factors stimulated the growth of this theory, none was more important than the computer. Psychologists began to wonder if the logical operations carried out by computers might tell us something about how the human mind works. They drew analogies between a computer's hardware and the brain and between computer software and cognition. The physical brain is said to be analogous to the computer's hardware; cognition is said to be analogous to its software.

This line of thinking helped to generate **information-processing theory,** which emphasizes that individuals manipulate information, monitor it, and strategize about it. According to this theory, individuals develop a gradually increasing capacity for processing information, which allows them to acquire increasingly complex knowledge and skills (Bjorklund, 2005; Mayer, 2004; Siegler & Alibali, 2005). Unlike Piaget's theory but like Vygotsky's theory, information-processing theory does not describe development as stagelike.

Vygotsky's theory A sociocultural cognitive theory that emphasizes how culture and social interaction guide cognitive development.

information-processing theory Emphasizes that individuals manipulate information, monitor it, and strategize about it. Central to this theory are the processes of memory and thinking.

Robert Siegler (1998, 2003; Siegler & Alibali, 2005), a leading expert on children's information processing, states that thinking is information processing. He says that when individuals perceive, encode, represent, store, and retrieve information, they are thinking. Siegler especially emphasizes that an important aspect of development is to learn good strategies for processing information. For example, becoming a better reader might involve learning to monitor the key themes of the material being read.

Evaluating the Cognitive Theories These are some contributions of cognitive theories:

- The cognitive theories present a positive view of development, emphasizing conscious thinking.
- The cognitive theories (especially Piaget's and Vygotsky's) emphasize the individual's active construction of understanding.
- Piaget's and Vygotsky's theories underscore the importance of examining developmental changes in children's thinking.
- The information-processing theory offers detailed descriptions of cognitive processes.

These are some criticisms of cognitive theories:

- There is skepticism about the pureness of Piaget's stages.
- The cognitive theories do not give adequate attention to individual variations in cognitive development.
- The information-processing theory does not provide an adequate description of developmental changes in cognition.
- Psychoanalytic theorists argue that the cognitive theories do not give enough credit to unconscious thought.

Behavioral and Social Cognitive Theories

Behaviorists essentially propose that scientifically we can study only what can be directly observed and measured. At about the same time as Freud was interpreting patients' unconscious minds through their early childhood experiences, Ivan Pavlov and John B. Watson were conducting detailed observations of behavior in controlled laboratory settings. Out of the behavioral tradition grew the belief that development is observable behavior that can be learned through experience with the environment. The three versions of the behavioral approach that we will explore are Pavlov's classical conditioning, Skinner's operant conditioning, and Bandura's social cognitive theory.

Pavlov's Classical Conditioning In the early 1900s, the Russian physiologist Ivan Pavlov (1927) knew that dogs innately salivate when they taste food. He became curious when he observed that dogs salivate to various sights and sounds before eating their food. For example, when an individual paired the ringing of a bell with the food, the bell ringing subsequently elicited the salivation response from the dogs when it was presented by itself. With this experiment, Pavlov discovered the principle of *classical conditioning,* in which a neutral stimulus (in our example, ringing a bell) acquires the ability to produce a response originally produced by another stimulus (in our example, food).

In the early twentieth century, John Watson wanted to show that Pavlov's concept of classical conditioning could be applied to human beings. He showed an infant named Albert a white rat to see if he was afraid of it. He was not. As Albert played with the rat, a loud noise was sounded behind his head. As you might imagine, the noise caused little Albert to cry. After several pairings of the loud noise and the white rat, Albert began to cry at the sight of the rat even when the noise was not sounded (Watson & Rayner, 1920). Today, we could not ethically conduct such an experiment, for reasons that we will discuss later in the chapter.

Many of our fears—fear of the dentist from a painful experience, fear of driving from being in an automobile accident, fear of heights from falling off a high chair when we were infants, and fear of dogs from being bitten—can be learned through classical conditioning.

Skinner's Operant Conditioning In B. F. Skinner's (1938) *operant conditioning,* the consequences of a behavior produce changes in the probability of the behavior's occurrence. A behavior followed by a rewarding stimulus is more likely to recur, whereas a behavior followed by a punishing stimulus it is less likely to recur. For example, when a person smiles at a child after the child has done something, the child is more likely to engage in the activity than if the person gives the child a nasty look.

For Skinner, such rewards and punishments shape individuals' development. For example, Skinner's approach argues that shy people learned to be shy as a result of experiences they had while growing up. It follows that modifications in an environment can help a shy person become more socially oriented.

Bandura's Social Cognitive Theory Some psychologists agree with the behaviorists' notion that development is learned and is influenced strongly by environmental interactions. However, they stress that Skinner went too far in declaring that cognition is unimportant in understanding development (Mischel, 2004). **Social cognitive theory** is the view of psychologists who emphasize behavior, environment, and cognition as the key factors in development.

American psychologist Albert Bandura (1925–) is the leading architect of social cognitive theory. Bandura (1986, 2001, 2004) emphasizes that cognitive processes have important links with the environment and behavior. His early research program focused heavily on observational learning (also called imitation or modeling), which is learning that occurs through observing what others do. What is *cognitive* about observational learning in Bandura's view? He proposes that people cognitively represent the behavior of others and then sometimes adopt this behavior themselves. For example, a young boy might observe his father's aggressive outbursts and hostile interchanges with people; when observed with his peers, the young boy's style of interaction is highly aggressive, showing the same characteristics as his father's behavior. A girl might adopt the dominant and sarcastic style of her teacher. When observed interacting with her younger brother, she says, "You are so slow. How can you do this work so slowly?" Social cognitive theorists stress that people acquire a wide range of such behaviors, thoughts, and feelings through observing others' behavior and that these observations form an important part of life-span development.

Bandura's (1998, 2001, 2004) most recent model of learning and development involves behavior, the person/cognition, and the environment. An individual's confidence that he or she can control his or her success is an example of a person factor, and developing strategies is an example of a cognitive factor. As shown in figure 2.4, behavior, person/cognitive, and environmental factors operate interactively. Behavior can influence person factors and vice versa. The person's cognitive activities can influence the environment, the environment can change the person's cognition, and so on.

Let's consider how Bandura's model might work in the case of a college student's achievement behavior. As the student diligently studies and gets good grades, her behavior produces positive thoughts about her abilities. As part of her effort to make good grades, she plans and develops a number of strategies to make her studying more efficient. In these ways, her behavior has influenced her thought and her thought has influenced her behavior. At the beginning of the term, her college made a special effort to involve students in a study skills program. She decided to join. Her success, along with that of other students who attended the program, has led the college to expand the program next semester. In these ways, environment influenced

B. F. Skinner was a tinkerer who liked to make new gadgets. The younger of his two daughters, Deborah, was raised in Skinner's enclosed Air-Crib, which he invented because he wanted to control her environment completely. The Air-Crib was soundproofed and temperature controlled. Debbie, shown here as a child with her parents, is currently a successful artist, is married, and lives in London. *What do you think about Skinner's Air-Crib?*

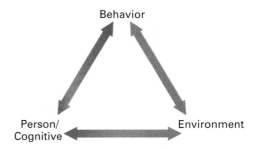

FIGURE 2.4 Bandura's Social Cognitive Model
The arrows illustrate how relations between behavior, person/cognitive, and environment are reciprocal rather than unidirectional.

social cognitive theory The view of psychologists who emphasize behavior, environment, and cognition as the key factors in development.

Albert Bandura. Bandura has been one of the leading architects of social cognitive theory. _What is the nature of his theory?_

Albert Bandura

behavior, and behavior changed the environment. And the college administrators' expectations that the study skills program would work made it possible in the first place. The program's success has spurred expectations that this type of program could work in other colleges. In these ways, cognition changed the environment, and the environment changed cognition.

Evaluating the Behavioral and Social Cognitive Theories   Contributions of the behavioral and social cognitive theories include:

- The importance of scientific research
- The environmental determinants of behavior
- The importance of observational learning (Bandura)
- Person/cognitive factors (social cognitive theory)

Criticisms of the behavioral and social cognitive theories include:

- Too little emphasis on cognition (Pavlov, Skinner)
- Too much emphasis on environmental determinants
- Inadequate attention to developmental changes
- Too mechanical and inadequate consideration of the spontaneity and creativity of humans

Behavioral and social cognitive theories emphasize the importance of environmental experiences in human development. Next we turn our attention to a theory that underscores the importance of biological foundations of development—ethological theory.

Ethological Theory

Ethology stresses that behavior is strongly influenced by biology, is tied to evolution, and is characterized by critical or sensitive periods. Ethologists believe that the presence or absence of certain experiences at particular times in the life span influences individuals well beyond the time they first occur and that most psychologists underestimate the importance of these special time frames in early development. Ethologists also stress the powerful roles that evolution and biological foundations play in development (Rosenzweig, 2000).

Ethology emerged as an important view because of the work of European zoologists, especially Konrad Lorenz (1903–1989). Working mostly with greylag geese, Lorenz (1965) studied a behavior pattern that was considered to be programmed within the birds' genes. A newly hatched gosling seemed to be born with the instinct to follow its mother. Observations showed that the gosling was capable of such behavior as soon as it hatched. Lorenz proved that it was incorrect to assume that such behavior was programmed in the animal. In a remarkable set of experiments, Lorenz separated the eggs laid by one goose into two groups. One group he returned to the goose to be hatched by her. The other group was hatched in an incubator. The goslings in the first group performed as predicted. They followed their mother as soon as they hatched. However, those in the second group, which saw Lorenz when they first hatched, followed him everywhere, as though he were their mother. Lorenz marked the goslings and then placed both groups under a box. Mother goose and "mother" Lorenz stood aside as the box lifted. Each group of goslings went directly to its "mother." Lorenz called this process _imprinting_, the rapid, innate learning within a limited critical period of time that involves attachment to the first moving object seen.

The ethological view of Lorenz and the European zoologists forced American developmental psychologists to recognize the importance of the biological basis of behavior. However, ethological research and theory lacked some ingredients that would elevate it to the ranks of the other theories discussed so far in this chapter. In particular, there was little or nothing in the classical ethological view about the

ethology Stresses that behavior is strongly influenced by biology, is tied to evolution, and is characterized by critical or sensitive periods.

Konrad Lorenz, a pioneering student of animal behavior, is followed through the water by three imprinted greylag geese. Describe Lorenz's experiment with the geese. *Do you think his experiment would have the same results with human babies? Explain.*

nature of social relationships across the human life span, something that any major theory of development must explain. Also, its concept of *critical period,* a fixed time period very early in development during which certain behaviors optimally emerge, seemed to be overdrawn. Classical ethological theory was weak in stimulating studies with humans. Recent expansion of the ethological view, however, has improved its status as a viable developmental perspective.

One of the most important applications of ethological theory to human development involves John Bowlby's (1969, 1989) theory of attachment. Bowlby argued that attachment to a caregiver over the first year of life has important consequences throughout the life span. In his view, if this attachment is positive and secure, the individual will likely develop more positively in childhood and adulthood. If the attachment is negative and insecure, life-span development will likely not be optimal. In chapter 7, "Socioemotional Development in Infancy," we will explore the concept of infant attachment in much greater detail.

Contributions of ethological theory include:

- Increased focus on the biological and evolutionary basis of development
- Use of careful observations in naturalistic settings
- Emphasis on sensitive periods of development

These are some criticisms of ethological theory:

- Concepts of critical and sensitive periods perhaps too rigid
- Too strong an emphasis on biological foundations
- Inadequate attention to cognition
- Better at generating research with animals than with humans

Another theory that emphasizes the biological aspects of human development—evolutionary psychology—will be presented in chapter 3, "Biological Beginnings," along with views on the role of heredity in development. Also, we will examine a number of biological theories of aging in chapter 18, "Physical Development in Late Adulthood."

Ecological Theory

While ethological theory stresses biological factors, ecological theory emphasizes environmental factors. One ecological theory that has important implications for understanding life-span development was created by Urie Bronfenbrenner (1917–).

Ecological theory is Bronfenbrenner's (1986, 2000, 2004; Bronfenbrenner & Morris, 1998) environmental system of development. It consists of five environmental systems ranging from the fine-grained inputs of direct interactions with people to the broad-based inputs of culture (see figure 2.5):

www.mhhe.com/santrockld10

Exploring Ethology
Bronfenbrenner's Theory

ecological theory Bronfenbrenner's environmental systems theory that focuses on five environmental systems: microsystem, mesosystem, exosystem, macrosystem, and chronosystem.

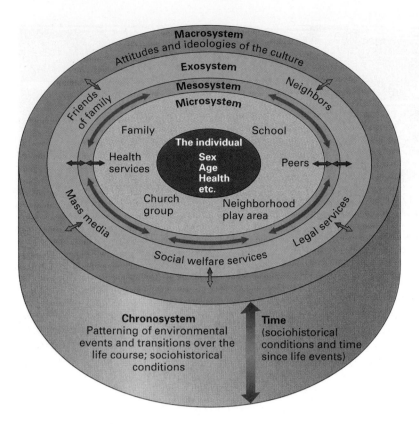

FIGURE 2.5 Bronfenbrenner's Ecological Theory of Development
Bronfenbrenner's ecological theory consists of five environmental systems: microsystem, mesosystem, exosystem, macrosystem, and chronosystem.

- *Microsystem:* The setting in which the individual lives. These contexts include the person's family, peers, school, and neighborhood. It is in the microsystem that the most direct interactions with social agents take place—with parents, peers, and teachers, for example. The individual is viewed not as a passive recipient of experiences in these settings, but as someone who helps to construct the settings.
- *Mesosystem:* Involves relations between microsystems or connections between contexts. Examples are the relation of family experiences to school experiences, school experiences to church experiences, and family experiences to peer experiences. For example, children whose parents have rejected them may have difficulty developing positive relations with teachers.
- *Exosystem:* Is involved when experiences in another social setting—in which the individual does not have an active role—influence what the individual experiences in an immediate context. For example, work experiences can affect a woman's relationship with her husband and their child. The mother might receive a promotion that requires more travel, which might increase marital conflict and change patterns of parent-child interaction.
- *Macrosystem:* The culture in which individuals live. Remember from chapter 1 that culture refers to the behavior patterns, beliefs, and all other products of a group of people that are passed on from generation to generation. Remember also that cross-cultural studies—the comparison of one culture with one or more other cultures—provide information about the generality of development.
- *Chronosystem:* The patterning of environmental events and transitions over the life course, as well as sociohistorical circumstances. For example, in studying the effects of divorce on children, researchers have found that the negative effects often peak in the first year after the divorce (Hetherington, 1993). By two years after the divorce, family interaction is less chaotic and more stable.

With regard to sociocultural circumstances, women today are much more likely to be encouraged to pursue a career than they were 20 or 30 years ago. Bronfenbrenner (2000, 2004; Bronfenbrenner & Morris, 1998) has added biological influences to his theory and now describes it as a bioecological theory. Nonetheless, ecological, environmental contexts still predominate in Bronfenbrenner's theory (Ceci, 2000).

The contributions of ecological theory include:

- A systematic examination of macro and micro dimensions of environmental systems
- Attention to connections between environmental settings (mesosystem)
- Consideration of sociohistorical influences on development (chronosystem)

These are some criticisms of ecological theory:

- Too little attention to biological foundations of development, even with the added discussion of biological influences in recent years
- Inadequate attention to cognitive processes

The macrosystem in Bronfenbrenner's theory involves cultural comparisons. The Diversity in Life-Span Development interlude examines cross-cultural variations in child rearing.

Urie Bronfenbrenner. Bronfenbrenner developed ecological theory, a perspective that is receiving increased attention. His theory emphasizes the importance of both micro and macro dimensions of the environment in which the child lives.

Diversity in Life-Span Development
Culture and Child Rearing

Child-rearing practices often reflect a culture's values. Indeed, researchers have found that child-rearing goals of parents depend less on their personal characteristics and more on the values of the culture in which the parents live (Chao & Tseng, 2002; Trommsdorff, 2002). Do you think children should be reared to be independent or to fit in with the group? Chances are that if you live in a Western culture such as the United States or Germany, you would endorse the belief that children should be reared to behave and think independently. However, if you live in an Eastern culture such as China or Japan, you are more likely to believe that children should be reared to fit in with the group and comply with what others think.

Chinese and Japanese children are reared to show a concern for social harmony (Keller, 2002). They (as well as children in African and Latino communal cultures) grow up with a stronger sense of "family self" than children in the United States and most other Western cultures, believing that what they do reflects not just on one's self but on one's family. Do something wrong or deviant and you shame your family; do something right and you bring honor to your family in these communal cultures. Related to the family self-orientation, researchers have found that U.S. adolescents are much less likely to say their parents are disappointed in them than are adolescents in Japan (Atkinson, 1988).

Keep in mind, though, that cultures as large and complex as the United States have residents with diverse views on child rearing. This is especially true today as a result of the dramatic increase in immigrants from Asian and Latino countries. Many Asians and Latinos who have immigrated to the United States have brought child-rearing views with them from their native country, views that in many cases conflict with the emphasis on independence in the American culture. Such differences in cultural values can pose difficulty when children and adolescents from communal cultures want more independence like their American peers and friends, but their parents and grandparents want to preserve their native culture's traditions. This may especially develop when immigrant adolescents want to date earlier and have more independence in their romantic relationships than their parents believe is appropriate. One recent study of Latina youth in a Midwestern town in the United States found that parents placed strict boundaries on their youths' romantic involvement (Raffaeilli & Ontai, 2001). The girls reported that their early dating experiences usually occurred without parental knowledge or permission and over half of the girls engaged in "sneak dating."

What are some examples of how cultural values shape child-rearing practices?

An Eclectic Theoretical Orientation

An **eclectic theoretical orientation** does not follow any one theoretical approach, but rather selects from each theory whatever is considered its best features. No single theory described in this chapter can explain entirely the rich complexity of life-span development. Each of the theories has made important contributions to our understanding of development, but none provides a complete description and explanation. Psychoanalytic theory best explains the unconscious mind. Erikson's theory best describes the changes that occur in adult development. Piaget's, Vygotsky's, and the information-processing views provide the most complete description of cognitive development. The behavioral and social cognitive and ecological theories have been the most adept at examining the environmental determinants of development. The ethological theories have made us aware of biology's role and the importance of sensitive periods in development. It is important to recognize that, although theories are helpful guides, relying on a single theory to explain development is probably a mistake.

eclectic theoretical orientation An orientation that does not follow any one theoretical approach, but rather selects from each theory whatever is considered the best in it.

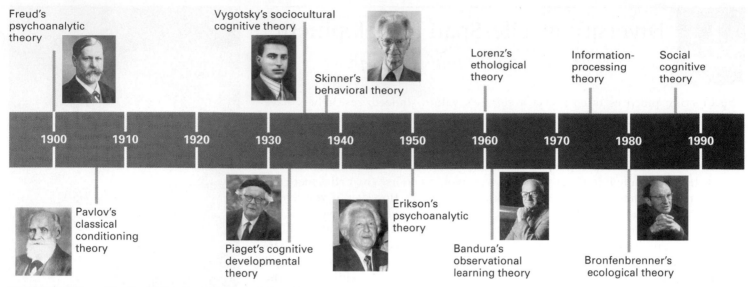

FIGURE 2.6 Time Line for Major Developmental Theories

An attempt was made in this chapter to present five theoretical perspectives objectively. The same eclectic orientation will be maintained throughout the book. In this way, you can view the study of development as it actually exists—with different theorists making different assumptions, stressing different empirical problems, and using different strategies to discover information. The theories that we have discussed were conceived at different points in the twentieth century. For a chronology of when these theories were proposed, see figure 2.6. Figure 2.7 compares the main theoretical perspectives in terms of how they view important developmental issues in life-span development.

Theory	Issues		
	Continuity/discontinuity, early versus later experiences	**Biological and environmental factors**	**Importance of cognition**
Psychoanalytic	Discontinuity between stages—continuity between early experiences and later development; early experiences very important; later changes in development emphasized in Erikson's theory	Freud's biological determination interacting with early family experiences; Erikson's more balanced biological-cultural interaction perspective	Emphasized, but in the form of unconscious thought
Cognitive	Discontinuity between stages in Piaget's theory; continuity between early experiences and later development in Piaget's and Vygotsky's theory; no stages in Vygotsky's theory or information-processing theory	Piaget's emphasis on interaction and adaptation; environment provides the setting for cognitive structures to develop; information-processing view has not addressed this issue extensively but mainly emphasizes biological-environmental interaction	The primary determinant of behavior
Behavioral and social cognitive	Continuity (no stages); experience at all points of development important	Environment viewed as the cause of behavior in both views	Strongly deemphasized in the behavioral approach but an important mediator in social cognitive theory
Ethological	Discontinuity but no stages; critical or sensitive periods emphasized; early experiences very important	Strong biological view	Not emphasized
Ecological	Little attention to continuity/discontinuity; change emphasized more than stability	Strong environmental view	Not emphasized

FIGURE 2.7 A Comparison of Theories and Issues in Life-Span Development

Review and Reflect: Learning Goal 1

1 Describe theories of life-span development

REVIEW

- How can theory and hypothesis be defined? What are two main psychoanalytic theories? What are some contributions and criticisms of the psychoanalytic theories?
- What are three main cognitive theories? What are some contributions and criticisms of the cognitive theories?
- What are three main behavioral and social cognitive theories? What are some contributions and criticisms of the behavioral and social cognitive theories?
- What is the nature of ethological theory? What are some contributions and criticisms of the theory?
- What characterizes ecological theory? What are some contributions and criticisms of the theory?
- What is an eclectic theoretical orientation?

REFLECT

- Which of the life-span theories do you think best explains your own development? Why?

2 RESEARCH IN LIFE-SPAN DEVELOPMENT

Types of Research   **Time Span of Research**

Generally, research in life-span development is designed to test hypotheses, which in some cases, are derived from the theories just described. Through research, theories are modified to reflect new data and occasionally new theories arise. What types of research are conducted in life-span development? If researchers want to study people of different ages, what research designs can they use? These are the questions that we will examine next.

Types of Research

This section describes the major methods used to gather data about life-span development. For this purpose, there are three basic types of research: descriptive, correlational, and experimental. Each has strengths and weaknesses.

Descriptive Research   Some important theories have grown out of **descriptive research,** which has the purpose of observing and recording behavior. For example, a psychologist might observe the extent to which people are altruistic or aggressive toward each other. By itself, descriptive research cannot prove what causes some phenomenon, but it can reveal important information about people's behavior and attitudes. Descriptive research methods include observation, surveys and interviews, standardized tests, case studies, life-history records, and physiological measures.

Observation   Scientific observation requires an important set of skills (McMillan, 2004). Unless we are trained observers and practice our skills regularly, we might not know what to look for, we might not remember what we saw, we might not

Science refines everyday thinking.

—**ALBERT EINSTEIN**
German-born American Physicist, 20th Century

descriptive research Has the purpose of observing and recording behavior.

realize that what we are looking for is changing from one moment to the next, and we might not communicate our observations effectively.

For observations to be effective, they have to be systematic (Elmes, Kantowitz, & Roedinger, 2005; Nadelman, 2004). We have to have some idea of what we are looking for. We have to know whom we are observing, when and where we will observe, and how the observations will be made. In what form they will be recorded: In writing? Tape recording? Video?

Where should we make our observations? We have two choices: the laboratory and the everyday world.

When we observe scientifically, we often need to control certain factors that determine behavior but are not the focus of our inquiry (Lammers & Badia, 2005). For this reason, some research in life-span development is conducted in a **laboratory,** a controlled setting with many of the complex factors of the "real world" removed.

An experiment conducted by Albert Bandura (1965) revealed that children behaved more aggressively after observing a model being rewarded for aggression. Bandura conducted this study in a laboratory with adults the child did not know. Thus, he controlled when the child witnessed aggression, how much aggression the child saw, and what form the aggression took. Bandura would not have had as much control over the experiment, or as much confidence in the results, if the study had been conducted in the children's homes and if familiar people had been present, such as the child's parents, siblings, or friends.

Laboratory research does have some drawbacks. First, it is almost impossible to conduct research without the participants' knowing they are being studied. Second, the laboratory setting is unnatural and therefore can cause the participants to behave unnaturally.

Another drawback of laboratory research is that people who are willing to come to a university laboratory may not fairly represent groups from diverse cultural backgrounds. Those who are unfamiliar with university settings, and with the idea of "helping science," may be intimidated by the setting.

Still another problem is that some aspects of life-span development are difficult if not impossible to examine in the laboratory. Laboratory studies of certain types of stress may even be unethical.

laboratory A controlled setting in which many of the complex factors of the "real world" are removed.

In this research study, mother-child interaction is being videotaped. Later, researchers will code the interaction using precise categories.

Naturalistic observation provides insights that we sometimes cannot achieve in the laboratory (Billman, 2003; Langston, 2002). **Naturalistic observation** means observing behavior in real-world settings, making no effort to manipulate or control the situation. Life-span researchers conduct naturalistic observations at sporting events, day-care centers, work settings, malls, and other places people live in and frequent.

Naturalistic observation was used in one study that focused on conversations in a children's science museum (Crowley & others, 2001). Parents were three times as likely to engage boys than girls in explanatory talk while visiting different exhibits at the science museum, suggesting a gender bias that encourages boys more than girls in science (see figure 2.8). In another study, Mexican American parents who had completed high school used more explanations with their children when visiting a science museum than Mexican American parents who had not completed high school (Tenenbaum & others, 2002).

Survey and Interview

Sometimes the best and quickest way to get information about people is to ask them for it. One technique is to *interview* them directly. A related method that is especially useful when information from many people is needed is the *survey*, sometimes referred to as a questionnaire. A standard set of questions is used to obtain peoples' self-reported attitudes or beliefs about a particular topic. In a good survey, the questions are clear and unbiased, allowing respondents to answer unambiguously.

Surveys and interviews can be used to study a wide range of topics from religious beliefs to sexual habits to attitudes about gun control to beliefs about how to improve schools. Surveys and interviews can be conducted in person or over the telephone. In addition, some surveys are now being conducted over the Internet.

Some survey and interview questions are unstructured and open-ended, such as "Could you elaborate on your optimistic tendencies?" or "How fulfilling would you say your marriage is?" Such questions allow for unique responses from each person surveyed. Other survey and interview questions are more structured and specific. For example, one national poll on beliefs about what needs to be done to improve U.S. schools asked: "Of the following four possibilities, which one do you think offers the most promise for improving public schools in the community: a qualified, competent teacher in every classroom; free choice for parents among a number of private, church-related, and public schools; rigorous academic standards; the elimination of social promotion; or don't know?" (Rose & Gallup, 2000). More than half of the respondents said that the most important way to improve schools is to have a qualified, competent teacher in every classroom.

One problem with surveys and interviews is the tendency of participants to answer questions in a way that they think is socially acceptable or desirable rather than telling what they truly think or feel (Best & Kahn, 2003). For example, on a survey or in an interview some individuals might say that they do not take drugs even though they do.

Standardized Test

A **standardized test** has uniform procedures for administration and scoring. Many standardized tests allow a person's performance to be compared with the performance of other individuals (Aiken, 2003; Gregory, 2004). One widely used standardized test in psychology is the Stanford-Binet intelligence test, which is described in chapter 10, "Physical and Cognitive Development in Middle and Late Childhood."

The main advantage of standardized tests is that they provide information about individual differences among people. One problem with standardized tests is that they do not always predict behavior in nontest situations. Another problem is that standardized tests are based on the belief that a person's behavior is consistent and stable, yet personality and intelligence—two primary targets of

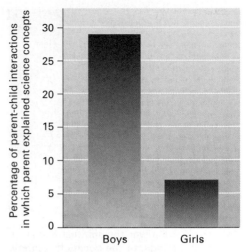

FIGURE 2.8 Parents' Explanations of Science to Sons and Daughters at a Science Museum

In a naturalistic observation study at a children's science museum, parents were three times more likely to explain science to boys than to girls (Crowley & others, 2001). The gender difference occurred regardless of whether the father, the mother, or both parents were with the child, although the gender difference was greatest for fathers' science explanations to sons and daughters.

"Would you say Attila is doing an excellent job, a good job, a fair job, or a poor job?"

naturalistic observation Observing behavior in real-world settings.

standardized test A test with uniform procedures for administration and scoring. Many standardized tests allow a person's performance to be compared with the performance of other individuals.

Mahatma Gandhi was the spiritual leader of India in the middle of the twentieth century. Erik Erikson conducted an extensive case study of his life to determine what contributed to his identity development. *What are some limitations of the case study approach?*

standardized testing—can vary with the situation. For example, a person may perform poorly on a standardized intelligence test in an office setting but score much higher at home, where he or she is less anxious.

This criticism is especially relevant for members of minority groups, some of whom have been inaccurately classified as mentally retarded on the basis of their scores on intelligence tests (Valencia & Suzuki, 2001). In addition, cross-cultural psychologists caution that many psychological tests developed in Western cultures might not be appropriate in other cultures (Matsumoto, 2004). People in other cultures may have had experiences that cause them to interpret and respond to questions much differently from the people for whom the test was standardized.

Case Study A **case study** is an in-depth look at a single individual. Case studies are performed mainly by mental health professionals when, for either practical or ethical reasons, the unique aspects of an individual's life cannot be duplicated and tested in other individuals (Dattilio, 2001). A case study provides information about one person's fears, hopes, fantasies, traumatic experiences, upbringing, family relationships, health, or anything that helps the psychologist understand the person's mind and behavior.

An example of a case study is Erik Erikson's (1969) analysis of India's spiritual leader Mahatma Gandhi. Erikson studied Gandhi's life in great depth to gain insights into how his positive spiritual identity developed, especially during his youth. In putting the pieces of Gandhi's identity development together, Erikson described the contributions of culture, history, family, and various other factors that might affect the way other people develop an identity.

Other vivid case studies appear in later chapters. One involves Michael Rehbein, who had much of the entire left side of his brain removed at 7 years of age to end severe epileptic seizures. Another concerns a modern-day "wild child" named Genie, who lived in near isolation during her childhood.

Case histories provide dramatic, in-depth portrayals of people's lives, but remember that we must be cautious when generalizing from this information. The subject of a case study is unique, with a genetic makeup and personal history that no one else shares. In addition, case studies involve judgments of unknown reliability. Psychologists who conduct case studies rarely check to see if other psychologists agree with their observations.

Life-History Record A **life-history record** documents a lifetime chronology of events and activities. It often involves a combination of data records on education, work, family, and residence. The record may be generated with information from archival materials (public records or historical documents) or interviews, which might include obtaining a life calendar from the respondent. Life calendars record the age (year and month) at which transitions occur in a variety of activity domains and life events, thus portraying an unfolding life course. In compiling life-history records, researchers increasingly use a wide array of materials, including written and oral reports from the subject, vital records, observation, and public documents (Clausen, 1993). One of the advantages of the multiple-materials approach is that information from varied sources can be compared and discrepancies sometimes can be resolved, resulting in a more accurate life-history record.

Physiological Measures Researchers are increasingly using physiological measures when they study development at different points in the life span. One type of physiological measure involves an assessment of the hormones in the bloodstream. For example, as puberty unfolds, the blood levels of certain hormones increase. To determine the nature of these hormonal changes, researchers take blood samples from willing adolescents (Susman & Rogol, 2004).

Another physiological measure that is increasingly being used is neuroimaging, especially *functional magnetic resonance imaging (fMRI)*, in which electromagnetic waves

case study An in-depth look at a single individual.

life-history record A record of information about a lifetime chronology of events and activities that often involve a combination of data records on education, work, family, and residence.

are used to construct images of a person's brain tissue and biochemical activity (Fox & Schott, 2004). We will have much more to say about neuroimaging and other physiological measures at various points in this book.

Correlational Research   In **correlational research,** the goal is to describe the strength of the relationship between two or more events or characteristics. The more strongly the two events are correlated (that is, related or associated), the more effectively we can predict one event from the other (Leary, 2004). For example, if researchers find that low-involved, permissive parenting is correlated with a child's lack of self-control, it suggests that low-involved, permissive parenting might be one source of the lack of self-control. This form of research is a key method of data analysis, which you may recall, is the third step in the scientific method.

A caution is in order, however. *Correlation does not equal causation.* The correlational finding just mentioned does not mean that permissive parenting necessarily causes low self-control in children. It could mean that, but it also could mean that a child's lack of self-control caused the parents to simply throw up their arms in despair and give up trying to control the child. It also could mean that other factors, such as heredity or poverty, caused the correlation between permissive parenting and low self-control in children. Figure 2.9 illustrates these possible interpretations of correlational data.

Throughout this book you will read about numerous correlational research studies. Keep in mind how easy it is to assume causality when two events or characteristics merely are correlated.

Experimental Research   An **experiment** is a carefully regulated procedure in which one or more factors believed to influence the behavior being studied are manipulated while all other factors are held constant. If the behavior under study changes when a factor is manipulated, we say that the manipulated factor has caused the behavior to change (Kirk, 2003; Mitchell & Jolley, 2004). In other words, the experiment has demonstrated cause and effect. The cause is the factor that was manipulated. The effect is the behavior that changed because of the manipulation. Nonexperimental research methods (descriptive and correlational research) cannot establish cause and effect because they do not involve manipulating factors in a controlled way.

Experiments include two types of changeable factors, or variables: independent and dependent. An *independent variable* is a manipulated, influential, experimental factor. It is a potential cause. The label "independent" is used because this variable

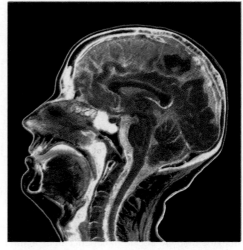

This fMRI scan of a 51-year-old male shows atrophy in the cerebral cortex of the brain, which occurs in various disorders including stroke and Alzheimer disease. The area of the upper cerebral cortex (where higher level brain functioning such as thinking and planning occur) is colored dark red. Neuroimaging techniques such as the fMRI are helping researchers to learn more about how the brain functions as people develop and age, as well as what happens to the brain when aging diseases such as stroke and Alzheimer disease are present.

correlational research The goal is to describe the strength of the relationship between two or more events or characteristics.

experiment A carefully regulated procedure in which one or more of the factors believed to influence the behavior being studied are manipulated while all other factors are held constant.

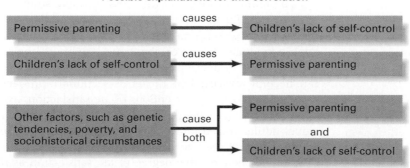

FIGURE 2.9 Possible Explanations for Correlational Data
An observed correlation between two events cannot be used to conclude that one event caused the other. Some possibilities are that the second event caused the first event or that a third, unknown event caused the correlation between the first two events.

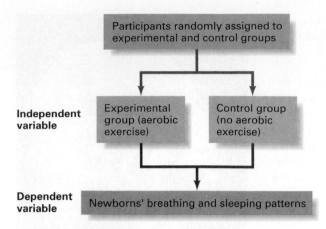

FIGURE 2.10 Principles of Experimental Research
Imagine that you decide to conduct an experimental study of the effects of aerobic exercise by pregnant women on their newborns' breathing and sleeping patterns. You would randomly assign pregnant women to experimental and control groups. The experimental-group women would engage in aerobic exercise over a specified number of sessions and weeks. The control group would not. Then, when the infants are born, you would assess their breathing and sleeping patterns. If the breathing and sleeping patterns of newborns whose mothers were in the experimental group are more positive than those of the control group, you would conclude that aerobic exercise caused the positive effects.

can be manipulated independently of other factors to determine its effect. Researchers have a vast array of options open to them in selecting independent variables, and one experiment may include several independent variables. A *dependent variable* is a factor that can change in an experiment, in response to changes in the independent variable. As researchers manipulate the independent variable, they measure the dependent variable for any resulting effect.

Experiments can involve one or more experimental groups and one or more control groups. An *experimental group* is a group whose experience is manipulated. A *control group* is a comparison group that is as much like the experimental group as possible and that is treated in every way like the experimental group except for the manipulated factor (independent variable). The control group serves as a baseline against which the effects of the manipulated condition can be compared.

Random assignment is an important principle for deciding whether each participant will be placed in the experimental group or in the control group (Smith & Davis, 2004). *Random assignment* means that researchers assign participants to experimental and control groups by chance. It reduces the likelihood that the experiment's results will be due to any preexisting differences between groups. Figure 2.10 illustrates the nature of experimental research.

Time Span of Research

A special concern of developmentalists is the time span of a research investigation. Studies that focus on the relation of age to some other variable are common in life-span development. We have several options: Researchers can study different individuals of different ages and compare them; they can study the same individuals as they age over time; or they can use some combination of these two approaches.

Cross-Sectional Approach The **cross-sectional approach** is a research strategy in which individuals of different ages are compared at one time. A typical cross-sectional study might include a group of 5-year-olds, 8-year-olds, and 11-year-olds. Another might include a group of 15-year-olds, 25-year-olds, and 45-year-olds. The different groups can be compared with respect to a variety of dependent variables: IQ, memory, peer relations, attachment to parents, hormonal changes, and so on. All of this can be accomplished in a short time. In some studies data are collected in a single day. Even in large-scale cross-sectional studies with hundreds of subjects, data collection does not usually take longer than several months to complete.

The main advantage of the cross-sectional study is that the researcher does not have to wait for the individuals to grow up or become older. Despite its time efficiency, the cross-sectional approach has its drawbacks. It gives no information about how individuals change or about the stability of their characteristics. The increases and decreases of development—the hills and valleys of growth and development—can become obscured in the cross-sectional approach. For example, in a cross-sectional approach to perceptions of life satisfaction, average increases and decreases might be revealed. But the study would not show how the life satisfaction of individual adults waxed and waned over the years. It also would not tell us whether adults who had positive or negative perceptions of life satisfaction as young adults maintained their relative degree of life satisfaction as middle-aged or older adults.

Longitudinal Approach The **longitudinal approach** is a research strategy in which the same individuals are studied over a period of time, usually several years

cross-sectional approach A research strategy in which individuals of different ages are compared at one time.

longitudinal approach A research strategy in which the same individuals are studied over a period of time, usually several years or more.

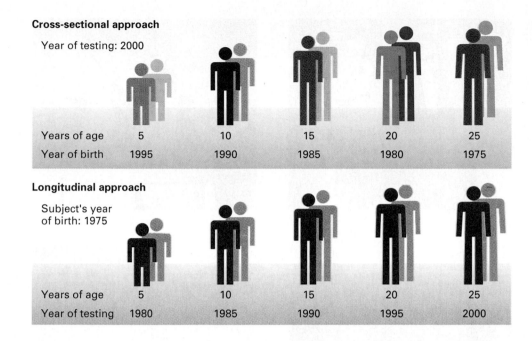

Cross-sectional approach

Year of testing: 2000

Years of age	5	10	15	20	25
Year of birth	1995	1990	1985	1980	1975

Longitudinal approach

Subject's year of birth: 1975

Years of age	5	10	15	20	25
Year of testing	1980	1985	1990	1995	2000

FIGURE 2.11 A Comparison of Cross-Sectional and Longitudinal Approaches

or more. For example, if a study of life satisfaction were conducted longitudinally, the same adults might be assessed periodically over a 70-year time span—at the ages of 20, 35, 45, 65, and 90, for example. Figure 2.11 compares the cross-sectional and longitudinal approaches.

Although longitudinal studies provide a wealth of information about such important issues as stability and change in development and the importance of early experience for later development, they are not without their problems (Raudenbush, 2001). They are expensive and time consuming. The longer the study lasts, the more participants drop out—they move, get sick, lose interest, and so forth. Participants can bias the outcome of a study, because those who remain may be dissimilar to those who drop out. Those individuals who remain in a longitudinal study over a number of years may be more compulsive and conformity-oriented, for example, or they might have more stable lives.

Sequential Approach Sometimes developmentalists also combine the cross-sectional and longitudinal approaches to learn about life-span development (Schaie, 1993). The **sequential approach** is the combined cross-sectional, longitudinal design. In most instances, this approach starts with a cross-sectional study that includes individuals of different ages. A number of months after the initial assessment, the same individuals are tested again—this is the longitudinal aspect of the design. At this later time, a new group of participants is assessed at each age level. The new groups at each level are added at the later time to control for changes that might have taken place in the original group—some might have dropped out of the study, or retesting might have improved their performance, for example. The sequential approach is complex, expensive, and time consuming, but it does provide information that is impossible to obtain from cross-sectional or longitudinal approaches alone. The sequential approach has been especially helpful in examining cohort effects in life-span development, which we will discuss next.

Cohort Effects A *cohort* is a group of people who are born at a similar point in history and share similar experiences as a result, such as living through the Great Depression of the 1930s or growing up in the same city around the same time. Other

sequential approach A combined cross-sectional, longitudinal design.

(a) (b) (c)

(d) (e) (f)

FIGURE 2.12 Cohort Effects

Cohort effects are due to a person's time of birth or generation but not actually to age. Think for a moment about growing up in (a) the Roaring Twenties, (b) the Great Depression, (c) the 1940s and World War II, (d) the 1950s, (e) the late 1960s, and (f) today. *How might your development be different depending on which of these time frames has dominated your life? your parents' lives? your grandparents' lives?*

examples of the ways in which cohorts can differ include years of education, child-rearing practices, health, attitudes toward sex, religious values, and economic status (see figure 2.12). In life-span development research, **cohort effects** are due to a person's time of birth, era, or generation but not to actual age. Cohort effects are important because they can powerfully affect the dependent measures in a study ostensibly concerned with age. Researchers have shown it is especially important to be aware of cohort effects in the assessment of adult intelligence (Schaie, 1996). Individuals born at different points in time—such as 1920, 1940, and 1960—have had varying opportunities for education, with individuals born in earlier years having had less access.

Cross-sectional studies can show how different cohorts respond but they can confuse age changes and cohort effects. Longitudinal studies are effective in studying age changes but only within one cohort. With sequential studies, both age changes in one cohort can be examined and compared with age changes in another cohort.

A point that is important to make is that theories often are linked with a particular research method or methods. Thus, method(s) researchers use are associated with their particular theoretical approach. Figure 2.13 illustrates the connections between research methods and theories.

So far we have discussed many aspects of scientific research in life-span development. In the Research in Life-Span Development interlude, you can read about the research journals in which this research is published.

cohort effects Effects due to a person's time of birth, era, or generation but not to actual age.

Research Method	Theory
Observation	• All theories emphasize some form of observation. • Behavioral and social cognitive theories place the strongest emphasis on laboratory observation. • Ethological theory places the strongest emphasis on naturalistic observation.
Survey/interview	• Psychoanalytic and cognitive studies (Piaget, Vygotsky) often use interviews. • Behavioral, social cognitive, and ethological theories are the least likely to use surveys or interviews.
Standardized test	• None of the theories discussed emphasize the use of this method.
Case study	• Psychoanalytic theories (Freud, Erikson) are the most likely to use this method.
Life-history record	• This method is most likely to be advocated by ecological theory and psychoanalytic theories.
Correlational research	• All of the theories use this research method, although psychoanalytic theories are the least likely to use it.
Experimental research	• The behavioral and social cognitive theories and the information-processing theories are the most likely to use the experimental method. • Psychoanalytic theories are the least likely to use it.
Cross-sectional/ longitudinal/ sequential methods	• No theory described uses these methods more than any other. • The sequential method is the least likely to be used by any theory.

FIGURE 2.13 Connections of Research Methods to Theories

Research in Life-Span Development
Research Journals

Regardless of whether you pursue a career in life-span development, psychology, or some related scientific field, you can benefit by learning about the journal process. As a student you might be required to look up original research in journals. As a parent, teacher, or nurse you might want to consult journals to obtain information that will help you understand and work more effectively with people. And as an inquiring person, you might look up information in journals after you have heard or read something that piqued your curiosity.

A journal publishes scholarly and academic information, usually in a specific domain—like physics, math, sociology, or, our current interest, life-span development. Scholars in these fields publish most of their research in journals, which are the source of core information in virtually every academic discipline.

An increasing number of journals publish information about life-span development. Among the leading journals in life-span development are *Developmental Psychology, Child Development, Pediatrics, Pediatric Nursing, The Journals of Gerontology, Infant Behavior and Development, Journal of Research on Adolescence, Journal of Adult Development, Journal of Gerontological Nursing, Psychology and Aging, Human Development*, and many others. Also, a number of journals that do not

Child Development
Developmental Psychology
The Journals of Gerontology

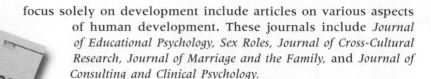

focus solely on development include articles on various aspects of human development. These journals include *Journal of Educational Psychology, Sex Roles, Journal of Cross-Cultural Research, Journal of Marriage and the Family,* and *Journal of Consulting and Clinical Psychology.*

Every journal has a board of experts who evaluate articles submitted for publication. Each submitted paper is accepted or rejected on the basis of such factors as its contribution to the field, methodological excellence, and clarity of writing. Some of the most prestigious journals reject as many as 80 to 90 percent of the articles submitted.

Journal articles are usually written for other professionals in the specialized field of the journal's focus; therefore, they often contain technical language and terms specific to the discipline that are difficult for nonprofessionals to understand. Their organization often takes this course: abstract, introduction, method, results, discussion, and references.

The *abstract* is a brief summary that appears at the beginning of the article. The abstract lets readers quickly determine whether the article is relevant to their interests. The *introduction* introduces the problem or issue that is being studied. It includes a concise review of research relevant to the topic, theoretical ties, and one or more hypotheses to be tested. The *method* section consists of a clear description of the subjects evaluated in the study, the measures used, and the procedures that were followed. The method section should be sufficiently clear and detailed so that by reading it another researcher could repeat or replicate the study. The *results* section reports the analysis of the data collected. In most cases, the results section includes statistical analyses that are difficult for nonprofessionals to understand. The *discussion* section describes the author's conclusions, inferences, and interpretation of what was found. Statements are usually made about whether the hypotheses presented in the introduction were supported, limitations of the study, and suggestions for future research. The last part of the journal article, called *references,* includes bibliographic information for each source cited in the article. The references section is often a good source for finding other articles relevant to the topic that interests you.

Where do you find journals such as those we have described? Your college or university library likely has some of them, and some public libraries also carry journals. Online resources such as PsycINFO, which can facilitate the search for journal articles, are available to students on many campuses.

Review and Reflect: Learning Goal 2

 Explain how research on life-span development is conducted

REVIEW

- How is research on life-span development conducted?
- What are some ways that researchers study the time span of people's lives?

REFLECT

- You have learned that correlation does not equal causation. Develop an example of two variables (two sets of observations) that are correlated but that you believe almost certainly have no causal relationship.

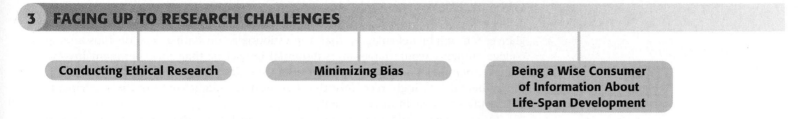

3 **FACING UP TO RESEARCH CHALLENGES**

Conducting Ethical Research

Minimizing Bias

Being a Wise Consumer of Information About Life-Span Development

The scientific foundation of research in life-span development helps to minimize the effect of research bias and maximize the objectivity of the results. Still, some subtle challenges remain to be fully resolved. One is to ensure that research is conducted in an ethical way; another is to recognize, and try to overcome, researchers' deeply buried personal biases. Another challenge is to be a wise consumer of information about life-span development.

Conducting Ethical Research

The explosion in technology has forced society to grapple with looming ethics questions that were unimaginable only a few decades ago. The same line of research that enables previously sterile couples to have children might also someday let prospective parents "call up and order" the characteristics they prefer in their children or tip the balance of males and females in the world. Should embryos left over from procedures for increasing fertility be saved or discarded? Should people with heritable fatal diseases (such as Huntington disease) be discouraged from having children? Should children who appear to have attention deficit hyperactivity disorder be medicated? Should physicians be required to resuscitate a 95-year-old person who has gone into cardiac arrest?

Ethics in research may affect you more personally if you serve at some point, as is quite likely, as a participant in a study. In that event, you need to know about your rights as a participant and about the responsibilities researchers have in assuring that these rights are safeguarded. The failure to consider participants' well-being can have life-altering consequences for them. For example, one investigation of young dating couples asked them to complete a questionnaire that coincidentally stimulated some of the participants to think about potentially troublesome issues (Rubin & Mitchell, 1976). One year later, when the researchers followed up with the original sample, 9 of 10 participants said they had discussed their answers with their dating partner. In most instances, the discussions helped to strengthen the relationships. In some cases, though, the participants used the questionnaire as a springboard to discuss previously hidden problems or concerns. One participant said, "The study definitely played a role in ending my relationship with Larry." In this case, the couple had different views about how long they expected to be together. She was thinking of a short-term dating relationship only, while he was thinking in terms of a lifetime. Their answers to the questions brought the disparity in their views to the surface and led to the end of their relationship. Researchers have a responsibility to anticipate the personal problems their study might cause and to at least inform the participants of the possible fallout.

If you ever become a researcher in life-span development yourself, you will need an even deeper understanding of ethics. You may never become a researcher in the field of psychology, but you may carry out one or more experimental projects in psychology courses. Even smart, conscientious students frequently do not consider the rights of the participants who serve in their experiments. A student might think, "I volunteer in a home for the mentally retarded several hours per week. I can use the residents of the home in my study to see if a particular treatment helps improve their memory for everyday tasks." But without proper permissions, the most well-meaning, kind, and considerate studies still violate the rights of the participants.

www.mhhe.com/santrockld10

Psychologists' Ethical Principles

Ethics Guidelines   Safeguarding the rights of research participants is a challenge because the potential harm is not always obvious (Gall, Borg, & Gall, 2003). At first glance, you might not imagine that a questionnaire on dating relationships among college students would have any substantial impact or that an experiment involving treatment of memory loss in older adults would be anything but beneficial. But researchers increasingly recognize that lasting harm might come to the participants in a study of life-span development.

Today colleges and universities have review boards that evaluate the ethical nature of research conducted at their institutions. Proposed research plans must pass the scrutiny of a research ethics committee before the research can be initiated.

In addition, the American Psychological Association (APA) has developed ethics guidelines for its members. The code of ethics instructs psychologists to protect their participants from mental and physical harm. The participants' best interests need to be kept foremost in the researcher's mind (Rosnow & Rosenthal, 2005). APA's guidelines address four important issues:

- *Informed Consent* All participants must know what their participation will involve and what risks might develop. For example, participants in a study on dating should be told beforehand that a questionnaire might stimulate thoughts about issues in their relationship that they have not considered. Participants also should be informed that in some instances a discussion of the issues might improve their relationship, but in others might worsen the relationship and even end it. Even after informed consent is given, participants must retain the right to withdraw from the study at any time and for any reason.
- *Confidentiality* Researchers are responsible for keeping all of the data they gather on individuals completely confidential and, when possible, completely anonymous.
- *Debriefing* After the study has been completed, participants should be informed of its purpose and the methods that were used. In most cases, the experimenter also can inform participants in a general manner beforehand about the purpose of the research without leading participants to behave in a way they think that the experimenter is expecting. When preliminary information about the study is likely to affect the results, participants can at least be debriefed after the study has been completed.
- *Deception* This is an ethical issue that researchers debate extensively (Leary, 2004). In some circumstances, telling the participants beforehand what the research study is about substantially alters the participants' behavior and invalidates the researcher's data. In all cases of deception, however, the psychologist must ensure that the deception will not harm the participants and that the participants will be told the complete nature of the study (debriefed) as soon as possible after the study is completed.

Minimizing Bias

Studies of life-span development are most useful when they are conducted without bias or prejudice toward any particular group of people. Of special concern is bias based on gender and bias based on culture or ethnicity.

Gender Bias   For most of its existence, our society has had a strong gender bias, a preconceived notion about the abilities of women and men that prevented individuals from pursuing their own interests and achieving their potential (Helgeson, 2005). Gender bias also has had a less obvious effect within the field of life-span development (Etaugh & Bridges, 2001). For example, it is not unusual for conclusions to be drawn about females' attitudes and behaviors from research conducted with males as the only participants (Matlin, 2004).

Florence Denmark and her colleagues (1988) argue as well that when gender differences are found, they sometimes are unduly magnified. For example, a researcher might report in a study that 74 percent of the men had high achievement expectations versus only 67 percent of the women and go on to talk about the differences in some detail. In reality, this might be a rather small difference. It also might disappear if the study were repeated or the study might have methodological problems that don't allow such strong interpretations.

Cultural and Ethnic Bias   The realization that research on life-span development needs to include more people from diverse ethnic groups has also been building (Graham, 1992). Historically, people from ethnic minority groups (African American, Latino, Asian American, and Native American) have been discounted from most research in the United States and simply thought of as variations from the norm or average. Because their scores don't always fit the norm, minority individuals have been viewed as confounds or "noise" in data. Consequently, researchers have deliberately excluded them from the samples they have selected. Given the fact that individuals from diverse ethnic groups were excluded from research on life-span development for so long, we might reasonably conclude that people's real lives are perhaps more varied than research data have indicated in the past (Ponterotto & others, 2001).

Researchers also have tended to overgeneralize about ethnic groups (Jenkins & others, 2003; Trimble, 1989). **Ethnic gloss** is using an ethnic label such as African American or Latino in a superficial way that portrays an ethnic group as being more homogeneous than it really is. For example, a researcher might describe a research sample like this: "The participants were 60 Latinos." A more complete description of the Latino group might be something like this: "The 60 Latino participants were Mexican Americans from low-income neighborhoods in the southwestern area of Los Angeles. Thirty-six were from homes in which Spanish is the dominant language

ethnic gloss Using an ethnic label such as African American or Latino in a superficial way that portrays an ethnic group as being more homogeneous than it really is.

Look at these two photographs, one of all White males, the other of a diverse group of females and males from different ethnic groups, including some White individuals. Consider a topic in psychology, such as parenting, love, or cultural values. *If you were conducting research on this topic, might the results of the study be different depending on whether the participants in your study were the individuals in the photograph on the left or those on the right?*

Careers in Life-Span Development

Pam Reid, Educational and Developmental Psychologist

When she was a child, Pam Reid liked to play with chemistry sets. Pam majored in chemistry during college and wanted to become a doctor. However, when some of her friends signed up for a psychology class as an elective, she also decided to take the course. She was intrigued by learning about how people think, behave, and develop—so much so that she changed her major to psychology. Pam went on to obtain her Ph.D. in psychology (American Psychological Association, 2003, p. 16).

For a number of years, Pam was a professor of education and psychology at the University of Michigan, where she also was a research scientist at the Institute for Research on Women and Gender. Her main focus has been on how children and adolescents develop social skills with a special interest in the development of African American girls (Reid & Zalk, 2001). In 2004, Pam became provost and executive vice-president at Roosevelt University in Chicago.

Pam Reid (*back row, center*) with graduate students she mentored at the University of Michigan.

Watch the video, "Self-Report Bias in Surveys," to learn how life-span development researchers minimize racial, ethnic, and cultural bias in their studies.

spoken, 24 from homes in which English is the main language spoken. Thirty were born in the United States, 30 in Mexico. Twenty-eight described themselves as Mexican American, 14 as Mexican, 9 as American, 6 as Chicano, and 3 as Latino." Ethnic gloss can cause researchers to obtain samples of ethnic groups that are not representative of the group's diversity, which can lead to overgeneralization and stereotyping.

Pam Reid is a leading researcher who studies gender and ethnic bias in development. To read about Pam's interests, see the Careers in Life-Span Development insert.

Being a Wise Consumer of Information About Life-Span Development

Television, radio, newspapers, and magazines all frequently report on life-span development research that is likely to be of interest to the general public. Much of the information has been published in professional journals or presented at national meetings, and most major colleges and universities have a media relations department that contacts the press about current research by their faculty.

You should be aware, however, that not all information about life-span development presented for public consumption comes from professionals with excellent credentials and reputations at colleges or universities or in applied mental health settings (Stanovich, 2004). Because journalists, television reporters, and other media personnel are not usually trained in psychological and adjustment research, they often have trouble sorting through the widely varying material they find and making sound decisions about the best information to present to the public. In addition, the media often focus on sensationalistic and dramatic findings about life-span development to capture your attention. They tend to go beyond what actual research articles and clinical findings really demonstrate.

Even when the media present the results of excellent research, they have trouble adequately informing people about what has been found and the implications for people's lives. For example, this entire book is designed to carry out the task of carefully introducing, defining, and elaborating on key concepts and issues, research, and clinical findings. The media, however, do not have the luxury of so much time and space to detail and specify the limitations and qualifications of research. They often have only a few minutes or a few lines to summarize as best they can the complex findings of a study or a life-span concept.

In the end, you have to take responsibility for evaluating the reports on life-span research that you encounter in the media. To put it another way, you have to consume life-span development information wisely. Five guidelines to help you be a wise consumer of information about psychological and adjustment research are presented here:

1. *Distinguish between group results and individual needs.* People who learn about life-span development research through the media are likely to apply the results to their individual circumstances. Yet most research focuses on groups, and individual variations in participants' responses are seldom emphasized. As a result, the ill-informed consumer of life-span research may get the wrong idea about the "normality" of his or her circumstances. For example, researchers interested in the effects of divorce on an adult's ability to cope with stress might conduct a study of 50 divorced women and 50 married women. They might conclude that the divorced women, as a group, cope more poorly with stress than the married women in the study do. In this particular study, however, some of the divorced women were likely to be coping better than some of the married women. Indeed, of the 100 women in the study, the 2 or 3 women who were coping the best with stress may have been divorced women. It would be accurate to report the findings as showing that divorced women (as a group) coped less effectively with stress than married women (as a group) did. But it would not be sensible to conclude, after reading a summary of the results of the study, that your divorced sister may not be coping with stress as well as she thinks and recommend that she see a therapist.

   The failure of the media to distinguish adequately between research on groups and the individual needs of consumers is not entirely their fault. Researchers have not made the difference clear, either. They often fail to examine the overlap in the data on the groups they are comparing and look for only the differences. And then too often they highlight only these differences in their reports as well.

   Remember, if you read a report in a research journal or the media which states that the divorced women coped more poorly with stress than the married women did, you cannot conclude that all divorced women coped more poorly with stress. The only conclusion you can reasonably draw is that more married women coped better than divorced women did.

2. *Don't overgeneralize from a small sample.* Media presentations of life-span information often don't have the space or time to go into details about the nature of the sample used in the study. Sometimes you will get basic information about the sample's size—whether it is based on 10 participants, 50 participants, or 200 participants, for example. If you can't learn anything else about the sample, at least pay attention to its number.

   Small or very small samples require caution in generalizing to a larger population of individuals. For example, a sample of only 10 or 20 divorced women may have some unique characteristics that would make the study's finding inapplicable to many women. The women in the sample might all have high incomes, be White, be childless, live in a small southern town, and be undergoing psychotherapy. Divorced women who have moderate to low incomes, are from other ethnic backgrounds, have children, are living in different contexts, and are not undergoing psychotherapy might have given very different responses.

3. *Look for answers beyond a single study.* The media might identify an interesting piece of research or a clinical finding and claim that it is something phenomenal with far-reaching implications. Although such pivotal studies do occur, they are rare. It is safer to assume that no single study will provide conclusive answers to an important question, especially answers that apply to all people. In fact, in most life-span domains that prompt many investigations, conflicting results are common. Answers to questions in research usually emerge after many scientists have conducted similar investigations that yield similar conclusions.

   If one study reports that a particular therapy conducted by a particular therapist has been especially effective with divorced adults, you should not conclude that the therapy will work as effectively with all divorced adults and with other therapists until more studies are conducted. Remember that you should not take a report of one research study as the absolute, final answer to a problem.

4. ***Don't attribute causes where none have been found.*** Drawing causal conclusions from correlational studies is one of the most common mistakes made by the media. When a true experiment has not been conducted—that is, when participants have not been randomly assigned to treatments or experiences—two variables or factors might have only a noncausal relationship to each other. Remember from the discussion of correlation earlier in the chapter that causal interpretations cannot be made when two or more factors are simply correlated. We cannot say that one causes the other.

In the case of divorce, imagine that you read this headline: "Low income causes divorced women to have a high degree of stress." You can instantly conclude that the story is about a correlational study, not an experimental study. The word "causes" is used in error. Why? Because for ethical and practical reasons, women participants cannot be randomly assigned to become divorced or stay married, and divorced women cannot be randomly assigned to be poor or rich. A more accurate heading would probably be "Low-income divorced women have a high degree of stress," meaning that the researchers found a correlation between being divorced, having a low income, and having a lot of stress. Be skeptical of words indicating causation until you know more about the research they are describing.

5. ***Evaluate the source of the information about life-span development.*** Remember that studies conducted by researchers are not automatically accepted by the rest of the research community. The researchers usually must submit their findings to a journal for review by their colleagues, who make a decision about whether to publish the paper or not depending on the care taken in conducting the research. Although the quality of research and findings is not uniform among all psychology journals, in most cases journals submit the findings to far greater scrutiny than the popular media do.

Within the media, though, you can usually draw a distinction. The reports of life-span research in respected newspapers, such as the *New York Times* and *Washington Post*, as well as in credible magazines such as *Time* and *Newsweek*, are far more trustworthy than reports in tabloids, such as the *National Enquirer* and *Star.* But regardless of the source—serious publication, tabloid, or even academic journal—you are responsible for reading the details of the research behind the findings that are presented and analyzing the study's credibility.

Review and Reflect: Learning Goal 3

 Discuss research challenges in life-span development

REVIEW

- What are researchers' ethical responsibilities to the people they study?
- How can gender, cultural, and ethnic bias affect the outcome of a research study?
- What is involved in being a wise consumer of information about life-span development?

REFLECT

- Imagine that you are conducting a research study on the sexual attitudes and behaviors of adolescents. What ethical safeguards should you use in conducting the study?

Reach Your Learning Goals

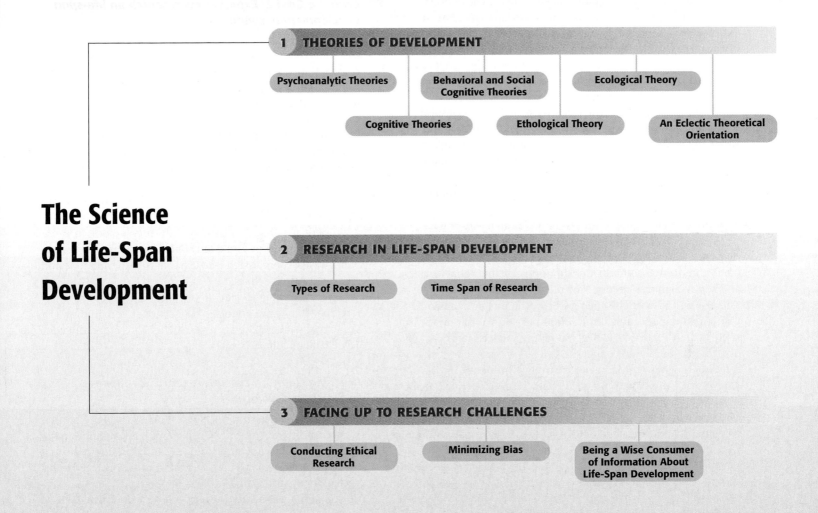

The Science of Life-Span Development

1 THEORIES OF DEVELOPMENT
- Psychoanalytic Theories
- Behavioral and Social Cognitive Theories
- Ecological Theory
- Cognitive Theories
- Ethological Theory
- An Eclectic Theoretical Orientation

2 RESEARCH IN LIFE-SPAN DEVELOPMENT
- Types of Research
- Time Span of Research

3 FACING UP TO RESEARCH CHALLENGES
- Conducting Ethical Research
- Minimizing Bias
- Being a Wise Consumer of Information About Life-Span Development

Summary

 Learning Goal 1: Describe theories of life-span development

- The scientific method involves four main steps: (1) conceptualize a problem, (2) collect data, (3) analyze data, and (4) draw conclusions. A theory is an interrelated, coherent set of ideas that helps to explain and to make predictions. Theory is often involved in conceptualizing a problem. Hypotheses are specific assumptions and predictions, often derived from theory, that can be tested to determine their accuracy. Psychoanalytic theory describes development as primarily unconscious and as heavily colored by emotion. Psychoanalytic theorists believe that behavior is merely a surface characteristic and that early experiences with parents shape development. The two main psychoanalytic theories in developmental psychology are Freud's and Erikson's. Freud said that personality is made up of three structures—id, ego, and superego. The conflicting demands of these structures produce anxiety. Freud also proposed that individuals go through five psychosexual stages— oral, anal, phallic, latency, and genital. Erikson's theory

emphasizes these eight psychosocial stages of development: trust versus mistrust, autonomy versus shame and doubt, initiative versus guilt, industry versus inferiority, identity versus identity confusion, intimacy versus isolation, generativity versus stagnation, and integrity versus despair. Contributions of psychoanalytic theories include an emphasis on early experiences and family relationships. Criticisms include the main concepts being difficult to test scientifically and too much emphasis on sexuality.

- The three main cognitive theories are Piaget's cognitive developmental theory, Vygotsky's sociocultural theory, and information-processing theory. Cognitive theories emphasize conscious thoughts. Piaget proposed a cognitive developmental theory in which children use the processes of organization and adaptation (assimilation and accommodation) to understand their world. In Piaget's theory, children go through four cognitive stages: sensorimotor, preoperational, concrete operational, and formal operational. Vygotsky's sociocultural cognitive theory emphasizes how culture and

71

social interaction guide cognitive development. The information-processing theory emphasizes that individuals manipulate information, monitor it, and strategize about it. Contributions of cognitive theories include a positive view of development and an emphasis on the active construction of understanding. Criticisms include skepticism about the pureness of Piaget's stages and too little attention to individual variations.

- Three versions of the behavioral approach are Pavlov's classical conditioning, Skinner's operant conditioning, and Bandura's social cognitive theory. In Pavlov's classical conditioning, a neutral stimulus acquires the ability to produce a response originally produced by another stimulus. In Skinner's operant conditioning, the consequences of a behavior produce changes in the probability of the behavior's recurrence. In Bandura's social cognitive theory, observational learning is a key aspect of life-span development. Bandura emphasizes reciprocal interactions among the person (cognition), behavior, and environment. Contributions of the behavioral and social cognitive theories include an emphasis on scientific research and environmental determinants of behavior. Criticisms include too little emphasis on cognition in Pavlov's and Skinner's views and giving inadequate attention to developmental changes.

- Ethology stresses that behavior is strongly influenced by biology, is tied to evolution, and is characterized by critical or sensitive periods. Contributions of ethological theory include a focus on the biological and evolutionary basis of development, and the use of careful observations in naturalistic settings. Criticisms include a belief that the critical and sensitive period concepts might be too rigid and too much emphasis on biological foundations.

- Ecological theory is Bronfenbrenner's environmental systems view of development. It consists of five environmental systems: microsystem, mesosystem, exosystem, macrosystem, and chronosystem. Contributions of the theory include a systematic examination of macro and micro dimensions of environmental systems, and attention to connections between environmental systems. Criticisms include giving inadequate attention to biological factors, as well as too little emphasis on cognitive factors.

- An eclectic theoretical orientation does not follow any one theoretical approach, but rather selects from each theory whatever is considered the best in it.

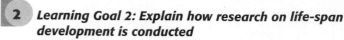

Learning Goal 2: Explain how research on life-span development is conducted

- Three main types of research are (1) descriptive, (2) correlational, and (3) experimental. Five types of descriptive research are observation (in a laboratory or a naturalistic setting), survey (questionnaire) or interview, standardized test, case study, life-history record, and physiological measures. In correlational research, the goal is to describe the strength of the relationship between two or more events or characteristics. Experimental research involves conducting an experiment, which can determine cause and effect. An independent variable is the manipulated, influential, experimental factor. A dependent variable is a factor that can change in an experiment, in response to changes in the independent variable. Experiments can involve one or more experimental groups and control groups. In random assignment, researchers assign participants to experimental and control groups by chance.

- When researchers decide about the time span of their research, they can conduct cross-sectional, longitudinal, or sequential studies. Life-span researchers are especially concerned about cohort effects.

Learning Goal 3: Discuss research challenges in life-span development

- Researchers' ethical responsibilities include seeking participants' informed consent, ensuring their confidentiality, debriefing them about the purpose and potential personal consequences of participating, and avoiding unnecessary deception of participants.

- Researchers need to guard against gender, cultural, and ethnic bias in research. Every effort should be made to make research equitable for both females and males. More individuals from ethnic minority backgrounds need to be included as participants in life-span research. A special concern is ethnic gloss.

- Five guidelines for being a wise consumer of information about life-span development are: (1) distinguish between group results and individual needs, (2) don't overgeneralize from a small sample, (3) look for answers beyond a single study, (4) don't attribute causes where none have been found, and (5) evaluate the source of the information about life-span development.

Key Terms

theory 41
hypotheses 41
psychoanalytic theory 42
Erikson's theory 43
Piaget's theory 45
assimilation 45
accommodation 46
Vygotsky's theory 47

information-processing
  theory 47
social cognitive theory 49
ethology 50
ecological theory 51
eclectic theoretical
  orientation 53
descriptive research 55

laboratory 56
naturalistic observation 57
standardized test 57
case study 58
life-history record 58
correlational research 59
experiment 59
cross-sectional approach 60

longitudinal approach 60
sequential approach 61
cohort effects 62
ethnic gloss 67

Key People

Sigmund Freud 42   Lev Vygotsky 47   B. F. Skinner 49   Konrad Lorenz 50
Erik Erikson 43   Robert Siegler 48   Albert Bandura 49   Urie Bronfenbrenner 51
Jean Piaget 45   Ivan Pavlov 48

E-Learning Tools

To help you master the material in this chapter, you'll find a number of valuable study tools on the LifeMap CD-ROM that accompanies this book and on the Online Learning Center for *Life-Span Development*, tenth edition, at www.mhhe.com/santrockld10.

Video Clips

In the margins of this book there are icons directing you to the LifeMap CD-ROM that accompanies the book. There you'll find a video for chapter 2 called "Self-Report Bias in Surveys." Anyone who conducts a survey must deal with at least two forms of bias: the researcher's own bias in the phrasing of questions, and the reliability of the answers supplied to those questions. As this segment demonstrates, forms of bias may involve differences of gender, culture, and ethnicity.

Self-Assessment

Connect to www.mhhe.com/santrockld10 to reflect on how you've become the person you are today by completing the self-assessment, *Models and Mentors in My Life*.

Taking It to the Net

Connect to www.mhhe.com/santrockld10 to research the answers to these questions.

1. Like many students of life-span psychology, Ymelda has a hard time with Freud's sometimes reductionist emphasis on sex. To what extent are Freud's theoretical insights limited by that preoccupation with sex?

2. Juan's life-span psychology teacher asked the class to read about Albert Bandura's famous "Bobo" doll experiment and determine if there were any gender differences in the responses of boys and girls (a) who saw aggressive behavior rewarded and (b) who saw aggressive behavior punished. What should Juan's conclusions be?

3. A requirement for Wanda's methods course is to design and carry out an original research project. Among the many decisions she must make is what type of data she will collect. She decides to research adapting to college life. Her instructor asks if she will use an interview or a survey. What are the distinctions between surveys and interviews, and what are the benefits and difficulties of each? What ethical considerations need to be taken into account?

Health and Well-Being, Parenting, and Education Exercises

Build your decision-making skills by trying your hand at the health and well-being, parenting, and education exercises.

Connect to www.mhhe.com/santrockld10 to research the answers and complete the exercises.

C H A P T E R

There are one hundred
and ninety-three living
species of monkeys and
apes. One hundred and
ninety-two of them are
covered with hair. The
exception is the naked
ape, self-named Homo
sapiens.

—DESMOND MORRIS
*British Zoologist,
20th Century*

Biological Beginnings

Learning Goals

1 Discuss the evolutionary perspective on life-span development

2 Describe what genes are and how they influence human development

3 Identify some important reproductive challenges and choices

4 Explain some of the ways that heredity and environment interact to produce individual differences in development

Images of Life-Span Development
The Jim and Jim Twins

Jim Lewis (*left*) and Jim Springer (*right*).

Jim Springer and Jim Lewis are identical twins. They were separated at 4 weeks of age and did not see each other again until they were 39 years old. Both worked as part-time deputy sheriffs, vacationed in Florida, drove Chevrolets, had dogs named Toy, and married and divorced women named Betty. One twin named his son James Allan, and the other named his son James Alan. Both liked math but not spelling, enjoyed carpentry and mechanical drawing, chewed their fingernails down to the nubs, had almost identical drinking and smoking habits, had hemorrhoids, put on 10 pounds at about the same point in development, first suffered headaches at the age of 18, and had similar sleep patterns.

But Jim and Jim have some differences. One wears his hair over his forehead, the other slicks it back and has sideburns. One expresses himself best orally; the other is more proficient in writing. But, for the most part, their profiles are remarkably similar.

Another pair, Daphne and Barbara, are called the "giggle sisters" because, after being reunited, they were always making each other laugh. A thorough search of their adoptive families' histories revealed no gigglers. And the identical sisters handled stress by ignoring it, avoided conflict and controversy whenever possible, and showed no interest in politics.

Two other identical twin sisters were separated at 6 weeks and reunited in their fifties. Both had nightmares, which they describe in hauntingly similar ways: both dreamed of doorknobs and fishhooks in their mouths as they smothered to death! The nightmares began during early adolescence and stopped within the past 10 to 12 years. Both women were bed wetters until about 12 or 13 years of age, and their educational and marital histories are remarkably similar.

These sets of twins are part of the Minnesota Study of Twins Reared Apart, directed by Thomas Bouchard and his colleagues (1990, 1995, 2004). The study brings identical twins (identical genetically because they come from the same fertilized egg) and fraternal twins (more dissimilar genetically than identical twins because they come from different fertilized eggs) from all over the world to Minneapolis to investigate their lives. There the twins complete a number of personality tests and provide detailed medical histories, including information about diet and smoking, exercise habits, chest X-rays, heart stress tests, and EEGs (brain-wave tests). The twins are interviewed and asked more than 15,000 questions about their family and childhood environment, personal interests, vocational orientation, values, and aesthetic judgments. They also are given ability and intelligence tests.

Critics of the Minnesota identical twins study point out that some of the separated twins were together for several months prior to their adoption, that some of the twins had been reunited prior to their testing (in some cases, a number of years earlier), that adoption agencies often place twins in similar homes, and that even strangers who spend several hours together and start comparing their lives are likely to come up with some coincidental similarities (Adler, 1991; Joseph, 2001). Still, the Minnesota study of identical twins indicates the increased interest scientists have recently shown in the genetic basis of human development and points to the need for further research on genetic and environmental factors (Bouchard & others, 2004).

PREVIEW
The examples of Jim and Jim, the giggle sisters, and the identical twins who had the same nightmares stimulate us to think about our genetic heritage and the biological foundations of our existence. Organisms are not like billiard balls, moved by simple, external forces to predictable positions on life's pool table. Environmental experiences and biological foundations work together to make us who we are. Our coverage of life's biological beginnings in this chapter focuses on evolution, genetic foundations, reproductive challenges and choices, and the interaction of heredity and environment.

1 THE EVOLUTIONARY PERSPECTIVE

> **Natural Selection and Adaptive Behavior**

> **Evolutionary Psychology**

In evolutionary time, humans are relative newcomers to Earth, yet we have established ourselves as the most successful and dominant species. If we consider evolutionary time as a calendar year, humans arrived here in the last moments of December (Sagan, 1977). As our earliest ancestors left the forest to feed on the savannahs, and then to form hunting societies on the open plains, their minds and behaviors changed. How did this evolution come about?

Natural Selection and Adaptive Behavior

Natural selection is the evolutionary process that favors individuals of a species that are best adapted to survive and reproduce. To understand natural selection, let's return to the middle of the nineteenth century, when the British naturalist Charles Darwin was traveling around the world, observing many different species of animals in their natural surroundings. Darwin, who published his observations and thoughts in *On the Origin of Species* (1859), noted that most organisms reproduce at rates that would cause enormous increases in the population of most species and yet populations remain nearly constant. He reasoned that an intense, constant struggle for food, water, and resources must occur among the many young born each generation, because many of the young do not survive. Those that do survive and reproduce pass on some of their characteristics to the next generation. Darwin believed that these survivors are probably superior in a number of ways to those who do not survive. In other words, the survivors are better *adapted* to their world than are the nonsurvivors (Enger, Ross, & Bailey, 2005; Freeman & Herron, 2004). The best-adapted individuals survive to leave the most offspring. Over the course of many generations, organisms with the characteristics needed for survival would make up an increased percentage of the population. Over many, many generations, this could produce a gradual modification of the whole population. If environmental conditions change, however, other characteristics might become favored by natural selection, moving the species in a different direction (Krogh, 2005).

All organisms must adapt to particular places, climates, food sources, and ways of life. An example of adaptation is an eagle's claws, which facilitate predation. *Adaptive behavior* is behavior that promotes an organism's survival in the natural habitat (Raven & others, 2005). For example, in the human realm, attachment between a caregiver and a baby ensures the infant's closeness to a caregiver for feeding and protection from danger, thus increasing the infant's chances of survival.

Evolutionary Psychology

Although Darwin introduced the theory of evolution by natural selection in 1859, his ideas only recently have become a popular framework for explaining behavior. Psychology's newest approach, **evolutionary psychology,** emphasizes the importance of adaptation, reproduction, and "survival of the fittest" in shaping behavior. "Fit" in this sense refers to the ability to bear offspring that survive long enough to bear offspring of their own. In this view, the evolutionary process of natural selection has favored behaviors that increase our reproductive success, our ability to pass our genes to the next generation (Cosmides & others, 2003; Gaulin & McBurney, 2004).

David Buss (1995, 2000, 2004) has been especially influential in stimulating new interest in how evolution can explain human behavior. He believes that just as evolution shapes our physical features, such as body shape and height, it also pervasively influences how we make decisions, how aggressive we are, our fears, and our mating patterns. For example, assume that our ancestors were hunters and gatherers on the plains and that men did most of the hunting and women stayed close to home gathering seeds and plants for food. If you have to travel some distance from your home in an effort to find and slay a fleeing animal, you need not only certain physical traits but also ability for certain types of spatial thinking. Men born with these traits would be more likely than men without them to survive, to bring home lots of food, and to be considered attractive mates—and thus to reproduce and pass on these characteristics to their children. In other words, some traits would provide a reproductive advantage for males and, over many generations, men with good spatial thinking skills might become more numerous in the population. Critics point out that this example based on evolutionary theory may or may not have actually happened.

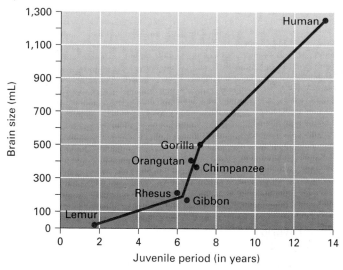

FIGURE 3.1 The Brain Sizes of Various Primates and Humans in Relation to the Length of the Juvenile Period

Evolutionary Developmental Psychology   Much of the thinking about evolutionary psychology has not had a developmental focus. Recently, however, interest has grown in applying the concepts of evolutionary psychology to the changes that take place as people develop. Here are a few ideas proposed by evolutionary developmental psychologists (Bjorklund & Pellegrini, 2002, pp. 336–340):

- *An extended "juvenile" period evolved because humans require time to develop a large brain and learn the complexity of human social communities.* Humans take longer to become reproductively mature than any other mammal (see figure 3.1). During this time they develop a large brain and the experiences required for mastering the complexities of human society.

- *"Many aspects of childhood function as preparations for adulthood and were selected over the course of evolution"* (p. 337). For example, through play children learn much that can help them adapt as adults. Beginning in the preschool years, boys in all cultures engage in more rough-and-tumble play than girls. Perhaps rough-and-tumble play is preparation for adult fighting and hunting by males. Girls engage in play that involves more imitation of parents, such as caring for dolls, and less physical dominance than boys do. This, according to evolutionary psychologists, is an evolved tendency that prepares females for becoming the primary caregivers for their offspring.

- *Some characteristics of childhood were selected to be adaptive at specific points in development and not as preparation for adulthood.* For example, some aspects of play may function, not as a foundation for adulthood, but to help children adapt to their immediate circumstances, perhaps to learn about their current environment.

evolutionary psychology Emphasizes the importance of adaptation, reproduction, and "survival of the fittest" in shaping behavior.

- *Many evolved psychological mechanisms are domain-specific.* That is, they apply to a specific aspect of a person's psychological makeup. According to evolutionary psychology, domain-specific information processing evolved as our ancestors dealt with certain recurring problems. Rather it consists of a set of specialized modules, such as a module for physical knowledge, a module for mathematical knowledge, and a module for language. Also in this view, "infants enter the world 'prepared' to process and learn some information more readily than others, and these preparations serve as a foundation for social and cognitive development across childhood and adolescence" (p. 338).

- *Evolved mechanisms are not always adaptive in contemporary society.* Some behaviors that were adaptive for our prehistoric ancestors may not serve us well today. For example, the food-scarce environment of our ancestors likely led to humans' propensity to gorge when food is available and to crave high-caloric foods, a trait that has led to an epidemic of obesity in recent times, when food is plentiful.

Evolution and Life-Span Development In evolutionary theory, what matters is that individuals live long enough to reproduce and pass on their characteristics. So why do humans live so long after reproduction? Currently, there is a great deal of interest in evolutionary explanations of aging (Gavrilova & Gavrilova, 2002; Siegfried, 2002). Perhaps evolution favored a longer life because having older people around improves the survival of more babies. For example, an evolutionary advantage may have existed because grandparents cared for the young while parents were out hunting and gathering food.

According to life-span developmentalist Paul Baltes (2000, 2003; Baltes & Smith, 2003), the benefits conferred by evolutionary selection decrease with age. Natural selection has not weeded out many harmful conditions and nonadaptive characteristics that appear among older adults. Why? Natural selection operates primarily on characteristics that are tied to reproductive fitness, which extends through the earlier part of adulthood. Thus, says Baltes, selection primarily operates during the first half of life.

As an example, consider Alzheimer disease, an irreversible brain disorder characterized by gradual deterioration. This disease typically does not appear until age 70 or later. If it were a disease that struck 20-year-olds, perhaps natural selection would have eliminated it eons ago.

Thus, unaided by evolutionary pressures against nonadaptive conditions, we suffer the aches, pains, and infirmities of aging. And as the benefits of evolutionary selection decrease with age, argues Baltes, the need for culture increases (see figure 3.2). That is, as older adults weaken biologically, they need culture-based resources such as cognitive skills, literacy, medical technology, and social support. For example, help and training from other people may be needed for older adults to maintain their cognitive skills (Hoyer & Roodin, 2003).

Evaluating Evolutionary Psychology Although the popular press gives a lot of attention to the ideas of evolutionary psychology, it remains just one theoretical approach. Like the theories described in chapter 2, it has limitations, weaknesses, and critics. Albert Bandura (1998), whose social cognitive theory was described in chapter 2, acknowledges the important influence of evolution on human adaptation. However, he rejects what he calls "one-sided evolutionism," which sees social behavior as the product of evolved biology. An alternative is a *bidirectional view,* in which environmental and biological conditions influence each other. For example, evolutionary pressures created changes in biological structures that allowed the use of tools, which enabled organisms to manipulate,

Evolution
Evolutionary Psychology
Handbook of Evolutionary Psychology
Evolutionary Psychology Resources

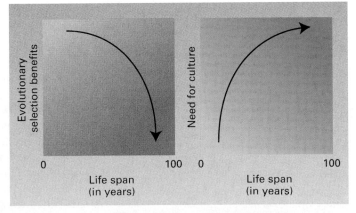

FIGURE 3.2 Baltes' View of Evolution and Culture Across the Life Span
Evolutionary selection benefits decrease with age, whereas the need for culture increases with age.

alter, and construct new environmental conditions. In turn, environmental innovations produced new selection pressures for the evolution of specialized biological systems for consciousness, thought, and language.

People have used their biological capacities to produce diverse cultures—aggressive, pacific, egalitarian, or autocratic. As American scientist Steven Jay Gould (1981) concluded, in most domains of human functioning, biology allows a broad range of cultural possibilities.

Review and Reflect: Learning Goal 1

 1 **Discuss the evolutionary perspective on life-span development**

REVIEW

- How can natural selection and adaptive behavior be defined?
- What is evolutionary psychology? What are some basic ideas about human development proposed by evolutionary psychologists?

REFLECT

- Which is more persuasive to you: the views of evolutionary psychologists or their critics? Why?

---

2 **GENETIC FOUNDATIONS**

The Genetic Process   **Genetic Principles**   **Chromosome and Gene-Linked Abnormalities**

Every species has a mechanism for transmitting characteristics from one generation to the next. This mechanism is explained by the principles of genetics. Each of us carries a "genetic code" that we inherited from our parents, and it is a distinctly human code. Because it carries this human code, a fertilized human egg cannot grow into an egret, eagle, or elephant.

The Genetic Process

Each of us began life as a single cell weighing about one twenty-millionth of an ounce! This tiny piece of matter housed our entire genetic code—instructions that orchestrated growth from that single cell to a person made of trillions of cells, each containing a perfect replica of the original genetic code. That code is carried by our genes. What are genes and what do they do?

chromosomes Threadlike structures that contain the remarkable substance DNA; there are 23 pairs of chromosomes.

DNA A complex molecule that contains genetic information.

genes Units of hereditary information composed of DNA. Genes direct cells to reproduce themselves and to assemble proteins.

DNA and the Collaborative Gene   The nucleus of each human cell contains **chromosomes,** which are threadlike structures that contain the remarkable substance deoxyribonucleic acid, or DNA. **DNA** is a complex molecule that contains genetic information. It has a double helix shape, like a spiral staircase. **Genes,** the units of hereditary information, are short segments of DNA, as you can see in figure 3.3. They direct cells to reproduce themselves and to assemble proteins. Proteins, in turn, serve as the building blocks of cells as well as regulators that direct the body's processes.

Each gene has its own function and each gene has its own location, its own designated place on a particular chromosome. Today, a great deal of enthusiasm surrounds efforts to discover the specific locations of genes that are linked to certain

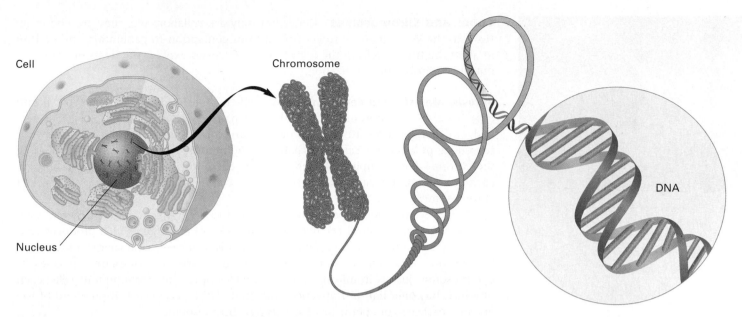

FIGURE 3.3 Cells, Chromosomes, Genes, and DNA
(*Left*) The body contains trillions of cells, which are the basic structural units of life. Each cell contains a central structure, the nucleus. (*Middle*) Chromosomes and genes are located in the nucleus of the cell. Chromosomes are made up of threadlike structures composed of DNA molecules. (*Right*) A gene, a segment of DNA that contains the hereditary code. The structure of DNA is a spiraled double chain.

functions (Prescott, Harley, & Klein, 2005). An important step in this direction was accomplished when the Human Genome Project and the Celera Corporation completed a preliminary map of the human *genome*—all of the approximately 30,000 human genes (U.S. Department of Energy, 2001).

One of the big surprises of the Human Genome Project was the recent finding that humans have only about 20,000 to 25,000 genes (International Human Genome Sequencing Consortium, 2004). Scientists had thought that humans had as many as 100,000 or more genes. They also had believed that each gene programmed just one protein. In fact, humans appear to have far more proteins than they have genes, so there cannot be a one-to-one correspondence between them (Commoner, 2002; Moore, 2001). Each segment of DNA is not translated, in automation-like fashion, into one and only one protein. It does not act independently, as developmental psychologist David Moore (2001) emphasized by titling his recent book *The Dependent Gene*. Rather than being an independent source of developmental information, DNA collaborates with other sources of information to specify our characteristics. The collaboration operates at many points. Small pieces of DNA are mixed, matched, and linked by the cellular machinery (Weaver, 2005). That machinery is sensitive to its context; that is, it is influenced by what is going on around it. Whether or not a gene is turned "on," working to assemble proteins, is also a matter of collaboration. The activity of genes (*genetic expression*) is affected by their environment (Gottlieb, 2003, 2004). For example, hormones that circulate in the blood make their way into the cell where they can turn genes "on" and "off." And the flow of hormones can be affected by environmental conditions, such as light, day length, nutrition, and behavior. Numerous studies have shown that external events outside of the cell and the person, as well as events inside the cell, can excite or inhibit gene expression (Gottlieb, Wahlsten, & Lickliter, 1998; Mauro & others, 1994).

In short, a single gene is rarely the source of a protein's genetic information, much less of an inherited trait (Gottlieb, 2003, 2004; Moore, 2001). Rather than being a group of independent genes, the human genome consists of many dependent genes.

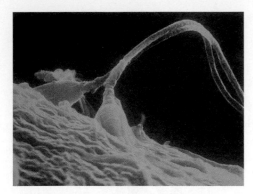

FIGURE 3.4 Union of Sperm and Egg

Landmarks in the History
of Genetics
Heredity Resources
Genetics Journals and News

mitosis Cellular reproduction in which the cell's nucleus duplicates itself with two new cells being formed, each containing the same DNA as the parent cell, arranged in the same 23 pairs of chromosomes.

meiosis A specialized form of cell division that produces cells with only one copy of each chromosome. Meiosis forms eggs and sperm (or gametes).

fertilization A stage in the reproduction process whereby an egg and a sperm fuse to create a single cell, called a zygote.

zygote A single cell formed through fertilization.

genotype A person's genetic heritage; the actual genetic material.

phenotype The way an individual's genotype is expressed in observed and measurable characteristics.

Genes and Chromosomes Genes not only are collaborative; they are enduring. How do the genes manage to get passed from generation to generation and end up in all of the trillion cells in the body? Three processes explain the heart of the story: mitosis, meiosis, and fertilization.

Mitosis, Meiosis, and Fertilization All cells in your body (except the sperm and egg) have 46 chromosomes arranged in 23 pairs. Why pairs? Because you inherited one chromosome from your mother and one from your father. These cells reproduce by a process called **mitosis.** During mitosis, the cell's nucleus—including the chromosomes—duplicates itself and the cell divides. Two new cells are formed, each containing the same DNA as the parent cell, arranged in the same 23 pairs of chromosomes.

However, in order to pass genetic material to offspring from two different parents, a specialized form of cell division—**meiosis**—is required, which produces cells with only one copy of each chromosome. Meiosis forms eggs and sperm (or *gametes*). During meiosis, a cell of the testes (in men) or ovaries (in women) duplicates its chromosomes just as in mitosis, but then divides *twice,* thus forming four cells, each of which has only half of the genetic material of the parent cell. By the end of the process, each egg or sperm has 23 *unpaired* chromosomes.

The next stage in the process of reproduction is **fertilization,** whereby an egg and a sperm fuse to create a single cell, called a **zygote** (see figure 3.4). In the zygote, the two sets of unpaired chromosomes from the egg and sperm combine to form one set of paired chromosomes—one member of each pair from the mother's egg and the other member from the father's sperm. In this manner, each parent contributes half of the offspring's genetic material.

Sources of Variability Combining the genes of two parents in offspring increases genetic variability in the population, which is valuable for a species because it provides more characteristics for natural selection to operate on (Halliburton, 2004). Passing along accurate copies of the genes is also essential. However, the chromosomes in the zygote are not exact copies of the chromosomes of the mother's ovaries and the father's testes. During the formation of the sperm and egg in meiosis, the members of each pair of chromosomes are separated, but whether the gamete receives the maternal or the paternal chromosome is a matter of chance. In addition, before the pairs separate, pieces of the two parents' chromosomes are exchanged, creating a new combination of genes on each. Thus, when chromosomes from the mother's egg and the father's sperm are brought together in the zygote, the result is a truly unique combination of genes.

Figure 3.5 shows 23 paired chromosomes of a male and a female. The members of each pair of chromosomes are both similar and different: Each chromosome in the pair contains varying forms of the same genes, at the same location on the chromosome. A gene for hair color, for example, is located on both members of one pair of chromosomes, in the same location on each. However, one of those chromosomes might carry the gene for blond hair; the other chromosome in the pair might carry the gene for brown hair.

Do you notice any obvious differences between the chromosomes of the male and the chromosomes of the female in figure 3.5? The difference lies in the 23rd pair. Ordinarily, females have two chromosomes called *X chromosomes;* males have an X and a *Y chromosome.* The presence of a Y chromosome is what makes an individual male.

Genetic Principles

All of a person's genetic material makes up his or her **genotype.** However, not all of the genetic material is apparent in our observed and measurable characteristics. A **phenotype** consists of observable characteristics. Phenotypes include physical characteristics (such as height, body style, and hair color) and psychological characteristics

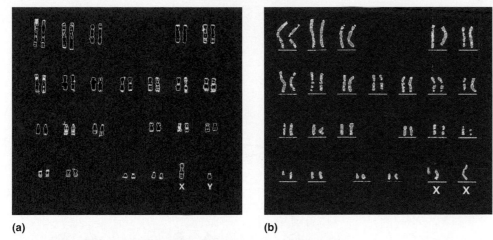

(a)   (b)

FIGURE 3.5 The Genetic Difference Between Males and Females
Set (*a*) shows the chromosome structure of a male, and set (*b*) shows the chromosome structure of a female. The last pair of 23 pairs of chromosomes is in the bottom right box of each set. Notice that the Y chromosome of the male is smaller than the X chromosome of the female. To obtain this kind of chromosomal picture, a cell is removed from a person's body, usually from the inside of the mouth. The chromosomes are stained by chemical treatment, magnified extensively, and then photographed.

(such as personality and intelligence). For each genotype, a range of phenotypes can be expressed. An individual can inherit the genetic potential to grow very large, but good nutrition will also be important to achieving that potential.

What determines the phenotype that is expressed? Much is unknown about the answer to this question (Lewis, 2005). However, a number of genetic principles have been discovered, among them those of dominant-recessive genes, sex-linked genes, genetic imprinting, and polygenically determined characteristics.

Dominant-Recessive Genes Principle   According to the *dominant-recessive genes principle,* if one gene of a pair is dominant and one is recessive, the dominant gene exerts its effect, overriding the potential influence of the other, recessive gene. A recessive gene exerts its influence only if the two genes of a pair are both recessive. If you inherit a recessive gene for a trait from each of your parents, you will show the trait. If you inherit a recessive gene from only one parent, you may never know you carry the gene. Brown hair, farsightedness, and dimples rule over blond hair, nearsightedness, and freckles in the world of dominant-recessive genes. Can two brown-haired parents have a blond-haired child? Yes, they can. Suppose that in each parent the gene pair that governs hair color includes a dominant gene for brown hair and a recessive gene for blond hair. Since dominant genes override recessive genes, the parents have brown hair, but both are carriers of blondness and pass on their recessive genes for blond hair. With no dominant gene to override them, the recessive genes can make the child's hair blond. Figure 3.6 illustrates the dominant-recessive genes principle.

Sex-Linked Genes   *X-linked inheritance* is the term used to describe the inheritance of an altered (*mutated*) gene that is carried on the X chromosome (Klug & Cummings, 2005). Most such mutated genes are recessive, but remember that males have only one X chromosome. When there is an alteration of the X chromosome, males have no "backup" copy and therefore may develop an X-linked disease. However, females have a second X chromosome, which is likely to be unchanged. As a result, they are not likely to have the X-linked disease. Thus, most individuals who have X-linked diseases are males. Females who have one changed copy of the X gene are known as "carriers," and they usually do not show any signs of the X-linked disease. Hemophilia

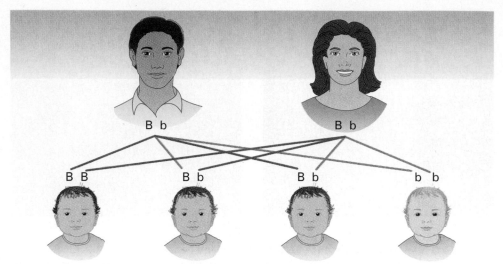

B = Gene for brown hair   b = Gene for blond hair

FIGURE 3.6 How Brown-Haired Parents Can Have a Blond-Haired Child
Although both parents have brown hair, each parent can have a recessive gene for blond hair. In this example, both parents have brown hair, but each parent carries the recessive gene for blond hair. Therefore, the odds of their child having blond hair are one in four—the probability the child will receive a recessive gene (*b*) from each parent.

and fragile X syndrome, which we will discuss later in the chapter, are examples of X-linked inheritance (Gonzales-del Angel & others, 2000).

Genetic Imprinting   *Genetic imprinting* occurs when genes have differing effects depending on whether they are inherited from the mother or the father (Jirtle, Sander, & Barret, 2000). An imprinted gene dominates one that has not been imprinted. For example, individuals who inherit Huntington disease from their fathers show symptoms of the disease at an earlier age than when they inherit from their mother (Navarrette, Martinez, & Salamanca, 1994). We will further discuss Huntington disease later in chapter.

Polygenic Inheritance   Genetic transmission is usually more complex than the simple examples we have examined thus far (Lewis, 2005). *Polygenic inheritance* occurs when many genes interact to influence a characteristic. Few psychological characteristics, for example, are the result of a single gene or pairs of genes. Most are determined by the interaction of many different genes; they are said to be *polygenically determined*. There are about 20,000 to 25,000 human genes, so you can imagine that possible combinations are staggering in number.

Calvin and Hobbes   by Bill Watterson

Name	Description	Treatment	Incidence
Down syndrome	An extra chromosome causes mild to severe retardation and physical abnormalities.	Surgery, early intervention, infant stimulation, and special learning programs	1 in 1,900 births at age 20 1 in 300 births at age 35 1 in 30 births at age 45
Klinefelter syndrome (XXY)	An extra X chromosome causes physical abnormalities.	Hormone therapy can be effective	1 in 800 male births
Fragile X syndrome	An abnormality in the X chromosome can cause mental retardation, learning disabilities, or short attention span.	Special education, speech and language therapy	More common in males than in females
Turner syndrome (XO)	A missing X chromosome in females can cause mental retardation and sexual underdevelopment.	Hormone therapy in childhood and puberty	1 in 2,500 female births
XYY syndrome	An extra Y chromosome can cause above-average height.	No special treatment required	1 in 1,000 male births

FIGURE 3.7 Some Chromosome Abnormalities
Note: Treatment does not necessarily erase the problem but may improve the individual's adaptive behavior and quality of life.

Chromosome and Gene-Linked Abnormalities

In some cases, abnormalities characterize the genetic process. Some of these abnormalities involve whole chromosomes that do not separate properly during meiosis. Other abnormalities are produced by inheriting harmful genes.

Chromosome Abnormalities Sometimes, when a gamete is formed, the sperm or ovum does not have its normal set of 23 chromosomes. The most notable examples involve Down syndrome and abnormalities of the sex chromosomes (see figure 3.7).

Down Syndrome An individual with **Down syndrome** has a round face, a flattened skull, an extra fold of skin over the eyelids, a protruding tongue, short limbs, and retardation of motor and mental abilities. The syndrome is caused by the presence of an extra copy of chromosome 21. It is not known why the extra chromosome is present, but the health of the male sperm or female ovum may be involved (Davison, Gardiner, & Costa, 2001; MacLean, 2000). Down syndrome appears approximately once in every 1,000 live births. Women between the ages of 16 and 34 are less likely to give birth to a child with Down syndrome than are younger or older women (Morris & others, 2003). African American children are rarely born with Down syndrome.

Sex-Linked Chromosome Abnormalities Recall that a newborn normally has either an X and a Y chromosome, or two X chromosomes. Human embryos must possess at least one X chromosome to be viable. The most common sex-linked chromosome abnormalities involve the presence of an extra chromosome (either an X or Y) or the absence of one X chromosome in females.

    Klinefelter syndrome is a chromosome disorder in which males have an extra X chromosome, making them XXY instead of XY (Lowe & others, 2001). Males with this disorder have undeveloped testes, usually develop enlarged breasts, and become tall. Klinefelter syndrome occurs approximately once in every 800 live male births.

    Fragile X syndrome is a chromosome disorder that results from an abnormality in the X chromosome, which becomes constricted and often breaks.

These athletes, many of whom have Down syndrome, are participating in a Special Olympics competition. Notice the distinctive facial features of the individuals with Down syndrome, such as a round face and a flattened skull. *What causes Down syndrome?*

Down syndrome A chromosomally transmitted form of mental retardation, caused by the presence of an extra copy of chromosome 21.

Klinefelter syndrome A chromosome disorder in which males have an extra X chromosome, making them XXY instead of XY.

fragile X syndrome A chromosome disorder involving an abnormality in the X chromosome, which becomes constricted and often breaks.

Genetic Disorders
Prenatal Testing and Down Syndrome

Turner syndrome A chromosome disorder in females in which either an X chromosome is missing, making the person XO instead of XX, or the second X chromosome is partially deleted.

XYY syndrome A chromosome disorder in which males have an extra Y chromosome.

phenylketonuria (PKU) A genetic disorder in which an individual cannot properly metabolize phenylalanine, an amino acid. PKU is now easily detected but, if left untreated, results in mental retardation and hyperactivity.

Mental deficiency often is an outcome but it may take the form of mental retardation, a learning disability, or a short attention span (Lewis, 2005). This disorder occurs more frequently in males than in females, possibly because the second X chromosome in females negates the disorder's negative effects (O'Donnell & Warren, 2003).

Turner syndrome is a chromosome disorder in females in which either an X chromosome is missing, making the person XO instead of XX, or the second X chromosome is partially deleted. These females are short in stature and have a webbed neck. They might be infertile and have difficulty in mathematics, but their verbal ability is often quite good (Rae & others, 2004). Turner syndrome occurs in approximately 1 of every 2,500 live female births.

The **XYY syndrome** is a chromosome disorder in which the male has an extra Y chromosome. Early interest in this syndrome focused on the belief that the extra Y chromosome found in some males contributed to aggression and violence. However, researchers subsequently found that XYY males are no more likely to commit crimes than are XY males (Witkin & others, 1976).

Gene-Linked Abnormalities Abnormalities can be produced by an uneven number of chromosomes; they also can result from harmful genes. More than 7,000 such genetic disorders have been identified, although most of them are rare.

Phenylketonuria (PKU) is a genetic disorder in which the individual cannot properly metabolize phenylalanine, an amino acid. Phenylketonuria is now easily detected, but, if it is left untreated, mental retardation and hyperactivity result. The disorder is treated by diet to prevent an excess accumulation of phenylalanine. Phenylketonuria involves a recessive gene and occurs about once in

Name	Description	Treatment	Incidence
Cystic fibrosis	Glandular dysfunction that interferes with mucus production; breathing and digestion are hampered, resulting in a shortened life span.	Physical and oxygen therapy, synthetic enzymes, and antibiotics; most individuals live to middle age.	1 in 2,000 births
Diabetes	Body does not produce enough insulin, which causes abnormal metabolism of sugar.	Early onset can be fatal unless treated with insulin.	1 in 2,500 births
Hemophilia	Delayed blood clotting causes internal and external bleeding.	Blood transfusions/injections can reduce or prevent damage due to internal bleeding.	1 in 10,000 males
Huntington disease	Central nervous system deteriorates, producing problems in muscle coordination and mental deterioration.	Doesn't usually appear until age 35 or older; death likely 10 to 20 years after symptoms appear.	1 in 20,000 births
Phenylketonuria (PKU)	Metabolic disorder that, left untreated, causes mental retardation.	Special diet can result in average intelligence and normal life span.	1 in 10,000 to 1 in 20,000 births
Sickle-cell anemia	Blood disorder that limits the body's oxygen supply; it can cause joint swelling, as well as heart and kidney failure.	Penicillin, medication for pain, antibiotics, and blood transfusions.	1 in 400 African American children (lower among other groups)
Spina bifida	Neural tube disorder that causes brain and spine abnormalities.	Corrective surgery at birth, orthopedic devices, and physical/medical therapy.	2 in 1,000 births
Tay-Sachs disease	Deceleration of mental and physical development caused by an accumulation of lipids in the nervous system.	Medication and special diet are used, but death is likely by 5 years of age.	One in 30 American Jews is a carrier.

FIGURE 3.8 Some Gene-Linked Abnormalities

every 10,000 to 20,000 live births. Phenylketonuria accounts for about 1 percent of institutionalized mentally retarded individuals, and it occurs primarily in Whites.

The story of phenylketonuria has important implications for the nature-nurture issue. Although phenylketonuria is a genetic disorder (nature), how or whether a gene's influence in phenylketonuria is played out can depend on environmental influences since the disorder can be treated (nurture) (Luciana, Sullivan, & Nelson, 2001; Merrick, Aspler, & Schwartz, 2001). That is, the presence of a genetic defect *does not* inevitably lead to the development of the disorder *if* the individual develops in the right environment (one free of phenylalanine).

Sickle-cell anemia, which occurs most often in African Americans, is a genetic disorder that impairs the body's red blood cells. A red blood cell is usually shaped like a disk, but in sickle-cell anemia, a recessive gene causes the cell to become a hook-shaped "sickle." These cells die quickly, causing anemia and early death of the individual, because of their failure to carry oxygen to the body's cells. About 1 in 400 African American babies is affected. One in 10 African Americans is a carrier, as is 1 in 20 Latin Americans.

Other diseases that result from genetic abnormalities include cystic fibrosis, diabetes, hemophilia, Huntington disease, spina bifida, and Tay-Sachs disease. Figure 3.8 provides further information about some of the genetic abnormalities we have discussed. The work of the Human Genome Project and similar research holds out the promise that someday scientists may identify why these and other genetic abnormalities occur and discover how to cure them. The Human Genome Project has already linked specific DNA variations with increased risk of a number of diseases and conditions, including Huntington disease (in which the central nervous system deteriorates), some forms of cancer, asthma, diabetes, hypertension, and Alzheimer disease (Knowles, 2004).

Every individual carries DNA variations that might predispose that person to serious physical disease or mental disorder. Identifying the flaws could enable doctors to predict an individual's disease risks, recommend healthy lifestyle regimens, and prescribe the safest and most effective drugs. A decade or two from now, parents of a newborn baby may be able to leave the hospital with a full genome analysis of their offspring that reveals disease risks.

However, this knowledge might bring important costs as well as benefits. Who would have access to a person's genetic profile? An individual's ability to land and hold jobs or obtain insurance might be threatened if it is known that a person is considered at risk for some disease. For example, should an airline pilot or a neurosurgeon who is predisposed to develop a disorder that makes one's hands shake be required to leave that job early? To think further about such issues, see figure 3.9.

Genetic counselors, usually physicians or biologists who are well-versed in the field of medical genetics, are familiar with the kinds of problems just described, the

Careers in Life-Span Development

Holly Ishmael, Genetic Counselor

Holly Ishmael is a genetic counselor at Children's Mercy Hospital in Kansas City. She obtained an undergraduate degree in psychology from Sarah Lawrence College and then a master's degree in genetic counseling from the same college. She uses many of the principles discussed in this chapter in her genetic counseling work.

Genetic counselors have specialized graduate degrees in the areas of medical genetics and counseling. They enter graduate school in these areas with undergraduate backgrounds from a variety of disciplines, including biology, genetics, psychology, public health, and social work. Genetic counselors, like Holly, work as members of a health-care team, providing information and support to families with birth defects or genetic disorders. They identify families at risk by analyzing inheritance patterns and explore options with the family. Some genetic counselors, like Holly, become specialists in prenatal and pediatric genetics; others might specialize in cancer genetics or psychiatric genetic disorders.

Holly says, "Genetic counseling is a perfect combination for people who want to do something science-oriented, but need human contact and don't want to spend all of their time in a lab or have their nose in a book" (Rizzo, 1999, p. 3).

There are approximately thirty graduate genetic counseling programs in the United States. If you are interested in this profession, you can obtain further information from the National Society of Genetic Counselors at www.nsgc.org.

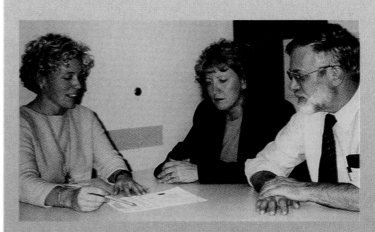

Holly Ishmael (*left*) in a genetic counseling session.

sickle-cell anemia A genetic disorder that affects the red blood cells and occurs most often in people of African descent.

FIGURE 3.9 Exploring Your Genetic Future

	Yes	No	Undecided
1. Would you want you or your loved one to be tested for a gene that increases your risk for a disease, but does not determine whether you will actually develop the disease?	☐	☐	☐
2. Would you want you and your mate to be tested before having offspring to determine your risk for having a child who is likely to contract various diseases?	☐	☐	☐
3. Should testing of unborn children be restricted to traits that are commonly considered to have negative outcomes, such as disease?	☐	☐	☐
4. Should altering a newly conceived person's genes to improve qualities such as intelligence, appearance, and strength be allowed?	☐	☐	☐
5. Should employers be permitted access to your genetic information?	☐	☐	☐
6. Should life insurance companies have access to your genetic information?	☐	☐	☐

odds of encountering them, and helpful strategies for offsetting some of their effects. To read about the career and work of a genetic counselor, see the Careers in Life-Span Development insert. ◀ page 87

Review and Reflect: Learning Goal 2

2 **Describe what genes are and how they influence human development**

REVIEW

- How does the genetic process work?
- What are some important genetic principles?
- What are some chromosome and gene-linked abnormalities?

REFLECT

- What are some possible ethical issues regarding genetics and development that might arise in the future?

3 **REPRODUCTIVE CHALLENGES AND CHOICES**

| **Prenatal Diagnostic Tests** | **Infertility and Reproductive Technology** | **Adoption** |

Earlier in this chapter we discussed several principles of genetics, including the role of meiosis in reproduction. Having also examined a number of genetic abnormalities that can occur, we now have some background to consider challenges and choices facing prospective parents.

Prenatal Diagnostic Tests

Scientists have developed a number of tests to determine whether a fetus is developing normally. These tests include amniocentesis, ultrasound sonography, chorionic villus sampling, and a maternal blood test.

Amniocentesis is a prenatal medical procedure in which a sample of amniotic fluid is withdrawn by syringe and tested for any chromosome or metabolic disorders. The amnionic fluid is found within the amnion, a thin, membranous sac in which the embryo is suspended. Amniocentesis is performed between the 12th and 16th weeks of pregnancy. The later amniocentesis is performed, the better its diagnostic potential (Welsh, Blessed, & Lacoste, 2003). The earlier it is performed, the more useful it is in deciding how to handle a pregnancy (Pinette & others, 2004). Amniocentesis does carry a small risk of miscarriage: about 1 woman in every 200 to 300 miscarries after amniocentesis.

Ultrasound sonography is a prenatal medical procedure in which high-frequency sound waves are directed into the pregnant woman's abdomen. The echo from the sounds is transformed into a visual representation of the fetus' inner structures. This technique can detect disorders such as microencephaly, a form of mental retardation involving an abnormally small brain, as well as giving clues to the baby's sex (Bahado-Singh & others, 2003). Ultrasound sonography is often used during an amniocentesis procedure because placement of the syringe requires knowledge of the precise location of the fetus in the mother's abdomen. Although considered one of the safest prenatal tests available, when ultrasound sonography is used five or more times, the risk of low birth weight may be increased.

As scientists have searched for more accurate, safer assessments of high-risk prenatal conditions, they have developed a new test. *Chorionic villus sampling* is a prenatal medical procedure in which a small sample of the placenta (the vascular organ that links the fetus to the mother's uterus) is removed at some point between the 8th and 11th weeks of pregnancy (Zoppi & others, 2001). Diagnosis takes approximately 10 days. Chorionic villus sampling allows a decision about abortion to be made near the end of the first 12 weeks of pregnancy, a point when abortion is safer and less traumatic than after amniocentesis, which is done between 12 and 16 weeks of pregnancy. Chorionic villus sampling has a slightly higher risk of miscarriage than amniocentesis and is linked with a slight risk of limb deformities (Papp & Papp, 2003). Both techniques provide valuable information about the presence of birth defects, but they also raise difficult issues for parents about whether an abortion should be obtained if birth defects are present.

Maternal blood screening identifies pregnancies that are at higher risk for birth defects such as spina bifida (a typically fatal defect in the spinal cord) and Down syndrome (Erdem & others, 2002). When maternal blood testing first began in the 1980s, the maternal blood screening test only measured alpha-fetoprotein (AFP). The test is now called the *triple screen* because it currently measures three substances in the mother's blood: alpha-fetoprotein, estriol, and human chorionic gonadotropin. This test is administered to women 16 to 18 weeks into pregnancy. After an abnormal triple screen result, the next step is usually an ultrasound examination; if that does not provide an explanation of the abnormal triple screen results, amniocentesis is typically used.

Infertility and Reproductive Technology

Approximately 10 to 15 percent of couples in the United States experience *infertility*, which is defined as the inability to conceive a child after 12 months of regular intercourse without contraception. The cause of infertility can rest with the woman or the man (Pasch, 2001). The woman may not be ovulating (releasing eggs to be fertilized), she may be producing abnormal ova, her fallopian tubes by which ova

A 6-month-old infant poses with the ultrasound sonography record taken four months into the baby's prenatal development. *What is ultrasound sonography?*

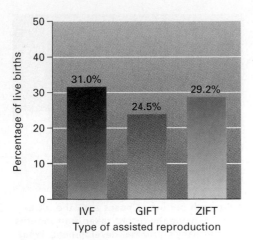

FIGURE 3.10 Success Rates of Three Different Assisted Reproduction Techniques

Note: The results were combined across the ages of the couples because there was little variation in success rates based on age.

Amniocentesis
Obstetric Ultrasound
Genetic Counseling

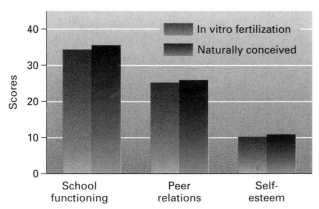

FIGURE 3.11 Socioemotional Functioning of Children Conceived Through In Vitro Fertilization or Naturally Conceived

In one study, comparisons of the socioemotional functioning of young adolescents who had either been conceived through in vitro fertilization (IVF) or naturally conceived revealed no differences between the two groups (Golombok & others, 2001). Although the means for the naturally conceived group were slightly higher, this is likely due to chance. The mean scores shown for the different measures are in the normal range of functioning.

normally reach the womb may be blocked, or she may have a disease that prevents implantation of the embyro into the uterus. The man may produce too few sperm, the sperm may lack motility (the ability to move adequately), or he may have a blocked passageway (Oehninger, 2001). In one study, long-term use of cocaine by men was related to low sperm count, low motility, and a higher number of abnormally formed sperm (Bracken & others, 1990). Cocaine-related infertility appears to be reversible if users stop taking the drug for at least one year.

In some cases of infertility, surgery may correct the cause; in others, hormone-based drugs may improve the probability of having a child. Of the 2 million couples who seek help for infertility every year in the United States, about 40,000 try high-tech assisted reproduction. The three most common techniques are:

- *In vitro fertilization (IVF).* Eggs and sperm are combined in a laboratory dish. If any eggs are successfully fertilized, one or more of the resulting embryos is transferred into the woman's uterus or womb.
- *Gamete intrafallopian transfer (GIFT).* A doctor inserts eggs and sperm directly into a woman's fallopian tube.
- *Zygote intrafallopian transfer (ZIFT).* This is a two-step procedure. First, eggs are fertilized in the laboratory. Then, any resulting zygotes are transferred to a fallopian tube.

The success rates for these three assisted reproduction techniques, based on a national study in the United States in 2000 by the Centers for Disease Control and Prevention, is shown in figure 3.10. IVF is by far the most common technique used (98 percent of all cases in the national study) and had the highest success rate in the national study of slightly more than 30 percent.

One consequence of fertility treatments is an increase in multiple births. Approximately 25 percent of pregnancies achieved by fertility treatments now result in multiple births. Though parents may be thrilled at the prospect of having children, they also face serious risks. Any multiple birth increases the likelihood that the babies will have life-threatening and costly problems, such as extremely low birth weight. Multiple births also pose risks for mothers, such as a higher risk of hypertension and anemia. A recent study revealed that guidelines developed by the medical profession have reduced the number of multiple births involving IVF (Jain, Missmer, & Hornstein, 2004). For example, in 1997 11.4 percent of IVF mothers carried triplets or more but in 2000 this figure had dropped to 7.7 percent, although the percentage of pregnancies with twins did not change. One of the most important guidelines issued called for doctors to limit the number of embryos transferred to no more than two in the youngest women with the healthiest eggs.

The creation of families by means of the new reproductive technologies raises important questions about the psychological consequences for children. However, studies support the idea that "test-tube" babies function well and typically do not differ from naturally conceived children in various behaviors and psychological characteristics (Golombok, MacCallum, & Goodman, 2001; Hahn & Dipietro, 2001) (see figure 3.11).

A summary of some infertility causes and solutions is presented in figure 3.12.

Adoption

Although surgery and fertility drugs can sometimes solve the infertility problem, another choice is to adopt a child (Bass, Shields, & Behrman, 2004; Moody, 2001; Smit, 2002). Adoption is the social and legal process by which a parent-child relationship is established between persons unrelated at birth. It is estimated that approximately 2 to 4 percent of children in the United States are adopted (Stolley, 1993).

Men

Problem	Possible causes	Treatment
Low sperm count	Hormone imbalance, varicose vein in scrotum, possibly environmental pollutants, lead, arsenic Drugs (cocaine, marijuana, some steroids and antibiotics) Y chromosome gene deletions	Hormone therapy, surgery, avoiding excessive heat
Immobile sperm	Abnormal sperm shape Infection Malfunctioning prostate	None Antibiotics Hormones
Antibodies against sperm	Problem in immune system	Drugs

Women

Problem	Possible causes	Treatment
Ovulation problems	Pituitary or ovarian tumor Underactive thyroid	Surgery Drugs
Antisperm secretions	Unknown	Acid or alkaline douche, estrogen therapy
Blocked fallopian tubes	Infection caused by IUD or abortion or by sexually transmitted infection	Eggs surgically removed from ovary and placed in uterus
Endometriosis (tissue buildup in uterus)	Delayed parenthood until the thirties	Hormones, surgical removal of uterine tissue buildup

FIGURE 3.12 Fertility Problems, Possible Causes, and Treatments

Researchers have found that adopted children and adolescents often show more psychological and school-related problems than nonadopted children (Brodzinsky, Lang, & Smith, 1995; Brodzinsky & Pinderhughes, 2002). For example, adopted adolescents are referred to psychological treatment two to five times as often as their nonadopted peers (Grotevant & McRoy, 1990).

In one study of 4,682 adopted adolescents and the same number of nonadopted adolescents, adoptees showed lower levels of adjustment (Sharma, McGue, & Benson, 1996). In another study, adopted adolescents had more school adjustment problems, were more likely to use illicit drugs, and were more likely to engage in delinquent behavior (Sharma, McGue, & Benson, 1998). However, adopted siblings were less withdrawn and engaged in more prosocial behavior (such as being altruistic, caring, and supportive of others) than nonadopted siblings. In one study of 1,587 adopted and 87,165 nonadopted adolescents, the adopted adolescents were at higher risk for all of the domains sampled, including school achievement and problems, substance abuse, psychological well-being, and physical health (Miller & others, 2000). In this study, the effects of adoption were more negative when the adoptive parents had low levels of education. Also, in this study, when a subsample consisting of the most negative problem profiles was examined, the differences between adopted and nonadopted even widened with the adopted adolescents far more likely to have the most problems.

Research has documented that early adoption often has better outcomes for the child than later adoption. In one study, the later adoption occurred, the more problems the adoptees had. Infant adoptees had the fewest adjustment difficulties; those adopted after they were 10 years of age had the most problems (Sharma, McGue, & Benson, 1996). At age 6, children adopted from an orphanage in the first six months of their lives showed no lasting negative effects of their early experience. However, children from the orphanage who were adopted after they were 6 months of age had abnormally high levels of cortisol, a stress-regulating hormone, indicating that their stress regulation had not developed adequately (Chisholm, 1998).

Infertility Resources

Although adoption is associated with increased academic and psychological difficulties, the changes in adoption practices over the last several decades, which we will discuss shortly, make it difficult to generalize about the average adopted child or average adopted family. Further, despite the overall group differences in adopted and nonadopted children, the vast majority of adopted children (including those adopted at older ages, transracially—adopting a child of a different race—and across national borders) adjust effectively and their parents report considerable satisfaction in their adoption decision (Brodzinsky & Pinderhughes, 2002).

In addition, researchers have found that children whose biological parents could not or would not provide adequate care for them benefit from adoption. For example, there is consistent evidence that adopted children fare much better than children who reside in long-term foster care or in institutional-type environments (Brodzinsky & Pinderhughes, 2002).

Many of the keys to effectively parenting adopted children are no different from those for effectively parenting biological children: Be supportive and caring, be involved and monitor the child's behavior and whereabouts, be a good communicator, and help the child learn to develop self-control. However, there are some unique circumstances that parents of adopted children face. These include recognizing the differences involved in adoptive family life, providing child rearing that supports open communication about these differences, showing respect for the birth family, and supporting the child's search for self and identity.

David Brodzinsky and Ellen Pinderhughes (2002, pp. 288–292) recently described some of the challenges that parents face when their children are at different points in development and the best ways to handle these:

- *Infancy* Developing a positive attachment bond between an infant and parents is an important aspect of infancy. Although researchers have found few differences in the attachment of adopted and nonadopted infants, attachment can be compromised "when parents have difficulty in claiming the child as their own either because of unresolved fertility issues, lack of support from family and friends, and/or when their expectations about the child have not been met" (p. 288). Working with competent adoption agencies or counselors can benefit prospective adoptive parents. The agencies and counselors can provide education and support that is helpful in producing realistic parental expectations, especially in circumstances in which the child has special needs.

- *Early Childhood* During infancy, the primary focus of adoptive parents is often to integrate the child into the family and develop a strong parent-child attachment bond. In early childhood, there is a growing recognition by adoptive parents that they need to begin the process of family differentiation. Early childhood is when most parents begin to talk with their child about adoption. "Although not as common today as in the past, some parents consciously decide not to tell their children about the adoption" (p. 289). This may increase the child's psychological risk if he or she finds out about the adoption at a later point in development. Many children begin to ask where they came from when they are approximately 4 to 6 years of age. This is a natural time to begin to respond in simple ways to children about their adopted status (Warshak, 2003).

- *Middle and Late Childhood* During the elementary school years, "children now begin to express much more curiosity about their origins: *Where did I come from? What did my birthmother and birthfather look like? Why didn't they keep me? Where are they now? Can I meet them?*" (p. 290). As children get older, the explanations offered by adoptive parents are often no longer as readily accepted as they were earlier in the child's life. Also, as they grow older, children may become more ambivalent about being adopted. It is important for adoptive parents to recognize that this ambivalence is normal. Open communication on the part of adoptive parents helps to prevent the development of a barrier between the biological and adoptive families. Clinical psychologists report that one problem that sometimes surfaces is the desire of adoptive parents to make life too perfect for the adoptive child and to present a perfect image of themselves to the child. The result too often is that adopted children feel that they cannot release any angry feelings and openly discuss problems (Warshak, 2003).

- *Adolescence* The development of more abstract and logical thinking in adolescence provides the foundation for adopted children to reflect on their adopted status in more complex ways. As pubertal change focuses adolescents' attention on their bodies, many adopted adolescents "become preoccupied with the lack of physical resemblance between themselves and others in the family" (p. 291). The search for identity that characterizes adolescence may also give rise to extensive exploration of the fact that they are adopted and how this fits into their identity. Adoptive parents "need to be aware of these many complexities and provide teenagers with the support they need to cope with these adoption-related tasks" (p. 292).

As we see next in the Diversity in Life-Span Development interlude, increased diversity has not only characterized adopted children but adoptive parents as well.

Diversity in Life-Span Development

The Increased Diversity of Adopted Children and Adoptive Parents

A number of changes began occurring in adoption practice in the last several decades of the twentieth century. These changes include (Brodzinsky & Pinderhughes, 2002, pp. 280–282):

- Until the 1960s, most U.S. adopted children were healthy, European American infants, adopted within a few days or weeks of birth. However, in recent decades, societal changes "led to a growing number of unmarried mothers deciding to keep their babies. These changes, along with the legalization of abortion and the ready availability of contraception, resulted in a dramatic decrease in the number of healthy, European American infants available for adoption" (p. 280).
- "With fewer healthy, European babies available for adoption in the United States, many prospective adoptive parents have explored other options" (p. 281). These options included transracial adoption and adopting children from other countries (Hjern, Vinnerljung, & Lindblad, 2004).
- "Still other prospective adoptive parents began considering adopting foster children whose history and personal characteristics (such as older age at placement, minority [ethnic] status, exposure to neglect and/or abuse, chronic medical problems, and/or physical or mental health problems) were once thought to be barriers to adoption" (p. 281).
- Changes have also characterized adoptive parents. Until the last several decades of the twentieth century, most adoptive parents were of middle- and upper-socioeconomic-status background, "married, infertile, European American couples, usually in their 30s and 40s, and free of any form of disability. Adoption agencies routinely *screened out* couples who did not have these characteristics. Today, however, adoption agency policy and practice have moved in the direction of *screening in* as many different types of adoption applicants as possible. For example, public agencies (in the United States) now have no income requirement for adoptive parents and offer financial and medical subsidies for

What changes in adopted children and adoptive parents have taken place in the last several decades?

View the video, "Interview with Adoptive Parents," to appreciate the complexities and barriers adoptive parents encounter during the adoption process.

children with special needs, which in turn has supported the efforts of low-income couples to adopt children, especially those who otherwise might not find permanent homes" (p. 281). Many agencies now permit single adults, older adults, and gay and lesbian adults to adopt children (Rampage & others, 2003).

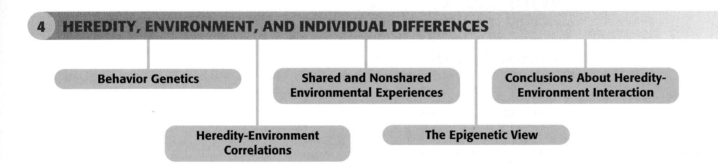

Review and Reflect: Learning Goal 3

 3 Identify some important reproductive challenges and choices

REVIEW

- What are some common prenatal diagnostic tests?
- What are some causes of infertility? What types of reproductive technology are used to improve the success rates of having children for infertile couples?
- How does adoption affect children's development?

REFLECT

- We discussed a number of studies indicating that adoption is linked with negative outcomes for children. Does that mean that all adopted children have more negative outcomes than all nonadopted children? Explain.

4 HEREDITY, ENVIRONMENT, AND INDIVIDUAL DIFFERENCES

Behavior Genetics

Shared and Nonshared Environmental Experiences

Conclusions About Heredity-Environment Interaction

Heredity-Environment Correlations

The Epigenetic View

As we have described genes and how they work, one theme is apparent: Heredity and environment interact to produce development (McGuire, 2001). Whether we are studying how genes produce proteins, their influence on how tall a person is, or how PKU might affect an individual, we end up discussing heredity-environment interactions. Is it possible, though, to untangle the influence of heredity from that of environment and discover the role of each in producing individual differences in development? When heredity and environment interact, how does heredity influence the environment, and vice versa?

Behavior Genetics

Behavior genetics is the field that seeks to discover the influence of heredity and environment on individual differences in human traits and development (DiLalla, 2004; Gottesman, 2004; Maxson, 2003). If you think about all of the people you know, you have probably realized that people differ in terms of their level of introversion/extraversion. What behavior geneticists try to do is to figure out what is responsible for such differences—that is, to what extent do people differ because of differences in genes, environment, or a combination of these?

To study the influence of heredity on behavior, behavior geneticists often use either twins or adoption situations (Goldsmith, Lemery, & Essex, 2004). In the most common **twin study,** the behavioral similarity of identical twins is compared with the behavioral similarity of fraternal twins. *Identical twins* (called monozygotic twins)

behavior genetics The field that seeks to discover the influence of heredity and environment on individual differences in human traits and development.

twin study A study in which the behavioral similarity of identical twins is compared with the behavioral similarity of fraternal twins.

develop from a single fertilized egg that splits into two genetically identical replicas, each of which becomes a person. *Fraternal twins* (called dizygotic twins) develop from separate eggs and separate sperm. Although fraternal twins share the same womb, they are no more alike genetically than are nontwin brothers and sisters, and they may be of different sexes.

By comparing groups of identical and fraternal twins, behavior geneticists capitalize on the basic knowledge that identical twins are more similar genetically than are fraternal twins (Bertelsen, 2004; Jacob & others, 2001). In one twin study, the extraversion and neuroticism (psychological instability) of 7,000 pairs of Finnish identical and fraternal twins were compared (Rose & others, 1988). On both of these personality traits, the identical twins were much more similar than the fraternal twins were, suggesting an important role for heredity in both traits. However, several issues complicate interpretation of twin studies. For example, perhaps the environments of identical twins are more similar than the environments of fraternal twins. Adults might stress the similarities of identical twins more than those of fraternal twins, and identical twins might perceive themselves as a "set" and play together more than fraternal twins do. If so, observed similarities in identical twins could be more strongly influenced by the environment than the results suggested.

In an **adoption study,** investigators seek to discover whether the behavior and psychological characteristics of adopted children are more like those of their adoptive parents, who have provided a home environment, or more like those of their biological parents, who have contributed their heredity. Another form of the adoption study involves comparing adopted and biological siblings.

Twin studies are among those that are used to estimate life expectancy. In the Research in Life-Span Development interlude, we explore these twins studies and other efforts to pin down the role of genes in longevity.

Behavior Genetics
Twin Research

Research in Life-Span Development
Genes and Longevity

Researchers are now exploring the possibility that genetics might play a stronger role in people being able to reach a very old age. One effort in this regard involves the study of centenarians—individuals 100 years old and older. A major investigation is the New England Centenarian Study conducted by Thomas Perls and his colleagues (Perls, 2004; Perls & Terry, 2003; Perls & others, 2000; Terry & others, 2004). In one study, 444 centenarians' pedigrees containing 2,092 siblings were analyzed (Perls & others, 2002). Sibling death rates and survival probabilities were compared with U.S. national levels. A lifelong reduction of mortality risk, even in very old age, of approximately half was found in the siblings. One interpretation of these findings is that because siblings are more closely related genetically than people in general, these results were likely due to the closer genetic relatedness of the siblings. However, some environmental and behavioral factors that siblings have in common early in life may remain strong throughout life, such as socioeconomic status and lifestyle.

Another research strategy involves studying the children of centenarians, and in one recent investigation they appeared to be unusually healthy (Terry & others, 2003). The health histories of 177 unrelated children of centenarians were compared with those of a matched control group. The control group consisted of children whose parents were born in the same year as the centenarians but at least one of the parents had died at average life expectancy. The offspring of the centenarians had reduced prevalence rates of 56 percent for heart

adoption study A study in which investigators seek to discover whether the behavior and psychological characteristics of adopted children are more like their adoptive parents, who have provided a home environment, or more like their biological parents, who have contributed their heredity. Another form of the adoption study is to compare adopted and biological siblings.

disease, 66 percent for hypertension, and 59 percent for diabetes. Thus, the offspring of centenarians show markedly reduced prevalence of diseases associated with aging. One possibility is that individuals who reach extreme old age lack many of the so-called "disease genes" that significantly increase the risk of premature death by predisposing individuals to various life-threatening diseases (Perls & Terry, 2003).

Heredity-Environment Correlations

The difficulties that researchers encounter when they interpret the results of twin studies and adoption studies reflect the complexities of heredity-environment interaction (DiLalla, 2004). Some of these interactions are *heredity-environment correlations,* which means that individuals' genes influence the types of environments to which they are exposed. In a sense, individuals "inherit" environments that are related or linked to genetic propensities (Brooker, 2005; Plomin & others, 2001). Behavior geneticist Sandra Scarr (1993) described three ways that heredity and environment are correlated (see figure 3.13):

- **Passive genotype-environment correlations** occur because biological parents, who are genetically related to the child, provide a rearing environment for the child. For example, the parents might have a genetic predisposition to be intelligent and read skillfully. Because they read well and enjoy reading, they provide their children with books to read. The likely outcome is that their children, given their own inherited predispositions from their parents and their book-filled environment, will become skilled readers.
- **Evocative genotype-environment correlations** occur because a child's characteristics elicit certain types of environments. For example, cooperative, attentive children evoke more pleasant and instructional responses from the adults around them than uncooperative, distractible children do.
- **Active (niche-picking) genotype-environment correlations** occur when children seek out environments that they find compatible and stimulating. *Niche-picking* refers to finding a setting that is suited to one's abilities. Children select from their surrounding environment some aspect that they respond to, learn about, or ignore. Their active selections of environments are related to their particular genotype. For example, outgoing children tend to seek out social contexts in which to interact with people, whereas shy children don't. Children who are musically inclined are likely to select musical environments in which they can successfully perform their skills.

passive genotype-environment correlations Correlations that exist when the natural parents, who are genetically related to the child, provide a rearing environment for the child.

evocative genotype-environment correlations Correlations that exist when the child's characteristics elicit certain types of environments.

active (niche-picking) genotype-environment correlations Correlations that exist when children seek out environments they find compatible and stimulating.

Heredity-Environment Correlation	Description	Examples
Passive	Children inherit genetic tendencies from their parents and parents also provide an environment that matches their own genetic tendencies.	Musically inclined parents usually have musically inclined children and they are likely to provide an environment rich in music for their children.
Evocative	The child's genetic tendencies elicit stimulation from the environment that supports a particular trait. Thus genes evoke environmental support.	A happy, outgoing child elicits smiles and friendly responses from others.
Active (niche-picking)	Children actively seek out "niches" in their environment that reflect their own interests and talents and are thus in accord with their genotype.	Libraries, sports fields, and a store with musical instruments are examples of environmental niches children might seek out if they have intellectual interests in books, talent in sports, or musical talents, respectively.

FIGURE 3.13 Exploring Heredity-Environment Correlations

Scarr believes that the relative importance of the three genotype-environment correlations changes as children develop from infancy through adolescence. In infancy, much of the environment that children experience is provided by adults. Thus, passive genotype-environment correlations are more common in the lives of infants and young children than they are for older children and adolescents who can extend their experiences beyond the family's influence and create their environments to a greater degree.

Critics argue that the concept of heredity-environment correlation gives heredity too much influence in determining development (Gottlieb, 2003, 2004). Heredity-environment correlation stresses that heredity determines the types of environments children experience. Next, we will examine a view that emphasizes the importance of the nonshared environment of siblings and their heredity as important influences on their development.

Shared and Nonshared Environmental Experiences

Behavior geneticists believe that another way of analyzing the environment's role in heredity-environment interaction is to consider experiences that children share in common with other children living in the same home, as well as experiences that are not shared (Feinberg & Hetherington, 2001; Plomin, Ashbury, & Dunn, 2001).

Shared environmental experiences are siblings' common experiences, such as their parents' personalities or intellectual orientation, the family's socioeconomic status, and the neighborhood in which they live. By contrast, **nonshared environmental experiences** are a child's unique experiences, both within the family and outside the family, that are not shared with a sibling. Even experiences occurring within the family can be part of the "nonshared environment." For example, parents often interact differently with each sibling, and siblings interact differently with parents (Hetherington, Reiss, & Plomin, 1994; Reiss & others, 2000). Siblings often have different peer groups, different friends, and different teachers at school.

Behavior geneticist Robert Plomin (1993) has found that common rearing, or shared environment, accounts for little of the variation in children's personality or interests. In other words, even though two children live under the same roof with the same parents, their personalities are often very different. Further, behavior geneticists argue that heredity influences the nonshared environments of siblings in the manner we described earlier in the concept of heredity-environment correlations (Plomin & others, 2001). For example, a child who has inherited a genetic tendency to be athletic is likely to spend more time in environments related to sports, whereas a child who has inherited a tendency to be musically inclined is more likely to spend time in environments related to music.

The Epigenetic View

The heredity-environment correlation view emphasizes how heredity directs the kind of environmental experiences individuals have. However, earlier in the chapter we discussed how genes are collaborative, not determining an individual's traits in an independent manner, but rather in an interactive manner with the environment (Moore, 2001). In line with the concept of a collaborative gene, Gilbert Gottlieb (1998, 2003, 2004) proposed the **epigenetic view,** which emphasizes that development is the result of an ongoing, bidirectional interchange between heredity and the environment. Figure 3.14 compares the heredity-environment correlation and epigenetic views of development.

Let's look at an example that reflects the epigenetic view. A baby inherits genes from both parents at conception (called the genotype). During prenatal development, toxins, nutrition, and stress can influence some genes to stop functioning while others become stronger or weaker. During infancy, environmental experiences such as toxins, nutrition, stress, learning, and encouragement continue to modify genetic activity.

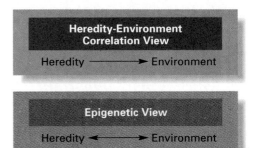

FIGURE 3.14 Comparison of the Heredity-Environment Correlation and Epigenetic Views

shared environmental experiences
Siblings' common environmental experiences, such as their parents' personalities and intellectual orientation, the family's socioeconomic status, and the neighborhood in which they live.

nonshared environmental experiences
The child's own unique experiences, both within the family and outside the family, that are not shared by another sibling. Thus, experiences occurring within the family can be part of the "nonshared environment."

epigenetic view Emphasizes that development is the result of an ongoing, bidirectional interchange between heredity and environment.

Conclusions About Heredity-Environment Interaction

Heredity and environment operate together—or cooperate—to produce a person's intelligence, temperament, height, weight, ability to pitch a baseball, ability to read, and so on (Gottlieb, 2004; Overton, 2004). If an attractive, popular, intelligent girl is elected president of her senior class in high school, is her success due to heredity or to environment? Of course, the answer is both.

The relative contributions of heredity and environment are not additive (McLearn, 2004). That is, we can't say that such-and-such a percentage of nature and such-and-such a percentage of experience make us who we are. Nor is it accurate to say that full genetic expression happens once, around conception or birth, after which we carry our genetic legacy into the world to see how far it takes us. Genes produce proteins throughout the life span, in many different environments. Or they don't produce these proteins, depending in part on how harsh or nourishing those environments are.

The emerging view is that many complex behaviors likely have some *genetic loading* that gives people a propensity for a particular developmental trajectory (Plomin & others, 2001). However, the actual development requires more: an environment. And that environment is complex and information-filled, just like the mixture of genes we inherit (Sternberg & Grigorenko, 2001). Environmental influences range from the things we lump together under "nurture" (such as parenting, family dynamics, schooling, and neighborhood quality) to biological encounters (such as viruses, birth complications, and even biological events in cells) (Greenough, 1997, 1999; Greenough & others, 2001).

The most recent nature-nurture controversy erupted when Judith Harris (1998) published *The Nurture Assumption*. In this provocative book, she argued that what parents do does not make a difference in their children's and adolescents' behavior. Yell at them. Hug them. Read to them. Ignore them. Harris says it won't influence how they turn out. She argues that genes and peers are far more important than parents in children's and adolescents' development.

Genes and peers do matter, but Harris' descriptions of peer influences do not take into account the complexity of peer contexts and developmental trajectories (Hartup, 1999). In addition, Harris is wrong in saying that parents don't matter. For example, in the early child years parents play an important role in selecting children's peers and indirectly influencing children's development (Baumrind, 1999). A huge parenting literature with many research studies documents the importance of parents in children's development (Collins & others, 2000, 2001; Maccoby, 2002). We will discuss parents' important roles throughout this book.

The interaction of heredity and environment is so extensive that to ask which is more important, nature or nurture, is like asking which is more important to a rectangle, height or width.

—WILLIAM GREENOUGH
Contemporary Developmental Psychologist, University of Illinois at Urbana

Review and Reflect: Learning Goal 4

 4 **Explain some of the ways that heredity and environment interact to produce individual differences in development**

REVIEW
- What is behavior genetics?
- What are three types of heredity-environment correlations and what is an example of each?
- What is meant by the concepts of shared and nonshared environmental experiences?
- What is the epigenetic view of development?
- What conclusions can be reached about heredity-environment interaction?

REFLECT
- Someone tells you that they have analyzed their genetic background and environmental experiences and reached the conclusion that environment definitely has had little influence on their intelligence. What would you say to this person about their ability to make this self-diagnosis?

Reach Your Learning Goals

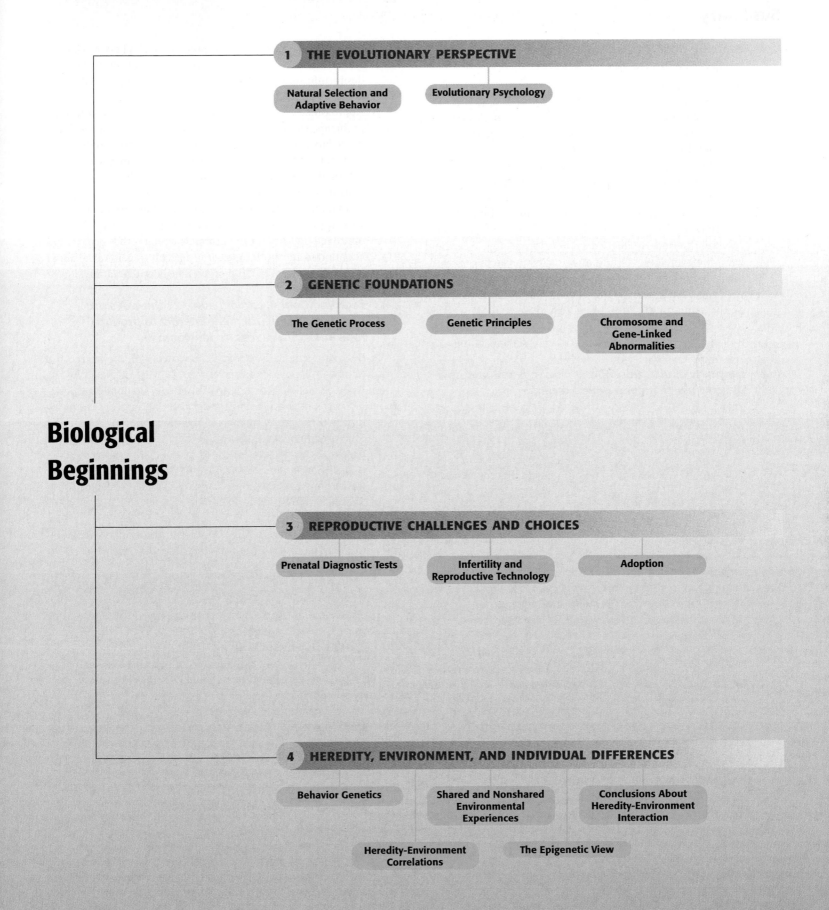

Biological Beginnings

1 THE EVOLUTIONARY PERSPECTIVE

Natural Selection and Adaptive Behavior

Evolutionary Psychology

2 GENETIC FOUNDATIONS

The Genetic Process

Genetic Principles

Chromosome and Gene-Linked Abnormalities

3 REPRODUCTIVE CHALLENGES AND CHOICES

Prenatal Diagnostic Tests

Infertility and Reproductive Technology

Adoption

4 HEREDITY, ENVIRONMENT, AND INDIVIDUAL DIFFERENCES

Behavior Genetics

Shared and Nonshared Environmental Experiences

Conclusions About Heredity-Environment Interaction

Heredity-Environment Correlations

The Epigenetic View

Summary

 ### Learning Goal 1: Discuss the evolutionary perspective on life-span development

- Natural selection is the process that favors the individuals of a species that are best adapted to survive and reproduce. The process of natural selection was proposed by Charles Darwin. In evolutionary theory, adaptive behavior is behavior that promotes the organism's survival in the natural habitat.
- Evolutionary psychology holds that adaptation, reproduction, and "survival of the fittest" are important in shaping behavior. Biological evolution shaped human beings into a culture-making species. Ideas proposed by evolutionary developmental psychology include the view that an extended "juvenile period" is needed to develop a large brain and learn the complexity of human social communities. According to Baltes, the benefits of evolutionary selection decrease with age mainly because of a decline in reproductive fitness. At the same time, cultural needs increase. Bandura argues for a bidirectional link between biology and environment. Biology allows for a broad range of cultural possibilities.

 ### Learning Goal 2: Describe what genes are and how they influence human development

- The nucleus of each human cell contains 46 chromosomes, which are composed of DNA. Genes, hereditary units composed of short segments of DNA, direct cells to reproduce and manufacture proteins that maintain life. Genes do not act independently to produce a trait or behavior. Rather, genes act collaboratively. Mitosis and meiosis are two important ways in which new cells are formed. In the process of reproduction, an egg and a sperm unite to form a zygote. Sources of genetic variability occur during meiosis and include the random separation of maternal and paternal chromosomes.
- Genetic principles include those involving genotype and phenotype, dominant-recessive genes, sex-linked genes, genetic imprinting, and polygenic inheritance.
- Chromosome abnormalities occur when chromosomes do not divide evenly. Down syndrome is the result of a chromosome abnormality caused by the presence of an extra copy of chromosome 21. Sex-linked chromosome abnormalities include Klinefelter syndrome (XXY), fragile X syndrome, Turner syndrome (XO), and XYY syndrome. Gene-linked abnormalities involve harmful genes. Gene-linked disorders include phenylketonuria (PKU) and sickle-cell anemia.

 ### Learning Goal 3: Identify some important reproductive challenges and choices

- Amniocentesis, ultrasound sonography, chorionic villus sampling, and the maternal blood test are used to determine the presence of defects once pregnancy has begun. Genetic counseling has increased in popularity as more couples desire information about their risk of having a child with defective characteristics.
- Approximately 15 percent of U.S. couples have infertility problems, some of which can be corrected through surgery or fertility drugs. Additional options include in vitro fertilization and other more recently developed techniques.
- Although adopted children and adolescents have more problems than their nonadopted counterparts, the vast majority of adopted children adapt effectively. When adoption occurs very early in development, the outcomes for the child are improved. Because of the dramatic changes that occurred in adoption in recent decades, it is difficult to generalize about the average adopted child or average adoptive family.

 ### Learning Goal 4: Explain some of the ways that heredity and environment interact to produce individual differences in development

- Behavior genetics is the field concerned with the degree and nature of behavior's hereditary basis. Methods used by behavior geneticists include twin studies and adoption studies.
- In Scarr's heredity-environment correlations view, heredity directs the types of environments that children experience. She describes three genotype-environment correlations: passive, evocative, and active (niche-picking). Scarr believes that the relative importance of these three genotype-environment correlations changes as children develop.
- Shared environmental experiences refer to siblings' common experiences, such as their parents' personalities and intellectual orientation, the family's socioeconomic status, and the neighborhood in which they live. Nonshared environmental experiences involve the child's unique experiences, both within a family and outside a family, that are not shared with a sibling. Many behavior geneticists argue that differences in the development of siblings are due to nonshared environmental experiences (and heredity) rather than shared environmental experiences.
- The epigenetic view emphasizes that development is the result of an ongoing, bidirectional interchange between heredity and environment.
- Many complex behaviors have some genetic loading that gives people a propensity for a particular developmental trajectory. However, actual development also requires an environment and that environment is complex. The interaction of heredity and environment is extensive. Much remains to be discovered about the specific ways that heredity and environment interact to influence development.

Key Terms

evolutionary psychology 78
chromosomes 80
DNA 80
genes 80
mitosis 82
meiosis 82
fertilization 82
zygote 82

genotype 82
phenotype 82
Down syndrome 85
Klinefelter syndrome 85
fragile X syndrome 85
Turner syndrome 86
XYY syndrome 86
phenylketonuria (PKU) 86

sickle-cell anemia 87
behavior genetics 94
twin study 94
adoption study 95
passive genotype-environment
  correlations 96
evocative genotype-
  environment correlations 96

active (niche-picking)
  genotype-environment
  correlations 96
shared environmental
  experiences 97
nonshared environmental
  experiences 97
epigenetic view 97

Key People

Charles Darwin 77
David Buss 78
Paul Baltes 79
Albert Bandura 79

Steven Jay Gould 80
David Moore 81
David Brodzinsky and Ellen
  Pinderhughes 92

Thomas Perls 95
Sandra Scarr 96
Robert Plomin 97

Gilbert Gottlieb 97
Judith Harris 98

E-Learning Tools

To help you master the material in this chapter, you'll find a number of valuable study tools on the LifeMap CD-ROM that accompanies this book and on the Online Learning Center for *Life-Span Development,* tenth edition, at www.mhhe.com/santrockld10.

Video Clips

In the margins of this book there are icons directing you to the LifeMap CD-ROM that accompanies the book. There you'll find a video for chapter 3 called "Interview with Adoptive Parents." This segment looks at the complicated process of adopting a child from the point of view of the adoptive parents.

Self-Assessment

Connect to www.mhhe.com/santrockld10 to examine your biological heritage by completing the self-assessments, *Prenatal Genetic Screening Questionnaire* and *My Family Health Tree.*

Taking It to the Net

Connect to www.mhhe.com/santrockld10 to research the answers to these questions.

1. Ahmahl, a biochemistry major, is writing a psychology paper on the potential dilemmas that society and scientists may face as a result of the decoding of the human genome. What are some of the main issues or concerns that Ahmahl should address in his class paper?

2. Brandon and Katie are thrilled to learn that they are expecting their first child. They are curious about the genetic make-up of their unborn child and want to know (a) what disorders might be identified through prenatal genetic testing? and (b) which tests, if any, Katie should undergo to help determine this information?

3. Leslie has been a preschool teacher for many years, and has always believed that young children's minds and personalities are a "blank slate." Leslie's new co-worker, Pat, is freshly out of college and argues that evolutionary psychology has identified many behavioral tendencies that are inborn. Might there be a middle ground between the two perspectives?

Health and Well-Being, Parenting, and Education Exercises

Build your decision-making skills by trying your hand at the health and well-being, parenting, and education exercises.

Connect to www.mhhe.com/santrockld10 to research the answers and complete the exercises.

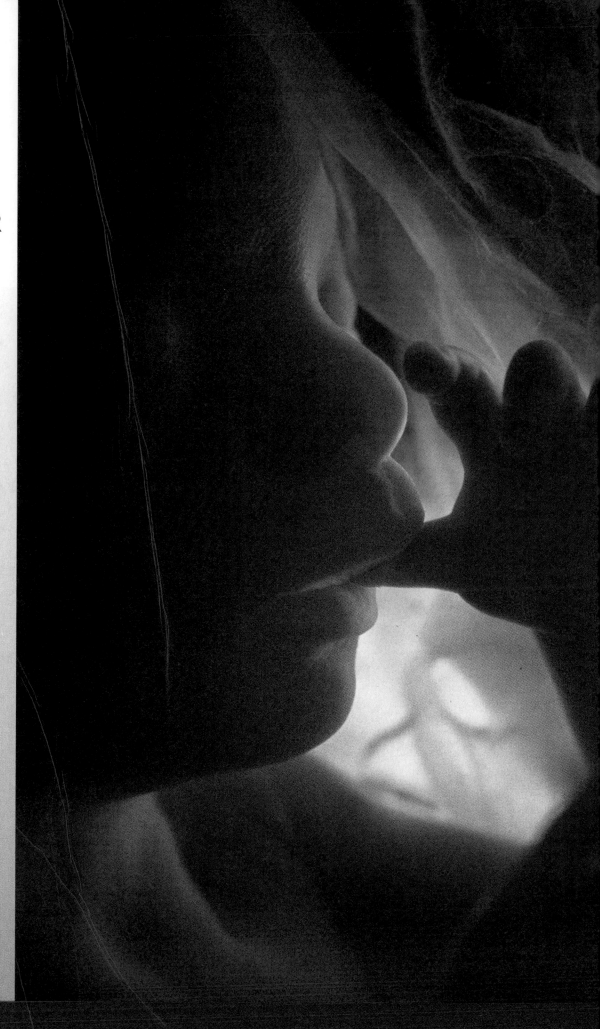

CHAPTER

There was a star danced, and under that I was born.

—WILLIAM SHAKESPEARE
*English Playwright,
17th Century*

Prenatal Development and Birth

Images of Life-Span Development
Tanner Roberts' Birth: A Fantastic Voyage

Tanner Roberts was born in a suite at St. Joseph's Medical Center in Burbank, California. Let's examine what took place in the hours leading up to his birth.

It is day 266 of his mother Cindy's pregnancy. She is in the frozen-food aisle of a convenience store and feels a sharp pain, starting in the small of her back and reaching around her middle, which causes her to gasp. For weeks, painless Braxton Hicks spasms (named for the gynecologist who discovered them) have been flexing her uterine muscles. But these practice contractions were not nearly as intense and painful as the one she just experienced. After six hours of irregular spasms, her uterus settles into a more predictable rhythm.

At 3 A.M., Cindy and her husband, Tom, are wide awake. They time Cindy's contractions with a stopwatch. The contractions are now only six minutes apart. It's time to call the hospital. A short time later, Tom and Cindy arrive at the hospital's labor-delivery suite. A nurse puts a webbed belt and fetal monitor around Cindy's middle to measure her labor. The monitor picks up the fetal heart rate. With each contraction of the uterine wall, Tanner's heartbeat jumps from its resting state of about 140 beats to 160 to 170 beats per minute. When the cervix is dilated to more than 4 centimeters, or almost half open, Cindy receives her first medication. As Demerol begins to drip in her veins, the pain of her contractions is less intense. Tanner's heart rate dips to 130 and then 120.

Contractions are now coming every three to four minutes, each one lasting about 25 seconds. The Demerol does not completely obliterate Cindy's pain. She hugs her husband as the nurse urges her to "relax those muscles. Breathe deep. Relax. You're almost there."

Each contraction briefly cuts off Tanner's source of oxygen, his mother's blood. However, in the minutes of rest between contractions, Cindy's deep breathing helps rush fresh blood to the baby's heart and brain.

At 8 A.M., Cindy's cervix is almost completely dilated and the obstetrician arrives. Using a tool made for the purpose, he reaches into the birth canal and tears the membranes of the amniotic sac, and about half a liter of clear fluid flows out. Contractions are now coming every two minutes, and each one is lasting a full minute.

By 9 A.M., the labor suite has been transformed into a delivery room. Tanner's body is compressed by his mother's contractions and pushes. As he nears his entrance into the world, the compressions help press the fluid from his lungs in preparation for his first breath. Squeezed tightly in the birth canal, the top of Tanner's head emerges. His face is puffy and scrunched. Although fiercely squinting because of the sudden light, Tanner's eyes are open. Tiny bubbles of clear mucus are on his lips. Before any more of his body emerges, the nurse cradles Tanner's head and suctions his nose and mouth. Tanner takes his first breath, a large gasp followed by whimpering, and then a loud cry. Tanner's body is wet but only slightly bloody as the doctor lifts him onto his mother's abdomen. The umbilical cord, still connecting Tanner with his mother, slows and stops pulsating. The obstetrician cuts it, severing Tanner's connection to his mother's womb. Now Tanner's blood flows not to his mother's body for nourishment, but to his own lungs, intestines, and other organs. (Warrick, 1992, pp. E1, 12, 13)

PREVIEW

This chapter chronicles the truly remarkable developments from conception through birth. Imagine . . . at one time you were an organism floating in a sea

of fluid in your mother's womb. Let's now explore what your development was like from the time you were conceived through the time you were born.

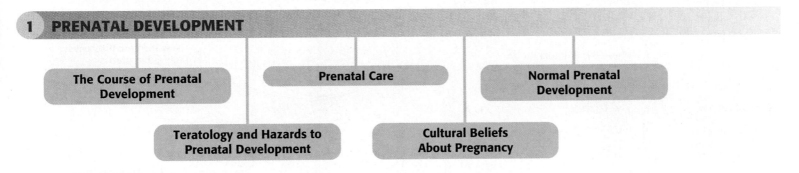

Imagine how Tanner Roberts came to be. Out of thousands of eggs and millions of sperm, one egg and one sperm united to produce him. Had the union of sperm and egg come a day or even an hour earlier or later, a different sperm may have fertilized the egg and Tanner might have been very different—maybe even of the opposite sex. Conception occurs when a single sperm cell from the male unites with an ovum (egg) in the female's fallopian tube in a process called fertilization. Remember from chapter 3 that the fertilized egg is called a zygote.

The Course of Prenatal Development

The course of prenatal development lasts approximately 266 days, beginning with fertilization and ending with birth. Prenatal development is divided into three periods: germinal, embryonic, and fetal.

The Germinal Period The **germinal period** is the period of prenatal development that takes place in the first two weeks after conception. It includes the creation of the zygote, continued cell division, and the attachment of the new organism to the uterine wall. By approximately one week after conception, the differentiation of cells has already commenced. At this stage the group of cells, now called the **blastocyst,** consists of an inner mass of cells that will eventually develop into the embryo, and the **trophoblast,** an outer layer of cells that will become part of the placenta. *Implantation,* the attachment of the blastocyst to the uterine wall, takes place about 10 to 14 days after conception. Figure 4.1 illustrates some of the most significant developments during the germinal period.

The Embryonic Period The **embryonic period** is the period of prenatal development that occurs from two to eight weeks after conception. During the embryonic period, the rate of cell differentiation intensifies, support systems for cells form, and organs appear. After the blastocyst attaches to the uterine wall, the mass of cells is called an *embryo* and three layers of cells are formed. The embryo's *endoderm* is the inner layer of cells, which will develop into the digestive and respiratory systems. The outer layer of cells is divided into two parts. The *ectoderm* is the outermost layer, which will become the nervous system, sensory receptors (ears, nose, and eyes, for example), and skin parts (hair and nails, for example). The *mesoderm* is the middle layer, which will become the circulatory system, bones, muscles, excretory system, and reproductive system. Every body part eventually develops from these three layers.

As the embryo's three layers form, life-support systems for the embryo mature and develop rapidly. These life-support systems include the placenta, the umbilical cord, and the amnion. The **placenta** consists of a disk-shaped group of tissues in which small blood vessels from the mother and the offspring intertwine but do not

germinal period The period of prenatal development that takes place in the first two weeks after conception. It includes the creation of the zygote, continued cell division, and the attachment of the zygote to the uterine wall.

blastocyst The inner mass of cells that develops during the germinal period. These cells later develop into the embryo.

trophoblast An outer layer of cells that develops in the germinal period. These cells will become part of the placenta.

embryonic period The period of prenatal development that occurs from two to eight weeks after conception. During the embryonic period, the rate of cell differentiation intensifies, support systems for the cells form, and organs appear.

placenta A disk-shaped group of tissues in which small blood vessels from the mother and offspring intertwine but do not join.

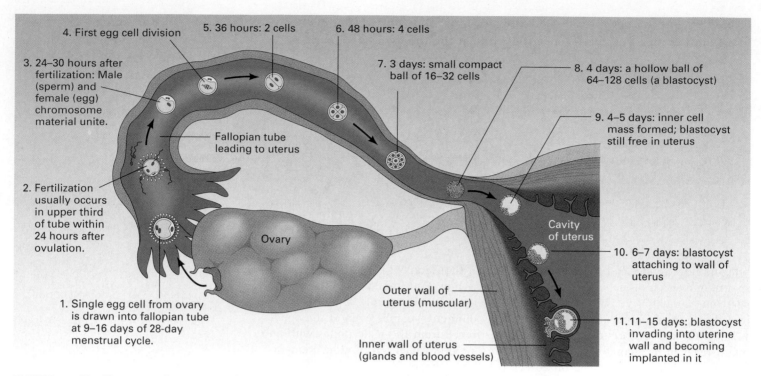

FIGURE 4.1 Significant Developments in the Germinal Period

**The Visible Embryo
The Trimesters**

umbilical cord Contains two arteries and one vein; connects the baby to the placenta.

amnion The life-support system that is a bag or envelope containing a clear fluid in which the developing embryo floats.

organogenesis Organ formation that takes place during the first two months of prenatal development.

fetal period The prenatal period of development that begins two months after conception and lasts for seven months, on average.

join. The **umbilical cord,** which contains two arteries and one vein, connects the baby to the placenta. Very small molecules—oxygen, water, salt, food from the mother's blood, as well as carbon dioxide and digestive wastes from the embryo's blood—pass back and forth between the mother and infant. Large molecules cannot pass through the placental wall; these include red blood cells and many harmful substances, such as most bacteria, maternal wastes, and hormones. The mechanisms that govern the transfer of substances across the placental barrier are complex and are still not entirely understood (Jimenez & others, 2004; Wehrens & others, 2004). Figure 4.2 provides an illustration of the placenta, the umbilical cord, and the nature of blood flow in the expectant mother and developing child in the uterus. The **amnion,** a bag or an envelope that contains a clear fluid in which the developing embryo floats, is another part of the life-support system. Like the umbilical cord, the amnion develops from the fertilized egg, not from the mother's own body. The amniotic fluid provides an environment that is temperature and humidity controlled, as well as shockproof.

By the time most women even know they are pregnant, some important embryonic developments have taken place. In the third week, the neural tube, which eventually becomes the spinal cord and brain, forms. At about 21 days, eyes begin to appear, and at 24 days the cells for the heart begin to differentiate. During the fourth week, the urogenital system becomes apparent, and arm and leg buds emerge. Four chambers of the heart take shape, and blood vessels appear. From the fifth to the eighth week, arms and legs differentiate further; at this time, the face starts to form but still is not very recognizable. The intestinal tract develops and the facial structures fuse. At eight weeks, the developing organism weighs about $1/30$ ounce and is just over 1 inch long.

Organogenesis is the process of organ formation that takes place during the first two months of prenatal development. When organs are being formed, they are especially vulnerable to environmental changes. Later in the chapter, we will describe the environmental hazards that can adversely affect organogenesis.

The Fetal Period The **fetal period** is the prenatal period of development that begins two months after conception and lasts for seven months, on average. Growth

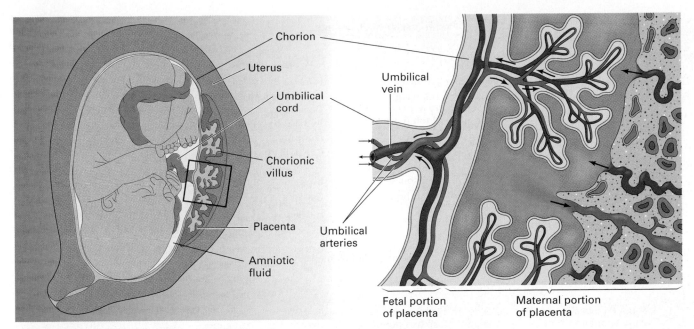

FIGURE 4.2 The Placenta and the Umbilical Cord

Maternal blood flows through the uterine arteries to the spaces housing the placenta, and it returns through the uterine veins to the maternal circulation. Fetal blood flows through the umbilical arteries into the capillaries of the placenta and returns through the umbilical vein to the fetal circulation. The exchange of materials takes place across the layer separating the maternal and fetal blood supplies, so the bloods never come into contact. *Note:* The area bound by the square is enlarged in the right half of the illustration. Arrows indicate the direction of blood flow.

and development continue their dramatic course during this time. Three months after conception, the fetus is about 3 inches long and weighs about 1 ounce. It has become active, moving its arms and legs, opening and closing its mouth, and moving its head. The face, forehead, eyelids, nose, and chin are distinguishable, as are the upper arms, lower arms, hands, and lower limbs. The genitals can be identified as male or female. By the end of the fourth month, the fetus has grown to 6 inches in length and weighs 4 to 7 ounces. At this time, a growth spurt occurs in the body's lower parts. Prenatal reflexes are stronger; arm and leg movements can be felt for the first time by the mother.

By the end of the fifth month, the fetus is about 12 inches long and weighs close to a pound. Structures of the skin have formed—toenails and fingernails, for example. The fetus is more active, showing a preference for a particular position in the womb. By the end of the sixth month, the fetus is about 14 inches long and has gained another half pound to a pound. The eyes and eyelids are completely formed, and a fine layer of hair covers the head. A grasping reflex is present and irregular breathing movements occur. By the end of the seventh month, the fetus is about 16 inches long, and having gained another pound, now weighs about 3 pounds. During the eighth and ninth months, the fetus grows longer and gains substantial weight—about another 4 pounds. At birth, the average American baby weighs $7\frac{1}{2}$ pounds and is about 20 inches long. In these last two months, fatty tissues develop, and the functioning of various organ systems—heart and kidneys, for example—steps up.

We have described a number of changes in prenatal development in terms of germinal, embryonic, and fetal periods. Another way to divide prenatal development is in terms of equal periods of three months, called *trimesters*. An overview of some of the main changes in prenatal development in the three trimesters is presented in figure 4.3. Remember that the three trimesters are not the same as the three prenatal periods we have discussed—germinal, embryonic, and fetal. The germinal and embryonic periods occur in the first trimester. The fetal period begins toward the end of the first trimester and continues through the second and third trimesters. An important point that needs to be made is that the first time a fetus

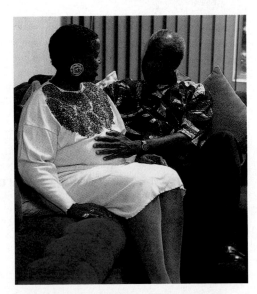

Lines of communication should be open between the expectant mother and her partner during pregnancy. *What are some examples of good partner communication during pregnancy?*

First trimester (first 3 months)			
Prenatal growth	**Conception to 4 weeks** • Is less than 1/10 inch long • Beginning development of spinal cord, nervous system, gastrointestinal system, heart, and lungs • Amniotic sac envelopes the preliminary tissues of entire body • Is called a "zygote"	**8 weeks** • Is just over 1 inch long • Face is forming with rudimentary eyes, ears, mouth, and tooth buds • Arms and legs are moving • Brain is forming • Fetal heartbeat is detectable with ultrasound • Is called an "embryo"	**12 weeks** • Is about 3 inches long and weighs about 1 ounce • Can move arms, legs, fingers, and toes • Fingerprints are present • Can smile, frown, suck, and swallow • Sex is distinguishable • Can urinate • Is called a "fetus"

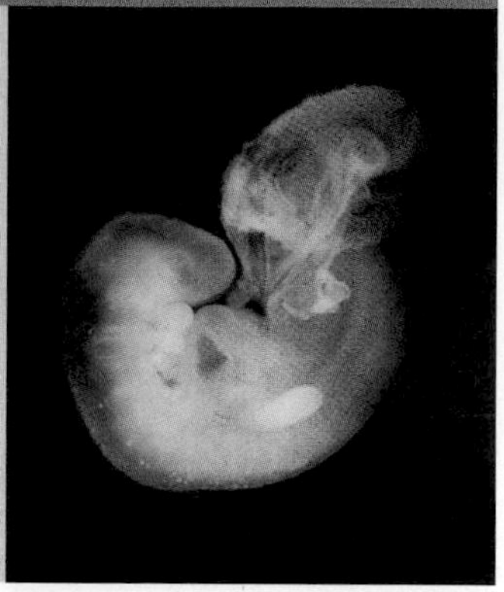

Second trimester (middle 3 months)			
Prenatal growth	**16 weeks** • Is about 6 inches long and weighs about 4 to 7 ounces • Heartbeat is strong • Skin is thin, transparent • Downy hair (lanugo) covers body • Fingernails and toenails are forming • Has coordinated movements; is able to roll over in amniotic fluid	**20 weeks** • Is about 12 inches long and weighs close to 1 pound • Heartbeat is audible with ordinary stethoscope • Sucks thumb • Hiccups • Hair, eyelashes, eyebrows are present	**24 weeks** • Is about 14 inches long and weighs 1 to 1½ pounds • Skin is wrinkled and covered with protective coating (vernix caseosa) • Eyes are open • Waste matter is collected in bowel • Has strong grip

Third trimester (last 3 months)			
Prenatal growth	**28 weeks** • Is about 16 inches long and weighs about 3 pounds • Is adding body fat • Is very active • Rudimentary breathing movements are present	**32 weeks** • Is 16½ to 18 inches long and weighs 4 to 5 pounds • Has periods of sleep and wakefulness • Responds to sounds • May assume the birth position • Bones of head are soft and flexible • Iron is being stored in liver	**36 to 38 weeks** • Is 19 to 20 inches long and weighs 6 to 7½ pounds • Skin is less wrinkled • Vernix caseosa is thick • Lanugo is mostly gone • Is less active • Is gaining immunities from mother

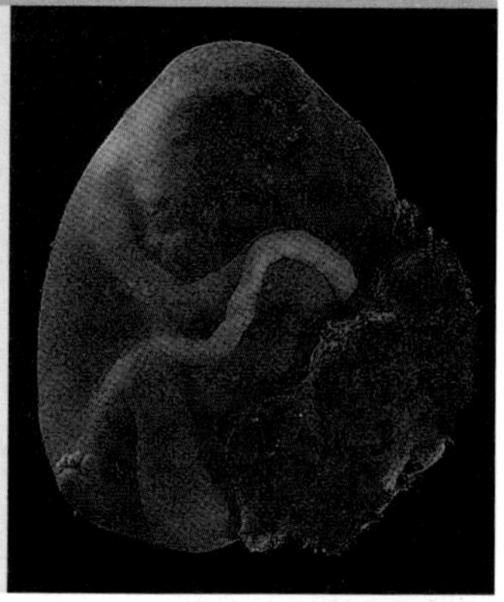

FIGURE 4.3 The Three Trimesters of Prenatal Development

has a chance of surviving outside of the womb—that is, when it is viable—is the beginning of the third trimester (at about seven months). Even when infants are born in the seventh month, they usually need assistance in breathing.

Teratology and Hazards to Prenatal Development

Some expectant mothers carefully tiptoe about in the belief that everything they do and feel has a direct effect on their unborn child. Others behave casually, assuming that their experiences will have little effect. The truth lies somewhere between these two extremes. Although living in a protected, comfortable environment, the fetus is not totally immune to the larger world surrounding the mother. The environment can affect the child in many well-documented ways. Thousands of babies born deformed or mentally retarded every year are the result of events that occurred in the mother's life, as early as one or two months *before* conception (Bailey, Forget, & Koren, 2002).

A **teratogen** (the word comes from the Greek word *tera*, meaning "monster") is any agent that causes a birth defect. The field of study that investigates the causes of birth defects is called *teratology*. Teratogens include drugs, incompatible blood types, environmental pollutants, infectious diseases, nutritional deficiencies, maternal stress, and advanced maternal and paternal age. So many teratogens exist that practically every fetus is exposed to at least some teratogens. For this reason, determining which teratogen causes which birth defect is difficult. In addition, it may take a long time for the effects of a teratogen to show up. Only about half of all potential effects appear at birth.

The dose, the time of exposure to a particular agent, and genetic susceptibility influence the severity of the damage to an unborn child and the type of defect that occurs:

- *Dose* The dose effect is what you might expect—the greater the dose of an agent, such as a drug, the greater the effect.
- *Time of Exposure* Teratogens do more damage at some points in development than at others (Brent & Fawcett, 2000). Damage during the germinal stage may even prevent implantation from occurring. After that, the embryonic period is a more vulnerable time than the fetal period. As figure 4.4 shows, sensitivity to teratogens is first noticed at about three weeks after conception. The probability of a structural defect is greatest early in the embryonic period, when organs are being formed. After organogenesis is complete, teratogens are less likely to cause anatomical defects. Exposure later, during the fetal period, is more likely to stunt growth or to create problems in the way organs function. The precision of the timing of organogenesis is evident; teratologists point out that the vulnerability of the eyes is greatest at 24 to 40 days, the heart at 20 to 40 days, and the legs at 24 to 36 days.

  In chapter 2, we introduced the concept of *critical period* in our discussion of Lorenz's ethological theory. Recall that a critical period is a fixed time period very early in development during which certain experiences or events can have a long-lasting effect on development. As shown in figure 4.4, each body structure has its own critical period of formation. Thus, the critical period for the central nervous system (week 3) is earlier than for arms and legs (weeks 4 and 5).

- *Genetic Susceptibility* The type or severity of abnormalities caused by a teratogen is linked to the genotype of the pregnant woman and the genotype of the fetus. For example, variation in maternal metabolism of a particular drug can influence the degree to which the drug effects are transmitted to the fetus. Differences in placental membranes and placental transport also affect fetal exposure. The genetic susceptibility of the fetus to a particular teratogen can also affect the extent to which the fetus is vulnerable (Pellizzer & others, 2004).

Prescription and Nonprescription Drugs   Some pregnant women take prescription and nonprescription drugs without thinking about the possible effects on the fetus (Addis, Magrini, & Mastroiacovo, 2001). Occasionally, a rash of deformed babies is born, bringing to light the damage drugs can have on a developing fetus. This happened in 1961, when many pregnant women took a popular tranquilizer, thalidomide, to alleviate their morning sickness. In adults, the effects of thalidomide were mild; in embryos, however, they were devastating. Not all infants were affected in the same way. If the mother took thalidomide on day 26 (probably before she knew she was pregnant), an arm might not grow. If she took the drug two days later, the arm might not grow past the elbow. The thalidomide tragedy shocked the medical community and parents into the stark realization that the mother does not have to be a chronic drug user for the fetus to be harmed. Taking the wrong drug at the wrong time is enough to physically handicap the offspring for life (Rodier, 2004; Sorokin, 2002; Stanwood & Levitt, 2004).

The history of man for nine months preceding his birth would, probably, be far more interesting, and contain events of greater moment than all three score and ten years that follow it.

—SAMUEL TAYLOR COLERIDGE
English Poet, Essayist, 19th Century

www.mhhe.com/santrockld10

Health and Prenatal Development
Exploring Teratology
High-Risk Situations

teratogen From the Greek word *tera*, meaning "monster." Any agent that causes a birth defect. The field of study that investigates the causes of birth defects is called *teratology*.

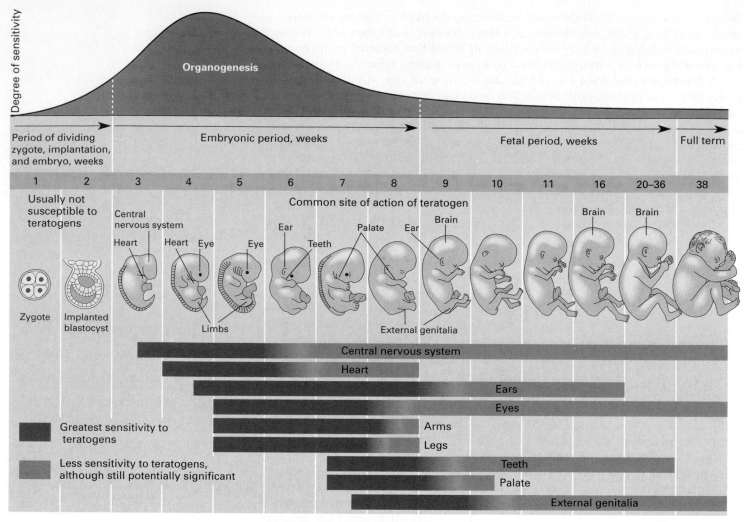

FIGURE 4.4 Teratogens and the Timing of Their Effects on Prenatal Development
The danger of structural defects caused by teratogens is greatest early in embryonic development.
The period of organogenesis (red color) lasts for about six weeks. Later assaults by teratogens
(blue-green color) mainly occur in the fetal period and instead of causing structural damage are
more likely to stunt growth or cause problems of organ function.

Prescription drugs that can function as teratogens include antibiotics, such as streptomycin and tetracycline; some antidepressants; certain hormones, such as progestin and synthetic estrogen; and Accutane (which often is prescribed for acne) (Andrade & others, 2004; Kallen, 2004; Webster & Freeman, 2003).

Nonprescription drugs that can be harmful include diet pills, aspirin, and caffeine (Cnattingius & others, 2000). Let's explore the research on caffeine. A review of studies on caffeine consumption during pregnancy concluded that a small increase in the risks for spontaneous abortion and low birth weight occurs for pregnant women consuming more than 300 milligrams of caffeine (approximately two to three cups of brewed coffee or 12-ounce cans of cola) per day (Fernandes & others, 1998). In computing daily caffeine intake, other foods such as tea and chocolate also need to be included. In one study, pregnant women who drank caffeinated coffee were more likely to have preterm deliveries and newborns with a lower birth weight than their counterparts who did not drink caffeinated coffee (Eskenazi & others, 1999). In this study, no effects were found for pregnant women who drank decaffeinated coffee. Taking into account such results, the U.S. Food and Drug Administration recommends that pregnant women either not consume caffeine or consume it only sparingly.

Psychoactive Drugs *Psychoactive drugs* are drugs that act on the nervous system to alter states of consciousness, modify perceptions, and change moods. A number of psychoactive drugs, including alcohol and nicotine, as well as illegal drugs such as cocaine, marijuana, and heroin, have been studied to determine their links to prenatal and child development (Caulfield, 2001; Fogel, 2001).

Alcohol Heavy drinking by pregnant women can be devastating to offspring (Barr & Streissguth, 2001; O'Leary, 2004). **Fetal alcohol syndrome (FAS)** is a cluster of abnormalities that appears in the offspring of some mothers who drink alcohol heavily during pregnancy. The abnormalities include facial deformities and defective limbs, face, and heart. Most of these children are below average in intelligence, and some are mentally retarded (Bookstein & others, 2002; O'Leary, 2004). Although many mothers of FAS infants are heavy drinkers, many mothers who are heavy drinkers do not have children with FAS or have one child with FAS and other children who do not have it. Figure 4.5 shows a child with fetal alcohol syndrome. Although no serious malformations such as those produced by FAS are found in infants born to mothers who are moderate drinkers, in one study, children whose mothers drank moderately (one to two drinks a day) during pregnancy were less attentive and alert, even at 4 years of age (Streissguth & others, 1984). A recent study found that moderate alcohol drinking by pregnant women (three or fewer drinks a day) was linked with increased risk of preterm birth (Parazzini & others, 2003). Also, in a longitudinal study, the more alcohol mothers drank in the first trimester of pregnancy, the more 14-year-olds fell behind on growth markers such as weight, height, and head size (Day & others, 2002).

What are some guidelines for alcohol use during pregnancy? Moderate drinking of one or two servings of beer or wine or one serving of hard liquor a few days a week can have negative effects on the fetus, although it is generally agreed that this level of alcohol use will not cause fetal alcohol syndrome (Willford & others, 2004). The U.S. Surgeon General recommends that *no* alcohol be consumed during pregnancy.

Nicotine Cigarette smoking by pregnant women can also adversely influence prenatal development, birth, and postnatal development. Fetal and neonatal deaths are higher among smoking mothers (Mathews, Menacker, & MacDorman, 2003). There also are higher incidences of preterm births and lower birth weights (Ashmead, 2003).

In one study, urine samples from 22 of 31 newborns of smoking mothers contained substantial amounts of one of the strongest carcinogens (NNK) in tobacco smoke; the urine samples of the newborns whose mothers did not smoke were free of the carcinogen (Lackmann & others, 1999). A recent study found that prenatal exposure to heavy maternal smoking induced nicotine withdrawal symptoms in newborns (Godding & others, 2004). In another study, prenatal exposure to cigarette smoking was related to poorer language and cognitive skills at 4 years of age (Fried & Watkinson, 1990). Respiratory problems and sudden infant death syndrome (SIDS, also known as crib death) are more common among the offspring of mothers who smoked during pregnancy (Sawnani & others, 2004; Stocks & Dezateux, 2003). And a recent study revealed a link between maternal smoking during pregnancy and increased incidence of attention deficit hyperactivity disorder in almost 3,000 children 5 to 16 years of age (Thapar & others, 2003). Intervention programs designed to help pregnant women stop smoking can reduce some of smoking's negative behaviors, especially by raising birth weights (Klesges & others, 2001).

Illegal Drugs Among the illegal drugs that have been studied to determine their effects on prenatal and child development are cocaine, marijuana, and heroin.

Cocaine Does cocaine use during pregnancy harm the developing embryo and fetus? The most consistent finding is that cocaine exposure during prenatal development is associated with reduced birth weight, length, and head circumference

FIGURE 4.5 Fetal Alcohol Syndrome
Notice the wide-set eyes, flat bones, and thin upper lip.

www.mhhe.com/santrockld10

Fetal Alcohol Syndrome
Smoking and Pregnancy

fetal alcohol syndrome (FAS) A cluster of abnormalities that appears in the offspring of mothers who drink alcohol heavily during pregnancy.

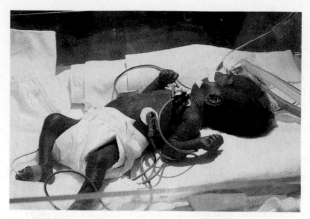

This baby was exposed to cocaine prenatally. *What are some of the possible effects on development of being exposed to cocaine prenatally?*

(Smith & others, 2001). Also, in one study, prenatal cocaine exposure was associated with impaired motor development at 2 years of age (Arendt & others, 1999). In a recent study, 1-month-old infants, exposed to cocaine during pregnancy, had lower arousal, less effective self-regulation, higher excitability, and lower quality of reflexes (Lester & others, 2002). Other studies link cocaine use with impaired information processing and language development (Bandstra & others, 2004; Morrow & others, 2003; Singer & others, 1999). In one study, for example, prenatal cocaine exposure was moderately related to poor attentional skills through 5 years of age (Bandstra & others, 2000). In another study, prenatal exposure to cocaine was related to impaired processing of auditory information after birth (Potter & others, 2000).

A cautious interpretation of these findings has been emphasized (Chavkin, 2001; Frank & others, 2001; Vidaeff & Mastrobattista, 2003). Why? Because other factors (such as poverty, malnutrition, and other substance abuse) in the lives of pregnant women who use cocaine often cannot be ruled out as possible contributors to the problems found in their children (Kaugers, Russ, & Singer, 2000). For example, cocaine users are more likely than nonusers to smoke cigarettes, use marijuana, drink alcohol, and take amphetamines.

However, despite these cautions in interpretation, the weight of recent research evidence indicates that children born to cocaine-using mothers are likely to have neurological and cognitive deficits (Lewis & others, 2004; Mayes, 2003). Because of the potential harmful effect of cocaine to the pregnant mother, and to the fetus, its use is not recommended.

Marijuana In spite of marijuana being used by a number of women of reproductive age, there has not been extensive research investigation of its effects on their offspring. In a recent review of the research that has been done, it was concluded that marijuana use during pregnancy is not linked to the offspring's general intelligence but that a child's attention may be impaired (Fried, 2002). Also, the National Institute of Drug Abuse's (2001) review of marijuana effects concluded that babies born to mothers who used marijuana during pregnancy are smaller than babies born to mothers who did not use the drug. Further, in a longitudinal study, prenatal marijuana exposure was related to learning and memory difficulties at age 11 (Richardson & others, 2002). However, because of the small numbers of studies, it is difficult to reach conclusions about the effects of marijuana use by mothers during pregnancy on the child's development. Nonetheless, marijuana is not recommended for use by pregnant women.

Heroin It is well documented that infants whose mothers are addicted to heroin show several behavioral difficulties (Hulse & others, 2001). The young infants of these mothers are addicted and show withdrawal symptoms characteristic of sudden opiate abstinence, such as tremors, irritability, abnormal crying, disturbed sleep, and impaired motor control. Behavioral problems are still often present at the first birthday, and attention deficits may appear later in the child's development. The most common treatment for heroin addiction, methadone, is associated with very severe withdrawal symptoms in newborns (Crandall, Crosby, & Carlson, 2004).

Incompatible Blood Types The incompatibility of the mother's and fetus' blood types is another risk to prenatal development. Variations in the surface structure of red blood cells distinguish different blood types. One type of surface marker borne by red blood cells identifies a person's blood group as A, B, O, or AB. The second type, called the *Rh factor,* is said to be positive if the Rh marker is present or negative if the individual's red blood cells do not carry this marker. If a pregnant woman is Rh negative and the father is Rh positive, the fetus may be Rh positive (Weiss, 2001). When the fetus' blood is Rh positive and the mother's is Rh negative, the mother's immune system may produce antibodies that will attack the fetus. This can result in any number of problems, including miscarriage or stillbirth, anemia, jaundice, heart defects, brain damage, or death soon after birth (Narang & Jain, 2001).

Generally, the first Rh-positive baby of an Rh-negative mother is not at risk because the mother's blood typically does not come into direct contact with the baby except during delivery, so her body isn't stimulated to produce antibodies. But with each subsequent Rh-positive pregnancy the risk becomes greater. A vaccine (RhoGAM) may be given to the mother within three days of the child's birth to prevent her body from making antibodies that will attack future Rh-positive fetuses. Also, babies affected by Rh incompatibility can be given blood transfusions before or right after birth (Mannessier & others, 2000).

Environmental Hazards Radiation, chemicals, and other hazards in our modern industrial world can endanger the fetus (Blaasaas, Tynes, & Lie, 2004; Grigorenko, 2001; Rodier, 2004; Urbano & Tait, 2004). For instance, radiation can cause a gene mutation (an abrupt, permanent change in DNA). Chromosomal abnormalities are higher among the offspring of fathers exposed to high levels of radiation in their occupations (Schrag & Dixon, 1985). X-ray radiation also can affect the developing embryo and fetus, especially in the first several weeks after conception, when women do not yet know they are pregnant (Barnett & Maulik, 2001). Possible effects of radiation include microencephaly, mental retardation, and leukemia. It is important for women and their physicians to weigh the risk of an X-ray when an actual or potential pregnancy is involved (Brent, 2004; Shaw, 2001); however, a routine diagnostic X-ray of a body area other than the abdomen, with the woman's abdomen protected by a lead apron, is generally considered safe.

Environmental pollutants and toxic wastes are also sources of danger to unborn children (Guo & others, 2004; Rodier, 2004). Researchers have found that various hazardous wastes and pesticides cause defects in animals exposed to high doses. Among the dangerous pollutants and wastes are carbon monoxide, mercury, and lead. Some children are exposed to lead because they live in houses in which lead-based paint flakes off the walls or near busy highways, where there are heavy automobile emissions from leaded gasoline. Researchers believe that early exposure to lead affects children's mental development (Markowitz, 2000). For example, in one study, 2-year-olds who prenatally had high levels of lead in their umbilical-cord blood performed poorly on a test of mental development (Bellinger & others, 1987).

Some fish contain high levels of mercury, which is released into the air both naturally and by industrial pollution (Fitzgerald & others, 2004). When mercury falls into the water it can become toxic, accumulating in large fish, such as shark, swordfish, king mackerel, tilefish, and some species of large tuna (Stephenson, 2004). Mercury is easily transferred across the placenta, and the embryo's developing brain and nervous system are highly sensitive to the metal (Grandjean & others, 2003; Patterson, Ryan, & Dickey, 2004; Vreugdenhil & others, 2004). The U.S. Food and Drug Administration (2004) recommends that pregnant women, as well as mothers who are nursing or trying to conceive and young children, should also avoid eating these fish.

Researchers also have found that manufacturing chemicals known as PCBs are harmful to prenatal development (Jacobson & Jacobson, 2003). In one study, the extent to which pregnant women ate PCB-polluted fish from Lake Michigan was examined, and subsequently their newborns were observed (Jacobson & others, 1984). The women who had eaten more PCB-polluted fish were more likely to have smaller, preterm infants who were more likely to react slowly to stimuli. And, in another study, prenatal exposure to PCBs was associated with problems in visual discrimination and short-term memory in 4-year-old children (Jacobson & others, 1992).

Yet another recent environmental concern for expectant mothers is prolonged exposure to heat produced by saunas or hot tubs. By raising the mother's body temperature, a sauna or a hot tub can cause a fever that endangers the fetus. The high temperature of a fever may interfere with cell division and may cause birth defects or even fetal death if the fever occurs repeatedly for prolonged periods of time. If the expectant mother feels uncomfortably hot in a sauna or hot tub, she should get out, even if she has been there only for a short time.

An explosion at the Chernobyl nuclear power plant in the Ukraine produced radioactive contamination that spread to surrounding areas. Thousands of infants were born with health problems and deformities as a result of the nuclear contamination, including this boy whose arm did not form. *Other than radioactive contamination, what are some other types of environmental hazards to prenatal development?*

Other Maternal Factors So far we have discussed a number of drugs and environmental hazards that can have harmful effects on prenatal and child development. Here we will explore these other potentially harmful maternal factors: infectious diseases, nutrition, emotional states and stress, and age.

Infectious Diseases Maternal diseases and infections can produce defects in offspring by crossing the placental barrier, or they can cause damage during the birth process itself (Iannucci, 2000). Rubella (German measles) is one disease that can cause prenatal defects. The greatest damage occurs if a mother contracts rubella in the third or fourth week of pregnancy, although infection during the second month is also damaging. A rubella outbreak in 1964–1965 resulted in 30,000 prenatal and neonatal (newborn) deaths, and more than 20,000 affected infants were born with malformations, including mental retardation, blindness, deafness, and heart problems. Elaborate preventive efforts ensure that rubella will never again have such disastrous effects. A vaccine that prevents German measles is now routinely administered to children, and women who plan to have children should have a blood test before they become pregnant to determine if they are immune to the disease (Bar-Oz & others, 2004; Signore, 2001; Ward, Lambert, & Lester, 2001).

Syphilis (a sexually transmitted infection) is more damaging later in prenatal development—four months or more after conception. Rather than affecting organogenesis, as rubella does, syphilis damages organs after they have formed. Damage includes eye lesions, which can cause blindness, and skin lesions. When syphilis is present at birth, problems can develop in the central nervous system and gastrointestinal tract (Hollier & others, 2001). Most states require that pregnant women be given a blood test to detect the presence of syphilis.

Another infection that has received widespread attention recently is genital herpes. Newborns contract this virus when they are delivered through the birth canal of a mother with genital herpes (Qutub & others, 2001). About one-third of babies delivered through an actively infected birth canal die; another one-fourth become brain damaged. If an active case of genital herpes is detected in a pregnant woman close to her delivery date, a cesarean section can be performed (in which the infant is delivered through an incision in the mother's abdomen) to keep the virus from infecting the newborn.

AIDS is a sexually transmitted infection caused by the human immunodeficiency virus (HIV), which destroys the body's immune system. In the early 1990s, before preventive treatments were available, 1,000 to 2,000 infants were born with HIV infection each year in the United States. Since then, dramatic reductions in the transmission of AIDS from mothers to the fetus/newborn have occurred (Blair & others, 2004; Gerrard & Chudasama, 2003). Only about one-third as many cases of newborns with AIDS appear in the United States today as in the early 1990s. This decline is due to the increase in counseling and voluntary testing of pregnant women for HIV and to the use of zidovudine (AZT) by infected women during pregnancy, and for the infant after birth (Rovira & others, 2001; Sullivan, 2003).

A mother can infect her offspring with AIDS in three ways: (1) during gestation across the placenta, (2) during delivery through contact with maternal blood or fluids, and (3) postpartum (after birth) through breast feeding. The transmission of AIDS through breast feeding is especially a problem in many developing countries (Chama, Audu, & Kyari, 2004; UNICEF, 2004).

Babies born to HIV-infected mothers can be (1) infected and symptomatic (show AIDS symptoms), (2) infected but asymptomatic (not show AIDS symptoms), or (3) not infected at all. An infant who is infected and asymptomatic may still develop HIV symptoms up until 15 months of age.

Nutrition A developing fetus depends completely on its mother for nutrition, which comes from the mother's blood. The nutritional status of the fetus is determined by the mother's total caloric intake, and also by appropriate levels of proteins, vitamins, and minerals (Matthews, Youngman, & Neil, 2004; Ramakrishnan, 2004). The mother's nutrition even influences her ability to reproduce. In extreme instances of malnutrition, women stop menstruating, thus precluding conception. Children born to malnourished mothers are more likely to be malformed.

Researchers have also found that being overweight before and during pregnancy can be a risk factor for the fetus and the child. In two recent studies, obese women had a significant risk of late fetal death, although the risk of preterm delivery was reduced in these women (Cnattingius & others, 1998; Kumari, 2001).

One aspect of maternal nutrition that is important for normal prenatal development is folic acid, a B-complex vitamin (Cleves & others, 2004). A lack of folic acid is linked with neural tube defects such as spina bifida in offspring (Evans & others, 2004; Faber & others, 2004). The U.S. Public Health Service now recommends that pregnant women consume a minimum of 400 micrograms of folic acid per day (that is about twice the amount the average woman gets in one day). Orange juice and spinach are examples of foods rich in folic acid.

Because the fetus depends entirely on its mother for nutrition, it is important for the pregnant woman to have good nutritional habits. In Kenya, this government clinic provides pregnant women with information about how their diet can influence the health of their fetus and offspring. *What might the information about diet be like?*

Emotional States and Stress   Tales abound about how a pregnant woman's emotional state affects the fetus. For centuries it was thought that frightening experiences—such as a severe thunderstorm or a family member's death—leave birthmarks on the child or affect the child in more serious ways. In fact, a mother's stress can be transmitted to the fetus, but we have a better grasp of how this takes place (Federenko & Wadhwa, 2004; Loveland & others, 2004; Relier, 2001). When a pregnant woman experiences intense fears, anxieties, and other emotions, physiological changes occur that may also affect her fetus (Monk & others, 2004; Niederhofer & Reieter, 2004). For example, producing adrenaline in response to fear restricts blood flow to the uterine area and can deprive the fetus of adequate oxygen.

Researchers have been uncovering links between fetal health and various states in the mother, although the mechanisms that link the two are still far from certain. Women under stress are about four times more likely than their low-stress counterparts to deliver babies prematurely (Dunkel-Schetter, 1998; Dunkel-Schetter & others, 2001). Why? Maternal stress may increase the level of corticotrophin-releasing hormone (CRH) early in pregnancy (Hobel & others, 1999). CRH, in turn, has been linked to premature delivery. A mother's stress may also influence the fetus indirectly by increasing the likelihood that the mother will engage in unhealthy behaviors, such as taking drugs and engaging in poor prenatal care.

The mother's emotional state during pregnancy can influence the birth process, too. An emotionally distraught mother might have irregular contractions and a more difficult labor, which can cause irregularities in the supply of oxygen to the fetus or other problems after birth. Babies born after extended labor also may adjust more slowly to their world and be more irritable.

Positive emotional states also appear to make a difference to the fetus. Pregnant women who are optimistic thinkers have less adverse outcomes than pregnant women who are pessimistic thinkers (Lobel & others, 2002). Optimists are more likely to believe that they have control over the outcomes of their pregnancies.

Maternal Age   When possible harmful effects on the fetus and infant are considered, two maternal ages are of special interest: adolescence and the mid-thirties and beyond (Abel, Kruger, & Burd, 2002). Approximately 1 of every 5 births in the United States is to an adolescent; in some urban areas, the figure reaches as high as 1 in every 2 births. Infants born to adolescents are often premature (Ekwo & Moawad, 2000). The mortality rate of infants born to adolescent mothers is double that of infants born to mothers in their twenties. Although this high rate probably reflects the immaturity of the mother's reproductive system, poor nutrition, lack of prenatal care, and low socioeconomic status may also play a role (Lenders, McElrath, & Scholl, 2000).

What are some of the risks for infants born to adolescent mothers?

Reproductive Health Links
Exploring Pregnancy
Childbirth Classes
Prenatal Care
Health-Care Providers

Prenatal care decreases the probability that a child born to an adolescent girl will have physical problems. However, adolescents are the least likely of women in all age groups to obtain prenatal assistance from clinics, pediatricians, and health services.

Key dangers to the fetus when the mother is 35 years or older include the increased risk for low birth weight and for Down syndrome. As we discussed earlier in the chapter, the risk for Down syndrome is related to the mother's age (Holding, 2002). One recent study found that low birth weight delivery increased 11 percent and preterm delivery increased 14 percent in women 35 years and older (Tough & others, 2002). A baby with Down syndrome rarely is born to a mother 16 to 34 years of age.

We still have much to learn about the role of the mother's age in pregnancy and childbirth. As women remain active, exercise regularly, and are careful about their nutrition, they may remain fertile at older ages than was thought possible in the past.

Paternal Factors   So far, we have been considering maternal factors during pregnancy that can influence prenatal development and the development of the child. Might there also be some paternal risk factors? Indeed, there are several. Men's exposure to lead, radiation, certain pesticides, and petrochemicals may cause abnormalities in sperm that lead to miscarriage or diseases, such as childhood cancer (Trasler, 2000; Trasler & Doerkson, 2000). When fathers have a diet low in vitamin C, their offspring have a higher risk of birth defects and cancer (Fraga & others, 1991). Also, it has been speculated that, when fathers take cocaine, it may attach itself to sperm and cause birth defects, but the evidence for this is not yet strongly established.

The father's smoking during the mother's pregnancy also can cause problems for the offspring. In one investigation, the newborns of fathers who smoked around their wives during the pregnancy were 4 ounces lighter at birth for each pack of cigarettes smoked per day than were the newborns whose fathers did not smoke during their wives' pregnancy (Rubin & others, 1986). In another study, in China, the longer the fathers smoked, the stronger the risk was for their children to develop cancer (Ji & others, 1997). In such studies, it is very difficult to tease apart prenatal and postnatal effects.

The father's age also makes a difference. When fathers are older, their offspring face increased risk for certain birth defects, including Down syndrome (about 5 percent of these children have older fathers), dwarfism, and Marfan syndrome, which involves head and limb deformities.

There are also risks to offspring when both the mother and father are older. In one recent study, the risk of an adverse pregnancy outcome, such as miscarriage, was much greater when the woman was 35 years or older and the man was 40 years of age or older (de la Rochebrochard & Thonneau, 2002).

Prenatal Care

Prenatal care varies enormously, but usually involves a package of medical care services in a defined schedule of visits (McCormick, 2001; Parmet, Lynn, & Glass, 2004). In addition to medical care, prenatal care programs often include comprehensive educational, social, and nutritional services (Willis & others, 2004). Prenatal care usually includes screening for manageable conditions and/or treatable diseases that can affect the baby or the mother. The education an expectant woman receives about pregnancy, labor and delivery, and caring for the newborn can be extremely valuable, especially for first-time mothers (Chang & others, 2003; Cosey & Bechtel, 2001). Prenatal care is also very important for women in poverty because it links them with other social services. The legacy of prenatal care continues after birth, because women who receive this type of care are more likely to seek preventive care for their infants (Bates & others, 1994).

Inadequate prenatal care can occur for a variety of reasons, including the health-care system, provider practices, and individual and social characteristics (Lewallen, 2004; Malulik, 2003; Thompson & others, 2003). One recent study found that U.S. women who had no prenatal care were far more likely to have infants who were low birth weight, had increased mortality, and a number of other physical problems than their counterparts who received prenatal care (Herbst & others, 2003).

Motivating positive attitudes toward pregnancy is also important. Women who have unplanned or unwanted pregnancies, or who have negative attitudes about being pregnant, are more likely to delay prenatal care or to miss appointments (Joseph, 1989).

Next, in the Diversity in Life-Span Development interlude, we will compare prenatal care in different countries.

Diversity in Life-Span Development

Prenatal Care in the United States and Around the World

As advanced a nation as the United States has become economically and technologically, it still has more low birth weight infants than a number of other countries (Grant, 1997; Smulian & others, 2002). Only 4 percent of the infants born in Sweden, Finland, the Netherlands, and Norway are low birth weight, and only 5 percent of those born in New Zealand, Australia, France, and Japan are low birth weight. In the United States, almost 8 percent of all infants are low birth weight. In some developing countries, such as Bangladesh, where poverty is rampant and the health and nutrition of mothers is poor, the percentage of low birth weight infants reaches as high as 50 percent.

In the United States, discrepancies occur between the prenatal development and birth of African American infants and non-Latino White infants (Dubay & others, 2001). African American infants are twice as likely to be born prematurely, have low birth weight, and have mothers who received late or no prenatal care. They are three times as likely to have their mothers die in childbirth and five times as likely to be born to unmarried teenage mothers (Edelman, 1995).

In many of the countries with a lower percentage of low birth weight infants than the United States, either free or very low cost prenatal and postnatal care is available to mothers. This care includes paid maternity leave from work that ranges from 9 to 40 weeks. In Norway and the Netherlands, prenatal care is coordinated with a general practitioner, an obstetrician, and a midwife. One recent national study found that in the United States, the absence of prenatal care increased the risk for preterm birth by almost threefold for both non-Latino White and African American women (Vintzileos & others, 2002). Another recent study found that the later prenatal care begins, the greater the risk of congenital malformations (Carmichael, Shaw, & Nelson, 2002).

For many years, there was a discrepancy in the prenatal care obtained by non-Latino White and African American expectant mothers. For example, in the 1980s, more than one-fifth of all non-Latino White mothers and one-third of all African American mothers did not receive prenatal care in the first trimester of their pregnancy, and 5 percent of White mothers and 10 percent of African American mothers received no prenatal care at all. However, from 1990 to 2001, the use of timely prenatal care increased for women from a variety of ethnic backgrounds in the United States, although this care still characterized non-Latino White women more than African American and Latino women (MacDorman & others, 2002) (see figure 4.6). Other researchers also have found that the discrepancy in prenatal care

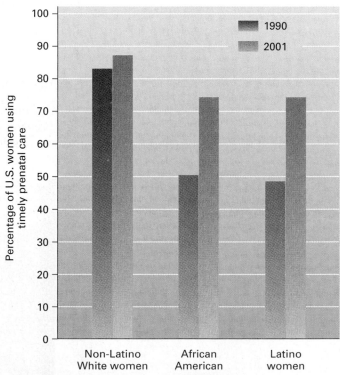

FIGURE 4.6 Percentage of U.S. Women Using Timely Prenatal Care: 1990 to 2001

From 1990 to 2001, the use of timely prenatal care increased by 6 percent (to 88.5) for non-Latino White women, by 23 percent (to 74.5) for African American women, and by 26 percent (to 75.7) for Latino women in the United States (MacDorman & others, 2002).

for non-Latino White and African American women is decreasing (Alexander, Kogan, & Nabukera, 2002).

Many infant-development researchers believe that the United States needs more comprehensive medical and educational services to improve the quality of prenatal care and to reduce the percentage of low birth weight infants (Maulik, 2003; Parmet, Lynn, & Glass, 2004; Thompson & others, 2003).

Cultural Beliefs About Pregnancy

All cultures have beliefs and rituals that surround life's major events, including pregnancy. Some cultures treat pregnancy simply as a natural occurrence; others see it as a medical condition. Obtaining medical care during pregnancy may not seem important to a woman whose culture defines pregnancy as a natural condition.

How expectant mothers behave during pregnancy may depend in part on the prevalence of traditional home-care remedies and folk beliefs, the importance of indigenous healers, and the influence of health-care professionals in their culture. For example, some Filipinos will not take any medication during pregnancy. Many Mexican American women seek advice about their pregnancy from their mothers and from older women in the community. They may also call on an indigenous healer known as a *curandero*. In various cultures pregnant women may turn to herbalists, faith healers, root doctors, or spiritualists for help.

When health-care professionals work with expectant mothers, cultural assessment should be an important component of their care. In other words, health-care providers should identify beliefs, values, and behaviors related to childbearing. In particular, ethnic background, degree of affiliation with the ethnic group, patterns of decision making, religious preference, language, communication style, and etiquette may all affect a woman's attitudes about the care needed during pregnancy. Health-care workers should assess whether a woman's beliefs or practices pose a threat to her or the fetus. If they do, health-care professionals should consider a culturally sensitive way to handle the problem.

Normal Prenatal Development

Much of our discussion so far in this chapter has focused on what can go wrong with prenatal development. It is important to keep in mind that most of the time, prenatal development does not go awry and development occurs along the positive

In India, a midwife checks on the size, position, and heartbeat of a fetus. Midwives deliver babies in many cultures around the world. *What are some cultural variations in prenatal care?*

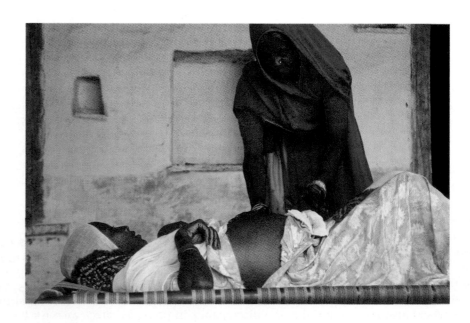

path that we described at the beginning of the chapter (Lester, 2000). Nonetheless, prospective mothers and those who are pregnant should take steps to avoid the vulnerabilities to fetal development that we have described.

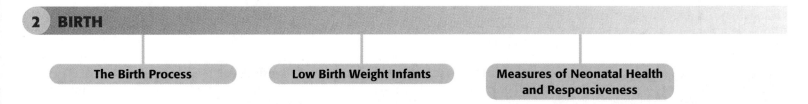

2 BIRTH

The Birth Process | Low Birth Weight Infants | Measures of Neonatal Health and Responsiveness

As we saw in the opening story about Tanner Roberts, many changes take place during the birth of a baby. Let's further explore the birth process.

The Birth Process

Here we will examine the stages of birth, the transition from fetus to newborn, childbirth strategies, low birth weight infants, and measures of neonatal (newborn) health and responsiveness.

Stages of Birth Childbirth—or labor—occurs in three stages. For a woman having her first child, the first stage lasts an average of 12 to 24 hours; it is the longest of the three stages. In the first stage, uterine contractions are 15 to 20 minutes apart at the beginning and last up to a minute. These contractions cause the woman's cervix, the opening into the birth canal, to stretch and open. As the first stage progresses, the contractions come closer together, appearing every two to five minutes. Their intensity increases, too. By the end of the first birth stage, contractions dilate the cervix to an opening of about 4 inches, so that the baby can move from the uterus to the birth canal.

The second birth stage begins when the baby's head starts to move through the cervix and the birth canal. It terminates when the baby completely emerges from the mother's body. For a first birth, this stage lasts approximately $1^1/_2$ hours. With each contraction, the mother bears down hard to push the baby out of her body. By the time the baby's head is out of the mother's body, the contractions come almost every minute and last for about a minute.

Afterbirth is the third stage, at which time the placenta, umbilical cord, and other membranes are detached and expelled. This final stage is the shortest of the three birth stages, lasting only minutes.

We must respect this instant of birth, this fragile moment. The baby is between two worlds, on a threshold, hesitating. . .

—**Frederick Leboyer**
French Obstetrician, 20th Century

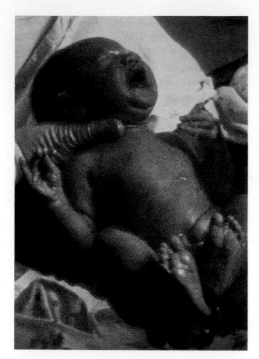

After the long journey of prenatal development, birth takes place. During birth the baby is on a threshold between two worlds. *What is the fetus/newborn transition like?*

A woman in the African !Kung culture giving birth in a sitting position. Notice the help and support being given by another woman. *What are some cultural variations in childbirth?*

doula A caregiver who provides continuous physical, emotional, and educational support for the mother before, during, and after childbirth.

The Transition from Fetus to Newborn   Being born involves considerable stress for the baby. During each contraction, when the placenta and umbilical cord are compressed as the uterine muscles draw together, the supply of oxygen to the fetus is decreased. If the delivery takes too long, anoxia can develop. *Anoxia*, the condition in which the fetus/newborn has an insufficient supply of oxygen, can cause brain damage.

The baby has considerable capacity to withstand the stress of birth. Large quantities of adrenaline and noradrenalin, hormones that protect the fetus in the event of oxygen deficiency, are secreted in stressful circumstances. These hormones increase the heart's pumping activity, speed up heart rate, channel blood flow to the brain, and raise the blood-sugar level. Never again in life will such large amounts of these hormones be secreted. This circumstance underscores how stressful it is to be born and also how well prepared and adapted the fetus is for birth (Committee on Fetus and Newborn, 2000; Van Beveren, 2002).

As we saw in the case of Tanner Roberts at the beginning of the chapter, the umbilical cord is cut immediately after birth, and the baby is on its own. Now 25 million little air sacs in the lungs must be filled with air. The first breaths may be the hardest ones an individual takes. Before birth, oxygen came from the mother via the umbilical cord, but now the baby has to be self-sufficient and breathe on its own.

At the time of birth, the baby is covered with what is called *vernix caseosa,* a protective skin grease. This vernix consists of fatty secretions and dead cells, thought to function in protecting the baby's skin against heat loss before and during birth. After the baby and mother have met and become acquainted with each other, the baby is taken to be cleaned, examined, weighed, and evaluated. Later in the chapter, we will discuss several measures that are used to examine the newborn's health and responsiveness.

Childbirth Strategies   Among the childbirth decisions that need to be made are what the setting will be, who the attendants will be, and which childbirth technique will be used. Here we will discuss the options available to expectant parents.

Childbirth Setting and Attendants   In the United States, 99 percent of births take place in hospitals, and more than 90 percent are attended by physicians (Ventura & others, 1997). Most hospitals have replaced the sterile "delivery room" of the early twentieth century with a homelike birthing center, and it is the norm for fathers or birth coaches to be with the mother throughout labor and delivery. Medical policies often allow the mother and her obstetrician to choose from a full range of birth experiences, from a totally unmedicated, natural birth to the most complex, intensive medical care. An in-hospital birthing center offers a compromise between a technological, depersonalized hospital birth (which cannot offer the emotional experience of a home birth) and a birth at home (which cannot offer the medical backup of a hospital). Some women with good medical histories and low risk for problem delivery choose a home delivery or a delivery in a freestanding birthing center, which is usually staffed by nurse-midwives (Wong, Perry, & Hockenberry, 2001).

Midwifery is the norm throughout most of the world but only about 6 percent of women who deliver a baby in the United States are attended by a midwife (Tritten, 2004; Ventura & others, 1997). In the United States, most midwives are nurses who have been specially trained in delivering babies (Hyde & Roche-Reid, 2004; O'Dowd, 2004). Compared to physicians, certified nurse-midwives generally spend more time with patients during prenatal visits, place more emphasis on patient counseling and education, provide more emotional support, and are more likely to be with the patient one-on-one during the entire labor and delivery process.

In many countries around the world, babies are more likely to be delivered at home than they are in the United States. For example, in Holland, 35 percent of the babies are born at home, and more than 40 percent are delivered by midwives rather than doctors (Treffers & others, 1990).

In many countries, a doula attends a childbearing woman. *Doula* is a Greek word that means "a woman who helps." A **doula** is a caregiver who provides continuous physical, emotional, and educational support for the mother before, during, and after childbirth. Doulas remain with the mother throughout labor, assessing and responding to her needs. Researchers have found positive effects when a doula is present at the birth of a child (Stein, Kennell, & Fulcher, 2003). In one study, the mothers who received doula support reported less labor pain than the mothers who did not receive doula support (Klaus, Kennell, & Klaus, 1993). Doulas typically function as part of a "birthing team," serving as an adjunct to the midwife or the hospital obstetric staff (McGrath & others, 1999; Pascali-Bonaro, 2002).

In the United States, most doulas work as independent providers hired by the expectant woman. Managed care organizations are increasingly offering doula support as a part of regular obstetric care. In many cultures, the practice of a knowledgeable woman helping a mother in labor is not officially labeled "doula" support but is simply an accepted centuries-old custom.

Other customs surrounding who will attend the mother during labor and delivery are vastly different from those in Western culture. In the East African Nigoni culture, men are completely excluded from the childbirth process. In this culture, women even conceal their pregnancy from their husband as long as possible. In the Nigoni culture, when a woman is ready to give birth, female relatives move into the woman's hut and the husband leaves, taking his belongings (clothes, tools, weapons, and so on) with him. He is not permitted to return until after the baby is born. In some cultures, childbirth is a more open, community affair than in the United States. For example, in the Pukapukan culture in the Pacific Islands, women give birth in a shelter that is open for villagers to observe.

Methods of Childbirth Among the methods of delivery are medicated, natural and prepared, and cesarean. The American Academy of Pediatrics recommends the least possible medication during delivery, although it is up to the mother or attending medical personnel to decide whether drugs are needed.

There are three basic kinds of drugs that are used for labor: analgesia, anesthesia, and oxytocics. *Analgesia* is used to relieve pain. Analgesics include tranquilizers, barbiturates, and narcotics (such as Demerol). *Anesthesia* is used in late first-stage labor and during expulsion of the baby to block sensation in an area of the body or to block consciousness. There is a trend toward not using general anesthesia, which blocks consciousness, in normal births because it can be transmitted through the placenta to the fetus. However, an epidural anesthesia does not cross the placenta. An *epidural block* is regional anesthesia that numbs the woman's body from the waist down. Even this drug, thought to be relatively safe, has come under recent criticism because it is associated with fever, extended labor, and increased risk for cesarean delivery (Ransjo-Arvidson & others, 2001). *Oxytocics* are synthetic hormones that are used to stimulate contractions. Pitocin is the most commonly used oxytocic (Carbonne, Tsatsarius, & Goffinet, 2001; Gard & others, 2002).

It is difficult to predict how a particular drug will affect an individual pregnant woman and her fetus. Though we have many commonalities as human beings, we also vary a great deal. Thus, a particular drug might have only a minimal effect on

Careers in Life-Span Development

Linda Pugh, Perinatal Nurse

Perinatal nurses work with childbearing women to support health and growth during the childbearing experience. Linda Pugh, Ph.D., R.N.C., is a perinatal nurse on the faculty at The Johns Hopkins University School of Nursing. She is certified as an inpatient obstetric nurse and specializes in the care of women during labor and delivery. She teaches undergraduate and graduate students, educates professional nurses, and conducts research. In addition, Linda consults with hospitals and organizations about women's health issues and topics we discuss in this chapter.

Her research interests include nursing interventions with low-income breast feeding women, discovering ways to prevent and ameliorate fatigue during childbearing, and using breathing exercises during labor.

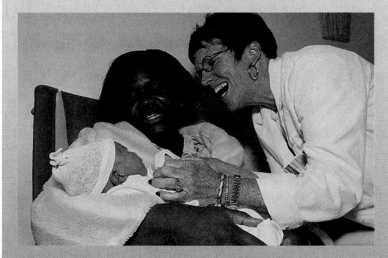

Linda Pugh (*right*), a perinatal nurse, with a mother and her newborn.

www.mhhe.com/santrockld10

Childbirth Strategies
Childbirth Setting and Attendants
Midwifery
Doula
Fathers and Childbirth
Siblings and Childbirth

Many husbands, or coaches, take childbirth classes with their wives or friends as part of prepared or natural childbirth. This is a Lamaze training session. *What is the nature of the Lamaze method? Who devised it?*

one fetus yet have a much stronger effect on another fetus. The drug's dosage also is a factor. Stronger doses of tranquilizers and narcotics given to decrease the mother's pain have a potentially more negative effect on the fetus than mild doses. It is important for the mother to assess her level of pain and have a voice in the decision of whether she should receive medication or not (Young, 2001).

Though the trend at one time was toward a natural childbirth without any medication, today the emphasis is on using some medication but keeping it to a minimum when possible. The emphasis today also is on broadly educating the pregnant woman so that she can be reassured and confident. The emphasis on education is reflected in the techniques of natural childbirth and prepared childbirth.

Natural childbirth was developed in 1914 by an English obstetrician, Grantley Dick-Read. Its purpose is to reduce the mother's pain by decreasing her fear through education about childbirth and by teaching her to use breathing methods and relaxation techniques during delivery. Dick-Read believed that the doctor's relationship with the mother is an important dimension of reducing her perception of pain. He said the doctor should be present during her active labor prior to delivery and should provide reassurance.

Prepared childbirth was developed by French obstetrician Ferdinand Lamaze. This childbirth strategy is similar to natural childbirth but includes a special breathing technique to control pushing in the final stages of labor, as well as a more detailed anatomy and physiology course. The Lamaze method has become very popular in the United States. The pregnant woman's husband or a friend usually serves as a coach, who attends childbirth classes with her and helps her with her breathing and relaxation during delivery.

Many other prepared childbirth techniques also have been developed. They usually include elements of Dick-Read's natural childbirth or Lamaze's method, plus one or more other components. For instance, the Bradley method places special emphasis on the father's role as a labor coach. Virtually all of the prepared childbirth methods emphasize some degree of education, relaxation and breathing exercises, and support. In recent years, new ways of teaching relaxation have been offered, including guided mental imagery, massage, and meditation. In sum, the current belief in prepared childbirth is that, when information and support are provided, women *know* how to give birth. To read about one nurse whose research focuses on discovering ways to prevent and reduce fatigue during childbearing and the use of breathing exercises during labor, see the Careers in Life-Span Development insert.

In a *cesarean delivery,* the baby is removed from the mother's uterus through an incision made in her abdomen. This method also is sometimes known as a cesarean section or C-section. A cesarean section is usually performed if the baby is in a **breech position,** which causes the baby's buttocks to be the first part to emerge from the vagina. Normally, the crown of the baby's head comes through the vagina first, but in 1 of every 25 deliveries, the baby's head is still in the uterus when the rest of the body is out. Breech births can cause respiratory problems.

Cesarean deliveries also are performed if the baby is lying crosswise in the uterus, if the baby's head is too large to pass through the mother's pelvis, if the baby develops complications, or if the mother is bleeding vaginally.

The benefits and risks of cesarean sections continue to be debated (Green & others, 2001; Papp, 2003; Peskin & Reine, 2002). Cesarean deliveries are safer than breech deliveries, but they involve a higher infection rate, longer hospital stay, and the greater expense and stress that accompany any surgery.

Some critics believe that too many babies are delivered by cesarean section in the United States. More cesarean sections are performed in the United States than in any other country in the world. In the 1980s, births by cesarean section increased almost

natural childbirth Developed in 1914 by Dick-Read, this method attempts to reduce the mother's pain by decreasing her fear through education about childbirth and relaxation techniques during delivery.

prepared childbirth Developed by French obstetrician Ferdinand Lamaze, this childbirth strategy is similar to natural childbirth but includes a special breathing technique to control pushing in the final stages of labor and a more detailed anatomy and physiology course.

breech position The baby's position in the uterus that causes the buttocks to be the first part to emerge from the vagina.

50 percent in the United States, with almost one-fourth of babies delivered in this way. In the early 1990s, cesarean births decreased but recently have increased once again (National Center for Health Statistics, 2002).

Low Birth Weight Infants

Low birth weight infants weigh less than $5^1/_2$ pounds at birth. *Very low birth weight* newborns weigh under 3 pounds, and *extremely low birth weight* infants weigh under 2 pounds (Tang & others, 2004). Another way of classifying newborns involves whether they are preterm or small for date.

Preterm infants are those born three weeks or more before the pregnancy has reached its full term—in other words, 35 or fewer weeks after conception. A short gestation period does not necessarily harm an infant. The neurological development of the preterm baby continues after birth on approximately the same timetable as if the infant were still in the womb. For example, consider a preterm baby born 30 weeks after conception. At 38 weeks, appoximately two months after birth, this infant shows the same level of brain development as a 38-week fetus who is yet to be born. But most preterm babies are also low birth weight babies. In one recent study, weekly injections of the hormone progesterone, which is naturally produced by the ovaries, lowered the rate of preterm births by one-third (Meis & Peaceman, 2003). Researchers are recommending that further research be conducted to determine the safest and most effective way to administer the drug.

Small for date infants (also called *small for gestational age infants*) are those whose birth weight is below normal when the length of the pregnancy is considered. They weigh less than 90 percent of all babies of the same gestational age. Small for date infants may be preterm or full term. One recent study found that small for date infants had more than a fourfold risk for death (Regev & others, 2003).

The incidence of low birth weight varies considerably from country to country. The U.S. low birth weight rate of 7.8 percent is considerably higher than that of many other developed countries (National Center for Health Statistics, 2004; UNICEF, 2004) (see figure 4.7). In the developing world, low birth weight stems mainly from the mother's poor health and nutrition. Diarrhea and diseases such as malaria, which are common in developing countries, can impair fetal growth if the mother becomes ill while she is pregnant. In developed countries, cigarette smoking during pregnancy is the leading cause of low birth weight (UNICEF, 2004). In both developed and developing countries, adolescents who give birth when their bodies have not fully matured are at risk for having low birth weight babies. In the United States, the increase in the number of low birth weight infants is thought to be due to the increasing number of adolescents having babies, the use of drugs, and poor nutrition.

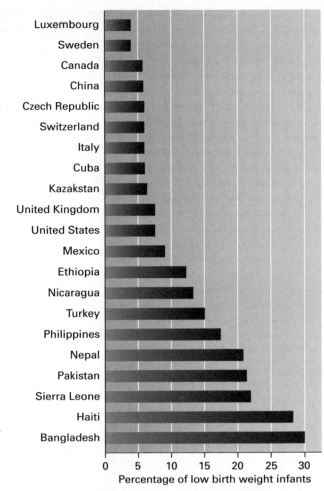

FIGURE 4.7 Low Birth Weight Rates by Country
The graph shows the percentage of children born with low birth weight in a wide range of countries around the world (UNICEF, 2001).

Consequences of Low Birth Weight Although most low birth weight infants are normal and healthy, as a group they have more health and developmental problems than normal birth weight infants (Chaudhari & others, 2004; Gale & Martyn, 2004). The number and severity of these problems increase as birth weight decreases (Kilbride, Thorstad, & Daily, 2000, 2004). Survival rates for infants who are born very early and very small have risen, but this improvement has brought increases in rates of severe brain damage (Yu, 2000). The lower the brain weight, the greater the likelihood of brain injury (Watenberg & others, 2002). Approximately 7 percent of moderately low birth weight infants (3 pounds 5 ounces to 5 pounds 8 ounces) have brain injuries. This figure increases to 20 percent for the smallest newborns (1 pound 2 ounces to 3 pounds 5 ounces). Low birth weight infants are also more likely than normal birth weight infants to have lung or liver diseases.

At school age, children who were born low in birth weight are more likely than their normal birth weight counterparts to have a learning disability, attention deficit

low birth weight infants Infants that weigh less than $5^1/_2$ pounds at birth.

preterm infants Infants born three weeks or more before the pregnancy has reached its full term.

small for date infants Also called small for gestational age infants, these infants' birth weights are below normal when the length of pregnancy is considered. Small for date infants may be preterm or full term.

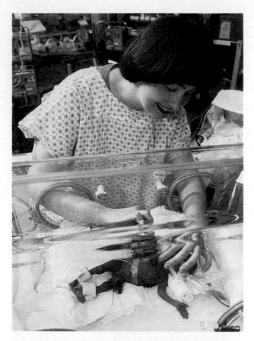

A "kilogram kid," weighing less than 2.3 pounds at birth. *What are some long-term outcomes for weighing so little at birth?*

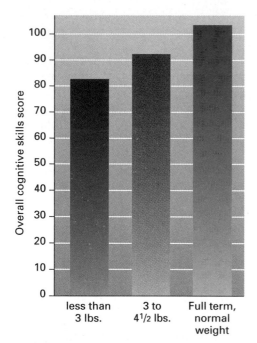

FIGURE 4.8 Comparison of the Overall Cognitive Processing Skills of Middle School Students Who Were Born with Low Birth Weight or Normal Birth Weight

The overall cognitive skills score was a composite score arrived at by combining students' scores on several cognitive measures such as the Kaufman Assessment Battery for Children (an intelligence test), analogies (a task that requires individuals to understand how concepts are similar), and other tests.

hyperactivity disorder, or breathing problems such as asthma (Taylor, Klein, & Hack, 1994). Very low birth weight children have more learning problems and lower levels of achievement in reading and math than moderately low birth weight children. Approximately 50 percent of all low birth weight children are enrolled in special education programs. One recent study of extremely low birth weight infants in four locations (New Jersey, Ontario, Bavaria, and Holland) found that when they were 8 to 11 years old more than half required special education and/or repeated a grade (Saigal & others, 2003).

Do these negative outcomes of low birth weight continue into adolescence? In one study, the outcomes at middle-school age of being very low birth weight (under 3 pounds) were examined (Taylor & others, 2000). When compared with a control group who was born full term, the low birth weight adolescents had lower cognitive skills, weaker academic records, and showed more behavioral problems (see figure 4.8). However, another recent study found that the majority of very low birth weight infants (weighing just over 2 pounds on average) had improved IQ scores from 3 years of age (average IQ = 90) to 8 years of age (average IQ = 95) (Ment & others, 2003). Despite the improvement, the IQ scores of the very low birth weight infants were still in the low average range. The very low birth weight infants who improved the most had received early speech therapy and had highly educated mothers.

Not all of these adverse consequences can be attributed solely to being born low in birth weight. Some of the less severe but more common developmental and physical delays occur because many low birth weight children come from disadvantaged environments (Fang, Madhaven, & Alderman, 1999).

Some of the devastating effects of being born low in birth weight can be reversed (Doyle & others, 2004). Intensive enrichment programs that provide medical and educational services for both the parents and children can improve short-term outcomes for low birth weight children. Federal laws mandate that services for school-age children be expanded to include family-based care for infants. At present, these services are aimed at children born with severe disabilities. The availability of services for moderately low birth weight children who do not have severe physical problems varies, but most states do not provide these services.

Kangaroo Care and Massage Therapy **Kangaroo care** is a way of holding a preterm infant so that there is skin-to-skin contact. The baby, wearing only a diaper, is held upright against the parent's bare chest. Kangaroo care is typically practiced for two to three hours per day, skin-to-skin over an extended time period in early infancy (Feldman & others, 2003; White-Traut, 2004).

The label *kangaroo care* was chosen to describe this strategy because the method is similar to how a kangaroo is carried by its mother. It is estimated that more than 200 neonatal intensive-care units practice kangaroo care today compared with less than 70 in the early 1990s. One recent survey found that 82 percent of neonatal intensive-care units use kangaroo care in the United States today (Engler & others, 2002).

Why use kangaroo care with preterm infants? Researchers have found that the close physical contact with the parent can help to stabilize the preterm infant's heartbeat, temperature, and breathing (Ferber & Makhoul, 2004; Ludington-Hoe & others, 2004; Reid, 2004). Preterm infants often have difficulty coordinating their breathing and heart rate. Researchers also have found that mothers who use kangaroo care often have more success with breast feeding and improve their milk supply. Further, researchers have found that preterm infants who experience kangaroo care have longer periods of sleep, gain more weight, decrease their crying, have longer periods of alertness, and earlier hospital discharge (Chwo & others, 2002; Feldman & others, 2003; Lehtonen & Martin, 2004; Ludington-Hoe, Cong, & Hashemi, 2002). One recent study compared 26 low birth weight infants who received kangaroo care with 27 low birth weight infants who received standard medical/nursing care (Ohgi & others, 2002). At both 6 and 12 months of age, the kangaroo care infants were able to better regulate their body states, had better orientation, and had a more positive mood. Another recent study found that kangaroo care preterm infants had better control of their arousal, more effectively attended to stimuli, and showed sustained exploration in a toy session than a control group of preterm infants who did not receive kangaroo care (Feldman & others, 2002). Increasingly kangaroo care is being recommended for full-term infants as well.

Throughout history and in many cultures, infant massage has been used by care-givers. In India, Africa, and Asia, infants are routinely massaged by parents or other family members for several months after birth. Many preterm infants experience less touch than full-term infants because they are isolated in temperature-controlled incubators (Beachy, 2003). However, the research of Tiffany Field has led to a surge of interest in the role that massage might play in improving the developmental outcomes of preterm infants. To read about her research, see the Research in Life-Span Development interlude.

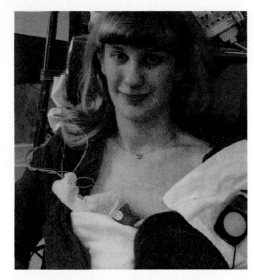

New mother learning how to practice kangaroo care. *What is kangaroo care?*

Research in Life-Span Development
Tiffany Field's Research on Massage Therapy

Interest using touch and massage to improve the growth, health, and well-being of infants has been stimulated by the research of Tiffany Field (1998, 2001, 2002, 2003; Field, Hernandez-Reif, & Freedman, 2004; Field & others, 2003), director of the Touch Research Institute at the University of Miami School of Medicine. In her first study in this area, massage therapy consisting of firm stroking with the palms of the hands was given three times per day for 15-minute periods to preterm infants (Field & others, 1986). The massage therapy led to 47 percent greater weight gain than standard medical treatment (see figure 4.9). The

kangaroo care A way of holding a preterm infant so that there is skin-to-skin contact.

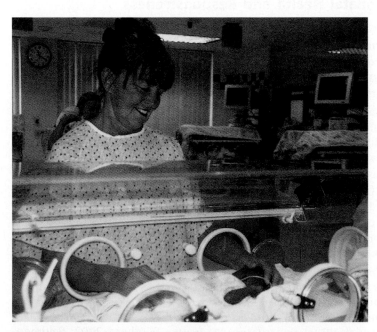

Shown here is Tiffany Field massaging a newborn infant. *What types of infants has massage therapy been shown to help?*

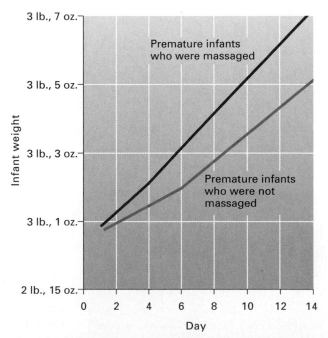

FIGURE 4.9 Weight Gain Comparison of Premature Infants Who Were Massaged or Not Massaged
The graph shows that the mean daily weight gain of premature infants who were massaged was greater than for premature infants who were not massaged.

massaged infants also were more active and alert than preterm infants who were not massaged, and they performed better on developmental tests.

In later studies, Field demonstrated the benefits of massage therapy for infants who faced a variety of problems. For example, in one study, Field (1992) gave massage to preterm infants who were exposed to cocaine in utero. These infants gained weight and improved their scores on developmental tests. In another investigation, newborns born to HIV-positive mothers were randomly assigned to a massage therapy group or to a control group that did not receive the therapy (Scafidi & Field, 1996). Infants in the massage therapy group received three 15-minute massages daily for 10 days. The massaged infants showed superior performance on a wide range of assessments, including daily weight gain. Another study investigated 1- to 3-month-old infants born to depressed adolescent mothers (Field & others, 1996). The infants of depressed mothers who received massage therapy had lower stress—as well as improved emotionality, sociability, and soothability—compared with the non-massaged infants of depressed mothers.

In other studies by Field and her colleagues, infants are not the only ones who may benefit from massage therapy. They have demonstrated the benefits of massage therapy with women in reducing labor pain (Field, Hernandez-Reif, Taylor, & others, 1997), with children who have arthritis (Field, Hernandez-Reif, Seligman, & others, 1997), with autistic children's attentiveness (Field, Lasko, & others, 1997), and with adolescents who have attention deficit hyperactivity disorder (Field, Quintino, & others, 1998). Field and her colleagues also are studying the amount of touch a child normally receives in early childhood education programs. They hope that positive forms of touch will return to school systems, where touching has been outlawed because of the fear of sexual abuse lawsuits.

Measures of Neonatal Health and Responsiveness

Almost immediately after birth, a newborn is weighed, cleaned up, and tested for signs of developmental problems that might require urgent attention. The **Apgar Scale** is widely used to assess the health of newborns at one and five minutes after birth. The Apgar Scale evaluates infants' heart rate, respiratory effort, muscle tone, body color, and reflex irritability. An obstetrician or a nurse does the evaluation and gives the newborn a score, or reading, of 0, 1, or 2 on each of these five health signs (see figure 4.10). A total score of 7 to 10 indicates that the newborn's condition is good. A score of 4 to 6 indicates there may be developmental difficulties. A score of 3 or below signals an emergency and indicates that the baby might not survive. The Apgar Scale is especially good at assessing the newborn's ability to respond to the stress of delivery, labor, and the new environment (Casey, McIntire, & Leveno, 2001). The Apgar Scale also identifies high-risk infants who need resuscitation.

To evaluate the newborn more thoroughly, the **Brazelton Neonatal Behavioral Assessment Scale** is performed within 24 to 36 hours after birth. This scale measures the newborn's neurological development, reflexes, and reactions to people. When the Brazelton is given, the newborn is treated as an active participant, and the score attained is based on the newborn's best performance. Sixteen reflexes, such as sneezing, blinking, and rooting, are assessed, along with reactions to circumstances, such as the infant's reaction to a rattle. (We will have more to say about reflexes in chapter 5, when we discuss physical development in infancy.) The examiner rates the newborn on each of 27 items. As an indication of how detailed the ratings are, consider item 15: "cuddliness." Nine categories are involved in assessing this item, and scoring is done on a continuum

Apgar Scale A widely used method to assess the health of newborns at one and five minutes after birth. The Apgar Scale evaluates infants' heart rate, respiratory effort, muscle tone, body color, and reflex irritability.

Brazelton Neonatal Behavioral Assessment Scale A test performed within 24 to 36 hours after birth to assess newborns' neurological development, reflexes, and reactions to people.

Score	0	1	2	
Heart rate	Absent	Slow—less than 100 beats per minute	Fast—100–140 beats per minute	
Respiratory effort	No breathing for more than one minute	Irregular and slow	Good breathing with normal crying	
Muscle tone	Limp and flaccid	Weak, inactive, but some flexion of extremities	Strong, active motion	
Body color	Blue and pale	Body pink, but extremities blue	Entire body pink	
Reflex irritability	No response	Grimace	Coughing, sneezing and crying	

FIGURE 4.10 The Apgar Scale

that ranges from the infant's being very resistant to being held to the infant's being extremely cuddly and clinging. The Brazelton scale is used not only as a sensitive index of neurological competence in the week after birth, but also as a measure in many research studies on infant development (Ohgi & others, 2003). In scoring the Brazelton scale, T. Berry Brazelton and his colleagues (Brazelton, Nugent, & Lester, 1987) organize the 27 items into four categories—physiological, motoric, state, and interaction. They also classify the baby in global terms, such as "worrisome," "normal," or "superior," based on these categories (Nugent & Brazelton, 2000).

A very low Brazelton score can indicate brain damage, or it can reflect stress to the brain that may heal in time. However, if an infant merely seems sluggish in responding to social circumstances, parents are encouraged to give the infant attention and become more sensitive to the infant's needs. Parents are shown how the newborn can respond to people and how to stimulate such responses. Researchers have found that the social interaction skills of both high-risk infants and healthy, responsive infants can be improved through such communication with parents (Worobey & Belsky, 1982).

Review and Reflect: Learning Goal 2

2 Discuss the birth process

REVIEW

- What are the three main stages of birth? What is the transition from fetus to newborn like for the infant? What are some different birth strategies?
- What are the outcomes for children if they are born preterm or with a low birth weight?
- What are two measures of neonatal health and responsiveness?

REFLECT

- If you are a female, which birth strategy do you prefer? Why? If you are a male, how involved would you want to be in helping your partner through pregnancy and the birth of your baby?

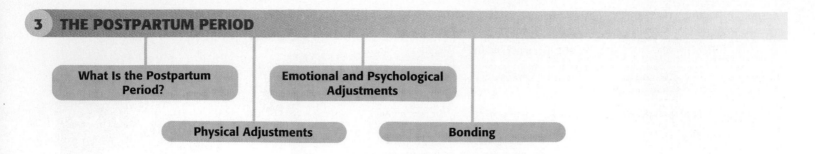

3 THE POSTPARTUM PERIOD

What Is the Postpartum Period?

Physical Adjustments

Emotional and Psychological Adjustments

Bonding

The weeks immediately following childbirth present a number of challenges for new parents and their offspring. Many health professionals believe that the best way to meet these challenges is with a family-centered approach that uses the family's resources to support an early and smooth adjustment to the newborn by all family members.

What Is the Postpartum Period?

Postpartum Adjustment
Postpartum Resources

The **postpartum period** is the period after childbirth or delivery. It is a time when the woman adjusts, both physically and psychologically, to the process of childbearing. It lasts for about six weeks or until the body has completed its adjustment and has returned to a near prepregnant state. Some health professionals refer to the postpartum period as the "fourth trimester." Though the time span of the postpartum period does not necessarily cover three months, the term of "fourth trimester" suggests continuity and the importance of the first several months after birth for the mother.

The postpartum period is influenced by what preceded it. During pregnancy, the woman's body gradually adjusted to physical changes, but now it is forced to respond quickly. The method of delivery and circumstances surrounding the delivery affect the speed with which the woman's body readjusts during the postpartum period. The postpartum period involves a great deal of adjustment and adaptation (Krystal, 2004; Plackslin, 2000). The mother has to recover from childbirth; the mother has to learn how to take care of the baby; the mother needs to learn to feel good about herself as a mother; and those close to the mother—such as her husband, a partner, grandparents, siblings, or friends—need to provide help and support.

Physical Adjustments

A woman's body makes numerous physical adjustments in the first days and weeks after childbirth. She may have a great deal of energy or feel exhausted and let down. Most new mothers feel tired and need rest. Though these changes are normal, the fatigue can undermine the new mother's sense of well-being and confidence in her ability to cope with a new baby and a new family life.

Involution is the process by which the uterus returns to its prepregnant size five or six weeks after birth. Immediately following birth, the uterus weighs 2 to 3 pounds. By the end of five or six weeks, the uterus weighs 2 to $3^{1}/_{2}$ ounces. Nursing the baby helps contract the uterus at a rapid rate.

After delivery, a woman's body undergoes sudden and dramatic changes in hormone production. When the placenta is delivered, estrogen and progesterone levels drop steeply and remain low until the ovaries start producing hormones again. The woman will probably begin menstruating again in four to eight weeks if she is not breast feeding. If she is breast feeding, she might not menstruate for several months to a year or more, though ovulation can occur during this time. The first several menstrual periods following delivery might be heavier than usual, but periods soon return to normal.

Some women and men want to resume sexual intercourse as soon as possible after the birth. Others feel constrained or afraid. A sore perineum (the area between the anus and vagina in the female), a demanding baby, lack of help, and extreme

postpartum period The period after childbirth when the mother adjusts, both physically and psychologically, to the process of childbirth. This period lasts for about six weeks or until her body has completed its adjustment and returned to a near prepregnant state.

fatigue affect a woman's ability to relax and to enjoy making love. Physicians often recommend that women refrain from having sexual intercourse for approximately six weeks following the birth of the baby.

If the woman regularly engaged in conditioning exercises during pregnancy, exercise will help her recover her former body contour and strength during the postpartum period. With a caregiver's approval, the new mother can begin some exercises as soon as one hour after delivery. In addition to recommending exercise in the postpartum period for women, health professionals also increasingly recommend that women practice the relaxation techniques they used during pregnancy and childbirth. Five minutes of slow breathing on a stressful day in the postpartum period can relax and refresh the new mother, as well as the new baby.

Emotional and Psychological Adjustments

Emotional fluctuations are common for mothers in the postpartum period. These emotional fluctuations may be due to any of a number of factors: hormonal changes, fatigue, inexperience or lack of confidence with newborn babies, or the extensive time and demands involved in caring for a newborn. For some women, the emotional fluctuations decrease within several weeks after the delivery and are a minor aspect of their motherhood. For others, they are more long-lasting and can produce feelings of anxiety, depression, and difficulty in coping with stress (Barnes, 2002; Dennis, 2004; Goodman, 2004). Mothers who have such feelings, even when they are getting adequate rest, may benefit from professional help in dealing with their problems. Here are some of the signs that can indicate a need for professional counseling about postpartum adaptation:

- Excessive worrying
- Depression
- Extreme changes in appetite
- Crying spells
- Inability to sleep

As shown in figure 4.11, about 70 percent of new mothers have what are called "postpartum blues." About two to three days after birth, they begin to feel depressed, anxious, and upset. These feelings may come and go for several days after the birth, often peaking about three to five days after the birth. These feelings, even without treatment, usually go away after one or two weeks. However, women with **postpartum depression** have such strong feelings of sadness, anxiety, or despair that they have trouble coping with their daily tasks. Postpartum depression involves a major depressive episode that typically occurs about four weeks after delivery. Without treatment, postpartum depression may become worse and last for many months (Bonari & others, 2004; Clay & Seehusen, 2004; Teissedre & Chabrol, 2004). As shown in figure 4.11, postpartum depression occurs in approximately 10 percent of new mothers. Between 25 to 50 percent of these depressed new mothers have episodes that last six months or longer (Beck, 2002). If untreated, approximately 25 percent of these women are still depressed a year later.

Though the hormonal changes occurring after childbirth are believed to play a role in postpartum depression, the precise nature of this hormonal role has not been identified (Dennis & Stewart, 2004; Flores & Hendrick, 2002; McCoy, Beal, & Watson, 2003). Estrogen has been shown to have positive effects in treating postpartum depression for some women, but some possible negative side effects of estrogen are problematic (Grigoriadis & Kennedy, 2002; Tsigos & Chrousos, 2002). Several antidepressant drugs have been shown to be effective in treating postpartum depression and appear to be safe for breast feeding women (Sharma, 2002). Psychotherapy, especially cognitive therapy, has also been found to be an effective treatment of postpartum depression (Beck, 2002; Kennedy, Beck, & Driscoll, 2002).

One recent study found that postpartum depression not only affects the new mother but also her child (Righetti-Veltema & others, 2002). A sample of 570 women

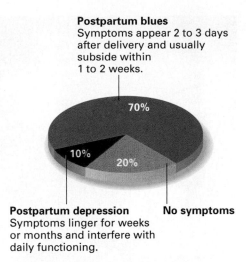

Postpartum blues
Symptoms appear 2 to 3 days after delivery and usually subside within 1 to 2 weeks.

70%

10%   20%

Postpartum depression
Symptoms linger for weeks or months and interfere with daily functioning.

No symptoms

FIGURE 4.11 Percentage of U.S. Women Who Experience Postpartum Blues and Postpartum Depression

 Watch the video, "Transitions to Parenting—Heterosexual Married Couples," for an interview with an expectant couple discussing some of the difficult postpartum adjustments that new parents can expect to face.

postpartum depression Characteristic of women who have such strong feelings of sadness, anxiety, or despair that they have trouble coping with daily tasks in the postpartum period.

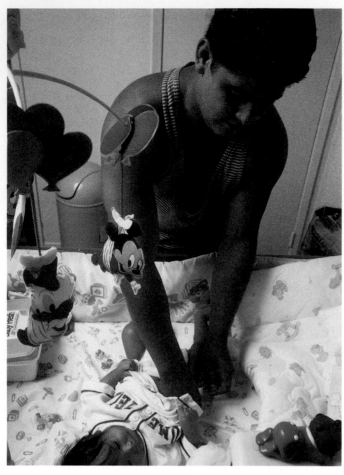

The postpartum period is a time of considerable adjustment and adaptation for both the mother and the father. Fathers can provide an important support system for mothers, especially in helping mothers care for young infants. *As part of supporting the mother, what kinds of tasks might the father of a newborn do?*

bonding The formation of a close connection, especially a physical bond between parents and their newborn, in the period shortly after birth.

and their infants were assessed three months after delivery. Ten percent of the mothers were classified as experiencing postpartum depression on the basis of their responses to the Edinburgh Postnatal Depression Scale. The negative effects on the infant involved eating or sleeping problems. The depressed mothers had less vocal and visual communication with their infant, touched the infant less, and smiled less at the infant than nondepressed mothers.

The father also undergoes considerable adjustment in the postpartum period, although in many cases he will be away at work all day, whereas the mother will be at home, at least in the first few weeks. One of the most common reactions of the husband is the feeling that the baby comes first and gets all of the attention. In some marriages, the man may have had that relationship with his wife and now feels that he has been replaced by the baby.

One strategy to help the father's postpartum reaction is for the parents to set aside some special time to be together with each other. The father's postpartum reaction also likely will be improved if he has taken childbirth classes with his wife and is an active participant in caring for the baby (Schachman, Lee, & Lederma, 2004).

Important factors for both the mother and the father are the time and thought that go into being a competent parent of a young infant (Cowan & Cowan, 2000; McVeigh, Baafi, & Williamson, 2002). It is important for both the mother and the father to become aware of the young infant's developmental needs—physical, psychological, and emotional. Both the mother and the father need to develop a sensitive, comfortable relationship with the baby.

Bonding

A special component of the parent-infant relationship is **bonding,** the formation of a connection, especially a physical bond between parents and the newborn in the period shortly after birth. Some physicians believe that the period shortly after birth is critical in development. During this time, the parents and child need to form an important emotional attachment that provides a foundation for optimal development in years to come (Kennell & McGrath, 1999). Special interest in bonding stems from concern by pediatricians that the circumstances surrounding delivery often separate mothers and their infants, preventing or making difficult the development of a bond. The pediatricians argued that giving the mother drugs to make her delivery less painful can contribute to the lack of bonding. The drugs can make the mother drowsy, thus interfering with her ability to respond to and stimulate the newborn. Advocates of bonding also assert that preterm infants are isolated from their mothers to an even greater degree than are full-term infants, thereby increasing their difficulty in bonding.

Is there evidence that such close contact between mothers and newborns is critical for optimal development later in life? Although some research supports the bonding hypothesis (Klaus & Kennell, 1976), a body of research challenges the significance of the first few days of life as a critical period (Bakeman & Brown, 1980; Rode & others, 1981). Indeed, the extreme form of the bonding hypothesis—that the newborn must have close contact with the mother in the first few days of life to develop optimally—simply is not true.

Nonetheless, the weakness of the maternal-infant bonding research should not be used as an excuse to keep motivated mothers from interacting with their infants in the postpartum period. Such contact brings pleasure to many mothers. In some mother-infant pairs—including preterm infants, adolescent mothers, or mothers from disadvantaged circumstances—the practice of bonding may set in motion a climate for improved interaction after the mother and infant leave the hospital.

In recognition of the belief that bonding may have a positive effect on getting the parent-infant relationship off to a good start, many hospitals now offer a *rooming-in* arrangement, in which the baby remains in the mother's room most of the time during the hospital stay. However, if parents choose not to use this rooming-in arrangement, the weight of the research evidence suggests that it will not harm the infant emotionally (Lamb, 1994).

Review and Reflect: Learning Goal 3

3 **Explain the changes that take place in the postpartum period**

REVIEW

- What does the postpartum period involve?
- What physical adjustments does the woman's body make in this period?
- What emotional and psychological adjustments characterize the postpartum period?
- Is bonding critical for optimal development?

REFLECT

- If you are a female, what can you do to adjust effectively in the postpartum period? If you are a male, what can you do to help in the postpartum period?

Reach Your Learning Goals

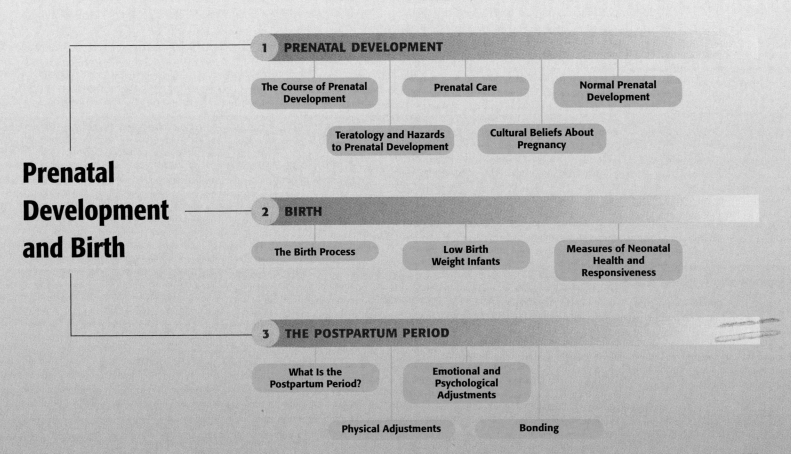

Prenatal Development and Birth

1 PRENATAL DEVELOPMENT

- The Course of Prenatal Development
- Prenatal Care
- Normal Prenatal Development
- Teratology and Hazards to Prenatal Development
- Cultural Beliefs About Pregnancy

2 BIRTH

- The Birth Process
- Low Birth Weight Infants
- Measures of Neonatal Health and Responsiveness

3 THE POSTPARTUM PERIOD

- What Is the Postpartum Period?
- Emotional and Psychological Adjustments
- Physical Adjustments
- Bonding

Summary

1 *Learning Goal 1: Describe prenatal development*

- Prenatal development is divided into three periods: germinal (conception until two weeks later), which ends when the blastocyst attaches to the uterine wall; embryonic (two to eight weeks after conception), during which the embryo differentiates into three layers, life-support systems develop, and organ systems form (organogenesis); and fetal (two months after conception until about nine months, or when the infant is born), a time when organ systems mature to the point at which life can be sustained outside the womb.

- Teratology is the field that investigates the causes of congenital (birth) defects. Any agent that causes birth defects is called a teratogen. The dose, time of exposure, and genetic susceptibility influence the severity of the damage to an unborn child and the type of defect that occurs. Prescription drugs that can be harmful include antibiotics, some antidepressants, and certain hormones. Nonprescription drugs that can be harmful include diet pills, aspirin, and coffee. Fetal alcohol syndrome (FAS) is a cluster of abnormalities that appear in offspring of some mothers who drink heavily during pregnancy. When pregnant women drink moderately, negative effects on their offspring have been found. Cigarette smoking by pregnant women can have serious adverse effects on prenatal and child development (such as low birth weight). Illegal drugs that are potentially harmful to offspring include marijuana, cocaine, and heroin. Incompatibility of the mother's and the fetus' blood types can also be harmful to the fetus. Potential environmental hazards include radiation, environmental pollutants, toxic wastes, and prolonged exposure to heat in saunas and hot tubs. Rubella (German measles) can be harmful. Syphilis, genital herpes, and AIDS are other teratogens. A developing fetus depends entirely on its mother for nutrition. One nutrient that is especially important early in development is folic acid. High anxiety and stress in the mother are linked with less than optimal prenatal and birth outcomes. Maternal age can negatively affect the offspring's development if the mother is an adolescent or over 30. Paternal factors that can adversely affect prenatal development include exposure to lead, radiation, certain pesticides, and petrochemicals.

- Prenatal care varies extensively but usually involves medical care services with a defined schedule of visits.

- Specific actions in pregnancy are often determined by cultural beliefs. Certain behaviors are expected if a culture views pregnancy as a medical condition or a natural occurrence. For example, prenatal care may not be a priority for expectant mothers who view pregnancy as a natural occurrence.

- It is important to remember that, although things can and do go wrong during pregnancy, most of the time pregnancy and prenatal development go well. Avoiding teratogens helps ensure a positive outcome.

2 *Learning Goal 2: Discuss the birth process*

- Childbirth occurs in three stages. The first stage, which lasts about 12 to 24 hours for a woman having her first child, is the longest stage. The cervix dilates to about 4 inches at the end of the first stage. The second stage begins when the baby's head moves through the cervix and ends with the baby's complete emergence. The third stage is afterbirth, which involves expulsion of the placenta. Being born involves considerable stress for the baby, but the baby is well prepared and adapted to handle the stress. Anoxia—insufficient oxygen supply to the fetus/newborn—is a potential hazard. Childbirth strategies involve the childbirth setting and attendants. In the United States, births are attended primarily by physicians and in some cases midwives. In many countries, a doula attends a childbearing woman. Methods of delivery include medicated, natural and prepared, and cesarean.

- Low birth weight infants weigh less than $5\frac{1}{2}$ pounds at birth and they may be preterm (born three weeks or more before the pregnancy has reached full term) or small for date (also called small for gestational age, which refers to infants whose birth weight is below norm when the length of pregnancy is considered). Small for date infants may be preterm or full term. Although most low birth weight infants are normal and healthy, as a group they have more health and developmental problems than normal birth weight infants. Kangaroo care and massage therapy have been shown to have benefits for preterm infants.

- For many years, the Apgar Scale has been used to assess the newborn's health. The Brazelton Neonatal Behavioral Assessment Scale examines the newborn's neurological development, reflexes, and reactions to people.

3 *Learning Goal 3: Explain the changes that take place in the postpartum period*

- The postpartum period is the name given to the period after childbirth or delivery. In this period, the woman's body adjusts physically and psychologically to the process of childbearing. The period lasts for about six weeks or until the body has completed its adjustment.

- Physical adjustments in the postpartum period include fatigue, involution (the process by which the uterus returns to its pre-pregnant size five or six weeks after birth), hormonal changes, deciding when to resume sexual intercourse, and exercises to recover body contour and strength.

- Emotional fluctuations on the part of the mother are common in this period, and they can vary a great deal from one mother to the next. Postpartum depression characterizes women who have such strong feelings of sadness, anxiety, or despair that they have trouble coping with daily tasks in the postpartum period. Postpartum depression occurs in about 10 percent of new mothers. The father and others close to the mother also may experience postpartum adjustment.

- Bonding is the formation of a close connection, especially a physical bond between parents and the newborn shortly after birth. Early bonding has not been found to be critical in the development of a competent infant.

Key Terms

germinal period 105
blastocyst 105
trophoblast 105
embryonic period 105
placenta 105
umbilical cord 106
amnion 106

organogenesis 106
fetal period 106
teratogen 109
fetal alcohol syndrome
  (FAS) 111
doula 120
natural childbirth 122

prepared childbirth 122
breech position 122
low birth weight infants 123
preterm infants 123
small for date infants 123
kangaroo care 125
Apgar Scale 126

Brazelton Neonatal Behavioral
  Assessment Scale 126
postpartum period 128
postpartum depression 129
bonding 130

Key People

Grantley Dick-Read 122

Ferdinand Lamaze 122

Tiffany Field 125

T. Berry Brazelton 127

E-Learning Tools

To help you master the material in this chapter, you'll find a number of valuable study tools on the LifeMap CD-ROM that accompanies this book and on the Online Learning Center for *Life-Span Development,* tenth edition, at www.mhhe.com/santrockld10.

Video Clips

In the margins of this book there are icons directing you to the LifeMap CD-ROM that accompanies the book. There you'll find a video for chapter 4 called "Transitions to Parenting—Heterosexual Married Couples." In an interview conducted only weeks before the birth of their first child, a couple anticipates some of the transitional issues that all parents must deal with in the weeks immediately following the birth of the child.

Self-Assessment

Connect to www.mhhe.com/santrockld10 to learn more about how alcohol can affect an unborn baby by completing the self-assessment, *Pregnancy Screening for Alcohol Use.*

Taking It to the Net

Connect to www.mhhe.com/santrockld10 to research the answers to these questions.

1. Denise's sister, Doreen, is pregnant for the first time. Doreen is not known for her healthy lifestyle; she rarely exercises, smokes frequently, and is a social drinker. What are some lifestyle activities that Denise can encourage Doreen to adopt in order to give birth to a healthy baby?
2. Sienne told her fiancé, Jackson, that he had better stop smoking before they begin trying to conceive a child. Why is Sienne concerned about Jackson's smoking and its effect on their children before they have even started planning their family?
3. Hannah, who gave birth to a healthy baby boy—her first child—two weeks ago, suddenly appears to her husband Sean to be melancholy and lethargic. She is also having trouble sleeping. How can Sean determine if Hannah is just going through a natural period of postbaby "blues" or if she might be suffering from postpartum depression?

Health and Well-Being, Parenting, and Education Exercises

Build your decision-making skills by trying your hand at the health and well-being, parenting, and education exercises.

Connect to www.mhhe.com/santrockld10 to research the answers and complete the exercises.

C H A P T E R

A baby is the most complicated object made by unskilled labor.
—Anonymous

Physical Development in Infancy

Images of Life-Span Development
Breast and Bottle Feeding in the Third World

Latonya is a newborn baby in the African country of Ghana. The culture into which she was born discourages breast feeding. She has been kept apart from her mother and bottle fed in her first days of infancy. Manufacturers of infant formula provide the hospital where she was born with free or subsidized milk powder. Her mother has been persuaded to bottle feed rather than breast feed her. When her mother bottle feeds Latonya, she overdilutes the milk formula with unclean water. Latonya's feeding bottles also have not been sterilized. Latonya becomes very sick. She dies before her first birthday.

By contrast, Ramona's mother is breast feeding her. Ramona was born at a Nigerian hospital where a "baby-friendly" program has been initiated. In this program, babies are not separated from their mothers at birth, and the mothers are encouraged to breast feed them. The mothers are told of the perils of bottle feeding that involve unsafe water and unsterilized bottles. They also are informed about the advantages of breast milk, including its nutritious and hygienic qualities, its ability to immunize babies against common illnesses, and its role in reducing the mother's risk of breast and ovarian cancer. At 1 year of age, Ramona is very healthy.

In recent years, the World Health Organization and UNICEF have tried to reverse the trend of bottle feeding infants, which has emerged in many impoverished countries. Together, both organizations have instituted the baby-friendly program in many countries. They have also persuaded the International Association of Infant Formula Manufacturers to stop marketing their baby formulas to hospitals in countries where the governments support the baby-friendly initiatives. For the hospitals themselves, costs have fallen as infant formula, feeding bottles, and separate nurseries become unnecessary. For example, baby-friendly Jose Fabella Memorial Hospital in the Philippines reported saving 8 percent of its annual budget.

Hospitals play a vital role in convincing mothers to breast feed their babies. For many years, maternity units favored bottle feeding and did not give mothers adequate information about the benefits of breast feeding. With the initiatives of the World Health Organization and UNICEF, practices are changing, but many places in the world still have not implemented the baby-friendly initiatives (UNICEF, 2004).

The advantages of breast feeding—especially in impoverished countries—are substantial. However, these advantages are now counterbalanced by the risk of passing HIV to the baby through breast milk because the majority of mothers don't know whether or not they are infected (Dabis & others, 2004; Henderson, Martines, & de Zoysa, 2004). In some areas of Africa, more than 30 percent of mothers carry HIV.

PREVIEW

It is very important for infants to get a healthy start. In this chapter we will explore these aspects of the infant's development: physical growth, motor development, and sensory and perceptual development.

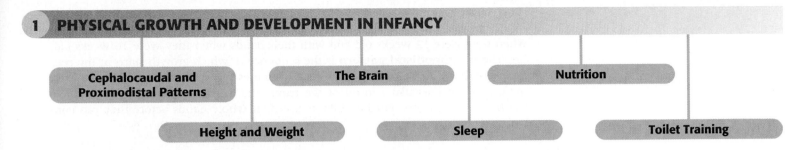

1 PHYSICAL GROWTH AND DEVELOPMENT IN INFANCY

- Cephalocaudal and Proximodistal Patterns
- The Brain
- Nutrition
- Height and Weight
- Sleep
- Toilet Training

Infants' physical development in the first two years of life is extensive. At birth, neonates have a gigantic head (relative to the rest of the body), which flops around uncontrollably, and some basic reflexes. In the span of 12 months, infants become capable of sitting anywhere, standing, stooping, climbing, and usually walking. During the second year, growth decelerates, but rapid increases in such activities as running and climbing take place. Let's now examine in greater detail the sequence of physical development in infancy.

Cephalocaudal and Proximodistal Patterns

An extraordinary proportion of the total body is occupied by the head during prenatal development and early infancy (see figure 5.1). The **cephalocaudal pattern** is the sequence in which the earliest growth always occurs at the top—the head— with physical growth in size, weight, and feature differentiation gradually working its way down from top to bottom (for example, shoulders, middle trunk, and so on). This same pattern occurs in the head area, because the top parts of the head—the eyes and brain—grow faster than the lower parts, such as the jaw. Later in the chapter you will see that sensory and motor development generally proceeds according to the cephalocaudal principle. For example, infants see objects before they can control their trunk, and they can use their hands long before they can crawl or walk.

Sensory and motor development generally proceed according to the cephalocaudal principle. For example, infants see objects before they can control their torso, and they can use their hands long before they can crawl or walk. However, one recent

cephalocaudal pattern The sequence in which the earliest growth always occurs at the top—the head—with physical growth in size, weight, and feature differentiation gradually working from top to bottom.

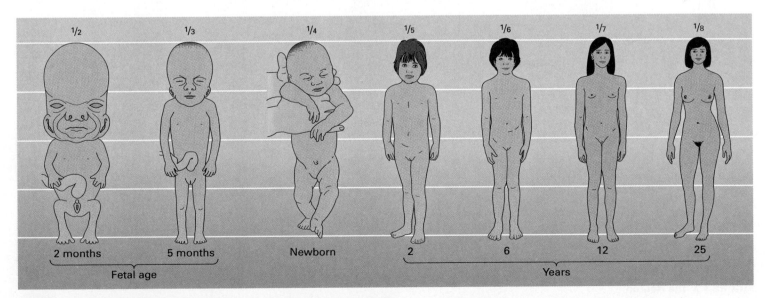

| 1/2 | 1/3 | 1/4 | 1/5 | 1/6 | 1/7 | 1/8 |

| 2 months | 5 months | Newborn | 2 | 6 | 12 | 25 |

Fetal age — Years

FIGURE 5.1 Changes in Proportions of the Human Body During Growth
As individuals develop from infancy through adulthood, one of the most noticeable physical changes is that the head becomes smaller in relation to the rest of the body. The fractions listed refer to head size as a proportion of total body length at different ages.

study found that infants reached for toys with their feet prior to using their hands (Galloway & Thelen, 2004). On average, infants first touched the toy with their feet when they were 12 weeks old and with their hands when they were 16 weeks old.

The **proximodistal pattern** is the sequence in which growth starts at the center of the body and moves toward the extremities. An example of this is the early maturation of muscular control of the trunk and arms, as compared with that of the hands and fingers. Further, infants use their whole hands before they can control several fingers.

Height and Weight

The average North American newborn is 20 inches long and weighs 7½ pounds. Ninety-five percent of full-term newborns are 18 to 22 inches long and weigh between 5½ and 10 pounds.

In the first several days of life, most newborns lose 5 to 7 percent of their body weight before they learn to adjust to neonatal feeding. Once infants adjust to sucking, swallowing, and digesting, they grow rapidly, gaining an average of 5 to 6 ounces per week during the first month. They have doubled their birth weight by the age of 4 months and have nearly tripled it by their first birthday. Infants grow about 1 inch per month during the first year, reaching approximately 1½ times their birth length by their first birthday.

Infants' rate of growth is considerably slower in the second year of life. By 2 years of age, infants weigh approximately 26 to 32 pounds, having gained a quarter to half a pound per month during the second year; now they have reached about one-fifth of their adult weight. At 2 years of age, the average infant is 32 to 35 inches in height, which is nearly half of their adult height.

proximodistal pattern The sequence in which growth starts at the center of the body and moves toward the extremities.

neuron Nerve cell that handles information processing at the cellular level.

The Brain

As an infant walks, talks, runs, shakes a rattle, smiles, and frowns, changes are occurring in its brain. Consider that the infant begins life as a single cell and nine months later is born with a brain and nervous system that contains tens of billions of nerve cells, or neurons. A **neuron** is a nerve cell that handles information processing at the cellular level (see figure 5.2).

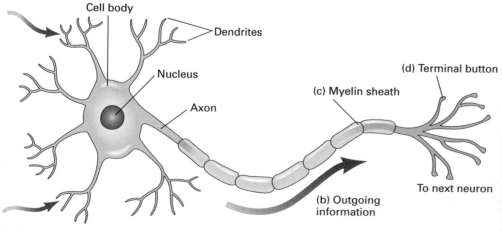

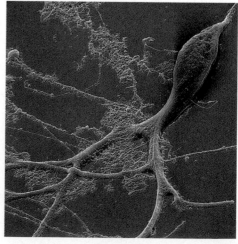

Cell body

Dendrites

Nucleus

(d) Terminal button

(c) Myelin sheath

Axon

To next neuron

(b) Outgoing information

(a) Incoming information

FIGURE 5.2 The Neuron

(*a*) The dendrites of the cell body receive information from other neurons, muscles, or glands through the axon. (*b*) Axons transmit information away from the cell body. (*c*) A myelin sheath covers most axons and speeds information transmission. (*d*) As the axon ends, it branches out into terminal buttons. At the right is an actual photograph of a neuron.

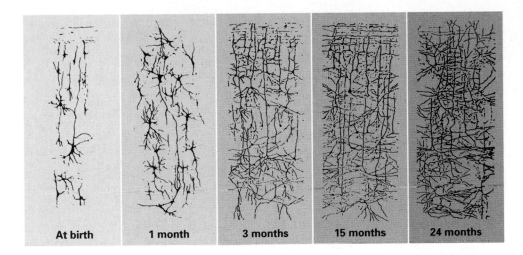

At birth **1 month** **3 months** **15 months** **24 months**

FIGURE 5.3 The Development of Dendritic Spreading
Note the increase in connectedness between neurons over the course of the first two years of life.

The Brain's Development Brain development occurs extensively in utero and continues through infancy and later. Because the brain is still developing so rapidly in infancy, the infant's head should be protected from falls or other injuries and the baby should never be shaken. *Shaken baby syndrome,* which includes brain swelling and hemorrhaging, affects hundreds of babies in the United States each year (Harding, Risdon, & Krous, 2004; Minns & Busuttil, 2004).

At birth, the newborn's brain is about 25 percent of its adult weight. By the second birthday, the brain is about 75 percent of its adult weight. However, the brain's areas do not mature uniformly. Some areas, such as the primary motor areas, develop earlier than others, such as the primary sensory areas.

A *myelin sheath,* which is a layer of fat cells, encases many axons (see figure 5.2). The myelin sheath insulates nerve cells and also helps nerve impulses travel faster. *Myelination,* the process of encasing axons with fat cells, begins prenatally and continues after birth. Myelination for visual pathways occurs rapidly after birth, being completed in the first six months. Auditory myelination is not completed until 4 or 5 years of age. Some aspects of myelination continue even into adolescence.

One of the most dramatic changes in the brain in the first two years of life is the spreading connections of dendrites to each other. Figure 5.3 illustrates these changes. Whereas myelination speeds up neural transmissions, the expansion of dendritic connections facilitates the spreading of neural pathways in infant development.

Another important aspect of the brain's development at the cellular level is the dramatic increase in connections between neurons. *Synapses* are tiny gaps between neurons where chemical interactions connect axons and dendrites, allowing information to pass from neuron to neuron. As the infant develops, synaptic connections between axons and dendrites proliferate.

Researchers have discovered an intriguing aspect of synaptic connections. Nearly twice as many of these connections are made as will ever be used (Huttenlocher & Dabholkar, 1997). The connections that are used become strengthened and survive, while the unused ones are replaced by other pathways or disappear (Casey, Durston, & Fossella, 2001). In the language of neuroscience, these connections will be "pruned." Figure 5.4 vividly illustrates the dramatic growth and later pruning of synapses in the visual, auditory, and prefrontal cortex areas of the brain (Huttenlocher & Dabholkar, 1997). These areas are critical for higher-level cognitive functioning in areas like learning, memory, and reasoning.

As shown in figure 5.4, "blooming and pruning" vary considerably by brain region in humans (Thompson & Nelson, 2001). For example, the peak of synaptic overproduction in the visual cortex occurs at about the fourth postnatal month, followed by a gradual retraction until the middle to end of the preschool years (Huttenlocher & Dabholkar, 1997). In areas of the brain involved in hearing and

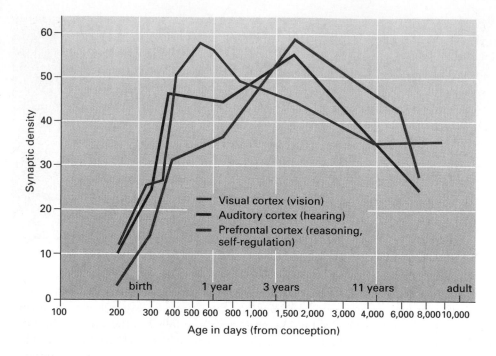

Neural Processes
Charles Nelson's Research

language, a similar, though somewhat later, course is detected. However, in the prefrontal cortex, the area of the brain where higher-level thinking and self-regulation occur, the peak of overproduction takes place at about 1 year of age; it is not until middle to late adolescence that the adult density of synapses is achieved. Both heredity and environment are thought to influence the timing and course of synaptic overproduction and subsequent retraction.

Using the electroencephalogram (EEG), which measures the brain's electrical activity, researchers have found that a spurt in EEG activity occurs at about 1½ to 2 years of age (Fischer & Bidell, 1998; Fischer & Rose, 1995). Other spurts seem to take place at about 9, 12, 15, and 18 to 20 years of age. Researchers believe that these spurts of brain activity may coincide with important changes in cognitive development. For example, the increase in EEG brain activity at 1½ to 2 years of age is likely associated with an increase in conceptual and language growth.

Studying the brain's development in infancy is not as easy as it might seem, because even the latest brain-imaging technologies cannot make out fine details in adult brains and cannot be used with babies. Positron-emission tomography (PET) scans pose a radiation risk to babies, and infants wriggle too much to capture accurate images using magnetic resonance imaging (MRI) (Marcus, Mulrine, & Wong, 1999). However, one researcher, Charles Nelson (1999, 2003), is finding out more about the brain's development in infancy. By attaching up to 128 electrodes to a baby's scalp, Nelson has found that even newborns produce distinctive brain waves that reveal they can distinguish their mother's voices from another woman's, even while they are asleep (see figure 5.5). In other research, Nelson allowed infants to feel a specific wooden toy and found that by 8 months of age babies can distinguish the picture of that wooden toy from pictures of other toys. This achievement coincides with the development of neurons in the brain's hippocampus, an important structure in memory, allowing the infant to remember specific items and events.

The Brain's Lobes and Hemispheres The highest level of the brain is the forebrain. It consists of a number of structures, including the *cerebral cortex*, which makes up about 80 percent of the brain's volume and covers the lower portions of the brain like a cap. The cerebral cortex plays a critical role in many important human functions, such as perception, language, and thinking.

FIGURE 5.5 Measuring the Brain's Activity in Research on Infant Memory
In Charles Nelson's research, electrodes are attached to a baby's scalp to measure the brain's activity to determine its role in the development of an infant's memory. *Why is it so difficult to measure infants' brain activity?*

The cerebral cortex is divided into two halves, or hemispheres (see figure 5.6). Each hemisphere is divided into four main areas called lobes:

- The *frontal lobes* are involved in voluntary movement and thinking.
- The *occipital lobes* are involved in vision.
- The *temporal lobes* are involved in hearing.
- The *parietal lobes* are involved in processing information about body sensations.

The frontal lobes are immature in the newborn. However, as neurons in the frontal lobes become myelinated and interconnected during the first year of life, infants develop an ability to regulate their physiological states, such as sleep, and gain more control over their reflexes. Cognitive skills that require deliberate thinking do not emerge until later (Bell & Fox, 1992). Indeed, as we saw earlier, the prefrontal region of the frontal lobe has the most prolonged development of any brain region with changes detectable at least into the adolescent years (Johnson, 2001).

Lateralization is the specialization of function in one hemisphere of the cerebral cortex or the other. Researchers continue to be interested in the degree to which each is involved in various aspects of thinking, feeling, and behavior (Gandour & others, 2003; Zald, 2003).

The most extensive research on the brain's hemispheres has focused on language (Wood & others, 2004). At birth, the hemispheres already have started to specialize: Newborns show greater electrical brain activity in the left hemisphere than the right hemisphere when they are listening to speech sounds (Hahn, 1987). Speech and grammar are localized to the left hemisphere in most people. But it is merely a popular myth that the left hemisphere is the exclusive location of language and logical thinking or that the right hemisphere is the exclusive location of emotion and creative thinking. Some aspects of language, such as appropriate language use in different contexts, and the use of metaphor and humor, involves the right hemisphere. Thus, language does not occur exclusively in the brain's left hemisphere (Johnson, 2000, 2001; Knect & others, 2003; Tremblay, Monetta, & Joanette, 2004).

Further, most neuroscientists agree that complex functions, such as reading, performing music, and creating art, are the outcome of communication between both sides of the brain. They believe that labeling people as "left-brained" because they are logical thinkers and "right-brained" because they are creative thinkers does not correspond to the way the brain's hemispheres actually work.

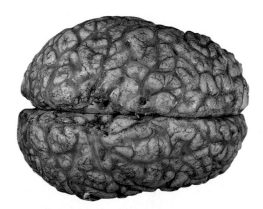

FIGURE 5.6 The Human Brain's Hemispheres
The two halves (hemispheres) of the human brain are clearly seen in this photograph.

lateralization Specialization of function in one hemisphere of the cerebral cortex or the other.

FIGURE 5.7 Early Deprivation and Brain Activity

These two photographs are PET (positron-emission tomography) scans (which use radioactive tracers to image and analyze blood flow and metabolic activity in the body's organs) of the brains of (*a*) a normal child and (*b*) an institutionalized Romanian orphan who experienced substantial deprivation since birth. In PET scans, the highest to lowest brain activity is reflected in the colors of red, yellow, green, blue, and black, respectively. As can be seen, red and yellow show up to a much greater degree in the PET scan of the normal child than the deprived Romanian orphan.

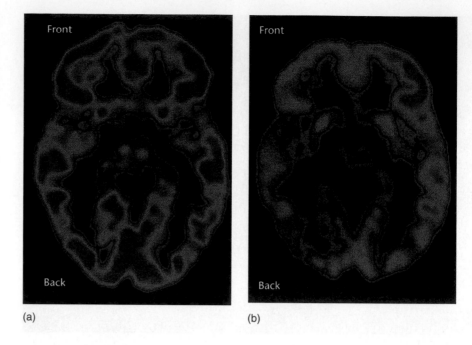

(a)　　　　　　　　　　　　　(b)

Development of the Brain
Early Development of the Brain
Early Experience and the Brain

Early Experience and the Brain   Until the middle of the twentieth century, scientists believed that the brain's development was determined almost exclusively by genetic factors. Researcher Mark Rosenzweig (1969) was curious about whether early experiences change the brain's development. He conducted a number of experiments with rats and other animals to investigate this possibility. Animals were randomly assigned to grow up in different environments. Animals in an enriched early environment lived in cages with stimulating features, such as wheels to rotate, steps to climb, levers to press, and toys to manipulate. In contrast, other animals had the early experience of growing up in standard cages or in barren, isolated conditions. The results were stunning. The brains of the animals growing up in the enriched environment developed better than the brains of the animals reared in standard or isolated conditions. The brains of the "enriched" animals weighed more, had thicker layers, had more neuronal connections, and had higher levels of neurochemical activity. Similar findings occurred when older animals were reared in vastly different environments, although the results were not as strong as for the younger animals. Such results give hope that enriching the lives of infants and young children who live in impoverished environments can produce positive changes in their development.

Depressed brain activity has recently been found in children who grow up in a deprived environment (Cicchetti, 2001). As shown in figure 5.7, a child who grew up in the unresponsive and nonstimulating environment of a Romanian orphanage showed considerably depressed brain activity compared with a normal child.

The profusion of connections described earlier provides the growing brain with flexibility and resilience. Consider 16-year-old Michael Rehbein. At age 4½, he began to experience uncontrollable seizures—as many as 400 a day. Doctors said that the only solution was to remove the left hemisphere of his brain where the seizures were occurring. The first major surgery was at age 7 and another at age 10. Recovery was slow but his right hemisphere began to reorganize and take over functions that normally occur in the brain's left hemisphere. One of these functions was speech (see figure 5.8).

Neuroscientists believe that what wires the brain—or rewires it, in the case of Michael Rehbein—is repeated experience (Nash, 1997). Each time a baby tries to touch an attractive object or gazes intently at a face, tiny bursts of electricity shoot through the brain, knitting neurons together into circuits. What results are some of the behavioral milestones that we discuss in this and other chapters. For example, at about 2 months of age, the motor-control centers of the brain develop to the point at which infants can suddenly reach out and grab a nearby object. At about 4 months, the neural connections necessary for depth perception begin to form. And at about 12 months the brain's speech centers are poised to produce one of infancy's magical moments: when the infant utters his or her first word.

In sum, neural connections are formed early in life. The infant's brain literally is waiting for experiences to determine how connections are made (Greenough, 2001; Johnson, 2000, 2001, 2005). Before birth, it appears that genes mainly direct how the brain establishes basic wiring patterns. Neurons grow and travel to distant places awaiting further instructions. After birth, environmental experiences guide the brain's development. The inflowing stream of sights, sounds, smells, touches, language, and eye contact help shape the brain's neural connections (Black, 2001; Neville & Bavelier, 2002).

Sleep

When we were infants, sleep consumed more of our time than it does now. Newborns sleep 16 to 17 hours a day, although some sleep more and others less. The range is from about 10 hours to about 21 hours, and the longest period of sleep is not always between 11 P.M. and 7 A.M. Although total sleep remains somewhat consistent for young infants, their periods of sleep during the day do not always follow a rhythmic pattern. An infant may change from sleeping several long bouts of 7 or 8 hours to three or four shorter sessions only a few hours in duration. By about 1 month of age, many American infants have begun to sleep longer at night, and by about 4 months of age, they usually have moved closer to adultlike sleep patterns, spending the most time sleeping at night and the most time awake during the day (Daws, 2000).

Cultural variations influence infant sleeping patterns. For example, in the Kipsigis culture in the African country of Kenya, infants sleep with their mothers at night and are permitted to nurse on demand (Super & Harkness, 1997). During the day they are strapped to their mothers' backs, accompanying them on daily rounds of chores and social activities. As a result, the Kipsigis infants do not sleep through the night until much later than American infants do. During the first eight months of postnatal life, Kipsigis infants rarely sleep longer than three hours at a stretch, even at night. This sleep pattern contrasts with that of American infants, many of whom begin to sleep up to eight hours a night by 8 months of age.

REM Sleep Researchers are intrigued by the various forms of infant sleep. They are especially interested in *REM (rapid eye movement) sleep*. Most adults spend about one-fifth of their night in REM sleep, and REM sleep usually appears about one hour after non-REM sleep. However, about half of an infant's sleep is REM sleep, and infants often begin their sleep cycle with REM sleep rather than non-REM sleep. By the time infants reach 3 months of age, the percentage of time they spend in REM sleep falls to about 40 percent, and REM sleep no longer begins their sleep cycle. The large amount of REM sleep may provide infants with added self-stimulation, since they spend less time awake than do older children (Zuk & Zuk, 2002). REM sleep also might promote the brain's development in infancy (McNamara & Sullivan, 2000). Figure 5.9 illustrates the average number of total hours spent in sleep, and the amount of time spent in REM sleep, across the human life span. As can be seen, infants sleep far more than children and adults, and a much greater amount of time is taken up by REM sleep in infancy than at any other point in the life span.

Shared Sleeping Cultures also vary in their approach to newborns' sleeping arrangements (Berkowitz, 2004; Cortesi & others, 2004; Owens, 2004). Sharing a

(a)

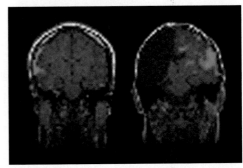

(b)

FIGURE 5.8 Plasticity in the Brain's Hemispheres

(*a*) Michael Rehbein at 14 years of age.
(*b*) Michael's right hemisphere (*right*) has reorganized to take over the language functions normally carried out by corresponding areas in the left hemisphere of an intact brain (*left*). However, the right hemisphere is not as efficient as the left, and more areas of the brain are recruited to process speech.

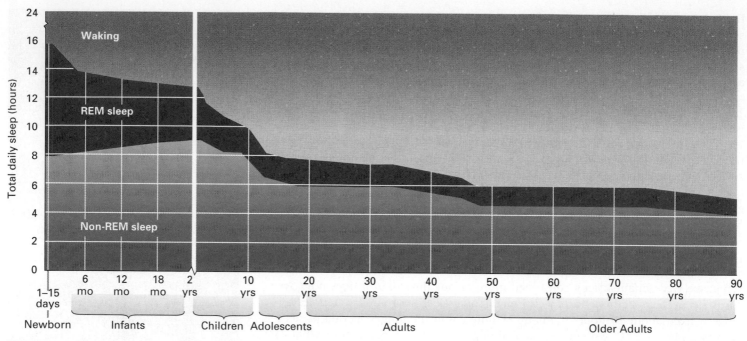

FIGURE 5.9 Sleep Across the Human Life Span

bed with a mother is a common practice in many cultures, whereas in others new-borns sleep in a crib, either in the same room as the parents or in a separate room. In the United States, sleeping in a crib in a separate room is the most frequent sleeping arrangement for an infant. In one cross-cultural study, American mothers said they have their infants sleep in a separate room to promote the infants' self-reliance and independence (Morelli & others, 1992). By contrast, Mayan mothers in rural Guatemala had infants sleep in their bed until the birth of a new sibling, at which time the infant would sleep with another family member or in a separate bed in the mother's room. The Mayan mothers believed that the co-sleeping arrangement with their infants enhanced the closeness of their relationship with the infants and were shocked when told that American mothers have their babies sleep alone.

Some child experts believe that shared sleeping is beneficial, promoting breast feeding, responding more quickly to the baby's cries, and detecting potentially dangerous breathing pauses in the baby (McCoy & others, 2004; McKenna, Mosko, & Richard, 1997). However, the American Academy of Pediatrics Task Force on Infant Positioning and SIDS (AAPTFIPS) (2000) discourages shared sleeping. The Task Force concluded that in some instances bed sharing might lead to sudden infant death syndrome (SIDS), not to mention the risk of a sleeping mother rolling over onto her baby.

One recent study found physiological responses indicative of greater stress in co-sleeping infants than non-co-sleeping infants (Hunsley & Thoman, 2002). Thus, shared sleeping remains a controversial issue, with some experts recommending it and others arguing against it. Whatever the sleeping arrangements, it is recommended that the infant's bedding provide firm support and cribs should have side rails.

S leep that knits up the ravelled sleave of care . . . Balm of hurt minds, nature's second course. Chief nourisher in life's feast.

—**WILLIAM SHAKESPEARE**
English Playwright, 17th Century

sudden infant death syndrome (SIDS)
A condition that occurs when an infant stops breathing, usually during the night, and suddenly dies without an apparent cause.

SIDS **Sudden infant death syndrome (SIDS)** is a condition that occurs when infants stop breathing, usually during the night, and die suddenly without an apparent cause. SIDS remains the highest cause of infant death in the United States with nearly 3,000 infant deaths annually attributed to SIDS. Risk of SIDS is highest at 4 to 6 weeks of age (Matthews, Menacker, & MacDorman, 2003).

Since 1992, The American Academy of Pediatrics (AAP) has recommended that infants be placed to sleep on their backs to reduce the risk of SIDS. Since that time, the frequency of prone sleeping has decreased from 70 percent to 20 percent of U.S. infants (AAPTFIPS, 2000). Researchers have found that SIDS decreases when infants sleep on their backs rather than their stomachs or sides (Ige & Shelton, 2004; Lipsitt, 2003; Moon, Oden, & Grady, 2004). Among the reasons given for prone sleeping being a high risk factor for SIDS are that it impairs the infant's arousal from sleep and restricts the infant's ability to swallow effectively (Horne, Parslow, & Harding, 2004; Horne & others, 2002; Tuladhar & others, 2003).

In addition to sleeping in a prone position, researchers have found that the following are risk factors for SIDS (AAPTFIPS, 2000; Kahn & others, 2002):

- Low birth weight infants are 5 to 10 times more likely to die of SIDS than are their normal-weight counterparts (Horne & others, 2002).
- Infants whose siblings have died of SIDS are two to four times as likely to die of it (Lenoir, Mallet, & Calenda, 2000).
- Six percent of infants with sleep apnea, a temporary cessation of breathing in which the airway is completely blocked, usually 10 seconds or longer, die of SIDS (McNamara & Sullivan, 2000).
- African American and Eskimo infants are four to six times as likely as all others to die of SIDS (Daley, 2004; Unger & others, 2003).
- SIDS is more common in lower socioeconomic groups (Mitchell & others, 2000).
- SIDS is more common in infants who are passively exposed to cigarette smoke (Chong, Yip, & Karlberg, 2004; Horne & others, 2004).
- SIDS is more common if infants sleep in soft bedding (Flick & others, 2001).

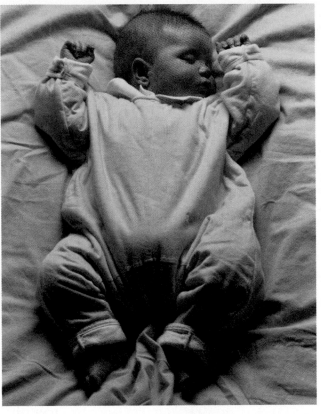

Is this a good sleep position for infants? Why or why not?

SIDS

Nutrition

Our coverage of infant nutrition begins with information about nutritional needs and eating behavior, then turns to the issue of breast versus bottle feeding, and concludes with an overview of malnutrition.

Nutritional Needs and Eating Behavior The importance of adequate nutrients consumed in a loving and supportive environment during the infant years cannot be overstated (Samour, Helm, & Lang, 2000). From birth to 1 year of age, human infants nearly triple their weight and increase their length by 50 percent. Individual differences among infants in terms of their nutrient reserves, body composition, growth rates, and activity patterns make defining actual nutrient needs difficult. However, because parents need guidelines, nutritionists recommend that infants consume approximately 50 calories per day for each pound they weigh—more than twice an adult's requirement per pound.

Some years ago, controversy surrounded the issue of whether a baby should be fed on demand or on a regular schedule. Behaviorist John Watson (1928) argued that scheduled feeding is superior because it increases the child's orderliness. An example of his recommended schedule for newborns was 4 ounces of formula every six hours. In recent years, demand feeding—in which the timing and amount of feeding are determined by the infant—has become more popular.

Today, Americans are extremely nutrition-conscious. Does the same type of nutrition that makes us healthy adults also make young infants healthy? Some affluent, well-educated parents almost starve their babies by feeding them the low-fat, low-calorie diet they themselves eat. Diets designed for adult weight loss and prevention of heart disease may actually retard growth and development in babies. Fat is very important for babies. Nature's food—breast milk—is not low in fat or

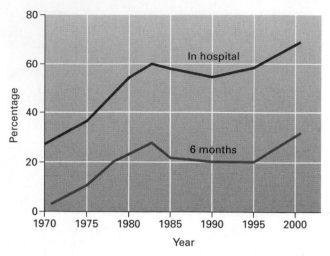

FIGURE 5.10 Trends in Breast Feeding in the United States: 1970–2001

calories. No child under the age of 2 should be consuming skim milk. In one investigation, seven babies 7 to 22 months of age were found to be undernourished by their unwitting health-conscious parents (Lifshitz & others, 1987). In some instances, the parents had been fat themselves and were determined that their child was not going to be. The well-meaning parents substituted vegetables, skim milk, and other low-fat foods for what they called junk food. However, for growing infants, high-calorie, high-energy foods are part of a balanced diet.

A recent national study of more than 3,000 randomly selected 4- to 24-month-olds documented that many U.S. parents aren't feeding their babies enough fruits and vegetables, but are feeding them too much junk food (Fox & others, 2004). Up to one-third of the babies ate no vegetables and fruit, frequently ate French fries, and almost half of the 7- to 8-month-old babies were fed desserts, sweets, or sweetened drinks. By 15 months, French fries were the most common vegetables the babies ate.

Breast Versus Bottle Feeding Human milk or an alternative formula is the baby's source of nutrients and energy for the first 4 to 6 months of life. For years, debate has focused on whether breast feeding is better for the infant than bottle feeding. The growing consensus is that breast feeding is better for the baby's health (Blum, 2000; Kramer, 2003; More, 2003). As shown in figure 5.10, the prevalence of initiating breast feeding in the hospital and breast feeding at six months after birth in the United States reached an all-time high of 69 percent and 32.5 percent, respectively, in 2001, the latest year for which figures were available (Ryan, Wenjun, & Acosta, 2002).

What are some of the benefits of breast feeding? They include these benefits during the first two years of life and later (AAP Work Group on Breastfeeding [AAPWGB], 1997; London & others, 2000):

- Appropriate weight gain and lowered risk of childhood obesity (Bergmann & others, 2003; Meier & others, 2004). A recent review of 11 studies found that breast feeding reduces the risk of childhood obesity to a moderate extent (Dewey, 2003).
- Fewer allergies (Oddy & others, 2004; Prescott, 2003)
- Prevention or reduction of diarrhea, respiratory infections (such as pneumonia and bronchitis), bacterial and urinary tract infections, and otitis media (a middle ear infection) (Marild & others, 2004; Nash, 2003; Pardo-Crespo & others, 2004).
- Denser bones in childhood and adulthood (Gibson & others, 2000)
- Reduced childhood cancer and reduced incidence of breast cancer in mothers and their female offspring (Bernier & others, 2000; Eisinger & Burke, 2003; Lee & others, 2003)
- Lower incidence of SIDS—in one study, for every month of exclusive breast feeding, the rate of SIDS was cut in half (Fredrickson, 1993)
- Improved neurological and cognitive development (Brody, 1994)
- Improved visual acuity (Makrides & others, 1995)

Human milk or an alternative formula is a baby's source of nutrients for the first four to six months. The growing consensus is that breast feeding is better for the baby's health, although controversy still swirls about the issue of breast feeding versus bottle feeding. *Why is breast feeding strongly recommended by pediatricians?*

Which women are least likely to breast feed? They include mothers who work full-time outside of the home, mothers under age 25, mothers without a high school education, African American mothers, and mothers in low-income circumstances (Ryan, 1997). In one study of low-income mothers in Georgia, interventions (such as counseling focused on the benefits of breast feeding and the free loan of a breast pump) increased the incidence of breast feeding (Ahluwalia & others,

2000). Increasingly, mothers who return to work in the infant's first year of life use a breast pump to extract breast milk that can be stored for later feeding of the infant when the mother is not present.

The AAP Work Group on Breastfeeding strongly endorses breast feeding throughout the first year of life (AAPWGB, 1997). Are there circumstances when mothers should not breast feed? Yes, a mother should not breast feed (1) when the mother is infected with AIDS or some other infectious disease that can be transmitted through her milk, (2) if she has active tuberculosis, or (3) if she is taking any drug that may not be safe for the infant (AAPWGB, 1997; Brown, 2003; Mathew, 2004; Sedgh & others, 2004).

Some women cannot breast feed their infants because of physical difficulties; others feel guilty if they terminate breast feeding early (Mozingo & others, 2000). Mothers may also worry that they are depriving their infants of important emotional and psychological benefits if they bottle feed rather than breast feed. Some researchers have found, however, that there are no psychological differences between breast fed and bottle fed infants (Ferguson, Harwood, & Shannon, 1987; Young, 1990). To read about a program that gives infants a healthy start in life, see the Diversity in Life-Span Development interlude.

 Watch the video "Nutritional Benefits of Breast Feeding" to learn the health advantages of breast feeding over bottle feeding for infants.

Diversity in Life-Span Development
A Healthy Start

The Hawaii Family Support/Healthy Start Program began in 1985 (Allen, Brown, & Finlay, 1992). It was designed by the Hawaii Family Stress Center in Honolulu, which had been making home visits to improve family functioning and reduce child abuse for more than a decade. Participation in the program is voluntary. Families of newborns are screened for family risk factors, including unstable housing, histories of substance abuse, depression, parents' abuse as children, late or no prenatal care, fewer than 12 years of schooling, poverty, and unemployment. Workers screen for early identification by interviewing new mothers in the hospital. They also screen families referred by physicians, nurses, and others. Because the demand for services outstrips available resources, only families with a substantial number of risk factors can participate.

Each new participating family receives a weekly visit from a family support worker. Each of the program's eight home visitors works with approximately 25 families at a time. The worker helps the family cope with any immediate crisis, such as unemployment or substance abuse. The family is linked directly with a pediatrician to ensure that the children receive regular health care. Infants are screened for developmental delays and are immunized on schedule. Pediatricians who have been educated about the program are notified when a child is enrolled in Healthy Start and when a family at risk stops participating.

The Family Support/Healthy Start Program is staffed by several specialized support workers. A child development specialist works with families of children with special needs. To serve other families, one of the program's male family support workers may visit a father to talk specifically about his role in the family. The support workers encourage parents to participate in group activities held each week at the program center located in a neighborhood shopping center.

Over time, parents are encouraged to assume more responsibility for their family's health and well-being. Families can participate in Healthy Start until the child is 5 years old and enters public school.

The Hawaii Family Support/Healthy Start Program provides many home-visitor services for overburdened families of newborns and young children. This program has been very successful in reducing abuse and neglect in families. *What are some examples of the home-visitor services in this program?*

This Honduran child has kwashiorkor. Notice the tell-tale sign of kwashiorkor—a greatly expanded abdomen. *What are some other characteristics of kwashiorkor?*

Toilet Training

marasmus A wasting away of body tissues in the infant's first year, caused by severe protein-calorie deficiency.

kwashiorkor A condition caused by a deficiency in protein in which the child's abdomen and feet become swollen with water; usually appears between 1 to 3 years of age.

Malnutrition in Infancy Early weaning of infants from breast milk to inadequate sources of nutrients, such as unsuitable and unsanitary cow's milk formula, can cause protein deficiency and malnutrition in infants (Kramer, 2003). Something that looks like milk but is not, usually a form of tapioca or rice, is also often substituted for breast milk. In many of the world's developing countries, mothers used to breast feed their infants for at least two years. To become more modern, they stopped breast feeding much earlier and replaced it with bottle feeding. Comparisons of breast fed and bottle fed infants in such countries as Afghanistan, Haiti, Ghana, and Chile document that the mortality rate of bottle fed infants is as much as five times that of breast fed infants (Grant, 1997).

Two life-threatening conditions that can result from malnutrition are marasmus and kwashiorkor. **Marasmus** is caused by a severe protein-calorie deficiency and results in a wasting away of body tissues in the infant's first year. The infant becomes grossly underweight and his or her muscles atrophy. **Kwashiorkor,** caused by severe protein deficiency, usually appears between 1 and 3 years of age. Children with kwashiorkor sometimes appear to be well fed even though they are not because the disease can cause the child's abdomen and feet to swell with water. Kwashiorkor causes a child's vital organs to collect the nutrients that are present and deprive other parts of the body of them. The child's hair also becomes thin, brittle, and colorless, and the child's behavior often becomes listless.

Even if not fatal, severe and lengthy malnutrition is detrimental to physical, cognitive, and social development (Grantham-McGregor, Ani, & Fernald, 2001; Nolen & others, 2002). In one investigation, two groups of extremely malnourished 1-year-old South African infants were studied (Bayley, 1970). The children in one group were given adequate nourishment during the next six years; no intervention took place in the lives of the other group. After the seventh year, the poorly nourished group of children performed much worse on tests of intelligence than did the adequately nourished group. Another study linked the diets of rural Guatemalan infants with their social development at the time they entered elementary school (Barrett, Radke-Yarrow, & Klein, 1982). Children whose mothers had been given nutritious supplements during pregnancy and who themselves had been given more nutritious, high-calorie foods in their first two years of life were more active, more involved, more helpful with their peers, less anxious, and happier than their counterparts who had not been given nutritional supplements. The results suggest how important it is for parents to be attentive to the nutritional needs of their infants.

In further research on early supplementary feeding and children's cognitive development, Ernesto Pollitt and his colleagues (1993) conducted a longitudinal investigation over two decades in rural Guatemala. They found that early nutritional supplements in the form of protein and increased calories can have positive long-term effects on cognitive development. The researchers also found that the relation of nutrition to cognitive performance is moderated both by the time period during which the supplement is given and by the sociodemographic context. For example, the children in the lowest socioeconomic groups benefited more than did the children in higher socioeconomic groups. Although there still was a positive nutritional influence when supplementation began after 2 years of age, the effect on cognitive development was less powerful.

To adequately develop physically, as well as cognitively and socioemotionally, children need a nurturant, supportive environment (Chopra, 2003). One individual who has stood out as an advocate of caring for children is T. Berry Brazelton, who is featured in the Careers in Life-Span Development insert.

Toilet Training

The ability to control elimination depends on both muscular maturation and motivation (Schum & others, 2001; Sun & Rugolotto, 2004). Children must be able to control their muscles to eliminate at the appropriate time, and they must want to eliminate in the toilet or potty, rather than in their diapers or pants. Many toddlers are physically unable to control elimination at 2 years of age. When toilet training is initiated, it should be accomplished in a warm, relaxed, supportive manner (Michel, 2000; Weaver & Dobson, 2004).

Many parents today are being encouraged to use a "readiness" approach to toilet training—that is, wait until children show signs that they are ready for toilet training. Pediatricians note that this approach delays toilet training until an older age today more than in earlier generations (AAP, 2001; Blum, Taubman, & Nemeth, 2004). One recent study of almost 500 U.S. children found that 50 percent of the girls were toilet trained by 35 months and 50 percent of the boys by 39 months (Schum & others, 2001). In another recent study, earlier toilet training was not associated with constipation, stool withholding, or stool toileting refusal (Blum, Taubman, & Nemeth, 2003). However, initiation of intensive training before 27 months of age was not related to earlier completion of toilet training, suggesting little benefit in beginning intensive toilet training prior to this age. Also, a recent survey of pediatricians found that less than 30 percent recommended an early, intense toilet training effort (Polaha, Warzak, & Dittmer-Memahon, 2002).

However, some developmentalists argue that delaying toilet training until the twos and threes can make it a battleground because many children at these ages are pushing so strongly for autonomy. Another argument is that late toilet training can be difficult for children who go to day care, because older children in diapers or training pants can be stigmatized by peers.

Careers in Life-Span Development

T. Berry Brazelton, Pediatrician

T. Berry Brazelton is America's best-known pediatrician as a result of his numerous books, television appearances, and newspaper and magazine articles about parenting and children's health. He takes a family-centered approach to child development issues and communicates with parents in easy-to-understand ways.

Dr. Brazelton founded the Child Development Unit at Boston Children's Hospital and created the Brazelton Neonatal Behavioral Assessment Scale, a widely used measure of the newborn's health and well-being (which you read about in chapter 4). He also has conducted a number of research studies on infants and children and has been president of the Society for Research in Child Development, a leading research organization.

T. Berry Brazelton, pediatrician, with a young child.

Review and Reflect: Learning Goal 1

1 **Discuss physical growth and development in infancy**

REVIEW

- What are cephalocaudal and proximodistal patterns?
- What changes in height and weight take place in infancy?
- What are some key features of the brain and its development in infancy?
- What changes occur in sleep during infancy?
- What are infants' nutritional needs?
- When should toilet training be instituted?

REFLECT

- What three pieces of advice about the infant's physical development would you want to give a friend who has just had a baby? Why those three?

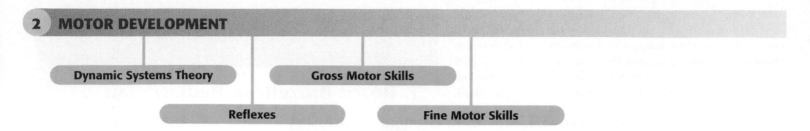

2   MOTOR DEVELOPMENT

> Dynamic Systems Theory
>
> Reflexes
>
> Gross Motor Skills
>
> Fine Motor Skills

The study of motor development has seen a renaissance in the last 15 years with new insights in terms of understanding how infants acquire motor skills. Many of these insights have been fueled by the dynamic systems view.

Dynamic Systems Theory

Developmentalist Arnold Gesell (1934) concluded that his painstaking observations had revealed how people develop their motor skills. He discovered that infants and children develop motor skills in a fixed order and within specific time frames. Most babies do go through a series of developmental milestones such as learning to crawl and learning to walk in a fixed sequence. These observations, according to Gesell, show that motor development comes about through the unfolding of a genetic plan, or *maturation*.

Later studies, however, demonstrated that motor development is not the consequence of nature or nurture alone. In the 1990s, the study of motor development experienced a renaissance as psychologists developed new insights into *how* motor skills develop (Smith & Samuelson, 2003; Thelen & Smith, 1998). One increasingly influential theory is the dynamic systems theory proposed by Esther Thelen.

According to **dynamic systems theory,** infants assemble motor skills for perceiving and acting. Notice that perception and action are coupled according to this theory (Thelen, 1995, 2000, 2001; Thelen & Smith, 1998; Thelen & Whitmeyer, 2005). In order to develop motor skills, infants must perceive something in the environment that motivates them to act and use their perceptions to fine-tune their movements. Motor skills represent solutions to the infant's goals.

How is a motor skill developed according to this theory? When infants are motivated to do something, they create a new motor behavior to complete the new desired act. The new behavior is the result of many converging factors: (1) the development of the nervous system and the body's physical properties, including its possibilities for movement; (2) the goal the child is motivated to reach; and (3) the environmental support for the skill. For example, babies learn to walk only when maturation of the nervous system allows them to control certain leg muscles, when their legs have grown enough to support their weight, and when they want to move.

Mastering a motor skill requires the infant's active efforts to coordinate several components of the skill (Spencer & others, 2000). Infants explore and select possible solutions to the demands of a new task; they assemble adaptive patterns by modifying their current movement patterns. The first step occurs when the infant is motivated by a new challenge—such as the desire to cross a room—and gets into the "ball park" of the task demands by taking a couple of stumbling steps. Then the infant "tunes" these movements to make them smoother and more effective. The tuning is achieved through repeated cycles of action and perception of the consequences of that action. According to the dynamic systems view, even universal milestones, such as crawling, reaching, and walking, are learned through this process of adaptation: Infants modulate their movement patterns to fit a new task by exploring and selecting possible configurations.

Thus, according to dynamic systems theory, motor development is not a passive process in which genes dictate the unfolding of a sequence of skills over time. Rather, the infant actively puts together a skill in order to achieve a goal within the

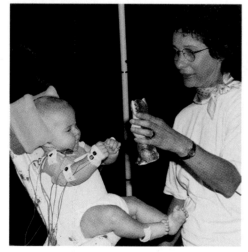

Esther Thelen is shown conducting an experiment to discover how infants learn to control their arms to reach and grasp for objects. A computer device is used to monitor the infant's arm movements and to track muscle patterns. Thelen's research is conducted from a dynamic systems perspective. *What is the nature of this perspective?*

dynamic systems theory The perspective on motor development that seeks to explain how motor behaviors are assembled for perceiving and acting.

constraints set by the infant's body and environment. Nature and nurture, the infant and the environment, are all working together as part of an ever-changing system.

Let's look at two babies—Gabriel and Hannah—to see how dynamic systems theory describes and explains their behavior and development (Thelen & others, 1993). Each child improvises ways to reach out with one of their arms from a sitting position and wrap their fingers around a new toy. Gabriel and Hannah make all sorts of split-second adjustments to keep each reaching motion on course. Their rapid arm extension requires holding their bodies steady so that their arm and upper torso don't plow into the toy. Muscles in their arm and shoulder contract and stretch in a host of combinations and exert a variety of forces. Their arm movements are not exact, machinelike motions that can be precisely planned out in advance but rather adapt to the goal and context at hand—how to pick up the new toy.

As we examine the course of motor development, we will describe how dynamic systems theory applies to some specific skills. To begin, though, we describe how the story of motor development begins with reflexes.

Reflexes

The newborn is not a completely helpless organism. Among other things, he or she has some basic reflexes, which are genetically carried survival mechanisms. For example, newborns naturally hold their breath and contract their throats to keep water out. Reflexes are built-in reactions to stimuli; they govern the newborn's movements, which are automatic and beyond the newborn's control. They allow infants to respond adaptively to their environment before they have had the opportunity to learn. For example, the sucking and rooting reflexes have survival value for newborn mammals, who must find a mother's breast to obtain nourishment. The **sucking reflex** occurs when newborns automatically suck an object placed in their mouth. This reflex enables newborns to get nourishment before they have associated a nipple with food. The **rooting reflex** occurs when the infant's cheek is stroked or the side of the mouth is touched. In response, the infant turns its head toward the side that was touched in an apparent effort to find something to suck. The sucking and rooting reflexes both disappear when the infant is 3 to 4 months old. They are replaced by the infant's voluntary eating.

The **Moro reflex** is a neonatal startle response that occurs in reaction to a sudden, intense noise or movement. When startled, the newborn arches its back, throws back its head, and flings out its arms and legs. Then the newborn rapidly closes its arms and legs to the center of its body. Steady pressure on any part of the infant's body calms the infant after it has been startled. The Moro reflex is believed to be a way of grabbing for support while falling; it would have had survival value for our primate ancestors. This reflex, which is normal in all newborns, also tends to disappear at 3 to 4 months of age.

Some reflexes present in the newborn—coughing, blinking, and yawning, for example—persist throughout life. They are as important for the adult as they are for the infant. Other reflexes, though, disappear several months following birth, as the infant's brain matures, and voluntary control over many behaviors develops. The movements of some reflexes eventually become incorporated into more complex, voluntary actions. One important example is the **grasping reflex,** which occurs when something touches the infant's palms. The infant responds by grasping tightly. By the end of the third month, the grasping reflex diminishes, and the infant shows a more voluntary grasp, which is often produced by visual stimuli. For example, when an infant sees a mobile whirling above its crib, it may reach out and try to grasp it. As its motor development becomes smoother, the infant will grasp objects, carefully manipulate them, and explore their qualities. An overview of the reflexes we have discussed, along with others, is given in figure 5.11.

Sucking is a reflex that serves as the infant's route to nourishment. The sucking capabilities of newborns vary considerably. Some newborns are efficient at forceful

www.mhhe.com/santrockld7o

Esther Thelen's Research

*T*he experiences of the first three years of life are almost entirely lost to us, and when we attempt to enter into a small child's world, we come as foreigners who have forgotten the landscape and no longer speak the native tongue.

—**Selma Fraiberg**
Developmentalist and Child Advocate, 20th Century

sucking reflex A newborn's built-in reaction to automatically suck an object placed in its mouth. The sucking reflex enables the infant to get nourishment before he or she has associated a nipple with food.

rooting reflex A newborn's built-in reaction that occurs when the infant's cheek is stroked or the side of the mouth is touched. In response, the infant turns his or her head toward the side that was touched, in an apparent effort to find something to suck.

Moro reflex A neonatal startle response that occurs in reaction to a sudden, intense noise or movement. When startled, the newborn arches its back, throws its head back, and flings out its arms and legs. Then the newborn rapidly closes its arms and legs to the center of the body.

grasping reflex A neonatal reflex that occurs when something touches the infant's palms. The infant responds by grasping tightly.

Reflex	Stimulation	Infant's Response	Developmental Pattern
Blinking	Flash of light, puff of air	Closes both eyes	Permanent
Babinski	Sole of foot stroked	Fans out toes, twists foot in	Disappears after 9 months to 1 year
Grasping	Palms touched	Grasps tightly	Weakens after 3 months, disappears after 1 year
Moro (startle)	Sudden stimulation, such as hearing loud noise or being dropped	Startles, arches back, throws head back, flings out arms and legs and then rapidly closes them to center of body	Disappears after 3 to 4 months
Rooting	Cheek stroked or side of mouth touched	Turns head, opens mouth, begins sucking	Disappears after 3 to 4 months
Stepping	Infant held above surface and feet lowered to touch surface	Moves feet as if to walk	Disappears after 3 to 4 months
Sucking	Object touching mouth	Sucks automatically	Disappears after 3 to 4 months
Swimming	Infant put face down in water	Makes coordinated swimming movements	Disappears after 6 to 7 months
Tonic neck	Infant placed on back	Forms fists with both hands and usually turns head to the right (sometimes called the "fencer's pose" because the infant looks like it is assuming a fencer's position)	Disappears after 2 months

FIGURE 5.11 Infant Reflexes

sucking and obtaining milk; others are not as adept and get tired before they are full. Most infants take several weeks to establish a sucking style that is coordinated with the way the mother is holding the infant, the way milk is coming out of the bottle or breast, and the infant's sucking speed and temperament.

Pediatrician T. Berry Brazelton (1956) observed infants for more than a year to determine the incidence of their sucking when they were nursing and how their sucking changed as they grew older. Over 85 percent of the infants engaged in considerable sucking behavior unrelated to feeding. They sucked their finger, their fists, and pacifiers. By the age of 1 year, most had stopped the sucking behavior. However, as many as 40 percent of children continue to suck their thumbs after they have started school (Kessen, Haith, & Salapatek, 1970). Most developmentalists do not attach a great deal of significance to this behavior and are not aware of parenting strategies that might contribute to it. Individual differences in children's biological makeup may be involved to some degree in the continuation of sucking behavior.

Gross Motor Skills

Ask any parents about their baby, and sooner or later you are likely to hear about one or more motor milestones, such as "Cassandra just learned to crawl," "Jesse is finally sitting alone," or "Angela took her first step last week." It is no wonder that parents proudly announce such milestones. They reflect the transformation of babies from being unable to lift their heads to being able to grab things off the grocery store shelf, to chase a cat, and to participate actively in the family's social life (Thelen, 1995, 2000). These milestones are reached through the development of gross motor skills.

Gross motor skills involve large-muscle activities, such as moving one's arms and walking. How do gross motor skills develop through the human life span?

gross motor skills Motor skills that involve large-muscle activities, such as walking.

The Development of Posture Gross motor skills, as well as many other activities, require postural control (Adolph, 2002, 2005; Thelen, 1995, 2000). Infants need to control their heads to stabilize their gaze and to track moving objects.

Newborn infants cannot voluntarily control their posture. Within a few weeks, though, they can hold their heads erect, and soon they can lift their heads while prone. By 2 months of age, babies can sit while supported on a lap or an infant seat, but they cannot sit independently until 6 or 7 months of age. Standing also develops gradually across the first year of life. By about 8 months of age, infants usually learn to pull themselves up and hold on to a chair, and they often can stand alone by 10 to 12 months of age.

In Thelen's (1995, 2000) view, posture refers to more than just holding the body still and straight, however. Posture, like other movements, is a dynamic process that is linked with several sensory modalities: proprioception from the skin, joints, and muscles; vestibular organs in the inner ear that regulate balance and equilibrium; and cues from vision and hearing (Spencer & others, 2000).

Learning to Walk   Locomotion and postural control are closely linked, especially in walking upright (Adolph, 2005; Adolph, Vereijken, & Shrout, 2003; Berger & Adolph, 2003). Walking upright requires balancing on one leg while swinging the other leg forward and simultaneously shifting the weight from one leg to the other (Thelen, 2000).

Although infants usually learn to walk about their first birthday, the neural pathways that control the leg alternation component of walking are in place from a very early age, possibly even at birth or before. Infants engage in frequent alternating kicking movements when they are lying on their backs throughout the first 6 months of life. Also when 1- to 2-month-olds are given support with their feet in contact with a motorized treadmill, they show well-coordinated, alternating steps.

If infants can produce forward stepping movements so early, why does it take them so long to learn to walk? Because the key skills in learning to walk require so many concurrent movements, infants need about a year to solve this difficult biomechanical problem.

In learning to locomote, infants learn what kinds of places and surfaces afford safe locomotion (Adolph, 2005; Adolph, Weise, & Marin, 2003). Karen Adolph's (1997) research investigated how experienced and inexperienced crawling infants and walking infants descend steep slopes (see figure 5.12). Newly crawling infants, who averaged about 8½ months in age, rather indiscriminately went down the steep slopes,

Newly crawling infant

Experienced walker

FIGURE 5.12 The Role of Experience in Crawling and Walking Infants' Judgments of Whether to Go Down a Slope
Karen Adolph (1997) found that locomotor experience rather than age was the primary predictor of adaptive responding on slopes of varying steepness. Newly crawling and walking infants could not judge the safety of the various slopes. With experience, they learned to avoid slopes where they would fall. When expert crawlers began to walk, they again made mistakes and fell, even though they had judged the same slope accurately when crawling. Adolph referred to this as the *specificity of learning* because it does not transfer across crawling and walking.

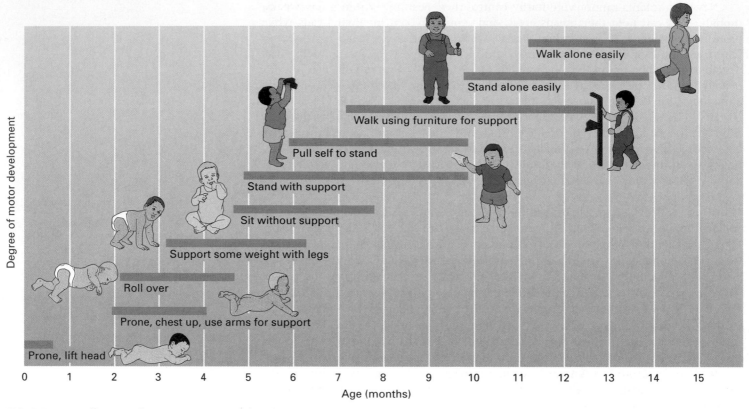

FIGURE 5.13 Milestones in Gross Motor Development

often falling in the process (with their mothers next to the slope to catch them). However, with further weeks of practice, the crawling babies became more adept at judging which slopes were too steep to crawl down and which ones they could navigate safely. Likewise, newly walking infants were unable to judge the safety of the various slopes but experienced infant walkers accurately matched locomotor skills with the steepness of the slopes. They rarely fell downhill, either refusing to go down the steep slopes or going down backward in a cautious manner. Experienced walkers perceptually assessed the situation—looking, swaying, touching, and thinking before they moved down the slope. With experience both the crawlers and the walkers learned to avoid the risky slopes whereon they would fall by integrating perceptual information with the development of new motor behaviors. In this research, we again see the importance of perceptual-motor coupling in the development of motor skills.

Practice is especially important in learning to walk (Adolph, 2005). "Thousands of daily walking steps, each step slightly different from the last because of variations in the terrain and the continually varying biomechanical constraints on the body, may help infants to identify the relevant combinations of . . . strength and balance" required to improve their walking skill (Adolph, Vereijken, & Shrout, 2003, p. 495).

Figure 5.13 summarizes important accomplishments in gross motor skills during the first year, culminating in the ability to walk easily. These motor accomplishments bring increasing independence. Older infants can explore their environment more extensively and initiate interaction with caregivers and peers more readily than when they were younger.

The timing of these milestones varies by as much as two to four months, especially among older infants, and experiences can modify the onset of these motor accomplishments. Also, in some instances, the sequence does not always hold. For example, many American infants do not crawl on their belly or their hands and knees. They may discover an idiosyncratic form of locomotion prior to walking such as rolling, or they might never locomote until they get upright (Adolph, 2002). In the African Mali tribe, crawling is not even the norm (Bril, 1999).

www.mhhe.com/santrockld10

Developmental Milestones
Karen Adolph's Research

Development in the Second Year In the second year of life, toddlers become more motorically skilled and mobile. No longer content with being in a playpen, they want to move all over the place. Child development experts believe that motor activity during the second year is vital to the child's competent development and that few restrictions, except for safety, should be placed on their motoric adventures (Fraiberg, 1959).

By 13 to 18 months, toddlers can pull a toy attached to a string and use their hands and legs to climb up a number of steps. By 18 to 24 months, toddlers can walk quickly or run stiffly for a short distance, balance on their feet in a squat position while playing with objects on the floor, walk backward without losing their balance, stand and kick a ball without falling, stand and throw a ball, and jump in place.

Can parents give their babies a head start on becoming physically fit and physically talented through structured exercise classes? Physical fitness classes for babies range from passive fare—with adults putting infants through the paces—to programs called "aerobic" because they demand crawling, tumbling, and ball skills. Pediatricians point out that when an adult is stretching and moving an infant's limbs, it is easy for them to go beyond the infant's physical limits without knowing. Pediatricians also recommend that exercise for infants should not be of the intense, aerobic variety. Babies cannot adequately stretch their bodies to achieve aerobic benefits.

Cultural Variations in Guiding Infants' Motor Development Most infancy experts recommend against structured exercise classes for babies, but there are other ways of guiding infants' motor development. Caregivers in some cultures do handle babies vigorously, which might advance motor development.

Mothers in developing cultures tend to stimulate their infants' motor skills more than mothers in more advanced cultures (Hopkins, 1991). For example, Jamaican mothers regularly massage their infants and stretch their arms and legs; this practice is linked to advanced motor development (Hopkins, 1991). Mothers in the Gusii culture of Kenya also encourage vigorous movement in their babies (Hopkins & Westra, 1988). We can only speculate about the reasons for this cultural difference. Perhaps this stimulation in developing countries improves the infants' chances of survival, or perhaps caregivers recognize that motor skills are required for important jobs in the culture.

Do these cultural variations make a difference in the infant's motor development? When caregivers provide babies with physical guidance by physically handling them in special ways, such as stroking, massaging, or stretching, or by giving

> *A baby is an angel whose wings decrease as his legs increase.*
> —FRENCH PROVERB

 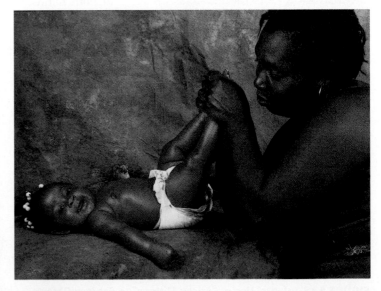

(Left) In the Algonquin culture in Quebec, Canada, babies are strapped to a cradle board for much of their infancy. **(Right)** In Jamaica, mothers massage and stretch their infants' arms and legs. *To what extent do cultural variations in infants' activities influence the time at which they reach motor milestones?*

them opportunities for exercise, the infants often attain motor milestones earlier than infants whose caregivers have not provided these physical activities. For example, Jamaican mothers expect their infants to sit and walk alone 2 to 3 months earlier than English mothers do (Hopkins & Westra, 1990).

Nonetheless, even when infants' activity is restricted, they still often develop normal motor skills. For example, Algonquin infants in Quebec, Canada, spend much of their first year strapped to a cradleboard. Despite their inactivity, these infants still sit up, crawl, and walk within an age range similar to infants in cultures who have had much greater opportunity for activity.

 To view a profile of a 1-year-old and her gross motor development, watch the video "Gross Motor Ability at 1 Year."

Fine Motor Skills

Whereas gross motor skills involve large muscle activity, **fine motor skills** involve finely tuned movements. Grasping a toy or anything that requires finger dexterity demonstrates fine motor skills.

Infants have hardly any control over fine motor skills at birth, but they have many components of what will become finely coordinated arm, hand, and finger movements (Rosenblith, 1992). A significant achievement in their interactions with their surroundings comes with the onset of reaching and grasping (Keen, 2005; McCarty & Ashmead, 1999).

For many years it was believed that when infants reach for an object, they must continuously have sight of the hand and the target (White, Castle, & Held, 1964). However, Rachel Clifton and her colleagues (1993) demonstrated that infants do not have to see their own hands in order to reach for an object. They concluded that proprioceptive cues from muscles, tendons, and joints, not sight of the limb, guide reaching by 4-month-old infants.

The development of reaching and grasping becomes more refined during the first two years of life (Keen, 2005). Initially, infants move their shoulders and elbows crudely, but later they move their wrists, rotate their hands, and coordinate their thumb and forefinger.

fine motor skills Motor skills that involve more finely tuned movements, such as finger dexterity.

These coordinated movements are eventually mastered because the infant's grasping system is very flexible. Infants vary their grip on an object depending on its size and shape, as well as the size of their own hands relative to the object's size. Infants grip small objects with their thumb and forefinger (and sometimes their middle finger, too), whereas they grip large objects with all of the fingers of one hand or both hands.

Perceptual-motor coupling is necessary for the infant to coordinate grasping (Keen, 2005). In studies of grasping, age differences have been found in regard to which perceptual system is most likely to be used to coordinate grasping. Four-month-old infants rely greatly on touch to determine how they will grip an object; eight-month-olds are more likely to use vision as a guide (Newell & others, 1989). This developmental change resulted in increased efficiency because vision allows infants to preshape their hands as they reach for an object.

Experience plays a role in reaching and grasping. In one recent study, 3-month-old infants participated in a series of play sessions wearing "sticky mittens" ("mittens with palms that stuck to the edges of toys and allowed the infants to pick up the toys") (Needham, Barrett, & Peterman, 2002, p. 279) (see figure 5.14). Following the mitten sessions, these infants grasped and manipulated objects earlier in their development than a control group of infants who did not receive the "mitten" experience. The experienced infants looked at the objects longer, swatted at them more during visual contact, and were more likely to mouth the objects.

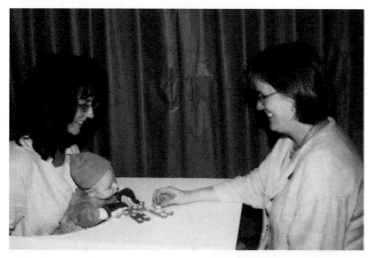

FIGURE 5.14 Infants' Use of "Sticky Mittens" to Explore Objects
Amy Needham (2002) and her colleagues found that "sticky mittens" enhanced young infants' object exploration skills.

Review and Reflect: Learning Goal 2

2 **Describe infants' motor development**

REVIEW

- What is dynamic systems theory?
- What are some reflexes that infants have?
- How do gross motor skills develop in infancy?
- How do fine motor skills develop in infancy?

REFLECT

- Which view of infant motor development do you prefer—the traditional maturational view or the dynamic systems view? Why?

3   SENSORY AND PERCEPTUAL DEVELOPMENT

```
What Are Sensation          Visual Perception          Intermodal Perception
and Perception?

        The Ecological View          Other Senses          Perceptual-Motor Coupling
```

Right now, I am looking at my computer screen to make sure the words are being printed accurately as I am typing them. My perceptual and motor skills are working together. Recall that even control of posture uses information from the senses. And when people grasp an object, they use perceptual information about the object to adjust their motions.

How do these sensations and perceptions develop? Can a newborn see? Do infants feel pain? If so, what can it perceive? What about the other senses—hearing, smell, taste, and touch? What are they like in the newborn, and how do they develop? Can an infant put together information from two modalities, such as sight and sound? These are among the intriguing questions that we will explore in this section.

What Are Sensation and Perception?

How does a newborn know that her mother's skin is soft rather than rough? How does a 5-year-old know what color his hair is? How does a 10-year-old know that a firecracker is louder than a cat's meow? Infants and children "know" these things because of information that comes through the senses. Without vision, hearing, touch, taste, smell, and other senses, we would be isolated from the world; we would live in dark silence, a tasteless, colorless, feelingless void.

Sensation occurs when information interacts with sensory *receptors*—the eyes, ears, tongue, nostrils, and skin. The sensation of hearing occurs when sound waves are collected by the outer ear and transmitted through the bones of the inner ear to the auditory nerve. The sensation of vision occurs as rays of light contact the eyes, become focused on the retina, and are transmitted by the optic nerve to the visual centers of the brain.

Perception is the interpretation of what is sensed. The sound waves that contact the ears may be interpreted as either noise or musical sounds, for example. The physical energy transmitted to the retina of the eye may be interpreted as a particular color, pattern, or shape.

sensation The product of the interaction between information and the sensory receptors—the eyes, ears, tongue, nostrils, and skin.

perception The interpretation of what is sensed.

Newborns' Senses
Richard Aslin's Research
Leslie Cohen's Research
Albert Yonas' Research
International Society on
Infant Studies

The Ecological View

For the past several decades, much of the research on perceptual development in infancy has been guided by the ecological view of Eleanor and James J. Gibson (E. Gibson, 1969, 1989, 2001; J. Gibson, 1966, 1979). They argue that we do not have to assemble bits and pieces of data from sensations and build up representations of the world in our minds. The environment itself is rich with information; our perceptual system selects from that rich output.

According to the Gibsons' **ecological view,** we directly perceive information that exists in the world around us. Perception brings us into contact with the environment to interact with and adapt to it. Perception is designed for action. Perception gives people such information as when to duck, when to turn their bodies through a narrow passageway, and when to put their hands up to catch something.

In the Gibsons' view, all objects have **affordances,** which provide opportunities for interaction with the objects to perform specific activities. A pot may afford a chef something to cook with and may afford a toddler something to bang. Adults immediately know whether a chair is appropriate for sitting, a surface is safe for walking, or an object is within reach. We directly and accurately perceive these affordances by sensing information from the environment—the light or sound reflecting from the surfaces of the world—and from our own bodies through receptors in the muscles, joints, and skin, among others.

Through perceptual development, children become more efficient at discovering and using affordances. An important developmental question is, What affordances can infants or children detect and use? In one study, for example, when babies who could walk were faced with a squishy waterbed, they stopped and explored it, then chose to crawl rather than walk across it (Gibson & others, 1987). They combined perception and action to adapt to the demands of the task.

Similarly, as we described earlier in the section on motor development, infants who were just learning to crawl or just learning to walk were less cautious when confronted with a steep slope than experienced crawlers or walkers were (Adolph, 1997; Adolph & Avolio, 2000). The more experienced crawlers and walkers perceived that a slope *affords* the possibility for not only faster locomotion but also for falling. Again, infants coupled perception and action to make a decision about what do in their environment.

Studying the infant's perception has not been an easy task. The Research in Life-Span Development interlude describes some of the ingenious ways researchers study the newborn's perception.

Research in Life-Span Development

Studying the Newborn's Perception

The creature has poor motor coordination and can move itself only with great difficulty. Although it cries when uncomfortable, it uses few other vocalizations. In fact, it sleeps most of the time, about 16 to 17 hours a day. You are curious about this creature and want to know more about what it can do. You think to yourself, "I wonder if it can see. How can I find out?"

You obviously have a communication problem with the creature. You must devise a way that will allow the creature to "tell" you that it can see. While examining the creature one day, you make an interesting discovery. When you move a large object toward it, it moves its head backward, as if to avoid a collision with the object. The creature's head movement suggests that it has at least some vision.

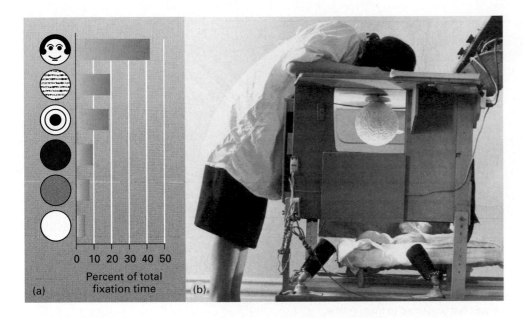

FIGURE 5.15 Fantz' Experiment on Infants' Visual Perception
(*a*) Infants 2 to 3 months old preferred to look at some stimuli more than others. In Fantz' experiment, infants preferred to look at patterns rather than at color or brightness. For example, they looked longer at a face, a piece of printed matter, or a bull's-eye than at red, yellow, or white discs. (*b*) Fantz used a "looking chamber" to study infants' perception of stimuli.

In case you haven't already guessed, the creature you have been reading about is the human infant, and the role you play is that of a researcher interested in devising techniques to learn about the infant's visual perception. After years of work, scientists have developed research methods and tools sophisticated enough to examine the subtle abilities of infants and to interpret their complex actions (Bendersky & Sullivan, 2002; Kellman & Banks, 1998).

Visual Preference Method

Robert Fantz (1963) was a pioneer in the effort to understand the infant's visual perception. Fantz made an important discovery that advanced the ability of researchers to investigate infants' visual perception: Infants look at different things for different lengths of time. Fantz placed infants in a "looking chamber," which had two visual displays on the ceiling above the infant's head. An experimenter viewed the infant's eyes by looking through a peephole. If the infant was fixating on one of the displays, the experimenter could see the display's reflection in the infant's eyes. This allowed the experimenter to determine how long the infant looked at each display. Fantz (1963) found that infants only 2 days old look longer at patterned stimuli, such as faces and concentric circles, than at red, white, or yellow discs. Infants 2 to 3 years old preferred to look at patterns—a face, a piece of printed matter, or a bull's-eye—longer than at red, yellow, or white discs (see figure 5.15). Fantz' research method—studying whether infants can distinguish one stimulus from another by measuring the length of time they attend to different stimuli—is referred to as the **visual preference method.**

Habituation and Dishabituation

Another way that researchers have studied infant perception is to present a stimulus (such as a sight or a sound) a number of times. If the infant reduces its attention to the stimulus after a number of presentations, it indicates that the infant is no longer interested in the stimulus. This research method is referred to as **habituation**—decreased responsiveness to a stimulus after repeated presentations of the stimulus. **Dishabituation** is the recovery of a habituated response after a change in stimulation. Among the measures researchers use to study whether habituation is occurring are sucking behavior (sucking behavior stops when the young infant attends to a novel object), heart and respiration rates, and the length of time

visual preference method A method used to determine whether infants can distinguish one stimulus from another by measuring the length of time they attend to different stimuli.

habituation Decreased responsiveness to a stimulus after repeated presentation of the stimulus.

dishabituation Recovery of a habituated response after a change in stimulation.

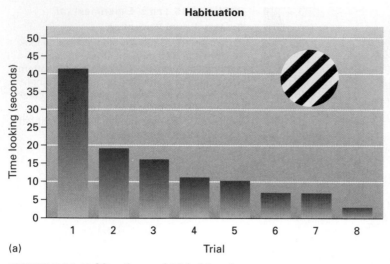

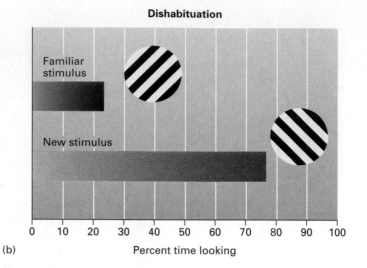

FIGURE 5.16 Habituation and Dishabituation

In the first part of one study, 7-hour-old newborns were shown the stimulus in (*a*). As indicated, the newborns looked at it an average of 41 seconds when it was first presented to them (Slater, Morison, & Somers, 1988). Over seven more presentations of the stimulus, they looked at it less and less. In the second part of the study, infants were presented with both the familiar stimulus to which they had just become habituated to (*a*) and a new stimulus (shown in *b*, which was rotated 90 degrees). The newborns looked at the new stimulus three times as much as the familiar stimulus.

the infant looks at an object. Newborn infants can habituate to repeated sights, sounds, smells, or touches (Rovee-Collier, 2002). Figure 5.16 shows the results of one study of habituation and dishabituation with newborns (Slater, Morison, & Somers, 1988).

Tracking

A valuable technique to determine if an infant can see or hear is called *tracking*. Newborns typically "turn their eyes and heads in the direction of an interesting sound or sight, especially the human voice and face. Many assessments of newborns and infants observe tracking to determine the infant's early visual integrity. Similarly newborns, as well as older infants, show reactions to sounds that are made from objects out of view. A startle is a normal reaction to a loud noise. A reduction in movement and head turning indicate the ability to hear softer sounds" (Bendersky & Sullivan, 2002, pp. 18–19).

Equipment

Videotape equipment allows researchers to investigate elusive behaviors. High-speed computers make it possible to perform complex data analysis in minutes. Other equipment records respiration, heart rate, body movement, visual fixation, and sucking behavior, which provide clues to what the infant is perceiving. For example, some researchers use equipment that detects if a change in infants' respiration follows a change in the pitch of a sound. If so, it suggests that the infants heard the pitch change. Thus, scientists have become ingenious at assessing the development of infants, discovering ways to "interview" them even though they cannot yet talk.

Visual Perception

Some important changes in visual perception with age can be traced to differences in how the eye itself functions over time. These changes in the eye's functioning influence, for example, how clearly an infant can see an object and differentiate its colors.

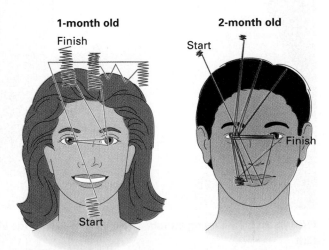

FIGURE 5.17 Visual Acuity During the First Months of Life
The four photographs represent a computer estimation of what a picture of a face looks like to a
1-month-old, 2-month-old, 3-month-old, and 1-year-old (which approximates that of an adult).

Visual Acuity and Color Psychologist William James (1890/1950) called the newborn's perceptual world a "blooming, buzzing confusion." A century later, we can safely
say that he was wrong. Even the newborn perceives a world with some order. That
world, however, is far different than the one perceived by the toddler or the adult.

Just how well can infants see? Newborns cannot see small things that are far
away. The newborn's vision is estimated to be 20/600 on the well-known Snellen
chart, with which you are tested when you have your eyes examined (Banks &
Salapatek, 1983). In other words, an object 20 feet away is only as clear to the newborn as it would be if it were 600 feet away from an adult with normal vision
(20/20). By 6 months of age, though, vision is 20/100 or better, and, by about the
first birthday, the infant's vision approximates that of an adult (Banks & Salapatek,
1983). Figure 5.17 shows a computer estimation of what a picture of a face looks
like to an infant at different ages from a distance of about 6 inches. Notice that the
clarity of the images improves as the infant ages.

The infant's color vision also improves. At birth, babies can distinguish between
green and red (Adams, 1989). Adultlike functioning of all of the eye's color-sensitive
receptors (*cones*) is present by 2 months of age.

Perceiving Patterns What does the world look like to infants? Do they recognize patterns? As we saw in the Research in Life-Span Development interlude,
Robert Fantz (1963) used his "looking chamber" to reveal that infants look at different things for different lengths of time. Even 2- to 3-month-old infants prefer to
look at patterned displays than nonpatterned displays. For example, they
prefer to look at a normal human face rather than one with scrambled
features, and prefer to look at a bull's-eye target or black and white stripes
rather than a plain circle.

Even very young infants soon change the way they gather information from the visual world. By using a special mirror arrangement,
researchers projected an image of human faces in front of infants' eyes so
that the infants' eye movements could be photographed (Maurer &
Salapatek, 1976). Figure 5.18 shows the plotting of eye fixations of a
1-month-old and a 2-month-old infant. Notice that the 2-month-old
scanned a much wider area of the face than the 1-month-old did. The older
infant also spent more time examining the internal details of the face,
whereas the younger infant concentrated on the outer contours of the face.

Perceptual Constancy Some perceptual accomplishments are especially intriguing because they indicate that the infant's perception is better than it should be based on sensory information (Bower, 2002; Slater,
Field, & Hernandez-Reif, 2002). This is the case in *perceptual constancy*, in
which sensory stimulation is changing but perception of the physical

**FIGURE 5.18 How 1- and 2-Month-Old Infants Scan the
Human Face**

world remains constant. Two types of perceptual constancy are size constancy and shape constancy.

Size constancy is the recognition that an object remains the same even though the retinal image of the object changes. The size of an object's image on the retina is not sufficient to determine its actual size. The farther away from us an object is, the smaller its image is on our eyes. For example, a bicycle standing right in front of a child appears smaller than the car parked across the street, even though the bicycle casts a larger image on the child's eyes than the car does.

But what about babies? Do they have size constancy? Researchers have found that babies as young as 3 months of age show size constancy (Bower, 1966; Day & McKenzie, 1973). However, at 3 months of age, this ability is not fully mature. Further progress in perceiving size constancy continues until 10 or 11 years of age (Kellman & Banks, 1998).

Shape constancy is the recognition that an object's shape remains the same even though its orientation to us changes. Look around the room you are in right now. You likely see objects of varying shapes, such as tables and chairs. If you get up and walk around the room, you will see these objects from different sides and angles. Even though your retinal images of the objects change as you walk and look, you will still perceive the objects as the same shape.

Do babies have shape constancy? As with size constancy, researchers have found that babies as young as 3 months of age have shape constancy (Bower, 1966; Day & McKenzie, 1973). Three-month-old infants, however, do not have shape constancy for irregularly shaped objects, such as tilted planes (Cook & Birch, 1984).

Why is it important for infants to develop perceptual constancy early in their lives? If infants did not develop perceptual constancy, each time they saw an object from a different distance or in a different orientation, they would perceive it as a different object. Thus, the development of perceptual constancy allows the infant to perceive its world as stable.

size constancy The recognition that an object remains the same even though the retinal image of the object changes.

shape constancy The recognition that an object's shape remains the same even though its orientation to us changes.

Depth Perception How early can infants perceive depth? To investigate this question, Eleanor Gibson and Richard Walk (1960) conducted a classic experiment. They constructed a miniature cliff with a drop-off covered by glass. The motivation for this experiment arose when Gibson was eating a picnic lunch on the edge of the Grand Canyon. She wondered whether an infant looking over the canyon's rim would perceive the dangerous dropoff and back up. She also was worried that her own two young children would play too close to the canyon's edge and fall off. In their laboratory, Gibson and Walk placed infants on the edge of a visual cliff and had their mothers coax them to crawl onto the glass (see figure 5.19). Most infants would not crawl out on the glass, choosing instead to remain on the shallow side, indicating that they could perceive depth. However, because the 6- to 14-month-old infants had extensive visual experience, this research did not answer the question of whether depth perception is innate.

Exactly how early in life does depth perception develop? This question is difficult to answer. Research with 2- to 4-month-old infants shows differences in heart rate when they are placed directly on the deep side of the visual cliff instead of on the shallow side (Campos, Langer, & Krowitz, 1970). However, an alternative interpretation is that young infants respond to differences in some visual characteristics of the deep and shallow cliffs, with no actual knowledge of depth.

An important contributor to depth perception is *binocular vision*, which involves the fact that we have two eyes separated by several inches that give us slightly different views of the

FIGURE 5.19 Examining Infants' Depth Perception on the Visual Cliff
Eleanor Gibson and Richard Walk (1960) found that most infants would not crawl out on the glass, which indicated that they had depth perception.

world. The brain combines these images so that we see one rather than two views of the world. Newborns do not have binocular vision; it develops at about 3 to 4 months of age and it provides a powerful cue to depth (Slater, Field, & Hernandez-Reif, 2002).

Visual Expectations   Infants not only see forms and figures at an early age but also develop expectations about future events in their world by the time they are 3 months of age (Adler & Haith, 2003). Marshall Haith and his colleagues (Canfield & Haith, 1991; Haith, Hazen, & Goodman, 1988) studied whether babies would form expectations about where an interesting picture would appear. The pictures were presented to the infants in either a regular alternating sequence (such as left, right, left, right) or an unpredictable sequence (such as right, right, left, right). When the sequence was predictable, the 3-month-old infants began to anticipate the location of the picture, looking at the side on which it was expected to appear. The young infants formed this visual expectation in less than one minute. However, younger infants did not develop expectations about where a picture would be presented.

Elizabeth Spelke (1991, 2000; Spelke & Hespos, 2001) also has demonstrated that young infants form visual expectations. She placed babies before a puppet stage and showed them a series of unexpected actions—for example, one ball seemed to roll through a solid barrier, another seemed to leap between two platforms, and a third appeared to hang in midair (Spelke, 1979). Spelke measured the babies' looking times and recorded longer intervals for unexpected than expected actions. She concluded that, by 4 months of age, even though infants do not yet have the ability to talk about objects, move around objects, manipulate objects, or even see objects with high resolution, they can recognize the solidity of objects and the continuity of objects. However, she has found that at 4 months of age, infants do not expect an object to obey gravitational constraints (Spelke & others, 1992).

By 6 to 8 months, infants have learned to perceive gravity and support—that an object hanging on the end of a table should fall, that ball-bearings will travel farther when rolled down a longer rather than a shorter ramp, and that cup handles will not fall when attached to a cup (Slater, Field, & Hernandez-Reif, 2002). As infants develop, their experiences and actions on objects help them to understand physical laws.

Other Senses

Considerable development also takes place in other sensory systems during infancy. We will explore development in hearing, touch and pain, smell, and taste.

Hearing   Can the fetus hear? What kind of changes in hearing take place in infancy?

During the last two months of pregnancy, the fetus can hear sounds as it nestles in its mother's womb: It hears the mother's voice, music, and so on (Kisilevsky, 1995; Smith, Muir, & Kisilevsky, 2001). Two psychologists wanted to find out if a fetus that heard Dr. Seuss' classic story *The Cat in the Hat* while still in the mother's womb would prefer hearing the story after birth (DeCasper & Spence, 1986). During the last months of pregnancy, sixteen women read *The Cat in the Hat* to their fetuses. Then shortly after they were born, the mothers read either *The Cat in the Hat* or a story with a different rhyme and pace, *The King, the Mice and the Cheese* (which was not read to them during prenatal development). The infants sucked on a nipple in a different way when the mothers read the two stories, suggesting that the infants recognized the pattern and tone of *The Cat in the Hat* (see figure 5.20). This study illustrates that an infant's brain has a remarkable ability to learn even before birth and reflects the ingenuity of researchers in assessing development.

A recent study examined the ability of human fetuses to recognize their own mother's voice (Kisilevsky & others, 2003). Sixty term fetuses (mean gestational age, 38.4 weeks) were assigned to one of two conditions in which they were exposed to a tape recording of their mother or a female stranger reading a passage. Voice stimuli

FIGURE 5.20 Hearing in the Womb
(*a*) Pregnant mothers read *The Cat in the Hat* to their fetuses during the last few months of pregnancy. (*b*) When they were born, the babies preferred listening to a recording of their mothers reading *The Cat in the Hat*, as evidenced by their sucking on a nipple that produced this recording, rather than another story, *The King, the Mice and the Cheese.*

(a)

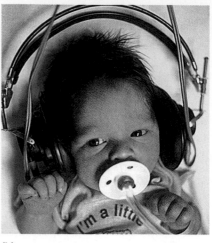

(b)

were delivered through a loudspeaker held just above the mother's abdomen. Fetal heart rate was monitored and increased in response to the mother's voice but decreased in response to the stranger's voice. This finding indicates that experience influences fetal voice processing.

Hearing changes in infancy involve perception of a sound's loudness, pitch, and localization. Immediately after birth, infants cannot hear soft sounds quite as well as adults can; a stimulus must be louder to be heard by a newborn than by an adult (Trehub & others, 1991). For example, an adult can hear a whisper from about 4 to 5 feet away, but a newborn requires that sounds be closer to a normal conversational level to be heard at that distance. Infants are also less sensitive to the pitch of a sound than adults are. *Pitch* is the perception of the frequency of a sound. A soprano voice sounds high pitched, a bass voice low pitched. Infants are less sensitive to low-pitched sounds and are more likely to hear high-pitched sounds (Aslin, Jusczyk, & Pisoni, 1998). By 2 years of age, infants have considerably improved their ability to distinguish sounds with different pitches. It is important to be able to *localize* sounds, detecting their origins. Even newborns can determine the general location from where a sound is coming but by 6 months of age, they are more proficient at localizing sounds; this ability continues to improve in the second year (Litovsky & Ashmead, 1997; Morrongiello, Fenwick, & Chance, 1990).

Newborns are especially sensitive to the sounds of human speech. They will suck more rapidly on a nipple in order to listen to some sounds rather than others. Their sucking behavior indicates that they prefer a recording of their mother's voice to the voice of an unfamiliar woman, their mother's native language to a foreign language, and the classical music of Beethoven to the rock music of Aerosmith (Flohr & others, 2001; Spence & DeCasper, 1987).

Touch and Pain   Do newborns respond to touch? Can they feel pain?

Newborns do respond to touch. A touch to the cheek produces a turning of the head; a touch to the lips produces sucking movements.

An important ability that develops in infancy is to connect information about vision with information about touch. One-year-olds clearly can do this, and it appears that 6-month-olds can, too (Acredolo & Hake, 1982). Whether still-younger infants can coordinate vision and touch is yet to be determined.

If and when you have a son and need to consider whether he should be circumcised, the issue of an infant's pain perception probably will become important to you. Circumcision is usually performed on young boys about the third day after birth. Will your young son experience pain if he is circumcised when he is 3 days old? An investigation by Megan

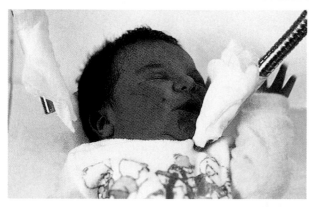

FIGURE 5.21 Newborns' Preference for the Smell of Their Mother's Breast Pad

In the experiment by MacFarlane (1975), 6-day-old infants preferred to smell their mother's breast pad rather than a clean one that had never been used, but 2-day-old infants did not show the preference, indicating that this odor preference requires several days of experience to develop.

Gunnar and her colleagues (1987) found that newborn infant males cried intensely during circumcision. The circumcised infant also displays amazing resiliency. Within several minutes after the surgery, they can nurse and interact in a normal manner with their mothers. And, if allowed to, the newly circumcised newborn drifts into a deep sleep, which seems to serve as a coping mechanism.

For many years, doctors performed operations on newborns without anesthesia. This practice was accepted because of the dangers of anesthesia and because of the supposition that newborns do not feel pain. As researchers demonstrated that newborns can feel pain, the practice of operating on newborns without anesthesia is being challenged. Anesthesia now is used in some circumcisions.

Smell As with the other senses, most research on developmental changes in smell focuses on early infancy and aging. Newborns can differentiate odors. The expressions on their faces seem to indicate that they like the way vanilla and strawberry smell but do not like the way rotten eggs and fish smell (Steiner, 1979). In one investigation, 6-day-old infants who were breast fed showed a clear preference for smelling their mother's breast pad (MacFarlane, 1975) (see figure 5.21). However, when they were 2 days old, they did not show this preference (compared with a clean breast pad), indicating that they require several days of experience to recognize this odor.

Taste Sensitivity to taste might be present even before birth. When saccharin was added to the amniotic fluid of a near-term fetus, swallowing increased (Windle, 1940). In one study, even at only 2 hours of age, babies made different facial expressions when they tasted sweet, sour, and bitter solutions (Rosenstein & Oster, 1988) (see figure 5.22). At about 4 months of age, infants begin to prefer salty tastes, which as newborns they had found to be aversive (Harris, Thomas, & Booth, 1990).

Intermodal Perception

Imagine yourself playing basketball or tennis. You are experiencing many visual inputs: the ball coming and going, other players moving around, and so on. However, you are experiencing many auditory inputs as well: the sound of the ball bouncing or being hit, the grunts and groans, and so on. There is good correspondence between much of the visual and auditory information: When you see the ball bounce, you hear a bouncing sound; when a player stretches to hit a ball, you hear a groan.

We live in a world of objects and events that can be seen, heard, and felt. When mature observers simultaneously look at and listen to an event, they experience a unitary episode. All of this is so commonplace that it scarcely seems worth mentioning. But consider the task of very young infants with little practice at perceiving. Can they put vision and sound together as precisely as adults do?

Intermodal perception involves integrating information from two or more sensory modalities, such as vision and hearing. To test intermodal perception, Elizabeth Spelke (1979) showed 4-month-old infants two films simultaneously. In each film, a puppet jumped up and down, but in one of the films the soundtrack matched the puppet's dancing movements; in the other film, it did not. By measuring the infant's gaze, Spelke found that the infants looked more at the puppet whose actions were synchronized with the sound track, suggesting that they recognized the visual-sound correspondence. Young infants can also coordinate visual-auditory information involving people. In one study, as early as at 3½ months old, infants looked more at their mother when they also heard her voice and longer at their father when they also heard his voice (Spelke & Owsley, 1979).

Might auditory-visual relations be coordinated even in newborns? Newborns do turn their eyes and their head toward the sound of a voice or rattle when the sound is maintained for several seconds (Clifton & others, 1981), but the newborn can localize a sound and look at an object only in a crude way (Bechtold, Bushnell, & Salapatek, 1979). Improved accuracy at auditory-visual coordination likely requires a sharpening through experience with visual and auditory stimuli.

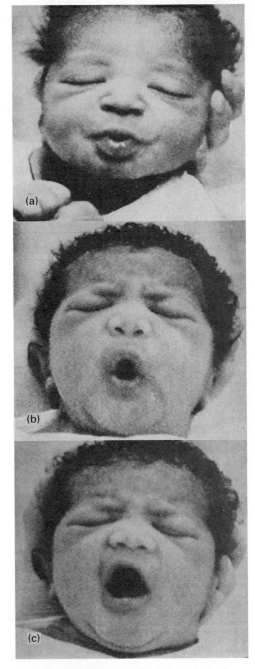

(a)

(b)

(c)

FIGURE 5.22 Newborns' Facial Responses to Basic Tastes
Facial expressions elicited by (*a*) a sweet solution, (*b*) a sour solution, and (*c*) a bitter solution.

intermodal perception The ability to relate and integrate information from two or more sensory modalities, such as vision and hearing.

In sum, crude exploratory forms of intermodal perception exist in newborns. These exploratory forms of intermodal perception become sharpened with experience in the first year of life (Lewkowicz, 2003). In the first six months, infants have difficulty connecting sensory input from different modes, but in the second half of the first year they show an increased ability to make this connection mentally. Thus, babies are born into the world with some innate abilities to perceive relations among sensory modalities, but their intermodal abilities improve considerably through experience (Banks, 2005). As with all aspects of development, in perceptual development, nature and nurture interact and cooperate (Condry, Smith, & Spelke, 2001; Lickliter & Bahrick, 2000).

Perceptual-Motor Coupling

As we come to the end of this chapter, we return to the important theme of perceptual-motor coupling. The distinction between perceiving and doing has been a time-honored tradition in psychology. However, a number of experts on perceptual and motor development question whether this distinction makes sense (Bertenthal, 2005; Gibson, 2001; Keen, 2005; Thelen & Whitmeyer, 2005). The main thrust of research in Esther Thelen's dynamic systems approach is to explore how people assemble motor behaviors for perceiving and acting. The main theme of the ecological approach of Eleanor and James J. Gibson is to discover how perception guides action. Action can guide perception and perception can guide action. Only by moving one's eyes, head, hands, and arms and by moving from one location to another can an individual fully experience his or her environment and learn how to adapt to it. Perception and action are coupled.

Babies, for example, continually coordinate their movements with perceptual information to learn how to maintain balance, reach for objects in space, and move across various surfaces and terrains (Thelen, 2000; Thelen & Whitmeyer, 2005). They are motivated to move by what they perceive. Consider the sight of an attractive toy across the room. In this situation, infants must perceive the current state of their bodies and learn how to use their limbs to reach the toy. Although their movements at first are awkward and uncoordinated, babies soon learn to select patterns that are appropriate for reaching their goals.

Equally important is the other part of the perception-action coupling. That is, action educates perception. For example, watching an object while exploring it manually helps infants to discriminate its properties of texture, size, and hardness. Locomoting in the environment teaches babies about how objects and people look from different perspectives, or whether surfaces will support their weight. Individuals perceive in order to move and move in order to perceive. Perceptual and motor development do not occur in isolation from one another but instead are coupled (Bornstein, Arterberry, & Mash, 2005; Thelen & Whitmeyer, 2005).

Review and Reflect: Learning Goal 3

 3 **Explain sensory and perceptual development in infancy**

REVIEW

- What are sensation and perception?
- What is the ecological view of perception?
- How does visual perception develop in infancy?
- How do hearing, touch and pain, smell, and taste develop in infancy?
- What is intermodal perception?
- How is perceptual-motor development coupled?

REFLECT

- How much sensory stimulation should caregivers provide for infants? A little? A lot? Could an infant be given too much sensory stimulation? Explain.

Reach Your Learning Goals

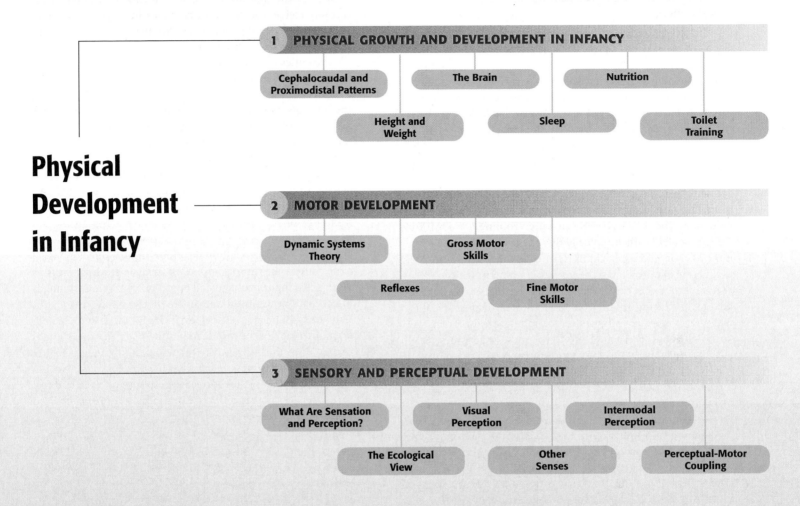

Physical Development in Infancy

1 PHYSICAL GROWTH AND DEVELOPMENT IN INFANCY

- Cephalocaudal and Proximodistal Patterns
- The Brain
- Nutrition
- Height and Weight
- Sleep
- Toilet Training

2 MOTOR DEVELOPMENT

- Dynamic Systems Theory
- Gross Motor Skills
- Reflexes
- Fine Motor Skills

3 SENSORY AND PERCEPTUAL DEVELOPMENT

- What Are Sensation and Perception?
- Visual Perception
- Intermodal Perception
- The Ecological View
- Other Senses
- Perceptual-Motor Coupling

Summary

1 Learning Goal 1: Discuss physical growth and development in infancy

- The cephalocaudal pattern is the sequence in which growth proceeds from top to bottom. The proximodistal pattern is the sequence in which growth starts at the center of the body and moves toward the extremities.

- The average North American newborn is 20 inches long and weighs $7\frac{1}{2}$ pounds. Infants grow about 1 inch per month in the first year and nearly triple their weight by their first birthday. The rate of growth slows in the second year.

- One of the most dramatic changes in the brain in the first two years of life is dendritic spreading, which increases the connections between neurons. Myelination, which speeds the conduction of nerve impulses, continues through infancy and even into adolescence. The cerebral cortex has two hemispheres (left and right). Lateralization refers to specialization of function in one hemisphere or the other. Research with animals suggests that the environment plays a key role in early brain development. Neural connections are formed early in an infant's life. Before birth, genes mainly direct neurons to different locations. After birth, the inflowing stream of sights, sounds, smells, touches, language, and eye contact help shape the brain's neural connections.

- Newborns usually sleep 16 to 17 hours a day. By 4 months of age, many American infants approach adultlike sleeping patterns. REM sleep—during which dreaming occurs—is present more in early infancy than in childhood and adulthood. Sleeping arrangements for infants vary across cultures. In America, infants are more likely to sleep alone than in many other cultures. Some experts believe shared sleeping can lead to sudden infant death syndrome (SIDS), a condition that occurs when a sleeping infant suddenly stops breathing and dies without an apparent cause.

- Infants need to consume about 50 calories per day for each pound they weigh. The growing consensus is that breast feeding is superior to bottle feeding. Severe infant malnutrition is still prevalent in many parts of the world. A special concern in impoverished countries is early weaning from breast milk.

- Toilet training is expected to be attained by about 3 years of age in North America. Toilet training should be carried out in a relaxed, supportive manner.

167

Learning Goal 2: Describe infants' motor development

- The study of motor development has experienced a renaissance in recent years. Much of this renaissance is captured by Thelen's dynamic systems theory, which seeks to explain how motor behaviors are assembled for perceiving and acting. Perception and action are coupled. According to this theory, motor skills are the result of many converging factors, such as the development of the nervous system, the body's physical properties and its movement possibilities, the goal the child is motivated to reach, and environmental support for the skill. In the dynamic systems view, motor development is far more complex than the result of a genetic blueprint.

- Reflexes—automatic movements—govern the newborn's behavior. They include the sucking, rooting, and Moro reflexes—all of which typically disappear after three to four months. For infants, sucking is an especially important reflex because it provides a means of obtaining nutrition.

- Gross motor skills involve large-muscle activities. Key skills developed during infancy include control of posture and walking. A number of gross motor milestones occur in infancy, although the actual month of these milestones may vary as much as two to four months, especially in older infants. Although infants usually learn to walk by their first birthday, the neural pathways that allow walking begin to form earlier.

- Fine motor skills involve finely tuned movements. The onset of reaching and grasping marks a significant accomplishment, and this becomes more refined during the first two years of life.

 Learning Goal 3: Explain sensory and perceptual development in infancy

- Sensation occurs when information interacts with sensory receptors. Perception is the interpretation of sensation.

- Created by the Gibsons, the ecological view states that we directly perceive information that exists in the world around us. Perception brings people in contact with the environment to interact with and adapt to it. Affordances provide opportunities for interaction offered by objects that are necessary to perform activities.

- Researchers have developed a number of methods to assess the infant's perception, including the visual preference method (which Fantz used to determine young infants' interest in looking at patterned over nonpatterned displays), habituation and dishabituation, and tracking. The infant's visual acuity increases dramatically in the first year of life. In color vision, newborns can distinguish green and red. All three color-sensitive receptors function in adultlike ways by 2 months of age. Young infants systematically scan human faces. By 3 months of age, infants show size and shape constancy. As visual perception develops, infants develop visual expectations. In Gibson and Walk's classic study, infants as young as 6 months of age had depth perception. Crawling is linked with decisions infants make on the visual cliff.

- The fetus can hear several weeks prior to birth. Immediately after birth, newborns can hear, but their sensory threshold is higher than that of adults. Developmental changes in the perception of loudness, pitch, and localization of sound occur during infancy. Newborns can respond to touch and feel pain. Newborns can differentiate odors, and sensitivity to taste may be present before birth.

- Infants as young as 2 months of age have intermodal perception—the ability to relate and integrate information from two or more sensory modalities. Crude, exploratory forms of intermodal perception are present in newborns and become sharpened over the first year of life.

- Perception and action are often not isolated but rather are coupled. Individuals perceive in order to move and move in order to perceive.

Key Terms

cephalocaudal pattern 137	kwashiorkor 148	gross motor skills 152	visual preference method 159
proximodistal pattern 138	dynamic systems theory 150	fine motor skills 156	habituation 159
neuron 138	sucking reflex 151	sensation 157	dishabituation 159
lateralization 141	rooting reflex 151	perception 157	size constancy 162
sudden infant death syndrome (SIDS) 144	Moro reflex 151	ecological view 158	shape constancy 162
	grasping reflex 151	affordances 158	intermodal perception 165
marasmus 148			

Key People

Charles Nelson 140	Karen Adolph 153	Robert Fantz 159	Marshall Haith 163
Mark Rosenzweig 142	Rachel Clifton 156	William James 161	Elizabeth Spelke 163
Ernesto Pollitt 148	Eleanor and James	Richard Walk 162	
T. Berry Brazelton 148	J. Gibson 158		
Esther Thelen 150			

 **E-Learning Tools**

To help you master the material in this chapter, you'll find a number of valuable study tools on the LifeMap CD-ROM that accompanies this book and on the Online Learning Center for *Life-Span Development*, tenth edition, at www.mhhe.com/santrockld10.

Video Clips

In the margins of this book there are icons directing you to the LifeMap CD-ROM that accompanies the book. There you'll find two videos for chapter 5. The first video is called "Nutritional Benefits of Breast Feeding." Is breast feeding better for the infant than bottle feeding? In this segment, a dietician details some of the benefits of breast feeding. The second video is called "Gross Motor Ability at 1 Year." A profile of one-year-old Cindy illustrates some of the advances in gross motor skills that have occurred during the first year of life.

Self-Assessment

Connect to www.mhhe.com/santrockld10 to examine your understanding of physical development in infancy by completing the self-assessment, *My Beliefs About Nurturing a Baby's Physical Development.*

Taking It to the Net

Connect to www.mhhe.com/santrockld10 to research the answers to these questions.

1. Beginning in the 1990s, a number of products were marketed to parents based on widely publicized research findings about how certain kinds of music could influence a child's cognitive development (popularly known as the "Mozart Effect"). Ben is a marketing manager for a company that publishes these products. He feels it's his responsibility to understand how these claims can be supported by what we currently know about child cognitive development. He would like to promote a CD recording of Mozart designed to be played in the nursery without making a glib causal connection between listening to a certain kind of music and a child's intelligence. How might Ben qualify the claims his company makes for the CD?

2. Huy grew up in a traditional Chinese family, where co-sleeping until adolescence was the norm. He sees no problem with allowing his infant daughter to sleep with him and his wife. His wife, Lori, who was born and raised in the United States, is concerned that allowing the baby to sleep in their bed places her at risk for SIDS. Is co-sleeping a significant risk factor for SIDS? What else can Huy and Lori do to reduce the risk?

3. Marianne has landed a part-time job as a nanny for Jack, a two-month old boy. What can Marianne expect to see in terms of the child's sensory and motor development as she observes and interacts with Jack over the next six months?

Health and Well-Being, Parenting, and Education Exercises

Build your decision-making skills by trying your hand at the health and well-being, parenting, and education exercises.

Connect to www.mhhe.com/santrockld10 to research the answers and complete the exercises.

CHAPTER 6

I wish I could travel down by the road that crosses the baby's mind where reason makes kites of her laws and flies them. . . .

—RABINDRANATH TAGORE
Bengali Poet, Essayist, 20th Century

Cognitive Development in Infancy

Learning Goals

1 Summarize the cognitive processes in Piaget's theory and the stage of sensorimotor development

2 Describe how infants learn and remember

3 Discuss the assessment of intelligence in infancy

4 Explain language development in infancy

Images of Life-Span Development
Laurent, Lucienne, and Jacqueline

The Swiss psychologist Jean Piaget was a meticulous observer of his three children—Laurent, Lucienne, and Jacqueline. His observations of their behavior fill his books on cognitive development. The following examples provide a glimpse of Piaget's detailed observations of his children's cognitive development in infancy (Piaget, 1952):

- At 21 days of age, "Laurent found his thumb after three attempts: prolonged sucking begins each time. But, once he has been placed on his back, he does not know how to coordinate the movement of the arms with that of the mouth and his hands draw back even when his lips are seeking them" (p. 27).
- During the third month, thumb sucking becomes less important to Laurent because of new visual and auditory interests. But, when he cries, his thumb goes to the rescue.
- Toward the end of Lucienne's fourth month, while she is lying in her crib, Piaget hangs a doll above her feet. Lucienne thrusts her feet at the doll and makes it move. "Afterward, she looks at her motionless foot for a second, then recommences. There is no visual control of her foot, for the movements are the same when Lucienne only looks at the doll or when I place the doll over her head. On the other hand, the tactile control of the foot is apparent: after the first shakes, Lucienne makes slow foot movements as though to grasp and explore" (p. 159).
- At 11 months, "Jacqueline is seated and shakes a little bell. She then pauses abruptly in order to delicately place the bell in front of her right foot; then she kicks hard. Unable to recapture it, she grasps a ball which she then places at the same spot in order to give it another kick" (p. 225).
- At 1 year, 2 months, "Jacqueline holds in her hands an object which is new to her: a round, flat box which she turns all over, shakes, (and) rubs against the bassinet. She lets it go and tries to pick it up. But she only succeeds in touching it with her index finger, without grasping it. She nevertheless makes an attempt and presses on the edge. The box then tilts up and falls again" (p. 273). Jacqueline shows an interest in this result and studies the fallen box.
- At 1 year, 8 months, "Jacqueline arrives at a closed door with a blade of grass in each hand. She stretches out her right hand toward the (door)knob but sees that she cannot turn it without letting go of the grass. She puts the grass on the floor, opens the door, picks up the grass again, and enters. But when she wants to leave the room, things become complicated. She puts the grass on the floor and grasps the doorknob. But then she perceives that in pulling the door toward her she will simultaneously chase away the grass which she placed between the door and the threshold. She therefore picks it up in order to put it outside the door's zone of movement" (p. 339).

For Piaget, these observations reflect important changes in the infant's cognitive development. Later in the chapter, you will learn that Piaget believed that infants go through six substages of development and that the behaviors you have just read about characterize those substages.

PREVIEW

The excitement and enthusiasm about infant cognition have been fueled by an interest in what an infant knows at birth and soon after, by continued fascination about innate and learned factors in the infant's cognitive development,

and by controversies about whether infants construct their knowledge (Piaget's view) or whether they know their world more directly. In this chapter we will study Piaget's theory of infant development, learning and remembering, individual differences in intelligence, and language development.

1 PIAGET'S THEORY OF INFANT DEVELOPMENT

Cognitive Processes	The Sensorimotor Stage of Development

Piaget proposed that, just as our physical bodies have structures that enable us to adapt to the world, we build mental structures that help us to adapt to the world. *Adaptation* involves adjusting to new environmental demands. Yet Piaget also stressed that information is not simply poured into children's minds from the environment. Rather, children actively construct their own cognitive worlds. Piaget sought to explain how children think differently about their world at successive points in their development and how these systematic changes occur.

Cognitive Processes

Poet Nora Perry asked, "Who knows the thoughts of the child?" As much as anyone, Piaget knew. Through careful observations of his own three children—Laurent, Lucienne, and Jacqueline—and inquisitive interviews of other children, Piaget developed a theory that changed our ideas of how children think about the world.

What processes do children use as they construct their knowledge of the world? Piaget believed that these processes are especially important in this regard: schemes, assimilation and accommodation, organization, equilibrium and equilibration.

Schemes Piaget (1952) said that as the child seeks to construct an understanding of the world, the developing brain creates **schemes,** which are actions or mental representations that organize knowledge. In Piaget's theory, behavioral schemes (physical activities) characterize infancy and mental schemes (cognitive activities) develop in childhood (Lamb, Bornstein, & Teti, 2002). A baby's schemes are structured by simple actions, such as sucking, looking, and grasping, that can be performed on objects. Older children have schemes that include strategies and plans for solving problems. For example, a 5-year-old might have a scheme that involves the strategy of classifying objects by size, shape, or color. By the time we have reached adulthood, we have constructed an enormous number of diverse schemes, ranging from how to drive a car to balancing a budget to the concept of fairness.

Assimilation and Accommodation To explain how children use and adapt their schemes, Piaget offered two concepts: assimilation and accommodation, which we initially described in chapter 2, "The Science of Life-Span Development." Recall that *assimilation* occurs when children incorporate new information into their existing knowledge (schemes), while *accommodation* occurs when children adjust their schemes to fit new information and experiences. Think about a toddler who has learned the word *car* to identify the family's car. The toddler might call all moving vehicles on roads "cars," including motorcycles and trucks; the child has assimilated these objects to his or her existing scheme. But the child soon learns that motorcycles and trucks are not cars and fine-tunes the category to exclude motorcycles and trucks, accommodating the scheme.

W̶e are born capable of learning.
—**Jean-Jacques Rousseau**
Swiss-Born French Philosopher, 18th Century

schemes In Piaget's theory, actions or mental representations that organize knowledge.

Assimilation and accommodation operate even in very young infants. Newborns reflexively suck everything that touches their lips; they assimilate all sorts of objects into their sucking scheme. By sucking different objects, they learn about their taste, texture, shape, and so on. After several months of experience, though, they construct their understanding of the world differently. Some objects, such as fingers and the mother's breast, can be sucked, and others, such as fuzzy blankets, should not be sucked. In other words, they accommodate their sucking scheme.

Organization To make sense out of their world, Piaget said, children cognitively organize their experiences. **Organization** is Piaget's concept of grouping isolated behaviors into a higher-order system. Items are grouped into categories. Every level of thought is organized. Continual refinement of this organization is an inherent part of development. A boy who has only a vague idea about how to use a hammer may also have a vague idea about how to use other tools. After learning how to use each one, he must relate these uses, or organize his knowledge, if he is to become skilled in using tools. In the same way, children continually integrate and coordinate the many other branches of knowledge that often develop independently.

Equilibrium and Equilibration **Equilibration** is a mechanism that Piaget proposed to explain how children shift from one stage of thought to the next. The shift occurs as children experience cognitive conflict, or disequilibrium, in trying to understand the world. Eventually, they resolve the conflict and reach a balance, or equilibrium, of thought. Piaget saw considerable movement between states of cognitive equilibrium and disequilibrium as assimilation and accommodation work in concert to produce cognitive change. For example, if a child believes that the amount of a liquid changes simply because the liquid is poured into a container with a different shape—for instance, from a container that is short and wide into a container that is tall and narrow—she might be puzzled by such issues as where the "extra" liquid came from and whether there is actually more liquid to drink. The child will eventually resolve these puzzles as her thought becomes more advanced. In the everyday world, the child is constantly faced with such counterexamples and inconsistencies.

Recall from chapter 2 that Piaget also argued people go through four stages in understanding the world. Each of the stages is age related and consists of distinct ways of thinking. Remember, it is the different way of understanding the world that makes one stage more advanced than another; knowing more information does not make a child's thinking more advanced, in the Piagetian view. This is what Piaget meant when he said a child's cognition is *qualitatively* different in one stage compared with another.

Piaget's theory is a general, unifying story of how biology and experience sculpt the infant's cognitive development: Assimilation and accommodation always take the child to a higher ground. For Piaget, the motivation for change is an internal search for equilibrium. As a result of this change toward becoming more cognitively competent, Piaget theorized that individuals go through four stages of development: sensorimotor, preoperational, concrete operational, and formal operational. A different way of understanding the world makes one stage more advanced than another. Here our focus is on Piaget's stage of infant cognitive development. In later chapters (8, 10, and 12) we will explore the last three Piagetian stages.

The Sensorimotor Stage of Development

The **sensorimotor stage** lasts from birth to about 2 years of age. In this stage, infants construct an understanding of the world by coordinating sensory experiences (such as seeing and hearing) with physical, motoric actions—hence the term "sensorimotor." At the beginning of this stage, newborns have little more than reflexive patterns with which to work. At the end of the stage, 2-year-olds have complex sensorimotor patterns and are beginning to operate with primitive symbols. First we will summarize Piaget's descriptions of how infants develop. Later we will consider criticisms of his view.

Watch the video "Brain and Infant Cognition" as you consider the debate over innate versus learned factors in an infant's cognitive development.

organization Piaget's concept of grouping isolated behaviors into a higher-order, more smoothly functioning cognitive system; the grouping or arranging of items into categories.

equilibration A mechanism that Piaget proposed to explain how children shift from one stage of thought to the next. The shift occurs as children experience cognitive conflict, or disequilibrium, in trying to understand the world. Eventually, they resolve the conflict and reach a balance, or equilibrium, of thought.

sensorimotor stage The first of Piaget's stages, which lasts from birth to about 2 years of age; infants construct an understanding of the world by coordinating sensory experiences (such as seeing and hearing) with motoric actions.

Substage	Age	Description	Example
1 Simple reflexes	Birth to 1 month	Coordination of sensation and action through reflexive behaviors.	Rooting, sucking, and grasping reflexes; newborns suck reflexively when their lips are touched.
2 First habits and primary circular reactions	1 to 4 months	Coordination of sensation and two types of schemes: habits (reflex) and primary circular reactions (reproduction of an event that initially occurred by chance). Main focus is still on the infant's body.	Repeating a body sensation first experienced by chance (sucking thumb, for example); then infants might accommodate actions by sucking their thumb differently than they suck on a nipple.
3 Secondary circular reactions	4 to 8 months	Infants become more object-oriented, moving beyond self-preoccupation; repeats actions that bring interesting or pleasurable results.	An infant coos to make a person stay near; as the person starts to leave, the infant coos again.
4 Coordination of secondary circular reactions	8 to 12 months	Coordination of vision and touch—hand-eye coordination; coordination of schemes and intentionality.	Infant manipulates a stick in order to bring an attractive toy within reach.
5 Tertiary circular reactions, novelty, and curiosity	12 to 18 months	Infants become intrigued by the many properties of objects and by the many things they can make happen to objects; they experiment with new behavior.	A block can be made to fall, spin, hit another object, and slide across the ground.
6 Internalization of schemes	18 to 24 months	Infants develop the ability to use primitive symbols and form enduring mental representations.	An infant who has never thrown a temper tantrum before sees a playmate throw a tantrum; the infant retains a memory of the event, then throws one himself the next day.

FIGURE 6.1 Piaget's Six Substages of Sensorimotor Development

Substages Piaget divided the sensorimotor stage into six substages: (1) simple reflexes; (2) first habits and primary circular reactions; (3) secondary circular reactions; (4) coordination of secondary circular reactions; (5) tertiary circular reactions, novelty, and curiosity; and (6) internalization of schemes (see figure 6.1).

Simple reflexes constitute the first sensorimotor substage, which corresponds to the first month after birth. In this substage, sensation and action are coordinated primarily through reflexive behaviors. These include the rooting and sucking reflexes, which the infant has at birth. In this substage, the infant develops an ability to produce behaviors that resemble reflexes in the absence of the usual stimulus for the reflex. For example, when the baby was just born, a bottle or nipple would produce sucking only when it was placed directly in the baby's mouth or touched to the lips. But soon the infant might suck when a bottle or nipple is only nearby. Reflexlike actions in the absence of a triggering stimulus demonstrate that the infant is initiating action and is actively structuring experiences in the first month of life.

First habits and primary circular reactions make up the second sensorimotor substage, which develops between 1 and 4 months of age. In this substage, the infant learns to coordinate sensation and two types of schemes: habits and primary circular reactions. A *habit* is a scheme based on a reflex that has become completely separated from its eliciting stimulus. For example, infants in substage 1 might suck when bottles are put to their lips or when they see a bottle. Infants in substage 2 might suck even when no bottle is present. A *circular reaction* is a repetitive or stereotyped action.

A *primary circular reaction* is a scheme based on the attempt to reproduce an event that initially occurred by chance. For example, suppose an infant accidentally sucks his fingers when they are placed near his mouth. Later, he searches for his fingers to suck them again, but the fingers do not cooperate because the infant cannot coordinate visual and manual actions.

www.mhhe.com/santrockld10

Piaget's Stages

simple reflexes Piaget's first sensorimotor substage, which corresponds to the first month after birth. In this substage, the basic means of coordinating sensation and action is through reflexive behaviors, such as rooting and sucking, which the infant has at birth.

first habits and primary circular reactions Piaget's second sensorimotor substage, which develops between 1 and 4 months of age. In this substage, infants' reflexes evolve into adaptive schemes that are more refined and coordinated.

Habits and circular reactions are stereotyped—that is, the infant repeats them the same way each time. During this substage, the infant's own body remains the infant's center of attention. There is no outward pull by environmental events.

Secondary circular reactions constitute the third sensorimotor substage, which develops between 4 and 8 months of age. In this substage, the infant becomes more object-oriented, moving beyond preoccupation with the self. By chance, an infant might shake a rattle. The infant repeats this action for the sake of experiencing fascination. The infant also imitates some simple actions, such as the baby talk or burbling of adults, and some physical gestures. However, the baby imitates only actions that he or she is already able to produce. Although directed toward objects in the world, the infant's schemes lack an intentional, goal-directed quality.

Coordination of secondary circular reactions is Piaget's fourth sensorimotor substage, which develops between 8 and 12 months of age. The critical requirement for the infant to progress into this substage is the coordination of vision and the sense of touch, or hand-eye coordination. Actions become more outwardly directed. Significant changes in this substage involve the coordination of schemes and intentionality. Infants readily combine and recombine previously learned schemes in a coordinated way. They might look at an object and grasp it simultaneously, or they might visually inspect a toy, such as a rattle, and finger it simultaneously, in obvious tactile exploration. Actions are even more outwardly directed than before. Related to this coordination is the second achievement—the presence of intentionality. For example, infants might manipulate a stick in order to bring a desired toy within reach, or they might knock over one block to reach and play with another one.

Tertiary circular reactions, novelty, and curiosity make up Piaget's fifth sensorimotor substage, which develops between 12 and 18 months of age. In this substage, infants become intrigued by the many properties of objects and by the many things that they can make happen to objects. A block can be made to fall, spin, hit another object, and slide across the ground. *Tertiary circular reactions* are schemes in which the infant purposely explores new possibilities with objects, continually doing new things to them and exploring the results. Piaget says that this stage marks the starting point for human curiosity and interest in novelty.

Internalization of schemes is Piaget's sixth and final sensorimotor substage, which develops between 18 and 24 months of age. In this substage, the infant develops the ability to use primitive symbols and form enduring mental representations. For Piaget, a *symbol* is an internalized sensory image or word that represents an event. Primitive symbols permit the infant to think about concrete events without directly acting them out or perceiving them. Moreover, symbols allow the infant to manipulate and transform the represented events in simple ways. In a favorite Piagetian example, Piaget's young daughter saw a matchbox being opened and closed. Later, she mimicked the event by opening and closing her mouth. This was an obvious expression of her image of the event.

Object Permanence Imagine what your life would be like if you could not distinguish between yourself and your world. It would be chaotic and unpredictable. This is what the life of a newborn must be like, according to Piaget. There is no differentiation between the self and world; objects have no separate, permanent existence.

By the end of the sensorimotor period, however, both are present. **Object permanence** is the understanding that objects and events continue to exist even when they cannot be seen, heard, or touched. Acquiring the sense of object permanence is one of the infant's most important accomplishments.

How could Piaget or other developmentalists know whether an infant had a sense of object permanence or not? The principal way that object permanence is studied is by watching an infant's reaction when an interesting object disappears (see figure 6.2). If infants search for the object, it is assumed that they believe it continues to exist.

Object permanence is just one of the basic concepts about the physical world developed by babies (Bremner, 2004). To Piaget, children, even infants, are much like little scientists, examining the world to see how it works.

---

secondary circular reactions Piaget's third sensorimotor substage, which develops between 4 and 8 months of age. In this substage, the infant becomes more object-oriented, or focused on the world, moving beyond preoccupation with the self in sensorimotor interactions.

coordination of secondary circular reactions Piaget's fourth sensorimotor substage, which develops between 8 and 12 months of age. In this substage, several significant changes take place involving the coordination of schemes and intentionality.

tertiary circular reactions, novelty, and curiosity Piaget's fifth sensorimotor substage, which develops between 12 and 18 months of age. In this substage, infants become intrigued by the variety of properties that objects possess and by the multiplicity of things they can make happen to objects.

internalization of schemes Piaget's sixth and final sensorimotor substage, which develops between 18 and 24 months of age. In this substage, the infant's mental functioning shifts from a purely sensorimotor plane to a symbolic plane, and the infant develops the ability to use primitive symbols and form enduring mental representations.

object permanence The Piagetian term for one of an infant's most important accomplishments: understanding that objects and events continue to exist, even when they cannot directly be seen, heard, or touched.

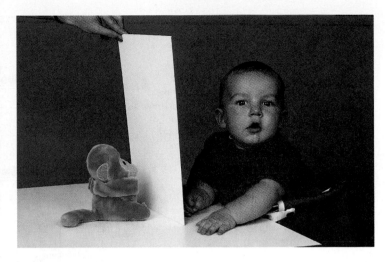

FIGURE 6.2 Object Permanence
Piaget argued that object permanence is one of infancy's landmark cognitive accomplishments. For this 5-month-old boy, "out- of- sight" is literally out of mind. The infant looks at the toy monkey (*left*), but, when his view of the toy is blocked (*right*), he does not search for it. Several months later, he will search for the hidden toy monkey, reflecting the presence of object permanence.

The Research in Life-Span Development interlude describes some of the ways in which adult scientists try to discover what these "baby scientists" are finding out about the world.

Research in Life-Span Development
Object Permanence and Causality

Two accomplishments of infants that Piaget examined were the development of object permanence and the child's understanding of causality. Let's examine two research studies that address these topics.

In both studies, Renee Baillargeon and her colleagues used a research method that involves *violation of expectations*. In this method, infants see an event happen as it normally would. Then, the event is changed in a way that violates what the infant expects to see. When infants look longer at the event that violates their expectations, it indicates they are surprised by it.

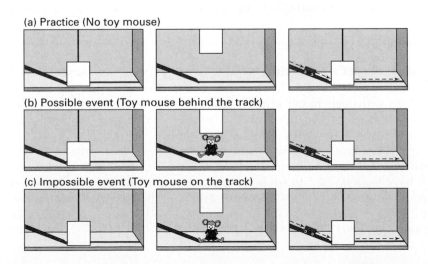

(a) Practice (No toy mouse)

(b) Possible event (Toy mouse behind the track)

(c) Impossible event (Toy mouse on the track)

FIGURE 6.3 Using the Violation of Expectations Method to Study Object Permanence in Infants

FIGURE 6.4 The Infants' Understanding of Causality

After young infants saw how far the medium-sized cylinder (*a*) pushed a toy bug, they showed more surprise at the event in (*c*) that showed a very small cylinder pushing the toy bug as far as the large cylinder (*b*). Their surprise, demonstrated by looking at (*c*) longer than (*b*), demonstrated that they understood the size of a cylinder was a causal factor in determining how far the toy bug would be pushed when it was hit by the cylinder.

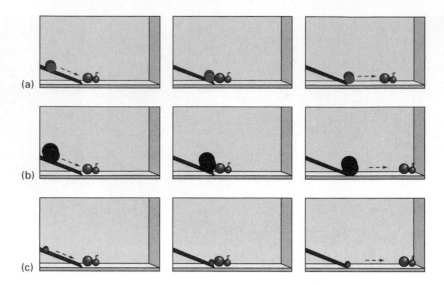

In one study focused on object permanence, researchers showed infants a toy car that moved down an inclined track, disappeared behind a screen, and then reemerged at the other end, still on the track (Baillargeon & DeVos, 1991) (see figure 6.3) (*a*). After this sequence was repeated several times, the infants then saw something different take place. In a "possible event" a toy mouse was placed *behind* the track but was hidden by the screen while the car rolled by (*b*). Then, in an "impossible event," the toy mouse was placed *on* the track but was secretly removed after the screen was lowered so that the car seemed to go through the mouse (*c*). In this study, infants as young as 3½ months of age looked longer at the impossible event than at the possible event, indicating that they were surprised by it. Their surprised look suggested they remembered not only that the toy mouse still existed (object permanence) but its location.

Another study focused on the infant's understanding of causality. Researchers found that even young infants comprehend that the size of a moving object determines how far it will move a stationary object that it collides with (Kotovsky & Baillargeon, 1994) (see figure 6.4). In this research, a cylinder rolls down a ramp and hits a toy bug at the bottom of the ramp. By 5½ and 6½ months of age, infants understand that the bug will roll farther if it is hit by a large cylinder than if it is hit by a small cylinder after they have observed how far it will be pushed by a medium-sized cylinder. Thus, by the middle of the first year of life these infants understood that the size of the cylinder was a causal factor in determining how far the bug would move if it were hit by the cylinder.

Evaluating Piaget's Sensorimotor Stage Piaget opened up a new way of looking at infants with his view that their main task is to coordinate their sensory impressions with their motor activity. However, the infant's cognitive world is not as neatly packaged as Piaget portrayed it, and some of Piaget's explanations for the cause of change are debated.

Piaget constructed his view of infancy mainly by observing the development of his own three children. In the past several decades, sophisticated experimental techniques have been devised to study infants, and there have been a large number of research studies on infant development. Much of the new research suggests that Piaget's view of sensorimotor development needs to be modified (Gounin-Decarie, 1996; Mandler, 2003).

A number of theorists, such as Eleanor Gibson (1989) and Elizabeth Spelke (1991; Spelke & Newport, 1998), argue that infants' perceptual abilities are highly developed very early in development. For example, in chapter 5 we discussed Spelke's research that demonstrated the presence of intermodal perception—the ability to coordinate information from two more sensory modalities, such as vision and hearing. As discussed earlier in this chapter, research by Renée Baillargeon (1995, 2004) and her colleagues (Aguiar & Baillargeon, 2002) documents that infants as young as 3 to 4 months expect objects to be *substantial* (in the sense that other objects cannot move through them) and *permanent* (in the sense that objects continue to exist when they are hidden).

In sum, researchers believe that infants see objects as bounded, unitary, solid, and separate from their background, possibly at birth or shortly thereafter, but definitely by 3 to 4 months of age, much earlier than Piaget envisioned. Young infants still have much to learn about objects, but the world appears both stable and orderly to them and thus capable of being conceptualized. Infants are continually trying to structure and make sense of their world (Meltzoff, 2004; Meltzoff & Gopnik, 1997).

Piaget claimed that certain processes are crucial in stage transitions, but the data do not always support his explanations. For example, in Piaget's theory, an important feature in the progression into substage 4, coordination of secondary circular reactions, is an infant's inclination to search for a hidden object in a familiar location (A) rather than to look for the object in a new location ($\overline{\text{B}}$). The **A$\overline{\text{B}}$ error** occurs when infants make the mistake of selecting the familiar hiding place rather than the new hiding place as they progress into substage 4. Researchers have found, however, that the A$\overline{\text{B}}$ error does not show up consistently (Corrigan, 1981; Sophian, 1985). The evidence indicates that A$\overline{\text{B}}$ errors are sensitive to the delay between hiding the object at $\overline{\text{B}}$ and the infant's attempt to find it (Diamond, 1985). Thus, the A$\overline{\text{B}}$ error might be due to a failure in memory.

Many of today's researchers assert that Piaget wasn't specific enough about how infants learn about their world and that infants are more competent than Piaget thought (Mandler, 2000, 2003, 2004; Meltzoff, 2004). As they have examined the specific ways that infants learn, the field of infant cognition has become very specialized. There are many researchers working on different questions, with no general theory emerging that can connect all of the different findings (Nelson, 1999). Their theories are local theories, focused on specific research questions, rather than grand theories like Piaget's (Kuhn, 1998). If there is a unifying theme, it is that investigators in infant development struggle with how developmental changes in cognition take place and the big issue of nature and nurture.

www.mhhe.com/santrockld7e

Cognitive Milestones

Infants are creating concepts and organizing their world into conceptual domains that will form the backbone of their thought throughout life.

—**Jean Mandler**
Contemporary Psychologist,
University of California–San Diego

 Review and Reflect: Learning Goal 1

1 Summarize the cognitive processes in Piaget's theory and the stage of sensorimotor development

REVIEW

- What cognitive processes are important in Piaget's theory?
- What are some characteristics of Piaget's stage of sensorimotor development? What are some contributions and criticisms of Piaget's sensorimotor stage?

REFLECT

- What are some implications of Piaget's theory of infant development for parenting?

A$\overline{\text{B}}$ error Occurs when infants make the mistake of selecting the familiar hiding place (A) rather than the new hiding place ($\overline{\text{B}}$) as they progress into substage 4 in Piaget's sensorimotor stage.

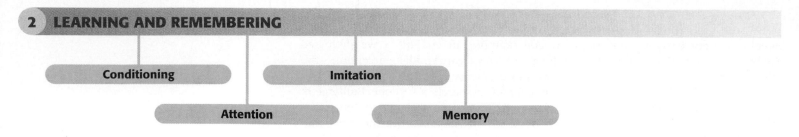

2 **LEARNING AND REMEMBERING**

Conditioning   Imitation

Attention   Memory

In this section, we will explore these aspects of how infants learn and remember: conditioning, attention, imitation, and memory. In contrast to Piaget's theory, the approaches we will consider here do not describe infant development in terms of stages.

Conditioning

In chapter 2, "The Science of Life-Span Development," we described Pavlov's classical conditioning and Skinner's operant conditioning. Researchers have demonstrated both types of conditioning in infants. Here we will examine some aspects of operant conditioning (in which the consequences of the behavior produce changes in the probability of the behavior's occurrence) in infants. For example, if an infant's behavior is followed by a rewarding stimulus, the behavior is likely to recur.

Operant conditioning has been especially helpful to researchers in their efforts to determine what infants perceive (Kraebel, Fable, & Gerhardstein, 2004). For example, infants will suck faster on a nipple when the sucking behavior is followed by a visual display, music, or a human voice (Rovee-Collier, 1987; Rovee-Collier & Barr, 2004).

attention The focusing of mental resources.

Carolyn Rovee-Collier (1987) has also demonstrated how infants can retain information from the experience of being conditioned. In a characteristic experiment, she places a 2½-month-old baby in a crib under an elaborate mobile (see figure 6.5). She then ties one end of a ribbon to the baby's ankle and the other end to the mobile. Subsequently, she observes that the baby kicks and makes the mobile move. The movement of the mobile is the reinforcing stimulus (which increases the baby's kicking behavior) in this experiment. Weeks later, the baby is returned to the crib, but its foot is not tied to the mobile. The baby kicks, which suggests it has retained the information that if it kicks a leg, the mobile will move.

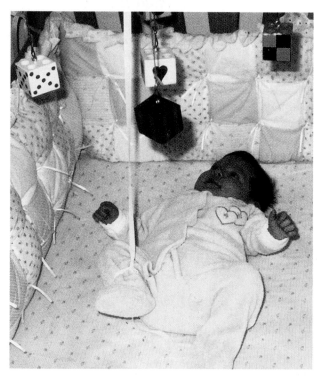

FIGURE 6.5 The Technique Used in Rovee-Collier's Investigation of Infant Memory
In Rovee-Collier's experiment, operant conditioning was used to demonstrate that infants as young as 2½ months of age can retain information from the experience of being conditioned.

Attention

Attention, the focusing of mental resources on select information, improves cognitive processing on many tasks. Even newborns can detect a contour and fixate on it. Older infants scan patterns more thoroughly. By 4 months, infants can selectively attend to an object.

Closely linked with attention are the processes of habituation and dishabituation that we discussed in chapter 5, "Physical Development in Infancy." Recall that if a stimulus—a sight or sound—is presented to infants several times in a row, they usually pay less attention to it each time, suggesting they are bored with it. This is the process of *habituation*—decreased responsiveness to a stimulus after repeated presentations of the stimulus. *Dishabituation* is the increase in responsiveness after a change in stimulation. Researchers study habituation to determine the extent to which infants can see, hear, smell, taste, and experience touch (Slater, 2004). Studies of habituation can indicate whether infants recognize something they have previously experienced. Among the measures researchers use to study whether habituation is occurring are sucking behavior (sucking stops when an infant attends to a novel object), heart rates, and the length of time the infant looks at an object. Newborn infants can habituate to repetitive stimulation in virtually every sensory modality—vision, hearing, and so on.

Infants' attention is so strongly governed by novelty and habituation that when an object becomes familiar, attention becomes shorter, making infants more vulnerable to distraction (Oakes, Kannass, & Shaddy, 2002). One recent study found that 10-month-olds were more distractible than 26-month-olds (Ruff & Capozzoli, 2003). Another recent study revealed that infants who were labeled "short lookers," because of the brief time they focused attention, had better memory at 1 year of age than did "long lookers," who had more sustained attention (Courage, Howe, & Squires, 2004).

A knowledge of habituation and dishabituation can benefit parent-infant interaction. Infants respond to changes in stimulation. If stimulation is repeated often, the infant's response will decrease to the point that the infant no longer responds to the parent. In parent-infant interaction, it is important for parents to do novel things and to repeat them often until the infant stops responding. The wise parent senses when the infant shows an interest and realizes that many repetitions of the stimulus may be necessary for the infant to process the information. The parent stops or changes behaviors when the infant redirects her attention (Rosenblith, 1992).

Imitation

Can infants imitate someone else's emotional expressions? If an adult smiles, will the baby follow with a smile? If an adult protrudes her lower lip, wrinkles her forehead, and frowns, will the baby show a sad face? If an adult opens his mouth, widens his eyes, and raises his eyebrows, will the baby follow suit? Can infants only a few days old do these things?

Infant development researcher Andrew Meltzoff (2002, 2004; Meltzoff & Moore, 1999) has conducted numerous studies of infants' imitative abilities. He sees infants' imitative abilities as biologically based, because infants can imitate a facial expression within the first few days after birth. This occurs before they have had the opportunity to observe social agents in their environment protruding their tongues and engaging in other behaviors. He also emphasizes that the infant's imitative abilities do not resemble what ethologists conceptualize as a hardwired, reflexive, innate releasing mechanism but rather involve flexibility, adaptability, and intermodal perception. In Meltzoff's observations of infants in the first 72 hours of life, the infants gradually displayed a full imitative response of an adult's facial expression, such as protruding the tongue or opening the mouth wide (see figure 6.6).

deferred imitation Imitation that occurs after a time delay of hours or days.

Not all experts on infant development accept Meltzoff's conclusions that newborns are capable of imitation. Some say that these babies were engaging in little more than automatic responses to a stimulus.

Meltzoff also has studied **deferred imitation,** which occurs after a time delay of hours or days. Piaget held that deferred imitation doesn't occur until about 18 months of age. Meltzoff's research suggested that it occurs much earlier. In one study, Meltzoff (1988) demonstrated that 9-month-old infants could imitate actions—such as pushing a recessed button in a box, which produced a beeping sound—that they had seen performed 24 hours earlier.

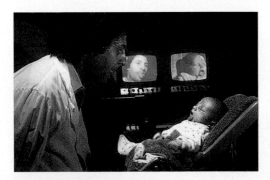

FIGURE 6.6 Infant Imitation
Infant development researcher Andrew Meltzoff protrudes his tongue in an attempt to get the infant to imitate his behavior.

Infant Cognition
Rovee-Collier's Research
Patricia Bauer's Infant Memory Studies

Memory

Memory, a central feature of cognitive development, involves the retention of information over time. Sometimes information is retained only for a few seconds, and at other times it is retained for a lifetime.

Can infants remember? Some researchers such as Rovee-Collier have concluded that infants as young as 2 to 6 months of age can remember some experiences through 1½ to 2 years of age (Rovee-Collier & Barr, 2004). However, critics such as Jean Mandler (2000), a leading expert on infant cognition, argue that the infants in Rovee-Collier's experiments are displaying only implicit memory. **Implicit memory** refers to memory without conscious recollection—memories of skills and routine procedures that are performed automatically. In contrast, **explicit memory** refers to the conscious memory of facts and experiences.

When people think about memory, they are usually referring to explicit memory. Most researchers find that babies do not show explicit memory until the second half of the first year (Bauer & others, 2003; Mandler & McDonough, 1995). Then, explicit memory improves substantially during the second year of life (Bauer, 2004; Carver & Bauer, 2001). In one longitudinal study, infants were assessed several times during their second year (Bauer & others, 2000). Older infants showed more accurate memory and required fewer prompts to demonstrate their memory than younger infants. In sum, most of infants' conscious memories are fragile and short-lived, except for memory of perceptual-motor actions, which can be substantial (Mandler, 2000, 2003).

Let's examine another aspect of memory. Do you remember your third birthday party? Probably not. Most adults can remember little if anything from the first three years of their life (Neisser, 2004). When adults do seem to be able to recall something from their infancy, it likely is something they have been told by relatives or something they saw in a photograph or a home movie. This phenomenon is called *infantile* or *childhood amnesia*. Even elementary school children do not remember much of their early child years. In one study, about three years after leaving preschool, children were much poorer at remembering their former classmates than their teacher was (Lie & Newcombe, 1999). In another study, 10-year-olds were shown pictures of their preschool classmates and they recognized only about 20 percent of them (Newcombe & Fox, 1994).

What is the cause of infantile amnesia? One reason for the difficulty older children and adults have in recalling events from their infant and early childhood years is the immaturity of the prefrontal lobes of the brain, which are thought to play an important role in memory for events (Boyer & Diamond, 1992).

memory A central feature of cognitive development, pertaining to all situations in which an individual retains information over time.

implicit memory Memory without conscious recollection; involves skills and routine procedures that are automatically performed.

explicit memory Conscious memory of facts and experiences.

Review and Reflect: Learning Goal 2

2 **Describe how infants learn and remember**

REVIEW

- How do infants learn through conditioning?
- What is attention? What characterizes attention in infants?
- How is imitation involved in infant learning?
- To what extent can infants remember?

REFLECT

- If a friend told you that she remembers being abused by her parents when she was 2 years old, would you believe her? Explain your answer.

3   INDIVIDUAL DIFFERENCES IN INTELLIGENCE

So far, we have discussed how the cognitive development of infants generally progresses. We have emphasized what is typical of the largest number of infants or the average infant, but the results obtained for *most* infants do not apply to *all* infants. It is advantageous to know whether an infant is developing at a slow, normal, or advanced pace during the course of infancy. If an infant advances at an especially slow rate, then some form of enrichment may be necessary. If an infant develops at an advanced pace, parents may be advised to provide toys that stimulate cognitive growth in slightly older infants. Individual differences in infant cognitive development have been studied primarily through the use of developmental scales, or infant intelligence tests. For example, the Brazelton Neonatal Behavioral Assessment Scale, which we discussed in chapter 4, is widely used to evaluate newborns.

The infant testing movement grew out of the tradition of IQ testing of older children. However, the measures for assessing infants are necessarily less verbal than IQ tests that assess the intelligence of older children. The infant developmental scales contain far more perceptual motor items. They also include measures of social interaction.

The most important early contributor to the developmental testing of infants was Arnold Gesell (1934). He developed a measure that was used as a clinical tool to help distinguish potentially normal babies from abnormal ones. This was especially useful to adoption agencies, which had large numbers of babies awaiting placement. Gesell's examination was used widely for many years and is still frequently used by pediatricians to assess infants. The current version of the Gesell test has four categories of behavior: motor, language, adaptive, and personal-social. The **developmental quotient (DQ)** is an overall developmental score that combines subscores in motor, language, adaptive, and personal-social domains in the Gesell assessment of infants.

The **Bayley Scales of Infant Development,** developed by Nancy Bayley, are widely used in the assessment of infant development. The current version has three components: a mental scale, a motor scale, and an infant behavior profile. Unlike Gesell, whose scales were clinically motivated, Bayley (1969) wanted to develop scales that would assess infant behavior and predict later development. The early version of the Bayley scales covered only the first year of development. In the 1950s, the scales were extended to assess older infants. In 1993, the Bayley-II was published, with updated norms for diagnostic assessment at a younger age.

Because our discussion in this chapter centers on the infant's cognitive development, our primary interest is in Bayley's mental scale. It includes assessment of:

- Auditory and visual attention to stimuli
- Manipulation, such as combining objects or shaking a rattle
- Examiner interaction, such as babbling and imitation
- Relation with toys, such as banging spoons together
- Memory involved in object permanence, as when the infant finds a hidden toy

How well should a 6-month-old perform on the Bayley mental scale? The 6-month-old infant should be able to vocalize pleasure and displeasure, persistently search for objects that are just out of immediate reach, and approach a mirror that is placed in front of the infant by the examiner. How well should a 12-month-old perform? By 12 months of age, the infant should be able to inhibit behavior when commanded to do so, imitate words the examiner says (such as *Mama*), and respond to simple requests (such as "Take a drink").

www.mhhe.com/santrockld10

Bayley Scales of Infant Development (2nd ed.)

developmental quotient (DQ) An overall developmental score that combines subscores in motor, language, adaptive, and personal-social domains in the Gesell assessment of infants.

Bayley Scales of Infant Development Scales developed by Nancy Bayley that are widely used in the assessment of infant development. The current version has three components: a mental scale, a motor scale, and an infant behavior profile.

Careers in Life-Span Development

Toosje Thyssen VanBeveren, Infant Assessment Specialist

Toosje Thyssen VanBeveren is a developmental psychologist at the University of Texas Medical Center in Dallas. She has a master's degree in child clinical psychology and a Ph.D. in human development.

Currently, Toosje is involved in a program called New Connections. This 12-week program is a comprehensive intervention for young children (0 to 6 years of age) who were affected by substance abuse prenatally and for their caregivers.

In the New Connections program, Toosje conducts assessments of infants' developmental status and progress, identifying delays and deficits. She might refer the infants to a speech, physical, or occupational therapist and monitor the infants' therapeutic services and developmental progress. Toosje trains the program staff and encourages them to use the exercises she recommends. She also discusses the child's problems with the primary caregivers, suggests activities they can carry out with their children, and assists them in enrolling their infants in appropriate programs.

During her graduate work at the University of Texas at Dallas, Toosje was author John Santrock's teaching assistant in his undergraduate course on life-span development for four years. As a teaching assistant, she attended classes, graded exams, counseled students, and occasionally gave lectures. Each semester, Toosje returns to give a lecture on prenatal development and infancy in the life-span class. She also teaches part-time in the psychology department at UT-Dallas. She teaches an undergraduate course, "The Child in Society," and a graduate course, "Infant Development."

In Toosje's words, "My days are busy and full. The work is often challenging. There are some disappointments but mostly the work is enormously gratifying."

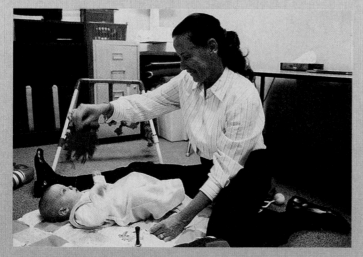

Toosje Thyssen VanBeveren conducting an infant assessment.

Another assessment tool, the Fagan Test of Infant Intelligence, is increasingly being used (Fagan, 1992). This test focuses on the infant's ability to process information, including encoding the attributes of objects, detecting similarities and differences between objects, forming mental representations, and retrieving these representations. The Fagan test estimates babies' intelligence by comparing the amount of time they look at a new object with the amount of time they spend looking at a familiar object. This test elicits similar performances from infants in different cultures and is correlated with measures of intelligence in older children. Toosje Thyssen VanBeveren is an infant assessment specialist who administers tests like the Bayley scales and the Fagan Test of Infant Intelligence. To read about her work with infants, see the Careers in Life-Span Development insert.

Tests of infant intelligence have been valuable in assessing the effects of malnutrition, drugs, maternal deprivation, and environmental stimulation on the development of infants. However, they do not correlate highly with IQ scores obtained later in childhood. This shortcoming is not surprising because the test items are considerably less verbal than the items on intelligence tests given to older children. Yet specific aspects of infant intelligence are related to specific aspects of childhood intelligence. For example, in one study, infant language abilities assessed by the Bayley test predicted language, reading, and spelling ability at 6 to 8 years of age (Siegel, 1989). Infant perceptual-motor skills predicted visuospatial, arithmetic, and fine motor skills at 6 to 8 years of age. These results indicate that an item analysis of infant scales like Bayley's can provide information about the development of specific intellectual functions.

The explosion of interest in infant development has produced many new measures, especially using tasks that evaluate the way infants process information. Evidence is accumulating that measures of habituation and dishabituation predict intelligence in childhood (McCall & Carriger, 1993). Less cumulative attention by an infant in the habituation situation and greater amounts of attention in the dishabituation situation reflect more efficient information processing. A recent review concluded that when measured between 3 and 12 months, both habituation and dishabituation are related to higher IQ scores on tests given at various times between infancy and adolescence (average correlation = .37) (Kavšek, 2004).

It is important, however, not to go too far and think that the connections between early infant cognitive development and later childhood cognitive development are so strong that no discontinuity takes place. Some important changes in cognitive development take place after infancy, changes that underscore the discontinuity of cognitive development. We will describe these changes in cognitive development in subsequent chapters, which focus on later periods of development.

Discuss the assessment of intelligence in infancy

REVIEW

- How is infant intelligence measured?

REFLECT

- Parents have their 1-year-old infant assessed with a developmental scale and the infant does very well on it. How confident should they be that the infant is going to be a genius when he or she grows up?

4 LANGUAGE DEVELOPMENT

What Is Language?

Language's Rule Systems

How Language Develops

Biological and Environmental Influences

In 1799, a naked boy was observed running through the woods near the village of Aveyron in France. The boy was captured and cared for by a scientist who gave him the name of Victor. Also known as the Wild Boy of Aveyron, he was believed to be about 11 years old and to have lived in the woods alone since early childhood. When found, he made no effort to communicate. Even after several years of tutoring, he never learned to communicate effectively. Sadly, a modern-day "wild child" was discovered in Los Angeles in 1970. She had been hidden in a closet since infancy. Given the name Genie, she was helped and studied by psychologist Susan Curtiss. Despite intensive intervention, Genie never acquired more than a primitive form of language. Both cases—the Wild Boy of Aveyron and Genie—raise questions about the biological and environmental determinants of language, topics that we will examine in greater detail later in this chapter. First, though, we need to explore what language is and its rule systems.

What Is Language?

Language is a form of communication—whether spoken, written, or signed—that is based on a system of symbols. Language consists of the words used by a community and the rules for varying and combining them.

Think how important language is in our everyday lives. We need language to speak with others, listen to others, read, and write. Our language enables us to describe past events in detail and to plan for the future. Language lets us pass down information from one generation to the next and create a rich cultural heritage.

All human languages have some common characteristics. These include infinite generativity and organizational rules. **Infinite generativity** is the ability to produce an endless number of meaningful sentences using a finite set of words and rules. Let's further explore what these rules involve.

Language's Rule Systems

Language is highly ordered and organized. The organization involves five systems of rules: phonology, morphology, syntax, semantics, and pragmatics. When

language A form of communication, whether spoken, written, or signed, that is based on a system of symbols.

infinite generativity The ability to produce an endless number of meaningful sentences using a finite set of words and rules.

we say "rules," we mean that language is orderly and the rules describe the way language works.

Phonology Every language is made up of basic sounds. **Phonology** is the sound system of the language, including the sounds that are used and how they may be combined. For example, English has the initial consonant cluster *spr* as in *spring*, but no words begin with the cluster *rsp*. Phonology provides a basis for constructing a large and expandable set of words out of two or three dozen phonemes.

The basic unit of sound in a language is a *phoneme;* it is the smallest unit of sound that affects meaning (Stoel-Gammon & Menn, 2005). An example of a phoneme is the sound represented by the letter *p,* as in the words *pot* and *spot*. The /p/ sound is slightly different in the two words, but this variation is not distinguished in English, and the /p/ sound is therefore a single phoneme. In some languages, such as Hindi, this variation represents separate phonemes.

Morphology **Morphology** refers to the units of meaning involved in word formation. A *morpheme* is a minimal unit of meaning; it is a word, or a part of a word, that cannot be broken into smaller meaningful parts. Every word in the English language is made up of one or more morphemes. Some words consist of a single morpheme (for example, *help*), whereas others are made up of more than one morpheme (for example, *helper,* which has two morphemes, *help + er,* with the morpheme *-er* meaning "one who," in this case "one who helps"). Thus, not all morphemes are words by themselves (for example, *-pre, -tion,* and *-ing*).

Just as the rules that govern phonology describe the sound sequences that can occur in a language, the rules of morphology describe the way meaningful units (morphemes) can be combined in words (Ravid, Levie, & Ben-Zvi, 2004; Tager-Flusberg, 2005). Morphemes have many jobs in grammar, such as marking tense (for example, *she walks* versus *she walked*) and number (*she walks* versus *they walk*).

Syntax **Syntax** involves the way words are combined to form acceptable phrases and sentences (O'Grady, 2005). If someone says to you, "Bob slugged Tom" or "Bob was slugged by Tom," you know who did the slugging and who was slugged in each case because you have a syntactic understanding of these sentence structures. You also understand that the sentence "You didn't stay, did you?" is a grammatical sentence, but that "You didn't stay, didn't you?" is unacceptably ambiguous.

If you learn another language, English syntax will not get you very far. For example, in English an adjective usually precedes a noun (as in *blue sky*), whereas in Spanish the adjective usually follows the noun *(cielo azul)*. Despite the differences in their syntactic structures, however, the world's languages have much in common. For example, consider the following short sentences:

The cat killed the mouse.
The mouse ate the cheese.
The farmer chased the cat.

FRANK & ERNEST reprinted by permission of Newspaper Enterprise Association, Inc.

In many languages it is possible to combine these sentences into more complex sentences. For example:

The farmer chased the cat that killed the mouse.
The mouse the cat killed ate the cheese.

However, no language we know of permits sentences like the following one:

The mouse the cat the farmer chased killed ate the cheese.

Can you make sense of this sentence? If you can, you probably can do it only after wrestling with it for several minutes. You likely could not understand it at all if someone uttered it during a conversation. It appears that language users cannot process subjects and objects arranged in too complex a fashion in a sentence. That is good news for language learners, because it means that all syntactic systems adhere to some common ground. Such findings are also considered important by researchers who are interested in the universal properties of syntax (de Jong, 2004).

Semantics **Semantics** refers to the meaning of words and sentences. Every word has a set of semantic features, or required attributes related to meaning (Pan, 2005). *Girl* and *women,* for example, share many semantic features but they differ semantically in regard to age.

Speakers of a language know the meanings of thousands of words, and store these words in semantic networks. We know, for example, that a lemon is a type of citrus, that citrus is a type of fruit, and that fruit is a category of food. We also know that there are other categories of food, such as grain, fish, and meat.

Pragmatics A final set of language rules involves **pragmatics,** the appropriate use of language in different contexts (Bryant, 2005). The domain of language is broad. When you take turns speaking in a discussion or use a question to convey a command ("Why is it so noisy in here? What is this, Grand Central Station?"), you are demonstrating knowledge of pragmatics. You also apply the pragmatics of English when you use polite language in appropriate situations (for example, when talking to your teacher) or tell stories that are interesting, jokes that are funny, and lies that convince.

Pragmatic rules can be complex and differ from one culture to another. If you were to study the Japanese language, you would come face-to-face with countless pragmatic rules about conversing with individuals of various social levels and with various relationships to you. Some of these pragmatic rules concern the ways of saying thank you. Indeed, the pragmatics of saying thank you are complex even in our own culture. Preschoolers' use of the phrase *thank you* varies with sex, socioeconomic status, and the age of the individual they are addressing.

At this point, we have discussed five important rule systems involved in language. An overview of these rule systems is presented in figure 6.7.

How Language Develops

According to an ancient historian, in the thirteenth century, the German Emperor Frederick II had a cruel idea. He wanted to know what language children would speak if no one talked to them. He selected several newborns and threatened their caregivers with death if they ever talked to the infants. Frederick never found out what language the children spoke because they all died. As we move forward in the twenty-first century, we are still curious about infants' development of language, although our experiments and observations are, to say the least, far more humane than the evil Frederick's.

Whatever language they learn, infants all over the world follow a similar path in language development. What are some key milestones in this development?

semantics The meaning of words and sentences.

pragmatics The appropriate use of language in different contexts.

Rule System	Description	Examples
Phonology	The sound system of a language. A phoneme is the smallest sound unit in a language.	The word *chat* has three phonemes or sounds: /ch/ /a/ /t/. An example of phonological rule in the English language is while the phoneme /r/ can follow the phonemes /t/ or /d/ in an English consonant cluster (such as *track* or *drab*), the phoneme /l/ cannot follow these letters.
Morphology	The system of meaningful units involved in word formation.	The smallest sound units that have a meaning are called morphemes, or meaning units. The word *girl* is one morpheme, or meaning unit; it cannot be broken down any further and still have meaning. When the suffix *s* is added, the word becomes *girls* and has two morphemes because the *s* changed the meaning of the word, indicating that there is more than one girl.
Syntax	The system that involves the way words are combined to form acceptable phrases and sentences.	Word order is very important in determining meaning in the English language. For example, the sentence "Sebastian pushed the bike" has a different meaning than "The bike pushed Sebastian."
Semantics	The system that involves the meaning of words and sentences.	Knowing the meaning of individual words—that is, vocabulary. For example, semantics includes knowing the meaning of such words as *orange*, *transportation*, and *intelligent*.
Pragmatics	The system of using appropriate conversation and knowledge of how to effectively use language in context.	An example is using polite language in appropriate situations, such as being mannerly when talking with one's teacher. Taking turns in a conversation involves pragmatics.

FIGURE 6.7 The Rule Systems of Language

Babbling and Other Vocalizations Babies actively produce sounds from birth onward (Lock, 2004; Volterra & others, 2005). The purpose of these early communications is to attract attention from caregivers and others in the environment. Babies' sounds and gestures go through this sequence during the first year:

- *Crying.* Babies cry even at birth and crying can signal distress. However, as we will discuss in chapter 7, there are different types of cries that signal different things.
- *Cooing.* Babies first coo at about 1 to 2 months. These are gurgling sounds made in the back of the throat and usually express pleasure during interaction with the caregiver.
- *Babbling.* This first occurs in the middle of the first year and includes strings of consonant-vowel combinations, such as "*ba, ba, ba, ba.*"
- *Gestures.* Infants start using gestures, such as showing and pointing, at about 8 to 12 months of age. They may wave bye-bye, nod to mean "yes," show an empty cup to want more milk, and point to a dog to draw attention to it.

Deaf infants, born to deaf parents who use sign language, babble with their hands and fingers at about the same age as hearing children babble vocally (Bloom, 1998). Such similarities in timing and structure between manual and vocal babbling indicate the presence of a unified language capacity that underlies signed and spoken language.

Recognizing Language Sounds Long before they begin to learn words, infants can make fine distinctions among the sounds of the language (Lock, 2004). Patricia Kuhl's (1993, 2000) research has demonstrated that from birth up to about 7 months of age, infants are "citizens of the world," recognizing when sounds change most of the time no matter what language the syllables come from. But over the next several months, infants get even better at perceiving the changes in sounds from their "own" language, the one their parents speak, and gradually lose the ability to recognize changes in sounds that don't exist in their native tongue (see figure 6.8).

In Kuhl's research, syllables that consist of phonemes from languages all over the world are piped through a speaker for infants to hear. A string of identical

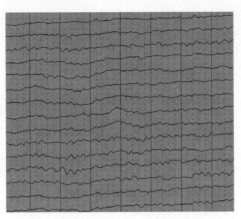

FIGURE 6.8 From Universal to Specialized Linguist
The people of the world speak thousands of languages and babies are born with the ability to learn any of them. In her research, Patricia Kuhl monitors infants' brain waves (an example of a brain wave recording is shown on the right) as they listen to different sounds. She has discovered that up to about the age of 7 months, infants can distinguish between two sounds in a language such as Mandarin Chinese— a subtle difference that English-speaking parents cannot detect. However, by 11 months of age, unused neuronal connections have begun to be pruned away. As infants' brains process a single language over time, they cease to be "universal linguists."

syllables is played and then the sound changes. A box with a toy bear in it is placed where the infant can see it. If the infant turns its head when the sounds of the syllables change, the darkened box lights up and the bear briefly dances and drums. That is, if the infant turns its head to look at the box as soon as it notices the sound changing, the infant is rewarded by getting to see the bear's performance.

An example involves the English /r/ and /l/ sounds, which distinguish words such as *rake* and *lake* (Iverson & Kuhl, 1996; Iverson & others, 2003). In the United States, infants from English-speaking homes detect the changes from *ra* to *la* when they are 6 months old and get better at it by 12 months of age. However, in Japanese there is no such /r/ or /l/ sound. In Japan, 6-month-old infants perform as well as their American counterparts in recognizing the /r/ and /l/ distinction, but by 12 months of age they lose this ability.

An important task for infants is to fish out individual words from the nonstop stream of sound that makes up ordinary speech (Brownlee, 1998; Jusczyk, 2000). To do so, they must find the boundaries between words, which is very difficult for infants because adults don't pause between words when they speak. Still, infants begin to detect word boundaries by 8 months of age. For example, in one study, 8-month-old infants listened to recorded stories that contained unusual words, such as *hornbill* and *python* (Jusczyk & Hohne, 1997). Two weeks later, the researchers tested the infants with two lists of words, one made up of words in the stories, the other of new, unusual words that did not appear in the stories. The infants listened to the familiar words for a second longer, on average, than to new words.

First Words The infant's first word is a milestone eagerly anticipated by every parent. This event usually occurs between 10 and 15 months of age and on average at about 13 months. However, as we have seen, long before babies say their first words, they have been communicating with their parents, often by gesturing and using their own special sounds. The appearance of first words is a continuation of this communication process (Berko Gleason, 2002, 2005).

A child's first words include those that name important people *(Dada)*, familiar animals *(kitty)*, vehicles *(car)*, toys *(ball)*, food *(milk)*, body parts *(eye)*, clothes *(hat)*, household items *(clock)*, and greeting terms *(bye)*. These were the first words of babies 50 years ago. They are the first words of babies today. Children often express various intentions with their single words, so that "cookie" might mean "That's a cookie" or "I want a cookie."

Between about 8 and 12 months of age, infants often indicate their first understanding of words. On average, infants understand about 50 words at about 13 months, but they can't say this many words until about 18 months (Menyuk, Liebergott, & Schultz, 1995). Thus, in infancy *receptive vocabulary* (words the child understands) considerably exceeds *spoken vocabulary* (words the child uses).

The infant's spoken vocabulary rapidly increases once the first word is spoken (Camaioni, 2004; Waxman, 2004). The average 18-month-old can speak about 50

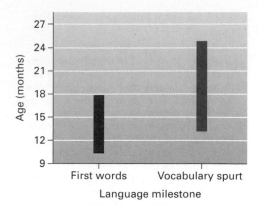

FIGURE 6.9 Variation in Language Milestones

www.mhhe.com/santrockld10

Language Milestones
The Naming Explosion

For a profile of a 2-year-old's language development and her communication with her mother, watch the video "Language Ability at 2 Years."

Around the world, young children learn to speak in two-word utterances, in most cases, at about 18 to 24 months of age. *What are some examples of these two-word utterances?*

telegraphic speech The use of short and precise words without grammatical markers such as articles, auxiliary verbs, and other connectives.

words, but by the age of 2 a child can speak about 200 words. This rapid increase in vocabulary that begins at approximately 18 months is called the *vocabulary spurt* (Bloom, Lifter, & Broughton, 1985).

The timing of a child's first word and vocabulary spurt varies (Bloom, 1998; Dale & Goodman, 2004). Figure 6.9 shows the range for these two language milestones in 14 children. On average, these children said their first word at 13 months and had a vocabulary spurt at 19 months. However, the ages for the first word of individual children varied from 10 to 17 months and for their vocabulary spurt from 13 to 25 months.

Children sometimes overextend or underextend the meanings of the words they use (Woodward & Markman, 1998). *Overextension* is the tendency to apply a word to objects that are not related to, or are inappropriate for, the word's meaning. For example, when children say "*Dada*" for "Father," they often also apply the word to other men, strangers, or boys. With time, overextensions decrease and eventually disappear. *Underextension* is the tendency to apply a word too narrowly; it occurs when children fail to name a relevant event or object. For example, a child might use the word *boy* to describe a 5-year-old neighbor but not apply the word to a male infant or to a 9-year-old male.

Two-Word Utterances By the time children are 18 to 24 months of age, they usually utter two-word utterances. To convey meaning with just two words, the child relies heavily on gesture, tone, and context. The wealth of meaning children can communicate with a two-word utterance includes the following (Slobin, 1972):

- Identification: "See doggie."
- Location: "Book there."
- Repetition: "More milk."
- Nonexistence: "All gone thing."
- Negation: "Not wolf."
- Possession: "My candy."
- Attribution: "Big car."
- Agent-action: "Mama walk."
- Action-direct object: "Hit you."
- Action-indirect object: "Give Papa."
- Action-instrument: "Cut knife."
- Question: "Where ball?"

These examples are from children whose first language is English, German, Russian, Finnish, Turkish, or Samoan.

Notice that the two-word utterances omit many parts of speech and are remarkably succinct. In fact, in every language, a child's first combinations of words have this economical quality; they are telegraphic. **Telegraphic speech** is the use of short and precise words without grammatical markers such as articles, auxiliary verbs, and other connectives. Telegraphic speech is not limited to two words. "Mommy give ice cream" and "Mommy give Tommy ice cream" also are examples of telegraphic speech.

We have discussed a number of language milestones in infancy. Figure 6.10 summarizes the time at which infants typically reach these milestones.

Biological and Environmental Influences

We have described how language develops, but we have not explained what makes this amazing development possible. Everyone who uses language in some way "knows" its rules and has the ability to create an infinite number of words and sentences. Where does this knowledge come from? Is it the product of biology? Or is language learned and influenced by experiences?

Biological Influences Some language scholars view the remarkable similarities in how children acquire language all over the world, despite the vast variation in language input they receive, as strong evidence that language has a biological basis. What role did evolution play in the biological foundations of language?

Evolution and the Brain's Role in Language The ability to speak and understand language requires a certain vocal apparatus as well as a nervous system with certain capabilities. The nervous system and vocal apparatus of humanity's predecessors changed over hundreds of thousands of years. Once equipped with these physical requirements for speaking, *Homo sapiens* went beyond the grunting and shrieking to develop speech. Although estimates vary, many experts believe that humans acquired language about 100,000 years ago. In evolutionary time, then, language is a very recent acquisition. It gave humans an enormous edge over other animals and increased the chances of human survival (Lachlan & Feldman, 2003; Pinker, 1994).

There is evidence that particular regions of the brain are predisposed to be used for language (Nakano & Blumstein, 2004; Pizzamiglio & others, 2005). Two regions involved in language were first discovered in studies of brain-damaged individuals. In 1861, a patient of Paul Broca, a French surgeon and anthropologist, received an injury to the left side of his brain. The patient became known as Tan because that was the only word he could speak after his brain injury. Tan suffered from **aphasia,** a loss or impairment of language ability caused by brain damage. Tan died several days after Broca evaluated him, and an autopsy revealed the location of the injury. Today, we refer to the part of the brain in which Broca's patient was injured as **Broca's area,** an area in the left frontal lobe of the brain next to the part that directs the muscle movements involved in speech production (see figure 6.11).

Another place in the brain where an injury can seriously impair language is **Wernicke's area,** a region of the brain's left hemisphere involved in language comprehension (see figure 6.11). Individuals with damage to Wernicke's area often produce fluent but incomprehensible speech.

Language Acquisition Device Linguist Noam Chomsky (1957) proposed that humans are biologically prewired to learn language at a certain time and in a certain way. He said that children are born into the world with a **language acquisition device (LAD),** a biological endowment that enables the child to detect certain features and rules of language, including phonology, syntax, and semantics. Children are prepared by nature with the ability to detect the sounds of language, for example, and follow rules such as how to form plurals and ask questions.

Chomsky's LAD is a theoretical construct, not a physical part of the brain. Is there evidence for the existence of a LAD? Supporters of the LAD concept cite the uniformity of language milestones across languages and cultures, evidence that children create language even in the absence of well-formed input, and biological substrates of language.

The Behavioral View and Environmental Influences As we said earlier, some language scholars view the similarities in children's language acquisition all over the world as strong evidence that language has a biological foundation. However, other language experts argue that experiences of the child, the particular language to be learned, and the context in which learning takes place can strongly influence language acquisition (Goorhuis-Brouwer & others, 2004; Marchman, 2003).

The Behavioral View According to behaviorists, language is a complex learned skill, much like playing the piano or dancing. Behaviorists argued that language represents chains of responses acquired through reinforcement (Skinner, 1957). A baby happens to babble "*Ma-ma*" and Mama rewards the baby with hugs and smiles; the

Age	Language Milestones
Birth	Crying
1 to 2 months	Cooing begins
6 months	Babbling begins
7 to 11 months	Change from universal linguist to language-specific listener
8 to 12 months	Use gestures, such as showing and pointing Comprehension of words appears
13 months	First word spoken
18 months	Vocabulary spurt starts
18 to 24 months	Uses two-word utterances Rapid expansion of understanding of words

FIGURE 6.10 Some Language Milestones in Infancy

In the wild, chimps communicate through calls, gestures, and expressions, which evolutionary psychologists believe might be the roots of true language.

aphasia A loss or impairment of language ability caused by brain damage.

Broca's area An area in the brain's left frontal lobe next to the part that directs the muscle movements involved in speech production.

Wernicke's area An area of the brain's left hemisphere that is involved in language comprehension.

language acquisition device (LAD) Chomsky's term that describes a biological endowment that enables the child to detect the features and rules of language, including phonology, syntax, and semantics.

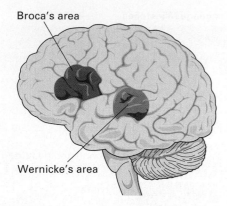

FIGURE 6.11 Broca's Area and Wernicke's Area

Broca's area is located in the frontal lobe of the brain's left hemisphere, and it is involved in the control of speech. Individuals with damage to Broca's area have problems saying words correctly. Also shown is Wernicke's area, a portion of the left hemisphere's temporal lobe that is involved in understanding language. Individuals with damage to this area have difficulty comprehending words; that is, they hear the words but don't know what they mean.

www.mhhe.com/santrockld10

Brain and Language Development

baby says "Mama" more and more. Bit by bit, the baby's language is built up. This view of language acquisition has several problems.

First, the evidence indicates that children learn the syntax of their native language even if they are not reinforced for doing so. Social psychologist Roger Brown (1973) spent long hours observing parents and their young children. He found that parents did not pay attention to the grammatical form of their children's utterances. They were just as likely to reinforce the ungrammatical utterances of the child as the grammatical ones.

Second, the behavioral view fails to explain the extensive orderliness of language. Because each child has a unique history of reinforcement, the behavioral view predicts that vast individual differences should appear in children's speech development. When children learn a certain aspect of a language, according to the behaviorist view, should depend on whether their parents or someone else has rewarded or punished them for something they have said. But as we have seen, a compelling fact about language is its orderly development. For example, all toddlers produce one-word utterances before two-word utterances.

Interaction with People   Although a purely behavioral view is not considered to be a viable explanation of language acquisition, interaction with others contributes in important ways to the development of children's language skills. Language is not learned in a social vacuum. Most children are bathed in language from a very early age (Fernald, 2001; Hart & Risley, 1995). We need this early exposure to language to acquire competent language skills. The Wild Boy of Aveyron did not learn to communicate effectively after a childhood devoid of social interactions with humans. Genie's language is rudimentary, even after years of extensive training. The support and involvement of caregivers and teachers greatly facilitate a child's language learning (Berko Gleason, 2000; Hoff, 2003). Of special concern are children who grow up in impoverished circumstances and are not exposed to guided participation in language. To read about the effects that poverty has on language development, see the Diversity in Life-Span Development interlude.

Diversity in Life-Span Development
Language Environment, Poverty, and Language Development

Let's examine three studies that focus on the language environment infants and young children experience and their vocabulary development. In one study, Janellen Huttenlocher and her colleagues (1991) observed mothers' speech when interacting with their infants. As indicated in figure 6.12, infants whose mothers spoke more often to them had markedly higher vocabularies. By the second birthday, vocabulary differences were substantial.

In another study, extensive conversations between 22 toddlers and their mothers were taped during the children's typical daily activities (Huttenlocher, Levine, & Vevea, 1998). Tapings were carried out every two to four months when the children were 16 to 26 months of age. The researchers found a remarkable link between the size of a child's vocabulary and the talkativeness of his or her mother. The mothers varied as much as tenfold in how much they talked. The toddler of the most talkative mother had a vocabulary more than four times the size of the vocabulary of the child with the quietest mother. This link

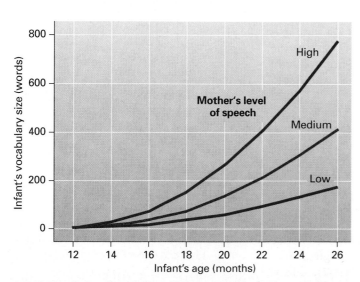

FIGURE 6.12 Level of Maternal Speech and Infant Vocabulary

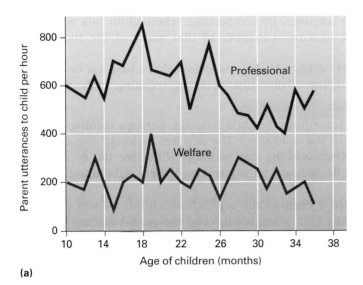

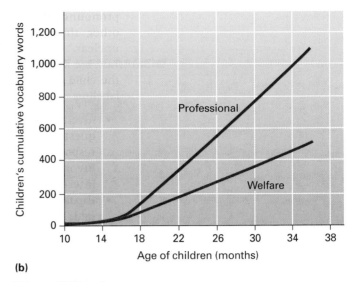

(a) (b)

FIGURE 6.13 Language Input in Professional and Welfare Families and Young Children's Vocabulary Development

(a) Parents from professional families talked with their young children more than parents from welfare families. (b) Children from professional families developed vocabularies that were twice as large as those from welfare families. Thus, by the time children go to preschool, they already have experienced considerable differences in language input in their families and developed different levels of vocabulary that are linked to the socioeconomic context in which they have lived.

might be due at least partly to genetics. However, Huttenlocher believes that is not the case, because the mothers did not vary much in their verbal IQs. Also, the children clearly were picking up what their mothers were saying, because the words each child used the most often mirrored those favored by the mother.

Young children's vocabularies are linked to the socioeconomic status of their families. Betty Hart and Todd Risley (1995) observed the language environments of children whose parents were professionals and children whose parents were on welfare. Compared with the professional parents, the welfare parents talked much less to their young children, talked less about past events, and provided less elaboration. All of the children learned to talk and acquired all of the forms of English. However, as indicated in figure 6.13, the children of the professional parents had a much larger vocabulary at 36 months of age than the children of the welfare parents.

In sum, the language environment of children is linked to their vocabulary development. When children grow up in impoverished circumstances, and when their parents do not use a large number of vocabulary words in communicating with them, their vocabulary development suffers.

One intriguing component of the young child's linguistic environment is **child-directed speech,** language spoken in a higher pitch than normal with simple words and sentences. Child-directed speech has the important function of capturing the infant's attention and maintaining communication. It is hard to use child-directed speech when not in the presence of a baby. As soon as you start talking to a baby, though, you shift into child-directed speech. Much of this is automatic and something most parents are not aware they are doing. Older children also modify their speech when talking to babies and younger children who are learning language. Even 4-year-olds speak in simpler ways to 2-year-olds than to their 4-year-old friends.

Patricia Kuhl (2002; Liu, Kuhl, & Tsao, 2003) says that child-directed speech plays an important role because it is clearer speech, which likely helps infants to

child-directed speech Language spoken in a higher pitch than normal with simple words and sentences.

CHAPTER

*We never know the love
of our parents until we
have become parents.*
—Henry Ward Beecher
American Writer, 19th Century

Socioemotional Development in Infancy

Images of Life-Span Development
The Story of Tom's Fathering

Many fathers are spending more time with their infants today than in the past.

Tom is a 1-year-old infant who is being reared by his father during the day. His mother works full-time at her job away from home, and his father is a writer who works at home; they prefer this arrangement over putting Tom in day care. Tom's father is doing a great job of caring for him. Tom's father keeps Tom nearby while he is writing and spends lots of time talking to him and playing with him. From their interactions, it is clear that they genuinely enjoy each other.

Tom's father is a far cry from the emotionally distant, conformist, traditional-gender-role fathers of the 1950s. He looks to the future and imagines the Little League games Tom will play in and the many other activities he can enjoy with Tom. Remembering how little time his own father spent with him, he is dedicated to making sure that Tom has an involved, nurturing experience with his father. Of course, not all fathers in the 1950s behaved like Tom's grandfather, and not all fathers today are as emotionally involved with their children as Tom is (Day & Lamb, 2004).

When Tom's mother comes home in the evening, she spends considerable time with him. Tom shows a positive attachment to both his mother and his father. By cooperating, his parents have successfully juggled their careers and work schedules to provide 1-year-old Tom with excellent child care.

PREVIEW

In chapters 5 and 6, you read about how the infant perceives, learns, and remembers. Infants also are socioemotional beings, capable of displaying emotions and initiating social interaction with people close to them. The main topics that we will explore in this chapter are emotional and personality development, attachment, and the social contexts of the family and child care.

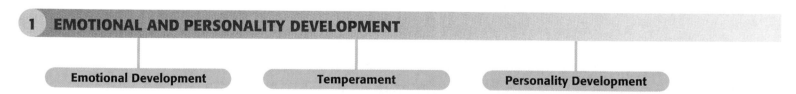

1 EMOTIONAL AND PERSONALITY DEVELOPMENT

Emotional Development	Temperament	Personality Development

Anyone who has been around infants for even a brief period of time detects that they are emotional beings. Not only do we notice infants' expressions of emotions, but we also sense that they vary in their temperament. Some are shy and others are outgoing. Some are active and others much less so. Let's explore these and other aspects of emotional and personality development in infants.

Emotional Development

Infants can express a number of emotions. We will see what these are and how they develop, but first we need to define *emotion*.

What Is Emotion?   Defining *emotion* is difficult because it is not easy to tell when a child or an adult is in an emotional state. For our purposes, we will define **emotion** as feeling, or affect, that occurs when a person is in a state or an inter-action that is important to them, especially to their well-being (Campos, 2004; Campos, Frankel, & Camras, 2004). Emotion is characterized by behavior that reflects (expresses) the pleasantness or unpleasantness of the state a person is in or the transactions being experienced (Austin & Chorpita, 2004). Emotions also can be more specific and take the form of joy, fear, anger, and so on, depending on how a transaction affects the person (for example, is the transaction a threat, a frustration, a relief, something to be rejected, something unexpected, and so on). And emotions can vary in how intense they are. For example, an infant may show intense fear or only mild fear in a particular situation.

When we think about children's emotions, a few dramatic feelings, such as rage, fear, and glorious joy, usually spring to mind. However, emotions can be subtle as well—the feeling a mother has when she holds her baby, the mild irritation of bore-dom, and the uneasiness of being in a new situation.

Biological and Environmental Influences   Emotions are influenced by biolog-ical foundations and environmental experiences. In *The Expression of Emotions in Man and Animals*, Charles Darwin (1872/1965) stated that the facial expressions of humans are innate, not learned; are the same in all cultures around the world; and evolved from the emotions of animals. Darwin compared the similarity of human snarls of anger with the growls of dogs and the hisses of cats. Today, psychologists still emphasize that emotions, especially facial expressions of emotions, have a strong biological foundation (Goldsmith, 2002). For example, children who are blind from birth and have never observed the smile or frown on another person's face smile and frown in the same way that children with normal vision do.

The biological foundations of emotion involve the development of the nervous system (Goldsmith & Davidson, 2004; Lewis & Stieben, 2004). Emotions are linked with early developing regions of the human nervous system, including structures of the limbic system and the brain stem (Thompson, Easterbrooks, & Walker, 2003). The capacity of infants to show distress, excitement, and rage reflects the early emergence of these biologically rooted emotional brain systems. Significant advances in emotional responding occur during infancy and childhood as a result of develop-mental changes in neurobiological systems, including the frontal regions of the cere-bral cortex that can exert control over the more primitive limbic system (Porges, Doussard-Roosevelt, & Maiti, 1994). The maturation of the cerebral cortex allows for fewer unpredictable mood swings and greater self-regulation of emotion as children develop.

Caregivers play a role in the infant's neurobiological regulation of emotions (Thompson, Easterbrooks, & Walker, 2003). For example, by soothing the infant when the infant cries and shows distress, caregivers help infants to modulate their emotion and reduce the level of stress hormones (Gunnar, 2000; Gunnar & Davis, 2003).

Emotions are the first language with which parents and infants communicate before the infant acquires speech (Maccoby, 1992). Infants react to their parents' facial expressions and tone of voice. In return, parents "read" what the infant is trying to communicate, responding appropriately when their infants are either dis-tressed or happy. Sensitive, responsive parents help their infants grow emotion-ally, whether the infants respond in distressed or happy ways (Campos, 2001; Thompson, 1998).

Blossoms are scattered by the wind
And the wind cares nothing, but
The blossoms of the heart
No wind can touch.

—YOUSHIDA KENKO
Buddhist Monk, 14th Century

International Society for Research on Emotions

emotion Feeling, or affect, that occurs when a person is in a state or interaction that is important to them. Emotion is characterized by behavior that reflects (expresses) the pleasantness or unpleasantness of the state a person is in or the transactions being experienced.

First appearance	Emotion
Primary Emotions	
3 months	Joy Sadness Disgust
2 to 6 months	Anger
First 6 months	Surprise
6 to 8 months	Fear (peaks at 18 months)
Self-Conscious Emotions	
1½ to 2 years	Empathy Jealousy Embarrassment
2½ years	Pride Shame Guilt

FIGURE 7.1 The First Appearance of Different Emotions

The initial aspects of infant attachment to parents are based on emotion-linked interchanges, as when an infant cries and the caregiver sensitively responds. By the end of the first year, a mother's facial expression—either smiling or fearful—influences whether an infant will explore an unfamiliar environment. And, when children hear their parents quarreling, they often react with distress and inhibit their play (Cummings, 1987). Exceptionally well-functioning families often include humor in their interactions, sometimes making each other laugh and developing light, pleasant mood states to defuse conflicts. And, when a positive mood has been induced in the child, the child is more likely to comply with a parent's directions. In sum, biological evolution has endowed human beings to be *emotional*, but embeddedness in culture and relationships with others provides diversity in emotional experiences (Saarni, 2000).

Early Developmental Change in Emotion In research on emotional development, two broad types of emotions are studied (Lewis, 2002) (see figure 7.1):

- **Primary emotions** are present in humans and other animals. The primary emotions include surprise, joy, anger, sadness, fear, and disgust. They appear in the first six to eight months of life.
- **Self-conscious emotions** require cognition, especially consciousness. The self-conscious emotions include empathy, jealousy, and embarrassment, which first appear at about 1½ to 2 years (in the middle of the second year of life following the emergence of consciousness), and pride, shame, and guilt, which first appear at about 2½ years of age (in the middle of the third year of life). In developing this second set of self-conscious emotions (referred to as *self-conscious evaluative emotions*), children acquire and are able to use societal standards and rules to evaluate their behavior.

Figure 7.2 shows infants expressing a number of the emotions we have described. Although we have provided specific ages for the initial onset of different emotions, these should be thought of as general ages, and developmentalists continue to debate just when specific emotions first appear (Campos, 2004; Lewis, 2002). Let's now look in greater detail at two emotion-linked behaviors in infancy: crying and smiling.

Crying Crying is the most important mechanism newborns have for communicating with their world. The first cry verifies that the baby's lungs have filled with air. Cries also may tell physicians and researchers something about the central nervous system.

primary emotions Emotions that are present in humans and other animals, including surprise, joy, anger, sadness, fear, and disgust; appear in first six to eight months of life.

self-conscious emotions Emotions that require cognition, especially consciousness; include empathy, jealousy, embarrassment, pride, shame, and guilt; appear for the first time from the middle of the second year through the middle of the third year of life.

Joy   Sadness   Anger

Fear   Surprise   Pride

FIGURE 7.2 Expression of Different Emotions in Infants

Babies have at least three types of cries:

- **Basic cry:** A rhythmic pattern that usually consists of a cry, followed by a briefer silence, then a shorter inspiratory whistle that is somewhat higher in pitch than the main cry, then another brief rest before the next cry. Some infancy experts believe that hunger is one of the conditions that incites the basic cry.
- **Anger cry:** A variation of the basic cry in which more excess air is forced through the vocal cords.
- **Pain cry:** A sudden long, initial loud cry followed by breath holding; no preliminary moaning is present. The pain cry is stimulated by a high-intensity stimulus.

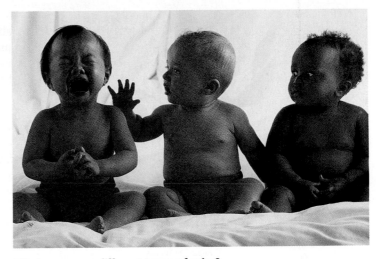

What are some different types of cries?

Most adults can determine whether an infant's cries signify anger or pain (Zeskind, Klein, & Marshall, 1992). Parents can distinguish the cries of their own baby better than those of another baby.

To soothe or not to soothe—should a crying baby be given attention and soothed, or does this spoil the infant? Many years ago, the behaviorist John Watson (1928) argued that parents spend too much time responding to infant crying. As a consequence, he said, parents reward crying and increase its incidence. More recently, behaviorist Jacob Gewirtz (1977) found that a caregiver's quick, soothing response to crying increased crying. In contrast, infancy experts Mary Ainsworth (1979) and John Bowlby (1989) stress that a caregiver cannot respond too much to infant crying in the first year of life. They believe that a quick, comforting response to the infant's cries is an important ingredient in the development of a strong bond between the infant and caregiver. In one of Ainsworth's studies, infants whose mothers responded quickly when they cried at 3 months of age cried less later in the first year of life (Bell & Ainsworth, 1972).

Controversy still characterizes the question of whether or how parents should respond to an infant's cries (Alvarez, 2004; Hiscock & Jordan, 2004; Lewis & Ramsay, 1999). However, developmentalists increasingly argue that an infant cannot be spoiled in the first year of life, which suggests that parents should soothe a crying infant rather than be unresponsive. This reaction should help infants develop a sense of trust and secure attachment to the caregiver.

Smiling   Smiling is another important communicative affective behavior of the infant. Two types of smiling can be distinguished in infants:

- **Reflexive smile:** A smile that does not occur in response to external stimuli and appears during the first month after birth, usually during sleep.
- **Social smile:** A smile that occurs in response to an external stimulus, typically a face in the case of the young infant.

Social smiling does not occur until 2 to 3 months of age (Emde, Gaensbauer, & Harmon, 1976), although some researchers argue that infants grin in response to voices as early as 3 weeks of age (Sroufe & Waters, 1976). The power of the infant's smiles has been appropriately captured by British theorist John Bowlby (1969): "Can we doubt that the more and better an infant smiles the better he is loved and cared for? It is fortunate for their survival that babies are so designed by nature that they beguile and enslave mothers."

Fear   The most frequent expression of an infant's fear involves **stranger anxiety,** in which an infant shows a fear and wariness of strangers. However, not all infants show distress when they encounter a stranger and whether an infant shows stranger anxiety also depends on the social context and the characteristics of the stranger.

basic cry A rhythmic pattern usually consisting of a cry, a briefer silence, a shorter inspiratory whistle that is higher pitched than the main cry, and then a brief rest before the next cry.

anger cry A cry similar to the basic cry, with more excess air forced through the vocal cords.

pain cry A sudden appearance of loud crying without preliminary moaning, followed by breath holding.

reflexive smile A smile that does not occur in response to external stimuli. It happens during the month after birth, usually during sleep.

social smile A smile in response to an external stimulus, which, early in development, typically is a face.

stranger anxiety An infant's fear and wariness of strangers; it tends to appear in the second half of the first year of life.

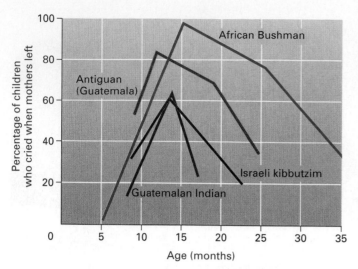

FIGURE 7.3 Separation Anxiety in Four Cultures

Note that separation anxiety peaked at about the same time in all four cultures in this study (13 to 15 months of age). However, a higher percentage (100 percent) of infants in an African Bushman culture engaged in separation anxiety compared with only about 60 percent of infants in Guatemalan Indian and Israeli kibbutzim cultures.

Stranger anxiety usually emerges gradually. It first appears at about 6 months of age in the form of wary reactions. By age 9 months, the fear of strangers is often more intense, and it continues to escalate through the infant's first birthday (Emde, Gaensbauer, & Harmon, 1976).

Infants show less stranger anxiety when they are in familiar settings. For example, in one study, 10-month-olds showed little stranger anxiety when they met a stranger in their own home but much greater fear when they encountered a stranger in a research laboratory (Sroufe, Waters, & Matas, 1974). Also, infants show less stranger anxiety when they are sitting on their mothers' laps than when placed in an infant seat several feet away from their mothers (Bohlin & Hagekull, 1993). Thus, it appears that, when infants have a sense of security, they are less likely to show stranger anxiety. In terms of parenting, this research suggests that providing an infant with the opportunity to adjust may help the child transition more smoothly into a new caregiving arrangement with strangers. For example, parents may want to take their infant for several brief visits with the new care provider before leaving the infant with the provider for a more extended period of time.

Who the stranger is and how the stranger behaves also influence stranger anxiety in infants. Infants are less fearful of child strangers than adult strangers. They also are less fearful of friendly, outgoing, smiling strangers than of passive, unsmiling strangers (Bretherton, Stolberg, & Kreye, 1981).

In addition to stranger anxiety, infants experience fear of being separated from their caregivers. The result is **separation anxiety**—an infant's distressed reaction when the caregiver leaves. Separation anxiety, typically expressed by crying, tends to peak at about 15 months among U.S. infants. In fact, in one study, separation anxiety peaked at about 13 to 15 months in four different cultures (Kagan, Kearsley, & Zelazo, 1978). As indicated in figure 7.3, the percentage of infants who displayed separation anxiety varied across cultures, but the infants reached a peak of separation anxiety at about the same age—just before the middle of the second year of life.

Social Referencing Social referencing involves "reading" emotional cues in others to help determine how to act in a particular situation. The development of social referencing helps infants to interpret ambiguous situations more accurately, as when they encounter a stranger and need to know whether to fear the person (Hertenstein & Campos, 2004; Mumme, Fernald, & Herrera, 1996).

Infants become better at social referencing in the second year of life. At this age, they tend to "check" with their mother before they act; they look at her to see if she is happy, angry, or fearful. For example, in one study, 14- to 22-month-old infants were more likely to look at their mothers' faces as a source of information for how to act in a situation than were 6- to 9-month-old infants (Walden, 1991).

Emotional Regulation and Coping During the first year of life, the infant gradually develops an ability to inhibit, or minimize, the intensity and duration of emotional reactions (Cole, Martin, & Dennis, 2004; Eisenberg, 2001; Eisenberg, Spinrad, & Smith, 2004). From early in infancy, babies put their thumbs in their mouths as a self-soothing strategy. At first, infants mainly depend on caregivers to help them soothe their emotions, as when a caregiver rocks an infant to sleep, sings lullabyes to the infant, gently strokes the infant, and so on. Many developmentalists stress that it is a good strategy for a caregiver to soothe an infant before the infant gets into an intense, agitated, uncontrolled state (Calkins, 2004; Thompson, 1994).

separation anxiety An infant's distressed reaction when the caregiver leaves.

social referencing "Reading" emotional cues in others to help determine how to act in a particular situation.

Later in infancy, when they become aroused, infants sometimes redirect their attention or distract themselves in order to reduce their arousal (Grolnick, Bridges, & Connell, 1996). By 2 years of age, toddlers can use language to define their feeling states and the context that is upsetting them (Kopp & Neufeld, 2002). A toddler might say, "Feel bad. Dog scare." This type of communication may help caregivers to help the child in regulating emotion.

Contexts can influence emotional regulation (Kopp & Neufeld, 2002; Raver, 2004; Saarni, 1999). Infants often are affected by fatigue, hunger, time of day, the people around them, and where they are. Infants must learn to adapt to different contexts that require emotional regulation. Further, new demands appear as the infant becomes older and parents modify their expectations. For example, a parent may take it in stride if a 6-month-old infant screams in a restaurant but may react very differently when a $1\frac{1}{2}$-year-old starts screaming.

"Oh, he's cute, all right, but he's got the temperament of a car alarm."

Temperament

Emotional responses to similar situations vary among infants. One infant might be cheerful and happy much of the time; another baby might cry a lot and more often display a negative mood. These behaviors reflect differences in **temperament,** an individual's behavioral style and characteristic way of emotionally responding (Rothbart & Putnam, 2002). Let's now explore how temperament can be classified, biological and environmental influences, the roles of culture and gender in temperament, the concept of goodness of fit, and the implications of temperamental variations for parenting.

Classifying Temperament How would you describe your temperament or the temperament of a friend? Researchers have described and classified the temperament of individuals in different ways. Here we will examine three ways of describing and classifying temperament.

Chess and Thomas' Classification Psychiatrists Alexander Chess and Stella Thomas (Chess & Thomas, 1977; Thomas & Chess, 1991) identified three basic types, or clusters, of temperament:

- **Easy child:** This child is generally in a positive mood, quickly establishes regular routines in infancy, and adapts easily to new experiences.
- **Difficult child:** This child reacts negatively and cries frequently, engages in irregular daily routines, and is slow to accept change.
- **Slow-to-warm-up child:** This child has a low activity level, is somewhat negative, and displays a low intensity of mood.

In their longitudinal investigation, Chess and Thomas (1977) found that 40 percent of the children they studied could be classified as easy, 10 percent as difficult, and 15 percent as slow to warm up. Notice that 35 percent did not fit any of the three patterns. Researchers have found that these three basic clusters of temperament are moderately stable across the childhood years.

Kagan's Behavioral Inhibition Another way of classifying temperament focuses on the differences between a shy, subdued, timid child and a sociable, extraverted, bold child. Jerome Kagan (1997, 2000, 2002, 2003; Kagan & Snidman, 1991) regards shyness with strangers (peers or adults) as one feature of a broad temperament category called *inhibition to the unfamiliar,* which is similar to the "slow-to-warm-up child." Inhibited children react to many aspects of unfamiliarity with initial avoidance, distress, or subdued affect, especially beginning about 7 to 9 months of age.

temperament An individual's behavioral style and characteristic way of emotionally responding.

easy child A child who is generally in a positive mood, who quickly establishes regular routines in infancy, and who adapts easily to new experiences.

difficult child A child who tends to react negatively and cry frequently, who engages in irregular daily routines, and who is slow to accept new experiences.

slow-to-warm-up child A child who has a low activity level, is somewhat negative, and displays a low intensity of mood.

What are some ways that developmentalists have classified infants' temperaments? Which classification makes the most sense to you, based on your observations of infants?

Infant Temperament

Kagan has found that inhibition shows considerable stability from infancy through early childhood. One recent study classified toddlers into extremely inhibited, extremely uninhibited, and intermediate groups (Pfeifer & others, 2002). Follow-up assessments occurred at 4 and 7 years of age. Continuity was demonstrated for both inhibition and lack of inhibition, although a substantial number of the inhibited children moved into the intermediate groups at 7 years of age.

Rothbart and Bates' Classification New classifications of temperament continue to be forged (Wachs & Kohnstamm, 2001). Mary Rothbart and John Bates (1998) have proposed the following framework for classifying temperament:

- *Positive affect and approach.* Kagan's uninhibited children fit into this category.
- *Negative affectivity.* Children with this temperament are easily distressed; they may fret and cry often. Kagan's inhibited children fit this category.
- *Effortful control (self-regulation).* Infants who are high on effortful control show an ability to keep their arousal from getting too high and have strategies for soothing themselves. By contrast, children low on effortful control are often unable to control their arousal; they become easily agitated and intensely emotional (Eisenberg & Spinrad, 2004; Eisenberg & others, 2002; Rothbart, 2004; Rothbart, Ellis, & Posner, 2004; Rothbart & others, 2003).

Biological Foundations and Experience Physiological characteristics are associated with different temperaments (Fox & others, 2004; Rothbart & Bates, 1998; Thompson & Goodvin, 2005). For example, the brain's limbic system is linked with positive affect and approach, especially through the neural circuits involved in reward. Conversely, the amygdala in the brain plays an important role in fear and inhibition (Kagan, 2003; LeDoux, 2000, 2002). Inhibition is also associated with a unique physiological pattern that includes high and stable heart rate, high cortisol levels, and high activity in the right frontal lobe of the brain (Kagan, 2003). Neurotransmitters also are linked to temperament. For example, low levels of the neurotransmitter serotonin may increase an individual's vulnerability to fear and frustration, which can contribute to negative affectivity, such as depression (Hariri & others, 2002).

Heredity contributes to temperament's biological foundations. Twin and adoption studies have found a heritability index in the range of .50 to .60, suggesting a moderate influence of heredity on temperament (Plomin & others, 1994). However, the strength of the association usually declines as infants become older (Goldsmith & Gottesman, 1981). This finding supports the belief that temperament becomes more malleable with experience. Alternatively, it may be that, as a child becomes older, behavior indicators of temperament are more difficult to spot.

Kagan (1997, 2003) argues that children inherit a physiology that biases them to develop a particular type of temperament. However, through experience they may learn to modify their temperament to some degree. For example, children may inherit a physiology that biases them to be fearful and inhibited but they may learn to reduce their fear and inhibition.

Gender, Culture, and Temperament Gender may be an important factor shaping the context that influences the fate of temperament. Parents may react differently to a child's temperament depending on whether the child is a boy or a girl and on the culture in which they live (Kerr, 2001). For example, in one study, mothers were more responsive to the crying of irritable girls than to the crying of irritable boys (Crockenberg, 1986).

Similarly, the reaction to an infant's temperament may depend in part on culture. For example, an active temperament might be valued in some cultures (such as the United States) but not in other cultures (such as China). Indeed, children's temperament can vary across cultures (Campos, Frankel, & Camras, 2004; Putnam, Sanson, & Rothbart, 2002). Behavioral inhibition is more highly valued in China than in North America, and researchers have found that Chinese children are more inhibited than Canadian infants (Chen & others, 1998). The cultural differences in temperament were linked to parent attitude and behaviors. Canadian mothers of inhibited 2-year-olds were less accepting of their infants' inhibited temperament, whereas Chinese mothers were more accepting.

How might an infant's temperament vary across cultures?

In short, many aspects of a child's environment can encourage or discourage the persistence of temperament characteristics. One useful way of thinking about these relationships applies the concept of goodness of fit, which we examine next.

Goodness of Fit **Goodness of fit** refers to the match between a child's temperament and the environmental demands with which the child must cope (Matheny & Phillips, 2001). Consider an active child who is made to sit still for long periods of time or a slow-to-warm-up child who is abruptly pushed into new situations on a regular basis. Both children face a lack of fit between their temperament and environmental demands. Lack of fit can produce adjustment problems for the child.

Some temperament characteristics pose more parenting challenges than others, at least in modern Western societies (Sanson, Smart, & Hemphill, 2004). Children's proneness to distress, as exhibited by frequent crying and irritability, can contribute to the emergence of avoidant or coercive parental responses. In one research study, though, extra support and training for mothers of distress-prone infants improved the quality of mother-infant interaction (van den Boom, 1989).

Parenting and the Child's Temperament Many parents don't become believers in temperament's importance until the birth of their second child. Many parents view the first child's behavior as being solely a result of how they socialized the child. However, management strategies that worked with the first child might not be as effective with the second child. Problems experienced with the first child (such as those involved in feeding, sleeping, and coping with strangers) might not exist with the second child, but new problems might arise. Such experiences strongly suggest that children differ from each other very early in life, and that these differences have important implications for parent-child interaction (Kwak & others, 1999; Rothbart & Putnam, 2002).

What are the implications of temperamental variations for parenting? Although answers to this question are necessarily speculative because of the incompleteness of the research literature, the following conclusions regarding the best parenting strategies to use in relation to children's temperament have been reached by temperament experts Ann Sanson and Mary Rothbart (1995):

- *Attention to and respect for individuality.* Parents need to be sensitive and flexible to the infant's signals and needs because it is difficult to generate general prescriptions for "good" parenting. A goal may be accomplished in one way with one child and in another way with another child, depending on the child's temperament.
- *Structuring the child's environment.* Crowded, noisy environments can pose greater problems for some children (such as a "difficult child") than others (such as an

goodness of fit Refers to the match between a child's temperament and the environmental demands with which the child must cope.

"easygoing" child). We also may expect that a fearful, withdrawing child would benefit from slower entry into new contexts.

- *The "difficult child" and packaged parenting programs.* Programs for parents often focus on dealing with children who have "difficult" temperaments. Even though acknowledgment that some children are harder to parent is often helpful, and advice on how to handle particular difficult characteristics can also be useful, whether a particular characteristic of a given temperament is difficult depends on its fit with the environment. To label a child "difficult" poses the danger of becoming a self-fulfilling prophecy. If a child is identified as "difficult," labeling the child as such may maintain that categorization.

Some critics argue that too often we are prone to pigeon-holing children into categories without examining the context in which temperament occurs (Wachs, 2000). Therefore, caregiving behavior needs to be taken into account when considering a child's temperament (Kochanska & others, 2004). Research does not yet allow for many highly specific recommendations, but, in general, caregivers should (1) be sensitive to the individual characteristics of the child, (2) be flexible in responding to these characteristics, and (3) avoid negative labeling of the child.

Personality Development

We have explored some important aspects of emotional development and temperament, which reveal individual variations in infants. Let's now examine the characteristics that often are thought of as central to the infant's personality development: trust and the development of self and independence.

Trust According to Erik Erikson (1968), the first year of life is characterized by the trust-versus-mistrust stage of development. Following a life of regularity, warmth, and protection in the mother's womb, the infant faces a world that is less secure. Erikson proposed that infants learn trust when they are cared for in a consistent, warm manner. If the infant is not well fed and kept warm on a consistent basis, a sense of mistrust is likely to develop.

Trust versus mistrust is not resolved once and for all in the first year of life. It arises again at each successive stage of development, which can have positive or negative outcomes. For example, children who leave infancy with a sense of trust can still have their sense of mistrust activated at a later stage, perhaps if their parents are separated or divorced under conflicting circumstances.

Self Development in Infancy
Seeking Independence

The Developing Sense of Self and Independence Individuals carry with them a sense of who they are and what makes them different from everyone else. They cling to this identity and begin to feel secure in the knowledge that their identity is becoming more stable. Real or imagined, the sense of self is a strong motivating force in life. When does the individual begin to sense a separate existence from others?

The Self Infants are not "given" a self by their parents or the culture. Rather, they find and construct selves (Rochat, 2002). Studying the self in infancy is difficult mainly because infants are unable to describe with language their experiences of themselves.

To determine whether infants can recognize themselves, psychologists have used mirrors. In the animal kingdom, only the great apes learn to recognize their reflection in the mirror, but the majority of human infants accomplish this feat toward the end of the second year of life. How does the mirror technique work? The mother puts a dot of rouge on her infant's nose. The observer watches to see how often the infant touches its nose. Next, the infant is placed in front of a mirror, and observers detect whether nose touching increases. In two independent investigations in the

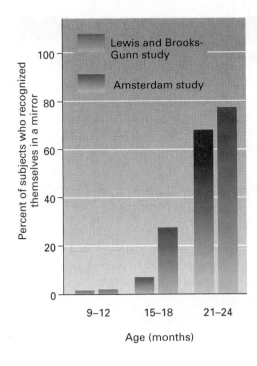

FIGURE 7.4 The Development of Self-Recognition in Infancy
The graph shows the findings of two studies in which infants less than 1 year of age did not recognize themselves in the mirror. A slight increase in the percentage of infant self-recognition occurred around 15 to 18 months of age. By 2 years of age, a majority of children recognized themselves.

second half of the second year of life, a majority of infants recognized their own image and coordinated the image they saw with the actions of touching their own bodies (Amsterdam, 1968; Lewis & Brooks-Gunn, 1979) (see figure 7.4).

Independence   Not only does the infant develop a sense of self in the second year of life, but independence also becomes a more central theme in the infant's life. The theories of Margaret Mahler and Erik Erikson have important implications for both self-development and independence. Mahler (1979) argues that the child goes through a separation and then an individuation process. *Separation* involves the infant's movement away from the mother. *Individuation* involves the development of self.

Erikson (1968), like Mahler, stressed that independence is an important issue in the second year of life. Erikson describes the second stage of development as the stage of autonomy versus shame and doubt. Autonomy builds as the infant's mental and motor abilities develop. At this point in development, not only can infants walk, but they can also climb, open and close, drop, push and pull, and hold and let go. Infants feel pride in these new accomplishments and want to do everything themselves, whether the activity is flushing a toilet, pulling the wrapping off a package, or deciding what to eat. It is important for parents to recognize the motivation of toddlers to do what they are capable of doing at their own pace. Then they can learn to control their muscles and their impulses themselves. But when caregivers are impatient and do for toddlers what they are capable of doing themselves, shame and doubt develop. Every parent has rushed a child from time to time. It is only when parents consistently overprotect toddlers or criticize accidents (wetting, soiling, spilling, or breaking, for example) that children develop an excessive sense of shame and doubt about their ability to control themselves and their world.

Erikson also believed that the stage of autonomy versus shame and doubt has important implications for the development of independence and identity during adolescence. The development of autonomy during the toddler years gives adolescents the courage to be independent individuals who can choose and guide their own future.

Erikson believed that autonomy versus shame and doubt is the key developmental theme of the toddler years. *What are some good strategies for parents to use with their toddlers?*

Review and Reflect: Learning Goal 1

1 **Discuss emotional and personality development in infancy**

REVIEW

- What is the nature of an infant's emotions and how do they change?
- What is temperament and how does it develop in infancy?
- What are some important aspects of personality in infancy and how do they develop?

REFLECT

- How would you describe your temperament? Does it fit one of Chess and Thomas' three styles—easy, slow to warm up, or difficult? If you have siblings, is your temperament similar or different from theirs?

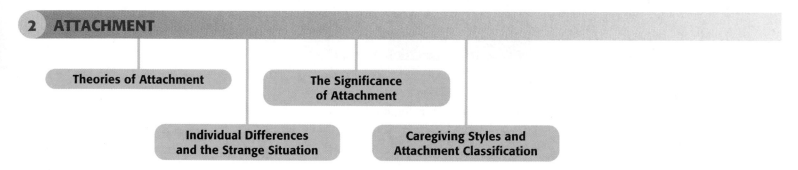

2 ATTACHMENT

Theories of Attachment

The Significance of Attachment

Individual Differences and the Strange Situation

Caregiving Styles and Attachment Classification

So far, we have discussed how emotions and emotional styles in infancy set the tone of our experiences in life. But emotions also write the lyrics because they are at the core of infants' relationships with their caregivers. Foremost among these relationships is **attachment,** a close emotional bond between an infant and a caregiver. Consider the situation in which a small curly haired girl named Danielle, age 11 months, begins to whimper. After a few seconds, she begins to wail. Soon her mother comes into the room, and Danielle's crying ceases. Quickly, Danielle crawls over to where her mother is seated and reaches out to be held. Danielle has just demonstrated attachment to her mother.

Theories of Attachment

There is no shortage of theories about infant attachment. Three theorists initially discussed in chapter 2—Freud, Erikson, and Bowlby—proposed influential views.

Freud believed that infants become attached to the person or object that provides oral satisfaction. For most infants, this is the mother because she is most likely to feed the infant. Is feeding as important as Freud thought? A classic study by Harry Harlow (1958) reveals that the answer is no (see figure 7.5). Harlow removed infant monkeys from their mothers at birth; for six months they were reared by surrogate (substitute) "mothers." One surrogate mother was made of wire, the other of cloth. Half of the infant monkeys were fed by the wire mother, half by the cloth mother. Periodically, the amount of time the infant monkeys spent with either the wire or the cloth mother was computed. Regardless of which mother fed them, the infant monkeys spent far more time with the cloth mother. This study clearly demonstrated that feeding is not the crucial element in the attachment process and that contact comfort is important.

Erik Erikson (1968) believed that the first year of life is the key time for the development of attachment. Recall his proposal (discussed in chapter 2) that the

attachment A close emotional bond between an infant and a caregiver.

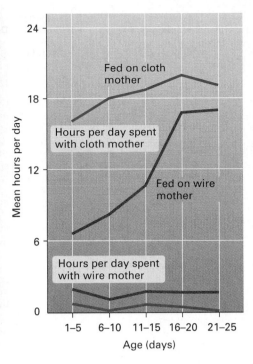

FIGURE 7.5 Contact Time with Wire and Cloth Surrogate Mothers
Regardless of whether the infant monkeys were fed by a wire or a cloth mother, they overwhelmingly preferred to spend contact time with the cloth mother.

first year of life represents the stage of trust versus mistrust. A sense of trust requires a feeling of physical comfort and minimal fear or apprehension about the future. Trust in infancy sets the stage for a lifelong expectation that the world will be a good and pleasant place to be. Erikson also believed that responsive, sensitive parenting contributes to an infant's sense of trust.

The ethological perspective of British psychiatrist John Bowlby (1969, 1989) also stresses the importance of attachment in the first year of life and the responsiveness of the caregiver. Bowlby believes that an infant and its primary caregiver form an attachment. He argues that the newborn is biologically equipped to elicit attachment behavior. The baby cries, clings, coos, and smiles. Later, the infant crawls, walks, and follows the mother. The immediate result is to keep the primary caregiver nearby; the long-term effect is to increase the infant's chances of survival.

Attachment does not emerge suddenly but rather develops in a series of phases, moving from a baby's general preference for human beings to a partnership with primary caregivers. Following are four such phases based on Bowlby's conceptualization of attachment (Schaffer, 1996):

- *Phase 1: From birth to 2 months.* Infants instinctively direct their attachment to human figures. Strangers, siblings, and parents are equally likely to elicit smiling or crying from the infant.
- *Phase 2: From 2 to 7 months.* Attachment becomes focused on one figure, usually the primary caregiver, as the baby gradually learns to distinguish familiar from unfamiliar people.
- *Phase 3: From 7 to 24 months.* Specific attachments develop. With increased locomotor skills, babies actively seek contact with regular caregivers, such as the mother or father.
- *Phase 4: From 24 months on.* Children become aware of others' feelings, goals, and plans and begin to take these into account in forming their own actions.

Individual Differences and the Strange Situation

Although attachment to a caregiver intensifies midway through the first year, isn't it likely that some babies have a more positive attachment experience than others? Mary Ainsworth thought so. Ainsworth (1979) created the **Strange Situation,** an

 Watch the video "Attachment Theory" for an overview of the theories of infant attachment offered by Freud, Erikson, and Bowlby.

Strange Situation An observational measure of infant attachment that requires the infant to move through a series of introductions, separations, and reunions with the caregiver and an adult stranger in a prescribed order.

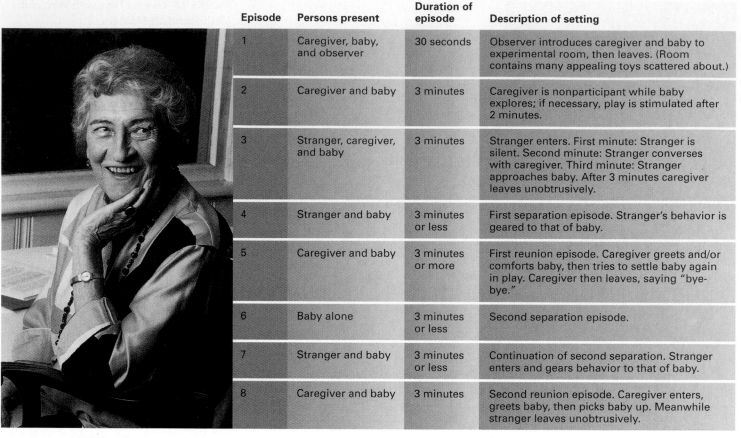

Episode	Persons present	Duration of episode	Description of setting
1	Caregiver, baby, and observer	30 seconds	Observer introduces caregiver and baby to experimental room, then leaves. (Room contains many appealing toys scattered about.)
2	Caregiver and baby	3 minutes	Caregiver is nonparticipant while baby explores; if necessary, play is stimulated after 2 minutes.
3	Stranger, caregiver, and baby	3 minutes	Stranger enters. First minute: Stranger is silent. Second minute: Stranger converses with caregiver. Third minute: Stranger approaches baby. After 3 minutes caregiver leaves unobtrusively.
4	Stranger and baby	3 minutes or less	First separation episode. Stranger's behavior is geared to that of baby.
5	Caregiver and baby	3 minutes or more	First reunion episode. Caregiver greets and/or comforts baby, then tries to settle baby again in play. Caregiver then leaves, saying "bye-bye."
6	Baby alone	3 minutes or less	Second separation episode.
7	Stranger and baby	3 minutes or less	Continuation of second separation. Stranger enters and gears behavior to that of baby.
8	Caregiver and baby	3 minutes	Second reunion episode. Caregiver enters, greets baby, then picks baby up. Meanwhile stranger leaves unobtrusively.

FIGURE 7.6 The Ainsworth Strange Situation

Mary Ainsworth (*left*) developed the Strange Situation to assess whether infants are securely or insecurely attached to their caregiver. The episodes involved in the Ainsworth Strange Situation are described here.

observational measure of infant attachment in which the infant experiences a series of introductions, separations, and reunions with the caregiver and an adult stranger in a prescribed order (see figure 7.6). In using the Strange Situation, researchers hope that their observations will provide information about the infant's motivation to be near the caregiver and the degree to which the caregiver's presence provides the infant with security and confidence.

Based on how babies respond in the Strange Situation, they are described as being securely or insecurely attached (there are three types of insecure attachment) to the caregiver:

- **Securely attached babies** use the caregiver as a secure base from which to explore the environment. When in the presence of their caregiver, securely attached infants explore the room and examine toys that have been placed in it. When the caregiver departs, securely attached infants might mildly protest, and when the caregiver returns these infants reestablish positive interaction with her, perhaps by smiling or climbing on her lap. Subsequently, they often resume playing with the toys in the room.
- **Insecure avoidant babies** show insecurity by avoiding the mother. In the Strange Situation, these babies engage in little interaction with the caregiver, often display distress by crying when she leaves the room, usually do not reestablish contact with her on her return, and may even turn their back on her at this point. If contact is established, the infant usually leans away or looks away.
- **Insecure resistant babies** often cling to the caregiver and then resist her by fighting against the closeness, perhaps by kicking or pushing away. In the

securely attached babies Babies that use the caregiver as a secure base from which to explore the environment.

insecure avoidant babies Babies that show insecurity by avoiding the caregiver.

insecure resistant babies Babies that often cling to the caregiver, then resist her by fighting against the closeness, perhaps by kicking or pushing away.

Strange Situation, these babies often cling anxiously to the caregiver and don't explore the playroom. When the caregiver leaves, they often cry loudly and push away if she tries to comfort them on her return.

- **Insecure disorganized babies** are disorganized and disoriented. In the Strange Situation, these babies might appear dazed, confused, and fearful. To be classified as disorganized, strong patterns of avoidance and resistance must be shown or certain select behaviors, such as extreme fearfulness around the caregiver, must be present.

Some critics believe that behavior in the Strange Situation—like other laboratory assessments—might not indicate what infants would do in a natural environment. Furthermore, as a measure of attachment it may vary with family circumstances and be culturally biased. For example, Strange Situation classifications of attachment are more stable when family economic and stressful circumstances are stable and less stable when those circumstances vary (Thompson, Easterbrooks, & Walker, 2003). Regarding cultural variations, German and Japanese babies often show different patterns of attachment than American infants. As shown in figure 7.7, German infants are more likely to show an avoidant attachment pattern and Japanese infants are less likely to show this pattern than U.S. infants (van IJzendoorn & Kroonenberg, 1988). The avoidant pattern in German babies likely occurs because their caregivers encourage them to be more independent (Grossmann & others, 1985). Also as shown in figure 7.7, Japanese babies are more likely than American babies to be categorized as resistant. This may have more to do with the Strange Situation as a measure of attachment than with attachment insecurity itself. Japanese mothers rarely let anyone unfamiliar with their babies care for them. Thus, the Strange Situation might create considerably more stress for Japanese infants than for American infants, who are more accustomed to separation from their mothers (Takahashi, 1990).

Even though there are cultural variations in attachment classification, the most frequent classification in every culture studied so far is secure attachment (van IJzendoorn & Kroonenberg, 1988). Further, researchers have found that infants' behaviors in the Strange Situation are closely related to how they behave at home in response to separation and reunion with their mothers (Pederson & Moran, 1996). Thus, many infant researchers believe the Strange Situation continues to show merit as a measure of infant attachment.

The Significance of Attachment

Do individual differences in attachment matter? Ainsworth believes that secure attachment in the first year of life provides an important foundation for psychological development later in life. The securely attached infant moves freely away from the mother but keeps track of where she is through periodic glances. The securely attached infant responds positively to being picked up by others and, when put back down, freely moves away to play. An insecurely attached infant, by contrast, avoids the mother or is ambivalent toward her, fears strangers, and is upset by minor, everyday separations.

If early attachment to a caregiver is important, it should relate to a child's social behavior later in development. For some children, early attachments seem to foreshadow later functioning (Carlson & others, 2004; Schneider, Atkinson & Tardif, 2001; Sroufe, 2001; Sroufe & others, 2005). For other children, there is little continuity (Thompson, Easterbrooks, & Walker, 2003). Consistency in

What is the nature of secure and insecure attachment?

www.mhhe.com/santrockld10

Harry Harlow
Forming a Secure Attachment
Attachment Research

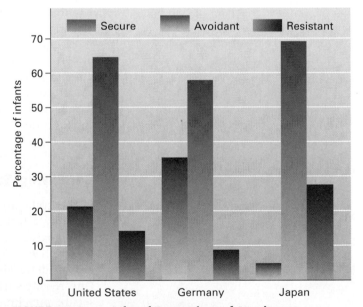

FIGURE 7.7 Cross-Cultural Comparison of Attachment
In one study, infant attachment in three countries—the United States, Germany, and Japan—was measured in the Ainsworth Strange Situation (van IJzendoorn & Kroonenberg, 1988). The dominant attachment pattern in all three countries was secure attachment. However, German infants were more avoidant and Japanese infants were less avoidant and more resistant than U.S. infants.

insecure disorganized babies Babies that show insecurity by being disorganized and disoriented.

caregiving over a number of years is likely an important factor in connecting early attachment and the child's functioning later in development.

Not all research reveals the power of infant attachment to predict subsequent development. In one longitudinal study, attachment classification in infancy did not predict attachment classification at 18 years of age (Lewis, 1997). In this study, the best predictor of an insecure attachment classification at 18 was the occurrence of parent divorce in intervening years.

Not all developmentalists believe that attachment in infancy is the only path to competence in life. Indeed, some developmentalists believe that too much emphasis has been placed on the attachment bond in infancy. Jerome Kagan (1987, 2000), for example, believes that infants are highly resilient and adaptive; he argues that they are evolutionarily equipped to stay on a positive developmental course, even in the face of wide variations in parenting. Kagan and others stress that genetic and temperament characteristics play more important roles in a child's social competence than the attachment theorists, such as Bowlby and Ainsworth, are willing to acknowledge (Bakermans-Kranenburg & others, 2004). For example, infants may have inherited a low tolerance for stress. This, rather than an insecure attachment bond, may be responsible for their inability to get along with peers.

Another criticism of attachment theory is that it ignores the diversity of socializing agents and contexts that exists in an infant's world. In some cultures, infants show attachments to many people. Among the Hausa (who live in Nigeria), both grandmothers and siblings provide a significant amount of care for infants (Harkness & Super, 1995). Infants in agricultural societies tend to form attachments to older siblings, who are assigned a major responsibility for younger siblings' care.

Researchers recognize the importance of competent, nurturant caregivers in an infant's development (McHale & others, 2001; Parke, 2004). At issue, though, is whether or not secure attachment, especially to a single caregiver, is critical (Thompson, 2000).

Despite such criticisms, there is ample evidence that security of attachment is important to development (Atkinson & Goldberg, 2004; Carlson, Sroufe, & Egeland, 2004; Egeland & Carlson, 2004; Fish, 2004; Sroufe & others, 2005; Thompson, Easterbrooks, & Walker, 2003). Secure attachment in infancy is important because it reflects a positive parent-infant relationship and provides the foundation that supports healthy socioemotional development in the years that follow.

Caregiving Styles and Attachment Classification

Is the style of caregiving linked with the quality of the infant's attachment? Securely attached babies have caregivers who are sensitive to their signals and are consistently available to respond to their infants' needs (Gao, Elliot, & Waters, 1999; Main, 2000). These caregivers often let their babies have an active part in determining the onset and pacing of interaction in the first year of life. One recent study found that maternal sensitivity in parenting was linked with secure attachment in infants in two different cultures: the United States and Colombia (Carbonell & others, 2002).

How do the caregivers of insecurely attached babies interact with them? Caregivers of avoidant babies tend to be unavailable or rejecting (Berlin & Cassidy, 2000). They often don't respond to their babies' signals and have little physical contact with them. When they do interact with their babies, they may behave in an angry and irritable way. Caregivers of resistant babies tend to be inconsistent; sometimes they respond to their babies' needs, and sometimes they don't. In general, they tend not to be very affectionate with their babies and show little synchrony when interacting with them. Caregivers of disorganized babies often neglect or physically abuse them (Barnett, Baniban, & Cicchetti, 1999). In some cases, these caregivers are depressed.

Review and Reflect: Learning Goal 2

2   Describe how attachment develops in infancy

REVIEW

- What is attachment? What is Bowlby's theory of attachment?
- What are some individual variations in attachment? What is the Strange Situation?
- What is the significance of attachment?
- How are caregiving styles related to attachment classifications?

REFLECT

- How might the infant's temperament be related to the way in which attachment is classified? Look at the temperament categories we described and reflect on how these might be more likely to show up in infants in some attachment categories than in others.

---

3   SOCIAL CONTEXTS

The Family	**Child Care**

Now that we have explored the infant's emotional and personality development and attachment, let's examine the social contexts in which these occur. We will begin by studying a number of aspects of the family and then turn to a social context in which infants increasingly spend time—child care.

The Family

Most of us began our lives in families and spent thousands of hours during our childhood interacting with our parents. Some of you are already parents; others of you may become parents. What is the transition to parenthood like?

The Transition to Parenthood   When people become parents through pregnancy, adoption, or stepparenting, they face disequilibrium and must adapt (Heincke, 2002). Parents want to develop a strong attachment with their infant, but they still want to maintain strong attachments to their spouse and friends, and possibly continue their careers. Parents ask themselves how this new being will change their lives. A baby places new restrictions on partners; no longer will they be able to rush out to a movie on a moment's notice, and money may not be readily available for vacations and other luxuries. Dual-career parents ask, "Will it harm the baby to place her in day care? Will we be able to find responsible baby-sitters?"

In a longitudinal investigation of couples from late pregnancy until $3\frac{1}{2}$ years after the baby was born, couples enjoyed more positive marital relations before the baby was born than after (Cowan & Cowan, 2000). Still, almost one-third showed an increase in marital satisfaction. Some couples said that the baby had both brought them closer together *and* moved them further apart. They commented that being parents enhanced their sense of themselves and gave them a new, more stable identity as a couple. Babies opened men up to a concern with intimate relationships, and the demands of juggling work and family roles stimulated women to manage family tasks more efficiently and pay attention to their own personal growth.

One recent study examined the transition to parenting in young African American and Latino couples from 14 and 24 years of age (Florsheim & others, 2003).

Fathers and mothers who had positive relationships with their own parents were more likely to show positive adjustment to parenting than their counterparts who had negative relationships with their parents. Another recent study found that a shorter maternity leave (less than 12 weeks) was linked with a higher level of depression in mothers (Feldman, Sussman, & Zigler, 2004).

At some point during the early years of the child's life, parents face the difficult task of juggling their roles as parents and as self-actualizing adults. Until recently in our culture, nurturing our children and having a career were thought to be incompatible. Fortunately, we have come to recognize that the balance between caring and achieving, nurturing and working—although difficult to manage—can be accomplished (Hoffman & Youngblade, 1999; Lorensen & others, 2004).

Reciprocal Socialization
For many years, socialization between parents and children was viewed as a one-way process: Children were considered to be the products of their parents' socialization techniques. Today, however, we view parent-child interaction as reciprocal (Parke, 2004). **Reciprocal socialization** is socialization that is bidirectional. That is, children socialize parents just as parents socialize children. For example, the interaction of mothers and their infants is symbolized as a dance or a dialogue in which successive actions of the partners are closely coordinated. This coordinated dance or dialogue can assume the form of mutual synchrony in which each person's behavior depends on the partner's previous behavior (Feldman, Greenbaum, & Yirmiya, 1999). Or it can be reciprocal in the sense that actions of the partners are matched, as when one partner imitates the other or when there is mutual smiling.

When reciprocal socialization has been studied in infancy, mutual gaze, or eye contact, plays an important role in early social interaction. In one investigation, the mother and infant engaged in a variety of behaviors while they looked at each other. By contrast, when they looked away from each other, the rate of such behaviors dropped considerably (Stern & others, 1977). In sum, the behaviors of mothers and infants involve substantial interconnection, mutual regulation, and synchronization.

An important form of reciprocal socialization is **scaffolding,** in which parents time interactions in such a way that the infant experiences turn-taking with the parents. Scaffolding involves parental behavior that supports children's efforts, allowing them to be more skillful than they would be if they were to rely only on their own abilities. In using scaffolding, caregivers provide a positive, reciprocal framework in which they and their children interact. For example, in the game peek-a-boo, the mother initially covers the baby. Then she removes the cover and registers "surprise" at the infant's reappearance. As infants become more skilled at peek-a-boo, pat-a-cake, and so on, there are other caregiver games that exemplify scaffolding and turn-taking sequences. In one study, infants who had more extensive scaffolding experiences with their parents (especially in the form of turn-taking) were more likely to engage in turn-taking when they interacted with their peers (Vandell & Wilson, 1988).

The Family as a System
As a social system, the family can be thought of as a constellation of subsystems defined in terms of generation, gender, and role (Minuchin, 2001). Divisions of labor among family members define particular subunits, and attachments define others. Each family member is a participant in several subsystems. Some are *dyadic* (involving two people), some *polyadic* (involving more than two people). The father and child represent one dyadic subsystem, the mother and father another. The mother-father-child represent one polyadic subsystem, the mother and two siblings another.

Jay Belsky (1981) proposed an organizational scheme that highlights the reciprocal influences of family members and family subsystems (see figure 7.8). Belsky believes that marital relations, parenting, and infant behavior and development can have both direct and indirect effects on each other. An example of a direct effect is the influence of the parents' behavior on the child. An example of an indirect effect is how the relationship between the spouses mediates the way a parent acts toward the child (Hsu, 2004). For example, marital conflict might reduce the efficiency of parenting, in which case marital conflict would indirectly affect the child's behavior.

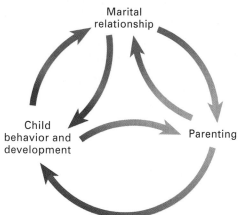

FIGURE 7.8 Interaction Between Children and Their Parents: Direct and Indirect Effects

reciprocal socialization Socialization that is bidirectional; children socialize parents, just as parents socialize children.

scaffolding Parents time interactions so that infants experience turn-taking with the parents.

Maternal and Paternal Caregiving   Can fathers take care of infants as competently as mothers can? Observations of fathers and their infants suggest that fathers have the ability to act sensitively and responsively with their infants (Parke, 2000, 2002, 2004). The strongest evidence of the plasticity of male caregiving abilities is based on male primates, which are notoriously low in their interest in offspring. When forced to live with infants whose female caregivers are absent, the adult male competently rears the infants. Remember, however, that although fathers can be active, nurturant, involved caregivers with their infants, many do not choose to follow this pattern (Chuang, Lamb, & Hwang, 2004; Day & Lamb, 2004; Lamb & Lewis, 2005; Marsiglio, 2004; Silverstein, 2001).

Do fathers behave differently toward infants than mothers do? Maternal interactions usually center on child-care activities—feeding, changing diapers, bathing. Paternal interactions are more likely to include play. Fathers engage in more rough-and-tumble play. They bounce infants, throw them up in the air, tickle them, and so on (Lamb, 1986, 2000). Mothers do play with infants, but their play is less physical and arousing than that of fathers.

In stressful circumstances, do infants prefer their mother or father? In one study, 20 12-month-olds were observed interacting with their parents (Lamb, 1977). With both parents present, the infants preferred neither their mother nor their father. The same was true when the infants were alone with the mother or the father. However, the entrance of a stranger, combined with boredom and fatigue, produced a shift in the infants' social behavior toward the mother. In stressful circumstances, then, infants show a stronger attachment to the mother.

In a more recent study, fathers were interviewed about their caregiving responsibilities when their children were 6, 15, 24, and 36 months of age (NICHD Early Child Care Research Network, 2000). A subset was videotaped during father-child play at 6 and 36 months. Caregiving activities (such as bathing, feeding, and dressing the child, and taking the child to day care) and sensitivity during play interactions (such as being responsive to the child's signals and needs, and expressing positive feelings) with their children were predicted by several factors. Fathers were more involved in caregiving when they worked fewer hours and mothers worked more hours, when fathers and mothers were younger, when mothers reported greater marital intimacy, and when the children were boys. Fathers who had less-traditional child-rearing beliefs and reported more marital intimacy were more sensitive during play.

Might the nature of parent-infant interaction be different in families that adopt nontraditional gender roles? This question was investigated by Michael Lamb and his colleagues (1982). They studied Swedish families in which the fathers were the primary caregivers of their firstborn, 8-month-old infants. The mothers were working full-time. In all observations, the mothers were more likely to discipline, hold, soothe, kiss, and talk to the infants than were the fathers. These mothers and fathers dealt with their infants differently, along the lines of American fathers and mothers following traditional gender roles. Having fathers assume the primary caregiving role did not substantially alter the way they interacted with their infants. This may be for biological reasons or because of deeply ingrained socialization patterns in cultures.

Child Care

Many parents worry whether child care will adversely affect their children. They fear that child care will reduce their infants' emotional attachment to them, retard the infants' cognitive development, fail to teach them how to control anger, and allow them to be unduly influenced by their peers. How extensive is child care? Are the worries of these parents justified?

Today far more young children are in child care than at any other time in history with about 2 million children currently receiving formal, licensed child care and more than 5 million children attending kindergarten. Also, uncounted millions of children are cared for by unlicensed baby-sitters.

www.mhhe.com/santrockld10

Family Resources
Maternal Resources
The Fatherhood Project

Child-care policies vary widely in countries around the world (Friedman, Randolph, & Kochanoff, 2004). In Sweden, mothers or fathers are given paid maternity or paternity leave for up to one year. For this reason, child care for Swedish infants under 1 year of age is usually not a major concern. Sweden and many other European countries have well-developed child-care policies. To learn about these policies, see the Diversity in Life-Span Development interlude.

Diversity in Life-Span Development
Child-Care Policy Around the World

Sheila Kammerman (1989, 2000a, b) has conducted extensive examinations of parental leave policies around the world. Parental leaves were first enacted as maternity policies more than a century ago to protect the physical health of working women at the time of childbirth. More recently, child-rearing, parental, and paternity leaves were created in response not only to the needs of working women (and parents), but also because of concern for the child's well-being. The European Union (EU) mandated a paid 14-week maternity leave in 1992 and a three-month parental leave in 1998.

Across cultures, policies vary in eligibility criteria, leave duration, benefit level, and the extent to which parents take advantage of these policies. The European policies just mentioned lead the way in creating new standards of parental leave. The United States is alone among advanced industrialized countries in the briefness of parental leave granted and among the few countries with unpaid leave (Australia and New Zealand are the others).

Sweden has one of the most extensive leave policies. Paid for by the government at 80 percent of wages, one year of parental leave is allowed (including maternity leave). Maternity leave may begin 60 days prior to expected birth of the baby and ends six weeks after birth. Another six months of parental leave can be used until the child's eighth birthday (Kammerman, 2000a). Virtually all eligible mothers take advantage of the leave policy and approximately 75 percent of eligible fathers take at least some part of the leave they are allowed. In addition, employed grandparents now also have the right to take time off to care for an ill grandchild. Spain is an example of a relatively poor country that still provides substantial parental leave. Spain allows a 16-week paid maternity leave (paid at 100 percent of wages) at childbirth with up to 6 weeks prior to childbirth allowed. Fathers are permitted two days of leave.

Although the United States allows a number of tax breaks for families with dependent children, the United States does not have a policy of paid leave for child care. With so many parents working outside the home, child care in the United States has become a major national concern. The type of child care that young children receive varies extensively (Burchinal & others, 1996; Scarr, 2000). Many child-care centers house large groups of children and have elaborate facilities. Some are commercial operations; others are nonprofit centers run by churches, civic groups, and employers. Child care is frequently provided in private homes, sometimes by child-care professionals or by mothers who want to earn extra money.

There is increasing interest in the role of child care in ethnic minority families (Johnson & others, 2003). Child-care patterns vary by ethnicity. For example, Latino families fall far below non-Latino White and African American families in using center care (11 percent, 20 percent, and 21 percent, respectively, in one recent study) (Smith, 2002). Despite indicating a preference for center-based care, African American and Latino families often rely on family-based care, especially by grandmothers. However, there has been a substantial increase in center-based care by African American mothers.

Researchers also have a special interest in the role of poverty in quality of child care (Chase-Lansdale, Coley, & Grining, 2001; Loeb & others, 2004; McLearn, 2004). In one study, child-care centers that served high-income children delivered better-quality care than did centers that served middle- and low-income children (Phillips & others, 1994). The indices of quality (such as teacher-child ratios) in subsidized centers for the poor were fairly good, but the quality of observed teacher-child interaction was lower than in high-income centers. A recent study found that extensive child care did not appear to be harmful to low-income children's development except when the care was of low quality (Votrub-Drzal & others, 2004). In this study, high-quality care, even when more than 45 hours a week, was related to lower incidences of internalizing problems (anxiety, for example) and externalizing problems (aggressive and destructive behaviors, for example).

What constitutes a high-quality child-care program for infants? The demonstration program developed by Jerome Kagan and his colleagues (Kagan, Kearsley, & Zelazo, 1978) at Harvard University is exemplary. The child-care center included a pediatrician, a nonteaching director, and an infant-teacher ratio of 3 to 1. Teachers' aides assisted at the center. The teachers and aides were trained to smile frequently, to talk with the infants, and to provide them with a safe environment, which included many stimulating toys. No adverse effects of child care were observed in this project. Most child-care environments are not as enriching as this center. Unfortunately, children who come from families with few psychological, social, and economic resources are more likely to experience poor-quality child care than are children from more-advantaged backgrounds (Lamb, 1994). To read about one individual who provides quality child care to individuals from impoverished backgrounds, see the Careers in Life-Span Development insert. In the Research in Life-Span Development interlude, you can read about an ongoing national study of child care and its effects.

Careers in Life-Span Development

Rashmi Nakhre, Day-Care Director

Rashmi Nakhre has two master's degrees—one in psychology, the other in child development—and is director of the Hattie Daniels Day Care Center in Wilson, North Carolina. Rashmi received the Distinguished Women of North Carolina Award for 1999–2000.

Rashmi first worked at the day-care center soon after she arrived in the United States 25 years ago. She says that she took the job initially because she needed the money but "ended up falling in love with my job." Rashmi has turned the Wilson, North Carolina, day-care center into a model for other centers. The center almost closed several years after she began working there because of financial difficulties. Rashmi played a major role in raising funds not only to keep it open but to improve it. The center provides quality day care for the children of many Latino migrant workers.

Rashmi Nakhre, day-care director, working with some of the children at her center.

Research in Life-Span Development

A National Longitudinal Study of Child Care

Aware of the growing use of child care, the National Institute of Child Health and Human Development (NICHD) developed a comprehensive, longitudinal study of child-care experiences. The study began in 1991, and data were collected on a diverse sample of almost 1,400 children and their families at 10 locations across the United States over a period of seven years. Researchers use multiple methods, such as trained observers, interviews, questionnaires, and testing, and measure many facets of children's development, including physical health, cognitive development, and socioemotional development. Following are some of the results of this extensive study to date (NICHD Early Child Care Research Network, 2001, 2002, 2003).

National Child Care
Information Center
NICHD Study of Early Child Care

- *Patterns of use.* There was high reliance on nonmaternal infant care, rapid entry into nonmaternal care postbirth, and considerable instability in nonmaternal care. By 4 months of age, nearly three-fourths of the infants had entered some form of nonmaternal child care. Almost half of the infants were cared for by a relative when they first entered care and only 12 percent were enrolled in child-care centers. Socioeconomic factors were linked to the amount and type of care. For example, mothers with higher incomes and families that were more dependent on the mother's income placed their infants in child care at an earlier age. Mothers who believed that maternal employment has positive effects on children were more likely to place their infant in nonmaternal care for longer hours. Low-income families were more likely than their more affluent counterparts to use child care, but infants from low-income families who were in child care averaged as many hours as other income groups. In the preschool years, mothers who were single, those with more education, and families with higher incomes used more hours of center care than other families. Minority families and mothers with less education used more hours of care by relatives.

- *Quality of care.* Quality of care was based on such characteristics as group size, child–adult ratio, physical environment, caregiver characteristics (such as formal education, specialized training, and child-care experience), and caregiver behavior (such as sensitivity to children). Infants from low-income families experienced lower quality of child care than infants from higher-income families. When quality of caregivers' care was high, children performed better on cognitive and language tasks, were more cooperative with their mothers during play, showed more positive and skilled interaction with peers, and had fewer behavior problems. Support was found for policies that improve state regulations for caregiver training and child–staff ratios, which were linked with higher cognitive and social competence at 54 months of age via positive caregiving by the child-care providers.

- *Amount of child care.* The quantity of child care predicted some child outcomes. When children spent more hours in child care in their first three years, interactions with the mother (at 6, 15, 24, and 36 months) were less positive. Also, mothers who were more insensitive and unresponsive had children who were less likely to show secure attachment to her at 15 and 36 months. Rates of illness were higher when more hours of child care were experienced.

- *Family and parenting influences.* The results of this large national study indicated that the influence of families and parenting is not weakened by extensive child care. Parents played a significant role in helping children to regulate their emotions, which was related to positive cognitive and social outcomes through the first grade.

In sum, there continues to be concern about some aspects of child care in the United States (Cohen, 2004; Marshall, 2004; Vandell, 2004). Experts increasingly recognize that child care may harm some children more than others (Langlois & Liben, 2003). Difficult children and those with poor self-control may be especially at risk in child care (Maccoby & Lewis, 2003). Thus, one intervention may involve teaching child-care providers how to foster self-regulatory skills in children (Fabes, Hanish, & Martin, 2003). Another intervention might involve more effort being invested in building attachment to the child-care center or school. For example, one study revealed that when children experienced their group, class, or school as a caring community, they showed increased concern for others, better conflict resolution skills, and a decrease in problem behaviors (Solomon & others, 2000).

What are some strategies parents can follow in regard to child care? Child-care expert Kathleen McCartney (2003, p. 4) offered this advice:

- *Recognize that the quality of your parenting is a key factor in your child's development.*

*W*e have all the knowledge necessary to provide absolutely first-rate child care in the United States. What is missing is the commitment and the will.

—EDWARD ZIGLER

Contemporary Developmental Psychologist, Yale University

- *Make decisions that will improve the likelihood you will be good parents.* "For some this will mean working full-time"—for personal fulfillment, income, or both. "For others, this will mean working part-time or not working outside the home."
- *Monitor your child's development.* "Parents should observe for themselves whether their children seem to be having behavior problems." They need to talk with child-care providers and their pediatrician about their child's behavior.
- *Take some time to find the best child care.* Observe different child-care facilities and be certain that you like what you see. "Quality child care costs money, and not all parents can afford the child care they want. However, state subsidies, and other programs like Head Start, are available for families in need."

Review and Reflect: Learning Goal 3

 3 **Explain how social contexts influence the infant's development**

REVIEW

- What are some important family processes in infant development?
- How does child care influence infant development?

REFLECT

- Imagine that a friend of yours is getting ready to put her baby in child care. What advice would you give to her? Do you think she should stay home with the baby? Why or why not? What type of child care would you recommend?

 View the video "Quality Child Indicators" to see how researchers address common anxieties about the possible consequences of formal child care.

Reach Your Learning Goals

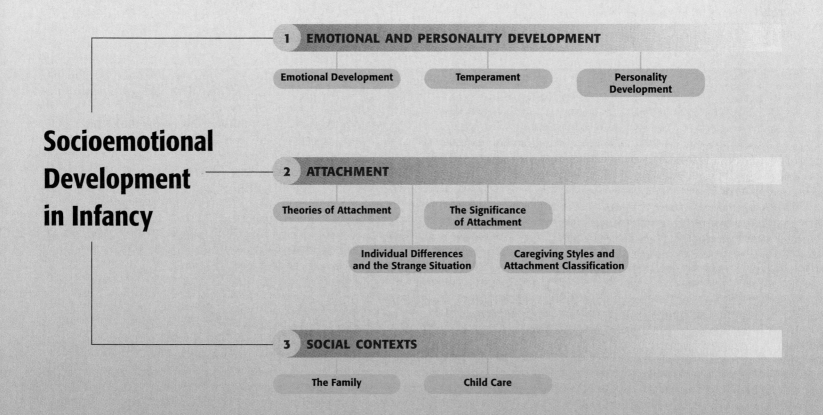

Socioemotional Development in Infancy

1 EMOTIONAL AND PERSONALITY DEVELOPMENT

- Emotional Development
- Temperament
- Personality Development

2 ATTACHMENT

- Theories of Attachment
- The Significance of Attachment
- Individual Differences and the Strange Situation
- Caregiving Styles and Attachment Classification

3 SOCIAL CONTEXTS

- The Family
- Child Care

Summary

 Learning Goal 1: Discuss emotional and personality development in infancy

- Emotion is feeling, or affect, that occurs when a person is in a state or an interaction that is important to them. Emotion is characterized by behavior that reflects (expresses) the pleasantness or unpleasantness of the person's state or the transaction being experienced. Emotions can vary in intensity and specificity. Darwin described the evolutionary basis of emotions, and today psychologists believe that emotions, especially facial expressions of emotions, have a biological foundation. Biological evolution endowed humans to be emotional, but embeddedness in culture and relationships provides diversity in emotional experiences. Emotions play key roles in parent-child relationships. Two broad types of emotions are primary emotions (surprise, joy, anger, sadness, fear, and disgust, which appear in the first six to eight months of life) and self-conscious emotions (empathy, jealousy, and embarrassment, which appear at about $1\frac{1}{2}$ to 2 years of age, and pride, shame, and guilt, which appear at about $2\frac{1}{2}$ years). Crying is the most important mechanism newborns have for communicating with their world. Babies have at least three types of cries—basic, anger, and pain cries. Controversy swirls about whether babies should be soothed when they cry, although increasingly experts recommend immediately responding in a caring way in the first year. Two types of smiling are reflexive and communicative. Two fears that infants develop are stranger anxiety and separation from a caregiver (which is reflected in separation anxiety). Social referencing increases in the second year of life. As infants develop, it is important for them to engage in emotional regulation.

- Temperament is an individual's behavioral style and characteristic way of emotional responding. Developmentalists are especially interested in the temperament of infants. Chess and Thomas classified infants as (1) easy, (2) difficult, or (3) slow to warm up. Kagan proposed that inhibition to the unfamiliar is an important temperament category. Rothbart and Bates' view of temperament emphasizes this classification: (1) positive affect and approach, (2) negative affectivity, and (3) effortful control (self-regulation). Physiological characteristics are associated with different temperaments, and a moderate influence of heredity has been found in studies of the heritability of temperament. Children inherit a physiology that biases them to have a particular type of temperament, but through experience they learn to modify their temperament style to some degree. Goodness of fit refers to the match between a child's temperament and the environmental demands the child must cope with. Goodness of fit can be an important aspect of a child's adjustment. Although research evidence is sketchy at this point in time, some general recommendations are that caregivers should (1) be sensitive to the individual characteristics of the child, (2) be flexible in responding to these characteristics, and (3) avoid negative labelling of the child.

- Erikson argued that an infant's first year is characterized by the stage of trust versus mistrust. At some point in the second half of the second year of life, the infant develops a sense of self. Independence becomes a central theme in the second year of life. Mahler argues that the infant separates herself from her mother and then develops individuation. Erikson stressed that the second year of life is characterized by the stage of autonomy versus shame and doubt.

 Learning Goal 2: Describe how attachment develops in infancy

- Attachment is a close emotional bond between two people. In infancy, feeding is not an important aspect of attachment to a caregiver, although contact comfort and trust are. Bowlby's ethological theory stresses that the caregiver and the infant instinctively trigger attachment. Attachment develops in four phases.

- Securely attached babies use the caregiver, usually the mother, as a secure base from which to explore the environment. Three types of insecure attachment are avoidant, resistant, and disorganized. Ainsworth argued that secure attachment in the first year of life is optimal for development. She created the Strange Situation, an observational measure of attachment.

- Ainsworth believes that secure attachment in the first year of life provides an important foundation for psychological development later in life. How strong the link is between early attachment and later development has varied somewhat across studies. Some critics argue that attachment theorists have not given adequate attention to genetics and temperament. Other critics stress that they have not adequately taken into account the diversity of social agents and contexts. Cultural variations in attachment have been found, but in all cultures studied to date secure attachment is the most common classification.

- Caregivers of secure babies are sensitive to the babies' signals and are consistently available to meet their needs. Caregivers of avoidant babies tend to be unavailable or rejecting. Caregivers of insecure resistant babies tend to be inconsistently available to their babies and usually are not very affectionate. Caregivers of disorganized babies often neglect or physically abuse their babies.

 Learning Goal 3: Explain how social contexts influence the infant's development

- The transition to parenthood requires considerable adaptation and adjustment on the part of parents. Children socialize parents just as parents socialize children. Mutual regulation and scaffolding are important aspects of reciprocal socialization. Belsky's model describes direct and indirect effects. The mother's primary role when interacting with the infant is caregiving; the father's is playful interaction.

- Child care has become a basic need of the American family. More children are in child care now than at any earlier point in history. The quality of child care is uneven, and child care remains a controversial topic. Quality child care can be achieved and seems to have few adverse effects on children. In the NICHD child-care study, infants from low-income families were more likely to receive the lowest quality of care. Also, higher quality of child care was linked with fewer child problems.

Key Terms

emotion 201
primary emotions 202
self-conscious emotions 202
basic cry 203
anger cry 203
pain cry 203
reflexive smile 203

social smile 203
stranger anxiety 203
separation anxiety 204
social referencing 204
temperament 205
easy child 205
difficult child 205

slow-to-warm-up child 205
goodness of fit 207
attachment 210
Strange Situation 211
securely attached babies 212
insecure avoidant babies 212
insecure resistant babies 212

insecure disorganized
  babies 213
reciprocal socialization 216
scaffolding 216

Key People

John Watson 203
Jacob Gewirtz 203
Mary Ainsworth 203, 211
John Bowlby 203, 211

Alexander Chess and
  Stella Thomas 205
Jerome Kagan 205, 214
Mary Rothbart and
  John Bates 206

Erik Erikson 208, 210
Margaret Mahler 209
Harry Harlow 210

Jay Belsky 216
Kathleen McCartney 220

E-LEARNING TOOLS

To help you master the material in this chapter, you'll find a number of valuable study tools on the LifeMap CD-ROM that accompanies this book and on the Online Learning Center for *Life-Span Development,* tenth edition, at www.mhhe.com/santrockld10.

Video Clips

In the margins of this book there are icons directing you to the LifeMap CD-ROM that accompanies the book. There you'll find two videos for chapter 7. The first video is called "Attachment Theory." This segment reviews the three main theories of infant attachment. In an interview, one researcher argues that attachment theory led to a revolution in developmental psychology. The second video is called "Quality Child Care Indicators." More children are placed in child care today than at any other time in history. This segment addresses some of the common anxieties about possible long-term effects of formal child care.

Self-Assessment

Connect to www.mhhe.com/santrockld10 to examine your understanding of infant emotions and socialization by completing the self-assessment, *My Beliefs About Nurturing a Baby's Socioemotional Development.*

Taking It to the Net

Connect to www.mhhe.com/santrockld10 to research the answers to these questions.

1. Catherine is conducting a class for new parents at a local clinic. What advice should Catherine give the parents about how parenting practices can affect a child's inborn temperament?

2. Dawn is a researcher for a biotech firm. She and her husband, Jeff, a corporate attorney, are expecting their first child. They both have worked hard to build their careers, and are looking forward to giving their baby the best possible upbringing. Although they are looking into various child-care programs, they are concerned about the potential negative effects. According to the research, does child care have a negative effect on attachment or future development? Does the quality of the program or the amount of time in child care make a difference?

3. Josiah, a middle-aged African American man, was raised by his mother in an economically depressed inner-city neighborhood. In spite of the economic hardship he and his mother experienced, Josiah has mostly fond memories of his childhood. He finished college, has a successful career, and is married and raising three children in a middle-class milieu. In 1965, the year after Josiah was born, Senator Daniel Patrick Moynihan published a controversial report on what he called the disintegration of the African American family structure in the United States. How might Josiah refute some of the Moynihan Report's categorical statements from his own perspective of having been raised in a single-parent African American household?

Health and Well-Being, Parenting, and Education Exercises

Build your decision-making skills by trying your hand at the health and well-being, parenting, and education exercises.

Connect to www.mhhe.com/santrockld10 to research the answers and complete the exercises.

CHAPTER

The greatest person
ever known
Is one all poets have
outgrown;
The poetry, innate and
untold,
Of being only four
years old.
—CHRISTOPHER MORLEY
American Novelist, 20th Century

Physical and Cognitive Development in Early Childhood

Images of Life-Span Development
Reggio Emilia's Children

A Reggio Emilia classroom in which young children explore topics that interest them.

The Reggio Emilia approach is an educational program for young children that was developed in the northern Italian city of Reggio Emilia. Children of single parents and children with disabilities have priority in admission; other children are admitted according to a scale of needs. Parents pay on a sliding scale based on income.

The children are encouraged to learn by investigating and exploring topics that interest them. A wide range of stimulating media and materials is available for children to use as they learn music, movement, drawing, painting, sculpting, collages, puppets and disguises, and photography, for example.

In this program, children often explore topics in a group, which fosters a sense of community, respect for diversity, and a collaborative approach to problem solving. Two co-teachers are present to serve as guides for children (Edwards, 2002). The Reggio Emilia teachers consider a project as an adventure, which can start from an adult's suggestion, from a child's idea, or from an event, such as a snowfall or something else unexpected. Every project is based on what the children say and do. The teachers allow children enough time to think and craft a project.

At the core of the Reggio Emilia approach is the image of children who are competent and have rights, especially the right to outstanding care and education. Parent participation is considered essential, and cooperation is a major theme in the schools. Many early childhood education experts believe the Reggio Emilia approach provides a supportive, stimulating context in which children are motivated to explore their world in a competent and confident manner (Firlik, 1996; Stegelin, 2003).

PREVIEW

Parents and educators who clearly understand how young children develop can play an active role in creating programs that foster their natural interest in learning, rather than stifling it. We will explore different approaches to early childhood education in this chapter, following a discussion of the physical, cognitive, and language changes in young children.

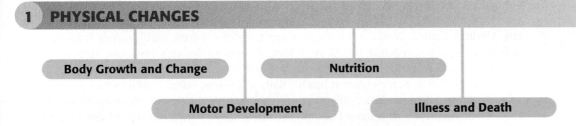

1   PHYSICAL CHANGES

Body Growth and Change

Motor Development

Nutrition

Illness and Death

Remember from chapter 5 that an infant's growth in the first year is rapid and follows cephalocaudal and proximodistal patterns. Around their first birthday, most infants begin to walk. During an infant's second year, the growth rate begins to slow down, but both gross and fine motor skills progress rapidly. The infant develops a sense of mastery through increased proficiency in walking and running. Improvement in fine motor skills—such as being able to turn the pages of a book one at a time—also contributes to the infant's sense of mastery in the second year. The growth rate continues to slow down in early childhood. Otherwise, we would be a species of giants.

Body Growth and Change

Growth in height and weight is the obvious physical change that characterizes early childhood. Unseen changes in the brain and nervous system are no less significant in preparing children for advances in cognition and language.

Height and Weight   The average child grows 2½ inches in height and gains between 5 and 7 pounds a year during early childhood. As the preschool child grows older, the percentage of increase in height and weight decreases with each additional year. Girls are only slightly smaller and lighter than boys during these years, a difference that continues until puberty. During the preschool years, both boys and girls slim down as the trunks of their bodies lengthen. Although their heads are still somewhat large for their bodies, by the end of the preschool years most children have lost their top-heavy look. Body fat also shows a slow, steady decline during the preschool years. The chubby baby often looks much leaner by the end of early childhood. Girls have more fatty tissue than boys; boys have more muscle tissue.

Preschool Growth and Development

Growth patterns vary individually. Think back to your preschool years. This was probably the first time you noticed that some children were taller than you, some shorter; some were fatter, some thinner; some were stronger, some weaker. Much of the variation was due to heredity, but environmental experiences were involved to some extent. A review of the height and weight of children around the world concluded that the two most important contributors to height differences are ethnic origin and nutrition (Meredith, 1978). The urban, middle-socioeconomic-status, and firstborn children were taller than rural, lower-socioeconomic-status, and later-born children. In the United States, African American children are taller than White children.

Why are some children unusually short? The culprits are congenital factors (genetic or prenatal problems), growth hormone deficiency, a physical problem that develops in childhood, or an emotional difficulty. Regarding congenital factors, preschool children whose mothers smoked regularly during pregnancy are half an inch shorter than their counterparts whose mothers did not smoke.

Growth hormone deficiency is the absence or deficiency of growth hormone produced by the pituitary gland to stimulate the body to grow. Growth hormone deficiency may occur during infancy or

The bodies of 5-year-olds and 2-year-olds are different. Notice that the 5-year-old not only is taller and weighs more, but also has a longer trunk and legs than the 2-year-old. *Can you think of some other physical differences between 2- and 5-year-olds?*

later in childhood (Berghout & others, 2004; Chernausek, 2004). It is estimated that as many as 10,000 to 15,000 U.S. children have growth hormone deficiency (Stanford University Medical Center, 2003). Without treatment, most children with growth hormone deficiency will not reach a height of 5 feet. Treatment for this hormone deficiency involves regular injections of growth hormone and usually lasts several years (Chemaitilly & others, 2003). Some children receive daily injections, others several times a week.

Children who are chronically sick are shorter than their counterparts who are rarely sick. Children who have been physically abused or neglected may not secrete adequate growth hormone, which can restrict their physical growth.

The Brain One of the most important physical developments during early childhood is the continuing development of the brain and nervous system (Byrnes, 2001). While the brain continues to grow in early childhood, it does not grow as rapidly as in infancy. The changes in the brain that do occur during early childhood enable children to plan their actions, attend to stimuli more effectively, and make considerable strides in language development.

Changes in Neurons Communication in the brain is characterized by the transmission of information between neurons, or nerve cells. Some of the brain's increase in size is due to the increase in the number and size of nerve endings within and between areas of the brain. These nerve endings continue to grow at least until adolescence.

Neurons communicate with each other through *neurotransmitters* (chemical substances) that carry information across *synapses* (gaps) between the neurons. The concentration of the neurotransmitter dopamine increases considerably from 3 to 6 years of age (Diamond, 2001). We will discuss the significance of this change shortly.

The brain's increase in size also is due to an increase in **myelination,** the process by which nerve cells are covered and insulated with a layer of fat cells. This has the effect of increasing the speed of information traveling through the nervous system (Nagy, Westerberg, & Klingberg, 2004). Some developmentalists believe myelination is important in the maturation of a number of children's abilities. For example, myelination in the areas of the brain related to hand-eye coordination is not complete until about 4 years of age. Myelination in the areas of the brain related to focusing attention is not complete until the end of the middle or late childhood.

Changes in Brain Structure Until recently, scientists have not had adequate technology to detect and map sensitive changes in the human brain as it develops. However, the creation of sophisticated brain-scanning techniques has allowed better detection of these changes (Pujol & others, 2004; Schalagar & others, 2002). Using these techniques, scientists recently have discovered that children's brains undergo dramatic anatomical changes between the ages of 3 and 15 (Thompson & others, 2000). By repeatedly obtaining brain scans of the same children for up to 4 years, they have found that children's brains experience rapid, distinct spurts of growth. The amount of brain material in some areas can nearly double in as little as a year, followed by a drastic loss of tissue as unneeded cells are purged and the brain continues to reorganize itself. The scientists have found that the overall size of the brain did not increase dramatically from age 3 to 15. What does dramatically change are local patterns within the brain.

Researchers also have found that from 3 to 6 years of age the most rapid growth takes place in the frontal lobe areas involved in planning and organizing new actions, and in maintaining attention to tasks (Blumenthal & others, 1999). From age 6 through puberty, the most growth takes place in the temporal and parietal lobes, especially areas that play major roles in language and spatial relations.

The Brain and Cognitive Development The increasing maturation of the brain, combined with opportunities to experience a widening world, contribute to children's emerging cognitive abilities (Cornish, 2004). Consider a child who is learning to read aloud. Input from the child's eyes is transmitted to the child's brain, then passed through

myelination The process by which the nerve cells are covered and insulated with a layer of fat cells, which increases the speed at which information travels through the nervous system.

many brain systems, which translate (process) the patterns of black and white into codes for letters, words, and associations. The output occurs in the form of messages to the child's lips and tongue. The child's own gift of speech is possible because brain systems are organized in ways that permit language processing.

The brain is organized in many neural circuits, which consist of neurons with certain functions. One neural circuit has an important function in attention and working memory (a type of memory similar to short-term memory that is like a mental workbench in performing many cognitive tasks) (Krimel & Goldman-Rakic, 2001). This neural circuit involves the *prefrontal cortex* and the neurotransmitter dopamine (Casey, Durston, & Fossella, 2001; Diamond, 2001) (see figure 8.1).

In sum, scientists are beginning to chart connections between children's cognitive development (attention and memory, for example), brain structures (prefrontal cortex, for example), and the transmission of information at the level of the neuron (the neurotransmitter dopamine, for example). As advances in technology allow scientists to "look inside" the brain and observe its activity, we will likely understand more precisely how the brain functions in cognitive development.

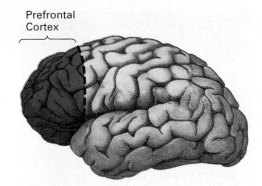

Prefrontal Cortex

FIGURE 8.1 The Prefrontal Cortex
This evolutionarily advanced portion (shaded in purple) of the brain shows extensive development from 3 to 6 years of age and is believed to play important roles in attention and working memory.

Motor Development

Running as fast as you can, falling down, getting right back up and running just as fast as you can . . . building towers with blocks . . . scribbling, scribbling, and scribbling some more . . . cutting paper with scissors . . . During your preschool years, you probably developed the ability to perform all of these activities.

Gross Motor Skills   The preschool child no longer has to make an effort simply to stay upright and to move around. As children move their legs with more confidence and carry themselves more purposefully, moving around in the environment becomes more automatic.

At 3 years of age, children enjoy simple movements, such as hopping, jumping, and running back and forth, just for the sheer delight of performing these activities. They take considerable pride in showing how they can run across a room and jump all of 6 inches. The run-and-jump will win no Olympic gold medals, but for the 3-year-old the activity is a source of considerable pride and accomplishment.

At 4 years of age, children are still enjoying the same kind of activities, but they have become more adventurous. They scramble over low jungle gyms as they display their athletic prowess. Although they have been able to climb stairs with one foot on each step for some time, they are just beginning to be able to come down the same way.

At 5 years of age, children are even more adventuresome than when they were 4. It is not unusual for self-assured 5-year-olds to perform hair-raising stunts on practically any climbing object. Five-year-olds run hard and enjoy races with each other and their parents. A summary of development in gross motor skills during early childhood is shown in figure 8.2.

Fine Motor Skills   At 3 years of age, children are still emerging from the infant ability to place and handle things. Although they have had the ability to pick up the tiniest objects between their thumb and forefinger for some time, they are still somewhat clumsy at it. Three-year-olds can build surprisingly high block towers, each block placed with intense concentration but often not in a completely straight line. When 3-year-olds play

What changes characterize gross motor skills in early childhood?

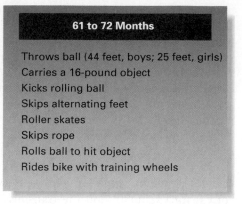

37 to 48 Months	49 to 60 Months	61 to 72 Months
Throws ball underhanded (4 feet)	Bounces and catches ball	Throws ball (44 feet, boys; 25 feet, girls)
Pedals tricycle 10 feet	Runs 10 feet and stops	Carries a 16-pound object
Catches large ball	Pushes/pulls a wagon/doll buggy	Kicks rolling ball
Completes forward somersault (aided)	Kicks 10-inch ball toward target	Skips alternating feet
Jumps to floor from 12 inches	Carries 12-pound object	Roller skates
Hops three hops with both feet	Catches ball	Skips rope
Steps on footprint pattern	Bounces ball under control	Rolls ball to hit object
Catches bounced ball	Hops on one foot four hops	Rides bike with training wheels

FIGURE 8.2 The Development of Gross Motor Skills in Early Childhood
The skills are listed in the approximate order of difficulty within each age period.

with a simple jigsaw puzzle, they are rather rough in placing the pieces. Even when they recognize the hole a piece fits into, they are not very precise in positioning the piece. They often try to force the piece in the hole or pat it vigorously.

By 4 years of age, children's fine motor coordination has improved substantially and become much more precise. Sometimes 4-year-old children have trouble building high towers with blocks because, in their desire to place each of the blocks perfectly, they may upset those already stacked. By age 5, children's fine motor coordination has improved further. Hand, arm, and body all move together under better command of the eye. Mere towers no longer interest the 5-year-old, who now wants to build a house or a church, complete with steeple, though adults might still need to be told what each finished project is meant to be. A summary of the development of fine motor skills in early childhood is shown in figure 8.3.

Handedness For centuries, left-handers have suffered unfair discrimination in a world designed for right-handers. For many years, teachers forced all children to write with their right hand, even if they had a left-hand tendency. Fortunately, today most teachers let children write with the hand they favor (Wenze & Wenze, 2004).

Origin and Development of Handedness What is the origin of hand preference? Genetic inheritance seems to be a strong influence. In one study, the handedness of adopted children was not related to the handedness of their adopted parents, but it was related to the handedness of their biological parents (Carter-Saltzman, 1980).

Right-handedness is dominant in all cultures (it appears in a ratio of about 9 right-handers to 1 left-hander) and it appears before the impact of culture. For

37 to 48 Months	49 to 60 Months	61 to 72 Months
Approximates a circle in drawing	Strings and laces shoelace	Folds paper into halves and quarters
Cuts paper	Cuts following a line	Traces around hand
Pastes using pointer finger	Strings 10 beads	Draws rectangle, circle, square, and triangle
Builds three-block bridge	Copies figure X	Cuts interior piece from paper
Builds eight-block tower	Opens and places clothespins (one-handed)	Uses crayons appropriately
Draws 0 and +	Builds a five-block bridge	Makes clay object with two small parts
Dresses and undresses doll	Pours from various containers	Reproduces letters
Pours from pitcher without spilling	Prints first name	Copies two short words

FIGURE 8.3 The Development of Fine Motor Skills in Early Childhood
The skills are listed in the approximate order of difficulty within each age period.

example, in one study, ultrasound observations of fetal thumb sucking showed that 9 of 10 fetuses were more likely to be sucking their right hand's thumb (Hepper, Shahidullah, & White, 1990). Newborns also show a preference for one side of their body over the other. In one study, 65 percent of the infants turned their head to the right when they were lying on their back in a crib (Michel, 1981). Fifteen percent preferred to face toward the left and the remaining 20 percent showed no preference. These preferences for the right or the left were linked with handedness later in development.

Handedness, the Brain, and Language   Approximately 95 percent of right-handed individuals primarily process speech in the brain's left hemisphere (Springer & Deutsch, 1985). However, left-handed individuals show more variation. More than half of left-handers process speech in their left hemisphere, just like right-handers. However, about one-fourth of left-handers process speech equally in both hemispheres (Knecht & others, 2000).

Are there differences in the language development of left- and right-handers? The most consistent finding is that left-handers are more likely to have reading problems (Natsopoulos & others, 1998).

Handedness and Other Abilities   Although there is a tendency for left-handers to have more reading problems than right-handers, left-handedness is more common among mathematicians, musicians, architects, and artists (Michelangelo, Leonardo da Vinci, and Picasso were all left-handed) (Schacter & Ransil, 1996). Architects and artists who are left-handed benefit from the tendency of left-handers to have unusually good visual-spatial skills and the ability to imagine spatial layouts (Holtzen, 2000). Also, in one study of more than 100,000 students taking the Scholastic Aptitude Test (SAT), 20 percent of the top-scoring group was left-handed, twice the rate of left-handedness found in the general population (10 percent) (Bower, 1985).

Nutrition

What are a preschool child's energy needs? What is a preschooler's eating behavior like?

Energy Needs   Feeding and eating habits are important aspects of development during early childhood (Leavitt, Tonniges, & Rogers, 2003; Wardle & others, 2003). What children eat affects their skeletal growth, body shape, and susceptibility to disease. Recognizing that nutrition is important for the child's growth and development, the federal government provides money for school lunch programs.

Energy requirements for individual children are determined by the **basal metabolism rate (BMR),** which is the minimum amount of energy a person uses in a resting state. An average preschool child requires 1,700 calories per day, but energy needs of individual children of the same age, sex, and size vary. Although the reasons for these differences are not known, differences in physical activity, basal metabolism, and the efficiency with which children use energy are possible explanations.

Eating Behavior   Caregivers' special concerns involve the appropriate amount of fat in young children's diets (Troiano & Flegal, 1998). While some health-conscious parents may be providing too little fat in their infants' and children's diets, many parents are raising their children on diets with too much fat and too many calories. Our changing lifestyles, which demand that we often eat on the run and pick up fast-food meals, contribute to the increased fat levels in children's diets. The American Heart Association recommends that the daily limit for calories from fat should be approximately 35 percent, and many fast-food meals have fat content that is too high for good health.

Being overweight can be a serious problem in early childhood (Borra & others, 2003; Ruxton, 2004). The percentage of obese children in the United States has increased dramatically in recent decades, and the percentage is likely to grow unless changes occur in children's lifestyles (Dietz, 2004; Freeman-Fobbs, 2003; Ottley, 2004). Childhood obesity contributes to a number of health problems. For example, physicians are now seeing

Today, most teachers let children write with the hand they favor. *What are the main reasons children become left- or right-handed?*

www.mhhe.com/santrockld10

Handedness

This would be a better world for children if parents had to eat the spinach.

—GROUCHO MARX
American Comedian, 20th Century

basal metabolism rate (BMR) The minimum amount of energy a person uses in a resting state.

Exploring Childhood Obesity
Helping an Overweight Child
Preschoolers' Health
Child Health Guide

 Watch the video "Children and Nutrition" and consider the role of diet and nutrition in the healthy development of children.

Causes of death	Deaths per 100,000
Accidents (unintentional injuries) Motor vehicle **4.3** Other accidents **8.2**	12.5
Congenital malformations, deformations, and chromosomal abnormalities	3.6
Malignant neoplasms	2.8
Assault (homicide)	2.5
Diseases of the heart	1.2
Influenza and pneumonia	0.8

FIGURE 8.4 Main Causes of Death in Children 1 through 4 Years of Age
These figures are based on the number of deaths per 100,000 children 1 through 4 years of age in the United States in 1999 (National Vital Statistics Report, 2001).

Type II (adult-onset) diabetes, a condition directly linked with obesity and a low level of fitness, in children as young as 5 years of age (Perry, 2001; Tresaco & others, 2004).

Is being overweight associated with lower self-esteem in young children? In one recent study, the relation between weight status and self-esteem in 5-year-old girls was examined (Davison & Birth, 2001). The girls who were overweight had lower body self-esteem than those who were not overweight. Thus, as early as 5 years of age, being overweight is linked with lower self-esteem.

Prevention of obesity in children includes helping children and parents see food as a way to satisfy hunger and nutritional needs, not as proof of love or as a reward for good behavior (Borra & others, 2003; Golan & Crow, 2004). Snack foods should be low in fat, simple sugars, and salt, as well as high in fiber. Routine physical activity should be a daily occurrence (Anza, Greenberg, & Unger, 2004; Bendelius, 2004; Fox, 2004). The child's life should be centered around activities, not meals (Rothstein, 2001). We will have much more to say about children's obesity in chapter 10, "Physical and Cognitive Development in Middle and Late Childhood."

One of the most common nutritional problems in early childhood is iron deficiency anemia, which results in chronic fatigue (Carley, 2003). This is a problem that results from the failure to eat adequate amounts of quality meats and dark green vegetables. Young children from low-income families are most likely to develop iron deficiency anemia (Majumdar & others, 2003).

Illness and Death

What are the leading causes of death in young children in the United States? What are the greatest health risks for children today? How pervasive is death among young children around the world?

The United States If a pediatrician who stopped practicing 50 years ago were to study the illness and health records of young children today, the conclusion might seem to be more like science fiction than medical fact (Elias, 1998). The story of children's health in the past 50 years is a shift toward prevention and outpatient care.

In recent decades, vaccines have nearly eradicated disabling bacterial meningitis and have become available to prevent measles, rubella, mumps, and chicken pox. From 1950 to the present, there has been a dramatic decline in deaths of children under the age of 5 from birth immaturity, birth defects, accidents, cancer, homicide, and heart disease. The disorders most likely to be fatal during early childhood today are birth defects, cancer, and heart disease. Although the dangers of many contagious diseases for children have been greatly diminished, it still is important for parents to keep young children on an immunization schedule to prevent a resurgence of these diseases.

In the United States, accidents are the leading cause of death in young children (National Vital Statistics Reports, 2001) (see figure 8.4). Motor vehicle accidents, drowning, falls, and poisoning are high on the list of causes of these deaths.

Influences on children's safety in childhood include the acquisition and practice of individual skills and safety behaviors, family and home influences, school and peer influences, and the community's actions (Tinsley, 2003). Notice that these influences reflect Bronfenbrenner's ecological model of development that we described in chapter 2, "The Science of Life-Span Development." Figure 8.5 shows how these ecological contexts can influence children's safety, security, and injury prevention (Sleet & Mercy, 2003). We will have more to say about contextual influences on young children's health shortly.

Today, a special concern about children's illness and health is exposure to parental smoking. Estimates indicate that approximately 22 percent of children and adolescents in the United States are exposed to tobacco smoke in the home. An increasing number of studies reach the conclusion that children are at risk for health problems when they live in homes in which a parent smokes (Gehrman & Hovell, 2003; Johansson, Hermansson, & Ludvigsson, 2004). In one study, if the mother smoked, her children were twice as likely to develop respiratory problems (Etzel, 1988). Children exposed to tobacco smoke in the home are more likely to develop wheezing symptoms and asthma than children in nonsmoking homes (Berman & others, 2003; Drongowski & others, 2003; Murray & others, 2004).

Environmental tobacco smoke also affects the amount of vitamin C in children and adolescents. In a recent study, when parents smoked at home their 4- to 18-year-old children and adolescents had significantly lower levels of vitamin C in their blood than their counterparts in nonsmoking homes (Strauss, 2001). The more parents smoked, the less vitamin C the children and adolescents had. Children exposed to environmental smoke should be encouraged to eat foods rich in vitamin C or be given this vitamin as a supplement (Preston & others, 2003).

Another contemporary concern in the United States is the poor health status of many young children from low-income families (Richter, 2003; Wagstaff & others, 2004). Approximately 11 million preschool children in the United States are malnourished and therefore at risk for health problems. Many have less resistance to diseases, including minor ones, such as colds, and major ones, such as influenza, than other children. In addition, an estimated 3 million children under 6 years of age are thought to be at risk for lead poisoning (Brittle & Zint, 2003; Moya, Bearer, & Etzel, 2004). Lead can get into children's bloodstreams through food or water that is contaminated by lead, from putting lead-contaminated fingers in their mouths, or from inhaling dust from lead-based paint. The negative effects of lead in children's blood are lower intelligence and achievement, and attention deficit hyperactivity disorder (Breysse & others, 2004; Canfield & others, 2003). Children in poverty are at higher risk for lead poisoning than children living in higher-socioeconomic conditions.

The State of Illness and Health of the World's Children

Each year UNICEF produces a report entitled, *The State of the World's Children.* In the most recent report, UNICEF (2003) emphasized the importance of information about the under-5 mortality rate of a nation. UNICEF concluded that the under-5 mortality rate is the result of a wide range of factors, including the nutritional health and health knowledge of mothers, the level of immunization, dehydration, availability of maternal and child health services, income and food availability in the family, availability of clean water and safe sanitation, and the overall safety of the child's environment.

UNICEF (2003) reports annual data on the rank of nations' under-5 mortality rate. In 2001, 35 nations had a lower under-5 mortality rate than the United States with Sweden having the lowest rate of all nations. The relatively high under-5 mortality rate of the United States compared with other developed nations is due to such factors as poverty and inadequate health care.

The devastating effects on the health of young children occur in countries where poverty rates are high. The poor are the majority in nearly one of every five nations in the world (UNICEF, 2003). They often experience lives of hunger, malnutrition, illness, inadequate access to health care, unsafe water, and a lack of protection from harm (UNICEF, 2004).

In the last decade, there has been a dramatic increase in the number of young children who have died because of HIV/AIDS transmitted to them by their parents (Atinmo & Oyewole, 2004; UNICEF, 2002). Deaths of young children due to HIV/AIDS especially occur in countries with high rates of poverty and low levels of education. For example, the uneducated are four times more likely to believe that there is no way to avoid AIDS and three times more likely to be unaware that the virus can be transmitted from mother to child (UNICEF, 2002).

Individual

Development of social skills and ability to regulate emotions

Involvement in activities that promote positive attachment and prosocial skills

Acquisition of early academic skills and knowledge

Impulse control (such as not darting out into a street to retrieve a ball)

Frequent use of personal protection (such as bike helmets and safety seats)

Family/Home

High awareness and knowledge of child management and parenting skills

Caregiver participation in the child's education and social activities

Frequent parent protective behaviors (such as use of child safety seats)

Presence of home safety equipment (such as smoke alarms and cabinet locks)

School/Peers

Promotion of home/school partnerships

Availability of enrichment programs, especially for low-income families

Absence of playground hazards

Management support for safety and injury prevention

Injury prevention and safety promotion policies and programs

Community

Availability of positive activities for children and their parents

Active surveillance of environmental hazards

Effective prevention policies in place (such as pool fencing)

Commitment to emergency medical services and trauma care for children

Emphasis on safety themes

FIGURE 8.5 Contexts and Young Children's Safety, Security, and Injury Prevention

Harvard Center for Children's Health
UNICEF

Many of the deaths of young children around the world can be prevented by a reduction in poverty and improvements in nutrition, sanitation, education, and health services.

Review and Reflect: Learning Goal 1

 1 Identify physical changes in early childhood

REVIEW

- What characterizes body growth and change?
- What changes take place in motor development?
- What role does nutrition play in early childhood?
- What are some causes of illness and death among young children in the United States and around the world?

REFLECT

- What were your eating habits as a young child? In what ways are they similar or different to your current eating habits? Were your early eating habits a forerunner of whether or not you have weight problems today?

---

2 COGNITIVE CHANGES

Piaget's Preoperational Stage   **Vygotsky's Theory**   **Information Processing**

The cognitive world of the preschool child is creative, free, and fanciful. Preschool children's imaginations work overtime, and their mental grasp of the world improves. Our coverage of cognitive development in early childhood focuses on three theories: Piaget's, Vygotsky's, and information processing.

Piaget's Preoperational Stage

Remember from chapter 6 that during Piaget's sensorimotor stage of development the infant progresses in the ability to organize and coordinate sensations and perceptions with physical movements and actions. What kinds of changes take place in the preoperational stage?

The preoperational stage stretches from approximately 2 to 7 years of age. It is a time when stable concepts are formed, mental reasoning emerges, egocentrism begins strongly and then weakens, and magical beliefs are constructed. The label *preoperational* emphasizes that the child at this stage cannot yet think something through without acting it out.

What are operations? **Operations** are internalized sets of actions that allow children to do mentally what before they did physically. Mentally adding and subtracting numbers are examples of operations.

Thought in the preoperational stage is flawed and not well organized. Preoperational thought marks the beginning of children's ability to reconstruct at the level of thought what has been established in their behavior. Preoperational thought also involves a transition from primitive to more sophisticated use of symbols. Preoperational thought can be divided into two substages: symbolic function and intuitive thought.

Symbolic Function Substage The **symbolic function substage** is the first substage of preoperational thought, which occurs roughly between 2 and 4 years of

operations In Piaget's theory, internalized sets of actions that allow children to do mentally what they formerly did physically.

symbolic function substage Piaget's first substage of preoperational thought, in which the child gains the ability to mentally represent an object that is not present (between 2 and 4 years of age).

age. In this substage, the young child gains the ability to mentally represent an object that is not present. The ability to engage in symbolic thought is called *symbolic function,* and it vastly expands the child's mental world. Young children use scribbled designs to represent people, houses, cars, clouds, and so on. Other examples of symbolism in early childhood are language and the prevalence of pretend play. In sum, the ability to think symbolically and to represent the world mentally predominates in this early substage of preoperational thought (DeLoache, 2004). Even though young children make distinct progress during this substage, their thought still has several important limitations, two of which are egocentrism and animism.

Egocentrism, the inability to distinguish between one's own perspective and someone else's, is an important feature of preoperational thought. This telephone conversation between 4-year-old Mary, who is at home, and her father, who is at work, typifies Mary's egocentric thought:

> **Father:** Mary, is Mommy there?
> **Mary:** (Silently nods)
> **Father:** Mary, may I speak to Mommy?
> **Mary:** (Nods again silently)

Mary's response is egocentric in that she fails to consider her father's perspective before replying. A nonegocentric thinker would have responded.

Piaget and Barbel Inhelder (1969) studied young children's egocentrism by devising the three mountains task (see figure 8.6). The child walks around the model of the mountains and becomes familiar with what the mountains look like from different perspectives. During this walking tour, the child can see that there are different objects on the mountains. The child is then seated on one side of the table on which the mountains are placed. The experimenter moves a doll to different locations around the table, at each location asking the child to select from a series of photos the one photo that most accurately reflects the view the doll is seeing. Children in the preoperational stage often pick the view from where they are sitting rather than the doll's view. Perspective-taking does not develop uniformly in preschool children, who frequently show perspective skills on some tasks but not others.

Animism, another limitation of preoperational thought, is the belief that inanimate objects have lifelike qualities and are capable of action. A young child might show animism by saying, "That tree pushed the leaf off, and it fell down," or "The sidewalk made me mad; it made me fall down." A young child who uses animism fails to distinguish the appropriate occasions for using human and nonhuman perspectives (Gelman & Opfer, 2004).

Possibly because young children are not very concerned about reality, their drawings are fanciful and inventive. Suns are blue, skies are yellow, and cars float on clouds in their symbolic, imaginative world. One 3½-year-old looked at a scribble he had just drawn and described it as a pelican kissing a seal (see figure 8.7*a*). The symbolism is simple but strong, like abstractions found in some modern art. As the famous twentieth-century artist Pablo Picasso commented, "I used to draw like Raphael but it has taken me a lifetime to draw like young children." In the elementary school years, a child's drawings become more realistic, neat, and precise (see figure 8.7*b*). Suns are yellow, skies are blue, and cars travel on roads (Winner, 1986).

Intuitive Thought Substage   Tommy is 4 years old. Although he is starting to develop his own ideas about the world he lives in, his ideas are still simple, and he is not very good at thinking things out. He has difficulty understanding events he knows are taking place but which he cannot see. His fantasized thoughts bear little resemblance to reality. He cannot yet answer the question "What if . . . ?" in any reliable way. For example, he has only a vague idea of what would happen if a car were to hit him. He also has difficulty negotiating traffic because he cannot do the mental calculations necessary to estimate whether an approaching car will hit him when he crosses the road.

The **intuitive thought substage** is the second substage of preoperational thought, which occurs between approximately 4 and 7 years of age. In this substage,

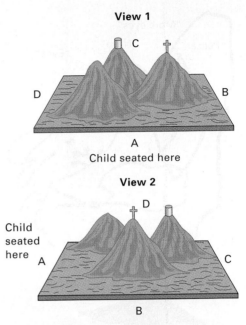

View 1

A
Child seated here

View 2

Child seated here

B

FIGURE 8.6 The Three Mountains Task
View 1 shows the child's perspective from where he or she is sitting. View 2 is an example of the photograph the child would be shown, mixed in with others from different perspectives. To correctly identify this view, the child has to take the perspective of a person sitting at spot B. Invariably, a preschool child who thinks in a preoperational way cannot perform this task. When asked what a view of the mountains looks like from position B, the child selects a photograph taken from location A, the child's view at the time.

Symbolic Thinking

egocentrism The inability to distinguish between one's own perspective and someone else's (salient feature of the first substage of preoperational thought).

animism The belief that inanimate objects have "lifelike" qualities and are capable of action.

intuitive thought substage Piaget's second substage of preoperational thought, in which children begin to use primitive reasoning and want to know the answers to all sorts of questions (between 4 and 7 years of age).

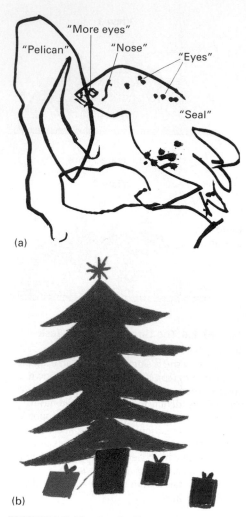

(a)

(b)

FIGURE 8.7 The Symbolic Drawings of Young Children

(*a*) A 3½-year-old's symbolic drawing. Halfway into this drawing, the 3½-year-old artist said it was "a pelican kissing a seal." (*b*) This 11-year-old's drawing is neater and more realistic but also less inventive.

centration The focusing of attention on one characteristic to the exclusion of all others.

conservation In Piaget's theory, awareness that altering an object's or a substance's appearance does not change its quantitative properties.

children begin to use primitive reasoning and want to know the answers to all sorts of questions. Piaget called this time period *intuitive* because, on the one hand, young children seem so sure about their knowledge and understanding, yet they are so unaware of how they know what they know. That is, they say they know something but know it without the use of rational thinking.

An important characteristic of preoperational thought is **centration**—the focusing, or centering, of attention on one characteristic to the exclusion of all others. Centration is most clearly evidenced in young children's lack of **conservation**—awareness that altering an object's or a substance's appearance does not change its quantitative properties. To adults, it is obvious that a certain amount of liquid stays the same, regardless of a container's shape, but this is not at all obvious to young children. Instead, they are struck by the height of the liquid in the container. In the conservation task—Piaget's most famous test—a child is presented with two identical beakers, each filled to the same level with liquid (see figure 8.8). The child is asked if these beakers have the same amount of liquid, and she usually says yes. Then the liquid from one beaker is poured into a third beaker, which is taller and thinner than the first two. The child is then asked if the amount of liquid in the tall, thin beaker is equal to that which remains in one of the original beakers. Children who are less than 7 or 8 years old usually say no and justify their answers in terms of the differing height or width of the beakers. Older children usually answer yes and justify their answers appropriately ("If you poured the milk back, the amount would still be the same").

In Piaget's theory, failing the conservation of liquid task is a sign that children are at the preoperational stage of cognitive development. Passing this test is a sign that they are at the concrete operational stage. In Piaget's view, the preoperational child fails to show conservation not only of liquid but also of number, matter, length, volume, and area (figure 8.9 portrays several of these). Children often vary in their performance on different conservation tasks. Thus, a child might be able to conserve volume but not number.

The child's inability to mentally reverse actions is an important characteristic of preoperational thought. For example, in the conservation of matter shown in

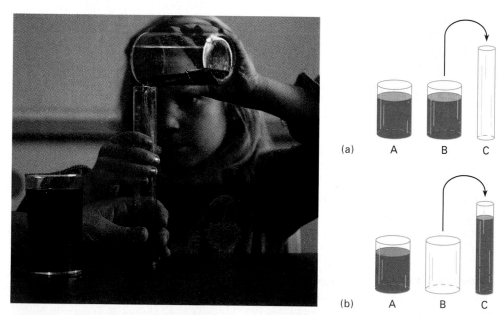

FIGURE 8.8 Piaget's Conservation Task

The beaker test is a well-known Piagetian test to determine whether a child can think operationally—that is, can mentally reverse actions and show conservation of the substance. (*a*) Two identical beakers are presented to the child. Then, the experimenter pours the liquid from B into C, which is taller and thinner than A or B. (*b*) The child is asked if these beakers (A and C) have the same amount of liquid. The preoperational child says "no." When asked to point to the beaker that has more liquid, the preoperational child points to the tall, thin beaker.

Type of Conservation	Initial Presentation	Manipulation	Preoperational Child's Answer
Number	Two identical rows of objects are shown to the child, who agrees they have the same number.	One row is lengthened and the child is asked whether one row now has more objects.	Yes, the longer row.
Matter	Two identical balls of clay are shown to the child. The child agrees that they are equal.	The experimenter changes the shape of one of the balls and asks the child whether they still contain equal amounts of clay.	No, the longer one has more.
Length	Two sticks are aligned in front of the child. The child agrees that they are the same length.	The experimenter moves one stick to the right, then asks the child if they are equal in length.	No, the one on the top is longer.

FIGURE 8.9 Some Dimensions of Conservation: Number, Matter, and Length

figure 8.9, preoperational children say that the longer shape has more clay because they assume that "longer is more." Preoperational children cannot mentally reverse the clay-rolling process to see that the amount of clay is the same in both the shorter ball shape and the longer stick shape.

Some developmentalists stress that Piaget was entirely correct in his estimate of when children's conservation skills emerge. For example, Rochel Gelman (1969) showed that when the child's attention to relevant aspects of the conservation task is improved, the child is more likely to conserve. Gelman has also demonstrated that attentional training on one dimension, such as number, improves the preschool child's performance on another dimension, such as mass. Thus, Gelman believes that conservation appears earlier than Piaget thought and that attention is especially important in explaining conservation.

Yet another characteristic of preoperational children is that they ask a barrage of questions. Children's earliest questions appear around the age of 3, and by the age of 5 they have just about exhausted the adults around them with "why" questions. The child's questions yield clues about mental development and reflect intellectual curiosity. These questions signal the emergence of the child's interest in reasoning and figuring out why things are the way they are. Here are some samples of the questions children ask during the questioning period of 4 to 6 years of age (Elkind, 1976):

- "What makes you grow up?"
- "Why does a lady have to be married to have a baby?"
- "Who was the mother when everybody was a baby?"

Vygotsky's Theory

In chapter 2, we described some basic ideas about Vygotsky's theory. Here we expand on Vygotsky's theory of development, beginning with his unique ideas about the zone of proximal development.

The Zone of Proximal Development The **zone of proximal development (ZPD)** is Vygotsky's (1962) term for the range of tasks that are too difficult for a child to master alone but that can be learned with the guidance and assistance of adults or more-skilled children. Thus, the lower limit of the ZPD is the level of problem solving reached by the child working independently. The upper limit is the level

"I still don't have all the answers, but I'm beginning to ask the right questions."

zone of proximal development (ZPD) Vygotsky's term for tasks too difficult for children to master alone but that can be mastered with assistance.

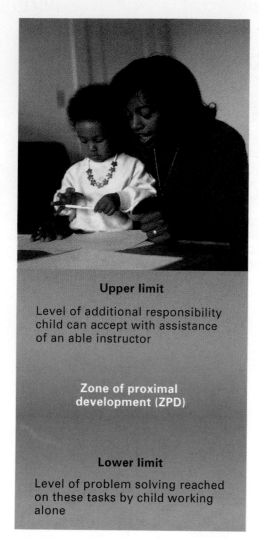

Upper limit

Level of additional responsibility child can accept with assistance of an able instructor

Zone of proximal development (ZPD)

Lower limit

Level of problem solving reached on these tasks by child working alone

FIGURE 8.10 Vygotsky's Zone of Proximal Development

Vygotsky's zone of proximal development has a lower limit and an upper limit. Tasks in the ZPD are too difficult for the child to perform alone. They require assistance from an adult or a more-skilled child. As children experience the verbal instruction or demonstration, they organize the information in their existing mental structures, so they can eventually perform the skill or task alone.

Vygotsky on Language and Thought
Vygotsky: Revolutionary Scientist

of additional responsibility the child can accept with the assistance of an able instructor (see figure 8.10). Vygotsky's emphasis on the ZPD underscores the importance of social influences, especially instruction, on children's cognitive development. For example, an adult helping a child put together a jigsaw puzzle falls into the ZPD. The ZPD captures the child's cognitive skills that are in the process of maturing and can be mastered only with the assistance of a more-skilled person (Bodrova & Leong, 2003; Rowe & Wertsch, 2004; Shamir & Tzuriel, 2004). Vygotsky (1962) called these skills the "buds" or "flowers" of development, to distinguish them from the "fruits" of development, tasks that the child already can accomplish independently.

Scaffolding   In chapter 7, we discussed the concept of scaffolding in socioemotional development. Here we describe its role in cognitive development. Closely linked to the idea of zone of proximal development, *scaffolding* involves changing the level of support. Over the course of a teaching session, a more-skilled person adjusts the amount of guidance to fit the child's current performance level. When the task the student is learning is new, the more-skilled person may use direct instruction. As the student's competence increases, less guidance is given.

Language and Thought   According to Vygotsky, children use speech not only for social communication, but also to help them solve tasks. Vygotsky (1962) further argued that young children use language to plan, guide, and monitor their behavior. This use of language for self-regulation is called *private speech*. For Piaget private speech is egocentric and immature, but for Vygotsky it is an important tool of thought during the early childhood years.

Vygotsky said that language and thought initially develop independently of each other and then merge. He emphasized that all mental functions have external, or social, origins. Children must use language to communicate with others before they can focus inward on their own thoughts. Children also must communicate externally and use language for a long period of time before they can make the transition from external to internal speech. This transition period occurs between 3 and 7 years of age and involves talking to oneself. After a while, the self-talk becomes second nature to children, and they can act without speaking aloud. When this occurs, children have internalized their egocentric speech in the form of *inner speech*, which becomes their thoughts.

Vygotsky argued that children who use a lot of private speech are more socially competent than those who don't (Santiago-Delefosse & Delefosse, 2002). He argued that *private speech* represents an early transition in becoming more socially communicative. For Vygotsky, when young children talk to themselves, they are using language to govern their behavior and guide themselves. For example, a child working on a puzzle might say to herself, "Which pieces should I put together first? I'll try those green ones first. Now I need some blue ones. No, that blue one doesn't fit there. I'll try it over here."

Piaget stressed that self-talk is egocentric and reflects immaturity. However, researchers have found support for Vygotsky's view that private speech plays a positive role in children's development (Winsler, Carlton, & Barry, 2000). Researchers have found that children use private speech more when tasks are difficult, when their errors have been pointed out to them, and when they are not sure how to proceed (Berk, 1994). They also have revealed that children who use private speech are more attentive and improve their performance more than children who do not use private speech (Berk & Spuhl, 1995).

Teaching Strategies   Vygotsky's theory already has been embraced by many teachers and has been successfully applied to education (Berninger & others, 2004; Goos, 2004; Rowe & Wertsch, 2004; Tudge & Scrimsher, 2003). Here are some ways Vygotsky's theory can be incorporated in classrooms:

1. *Use the child's zone of proximal development in teaching.* Teaching should begin toward the zone's upper limit, so that the child can reach the goal with help and move to a higher level of skill and knowledge. Offer just enough assistance. You might ask, "What can I do to help you?" Or simply observe the child's intentions and attempts,

smoothly providing support when needed. When the child hesitates, offer encouragement. And encourage the child to practice the skill. You may watch and appreciate the child's practice or offer support when the child forgets what to do.

2. *Use more-skilled peers as teachers.* Remember that it is not just adults that are important in helping children learn important skills. Children also benefit from the support and guidance of more-skilled children (John-Steiner & Mahn, 2003).

3. *Monitor and encourage children's use of private speech.* Be aware of the developmental change from externally talking to oneself when solving a problem during the preschool years to privately talking to oneself in the early elementary school years. In the elementary school years, encourage children to internalize and self-regulate their talk to themselves.

4. *Effectively assess the child's ZPD.* Vygotsky argued that formal, standardized tests are not the best way to assess children's learning. Rather, Vygotsky argued that assessment should focus on determining the child's zone of proximal development. The skilled helper presents the child with tasks of varying difficulty to determine the best level at which to begin instruction.

5. *Place instruction in a meaningful context.* In education today, there is an increased emphasis on moving away from abstract presentations of material to providing students with opportunities to experience learning in meaningful, real-world settings. Thus, instead of just teaching children to memorize math formulas, students work on math problems with real-world implications (Santrock, 2004).

6. *Transform the classroom with Vygotskian ideas.* What does a Vygotskian classroom look like? The Kamehameha Elementary Education Program (KEEP) is based on Vygotsky's theory (Tharp, 1994). The zone of proximal development is the key element of instruction in this program. Children might read a story and then interpret its meaning. Many of the learning activities take place in small groups. All children spend at least 20 minutes each morning in a setting called "Center One." In this context, scaffolding is used to improve children's literary skills. The instructor asks questions, responds to students' queries, and builds on the ideas that students generate. Thousands of children from low-income families have attended KEEP public schools—in Hawaii, on an Arizona Navajo Indian reservation, and in Los Angeles. Compared with a control group of non-KEEP children, the KEEP children participated more actively in classroom discussion, were more attentive in class, and had higher reading achievement (Tharp & Gallimore, 1988).

In one recent study with a foundation in Vygotsky's theory, pairs of children from two U.S. public schools worked together (Matusov, Bell, & Rogoff, 2001). One member of the pair was always from a school with a traditional format involving only occasional opportunities for children to cooperate in their schoolwork. The other member of the pair was always from a school that emphasizes collaboration throughout the school day. The children with the collaborative school background more often built on each other's ideas in a collaborative way than did the children with the traditional school background. The traditional school children primarily used a "quizzing" form of guidance based on asking known-answer questions and withholding information to test learner's understanding.

Evaluating Vygotsky's Theory Even though their theories were proposed at about the same time, most of the world learned about Vygotsky's theory later than they learned about Piaget's theory, so Vygotsky's theory has not yet been evaluated as thoroughly. Vygotsky's view of the importance of sociocultural influences on children's development fits with the current belief that it is important to evaluate the contextual factors in learning (Kozulin, 2000; Kozulin & others, 2003).

We already have mentioned several comparisons of Vygotsky's and Piaget's theories, such as Vygotsky's emphasis on the importance of inner speech in development and Piaget's view that such speech is immature. Although both theories are constructivist, Vygotsky's is a **social constructivist approach,** which emphasizes the social contexts of learning and the construction of knowledge through social interaction.

social constructivist approach An approach that emphasizes the social contexts of learning and that knowledge is mutually built and constructed. Vygotsky's theory reflects this approach.

In moving from Piaget to Vygotsky, the conceptual shift is from the individual to collaboration, social interaction, and sociocultural activity (Rogoff, 1998, 2003). The endpoint of cognitive development for Piaget is formal operational thought. For Vygotsky, the endpoint can differ depending on which skills are considered to be the most important in a particular culture. For Piaget, children construct knowledge by transforming, organizing, and reorganizing previous knowledge. For Vygotsky, children construct knowledge through social interaction (Tudge & Scrimsher, 2003). The implication of Piaget's theory for teaching is that children need support to explore their world and discover knowledge. The main implication of Vygotsky's theory for teaching is that students need many opportunities to learn with the teacher and more-skilled peers. In both Piaget's and Vygotsky's theories, teachers serve as facilitators and guides, rather than as directors and molders of learning. Figure 8.11 compares Vygotsky's and Piaget's theories.

Criticisms of Vygotsky's theory also have surfaced. Some critics say he overemphasized the role of language in thinking. Also, his emphasis on collaboration and guidance has potential pitfalls. Might facilitators be too helpful in some cases, as when a parent becomes too overbearing and controlling? Further, some children might become lazy and expect help when they might have done something on their own.

Piaget's cognitive development theory and Vygotsky's sociocultural cognitive theory have provided important insights about the way young children think and how this thinking changes developmentally. Next, we will explore a third major view on children's thinking—information processing.

Information Processing

Not only can we study stages of cognitive development, as Piaget did, but we can also study young children's cognitive processes. Two important aspects of preschool children's thinking are attention and memory. What are the limitations and advances in attention and memory during the preschool years?

	Vygotsky	Piaget
Sociocultural Context	Strong emphasis	Little emphasis
Constructivism	Social constructivist	Cognitive constructivist
Stages	No general stages of development proposed	Strong emphasis on stages (sensorimotor, preoperational, concrete operational, and formal operational)
Key Processes	Zone of proximal development, language, dialogue, tools of the culture	Schema, assimilation, accommodation, operations, conservation, classification, hypothetical-deductive reasoning
Role of Language	A major role; language plays a powerful role in shaping thought	Language has a minimal role; cognition primarily directs language
View on Education	Education plays a central role, helping children learn the tools of the culture	Education merely refines the child's cognitive skills that have already emerged
Teaching Implications	Teacher is a facilitator and guide, not a director; establish many opportunities for children to learn with the teacher and more-skilled peers	Also views teacher as a facilitator and guide, not a director; provide support for children to explore their world and discover knowledge

FIGURE 8.11 Comparison of Vygotsky's and Piaget's Theories

Attention In chapter 6, we discussed attention in the context of habituation, which is something like being bored. In habituation, the infant loses interest in a stimulus and no longer attends to it. Habituation involves a decrement in attention. Dishabituation is the recovery of attention. The importance of these aspects of attention in infancy for the preschool years was underscored by research showing that both a decrease and a recovery of attention, when measured in the first six months of infancy, were associated with higher intelligence in the preschool years (Bornstein & Sigman, 1986).

Recall that in chapter 6 we defined *attention* as the focusing of cognitive resources. The child's ability to pay attention changes significantly during the preschool years in three ways:

- *Control of attention.* Toddlers wander around, shift attention from one activity to another, and seem to spend little time focused on any one object or event. By comparison, the preschool child might be observed watching television for a half hour. In one study, young children's attention to television in the natural setting of the home was videotaped (Anderson & others, 1985). In 99 families comprising 460 individuals who were observed for 4,672 hours, visual attention to television dramatically increased during the preschool years.

- *Salient versus relevant dimensions.* One deficit in attention during the preschool years concerns those dimensions that stand out, or are *salient,* compared with those that are relevant to solving a problem or performing well on a task. For example, a problem might have a flashy, attractive clown that presents the directions for solving a problem. Preschool children are influenced strongly by the features of the task that stand out, such as the flashy, attractive clown. After the age of 6 or 7, children attend more efficiently to the dimensions of the task that are relevant, such as the directions for solving a problem. Developmentalists argue this change reflects a shift to cognitive control of attention, so that children act less impulsively and reflect more.

- *Planfulness.* When experimenters ask children to judge whether two complex pictures are the same, preschool children tend to use a haphazard comparison strategy, not examining all of the details before making a judgment. By comparison, elementary school age children are more likely to systematically compare the details across the pictures, one detail at a time (Vurpillot, 1968) (see figure 8.12).

Memory Memory—the retention of information over time—is a central process in children's cognitive development. Conscious memory comes into play as early as 7 months of age, although children and adults have little or no memory of events experienced before the age of 3. Among the interesting questions about memory in the preschool years are those involving short-term memory.

Short-Term Memory In **short-term memory,** individuals retain information for up to 30 seconds, assuming there is no rehearsal of the information. Using rehearsal (repeating information after it has been presented), we can keep information in short-term memory for a much longer period. One method of assessing short-term memory is the memory-span task. If you have taken an IQ test, you were probably exposed to one of these tasks. You simply hear a short list of stimuli—usually digits—presented at a rapid pace (one per second, for example). Then you are asked to repeat the digits. Research with the memory-span task suggests that short-term memory increases during early childhood. For example, in one investigation, memory span increased from about 2 digits in 2- to 3-year-old children to about 5 digits in 7-year-old children, yet between 7 and 13 years of age memory span increased only by 1½ digits (Dempster, 1981) (see figure 8.13). Keep in mind, though, that memory span varies from one individual to another; it is for this reason that IQ and various aptitude tests were developed.

Why are there differences in memory span because of age? Rehearsal of information is important; older children rehearse the digits more than younger children.

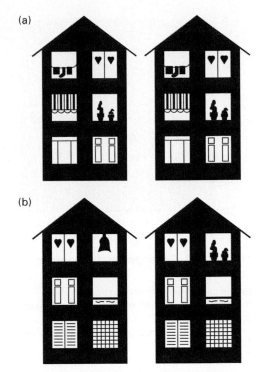

(a)

(b)

FIGURE 8.12 The Planfulness of Attention
In one study, children were given pairs of houses to examine, like the ones shown here (Vurpillot, 1968). For three pairs of houses, what was in the windows was identical (*a*). For the other three pairs, the windows had different items in them (*b*). By filming the reflection in the children's eyes, it could be determined what they were looking at, how long they looked, and the sequence of their eye movements. Children under 6 examined only a fragmentary portion of each display and made their judgments on the basis of insufficient information. By contrast, older children scanned the windows in more detailed ways and were more accurate in their judgments of which windows were identical.

short-term memory The memory component in which individuals retain information for up to 30 seconds, assuming there is no rehearsal of the information.

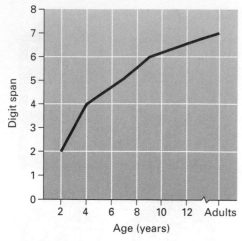

FIGURE 8.13 Developmental Changes in Memory Span

In one study, memory span increased about 3 digits from 2 years of age to 5 digits at 7 years of age (Dempster, 1981). By 12 years of age, memory span had increased on average another 1½ digits to 7 digits.

Four-year-old Jennifer Royal was the only eyewitness to one of her playmate's being shot to death. She was allowed to testify in open court and the clarity of her statements helped to convict the gunman. *What are some issues involved in whether young children should be allowed to testify in court?*

Speed and efficiency of processing information are important, too, especially the speed with which memory items can be identified (Schneider, 2004). For example, in one study, children were tested on their speed at repeating words presented orally (Case, Kurland, & Goldberg, 1982). Speed of repetition was a powerful predictor of memory span. Indeed, when the speed of repetition was controlled, the 6-year-olds' memory spans were equal to those of young adults.

The speed-of-processing explanation highlights a key point in the information-processing perspective: The speed with which a child processes information is an important aspect of the child's cognitive abilities (Halford, 2004; Schneider, 2004). In one recent study, faster processing speed on a memory-span task was linked with higher reading and mathematics achievement (Hitch, Towse, & Hutton, 2001).

How Accurate Are Young Children's Long-Term Memories? In chapter 6, we saw that most of an infant's memories are fragile and, for the most part, short-lived—except for the memory of perceptual-motor actions, which can be substantial (Mandler, 2000, 2004). Does their memory become more accurate when they grow into the early childhood years? Yes, it does. Young children can remember a great deal of information if they are given appropriate cues and prompts.

A current controversy focuses on whether young children should be allowed to testify in court. Increasingly, young children are being allowed to testify, especially if they are the only witnesses to abuse, a crime, and so forth. These conclusions have been reached about children as eyewitnesses (Bruck & Ceci, 1999):

- *Age differences in children's susceptibility to suggestion.* Preschoolers are more suggestible than older children and adults (Koriat, Goldsmith, & Pansky, 2000). Young children can be led, under certain circumstances, to incorporate false suggestions into their accounts of even intimate body touching by adults (Hyman & Loftus, 2001). Despite their greater resistance to suggestibility, there is concern, too, about the effects of suggestive interviews on older children.
- *Individual differences in susceptibility.* Some preschoolers are highly resistant to interviewers' suggestions, while others succumb immediately to the slightest suggestion (Ceci, 2003).
- *Young children's accuracy as eyewitnesses.* Despite the evidence that many young children's responses can be influenced by suggestible interviews, they are capable of recalling much that is relevant about an event (Howe, 1997). Children are more likely to accurately recall an event when the interviewer has a neutral tone, does not use misleading questions, and they are not motivated to make a false report (Bruck & Ceci, 1999).

To read further about false memories in children, see the Research in Life-Span Development interlude.

Research in Life-Span Development

How Parents Can Subtly Suggest False Events to Their Children

A series of studies by Deborah Poole and D. Stephen Lindsay (1995, 1996, 2001) reveal how parents can subtly influence their young children's memory for events. In one study, preschool children participated in four activities (such as lifting cans with pulleys) with "Mr. Science" in a university laboratory (Poole & Lindsay, 1995). Four months later, the children's parents were mailed a storybook with a description of their child's visit to see Mr. Science. The storybook described two of the activities in which the child had participated but it also described two in which the child had not participated. Each description also ended with this fabrication of what had happened when it was time to leave the laboratory: "Mr. Science wiped (child's name) hands and face with a wet-wipe. The cloth got close to (child's name) mouth and tasted real yucky."

Parents read the descriptions to their children three times. Later, the children told the experimenter that they had participated in the activities that actually had only been mentioned in the descriptions read by their parents. For example, when asked whether Mr. Science had put anything yucky in their mouths, more than half of the young children say that he had. Subsequently, when asked whether Mr. Science put something in their mouth or their mom just read this to them in a story, 71 percent of the young children said that it really happened.

This study shows how subtle suggestions can influence children's inaccurate reporting of nonevents, which, if pursued in follow-up questioning by an interviewer who suspected that something sexual had occurred, could lead to a sexual interpretation. This study also revealed the difficulty preschool children have in identifying the source of a suggestion (called *source-monitoring errors*). Children in this study confused their parent reading the suggestion to them with their experience of the suggestion.

In subsequent studies, Poole & Lindsay (1996, 2001) replicated their findings with children from a wider age range (3- to 8-year-olds) with the exception of the results for source monitoring. Three- and four-year-old children had difficulty reporting the source of the information (Mr. Science versus their mother), while older children were more accurate in source identification.

(Source: Bruck & Ceci, 1999, pp. 429–430)

In sum, whether a young child's eyewitness testimony is accurate or not may depend on a number of factors such as the type, number, and intensity of the suggestive techniques the child has experienced. It appears that the reliability of young children's reports has as much to do with the skills and motivation of the interviewer as with any natural limitations on young children's memory (Ceci, Fitneva, & Gilstrap, 2003).

Strategies In chapter 2, we mentioned that an especially important aspect of information-processing theory is the use of good strategies. Strategies consist of deliberate mental activities to improve the processing of information (Garton, 2004; Siegler & Alibali, 2005). For example, rehearsing information and organizing it are two typical strategies that older children and adults use to remember more effectively. For the most part, young children do not use rehearsal and organization to remember (Miller & Seier, 1994).

Do young children use any strategies at all? Problem-solving strategies in young children were the focus of research by Zhe Chen and Robert Siegler (2000). They placed young children at a table where an attractive toy was placed too far away for the child to reach it (they were not allowed to crawl on the table). On the table, between the child and the toy, were six potential tools (see figure 8.14). Only one of them was likely to be useful in obtaining the toy. After initially assessing the young children's attempts to obtain the toy on their own, the experimenters either modeled how to obtain the toy (using the appropriate tool) or gave the child a hint (telling the child to use the particular tool). These 2-year-olds learned the strategy and subsequently mapped the strategy onto new problems. Admittedly, this is a rather simple problem-solving strategy—selecting the best tool to use to obtain a desired toy—but it does document that children as young as 2 years of age can learn a strategy.

During early childhood, the relatively stimulus-driven toddler is transformed into a child capable of flexible, goal-directed problem solving (Zelazo & Müller, 2004; Zelazo & others, 2003). For example, 3- to 4-year-olds are somewhat cognitively inflexible because of lack of understanding of the concept of perspectives and, thus, cannot understand that a single stimulus can be redescribed in a different, incompatible way

FIGURE 8.14 The Toy-Retrieval Task in the Study of Young Children's Problem-Solving Strategies
The child needed to choose the target tool (in this illustration, the toy rake) to pull in the toy (in this case, the turtle).

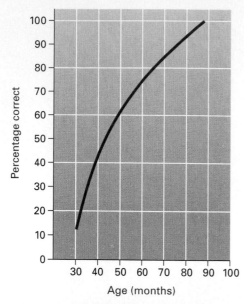

FIGURE 8.15 Developmental Changes in False-Belief Performance

False-belief performance dramatically increases from 2½ years of age through the middle of the elementary school years. In a summary of the results of many studies, 2½-year-olds gave incorrect responses about 80 percent of the time (Wellman, Cross, & Watson, 2001). At 3 years, 8 months, they were correct about 50 percent of the time, and after that, gave increasingly correct responses.

from two different perspectives (Perner & others, 2002). Consider a problem in which children must sort stimuli using the rule of *color*. In the course of the color sorting, a child may describe a red rabbit as a *red one* to solve the problem. However, in a subsequent task, the child may need to discover a rule that describes the rabbit as just a *rabbit* to solve the problem. If 3- to 4-year-olds fail to understand that it is possible to provide multiple descriptions of the same stimulus, they persist in describing the stimulus as a red rabbit. Researchers have found that at about 4 years of age, children acquire the concept of perspectives, which allows them to appreciate that a single description can be described in two different ways (Frye, 1999).

The Young Child's Theory of Mind Theory of mind refers to awareness of one's own mental processes and the mental processes of others. Even young children are curious about the nature of the human mind, and developmentalists have shown a flurry of interest in children's thoughts about what the human mind is like (Flavell, 2004; McCormick, 2003; Peterson & Slaughter, 2003; Wellman, 1997, 2000, 2004).

Children's theory of mind changes as they go through the early childhood years (Flavell, Miller, & Miller, 2002):

- *2 to 3 years of age.* Children begin to understand three mental states:
  Perceptions. The child realizes that another person sees what is in front of her eyes and not necessarily what is in front of the child's eyes.
  Desires. The child understands that if someone wants something, he will try to get it. A child might say, "I want my mommy."
  Emotions. The child can distinguish between positive (for example, happy) and negative (sad, for example) emotions. A child might say, "Tommy feels bad."
- *4 to 5 years of age.* Children come to understand that the mind can represent objects and events accurately or inaccurately. The realization that people can have *false beliefs*—beliefs that are not true—develops in a majority of children by the time they are 5 years old (Wellman, Cross, & Watson, 2001) (see figure 8.15). One study of false beliefs involved showing young children a Band-Aids box and asking them what was inside (Jenkins & Astington, 1996). To the children's surprise, the box actually contained pencils. When asked what a child who had never seen the box would think was inside, 3-year-olds typically responded "pencils." However, the 4- and 5-year-olds, grinning at the anticipation of other children's false beliefs who had not seen what was inside the box, were more likely to say "Band-Aids."
- *Beyond age 5.* It is only beyond the preschool years that children have a deepening appreciation of the mind itself rather than just an understanding of mental states (Wellman, 2004). Not until middle and late childhood do children see the mind as an active constructor of knowledge or processing center (Flavell, Green, & Flavell, 1998). In middle and late childhood, children move from understanding that beliefs can be false to an understanding of beliefs and mind as "interpretive," exemplified in an awareness that the same event can be open to multiple interpretations (Carpendale & Chandler, 1996).

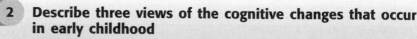

Review and Reflect: Learning Goal 2

2 **Describe three views of the cognitive changes that occur in early childhood**

REVIEW

- What characterizes Piaget's stage of preoperational thought?
- What is Vygotsky's theory of children's cognitive development?
- What are some important ways that young children process information?

REFLECT

- Should children be allowed to develop such concepts as conservation naturally or should the concepts be taught to them? Explain.

theory of mind Refers to the awareness of one's own mental processes and the mental processes of others.

Young children's understanding sometimes gets way ahead of their speech. One 3-year-old, laughing with delight as an abrupt summer breeze stirred his hair and tickled his skin, commented, "I got breezed!" Many of the oddities of young children's language sound like mistakes to adult listeners. However, from the children's point of view, they are not mistakes. They represent the way young children perceive and understand their world at that point in their development.

As children go through the early childhood years, their grasp of the rule systems that govern language increases (Hoff, 2003; Oates & Grayson, 2004; Tager-Flusberg, 2005). These rule systems include phonology (the sound system), morphology (rules for combining minimal units of meaning), syntax (rules for making sentences), semantics (the meaning system), and pragmatics (rules for use in social settings).

Children become increasingly capable of producing all the sounds of their language. They can even produce complex consonant clusters such as *str-* and *-mpt-*.

By the time children move beyond two-word utterances, they demonstrate a knowledge of morphology rules (Carlisle, 2004). Children begin using the plural and possessive forms of nouns (such as *dogs* and *dog's*). They put appropriate endings on verbs (such as *-s* when the subject is third-person singular and *-ed* for the past tense). They use prepositions (such as *in* and *on*), articles (such as *a* and *the*), and various forms of the verb *to be* (such as "I *was* going to the store"). Some of the best evidence for changes in children's use of morphological rules occurs in their overgeneralization of the rules. Have you ever heard a preschool child say "foots" instead of "feet," or "goed" instead of "went"? If you do not remember hearing such usage, talk to parents who have young children or to the young children themselves. You will hear some interesting morphological overgeneralizations.

In a classic experiment that was designed to study children's understanding of morphological rules, Jean Berko (1958) presented preschool children and first-grade children with cards such as the one shown in figure 8.16. Children were asked to look at the card while the experimenter read aloud the words on the card. Then the children were asked to supply the missing word. This might sound easy, but Berko was interested not just in the children's ability to recall the right word but also in their ability to say it "correctly" (with the ending that was dictated by morphological rules). "Wugs" would be the correct response for the card in figure 8.16.

Although the children's answers were not perfect, they were much better than chance. What makes Berko's study impressive is that most of the words were made up for the experiment. Thus, the children could not base their responses on remembering past instances of hearing the words. Instead, they were forced to rely on *rules*.

Young children also learn to manipulate syntax (Scott, 2004). They can generate questions, passives, clauses, and all the major syntactic structures of their language. As children move beyond the two-word stage, their knowledge of semantics or meanings also rapidly advances (McGregor, 2004). The speaking vocabulary of a 6-year-old child ranges from 8,000 to 14,000 words. Assuming that word learning began when the child was 12 months old, this translates into a rate of 5 to 8 new word meanings a day between the ages of 1 and 6. After five years of word learning, the 6-year-old child does not slow down. According to some estimates, the average child of this age is moving along at the awe-inspiring rate of 22 words a day! How would you fare if you were given the task of learning 22 new words every day? It is truly miraculous how quickly children learn language.

Although there are many differences between a 2-year-old's language and a 6-year-old's language, the most dramatic differences pertain to pragmatics. A

Language Development
Language Growth
Pragmatic Language

This is a wug.

Now there is another one.
There are two of them.
There are two _____.

FIGURE 8.16 Stimuli in Berko's Study of Young Children's Understanding of Morphological Rules
In Jean Berko's (1958) study, young children were presented cards, such as this one with a "wug" on it. Then the children were asked to supply the missing word; in supplying the missing word, they had to say it correctly too. "Wugs" is the correct response here.

How do children's language abilities develop during early childhood?

6-year-old is simply a much better conversationalist than a 2-year-old. What are some of the changes in pragmatics that are made in the preschool years? At about 3 years of age, children improve in their ability to talk about things that are not physically present. That is, they improve their command of the characteristic of language known as "displacement." Children become increasingly removed from the "here and now" and are able to talk about things that are not physically present, as well as things that happened in the past, or may happen in the future. Preschoolers can tell you what they want for lunch tomorrow, something that would not have been possible at the two-word stage in infancy. Preschool children also become increasingly able to talk in different ways to different people.

The advances in language that take place in early childhood lay the foundation for later development in the elementary school years, which we will discuss in chapter 10.

Review and Reflect: Learning Goal 3

3 **Summarize how language develops in early childhood**

REVIEW

- How does the grasp of language's rule systems change in early childhood?

REFLECT

- How are nature and nurture likely to be involved in the dramatic increase in a young child's spoken vocabulary?

4 EARLY CHILDHOOD EDUCATION

| Variations in Early Childhood Education | Education for Children Who Are Disadvantaged | Issues in Early Childhood Education |

Our exploration of early childhood education focuses on variations in programs, education for children who are disadvantaged, and some issues in early childhood education.

Variations in Early Childhood Education

There are many variations in the ways young children are educated. First we will explore the child-centered kindergarten, then turn to the Montessori approach. We will conclude this section by examining developmentally appropriate and inappropriate practices in education.

The Child-Centered Kindergarten   Kindergarten programs vary a great deal (Driscoll & Nagel, 2005; Estes, 2004; Spodek & Saracho, 2003). Some approaches place more emphasis on young children's social development, others on their cognitive development.

In the **child-centered kindergarten,** education involves the whole child and includes concern for the child's physical, cognitive, and socioemotional development. Instruction is organized around the child's needs, interests, and learning styles. The

child-centered kindergarten Education that involves the whole child by considering both the child's physical, cognitive, and social development and the child's needs, interests, and learning styles.

process of learning, rather than what is learned, is emphasized (White & Coleman, 2000). Each child follows a unique developmental pattern, and young children learn best through firsthand experiences with people and materials. Play is extremely important in the child's total development. *Experimenting, exploring, discovering,* and *trying out* are all words that describe excellent kindergarten programs.

Early Childhood Education
NAEYC
High/Scope: Active Learning

The Montessori Approach   Montessori schools are patterned after the educational philosophy of Maria Montessori, an Italian physician-turned-educator, who crafted a revolutionary approach to young children's education at the beginning of the twentieth century (Wentworth, 1999). Although some Montessori schools provide programs for school-age children, most specialize in early childhood education.

In the **Montessori approach,** children are given considerable freedom and spontaneity in choosing activities. They are allowed to move from one activity to another as they desire. The teacher acts as a facilitator rather than a director of learning. The teacher shows the child how to perform intellectual activities, demonstrates interesting ways to explore curriculum materials, and offers help when the child requests it.

Some developmentalists favor the Montessori approach, but others believe that it neglects children's social development. For example, while Montessori fosters independence and the development of cognitive skills, it deemphasizes verbal interaction between the teacher and child and peer interaction. Montessori's critics also argue that it restricts imaginative play.

Developmentally Appropriate and Inappropriate Practice in Education
Developmentally appropriate practice is based on knowledge of the typical development of children within an age span (age-appropriateness) and the uniqueness of the child (individual-appropriateness). Developmentally appropriate practice contrasts with developmentally inappropriate practice, which ignores the concrete, hands-on approach to learning. Direct teaching largely through abstract paper-and-pencil activities presented to large groups of young children is believed to be developmentally inappropriate.

One of the most comprehensive documents addressing the issue of developmentally appropriate practice in early childhood programs is the position statement by the National Association for the Education of Young Children (NAEYC) (Bredekamp, 1987, 1997; National Association for the Education of Young Children, 1986). This document reflects the expertise of many of the foremost experts in the field of early childhood education. In figure 8.17 you can examine some of the NAEYC recommendations for developmentally appropriate education.

In one study, the children who attended developmentally appropriate kindergartens displayed more appropriate classroom behavior and had better conduct records and better work and study habits in the first grade than did the children who attended developmentally inappropriate kindergartens (Hart & others, 1993, 1998). One recent study compared 182 children from five developmentally appropriate classrooms (hands-on activities and integrated curriculum tailored to meet age group, cultural, and individual learning styles) and five developmentally inappropriate kindergarten classrooms (academic, direct instruction emphasis with extensive use of workbooks/worksheets, seatwork, and rote drill/practice activities) in a Louisiana school system (Hart & others, 2003). Children from the two types of classrooms did not differ in pre-kindergarten readiness and the classrooms were balanced in terms of sex and socioeconomic status. Teacher ratings of child behavior and scores on the California Achievement Test were obtained through the third grade. Children who were in developmentally inappropriate classrooms had slower growth in vocabulary, math application, and math computation. In another recent study, the academic achievement of mostly African American and Latino children who were attending Head Start was assessed in terms of whether they were in schools emphasizing developmentally appropriate or inappropriate practices (Huffman & Speer, 2000). The young children in the developmentally appropriate classrooms were more advanced in letter/word identification and showed better performance in applying problems over time.

Montessori approach An educational philosophy in which children are given considerable freedom and spontaneity in choosing activities and are allowed to move from one activity to another as they desire.

developmentally appropriate practice
Education that focuses on the typical developmental patterns of children (age-appropriateness) and the uniqueness of each child (individual-appropriateness).

Component	Appropriate Practice	Inappropriate Practice
Curriculum goals	Experiences are provided in all developmental areas—physical, cognitive, social, and emotional.	Experiences are narrowly focused on cognitive development without recognition that all areas of the child's development are interrelated.
	Individual differences are expected, accepted, and used to design appropriate activities.	Children are evaluated only against group norms, and all are expected to perform the same tasks and achieve the same narrowly defined skills.
	Interactions and activities are designed to develop children's self-esteem and positive feelings toward learning.	Children's worth is measured by how well they conform to rigid expectations and perform on standardized tests.
Teaching strategies	Teachers prepare the environment for children to learn through active exploration and interaction with adults, other children, and materials.	Teachers use highly structured, teacher-directed lessons almost exclusively.
	Children select many of their own activities from among a variety the teacher prepares.	The teacher directs all activity, deciding what children will do and when.
	Children are expected to be mentally and physically active.	Children are expected to sit down, be quiet, and listen or do paper-and-pencil tasks for long periods of time. A major portion of time is spent passively sitting, watching, and listening.
Guidance of socioemotional development	Teachers enhance children's self-control by using positive guidance techniques, such as modeling and encouraging expected behavior, redirecting children to a more acceptable activity, and setting clear limits.	Teachers spend considerable time enforcing rules, punishing unacceptable behavior, demeaning children who misbehave, making children sit and be quiet, and refereeing disagreements.
	Children are provided many opportunities to develop social skills, such as cooperating, helping, negotiating, and talking with the person involved to solve interpersonal problems.	Children work individually at desks and tables most of the time and listen to the teacher's directions to the whole group.

FIGURE 8.17 NAEYC Recommendations for Developmentally Appropriate and Inappropriate Education

Head Start Resources
Poverty and Learning

Project Head Start A government-funded program that is designed to provide children from low-income families the opportunity to acquire the skills and experiences important for school success.

Education for Children Who Are Disadvantaged

For many years, children from low-income families did not receive any education before they entered the first grade. In the 1960s, an effort was made to try to break the cycle of poverty and poor education for young children in the United States through compensatory education. **Project Head Start** is a government-funded program designed to provide children from low-income families the opportunity to acquire the skills and experiences important for success in school. Project Head Start began in the summer of 1965, funded by the Economic Opportunity Act, and it continues to serve disadvantaged children today.

Evaluations support the positive influence of quality early childhood programs on both the cognitive and social worlds of disadvantaged young children (Reynolds, 1999; Warner & Sower, 2005). One high-quality early childhood education program (although not a Head Start program) is the Perry Preschool program in Ypsilanti, Michigan, a 2-year preschool program that includes weekly home visits from program personnel. In an analysis of the long-term effects of the program, young adults who attended the Perry Preschool have higher high school graduation rates, a higher employment rate, less need for welfare, a lower crime rate, and a lower teen pregnancy rate than in a control group from the same background who did not have the enriched early childhood education experience (Weikart, 1993).

Although educational intervention for children who are disadvantaged is important, Head Start programs are not all created equal (Zigler & Styfco, 2004). One estimate is that 40 percent of the 1,400 Head Start programs are of questionable quality (Zigler &

Styfco, 1994). Developing consistently high-quality Head Start programs should be a national priority.

One individual who is strongly motivated to make Head Start a valuable learning experience for young children from disadvantaged backgrounds is Yolanda Garcia. To read about her work, see the Careers in Life-Span Development insert.

Issues in Early Childhood Education

Two contemporary issues in early childhood education focus on what the curriculum should be and whether preschool matters.

Curriculum Controversy Currently, there is controversy about what the curriculum for U.S. early childhood education should be (Brewer, 2004; Hill, Stremmel, & Fu, 2005). On one side are those who advocate a child-centered, constructivist approach much like that emphasized by the National Association of Education for Young Children along the lines of developmentally appropriate practice. On the other side are those who advocate an academic, instructivist approach. In the academic instructivist approach, teachers directly instruct young children to learn basic academic skills, especially in reading and math.

In reality, many high-quality early childhood education programs include both academic and constructivist approaches. Many education experts, such as Lilian Katz (1999), though, worry about academic approaches that place too much pressure on young children to achieve and don't provide any opportunities to actively construct knowledge. Competent early childhood programs also should focus on cognitive development *and* socioemotional development, not exclusively on cognitive development (NAEYC, 2002).

Does Preschool Matter? Preschool is rapidly becoming a norm in early childhood education. Twenty-three states already have legislation pending to provide schooling for 4-year-old children, and there are many private preschool programs. The growth in preschool education may benefit many children, but is preschool really a good thing for all children? According to developmental psychologist David Elkind (1988), parents who are exceptionally competent and dedicated and who have both the time and the energy can provide the basic ingredients of early childhood education in their home. If parents have the competence and resources to provide young children with a variety of learning experiences and exposure to other children and adults (possibly through neighborhood play groups), along with opportunities for extensive play, then home schooling may sufficiently educate young children. However, if parents do not have the commitment, the time, the energy, and the resources to provide young children with an environment that approximates a good early childhood program, then it *does* matter whether a child attends preschool. Thus, the issue is not whether preschool is important but whether home schooling can closely duplicate what a competent preschool program can offer.

Careers in Life-Span Development

Yolanda Garcia, Director of Children's Services/Head Start

Yolanda Garcia has worked in the field of early childhood education and family support for three decades. She has been the Director of the Children's Services Department for the Santa Clara, California, County Office of Education since 1980. As director, she is responsible for managing child development programs for 2,500 3- to 5-year-old children in 127 classrooms. Her training includes two master's degrees, one in public policy and child welfare from the University of Chicago and another in education administration from San Jose State University.

Yolanda has served on many national advisory committees that have resulted in improvements in the staffing of Head Start programs. Most notably, she served on the Head Start Quality Committee that recommended the development of Early Head Start and revised performance standards for Head Start programs. Yolanda currently is a member of the American Academy of Science Committee on the Integration of Science and Early Childhood Education.

Yolanda Garcia, Director of Children's Services/Head Start, working with some Head Start children in Santa Clara, California.

What is the curriculum controversy in early childhood education?

In Japan, the goals of early childhood education are quite different from those of American programs. To read about the differences, see the Diversity in Life-Span Development interlude.

Diversity in Life-Span Development
Early Childhood Education in Japan

At a time of low academic achievement by children in the United States, many Americans are turning to Japan, a country of high academic achievement, for possible answers. However, the answers provided by Japanese preschools are not the ones Americans expected to find. In most Japanese preschools, surprisingly little emphasis is put on academic instruction. In one study, 300 Japanese and 210 American preschool teachers, child development specialists, and parents were asked about various aspects of early childhood education (Tobin, Wu, & Davidson, 1989). Only 2 percent of the Japanese respondents listed "to give children a good start academically" as one of their top three reasons for a society to have preschools. In contrast, over half the American respondents chose this as one of their top three choices. To prepare children for successful careers in first grade and beyond, Japanese schools do not teach reading, writing, and mathematics but rather skills like persistence, concentration, and the ability to function as a member of a group. The vast majority of young Japanese children are taught to read at home by their parents.

In the comparison of Japanese and American parents, more than 60 percent of the Japanese parents said that the purpose of preschool is to give children experience being a member of the group compared with only 20 percent of the U.S. parents (Tobin, Wu, & Davidson, 1989) (see figure 8.18). Lessons in living and working together grow naturally out of the Japanese culture. In many Japanese kindergartens, children wear the same uniforms, including caps, which are of different colors to indicate the classrooms to which they belong. They have identical sets of equipment, kept in identical drawers and shelves. This is not intended to turn the young children into robots, as some Americans have

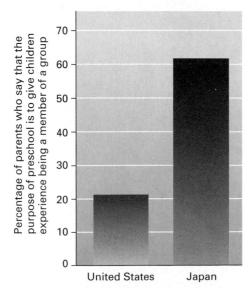

FIGURE 8.18 Comparison of Japanese and U.S. Parents' Views on the Purpose of Preschool

observed, but to impress on them that other people, just like themselves, have needs and desires that are equally important (Hendry, 1995).

As in America, there is diversity in Japanese early childhood education. Some Japanese kindergartens have specific aims, such as early musical training or the practice of Montessori strategies. In large cities, some kindergartens are attached to universities that have elementary and secondary schools. Some Japanese parents believe that, if their young children attend a university-based program, it will increase the children's chances of eventually being admitted to top-rated schools and universities. Several more progressive programs have introduced free play as an antidote for the heavy intellectual orientation in some Japanese kindergartens.

Review and Reflect: Learning Goal 4

 4 Evaluate different approaches to early childhood education

REVIEW

- What are some variations in early childhood education?
- What are the main efforts to educate young children who are disadvantaged?
- What are two contemporary issues related to early childhood education?

REFLECT

- Might preschool be more beneficial to children from middle-income than low-income families? Why?

Reach Your Learning Goals

Physical and Cognitive Development in Early Childhood

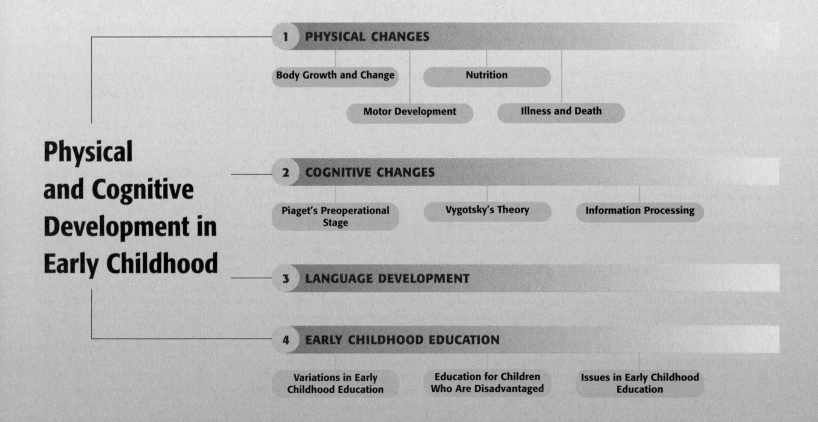

1 PHYSICAL CHANGES
- Body Growth and Change
- Motor Development
- Nutrition
- Illness and Death

2 COGNITIVE CHANGES
- Piaget's Preoperational Stage
- Vygotsky's Theory
- Information Processing

3 LANGUAGE DEVELOPMENT

4 EARLY CHILDHOOD EDUCATION
- Variations in Early Childhood Education
- Education for Children Who Are Disadvantaged
- Issues in Early Childhood Education

Summary

 Learning Goal 1: Identify physical changes in early childhood

- The average child grows 2½ inches in height and gains between 5 and 7 pounds a year during early childhood. Growth patterns vary individually, though. Some children are unusually short because of congenital problems, a physical problem that develops in childhood, or emotional problems. Some of the brain's increase in size in early childhood is due to increases in the number and size of nerve endings, some to myelination. Recently, researchers have found that changes in local patterns in the brain occur between 3 and 15 years of age. These changes often involve spurts of brain activity. From 3 to 6 years of age, the most rapid growth occurs in the frontal lobes; from 6 to puberty, the most substantial changes take place in the temporal and parietal lobes, especially those areas involving language and spatial relations. Increasing brain maturation contributes to improved cognitive abilities.

- Gross motor skills increase dramatically during early childhood. Children become increasingly adventuresome as their gross motor skills improve. Fine motor skills also improve substantially during early childhood. At one point, all children were taught to be right-handed. In today's world, the strategy is to allow children to use the hand they favor. Left-handed children are as competent in motor skills and intellect as right-handed children, although left-handers have more reading problems. Both genetic and environmental explanations of handedness have been given.

- Energy requirements vary according to basal metabolism, rate of growth, and level of activity. A special concern is that too many young children are being raised on diets that are too high in fat. The child's life should be centered on activities, not meals.

- In recent decades, vaccines have virtually eradicated many diseases that once resulted in the deaths of many young children. The disorders still most likely to be fatal for young children are birth defects, cancer, and heart disease, but accidents are the leading cause of death in young children. A special concern is the poor health status of many young children in low-income families. They often have less resistance to disease, including colds and influenza, than do their higher-socioeconomic-status counterparts. There has been a dramatic increase in HIV/AIDS in young children in developing countries in the last decade.

 Learning Goal 2: Describe three views of the cognitive changes that occur in early childhood

- Piaget's preoperational stage of thought is the beginning of the ability to reconstruct at the level of thought what has been established in behavior and a transition from primitive to more sophisticated use of symbols. In preoperational thought, the child's thoughts are flawed and not well organized. The symbolic function substage occurs between 2 and 4 years of age and is characterized by symbolic thought, egocentrism, and animism. The intuitive thought substage stretches from 4 to 7 years of age. It is called intuitive because children seem so sure about their knowledge yet are unaware of how they know what they know. The preoperational child lacks conservation and asks a barrage of questions.

- In Vygotsky's theory, the zone of proximal development (ZPD) describes the range of tasks that are too difficult for children to master alone but which can be learned with the guidance and assistance of adults or more-skilled children. Scaffolding involves changing the level of support over the course of a teaching session, with the more-skilled person adjusting guidance to fit the student's current performance level. Vygotsky believed that language plays a key role in guiding cognition. Applications of Vygotsky's theory in education focus on using the child's zone of proximal development, using scaffolding and more-skilled peers as teachers, monitoring and encouraging children's use of private speech, assessing the child's ZPD rather than IQ, and transforming the classroom with Vygotskian ideas. Comparisons of Vygotsky's and Piaget's theories involve constructivism, metaphors for learning, stages, key processes, role of language, views on education, and teaching implications. Vygotsky's theory is social constructivist, Piaget's cognitive constructivist.

- Information-processing theory emphasizes cognitive processes. The child's ability to attend to stimuli dramatically improves during early childhood. One deficit in attention in early childhood is that the child attends to the salient rather than the relevant features of a task. Significant improvement in short-term memory occurs during early childhood. With good prompts, young children's long-term memories can be accurate, although young children can be led into developing false memories. Young children usually don't use strategies to remember, but they can learn rather simple problem-solving strategies. Theory of mind is the awareness of one's own mental processes and the mental processes of others. Children begin to understand mental states involving perceptions, desires, and emotions at 2 to 3 years of age and at 4 to 5 years of age realize that people can have false beliefs.

3 **Learning Goal 3: Summarize how language develops in early childhood**

- Young children increase their grasp of language's rule systems. These include phonology, morphology, syntax, semantics, and pragmatics. Berko's classic experiment demonstrated that young children understand morphological rules.

4 **Learning Goal 4: Evaluate different approaches to early childhood education**

- The child-centered kindergarten emphasizes the education of the whole child, with particular attention to individual variation, the process of learning, and the importance of play in development. The Montessori approach, another well-known strategy for early childhood education, allows children to choose from a range of activities while teachers serve as facilitators. Developmentally appropriate practice focuses on the typical patterns of children (age-appropriateness) and the uniqueness of each child (individual-appropriateness). Such practice contrasts with developmentally inappropriate practice, which ignores the concrete, hands-on approach to learning.

- The U.S. government has tried to break the poverty cycle with programs such as Head Start. Model programs have been shown to have positive effects on children from poverty backgrounds.

- Controversy characterizes early childhood education curricula. On the one side are the child-centered, constructivist advocates, on the other are those who advocate an instructivist, academic approach. In terms of whether preschool matters, some parents can educate young children as effectively as a school does; however, most parents do not have the skills, time, and commitment to do so.

Key Terms

myelination 228
basal metabolism rate (BMR) 231
operations 234
symbolic function substage 234
egocentrism 235

animism 235
intuitive thought substage 235
centration 236
conservation 236
zone of proximal development (ZPD) 237

social constructivist approach 239
short-term memory 241
theory of mind 244
child-centered kindergarten 246

Montessori approach 247
developmentally appropriate practice 247
Project Head Start 248

Key People

Jean Piaget 234
Barbel Inhelder 235

Rochel Gelman 237
Lev Vygotsky 237

Zhe Chen and Robert Siegler 243

Jean Berko 245
Maria Montessori 247
David Elkind 249

E-Learning Tools

To help you master the material in this chapter, you'll find a number of valuable study tools on the LifeMap CD-ROM that accompanies this book and on the Online Learning Center for *Life-Span Development,* tenth edition, at www.mhhe.com/santrockld10.

Video Clips

In the margins of this book there are icons directing you to the LifeMap CD-ROM that accompanies the book. There you'll find a video for chapter 8 called "Children and Nutrition." Diet and physical activity, as this segment demonstrates, are important aspects of a healthy lifestyle. These lifestyle choices begin in early childhood.

Self-Assessment

Connect to www.mhhe.com/santrockld10 to examine your understanding of cognitive development in early childhood by completing the self-assessment, *What I Think Is Important in Early Childhood Education.*

Taking It to the Net

Connect to www.mhhe.com/santrockld10 to research the answers to these questions.

1. A child's grasp of elementary physics (conservation laws, for example) normally improves during Piaget's preoperational stage. Many adults, however, nevertheless retain a set of incorrect assumptions about motion and matter—what psychologists sometimes refer to as "intuitive physics." Julien is 5 years old. When asked to describe the trajectory a chess piece would follow as it spun off a revolving circular table, Julien answers that it would follow a curved trajectory (an answer inconsistent with Newton's first law of motion). What other misconceptions about the physical world might Julien be likely to retain past the age of 10?

2. Margaret and Zhang have a 3-year-old daughter. Zhang speaks both English and Mandarin Chinese, and he and Margaret would like to teach their daughter both languages as early as possible. Does research suggest that there is an optimal period for the acquisition of a second language? Should they introduce their daughter to one language first, and only then begin instruction in the second?

3. Beyonce, who is working in a prosecutor's office for her senior internship, has been asked to write a memo on the suggestibility of child witnesses and how likely a jury is to believe a child's testimony in court cases. How can she find information for the memo that provides research-based facts as well as guidelines for dealing with child witnesses that will be helpful for the prosecutors?

Health and Well-Being, Parenting, and Education Exercises

Build your decision-making skills by trying your hand at the health and well-being, parenting, and education exercises.

Connect to www.mhhe.com/santrockld10 to research the answers and complete the exercises.

CHAPTER

9

Let us play, for it is
yet day
And we cannot go to
sleep;
Besides, in the sky
the little birds fly
And the hills are all
covered with sheep.
—WILLIAM BLAKE
English Poet, 19th Century

Socioemotional Development in Early Childhood

Chapter Outline

Learning Goals

EMOTIONAL AND PERSONALITY DEVELOPMENT

1

The Self

Emotional Development

Moral Development

Gender

Discuss emotional and personality development in early childhood

FAMILIES

2

Parenting

Sibling Relationships and Birth Order

The Changing Family in a Changing Society

Explain how families can influence young children's development

PEER RELATIONS, PLAY, AND TELEVISION

3

Peer Relations

Play

Television

Describe the roles of peers, play, and television in young children's development

Images of Life-Span Development
Sara and Her Developing Moral Values

The following story reflects the developing values of a young girl (Kantrowitz, 1991). Sara Newland loves animals just like most children do. But Sara went beyond most children's love for animals when she heard about an endangered species during a trip to a zoo. She became motivated to help the endangered animals. Guided by her mother, Sara raised $35 by baking cookies and selling them near her apartment building in New York City. She mailed the money to the World Wildlife Fund and felt good about her contribution. However, several weeks later, her happiness turned to sadness when the fund wrote Sara and requested more money. Sara thought she had taken care of the endangered animal problem and was depressed that she had not. Sara's mother comforted her and talked with her about how big some of life's problems are, such as that of helping endangered species around the world, which require contributions from many people.

In elementary school, Sara has continued her goodwill and kindness. Now 9 years old, she helps out at a child-care center and takes meals to homeless individuals in her neighborhood. Sara communicates with her friends and others about the homeless and tells them not to be afraid of them but to think about how they can be helped. In Sara's words, "If everyone gave them food, they would have decent meals."

Sensitive parents can make a difference in encouraging young children's sense of morality and values. Some experts on moral development believe that a capacity for goodness is present from the start, which reflects the "innate goodness" view of the child, which we discussed in chapter 1. However, many developmentalists also believe that parents must nurture that goodness, just as they help their children become good readers, musicians, or athletes.

PREVIEW

In early childhood, children's emotional and personality development change in significant ways and their small worlds widen. In addition to the continuing influence of family relationships, peers take on a more significant role in children's development and play fills the days of many young children's lives.

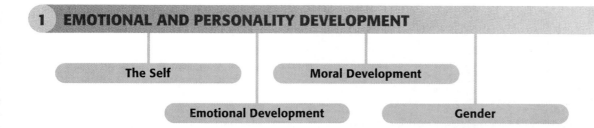

1 EMOTIONAL AND PERSONALITY DEVELOPMENT

- The Self
- Emotional Development
- Moral Development
- Gender

In the story that opened the chapter, Sara displayed a positive sense of morality through her motivation to help an endangered species and the homeless. Let's further explore young children's moral development and other aspects of their emotional and personality development, beginning with the self.

The Self

We learned in chapter 7 that toward the end of the second year of life children develop a sense of self. During early childhood, some important developments in the self take place. Among these developments are facing the issue of initiative versus guilt and enhancing self-understanding.

Initiative Versus Guilt According to Erik Erikson (1968), the psychosocial stage that characterizes early childhood is *initiative versus guilt*. By now, children have become convinced that they are persons of their own; during early childhood, they must discover what kind of person they will become. They intensely identify with their parents, who most of the time appear to them to be powerful and beautiful, although often unreasonable, disagreeable, and sometimes even dangerous. During early childhood, children use their perceptual, motor, cognitive, and language skills to make things happen. They have a surplus of energy that permits them to forget failures quickly and to approach new areas that seem desirable—even if they seem dangerous—with undiminished zest and some increased sense of direction. On their own *initiative*, then, children at this stage exuberantly move out into a wider social world.

The great governor of initiative is *conscience*. Children now not only feel afraid of being found out, but they also begin to hear the inner voices of self-observation, self-guidance, and self-punishment (Bybee, 1999). Their initiative and enthusiasm may bring them not only rewards but also punishments. Children's widespread disappointment at this stage leads to an unleashing of guilt that lowers self-esteem.

Whether children leave this stage with a sense of initiative that outweighs their sense of guilt depends in large part on how parents respond to their children's self-initiated activities. Children who are given the freedom and opportunity to initiate motor play, such as running, bike riding, sledding, skating, tussling, and wrestling, have their sense of initiative supported. Children's initiative is also supported when parents answer their children's questions and do not deride or inhibit fantasy or play activity. In contrast, if children are made to feel that their motor activity is bad, that their questions are a nuisance, and that their play is silly and stupid, then they often develop a sense of guilt over self-initiated activities that may persist through life's later stages (Elkind, 1970).

Self-Understanding **Self-understanding** is the child's representation of self, the substance and content of self-conceptions. For example, a 5-year-old girl understands that she is a girl, has blond hair, likes to ride her bicycle, has a friend, and is a swimmer. An 11-year-old boy understands that he is a student, a boy, a football player, a family member, a video-game lover, and a rock music fan. A child's self-understanding is based on the various roles and membership categories that define who children are. Though not the whole of personal identity, self-understanding provides its rational underpinnings (Damon & Hart, 1992).

The roots of self-understanding begin with self-recognition, which takes place by approximately 18 months of age. Because children can verbally communicate their ideas, research on self-understanding in childhood is not limited to visual self-recognition, as it was during infancy. Mainly by interviewing children, researchers have probed children's conceptions of many aspects of self-understanding (Moore & Lemmon, 2001). These include mind and body, self in relation to others, and pride and shame in self. In early childhood, children usually conceive of the self in physical terms. Most young children think the self is part of their body, usually their head. Young children usually confuse self, mind, and body. Because the self is a body part for them, they describe it along many material dimensions, such as size, shape, and color. Young children distinguish themselves from others through many different physical and material attributes. Says 4-year-old Sandra, "I'm different from Jennifer because I have brown hair and she has blond hair." Says 4-year-old Ralph,

self-understanding The child's cognitive representation of self, the substance and content of the child's self-conceptions.

"I am different from Hank because I am taller, and I am different from my sister because I have a bicycle."

In early childhood, children frequently think of themselves in terms of a physical self or an active self. That is, the *active dimension* is a central component of the self in early childhood (Keller, Ford, & Meacham, 1978). If we define the category *physical* broadly enough, we can include physical actions as well as body image and material possessions. For example, preschool children often describe themselves in terms of activities such as play.

Emotional Development

Children, like adults, experience many emotions during the course of a day. At times, children also try to make sense of other people's emotional reactions and feelings.

Young Children's Emotion Language and Understanding
Among the most important changes in emotional development in early childhood are the increased use of emotion language and the understanding of emotion (Kuebli, 1994). Preschoolers become more adept at talking about their own and others' emotions. Between 2 and 3 years of age, children continue to increase the number of terms they use to describe emotion (Ridgeway, Waters, & Kuczaj, 1985). However, in the preschool years, children are learning more than just the "vocabulary" of emotion terms, they also are learning about the causes and consequences of feelings (Denham, 1998).

At 4 to 5 years of age, children show an increased ability to reflect on emotions. In this developmental time frame, they also begin to understand that the same event can elicit different feelings in different people. Moreover, they show a growing awareness about controlling and managing emotions to meet social standards (Bruce, Olen, & Jensen, 1999). A summary of the characteristics of young children's emotion language and understanding is shown in figure 9.1.

Self-Conscious Emotions
Self-conscious emotions require that children be able to refer to themselves and be aware of themselves as distinct from others (Lewis, 2002). Pride, shame, embarrassment, and guilt are self-conscious emotions.

Recall from chapter 7, "Socioemotional Development in Infancy," that self-awareness appears in the last half of the second year of life. The self-conscious emotions do not appear to develop, at the very earliest, until this self-awareness is in place. Thus, emotions such as pride and guilt become more common in the early

FIGURE 9.1 Some Characteristics of Young Children's Emotion Language and Understanding

Approximate Age of Child	Description
2 to 3 years	Increase emotion vocabulary most rapidly
	Correctly label simple emotions in self and others and talk about past, present, and future emotions
	Talk about the causes and consequences of some emotions and identify emotions associated with certain situations
	Use emotion language in pretend play
4 to 5 years	Show increased capacity to reflect verbally on emotions and to consider more complex relations between emotions and situations
	Understand that the same event may call forth different feelings in different people and that feelings sometimes persist long after the events that caused them
	Demonstrate growing awareness about controlling and managing emotions in accord with social standards

childhood years. They are especially influenced by parents' responses to children's behavior. For example, a young child may experience a twinge of guilt when a parent says, "You should feel bad about biting your sister." Shortly, we will further discuss guilt in the context of moral development.

In one study, girls showed more shame and pride than boys (Stipek, Recchia, & McClintic, 1992). This gender difference is interesting because girls are more at risk for internalizing disorders, such as anxiety and depression, in which feelings of shame and self-criticism often are evident (Cummings, Braungart-Rieker, & Du Rocher-Schudlich, 2003).

Emotion-Coaching and Emotion-Dismissing Parents In chapter 7, we described the importance of self-regulation of emotion in infancy. The self-regulation of emotion continues to be an important aspect of socioemotional development in the childhood years and parents can play an important role in helping young children regulate their emotions (Havighurst, Harley, & Prior, 2004). Depending on how they talk with their children about emotion, parents can be described as taking an *emotion-coaching* or an *emotion-dismissing* approach (Katz, 1999). *Emotion-coaching parents* monitor their children's emotions, view their children's negative emotions as opportunities for teaching, assist them in labeling emotions, and coach them in how to deal effectively with emotions. In contrast, *emotion-dismissing parents* view their role as to deny, ignore, or change negative emotions. Researchers have found that when interacting with their children, emotion-coaching parents are less rejecting, use more scaffolding and praise, and are more nurturant than are emotion-dismissing parents (Gottman & DeClaire, 1997). The children of emotion-coaching parents were better at soothing themselves when they got upset, more effective in regulating their negative affect, focused their attention better, and had fewer behavior problems than the children of emotion-dismissing parents.

Moral Development

Moral development involves the development of thoughts, feelings, and behaviors regarding rules and conventions about what people should do in their interactions with other people. Developmentalists study how children think, behave, and feel about such rules and regulations. We will begin our exploration of moral development in children by focusing on a cognitive view of moral development.

Piaget's View of Moral Reasoning Interest in how children think about moral issues was stimulated by Piaget (1932), who extensively observed and interviewed children from the ages of 4 through 12. Piaget watched children play marbles to learn how they thought about and used the game's rules. He also asked children about ethical issues—theft, lies, punishment, and justice, for example. Piaget concluded that children go through two distinct stages in how they think about morality and a transition between the two stages.

- From 4 to 7 years of age, children display **heteronomous morality,** the first stage of moral development in Piaget's theory. Children think of justice and rules as unchangeable properties of the world, removed from the control of people.
- From 7 to 10 years of age, children are in a transition showing some features of the first stage of moral reasoning and some features of the second stage, autonomous morality.
- From about 10 years of age and older, children show **autonomous morality,** the second stage of moral development. They become aware that rules and laws are created by people, and in judging an action, they consider the actor's intentions as well as the consequences.

A heteronomous thinker judges the rightness or goodness of behavior by considering the consequences of the behavior, not the intentions of the actor. For

moral development Development that involves thoughts, feelings, and actions regarding rules and conventions about what people should do in their interactions with other people.

heteronomous morality The first stage of moral development in Piaget's theory, occurring from approximately 4 to 7 years of age. Justice and rules are conceived of as unchangeable properties of the world, removed from the control of people.

autonomous morality The second stage of moral development in Piaget's theory, displayed by older children (about 10 years of age and older). The child becomes aware that rules and laws are created by people and that, in judging an action, one should consider the actor's intentions as well as the consequences.

example, the heteronomous thinker says that breaking twelve cups accidentally is worse than breaking one cup intentionally. For the moral autonomist, the actor's intentions assume paramount importance. The heteronomous thinker also believes that rules are unchangeable and are handed down by all-powerful authorities. When Piaget suggested to young children that they use new rules in a game of marbles, they resisted. By contrast, older children—moral autonomists—accept change and recognize that rules are merely convenient conventions, subject to change.

The heteronomous thinker also believes in **immanent justice,** Piaget's concept that if a rule is broken, punishment will be meted out immediately. The young child believes that a violation is connected automatically to its punishment. Thus, young children often look around worriedly after committing a transgression, expecting inevitable punishment. Immanent justice also implies that if something unfortunate happens to someone, the person must have transgressed earlier. Older children, who are moral autonomists, recognize that punishment occurs only if someone witnesses the wrongdoing and that, even then, punishment is not inevitable.

Piaget argued that, as children develop, they become more sophisticated in thinking about social matters, especially about the possibilities and conditions of cooperation. Piaget believed that this social understanding comes about through the mutual give-and-take of peer relations. In the peer group, where others have power and status similar to the child's, plans are negotiated and coordinated, and disagreements are reasoned about and eventually settled. Parent-child relations, in which parents have the power and children do not, are less likely to advance moral reasoning, because rules are often handed down in an authoritarian way. Later, in chapter 11, we will discuss another highly influential cognitive view of moral development, that of Lawrence Kohlberg.

Moral Behavior The study of moral behavior is emphasized by behavioral and social cognitive theorists (Grusec, 2005). The processes of reinforcement, punishment, and imitation are used to explain children's moral behavior. When children are rewarded for behavior that is consistent with laws and social conventions, they are likely to repeat that behavior. When models who behave morally are provided, children are likely to adopt their actions. And, when children are punished for immoral behavior, those behaviors are likely to be reduced or eliminated. However, because punishment may have adverse side effects, it needs to be used judiciously and cautiously.

Another important point needs to be made about the social cognitive view of moral development. Moral behavior is influenced extensively by the situation. What children do in one situation is often only weakly related to what they do in other situations. A child might cheat in math class but not in English class; a child might steal a piece of candy when others are not present but not steal it when they are present. More than half a century ago, morality's situational nature was observed in a comprehensive study of thousands of children in many different situations—at home, at school, and at church, for example. The totally honest child was virtually nonexistent; so was the child who cheated in all situations (Hartshorne & May, 1928–1930).

Social cognitive theorists also believe that the ability to resist temptation is closely tied to the development of self-control. Children must overcome their impulses toward something they want that is prohibited. To achieve this self-control, they must learn to be patient and to delay gratification. According to social cognitive theorists, cognitive factors are important in the child's development of self-control (Bandura, 2002).

Moral Feelings In chapter 2, we discussed Sigmund Freud's psychoanalytic theory. It describes the *superego* as one of the three main structures of personality—the id and ego being the other two. In Freud's classical psychoanalytic theory, the child's superego—the moral branch of personality—develops as the child resolves the Oedipus conflict and identifies with the same-sex parent in the early childhood years. Among the reasons children resolve the Oedipus conflict is the fear of losing their parents' love and of being punished for their unacceptable sexual wishes toward the

immanent justice The concept that, if a rule is broken, punishment will be meted out immediately.

opposite-sex parent. To reduce anxiety, avoid punishment, and maintain parental affection, children form a superego by identifying with the same-sex parent. Through their identification with the same-sex parent, children internalize the parents' standards of right and wrong that reflect societal prohibitions and turns inward the hostility that was previously aimed externally at the same-sex parent. This inwardly directed hostility is now felt self-punitively as guilt, which is experienced unconsciously (beyond the child's awareness). In the psychoanalytic account of moral development, the self-punitiveness of guilt is responsible for keeping the child from committing transgressions. That is, children conform to societal standards to avoid guilt.

Positive feelings, such as empathy, contribute to the child's moral development. *Empathy* is reacting to another's feelings with an emotional response that is similar to the other's feelings (Eisenberg, 2005; Hoffman, 2002). Although empathy is experienced as an emotional state, it often has a cognitive component. The cognitive component is the ability to discern another's inner psychological states, or what is called "perspective taking." Young infants have the capacity for some purely empathic responses, but for effective moral action children need to learn how to identify a wide range of emotional states in others. They also need to learn to anticipate what kinds of action will improve another person's emotional state.

What is moral is what you feel good after and what is immoral is what you feel bad after.

—**Ernest Hemingway**
American Author, 20th Century

Gender

While sex refers to the biological dimension of being male or female, **gender** refers to the social and psychological dimensions of being male or female. Two aspects of gender bear special mention:

- **Gender identity** is the sense of being male or female, which most children acquire by the time they are 3 years old.
- **Gender role** is a set of expectations that prescribes how females or males should think, act, and feel.

Gender Resources

Biological Influences   How might our biological foundations influence our gender behavior and thought? Among the possible influences are chromosomes, hormones, and evolution.

Chromosomes, Gonads, and Hormones   In chapter 3, you learned that humans normally have 46 chromosomes arranged in pairs. The 23rd pair consists of a combination of X and Y chromosomes, usually two X chromosomes in a female and an X and a Y in a male.

Just as chromosomes are important in understanding biological influences, so are hormones (Berenbaum & Bailey, 2003; Lippa, 2005). The two main classes of sex hormones are estrogens and androgens, which are secreted by the *gonads* (ovaries in females, testes in males). *Estrogens,* such as estradiol, influence the development of female physical sex characteristics. *Androgens,* such as testosterone, promote the development of male physical sex characteristics. In the first few weeks of gestation, female and male embryos look alike. Males start to differ from females when the Y chromosome in the male embryo triggers the development of testes (rather than ovaries); the testes secrete copious amounts of androgens, which lead to the development of male sex organs. Low levels of androgens in the female embryo allow the normal development of female sex organs.

A recent research study suggests that genetic males born with ambiguous genitals because of a rare birth defect and who are surgically assigned to be female frequently grow up feeling like boys and may eventually switch their gender back to male, even with no knowledge of their history (Reiner & Gearhart, 2004). In this research, 16 genetically male children 5 to 16 years of age were studied; 14 of them were raised as females. Children and parents were asked detailed questions about

gender The social and psychological dimension of being male or female.

gender identity The sense of being male or female, which most children acquire by the time they are 3 years old.

gender role A set of expectations that prescribes how females or males should think, act, and feel.

the children's play patterns, levels of aggression, career goals, and attitudes about gender roles. The families were followed for 34 to 98 months. In the most recent assessment, 8 of the 14 individuals raised as girls had declared themselves boys, including 4 who had not been told of their surgical transformation. The researchers concluded that nature is more important than nurture in the case of these children and the majority of children born with these problems should be left as the male sex. However, the issue is complex since 5 of the 16 children appeared happy living as girls, implying that in some cases nurture can trump nature. Further, other research and clinical reports indicate many genetic males raised as girls appear to be well adjusted (Gooren, 2002; Slijper & others, 1998).

The Evolutionary Psychology View   In chapter 3 we described the approach of evolutionary psychology, which emphasizes that adaptation during the evolution of humans produced psychological differences between males and females (Buss, 1995, 2000, 2004). Here we review and expand on that discussion.

Evolutionary psychologists argue that primarily because of their differing roles in reproduction, males and females faced different pressures in primeval environments when the human species was evolving. In particular, because having multiple sexual liaisons improves the likelihood that males will pass on their genes, natural selection favored males who adopted short-term mating strategies. These males competed with other males to acquire more resources in order to access females. Therefore, say evolutionary psychologists, males evolved dispositions that favor violence, competition, and risk taking.

In contrast, according to evolutionary psychologists, females' contributions to the gene pool were improved by securing resources for their offspring, which was promoted by obtaining long-term mates who could support a family (Jackson, 2004). As a consequence, natural selection favored females who devoted effort to parenting and chose mates who could provide their offspring with resources and protection. Females developed preferences for successful, ambitious men who could provide these resources.

This evolutionary unfolding, according to some evolutionary psychologists, explains key gender differences in sexual attitudes and sexual behavior. For example, in one study, men said that ideally they would like to have more than 18 sexual partners in their lifetime, whereas women stated that ideally they would like to have only 4 or 5 (Buss & Schmidt, 1993). In another study, 75 percent of the men but none of the women approached by an attractive stranger of the opposite sex consented to a request for sex (Clark & Hatfield, 1989).

Such gender differences, says David Buss (2000, 2004), are exactly the type predicted by evolutionary psychology. Buss argues that men and women differ psychologically in those domains in which they have faced different adaptive problems during evolutionary history. In all other domains, predicts Buss, the sexes will be psychologically similar.

Critics of evolutionary psychology argue that its hypotheses are backed by speculations about prehistory, not evidence, and that in any event people are not locked into behavior that was adaptive in the evolutionary past. Critics also claim that the evolutionary view pays little attention to cultural and individual variations in gender differences.

Social Influences   Many social scientists do not locate the cause of psychological gender differences in biological dispositions. Rather, they argue that these differences are due to social experiences (Denmark, Rabinowitz, & Sechzer, 2005).

In the United States, adults discriminate between the sexes shortly after the infant's birth. The "pink and blue" treatment might be applied to boys and girls before they leave the hospital. Soon afterward, differences in hairstyles, clothes, and toys become obvious. Adults and peers reward these differences throughout development. And boys and girls learn gender roles through imitation, or observational

First imagine that this is a photograph of a baby girl. *What expectations would you have for her?* Then imagine that this is a photograph of a baby boy. *What expectations would you have for him?*

learning, by watching what other people say and do. In recent years, the idea that parents are the critical socializing agents in gender-role development has come under fire. Parents are only one of many sources through which children learn gender roles (Beal, 1994; Fagot, Rodgers, & Leinbach, 2000). Culture, schools, peers, the media, and other family members provide other gender role models, yet it is important to guard against swinging too far in this direction because—especially in the early years of development—parents are important influences on gender development.

Social Theories of Gender Three main social theories of gender have been proposed—social role theory, psychoanalytic theory, and social cognitive theory. Alice Eagly (2000, 2001) proposed **social role theory,** which states that gender differences result from the contrasting roles of women and men. In most cultures around the world, women have less power and status than men have and they control fewer resources (Denmark, Rabinowitz, & Sechzer, 2005; Wood, 2001). Compared with men, women perform more domestic work, spend fewer hours in paid employment, receive lower pay, and are more thinly represented in the highest levels of organizations. In Eagly's view, as women adapted to roles with less power and less status in society, they showed more cooperative, less dominant profiles than men. Thus, the social hierarchy and division of labor are important causes of gender differences in power, assertiveness, and nurture (Eagly & Diekman, 2003).

The **psychoanalytic theory of gender** stems from Freud's view that the preschool child develops a sexual attraction to the opposite-sex parent. At 5 or 6 years of age, the child renounces this attraction because of anxious feelings. Subsequently, the child identifies with the same-sex parent, unconsciously adopting the same-sex parent's characteristics. However, developmentalists argue that gender development does not proceed as Freud proposed (Callan, 2001). Children become gender-typed much earlier than 5 or 6 years of age, and they become masculine or feminine even when the same-sex parent is not present in the family.

The social cognitive approach discussed in chapter 2 provides an alternative explanation of how children develop gender-typed behavior (see figure 9.2). According to the **social cognitive theory of gender,** children's gender development occurs through observation and imitation, and through the rewards and punishments children experience for gender-appropriate and gender-inappropriate behavior (Bussey & Bandura, 1999). Parents often use rewards and punishments to teach their daughters to be feminine ("Karen, you are being a good girl when you play gently with your doll") and their sons to be masculine ("Keith, a boy as big as you is not supposed to cry"). Children also learn about gender from observing other adults in the neighborhood and on television (Fagot, Rodgers, & Leinbach, 2000). As children get older, peers become increasingly important. Peers extensively reward and punish gender behavior (Lott & Maluso, 2001). For example, when children play in ways that the culture says are sex-appropriate, they tend to be rewarded by their peers. Those who engage in activities that are considered inappropriate tend to be criticized or abandoned by their peers.

social role theory A theory that gender differences result from the contrasting roles of men and women.

psychoanalytic theory of gender A theory deriving from Freud's view that the preschool child develops a sexual attraction to the opposite-sex parent, by approximately 5 or 6 years of age renounces this attraction because of anxious feelings, and subsequently identifies with the same-sex parent, unconsciously adopting the same-sex parent's characteristics.

social cognitive theory of gender A theory that emphasizes that children's gender development occurs through the observation and imitation of gender behavior and through the rewards and punishments children experience for gender-appropriate and gender-inappropriate behavior.

Theory	Processes	Outcomes
Freud's psychoanalytic theory	Sexual attraction to opposite-sex parent at 3 to 5 years of age; anxiety about sexual attraction and subsequent identification with same-sex parent at 5 to 6 years of age	Gender behavior similar to that of same-sex parent
Social cognitive theory	Rewards and punishments of gender-appropriate and -inappropriate behavior by adults and peers; observation and initiation of models' masculine and feminine behavior	Gender behavior

FIGURE 9.2 A Comparison of the Psychoanalytic and Social Cognitive Views of Gender Development
Parents influence their children's development by action and example.

From 4 to about 12 years of age, children spend most of their free playtime exclusively with others of their own sex (Maccoby, 2002). What kind of socialization takes place in these same-sex play groups? In one study, researchers observed preschoolers over six months (Martin & Fabes, 2001). The more time boys spent interacting with other boys, the more their activity level, rough-and-tumble play, and sex-typed choice of toys and games increased, and the less time boys spent near adults. By contrast, the more time preschool girls spent interacting with other girls, the more their activity level and aggression decreased, and the more their girl-type play activities and time spent near adults increased. After watching elementary school children repeatedly play in same-sex groups, two researchers characterized the playground as "gender school" (Luria & Herzog, 1985).

Parental Influences   Parents, by action and by example, influence their children's gender development (Lenton & Blair, 2004; Maccoby, 2003). Both mothers and fathers are psychologically important to their children's gender development (McHale, Crouter, & Whiteman, 2003). Mothers are more consistently given responsibility for nurturance and physical care. Fathers are more likely to engage in playful interaction and to be given responsibility for ensuring that boys and girls conform to existing cultural norms. And, whether or not they have more influence on them, fathers are more involved in socializing their sons than their daughters. Fathers seem to play an especially important part in gender-role development. They are more likely than mothers to act differently toward sons and daughters (Leaper, 2002). Thus, they contribute more to distinctions between the genders (Huston, 1983).

Many parents encourage boys and girls to engage in different types of play and activities (Fagot, 1995). Girls are more likely to be given dolls to play with during childhood. When old enough, they are more likely to be assigned baby-sitting duties. Girls are encouraged to be more nurturant and emotional than boys are. Fathers are more likely to engage in aggressive play with their sons than with their daughters.

Peer Influences   Parents provide the earliest discrimination of gender roles in development, but before long, peers join the societal process of responding to and modeling masculine and feminine behavior. There is increasing evidence that gender plays an important role in peer relations. This evidence involves the gender composition of children's groups, group size, and interaction in same-sex groups (Maccoby, 1998, 2002):

- *Gender composition of children's groups.* Around the age of 3, children already show a preference to spend time with same-sex playmates. From 4 to 12 years of age, this preference for playing in same-sex groups increases, and during the elementary school years children spend a large majority of their free time with children of their own sex (see figure 9.3).
- *Group size.* From about 5 years of age onward, boys are more likely to associate together in larger clusters than girls are. Boys are also more likely to participate in organized group games than girls are. In one study, same-sex groups of six children were permitted to use play materials in any way they wished (Benenson, Apostolaris, & Parnass, 1997). Girls were more likely than boys to play in dyads or triads, while boys were more likely to interact in larger groups and seek to attain a group goal.
- *Interaction in same-sex groups.* Boys are more likely than girls to engage in rough-and-tumble play, competition, conflict, ego displays, risk taking, and seeking dominance. By contrast, girls are more likely to engage in "collaborative discourse," in which they talk and act in a more reciprocal manner.

Peers often reject children who act in a manner that is more characteristic of the other gender (Matlin, 2004). However, researchers have found that there is greater pressure for boys to conform to a traditional male role than for girls to conform to a traditional female role (Fagot, Rogers, & Leinbach, 2000).

www.mhhe.com/santrockld1o

Fathers and Sons

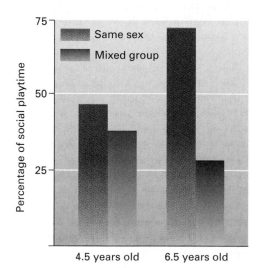

FIGURE 9.3 Developmental Changes in Percentage of Time Spent in Same-Sex and Mixed-Group Settings
Observations of children show that they are more likely to play in same-sex than mixed-sex groups. This tendency increases between 4 and 6 years of age.

Cognitive Influences Observation, imitation, rewards and punishment—these are the mechanisms by which gender develops according to social cognitive theory. Interactions between the child and the social environment are the main keys to gender development in this view. Some critics argue that this explanation pays too little attention to the child's own mind and understanding, and portrays the child as passively acquiring gender roles (Gelman, Taylor, & Nyugen, 2004; Martin & Dinella, 2001). Two cognitive theories—cognitive developmental theory and gender schema theory—stress that individuals actively construct their gender world:

- The **cognitive developmental theory of gender** states that children's gender typing occurs *after* children think of themselves as boys and girls. Once they consistently conceive of themselves as male or female, children prefer activities, objects, and attitudes consistent with this label.
- **Gender schema theory** states that gender typing emerges as children gradually develop gender schemas of what is gender-appropriate and gender-inappropriate in their culture. A *schema* is a cognitive structure, a network of associations that guide an individual's perceptions. A *gender schema* organizes the world in terms of female and male. Children are internally motivated to perceive the world and to act in accordance with their developing schemas.

Initially proposed by Lawrence Kohlberg (1966), the cognitive developmental theory of gender holds that gender development depends on cognition, and it applies the ideas of Piaget that we discussed in chapter 6. As young children develop the conservation and categorization skills described by Piaget, said Kohlberg, they develop a concept of gender. What's more, they come to see that they will always be male or female. As a result, they begin to select models of their own sex to imitate. The little girl acts as if she is thinking, "I'm a girl, so I want to do girl things. Therefore, the opportunity to do girl things is rewarding."

Notice that in this view gender-typed behavior occurs only after children develop *gender constancy*, which is the understanding that sex remains the same, even though activities, clothing, and hairstyle might change (Ruble, 2000). However, researchers have found that children do not develop gender constancy until they are about 6 or 7 years old. Before this time, most little girls prefer girlish toys and clothes and games, and most little boys prefer boyish toys and games. Thus, contrary to Kohlberg's description of cognitive developmental theory, gender typing does not appear to depend on gender constancy.

Unlike cognitive developmental theory, gender schema theory does not require children to perceive gender constancy before they begin gender typing (see figure 9.4).

cognitive developmental theory of gender The theory that children's gender typing occurs after they have developed a concept of gender. Once they consistently conceive of themselves as male or female, children often organize their world on the basis of gender.

gender schema theory The theory that an individual's attention and behavior are guided by an internal motivation to conform to gender-based sociocultural standards and stereotypes.

Theory	Processes	Emphasis
Cognitive developmental theory	Development of gender constancy, especially around 6 to 7 years of age, when conservation skills develop; after children develop ability to consistently conceive of themselves as male or female, children often organize their world on the basis of gender, such as selecting same-sex models to imitate	Cognitive readiness facilitates gender identity
Gender schema theory	Sociocultural emphasis on gender-based standards and stereotypes; children's attention and behavior are guided by an internal motivation to conform to these gender-based standards and stereotypes, allowing children to interpret the world through a network of gender-organized thoughts	Gender schemas reinforce gender behavior

FIGURE 9.4 The Development of Gender Behavior According to the Cognitive Developmental and Gender Schema Theories of Gender Development

Instead, gender schema theory states that gender typing occurs when children are ready to encode and organize information along the lines of what is considered appropriate for females and males in their society (Martin & Dinella, 2001; Martin & Halverson, 1981; Martin & Ruble, 2004). Bit by bit, children pick up what is gender-appropriate and gender-inappropriate in their culture, and they develop gender schemas that shape how they perceive the world and what they remember. Children are motivated to act in ways that conform with these gender schemas. Thus, gender schemas fuel gender typing. To read about how gender schemas extend to young children's judgments about occupations, see the Research in Life-Span Development interlude.

Research in Life-Span Development
Young Children's Gender Schemas of Occupations

In one study, researchers interviewed children 3 to 7 years old about ten traditionally masculine occupations, such as airplane pilot or car mechanic, and feminine occupations, such as clothes designer or secretary, using questions such as these (Levy, Sadovsky, & Troseth, 2000):

- *Example of a traditionally masculine occupation item:* An airplane pilot is a person who flies an airplane for other people. Who do you think would do the best job as an airplane pilot, a man or a woman?
- *Example of a traditionally feminine occupation item:* A clothes designer is a person who draws up and makes clothes for other people. Who do you think would do the best job as a clothes designer, a man or a woman?

As indicated in figure 9.5, the children expressed well-developed gender schemas, in this case reflected in stereotypes. They viewed men as more competent than women in masculine occupations and women as more competent than men in feminine occupations. Also, girls were much more likely to rate women as more competent in feminine occupations than they were to rate men as more competent in masculine occupations. Conversely, boys were more likely to rate men as more competent in masculine occupations than they were to rate women as more competent in feminine occupations. These findings demonstrate that children as young as 3 to 4 years of age have strong gender schemas regarding the perceived competencies of men and women in gender-typed occupations.

The researchers also asked the children to select from a list of emotions how they would feel if they grew up to have each of the ten occupations. Girls said they would be happy with the feminine occupations and angry or disgusted with the masculine occupations. As expected, boys said they would be happy if they grew up to have the masculine occupations but angry and disgusted with the feminine occupations. However, boys' emotions were more intense (more angry and disgusted) in their avoidance of the feminine occupations than girls' avoidance of masculine occupations. This finding supports other research that indicates gender roles often constrict boys more than girls (Matlin, 2004).

	Boys	Girls
"Masculine" Occupations		
Percentage who judged men more competent	87	70
Percentage who judged women more competent	13	30
"Feminine" Occupations		
Percentage who judged men more competent	35	8
Percentage who judged women more competent	64	92

FIGURE 9.5 Children's Judgments About the Competence of Men and Women in Gender-Stereotyped Occupations

In sum, cognitive factors contribute to the way children think and act as males and females. Through biological, social, and cognitive processes, children develop their gender attitudes and behaviors (Bannon, 2004).

Review and Reflect: Learning Goal 1

 Discuss emotional and personality development in early childhood

REVIEW

- What are changes in the self during early childhood?
- What changes take place in emotional development in early childhood?
- What are some key aspects of moral development in young children?
- How does gender develop in young children?

REFLECT

- Which theory of gender development do you like the best? What might an eclectic theoretical view of gender development be like? (You might want to review the discussion of an eclectic theoretical orientation in chapter 2.)

---

2 FAMILIES

| Parenting | Sibling Relationships and Birth Order | The Changing Family in a Changing Society |

In chapter 7, we learned that attachment is an important aspect of family relationships during infancy. Remember that some experts propose that attachment to a caregiver during the first several years of life is the key ingredient in the child's socioemotional development. We also learned that other experts maintain that secure attachment has been overemphasized and that the child's temperament, other social agents and contexts, and the complexity of the child's social world are also important in determining the child's social competence and well-being. Some developmentalists also emphasize that the infant years have been overdramatized as determinants of life-span development. They argue that social experiences in the early childhood years and later deserve more attention than they have sometimes been given.

In this section, we will discuss early childhood experiences beyond attachment. We will explore the different types of parenting styles, sibling relationships, and the ways in which more children are now experiencing socialization in a greater variety of family structures than at any other point in history.

Parenting

An important dimension of parenting is the styles parents use when they interact with their children. Other considerations include punishment, child abuse, coparenting, and time and effort.

Parenting Styles Parenting requires interpersonal skills and makes emotional demands, yet there is little in the way of formal education for this task. Most parents learn parenting practices from their own parents—some they accept, some they discard. In addition, two parents may bring different views of parenting to the marriage. Unfortunately, when parenting methods are passed on from one generation to the next, both desirable and undesirable practices are perpetuated.

Calvin and Hobbes

WHAT ASSURANCE DO I HAVE THAT YOUR PARENTING ISN'T SCREWING ME UP?

Parents want their children to grow into socially mature individuals, and they may feel frustrated in trying to discover the best way to accomplish this. Developmentalists have long searched for the ingredients of parenting that promote competent socioemotional development.

The work of Diana Baumrind (1971) has especially been prominent. She suggests that parents should be neither punitive nor aloof. Rather, they should develop rules for their children and be affectionate with them. She identified four types of parenting styles:

- **Authoritarian parenting** is a restrictive, punitive style in which parents exhort the child to follow their directions and respect their work and effort. The authoritarian parent places firm limits and controls on the child and allows little verbal exchange. For example, an authoritarian parent might say, "You do it my way or else." Authoritarian parents also might spank the child frequently, enforce rules rigidly but not explain them, and show rage toward the child. Children of authoritarian parents are often unhappy, fearful, and anxious about comparing themselves with others; they often fail to initiate activity, and have weak communication skills.
- **Authoritative parenting** encourages children to be independent but still places limits and controls on their actions. Extensive verbal give-and-take is allowed, and parents are warm and nurturant toward the child. An authoritative parent might put his arm around the child in a comforting way and say, "You know you should not have done that. Let's talk about how you can handle the situation better next time." Authoritative parents support children's constructive behavior. They also expect mature, independent, and age-appropriate behavior of children. Children whose parents are authoritative are often cheerful, self-controlled, self-reliant, and achievement-oriented; they maintain friendly relations with peers, cooperate with adults, and cope well with stress.
- **Neglectful parenting** is a style in which the parent is very uninvolved in the child's life. Children whose parents are neglectful develop the sense that other aspects of the parents' lives are more important than they are. These children tend to be socially incompetent. Many have poor self-control and don't handle independence well. They frequently have low self-esteem, are immature, and may be alienated from the family. In adolescence, they may show patterns of truancy and delinquency.
- **Indulgent parenting** is a style of parenting in which parents are very involved with their children but place few demands or controls on them. These parents let their children do what they want. Children never learn to control their own behavior and always expect to get their way. Some parents deliberately rear their children in this way because they believe that the combination of warm involvement and few restraints will produce a creative, confident child. However, children whose parents are indulgent rarely learn respect for others and have difficulty controlling their behavior. They might be domineering, egocentric, noncompliant, and have difficulties in peer relations.

www.mhhe.com/santrockld10

Parenting

authoritarian parenting A restrictive punitive style in which parents exhort the child to follow their directions and to respect work and effort. The authoritarian parent places firm limits and controls on the child and allows little verbal exchange. Authoritarian parenting is associated with children's social incompetence.

authoritative parenting A parenting style in which parents encourage their children to be independent but still place limits and controls on their actions. Extensive verbal give-and-take is allowed, and parents are warm and nurturant toward the child. Authoritative parenting is associated with children's social competence.

neglectful parenting A style of parenting in which the parent is very uninvolved in the child's life; it is associated with children's social incompetence, especially a lack of self-control.

indulgent parenting A style of parenting in which parents are highly involved with their children but place few demands or controls on them. Indulgent parenting is associated with children's social incompetence, especially a lack of self-control.

These four styles of parenting involve combinations of acceptance and responsiveness on the one hand and demand and control on the other. How these dimensions combine to produce authoritarian, authoritative, neglectful, and indulgent parenting is shown in figure 9.6. Research studies continue to document more positive links between authoritative parenting and the well-being of children and adolescents than for the other three types of parenting styles (Slicker & Thornberry, 2003).

Do the benefits of authoritative parenting transcend the boundaries of ethnicity, socioeconomic status, and household composition? Although occasional exceptions to patterns have been found, the evidence linking authoritative parenting with competence on the part of the child has been found in research across a wide range of ethnic groups, social strata, cultures, and family structures (Steinberg & Silk, 2002).

Nonetheless, researchers have found that in some ethnic groups, aspects of the authoritarian style may be associated with more positive child outcomes than Baumrind predicts. Aspects of traditional Asian child rearing practices are often continued by Asian American families (Ishii-Kuntz, 2004). In some cases, these practices have been described as authoritarian. However, Ruth Chao (2001; Chao & Tseng, 2002) argues that the style of parenting used by many Asian American parents is best conceptualized as a type of training in which parents are concerned and involved in their children's lives rather than reflecting strict or authoritarian control. Thus, the parenting style Chao describes, *training,* is based on a type of parental control that is distinct from the more "domineering" control reflected in the authoritarian parenting style. Positive outcomes of the training parenting style in Asian American families are evident in the high academic achievement of Asian American children (Stevenson & Zusho, 2002; Tseng, 2004).

Latino childrearing practices encourage the development of a self and identity that is embedded in the family and requires respect and obedience (Harwood & others, 2002; Martinez & Halgunseth, 2004). As in African American families, there is a high level of cross-generational and coresidence arrangements and assistance (Zinn & Well, 2000).

Researchers have found that African American parents are more likely than non-Latino White parents to use physical punishment (Horn, Joseph, & Cheng, 2004). However, the use of physical punishment is linked with more externalized child problems (such as acting out and high levels of aggression) in non-Latino White families but not African American families (Deater-Deckard & Dodge, 1997). One explanation of this finding is the need for African American parents to enforce rules in the dangerous environments in which they are more likely to live (Harrison-Hale, McLoyd, & Smedley, 2004). In this context, requiring obedience to parental authority may be an adaptive strategy to keep children from engaging in antisocial behavior that can have serious consequences for the victim or the perpetrator. As we see next, though, overall, there are concerns about the use of physical punishment in disciplining children.

Punishment For centuries, corporal (physical) punishment, such as spanking, has been considered a necessary and even desirable method of disciplining children (Greven, 1991). Use of corporal punishment is legal in every state in America, and it is estimated that 70 to 90 percent of American parents have spanked their children (Straus, 2001).

Despite the widespread use of corporal punishment, there have been surprisingly few research studies on physical punishment and those that have been conducted are correlational (Baumrind, Larzelere, & Cowan, 2002; Kazdin & Benjet, 2003). Clearly, it would be highly unethical to randomly assign parents to either spank or not spank

	Accepting, responsive	Rejecting, unresponsive
Demanding, controlling	Authoritative	Authoritarian
Undemanding, uncontrolling	Indulgent	Neglectful

FIGURE 9.6 Classification of Parenting Styles
The four types of parenting styles (authoritative, authoritarian, indulgent, and neglectful) involve the dimensions of acceptance and responsiveness, on the one hand, and demand and control on the other. For example, authoritative parenting involves being both accepting/responsive and demanding/controlling.

their children in an experimental study. Recall that cause and effect cannot be determined in a correlational study. In one correlational study, spanking by parents was linked with children's antisocial behavior, including cheating, telling lies, being mean to others, bullying, getting into fights, and being disobedient (Straus, Sugarman, & Giles-Sims, 1997). In a recent study of White, African American, and Latino families, spanking by parents predicted an increase in children's problems over time in all three groups (McLoyd & Smith, 2002). However, when parents showed strong emotional support of the child, the link between spanking and child problems was reduced.

A recent research review concluded that corporal punishment by parents is associated with children's higher levels of immediate compliance and aggression, and lower levels of moral internalization and mental health (Gershoff, 2002). Some critics, though, argue that the research evidence is not yet sound enough to warrant a blanket injunction against corporal punishment (Baumrind, Larzelere, & Cowan, 2002; Kazdin & Benjet, 2003).

Here are some of the reasons why spanking or other forms of intense punishment with children should be avoided:

- When intense punishment such as yelling, screaming, or spanking is used, the adult is presenting the child with an out-of-control model for handling stressful situations. The children may imitate this aggressive, out-of-control behavior.
- Punishment can instill fear, rage, or avoidance in children. For example, spanking the child may cause the child to avoid being around the parent and fear the parent.
- Punishment tells children what not to do rather than what to do. When parents make punishing statements to children, such as "No, don't do that!" it should be accompanied by positive feedback, such as "But why don't you try this?"
- Punishment can be abusive. When parents discipline their children, they might not intend to be abusive but become so aroused when they are punishing the child that they become abusive (Baumrind, Larzelere, & Cowan, 2002).

Because of reasons such as these, a law was passed in Sweden in 1979 forbidding parents to physically punish (spank or slap, for example) when disciplining their children. The law is still in effect and since it was enacted youth rates of juvenile delinquency, alcohol abuse, rape, and suicide have dropped in Sweden (Durrant, 2000). The improved picture for Swedish youth may have occurred for other reasons, such as changing societal attitudes and opportunities for youth. Nonetheless, the Swedish experience suggests that physical punishment of children may not be necessary to improve the well-being of youth. Joining Sweden in forbidding parents to physically punish their children, these countries have also passed anti-spanking laws: Finland (1984), Denmark (1986), Norway (1987), Austria (1989), Cyprus (1994), Latvia (1998), Croatia (1999), Germany (2000), and Israel (2000).

A recent cross-cultural comparison found that individuals in the United States and Canada were among the most favorable toward corporal punishment and remembered it being used by their parents (Curran & others, 2001) (see figure 9.7). People in Sweden especially had an unfavorable attitude toward corporal punishment and were less likely than people in the other countries to remember it being used by their parents.

The use of physical punishment by parents may be linked to an individual's hostility or marital conflict. One longitudinal study found that high rates of individual hostility or marital hostility assessed during the prenatal period were linked with the use of more frequent and severe physical punishment of children at 2 and 5 years of age (Kanoy & others, 2003).

Most child psychologists recommend reasoning with the child, especially explaining the consequences of the child's actions for others, as the best way to handle children's misbehaviors (Straus, 2001). Time-out, in which the child is removed from a setting where the child experiences positive reinforcement, can also be effective. For example, when the child has misbehaved, a parent might take away TV viewing for a specified period of time.

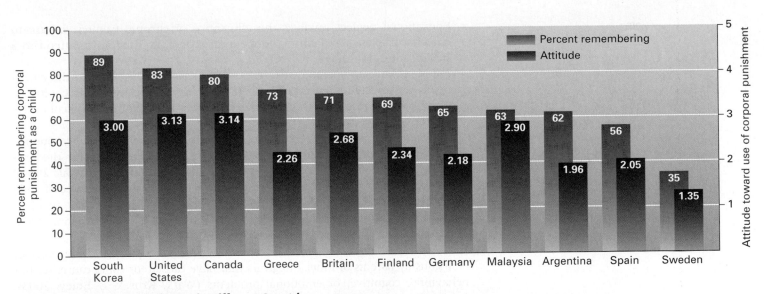

FIGURE 9.7 Corporal Punishment in Different Countries
A 5-point scale was used to assess attitudes toward corporal punishment with scores closer to 1 indicating an attitude against its use and scores closer to 5 suggesting an attitude for its use.

Child Abuse Unfortunately, punishment sometimes leads to the abuse of infants and children. In 2000, approximately 879,000 U.S. children were found to be victims of child abuse (U.S. Department of Health and Human Services, 2003). Eighty-four percent of these children were abused by a parent or parents. Laws in many states now require doctors and teachers to report suspected cases of child abuse, yet many cases go unreported, especially those of battered infants.

Many people have difficulty understanding parents who abuse or neglect their children. Our response is often outrage and anger at the parent. This outrage focuses attention on parents as bad, sick, monstrous, sadistic individuals who cause their children to suffer. Experts on child abuse argue that this view is too simple and deflects attention from the social context of the abuse and the parents' coping skills. It is important to recognize that child abuse is a diverse condition, that it is usually mild to moderate in severity, and that it is only partially caused by personality characteristics of the parent (Azar, 2002; Field, 2000). Although too often the abuser is a raging, uncontrolled physical abuser, in many cases the abuser is an overwhelmed single mother in poverty who neglects the child.

Whereas the public and many professionals use the term *child abuse* to refer to both abuse and neglect, developmentalists increasingly use the term *child maltreatment* (Cicchetti, 2001; Kotch, 2003). This term does not have quite the emotional impact of the term *abuse* and acknowledges that maltreatment includes diverse conditions.

The four main types of child maltreatment are physical abuse, child neglect, sexual abuse, and emotional abuse (National Clearinghouse on Child Abuse and Neglect Information, 2002, 2004):

- *Physical abuse* is characterized by the infliction of physical injury as a result of punching, beating, kicking, biting, burning, shaking, or otherwise physically harming a child (Herman-Giddens, 2004). The parent or other person may not have intended to hurt the child; the injury may have resulted from excessive physical punishment.
- *Child neglect* is characterized by failure to provide for the child's basic needs (Dubowitz, Pitts, & Black, 2004; Wark, Kruczek, & Boley, 2003). Neglect can be physical, educational, or emotional:
  - Physical neglect includes refusal of, or delay in, seeking health care; abandonment; expulsion from the home or refusal to allow a runaway to return home; and inadequate supervision.

Child maltreatment involves grossly inadequate and destructive aspects of parenting.

—**DANTE CICCHETTI**
Contemporary Developmental Psychologist, University of Rochester

Child Abuse Prevention Network
International Aspects
of Child Abuse
National Clearinghouse
on Child Abuse and Neglect

- Educational neglect involves the allowance of chronic truancy, failure to enroll a child of mandatory school age in school, and failure to attend to a special education need.
- Emotional neglect includes such actions as marked inattention to the child's needs for affection; refusal of or failure to provide necessary psychological care; spouse abuse in the child's presence; and allowing drug or alcohol use by the child.
- *Sexual abuse* includes fondling a child's genitals, intercourse, incest, rape, sodomy, exhibitionism, and commercial exploitation through prostitution or the production of pornographic materials (Hobbins, 2004; Hulme & Agrawal, 2004). Many experts observe that sexual abuse is the most underreported type of child maltreatment because of the secrecy or "conspiracy of silence" that so often characterizes sex-ual abuse cases (Bonanno & others, 2003; Kogan, 2004; Roberts & others, 2004).
- *Emotional abuse (psychological abuse/verbal abuse/mental injury)* includes acts or omissions by parents or other caregivers that have caused, or could cause, serious behavioral, cognitive, or emotional problems (Wark, Krusek, & Boley, 2003). Some cases of emotional abuse, even without any harm evident in the child's behavior or condition, are serious enough to warrant intervention by child protective services. For example, parents or others may use unusual types of punishment, such as confining a child in a dark closet. Less severe acts, such as frequent belittling and rejection of the child, are often difficult to prove and make it difficult for child protective services to intervene.

Although any of these forms of child maltreatment may be found separately, they often occur in combination. Emotional abuse is almost always present when other forms of abuse are identified.

The Cultural Context of Abuse   Culture influences the incidence of child abuse (Sebre & others, 2004). The extensive violence that takes place in American culture is reflected in the occurrence of violence in the family (Azar, 2002). A regular diet of violence appears on television screens, and parents often resort to power assertion as a disciplinary technique. In China, where physical punishment is rarely used to discipline children, the incidence of reported child abuse is very low. In the United States, many abusing parents report that they do not have sufficient resources or help from others, which may be a realistic evaluation of the situation of many low-income families.

Family Influences   To understand abuse in the family, the interactions of all family members need to be considered, regardless of who performs the violent acts against the child (Bugental & Happaney, 2004; Kim & Cicchetti, 2004; Margolin, 1994). For example, even though the father may be the one who physically abuses the child, contributions by the mother, the child, and siblings also should be evaluated. Many parents who abuse their children come from families in which physical punishment was used. These parents view physical punishment as a legitimate way of controlling the child's behavior.

Were parents who abuse children abused by their own parents? About one-third of parents who were abused themselves when they were young also abuse their own children (Cicchetti & Toth, 1998). Thus, some, but not a majority, of parents are locked into an intergenerational transmission of abuse. Mothers who break out of the intergenerational transmission of abuse often have at least one warm, caring adult in their background; have a close, positive marital relationship; and have received therapy (Egeland, Jacobvitz, & Sroufe, 1988).

Developmental Consequences of Abuse   Among the developmental consequences of child maltreatment are poor emotion regulation, attachment problems, problems in peer relations, difficulty in adapting to school, and other psychological problems (Brown & others, 2004; Haugaard & Hazen, 2004; Shonk & Cicchetti, 2001). Maltreated infants may show excessive negative affect or blunted positive affect. Maltreated children appear to be poorly equipped to develop successful peer relations, due to their aggressiveness, avoidance, and aberrant responses to both distress and positive approaches from peers (Bolger & Patterson, 2001; Mueller & Silverman, 1989).

Being physically abused has been linked with children's anxiety, personality problems, depression, conduct disorder, and delinquency (Malmgren & Meisel, 2004; Maughan & Cicchetti, 2002; Shonk & Cicchetti, 2001). Later, during the adult years, maltreated children show increased violence toward other adults, dating partners, and marital partners, as well as increased substance abuse, anxiety, and depression (Grogan-Kaylor, 2003; Malinosky-Rummell & Hansen, 1993). In sum, maltreated children are at risk for developing a wide range of problems and disorders (Arias, 2004; Bissada & Briere, 2001; Haugaard & Hazen, 2004).

Coparenting   A dramatic increase in research on *coparenting* has occurred in the last two decades. The theme of this research is that poor coordination between parents, undermining of the other parent, lack of cooperation and warmth, and disconnection by one parent are conditions that place children at risk for problems (Doherty & Beaton, 2004; McHale, Kuersten-Hogan, & Rao, 2004; McHale & others, 2002; Van Egeren & Hawkins, 2004). For example, in one study, 4-year-old children from families characterized by low levels of mutuality and support in coparenting were more likely than their classmates to show difficulties in social adjustment on the playground (McHale, Johnson, & Sinclair, 1999). By contrast, parental cooperation and warmth are linked with children's prosocial behavior and competence in peer relations.

Good Parenting Takes Time and Effort   In U.S. society today, there is an unfortunate theme which suggests that parenting can be accomplished quickly, with little or no inconvenience (Sroufe, 2000). One example is the practice of playing Mozart CDs in the hope that they will enrich infants' and young children's brains. One-minute bedtime stories are being marketed successfully for parents to read to their children (Walsh, 2000). Most of these are brief summaries of longer stories. There are one-minute bedtime bear books, puppy books, and so on. Parents who find these quick books appealing know it is good to read to their children, but they don't want to spend a lot of time doing it.

Judith Harris' (1998) book *The Nurture Assumption* (which states that heredity and peer relations are the key factors in children's development) fits into this theme that parents don't need to spend much time with their children. Why did this idea become so popular? Perhaps in part because it made people who don't spend much time with their children feel less guilty.

What is wrong with these quick-fix approaches to parenting? Good parenting takes a lot of time and a lot of effort (Magnuson & Duncan, 2004; Powell, 2005). You can't do it in a minute here and a minute there. You can't do it with CDs.

Parents who do not spend enough time with their children or who have problems in child rearing can benefit from counseling and therapy. To read about the work of marriage and family counselor Darla Botkin, see the Careers in Life-Span Development insert.

Sibling Relationships and Birth Order

What are sibling relationships like? How extensively does birth order influence behavior?

Sibling Relationships   Any of you who have grown up with siblings (brothers or sisters) probably have a rich memory of aggressive, hostile interchanges. But

Watch the video "When a Second Baby Comes Along" to learn more about the connection between personality traits and birth order.

Careers in Life-Span Development

Darla Botkin, Marriage and Family Therapist

Darla Botkin is a marriage and family therapist who teaches, conducts research, and engages in therapy in the area of marriage and family therapy. She is on the faculty of the University of Kentucky. Darla obtained a bachelor's degree in elementary education with a concentration in special education and then went on to receive a master's degree in early childhood education. She spent the next six years working with children and their families in a variety of settings, including child care, elementary school, and Head Start. These experiences led Darla to recognize the interdependence of the developmental settings that children and their parents experience (such as home, school, and work). She returned to graduate school and obtained a Ph.D. in family studies from the University of Tennessee. She then became a faculty member in the Family Studies program at the University of Kentucky. Completing further coursework and clinical training in marriage and family therapy, she became certified as a marriage and family therapist.

Darla's current interests include working with young children in family therapy, gender and ethnic issues in family therapy, and the role of spirituality in family wellness.

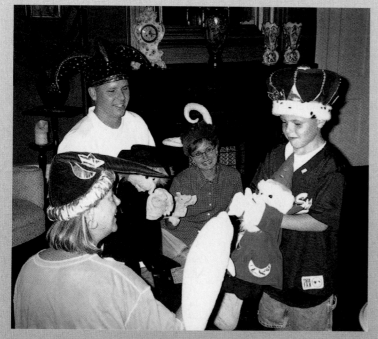

Darla Botkin (*left*), conducting a family therapy session.

sibling relationships also have many pleasant, caring moments (Zukow-Goldring, 2002). Children's sibling relationships include helping, sharing, teaching, fighting, and playing (Bank, Burraston, & Snyder, 2004). Children can act as emotional supports, rivals, and communication partners. More than 80 percent of American children have one or more siblings. Because there are so many possible sibling combinations, it is difficult to generalize about sibling influences. Among the factors to consider are the number of siblings, the ages of siblings, birth order, age spacing, the sex of siblings, and whether sibling relationships are different from parent-child relationships (Brody, 2004; Conger & Bryant, 2004; Teti, 2002).

Birth Order   Birth order is a special interest of many sibling researchers. When differences in birth order are found, they usually are explained by variations in interactions with parents and siblings associated with the unique experiences of being in a particular position in the family. This is especially true in the case of the firstborn child (Teti & others, 1993). Parents have higher expectations for firstborn children than for later-born children. They put more pressure on them for achievement and responsibility. They also interfere more with their activities (Rothbart, 1971).

Given the differences in family dynamics involved in birth order, it is not surprising that firstborns and later-borns have different characteristics (Dunn, 2004; Zajonc, 2001). Firstborn children are more adult-oriented, helpful, conforming, anxious, and self-controlled than their siblings. Parents give more attention to firstborns and this is related to firstborns' nurturant behavior (Stanhope & Corter, 1993). Parental demands and high standards established for firstborns result in these children's excelling in academic and professional endeavors. Firstborns are over-represented in *Who's Who* and among Rhodes scholars, for example. However, some of the same pressures placed on firstborns for high achievement may be the reason they also have more guilt, anxiety, and difficulty in coping with stressful situations, as well as higher admission to child guidance clinics.

What is the only child like? The popular conception is that the only child is a "spoiled brat," with undesirable characteristics such as dependency, lack of self-control, and self-centered behavior. But researchers present a more positive portrayal of the only child, who often is achievement-oriented and displays a desirable personality, especially in comparison with later-borns and children from large families (Falbo & Poston, 1993; Jiao, Ji, & Jing, 1996).

Keep in mind, though, that birth order by itself often is not a good predictor of behavior. When factors such as age spacing, sex of the siblings, heredity, temperament, parenting styles, peer influences, school influences, socio-cultural factors, and so forth are taken into account, they often are more important in determining a child's behavior than birth order.

The Changing Family in a Changing Society

More children are growing up in diverse family structures than ever before. Many mothers spend the greatest part of their day away from their children, even their infants. More than one of every two mothers with a child under the age of 5 is in the labor force; more than two of every three with a child from 6 to 17 years of age is. And the increasing number of children growing up in single-parent families is staggering (Martin, Emery, & Peris, 2004). As shown in figure 9.8, the United States has the highest percentage of single-parent families, compared with virtually all other countries.

Working Parents   Because household operations have become more efficient and family size has decreased in America, it is not certain that when both parents work outside the home, children receive less attention than children in the past whose mothers were not employed. Outside employment—at least for parents with school-age children—might simply be filling time previously taken up by added household burdens and more children. It also cannot be assumed that if the mother does not work, the child will benefit from the time freed up by streamlined household operations and smaller families. Mothering does not always have a positive effect on the child. The educated, nonworking mother may overinvest her energies in her children. This attention can foster an excess of worry and discourage the child's independence. In such situations, the mother may give more parenting than the child can profitably handle.

As Lois Hoffman (1989) commented, maternal employment is a part of modern life. It is not an aberrant aspect of it but a response to other social changes. The needs of the growing child require the mother to loosen her hold on the child. This task may be easier for the working woman, whose job creates an additional source of identity and self-esteem for her.

A number of researchers have found no detrimental effects of maternal employment on children's development (Gottfried, Gottfried, & Bathurst, 2002; Hoffman & Youngblade, 1999). However, in specific circumstances, work can produce positive or negative effects on parenting (Crouter & Booth, 2004; Zaslow, 2004). In some families, work-related stress can spill over and harm parenting. In others, a greater sense of overall well-being produced by work can lead to more positive parenting.

In contrast, researchers are consistently finding that when a child's mother works in the first year of life it can have a negative effect on the child's later development (Belsky & Eggebeen, 1991; Hill & others, 2001). For example, a recent major longitudinal study found that the 3-year-old children of mothers who went to work before the children were 9 months old had poorer cognitive outcomes than 3-year-old children who had stayed at home with their mothers in the first nine months of the child's life (Brooks-Gunn, Han, & Waldfogel, 2002). The negative effects of

The one-child family is becoming much more common in China because of the strong motivation to limit the population growth in the People's Republic of China. The policy's effects on children have not been fully examined. *In general, what have researchers found the only child to be like?*

Big sisters are the crab grass in the lawn of life.
—CHARLES SCHULZ
American Cartoonist, 20th Century

Family and the Workplace

FIGURE 9.8 Single-Parent Families in Different Countries

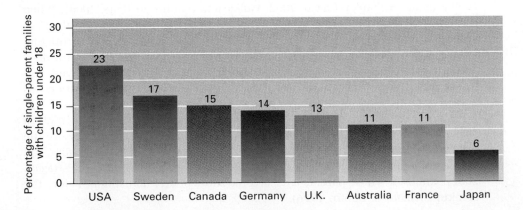

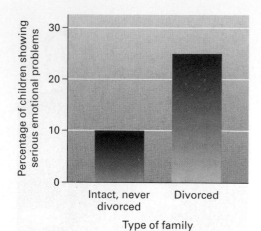

FIGURE 9.9 Divorce and Children's Emotional Problems

In Hetherington's research, 25 percent of children from divorced families showed serious emotional problems compared with only 10 percent of children from intact, never-divorced families. However, keep in mind that a substantial majority (75 percent) of the children from divorced families did not show serious emotional problems.

Divorce Resources
Father Custody

working mothers were less pronounced when the mothers worked less than 30 hours a week, the mothers were more sensitive (responsive and comforting) in their caregiving, and the child care the children received outside the home was higher in quality. Thus, when mothers do go back to work in the infant's first year of life, it clearly is important that they consider how many hours they are going to work, be sensitive in their caregiving, and get the best child care they can afford.

Children in Divorced Families Let's examine some important questions about children in divorced families:

- *Are children better adjusted in intact, never-divorced families than in divorced families?* Most researchers agree that children from divorced families show poorer adjustment than their counterparts in nondivorced families (Amato, 2004; Hetherington & Kelly, 2002; Hetherington & Stanley-Hagan, 2002; Martin, Emery, & Peris, 2004) (see figure 9.9). Those who have experienced multiple divorces are at greater risk. Children in divorced families are more likely than children in nondivorced families to have academic problems, to show externalized problems (such as acting out and delinquency) and internalized problems (such as anxiety and depression), to be less socially responsible, to have less competent intimate relationships, to drop out of school, to become sexually active at an early age, to take drugs, to associate with antisocial peers, and to have low self-esteem (Conger & Chao, 1996). Nonetheless, keep in mind that a majority of children in divorced families do not have significant adjustment problems. One recent study found that 20 years after their parents had divorced when they were children, approximately 80 percent of adults concluded that their parents' decision to divorce was a wise one (Ahrons, 2004).

- *Should parents stay together for the sake of the children?* Whether parents should stay in an unhappy or conflicted marriage for the sake of their children is one of the most commonly asked questions about divorce (Hetherington, 1999, 2000). If the stresses and disruptions in family relationships associated with an unhappy, conflictual marriage that erode the well-being of children are reduced by the move to a divorced, single-parent family, divorce can be advantageous. However, if the diminished resources and increased risks associated with divorce also are accompanied by inept parenting and sustained or increased conflict, not only between the divorced couple but also among the parents, children, and siblings, the best choice for the children would be for an unhappy marriage to be retained (Hetherington & Stanley-Hagan, 2002). These are "ifs," and it is difficult to determine how these will play out when parents either remain together in an acrimonious marriage or become divorced. Note that marital conflict may have negative consequences for children in the context of marriage or divorce (Clingempeel & Brand-Clingempeel, 2004; Cummings, Braungart-Rieker, & Du Rocher-Schudlich, 2003).

- *How much do family processes matter in divorced families?* Family processes matter a lot (Hetherington & Stanley-Hagan, 2002; Wallerstein & Johnson-Reitz, 2004). When divorced parents' relationship with each other is harmonious and when they use authoritative parenting, the adjustment of children improves (Hetherington, Bridges, & Insabella, 1998). A number of researchers have shown that a disequilibrium, which includes diminished parenting skills, occurs in the year following the divorce but that, by two years after the divorce, restabilization has occurred and parenting skills have improved (Hetherington, 1989).

- *What factors are involved in the child's individual risk and vulnerability in a divorced family?* Among the factors involved in the child's risk and vulnerability are the child's adjustment prior to the divorce, as well as the child's personality and temperament, gender, and custody situation (Hetherington & Stanley-Hagan, 2002). Children whose parents later divorce show poorer adjustment before the breakup (Amato & Booth, 1996).

Personality and temperament also play a role in children's adjustment in divorced families. Children who are socially mature and responsible, who show few behavioral problems, and who have an easy temperament are better able to cope with their parents' divorce. Children with a difficult temperament often have problems in coping with their parents' divorce (Hetherington, 2000).

Earlier studies reported gender differences in response to divorce, with divorce being more negative for girls than boys in mother-custody families. However, more recent studies have shown that gender differences are less pronounced and consistent than was previously believed. Some of the inconsistency may be due to the increase in father custody, joint custody, and increased involvement of noncustodial fathers, especially in their sons' lives (Palmer, 2004). One recent analysis of studies found that children in joint-custody families were better adjusted than children in sole-custody families (Bauserman, 2002). Some studies have shown that boys adjust better in father-custody families, girls in mother-custody families, whereas other studies have not (Maccoby & Mnookin, 1992; Santrock & Warshak, 1979).

Gay and Lesbian Parents Increasingly, gay and lesbian couples are creating families that include children. This is controversial to many heterosexual individuals who view a gay or lesbian family as damaging to the development of a child. Approximately 20 percent of lesbians and 10 percent of gay men are parents, most of whom have children from a heterosexual marriage that ended in a divorce (Patterson, 2002). There may be more than 1 million gay and lesbian parents in the United States today.

An important aspect of lesbian and gay families with children is the sexual identity of parents at the time of a child's birth or adoption (Patterson, 2002). The largest group of children with lesbian and gay parents are likely those who were born in the context of heterosexual relationships with one or both parents only later identifying themselves as gay or lesbian. Gay and lesbian parents may be single or they may have same-gender partners. In addition, lesbians and gay men are increasingly choosing parenthood through donor insemination and surrogates. Custodial arrangements also may vary.

Another issue focuses on custody arrangements for children (Peplau & Beals, 2004). Many lesbian mothers and gay fathers have lost custody of their children to heterosexual spouses following divorce. For this reason, many lesbian mothers and gay fathers are noncustodial parents.

Researchers have found few differences among children growing up with lesbian mothers or gay fathers and children growing up with heterosexual parents (Patterson, 2002). For example, children growing up in gay or lesbian families are just as popular with their peers, and there are no differences in the adjustment and mental health of children living in these families when they are compared with children in heterosexual families (Hyde & DeLamater, 2005). Also, the overwhelming majority of children growing up in a gay or lesbian family have a heterosexual orientation (Tasker & Golombok, 1997, 1998).

Cultural, Ethnic, and Socioeconomic Variations in Families Parenting can be influenced by culture, ethnicity, and socioeconomic status. What have cross-cultural studies found about parenting?

Cross-Cultural Studies Cultures vary on a number of issues involving families, such as what the father's role in the family should be, the extent to which support systems are available to families, and the ways in which children should be disciplined (Harkness & Super, 2002; Parke & others, 2005). Although there are cross-cultural variations in parenting (Whiting & Edwards, 1988), in one study of parenting behavior in 186 cultures around the world, the most common pattern was a warm and

What are some characteristics of families within different ethnic groups?

www.mhhe.com/santrockld10

Family Diversity

View the video "Cultural Variation in Father's Role" to learn what researchers think about the development functions fathers fulfill across cultures.

controlling style, one that was neither permissive nor restrictive (Rohner & Rohner, 1981). The investigators commented that the majority of cultures have discovered, over many centuries, a "truth" that only recently emerged in the Western world—namely, that children's healthy social development is most effectively promoted by love and at least some moderate parental control.

Ethnicity Families within different ethnic groups in the United States differ in their size, structure, composition, reliance on kinship networks, and levels of income and education (Coll & Pachter, 2002; Diggs & Socha, 2004; Leyendecker & others, 2005; Parke, 2004). Large and extended families are more common among minority groups than among the White majority (Gonzalez & others, 2004; Martinez & Halgunseth, 2004). For example, 19 percent of Latino families have three or more children, compared with 14 percent of African American and 10 percent of White families. African American and Latino children interact more with grandparents, aunts, uncles, cousins, and more-distant relatives than do White children.

Single-parent families are more common among African Americans and Latinos than among White Americans (Tucker, Subramanian, & James, 2004; Weinraub, Houruath, & Gringlas, 2002). In comparison with two-parent households, single parents often have more limited resources of time, money, and energy (Gyamfi, Brooks-Gunn, & Jackson, 2001). Ethnic minority parents also are less educated and more likely to live in low-income circumstances than their White counterparts (Harrison-Hale, McLoyd, & Smedley, 2004). Still, many impoverished ethnic minority families manage to find ways to raise competent children (Coll & Pachter, 2002; Fuligni & Yoshikawa, 2004).

Some aspects of home life can help protect ethnic minority children from injustice. The community and the family can filter out destructive racist messages, and parents can present different frames of reference as alternatives to those presented by the majority. The extended family also can serve as an important buffer to stress (McAdoo, 2002). To read further about ethnic minority parenting, see the Diversity in Life-Span Development interlude.

Diversity in Life-Span Development
Acculturation and Ethnic Minority Parenting

Ethnic minority children and their parents "are expected to transcend their own cultural background and to incorporate aspects of the dominant culture" into children's development. "Young children's expectations and opportunities for *acculturation*" (the process through which cultural adaptation and change occurs) are mainly influenced by their parents and the extended-family system. The level of family acculturation can affect parenting style by influencing expectations for children's development, parent-child interactions, and the role of the extended family (Ishii-Kuntz, 2004; Martinez & Halgunseth, 2004). The appropriateness of caregiving practices may involve conflict or confusion between less acculturated and more acculturated family members. For example, in one study, the level of acculturation and maternal education were the strongest predictors of maternal-infant interaction patterns in Latino families (Perez-Febles, 1992).

In early childhood, the family's level of acculturation continues to influence caregiving practices and important decisions about child care and early childhood education. In child-care centers, "school, church, and other community settings, ethnic minority children learn about the dominant cultural values and behaviors, and may be expected to adapt to unfamiliar cultural norms (such as being on the winning team, expressing emotions, and being responsible for one's self). For example, an African American mother might prefer to leave her children with extended family while she is at work because the kinship network is seen as a natural way to cope with maternal absence. This well-intentioned, culturally appropriate decision might, however, put the child at an educational and social disadvantage relative to other children of similar age who have the benefit of important preschool experiences that may ease the transition into early school years."

How is acculturation involved in ethnic minority parenting?

In middle and late childhood and adolescence, disparity among the acculturation of children, their parents, and the extended family can become magnified. In adolescence, individuals often make decisions about their acculturation status more independently from their family. When immigrant adolescents choose to adopt the values of the dominant U.S. culture (such as unchaperoned dating), they often clash with those of parents and extended-family members who have more traditional values.

It is important to recognize the complexity and individual variation in the acculturative aspects of ethnic minority parenting (Harrison-Hale, McLoyd, & Smedley, 2004; Leyendecker & others, 2005; Tucker, Subramanian, & James, 2004). This complexity and variation involve the generation of the family members, the recency of their migration, their socioeconomic status, national origin, and many aspects of the social context of the dominant culture in which they now live (such as racial attitudes, quality of schooling, and community support groups).

(Source: Garcia, Coll & Pachter, 2002, pp. 7–8)

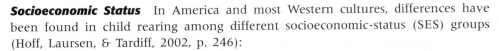

Socioeconomic Status In America and most Western cultures, differences have been found in child rearing among different socioeconomic-status (SES) groups (Hoff, Laursen, & Tardiff, 2002, p. 246):

- "Lower-SES parents (1) are more concerned that their children conform to society's expectations, (2) create a home atmosphere in which it is clear that parents have authority over children," (3) use physical punishment more in disciplining their children, and (4) are more directive and less conversational with their children.
- "Higher-SES parents (1) are more concerned with developing children's initiative" and delay of gratification, "(2) create a home atmosphere in which children are more nearly equal participants and in which rules are discussed as opposed to being laid down" in an authoritarian manner, (3) are less likely to use physical punishment, and (4) "are less directive and more conversational" with their children.

There also are socioeconomic differences in the way that parents think about education (Magnuson & Duncan, 2002; Hoff, Laursen, & Tardiff, 2002). Middle- and upper-income parents more often think of education as something that should be mutually encouraged by parents and teachers. By contrast, low-income parents are more likely to view education as the teacher's job. Thus, increased school-family linkages especially can benefit students from low-income families.

2 **Explain how families can influence young children's development**

REVIEW

- What aspects of parenting are linked with young children's development?
- How are sibling relationships and birth order related to young children's development?
- How is children's development affected by having two wage-earning parents, having divorced parents, and being part of a particular cultural, ethnic, and socioeconomic group?

REFLECT

- Which style or styles of parenting did your mother and father use in rearing you? What effects do you think their parenting styles have on your development?

---

3 **PEER RELATIONS, PLAY, AND TELEVISION**

| Peer Relations | Play | Television |

The family is an important social context for children's development. However, children's development also is strongly influenced by what goes on in other social contexts, such as peer relations, play, and television.

Peer Relations

As children grow older, peer relations consume an increasing amount of their time. What is the function of a child's peer group?

Peers are children of about the same age or maturity level. Same-age peer interaction fills a unique role in our culture. Age grading would occur even if schools were not age graded and children were left alone to determine the composition of their own societies (Hartup, 1983). One of the most important functions of the peer group is to provide a source of information and comparison about the world outside the family. Children receive feedback about their abilities from their peer group. Children evaluate what they do in terms of whether it is better than, as good as, or worse than what other children do. It is hard to make these judgments at home because siblings are usually older or younger.

How important are peers for development? When peer monkeys who have been reared together are separated, they become depressed and less advanced socially (Suomi, Harlow, & Domek, 1970). The human development literature contains a classic example of the importance of peers in social development. Anna Freud (Freud & Dann, 1951) studied six children from different families who banded together after their parents were killed in World War II. Intensive peer attachment was observed. The children formed a tightly knit group, dependent on one another and aloof with outsiders. Even though deprived of parental care, they neither became delinquent nor developed serious mental disorders.

Thus, good peer relations can be necessary for normal social development. Special concerns focus on children who are withdrawn and aggressive (Cillessen & Mayeux, 2004; Kupersmidt & DeRosier, 2004). Withdrawn children who are rejected by peers or are victimized and feel lonely are at risk for depression. Children who are aggressive with their peers are at risk for developing a number of problems, including delinquency and dropping out of school (Hay, Payne, & Chadwick, 2004; Sandstrom & Zakriski, 2004). We will have much more to say about peer relations in chapter 11, "Socioemotional Development in Middle and Late Childhood."

Play

An extensive amount of peer interaction during childhood involves play. Although peer interaction can involve play, social play is but one type of play. *Play* is a pleasurable activity that is engaged in for its own sake. Our coverage of play includes its functions, Parten's classic study of play, and types of play.

Play's Functions Play is essential to the young child's health. As today's children move into the twenty-first century and continue to experience pressure in their lives, play becomes even more crucial. Play increases affiliation with peers, releases tension, advances cognitive development, increases exploration, and provides a safe haven in which to engage in potentially dangerous behavior. Play increases the probability that children will converse and interact with each other. During this interaction, children practice the roles they will assume later in life (Sutton-Smith, 2000).

According to Freud and Erikson, play is an especially useful form of human adjustment, helping the child master anxieties and conflicts. Because tensions are relieved in play, the child can cope with life's problems. Play permits the child to work off excess physical energy and to release pent-up tensions. *Play therapy* allows the child to work off frustrations. Through play therapy, the therapist can analyze the child's conflicts and ways of coping with them (Drews, Carey, & Schaefer, 2003). Children may feel less threatened and be more likely to express their true feelings in the context of play.

Piaget (1962) maintained that play advances children's cognitive development. At the same time, he said that children's cognitive development *constrains* the way they play. Play permits children to practice their competencies and acquired skills in a relaxed, pleasurable way. Piaget thought that cognitive structures need to be exercised, and play provides the perfect setting for this exercise. For example, children who have just learned to add or multiply begin to play with numbers in different ways as they perfect these operations, laughing as they do so.

Vygotsky (1962), whose developmental theory was discussed in chapter 8, also considered play to be an excellent setting for cognitive development. He was especially interested in the symbolic and make-believe aspects of play, as when a child substitutes a stick for a horse and rides the stick as if it were a horse. For young children, the imaginary situation is real. Parents should encourage such imaginary play, because it advances the child's cognitive development, especially creative thought.

Daniel Berlyne (1960) described play as exciting and pleasurable in itself because it satisfies our exploratory drive. This drive involves curiosity and a desire for information about something new or unusual. Play is a means whereby children can safely explore and seek out new information—something they might not otherwise do. Play encourages this exploratory behavior by offering children the possibilities of novelty, complexity, uncertainty, surprise, and incongruity.

Parten's Classic Study of Play Many years ago, Mildred Parten (1932) developed an elaborate classification of children's play. Based on observations of children in free play at nursery school, Parten arrived at the following play categories:

- **Unoccupied play** is not play as it is commonly understood. The child may stand in one spot or perform random movements that do not seem to have a goal. In most nursery schools, unoccupied play is less frequent than other forms of play.
- **Solitary play** happens when the child plays alone and independently of others. The child seems engrossed in the activity and does not care much about anything

unoccupied play Play in which the child is not engaging in play as it is commonly understood and might stand in one spot, or perform random movements that do not seem to have a goal.

solitary play Play in which the child plays alone and independently of others.

Mildred Parten classified play into six categories. *Study this photograph. Which of Parten's categories are reflected in the behavior of the children?*

*A*nd that park grew up with me; that small world widened as I learned its secrets and boundaries, as I discovered new refuges in its woods and jungles: hidden homes and lairs for the multitudes of imagination, for cowboys and Indians. . . . I used to dawdle on half holidays along the bent and Devon-facing seashore, hoping for gold watches or the skull of a sheep or a message in a bottle to be washed up with the tide.

—DYLAN THOMAS
Welsh Poet, 20th Century

onlooker play Play in which the child watches other children play.

parallel play Play in which the child plays separately from others, but with toys like those the others are using or in a manner that mimics their play.

associative play Play that involves social interaction with little or no organization.

cooperative play Play that involves social interaction in a group with a sense of group identity and organized activity.

sensorimotor play Behavior engaged in by infants to derive pleasure from exercising their existing sensorimotor schemas.

else that is happening. Two- and three-year-olds engage more frequently in solitary play than older preschoolers do.

- **Onlooker play** takes place when the child watches other children play. The child may talk with other children and ask questions but does not enter into their play behavior. The child's active interest in other children's play distinguishes onlooker play from unoccupied play.
- **Parallel play** occurs when the child plays separately from others but with toys like those the others are using or in a manner that mimics their play. The older children are, the less frequently they engage in this type of play. However, even older preschool children engage in parallel play quite often.
- **Associative play** involves social interaction with little or no organization. In this type of play, children seem to be more interested in each other than in the tasks they are performing. Borrowing or lending toys and following or leading one another in line are examples of associative play.
- **Cooperative play** consists of social interaction in a group with a sense of group identity and organized activity. Children's formal games, competition aimed at winning, and groups formed by the teacher for doing things together are examples of cooperative play. Cooperative play is the prototype for the games of middle childhood. Little cooperative play is seen in the preschool years.

Types of Play   Parten's categories represent one way of thinking about the different types of play. However, today researchers and practitioners who are involved with children's play argue that other types of play are important in children's development. Whereas Parten's categories emphasize the role of play in the child's social world, the contemporary perspective on play emphasizes both the cognitive and the social aspects of play. Among the most widely studied types of children's play today are sensorimotor and practice play, pretense/symbolic play, social play, constructive play, and games (Bergen, 1988). We will consider each of these types of play in turn.

Sensorimotor and Practice Play   **Sensorimotor play** is behavior that is engaged in by infants to derive pleasure from exercising their existing sensorimotor schemas. The development of sensorimotor play follows Piaget's description of sensorimotor thought, which we discussed in chapter 6. Infants initially engage in exploratory and playful visual and motor transactions in the second quarter of the first year of life. Then, at 9 months of age, infants begin to select novel objects for exploration and play, especially those that are responsive, such as toys that make noise or bounce. At 12 months of age, infants enjoy making things work and exploring cause and effect.

Practice play involves the repetition of behavior when new skills are being learned or when physical or mental mastery and coordination of skills are required for games or sports. Sensorimotor play, which often involves practice play, is primarily confined to infancy, whereas practice play can be engaged in throughout life. During the preschool years, children often engage in play that involves practicing various skills. Although practice play declines in the elementary school years, practice play activities such as running, jumping, sliding, twirling, and throwing balls or other objects are frequently observed on the playgrounds at elementary schools.

Pretense/Symbolic Play **Pretense/symbolic play** occurs when the child transforms the physical environment into a symbol. Between 9 and 30 months of age, children increase their use of objects in symbolic play. They learn to transform objects—substituting them for other objects and acting toward them as if they were these other objects. For example, a preschool child treats a table as if it were a car and says, "I'm fixing the car," as he grabs a leg of the table.

Many experts on play consider the preschool years the "golden age" of symbolic/pretense play that is dramatic or sociodramatic in nature. This type of make-believe play often appears at about 18 months of age and reaches a peak at 4 to 5 years of age, then gradually declines.

Social Play **Social play** is play that involves interaction with peers. Parten's categories, described earlier, are oriented toward social play. Social play with peers increases dramatically during the preschool years.

Constructive Play **Constructive play** combines sensorimotor and repetitive activity with symbolic representation of ideas. Constructive play occurs when children engage in self-regulated creation or construction of a product or a problem solution. Constructive play increases in the preschool years as symbolic play increases and sensorimotor play decreases. In the preschool years, some practice play is replaced by constructive play. For example, instead of moving their fingers around and around in finger paint (practice play), children are more likely to draw the outline of a house or a person in the paint (constructive play). Some researchers have found that constructive play is the most common type of play during the preschool years (Rubin, Maioni, & Hornung, 1976).

Games **Games** are activities that are engaged in for pleasure that include rules and often competition with one or more individuals. Preschool children may begin to participate in social game play that involves simple rules of reciprocity and turn-taking. However, games take on a much stronger role in the lives of elementary school children. In one study, the highest incidence of game playing occurred between 10 and 12 years of age (Eiferman, 1971). After age 12, games decline in popularity (Bergen, 1988).

Television

Few developments in society in the second half of the twentieth century had a greater impact on children than television (Murray, 2000; Roberts, Henriksen, & Foehr, 2004; Van Evra, 2004). Many children spend more time in front of the television set than they do with their parents. Although it is only one of the many types of mass media that affect children's behavior, television is the most influential. The

A preschool "superhero" at play.

practice play Play that involves repetition of behavior when new skills are being learned or when physical or mental mastery and coordination of skills are required for games or sports.

pretense/symbolic play Play in which the child transforms the physical environment into a symbol.

social play Play that involves social interactions with peers.

constructive play Play that combines sensorimotor and repetitive activity with symbolic representation of ideas. Constructive play occurs when children engage in self-regulated creation or construction of a product or a problem solution.

games Activities engaged in for pleasure that include rules and often competition with one or more individuals.

"Mrs. Horton, could you stop by school today?"

Copyright © Martha Campbell.

persuasive capabilities of television are staggering (Kotler, Wright, & Huston, 2001). The 20,000 hours of television watched by the time the average American adolescent graduates from high school are greater than the number of hours spent in the classroom.

Television can have a negative influence on children by taking them away from homework, making them passive learners, teaching them stereotypes, providing them with violent models of aggression, and presenting them with unrealistic views of the world. However, television can have a positive influence on children's development by presenting motivating educational programs, increasing their information about the world beyond their immediate environment, and providing models of prosocial behavior (Clifford, Gunter, & McAleer, 1995; Fisch, 2004; Van Evra, 2004).

Just how much television do young children watch? They watch a lot. In the 1990s, children watched an average of 26 hours of television each week, which is more than any other activity except sleep (National Center for Children Exposed to Violence, 2001). As shown in figure 9.10, considerably more children in the United States than their counterparts in other developed countries watch television for long periods. For example, seven times as many 9-year-olds in the United States as their counterparts in Switzerland watch television more than 5 hours a day.

A special concern is the extent to which children are exposed to violence and aggression on television (Van Evra, 2004). Up to 80 percent of the prime-time shows include violent acts, including beatings, shootings, and stabbings. The frequency of violence increases on the Saturday morning cartoon shows, which average more than 25 violent acts per hour.

Effects of Television on Children's Aggression and Prosocial Behavior

What are the effects of television violence on children's aggression? Does television merely stimulate a child to go out and buy a *Star Wars* ray gun, or can it trigger an attack on a playmate? When children grow up, can television violence increase the likelihood they will violently attack someone?

In one longitudinal study of males, the amount of violence viewed on television at age 8 was significantly related to the seriousness of criminal acts performed as an adult (Huesmann, 1986). In another study, exposure to media violence at 6 to 10 years of age was linked with young adult aggressive behavior for both males and females (Huesmann & others, 2003). In yet another study, long-term exposure to television violence was significantly related to the likelihood of

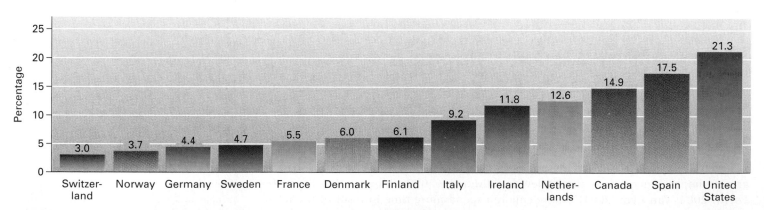

FIGURE 9.10 Percentage of 9-Year-Old Children Who Report Watching More Than Five Hours of Television per Weekday

aggression in 1,565 12- to 17-year-old boys (Belson, 1978). Boys who watched the most aggression on television were the most likely to commit a violent crime, swear, be aggressive in sports, threaten violence toward another boy, write slogans on walls, or break windows. These studies are *correlational,* so we can conclude from them that television violence is *associated with* aggressive behavior. In one experiment, children were randomly assigned to one of two groups: One group watched television shows taken directly from violent Saturday morning cartoon offerings on 11 different days; the second group watched television cartoon shows with all of the violence removed (Steur, Applefield, & Smith, 1971). The children were then observed during play at their preschool. The preschool children who saw the TV cartoon shows with violence kicked, choked, and pushed their playmates more than did the preschool children who watched nonviolent TV cartoon shows. Because the children were randomly assigned to the two conditions (TV cartoons with violence versus nonviolent TV cartoons), we can conclude that exposure to TV violence *caused* the increased aggression in the children in this investigation.

Children's Television Workshop
Television and Violence

In addition to television violence, there is increased concern about children who play violent video games, especially those that are highly realistic (Van Mierlo & Van den Buick, 2004; Vastag, 2004). Electronic games share some characteristics with other forms of audiovisual violence but differ from them in several important ways (Roberts, Henrikson, & Foehr, 2004). One difference is the electronic games' ability to immerse children so deeply that they experience an altered state of consciousness in which rational thought is suspended and arousing aggressive scripts are learned. Another difference is the direct rewards that game players receive ("winning points") for their actions.

Correlational studies indicate that children who extensively play violent electronic games are more aggressive than their counterparts who spend less time playing the games or do not play them at all (Cohen, 1995). Surveys have found that adolescents who frequently play violent electronic games are more likely to engage in delinquent behavior and are rated as more aggressive by their teachers than adolescents who are infrequent players (Anderson & Dill, 2000). Experiments have not yet been conducted to demonstrate increased aggression subsequent to playing violent video games, although a recent analysis of research studies concluded that playing violent video games is linked to aggression in both males and females (Anderson & Bushman, 2001).

A recent panel of leading experts concluded that media violence can have harmful short-term and long-term effects on children (Anderson & others, 2003). The effects are clearest for television but point in the same negative direction for video games. The experts outlined several explanations of how media violence may influence children:

- Children learn social behavior by observation, even though they are often unaware that learning has occurred. And they may imitate what they see.
- Frequent exposure to violence may make aggressive thoughts or social "scripts" more readily available in the child's mind, making it easier to summon aggression-related emotions or behaviors in a given situation.
- Media violence can produce physiological arousal, which may amplify an existing aggressive mood or tendency.
- Repeated exposure to media violence may desensitize a viewer, diminishing the unpleasant physical effects of seeing or thinking about violence.

Television also can teach children that it is better to behave in positive, prosocial ways than in negative, antisocial ways (Dorr, Rabin, & Irlin, 2002; Wilson, 2001). Aimee Leifer (1973) demonstrated that television is associated with prosocial behavior in young children. She selected a number of episodes from the television show *Sesame Street* that reflected positive social interchanges. She was especially interested

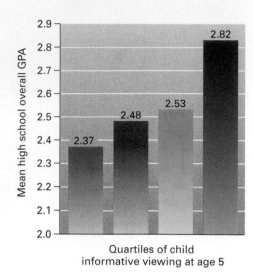

FIGURE 9.11 Educational TV Viewing and High School Grade Point Average for Boys

in situations that taught children how to use their social skills. For example, in one interchange, two men were fighting over the amount of space available to them. They gradually began to cooperate and to share the space. Children who watched these episodes copied these behaviors, and in later social situations they applied the prosocial lessons they had learned.

Television, Cognitive Development, and Achievement   Children bring various cognitive skills and abilities to their television viewing experience (Rabin & Dorr, 1995). Several important cognitive shifts take place between early childhood and middle and late childhood (Wilson, 2001). Preschool children often focus on the most striking perceptual features of a TV program and are likely to have difficulty in distinguishing reality from fantasy in the portrayals. As children enter elementary school, they are better able to link scenes together and draw causal conclusions from narratives. Judgments of reality also become more accurate in older children.

How does television influence children's creativity and verbal skills? In general television is negatively related to children's creativity (Williams, 1986), although educational programming for young children can promote creativity and imagination, possibly because it has a slower pace, and auditory and visual modalities are better coordinated (Anderson & others, 2001). Newer technologies, especially interactive television, hold promise for motivating children to learn and become more exploratory in solving problems (Singer, 1993).

In one recent longitudinal study, viewing educational programs as preschoolers was associated with a host of desirable characteristics in adolescence: getting higher grades, reading more books, placing a higher value on achievement, being more creative, and acting less aggressively (Anderson & others, 2001). These associations were more consistent for boys than girls. Figure 9.11 shows the results for boys' high school grade point average. In contrast, girls who were more frequent viewers of violent TV programs in the preschool years had lower grades in adolescence than girls who infrequently watched violent TV programs in the preschool years.

Review and Reflect: Learning Goal 3

3   **Describe the roles of peers, play, and television in young children's development**

REVIEW

- How do peers affect young children's development?
- What are some theories and types of play?
- How does television influence children's development?

REFLECT

- What guidelines would you recommend to parents that you think would help them to make television a more positive influence on their children's development? Consider factors such as the child's age, the child's activities other than TV, the parents' patterns of interaction with the children, and types of TV shows.

Reach Your Learning Goals

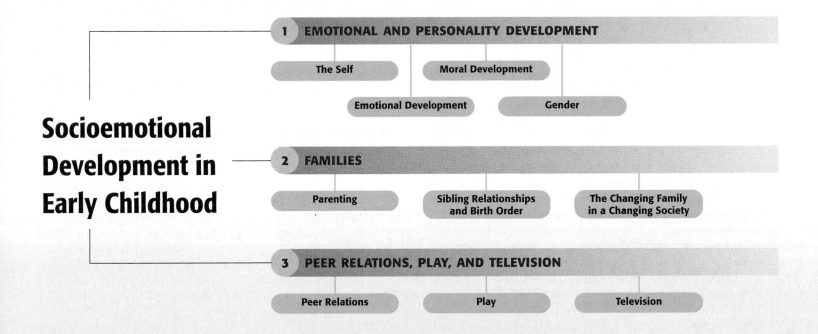

Socioemotional Development in Early Childhood

1 EMOTIONAL AND PERSONALITY DEVELOPMENT

The Self

Moral Development

Emotional Development

Gender

2 FAMILIES

Parenting

Sibling Relationships and Birth Order

The Changing Family in a Changing Society

3 PEER RELATIONS, PLAY, AND TELEVISION

Peer Relations

Play

Television

Summary

1 Learning Goal 1: Discuss emotional and personality development in early childhood

- In Erikson's theory early childhood is a period when development involves resolving the conflict of initiative versus guilt. Although a rudimentary form of self-understanding occurs at about 18 months in the form of self-recognition, in early childhood the physical self, or active self, emerges.

- Preschoolers become more adept at talking about their own and others' emotions. Two- and three-year-olds continue to increase the number of terms they use to describe emotion and learn more about the causes and consequences of feelings. At 4 to 5 years of age, children show an increased ability to reflect on emotions and understand that a single event can elicit different emotions in different people. They also show a growing awareness about controlling and managing emotions to meet social standards. Self-conscious emotions, such as pride, shame, and guilt, increase in early childhood. Emotion-coaching parents have children who engage in more effective self-regulation of their emotions than do emotion-dismissing parents.

- Moral development involves thoughts, feelings, and actions regarding rules and regulations about what people should do in their interactions with others. Developmentalists study how children think, behave, and feel about such rules and regulations. Piaget distinguished between the heteronomous morality of younger children and the autonomous morality of older children. Moral behavior is emphasized by behavioral and social cognitive theorists. According to these theories, there is considerable situational variability in moral behavior, and self-control is an important aspect of understanding chil-

dren's moral behavior. Freud's psychoanalytic theory emphasizes the importance of feelings with regard to the development of the superego, the moral branch of personality, which develops through the Oedipus conflict and identification with the same-sex parent. In Freud's view, children conform to societal standards to avoid guilt. Positive emotions, such as empathy, also are an important aspect of understanding moral feelings. Both positive and negative emotions contribute to children's moral development.

- Gender refers to the social and psychological dimensions of being male or female. Gender identity is acquired by 3 years of age for most children. A gender role is a set of expectations that prescribes how females or males should think, act, and feel. The 23rd pair of chromosomes may have two X chromosomes to produce a female, or one X and one Y chromosome to produce a male. The two main classes of sex hormones are estrogens, which are dominant in females, and androgens, which are dominant in males. Biology is not completely destiny in gender development; children's socialization experiences matter a great deal. Both psychoanalytic theory and social cognitive theory emphasize the adoption of parents' gender characteristics. Peers are especially adept at rewarding gender-appropriate behavior. Both cognitive developmental and gender schema theories emphasize the role of cognition in gender development.

2 Learning Goal 2: Explain how families can influence young children's development

- Authoritarian, authoritative, neglectful, and indulgent are four main parenting styles. Authoritative parenting is the most widely used style around the world and is the style most often associated with children's social competence. However, ethnic variations in parenting styles suggest that in African American and Asian American families, some aspects of control may benefit children. Latino parents often emphasize connectedness with the family and respect and obedience in their child rearing. Physical punishment is widely used by U.S. parents but there are a number of reasons why it is not a good choice. An understanding of child abuse requires information about cultural and familial influences. Child maltreatment places the child at risk for a number of developmental problems. Coparenting has positive effects on children's development. In today's society, an unfortunate theme is that parenting can be done quickly. However, good parenting takes extensive time and effort.

- Siblings interact with each other in positive and negative ways. Birth order is related in certain ways to child characteristics, but some critics argue that birth order by itself is not a good predictor of behavior.

- Sociocultural and economic factors affect children's development in many ways. In general, having both parents employed full-time outside the home has not been shown to have negative effects on children. However, in specific circumstances, when a mother works outside the home, such as when the infant is less than 1 year old, negative effects can occur. Divorce can have negative effects on children's adjustment, but so can an acrimonious relationship between parents who stay together for their children's sake. If divorced parents develop a harmonious relationship and practice authoritative parenting, children's adjustment improves. Approximately 20 percent of lesbians and 10 percent of gay men are parents. There is considerable diversity among lesbian mothers, gay fathers, and their children. Researchers have found few differences between children growing up in gay or lesbian families and children growing up in heterosexual families. Cultures vary on a number of issues regarding families. African American and Latino children are more likely than White American children to live in single-parent families and larger families and to have extended family connections. Lower-SES parents create a home atmosphere that involves more authority and physical punishment with children than higher-SES parents. Higher-SES parents are more concerned about developing children's initiative and delay of gratification.

 Learning Goal 3: Describe the roles of peers, play, and television in young children's development

- Peers are powerful socialization agents. Peers are children who are about the same age or maturity level. Peers provide a source of information and comparison about the world outside the family.

- Play's functions include affiliation with peers, tension release, advances in cognitive development, exploration, and provision of a safe haven. Parten developed the categories of unoccupied, solitary, onlooker, parallel, associative, and cooperative play. The contemporary perspective on play emphasizes both the cognitive and the social aspects of play. Among the most widely studied aspects of children's play today are sensorimotor play, practice play, pretense/symbolic play, social play, constructive play, and games.

- Television can have both negative influences (such as turning children into passive learners and presenting them with aggressive models) and positive influences (such as presenting motivating educational programs and providing models of prosocial behavior) on children's development. Children watch huge amounts of television. TV violence is not the only cause of children's aggression, but it can induce aggression. Prosocial behavior on TV is associated with increased positive behavior by children. Children's cognitive skills influence their TV-viewing experiences. Television viewing is negatively related to children's creativity and verbal skills.

Key Terms

self-understanding 257
moral development 259
heteronomous morality 259
autonomous morality 259
immanent justice 260
gender 261
gender identity 261
gender role 261

social role theory 263
psychoanalytic theory of
gender 263
social cognitive theory of
gender 263
cognitive developmental
theory of gender 265
gender schema theory 265

authoritarian parenting 268
authoritative parenting 268
neglectful parenting 268
indulgent parenting 268
unoccupied play 281
solitary play 281
onlooker play 282
parallel play 282

associative play 282
cooperative play 282
sensorimotor play 282
practice play 283
pretense/symbolic play 283
social play 283
constructive play 283
games 283

Key People

Erik Erikson 257
Jean Piaget 259
Sigmund Freud 260

Lawrence Kohlberg 265
Diana Baumrind 268
Ruth Chao 269

Lois Hoffman 275
Anna Freud 280
Lev Vygotsky 281

Daniel Berlyne 281
Mildred Parten 281

E-Learning Tools

To help you master the material in this chapter, you'll find a number of valuable study tools on the LifeMap CD-ROM that accompanies this book and on the Online Learning Center for *Life-Span Development,* tenth edition, at www.mhhe.com/santrockld10.

Video Clips

In the margins of this book there are icons directing you to the LifeMap CD-ROM that accompanies the book. There you'll find two videos for chapter 9. The first video is called "When a Second Baby Comes Along." Are there patterns among the personality traits of firstborn siblings? A researcher discusses the significance of birth order and offers some practical advice about preparing a child for a new brother or sister. The second video is called "Cultural Variations in Father's Role." A son will typically speak of his father as a role model, but the actual role that fathers play in their sons' and daughters' development continues to be a subject of research. This segment looks at some of that research.

Self-Assessment

Connect to www.mhhe.com/santrockld10 to examine your beliefs about caring for young children by completing the self-assessment, *My Parenting Style.*

Taking It to the Net

Connect to www.mhhe.com/santrockld10 to research the answers to these questions.

1. Doris and Ken are in the process of getting a divorce. Both of them want full custody of their two children: Kevin, age 10, and Chrissie, age 3. Although the divorce process has been very stressful for both of them, Doris and Ken share concerns about the effects their divorce might have on their children. What immediate effects can they expect, especially given the context of the custody battle? How might Kevin's reactions differ from Chrissie's? What might the long-term effects of the divorce be on their children?

2. Karen's mother is concerned about how best to help her daughter, Teresa, whose husband has abandoned her and their 5-year-old son. What are some of the challenges that Teresa may have to face and how can her mother help her through this difficult time?

3. Jonathan and Diedre want to shield their children from the violence on television, but they are not sure how to go about it—other than by not allowing any television viewing at all. What recommendations does the APA have for parents?

Health and Well-Being, Parenting, and Education Exercises

Build your decision-making skills by trying your hand at the health and well-being, parenting, and education exercises.

Connect to www.mhhe.com/santrockld10 to research the answers and complete the exercises.

CHAPTER

*The thirst to know and understand . . .
These are the good in life's rich hand.*

—SIR WILLIAM WATSON
English Poet, 20th Century

Physical and Cognitive Development in Middle and Late Childhood

Chapter Outline

Learning Goals

PHYSICAL CHANGES AND HEALTH   **1**

Body Growth and Proportion

Motor Development

Exercise and Sports

Health, Illness, and Disease

1 Describe physical changes and health in middle and late childhood

CHILDREN WITH DISABILITIES   **2**

Who Are Children with Disabilities?

Learning Disabilities

Attention Deficit Hyperactivity Disorder (ADHD)

Educational Issues

2 Identify children with different types of disabilities and issues in educating them

COGNITIVE CHANGES   **3**

Piaget's Theory

Information Processing

Intelligence

3 Explain cognitive changes in middle and late childhood

LANGUAGE DEVELOPMENT   **4**

Vocabulary and Grammar

Reading

Bilingualism

4 Discuss language development in middle and late childhood

Images of Life-Span Development
Zhang Liyin

A coach from a major sports school in China observed 5-year-old Zhang Liyin when she was playing in a kindergarten class in Beijing. The coach invited her to attend the sports school. Zhang was selected because of her body build, athletic skills, enthusiasm, and extraverted personality (Reilly, 1988).

The sports school is a privilege given to approximately 300,000 of China's 200 million students. There are approximately 3,000 sports schools in China and they are the only road to becoming an Olympic star in the country. A typical sports school has about 550 pupils between the ages of 5 and 16, all of whom live and study at the school. They get up at 7 A.M. and exercise for 30 minutes before breakfast, do school work the remainder of the morning, then train for 3 hours in the afternoon. At any point that a child shows a decline in potential, the child is asked to leave the sports school.

China will host the Olympic games in 2008 and China's leaders are intensifying the effort to develop champions for the 2008 games. Of course, China is not the only country where extensive training of young athletes takes place. In the United States, it is not unusual for parents to place their children in rigorous training programs for gymnastics, swimming, and other sports. Later in the chapter, we will further examine the nature of sports in children's lives.

Zhang Liyin (*third from left*) hopes to someday become an Olympic gymnastics champion. Attending the sports school is considered an outstanding privilege; only 300,000 of China's 200 million children are given this opportunity. *What positive and negative outcomes might children experience from playing sports? Are some sports programs, such as China's sports schools, too intense for children? Should children experience a more balanced life? Is there too much emphasis on sports in the United States?*

PREVIEW

Considerable progress in children's physical development continues to take place in the middle and late childhood years. Children grow taller, heavier, and stronger. They become more adept at using their physical skills. This chapter is about physical and cognitive development in middle and late childhood. To begin, we will explore some changes in physical development.

1   PHYSICAL CHANGES AND HEALTH

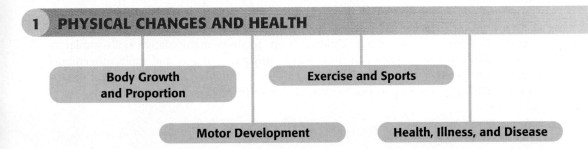

Continued change characterizes children's bodies during middle and late childhood, and their motor skills improve. It is important for children to engage in regular exercise and avoid illness and disease.

Body Growth and Proportion

The period of middle and late childhood involves slow, consistent growth. This is a period of calm before the rapid growth spurt of adolescence. During the elementary school years, children grow an average of 2 to 3 inches a year until, at the age of 11, the average girl is 4 feet, $10\frac{1}{4}$ inches tall, and the average boy is 4 feet, 9 inches tall. During the middle and late childhood years, children gain about 5 to 7 pounds a year. The weight increase is due mainly to increases in the size of the skeletal and muscular systems, as well as the size of some body organs. Muscle mass and strength gradually increase as "baby fat" decreases. The loose movements and knock-knees of early childhood give way to improved muscle tone. The increase in muscular strength is due to heredity and to exercise. Children also double their strength capabilities during these years. Because of their greater number of muscle cells, boys are usually stronger than girls.

Proportional changes are among the most pronounced physical changes in middle and late childhood. Head circumference, waist circumference, and leg length decrease in relation to body height (Hockenberry, 2005). A less noticeable physical change is that bones continue to ossify during middle and late childhood but yield to pressure and pull more than mature bones.

Motor Development

During middle and late childhood, children's motor skills become much smoother and more coordinated than they were in early childhood. For example, only one child in a thousand can hit a tennis ball over the net at the age of 3, yet by the age of 10 or 11 most children can learn to play the sport. Running, climbing, skipping rope, swimming, bicycle riding, and skating are just a few of the many physical skills elementary school children can master. In gross motor skills involving large activity, boys usually outperform girls.

As children move through the elementary school years, they gain greater control over their bodies and can sit and attend for longer periods of time. However, elementary school children are far from having physical maturity, so they need to be active. Elementary school children become more fatigued by long periods of

Every forward step we take we leave some phantom of ourselves behind.

—John Lancaster Spalding
American Educator, 19th Century

 Watch the video "Interactivity: Sensorimotor Neural Circuits" to learn how children obtain a progressively improved level of physical coordination.

sitting than by running, jumping, or bicycling. Physical action, such as batting a ball, skipping rope, or balancing on a beam, is essential for these children to refine their developing skills. An important principle of practice for elementary school children, therefore, is that they should be engaged in *active,* rather than passive, activities.

Increased myelination of the central nervous system is reflected in the improvement of fine motor skills during middle and late childhood. Children can more adroitly use their hands as tools. Six-year-olds can hammer, paste, tie shoes, and fasten clothes. By 7 years of age, children's hands have become steadier. At this age, children prefer a pencil to a crayon for printing, and reversal of letters is less common. Printing becomes smaller. At 8 to 10 years of age, the hands can be used independently with more ease and precision. Fine motor coordination develops to the point at which children can write rather than print words. Cursive letter size becomes smaller and more even. At 10 to 12 years of age, children begin to show manipulative skills similar to the abilities of adults. They can master the complex, intricate, and rapid movements needed to produce fine-quality crafts or to play a difficult piece on a musical instrument. Girls usually outperform boys in their use of fine motor skills.

Exercise and Sports

How much do children exercise? What are children's sports like?

Exercise It is becoming increasingly clear that exercise plays an important role in children's growth and development (Cooper, Nemet, & Galassetti, 2004; Fahey, Insel, & Roth, 2005; Kennedy, 2004; Watts & others, 2004). But are children getting enough exercise? In a 1997 national poll, only 22 percent of children in grades 4 through 12 were physically active for 30 minutes every day of the week (Harris, 1997). Their parents said their children were too busy watching TV, spending time on the computer, or playing video games to exercise much. Boys were more physically active at all ages than girls. In one historical comparison, the percentage of children involved in daily P.E. programs in schools decreased from 80 percent in 1969 to 20 percent in 1999 (Health Management Resources, 2001) (see figure 10.1). Further, a recent study found that 61 percent of 9- to 13-year-old U.S. children do not participate in any organized physical activity during their nonschool hours and that 23 percent do not engage in any free-time physical activity (Centers for Disease Control and Prevention, 2003).

Here are some ways to get children to exercise more:

- Offer more physical activity programs run by volunteers at school facilities.
- Improve physical fitness activities in schools.
- Have children plan community and school activities that really interest them.
- Encourage families to focus more on physical activity and parents to exercise more. In the national poll, more than 50 percent of the parents engaged in no vigorous physical activities on a regular basis.

Sports In the story that opened the chapter, you read about 6-year-old Zhang Liyin, who attends a sports school that is designed to produce future Olympians. By American standards, Zhang's life sounds rigid and punitive. Even though sports has a lofty status in American society, children are not being trained with the intensity that characterizes Zhang Liyin's school.

Nevertheless, sports have become an integral part of American culture. Thus, it is not surprising that more and more children become involved in sports every year. Both in public schools and in community agencies, children's sports programs that offer baseball, soccer, football, basketball, swimming, gymnastics, and other activities have changed the shape of many children's lives.

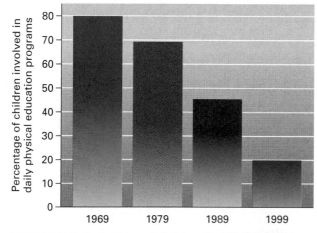

FIGURE 10.1 Percentage of Children Involved in Daily Physical Education Programs in the United States from 1969 to 1999

There has been a dramatic drop in the percentage of children participating in daily physical education programs in the United States from 80 percent in 1969 to only 20 percent in 1999.

Participation in sports can have both positive and negative consequences for children. Children's participation in sports can provide exercise, opportunities to learn how to compete, self-esteem, and a setting for developing peer relations and friendships. However, sports also can have negative outcomes for children: the pressure to achieve and win, physical injuries, a distraction from academic work, and unrealistic expectations for success as an athlete (Davis, 2004; Demorest & Landry, 2003, 2004). Few people challenge the value of sports for children when conducted as part of a school physical education or intramural program. However, some critics question the appropriateness of highly competitive, win-oriented sports teams in schools and communities.

There is a special concern for children in high-pressure sports settings involving championship play with accompanying media publicity. Some clinicians and child developmentalists observe that such activities not only put undue stress on the participants but also teach children the wrong values—namely, a win-at-all-costs philosophy (Pratt, Patel, & Greydanus, 2003). The possibility of exploiting children through highly organized, win-oriented sports programs is an ever-present danger. Overly ambitious parents, coaches, and community boosters can unintentionally create a highly stressful atmosphere in children's sports. When parental, agency, or community prestige becomes the central focus of the child's participation in sports, the danger of exploitation clearly is present. Programs oriented toward such purposes often require long and arduous training sessions over many months and years, frequently leading to sports specialization at too early an age. In such circumstances, adults often transmit a distorted view of the role of the sport in the child's life, communicating to the child that the sport is the most important aspect of the child's existence.

Health, Illness, and Disease

For the most part, middle and late childhood is a time of excellent health. Disease and death are less prevalent during this period than during others in childhood and in adolescence.

Accidents and Injuries The most common cause of severe injury and death in middle and late childhood is motor vehicle accidents, either as a pedestrian or as a passenger (Hockenberry, 2005). The use of safety-belt restraint greatly reduces the severity of motor vehicle injuries (Bolen, Bland, & Sacks, 1999). In addition, the school-age child's motivation to ride a bicycle increases the risk of accidents. Other serious injuries involve skateboards, roller skates, and other sports equipment.

Most accidents occur in or near the child's home or school. The most effective prevention strategy is to educate the child about the hazards of risk taking and improper use of equipment (Aitken & others, 2004; Philippakas & others, 2004). Wearing appropriate safety helmets, protective eye and mouth shields, and protective padding are recommended for children who engage in active sports (Briem & others, 2004).

Cancer Cancer is the second leading cause of death (with injuries the leading cause) in U.S. children 5 to 14 years of age. Three percent of all children's deaths in this age period are due to cancer. In the 15 to 24 age group, cancer accounts for 13 percent of all deaths. Currently, 1 in every 330 children in the United States develops cancer before the age of 19. Moreover, the incidence of cancer in children is increasing (Neglia & others, 2001).

Child cancers have a different profile from adult cancers. Adult cancers attack mainly the lungs, colon, breast, prostate, and pancreas. Child cancers mainly attack the white blood cells (leukemia), brain, bone, lymph system, muscles, kidneys, and nervous system. All are characterized by an uncontrolled proliferation of abnormal cells (Savell & others, 2004).

As indicated in figure 10.2, the most common cancer in children is leukemia, a cancer of the tissues that make blood cells. In leukemia, the

Child Health
Child Health Guide

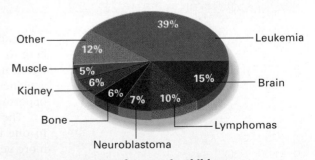

FIGURE 10.2 Types of Cancer in Children

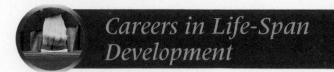

Careers in Life-Span Development

Sharon McLeod, Child Life Specialist

Sharon McLeod is a child life specialist who is clinical director of the Child Life and Recreational Therapy Department at the Children's Hospital Medical Center in Cincinnati.

Under Sharon's direction, the goals of the Child Life Department are to promote children's optimal growth and development, reduce the stress of health-care experiences, and provide support to child patients and their families. These goals are accomplished through therapeutic play and developmentally appropriate activities, educating and psychologically preparing children for medical procedures, and serving as a resource for parents and other professionals regarding children's development and health-care issues.

Sharon says that human growth and development provides the foundation for her profession of child life specialist. She also describes her best times as a student when she conducted field-work, had an internship, and experienced hands-on theories and concepts she learned in her courses.

Sharon McLeod, child life specialist, working with a child at Children's Hospital Medical Center in Cincinnati.

bone marrow manufactures an abundance of white blood cells that do not function properly. They invade the marrow and crowd out normal cells, making the child susceptible to bruising and infection. Lymphomas arise in the lymph system. Childhood lymphomas spread to the central nervous system and bone marrow (Carroll & others, 2003; Murray & others, 2004).

Child life specialists are among the health professionals who work to make the lives of children with diseases such as cancer less stressful. To read about the work of child life specialist Sharon McCleod, see the Careers in Life-Span Development insert.

Obesity In one recent analysis, the prevalence of being overweight among children from 6 to 11 years of age in the United States increased 325 percent from 1974 to 1999 (NHANES, 2001). Males are considered to be obese when their weight is 20 percent or more over their maximum desirable weight for their height, and females are considered obese when their weight is 25 percent over (Medline Plus, 2004). Girls are more likely to be obese than boys. Obesity at 6 years of age results in approximately a 25 percent probability that the child will be obese as an adult; obesity at age 12 results in approximately a 75 percent chance that the adolescent will be obese as an adult.

One recent national study found that from the late 1970s through the late 1990s, key dietary shifts took place among U.S. children: greater away-from-home consumption, large increases in total calories from salty snacks, soft drinks, and pizza; and large decreases in calories from low- and medium-fat milk and medium- and high-fat beef and pork (Nielsen, Siega-Riz, & Popkin, 2002). In this study, children's total caloric intake increased from the late 1970s to late 1990s. These dietary changes occurred for children as young as 2 years of age through the adult years. Also, one recent study found that time spent watching TV and the number of soft drinks consumed were both related to children's obesity (Giammattei & others, 2003).

Another recent national assessment found that most children's diets are poor or in need of improvement (Federal Interagency Forum on Child and Family Statistics, 2002). In this assessment, only 27 percent of 2- to 5-year-old children were categorized as having good diets. Their diets worsened as they became older—only 13 percent of 6- to 9-year-old children had healthy diets.

Inadequate levels of exercise are linked with being overweight (Ariza, Greenberg, & Unger, 2004; Fox, 2004; Williams, 2005). A child's activity level is influenced not only by heredity but also by a child's motivation to engage in energetic activities and caregivers who model an active lifestyle and provide children with opportunities to be active (Ruxton, 2004).

The context in which children eat can influence their eating habits and weight. In one recent study, children who ate with their families were more likely to eat more vegetables and low-fat foods (such as low-fat milk and salad dressing and lean meats), and drink fewer sodas than children who ate alone (Cullen, 2001). In this study, overweight children ate 50 percent of their meals in front of a TV, compared with only 35 percent of normal-weight children.

Obesity is a risk factor for many medical and psychological problems (Dietz, 2004; Etelson & others, 2003). Obese children can develop pulmonary problems and hip problems (Perez-Perdomo & others, 2003). Obese children also are prone to have high blood pressure, elevated blood cholesterol levels, and type 2 diabetes (Clinton-Smith, 2004; Hanevold & others, 2004; Ramchandani, 2004). Low self-esteem and depression are common outgrowths of obesity. Furthermore, obese children often have problems in peer relations and may be excluded from peer groups (Datar & Sturm, 2004; Janssen & others, 2004). One recent study found that obese children are often teased by their peers, have difficulty playing sports, and have health problems (Schwimmer, Burwinkle, & Varni, 2003). In chapter 14, we will discuss the most effective treatments for obesity, with a special focus on the importance of exercise.

Overweight Children
Heart Smart
Diseases and Illnesses
Medical Links
Cancer in Children

Review and Reflect: Learning Goal 1

1 Describe physical changes and health in middle and late childhood

REVIEW

- What are some changes in body growth and proportion in middle and late childhood?
- How do children's motor skills develop in middle and late childhood?
- What roles do exercise and sports play in children's lives?
- What are some characteristics of health, illness, and disease in middle and late childhood?

REFLECT

- Should parents be discouraged from coaching their children in sports or watching their children play in sports? Explain.

2 CHILDREN WITH DISABILITIES

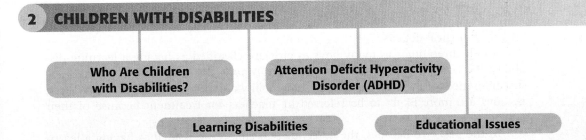

Who Are Children with Disabilities?

Learning Disabilities

Attention Deficit Hyperactivity Disorder (ADHD)

Educational Issues

The elementary school years are a time when children with disabilities become more sensitive about their differentness and how it is perceived by others.

Who Are Children with Disabilities?

Approximately 10 percent of children in the United States receive special education or related services. Figure 10.3 shows the approximate percentages of children with various disabilities who receive special education services (U.S. Department of Education, 2000). Within this group, a little more than half have a learning disability.

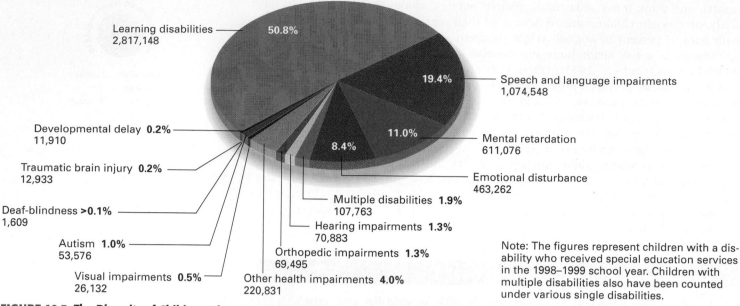

Learning disabilities
2,817,148 — 50.8%

Developmental delay 0.2%
11,910

Traumatic brain injury 0.2%
12,933

Deaf-blindness >0.1%
1,609

Autism 1.0%
53,576

Visual impairments 0.5%
26,132

Other health impairments 4.0%
220,831

Orthopedic impairments 1.3%
69,495

Hearing impairments 1.3%
70,883

Multiple disabilities 1.9%
107,763

8.4%

11.0%

19.4% — Speech and language impairments
1,074,548

Mental retardation
611,076

Emotional disturbance
463,262

Note: The figures represent children with a disability who received special education services in the 1998–1999 school year. Children with multiple disabilities also have been counted under various single disabilities.

FIGURE 10.3 The Diversity of Children Who Have a Disability

Substantial percentages of children also have speech or language impairments (19 percent of those with disabilities), mental retardation (11 percent), and serious emotional disturbance (8 percent).

Learning Disabilities

Bobby's second-grade teacher complains that his spelling is awful. Eight-year-old Tim says reading is really hard for him, and a lot of times the words don't make much sense. Alisha has good oral language skills but has considerable difficulty in computing correct answers to arithmetic problems. Each of these students has a learning disability.

After examining the research on learning disabilities, leading expert Linda Siegel (2003) recently concluded that a definition of **learning disabilities** should include these components: (1) a minimum IQ level; (2) a significant difficulty in a school-related area, especially reading and/or mathematics; and (3) exclusion of only severe emotional disorders, second-language background, sensory disabilities, and/or specific neurological deficits.

About three times as many boys as girls are classified as having a learning disability (U.S. Department of Education, 1996). Among the explanations for this gender difference are a greater biological vulnerability among boys and *referral bias*. That is, boys are more likely to be referred by teachers for treatment because of their behavior.

In the past two decades, the percentage of children classified as having a learning disability has increased substantially—from less than 30 percent of all children receiving special education and related services in 1977 to a little more than 50 percent today. Some experts say that the dramatic increase reflects poor diagnostic practices and overidentification. They suggest that teachers sometimes are too quick to label children with the slightest learning problem as having a learning disability, instead of recognizing that the problem may rest in their ineffective teaching. Other experts say the increase in children being labeled with a "learning disability" is justified (Hallahan & Kaufmann, 2003; Hallahan & others, 2005).

The most common problem that characterizes children with a learning disability involves reading (Rittey, 2003; Spafford & Grosser, 2005). **Dyslexia** is a category

**Exploring Disabilities
Learning Disabilities
Learning Disabilities Association**

learning disability Includes three components: (1) a minimum IQ level; (2) a significant difficulty in a school-related area (especially reading and/or mathematics); and (3) exclusion of only severe emotional disorders, second-language background, sensory disabilities, and/or specific neurological deficits.

dyslexia A category of learning disabilities involving a severe impairment in the ability to read and spell.

that is reserved for individuals who have a severe impairment in their ability to read and spell (Snowling, 2004; Vidyasagar, 2004).

Children with learning disabilities often have difficulties in handwriting, spelling, or composition. Their writing may be extremely slow, their writing products may be virtually illegible, and they may make numerous spelling errors because of their inability to match up sounds and letters.

About 5 percent of all school-age children in the United States receive special education or related services because of a learning disability. In the federal classification of children receiving special education and related services, attention deficit hyperactivity disorder (ADHD) is included in the learning disabilities category. Because of the significant interest in ADHD today, we will discuss it by itself next.

Attention Deficit Hyperactivity Disorder (ADHD)

Matthew has attention deficit hyperactivity disorder, and the outward signs are fairly typical. He has trouble attending to the teacher's instructions and is easily distracted. He can't sit still for more than a few minutes at a time, and his handwriting is messy. His mother describes him as very fidgety.

Attention deficit hyperactivity disorder (ADHD) is a disability in which children consistently show one or more of these characteristics over a period of time: (1) inattention, (2) hyperactivity, and (3) impulsivity. Children who are inattentive have difficulty focusing on any one thing and may get bored with a task after only a few minutes. Children who are hyperactive show high levels of physical activity and almost always seem to be in motion. Children who are impulsive have difficulty curbing their reactions and do not do a good job of thinking before they act. Depending on the characteristics that children with ADHD display, they can be diagnosed as (1) ADHD with predominantly inattention, (2) ADHD with predominantly hyperactivity/impulsivity, or (3) ADHD with both inattention and hyperactivity/impulsivity.

The number of children diagnosed and treated for ADHD has increased substantially, by some estimates doubling in the 1990s. The disorder occurs as much as four to nine times more in boys than in girls. There is controversy, however, about the increased diagnosis of ADHD (Terman & others, 1996). Some experts attribute the increase mainly to heightened awareness of the disorder. Others are concerned that many children are being diagnosed without undergoing extensive professional evaluation based on input from multiple sources.

Signs of ADHD may be present in the preschool years. Parents and preschool or kindergarten teachers may notice that the child has an extremely high activity level and a limited attention span. They may say the child is "always on the go," "can't sit still even for a second," or "never seems to listen." Many children with ADHD are difficult to discipline, have a low frustration tolerance, and have problems in peer relations (Farone & Doyle, 2001). Other common characteristics of children with ADHD include general immaturity and clumsiness.

Although signs of ADHD are often present during the preschool years, these signs are often not classified until the elementary school years (Stein & Perrin, 2003). The increased academic and social demands of formal schooling, as well as stricter standards for behavioral control, often illuminate the problems of the child with ADHD. Elementary school teachers typically report that the child with ADHD has difficulty working independently, completing seatwork, and organizing work. Restlessness and distractibility also are often noted. These problems are more likely to be observed during repetitive or taxing tasks, or tasks the child perceives to be boring (such as completing worksheets or doing homework) (Hoza & others, 2001).

It used to be thought that ADHD decreased in adolescence, but now it is thought that this often is not the case. Estimates suggest that ADHD decreases in only about

Many children with ADHD show impulsive behavior, such as this child who is jumping out of his seat and throwing a paper airplane at other children. *How would you handle this situation if you were a teacher and this were to happen in your classroom?*

www.mhhe.com/santrockld10

ADHD

attention deficit hyperactivity disorder (ADHD) A disability in which children consistently show one or more of the following characteristics: (1) inattention, (2) hyperactivity, and (3) impulsivity.

Public Law 94-142 mandates free, appropriate education for all children. *What characterizes this education?*

Education of Children
Who Are Exceptional
Inclusion

individualized education plan (IEP) A written statement that spells out a program tailored to a child with a disability. The plan should be (1) related to the child's learning capacity, (2) specially constructed to meet the child's individual needs and not merely a copy of what is offered to other children, and (3) designed to provide educational benefits.

least restrictive environment (LRE) The concept that a child with a disability must be educated in a setting that is as similar as possible to the one in which children who do not have a disability are educated.

inclusion Educating a child with special education needs full-time in the regular classroom.

one-third of adolescents. Increasingly, it is being recognized that these problems may continue into adulthood (Samuelsson, Lundberg, & Herkner, 2004).

Definitive causes of ADHD have not been found. However, a number of causes have been proposed, such as low levels of certain neurotransmitters (chemical messengers in the brain), prenatal and postnatal abnormalities, and environmental toxins, such as lead (Damico & others, 2004; Krause & others, 2003; Voeller, 2004). Thirty to 50 percent of children with ADHD have a sibling or parent who has the disorder (Farone & Doyle, 2001).

About 85 to 90 percent of children with ADHD are taking stimulant medication such as Ritalin or Adderall (which has fewer side effects than Ritalin) to enable them to control their behavior (Denney, 2001). Ritalin and Adderall are stimulants, and for most individuals, they speed up the nervous system and behavior. However, in many children with ADHD, the drug speeds up underactive areas of the prefrontal cortex that control attention, impulsivity, and planning, enhancing the children's ability to focus. This enhanced ability to focus their attention results in what *appears* to be a "slowing down" of behavior in these children (Reeves & Schweitzer, 2004). Researchers have found that a combination of medication (such as Ritalin) and behavior management improves the behavior of children with ADHD better than medication alone or behavior management alone (Chronis & others, 2004; Swanson & others, 2001). Critics argue that many physicians are too quick to prescribe stimulants for children with milder forms of ADHD (Marcovitch, 2004).

Educational Issues

The legal requirement that U.S. schools serve all children with a disability is a fairly recent development. Until laws were passed in the 1970s that mandated services for children with disabilities, most public schools either refused enrollment to children with disabilities or inadequately served them. In 1975, *Public Law 94-142*, the Education for All Handicapped Children Act, required that all students with disabilities be given a free, appropriate public education.

In 1990, Public Law 94-142 was renamed the *Individuals with Disabilities Education Act (IDEA)*. IDEA spells out broad mandates for services to all children with disabilities. These include the requirements that students with disabilities be given an individualized education plan (IEP) and education in the least restrictive environment (LRE) (Hardman, Drew, & Egan, 2005; Smith, 2004a).

An **individualized education plan (IEP)** is a written statement that spells out a program that is specifically tailored for the student with a disability (Friend, 2005). In general, the IEP should be (1) related to the child's learning capacity, (2) specifically constructed to meet the child's individual needs and not merely a copy of what is offered to other children, and (3) designed to provide educational benefits.

The **least restrictive environment (LRE)** is a setting that is as similar as possible to the one in which children who do not have a disability are educated. This provision of the IDEA has given a legal basis to efforts to educate children with a disability in the regular classroom (Dettmer, Dyck, & Thurston, 2002; Friend, 2005). The term **inclusion** describes educating a child with special education needs full-time in the regular classroom (Cole, Waldron, & Majd, 2004; Haager & Klingner, 2005).

Some experts on special education argue that the effort to use inclusion to educate children with disabilities has become too extreme in some cases (Kauffman & Hallahan, 2005; Kauffman, McGee, & Brigham, 2004). In their view, inclusion too often has meant making accommodations in the regular classroom that do not always benefit children with disabilities. They advocate a more individualized approach that does not always involve full inclusion but rather options such as special education outside the regular classroom.

Review and Reflect: Learning Goal 2

2 **Identify children with different types of disabilities and issues in educating them**

REVIEW

- Who are children with disabilities?
- What characterizes children with learning disabilities?
- How would you describe children with attention deficit hyperactivity disorder?
- What are some issues in educating children with disabilities?

REFLECT

- Think back on your own schooling and how children with learning disabilities or ADHD either were or were not diagnosed. Were you aware of such individuals in your classes? Were they helped by specialists? You may know one or more individuals with a learning disability or ADHD. Ask them about their educational experiences and whether they think schools could have done a better job of helping them.

3 **COGNITIVE CHANGES**

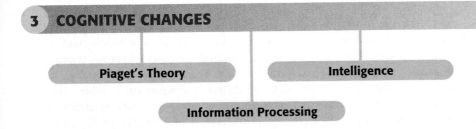

Do children enter a new stage of cognitive development in middle and late childhood? How do children process information in this age period? What is the nature of children's intelligence? Let's explore these questions.

Piaget's Theory

According to Piaget (1952), the preschool child's thought is preoperational. Preoperational thought involves the formation of stable concepts, the emergence of mental reasoning, the prominence of egocentrism, and the construction of magical belief systems. Thought during the preschool years is still flawed and not well organized. Piaget proposed that concrete operational thought does not appear until about the age of 7, but, as we learned in chapter 8, Piaget may have underestimated some of the cognitive skills of preschool children. For example, by carefully and cleverly designing experiments on understanding the concept of number, it was demonstrated that some preschool children show conservation, a concrete operational skill (Gelman, 1969). In chapter 8, we explored concrete operational thought by describing the preschool child's flaws in thinking about such concrete operational skills as conservation; here we will cover the characteristics of concrete operational thought again, this time emphasizing the competencies of elementary school children. Piaget suggested that concrete operational thought characterizes children from about 7 to 11 years of age. We will also consider applications of Piaget's ideas to children's education and an evaluation of Piaget's theory.

Remember that, according to Piaget, *concrete operational thought* is made up of operations—mental actions that allow children to do mentally what they had done physically before. Concrete operations are also mental actions that are reversible. In the well-known test of reversibility of thought involving conservation of matter, the

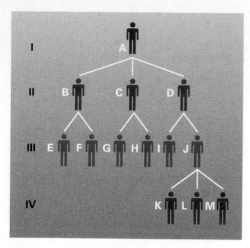

FIGURE 10.4 Classification: An Important Ability in Concrete Operational Thought
A family tree of four generations *(I to IV)*: The preoperational child has trouble classifying the members of the four generations; the concrete operational child can classify the members vertically, horizontally, and obliquely (up and down and across). For example, the concrete operational child understands that a family member can be a son, a brother, and a father, all at the same time.

Piaget and Education

seriation The concrete operation that involves ordering stimuli along a quantitative dimension (such as length).

transitivity The ability to logically combine relations to understand certain conclusions.

child is presented with two identical balls of clay. The experimenter rolls one ball into a long, thin shape; the other remains in its original ball shape. The child is then asked if there is more clay in the ball or in the long, thin piece of clay. By the time children reach the age of 7 or 8, most answer that the amount of clay is the same. To answer this problem correctly, children have to imagine the clay rolling back into a ball. This type of imagination involves a reversible mental action. Thus, a concrete operation is a reversible mental action on real, concrete objects. Concrete operations allow the child to coordinate several characteristics rather than focus on a single property of an object. In the clay example, the preoperational child is likely to focus on height *or* width. The concrete operational child coordinates information about both dimensions.

Many of the concrete operations Piaget identified focus on the way children reason about the properties of objects. One important skill that characterizes the concrete operational child is the ability to classify or divide things into different sets or subsets and to consider their interrelationships. An example of the concrete operational child's classification skills involves a family tree of four generations (see figure 10.4) (Furth & Wachs, 1975). This family tree suggests that the grandfather (A) has three children (B, C, and D), each of whom has two children (E through J), and that one of these children (J) has three children (K, L, and M). A child who comprehends the classification system can move up and down a level (vertically), across a level (horizontally), and up and down and across (obliquely) within the system. The concrete operational child understands that person J can at the same time be father, brother, and grandson, for example.

Some Piagetian tasks require children to reason about relations between classes. One such task is **seriation,** the concrete operation that involves ordering stimuli along a quantitative dimension (such as length). To see if students can serialize, a teacher might haphazardly place eight sticks of different lengths on a table. The teacher then asks the students to order the sticks by length. Many young children end up with two or three small groups of "big" sticks or "little" sticks, rather than a correct ordering of all eight sticks. Another mistaken strategy they use is to evenly line up the tops of the sticks but ignore the bottoms. The concrete operational thinker simultaneously understands that each stick must be longer than the one that precedes it and shorter than the one that follows it.

Another aspect of reasoning about the relations between classes is **transitivity,** which is the ability to logically combine relations to understand certain conclusions. In this case, consider three sticks (A, B, and C) of differing lengths. A is the longest, B is intermediate in length, and C is the shortest. Does the child understand that, if A > B and B > C, then A > C? In Piaget's theory, concrete operational thinkers do; preoperational thinkers do not.

Piaget and Education Piaget was not an educator and never pretended to be one. However, he provided a sound conceptual framework from which to view learning and education. Here are some more general principles in Piaget's theory that can be applied to teaching:

- *Take a constructivist approach.* Piaget emphasized that children learn best when they are active and seek solutions for themselves. Piaget opposed teaching methods that imply that children are passive receptacles. The educational implication of Piaget's view is that, in all subjects, students learn best by making discoveries, reflecting on them, and discussing them, rather than blindly imitating the teacher or doing things by rote.
- *Facilitate rather than direct learning.* Effective teachers design situations that allow students to learn by doing. These situations promote students' thinking and discovery. Teachers listen, watch, and question students to help them gain better understanding. Don't just examine *what* students think and the product of their learning. Rather, carefully observe them as they find out *how* they think. Ask

relevant questions to stimulate their thinking and ask them to explain their answers.

- *Consider the child's knowledge and level of thinking.* Students do not come to class with empty heads. They have many ideas about the physical and natural world. They have concepts of space, time, quantity, and causality. These ideas differ from the ideas of adults. Teachers need to interpret what a student is saying and respond in a mode of discourse that is not too far from the student's level.
- *Promote the student's intellectual health.* When Piaget came to lecture in the United States, he was asked, "What can I do to get my child to a higher cognitive stage sooner?" He was asked this question so often here compared with other countries that he called it the American question. For Piaget, children's learning occurs naturally. Children should not be pushed and pressured into achieving too much too early in their development, before they are maturationally ready. Some parents spend long hours every day holding up large flash cards with words on them to improve their baby's vocabulary. In the Piagetian view, this is not the best way for infants to learn. It places too much emphasis on speeding up intellectual development, involves passive learning, and will not work.
- *Turn the classroom into a setting of exploration and discovery.* What do actual classrooms look like when the teachers adopt Piaget's views? Several first- and second-grade math classrooms provide some good examples (Kamii, 1985, 1989). The teachers emphasize students' own exploration and discovery. The classrooms are less structured than what we think of as a typical classroom. Workbooks and predetermined assignments are not used. Rather, the teachers observe the students' interests and natural participation in activities to determine what the course of learning will be. For example, a math lesson might be constructed around counting the day's lunch money or dividing supplies among students. Teachers encourage peer interaction because students' different viewpoints can contribute to advances in thinking.

Piaget with his wife and three children; he often used his observations of his children to provide examples of his theory.

Evaluating Piaget's Theory   What were Piaget's main contributions? Has his theory withstood the test of time?

Contributions   Piaget was a giant in the field of developmental psychology, the founder of the present field of children's cognitive development. Psychologists owe him a long list of masterful concepts of enduring power and fascination: assimilation, accommodation, object permanence, egocentrism, conservation, and others. Psychologists also owe him the current vision of children as active, constructive thinkers (Vidal, 2000).

Piaget also was a genius when it came to observing children. His careful observations showed us inventive ways to discover how children act on and adapt to their world. Piaget showed us some important things to look for in cognitive development, such as the shift from preoperational to concrete operational thinking. He also showed us how children need to make their experiences fit their schemas (cognitive frameworks) yet simultaneously adapt their schemas to experience. Piaget also revealed how cognitive change is likely to occur if the context is structured to allow gradual movement to the next higher level and that a concept does not emerge suddenly, fully blown but, rather, through a series of partial accomplishments that lead to increasingly comprehensive understanding (Haith & Benson, 1998).

Criticisms   Piaget's theory has not gone unchallenged. Questions are raised about estimates of children's competence at different developmental levels; stages; the training of children to reason at higher levels; and culture and education.

- *Estimates of children's competence.* Some cognitive abilities emerge earlier than Piaget thought (Mandler, 2004; Miller, 2001). For example, as previously noted,

We owe to Piaget the present field of cognitive development with its image of the developing child, who through its own active and creative commerce with its environment, builds an orderly succession of cognitive structures enroute to intellectual maturity.

—JOHN FLAVELL
Contemporary Developmental Psychologist, Stanford University

An outstanding teacher and education in the logic of science and mathematics are important cultural experiences that promote the development of operational thought. *Might Piaget have underestimated the roles of culture and schooling in children's cognitive development?*

some aspects of object permanence emerge earlier than he thought. Even 2-year-olds are nonegocentric in some contexts. Some understanding of the conservation of number has been demonstrated as early as age 3, although Piaget did not think it emerged until 7. Young children are not as uniformly "pre" this and "pre" that (precausal, preoperational) as Piaget thought. Other cognitive abilities also can emerge later than Piaget thought. Many adolescents still think in concrete operational ways or are just beginning to master formal operations. Even many adults are not formal operational thinkers. In sum, recent theoretical revisions highlight more cognitive competencies of infants and young children and more cognitive shortcomings of adolescents and adults (Flavell, Miller, & Miller, 2002).

- *Stages.* Piaget conceived of stages as unitary structures of thought. Thus, his theory assumes developmental synchrony—that is, various aspects of a stage should emerge at the same time. However, some concrete operational concepts do not appear in synchrony. For example, children do not learn to conserve at the same time as they learn to cross-classify. Thus, most contemporary developmentalists agree that children's cognitive development is not as stagelike as Piaget thought.

- *Training children to reason at higher levels.* Some children who are at one cognitive stage (such as preoperational) can be trained to reason at a higher cognitive stage (such as concrete operational). This poses a problem for Piaget's theory. He argued that such training is only superficial and ineffective, unless the child is at a maturational transition point between the stages (Gelman & Williams, 1998).

- *Culture and education.* Culture and education exert stronger influences on children's development than Piaget proposed (Cole, 2005; Gelman & Brenneman, 1994). The age at which children acquire conservation skills is related to the extent to which their culture provides relevant practice. An outstanding teacher and education in the logic of math and science can promote concrete and formal operational thought.

Still, some developmental psychologists suggest we should not throw out Piaget altogether. These **neo-Piagetians** argue that Piaget got some things right but that his theory needs considerable revision. In their revision of Piaget, they give more emphasis to how children process information through attention, memory, and strategies (Case, 1999). They especially suggest that a more accurate vision of children's thinking requires more emphasis on strategies, the speed at which children process information, the particular cognitive task involved, and the division of cognitive problems into smaller, more precise steps (Case & Mueller, 2001).

Information Processing

Among the changes in information processing during middle and late childhood are those involving memory, critical thinking, creative thinking, and metacognition. Remember also, from chapter 8, that the attention of most children improves dramatically during middle and late childhood and that at this time children attend more to the task-relevant features of a problem than to the salient features.

neo-Piagetians Developmentalists who have elaborated on Piaget's theory, giving more emphasis to information-processing, strategies, and precise cognitive steps.

long-term memory A relatively permanent type of memory that holds huge amounts of information for a long period of time.

Memory   In chapter 8, we concluded that short-term memory increases considerably during early childhood but after the age of 7 does not show as much increase. Is the same pattern found for **long-term memory,** a relatively permanent and unlimited type of memory? Long-term memory increases with age during middle and late childhood.

Knowledge and Expertise   An especially important influence on memory is the knowledge that individuals have about a particular topic (National Research Council,

1999). The role of knowledge in memory has especially been studied in the context of experts and novices (Siegler & Alibali, 2005). Experts have acquired extensive knowledge that influences what they notice and how they organize, represent, and interpret information. This in turn affects their ability to remember, reason, and solve problems.

Expertise is a term that is used to describe organized factual knowledge about a particular content area. One child might have a great deal of knowledge about chess while another child is very knowledgeable about basketball. When individuals have expertise about a particular subject, their memory also tends to be good regarding material related to that subject.

One study found that 10- and 11-year-olds who were experienced chess players ("experts") were able to remember more information about chess pieces than college students who were not chess players ("novices") (Chi, 1978) (see figure 10.5). In contrast, when the college students were presented with other stimuli, they were able to remember them better than the children were. Thus, the children's expertise in chess gave them superior memories, but only in chess.

There are developmental changes in expertise. Older children usually have more expertise about a subject than younger children do, which can contribute to their better memory for the subject.

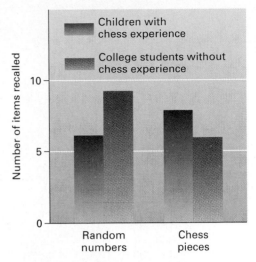

FIGURE 10.5 The Role of Expertise in Memory
Notice that when 10- to 11-year-old children and college students were asked to remember a string of random numbers that had been presented to them, the college students fared better. However, the 10- to 11-year-olds who had experience playing chess ("experts") had better memory for the location of chess pieces on a chess board than college students with no chess experience ("novices") (Chi, 1978).

Strategies If we know anything at all about long-term memory, it is that long-term memory depends on the learning activities individuals engage in when learning and remembering information (Mayer, 2003; Pressley, 2000; Schneider, 2004). **Strategies** are cognitive processes that do not occur automatically but require effort and work. They are under the learner's conscious control and can be used to improve memory (Siegler & Alibali, 2005). Strategies are also called *control processes.*

Two important strategies are creating mental images and elaborating on information. However, using imagery to remember verbal information works better for older children than for younger children (Schneider, 2004; Schneider & Pressley, 1997). In one study, 20 sentences were presented to first- through sixth-grade children to remember—such as "The angry bird shouted at the white dog" and "The policeman painted the circus tent on a windy day" (Pressley & others, 1987). Children were randomly assigned either to an imagery condition in which they were told to make a picture in their head for each sentence or a control condition in which they were told just to try hard. The instructions to form images helped older elementary school children (grades 4 through 6) but did not help the younger elementary school children (grades 1 through 3). However, mental imagery can help young school children to remember pictures (Schneider & Pressley, 1997).

Elaboration is an important strategy that involves engaging in more extensive processing of information. When individuals engage in elaboration, their memory benefits (Terry, 2003). Thinking of examples and referencing one's self are good ways to elaborate information. Thinking about personal associations with information makes the information more meaningful and helps children to remember it.

The use of elaboration changes developmentally (Pressley, 2003; Schneider, 2004; Schneider & Pressley, 1997). Adolescents are more likely to use elaboration spontaneously than children. Elementary school children can be taught to use elaboration strategies on a learning task, but they will be less likely than adolescents to use the strategies on other learning tasks in the future. Nonetheless, verbal elaboration can be an effective strategy for processing information even for young elementary school children.

Fuzzy Trace Theory Might something other than strategies be responsible for the improvement in memory during the elementary school years? Charles Brainerd and Valerie Reyna (1993; Reyna, 2004; Reyna & Brainerd, 1995) argue that fuzzy traces account for much of this improvement. Their **fuzzy trace theory** states that memory is best understood by considering two types of memory representations:

strategies Cognitive processes that do not occur automatically but require work and effort. These processes are under the learner's conscious control and can be used to improve memory. They are also called *control processes.*

elaboration An important strategy that involves engaging in more extensive processing of information.

fuzzy trace theory States that memory is best understood by considering two types of memory representations: (1) verbatim memory trace and (2) gist. In this theory, older children's better memory is attributed to the fuzzy traces created by extracting the gist of information.

(1) verbatim memory trace, and (2) gist. The *verbatim memory trace* consists of the precise details of the information, whereas *gist* refers to the central idea of the information. When gist is used, fuzzy traces are built up. Although individuals of all ages extract gist, young children tend to store and retrieve verbatim traces. At some point during the early elementary school years, children begin to use gist more and, according to the theory, this contributes to the improved memory and reasoning of older children because fuzzy traces are more enduring and less likely to be forgotten than verbatim traces.

Critical Thinking   Currently, both psychologists and educators have considerable interest in critical thinking, although it is not an entirely new idea (Santrock & Halonen, 2004). Famous educator John Dewey (1933) proposed a similar idea when he talked about the importance of getting students to think reflectively. **Critical thinking** involves thinking reflectively and productively, as well as evaluating the evidence. In this book, the second part of the Review and Reflect sections of each chapter challenges you to think critically about a topic or an issue related to the discussion.

Jacqueline and Martin Brooks (2001) lament that so few schools really teach students to think critically and develop a deep understanding of concepts. For example, many high school students read *Hamlet* but don't think deeply about it, never transforming their prior notions of power, greed, and relationships. Deep understanding occurs when students are stimulated to rethink their previously held ideas.

In Brooks and Brooks' view, schools spend too much time on getting students to give a single correct answer in an imitative way, rather than encouraging them to expand their thinking by coming up with new ideas and rethinking earlier conclusions. They observe that too often teachers ask students to recite, define, describe, state, and list, rather than to analyze, infer, connect, synthesize, criticize, create, evaluate, think, and rethink.

Brooks and Brooks point out that many successful students complete their assignments, do well on tests, and get good grades, yet they don't ever learn to think critically and deeply. They argue that our schools turn out students who think too superficially, staying on the surface of problems rather than stretching their minds and becoming deeply engaged in meaningful thinking.

Creative Thinking   Cognitively competent children not only think critically, but also creatively (Sternberg, Grigorenko, & Singer, 2004). **Creative thinking** is the ability to think in novel and unusual ways and to come up with unique solutions to problems. Thus, intelligence and creativity are not the same thing. This difference was recognized by J. P. Guilford (1967), who distinguished between **convergent thinking,** which produces one correct answer and characterizes the kind of thinking that is required on conventional tests of intelligence, and **divergent thinking,** which produces many different answers to the same question and characterizes creativity. For example, a typical item on a conventional intelligence test is "How many quarters will you get in return for 60 dimes?" In contrast, the following question has many possible answers: "What image comes to mind when you hear the phrase 'sitting alone in a dark room' or 'some unique uses for a paper clip'?"

It is important to recognize that children will show more creativity in some domains than others (Runco, 2004). A child who shows creative thinking skills in mathematics may not exhibit these skills in art, for example.

An important goal is to help children become more creative. What are the best strategies for accomplishing this goal?

- *Have children engage in brainstorming and come up with as many ideas as possible.* In **brainstorming,** individuals are encouraged to come up with creative ideas in a group, play off each other's ideas, and say whatever comes to mind. The more ideas children produce, the better their chance of creating something unique

critical thinking Thinking reflectively and productively, as well as evaluating the evidence.

creative thinking The ability to think in novel and unusual ways and to come up with unique solutions to problems.

convergent thinking Thinking that produces one correct answer and is characteristic of the kind of thinking tested by standardized intelligence tests.

divergent thinking Thinking that produces many answers to the same question and is characteristic of creativity.

brainstorming A technique in which individuals are encouraged to come up with creative ideas in a group, play off each other's ideas, and say practically whatever comes to mind.

(Runco, 2000). A recent review of research on brainstorming concluded that for many individuals, working alone can actually generate more ideas and better ideas than working in groups (Rickards & deCock, 2003). One reason for this is that in groups, some individuals loaf while others do most of the creative thinking. Nonetheless, there may be benefits to brainstorming, such as team building, that support its implementation.

- *Provide children with environments that stimulate creativity.* Some settings nourish creativity; others depress it. People who encourage children's creativity often rely on their natural curiosity. They provide exercises and activities that stimulate children to find insightful solutions to problems, rather than asking a lot of questions that require rote answers.
- *Don't overcontrol.* Teresa Amabile (1993) says that telling children exactly how to do things leaves them feeling that any originality is a mistake and any exploration is a waste of time. Letting children select their interests and supporting their inclinations are less likely to destroy their natural curiosity than dictating which activities they should engage in (Csikszentmihalyi, 2000).
- *Encourage internal motivation.* The excessive use of prizes, such as gold stars, money, or toys, can stifle creativity by undermining the intrinsic pleasure children derive from creative activities. Creative children's motivation is the satisfaction generated by the work itself (Amabile & Hennessey, 1992).
- *Foster flexible and playful thinking.* Creative thinkers are flexible and play with problems, which gives rise to a paradox. Although creativity takes effort, the effort goes more smoothly if students take it lightly.
- *Introduce children to creative people.* Teachers can invite creative people to their classrooms and ask them to describe what helps them become creative or to demonstrate their creative skills. A writer, poet, musician, scientist, and many others can bring their props and productions to the class, turning it into a theater for stimulating students' creativity.

Metacognition   **Metacognition** is cognition about cognition, or knowing about knowing (Flavell, 1999, 2004; Flavell, Miller, & Miller, 2002). One expert on children's thinking, Deanna Kuhn (1999), believes that metacognition should be a stronger focus of efforts to help children become better critical thinkers, especially at the middle school and high school levels. She distinguishes between first-order cognitive skills that enable children to know about the world (these have been the main focus of critical thinking programs) and second-order cognitive skills—*meta-knowing skills*—that entail knowing about one's own (and others') knowing.

The majority of developmental studies classified as "metacognitive" have focused on metamemory, or knowledge about memory (DeMarie, Abshier, & Ferron, 2001). This includes general knowledge about memory, such as knowing that recognition tests are easier than recall tests. It also encompasses knowledge about one's own memory, such as a student's ability to monitor whether she has studied enough for a test that is coming up next week.

By 5 or 6 years of age, children usually know that familiar items are easier to learn than unfamiliar ones, that short lists are easier than long ones, that recognition is easier than recall, and that forgetting is more likely to occur over time (Lyon & Flavell, 1993). However, in other ways young children's metamemory is limited. They don't understand that related items are easier to remember than unrelated ones and that remembering the gist of a story is easier than remembering information verbatim (Kreutzer, Leonard, & Flavell, 1975). By the fifth grade, students understand that gist recall is easier than verbatim recall. Young children also have an inflated opinion of their memory abilities. For example, in one study a majority of young children predicted that they would be able to recall all 10 items on a list of 10 items. When tested for this, none of the young children managed this feat (Flavell, Friedrichs, & Hoyt, 1970). As they move through the elementary school years, children give more realistic evaluations of their memory skills (Schneider & Pressley, 1997).

metacognition Cognition about cognition, or knowing about knowing.

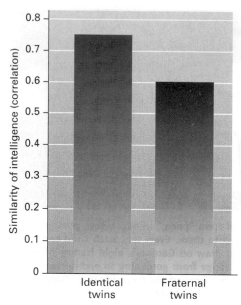

FIGURE 10.8 Correlation Between Intelligence Test Scores and Twin Status
The graph represents a summary of research findings that have compared the intelligence test scores of identical and fraternal twins. An approximate .15 difference has been found with a higher correlation for identical twins (.75) and a lower correlation for fraternal twins (.60).

if intelligence is genetically determined, Jensen reasoned, identical twins' IQs should be more similar than the intelligence of fraternal twins.

The studies on intelligence in identical twins that Jensen examined showed an average correlation of .82, a very high positive association. Investigations of fraternal twins, however, produced an average correlation of .50, a moderately high positive correlation. A difference of .32 is substantial. However, a more recent research review that included many studies conducted since Jensen's original review found that the difference in the average correlation of intelligence between identical and fraternal twins was .15, substantially less than what Jensen found (Grigorenko, 2000) (see figure 10.8).

Jensen also compared the correlation of IQ scores for identical twins reared together with those reared apart. The correlation for those reared together was .89, and for those reared apart was .78, a difference of .11. Jensen argued that if environmental factors were more important than genetic factors, the difference should have been greater.

Adoption studies have been inconclusive about the relative importance of heredity in intelligence. In most *adoption studies,* researchers determine whether the behavior of adopted children is more like that of their biological parents or their adopted parents. In one study, the educational levels attained by biological parents were better predictors of children's IQ scores than were the IQs of the children's adoptive parents (Scarr & Weinberg, 1983). Because of the stronger genetic link between the adopted children and their biological parents, the implication is that heredity is more important than environment. Environmental effects also have been found in studies of adoption. For example, moving children into an adoptive family with a better environment than the child had in the past increased the children's IQs by an average of 12 points (Lucurto, 1990).

How strong is the effect of heredity on intelligence? The concept of heritability attempts to tease apart the effects of heredity and environment in a population. **Heritability** is the fraction of the variance in a population that is attributed to genetics. The heritability index is computed using correlational techniques. Thus, the highest degree of heritabilty is 1.00 and correlations of .70 and above suggest a strong genetic influence. A committee of respected researchers convened by the American Psychological Association concluded that by late adolescence, the heritability of intelligence is about .75, which reflects a strong genetic influence (Neisser & others, 1996).

An important point to keep in mind about heritability is that it refers to a specific group (population), *not* to individuals (Okagaki, 2000). Researchers use the concept of heritability to try to describe why people differ. Heritability says nothing about why a single individual, like yourself, has a certain intelligence; nor does it say anything about differences *between* groups.

Most research on heredity and environment does not include environments that differ radically. Thus, it is not surprising that many genetic studies show environment to be a fairly weak influence on intelligence (Fraser, 1995).

The heritability index has several flaws. It is only as good as the data entered into its analysis and the interpretations made from it. The data are virtually all from traditional IQ tests, which some experts think are not always the best indicator of intelligence (Gardner, 2002; Sternberg, 2002). Also, the heritability index assumes that we can treat genetic and environmental influences as factors that can be separated, with each part contributing a distinct amount of influence. As we discussed in chapter 2, genes and the environment always work together. Genes always exist in an environment and the environment shapes their activity.

Today, most researchers agree that heredity does not determine intelligence to the extent Jensen claimed (Grigorenko, 2000; Sternberg & Grigorenko, 2004). For most people, this means modifications in environment can change their IQ scores considerably (Campbell & others, 2001). Although genetic endowment may always influence a person's intellectual ability, the environmental influences and opportunities we provide children and adults do make a difference (Sternberg & Preiss, 2005).

heritability The fraction of variance in a population that is attributed to genetics and is computed using correlational techniques.

In one study, researchers went into homes and observed how extensively parents from welfare and middle-income professional families talked and communicated with their young children (Hart & Risley, 1995). They found that the middle-income professional parents were much more likely to communicate with their young children than the welfare parents were. And how much the parents communicated with their children in the first three years of their lives was correlated with the children's Stanford-Binet IQ scores at age 3. The more parents communicated with their children, the higher the children's IQs were.

Schooling also influences intelligence (Ceci & Gilstrap, 2000; Christian, Bachnan, & Morrison, 2001). The biggest effects have been found when large groups of children have been deprived of formal education for an extended period, resulting in lower intelligence. One study examined the intelligence of children in South Africa whose schooling was delayed for four years because teachers were not available (Ramphal, 1962). Compared with children in nearby villages who had teachers, the children whose entry into school was delayed experienced a 5-point drop in IQ for every year of delay.

Another possible effect of education can be seen in rapidly increasing IQ test scores around the world (Daley & others, 2003; Flynn, 1999). IQ scores have been increasing so fast that a high percentage of people regarded as having average intelligence at the turn of the century would be considered below average in intelligence today (Howard, 2001) (see figure 10.9). If a representative sample of people today took the Stanford-Binet test used in 1932, about one-fourth would be defined as having very superior intelligence, a label usually accorded to fewer than 3 percent of the population (Horton, 2001). Because the increase has taken place in a relatively short time, it can't be due to heredity, but rather may be due to increasing levels of education attained by a much greater percentage of the world's population or to other environmental factors such as the explosion of information to which people are exposed. The worldwide increase in intelligence test scores that has occurred over a short time frame has been called the *Flynn effect,* after the researcher who discovered it—James Flynn.

Keep in mind that environmental influences are complex (Neisser & others, 1996; Sternberg, 2001). Growing up with all the "advantages," for example, does not guarantee success. Children from wealthy families may have easy access to excellent schools, books, travel, and tutoring, but they may take such opportunities for granted and fail to develop the motivation to learn and to achieve. In the same way, "poor" or "disadvantaged" does not automatically equal "doomed."

Researchers increasingly are interested in manipulating the early environment of children who are at risk for impoverished intelligence (Blair & Ramey, 1996; Ramey, Ramey, & Lanzi, 2001; Sternberg & Grigorenko, 2000). The emphasis is on prevention rather than remediation. Many low-income parents have difficulty providing an intellectually stimulating environment for their children. Programs that educate parents to be more sensitive caregivers and better teachers, as well as

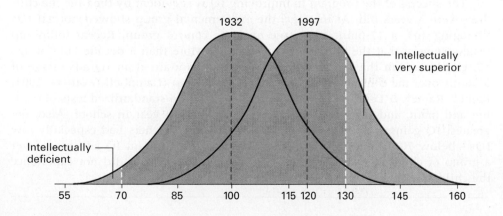

FIGURE 10.9 The Increase in IQ Scores from 1932 to 1997

As measured by the Stanford-Binet intelligence test, American children seem to be getting smarter. Scores of a group tested in 1932 fell along a bell-shaped curve with half below 100 and half above. Studies show that if children took that same test today, half would score above 120 on the 1932 scale. Very few of them would score in the "intellectually deficient" end, on the left side, and about one-fourth would rank in the "very superior" range.

support services such as quality child-care programs, can make a difference in a child's intellectual development.

A recent review of the research on early interventions concluded that (1) high-quality center-based interventions are associated with increases in children's intelligence and school achievement; (2) the interventions are most successful with poor children and children whose parents have little education; (3) the positive benefits continue through adolescence, but are not as strong as in early childhood or the beginning of elementary school; and (4) the programs that are continued into middle and late childhood have the best long-term results (Brooks-Gunn, 2003). To read further about environmental influences on intelligence, see the Research in Life-Span Development interlude.

Research in Life-Span Development

The Abecedarian Project

Each morning a young mother waited with her child for the bus that would take the child to school. The child was only 2 months old, and "school" was an experimental program at the University of North Carolina at Chapel Hill. There the child experienced a number of interventions designed to improve her intellectual development—everything from bright objects dangled in front of her eyes while she was a baby to language instruction and counting activities when she was a toddler (Wickelgren, 1999). The child's mother had an IQ of 40 and could not read signs or determine how much change she should receive from a cashier. Her grandmother had a similarly low IQ.

Today, at age 20, the child's IQ measures 80 points higher than her mother's did when the child was 2 months old. Not everyone agrees that IQ can be affected this extensively, but environment can make a substantial difference in a child's intelligence. As behavior geneticist Robert Plomin (1999) says, even something that is highly heritable (like intelligence) may be malleable through interventions.

The child we just described was part of the Abecedarian Intervention program at the University of North Carolina at Chapel Hill conducted by Craig Ramey and his associates (Ramey & Campbell, 1984; Ramey & Ramey, 1998; Ramey, Ramey, & Lanzi, 2001). They randomly assigned 111 young children from low-income, poorly educated families to either an intervention group, which received full-time, year-round child care along with medical and social work services, or a control group, which received medical and social benefits but no child care. The child-care program included gamelike learning activities aimed at improving language, motor, social, and cognitive skills.

The success of the program in improving IQ was evident by the time the children were 3 years old. At that age, the experimental group showed normal IQs averaging 101, a 17-point advantage over the control group. Recent follow-up results suggest that the effects are long-lasting. More than a decade later at age 15, children from the intervention group still maintained an IQ advantage of 5 points over the control-group children (97.7 to 92.6) (Campbell & others, 2001; Ramey, Ramey, & Lanzi, 2001). They also did better on standardized tests of reading and math, and were less likely to be held back a year in school. Also, the greatest IQ gains were made by the children whose mothers had especially low IQs—below 70. At age 15, these children showed a 10-point IQ advantage over a group of children whose mothers' IQs were below 70 but did not experience the child-care intervention.

Ethnicity and Culture In the United States, children from African American and Latino families score below children from White families on standardized intelligence tests. On the average, African American schoolchildren score 10 to 15 points lower on standardized intelligence tests than White American schoolchildren do (Brody, 2000; Lynn, 1996). These are *average scores,* however. About 15 to 25 percent of African American schoolchildren score higher than half of White schoolchildren do, and many White schoolchildren score lower than most African American schoolchildren. The reason is that the distribution of scores for African American and White schoolchildren overlap.

A controversy erupted in response to the book *The Bell Curve: Intelligence and Class Structure in American Life* (1994) by Richard Herrnstein and Charles Murray. Recall that the bell curve is the shape of a normal distribution graph, which represents large numbers of people who are sorted according to some shared characteristic, such as weight, taste in clothes, or IQ. Herrnstein and Murray note that predictions about any individual based exclusively on the person's IQ are virtually useless. Weak correlations between IQ and job success have predictive value only when they are applied to large groups of people. But within large groups, say Herrnstein and Murray, the pervasive influence of IQ on human society becomes apparent. The authors argued that America is developing a huge underclass of intellectually deprived individuals whose cognitive abilities will never match the future needs of most employers. They believe that this underclass, a large proportion of which is African American, may be doomed by their shortcomings to welfare dependency, poverty, and crime.

Significant criticisms have been leveled at *The Bell Curve.* The average score of African Americans is lower than the average score of Whites on IQ tests. However, as we have discussed, many experts raise serious questions about the ability of IQ tests to accurately measure a person's intelligence.

As African Americans have gained social, economic, and educational opportunities, the gap between African Americans and Whites on standardized intelligence tests has begun to narrow (Ogbu & Stern, 2001; Onwuegbuzi & Daley, 2001). This gap especially narrows in college, where African American and White students often experience more similar environments than in the elementary and high school years (Myerson & others, 1998). Also, when children from disadvantaged African American families are adopted into more-advantaged middle-socioeconomic-status families, their scores on intelligence tests more closely resemble national averages for middle-socioeconomic-status children than for lower-socioeconomic-status children (Scarr & Weinberg, 1983).

One potential influence on intelligence test performance is **stereotype threat,** the anxiety that one's behavior might confirm a negative stereotype about one's group (Steele & Aronson, 2004). For example, when African Americans take an intelligence test, they may experience anxiety about confirming the old stereotype that African Americans are "intellectually inferior." In one study, the verbal part of the GRE was given individually to African American and White students at Stanford University (Steele & Aronson, 1995). Half the students of each ethnic group were told that the researchers were interested in assessing their intellectual ability. The other half were told that the researchers were trying to develop a test and that it might not be reliable and valid (therefore, it would not mean anything in relation to their intellectual ability). The White students did equally well on the test in both conditions. However, the African American students did more poorly when they thought the test was assessing their intellectual ability; when they thought the test was just in the development stage and might not be reliable or valid, they performed as well as the White students.

Other studies have confirmed the existence of stereotype threat. African American students do more poorly on standardized tests if they believe they are being evaluated. If they believe the test doesn't count, they perform as well as White students (Aronson, 2002; Aronson & others, 1999; Aronson, Fried, & Good, 2002).

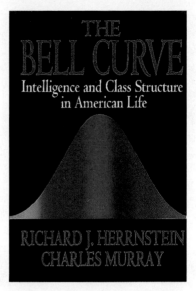

Herrnstein and Murray's *The Bell Curve* advocates a strong role for heredity in intelligence and claims that a large portion of underclass individuals, especially African Americans, are doomed because of their heredity. *What are some of the criticisms that have been leveled at Herrnstein and Murray's claims?*

www.mhhe.com/santrockld10

Two Views of *The Bell Curve*
Sternberg's Critique of *The Bell Curve*

stereotype threat The anxiety that one's behavior might confirm a negative stereotype about one's group.

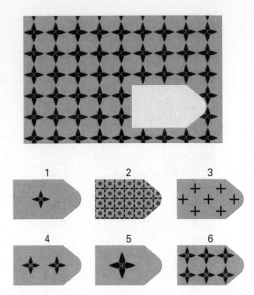

FIGURE 10.10 Sample Item from the Raven Progressive Matrices Test

Individuals are presented with a matrix arrangement of symbols, such as the one at the top of this figure, and must then complete the matrix by selecting the appropriate missing symbol from a group of symbols, such as the ones at the bottom.

However, some critics believe the extent to which stereotype threat explains the testing gap has been exaggerated (Sackett, Hardison, & Cullen, 2004).

Many of the early tests of intelligence were culturally biased, favoring urban children over rural children, children from middle-SES families over children from low-income families, and White children over minority children (Miller-Jones, 1989). The standards for the early tests were almost exclusively based on White middle-SES children. And some of the items were culturally biased. For example, one item on an early test asked what you should do if you find a 3-year-old in the street. The correct answer was "Call the police." However, children from impoverished inner-city families might not choose this answer if they have had bad experiences with the police. Children living in rural areas might not have police nearby. The contemporary versions of intelligence tests attempt to reduce such cultural bias.

Even if the content of test items is appropriate, however, another problem can characterize intelligence tests. Since many items are verbal, minority groups may encounter problems in understanding the language of the items.

Culture-fair tests are tests of intelligence that are intended to be free of cultural bias. Two types of culture-fair tests have been devised. The first includes items that are familiar to children from all socioeconomic and ethnic backgrounds, or items that at least are familiar to the children taking the test. For example, a child might be asked how a bird and a dog are different, on the assumption that all children have been exposed to birds and dogs. The second type of culture-fair test has no verbal questions. Figure 10.10 shows a sample question from the Raven Progressive Matrices Test. Even though tests such as the Raven Progressive Matrices are designed to be culture-fair, people with more education still score higher than those with less education do.

Why is it so hard to create culture-fair tests? Most tests tend to reflect what the dominant culture thinks is important (Aiken, 2003; Greenfield & others, 2003). If tests have time limits, that will bias the test against groups not concerned with time. If languages differ, the same words might have different meanings for different language groups. Even pictures can produce bias because some cultures have less experience with drawings and photographs (Anastasi & Urbina, 1996). Within the same culture, different groups could have different attitudes, values, and motivation, and this could affect their performance on intelligence tests. Items that ask why buildings should be made of brick are biased against children who have little or no experience with brick houses. Questions about railroads, furnaces, seasons of the year, distances between cities, and so on can be biased against groups who have less experience than others with these contexts.

These attempts to produce culture-fair tests remind us that conventional intelligence tests probably are culturally biased, yet the effort to create a truly culture-fair test has not yielded a successful alternative. It also is important to consider that what is viewed as intelligent in one culture may not be thought of as intelligent in another (Benson, 2003; Cole, 2005; Serpell, 2000). For example, people in Western cultures tend to view intelligence in terms of reasoning and thinking skills, whereas people in Eastern cultures see intelligence as a way for members of a community to successfully engage in social roles (Nisbett, 2003). One study found that Taiwanese Chinese conceptions of intelligence emphasize understanding and relating to others, including when to show and when not to show one's intelligence (Yang & Sternberg, 1997).

Robert Serpell (1974, 1993, 2000) has studied concepts of intelligence in rural African communities since the 1970s. He has found that people in rural African communities, especially those in which Western schooling is not common, tend to blur the distinction between being intelligent and being socially competent. In rural Zambia, for example, the concept of intelligence involves being both clever and responsible. Elena Grigorenko and her colleagues (2001) have also studied the concept of intelligence among rural Africans. They found that people in the Luo culture of rural Kenya view intelligence as consisting of four domains: (1) academic intelligence; (2) social qualities such as respect, responsibility, and consideration; (3) practical

culture-fair tests Tests of intelligence that are designed to be free of cultural bias.

thinking; and (4) comprehension. In another study in the same culture, children who scored highly on a test of knowledge about medicinal herbs—a measure of practical intelligence—tended to score poorly on tests of academic intelligence (Sternberg & others, 2001). These results indicated that practical and academic intelligence can develop independently and may even conflict with each other. They also suggest that the values of a culture may influence the direction in which a child develops. In a cross-cultural context, then, intelligence depends a great deal on environment.

The Use and Misuse of Intelligence Tests Psychological tests are tools. Like all tools, their effectiveness depends on the knowledge, skill, and integrity of the user. A hammer can be used to build a beautiful kitchen cabinet, or it can be used as a weapon of assault. Like a hammer, psychological tests can be used for positive purposes, or they can be badly abused. Here are some cautions about IQ that can help you avoid the pitfalls of using information about a child's intelligence in negative ways:

- *Avoid stereotyping and expectations.* A special concern is that the scores on an IQ test easily can lead to stereotypes and expectations about students. Sweeping generalizations are too often made on the basis of an IQ score. An IQ test should always be considered a measure of current performance. It is not a measure of fixed potential. Maturational changes and enriched environmental experiences can advance a student's intelligence.
- *Know that IQ is not a sole indicator of competence.* Another concern about IQ tests occurs when they are used as the main or sole assessment of competence. A high IQ is not the ultimate human value. As we have seen in this chapter, it is important to consider not only students' intellectual competence in such areas as verbal skills but also their creative and practical skills.
- *Use caution in interpreting an overall IQ score.* In evaluating a child's intelligence, it is wiser to think of intelligence as consisting of a number of domains. Keep in mind the different types of intelligence described by Sternberg and Gardner. Remember that, by considering the different domains of intelligence, you can find that every child has at least one or more strengths.

The Extremes of Intelligence
Intelligence tests have been used to discover indications of mental retardation or intellectual giftedness, the extremes of intelligence. At times, intelligence tests have been misused for this purpose. Keeping in mind the theme that an intelligence test should not be used as the sole indicator of mental retardation or giftedness, we will explore the nature of these intellectual extremes.

Mental Retardation **Mental retardation** is a condition of limited mental ability in which an individual has a low IQ, usually below 70 on a traditional intelligence test, and has difficulty adapting to everyday life. About 5 million Americans fit this definition of mental retardation.

There are several classifications of mental retardation. About 89 percent of the mentally retarded fall into the mild category, with IQs of 55 to 70. About 6 percent are classified as moderately retarded, with IQs of 40 to 54; these people can attain a second-grade level of skills and may be able to support themselves as adults through some types of labor. About 3.5 percent of the mentally retarded are in the severe category, with IQs of 25 to 39; these individuals learn to talk and engage in very simple tasks but require extensive supervision. Less than 1 percent have IQs below 25; they fall into the profoundly mentally retarded classification and need constant supervision (Drew & Hardman, 2000).

Mental retardation can have an organic cause, or it can be social and cultural in origin:

- **Organic retardation** is mental retardation that is caused by a genetic disorder or by brain damage; the word *organic* refers to the tissues or organs of the body, so there is some physical damage in organic retardation. Down syndrome,

A child with Down syndrome. *What causes a child to develop Down syndrome? In which major classification of mental retardation does the condition fall?*

mental retardation A condition of limited mental ability in which an individual has a low IQ, usually below 70 on a traditional test of intelligence, and has difficulty adapting to everyday life.

organic retardation Mental retardation that involves some physical damage and is caused by a genetic disorder or brain damage.

Careers in Life-Span Development

Sterling Jones, Supervisor of Gifted and Talented Education

Sterling Jones is program supervisor for gifted and talented children in the Detroit Public School System. Sterling has been working with children who are gifted for more than three decades. He believes that students' mastery of skills mainly depends on the amount of time devoted to instruction and the length of time allowed for learning. Thus, he believes that many basic strategies for challenging children who are gifted to develop their skills can be applied to a wider range of students than once believed. He has rewritten several pamphlets for use by teachers and parents, including *How to Help Your Child Succeed* and *Gifted and Talented Education for Everyone.*

Sterling has undergraduate and graduate degrees from Wayne State University and taught English for a number of years before becoming involved in the program for gifted children. He also has written materials on African Americans, such as *Voices from the Black Experience,* that are used in the Detroit schools.

Sterling Jones with some of the children in the gifted program in the Detroit Public School System.

cultural-familial retardation Retardation that is characterized by no evidence of organic brain damage, but the individual's IQ is between 50 and 70.

gifted Having above-average intelligence (an IQ of 130 or higher) and/or superior talent for something.

one form of mental retardation, occurs when an extra chromosome is present in an individual's genetic makeup. It is not known why the extra chromosome is present, but it may involve the health or age of the female ovum or male sperm. Most people who suffer from organic retardation have IQs that range between 0 and 50.

- **Cultural-familial retardation** is a mental deficit in which no evidence of organic brain damage can be found; individuals' IQs range from 50 to 70. Psychologists suspect that such mental deficits result from the normal variation that distributes people along the range of intelligence scores above 50, combined with growing up in a below-average intellectual environment.

Giftedness There have always been people whose abilities and accomplishments outshine others'—the whiz kid in class, the star athlete, the natural musician. People who are **gifted** have above-average intelligence (an IQ of 130 or higher) and/or superior talent for something. When it comes to programs for the gifted, most school systems select children who have intellectual superiority and academic aptitude. Children who are talented in the visual and performing arts (arts, drama, dance), athletics, or other special aptitudes tend to be overlooked (Olszewski-Kubilius, 2003; Smith, 2005; Winner, 2000).

There has been speculation that giftedness is linked with having a mental disorder. However, no relation between giftedness and mental disorder has been found. Recent studies support the conclusion that gifted people tend to be more mature, have fewer emotional problems than others, and grow up in a positive family climate (Davidson, 2000; Feldman, 2001).

What are the characteristics of children who are gifted? Lewis Terman (1925) conducted an extensive study of 1,500 children whose Stanford-Binet IQs averaged 150. A popular myth is that gifted children are maladjusted, but Terman found in his study that they were not only academically gifted but also socially well adjusted. Many of these gifted children went on to become successful doctors, lawyers, professors, and scientists.

Ellen Winner (1996) described three criteria that characterize gifted children, whether in art, music, or academic domains:

1. *Precocity.* Gifted children are precocious. They begin to master an area earlier than their peers. Learning in their domain is more effortless for them than for ordinary children. In most instances, these gifted children are precocious because they have an inborn high ability in a particular domain or domains.
2. *Marching to their own drummer.* Gifted children learn in a qualitatively different way than ordinary children. One way that they march to a different drummer is that they need minimal help, or scaffolding, from adults to learn. In many instances, they resist any kind of explicit instruction. They also often make discoveries on their own and solve problems in unique ways.

3. *A passion to master.* Gifted children are driven to understand the domain in which they have high ability. They display an intense, obsessive interest and an ability to focus. They are not children who need to be pushed by their parents. They motivate themselves, says Winner.

Is giftedness a product of heredity or environment? Likely both. Individuals who are gifted recall that they had signs of high ability in a particular area at a very young age, prior to or at the beginning of formal training (Howe & others, 1995). This suggests the importance of innate ability in giftedness. However, researchers also have found that individuals with world-class status in the arts, mathematics, science, and sports all report strong family support and years of training and practice (Bloom, 1985). Deliberate practice is an important characteristic of individuals who become experts in a particular domain. For example, in one study, the best musicians engaged in twice as much deliberate practice over their lives as the least successful ones did (Ericsson, Krampe, & Tesch, 1993).

One career opportunity in life-span development involves working with children who are gifted as a teacher or supervisor. To read about the work of a supervisor of gifted and talented education, see the Careers in Life-Span Development insert.

Children Who Are Gifted

Review and Reflect: Learning Goal 3

3 Explain cognitive changes in middle and late childhood

REVIEW

- What characterizes Piaget's stage of concrete operational thought? What are some contributions and criticisms of Piaget?
- How do children process information in the middle and late childhood years?
- What is intelligence? What are some different forms of intelligence? What are some issues related to intelligence?

REFLECT

- A CD-ROM, *Children's IQ and Achievement Test,* now lets parents test their child's IQ and how well the child is performing in relation to their grade in school. What might be some problems with parents giving their children an IQ test?

4 LANGUAGE DEVELOPMENT

| Vocabulary and Grammar | Reading | Bilingualism |

Children gain new skills as they enter school that make it possible to learn to read and write: These include increasingly using language in a displaced way, learning what a word is, and learning how to recognize and talk about sounds (Berko Gleason, 2003). They have to learn the *alphabetic principle,* that the letters of the alphabet represent sounds of the language. As children develop during middle and late childhood, changes in their vocabulary and grammar also take place (Hoff, 2003).

What are the main approaches to teaching children how to read?

Reading Research

Vocabulary and Grammar

During middle and late childhood, changes take place in the way children select words. When asked to say the first word that comes to mind when they hear a word, young children typically provide a word that often follows the word in a sentence. For example, when asked to respond to "dog" the young child may say "barks," or to the word "eat" say "lunch." At about 7 years of age, children begin to respond with a word that is the same part of speech as the stimulus word. For example, a child may now respond to the word "dog" with "cat" or "horse." To "eat," they now might say "drink." This is evidence that children now have begun to categorize their vocabulary by parts of speech (Berko Gleason, 2003). The process of categorizing becomes easier as children increase their vocabulary. Likewise, a larger vocabulary facilitates learning to read. Children who begin elementary school with a small vocabulary are at risk when it comes to learning to read (Berko Gleason, 2003).

Children make similar advances in grammar. The elementary school child's improvement in logical reasoning and analytical skills helps in the understanding of such constructions as the appropriate use of comparatives (*shorter, deeper*) and subjectives ("If you were president . . ."). During the elementary school years, children become increasingly able to understand and use complex grammar, such as the following sentence: *The boy who kissed his mother wore a hat.* They also learn to use language in a more connected way, producing connected discourse. They become able to relate sentences to one another to produce descriptions, definitions, and narratives that make sense. Children must be able to do these things orally before they can be expected to deal with them in written assignments.

Reading

Before learning to read, children learn to use language to talk about things that are not present; they learn what a word is; and they learn how to recognize sounds and talk about them (Berko Gleason, 2003). How should children be taught to read? Currently, debate focuses on the whole-language approach versus the basic-skills-and-phonics approach.

The **whole-language approach** stresses that reading instruction should parallel children's natural language learning. In some whole-language classes beginning readers are taught to recognize whole words or even entire sentences, and to use the context of what they are reading to guess at the meaning of words. Reading materials should be whole and meaningful—that is, children should be given material in its complete form, such as stories and poems, so that they learn to understand language's communicative function. Reading should be connected with listening and writing skills. Although there are variations in whole-language programs, most share the premise that reading should be integrated with other skills and subjects, such as science and social studies, and that it should focus on real-world material. Thus, a class might read newspapers, magazines, or books, and then write about and discuss them.

In contrast, the **basic-skills-and-phonics approach** emphasizes that reading instruction should teach phonics and its basic rules for translating written symbols into sounds. Early reading instruction should involve simplified materials. Only after children have learned correspondence rules that relate spoken phonemes to the alphabet letters that are used to represent them should they be given complex reading materials, such as books and poems.

Which approach is better? Children can benefit from both approaches (Smith, 2004a). Researchers have found strong evidence that the basic-skills-and-phonics approach should be used in teaching children to read but that students also

whole-language approach An approach to reading instruction based on the idea that instruction should parallel children's natural language learning. Reading materials should be whole and meaningful.

basic-skills-and-phonics approach The idea that reading instruction should teach both phonics and the basic rules for translating written symbols into sounds.

benefit from the whole-language approach (Fox & Hull, 2002; Heilman, Blair, & Rupley, 2002; Silva & Martins, 2003). Training for phonological awareness is best when it is integrated with reading and writing, is simple, and is conducted in small groups rather than with a whole class (Stahl, 2002).

Reading, like other important skills, takes time and effort (Popp, 2005). In a national assessment, children in the fourth grade had higher scores on a national reading test when they read 11 or more pages daily for school and homework (National Assessment of Educational Progress, 2000) (see figure 10.11). Teachers who required students to read a great deal on a daily basis had students who were more proficient at reading than teachers who required little reading by their students.

Bilingualism

Learning a second language is easier for children than for adolescents or adults. Adults make faster initial progress, but their eventual success in the second language is not as great as children's. For example, in one study, Chinese and Korean adults who immigrated to the United States at different ages were given a test of grammatical knowledge (Johnston & Newport, 1991). Those who began learning English when they were 3 to 7 years old scored as well as native speakers on the test, but those who arrived in the United States and started learning English in later childhood or adolescence had lower test scores (see figure 10.12). Children's ability to pronounce words with the correct accent in a second language also decreases with age, with an especially sharp drop occurring after the age of about 10 to 12 (Asher & Garcia, 1969). In sum, researchers have found that early bilingual exposure is optimal and ensures the least amount of damage to the home language and to the new language (Lesaux & Siegel, 2003; Lessow-Hurley, 2005; Petitto, Kovelman, & Harasymowycz, 2003).

Students in the United States are far behind their counterparts in many developed countries in learning a second language. For example, in Russia, schools have 10 grades, called *forms,* which roughly correspond to the 12 grades in American schools. Children begin school at age 7 in Russia and begin learning English in the third form. Because of this emphasis on teaching English, most Russian citizens under the age of 40 today are able to speak at least some English.

U.S. students may be missing more than the chance to acquire a skill by not learning to speak a second language (Soltero, 2004). *Bilingualism*—the ability to speak two languages—has a positive effect on children's cognitive development (Gibbons & Ng, 2004). Children who are fluent in two languages perform better than their single-language counterparts on tests of control of attention, concept formation, analytical reasoning, cognitive flexibility, and cognitive complexity (Bialystok, 1999, 2001). They also are more conscious of the structure of spoken and written language and better at noticing errors of grammar and meaning, skills that benefit their reading ability (Bialystok, 1993, 1997).

A current controversy related to bilingualism involves bilingual education. To read about this controversy, see the Diversity in Life-Span Development interlude.

Diversity in Life-Span Development

Bilingual Education

As many as 10 million children in the United States come from homes in which English is not the primary language. What is the best way to teach these children?

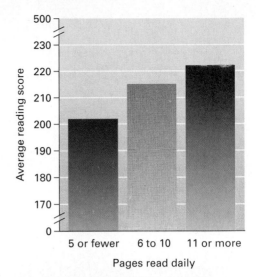

FIGURE 10.11 The Relation of Reading Achievement to Number of Pages Read Daily
In the recent analysis of reading in the fourth grade in the National Assessment of Educational Progress (2000), reading more pages daily in school and as part of homework assignments was related to higher scores on a reading test in which scores ranged from 0 to 500.

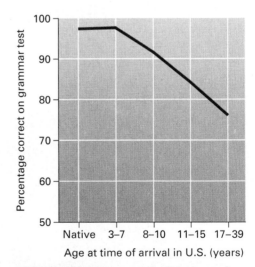

FIGURE 10.12 Grammar Proficiency and Age at Arrival in the United States
In one study, 10 years after arriving in the United States, individuals from China and Korea took a grammar test (Johnson & Newport, 1991). People who arrived before the age of 8 had a better grasp of grammar than those who arrived later.

For the last two decades, the preferred strategy has been *bilingual education,* which teaches academic subjects to immigrant children in their native language while slowly teaching English (Adamson, 2004; Brisk, 2005; Diaz-Rico, 2004; Farr, 2005). Advocates of bilingual education programs argue that if children who do not know English are taught only in English, they will fall behind in academic subjects. How, they ask, can 7-year-olds learn arithmetic or history taught only in English when they do not speak the language?

Critics of bilingual education argue that as a result of these programs, the children of immigrants are not learning English, which puts them at a permanent disadvantage in U.S. society. Since a California referendum in 1998 repealed bilingual education, a number of states have passed laws declaring English to be their official language, eliminating the obligation for schools to teach minority children in languages other than English. However, many such English-only initiatives are currently being challenged in state courts.

What have researchers found regarding outcomes of bilingual education programs? The results generally support bilingual education in that (1) children have difficulty in a subject when it is taught in a language they do not understand; and (2) when both languages are integrated in the classroom, children learn the second language more readily and participate more actively (Hakuta, 2000, 2001).

Some critics argue that too often it is believed that immigrant children need only one year of bilingual education. However, researchers have found that in general it takes immigrant children approximately three to five years to develop speaking proficiency and seven years to develop reading proficiency in English (Hakuta, Butler, & Witt, 2000). Also, it is important to recognize that individual variations characterize the ability of immigrant children to learn English. Children who come from lower-socioeconomic backgrounds have more difficulty than those from higher-socioeconomic backgrounds (Hakuta, 2001). Thus, immigrant children, especially those from low-socioeconomic backgrounds, may need more years of bilingual education than they currently are receiving.

Review and Reflect: Learning Goal 4

 4 **Discuss language development in middle and late childhood**

REVIEW

- What are some changes in vocabulary and grammar in the middle and late childhood years?
- What controversy characterizes how to teach children to read?
- What is bilingual education? What issues are involved in bilingual education?

REFLECT

- What are some of the key considerations in using a balanced approach to teaching reading?

Reach Your Learning Goals

Physical and Cognitive Development in Middle and Late Childhood

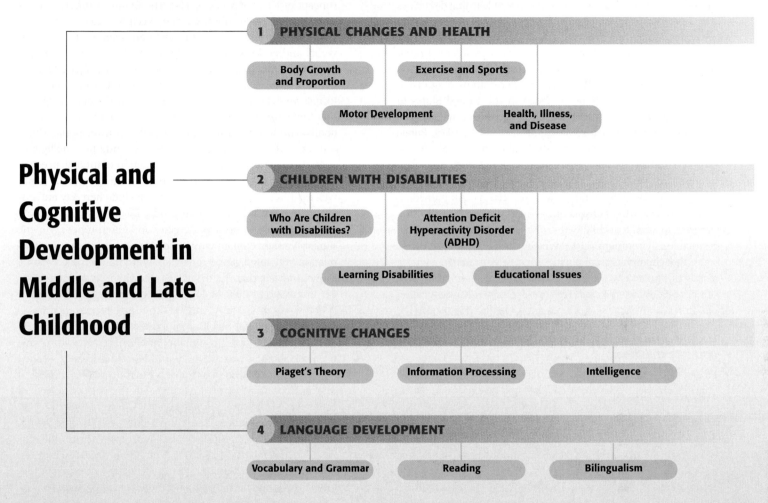

1 PHYSICAL CHANGES AND HEALTH

- Body Growth and Proportion
- Exercise and Sports
- Motor Development
- Health, Illness, and Disease

2 CHILDREN WITH DISABILITIES

- Who Are Children with Disabilities?
- Attention Deficit Hyperactivity Disorder (ADHD)
- Learning Disabilities
- Educational Issues

3 COGNITIVE CHANGES

- Piaget's Theory
- Information Processing
- Intelligence

4 LANGUAGE DEVELOPMENT

- Vocabulary and Grammar
- Reading
- Bilingualism

Summary

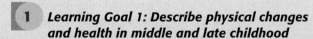

1 Learning Goal 1: Describe physical changes and health in middle and late childhood

- The period of middle and late childhood involves slow, consistent growth. During this period, children grow an average of 2 to 3 inches a year. Muscle mass and strength gradually increase. Among the most pronounced changes in body growth and proportion are decreases in head circumference, waist circumference, and leg length in relation to body height.
- During the middle and late childhood years, motor development becomes much smoother and more coordinated. Children gain greater control over their bodies and can sit and attend for longer periods of time. However, their lives should be activity-oriented and very active. Increased myelination of the central nervous system is reflected in improved motor skills. Improved fine motor skills appear in the form of handwriting development. Boys are usually better at gross motor skills, girls at fine motor skills.
- Most American children do not get nearly enough exercise. Children's participation in sports can have consequences that are either positive (exercise and self-esteem) or negative (pressure to win and physical injuries).

- For the most part, middle and late childhood is a time of excellent health. The most common cause of severe injury and death in childhood is motor vehicle accidents, with most occurring at or near the child's home or school. Cancer is the second leading cause of death in children (after accidents). Leukemia is the most common childhood cancer. Obesity in children poses serious health risks. The increase in the prevalence of obesity among children is linked to poor diet, inadequate exercise, and poor eating habits.

2 Learning Goal 2: Identify children with different types of disabilities and issues in educating them

- An estimated 10 percent of U.S. children with a disability receive special education or related services. Slightly more than 50 percent of these students are classified as having a learning disability. In the federal government classification, this classification includes attention deficit hyperactivity disorder, or ADHD.
- A learning disability includes three components: (1) a minimum IQ level; (2) a significant difficulty in a school-related area; and (3) exclusion of only severe emotional disorders,

second-language background, sensory disabilities, and/or specific neurological deficits. Dyslexia is a category of learning disabilities that involves a severe impairment in the ability to read and spell.

- Attention deficit hyperactivity disorder (ADHD) is a disability in which individuals consistently show problems in one or more of these areas: (1) inattention, (2) hyperactivity, and (3) impulsivity. ADHD has been increasingly diagnosed.

- A number of laws have been passed in the United States to ensure that children with a disability receive a free, appropriate education and are provided adequate services. In 1975, Public Law 94-142, the Education for All Handicapped Children Act, required that all children be given a free, appropriate public education. In 1990, Public Law 94-142 was renamed the Individuals with Disabilities Education Act (IDEA). An individual education plan (IEP) consists of a written plan that spells out a program tailored to a child with a disability. The concept of least restrictive environment (LRE), which is contained in the IDEA, states that children with disabilities must be educated in a setting that is as similar as possible to the one in which children without disabilities are educated. The term *inclusion* means educating children with disabilities full-time in the regular classroom.

Learning Goal 3: Explain cognitive changes in middle and late childhood

- Piaget said that the stage of concrete operational thought characterizes children from about 7 to 11 years of age. This stage involves operations, conservation, classification, seriation, and transitivity. Thought is not as abstract as later in development. Piaget's ideas have been applied extensively to education. Critics question Piaget's estimates of competence at different developmental levels, his stages concept, and other ideas. Neo-Piagetians argue that Piaget got some things right but that his theory needs considerable revision. Neo-Piagetians place more emphasis on how children process information, strategies, speed of information processing, and the division of cognitive problems into more precise steps.

- Long-term memory increases in middle and late childhood. Knowledge and expertise influence memory. Strategies, such as imagery and elaboration, can be used by children to improve their memory. Fuzzy trace theory has been proposed to explain developmental changes in memory. Critical thinking involves thinking reflectively and productively, as well as evaluating the evidence. A special concern is the lack of emphasis on critical thinking in many schools. Creative thinking is the ability to think in novel and unusual ways and to come up with unique solutions to problems. Guilford distinguished between convergent and divergent thinking. A number of strategies can be used to encourage children's creative thinking, including brainstorming. Metacognition is cognition about cognition, or knowing about knowing. Most metacognitive studies have focused on metamemory. Pressley views the key to education as helping students learn a rich repertoire of strategies.

- Intelligence consists of problem-solving skills and the ability to adapt to and learn from life's everyday experiences. Interest in intelligence often focuses on individual differences and assessment. Binet and Simon developed the first intelligence test. Bi-

net developed the concept of mental age and Stern created the concept of IQ as MA/CA × 100. The Stanford-Binet approximates a normal distribution. The Wechsler scales are widely used to assess intelligence and yield an overall IQ, as well as verbal and performance IQs. Spearman proposed that people have a general intelligence (*g*) and specific types of intelligence (*s*). Sternberg proposed that intelligence comes in three main forms: analytical, creative, and practical. Gardner proposes that there are eight types of intelligence: verbal, math, spatial, bodily-kinesthetic, interpersonal skills, intrapersonal skills, musical skills, and naturalist skills. The multiple-intelligence approaches have expanded our conception of intelligence, but critics argue that the research base for these approaches is not well established. Issues in intelligence include heredity and environment, ethnicity and culture, and the use and misuse of intelligence tests. In terms of heredity and environment, genetic similarity might explain why identical twins show stronger correlations on intelligence tests than fraternal twins do. Some studies indicate that the IQs of adopted children are more similar to the IQs of their biological parents than to those of their adoptive parents. Many studies show that intelligence has a reasonably strong heritability component. Criticisms of the heritability concept have been made. Intelligence test scores have risen considerably around the world in recent decades—called the Flynn effect—and this supports the role of environment in intelligence. Ramey's research revealed the positive effects of educational child care on intelligence. Cultures vary in the way they define intelligence. Early intelligence tests favored White, middle-socioeconomic-status individuals over urban individuals. Tests may be biased against certain groups because they are not familiar with a standard form of English, with the content tested, or with the testing situation. Tests are likely to reflect the values and experience of the dominant culture. In the United States, children from African American and Latino families score below children from White families on standardized intelligence tests. Mental retardation involves low IQ and problems in adapting to everyday life. One classification of mental retardation consists of organic or cultural-familial retardation. A child who is gifted has above-average intelligence and/or superior talent for something. Terman contributed to our understanding that gifted children are not more maladjusted than nongifted children. Three characteristics of gifted children are precocity, individuality, and a passion to master.

Learning Goal 4: Discuss language development in middle and late childhood

- Children become more analytical and logical in their approach to words and grammar. In terms of grammar, children now better understand comparatives and subjectives. They become increasingly able to use complex grammar and produce narratives that make sense.

- A current debate in reading focuses on the basic-skills-and-phonics approach versus the whole-language approach. The basic-skills-and-phonics approach advocates phonetics instruction and giving children simplified materials. The whole-language approach stresses that reading instruction should parallel children's natural language learning and giving children whole-language materials, such as books and poems.

- Bilingual education aims to teach academic subjects to immigrant children in their native languages (most often in Spanish) while gradually adding English instruction. Researchers have found that bilingualism does not interfere with performance in either language. Success in learning a second language is greater in childhood than in adolescence.

Key Terms

learning disability 298
dyslexia 298
attention deficit hyperactivity disorder (ADHD) 299
individualized education plan (IEP) 300
least restrictive environment (LRE) 300
inclusion 300
seriation 302

transitivity 302
neo-Piagetians 304
long-term memory 304
strategies 305
elaboration 305
fuzzy trace theory 305
critical thinking 306
creative thinking 306
convergent thinking 306
divergent thinking 306

brainstorming 306
metacognition 307
intelligence 308
individual differences 308
mental age (MA) 308
intelligence quotient (IQ) 308
normal distribution 308
triarchic theory of intelligence 310
heritability 312

stereotype threat 315
culture-fair tests 316
mental retardation 317
organic retardation 317
cultural-familial retardation 318
gifted 318
whole-language approach 320
basic-skills-and-phonics approach 320

Key People

Jean Piaget 301
Charles Brainerd and Valerie Reyna 305
John Dewey 306
Jacqueline and Martin Brooks 306
J. P. Guilford 306

Teresa Amabile 307
Deanna Kuhn 307
Michael Pressley 308
Alfred Binet 308
Theophile Simon 308
William Stern 308
David Wechsler 309

Charles Spearman 310
L. L. Thurstone 310
Robert J. Sternberg 310
Howard Gardner 310
Nathan Brody 311
Arthur Jensen 311
Craig Ramey 314

Richard Herrnstein and Charles Murray 315
Robert Serpell 316
Lewis Terman 318
Ellen Winner 318

E-Learning Tools

To help you master the material in this chapter, you'll find a number of valuable study tools on the LifeMap CD-ROM that accompanies this book and on the Online Learning Center for *Life-Span Development*, tenth edition, at www.mhhe.com/santrockld10.

Video Clips

In the margins of this book there are icons directing you to the LifeMap CD-ROM that accompanies the book. There you'll find a video for chapter 10 called "Interactivity: Sensorimotor Neural Circuits." One of the more noticeable developments of the middle and late childhood years is a refinement of motor skills. This segment looks at how different children achieve this new level of physical coordination.

Self-Assessment

Connect to www.mhhe.com/santrockld10 to learn more about various kinds of intelligence by completing the self-assessments, *Evaluating Myself on Gardner's Eight Types of Intelligence* and *How Emotionally Intelligent Am I?*

Taking It to the Net

Connect to www.mhhe.com/santrockld10 to research the answers to these questions.

1. Clarice and Henry's daughter Emma is in second grade. Emma's teacher recently told Clarice and Henry that Emma has been showing signs of ADHD in the classroom. These symptoms seem to occur only while Emma is at school. What should Clarice and Henry do to confirm the diagnosis before Ritalin or similar drugs are prescribed?

2. Noah's parents are upset to hear that their fourth grader may have dyslexia. Noah's father voices to his son's teacher his concern that people will think Noah is slow. What should Noah's teacher inform these parents about the nature and causes of dyslexia?

3. Elizabeth has chosen to be an elementary school teacher because she feels that children in the elementary school years are especially open to the influence of their teachers. She believes that talent is created and inspired, rather than being "essential" and simply waiting to be discovered. She likes the way Gardner's theory of multiple intelligences serves to classify the various talents children have. Can Stephen Jay Gould's classic critique of *The Bell Curve* and its methods also apply to Gardner's theory? Should Elizabeth be wary of a similar reductionism in her Gardner-inspired antiessentialist approach?

Health and Well-Being, Parenting, and Education Exercises

Build your decision-making skills by trying your hand at the health and well-being, parenting, and education exercises.

Connect to www.mhhe.com/santrockld10 to research the answers and complete the exercises.

CHAPTER

*Children are busy
becoming something they
have not quite grasped
yet, something which
keeps changing.*

—ALASTAIR REID
*American Poet,
20th Century*

Socioemotional Development in Middle and Late Childhood

Chapter Outline

EMOTIONAL AND PERSONALITY DEVELOPMENT

The Self

Emotional Development

Moral Development

Gender

FAMILIES

Parent-Child Issues

Societal Changes in Families

PEERS

Friends

Peer Status

Social Cognition

Bullying

SCHOOLS

Contemporary Approaches to Student Learning and Assessment

The Transition to Elementary School

Socioeconomic Status and Ethnicity

Cross-Cultural Comparisons of Achievement

Learning Goals

1 Discuss emotional and personality development in middle and late childhood

2 Describe parent-child issues and societal changes in families

3 Identify changes in peer relationships in middle and late childhood

4 Characterize the transition to elementary school and sociocultural aspects of schooling and achievement

This 14-year-old boy in Nepal is thought to be the sixth holiest Buddhist in the world. How might the moral reasoning of this boy be different than Kohlberg's theory predicts?

crucial in a given situation by presenting them with a series of dilemmas and a list of definitions of the major issues involved (Kohlberg's procedure does not make use of such a list). In the dilemma of Heinz and the druggist, individuals might be asked whether a community's laws should be upheld or whether Heinz should be willing to risk being injured or caught as a burglar. They might also be asked to list the most important values that govern human interaction. They are given six stories and asked to rate the importance of each issue in deciding what ought to be done. Then they are asked to list what they believe are the four most important issues. Rest argued that this method provides a more valid and reliable way to assess moral thinking than Kohlberg's method (Rest & others, 1999).

Culture and Moral Reasoning   Yet another criticism of Kohlberg's view is that it is culturally biased (Banks, 1993; Miller, 2005; Tappan, 2005; Wainryb, 2005). One review of 45 studies in 27 diverse world cultures provided support for the universality of Kohlberg's first four stages, although there was more cultural diversity at stages 5 and 6 (Snarey, 1987). In this review, it was also concluded that moral reasoning is more culture-specific than Kohlberg envisioned and that Kohlberg's scoring system does not recognize higher-level moral reasoning in certain cultural groups (Snarey, 1987). Examples of higher-level moral reasoning that would not be scored as such by Kohlberg's system are values related to communal equity and collective happiness in Israel, the unity and sacredness of all life-forms in India, and the relation of the individual to the community in New Guinea. These examples of moral reasoning would not be scored at the highest level in Kohlberg's system because they do not emphasize the individual's rights and abstract principles of justice. One study assessed the moral development of 20 adolescent male Buddhist monks in Nepal (Huebner & Garrod, 1993). The issue of justice, a basic theme in Kohlberg's theory, was not of paramount importance in the monks' moral views, and their concerns about the prevention of suffering and the role of compassion are not captured by Kohlberg's theory.

Families and Moral Development   Kohlberg believed that family processes are essentially unimportant in children's moral development. As noted earlier, he argued that parent-child relationships usually provide children with little opportunity for give-and-take or perspective taking. Rather, Kohlberg said that such opportunities are more likely to be provided by children's peer relations (Brabeck, 2000).

Did Kohlberg underestimate the contribution of family relationships to moral development? A number of developmentalists emphasize that *inductive discipline*, which uses reasoning and focuses children's attention on the consequences of their actions for others, positively influences moral development (Hoffman, 1970). They also stress that parents' moral values influence children's developing moral thoughts (Gibbs, 1993). Nonetheless, most developmentalists agree with Kohlberg and Piaget, that peers too play an important role in the development of moral reasoning.

Gender and the Care Perspective   Carol Gilligan (1982, 1992, 1996) argues that Kohlberg's theory is based on a male norm that puts abstract principles above relationships and concern for others. Kohlberg's theory takes a **justice perspective,** which is a moral perspective that focuses on the rights of the individual; individuals stand alone and independently make moral decisions. In contrast, Gilligan argues for a **care perspective,** which is a moral perspective that views people in terms of their connectedness with others and emphasizes interpersonal communication, relationships with others, and concern for others. According to Gilligan, Kohlberg greatly underplayed the care perspective, perhaps because he was a male, because most of his research was with males rather than females, and because he used male responses as a model for his theory.

In extensive interviews with girls from 6 to 18 years of age, Gilligan (1992, 1996) found that girls consistently interpret moral dilemmas in terms of human

justice perspective A moral perspective that focuses on the rights of the individual; individuals independently make moral decisions.

care perspective The moral perspective of Carol Gilligan, which views people in terms of their connectedness with others and emphasizes interpersonal communication, relationships with others, and concern for others.

relationships and base these interpretations on listening and watching other people. According to Gilligan, girls have the ability to sensitively pick up different rhythms in relationships and often are able to follow the pathways of feelings.

Gilligan suggests that girls reach a critical juncture in their development when they reach adolescence. Usually around 11 to 12 years of age, girls become aware that their intense interest in intimacy is not prized by the male-dominated culture, even though society values women as caring and altruistic. The dilemma arises when girls are presented with a choice that makes them look either selfish or selfless. Gilligan argues that, as adolescent girls experience this dilemma, they increasingly silence their "distinctive voice."

A meta-analysis (a statistical analysis that combines the results of many different studies) casts doubt on Gilligan's claim of substantial gender differences in moral judgment (Jaffee & Hyde, 2000). In this study, overall, only a small gender difference in care-based reasoning favored females, but this gender difference was greater in adolescence than in childhood. When differences occurred, they were better explained by the nature of the dilemma than by gender (for example, both males and females tended to use care reasoning when dealing with interpersonal dilemmas and justice reasoning when handling societal dilemmas).

Researchers have found that females consider care-oriented, relational moral dilemmas to be more salient or moral than males do (Eisenberg & Morris, 2004). In support of this idea, one recent study found that females rated prosocial dilemmas as more significant than males did (Wark & Krebs, 2000). Another recent study revealed that young adolescent girls used more care-based reasoning about dating dilemmas than boys (Weisz & Black, 2002).

Social Conventional Reasoning

Some theorists and researchers argue that it is important to distinguish between moral reasoning and social conventional reasoning, something they believe Kohlberg did not adequately do (Helwig & Turiel, 2004; Smetana, 2005; Smetana & Turiel, 2003; Turiel, 1998, 2003, 2005). **Social conventional reasoning** focuses on thoughts about social consensus and convention. In contrast, moral reasoning emphasizes ethical issues. Conventional rules are created to control behavioral irregularities and maintain the social system. Conventional rules are arbitrary and subject to individual judgment. For example, using a fork and spoon at meals is a social conventional rule, as is raising one's hand in class before speaking.

In contrast, moral rules are not arbitrary and determined by whim. They also are not created by social consensus. Rather, moral rules are obligatory, widely accepted, and somewhat impersonal (Turiel, 1998). Thus, rules pertaining to lying, cheating, stealing, and physically harming another person are moral rules because violation of these rules affronts ethical standards that exist apart from social consensus and convention. In sum, moral judgments involve concepts of justice, whereas social conventional judgments are concepts of social organization.

Prosocial Behavior and Altruism

Children's moral behavior can involve negative, antisocial acts—such as lying, cheating, and stealing—or it can involve *prosocial behavior*—the positive aspects of moral behavior, such as showing empathy to someone or behaving altruistically (Carlo, 2005; Hoffman, 2002). Whereas Kohlberg's and Gilligan's theories have focused primarily on the cognitive, thinking aspects of moral development, the study of prosocial moral behavior has placed more emphasis on its behavioral aspects (Grusec, Davidov, & Lundell, 2002).

Altruism is an unselfish interest in helping someone else. Human acts of altruism are plentiful—the hardworking laborer who places $5 in a Salvation Army kettle; rock concerts staged to feed the hungry, help farmers, and fund AIDS research; the child who takes in a wounded cat and cares for it, and so on.

William Damon (1988) described a developmental sequence of children's altruism, especially of sharing. Most sharing during the first three years of life is done not for reasons of empathy but for the fun of the social play ritual or out of mere

Carol Gilligan is shown with some of the students she has interviewed about the importance of relationships in a female's development. *What is Gilligan's view of moral development?*

Gilligan's Care Perspective

social conventional reasoning Thoughts about social consensus and convention, as opposed to moral reasoning that stresses ethical issues.

altruism Unselfish interest in helping another person.

imitation. Then, at about 4 years of age, a combination of empathic awareness and adult encouragement produces a sense of obligation on the part of the child to share with others. This obligation forces the child to share, even though the child may not perceive this as the best way to have fun. Most 4-year-olds are not selfless saints, however. Children believe they have an obligation to share but do not necessarily think they should be as generous to others as they are to themselves.

By the start of the elementary school years, children genuinely begin to express more objective ideas about fairness. It is common to hear 6-year-old children use the word *fair* as synonymous with *equal* or *same*. By the mid to late elementary school years, children also believe that equity means special treatment for those who deserve it. Missing from the factors that guide children's altruism is one that many adults might expect to be the most influential of all: the motivation to obey adult authority figures. Surprisingly, a number of studies have shown that adult authority has only a small influence on children's sharing (Eisenberg, 1982). Parental advice and prodding certainly foster standards of sharing, but the give-and-take of peer requests and arguments provides the most immediate stimulation of sharing.

Prosocial behavior occurs more often in adolescence than in childhood, although examples of caring for others and comforting someone in distress occur even during the preschool years (Eisenberg & Fabes, 1998; Eisenberg & Morris, 2004). The Research in Life-Span Development interlude focuses on a study that examines the consistency and development of prosocial behavior.

Research in Life-Span Development
The Consistency and Development of Prosocial Behavior

Nancy Eisenberg and her colleagues (1999) studied 32 individuals from the time they were 4 to 5 years of age to when they were in their early twenties. They were assessed on eleven occasions through a variety of procedures, including observations, interviews, parents' reports, and friends' reports. Observations of prosocial behavior in the preschool the children were attending focused on behaviors of sharing, helping, and offering comfort. In elementary school, the children were given an opportunity to anonymously donate to a charity for needy children money that had been given to them by the experimenter (8 nickels). Their helping behavior also was assessed in such tasks as giving them an opportunity to help the experimenter pick up dropped paper clips. In the later elementary school years, through adolescence, and into their early twenties, the individuals filled out a self-report scale of items that focused on altruism.

The results indicated that the observed prosocial behaviors in preschool (sharing, helping, and offering comfort) were related to the children's prosocial behavior in the elementary school years and in the early twenties. These findings support the view that prosocial behavior is rather stable from the early childhood years into at least the first part of early adulthood.

Gender

In chapter 9, we discussed the biological, cognitive, and social influences on gender development. Gender is such a pervasive aspect of an individual's identity that we will further consider its role in children's development here. Gender-related topics we will now examine are gender stereotypes, similarities and differences, and gender-role classification.

Carolina, when Lipsitz was directo[...]
And, in a 1987 national poll, teach[...]
number one reason that children l[...]

Although latchkey children m[...]
latchkey children vary enormously[...]
ing parents (Belle, 1999). Parents n[...]
their latchkey children's lives can [...]
experiences suggest that parental [...]
child cope more effectively with l[...]
pressure (Galambos & Maggs, 1989[...]
mal after-school program that incl[...]
ties was associated with better acad[...]
parison with other types of after-s[...]
self-care) (Posner & Vandell, 1994)[...]
after-school programs have warm [...]
ule, multiple activities, and oppo[...]
peers (Pierce, Hamm, & Vandell, 1[...]

Participation in five types of ou[...]
extracurricular activities, father care[...]
examined in one recent study to de[...]
achievement toward the end of the [...]
work, 2004). "Children who con[...]
during kindergarten and first grad[...]
than children who did not consist[...]
other types of out-of-school care [...]
grade" (p. 280). Parents who enrol[...]
more achievement-oriented and [...]
children than parents who don't p[...]

Review and Reflect: L[...]

2 Describe parent-child [...]

REVIEW
- What are some important[...]
- What are some societal c[...]
  development?

REFLECT
- What was your relationsh[...]
  tary school? How do you[...]

3 PEERS

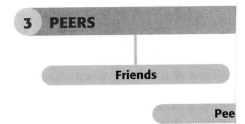

Friends

Pee[...]

During middle and late childhood[...]
their peers. First, we will explo[...]
aspects of peer relations.

sna[...]
exp[...]

and[...]
uni[...]
and[...]

imp[...]
pro[...]
mo[...]
bot[...]
con[...]
istic[...]
boy[...]
girl[...]
on[...]
mo[...]
mo[...]

mo[...]
cou[...]
is b[...]
nin[...]
siv[...]
hig[...]
hig[...]
and[...]
set[...]

has[...]
Rea[...]
siti[...]
thi[...]
To[...]
Bo[...]
sch[...]
tea[...]
be[...]
tle[...]

Ge[...]
tra[...]
in [...]
20[...]
ge[...]

be[...]
ing[...]
te[...]
be[...]
in[...]
Fo[...]
by[...]
are[...]

ev[...]

Gender Stereotypes Gender stereotypes are broad categories that reflect our general impressions and beliefs about females and males. Researchers have found that gender stereotyping is extensive (Lenton & Blair, 2004). In one far-ranging study of college students in 30 countries, males were widely believed to be dominant, independent, aggressive, achievement-oriented, and enduring, while females were widely believed to be nurturant, affiliative, less esteemed, and more helpful in times of distress (Williams & Best, 1982). Other research continues to find that gender stereotyping is pervasive (Arima, 2003; Best, 2001; Bigler, Averhart, & Liben, 2003).

In a subsequent study, women and men who lived in more highly developed countries perceived themselves as more similar than women and men who lived in less developed countries (Williams & Best, 1989). In the more highly developed countries, the women were more likely to attend college and be gainfully employed. Thus, as sexual equality increases, male and female stereotypes, as well as actual behavioral differences, may diminish. In this study, the women were more likely to perceive similarity between the sexes than the men were (Williams & Best, 1989). And the sexes were perceived more similarly in the Christian than in the Muslim societies.

Gender Similarities and Differences Let's now examine some of the similarities and differences between the sexes, keeping in mind that (1) the differences are averages—not all females versus all males; (2) even when differences are reported, there is considerable overlap between the sexes; and (3) the differences may be due primarily to biological factors, sociocultural factors, or both. First, we will examine physical similarities and differences, and then we will turn to cognitive and socioemotional similarities and differences.

Physical Development From conception on, females have a longer life expectancy than males, and females are less likely than males to develop physical or mental disorders. Estrogen strengthens the immune system, making females more resistant to infection, for example. Female hormones also signal the liver to produce more "good" cholesterol, which makes females' blood vessels more elastic than males'. Testosterone triggers the production of low-density lipoprotein, which clogs blood vessels. Males have twice the risk of coronary disease as females. Higher levels of stress hormones cause faster clotting in males, but also higher blood pressure than in females. Women have about twice the body fat of men, most concentrated around breasts and hips. In males, fat is more likely to go to the abdomen. On the average, males grow to be 10 percent taller than females. Male hormones promote the growth of long bones; female hormones stop such growth at puberty.

Does gender matter when it comes to brain structure and function? Human brains are much alike, whether the brain belongs to a male or a female (Halpern, 2001). However, researchers have found some differences between the brains of males and females (Goldstein & others, 2001; Kimura, 2000). The following are among the differences that have been discovered:

- One part of the hypothalamus responsible for sexual behavior is larger in men than in women (Swaab & others, 2001).
- Portions of the corpus callosum—the band of tissues through which the brain's two hemispheres communicate—are larger in females than males (Le Vay, 1991).
- An area of the parietal lobe that functions in visuospatial skills is larger in males than in females (Frederikse & others, 2000).
- The areas of the brain involved in emotional expression show more metabolic activity in females than in males (Gur & others, 1995).

Cognitive Development In a classic review of gender differences, Eleanor Maccoby and Carol Jacklin (1974) concluded that males have better math and visuospatial

*T*here is more difference within the sexes than between them.
—IVY COMPTON-BURNETT
English Novelist, 20th Century

gender stereotypes Broad categories that reflect our impressions and beliefs about females and males.

How does living in a stepfamily in[fluence a] child's development?

www.mhhe.com/santrockld10

Stepfamilies
Stepfamily Resources
Stepfamily Support

In his book *Savage Inequalities*, Jonathan Kozol (*above*) vividly portrayed the problems that children of poverty face in their neighborhood and at school. *What are some of these problems?*

www.mhhe.com/santrockld10

Interview with Jonathan Kozol
Diversity and Education

reading to them, and who don't have enough money to pay for educational materials and experiences, such as books and trips to zoos and museums. They might be malnourished and live in areas where crime and violence are a way of life. Many of the schools that children from impoverished backgrounds attend have fewer resources than do the schools in higher-income neighborhoods (Bradley & Corwyn, 2002). Schools in low-income areas are more likely to have more students with lower achievement test scores, lower graduation rates, and smaller percentages of students going to college.

Schools in low-income areas also are more likely to encourage rote learning, while schools in higher-income areas are more likely to work with children to improve their thinking skills (Spring, 2002). Thus far too many schools in low-income neighborhoods provide students with environments that are not conducive to effective learning, and many of the schools' buildings and classrooms are old, crumbling, and poorly maintained.

Jonathan Kozol (1991) vividly described some of the problems that children of poverty face in their neighborhood and at school in *Savage Inequalities*. Here are some of his observations in one inner-city area. East St. Louis, Illinois, which is 98 percent African American, has no obstetric services, no regular trash collection, and few jobs. Nearly one-third of the families live on less than $7,500 a year, and 75 percent of its population lives on welfare of some form. Blocks upon blocks of housing consist of dilapidated, skeletal buildings. Residents breathe the chemical pollution of nearby Monsanto Chemical Company. Raw sewage repeatedly backs up into homes. Lead from nearby smelters poisons the soil. Child malnutrition and fear of violence are common. The problems of the streets spill over into the schools, where sewage also backs up from time to time. Classrooms and hallways are old and unattractive, athletic facilities inadequate. Teachers run out of chalk and paper, the science labs are 30 to 50 years out of date, and the school's heating system has never worked correctly. A history teacher has 110 students but only 26 books.

Kozol says that anyone who visits places like East St. Louis, even for a brief time, comes away profoundly shaken. After all, these are innocent children who have done nothing wrong. Kozol's interest was in describing what life is like in the nation's inner-city neighborhoods and schools, which are predominantly African American and Latino. However, as indicated earlier, there are many non-Latino White children who live in poverty, although they often are in suburban or rural areas. Kozol argues that many inner-city schools are still segregated, are grossly underfunded, and do not provide adequate opportunities for children to learn effectively.

One trend in antipoverty programs is to conduct two-generational intervention (Huston, 1999; McLoyd, 1998, 1999, 2000). This involves providing services for children (such as educational child care or preschool education) and services for their parents (such as adult education, literacy training, and job skill training). Recent evaluations of the two-generational programs suggest that they have more positive effects on parents than they do on children (St. Pierre, Layzer, & Barnes, 1996). Also discouraging for children is that, when the two-generational programs show benefits, they are more likely to be in the form of health benefits than cognitive gains.

Ethnicity in Schools School segregation is still a factor in the education of children of color in the United States (Simons, Finlay, & Yang, 1991). Almost one-third of all African American and Latino students attend schools in which 90 percent or more of the students are from minority groups.

The school experiences of students from different ethnic groups vary considerably (Bennett, 2003; Nelson-LeGall & Kelly, 2001; Sheets, 2005). African American and Latino students are much less likely than non-Latino White or Asian American students to be enrolled in academic, college preparatory programs and are much

Average national reading score

more likely to be enrolled in remedial and special education programs. Asian American students are far more likely than other ethnic minority groups to take advanced math and science courses in high school. African American students are twice as likely as Latinos, Native Americans, or Whites to be suspended from school. Ethnic minorities of color constitute the majority in 23 of the 25 largest school districts in the United States, a trend that is increasing (Banks, 2002). However, 90 percent of the teachers in America's schools are non-Latino White, and the percentage of minority teachers is projected to decrease even further in the coming years.

American anthropologist John Ogbu (1989) proposed the view that ethnic minority students are placed in a position of subordination and exploitation in the American educational system. He believes that students of color, especially African Americans and Latinos, have inferior educational opportunities, are exposed to teachers and school administrators who have low academic expectations for them, and encounter negative stereotypes of ethnic minority groups (Ogbu, 2003; Ogbu & Stern, 2001). In one study of middle schools in predominantly Latino areas of Miami, Latino and White teachers more often than African American teachers rated African American students as having more behavioral problems (Zimmerman & others, 1995).

Like Ogbu, educational psychologist Margaret Beale Spencer (1990) says that a form of institutional racism permeates many American schools. That is, well-meaning teachers, acting out of misguided liberalism, fail to challenge children of color to achieve. Such teachers prematurely accept a low level of performance from these children, substituting warmth and affection for high standards of academic success.

Following are some strategies for improving relationships among ethnically diverse students (Santrock, 2006):

- *Turn the class into a jigsaw classroom.* When Eliot Aronson was a professor at the University of Texas at Austin, the school system contacted him for ideas on how to reduce the increasing racial tension in classrooms. Aronson (1986) developed the concept of the "jigsaw classroom," in which students from different cultural backgrounds are placed in a cooperative group in which they have to construct different parts of a project to reach a common goal. Aronson used the term *jigsaw* because he saw the technique as much like a group of students cooperating to put different pieces together to complete a jigsaw puzzle. How might this work? Team sports, drama productions, and music performances are examples of contexts in which students cooperatively participate to reach a common goal.
- *Encourage students to have positive personal contact with diverse other students.* Contact alone does not do the job of improving relationships with diverse others. For example, busing ethnic minority students to predominantly White schools, or vice versa, has not reduced prejudice or improved interethnic relations (Minuchin & Shapiro, 1983). What matters is what happens after children get to school. Especially beneficial in improving interethnic relations: sharing one's worries, successes, failures, coping strategies, interests, and other personal information with people of other ethnicities. When this happens, people are seen more as individuals than as members of a homogeneous cultural group.
- *Encourage students to engage in perspective taking.* Exercises and activities that help students see others' perspectives can improve interethnic relations. This helps students "step into the shoes" of peers who are culturally different and feel what it is like to be treated in fair or unfair ways.
- *Help students think critically and be emotionally intelligent when cultural issues are involved.* Students who learn to think critically and deeply about interethnic

Multicultural Education

Careers in Life-Span Development

James Comer, Child Psychiatrist

James Comer grew up in a low-income neighborhood in East Chicago, Indiana, and credits his parents with leaving no doubt about the importance of education. He obtained a BA degree from Indiana University. He went on to obtain a medical degree from Howard University College of Medicine, a Master of Public Health degree from the University of Michigan School of Public Health, and psychiatry training at the Yale University School of Medicine's Child Study Center. He currently is the Maurice Falk Professor of Child Psychiatry at the Yale University Child Study Center and an associate dean at the Yale University Medical School. During his years at Yale, James has concentrated his career on promoting a focus on child development as a way of improving schools. His efforts in support of healthy development of young people are known internationally.

James, perhaps, is best known for the founding of the School Development Program in 1968, which promotes the collaboration of parents, educators, and community to improve social, emotional, and academic outcomes for children.

James Comer (*left*) is shown with some of the inner-city African American children who attend a school that became a better learning environment because of Comer's intervention.

relations are likely to decrease their prejudice (Koppelman & Goodhart, 2005). Becoming more emotionally intelligent includes understanding the causes of one's feelings, managing anger, listening to what others are saying, and being motivated to share and cooperate.

- *Reduce bias.* Teachers can reduce bias by displaying images of children from diverse ethnic and cultural groups, selecting play materials and classroom activities that encourage cultural understanding, helping students resist stereotyping, and working with parents.
- *View the school and community as a team to help support teaching efforts.* James Comer (1988; Comer & others, 1996) proposes that a community, team approach is the best way to educate children. Three important aspects of the Comer Project for Change are (1) a governance and management team that develops a comprehensive school plan, assessment strategy, and staff development plan; (2) a mental health or school support team; and (3) a parent's program. Comer suggests that the entire school community should have a cooperative rather than an adversarial attitude. The Comer program is currently operating in more than 600 schools in 26 states. To read further about Comer's work and his career, see the Careers in Life-Span Development insert.
- *Be a competent cultural mediator.* Teachers can play a powerful role as a cultural mediator by being sensitive to racist content in materials and classroom interactions, learning more about different ethnic groups, being sensitive to children's ethnic attitudes, viewing students of color positively, and thinking of positive ways to get parents of color more involved as partners with teachers in educating children (Jones & Fuller, 2003; Taylor & Whittaker, 2003).

Cross-Cultural Comparisons of Achievement

American children are more achievement-oriented than their counterparts in many countries. However, in the past decade, the poor performance of American children in math and science has become well publicized. For example, in one cross-national comparison of the math and science achievement of 9- to 13-year-old students, the United States finished 13th (out of 15) in science and 15th (out of 16) in math achievement (Educational Testing Service, 1992). In this study, Korean and Taiwanese students placed first and second, respectively.

Critics of cross-national comparisons argue that, in many comparisons, virtually all U.S. children are being compared with a "select" group of children from other countries, especially in the secondary school comparisons. Therefore, they conclude, it is no wonder that American students don't fare so well. That criticism holds for some international comparisons. However, even when the top 25 percent of students in different countries have been compared, U.S. students move up some, but not a lot (Mullis, 1999). To read further about cross-cultural comparisons in achievement, see the Diversity in Life-Span Development interlude.

Diversity in Life-Span Development

Schooling and Achievement in U.S. and Asian Children

Harold Stevenson's (1995, 2000; Stevenson & Hofer, 1999) research explores reasons for the poor performance of American students. Stevenson and his colleagues have completed five cross-cultural comparisons of students in the United States, China, Taiwan, and Japan. In these studies, Asian students consistently outperform American students. And the longer the students are in school, the wider the gap between Asian and American students becomes—the lowest difference is in the first grade, the highest in the eleventh grade (the highest grade studied).

To learn more about the reasons for these large cross-cultural differences, Stevenson and his colleagues spent thousands of hours observing in classrooms, as well as interviewing and surveying teachers, students, and parents. They found that the Asian teachers spent more of their time teaching math than did the American teachers. For example, more than one-fourth of total classroom time in the first grade was spent on math instruction in Japan, compared with only one-tenth of the time in the U.S. first-grade classrooms. Also, the Asian students were in school an average of 240 days a year, compared with 178 days in the United States.

In addition to the substantially greater time spent on math instruction in the Asian schools than in the American schools, differences were found between the Asian and American parents. The American parents had much lower expectations for their children's education and achievement than did the Asian parents. Also, the American parents were more likely to say that their children's math achievement was due to innate ability; the Asian parents were more likely to say that their children's math achievement was the consequence of effort and training (Stevenson, Lee, & Stigler, 1986) (see figure 11.5). The Asian students were more likely to do math homework than were the American students, and the Asian parents were far more likely to help their children with their math homework than were the American parents (Chen & Stevenson, 1989).

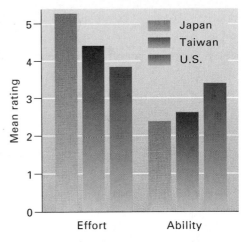

FIGURE 11.5 Mothers' Beliefs About the Factors Responsible for Children's Math Achievement in Three Countries

In one study, mothers in Japan and Taiwan were more likely to believe that their children's math achievement was due to effort rather than innate ability, while U.S. mothers were more likely to believe their children's math achievement was due to innate ability (Stevenson, Lee, & Stigler, 1986). If parents believe that their children's math achievement is due to innate ability and their children are not doing well in math, the implication is that they are less likely to think their children will benefit from putting forth more effort.

Review and Reflect: Learning Goal 4

4 Characterize the transition to elementary school and sociocultural aspects of schooling and achievement

REVIEW

- What are two major contemporary issues in educating children?
- What is the transition to elementary school like?
- How do socioeconomic status and ethnicity influence schooling?
- What are some cross-cultural comparisons of achievement?

REFLECT

- Should the United States be worried about the low performance of its students in mathematics and science in comparison to Asian students? Are Americans' expectations for students too low?

We [the United States] accept performances in students that are nowhere near where they should be.

—HAROLD STEVENSON
Contemporary Developmental Psychologist, University of Michigan

Reach Your Learning Goals

Socioemotional Development in Middle and Late Childhood

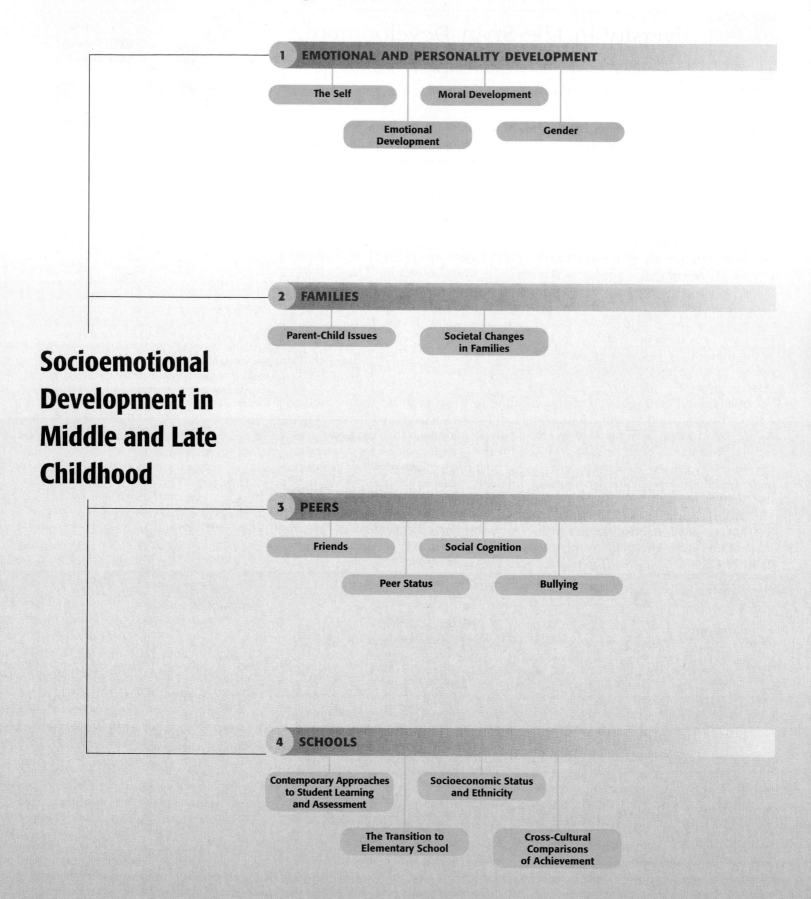

1 EMOTIONAL AND PERSONALITY DEVELOPMENT

- The Self
- Emotional Development
- Moral Development
- Gender

2 FAMILIES

- Parent-Child Issues
- Societal Changes in Families

3 PEERS

- Friends
- Peer Status
- Social Cognition
- Bullying

4 SCHOOLS

- Contemporary Approaches to Student Learning and Assessment
- The Transition to Elementary School
- Socioeconomic Status and Ethnicity
- Cross-Cultural Comparisons of Achievement

Summary

1 *Learning Goal 1: Discuss emotional and personality development in middle and late childhood*

- The internal self, the social self, and the socially comparative self become more prominent in middle and late childhood. Self-concept refers to domain-specific evaluations of the self. Self-esteem refers to global evaluations of the self and is also referred to as self-worth or self-image. Self-esteem is only moderately related to school performance but is more strongly linked to initiative. Four ways to increase self-esteem are to (1) identify the causes of low self-esteem, (2) provide emotional support and social approval, (3) help children achieve, and (4) help children cope. Erikson's fourth stage of development, industry versus inferiority, characterizes the middle and late childhood years.
- Developmental changes in emotion include increased understanding of complex emotions such as pride and shame, detecting that more than one emotion can be experienced in a particular situation, taking into account the circumstances that led up to an emotional reaction, improvements in the ability to suppress and conceal negative emotions, and using self-initiated strategies to redirect feelings. Emotional intelligence is a form of social intelligence that involves the ability to monitor one's own and others' feelings and emotions, to discriminate among them, and to use this information to guide one's own thinking and action. Goleman maintains that emotional intelligence involves four main areas: emotional self-awareness, managing emotions, reading emotions, and handling relationships. As children get older, they use a greater variety of coping strategies and more cognitive strategies.
- Kohlberg developed a provocative theory of moral reasoning. He argued that moral development consists of three levels—preconventional, conventional, and postconventional—and six stages (two at each level). Kohlberg believed that these stages were age-related. Influences on the Kohlberg stages include cognitive development, imitation and cognitive conflict, peer relations, and perspective taking. Criticisms of Kohlberg's theory have been made, especially by Gilligan, who advocates a stronger care perspective. Other criticisms focus on the inadequacy of moral reasoning to predict moral behavior, the assessment of moral reasoning, and culture and family influences. Some critics distinguish between moral reasoning and social conventional reasoning. Prosocial behavior involves positive moral behaviors. Altruism is an unselfish interest in helping others. Most sharing in the first three years is not done for empathy, but at about four years of age empathy contributes to sharing. By the start of the elementary school years, children express more objective ideas about fairness.
- Gender stereotypes are widespread around the world. A number of physical differences exist between males and females. Some experts, such as Hyde, argue that cognitive differences between males and females have been exaggerated. In terms of socioemotional differences, males are more physically aggressive than females, whereas females regulate their emotions better and engage in more prosocial behavior than males. There is controversy about how similar or different males and females are in a number of areas. Gender-role classification focuses on how masculine, feminine, or androgynous individuals are. Androgyny means having both positive feminine and masculine characteristics. It is important to think about gender in terms of context.

2 *Learning Goal 2: Describe parent-child issues and societal changes in families*

- Parents spend less time with children during middle and late childhood than in early childhood. New parent-child issues emerge and discipline changes. Control is more coregulatory.
- As in divorced families, children living in stepparent families have more adjustment problems than their counterparts in nondivorced families. However, a majority of children in stepfamilies do not have adjustment problems. Latchkey children may become vulnerable when they are not monitored by adults in the after-school hours.

3 *Learning Goal 3: Identify changes in peer relationships in middle and late childhood*

- Children's friendships serve six functions: companionship, stimulation, physical support, ego support, social comparison, and intimacy/affection. Intimacy and similarity are two common characteristics of friendship.
- Popular children are frequently nominated as a best friend and are rarely disliked by their peers. Average children receive an average number of both positive and negative nominations from their peers. Neglected children are infrequently nominated as a best friend but are not disliked by their peers. Rejected children are infrequently nominated as a best friend and are actively disliked by their peers. Controversial children are frequently nominated both as a best friend and as being disliked by peers. Rejected children are especially at risk for a number of problems.
- Social information-processing skills and social knowledge are two important dimensions of social cognition in peer relations.
- Significant numbers of children are bullied, and this can result in short-term and long-term negative effects for both the victims and bullies.

Learning Goal 4: Characterize the transition to elementary school and sociocultural aspects of schooling and achievement

- Contemporary approaches to student learning include direct instruction and constructivist. A number of learner-centered principles with a constructivist theme have been advocated by a team of experts convened by the American Psychological Association, the American Educational Research Association, and the National Council on Measurement in Education. Increased concern by the public and government in the United States has produced extensive state-mandated testing, which has both strengths and weaknesses, and is controversial. The most visible example of the increased state-mandated testing is the No Child Left Behind federal legislation.
- A special concern is that early schooling too often proceeds on the basis of negative feedback to children.
- Children in poverty face problems at home and at school that present barriers to their learning. It is important that teachers have positive expectations for and challenge children of color to achieve.
- American children are more achievement-oriented than children in many countries, but perform more poorly in math and science than many children in Asian countries, such as China, Taiwan, and Japan.

Key Terms

self-esteem 329
self-concept 329
emotional intelligence 331
preconventional reasoning 334
heteronomous morality 334
individualism, instrumental purpose, and exchange 334
conventional reasoning 334

mutual interpersonal expectations, relationships, and interpersonal conformity 334
social systems morality 334
postconventional reasoning 334
social contract or utility and individual rights 334

universal ethical principles 334
justice perspective 336
care perspective 336
social conventional reasoning 337
altruism 337
gender stereotypes 339
androgyny 341

intimacy in friendships 346
popular children 347
average children 347
neglected children 347
rejected children 347
controversial children 347
direct instruction approach 350

Key People

Erik Erikson 330
Daniel Goleman 331
Lawrence Kohlberg 332
James Rest 335
Carol Gilligan 336
William Damon 337

Nancy Eisenberg 338
Eleanor Maccoby 339
Carol Jacklin 339
Janet Shibley Hyde 340
Sandra Bem 341

William Pollack 341
Joan Lipsitz 344
Willard Hartup 346
John Coie 347
Kenneth Dodge 348

Jonathan Kozol 352
John Ogbu 353
Margaret Beale Spencer 353
Eliot Aronson 353
Harold Stevenson 355

E-Learning Tools

To help you master the material in this chapter, you'll find a number of valuable study tools on the LifeMap CD-ROM that accompanies this book and on the Online Learning Center for *Life-Span Development*, tenth edition, at www.mhhe.com/santrockld10.

Video Clips

In the margins of this book there are icons directing you to the LifeMap CD-ROM that accompanies the book. There you'll find two videos for chapter 11. The first video is called "Characteristics of Children Who Bully." How are bullies made? What causal factors distinguish those who are likely to bully from those likely to be bullied? This segment explores the power dynamics of childhood bullying. The second video is called "Schools and Public Policy." The transition to middle school can be a major paradigm shift for the student. In this segment, Dr. Jacquelynne Eccles describes how her study of the social parameters of middle school has led to changes in public policy.

Self-Assessment

Connect to www.mhhe.com/santrockld10 to reflect on your childhood by completing the self-assessment, *My Socioemotional Development as a Child*.

Taking It to the Net

Connect to www.mhhe.com/santrockld10 to research the answers to these questions.

1. Ling, a third-grade teacher, overheard a talk-show discussion on emotional intelligence. She has seen several books on the

subject in the local library but was unaware of its impact on learning. What is emotional intelligence and how can Ling and her students' parents facilitate this type of development in children?

2. Frank is researching the latest information on bullying after his younger brother told him of his recent experiences with bullies at his junior high school. What information is available on the prevalence of bullying, the make-up of the children who bully, and why this type of behavior is increasing?

3. Dimitri is a high school English teacher. He has heard about the controversy between direct-instruction and constructivist points of view, and he would like to try out both approaches in his classroom. How might Dimitri conduct his class differently according to each paradigm?

Health and Well-Being, Parenting, and Education Exercises

Build your decision-making skills by trying your hand at the health and well-being, parenting, and education exercises.

Connect to www.mhhe.com/santrockld10 to research the answers and complete the exercises.

C H A P T E R

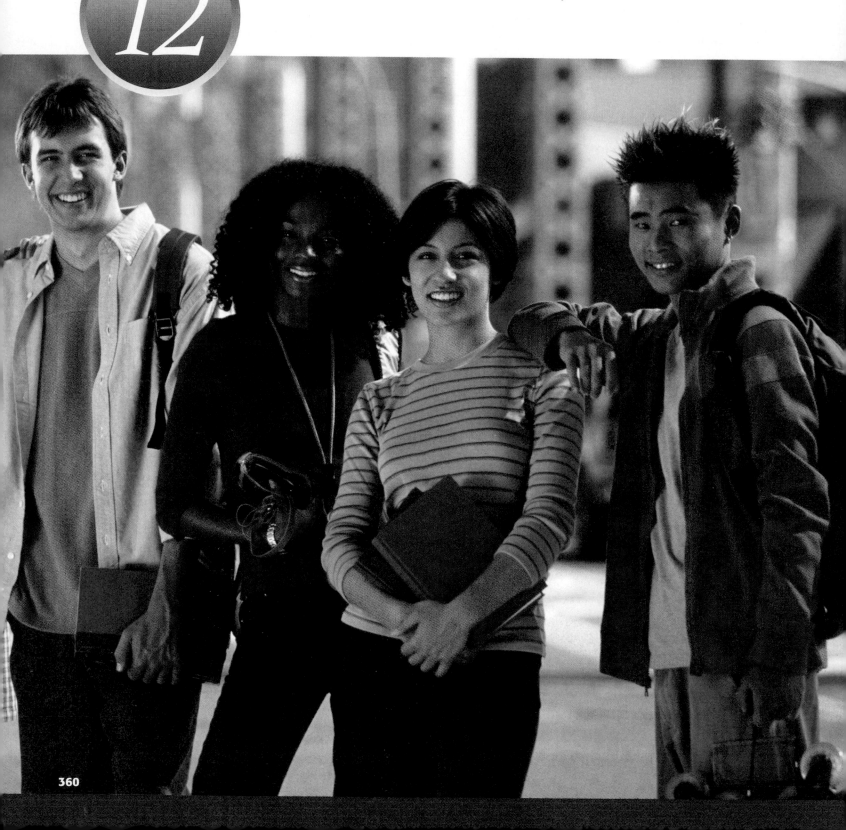

12

In youth, we clothe ourselves with rainbows,

and go brave as the zodiac.

—RALPH WALDO EMERSON
American Poet,
19th Century

Physical and Cognitive Development in Adolescence

Chapter Outline

Learning Goals

1 Discuss the nature of adolescence

2 Describe the changes involved in puberty, sexuality, and the brain

3 Identify adolescent problems in substance use and abuse, eating disorders, and health

4 Explain cognitive changes in adolescence

5 Summarize some key aspects of how schools influence adolescent development

Images of Life-Span Development
The Best of Times and the Worst of Times for Today's Adolescents

It is both the best of times and the worst of times for adolescents. Their world possesses powers and perspectives inconceivable 50 years ago: computers, longer life expectancies, the entire planet accessible through television, satellites, air travel. But so much knowledge and choice can be chaotic and dangerous. School curricula have been adapted to teach about new topics: AIDS, adolescent suicide, drug and alcohol abuse, incest. The hazards of the adult world, its sometimes fatal temptations, descend upon children so early that the ideal of childhood is demolished. Crack, for example, is far more addictive and deadly than marijuana, the drug of a different generation. Strange fragments of violence come flashing out of the television set and lodge in minds too young to understand them. The messages are powerful and contradictory. Rock videos suggest orgiastic sex. Public health officials counsel "safe sex." Television pours into the imaginations of children a bizarre version of reality. (Morrow, 1988, pp. 32–33)

Adolescence is not a time of rebellion, crisis, pathology, and deviance. A far more accurate vision of adolescence is of a time of evaluation, of decision making, of commitment, of carving out a place in the world. Most of the problems of today's youth are not with the youth themselves. What adolescents need is access to a range of legitimate opportunities and to long-term support from adults who care deeply about them (Hamburg & Hamburg, 2004).

PREVIEW

Adolescence is a transitional period in the human life span, linking childhood and adulthood. We begin the chapter by examining some general characteristics of adolescence followed by coverage of several adolescent problems and why adolescence is a critical juncture in health. Then we describe the significant cognitive changes that characterize adolescence and various aspects of schools for adolescents.

1 THE NATURE OF ADOLESCENCE

As in the development of children, genetic, biological, environmental, and social factors interact in adolescent development. The genes inherited from parents still influence thought and behavior during adolescence, but inheritance now interacts with the social conditions of the adolescent's world—with family, peers, friendships, dating, and school experiences. Adolescents have experienced thousands of hours of interaction with parents, peers, and teachers in their previous 10 to 13 years of development. Still new experiences and developmental tasks appear during adolescence. Relationships with parents take a different form, moments with peers become more intimate, and dating occurs for the first time, as do sexual exploration and possibly intercourse. The adolescent's thoughts are more abstract and idealistic. Biological changes trigger a heightened interest in body image. Adolescence, then, has both continuity and discontinuity with childhood.

There is a long history of worrying about how adolescents will turn out. In 1904, G. Stanley Hall proposed the "storm-and-stress" view that adolescence is a turbulent time charged with conflict and mood swings. Today's adolescents face demands and expectations, as well as risks and temptations, that appear to be more numerous and complex than those faced by adolescents only a generation ago. Nonetheless, contrary to the popular stereotype of adolescents as highly stressed and incompetent, the vast majority of adolescents successfully negotiate the path from childhood to adulthood. By some criteria, today's adolescents are doing better than their counterparts from a decade or two earlier. Today, more adolescents complete high school, especially African American adolescent girls. The majority of adolescents today have positive self-concepts and positive relationships with others.

A cross-cultural study by Daniel Offer and his colleagues (1988) supported the contention that most adolescents have positive images of themselves and contradicted the stereotype that most adolescents have problems or are disturbed in some way. The self-images of adolescents around the world were sampled—in the United States, Australia, Bangladesh, Hungary, Israel, Italy, Japan, Taiwan, Turkey, and West Germany. A healthy self-image characterized at least 73 percent of the adolescents studied. They appeared to be moving toward adulthood with a healthy integration of previous experiences, self-confidence, and optimism about the future. Although there were some differences among the adolescents, they were happy most of the time, they enjoyed life, they perceived themselves as able to exercise self-control, they valued work and school, they expressed confidence about their sexual selves, they expressed positive feelings toward their families, and they felt they had the capability to cope with life's stresses: not exactly a storm-and-stress portrayal of adolescence.

Public attitudes about adolescence emerge from a combination of personal experience and media portrayals, neither of which produce an objective picture of how normal adolescents develop (Feldman & Elliott, 1990). Some of the readiness to assume the worst about adolescents likely involves the short memories of adults. Many adults measure their current perceptions of adolescents by their memories of their own adolescence. Adults may portray today's adolescents as more troubled, less respectful, more self-centered, more assertive, and more adventurous than they were.

However, in matters of taste and manners, the young people of every generation have seemed radical, unnerving, and different from adults—different in how

Growing up has never been easy. However, adolescence is not best viewed as a time of rebellion, crisis, pathology, and deviance. A far more accurate vision of adolescence describes it as a time of evaluation, of decision making, of commitment, and of carving out a place in the world. Most of the problems of today's youth are not with the youth themselves. What adolescents need is access to a range of legitimate opportunities and to long-term support from adults who deeply care about them. *What might be some examples of such support and caring?*

Practical Resources and Research
Adolescent Issues
Profile of America's Youth
Trends in the Well-Being
of America's Youth

they look, in how they behave, in the music they enjoy, in their hairstyles, and in the clothing they choose. It is an enormous error, though, to confuse adolescents' enthusiasm for trying on new identities and enjoying moderate amounts of outrageous behavior with hostility toward parental and societal standards. Acting out and boundary testing are time-honored ways in which adolescents move toward accepting, rather than rejecting, parental values.

Although the majority of adolescents experience the transition from childhood to adulthood more positively than is portrayed by many adults and the media, too many adolescents today are not provided with adequate opportunities and support to become competent adults (Hamburg & Hamburg, 2004; Pittman & Diversi, 2003). In many ways, today's adolescents are presented with a less stable environment than adolescents of a decade or two ago. High divorce rates, high adolescent pregnancy rates, and increased geographic mobility of families contribute to this lack of stability in adolescents' lives. Today's adolescents are exposed to a complex menu of lifestyle options through the media, and, although the adolescent drug rate is beginning to show signs of decline, the rate of adolescent drug use in the United States is higher than that of any other country in the industrialized Western world. Many of today's adolescents face these temptations, as well as sexual activity, at increasingly young ages (Larson & Wilson, 2004).

Our discussion underscores an important point about adolescents: They do not make up a homogeneous group. Most adolescents negotiate the lengthy path to adult maturity successfully, but too large a group does not (Nichols & Good, 2004). Ethnic, cultural, gender, socioeconomic, age, and lifestyle differences influence the actual life trajectory of every adolescent. Different portrayals of adolescence emerge, depending on the particular group of adolescents being described (Call & others, 2003; Compas, 2004; Leventhal & Brooks-Gunn, 2004).

Review and Reflect: Learning Goal 1

1 **Discuss the nature of adolescence**

REVIEW

- What characterizes adolescent development?

REFLECT

- How much have adolescents changed or stayed the same over the last 30 to 40 years?

Now that we have considered some historical views of adolescents and have evaluated today's adolescents, let's turn our attention to the ways in which adolescents develop physically. We will begin with the dramatic changes of puberty.

2 PHYSICAL CHANGES

| Puberty | Adolescent Sexuality | The Brain |

One father remarked that the problem with his teenage son was not that he grew, but that he did not know when to stop growing. As we will see, there is considerable variation in the timing of the adolescent growth spurt. In addition to pubertal changes, other physical changes we will explore involve sexuality and the brain.

From *Penguin Dreams and Stranger Things,* by Berkeley Breathed. Copyright © 1985 by The Washington Post Company. By permission of Little, Brown & Company, Inc. and International Creative Management. Copyright © 1985 by Berkeley Breathed.

Puberty

Puberty can be distinguished from adolescence. For most of us, puberty ends long before adolescence is exited, although puberty is the most important marker of the beginning of adolescence. What is puberty? **Puberty** is a period of rapid physical maturation involving hormonal and bodily changes that occur primarily during early adolescence.

Imagine a toddler displaying all the features of puberty—a 3-year-old girl with fully developed breasts or a boy just slightly older with a deep voice. That is what we would see by the year 2250 if the age at which puberty arrives were to keep getting younger at its present pace. In Norway today, **menarche**—a girl's first menstruation—occurs at just over 13 years of age, compared with 17 years of age in the 1840s. In the United States—where children mature up to a year earlier than children in European countries—the average age of menarche declined significantly since the mid-nineteenth century (see figure 12.1). Fortunately, however, we are unlikely to see pubescent toddlers, since what has happened in the past century is likely the result of a higher level of nutrition and health. The available information suggests that menarche began to occur earlier at about the time of the Industrial Revolution, a period associated with increased standards of living and advances in medical science (Petersen, 1979).

Genetic factors also are involved in puberty. Puberty is not simply an environmental accident. As indicated earlier, although nutrition, health, and other factors affect puberty's timing and variations in its makeup, the basic genetic program is wired into the nature of the species (Sharp & others, 2004; Waylen & Wolke, 2004).

Another key factor that triggers puberty is body mass. Menarche occurs at a relatively consistent weight in girls. A body weight approximating 106 +/− 3 pounds can trigger menarche and the end of the pubertal growth spurt. For menarche to begin and continue, fat must make up 17 percent of the girl's body weight. However, both teenage anorexics whose weight drops dramatically, and female athletes in certain sports (such as gymnastics), may not menstruate (Phillips, 2003).

In summary, puberty's determinants include nutrition, health, heredity, and body mass. So far, our discussion of puberty has emphasized its dramatic changes. Keep in mind, though, that puberty is not a single, sudden event (Archibald,

puberty A period of rapid physical and sexual maturation that occurs mainly during early adolescence.

menarche A girl's first menstruation.

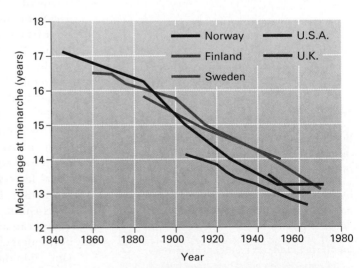

FIGURE 12.1 Median Ages at Menarche in Selected Northern European Countries and the United States from 1845 to 1969
Notice the steep decline in the age at which girls experienced menarche in five different countries. Recently the age at which girls experience menarche has been leveling off.

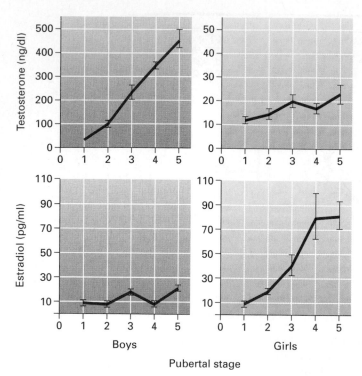

FIGURE 12.2 Hormone Levels by Sex and Pubertal Stage for Testosterone and Estradiol

The five stages range from the early beginning of puberty (stage 1) to the most advanced stage of puberty (stage 5). Notice the significant increase in testosterone in boys and the significant increase in estradiol in girls.

Graber, & Brooks-Gunn, 2003). We know whether a young boy or girl is going through puberty, but pinpointing puberty's beginning and end is difficult. Except for menarche, which occurs rather late in puberty, no single marker heralds puberty. For boys, the first whisker or first wet dream is an event that could mark its appearance, but both may go unnoticed.

Hormonal Changes Behind the first whisker in boys and the widening of hips in girls is a flood of **hormones,** powerful chemical substances secreted by the endocrine glands and carried through the body by the bloodstream. The endocrine system's role in puberty involves the interaction of the hypothalamus, the pituitary gland, and the gonads (sex glands). The **hypothalamus** is a structure in the higher portion of the brain that monitors eating, drinking, and sex. The **pituitary gland** is an important endocrine gland that controls growth and regulates other glands. The **gonads** are the sex glands—the testes in males, the ovaries in females. How does this hormonal system work? The pituitary sends a signal via gonadotropins (hormones that stimulate the testes or ovaries) to the appropriate gland to manufacture the hormone. Then the pituitary gland, through interaction with the hypothalamus, detects when the optimal level of hormones is reached and responds by maintaining gonadotropin secretion.

The concentrations of certain hormones increase dramatically during adolescence (Auchus & Rainey, 2004; Susman, Dorn, & Schiefelbein, 2003; Susman & Rogol, 2004). *Testosterone* is a hormone associated in boys with the development of genitals, an increase in height, and a change in voice. *Estradiol* is a hormone associated in girls with breast, uterine, and skeletal development. In one study, testosterone levels increased eighteen-fold in boys but only two-fold in girls during puberty; estradiol increased eight-fold in girls but only two-fold in boys (Nottelmann & others, 1987) (see figure 12.2). Note that both testosterone and estradiol are present in the hormonal makeup of both boys and girls but that testosterone dominates in male pubertal development, estradiol in female pubertal development.

The same influx of hormones that puts hair on a male's chest and imparts curvature to a female's breast may contribute to psychological development in adolescence (Cameron, 2004; Rowe & others, 2004). In one study of 108 normal boys and girls ranging in age from 9 to 14, a higher concentration of testosterone was present in boys who rated themselves as more socially competent (Nottelmann & others, 1987). In another study of 60 normal boys and girls in the same age range, girls with higher estradiol levels expressed more anger and aggression (Inoff-Germain & others, 1988). However, hormonal effects by themselves do not account for adolescent development (Graber & Brooks-Gunn, 2002; Rowe & others, 2004). For example, in one study, social factors accounted for two to four times as much variance as did hormonal factors in young adolescent girls' depression and anger (Brooks-Gunn & Warren, 1989). Behavior and moods also can affect hormones (Paikoff, Buchanan, & Brooks-Gunn, 1991). Stress, eating patterns, exercise, sexual activity, tension, and depression can activate or suppress various aspects of the hormonal system. In sum, the hormone-behavior link is complex (Susman & Rogol, 2004).

One additional aspect of the pituitary gland's role in development still needs to be described. Not only does the pituitary gland release gonadotropins that stimulate the testes and ovaries, but through interaction with the hypothalamus the pituitary gland also secretes hormones that either directly lead to growth and skeletal maturation or produce such growth effects through interaction with the thyroid gland, located in the neck region.

Height, Weight, and Sexual Maturation   Among the most noticeable physical changes during puberty are increases in height and weight, as well as sexual maturation.

Height and Weight   As indicated in figure 12.3, the growth spurt occurs approximately two years earlier for girls than for boys (Abbassi, 1998). The mean age at the beginning of the growth spurt in girls is 9 years of age; for boys, it is 11 years of age. The peak rate of pubertal change occurs at $11\frac{1}{2}$ years for girls and $13\frac{1}{2}$ years for boys. During their growth spurt, girls increase in height about $3\frac{1}{2}$ inches per year, boys about 4 inches.

Boys and girls who are shorter or taller than their peers before adolescence are likely to remain so during adolescence. In our society, there is a stigma attached to shortness in boys. At the beginning of the adolescent period, girls tend to be as tall as or taller than boys of their age, but by the end of the middle school years most boys have caught up or, in many cases, have even surpassed girls in height. And, even though height in the elementary school years is a good predictor of height later in adolescence, there is still room for the individual's height to change in relation to the height of his or her peers. As much as 30 percent of an individual's height in late adolescence is unexplained by his or her height in the elementary school years.

The rate at which adolescents gain weight follows approximately the same developmental timetable as the rate at which they gain height. Marked weight gains coincide with the onset of puberty. During early adolescence, girls tend to outweigh boys, but, just as with height, by about age 14 boys begin to surpass girls.

Sexual Maturation   Think back to the onset of your puberty. Of the striking changes that were taking place in your body, what was the first change that occurred? Researchers have found that male pubertal characteristics develop in this order: increase in penis and testicle size, appearance of straight pubic hair, minor voice change, first ejaculation (which usually occurs through masturbation or a wet dream), appearance of kinky pubic hair, onset of maximum growth, growth of hair in armpits, more detectable voice changes, and growth of facial hair. The normal range and average age of development for three sexual characteristics in boys—penis elongation, testes development, and growth of pubic hair—along with height spurt, are shown in figure 12.4.

What is the order of appearance of physical changes in females? First, either the breasts enlarge or pubic hair appears. Later, hair appears in the armpits. As these changes occur, the female grows in height, and her hips become wider than her shoulders. Her first menstruation comes rather late in the pubertal cycle. Initially, her menstrual cycles may be highly irregular. For the first several years, she may not ovulate every menstrual cycle; some girls do not ovulate at all until a year or two after menstruation begins. No voice changes comparable to those in pubertal males occur in pubertal females. By the end of puberty, the female's breasts have become more fully rounded. Two of the most noticeable aspects of female pubertal change are pubic hair and breast development. Figure 12.4 shows the normal range and average development of three sexual characteristics in girls—menarche, breast development, and the growth of pubic hair—along with height gain.

Individual Variations   The pubertal sequence may begin as early as 10 years of age or as late as $13\frac{1}{2}$ for most boys. It may end as early as 13 years or as late as 17 years for most boys. The normal range is wide enough that, given two boys of the same chronological age, one might complete the pubertal sequence before the other one has begun it. For girls, the age range of the first menstrual period is even wider. Menarche is considered within a normal range if it appears between the ages of 9 and 15.

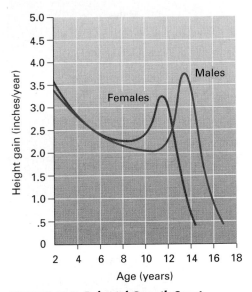

FIGURE 12.3 Pubertal Growth Spurt
On the average, the peak of the growth spurt that characterizes pubertal change occurs 2 years earlier for girls ($11\frac{1}{2}$) than for boys ($13\frac{1}{2}$).

www.mhhe.com/santrockld10

Biological Changes

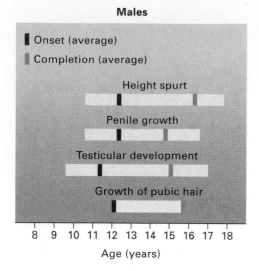

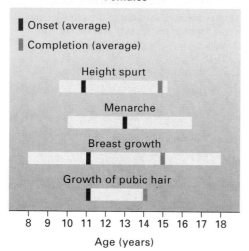

FIGURE 12.4 Normal Range and Average Development of Sexual Characteristics in Males and Females

Body Image One psychological aspect of physical change in puberty is certain: Adolescents are preoccupied with their bodies and develop individual images of what their bodies are like. Perhaps you looked in the mirror on a daily and sometimes even hourly basis to see if you could detect anything different about your changing body. Preoccupation with one's body image is strong throughout adolescence, but it is especially acute during puberty, a time when adolescents are more dissatisfied with their bodies than in late adolescence (Graber & Brooks-Gunn, 2001; Wright, 1989).

There are gender differences in adolescents' perceptions of their bodies. In general, throughout puberty, girls are less happy with their bodies and have more negative body images, compared with boys' feelings about their bodies (Brooks-Gunn & Paikoff, 1993). As pubertal change proceeds, girls often become more dissatisfied with their bodies, probably because their body fat increases, whereas boys become more satisfied as they move through puberty, probably because their muscle mass increases (Gross, 1984).

Early and Late Maturation Some of you entered puberty early, others late, and yet others on time. When adolescents mature earlier or later than their peers, might they perceive themselves differently? In the Berkeley Longitudinal Study some years ago, early-maturing boys perceived themselves more positively and had more successful peer relations than did their late-maturing counterparts (Jones, 1965). The findings for early-maturing girls were similar but not as strong as for boys. When the late-maturing boys were in their thirties, however, they had developed a stronger sense of identity than the early-maturing boys had (Peskin, 1967). Possibly this occurred because the late-maturing boys had more time to explore life's options or because the early-maturing boys continued to focus on their advantageous physical status instead of on career development and achievement.

More recent research confirms, though, that at least during adolescence it is advantageous to be an early-maturing rather than a late-maturing boy (Simmons & Blyth, 1987). The more recent findings for girls suggest that early-maturing girls experience more problems in school but also enjoy more independence and popularity with boys. The time that maturation is assessed also is a factor. In the sixth grade, early-maturing girls show greater satisfaction with their figures than do late-maturing girls, but by the tenth grade late-maturing girls are more satisfied (Simmons & Blyth, 1987) (see figure 12.5). One possible reason for this is that in late adolescence early-maturing girls are shorter and stockier, whereas late-maturing girls are taller and thinner. Late-maturing girls in late adolescence have bodies that more closely approximate the current American ideal of feminine beauty—tall and thin.

In the past decade, an increasing number of researchers have found that early maturation increases girls' vulnerability to a number of problems (Graber, 2003; Graber & others, 2004). Early-maturing girls are more likely to smoke, drink, be depressed, have an eating disorder, request earlier independence from their parents, and have older friends; and their bodies are likely to elicit responses from males that lead to earlier dating and earlier sexual experiences (Wiesner & Ittel, 2002). One recent study of 1,225 urban middle school girls found that those who entered puberty early experimented with alcohol and marijuana at much higher rates than their ethnic minority peers who developed later (Graber, 2003). In another study, early-maturing girls had lower educational and occupational attainment in adulthood (Stattin & Magnusson, 1990). Apparently as a result of their social and cognitive immaturity, combined with early physical development, early-maturing girls are easily lured into problem behaviors, not recognizing the possible long-term effects of these on their development (Petersen, 1993; Sarigiani & Petersen, 2000).

Some researchers now question whether the effects of puberty are as strong as once believed (Petersen, 1993). Puberty affects some adolescents more strongly than others and some behaviors more strongly than others. Body image, dating interest, and sexual behavior are affected by pubertal change. The recent questioning of puberty's effects suggests that, in terms of overall development and adjustment in the human life span, pubertal variations (such as early and late maturation) are less dramatic than commonly thought. In thinking about puberty's effects, keep in mind that an adolescent's world involves cognitive and socioemotional changes, as well as physical changes. As with all periods of development, these processes work in concert to produce who we are in adolescence.

Adolescent Sexuality

Adolescence is a time of sexual exploration and experimentation, of sexual fantasies and realities, of incorporating sexuality into one's identity. Adolescents have an almost insatiable curiosity about sexuality's mysteries. They think about whether they are sexually attractive, how to do sex, and what the future holds for their sexual lives. The majority of adolescents eventually manage to develop a mature sexual identity, but most experience times of vulnerability and confusion along life's sexual journey.

Adolescence is a bridge between the asexual child and the sexual adult (Feldman, 1999). Every society gives some attention to adolescent sexuality. In some societies, adults clamp down and protect adolescent females from males by chaperoning them. Other societies promote very early marriage. Yet other societies, such as those found in the United States, allow some sexual experimentation, although controversy abounds about just how far sexual experimentation should be allowed to go.

Television contributes to the sexual culture, and researchers have concluded that television teaches children and adolescents about sex (Collins & others, 2004; Galician, 2004; Gruber & Gruber, 2000; Ward & Caruthers, 2001). It is not just that TV shows have sexual content but advertisers also use sex to sell just about everything, from cars to detergents. And many adolescents not only are exposed to explicit sex in TV shows, but also in videos, the lyrics of popular music, and Internet websites (Roberts, Henriksen, & Foehr, 2004). A recent research review found that frequent watching of soap operas and music videos were linked with greater acceptance of casual attitudes about sex and higher expectations of engaging in sexual activity (Ward, 2003).

An important point to keep in mind is that sexual development and interest in sex are normal aspects of adolescent development and that the majority of adolescents have healthy sexual attitudes and engage in sexual practices that will not compromise their development. In our further discussion of adolescent sexuality, we will focus on the development of a sexual identity, the progression of adolescent sexual behaviors, risk factors for sexual problems, contraceptive use, sexually transmitted infections, and adolescent pregnancy. In chapter 14, "Physical and Cognitive Development in Early Adulthood," we will further explore these important aspects of sexuality: heterosexuality and homosexuality, sexually transmitted infections, and forcible sexual behavior and sexual harassment.

Developing a Sexual Identity Mastering emerging sexual feelings and forming a sense of sexual identity is multifaceted. This lengthy process involves learning to manage sexual feelings (such as sexual arousal and attraction), developing new forms of intimacy, and learning the skills to regulate sexual behavior to avoid undesirable consequences (Crockett, Raffaelli, & Moilanen, 2003). Developing a sexual identity also involves more than just sexual behavior. It includes interfaces with other developing identities. Sexual identities emerge in the context of physical factors, social factors, and cultural factors, with most societies placing constraints on the sexual behavior of adolescents.

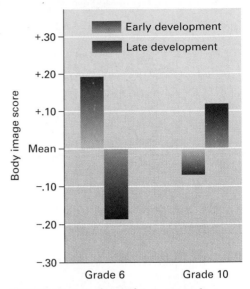

FIGURE 12.5 Early- and Late-Maturing Adolescent Girls' Perceptions of Body Image in Early and Late Adolescence

Sex is virtually everywhere in the American culture and is used to sell just about everything. *Is it surprising, then, that adolescents are so curious about sex and tempted to experiment with sex?*

An adolescent's sexual identity involves an indication of sexual orientation (homosexual, heterosexual, bisexual), and it also involves activities, interests, and styles of behavior (Buzwell & Rosenthal, 1996). For example, some adolescents have a high anxiety level about sex, others a low level. Some adolescents are strongly aroused sexually, others less so. Some adolescents are very active sexually, others not at all. Some adolescents are sexually inactive in response to their strong religious upbringing; others go to church regularly, yet their religious training does not inhibit their sexual activity (Thorton & Canburn, 1989).

Although the development of gay or lesbian identity has been widely studied in adults, few researchers have investigated the gay or lesbian identity (often referred to as the coming-out process) in adolescents. It is commonly believed that most gay and lesbian individuals quietly struggle with same-sex attractions in childhood, do not engage in heterosexual dating, and gradually recognize that they are gay or lesbian in mid to late adolescence (Diamond, 2003). Many youth do follow this developmental pathway but others do not (Diamond & Lucas, 2004). For example, many youth have no recollection of same-sex attractions and experience a more abrupt sense of their same-sex attraction in late adolescence (Savin-Williams, 2001). Researchers also have found that the majority of adolescents with same-sex attractions also experience some degree of other-sex attractions (Garofalo & others, 1999). Even though some adolescents who are attracted to same-sex individuals fall in love with these individuals, others claim that their same-sex attractions are purely physical (Savin-Williams, 2001; Savin-Williams & Diamond, 2004).

In sum, gay and lesbian youth have diverse patterns of initial attraction, often have bisexual attractions, and may have physical or emotional attraction to same-sex individuals but do not always fall in love with them (Diamond, 2003; Savin-Williams & Diamond, 2004). Of special concern is the lack of support that gay and lesbian adolescents receive from parents, teachers, counselors, and peers. We will discuss homosexuality, as well as heterosexuality, in greater depth in chapter 14, "Physical and Cognitive Development in Early Adulthood."

The Progression of Adolescent Sexual Behaviors Adolescents engage in a rather consistent progression of sexual behaviors (DeLamater & MacCorquodale, 1979). Necking usually comes first, followed by petting. Next comes intercourse, or, in some cases, oral sex, which has increased substantially in adolescence in recent years. In one study, 452 individuals 18 to 25 years of age were asked about their own past sexual experiences (Feldman, Turner, & Araujo, 1999). The following progression of sexual behaviors occurred: kissing preceded petting, which preceded sexual intercourse and oral sex (Feldman, Turner, & Araujo, 1999). Male adolescents reported engaging in these sexual behaviors approximately one year earlier than female adolescents.

Here is information from a national survey of adolescents that further reveals the timing of their sexual activities (Alan Guttmacher Institute, 1998):

- Most young adolescents have not had sexual intercourse: 8 in 10 girls and 7 in 10 boys are virgins at age 15.
- The probability that adolescents will have sexual intercourse increases steadily with age, but 1 in 5 individuals have not yet had sexual intercourse by age 19.
- Initial sexual intercourse occurs in the mid- to late-adolescent years for a majority of teenagers, about 8 years before they marry.
- The majority of adolescent females' first voluntary sexual partner are younger, the same age, or no more than 2 years older; 27 percent are 3 to 4 years older; and 12 percent are 5 or more years older.

In some areas of the United States, the percentages of sexually active young adolescents may be even greater. In an inner-city area of Baltimore, 81 percent of the males at age 14 said that they already had engaged in sexual intercourse. Other surveys in inner-city, low-income areas also reveal a high incidence of early sexual intercourse (Clark, Zabin, & Hardy, 1984).

What is the progression of sexual behaviors in adolescence?

In sum, by the end of adolescence the majority of U.S. adolescents have had sexual intercourse. Male, African American, and inner-city adolescents report being the most sexually active (Feldman, Turner, & Araujo, 1999). Although sexual intercourse can be a meaningful experience for older, mature adolescents, many adolescents are not emotionally prepared to handle sexual experiences, especially in early adolescence. In one study, the earlier boys and girls engaged in sexual intercourse, the more they were likely to show adjustment problems (Bingham & Crockett, 1996).

The timing of teenage sexual initiation varies by country and gender. In one study, among females, the proportion having first intercourse by age 17 ranged from 72 percent in Mali to 47 percent in the United States and 45 percent in Tanzania (Singh & others, 2000). The percentage of males who had their first intercourse by age 17 ranged from 76 percent in Jamaica to 64 percent in the United States and 63 percent in Brazil.

 Watch the video "Sex Among Teens at Age 15" to learn what some adolescents think about sex among their peers.

Risk Factors for Sexual Problems   Although most adolescents become sexually active at some point during adolescence, some adolescents engage in sex at early ages (before age 16) and experience a number of partners over time (Cavanaugh, 2004). These adolescents are the least effective users of contraception and are at risk for early, unintended pregnancy and for sexually transmitted infections. Early sexual activity also is linked with other risky behaviors such as excessive drinking, drug use, delinquency, and school-related problems (Dryfoos, 1990). In addition, adolescents who live in low-income neighborhoods often are more sexually active and have higher adolescent pregnancy rates than adolescents who live in more affluent circumstances. And as we saw earlier, African American adolescents engage in sexual activities sooner than other ethnic groups, while Asian American adolescents have the most restrictive sexual timetable.

Two other important factors in sexual risk taking are *self-regulation*—the ability to regulate one's emotions and behavior—and parent-adolescent relationships. One longitudinal study found that a lower level of self-regulation at 12 to 13 years of age was linked with a higher level of sexual risk taking four years later (Rafaelli & Crockett, 2003). Other researchers have also found a relation between low self-regulation and high sexual risk taking (Kahn & others, 2002). A recent research study also revealed that sexual risk taking in adolescence was related to low parental monitoring and poor parent-adolescent communication (Huebner & Howell, 2003).

Contraceptive Use   Sexual activity is a normal activity necessary for procreation, but it involves considerable risks if appropriate safeguards are not taken (Kelly, 2004). There are two kinds of risks that youth encounter: unintended/unwanted pregnancy and sexually transmitted infections. Both of these risks can be reduced significantly by using contraception and barriers (such as condoms) (Breheny & Stephens, 2004; Shafii & others, 2004). Gay and lesbian youth who do not experiment with heterosexual intercourse are spared the risk of pregnancy, but, like their heterosexual peers, they still face the risk of sexually transmitted infections.

The good news is that adolescents are increasing their use of contraceptives (Schaalma & others, 2004). Adolescent girls' contraceptive use at first intercourse rose from 48 percent to 65 percent during the 1980s (Forrest & Singh, 1990). By 1995, use at first intercourse reached 78 percent, with two-thirds of that figure involving condom use. A sexually active adolescent who does not use contraception has a 90 percent chance of pregnancy within one year (Alan Guttmacher Institute, 1998). The method of contraception used most frequently by adolescent girls is the pill (44 percent), followed by the condom (38 percent). About 10 percent use an injectable contraceptive, 4 percent use withdrawal, and 3 percent use an implant (Alan Guttmacher Institute, 1998). Approximately one-third of adolescent girls who rely on condoms also take the pill or practice withdrawal.

Although adolescent contraceptive use is increasing, many sexually active adolescents still do not use contraceptives, or they use them inconsistently (Ford, Sohn,

& Lepowski, 2001; Singh & others, 2004; Strong & others, 2005). Sexually active younger adolescents are less likely than older adolescents to take contraceptive precautions. Younger adolescents are more likely to use a condom or withdrawal, whereas older adolescents are more likely to use the pill or a diaphragm. In one study, adolescent females reported changing their behavior in the direction of safer sex practices more than did adolescent males (Rimberg & Lewis, 1994).

Sexually Transmitted Infections   **Sexually transmitted infections (STIs)** are contracted primarily through sexual contact, which is not limited to sexual intercourse. Oral-genital and anal-genital contact also can transmit STIs.

Every year more than 3 million American adolescents (about one-fourth of those who are sexually experienced) acquire an STI (Centers for Disease Control and Prevention, 2004). In a single act of unprotected sex with an infected partner, a teenage girl has a 1 percent risk of getting HIV, a 30 percent risk of acquiring genital herpes, and a 50 percent chance of contracting gonorrhea (Glei, 1999). Chlamydia (which can spread by sexual contact and infects the genitals of both sexes) is more common among adolescents than among young adults (Weinstock, Berman, & Cates, 2004). In some areas, as many as 25 percent of sexually active adolescents have contracted chlamydia (Donovan, 1993). In a cross-cultural study of sixteen developed countries, the incidence of chlamydia was high among adolescents in all of the countries (Panchaud & others, 2000). Adolescents also have a higher incidence of gonorrhea than do young adults.

In chapter 14, we will study sexually transmitted infections in more depth. Earlier we mentioned that when adolescents are sexually active and do not use contraception, one possible outcome is adolescent pregnancy. Let's further explore the nature of adolescent pregnancy.

Adolescent Pregnancy   In cross-cultural comparisons, the United States continues to have one of the highest adolescent pregnancy and childbearing rates in the industrialized world, despite a considerable decline in the 1990s (Centers for Disease Control and Prevention, 2002) (see figure 12.6). The U.S. adolescent pregnancy rate is eight times as high as in the Netherlands. Although U.S. adolescents are no more sexually active than their counterparts in the Netherlands, their adolescent pregnancy rate is dramatically higher.

There are encouraging trends, though, in U.S. adolescent pregnancy rates. In 2002, births to adolescent girls fell to a record low (National Center for Health Statistics, 2004). The rate of births to adolescent girls has dropped 25 percent since 1991. Reasons for the decline include increased contraceptive use, fear of sexually transmitted infections such as AIDS, and the economic prosperity of the 1990s, which may have motivated adolescents to delay starting a family so that they could take jobs. The greatest drop in U.S. adolescent pregnancy rates in the 1990s was for 15- to 17-year-old girls. There is a special concern about the continued high rate of adolescent pregnancy in Latinas (Child Trends, 2001).

The consequences of America's high adolescent pregnancy rate are cause for great concern. Adolescent pregnancy creates health risks for both the baby and the mother. Infants born to adolescent mothers are more likely to have low birth weights—a prominent factor in infant mortality—as well as neurological problems and childhood illness (Dryfoos, 1990). Adolescent mothers often drop out of school. Although many adolescent mothers resume their education later in life, they generally do not catch up economically with women who postpone childbearing until their twenties. One longitudinal study found that the children of women who had their first birth during their teens had lower achievement test scores and more behavioral problems than did children whose mothers had their first birth as adults (Hofferth & Reid, 2002).

The Alan Guttmacher Institute
CDC National Prevention Network
American Social Health Association
HIV/AIDS and Adolescents
Adolescent Pregnancy

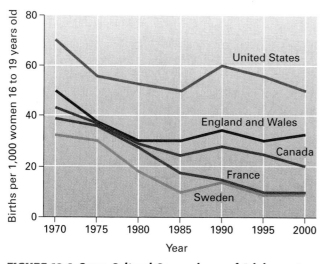

FIGURE 12.6 Cross-Cultural Comparisons of Adolescent Pregnancy Rates

sexually transmitted infections (STIs)
Infections that are contracted primarily through sexual contact, which is not limited to sexual intercourse. Oral-genital and anal-genital contact also can transmit STIs.

However, often it is not pregnancy alone that leads to negative consequences for an adolescent mother and her offspring (Hillis & others, 2004; Leadbetter & Way, 2001). Adolescent mothers are more likely to come from low-income backgrounds (Hoffman, Foster, & Furstenberg, 1993; Mehra & Agrawal, 2004). Many adolescent mothers also were not good students before they became pregnant. One recent study found that adolescent child-bearers were more likely to have a history of conduct problems, less educational attainment, and lower childhood socio-economic status than later child-bearers (Jaffee, 2002). However, in this study, early childbearing exacerbated the difficulties associated with these risks.

Keep in mind that not every adolescent female who bears a child lives a life of poverty and low achievement. Thus, although adolescent pregnancy is a high-risk circumstance and in general adolescents who do not become pregnant fare better than those who do, some adolescent mothers do well in school and have positive outcomes (Ahn, 1994; Barnet & others, 2004; Whitman & others, 2001). Serious, extensive efforts are needed to help pregnant adolescents and young mothers enhance their educational and occupational opportunities. Adolescent mothers also need help in obtaining competent child care and in planning for the future.

Family and consumer science educators teach life skills, such as effective decision making, to adolescents. To read about the work of one family and consumer science educator, see the Careers in Life-Span Development insert.

The Brain

In addition to the physical changes involved in puberty and sexuality, change also characterizes the brain during adolescence. What we know about brain development in adolescence is in its infancy, but as advances in technology take place, significant strides will also likely be made in charting developmental changes in the adolescent brain (Keating, 2003, 2004). What do we know now?

In chapter 8, "Physical and Cognitive Development in Early Childhood," we described how the pruning of synapses continues through late adolescence. Spurts in the brain's electrical activity seem to occur at about 9, 12, 15, and 18 to 20 years of age. These spurts may signal changes in cognitive development. During puberty, neural activity using the neurotransmitter dopamine increases while activity using the neurotransmitter serotonin decreases (Walker, 2002). What does this mean? Scientists do not know, but some have speculated that the increased risk for some mental disorders, such as schizophrenia, during adolescence and early adulthood may be due to this elevation of dopamine activity.

One of the most fascinating recent discoveries about the adolescent's brain focuses on developmental changes in the areas of the brain that involve emotion and higher-level cognitive functioning. The *amygdala* is a region of the brain that handles the processing of information about emotion; the prefrontal cortex is especially important in higher-level cognitive functioning (LeDoux, 2002). The amygdala matures earlier than the prefrontal cortex (see figure 12.7).

Careers in Life-Span Development

Lynn Blankenship, Family and Consumer Science Educator

Lynn Blankenship is a family and consumer science educator. She has an undergraduate degree in this area from the University of Arizona. She has taught for more than 20 years, the last 14 at Tucson High Magnet School.

Lynn was awarded the Tucson Federation of Teachers Educator of the Year Award for 1999–2000 and the Arizona Teacher of the Year in 1999.

Lynn especially enjoys teaching life skills to adolescents. One of her favorite activities is having students care for an automated baby that imitates the needs of real babies. She says that this program has a profound impact on students because the baby must be cared for around the clock for the duration of the assignment. Lynn also coordinates real-world work experiences and training for students in several child-care facilities in the Tucson area.

Lynn Blankenship (*center*) teaching life skills to students.

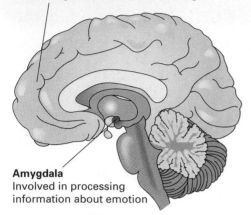

Prefrontal cortex
Involved in higher-order cognitive functioning, such as decision making

Amygdala
Involved in processing information about emotion

FIGURE 12.7 Developmental Changes in the Adolescent's Brain
The amygdala, which is responsible for processing information about emotion, matures earlier than the prefrontal cortex, which is responsible for making decisions and other higher-order cognitive functions. *What are some possible implications of these developmental changes in the brain for adolescents' behavior?*

In one study, researchers used functional magnetic resonance imaging (fMRI) to discover if the brain activity of adolescents (10- to 18-year-olds) differed from that of adults (20- to 40-years-olds) during the processing of emotional information (Baird & others, 1999). Participants viewed pictures of faces displaying fearful expressions while undergoing fMRI. When adolescents (especially the younger ones) processed emotional information, brain activity in the amygdala was more pronounced than in the prefrontal cortex, but the reverse occurred in adults. The researchers interpreted these findings to suggest that adolescents might be more likely to respond with "gut" reactions to emotional stimuli, whereas adults might be more likely to respond with rational, reasoned responses. The explanation for these results focused on the prefrontal cortex maturing later than the amygdala.

Thus, researchers are finding that the very last part of the brain to mature is the prefrontal cortex, where planning, setting priorities, suppressing impulses, and weighing the consequences of one's actions take place (Rubia & others, 2000). This means that the brain region for putting the brakes on risky, impulsive behavior and thinking before acting is still under construction during adolescence (Casey, Giedd, & Thomas, 2000; Giedd, 2004; Giedd & others, 1999). However, more research is needed to clarify these findings on possible developmental changes in brain activity and their links to adolescent thinking and behavior (Keating, 2004).

Review and Reflect: Learning Goal 2

2 Describe the changes involved in puberty, sexuality, and the brain

REVIEW

- What are some key aspects of puberty?
- What are some important aspects of sexuality in adolescence?
- What changes characterize the brain during adolescence?

REFLECT

- Did you experience puberty early or late? How did this timing affect your development?

3 ADOLESCENT PROBLEMS AND HEALTH

| Substance Use and Abuse | Eating Problems and Disorders | Adolescent Health |

In addition to the sexual problems that we just discussed, other problems that can develop during adolescence are substance abuse and eating disorders. We will discuss these problems here, and then in chapter 13 we will explore the adolescent problems of juvenile delinquency, depression, and suicide. In this section, we will also examine the impact of adolescence on health-related behaviors.

Substance Use and Abuse

The 1960s and 1970s were a time of marked increases in the use of illicit drugs. During the social and political unrest of those years, many youth turned to marijuana, stimulants, and hallucinogens. Adolescents also increased their alcohol consumption (Robinson & Greene, 1988). More precise data about drug use by adolescents have been collected in recent years (Fields, 2005).

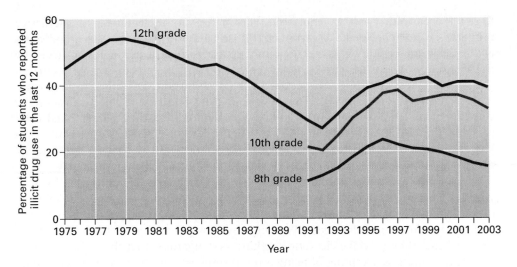

FIGURE 12.8 Trends in Drug Use by U.S. Eighth-, Tenth-, and Twelfth-Grade Students
This graph shows the percentage of U.S. eighth-, tenth-, and twelfth-grade students who reported having taken an illicit drug in the last 12 months from 1991 to 2003 for eighth- and tenth-graders, and from 1975 to 2003 for twelfth-graders (Johnston, O'Malley, & Bachman, 2004).

Trends in Drug Use   Each year since 1975, Lloyd Johnston, Patrick O'Malley, and Gerald Bachman, working at the Institute of Social Research at the University of Michigan, have carefully monitored the drug use of America's high school seniors in a wide range of public and private high schools. Since 1991, they also have surveyed drug use by eighth- and tenth-graders. The University of Michigan study is called the Monitoring the Future Study. In 2003, the study surveyed approximately 50,000 students in nearly 400 secondary schools.

The use of drugs among U.S. secondary school students declined in the 1980s but began to increase in the early 1990s. Since 1998, high school seniors' drug use has declined slightly (Johnston, O'Malley, & Bachman, 2004). Figure 12.8 shows the trends in illegal drug use by U.S. high school seniors from 1975 through 2003. The slight recent downturn in drug use by U.S. adolescents has been attributed to factors such as an increase in the perceived dangers of drug use. In addition, the tragedy of the terrorist attacks of 9/11/01 have had a sobering effect on youth.

Nonetheless, even with the recent decline, the United States still has the highest rate of adolescent drug use of any industrialized nation. Also, the University of Michigan survey likely underestimates the percentage of adolescents who take drugs because it does not include high school dropouts, who have a higher rate of drug use than do students who are still in school.

Alcohol   How extensive is alcohol use by adolescents? There have been sizeable drops at the eighth, tenth, and twelfth grades in the percentage of U.S. students saying that they had any alcohol to drink in the past 30 days (Johnston, O'Malley, & Bachman, 2004). The 30-day prevalence of alcohol use by eighth-graders has fallen from a 1996 high of 26 percent to 20 percent in 2003. From 2001 to 2003, 30-day prevalence among tenth-graders fell from 39 to 35 percent. Monthly prevalence among high school seniors was 72 percent in 1980 but had declined to 47 percent in 2003. Binge drinking (defined in the University of Michigan surveys as having five or more drinks in a row in the last two weeks) by twelfth-graders fell from 41 percent to 31 percent in 2003. Binge drinking by eighth- and tenth-graders also has declined in the twenty-first century (7 percent of eighth-graders and 18 percent of tenth-graders said they had been drunk in the last 30 days in 2003). A consistent sex difference occurs in binge drinking, with males engaging in this more than do females. In 1997, 39 percent of male high school seniors said they had been drunk in the last two weeks, compared with 29 percent of their female counterparts.

Although alcohol use by secondary school students has declined in recent years, college students show little drop in alcohol use and an increase in heavy drinking. Heavy drinking at parties among college males is common and is becoming more common (Wechsler & others, 2002).

National Clearinghouse for
Alcohol and Drug Information
Monitoring the Future

Cigarette Smoking Once adolescents begin to smoke cigarettes, the addictive properties of nicotine make it extremely difficult for them to stop. The good news is that cigarette smoking is decreasing among adolescents. In the national survey by the Institute of Social Research, the percentage of U.S. adolescents who are current cigarette smokers continued to decline in 2003 (Johnston, O'Malley, & Bachman, 2004). Cigarette smoking peaked in 1996 and 1997 and has declined considerably since then. In 1997, 36 percent of high school seniors said they had smoked cigarettes in the last 30 days, but in 2003 this figure had declined to 24 percent. Similar declines were found for tenth- and eighth-graders (30 percent in 1996 to 17 percent in 2003 and 21 percent in 1996 to 10 percent in 2003, respectively).

There are a number of explanations for the decline in cigarette use by U.S. youth. These include increasing prices, less tobacco advertising reaching adolescents, more antismoking advertisements, and an increase in negative publicity about the tobacco industry. Since the mid-1990s, an increasing percentage of adolescents have reported that they perceive cigarette smoking as dangerous, that they disapprove of it, that they are less accepting of being around smokers, and that they prefer to date nonsmokers (Johnston, O'Malley, & Bachman, 2004).

One recent study examined the risk factors for becoming a regular smoker in adolescence (Tucker, Ellickson, & Klein, 2003). Risk factors included having a friend who smoked, having a weak academic orientation, and experiencing low parental support.

The devastating effects of early smoking were brought home in a research study that found that smoking in the adolescent years causes permanent genetic changes in the lungs and forever increases the risk of lung cancer, even if the smoker quits (Weincke & others, 1999). The damage was much less likely among smokers in the study who started in their twenties. One of the remarkable findings in the study was that the early age of onset of smoking was more important in predicting genetic damage than how much the individuals smoked.

The Roles of Development, Parents, and Peers Most adolescents become drug users at some point in their development, whether limited to alcohol, caffeine, and cigarettes or extended to marijuana, cocaine, and hard drugs. A special concern involves adolescents using drugs as a way of coping with stress, which can interfere with the development of competent coping skills and responsible decision making. Researchers have found that drug use in childhood or early adolescence has more detrimental long-term effects on the development of responsible, competent behavior than when drug use occurs in late adolescence (Newcomb & Bentler, 1989). When they use drugs to cope with stress, many young adolescents enter adult roles of marriage and work prematurely, without adequate socioemotional growth, and experience greater failure in adult roles.

How early are adolescents beginning drug use? National samples of eighth- and ninth-grade students were included for the first time in 1991 in the Institute for Social Research survey of drug use (Johnston, O'Malley, & Bachman, 1992). Early in the drug use increase in the United States (late 1960s, early 1970s), drug use was much higher among college students than among high school students, who in turn had much higher rates of drug use than middle or junior high school students. However, today the rates for college and high school students are similar, and the rates for young adolescents are not as different from those of older adolescents as might be anticipated.

Parents, peers, and social support play important roles in preventing adolescent drug abuse (Hotton & Haans, 2004; Litt, 2003; Wills & others, 2004). Positive relationships with parents and others are important in reducing adolescents' drug use (Borawski & others, 2003; Little & others, 2004; Wood & others, 2004). In one recent study, parental control and monitoring were linked with a lower incidence of problem behavior by adolescents, including substance abuse (Fletcher, Steinberg, & Williams-Wheeler, 2004). Another study revealed that low parental involvement, peer pressure, and associating with problem-behaving friends were linked with higher use of drugs by adolescents (Simons-Morton & others, 2001). Also, a recent national survey revealed that parents who were more involved in setting limits, such as where adolescents went after school and what they were exposed to on TV and the Internet, were more likely to have adolescents who did not use drugs (National Center on Addiction and Substance Abuse, 2001). One longitudinal study linked the early onset of substance abuse with early childhood predictors (Kaplow & others, 2002). Risk factors at kindergarten for substance use at 10 to 12 years of age included being male, having a parent who abused substances, having a low level of verbal reasoning by parents, and having low social problem-solving skills. To read about a program designed to reduce young adolescents' drinking and smoking, see the Research in Life-Span Development interlude.

Research in Life-Span Development

Evaluation of a Family Program Designed to Reduce Drinking and Smoking in Young Adolescents

Few experimental studies have been conducted to determine if family programs can reduce drinking and smoking in young adolescents. In one recent experimental study, 1,326 families with 12- to 14-year-old adolescents living throughout the United States were interviewed (Bauman & others, 2002). After the baseline interviews, participants were randomly assigned either to go through the Family Matters program (experimental group) or to not experience the program (control group) (Bauman & others, 2002).

A description of the Family Matters program follows (Bauman & others, 2002, pp. 36–37). It "involves successive mailings of four booklets to families and telephone discussions with health educators after each mailing. Two weeks after family members read a booklet and complete the activities designed to reinforce its content, a health educator contacts the parent by telephone to encourage participation by all family members, answer any questions, and record information." The first booklet, "Why Families Matter," focuses on the negative consequences of adolescent substance abuse to the family. Booklet two, "Helping Families Matter to Teens," emphasizes "supervision, support, communication skills, attachment, time spent together, educational achievement, conflict reduction, and how well adolescence is understood." The third booklet, "Alcohol and Tobacco Rules Are Family Matters," asks parents to "list things that they do that might inadvertently encourage their child's use of tobacco or alcohol, identify rules that might influence the child's use,

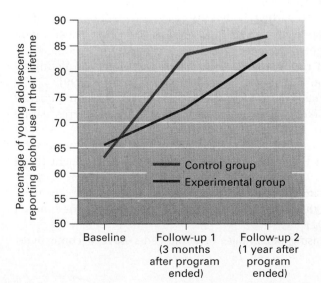

FIGURE 12.9 Young Adolescents' Reports of Alcohol Use in the Family Matters Program

Note that at baseline (before the program started) the young adolescents in the Family Matters program (experimental group) and their counterparts who did not go through the program (control group) reported approximately the same lifetime use of alcohol (slightly higher use by the experimental group). However, three months after the program ended, the experimental group reported lower alcohol use, and this reduction was still present one year after the program ended, although at a reduced level.

FIGURE 12.10 Young Adolescents' Reports of Cigarette Smoking in the Family Matters Program

Note that at baseline (before the program started) the young adolescents in the Family Matters program (experimental group) and their counterparts who did not go through the program (control group) reported approximately the same lifetime cigarette smoking (slightly higher use by the control group). However, three months after the program ended, the experimental group reported reduced cigarette smoking and this reduction was still present one year after the program ended.

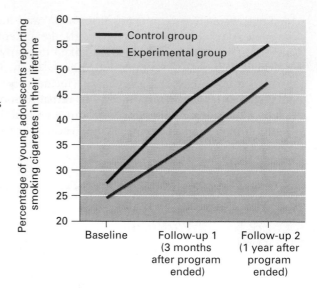

and consider ways to monitor use. Then adult family members and the child meet to agree upon rules and sanctions related to adolescent use." Booklet four, "Non-Family Influences That Matter," deals with what "the child can do to resist peer and media pressures for use." For example, "in one activity, the parents and adolescent practice what to do if a friend offers alcohol and tobacco and in another they watch favorite television shows to discuss tobacco and alcohol-related messages."

Two follow-up interviews with the parents and adolescents were conducted three months and one year after the experimental group completed the program. As shown in figures 12.9 and 12.10, adolescents in the Family Matters program reported lower alcohol and cigarette use both at three months and again one year after the program had been completed.

Substance abuse is a serious problem in adolescence. As we see next, eating disorders also can become serious problems in adolescence, especially for females.

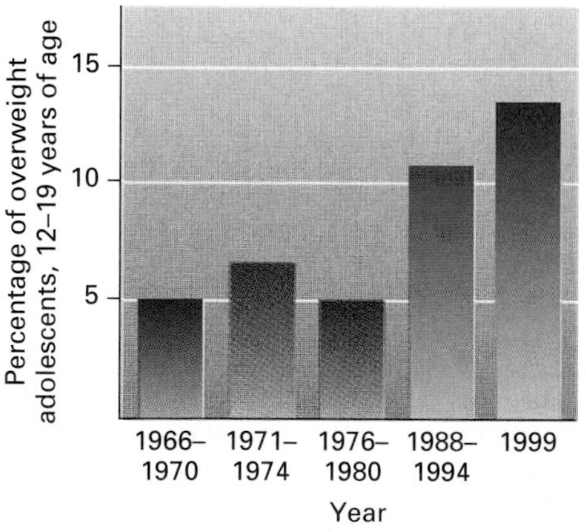

Eating Problems and Disorders

Eating disorders have become increasingly common in adolescence (Gowers & Bryant-Waugh, 2004; Irwin, 2004; Polivy & others, 2003). Here are some research findings involving adolescent eating disorders:

- Girls who felt negatively about their bodies in early adolescence were more likely to develop eating disorders, two years later, than their counterparts who did not feel negatively about their bodies (Attie & Brooks-Gunn, 1989).
- Negative parent-adolescent relationships were linked with increased dieting by girls over a one-year period (Archibald, Graber, & Brooks-Gunn, 1999).
- Girls who were both sexually active with their boyfriends and in pubertal transition were the most likely to be dieting or engaging in disordered eating patterns (Cauffman, 1994).
- Girls who were highly motivated to look like same-sex figures in the media were more likely than their peers to become very concerned about their weight (Field & others, 2001).
- Adolescent girls who watched four hours of television or more per day were more likely to be overweight than those who watched less than four hours a day (Dowda & others, 2001).
- Since the 1960s, an increasing percentage of adolescents have become overweight (see figure 12.11).

FIGURE 12.11 The Increase in Being Overweight in Adolescence from 1968 to 1999 in the United States

In this study, being overweight was determined by body mass index (BMI), which is computed by a formula that takes into account height and weight (National Center for Health Statistics, 2000). There was a substantial increase in the percentage of adolescents who were overweight from 1968 to 1999.

Let's now examine two eating disorders that may appear in adolescence: anorexia nervosa and bulimia nervosa.

Anorexia Nervosa   Although most U.S. girls have been on a diet at some point, slightly less than 1 percent ever develop anorexia nervosa (Walters & Kendler, 1994). **Anorexia nervosa** is an eating disorder that involves the relentless pursuit of thinness through starvation. Anorexia nervosa is a serious disorder that can lead to death (Agras & others, 2004). Three main characteristics of anorexia nervosa are:

- Weighing less than 85 percent of what is considered normal for their age and height.
- Having an intense fear of gaining weight. The fear does not decrease with weight loss.
- Having a distorted image of their body shape (Polivy & others, 2003; Striegel-Moore & others, 2004). Even when they are extremely thin, they see themselves as too fat. They never think they are thin enough, especially in the abdomen, buttocks, and thighs. They usually weigh themselves frequently, often take their body measurements, and gaze critically at themselves in mirrors (Seidenfeld, Sosin, & Rickert, 2004).

Anorexia nervosa typically begins in the early to middle teenage years, often following an episode of dieting and some type of life stress. It is about 10 times more likely to occur in females than males. When anorexia nervosa does occur in males, the symptoms and other characteristics (such as family conflict) are usually similar to those reported by females who have the disorder (Olivardia & others, 1995).

Most anorexics are White adolescent or young adult females from well-educated, middle- and upper-income families and are competitive and high-achieving (Schmidt, 2003). They set high standards, become stressed about not being able to reach the standards, and are intensely concerned about how others perceive them (Striegel-Moore, Silberstein, & Rodin, 1993). Unable to meet these high expectations, they turn to something they can control: their weight.

The fashion image in the American culture that emphasizes "thin is beautiful" contributes to the incidence of anorexia nervosa (Hsu, 2004; Polivy & others, 2003). This image is reflected in the saying, "You never can be too rich or too thin." The media portrays thin as beautiful in their choice of fashion models, which many adolescent girls want to emulate.

Bulimia Nervosa   Whereas anorexics control their eating by restricting it, most bulimics cannot (Mitchell & Mazzeo, 2004). **Bulimia nervosa** is an eating disorder in which the individual consistently follows a binge-and-purge pattern. The bulimic goes on an eating binge and then purges by self-inducing vomiting or using a laxative. Although many people binge and purge occasionally and some experiment with it, a person is considered to have a serious bulimic disorder only if the episodes occur at least twice a week for three months.

As with anorexics, most bulimics are preoccupied with food, have a strong fear of becoming overweight, and are depressed or anxious (Davison & Neale, 2004; Garcia-Alba, 2004; Quadflieg & Fichter, 2003). Unlike anorexics, people who binge-and-purge typically fall within a normal weight range, which makes bulimia more difficult to detect.

Approximately 1 to 2 percent of U.S. women are estimated to develop bulimia nervosa (Gotesdam & Agras, 1995), and about 90 percent of the cases are in women. Bulimia nervosa typically begins in late adolescence or early adulthood. Many women who develop bulimia nervosa were somewhat overweight before the onset of the disorder, and the binge eating often began during an episode of dieting. One recent study of adolescent girls found that increased dieting, pressure to be thin, exaggerated emphasis on appearance, body dissatisfaction, depression symptoms, low self-esteem, and low social support predicted binge eating two years later (Stice,

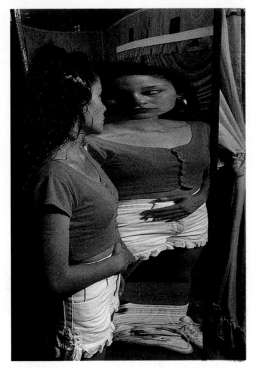

Anorexia nervosa has become an increasing problem for adolescent girls and young adult women. *What are some possible causes of anorexia nervosa?*

anorexia nervosa An eating disorder that involves the relentless pursuit of thinness through starvation.

bulimia nervosa An eating disorder in which the individual consistently follows a binge-and-purge pattern.

www.mhhe.com/santrockld10

Adolescent Health

Presnell, & Spangler, 2002). As with anorexia nervosa, about 70 percent of individuals who develop bulimia nervosa eventually recover from the disorder (Agras & others, 2004; Keel & others, 1999).

Let's now turn our attention to the role of adolescence in the development of health.

Adolescent Health

How important is adolescence in the development of health? What are the leading causes of death in adolescence?

Adolescence: A Critical Juncture in Health Adolescence is a critical juncture in the adoption of behaviors relevant to health (Blum & Nelson-Mmari, 2004; Roth & Brooks-Gunn, 2000; Spear & Kolbok, 2001). Many of the factors linked to poor health habits and early death in the adult years begin during adolescence. The early formation of healthy behavioral patterns, such as eating foods low in fat and cholesterol and engaging in regular exercise not only has immediate health benefits but contributes to the delay or prevention of major causes of premature disability and mortality in adulthood—heart disease, stroke, diabetes, and cancer (Jamner & others, 2004; Jessor, Turbin, & Costa, 1998; Sylvia, 2004).

In a comparison of adolescent health behavior in 28 countries, U.S. adolescents exercised less and ate more junk food than adolescents in most other countries (World Health Organization, 2000). Just two-thirds of U.S. adolescents exercised at least twice a week, compared with 80 percent or more of adolescents in Ireland, Austria, Germany, and the Slovak Republic. U.S. adolescents were more likely to eat fried food and less likely to eat fruits and vegetables than adolescents in most other countries studied. U.S. adolescents' eating choices were similar to those of adolescents in England. Eleven-year-olds in the United States were as likely as European 11-year-olds to smoke, but by age 15 U.S. adolescents were less likely to smoke.

Ethnic differences in exercise participation rates of U.S. adolescents is noteworthy (Frenn & others, 2003; Sanchez-Johnsen & others, 2004; Saxena, Borzekowski, & Rickert, 2002). In one recent study, the activity habits of more than 1,000 African American and more than 1,000 non-Latino White girls were examined annually from 9 to 10 years of age to 18 to 19 years of age (Kimm & others, 2002). (The study did not include boys because it was designed to determine why more African American women than non-Latino White women become obese.) At 9 to 10 years of age, most girls reported they were engaging in some physical activity outside of school. However, by 16 to 17 years of age, 56 percent of African American girls and 31 percent of non-Latino White girls were not engaging in any regular physical activity in their spare time. By 18 to 19 years of age, the figures were 70 percent and 29 percent, respectively. In sum, physical activity declines substantially in girls during adolescence and more in African American than non-Latino White girls (Kimm & Obarzanek, 2002).

Not only is there concern about nutrition and exercise in adolescence, there also has been a surge of interest in adolescent sleep patterns (Carskadon, 2002, 2004; Voelker, 2004). This interest focuses on the belief that many adolescents are not getting enough sleep and that their desire to stay up later at night and sleep longer in the morning has physiological underpinnings. These findings have implications for the hours during which adolescents learn most effectively in school (Dahl & Lewin, 2002). One recent study of 2,259 U.S. 11- to 14-year-olds found that not getting enough sleep was associated with lower self-esteem and higher levels of depression (Fredriksen & others, 2004).

Mary Carskadon and her colleagues (Carskadon, 2002, 2004; Acebo & Carskadon, 2002; Carskadon, Acebo, & Jenni, 2004) have conducted a number of research studies on adolescent sleep patterns. They found that when given the opportunity adolescents will sleep an average of nine hours and 25 minutes a night. Most get considerably less than nine hours of sleep, especially during the week. This shortfall creates a sleep deficit, which adolescents often attempt to make up on the weekend. The researchers also found that older adolescents tend to be more sleepy during the day than younger adolescents. They theorized that this sleepiness was not due to academic work or social pressures. Rather, their research suggests that adolescents' biological clocks undergo a shift as they get older, delaying their period of wakefulness by about one hour. A delay in the nightly release of the sleep-inducing hormone melatonin, which is produced in the brain's pineal gland, seems to underlie this shift. Melatonin is secreted at about 9:30 P.M. in younger adolescents and approximately an hour later in older adolescents.

Carskadon has suggested that early school starting times may cause grogginess, inattention in class, and poor performance on tests. Based on her research, school officials in Edina, Minnesota, decided to start classes at 8:30 A.M. rather than the usual 7:25 A.M. Since then, there have been fewer referrals for discipline problems and the number of students who report being ill or depressed has decreased. The school system reports that test scores have improved for high school students, but not for middle school students. This finding supports Carskadon's suspicion that early start times are likely to be more stressful for older than for younger adolescents.

Many health experts propose that improving adolescent health involves far more than trips to a doctor's office when sick. The health experts increasingly recognize that whether adolescents will develop a health problem or be healthy is primarily based on their behavior. The goals are to (1) reduce adolescents' health-compromising behaviors, such as drug abuse, violence, unprotected sexual intercourse, and dangerous driving; and (2) increase health-enhancing behaviors, such as eating nutritiously, exercising, wearing seat belts, and getting more sleep.

How might changing sleep patterns in adolescents affect their school performance?

Risk-Taking Behavior   One type of health-compromising behavior that increases in adolescence is risk taking. For example, beginning in early adolescence, individuals

> *seek* experiences that create high intensity feelings. Adolescents *like* intensity, excitement, and arousal. They are drawn to music videos that shock and bombard the senses. Teenagers flock to horror and slasher movies. They dominate queues waiting to ride the high-adrenaline rides at amusement parks. Adolescence is a time when sex, drugs, *very* loud music, and other high-stimulation experiences take on great appeal. It is a developmental period when an appetite for adventure, a predilection for risks, and a desire for novelty and thrills seem to reach naturally high levels. While these patterns of emotional changes are evident to some degree in most adolescents, it is important to acknowledge the wide range of individual differences during this period of development. (Dahl, 2004, p. 6)

What can be done to help adolescents satisfy their motivation for risk taking without compromising their health? As Laurence Steinberg (2004, p. 58) argues, one strategy is to limit

> opportunities for immature judgment to have harmful consequences. Thus, strategies such as raising the price of cigarettes, more vigilantly enforcing laws governing the sale of alcohol, expanding access to mental health and contraceptive services, and raising the driving age would likely be more effective in limiting adolescent smoking, substance abuse, suicide, pregnancy, and automobile fatalities than strategies aimed at making adolescents wiser, less impulsive, and less-short-sighted.

It also is important for parents, teachers, mentors, and other responsible adults to effectively monitor adolescents' behavior (Dahl, 2004). In many cases, adults decrease their monitoring of adolescents too early, leaving them to cope with tempting situations alone or with friends and peers (Masten, 2004). When adolescents are in tempting and dangerous situations with minimal adult supervision, their inclination to engage in risk-taking behavior combined with their lack of self-regulatory skills can make them vulnerable to a host of negative outcomes.

Leading Causes of Death in Adolescence Medical improvements have increased the life expectancy of today's adolescents compared with their counterparts who lived earlier in the twentieth century. Still, life-threatening factors continue to exist in adolescents' lives.

The three leading causes of death in adolescence are accidents, homicide, and suicide (Gould, 2001). More than half of all deaths in adolescents ages 10 to 19 are due to accidents, and most of those involve motor vehicles, especially for older adolescents. Risky driving habits, such as speeding, tailgating, and driving under the influence of alcohol or other drugs, may be more important causes of these accidents than is lack of driving experience. In about 50 percent of the motor vehicle fatalities involving an adolescent, the driver has a blood alcohol level of 0.10 percent, twice the level needed to be "under the influence" in some states. A high rate of intoxication is also often present in adolescents who die as pedestrians or while using recreational vehicles.

Homicide is the second leading cause of death in adolescence (National Center for Health Statistics, 2004). Homicide is especially high among African American male adolescents, who are three times more likely to be killed by guns than by natural causes (Simons, Finlay, & Yang, 1991). Suicide accounts for 6 percent of the deaths in the 10-to-14 age group, a rate of 1.3 per 100,000 people. In the 15-to-19 age group, suicide accounts for 12 percent of deaths or 9 per 100,000 people. Since the 1950s, the adolescent suicide rate has tripled. We will discuss suicide further in chapter 13.

Review and Reflect: Learning Goal 3

 3 **Identify adolescent problems in substance use and abuse, eating disorders, and health**

REVIEW

- What are some characteristics of adolescents' substance use and abuse and eating disorders?
- Why is adolescence a critical juncture in health? What are the leading causes of death in adolescence?

REFLECT

- What do you think should be done to reduce the use of drugs by adolescents?

4 ADOLESCENT COGNITION

| Piaget's Theory | Adolescent Egocentrism | Information Processing |

Adolescents' developing power of thought opens up new cognitive and social horizons. Let's examine what their developing power of thought is like, beginning with Piaget's theory (1952).

Piaget's Theory

What are Jean Piaget's ideas about cognitive development in adolescence? To answer this question, we will study Piaget's stage of formal operational thought.

Most significantly, formal operational thought is more abstract than concrete operational thought. Adolescents are no longer limited to actual, concrete experiences as anchors for thought. They can conjure up make-believe situations, events that are purely hypothetical possibilities or strictly abstract propositions, and can try to reason logically about them.

The abstract quality of the adolescent's thought at the formal operational level is evident in the adolescent's verbal problem-solving ability. Whereas the concrete operational thinker needs to see the concrete elements A, B, and C to be able to make the logical inference that, if A = B and B = C, then A = C, the formal operational thinker can solve this problem merely through verbal presentation.

Another indication of the abstract quality of adolescents' thought is their increased tendency to think about thought itself. One adolescent commented, "I began thinking about why I was thinking what I was. Then I began thinking about why I was thinking about what I was thinking about what I was." If this sounds abstract, it is, and it characterizes the adolescent's enhanced focus on thought and its abstract qualities.

Accompanying the abstract nature of formal operational thought in adolescence is thought full of idealism and possibilities. Although children frequently think in concrete ways, or in terms of what is real and limited, adolescents begin to engage in extended speculation about ideal characteristics—qualities they desire in themselves and in others. Such thoughts often lead adolescents to compare themselves with others in regard to such ideal standards. And, during adolescence, the thoughts of individuals are often fantasy flights into future possibilities. It is not unusual for the adolescent to become impatient with these newfound ideal standards and to become perplexed over which of many ideal standards to adopt.

At the same time that adolescents think more abstractly and idealistically, they also think more logically. Adolescents begin to think more as a scientist thinks, devising plans to solve problems and systematically testing solutions. This type of problem solving has an imposing name. **Hypothetical-deductive reasoning** is Piaget's formal operational concept that adolescents have the cognitive ability to develop hypotheses, or best guesses, about ways to solve problems, such as an algebraic equation. Then they systematically deduce, or conclude, which is the best path to follow in solving the equation. By contrast, children are more likely to solve problems in a trial-and-error fashion.

One example of hypothetical-deductive reasoning involves a modification of the familiar game Twenty Questions. Individuals are shown a set of 42 color pictures, displayed in a rectangular array (six rows of seven pictures each) and are asked to determine which picture the experimenter has in mind (that is, which is "correct"). The individuals are allowed to ask only questions to which the experimenter can answer yes or no. The object of the game is to select the correct picture by asking as few questions as possible. Adolescents who are deductive hypothesis testers formulate a plan and test a series of hypotheses, which considerably narrows the field of choices. The most effective plan is a "halving" strategy (Q: Is the picture in the right half of the array? A: No. Q: Okay. Is it in the top half? And so on.). A correct halving strategy guarantees the answer in seven questions or less. By contrast, concrete operational thinkers may persist with questions that continue to test some of

Might adolescents' ability to reason hypothetically and to evaluate what is ideal versus what is real lead them to engage in demonstrations, such as this protest related to better ethnic relations? What other causes might be attractive to adolescents' newfound cognitive abilities of hypothetical-deductive reasoning and idealistic thinking?

hypothetical-deductive reasoning Piaget's formal operational concept that adolescents have the cognitive ability to develop hypotheses, or best guesses, about ways to solve problems, such as an algebraic equation.

*T*he thoughts of youth are
long, long thoughts.

—Henry Wadsworth Longfellow
American Poet, 19th Century

Many adolescent girls spend long hours in front of the mirror, depleting cans of hairspray, tubes of lipstick, and jars of cosmetics. *How might this behavior be related to changes in adolescent cognitive and physical development?*

adolescent egocentrism The heightened self-consciousness of adolescents.

imaginary audience Involves adolescents' belief that others are as interested in them as they themselves are; attention-getting behavior motivated by a desire to be noticed, visible, and "on stage."

personal fable The part of adolescent egocentrism that involves an adolescent's sense of uniqueness and invincibility.

the same possibilities that previous questions could have eliminated. For example, they may ask whether the correct picture is in row 1 and are told that it is not. Later, they may ask whether the picture is *X*, which is in row 1.

Thus, formal operational thinkers test their hypotheses with judiciously chosen questions and tests. By contrast, concrete operational thinkers often fail to understand the relation between a hypothesis and a well-chosen test of it, stubbornly clinging to ideas that already have been discounted.

Some of Piaget's ideas on formal operational thought are being challenged (Byrnes, 2003; Eccles, Wigfield, & Byrnes, 2003; Keating, 2004; Kuhn, 2000). There is much more individual variation in formal operational thought than Piaget envisioned. Only about one in three young adolescents is a formal operational thinker. Many American adults never become formal operational thinkers, and neither do many adults in other cultures. Education in the logic of science and mathematics is an important cultural experience that promotes the development of formal operational thinking.

Also, for adolescents who become formal operational thinkers, assimilation (incorporating new information into existing knowledge) dominates the initial development of formal operational thought, and the world is perceived subjectively and idealistically. Later in adolescence, as intellectual balance is restored, these individuals accommodate (adjust to new information) to the cognitive upheaval that has occurred.

In addition to thinking more logically, abstractly, and idealistically, which characterizes Piaget's formal operational thought stage, in what other ways does adolescent cognition change? One important way involves adolescent egocentrism.

Adolescent Egocentrism

"Oh, my gosh! I can't believe it. Help! I can't stand it!" Tracy desperately yells. "What is wrong? What is the matter?" her mother asks. Tracy responds, "Everyone in here is looking at me." The mother queries, "Why?" Tracy says, "Look, this one hair just won't stay in place," as she rushes to the restroom of the restaurant. Five minutes later, she returns to the table in the restaurant after she has depleted an entire can of hairspray.

Adolescent egocentrism is the heightened self-consciousness of adolescents. David Elkind (1976) believes that adolescent egocentrism can be dissected into two types of social thinking—imaginary audience and personal fable. The notion of **imaginary audience** involves adolescents' belief that others are as interested in them as they themselves are, as well as attention-getting behavior—attempts to be noticed, visible, and "on stage." Tracy's comments and behavior that we described in the first paragraph of this section reflect the imaginary audience. Another adolescent might think that others are as aware of a small spot on his trousers as he is, possibly knowing that he has masturbated. Another adolescent, an eighth-grade girl, walks into her classroom and thinks that all eyes are riveted on her complexion. Adolescents especially sense that they are "on stage" in early adolescence, believing they are the main actors and all others are the audience.

According to Elkind, the **personal fable** is the part of adolescent egocentrism involving an adolescent's sense of uniqueness and invincibility. During a conversation between two 14-year-old girls, one named Margaret says, "Are you kidding, I won't get pregnant." And 13-year-old Adam describes himself, "No one understands me, particularly my parents. They have no idea of what I am feeling." The comments of Margaret and Adam reflect the personal fable. Adolescents' sense of personal uniqueness makes them feel that no one can understand how they really feel. For example, an adolescent girl thinks that her mother cannot possibly sense the hurt she feels because her boyfriend has broken up with her. As part of their effort to retain a sense of personal uniqueness, adolescents might craft a story about the self that is filled with fantasy, immersing themselves in a world that is far removed from reality. Personal fables frequently show up in adolescent diaries.

Adolescents also often show a sense of invincibility, believing that they themselves will never suffer the terrible experiences (such as deadly car wrecks) that can happen to other people. This sense of invincibility likely is involved in the reckless behavior of some adolescents, such as drag racing, drug use, suicide, and having sexual intercourse without using contraceptives or barriers against STIs.

Information Processing

Two of the most important aspects of changes in information processing in adolescence involve decision making and critical thinking.

Decision Making   Adolescence is a time of increased decision making—about the future, which friends to choose, whether to go to college, which person to date, whether to have sex, whether to buy a car, and so on (Byrnes, 1997, 2001, 2003; Galotti & Kozberg, 1996; Jacobs & Klaczynski, 2002; Kuhn, 2000). How competent are adolescents at making decisions? In some reviews, older adolescents are described as more competent than younger adolescents, who, in turn, are more competent than children (Keating, 1990). Compared with children, young adolescents are more likely to generate options, to examine a situation from a variety of perspectives, to anticipate the consequences of decisions, and to consider the credibility of sources.

The ability to make competent decisions does not guarantee that they will be made in everyday life, where breadth of experience often comes into play (Jacobs & Klaczynski, 2002; Jacobs & Potenza, 1990; Keating, 1990). For example, driver-training courses improve adolescents' cognitive and motor skills to levels equal to, or sometimes superior to, those of adults. However, driver training has not been effective in reducing adolescents' high rate of traffic accidents (Potvin, Champagne, & Laberge-Nadeau, 1988). An important research agenda is to study the ways adolescents make decisions in practical situations.

One strategy for improving adolescents' decision making is for parents to involve their adolescents in appropriate decision-making activities. In one study of more than 900 young adolescents and a subsample of their parents, adolescents were more likely to participate in family decision making when they perceived themselves as in control of what happens to them and if they thought that their input would have some bearing on the outcome of the decision-making process (Liprie, 1993).

Critical Thinking   Adolescence is an important transitional period in the development of critical thinking (Keating, 1990). In one study of fifth-, eighth-, and eleventh-graders, critical thinking increased with age but still only occurred in 43 percent of even the eleventh-graders, and many adolescents showed self-serving biases in their reasoning (Klaczynski & Narasimham, 1998).

Among the cognitive changes that allow improved critical thinking in adolescence are:

- Increased speed, automaticity, and capacity of information processing, which free cognitive resources for other purposes
- More breadth of content knowledge in a variety of domains
- Increased ability to construct new combinations of knowledge
- A greater range and more spontaneous use of strategies or procedures for applying or obtaining knowledge, such as planning, considering alternatives, and cognitive monitoring

Although adolescence is an important period in the development of critical-thinking skills, if a solid basis of fundamental skills (such as literacy and math skills) is not developed during childhood, such critical-thinking skills are unlikely to

Although driver-training courses can improve adolescents' cognitive and motor skills related to driving, these courses have not been effective in reducing adolescents' high rate of traffic accidents. *Why might this be so?*

mature in adolescence. For the subset of adolescents who lack such fundamental skills, potential gains in adolescent thinking are not likely.

Review and Reflect: Learning Goal 4

4 **Explain cognitive changes in adolescence**

REVIEW

- What is Piaget's theory of adolescent cognitive development?
- What is adolescent egocentrism?
- What are some important aspects of decision making and critical thinking in adolescence?

REFLECT

- Using Piaget's theory of cognitive development as a guide, suppose an 8-year-old and a 16-year-old are watching a political convention on television. How might their perceptions of the proceedings differ? What Piagetian concepts would these perceptions reflect?

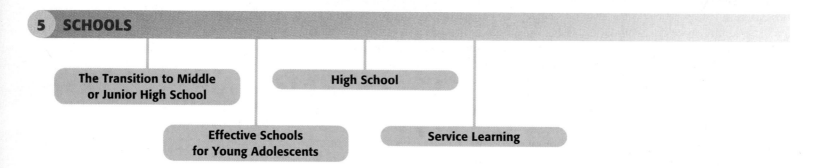

5 **SCHOOLS**

The Transition to Middle or Junior High School

High School

Effective Schools for Young Adolescents

Service Learning

The impressive changes in adolescents' cognition lead us to examine the nature of schools for adolescents. In chapter 11, we discussed different ideas about the effects of schools on children's development. Here we will focus more exclusively on the nature of secondary schools. Questions we will look at include: What is the transition from elementary to middle or junior high school like? What are effective schools for young adolescents?

The Transition to Middle or Junior High School

The emergence of junior high schools in the 1920s and 1930s was justified on the basis of the physical, cognitive, and social changes that characterize early adolescence, as well as the need for more schools for the growing student population. Old high schools became junior high schools, and new regional high schools were built. In most systems, the ninth grade remained a part of the high school in content, although physically separated from it in a 6-3-3 system. Gradually, the ninth grade was restored to the high school, as many school systems developed middle schools that include the seventh and eighth grades, or sixth, seventh, and eighth grades. The creation of middle schools was influenced by the earlier onset of puberty in recent decades.

One worry of educators and psychologists is that junior high and middle schools have simply become watered-down versions of high schools, mimicking their curricular and extracurricular schedules. The critics argue that unique curricular and extracurricular activities reflecting a wide range of individual differences in biological and psychological development in early adolescence should be incorporated into our junior high and middle schools. The critics also stress that many high schools foster passivity rather than autonomy and that schools should create a variety of pathways for students to achieve an identity.

The transition to middle school or junior high school from elementary schools interests developmentalists because, even though it is a normative experience for virtually all children, the transition can be stressful (Eccles, 2000, 2003; Seidman, 2000). Why? The transition takes place at a time when many changes—in the individual, in the family, and in school—are occurring simultaneously. These changes include puberty and related concerns about body image; the emergence of at least some aspects of formal operational thought, including accompanying changes in social cognition; increased responsibility and independence in association with decreased dependency on parents; change from a small, contained classroom structure to a larger, more impersonal school structure; change from one teacher to many teachers and from a small, homogeneous set of peers to a larger, more heterogeneous set of peers; and an increased focus on achievement and performance and their assessment. This list includes a number of negative, stressful features, but there can be positive aspects to the transition. Students are more likely to feel grown up, have more subjects from which to select, have more opportunities to spend time with peers and locate compatible friends, and enjoy increased independence from direct parental monitoring. They also may be more challenged intellectually by academic work.

When students make the transition from elementary school to middle or junior high school, they experience the **top-dog phenomenon,** the circumstance of moving from the top position (in elementary school, being the oldest, biggest, and most powerful students in the school) to the lowest position (in middle or junior high school, being the youngest, smallest, and least powerful students in the school). Researchers who have charted the transition from elementary to middle or junior high school find that the first year of middle or junior high school can be difficult for many students (Hawkins & Berndt, 1985). For example, in one study of the transition from sixth grade in an elementary school to the seventh grade in a junior high school, adolescents' perceptions of the quality of their school life plunged in the seventh grade (Hirsch & Rapkin, 1987). In the seventh grade, the students were less satisfied with school, were less committed to school, and liked their teachers less. The drop in school satisfaction occurred regardless of how academically successful the students were.

Schools for Adolescents
National Center for Education Statistics
United States Department of Education
Middle Schools

The transition from elementary to middle or junior high school occurs at the same time as a number of other developmental changes. *What are some of these other developmental changes?*

Effective Schools for Young Adolescents

In 1989 the Carnegie Corporation issued an extremely negative evaluation of our nation's middle schools. In the report, "Turning Points: Preparing American Youth for the 21st Century," the conclusion was put forth that most young adolescents attend massive, impersonal schools, learn from seemingly irrelevant curricula, trust few adults in school, and lack access to health care and counseling. The Carnegie Corporation (1989) report includes these recommendations:

- Develop smaller "communities" or "houses" to lessen the impersonal nature of large middle schools.
- Lower student-to-counselor ratios from several-hundred-to-1 to 10-to-1.
- Involve parents and community leaders in schools.
- Develop curricula that produce students who are literate, understand the sciences, and have a sense of health, ethics, and citizenship.
- Have teachers team teach in more flexibly designed curriculum blocks that integrate several disciplines, instead of presenting students with disconnected, rigidly separated 50-minute segments.

top-dog phenomenon The circumstance of moving from the top position in elementary school to the lowest position in middle or junior high school.

• Boost students' health and fitness with more in-school programs and help students who need public health care to get it.

In sum, middle schools throughout the nation need a major redesign if they are to be effective in educating adolescents for becoming competent adults in the twenty-first century (Eccles & Roeser, 2005).

High School

Just as there are concerns about U.S. middle school education, so are there concerns about U.S. high school education. Many students graduate from high school with inadequate reading, writing, and mathematical skills, including many who go on to college and have to enroll in remediation classes there. Other students drop out of high school and do not have skills that will allow them to advance in the work world.

High School Dropouts In the last half of the twentieth century, high school dropout rates declined overall (National Center for Education Statistics, 2001). For example, in the 1940s, more than half of U.S. 15- to 24-year-olds had dropped out of school; in 2000, this figure had decreased to only 10.9 percent. Figure 12.12 shows the trends in high school dropout rates from 1972 through 2000. Notice that the dropout rate of Latino adolescents remains high (27.8 percent of 15- to 24-year-old Latino adolescents had dropped out of school in 2000). The highest dropout rate in the United States, though, likely occurs for Native American youth—less than 50 percent finish their high school education.

Students drop out of schools for many reasons (Christensen & Thurlow, 2004). In one study, almost 50 percent of the dropouts cited school-related reasons for leaving school, such as not liking school or being expelled or suspended (Rumberger, 1995). Twenty percent of the dropouts (but 40 percent of the Latino students) cited economic reasons for leaving school. One-third of the female students dropped out for personal reasons, such as pregnancy or marriage.

A recent review of school-based dropout programs found that the most effective programs provided early reading programs, tutoring, counseling, and mentoring (Lehrer & others, 2003). They also emphasized the importance of creating caring environments and relationships, used block scheduling, and offered community-service opportunities.

Toward Effective High Schools Many high school graduates not only are poorly prepared for college, they also are poorly prepared for the demands of the modern, high-performance workplace. In a review of hiring practices at major companies, it was concluded that many companies now have sets of basic skills they want the individuals they hire to have. These include the ability to read at relatively high levels,

Reducing the Dropout Rate
High School Education

FIGURE 12.12 Trends in High School Dropout Rates

From 1972 through 2000, the school dropout rate for Latinos remained very high (27.8 percent of 15- to 24-year-olds in 2000). The African American dropout rate was still higher (13.1 percent) than the White non-Latino rate (6.9 percent) in 2000. The overall dropout rate declined considerably from the 1940s through the 1960s but has declined only slightly since 1972.

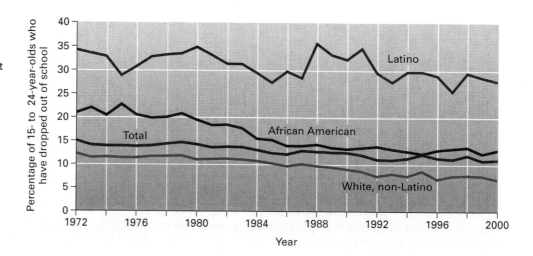

do at least elementary algebra, use personal computers for straightforward tasks such as word processing, solve semistructured problems in which hypotheses must be formed and tested, communicate effectively (orally and in writing), and work effectively in groups with persons of various backgrounds (Murnane & Levy, 1996).

An increasing number of educators believe that the nation's high schools need a new mission for the twenty-first century, which addresses the problems listed here (National Commission on the High School Senior Year, 2001):

- More support is needed to enable all students to graduate from high school with the knowledge and skills needed to succeed in post–secondary education and careers. Many parents and students, especially those in low-income and minority communities, are unaware of the knowledge and level of skills required to succeed in post–secondary education.
- High schools need to have higher expectations for student achievement. A special concern is the senior year of high school, which has become too much of a party-time rather than a time to prepare for one of life's most important transitions. Some students who have been accepted to college routinely ignore the academic demands of their senior year. Low academic expectations harm students from all backgrounds.
- U.S. high school students spend too much time working in low-level service jobs. Researchers have found that when tenth-graders work more than 14 hours a week their grades drop, and when eleventh-graders work 20 or more hours a week their grades drop (Greenberger & Steinberg, 1986). At the same time, shorter, higher-quality work experiences, including community service and internships, have been shown to benefit high school students.
- There has been too little coordination and communication across the different levels of the K–12, as well as between K–12 schools and institutions of higher education.
- At the middle and secondary school levels, every student needs strong, positive connections with adults, preferably many of them, as they explore options for school, post–secondary education, and work.

Are American secondary schools different from those in other countries? To explore this question, see the Diversity in Life-Span Development interlude.

Diversity in Life-Span Development
Cross-Cultural Comparisons of Secondary Schools

Secondary schools in different countries share a number of features, but differ on others (Cameron & others, 1983). Let's explore the similarities and differences in secondary schools in five countries: Australia, Brazil, Germany, Japan, and the United States.

Most countries mandate that children begin school at 6 to 7 years of age and stay in school until they are 14 to 17 years of age. Brazil requires students to go to school only until they are 14 years old, whereas Russia mandates that students stay in school until they are 17. Germany, Japan, Australia, and the United States require school attendance until at least 15 to 16 years of age, with some states, such as California, recently raising the mandatory age to 18.

Most secondary schools around the world are divided into two or more levels, such as middle school (or junior high school) and high school. However, Germany's schools are divided according to three educational ability tracks: (1) The main school provides a basic level of education, (2) the middle school gives students a more advanced education, and (3) the academic school prepares students for

Summary

 Learning Goal 1: Discuss the nature of adolescence

- Many stereotypes of adolescents are too negative. Most adolescents today successfully negotiate the path from childhood to adulthood. However, too many of today's adolescents are not provided with adequate opportunities and support to become competent adults. It is important to view adolescents as a heterogeneous group because different portraits of adolescents emerge, depending on the particular set of adolescents being described.

 Learning Goal 2: Describe the changes involved in puberty, sexuality, and the brain

- Puberty is a period of rapid physical maturation involving hormonal and bodily changes that occur primarily during early adolescence. Puberty's determinants include nutrition, health, heredity, and body mass. The endocrine system's influence on puberty involves an interaction of the hypothalamus, the pituitary gland, and the gonads (sex glands). Testosterone plays a key role in the pubertal development of males, whereas estradiol serves this function in females. The initial onset of the pubertal growth spurt occurs on the average at 9 years for girls and 11 for boys, reaching a peak change for girls at $11\frac{1}{2}$ and for boys at $13\frac{1}{2}$. Sexual maturation is a predominant feature of pubertal change. Individual variation in pubertal changes is substantial. Adolescents show considerable interest in their body image with girls having more negative body images than boys do. Early maturation favors boys, at least during early adolescence. Early-maturing girls are vulnerable to a number of risks.
- Mastering emerging sexual feelings and forming a sense of sexual identity involve multiple factors. National U.S. data indicate that by age 19, four of five individuals have had sexual intercourse. Risk factors for sexual problems include poverty, early sexual activity, low self-regulation, low parental monitoring, and poor parent-adolescent communication. Contraceptive use in adolescence is increasing. More than one in four adolescents has a sexually transmitted infection (STI). America's adolescent pregnancy rate is high but has been decreasing in recent years.
- Spurts in the brain's electrical activity seem to occur at about 9, 12, 15, and 18 to 20 years of age. Researchers recently have found that the prefrontal cortex, which is involved in higher-level cognitive processing, is not fully mature in adolescence, while the amygdala, which handles the processing of information about emotion, is more fully developed in adolescence. This means that the brain region responsible for putting the brakes on risky, impulsive behavior is still under construction in adolescence.

 Learning Goal 3: Identify adolescent problems in substance use and abuse, eating disorders, and health

- The 1960s and 1970s were times of marked increase in illicit drug use by adolescents. In the 1980s, adolescent drug use declined, but then increased through the mid-1990s, leveled off, and dropped considerably in 2003. Despite recent declines in use, the United States has the highest rate of drug use of any industrialized nation. Alcohol abuse is a major adolescent problem, although its rate has been dropping in recent years, as has cigarette smoking. Drug use in childhood or early adolescence has more negative outcomes than drug use that begins in late adolescence. Parents and peers play important roles in whether adolescents take drugs.
- Eating disorders have increased in adolescence with a substantial increase in the percentage of adolescents who are overweight. Two eating disorders that may emerge in adolescence are anorexia nervosa and bulimia nervosa.
- Adolescence is a critical juncture in health because many of the factors related to poor health habits and early death in the adult years begin during adolescence. Poor nutrition, lack of exercise, and inadequate sleep are concerns. Risk-taking behavior increases during adolescence. Among the strategies for keeping risk taking from compromising adolescents' health are to limit their opportunities for harm and monitor their behavior. The three leading causes of death in adolescence are accidents, homicide, and suicide.

 Learning Goal 4: Explain cognitive changes in adolescence

- Formal operational thought, Piaget's fourth stage of cognitive development, is more abstract, idealistic, and logical than concrete operational thought. Hypothetical-deductive reasoning is a term used to describe adolescents' more logical reasoning. Formal operational thought occurs in two phases—assimilation (early adolescence) and accommodation (middle years of adolescence). There is individual variation in adolescent cognition and Piaget did not give this adequate attention. Many young adolescents are not formal operational thinkers but rather are consolidating their concrete operational thought.
- Elkind describes the concept of adolescent egocentrism as the heightened self-consciousness of adolescents that consists of two parts: imaginary audience and personal fable.
- Changes in information processing in adolescence include increased decision making and critical thinking. Increased speed of processing, automaticity, and capacity, as well as more breadth of content knowledge and a greater range and spontaneous use of strategies, allow for improved critical thinking in adolescence.

5 **Learning Goal 5: Summarize some key aspects of how schools influence adolescent development**

- The transition to middle or junior high school coincides with many social, familial, and individual changes in the adolescent's life, and this transition is often stressful. The transition involves moving from the top-dog to the lowest position.
- In 1989, the Carnegie Foundation recommended a major redesign of U.S. middle schools that included an increase in

smaller "communities," lower student-to-counselor ratios, and an increase in parental and community involvement.

- The overall high school dropout rate declined considerably in the last half of the twentieth century, but the dropout rates of Latino and Native American youth remain very high. A number of strategies have been proposed for im-

proving U.S. high schools, including better support and higher expectations.

- Service learning involves educational experiences that promote social responsibility and service to the community. Researchers have found that service learning benefits students in a number of ways.

Key Terms

puberty 365
menarche 365
hormones 366
hypothalamus 366
pituitary gland 366

gonads 366
sexually transmitted infections (STIs) 372
anorexia nervosa 379

bulimia nervosa 379
hypothetical-deductive reasoning 383
adolescent egocentrism 384

imaginary audience 384
personal fable 384
top-dog phenomenon 387
service learning 390

Key People

Lloyd Johnston, Patrick O'Malley, and Gerald Bachman 375

Jean Piaget 383

David Elkind 384

E-LEARNING TOOLS

To help you master the material in this chapter, you'll find a number of valuable study tools on the LifeMap CD-ROM that accompanies this book and on the Online Learning Center for *Life-Span Development*, tenth edition, at www.mhhe.com/santrockld10.

Video Clips

In the margins of this book there are icons directing you to the LifeMap CD-ROM that accompanies the book. There you'll find two videos for chapter 12. The first video is called "Sex Among Teens at Age 15." These informal interviews with 15-year-olds offer a snapshot of contemporary adolescent attitudes toward sex. The second video is called "Eating Disorders." Obesity, anorexia nervosa, and bulimia are described in this segment, which also addresses the question of why these problems have become so common among adolescents.

Self-Assessment

Connect to www.mhhe.com/santrockld10 to reflect on your early teenage years by completing the self-assessment, *My Romantic and Sexual Involvement in Adolescence*.

Taking It to the Net

Connect to www.mhhe.com/santrockld10 to research the answers to these questions.

1. Sharon wonders why so much of the talk about adolescent pregnancy focuses on the girl's motivation and behavior. She wonders: What about the guys? How do adolescent males become absentee fathers?
2. Miguel plans to take a comparative literature class. His uncle, a high school literature teacher, looks at the course syllabus and says it is made up of titles that "pander to adolescent angst." He tells Miguel about the "Werther Effect," named after *The Sorrows of Young Werther*, a novella by Johann Wolfgang von Goethe that provoked a wave of adolescent suicides across Europe in the late 1700s. What elements of a story like *Werther* would appeal to the sensibilities of a typical adolescent?
3. Emory is petitioning his public school administrative board to expand the school system's service learning program. What pedagogical advantages of service learning should he emphasize in his presentation?

Health and Well-Being, Parenting, and Education Exercises

Build your decision-making skills by trying your hand at the health and well-being, parenting, and education exercises.

Connect to www.mhhe.com/santrockld10 to research the answers and complete the exercises.

In case you're worried about what's going to become of the younger generation, it's going to grow up and start worrying about the younger generation.

—ROGER ALLEN
Contemporary American Writer

Socioemotional Development in Adolescence

Chapter Outline

Learning Goals

THE SELF AND EMOTIONAL DEVELOPMENT

Self-Esteem

Identity

Emotional Development

1 Discuss changes in the self and emotional development during adolescence

FAMILIES

Autonomy and Attachment

Parent-Adolescent Conflict

2 Describe changes that take place in adolescents' relationships with their parents

PEERS

Friendships

Peer Groups

Dating and Romantic Relationships

3 Characterize the changes that occur in peer relations during adolescence

CULTURE AND ADOLESCENT DEVELOPMENT

Cross-Cultural Comparisons

Ethnicity

4 Explain how culture influences adolescent development

ADOLESCENT PROBLEMS

Juvenile Delinquency

Depression and Suicide

The Interrelation of Problems and Successful Prevention/Intervention Programs

5 Identify adolescent problems in socioemotional development and strategies for helping adolescents with problems

Images of Life-Span Development
A 15-Year-Old Girl's Self-Description

How do adolescents describe themselves? How would you have described yourself when you were 15 years old? What features would you have emphasized? Here is a self-portrait of one 15-year-old girl (Harter, 1990, pp. 352–53):

What am I like as a person? Complicated! I'm sensitive, friendly, outgoing, popular, and tolerant, though I can also be shy, self-conscious, and even obnoxious. Obnoxious! I'd like to be friendly and tolerant all of the time. That's the kind of person I want to be, and I'm disappointed when I'm not. I'm responsible, even studious now and then, but on the other hand, I'm a goof-off, too, because if you're too studious, you won't be popular. I don't usually do that well at school. I'm a pretty cheerful person, especially with my friends, where I can even get rowdy. At home I'm more likely to be anxious around my parents. They expect me to get all A's. It's not fair! I worry about how I probably should get better grades. But I'd be mortified in the eyes of my friends. So I'm usually pretty stressed-out at home, or sarcastic, since my parents are always on my case. But I really don't understand how I can switch so fast. I mean, how can I be cheerful one minute, anxious the next, and then be sarcastic? Which one is the real me? Sometimes, I feel phony, especially around boys. Say I think some guy might be interested in asking me out. I try to act different, like Madonna. I'll be flirtatious and fun-loving. And then everybody, I mean everybody else is looking at me like they think I'm totally weird. Then I get self-conscious and embarrassed and become radically introverted, and I don't know who I really am! Am I just trying to impress them or what? But I don't really care what they think anyway. I don't want to care, that is. I just want to know what my close friends think. I can be my true self with my close friends. I can't be my real self with my parents. They don't understand me. What do they know about what it's like to be a teenager? They still treat me like I'm still a kid. At least at school people treat you more like you're an adult. That gets confusing, though. I mean, which am I, a kid or an adult? It's scary, too, because I don't have any idea what I want to be when I grow up. I mean, I have lots of ideas. My friend Sheryl and I talk about whether we'll be flight attendants, or teachers, or nurses, veterinarians, maybe mothers, or actresses. I know I don't want to be a waitress or a secretary. But how do you decide all of this? I really don't know. I mean, I think about it a lot, but I can't resolve it. There are days when I wish I could just become immune to myself.

PREVIEW
Significant changes characterize socioemotional development in adolescence. These changes include increased efforts to understand one's self and emotional fluctuations. Changes also occur in the social contexts of adolescents' lives with transformations occurring in relationships with families and peers in cultural contexts. Adolescents also may develop socioemotional problems, such as delinquency and depression.

1 THE SELF AND EMOTIONAL DEVELOPMENT

| Self-Esteem | Identity | Emotional Development |

The 15-year-old girl's self-description that you just read reflects the increased interest in self-portrayal, search for an identity, and emotional swings in adolescence. Before we explore identity and emotional development in depth, let's examine how self-esteem changes in adolescence.

Self-Esteem

Recall from chapter 11 that *self-esteem* is the overall way we evaluate ourselves and that self-esteem is also referred to as self-image or self-worth. Controversy characterizes the extent to which self-esteem changes during adolescence and whether there are gender differences in adolescents' self-esteem. In one recent study, both boys and girls had particularly high self-esteem in childhood but their self-esteem dropped considerably during adolescence (Robins & others, 2002). The self-esteem of girls declined more than the self-esteem of boys during adolescence in this study. Another recent study also found that the self-esteem of girls declined during early adolescence, but that the self-esteem of boys increased in early adolescence (Baldwin & Hoffman, 2002). In this study, adolescent self-esteem was related to positive family relationships. Some critics argue that developmental changes and gender differences in self-esteem during adolescence have been exaggerated (Harter, 2002). For example, in one analysis of research studies on self-esteem in adolescence, it was concluded that girls have only slightly more negative self-esteem than do boys (Kling & others, 1999).

One explanation for the decline in the self-esteem among females during early adolescence focuses on girls' more negative body images during pubertal change compared with boys. Another explanation involves the greater interest young adolescent girls take in social relationships and society's failure to reward that interest. To read further about self-esteem in adolescence, see the Research in Life-Span Development interlude.

 Examine the video "Adolescent Self-Esteem" to learn about the tie between self-concept and self-esteem, and the way adolescents develop attitudes about themselves.

Research in Life-Span Development
Adolescents' Self-Images

One recent study examined the self-images of 675 adolescents (289 males and 386 females) from 13 to 19 years of age in Naples, Italy (Bacchini & Magliulo, 2003). Self-image was assessed using the Offer Self-Image Questionnaire (Offer & others, 1989), which consists of 130 items grouped into 11 scales that define five different aspects of self-image:

- The *psychological self* (made up of scales that assess impulse control, emotional tone, and body image)
- The *social self* (consists of scales that evaluate social relationships, morals, and vocational and educational aspirations)
- The *coping self* (comprised of scales to measure mastery of the world, psychological problems, and adjustment)
- The *familial self* (made up of only one scale that evaluates how adolescents feel about their parents)
- The *sexual self* (comprised of only one scale that examines adolescents' feelings and attitudes about sexual matters)

The adolescents had positive self-images with their scores being above a neutral score (3.5) on all 11 scales. For example, the adolescents' average body self-image score was 4.2. The aspect of their lives in which adolescents had the most positive self-image involved their educational and vocational aspirations (average score of 4.8). The lowest self-image score was for impulse control (average score of 3.9). These results support the view we expressed in chapter 12 that adolescents have a more positive perception of themselves than is commonly believed.

Gender differences were found on a number of the self-image scales with boys consistently having more positive self-images than did girls. Keep in mind, though, that as we indicated earlier, even though girls reported lower self-images than boys, their self-images still were mainly in the positive range.

Identity

By far the most comprehensive and provocative story of identity development has been told by Erik Erikson. As you may remember from chapter 2, identity versus identity confusion is the fifth stage in Erikson's eight stages of the life span, occurring at about the same time as adolescence. It is a time of being interested in finding out who one is, what one is all about, and where one is headed in life.

During adolescence, worldviews become important to the individual, who enters what Erikson (1968) calls a "psychological moratorium," a gap between the security of childhood and the autonomy of adulthood. Adolescents experiment with the numerous roles and identities they draw from the surrounding culture. Youth who successfully cope with these conflicting identities during adolescence emerge with a new sense of self that is both refreshing and acceptable (Bosma & Kunnen, 2001; Moshman, 1999). Adolescents who do not successfully resolve this identity crisis are confused, suffering what Erikson calls "identity confusion." This confusion takes one of two courses: The individuals withdraw, isolating themselves from peers and family, or they lose their identity in the crowd.

Identity is a self-portrait composed of many pieces. These pieces include:

- *Vocational/career identity,* or the career and work path a person wants to follow
- *Political identity,* or whether a person is conservative, liberal, or moderate
- *Religious identity,* or a person's spiritual beliefs
- *Relationship identity,* or whether a person is single, married, divorced, and so on
- *Achievement/intellectual identity,* or the extent to which the person is motivated to achieve and is intellectual
- *Sexual identity,* or whether a person is heterosexual, homosexual, or bisexual
- *Gender identity,* or the extent the individual is feminine, masculine, or androgynous
- *Cultural/ethnic identity,* or the ethnic groups one belongs to and the part of the world or country a person is from and how intensely the person identifies with their cultural heritage
- *Interest identity,* or the kind of things a person likes to do, which can include sports, music, hobbies, and so on
- *Personality identity,* or the individual's personality characteristics, such as being introverted or extraverted, anxious or calm, friendly or hostile, and so on
- *Physical identity,* or the individual's body image

Contemporary Views of Identity Contemporary views of identity development suggest several important considerations. First, identity development is a lengthy process; in many instances, it is a more gradual, less cataclysmic transition than Erikson's term *crisis* implies. Second, identity development is extraordinarily complex (Kroger, 2003; Moshman, 2005).

Identity formation neither begins nor ends with adolescence. It begins with the appearance of attachment, the development of a sense of self, and the emergence of independence in infancy, and it reaches its final phase with a life review and integration in old age. What is important about identity in adolescence, especially late

As long as one keeps searching, the answers come.

—JOAN BAEZ
American Folk Singer, 20th Century

Identity Development
Identity Development in Literature

FIGURE 13.1 Marcia's Four Statuses of Identity

Position on Occupation and Ideology	Identity Status			
	Identity diffusion	Identity foreclosure	Identity moratorium	Identity achievement
Crisis	Absent	Absent	Present	Present
Commitment	Absent	Present	Absent	Present

adolescence, is that for the first time physical development, cognitive development, and social development advance to the point at which the individual can sort through and synthesize childhood identities and identifications to construct a viable pathway toward adult maturity. Resolution of the identity issue at adolescence does not mean that identity will be stable through the remainder of one's life. A person who develops a healthy identity is flexible, adaptive, and open to changes in society, in relationships, and in careers. This openness assures numerous reorganizations of identity features throughout the life of the person who has achieved identity.

Identity formation does not happen neatly, and it usually does not happen suddenly. At the bare minimum, it involves commitment to a vocational direction, an ideological stance, and a sexual orientation. Synthesizing the identity components can be a long, drawn-out process, with many negations and affirmations of various roles and faces. Identities are developed in bits and pieces. Decisions are not made once and for all but have to be made again and again. And the decisions may seem trivial at the time: whom to date, whether or not to break up, whether or not to have intercourse, whether or not to take drugs, whether to go to college after high school or get a job, which major to choose, whether to study or whether to play, whether or not to be politically active, and so on. Over the years of adolescence, the decisions begin to form a core of what the individual is all about as a person—what is called "identity."

Identity Statuses and Development Canadian psychologist James Marcia (1980, 1994) analyzed Erikson's theory of identity development and concluded that it is important to distinguish between crisis and commitment in identity development. **Crisis** is a period of identity development during which the adolescent is choosing among meaningful alternatives. Most researchers now use the term *exploration* rather than *crisis*, although, in the spirit of Marcia's original formulation, we will use the term *crisis*. **Commitment** is defined as the part of identity development in which adolescents show a personal investment in what they are going to do.

The extent of an individual's crisis and commitment is used to classify him or her according to one of four identity statuses (see figure 13.1):

- **Identity diffusion** occurs when individuals have not yet experienced a crisis (that is, they have not yet explored meaningful alternatives) or made any commitments. Not only are they undecided about occupational and ideological choices, but they are also likely to show little interest in such matters.
- **Identity foreclosure** occurs when individuals have made a commitment but have not yet experienced a crisis. This occurs most often when parents hand down commitments to their adolescents, more often than not in an authoritarian manner. In these circumstances, adolescents have not had adequate opportunities to explore different approaches, ideologies, and vocations on their own.
- **Identity moratorium** occurs when individuals are in the midst of a crisis but their commitments are either absent or only vaguely defined.
- **Identity achievement** occurs when individuals have undergone a crisis and have made a commitment.

Let's explore some examples of Marcia's identity statuses. A 13-year-old adolescent has neither begun to explore her identity in any meaningful way nor made an identity commitment, so she is *identity diffused*. An 18-year-old boy's parents want him to be a

crisis Marcia's term for a period of identity development during which the adolescent is choosing among meaningful alternatives.

commitment Marcia's term for the part of identity development in which adolescents show a personal investment in what they are going to do.

identity diffusion Marcia's term for adolescents who have not yet experienced a crisis (explored meaningful alternatives) or made any commitments.

identity foreclosure Marcia's term for adolescents who have made a commitment but have not experienced a crisis.

identity moratorium Marcia's term for adolescents who are in the midst of a crisis, but their commitments are either absent or vaguely defined.

identity achievement Marcia's term for adolescents who have undergone a crisis and have made a commitment.

*O*nce formed, an identity furnishes individuals with a historical sense of who they have been, a meaningful sense of who they are now, and a sense of who they might become in the future.

—JAMES MARCIA

Contemporary Psychologist,
Simon Fraser University

medical doctor so he is planning on majoring in premedicine in college and really has not adequately explored any other options, so he is *identity foreclosed*. Nineteen-year-old Sasha is not quite sure what life paths she wants to follow, but she recently went to the counseling center at her college to find out about different careers, so she is in *identity moratorium* status. Twenty-one-year-old Marcelo extensively explored a number of different career options in college, eventually getting his degree in science education, and is looking forward to his first year of teaching high school students, so he is *identity achieved*. Our examples of identity statuses have focused on the career dimension, but remember that the whole of identity is made up of a number of dimensions.

Young adolescents are primarily in Marcia's identity diffusion, foreclosure, or moratorium status. At least three aspects of the young adolescent's development are important in identity formation: Young adolescents must establish confidence in parental support, develop a sense of industry, and gain a self-reflective perspective on their future. Some researchers believe the most important identity changes take place in the college years, rather than earlier in adolescence. For example, Alan Waterman (1992) has found that, from the years preceding high school through the last few years of college, the number of individuals who are identity achieved increases, along with a decrease in those who are identity diffused. College upperclassmen are more likely than college freshmen or high school students to be identity achieved. Many young adolescents are identity diffused. These developmental changes are especially true in regard to vocational choice. For religious beliefs and political ideology, fewer college students have reached the identity achieved status, with a substantial number characterized by foreclosure and diffusion. Thus, the timing of identity may depend on the particular role involved, and many college students are still wrestling with ideological commitments.

Many identity status researchers believe that a common pattern of individuals who develop positive identities is to follow what are called "MAMA" cycles of *Moratorium-Achievement-Moratorium-Achievement* (Marcia, 2002). These cycles may be repeated throughout life. Personal, family, and societal changes are inevitable, and, as they occur, the flexibility and skill required to explore new alternatives and develop new commitments are likely to facilitate an individual's coping skills.

Family Influences on Identity Parents are important figures in the adolescent's development of identity. In studies that relate identity development to parenting styles, democratic parents, who encourage adolescents to participate in family decision making, foster identity achievement. Autocratic parents, who control the adolescent's behavior without giving the adolescent an opportunity to express opinions, encourage identity foreclosure. Permissive parents, who provide little guidance to adolescents and allow them to make their own decisions, promote identity diffusion (Enright & others, 1980).

In addition to studying parenting styles, researchers have also examined the role of individuality and connectedness in the development of identity. The presence of a family atmosphere that promotes both individuality and connectedness is important in the adolescent's identity development (Cooper & Grotevant, 1989):

- **Individuality** consists of two dimensions: *self-assertion,* the ability to have and communicate a point of view, and *separateness,* the use of communication patterns to express how one is different from others.
- **Connectedness** consists of these two dimensions: *mutuality,* sensitivity to and respect for others' views, and *permeability*—openness to others' views.

In general, research findings reveal that identity formation is enhanced by family relationships that are both *individuated,* which encourages adolescents to develop their own point of view, and *connected,* which provides a secure base from which to explore the widening social worlds of adolescence.

Cultural and Ethnic Aspects of Identity Erikson was especially sensitive to the role of culture in identity development. He points out that, throughout the world,

individuality Individuality consists of two dimensions: self-assertion (the ability to have and communicate a point of view) and separateness (the use of communication patterns to express how one is different from others).

connectedness Connectedness consists of two dimensions: mutuality (sensitivity to and respect for others' views) and permeability (openness to others' views).

ethnic minority groups have struggled to maintain their cultural identities while blending into the dominant culture (Erikson, 1968). Erikson said that this struggle for an inclusive identity, or identity within the larger culture, has been the driving force in the founding of churches, empires, and revolutions throughout history.

For ethnic minority individuals, adolescence is often a special juncture in their development (Ontal-Grzebik & Raffaelli, 2004; Phinney, 2000; Spencer & others, 2001). Although children are aware of some ethnic and cultural differences, most ethnic minority individuals consciously confront their ethnicity for the first time in adolescence. In contrast to children, adolescents have the ability to interpret ethnic and cultural information, to reflect on the past, and to speculate about the future.

Jean Phinney (1996) defined **ethnic identity** as an enduring, basic aspect of the self that includes a sense of membership in an ethnic group and the attitudes and feelings related to that membership. Thus, for adolescents from ethnic minority groups, the process of identity formation has an added dimension due to exposure to alternative sources of identification—their own ethnic group and the mainstream or dominant culture. Researchers have found that ethnic identity increases with age and that higher levels of ethnic identity are linked with more positive attitudes not only toward one's own ethnic group but toward members of other ethnic groups as well (Phinney, Ferguson, & Tate, 1997). Many ethnic minority adolescents have bicultural identities—identifying in some ways with their ethnic minority group, in other ways with the majority culture (Comaz-Diaz, 2001; Phinney & Devich-Navarro, 1997).

The ease or difficulty with which ethnic minority adolescents achieve healthy identities depends on a number of factors (Ferrer-Wreder & others, 2002; Wren & Mendoza, 2004). Many ethnic minority adolescents have to confront issues of prejudice and discrimination, and barriers to the fulfillment of their goals and aspirations (Comaz-Diaz, 2001).

In one investigation, ethnic identity exploration was higher among ethnic minority than among White American college students (Phinney & Alipuria, 1990). In this same investigation, ethnic minority college students who had thought about and resolved issues involving their ethnicity had higher self-esteem than did their ethnic minority counterparts who had not. In another investigation, the ethnic identity development of Asian American, African American, Latino, and White American tenth-grade students in Los Angeles was studied (Phinney, 1989). Adolescents from each of the three ethnic minority groups faced a similar need to deal with their ethnic-group identification in a predominantly White American culture. In some instances, the adolescents from the three ethnic minority groups perceived different issues to be important in their resolution of ethnic identity. For Asian American adolescents, pressures to achieve academically and concerns about quotas that make it difficult to get into good colleges were salient issues. Many African American adolescent females discussed their realization that White American standards of beauty (especially hair and skin color) did not apply to them; African American adolescent males were concerned with possible job discrimination and the need to distinguish themselves from a negative societal image of African American male adolescents. For Latino adolescents, prejudice was a recurrent theme, as was the conflict in values between their Latino cultural heritage and the majority culture.

Researchers are also increasingly finding that a positive ethnic identity is related to positive outcomes for ethnic minority adolescents (Fridrich & Flannery, 1995; Umana-Taylor, 2004). For example, one recent study revealed that ethnic identity was linked with higher school engagement and lower aggression (Van Buren & Graham, 2003). Another recent study indicated that a stronger ethnic identity was related to higher self-esteem in African American, Latino, and Asian American youth (Bracey, Bamaca, & Umana-Taylor, 2004).

The contexts in which ethnic minority youth live influence their identity development (Spencer, 1999). Many ethnic minority youth in the United States live in

Michelle Chin, age 16: "Parents do not understand that teenagers need to find out who they are, which means a lot of experimenting, a lot of mood swings, a lot of emotions and awkwardness. Like any teenager, I am facing an identity crisis. I am still trying to figure out whether I am a Chinese American or an American with Asian eyes."

Many ethnic minority youth must bridge "multiple worlds" in constructing their identities.

—CATHERINE COOPER
Contemporary Psychologist, University of California at Santa Cruz

ethnic identity An enduring, basic aspect of the self that includes a sense of membership in an ethnic group and the attitudes and feelings related to that membership.

low-income urban settings where support for developing a positive identity is absent. Many of these youth live in pockets of poverty; are exposed to drugs, gangs, and criminal activities; and interact with other youth and adults who have dropped out of school and/or are unemployed. In such settings, effective organizations and programs for youth can make important contributions to developing a positive identity.

Ethnic identity often changes with succeeding generations (Phinney, 2003). The identity of first-generation immigrants is likely to be secure and unlikely to change considerably. They may or may not develop an "American" identity. The degree to which they begin to feel American appears to be related to learning English, developing social networks beyond their group, and becoming culturally competent in the new context. For second-generation immigrants, an "American" identity is more secure possibly because citizenship is granted with birth. Their ethnic identity is likely to be linked to retention of their ethnic language and social networks. For the third and later generations, the issues become more complex. Various historical, contextual, and political factors unrelated to acculturation may affect the extent to which their ethnic identity is retained (Ramirez, 2004). For non-European ethnic groups, racism and discrimination influence whether ethnic identity is retained (Cuéllar, Siles, & Bracamontes, 2004). However, today in the United States, non-European immigrants usually develop bicultural identities (Quintana, 2004; Ramirez, 2004). That is, they become American but also retain their ethnic identity.

Gender and Identity Development In Erikson's (1968) classic discussion of identity development, the division of labor between the sexes was reflected in his assertion that males' aspirations were mainly oriented toward career and ideological commitments, while females' were centered around marriage and childbearing. In the 1960s and 1970s, researchers found support for Erikson's assertion about gender differences in identity. For example, vocational concerns were more central to the identity of males, and affiliative concerns were more important in the identity of females. However, in the past two decades, as females have developed stronger vocational interests, sex differences are turning into sex similarities.

Some investigators believe the order of stages proposed by Erikson is different for females and males. One view is that for males identity formation precedes the stage of intimacy, while for females intimacy precedes identity. These ideas are consistent with the belief that relationships and emotional bonds are more important concerns of females, whereas autonomy and achievement are more important concerns of males (Gilligan, 1996). In one study, the development of a clear sense of self by adolescent girls was related to their concerns about care and response in relationships (Rogers, 1987).

The task of identity exploration may be more complex for females than for males, in that females may try to establish identities in more domains than males. In today's world, the options for females have increased and thus may at times be confusing and conflicting, especially for females who hope to successfully integrate family and career roles (Archer, 1994).

Emotional Development

Adolescence has long been described as a time of emotional turmoil (Hall, 1904). In its extreme form, this view is too stereotypical because adolescents are not constantly in a state of "storm and stress." Nonetheless, early adolescence is a time when emotional highs and lows increase (Rosenblum & Lewis, 2003; Scaramella & Conger, 2004). Young adolescents can be on top of the world one moment and down in the dumps the next. In many instances, the intensity of their emotions seems out of proportion to the events that elicit them (Steinberg & Levine, 1997). Young adolescents might sulk a lot, not knowing how to adequately express their feelings. With little or no provocation, they might blow up at their parents or siblings, which could involve using the defense mechanism of displacing their feelings onto another person.

Reed Larson and Maryse Richards (1994) found that adolescents reported more extreme emotions and more fleeting emotions than their parents did. For example,

www.mhhe.com/santrockld10

Cultural Identity in Canada
Exploring Ethnic Identities
An Adolescent Talks
About Ethnic Identity
Ethnic Identity Research

Watch the video "Girls and Body Image" for interviews with 14-year-old girls about their emerging images of themselves.

adolescents were five times more likely to report being "very happy" and three times more likely to report being "very sad" than their parents (see figure 13.2). These findings lend support to the perception of adolescents as moody and changeable (Rosenblum & Lewis, 2003).

Researchers have also found that from the fifth through the ninth grades, both boys and girls experience a 50 percent decrease in being "very happy" (Larson & Lampman-Petraitis, 1989). In this same study, adolescents were more likely than preadolescents to report mildly negative mood states.

It is important for adults to recognize that moodiness is a *normal* aspect of early adolescence and most adolescents make it through these moody times to become competent adults. Nonetheless, for some adolescents, such emotions can reflect serious problems. For example, rates of depressed moods become more elevated for girls during adolescence (Nolen-Hoeksema, 2004). We will have much more to say about depression later in the chapter.

As we saw in chapter 12, "Physical and Cognitive Development in Adolescence," significant hormonal changes characterize puberty. Emotional fluctuations in early adolescence may be related to the variability of hormones during this time period. Moods become less extreme as adolescents move into adulthood, and this decrease in emotional fluctuation may be due to adaptation to hormone levels over time (Rosenbaum & Lewis, 2003).

Researchers have discovered that pubertal change is associated with an increase in negative emotions (Archibald, Graber, & Brooks-Gunn, 2003; Brooks-Gunn, Graber, & Paikoff, 1994; Dorn, Williamson, & Ryan, 2002). However, most researchers conclude that hormonal influences are small and that when they occur they usually are associated with other factors, such as stress, eating patterns, sexual activity, and social relationships (Rosenbaum & Lewis, 2003; Susman, Dorn, & Schiefelbein, 2003; Susman & Rogol, 2004).

Indeed, environmental experiences may contribute more to the emotions of adolescence than hormonal changes. Recall from chapter 12 that in one study, social factors accounted for two to four times as much variance as hormonal factors in young adolescent girls' depression and anger (Brooks-Gunn & Warren, 1989). In sum, both hormonal changes and environmental experiences are involved in the changing emotional landscape of adolescence.

FIGURE 13.2 Self-Reported Extremes of Emotion by Adolescents, Mothers, and Fathers Using the Experience Sampling Method

In the study by Reed Larson and Maryse Richards (1994), adolescents and their mothers and fathers were beeped at random times by researchers using the experience sampling method. The researchers found that adolescents were more likely to report more emotional extremes than their parents.

Review and Reflect: Learning Goal 1

   Discuss changes in the self and emotional development during adolescence

REVIEW

- What are some changes in self-esteem that take place in adolescence?
- How does identity develop in adolescence?
- What factors affect emotional development in adolescence?

REFLECT

- Where are you in your identity development? Get out a sheet of paper and list each of the pieces of identity (vocational, political, religious, relationship achievement/intellectual, sexual, gender, cultural/ethnic, interest, personality, and physical) in a column on the left side of the paper. Then write the four identity statuses (diffused, foreclosed, moratorium, and achieved) across the top of the page. Next to each dimension of identity, place a check mark in the appropriate space that reflects your identity status for the particular aspect of identity. If you checked diffused or foreclosed for any of the dimensions, think about what you need to do to move on to a moratorium status in those areas.

2 FAMILIES

Autonomy and Attachment   **Parent-Adolescent Conflict**

In chapter 11, we discussed how, during middle and late childhood, parents spend less time with their children than in early childhood, that discipline involves an increased use of reasoning and deprivation of privileges, and that there is a gradual transfer of control from parents to children but still within the boundary of coregulation. Among the most important aspects of family relationships in adolescence are those that involve autonomy and attachment, and parent-adolescent conflict.

Autonomy and Attachment

The adolescent's push for autonomy and responsibility puzzles and angers many parents. Parents see their teenager slipping from their grasp. They may have an urge to take stronger control as the adolescent seeks autonomy and responsibility. Heated emotional exchanges may ensue, with either side calling names, making threats, and doing whatever seems necessary to gain control. Parents may seem frustrated because they *expect* their teenager to heed their advice, to want to spend time with the family, and to grow up to do what is right. Most parents anticipate that their teenager will have some difficulty adjusting to the changes that adolescence brings, but few parents can imagine and predict just how strong an adolescent's desires will be to spend time with peers or how much adolescents will want to show that it is they—not their parents—who are responsible for their successes and failures.

The ability to attain autonomy and gain control over one's behavior in adolescence is acquired through appropriate adult reactions to the adolescent's desire for control (Laursen & Collins, 2004; Zimmer-Gembeck & Collins, 2003). At the onset of adolescence, the average individual does not have the knowledge to make appropriate or mature decisions in all areas of life. As the adolescent pushes for autonomy, the wise adult relinquishes control in those areas in which the adolescent can make reasonable decisions but continues to guide the adolescent to make reasonable decisions in areas in which the adolescent's knowledge is more limited. Gradually, adolescents acquire the ability to make mature decisions on their own.

Gender differences characterize autonomy-granting in adolescence with boys being given more independence than girls. In one recent study, this was especially true in U.S. families with a traditional gender-role orientation (Bumpus, Crouter, & McHale, 2001).

Cultural differences also characterize adolescent autonomy. In one study, U.S. adolescents sought autonomy earlier than Japanese adolescents (Rothbaum & others, 2000). In the transition to adulthood, Japanese youth are less likely to live outside the home than Americans (Hendry, 1999).

Recall from chapter 7 that one of the most widely discussed aspects of socioemotional development in infancy is secure attachment to caregivers. In the past decade, researchers have explored whether secure attachment also might be an important concept in adolescents' relationships with their parents (Allen & others, 2003; Egeland & Carlson, 2004; Sroufe, 2001). For example, Joseph Allen and his colleagues (Allen, Hauser, & Borman-Spurrell, 1996; Allen & others, 1998, 2002) found that securely attached adolescents were less likely than those who were insecurely attached to engage in problem behaviors, such as juvenile delinquency and drug abuse. In other research, securely attached adolescents had better peer relations than their insecurely attached counterparts (Kobak, 1999; Laible, Carlo, & Raffaeli, 2000).

However, whereas adolescent-parent attachments are correlated with adolescent outcomes, the correlations are moderate, indicating that the success or failure of

> *When I was a boy of 14, my father was so ignorant I could hardly stand to have the man around. But when I got to be 21, I was astonished at how much he had learnt in 7 years.*
>
> —MARK TWAIN
> *American Writer and Humorist, 20th Century*

parent-adolescent attachments does not necessarily guarantee success or failure in peer relationships (Buhrmester, 2003). Clearly, secure attachment with parents can be an asset for the adolescent, fostering the trust to engage in close relationships with others and lay down the foundation for close relationship skills. But a significant minority of adolescents from strong, supportive families, nonetheless, struggle in peer relations for a variety of reasons, such as being physically unattractive, maturing late, and experiencing cultural and SES discrepancies. On the other hand, some adolescents from troubled families find a positive, fresh start with peer relations that can compensate for their problematic family backgrounds.

Parent-Adolescent Conflict

While attachment to parents remains strong during adolescence, the connectedness is not always smooth. Early adolescence is a time when conflict with parents escalates beyond childhood levels. This increase may be due to a number of factors: the biological changes of puberty, cognitive changes involving increased idealism and logical reasoning, social changes focused on independence and identity, maturational changes in parents, and expectations that are violated by parents and adolescents. The adolescent compares her parents to an ideal standard and then criticizes their flaws. A 13-year-old girl tells her mother, "That is the tackiest-looking dress I have ever seen. Nobody would be caught dead wearing that." The adolescent demands logical explanations for comments and discipline. A 14-year-old boy tells his mother, "What do you mean I have to be home at 10 P.M. because 'it's the way we do things around here'? Why do we do things around here that way? It doesn't make sense to me."

Many parents see their adolescent changing from a compliant child to someone who is noncompliant, oppositional, and resistant to parental standards. When this happens, parents tend to clamp down and put more pressure on the adolescent to conform to parental standards. Parents often expect their adolescents to become mature adults overnight, instead of understanding that the journey takes 10 to 15 years. Parents who recognize that this transition takes time handle their youth more competently and calmly than those who demand immediate conformity to adult standards. The opposite tactic—letting adolescents do as they please without supervision—is also unwise.

In one study, Reed Larson and Maryse Richards (1994) had mothers, fathers, and adolescents carry electronic pagers for a week and report their activities and emotions at random times. The result was a portrait of the hour-by-hour emotional realities lived by families with adolescents. Differences between the fast-paced daily realities lived by each family member created considerable potential for misunderstanding and conflict. Because each family member often was attending to different priorities, needs, and stressors, their realities often were out of sync. Even when they wanted to share leisure activity, their interests were at odds. One father said that his wife liked to shop, his daughter liked to play video games, and he liked to stay home. Although the main theme of this work was the stress of contemporary life, some of the families with adolescents were buoyant, and their lives were coordinated.

Although parent-adolescent conflict increases in early adolescence, it does not reach the tumultuous proportions G. Stanley Hall envisioned at the beginning of the twentieth century (Adams & Laursen, 2001; Collins & Laursen, 2004; Holmbeck, 1996; Steinberg & Silk, 2002). Rather, much of the conflict involves the everyday events of family life, such as keeping a bedroom clean, dressing neatly, getting home by a certain time, and not talking forever on the phone. The conflicts rarely involve major dilemmas, such as drugs and delinquency.

It is not unusual to hear parents of young adolescents ask, "Is it ever going to get better?" Things usually do get better as adolescents move from early to late adolescence. Conflict with parents often escalates during early adolescence, remains

It is not enough for parents to understand children. They must accord children the privilege of understanding them.

—MILTON SAPIRSTEIN
American Psychiatrist, 20th Century

Parenting Today's Adolescents
Parent-Adolescent Conflict
Reengaging Families with Adolescents

somewhat stable during the high school years, and then lessens as the adolescent reaches 17 to 20 years of age. Parent-adolescent relationships become more positive if adolescents go away to college than if they attend college while living at home (Sullivan & Sullivan, 1980).

The everyday conflicts that characterize parent-adolescent relationships may actually serve a positive developmental function. These minor disputes and negotiations facilitate the adolescent's transition from being dependent on parents to becoming an autonomous individual. For example, in one study, adolescents who expressed disagreement with their parents explored identity development more actively than did adolescents who did not express disagreement with their parents (Cooper & others, 1982). As previously mentioned, one way for parents to cope with the adolescent's push for independence and identity is to recognize that adolescence is a 10- to 15-year transitional period in the journey to adulthood, rather than an overnight accomplishment. Recognizing that conflict and negotiation can serve a positive developmental function can tone down parental hostility too. Understanding parent-adolescent conflict, though, is not simple (Conger & Ge, 1999).

In sum, the old model of parent-adolescent relationships suggested that as adolescents mature they detach themselves from parents and move into a world of autonomy apart from parents. The old model also suggested that parent-adolescent conflict is intense and stressful throughout adolescence. The new model emphasizes that parents serve as important attachment figures and support systems as adolescents explore a wider, more complex social world. The new model also emphasizes that, in most families, parent-adolescent conflict is moderate rather than severe and that the everyday negotiations and minor disputes are normal and can serve the positive developmental function of helping the adolescent make the transition from childhood dependency to adult independence (see figure 13.3).

Still, a high degree of conflict characterizes some parent-adolescent relationships. One estimate of the proportion of parents and adolescents who engage in prolonged, intense, repeated, unhealthy conflict is about one in five families (Montemayor, 1982). While this figure represents a minority of adolescents, it indicates that 4 to 5 million American families encounter serious, highly stressful parent-adolescent conflict. And this prolonged, intense conflict is associated with a number of adolescent problems—movement out of the home, juvenile delinquency, school dropout, pregnancy and early marriage, membership in religious cults, and drug abuse (Brook & others, 1990).

It should be pointed out that in some cultures there is less parent-adolescent conflict than in others. American psychologist Reed Larson (1999) spent six months in India studying middle-socioeconomic-status adolescents and their families.

Old Model	**New Model**
Autonomy, detachment from parents; parent and peer worlds are isolated	Attachment and autonomy; parents are important support systems and attachment figures; adolescent-parent and adolescent-peer worlds have some important connections
Intense, stressful conflict throughout adolescence; parent-adolescent relationships are filled with storm and stress on virtually a daily basis	Moderate parent-adolescent conflict common and can serve a positive developmental function; conflict greater in early adolescence

FIGURE 13.3 Old and New Models of Parent-Adolescent Relationships

He observed that in India there seems to be little parent-adolescent conflict and that many families likely would be described as "authoritarian" in Baumrind's categorization. Larson also observed that in India many adolescents do not go through a process of breaking away from their parents and that parents choose their youths' marital partners. Researchers also have found considerably less conflict between parents and adolescents in Japan than in the United States (Rothbaum & others, 2000).

We have seen that parents play very important roles in adolescent development (Collins & Laursen, 2004). Although adolescents are moving toward independence, they still need to stay connected with families (Bradshaw & Garbarino, 2004; Laursen & Collins, 2004; Roth & Brooks-Gunn, 2000). In the National Longitudinal Study on Adolescent Health (Council of Economic Advisors, 2000) of more than 12,000 adolescents, those who did not eat dinner with a parent five or more days a week had dramatically higher rates of smoking, drinking, marijuana use, getting into fights, and initiation of sexual activity. In another recent study, parents who played an active role in monitoring and guiding their adolescents' development were more likely to have adolescents with positive peer relations and lower drug use than parents who had a less active role (Mounts, 2002).

Competent adolescent development is most likely to happen when adolescents have parents who (Small, 1990):

- show them warmth and respect,
- demonstrate sustained interest in their lives,
- recognize and adapt to their cognitive and socioemotional development,
- communicate expectations for high standards of conduct and achievement, and
- display constructive ways of dealing with problems and conflict.

Review and Reflect: Learning Goal 2

 2 **Describe changes that take place in adolescents' relationships with their parents**

REVIEW

- How do autonomy and attachment develop in adolescence?
- What is the nature of parent-adolescent conflict?

REFLECT

- How much autonomy did your parents give you in adolescence? Too much? Too little? How intense was your conflict with your parents during adolescence? What were the conflicts mainly about? Would you behave differently toward your own adolescents than your parents did with you? If so, how?

3 PEERS

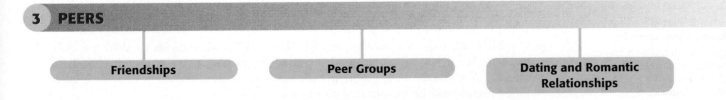

Friendships   Peer Groups   Dating and Romantic Relationships

In chapter 11, we discussed how children spend more time with their peers in middle and late childhood than in early childhood. We also found that friendships become more important in middle and late childhood and that popularity with peers is a strong

What changes take place in friendship during the adolescent years?

motivation for most children. Advances in cognitive development during middle and late childhood also allow children to take the perspective of their peers and friends more readily, and their social knowledge of how to make and keep friends increases.

Peer relations play powerful roles in the lives of adolescents. When you think back to your adolescent years, many of your most enjoyable moments probably were spent with peers—on the telephone, in school activities, in the neighborhood, at dances, or just hanging out. Peer relations undergo important changes in adolescence (Kerr & others, 2003). In childhood, the focus of peer relations is on being liked by classmates and being included in games or lunchroom conversations. Being overlooked or, worse yet, being rejected can have damaging effects on children's development that sometimes are carried forward to adolescence. Beginning in early adolescence, teenagers typically prefer to have a smaller number of friendships that are more intense and intimate than those of young children. Cliques are formed and shape the social lives of adolescents as they begin to hang out together.

Friendships

Harry Stack Sullivan (1953) was the most influential theorist to discuss the importance of adolescent friendships, and his ideas have withstood the test of time. He argued that there is a dramatic increase in the psychological importance and intimacy of close friends during early adolescence. In contrast to other psychoanalytic theorists' narrow emphasis on the importance of parent-child relationships, Sullivan contended that friends also play important roles in shaping children's and adolescents' well-being and development. In terms of well-being, he argued that all people have a number of basic social needs, including the need for tenderness (secure attachment), playful companionship, social acceptance, intimacy, and sexual relations. Whether or not these needs are fulfilled largely determines our emotional well-being. For example, if the need for playful companionship goes unmet, then we become bored and depressed; if the need for social acceptance is not met, we suffer a lowered sense of self-worth.

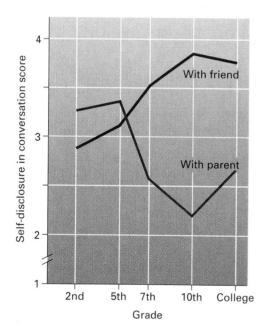

FIGURE 13.4 Developmental Changes in Self-Disclosing Conversations
Self-disclosing conversations with friends increased dramatically in adolescence while declining in an equally dramatic fashion with parents. However, self-disclosing conversations with parents began to pick up somewhat during the college years. The measure of self-disclosure involved a 5-point rating scale completed by the children and youth with a higher score representing greater self-disclosure. The data shown represent the means for each age group.

Developmentally, friends become increasingly depended on to satisfy these needs during adolescence; thus, the ups and downs of experiences with friends increasingly shape adolescents' state of well-being (Berndt, 2002). In particular, Sullivan argued that the need for intimacy intensifies during early adolescence, motivating teenagers to seek out close friends. He felt that, if adolescents fail to forge such close friendships, they experience painful feelings of loneliness, coupled with a reduced sense of self-worth.

Research findings support many of Sullivan's ideas. For example, adolescents report disclosing intimate and personal information to their friends more often than do younger children (Buhrmester, 1998) (see figure 13.4). Adolescents also say they depend more on friends than on parents to satisfy their needs for companionship, reassurance of worth, and intimacy.

Although most adolescents develop friendships with individuals who are close to their own age, some adolescents become best friends with younger or older individuals. A common fear, especially among parents, is that adolescents who have older friends will be encouraged to engage in delinquent behavior or early sexual behavior. Researchers have found that adolescents who interact with older youths do engage in these behaviors more frequently, but it is not known whether the older youth guide younger adolescents toward deviant behavior or whether the younger adolescents were already prone to deviant behavior before they developed the friendship with the older youth (Billy, Rodgers, & Udry, 1984).

Peer Groups

How much pressure is there to conform to peers during adolescence? Consider this statement made by an adolescent girl:

> Peer pressure is extremely influential in my life. I have never had very many friends, and I spend quite a bit of time alone. The friends I have are older. The closest friend I have had is a lot like me in that we are both sad and depressed a lot. I began to act even more depressed than before when I was with her. I would call her up and try to act even more depressed than I was because that is what I thought she liked. In that relationship, I felt pressure to be like her.

Conformity to peer pressure in adolescence can be positive or negative. Teenagers engage in all sorts of negative conformity behavior—use seedy language, steal, vandalize, and make fun of parents and teachers. However, a great deal of peer conformity is not negative and consists of the desire to be involved in the peer world, such as dressing like friends and wanting to spend large amounts of time with members of a clique. Such circumstances may involve prosocial activities as well, as when clubs raise money for worthy causes.

Young adolescents conform more to peer standards than children do. Investigators have found that, around the eighth and ninth grades, conformity to peers—especially to their antisocial standards—peaks (Leventhal, 1994). At this point, adolescents are most likely to go along with a peer to steal hubcaps off a car, draw graffiti on a wall, or steal cosmetics from a store counter. However, researchers have found that U.S. adolescents are more likely to put pressure on their peers to resist parental influence than Japanese adolescents are (Rothbaum & others, 2000).

Most adolescents conform to the mainstream standards of their peers. However, the rebellious or anticonformist adolescent reacts counter to the mainstream peer group's expectations, deliberately moving away from the actions or beliefs this group advocates.

Cliques and Crowds Cliques and crowds assume more important roles in the lives of adolescents than children (Brown, 2003, 2004). **Cliques** are small groups that range from 2 to about 12 individuals and average about 5 to 6 individuals. The clique members are usually of the same sex and about the same age. Cliques can form because adolescents engage in similar activities, such as being in a club or on a sports team. Some cliques also form because of friendship. Several adolescents may form a clique because they have spent time with each other and enjoy each other's company. Not necessarily friends, they often develop a friendship if they stay in the clique. What do adolescents do in cliques? They share ideas, hang out together, and often develop an in-group identity in which they believe that their clique is better than other cliques.

Crowds are a larger group structure than cliques. Adolescents are usually members of a crowd based on reputation and may or may not spend much time together. Crowds are less personal than cliques. Many crowds are defined by the activities adolescents engage in (such as "jocks" who are good at sports or "druggies" who take drugs) (Brown, 2004).

In one study, crowd membership was associated with adolescent self-esteem (Brown & Lohr, 1987). The crowds included jocks (athletically oriented), populars (well-known students who led social activities), normals (middle-of-the-road students who made up the masses), druggies or toughs (known for illicit drug use or other delinquent activities), and nobodies (low in social skills or intellectual abilities). The self-esteem of the jocks and the populars was highest, whereas that of the nobodies was lowest. One group of adolescents not in a crowd had self-esteem equivalent to that of the jocks and the populars; this group was the independents, who indicated that crowd membership was not important to them. Keep in mind that these data are correlational; self-esteem could increase an adolescent's

clique A small group that ranges from 2 to about 12 individuals, averaging about 5 to 6 individuals, and can form because adolescents engage in similar activities.

crowd A larger group structure than a clique, a crowd is usually formed based on reputation and members may or may not spend much time together.

probability of becoming a crowd member, just as crowd membership could increase the adolescent's self-esteem.

Adolescent Groups Versus Children Groups   Children groups differ from adolescent groups in several important ways. The members of children groups often are friends or neighborhood acquaintances, and their groups usually are not as formalized as many adolescent groups. During the adolescent years, groups tend to include a broader array of members. In other words, adolescents other than friends or neighborhood acquaintances often are members of adolescent groups. Try to recall the student council, honor society, or football team at your junior high school. If you were a member of any of these organizations, you probably remember that they were made up of many people you had not met before and that it was a more heterogeneous group than your childhood peer groups. For example, peer groups in adolescence are more likely to have a mixture of individuals from different ethnic groups than are peer groups in childhood.

Dating and Romantic Relationships

Adolescents spend considerable time either dating or thinking about dating, which has gone far beyond its original courtship function to become a form of recreation, a source of status and achievement, and a setting for learning about close relationships. One function of dating, though, continues to be mate selection.

Types of Dating and Developmental Changes   A number of developmental changes characterize dating (Florsheim, Moore, & Edgington, 2003). In one recent study, announcing that "I like someone" occurred by the sixth grade for 40 percent of the individuals sampled (Buhrmester, 2001) (see figure 13.5). However, it was not until the tenth grade that 50 percent of the adolescents had a sustained romantic relationship that lasted two months or longer. By their senior year, 25 percent still had not engaged in this type of sustained romantic relationship. Also, in this study, girls' early romantic involvement was linked with lower grades, less active participation in class discussion, and school-related problems. A rather large portion of adolescents in dating relationships say that their relationships have persisted 11 months or longer: 20 percent of adolescents 14 or younger, 35 percent of 15- to 16-year-olds, and almost 60 percent of 17- and 18-year-olds (Carver, Joyner, & Udry, 2003).

Adolescent Peer Relationships
Youth Connections

FIGURE 13.5 Age of Onset of Romantic Activity

In this study, announcing that "I like someone" occurred earliest, followed by going out with the same person three or more times, having an exclusive relationship for over two months, and finally planning an engagement or marriage (which characterized only a very small percentage of participants by the twelfth grade) (Buhrmester, 2001).

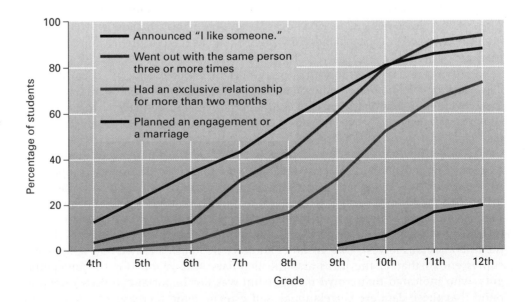

In their early romantic relationships, many adolescents are not moti-vated to fulfill attachment or even sexual needs. Rather, early romantic relationships serve as a context for adolescents to explore how attractive they are, how they should romantically interact with someone, and how all of this looks to the peer group (Brown, 1999). Only after adolescents acquire some basic competencies in interacting with romantic partners does the fulfillment of attachment and sexual needs become central functions of these relationships (Bouchey & Furman, 2003; Furman & Shaeffer, 2003).

In their early exploration of romantic relationships, today's adoles-cents often find comfort in numbers and begin hanging out together in mixed-sex groups. Sometimes they just hang out at someone's house or get organized enough to get someone to drive them to a mall or a movie (Peterson, 1997). A special concern is early dating and "going with" someone, which is associated with adolescent pregnancy and problems at home and school (Florsheim, Moore, & Edgington, 2003).

What are dating relationships like in adolescence?

Yet another form of dating recently has been added. *Cyberdating* is dating over the Internet (Thomas, 1998). One 10-year-old girl posted this ad on the Web:

> Hi! I'm looking for a Cyber Boyfriend! I'm 10. I have brown hair and brown eyes. I love swimming, playing basketball, and think kittens are adorable!!!

Cyberdating is especially becoming popular among middle school students. By the time they reach high school and are able to drive, dating usually has evolved into a more traditional real-life venture. Adolescents need to be cautioned about the potential hazards of cyberdating and not really knowing who is on the other end of the computer connection.

Dating in Gay and Lesbian Youth Most research on romantic relationships in adolescence has focused on heterosexual relationships. Recently, researchers have begun to study romantic relationships in gay, lesbian, and bisexual youth (Diamond & Savin-Williams, 2003; Savin-Williams & Diamond, 2004).

Most gay and lesbian youth have had some same-sex sexual experience, often with peers who are "experimenting" and then go on to a primarily heterosexual orientation. However, relatively few have same-sex romantic relationships because of limited opportunities and the social disapproval such relationships may generate from families or heterosexual peers (Diamond, 2003). Many sexual minority youth date other-sex peers, which can help them to clarify their sexual orientation or dis-guise it from others (Savin-Williams & Diamond, 2004). The importance of romance to gay and lesbian youth was underscored in a study that found that they rated the breakup of a current romance as their second most stressful problem, second only to disclosure of their sexual orientation to their parents (D'Augelli, 1991).

Dating Scripts **Dating scripts** are the cognitive models that guide individuals' dat-ing interactions. In one study of heterosexual adolescents, first dates were highly scripted along gender lines (Rose & Frieze, 1993). The males followed a proactive dat-ing script, the females a reactive one. The male's script involved initiating the date (ask-ing for and planning it), controlling the public domain (driving and opening doors), and initiating sexual interaction (making physical contact, making out, and kissing). The female's script focused on the private domain (concern about appearance, enjoy-ing the date), participating in the structure of the date established by the male (being picked up, having doors opened), and responding to his sexual overtures. These gen-der differences give males more power in the initial stage of a dating relationship.

In another study of heterosexual adolescents, male and female adolescents brought different motivations to the dating experience (Feiring, 1996). The 15-year-old girls were more likely to describe romance in terms of interpersonal qualities, the

dating scripts The cognitive models that individuals use to guide and evaluate dating interactions.

boys in terms of physical attraction. The young adolescents frequently mentioned the affiliative qualities of companionship, intimacy, and support as positive aspects of romantic relationships, but not love and security. Also, the young adolescents described physical attraction more in terms of cute, pretty, or handsome than in sexual terms (such as being a good kisser). Possibly the failure to discuss sexual interests was due to the adolescents' discomfort in talking about such personal feelings with an unfamiliar adult.

Sociocultural Contexts and Dating   The sociocultural context exerts a powerful influence on adolescents' dating patterns. Values and religious beliefs of people in various cultures often dictate the age at which dating begins, how much freedom in dating is allowed, whether dates must be chaperoned by adults or parents, and the roles of males and females in dating. For example, Latino and Asian American cultures have more conservative standards regarding adolescent dating than does the Anglo-American culture. Dating may be a source of cultural conflict for many immigrants and their families who have come from cultures in which dating begins at a late age, little freedom in dating is allowed, dates are chaperoned, and adolescent girl dating is especially restricted. One recent study found that Asian American adolescents were less likely to be involved in a romantic relationship in the past 18 months than African American or Latino adolescents (Carver, Joyner, & Udry, 2003).

In one recent study, Latina young adults in the midwestern United States reflected on their experiences in dating during adolescence (Raffaeli & Ontai, 2003). They said that their parents placed strict boundaries on their romantic involvement. As a result, the young women said that their adolescent dating experiences were filled with tension and conflict. Over half of the Latinas engaged in "sneak dating" without their parents' knowledge.

www.mhhe.com/santrockld10

Dating and Romantic Relationships
Teen Chat

Review and Reflect: Learning Goal 3

3   **Characterize the changes that occur in peer relations during adolescence**

REVIEW

- What changes take place in friendship during adolescence?
- What are adolescents' peer groups like?
- What is the nature of adolescent dating and romantic relationships?

REFLECT

- What were your peer relationships like during adolescence? What peer groups were you involved in? How did they influence your development? What were your dating and romantic relationships like in adolescence? If you could change anything about the way you experienced peer relations in adolescence, what would it be?

---

4   CULTURE AND ADOLESCENT DEVELOPMENT

Cross-Cultural Comparisons   **Ethnicity**

We live in an increasingly diverse world, one in which there is increasing contact between adolescents from different cultures and ethnic groups. In this section, we will explore how adolescents vary cross-culturally, rites of passage, and the nature of ethnic minority adolescents and their development.

Cross-Cultural Comparisons

What are the world's youth like? What traditions remain for adolescents around the globe? What circumstances are changing adolescents' lives?

Some experts argue that adolescence too often is thought of in a "Eurocentric" way (Nsamenang, 2002). Others note that advances in transportation and telecommunication are spawning a global youth culture in which adolescents everywhere wear the same type of clothing and have similar hairstyles, listen to the same music, and use similar slang expressions (Schegel, 2000). But cultural differences among adolescents have by no means disappeared (Larson & Wilson, 2004).

Consider some of the variations of adolescence around the world (Brown & Larson, 2002):

- Two-thirds of Asian Indian adolescents accept their parents' choice of a marital partner for them (Verma & Saraswathi, 2002).
- In the Philippines, many female adolescents sacrifice their own futures by migrating to the city to earn money that they can send home to their families.
- Street youth in Kenya and other parts of the world learn to survive under highly stressful circumstances (Nsamenang, 2002). In some cases abandoned by their parents, they may engage in delinquency or prostitution to provide for their economic needs.
- In the Middle East, many adolescents are not allowed to interact with the other sex, even in school (Booth, 2002).
- Whereas individuals in the United States are marrying later than in past generations, youth in Russia are marrying earlier to legitimize sexual activity (Stetsenko, 2002).

Thus, depending on the culture being observed, adolescence may involve many different experiences (Larson & Wilson, 2004).

Global Traditions and Changes in Adolescence Rapid global change is altering the experience of adolescence, presenting new opportunities and challenges to young people's health and well-being. Around the world, adolescents' experiences may differ depending on their gender, families, schools, and peers (Brown & Larson, 2002; Larson & Wilson, 2004). However, some adolescent traditions remain the same in various cultures.

Health Adolescent health and well-being has improved in some areas but not in others. Overall, fewer adolescents around the world die from infectious diseases and malnutrition now than in the past (Call & others, 2002; World Health Organization, 2002). However, a number of adolescent health-compromising behaviors (especially illicit drug use and unprotected sex) are increasing in frequency (Blum & Nelson-Mmari, 2004). Extensive increases in the rates of HIV in adolescents have occurred in many sub-Saharan countries (World Health Organization, 2002).

Gender Around the world, the experiences of male and female adolescents continue to be quite different (Brown & Larson, 2002; Larson & Wilson, 2004). Except in a few areas, such as Japan, the Philippines, and Western countries, males have far greater access to educational opportunities than females. In many countries, adolescent females have less freedom to pursue a variety of careers and engage in various leisure acts than males. Gender differences in sexual expression are widespread, especially in India, Southeast Asia, Latin America, and Arab countries where there are far more restrictions on the sexual activity of adolescent females than on males. These gender differences do appear to be narrowing over time, however. In some countries, educational and career opportunities for women are expanding and in some parts of the world control over adolescent girls' romantic and sexual relationships is weakening.

Muslim school in Middle East with boys only

Asian Indian adolescents in a marriage ceremony

Street youth in Rio De Janeiro

Family In some countries, adolescents grow up in closely knit families with extensive extended kin networks "that provide a web of connections and reinforce a traditional way of life" (Brown & Larson, 2002, p. 6). For example, in Arab countries, "adolescents are taught strict codes of conduct and loyalty" (p. 6). However, in Western countries such as the United States, adolescents are growing up in much larger numbers in divorced families and stepfamilies. Parenting in Western countries is less authoritarian than in the past.

Some of the trends that are occurring in many countries around the world "include greater family mobility, migration to urban areas, family members working in distant cities or countries, smaller families, fewer extended-family households, and increases in mothers' employment" (Brown & Larson, 2002, p. 7). Unfortunately, many of these changes may reduce the ability of families to provide time and resources for adolescents.

School In general, the number of adolescents in school in developing countries is increasing. However, schools in many parts of the world—especially Africa, South Asia, and Latin America—still do not provide education to all adolescents. Indeed, there has been a decline in recent years in the percentage of Latin American adolescents who have access to secondary and higher education (Welti, 2002). Furthermore, many schools do not provide students with the skills they need to be successful in adult work.

Peers Some cultures give peers a stronger role in adolescence than others (Brown, 2004; Brown & Larson, 2002). In most Western nations, peers figure prominently in adolescents' lives, in some cases taking on responsibilities that are otherwise assumed by parents. Among street youth in South America, the peer network serves as a surrogate family that supports survival in dangerous and stressful settings. In other regions of the world, such as in Arab countries, peers have a very restrictive role, especially for girls (Booth, 2002).

Activity	Nonindustrial, unschooled populations	Postindustrial, schooled populations		
		United States	Europe	East Asia
Household labor	5 to 9 hours	20 to 40 minutes	20 to 40 minutes	10 to 20 minutes
Paid labor	0.5 to 8 hours	40 to 60 minutes	10 to 20 minutes	0 to 10 minutes
Schoolwork	—	3.0 to 4.5 hours	4.0 to 5.5 hours	5.5 to 7.5 hours
Total work time	6 to 9 hours	4 to 6 hours	4.5 to 6.5 hours	6 to 8 hours
TV viewing	*Insufficient data*	1.5 to 2.5 hours	1.5 to 2.5 hours	1.5 to 2.5 hours
Talking	*Insufficient data*	2 to 3 hours	*Insufficient data*	45 to 60 minutes
Sports	*Insufficient data*	30 to 60 minutes	20 to 80 minutes	0 to 20 minutes
Structured voluntary activities	*Insufficient data*	10 to 20 minutes	10 to 20 minutes	0 to 10 minutes
Total free time	4 to 7 hours	6.5 to 8.0 hours	5.5 to 7.5 hours	4.0 to 5.5 hours

Note: The estimates in the table are averaged across a 7-day week, including weekdays and weekends. Time spent in maintenance activities like eating, personal care, and sleeping is not included. The data for nonindustrial, unschooled populations come primarily from rural peasant populations in developing countries.

FIGURE 13.6 Average Daily Time Use of Adolescents in Different Regions of the World

In sum, adolescents' lives are characterized by a combination of change and tradition. Researchers have found both similarities and differences in the experiences of adolescents in different countries (Larson & Wilson, 2004).

How Adolescents Around the World Spend Their Time Reed Larson and Suman Verma (Larson, 2001; Larson & Verma, 1999) have examined how adolescents spend their time in work, play, and developmental activities such as school. Figure 13.6 summarizes the average daily time use by adolescents in different regions of the world (Larson & Verma, 1999). U.S. adolescents spend about 60 percent as much time on schoolwork as East Asian adolescents do, which is mainly due to U.S. adolescents doing less homework.

What U.S. adolescents have in greater quantities than adolescents in other industrialized countries is discretionary time (Larson & Wilson, 2004). About 40 to 50 percent of U.S. adolescents' waking hours (not counting summer vacations) is spent in discretionary activities compared with 25 to 35 percent in East Asia and 35 to 45 percent in Europe. Whether this additional discretionary time is a liability or an asset for U.S. adolescents, of course, depends on how they use it.

According to Larson (2001), for optimal development, U.S. adolescents may have too much unstructured time because when adolescents are allowed to choose what they do with their time, they typically engage in unchallenging activities such as hanging out and watching TV. Although relaxation and social interaction are important aspects of adolescence, it seems unlikely that spending large numbers of hours per week in unchallenging activities fosters development. Structured voluntary activities may provide more promise for adolescent development than unstructured time, especially if adults give responsibility to adolescents, challenge them, and provide competent guidance in these activities (Larson, 2001).

Rites of Passage Another variation in the experiences of adolescents in different cultures is whether the adolescents go through a rite of passage. Some societies have elaborate ceremonies that signal the adolescent's move to maturity and achievement of adult status (Kottak, 2004). A **rite of passage** is a ceremony or ritual that marks an individual's transition from one status to another. Most rites of passage focus on the transition to adult status. In many primitive cultures, rites of passage are the avenue through which adolescents gain access

rite of passage A ceremony or ritual that marks an individual's transition from one status to another. Most rites of passage focus on the transition to adult status.

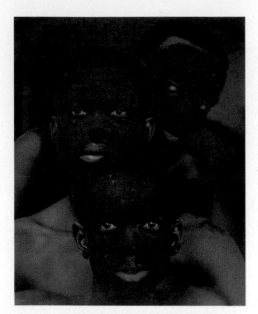

These Congolese Kota boys painted their faces as part of a rite of passage to adulthood. *What rites of passage do American adolescents have?*

to sacred adult practices, to knowledge, and to sexuality. These rites often involve dramatic practices intended to facilitate the adolescent's separation from the immediate family, especially the mother. The transformation is usually characterized by some form of ritual death and rebirth, or by means of contact with the spiritual world. Bonds are forged between the adolescent and the adult instructors through shared rituals, hazards, and secrets to allow the adolescent to enter the adult world. This kind of ritual provides a forceful and discontinuous entry into the adult world at a time when the adolescent is perceived to be ready for the change.

Africa has been the location of many rites of passage for adolescents, especially sub-Saharan Africa. Under the influence of Western culture, many of the rites are disappearing today, although some vestiges remain. In locations where formal education is not readily available, rites of passage are still prevalent.

Do we have such rites of passage for American adolescents? We certainly do not have universal formal ceremonies that mark the passage from adolescence to adulthood. Certain religious and social groups do have initiation ceremonies that indicate that an advance in maturity has been reached—the Jewish bar mitzvah, the Catholic confirmation, and social debuts, for example. School graduation ceremonies come the closest to being culture-wide rites of passage in the United States. The high school graduation ceremony has become nearly universal for middle-class adolescents and increasing numbers of adolescents from low-income backgrounds. Nonetheless, high school graduation does not result in universal changes; many high school graduates continue to live with their parents, continue to be economically dependent on them, and continue to be undecided about career and lifestyle matters. Another rite of passage for increasing numbers of American adolescents is sexual intercourse (Halonen & Santrock, 1999). By 19 years of age, four out of five American adolescents have had sexual intercourse.

Ethnicity

Earlier in this chapter, we explored the identity development of ethnic minority adolescents. Here we will examine other aspects of ethnicity, beginning with the difficulty of separating ethnicity and socioeconomic influences. First, we will examine the nature of ethnicity and socioeconomic status; second, we will examine the nature of differences and diversity; third, we will study the aspects of value conflicts, assimilation, and pluralism.

Ethnicity and Socioeconomic Status   Much of the research on ethnic minority adolescents has failed to tease apart the influences of ethnicity and socioeconomic status. Ethnicity and socioeconomic status can interact in ways that exaggerate the influence of ethnicity because ethnic minority individuals are overrepresented in the lower socioeconomic levels of American society. Consequently, researchers too often have given ethnic explanations of adolescent development that were largely due to socioeconomic status rather than ethnicity. For example, decades of research on group differences in self-esteem failed to consider the socioeconomic status of African American and White children and adolescents. When African American adolescents from low-income backgrounds are compared with White adolescents from middle-income backgrounds, the differences often are large but not informative because of the confounding of ethnicity and socioeconomic status (Scott-Jones, 1995).

Although some ethnic minority youth are from middle-income backgrounds, economic advantage does not entirely enable them to escape their ethnic minority status (Spencer & Dornbusch, 1990). Middle-income ethnic minority youth still encounter much of the prejudice, discrimination, and bias associated with being a member of an ethnic minority group. Often characterized as a "model minority" because of their strong achievement orientation and family cohesiveness, Japanese Americans still experience stress associated with ethnic minority status (Sue, 1990). Even though middle-income ethnic minority adolescents have more resources available to counter the destructive influences of prejudice and discrimination, they still cannot completely avoid the pervasive influence of negative stereotypes about ethnic minority groups.

Not all ethnic minority families are poor. However, poverty contributes to the stressful life experiences of many ethnic minority adolescents (Fox & others, 2004; Leventhal & Brooks-Gunn, 2004; Schellenach, Leadbetter, & Moore, 2004). Thus, many ethnic minority adolescents experience a double disadvantage: (1) prejudice, discrimination, and bias because of their ethnic minority status; and (2) the stressful effects of poverty.

Differences and Diversity There are legitimate differences between various ethnic minority groups, as well as between ethnic minority groups and the majority White group. Recognizing and respecting these differences are important aspects of getting along with others in a multicultural world. Historical, economic, and social experiences produce differences in ethnic groups (Coll, Meyer, & Brillion, 1995). Individuals living in a particular ethnic or cultural group adapt to the values, attitudes, and stresses of that culture. Their behavior, while possibly different from yours is nonetheless often functional for them. It is important for adolescents to take the perspective of individuals from ethnic and cultural groups that are different from theirs and think, "If I were in their shoes, what kind of experiences might I have had?" "How would I feel if I were a member of their ethnic or cultural group?" "How would I think and behave if I had grown up in their world?" Such perspective taking often increases an adolescent's empathy and understanding of individuals from ethnic and cultural groups different from their own (Gudykunst, 2004; Pang, 2005).

Another important dimension to continually keep in mind when studying ethnic minority adolescents is their diversity (Cauce & others, 2002; Pedersen, 2004). Ethnic minority groups are not homogeneous; they have different social, historical, and economic backgrounds. For example, Mexican, Cuban, and Puerto Rican immigrants are all Latinos, but they migrated for different reasons, came from varying socioeconomic backgrounds in their native countries, and experience different rates and types of employment in the United States.

The federal government now recognizes the existence of 511 different Native American tribes, each having a unique ancestral background with differing values and characteristics. Asian Americans include the Chinese, Japanese, Filipinos, Koreans, and Southeast Asians, each group having a distinct ancestry and language. As an indication of the diversity of Asian Americans, 90 percent of Korean American males graduate from high school, but only 71 percent of Vietnamese American males do.

Relatively high rates of minority immigration are contributing to the growth in the proportion of ethnic minorities in the U.S. population (McLoyd, 1998, 2000). Because immigrants often experience stressors uncommon to or less prominent among longtime residents (such as language barriers, dislocations and separations from support networks, dual struggle to preserve identity and to acculturate, and changes in SES status), adaptations in intervention programs may be required to achieve optimal cultural sensitivity when working with adolescents and their immigrant families (Chun & Akutsu, 2003).

Although the U.S. immigrant population has been growing, psychologists have been slow to study these families. In one recent study, the cultural values and intergenerational value discrepancies in immigrant (Vietnamese, Armenian, and Mexican) and nonimmigrant families (African American and European

Jason Leonard, age 15: "I want America to know that most of us black teens are not troubled people from broken homes and headed to jail. . . . In my relationships with my parents, we show respect for each other and we have values in our house. We have traditions we celebrate together, including Christmas and Kwanza."

www.mhhe.com/santrockld10

Changing Contexts

Careers in Life-Span Development

Carola Suarez-Orozco, Lecturer, Researcher, and Co-Director of Immigration Projects

Carola Suarez-Orozco is a researcher and lecturer in the Human Development and Psychology area at Harvard University. She also is co-director of the Harvard Immigration Projects. She obtained her undergraduate (development studies) and graduate (clinical psychology) degrees from the University of California at Berkeley.

Carola has worked both in clinical and public school settings in California and Massachusetts. She currently is codirecting a five-year longitudinal study of immigrant adolescents' (coming from Central America, China, and the Dominican Republic) adaptation to schools and society. One of the courses she teaches at Harvard is on the psychology of immigrant youth. Carola especially believes that more research needs to be conducted on the intersection of cultural and psychological factors in the adaptation of immigrant and ethnic minority youth.

Carola Suarez-Orozco, with her husband Marcelo, who also studies the adaptation of immigrants.

assimilation The absorption of ethnic minority groups into the dominant group, which often involves the loss of some or virtually all of the behavior and values of the ethnic minority group.

pluralism The coexistence of distinct ethnic and cultural groups in the same society. Individuals with a pluralistic stance usually advocate that cultural differences be maintained and appreciated.

American) were studied (Phinney, Ong, & Madden, 2000). Family obligations were endorsed more by parents than adolescents in all groups, and the intergenerational value discrepancy generally increased with time in the United States.

Parents and adolescents may be at different stages of acculturation, which can produce conflict over cultural values (Roosa & others, 2002; Samaniego & Gonzales, 1999; Santisteban & Mitrani, 2003). Research increasingly shows links between acculturation and adolescent problems (Gonzales & others, 2002). For example, more-acculturated Latino youths in the United States experience higher rates of conduct problems, substance abuse, and risky sexual behavior than their less-acculturated counterparts (Brook & others, 1998; Epstein, Botvin, & Díaz, 1998).

One individual who is deeply concerned about immigrant youth and conducts research to learn more about ways to help them cope with life in America is Carola Suarez-Orozco. To read about her work, see the Careers in Life-Span Development insert.

Value Conflicts, Assimilation, and Pluralism Stanley Sue (1990) believes that value conflicts are often involved when individuals respond to ethnic issues. These value conflicts have been a source of considerable controversy. According to Sue, without properly identifying the assumptions and effects of the conflicting values, it is difficult to resolve ethnic minority issues. Let's examine one of these value conflicts, assimilation versus pluralism, to see how it might influence an individual's response to an ethnic minority issue:

- **Assimilation** is the absorption of ethnic minority groups into the dominant group, which often means the loss of some or virtually all of the behavior and values of the ethnic group. Individuals who adopt an assimilation stance usually advocate that ethnic minority groups become more American.
- **Pluralism** is the coexistence of distinct ethnic and cultural groups in the same society. Individuals who adopt a pluralistic stance usually advocate that cultural differences be maintained and appreciated (Leong, 2000).

Sue believes that one way to resolve value conflicts about sociocultural issues is to conceptualize or redefine them in innovative ways. For example, in the assimilation/pluralism conflict, rather than assume that assimilation is necessary for the development of functional skills, one strategy is to focus on the fluctuating criteria defining those skills considered to be functional; another is to consider the possibility that developing functional skills does not prevent the existence of pluralism. For instance, the classroom instructor might use multicultural examples when teaching social studies and still be able to discuss both culturally universal and culturally specific approaches to American and other cultures. To read about a program that provides support for ethnic minority youth, see the Diversity in Life-Span Development interlude.

Diversity in Life-Span Development

El Puente

El Puente, which means "the bridge," was opened in New York City in 1983 because of community dissatisfaction with the health, education, and social services youth were receiving (Simons, Finlay, & Yang, 1991). El Puente emphasizes five areas of youth development: health, education, achievement, personal growth, and social growth.

El Puente is located in a former Roman Catholic church on the south side of Williamsburg in Brooklyn, a neighborhood made up primarily of low-income Latino families, many of which are far below the poverty line. Sixty-five percent of the residents receive some form of public assistance. The neighborhood has the highest school dropout rate for Latinos in New York City and the highest felony rate for adolescents in Brooklyn.

When the youth, ages 12 through 21, first enroll in El Puente, they meet with counselors and develop a four-month plan that includes the programs they are interested in joining. At the end of four months, the youth and staff develop a plan for continued participation. Twenty-six bilingual classes are offered in such subjects as the fine arts, theater, photography, and dance. In addition, El Puente sponsors a medical and fitness center, GED night school, and centers for mental health and social services.

These adolescents participate in the programs of El Puente, located in a predominantly low-income Latino neighborhood in Brooklyn, New York. *Which areas of youth development does the El Puente program stress?*

Review and Reflect: Learning Goal 4

4 **Explain how culture influences adolescent development**

REVIEW

• What are some comparisons of adolescents in different cultures? How do adolescents around the world spend their time? What are rites of passage?
• How does ethnicity influence adolescent development?

REFLECT

• What is your ethnicity? Have you ever been stereotyped because of your ethnicity? How different is your identity from the mainstream culture?

5 ADOLESCENT PROBLEMS

| Juvenile Delinquency | Depression and Suicide | The Interrelation of Problems and Successful Prevention/ Intervention Programs |

In chapter 12, we described these adolescent problems: substance abuse, sexually transmitted infections, and eating disorders. Here, we will examine the problems of juvenile delinquency, depression, and suicide.

Office of Juvenile Justice and
Delinquency Prevention
Justice Information Center
Preventing Crime

Juvenile Delinquency

The label **juvenile delinquent** is applied to an adolescent who breaks the law or engages in behavior that is considered illegal. Like other categories of disorders, juvenile delinquency is a broad concept; legal infractions range from littering to murder. Because the adolescent technically becomes a juvenile delinquent only after being judged guilty of a crime by a court of law, official records do not accurately reflect the number of illegal acts juvenile delinquents commit. Estimates of the number of juvenile delinquents in the United States are sketchy, but FBI statistics indicate that at least 2 percent of all youth are involved in juvenile court cases.

U.S. government statistics reveal that 8 of 10 cases of juvenile delinquency involve males (Snyder & Sickmund, 1999). Although males are still far more likely to engage in juvenile delinquency, in the last two decades there has been a greater increase in female delinquency than in male delinquency (Snyder & Sickmund, 1999). For both male and female delinquents, rates for property offenses are higher than for other rates of offenses (such as against persons, drug offenses, and public order offenses). Arrests of adolescent males for delinquency still are much higher than for adolescent females.

Delinquency rates among African Americans, other minority groups, and lower-socioeconomic-status youth are especially high in proportion to the overall population of these groups. However, such groups have less influence over the judicial decision-making process in the United States and, therefore, may be judged delinquent more readily than their White, middle-socioeconomic-status counterparts.

In the Pittsburgh Youth Study, a longitudinal study focused on more than 1,500 inner-city boys, three developmental pathways to delinquency were (Loeber & Farrington, 2001; Loeber & others, 1998; Stoutheimer-Loeber & others, 2002):

- *Authority conflict.* Youth on this pathway showed stubbornness prior to age 12, then moved on to defiance and avoidance of authority.
- *Covert.* This pathway included minor covert acts, such as lying, followed by property damage and moderately serious delinquency, then serious delinquency.
- *Overt.* This pathway included minor aggression followed by fighting and violence.

One issue in juvenile justice is whether an adolescent who commits a crime should be tried as an adult (Steinberg & Cauffman, 2001). In a recent study, trying adolescent offenders as adults increased rather than reduced their crime rate (Myers, 1999). The study evaluated more than 500 violent youth in Pennsylvania, which has adopted a "get tough" policy. Although these 500 offenders had been given harsher punishment than a comparison group retained in juvenile court, they were more likely to be rearrested—and rearrested more quickly—for new offenses once they were returned to the community. This suggests that the price of short-term public safety attained by prosecuting juveniles as adults might increase the number of criminal offenses over the long run.

Causes of Delinquency What causes delinquency? Many causes have been proposed, including heredity, identity problems, community influences, and family experiences. Erik Erikson (1968), for example, believes that adolescents whose development has restricted them from acceptable social roles or made them feel that they cannot measure up to the demands placed on them may choose a negative identity. Adolescents with a negative identity may find support for their delinquent image among peers, reinforcing the negative identity. For Erikson, delinquency is an attempt to establish an identity, although a negative one.

Although delinquency is less exclusively a phenomenon of lower socioeconomic status than it was in the past, some characteristics of lower-class culture might promote delinquency. The norms of many lower-SES peer groups and gangs are antisocial, or counterproductive, to the goals and norms of society at large. Getting into and staying out of trouble are prominent features of life for some adolescents in

juvenile delinquent An adolescent who breaks the law or engages in behavior that is considered illegal.

low-income neighborhoods (Flannery & others, 2003). Adolescents from low-income backgrounds may sense that they can gain attention and status by performing antisocial actions. Being "tough" and "masculine" are high-status traits for lower-SES boys, and these traits are often measured by the adolescent's success in performing and getting away with delinquent acts. A community with a high crime rate also lets the adolescent observe many models who engage in criminal activities. These communities may be characterized by poverty, unemployment, and feelings of alienation toward the middle class. Quality schooling, educational funding, and organized neighborhood activities may be lacking in these communities (Sabol, Coulton, & Korbin, 2004).

Family support systems are also associated with delinquency (Farrington, 2004; Feldman & Weinberger, 1994). Parents of delinquents are less skilled in discouraging antisocial behavior and in encouraging skilled behavior than are parents of non-delinquents. Parental monitoring of adolescents is especially important in determining whether an adolescent becomes a delinquent (Coley, Morris, & Hernandez, 2004; Patterson, DeBaryshe, & Ramsey, 1989). Family discord and inconsistent and inappropriate discipline also are associated with delinquency (Bor, McGee, & Fagan, 2004). An increasing number of studies have also found that siblings can have a strong influence on delinquency (Bank, Burraston, & Snyder, 2004; Conger & Reuter, 1996). In one recent study, high levels of hostile sibling relationships and older sibling delinquency were linked with younger sibling delinquency in both brother and sister pairs (Slomkowski & others, 2001). Having delinquent peers greatly increases the risk of becoming delinquent (Henry, Tolan, & Gorman-Smith, 2001).

Youth Violence   Youth violence is a special concern in the United States today (U.S. Department of Health and Human Services, 2001). In one study, 17 percent of U.S. high school students reported carrying a gun or other weapon the past 30 days (National Center for Health Statistics, 2000). In this same study, a smaller percentage (7 percent) reported bringing a gun or other weapon onto school property. Not all violence-related behaviors involve weapons. In this study, 44 percent of male and 27 percent of female high school students said they had been involved in one or more fights.

In the late 1990s, a series of school shootings gained national attention. In April 1999, in Littleton, Colorado, two Columbine High School students, Eric Harris, 18, and Dylan Klebold, 17, shot and killed 12 students and a teacher, wounded 23 others, and then killed themselves. In May 1998, slightly built Kip Kinkel strode into a cafeteria at Thurston High School in Springfield, Oregon, and opened fire on his fellow students, murdering two and injuring many others. Later that day, police went to Kip's home and found his parents lying dead on the floor, also victims of Kip's violence.

In 2001, 15-year-old Charles "Andy" Williams fired shots at Santana High School in Southern California, killing two classmates and injuring 13 others. According to students at the school, Andy was a victim of bullying and had joked the previous weekend of his violent plans, but no one took him seriously after he later said he was just kidding.

Is there any way psychologists can predict whether a youth will turn violent? It's a complex task, but researchers have pieced together some clues (Cowley, 1998). Violent youth are overwhelmingly male, and many are driven by feelings of powerlessness. Violence seems to infuse these youth with a sense of power. In one study based on data collected in the National Longitudinal Study of Adolescent Health, secure attachment to parents, living in an intact family, and attending church services with parents were linked with lower incidences of violent behavior in seventh-through twelfth-graders (Franke, 2000).

Small-town shooting sprees attract attention, but youth violence is far greater in poverty-infested areas of inner cities. Urban poverty fosters powerlessness and rage, and many inner-city neighborhoods provide almost daily opportunities to

> *Common parenting weaknesses in the families of antisocial boys include a lack of supervision, poor disciplining skills, limited problem-solving abilities, and a tendency to be uncommunicative with sons.*
>
> —GERALD PATTERSON
> *Contemporary American Psychologist, University of Oregon*

"Andy" Williams, escorted by police after being arrested for killing two classmates and injuring 13 others at Santana High School. *What factors might contribute to youth murders?*

observe violence. Many urban youth who live in poverty also lack adequate parent involvement and supervision (Tolan, 2001).

James Garbarino (1999, 2001) says there is a lot of ignoring that goes on in these kinds of situations. Parents often do not want to acknowledge what might be a very upsetting reality. Harris and Klebold were members of the "Trenchcoat Mafia" clique of Columbine outcasts. The two even had made a video for a school media class the previous fall that depicted them walking down the halls at the school shooting other students. Allegations were made that a year earlier the sheriff's department had been given information that Harris had bragged openly on the Internet that he and Klebold had built four bombs. Kip Kinkel had an obsession with guns and explosives, a history of abusing animals, and a nasty temper when crossed. When police examined his room, they found two pipe bombs, three larger bombs, and bomb-making recipes Kip had downloaded from the Internet. Clearly, some signs were present in these students' lives to suggest that they had some serious problems, but it is still very difficult to predict whether youth like these will act on their anger and sense of powerlessness to commit murder.

Garbarino (1999, 2001) has interviewed a number of youth killers. He concludes that nobody really knows precisely why a tiny minority of youth kill but that it might be a lack of a spiritual center. In the youth killers he interviewed, Garbarino often found a spiritual or emotional emptiness in which the youth sought meaning in the dark side of life.

Some interventions can reduce or prevent youth violence (Barton, 2004; Carnegie Council on Adolescent Development, 1995). Prevention efforts should include developmentally appropriate schools, supportive families, and youth and community organizations. At a more specific level, one promising strategy for preventing youth violence is the teaching of conflict management as part of health education in elementary and middle schools. To build resources for such programs, the Carnegie Foundation is supporting a national network of violence prevention practitioners based at the U.S. Department of Education, linked with a national research center on youth violence at the University of Colorado.

These are some of the Oregon Social Learning Center's recommendations for reducing youth violence (Walker, 1998, p. 1C):

- *Recommit to raising children safely and effectively.* This includes engaging in "parenting practices that produce healthy, well-adjusted children. Such practices involve consistent, fair discipline that is never harsh or severely punitive, careful monitoring and supervision, positive family management techniques, involvement in the child's daily life, daily debriefings about the child's experiences, and teaching problem-solving strategies."
- *Make prevention a reality.* Too often lip service is given to prevention strategies without investing in them at the necessary levels to make them effective.
- *"Give greater support to our schools, which are struggling to educate an increasingly diverse and at-risk student population."*
- *"Forge effective partnerships among families, schools, social service systems, public safety, churches, and other agencies to create the socializing experiences that will give all of our youth a chance to develop along positive lines."*

One individual whose goal is to reduce violence in adolescence and help at-risk adolescents cope more effectively with their lives is Rodney Hammond. To read about his work, see the Careers in Life-Span Development insert.

Depression and Suicide

What is the nature of depression in adolescence? What causes an adolescent to commit suicide?

Depression   Depression is more likely to occur in adolescence than in childhood and more likely to occur in adulthood than adolescence. Further, adolescent girls consistently have higher rates of depression than adolescent boys. (Graber, 2004; Logsdon, 2004; Nolen-Hoeksema, 2004). Among the reasons for this gender difference are that

- Females tend to ruminate in their depressed mood and amplify it.
- Females' self-images, especially their body images, are more negative than males'.
- Females face more discrimination than males do.
- Puberty occurs earlier for girls than for boys, and as a result girls experience a piling up of changes and life experiences in the middle school years, which can increase depression.

Certain family factors place adolescents at risk for developing depression (Eley & others, 2004; Graber, 2004; Seroczynski, Jacquez, & Cole, 2003). These include having a depressed parent, emotionally unavailable parents, parents who have high marital conflict, and parents with financial problems.

Poor peer relationships also are associated with adolescent depression (Bearman & Moody, 2004; Prinstein & Aikens, 2004). Not having a close relationship with a best friend, having less contact with friends, and experiencing peer rejection all increase depressive tendencies in adolescents. The experience of difficult changes or challenges also is associated with depressive symptoms in adolescence (Compas & Grant, 1993), and parental divorce increases depressive symptoms in adolescents. Also, when adolescents go through puberty at the same time as they move from elementary school to middle or junior high school, they report being depressed more than do adolescents who go through puberty after the school transition.

Suicide   Suicidal behavior is rare in childhood but escalates in early adolescence. Suicide is the third leading cause of death today among adolescents 13 through 19 years of age in the United States (National Center for Health Statistics, 2004). Although the incidence of suicide in adolescence has increased in recent decades, it still is a relatively rare event. In 2001, 1 in 10,000 U.S. 15- to 24-year-olds committed suicide (National Vital Statistics Reports, 2003).

Far more adolescents contemplate suicide or attempt suicide unsuccessfully (Borowsky, Ireland, & Resnick, 2001; Judge & Billick, 2004). In a national study, one-fifth of U.S. high school students said that they had seriously considered or attempted suicide in the last 12 months (National Center for Health Statistics, 2000). Less than 3 percent reported a suicide attempt that resulted in an injury, poisoning, or drug overdose that had been treated by a doctor. Females were more likely to attempt suicide than males but males were more likely to commit suicide. Males use more lethal

Careers in Life-Span Development

Rodney Hammond, Health Psychologist

Rodney Hammond described his college experiences:

> When I started as an undergraduate at the University of Illinois, Champaign-Urbana, I hadn't decided on my major. But to help finance my education, I took a part-time job in a child development research program sponsored by the psychology department. There, I observed inner-city children in settings designed to enhance their learning. I saw firsthand the contribution psychology can make, and I knew I wanted to be a psychologist. (American Psychological Association, 2003, p. 26)

Rodney Hammond went on to obtain a doctorate in school and community psychology with a focus on children's development. For a number of years, he trained clinical psychologists at Wright State University in Ohio and directed a program to reduce violence in ethnic minority youth. There, he and his associates taught at-risk youth how to use social skills to effectively manage conflict and to recognize situations that could lead to violence. Today, Rodney is Director of Violence Prevention at the Centers for Disease Control and Prevention in Atlanta. Rodney says that if you are interested in people and problem solving, psychology is a wonderful way to put these together.

(Source: American Psychological Association, 2003, pp. 26–27.)

Rodney Hammond, counseling an adolescent girl about the risks of adolescence and how to effectively cope with them.

Adolescent Depression
Suicide

means, such as a gun, in their suicide attempts, while adolescent females are more likely to cut their wrists or take an overdose of sleeping pills, which is less likely to result in death.

One issue focuses on whether homosexual adolescents are especially vulnerable to suicide. In one study of 12,000 adolescents, approximately 15 percent of gay and lesbian youth said that they had attempted suicide compared with 7 percent of heterosexual youth (Russell & Joyner, 2001). However, Richard Savin-Williams (2001) found that gay and lesbian adolescents were only slightly more likely than heterosexual adolescents to attempt suicide (Savin-Williams, 2001). He argues that most studies have exaggerated the suicide rates for gay adolescents because they only survey the most disturbed youth who are attending support groups or hanging out at shelters for gay youth.

Distal, or earlier, experiences often are involved in suicide attempts as well. The adolescent may have a long-standing history of family instability and unhappiness. Just as a lack of affection and emotional support, high control, and pressure for achievement by parents during childhood are related to adolescent depression, such combinations of family experiences also are likely to show up as distal factors in adolescents' suicide attempts. Adolescents who attempt suicide may also lack supportive friendships. One recent study found that social isolation was linked with suicide attempts in adolescent girls (Bearman & Moody, 2004).

Just as genetic factors are associated with depression, they also are associated with suicide. The closer a person's genetic relationship to someone who has committed suicide, the more likely that person is to also commit suicide.

What is the psychological profile of the suicidal adolescent? Suicidal adolescents often have depressive symptoms (Hallfors & others, 2004; Kaslow & others, 2004; Werth, 2004). Although not all depressed adolescents are suicidal, depression is the most frequently cited factor associated with adolescent suicide. A sense of hopelessness, low self-esteem, and high self-blame are also associated with adolescent suicide (Harter & Whitesell, 2001; O'Donnell & others, 2004).

The Interrelation of Problems and Successful Prevention/Intervention Programs

We have described some of the major adolescent problems in this chapter and in chapter 12: substance abuse; juvenile delinquency; school-related problems, such as dropping out of school; adolescent pregnancy and sexually transmitted infections; depression; and suicide.

The most at-risk adolescents have more than one problem. Researchers are increasingly finding that problem behaviors in adolescence are interrelated (Tubman & Windle, 1995). For example, heavy substance abuse is related to early sexual activity, lower grades, dropping out of school, and delinquency. Early initiation of sexual activity is associated with the use of cigarettes and alcohol, the use of marijuana and other illicit drugs, lower grades, dropping out of school, and delinquency. Delinquency is related to early sexual activity, early pregnancy, substance abuse, and dropping out of school. As many as 10 percent of all adolescents in the United States have serious multiple-problem behaviors (for example, adolescents who have dropped out of school, are behind in their grade level, are users of heavy drugs, regularly use cigarettes and marijuana, and are sexually active but do not use contraception). Another 15 percent of adolescents participate in many of these behaviors but with slightly lower frequency and less deleterious consequences. These high-risk youth often engage in two- or three-problem behaviors (Dryfoos, 1990).

In addition to understanding that many adolescents engage in multiple-problem behaviors, it also is important to develop programs that reduce adolescent problems. In a review of the programs that have been successful in preventing or reducing adolescent problems, adolescence researcher Joy Dryfoos (1990) described the common components of these successful programs:

1. *Intensive individualized attention.* In successful programs, high-risk children are attached to a responsible adult, who gives the child attention and deals with the child's specific needs. This theme occurs in a number of programs. In a successful substance-abuse program, a student assistance counselor is available full-time for individual counseling and referral for treatment.

2. *Community-wide multiagency collaborative approaches.* The basic philosophy of community-wide programs is that a number of different programs and services have to be in place. In one successful substance-abuse program, a community-wide health promotion campaign has been implemented that uses local media and community education, in concert with a substance-abuse curriculum in the schools.

3. *Early identification and intervention.* Reaching children and their families before children develop problems, or at the beginning of their problems, is a successful strategy. One preschool program serves as an excellent model for the prevention of delinquency, pregnancy, substance abuse, and dropping out of school. Operated by the High Schope Foundation in Ypsilanti, Michigan, the Perry Preschool has had a long-term positive impact on its students. This enrichment program, directed by David Weikart, serves disadvantaged African American children. They attend a high-quality two-year preschool program and receive weekly home visits from program personnel. Based on official police records, by age 19, individuals who had attended the Perry Preschool program were less likely to have been arrested and reported fewer adult offenses than a control group did. The Perry Preschool students also were less likely to drop out of school, and teachers rated their social behavior as more competent than that of a control group who had not received the enriched preschool experience.

One current program that seeks to prevent adolescent problems is called Fast Track (Dodge, 2001; Conduct Problems Prevention Research Group, 2002, 2004). High-risk children who show conduct problems at home and at kindergarten were identified. Then, during the elementary school years, the at-risk children and their families are given support and training in parenting, problem-solving and coping skills, peer relations, classroom atmosphere and curriculum, academic achievement, and home-school relations. Ten project interventionists work with the children, their families, and schools to increase the protective factors and decrease the risk factors in these areas. Thus far, results show that the intervention effectively improved parenting practices and children's problem-solving and coping skills, peer relations, reading achievement, and problem behavior at home and school during the elementary school years compared with a control group of high-risk children who did not experience the intervention.

Review and Reflect: Learning Goal 5

5 **Identify adolescent problems in socioemotional development and strategies for helping adolescents with problems**

REVIEW

- What is juvenile delinquency? What causes it? What is the nature of youth violence?
- What is the nature of depression and suicide in adolescence?
- How are adolescent problems interrelated? What are some components of successful prevention/intervention programs with adolescents?

REFLECT

- Are the consequences of choosing a course of risk taking in adolescence today more serious than in the past? If so, why?

Reach Your Learning Goals

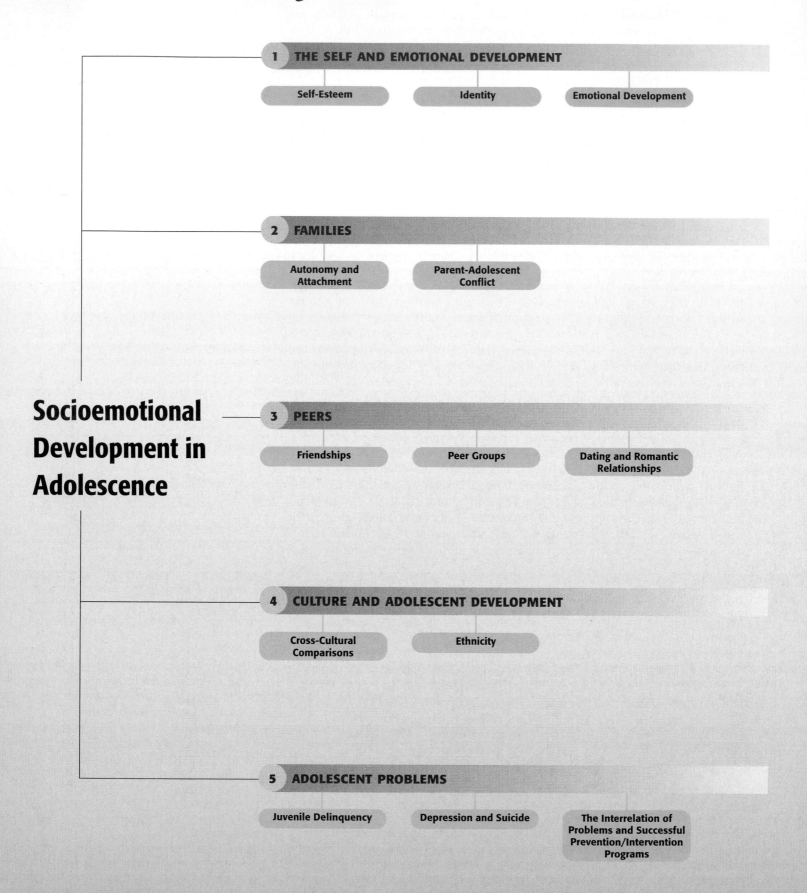

Socioemotional Development in Adolescence

1 THE SELF AND EMOTIONAL DEVELOPMENT

- Self-Esteem
- Identity
- Emotional Development

2 FAMILIES

- Autonomy and Attachment
- Parent-Adolescent Conflict

3 PEERS

- Friendships
- Peer Groups
- Dating and Romantic Relationships

4 CULTURE AND ADOLESCENT DEVELOPMENT

- Cross-Cultural Comparisons
- Ethnicity

5 ADOLESCENT PROBLEMS

- Juvenile Delinquency
- Depression and Suicide
- The Interrelation of Problems and Successful Prevention/Intervention Programs

Summary

 Learning Goal 1: Discuss changes in the self and emotional development during adolescence

- Some researchers have found that self-esteem declines in early adolescence for both boys and girls, but the drop for girls is greater. Other researchers caution that these declines are often exaggerated and actually are small in nature.
- Erikson's theory is the most comprehensive view of identity development. Identity versus identity confusion is the fifth stage in Erikson's theory. Identity is a self-portrait composed of many pieces. Identity development is extraordinarily complex. For the first time in development, during adolescence, individuals are physically, cognitively, and socially mature enough to synthesize their lives and pursue a path toward adult maturity. Marcia proposed that four statuses of identity exist, based on a combination of conflict and commitment: diffusion, foreclosure, moratorium, and achievement. Some experts believe the main identity changes take place in late adolescence or youth. Individuals often follow "*moratorium-achievement-moratorium-achievement*" cycles. Both individuation and connectedness in parent-adolescent relationships are linked with progress in adolescent identity development. Erikson argued that throughout the world ethnic minority groups have struggled to maintain their cultural identities while blending into the majority culture. Adolescence is often a special juncture in ethnic minority identity development. Erikson's theory argues for gender differences in identity, but some researchers have found gender similarities rather than differences. Others argue that relationships are more central in the identity development of females than of males.
- Adolescents report more extreme and fleeting emotions than their parents, and as individuals go through early adolescence they are less likely to report being very happy. However, it is important to view moodiness as a normal aspect of early adolescence. Although pubertal change is associated with an increase in negative emotions, hormonal influences are often small and environmental experiences may contribute more to the emotions of adolescence than hormonal changes.

 Learning Goal 2: Describe changes that take place in adolescents' relationships with their parents

- Many parents have a difficult time handling the adolescent's push for autonomy, even though the push is one of the hallmarks of adolescence. Adolescents do not simply move into a world isolated from parents; attachment to parents increases the probability that an adolescent will be socially competent.
- Parent-adolescent conflict increases in adolescence. The conflict is usually moderate rather than severe, and the increased conflict may serve the positive developmental function of promoting autonomy and identity. A subset of adolescents experiences high parent-adolescent conflict, which is linked with negative outcomes.

 Learning Goal 3: Characterize the changes that occur in peer relations during adolescence

- Harry Stack Sullivan was the most influential theorist to discuss the importance of adolescent friendships. He argued that there is a dramatic increase in the psychological importance and intimacy of close friends in early adolescence.
- The pressure to conform to peers is strong during adolescence, especially during the eighth and ninth grades. Cliques and crowds assume more importance in the lives of adolescents than in the lives of children. Membership in certain crowds—especially jocks and populars—is associated with increased self-esteem. Independents also show high self-esteem. Children groups are less formal and less heterogeneous than adolescent groups.
- Dating takes on added importance in adolescence, and it can have many functions. Younger adolescents often begin to hang out together in mixed-sex groups. A special concern is early dating, which is linked with developmental problems. Many gay and lesbian youth date other-sex peers, which can help them to clarify their sexual orientation or disguise it from others. Male dating scripts are proactive, those of females reactive. Culture can exert a powerful influence on adolescent dating.

 Learning Goal 4: Explain how culture influences adolescent development

- As in other periods of development, culture influences adolescents' development. There are both similarities and differences in adolescents across different countries. Much of what has been written and researched about adolescence comes from American and European scholars. With technological advances, a youth culture with similar characteristics may be emerging. However, there still are many variations in adolescents across cultures. In some countries, traditions are being continued in the socialization of adolescents, whereas in others, substantial changes in the experiences of adolescents are taking place. These traditions and changes involve health and well-being, gender, families, schools, and peers. Adolescents often fill their time with different activities, depending on the culture in which they live. Ceremonies mark an individual's transition from one status to another, especially into adulthood. In primitive cultures, rites of passage are often well defined. In contemporary America, rites of passage to adulthood are ill-defined.

- Much of the research on ethnic minority adolescents has not teased apart the influences of ethnicity and social class. Because of this failure, too often researchers have given ethnic explanations that were largely due to socioeconomic factors. While not all ethnic minority families are poor, poverty contributes to the stress of many ethnic minority adolescents. There are legitimate differences between many ethnic groups, as well as between ethnic groups and the White majority. Recognizing these differences is an important aspect of getting along with others in a diverse, multi-cultural world. Too often, differences between ethnic groups and the White majority have been interpreted as deficits on the part of the ethnic minority group. Another important dimension of ethnic minority groups is their diversity. Ethnic minority groups are not homogeneous; they have different social, historical, and economic backgrounds. Failure to recognize diversity and individual variations results in the stereotyping of an ethnic minority group. Value conflicts are often involved when individuals respond to ethnic issues. One prominent value conflict involves assimilation versus pluralism.

 Learning Goal 5: Identify adolescent problems in socioemotional development and strategies for helping adolescents with problems

- A juvenile delinquent is an adolescent who breaks the law or engages in conduct that is considered illegal. Heredity, identity problems, community influences, and family experiences have been proposed as causes of juvenile delinquency. An increasing concern is the high rate of violence among youth.
- Adolescents have a higher rate of depression than children. Female adolescents are more likely to have mood and depressive disorders than male adolescents are. Adolescent suicide is the third leading cause of death in U.S. adolescents. Both proximal (recent) and distal (earlier) factors are likely involved in suicide's causes.
- Researchers are increasingly finding that problem behaviors in adolescence are interrelated. Dryfoos found a number of common components in programs designed to prevent or reduce adolescent problems: They provide individual attention to high-risk adolescents, they develop community-wide intervention, and they include early identification and intervention.

Key Terms

crisis 399
commitment 399
identity diffusion 399
identity foreclosure 399

identity moratorium 399
identity achievement 399
individuality 400
connectedness 400

ethnic identity 401
clique 409
crowd 409
dating scripts 411

rite of passage 415
assimilation 418
pluralism 418
juvenile delinquent 420

Key People

Erik Erikson 398
James Marcia 399
Alan Waterman 400

Reed Larson and Maryse Richards 402
G. Stanley Hall 405

Harry Stack Sullivan 408
Stanley Sue 418

Richard Savin-Williams 424
Joy Dryfoos 424

 ## E-Learning Tools

To help you master the material in this chapter, you'll find a number of valuable study tools on the LifeMap CD-ROM that accompanies this book and on the Online Learning Center for *Life-Span Development*, tenth edition, at www.mhhe.com/santrockld10.

Video Clips

In the margins of this book there are icons directing you to the LifeMap CD-ROM that accompanies the book. There you'll find two videos for chapter 13. The first is called "Adolescent Self-Esteem." In this segment, Dr. Susan Harter examines the connection between self-concept and self-esteem and the way adolescents form attitudes about themselves. The second video is called "Girls and Body Image." Interviews with 14-year-old girls, about their emerging image of themselves as female, test the validity of the so-called "gender intensification hypothesis."

Self-Assessment

Connect to www.mhhe.com/santrockld10 to reflect on your feelings and your early teenage years by completing the self-assessments, *My Self-Esteem, How Much Did My Parents Monitor My Behavior in Adolescence?,* and *Am I Depressed?*

Taking It to the Net

Connect to www.mhhe.com/santrockld10 to research the answers to these questions.

1. Shelley's mother is Euro-American, and her father is Japanese. Many people who do not know Shelley have a hard time identifying her ethnic background, and she is constantly asked, "What are you?" There are a couple of other students of color at her school, although few of them openly identify as biracial or multiracial. Shelley is now in the process of figuring out who she is. What are some of the challenges biracial or multiracial adolescents face? How might the process of identity development progress?

2. Fourteen-year-old Denise, an only child, and her mother, Doris, always had a great relationship—until recently. Now it seems that they are constantly arguing. Doris is nevertheless struggling to understand her daughter's point of view. How can she tell if Denise's behavior is normal for a 14-year-old?

3. The local school board seeks to prevent violent and tragic incidents like those in Littleton, Colorado, and Springfield, Oregon. It has asked its principals and teachers to study an APA publication that identifies warning signs of violence and suggests interventions. What will they learn from it, and how can they try and prevent similar situations in their own school district if possible?

Health and Well-Being, Parenting, and Education Exercises

Build your decision-making skills by trying your hand at the health and well-being, parenting, and education exercises.

Connect to www.mhhe.com/santrockld10 to research the answers and complete the exercises.

CHAPTER

14

> *Whatever you can do, or*
> *dream you can, begin it.*
> *Boldness has genius,*
> *power, and magic.*
> —Johann Wolfgang von Goethe
> *German Playwright and Novelist,*
> *19th Century*

Physical and Cognitive Development in Early Adulthood

Chapter Outline		*Learning Goals*
THE TRANSITION FROM ADOLESCENCE TO ADULTHOOD	**1**	Describe the transition from adolescence to adulthood
Becoming an Adult		
The Transition from High School to College		
PHYSICAL DEVELOPMENT	**2**	Identify the changes in physical development in young adults
The Peak and Slowdown in Physical Performance		
Eating and Weight		
Regular Exercise		
Substance Abuse		
SEXUALITY	**3**	Discuss sexuality in young adults
Sexual Orientation		
Sexually Transmitted Infections		
Forcible Sexual Behavior and Sexual Harassment		
COGNITIVE DEVELOPMENT	**4**	Characterize cognitive changes in early adulthood
Cognitive Stages		
Creativity		
CAREERS AND WORK	**5**	Explain the key dimensions of careers and work in early adulthood
Developmental Changes		
Personality Types		
Values and Careers		
Monitoring the Occupational Outlook		
The Impact of Work		

Images of Life-Span Development
Florence Griffith Joyner

"When you have been second best for so long, you can either accept it or try to become the best. I made the decision to try to be the best" —Florence Griffith Joyner, Olympic gold medalist.

Florence Griffith Joyner, also known as "Flo-Jo," smashed Olympic and world records in the 100-meter and 200-meter dashes at 28 years of age. This was especially unusual because earlier sprint champions were in their early twenties. Through better weight training, eating habits, and remarkable self-discipline, Flo-Jo was able to accomplish her track goals at an age at which many thought such achievements were impossible. In college, Flo-Jo had to juggle many aspects of her life to be successful. In addition to being a full-time college student, she also worked and commuted to school. Nonetheless, she not only became the NCAA champion in the 200-meter dash but she also managed to achieve high grades.

Flo-Jo grew up in poverty in the Watts area in Los Angeles. She never forgot her past and frequently gave back to the community. She often returned to speak to children and urged them to place academics ahead of athletics in their lives.

Florence Griffith Joyner unfortunately died an early death at the age of 38, apparently as the result of a seizure. A book she wrote prior to her death was later published (Griffith Joyner & Hanc, 1999). In it, she talked about the importance of finding a career that you like and making a deep commitment to be the best you can be in life and work.

PREVIEW

In this chapter, we will explore many aspects of physical and cognitive development in early adulthood. These include some of the areas that were so important in Flo-Jo's life: seeking to reach peak physical performance, achieving, finding the right career match, and juggling roles. However, we will begin where we left off in section 6, "Adolescence," and address the transition from adolescence to adulthood.

---

1 THE TRANSITION FROM ADOLESCENCE TO ADULTHOOD

Becoming an Adult

The Transition from High School to College

As singer Bob Dylan asks, "How many roads must a man walk down before you call him a man?" When does an adolescent become an adult? In chapter 12, we saw that it is not easy to tell when a girl or a boy enters adolescence. The task of determining when an individual becomes an adult is more difficult.

Becoming an Adult

An important transition occurs from adolescence to adulthood (Arnett, 2004; Gutman, 2002; Montgomery & Cote, 2003). It has been said that adolescence begins in biology and ends in culture. That is, the transition from childhood to adolescence begins with the onset of pubertal maturation, whereas the transition from adolescence to adulthood is determined by cultural standards and experiences.

Around the world, youth are increasingly expected to delay their entry into adulthood, in large part because contemporary society requires adults who are more educated and skilled than previous generations (Mortimer & Larson, 2002). Thus, the transition between adolescence and adulthood can be a long one. **Emerging adulthood** is the term now given to the transition from adolescence to adulthood (Arnett, 2000; 2004). The age range for emerging adulthood is approximately 18 to 25 years of age. Experimentation and exploration characterize the emerging adult. At this point in their development, many individuals are still exploring which career path they want to follow, what they want their identity to be, and which lifestyle they want to adopt (for example, single, cohabiting, or married).

In the United States, the most widely recognized marker of entry into adulthood is holding a more or less permanent, full-time job, which usually happens when an individual finishes school—high school for some, college for others, graduate or professional school for still others. However, other criteria are far from clear. Economic independence is one marker of adult status but achieving it is often a long process. College graduates are increasingly returning to live with their parents as they attempt to establish themselves economically. A recent longitudinal study found that at age 25 only slightly more than half of the participants were fully financially independent of their family of origin (Cohen & others, 2003). The most dramatic findings in this study, though, involved the extensive variability in the individual trajectories of adult roles across ten years from 17 to 27 years of age; many of the participants moved back and forth between increasing and decreasing dependency.

Taking responsibility for oneself is likely an important marker of adult status for many individuals. One recent study found that increased responsibility was a marker for adult status (Shulman & Ben-Artzi, 2003). And in another study, more than 70 percent of college students said that being an adult means accepting responsibility for the consequences of one's actions, deciding on one's own beliefs and values, and establishing a relationship with parents as an equal adult (Arnett, 1995).

Is there a specific age at which individuals become adults? One study examined emerging adults' perception of whether they were adults (Arnett, 2000). The majority of the 18- to 25-year-olds responded neither "yes" nor "no," but "in some respects yes, in some respects no" (see figure 14.1). In this study, not until the late twenties and early thirties did a clear majority of respondents agree that they had reached adulthood. Thus, these emerging adults saw themselves as neither adolescents nor full-fledged adults.

In another study, however, 21-year-olds said that they had reached adult status when they were 18 to 19 years old (Scheer, 1996). In this study, both social status factors (financial status and graduation/education) and cognitive factors (being responsible and making independent decisions) were cited as markers for reaching adulthood. Clearly, reaching adulthood involves more than just attaining a specific chronological age.

The new freedoms and responsibilities of emerging adulthood represent major changes in individuals' lives. Although change characterizes the transition from adolescence to adulthood, keep in mind that considerable continuity still glues these periods together. For example, one recent longitudinal study found that religious views and behaviors of emerging adults were especially stable, and to a lesser degree, their attitudes toward drugs were stable as well (Bachman & others, 2002).

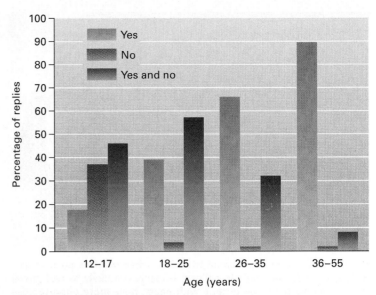

FIGURE 14.1 Self-Perceptions of Adult Status

In one study, individuals were asked, "Do you feel that you have reached adult status?" and were given a choice of answering "yes," "no," or "in some respects yes, in some respects no" (Arnett, 2000). As indicated in the graph, the majority of the emerging adults (18 to 25) responded "in some respects yes, in some respects no."

emerging adulthood The transition from adolescence to adulthood (approximately 18 to 25 years of age) that involves experimentation and exploration.

The transition from high school to college often involves positive as well as negative features. In college, students are likely to feel grown up, be able to spend more time with peers, have more opportunities to explore different lifestyles and values, and enjoy greater freedom from parental monitoring. However, college involves a larger, more impersonal school structure and an increased focus on achievement and its assessment. *What was your transition to college like?*

What we have said about the determinants of adult status mainly characterize individuals in industrialized societies, especially Americans. Are the criteria for adulthood the same in developing countries as they are in the United States? In developing countries, marriage is more often a significant marker for entry into adulthood, and this usually occurs much earlier than the adulthood markers in the United States (Arnett, 2000, 2004). Further, a recent study found that a majority of Chinese college students in their early twenties said that they had reached adult status (Nelson, Badger, & Wu, 2004).

At some point in the late teens through the early twenties, then, individuals reach adulthood. In becoming an adult, they accept responsibility for themselves, become capable of making independent decisions, and gain financial independence from their parents (Arnett, 2000, 2004).

The Transition from High School to College

Just as the transition from elementary school to middle or junior high school involves change and possible stress, so does the transition from high school to college. In many instances, there are parallel changes in the two transitions. Going from being a senior in high school to being a freshman in college replays the top-dog phenomenon of transferring from the oldest and most powerful group of students to the youngest and least powerful group of students that occurred earlier as adolescence began.

The transition from high school to college involves movement to a larger, more impersonal school structure; interaction with peers from more diverse geographical and sometimes more diverse ethnic backgrounds; and increased focus on achievement and its assessment.

But, as with the transition from elementary to middle or junior high school, the transition from high school to college can involve positive features. Students are more likely to feel grown up, have more subjects from which to select, have more time to spend with peers, have more opportunities to explore different lifestyles and values, enjoy greater independence from parental monitoring, and be

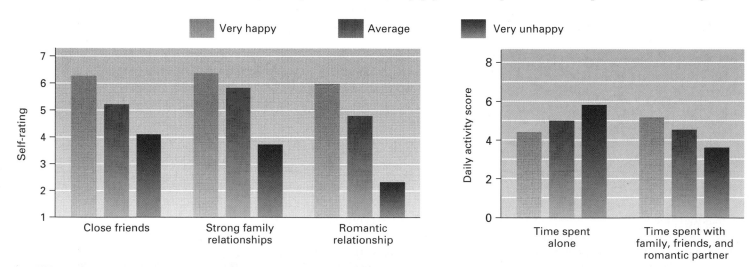

FIGURE 14.2 Characteristics of Very Happy College Students (Diener & Seligman, 2002)
Self-ratings were made on a scale of 1 to 7, with 1 being much below the average of college students on the campus studied (University of Illinois), and 7 being much above the average of college students on the campus. Daily activity scores reflect mean times with 1 representing no time, and 8 reflecting 8 hours per day.

challenged intellectually by academic work (Santrock & Halonen, 2006).

Stress Today's college students experience more stress and are more depressed than in the past, according to a national study of more than 300,000 freshmen at more than 500 colleges and universities (Sax & others, 2003). In 2002, 27 percent (up from 16 percent in 1985) said they frequently "felt overwhelmed with what I have to do." And college freshmen in 2003 indicated that they felt more depressed than their counterparts from the 1980s had indicated. The pressure to succeed in college, get a great job, and make lots of money were pervasive concerns of these students.

In one study, the academic circumstances creating the most stress for students were tests and finals, grades and competition, professors and class environment, too many demands, papers and essay exams, career and future success, and studying (Murphy, 1996). The personal circumstances that caused the most stress for students were intimate relationships, finances, parental conflicts and expectations, and roommate conflicts.

Let's examine some ways to cope with stress, beginning with the negative ways:

- Repress it so you don't have to think about it.
- Take it out on other people when you feel angry or depressed.
- Keep your feelings to yourself.
- Tell yourself the problem will go away.
- Refuse to believe what is happening.
- Try to reduce the tension by drinking and eating more.

Fortunately, you can cope with stress in these positive ways:

- See stress as a challenge to be overcome rather than an overwhelming threat (Steptoe & Ayers, 2005).
- Have good coping resources, such as friends, family, and a mentor. One recent study found that first-year students showed better adaptation to college when they had less family conflict (Feenstra & others, 2001).
- Develop an optimistic outlook and think positively. Thinking optimistically gives you the sense that you are controlling your environment rather than letting it control you. One recent study found that greater optimism, assessed at the beginning of the first semester of college, was linked with less stress and depression over the course of the semester (Brisette, Scheier, & Carver, 2002).
- Learn how to relax.
- Seek counseling. Most college campuses have a counseling center with access to mental health professionals who can help you to learn effective ways to cope with stress.

Happiness What makes college students happy? One recent study of 222 undergraduates compared the upper 10 percent of college students who were very happy with average and very unhappy college students (Diener & Seligman, 2002). The very happy college students were highly social, more extraverted, and had stronger romantic and social relationships than the less happy college students, who spent more time alone (see figure 14.2).

Careers in Life-Span Development

Grace Leaf, College/Career Counselor

Grace Leaf is a counselor at Spokane Community College in Washington. She has a master's degree in educational leadership and is working toward a doctoral degree in educational leadership at Gonzaga University in Washington. Her job involves teaching orientation for international students, conducting individual and group advising, and doing individual and group career planning. Grace tries to connect students with goals and values and help them design an educational program that fits their needs and visions.

Grace Leaf, counseling college students at Spokane Community College about careers.

The American College Freshman

Education The United States is becoming a more educated country. In 2001, 29 percent of 25- to 29-year-olds had at least a bachelor's degree, compared with only 17 percent in 1971 (U.S. Department of Education, 2003). Total college enrollment is expected to increase in the next decade as increasing numbers of high school graduates pursue higher education. In the last several decades, there has been a dramatic increase in the number of individuals who attend community colleges rather than four-year colleges, and the community college movement continues to expand.

What is college attendance like around the world? Canada has the largest percentage of 18- to 21-year-olds enrolled in college (41 percent), followed by Belgium (40 percent), France (36 percent), the United States (35 percent), Ireland (31 percent), and New Zealand (25 percent) (U.S. Department of Education, 1999). The greatest percentage increase in college attendance is taking place in Africa—128 percent from 1980 through 1996.

These figures do not include the many returning students who make up an increasing percentage of the college population in the United States. Returning students either did not go to college right out of high school or went to college, dropped out, and now have returned. More than one of every five full-time college students today is a returning student, and about two-thirds of part-time college students are returning students (Sax & others, 2003). Many returning students have to balance their course work with commitments to a partner, children, job, and community responsibilities. Despite the many challenges that returning students face, they bring many strengths to campus, such as life experiences that can be applied to a wide range of issues and topics.

College counselors can provide good information about coping with stress and academic matters. To read about the work of college counselor Grace Leaf, see the Careers in Life-Span Development insert.

Review and Reflect: Learning Goal 1

 1 **Describe the transition from adolescence to adulthood**

REVIEW

- What are the criteria for becoming an adult? What is the nature of emerging adulthood?
- What is the transition from high school to college like?

REFLECT

- What do you think is the most important criterion for becoming an adult? Does it make sense to describe becoming an adult in terms of "emerging adulthood" over a period of years or is there a specific age at which someone becomes an adult? Explain.

2 PHYSICAL DEVELOPMENT

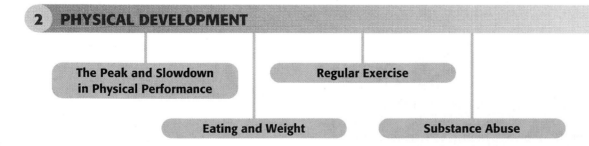

| The Peak and Slowdown in Physical Performance | Regular Exercise |
| Eating and Weight | Substance Abuse |

For most individuals, physical status not only reaches its peak in early adulthood, it also begins to decline during this period. Interest in health has increased among young adults, with special concerns about diet, weight, exercise, and addiction.

The Peak and Slowdown in Physical Performance

Most of us reach our peak physical performance under the age of 30, often between the ages of 19 and 26. This peak of physical performance occurs not only for the average young adult, but for outstanding athletes as well. Even though athletes as a group keep getting better than their predecessors—running faster, jumping higher, and lifting more weight—the age at which they reach their peak performance has remained virtually the same (Schultz & Curnow, 1988).

Most swimmers and gymnasts reach their peak performance in their late teens. Golfers and marathon runners tend to peak in their late twenties. In other areas of athletics, peak performance is often in the early to mid-twenties.

Not only do we reach our peak physical performance during early adulthood, but during this time we are also the healthiest. Few young adults have chronic health problems, and they have fewer colds and respiratory problems than when they were children. Most college students know what it takes to prevent illness and promote health. In one study, college students' ranking of health-protective activities—nutrition, sleep, exercise, watching one's weight, and so on—virtually matched that of licensed nurses (Turk, Rudy, & Salovey, 1984).

Although most college students know what it takes to prevent illness and promote health, they don't fare very well when it comes to applying this information to themselves. In one study, college students reported that they probably would never have a heart attack or drinking problem, but that other college students would (Weinstein, 1984). The college students also said no relation exists between their risk of heart attack and how much they exercise, smoke, or eat meat or high-cholesterol food such as eggs, even though they correctly recognized that factors such as family history influence risk. Many college students, it seems, have unrealistic, overly optimistic beliefs about their future health risks.

In early adulthood, few individuals stop to think about how their personal lifestyles will affect their health later in their adult lives. As young adults, many of us develop a pattern of not eating breakfast, not eating regular meals, and relying on snacks as our main food source during the day, eating excessively to the point where we exceed the normal weight for our age, smoking moderately or excessively, drinking moderately or excessively, failing to exercise, and getting by with only a few hours of sleep at night. These poor personal lifestyles were associated with poor health in one investigation of 7,000 individuals from the ages of 20 to 70 (Belloc & Breslow, 1972). In the Berkeley Longitudinal Study—in which individuals were evaluated over a period of 40 years—physical health at age 30 predicted life satisfaction at age 70, more so for men than women (Mussen, Honzik, & Eichorn, 1982).

There are some hidden dangers in the peaks of performance and health in early adulthood. Young adults can draw on physical resources for a great deal of pleasure, often bouncing back easily from physical stress and abuse. However, this can lead them to push their bodies too far. The negative effects of abusing one's body may not show up in the first part of early adulthood, but they probably will surface later in early adulthood or in middle adulthood (Csikszentmihalyi & Rathunde, 1998).

How are gender and ethnicity linked to health behavior and beliefs in young adults? One recent study found that male college students engaged in riskier health behaviors than did female college students (Courtenay, McCreary, & Merighi, 2002). Among various ethnic groups in this study, Asian Americans reported the most risky health behaviors, especially in cigarette smoking. Latinos showed the greatest dietary health risks, which was most notable in their high fat intake.

Not only do we reach our peak in physical performance during early adulthood, but it is during this age period that we also begin to decline in physical performance. Muscle tone and strength usually begin to show signs of decline around the age of 30. Sagging chins and protruding abdomens also may begin to appear for the first time. The lessening of physical abilities is a common complaint among the just-turned

After thirty, a body has a mind of its own.
—BETTE MIDLER
American Actress, 20th Century

thirties. Says one 30-year-old, "I played tennis last night. My knees are sore and my lower back aches. Last month, it was my elbow that hurt. Several years ago it wasn't that way. I could play all day and not be sore the next morning." Sensory systems show little change in early adulthood, but the lens of the eye loses some of its elasticity and becomes less able to change shape and focus on near objects. Hearing peaks in adolescence, remains constant in the first part of early adulthood, and then begins to decline in the last part of early adulthood. And in the mid to late twenties, the body's fatty tissue increases.

The health profile of our nation's young adults can be improved by reducing the incidence of certain health-impairing lifestyles, such as overeating, and by engaging in health-improving lifestyles that include good eating habits, exercising regularly, and not abusing drugs (Hahn, Payne, & Mauer, 2005; Robbins, Powers, & Burgess, 2005).

Eating and Weight

In chapters 8 and 10, we explored obesity in childhood and examined the eating disorders of anorexia nervosa and bulimia nervosa in adolescence (chapter 12). Now, we will turn our attention to obesity in the adult years and the extensive preoccupation that many adults have with dieting.

Obesity   Obesity is a serious and pervasive health problem for many individuals (Centers for Disease Control and Prevention, 2005; International Obesity Task Force, 2004; Steiger, Bruce, & Israel, 2003). The prevalence of obesity in U.S. adults increased from 19 percent to 25 percent in 2002. More than 60 percent of U.S. adults are either overweight or obese (National Center for Health Statistics, 2004).

Obesity is linked to increased risk of hypertension, diabetes, and cardiovascular disease (Stunkard, 2000). For individuals who are 30 percent overweight, the probability of dying in middle adulthood increases by about 40 percent. *Body mass index*, a measure of weight in relation to height, is often used to determine whether an individual is underweight, a healthy weight, overweight, or obese (see figure 14.3).

What factors are involved in obesity? The possible culprits are heredity, leptin, set point and metabolism, environmental factors, ethnicity, and gender.

Heredity   Until recently, the genetic component of obesity had been underestimated by scientists. Some individuals do inherit a tendency to be overweight. Researchers have documented that animals can be inbred to have a propensity for obesity (Blundell, 1984). Further, identical human twins have similar weights, even when they are reared apart (Collaku & others, 2004). Estimates of the variance in body mass that can be explained by heredity range from 25 to 70 percent.

Leptin   Leptin (from the Greek word *leptos*, which means "thin") is a protein that is involved in satiety (the condition of being full to satisfaction) and released by fat cells, resulting in decreased food intake and increased energy expenditure (Obwerbauer & others, 2001). Leptin acts as an antiobesity hormone (Misra & others, 2001).

Initial research focused on a strain of mice called the *ob mouse*. Because of a genetic mutation, the fat cells of *ob* mice cannot produce leptin. The *ob* mice also have a low metabolism, overeat, and get extremely fat. A particular gene called *ob* normally produces leptin. But when *ob* mice are given daily

Weight (pounds)

Height	120	130	140	150	160	170	180	190	200	210	220	230	240	250
4'6"	29	31	34	36	39	41	43	46	48	51	53	56	58	60
4'8"	27	29	31	34	36	38	40	43	45	47	49	52	54	56
4'10"	25	27	29	31	34	36	38	40	42	44	46	48	50	52
5'0"	23	25	27	29	31	33	35	37	39	41	43	45	47	49
5'2"	22	24	26	27	29	31	33	35	37	38	40	42	44	46
5'4"	21	22	24	26	28	29	31	33	34	36	38	40	41	43
5'6"	19	21	23	24	26	27	29	31	32	34	36	37	39	40
5'8"	18	20	21	23	24	26	27	29	30	32	34	35	37	38
5'10"	17	19	20	22	23	24	26	27	29	30	32	33	35	36
6'0"	16	18	19	20	22	23	24	26	27	28	30	31	33	34
6'2"	15	17	18	19	21	22	23	24	26	27	28	30	31	32
6'4"	15	16	17	18	20	21	22	23	24	26	27	28	29	30
6'6"	14	15	16	17	19	20	21	22	23	24	25	27	28	29
6'8"	13	14	15	17	18	19	20	21	22	23	24	25	26	28

■ Underweight   ■ Healthy weight   ■ Overweight   ■ Obese

FIGURE 14.3 Determining Your Body Mass Index

Body mass index is a measure of weight in relation to height. Anyone with a BMI of 25 or more is considered overweight. People who have a body mass index of 30 or more (a BMI of 30 is roughly 30 pounds over a healthy weight) are considered obese. BMI has some limitations: It can overestimate body fat in people who are very muscular, and it can underestimate body fat in people who have lost muscle mass, such as the elderly.

injections of leptin, their metabolic rate increases, they become more active, and they eat less. Consequently, their weight falls to normal. Figure 14.4 shows an untreated *ob* mouse and an *ob* mouse that has received injections of leptin. In humans, leptin concentrations have been linked with weight, percentage of body fat, weight loss in a single diet episode, and cumulative percentage of weight loss in all diet episodes (Benini & others, 2001; De Graaf & others, 2004). Today, scientists are interested in the possibility that leptin might help obese individuals lose weight.

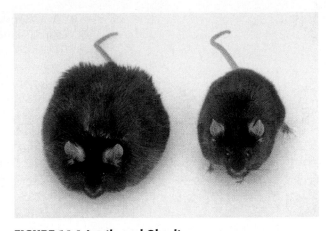

FIGURE 14.4 Leptin and Obesity
The *ob* mouse on the left is untreated; the one on the right has been given injections of leptin.

Set Point The amount of stored fat in your body is an important factor in your *set point,* the weight maintained when no effort is made to gain or lose weight. Fat is stored in what are called adipose cells. When these cells are filled, you do not get hungry. When people gain weight—because of genetic predisposition, childhood eating patterns, or adult overeating—the number of their fat cells increases, and they might not be able to get rid of them. A normal-weight individual has 30 to 40 billion fat cells. An obese individual has 80 to 120 billion fat cells. Some scientists have proposed that these fat cells can shrink but might not go away.

Environmental Factors The human gustatory system and taste preferences developed at a time when reliable food sources were scarce. Our earliest ancestors probably developed a preference for sweets because ripe fruit, which is a concentrated source of sugar (and calories), was so accessible. Today many people still have a "sweet tooth," but unlike our ancestors' ripe fruit that contained sugar *plus* vitamins and minerals, the soft drinks and candy bars we snack on today often fill us with empty calories.

Strong evidence of the environment's influence on weight is the doubling of the rate of obesity in the United States since 1900. This dramatic increase in obesity likely is due to greater availability of food (especially food high in fat), energy-saving devices, and declining physical activity. One recent study found that in 2000, U.S. women ate 335 calories more a day and men 168 more a day than they did in the early 1970s (National Center for Health Statistics, 2004).

Sociocultural factors are involved in obesity, which is six times more prevalent among women with low incomes than among women with high incomes. Americans also are more obese than Europeans and people in many other areas of the world (Williams, 2005).

Ethnicity and Gender A recent study found that African American and Latino women in their twenties and thirties become obese faster than their White counterparts, and Latino men become obese faster than White and African American men (McTigue, Garrett, & Popkin, 2002). Two possibilities might explain these findings (Brownell, 2002). There may be some biological vulnerability that makes some ethnic-gender groups more susceptible to obesity. Also, some individuals may be at risk for obesity because of their environment, as when their exposure to junk food and fast food is high and their opportunities to be active are minimal.

Dieting Ironically, while obesity is on the rise, dieting has become an obsession with many Americans. The topic of dieting is of great interest to many diverse groups in the United States, including the public, health professionals, policy makers, the media, and the powerful diet and food industries. On one side are the societal norms that promote a very lean, aesthetic body. This ideal is supported by $30 billion a year in sales of diet books, programs, videos, foods, and pills. On the other side are health professionals and a growing minority of the press. Although they recognize the alarmingly high rate of obesity, they are frustrated by high relapse rates and the obsession with excessive thinness that can lead to chronic dieting and serious health risks (Brownell, 2000).

www.mhhe.com/santrockld10

Why People Are Getting Fatter
Obesity

Many people live their lives as one big long diet, interrupted by occasional hot fudge sundaes or chocolate chip cookies. They are **restrained eaters,** individuals who chronically restrict their food intake to control their weight. Restrained eaters are often on diets, are very conscious of what they eat, and tend to feel guilty after splurging on sweets. An interesting characteristic of restrained eaters is that when they stop dieting, they tend to binge eat—that is, eat large quantities of food in a short time (Lowe & Timko, 2004; McFarlane, Polivy, & Herman, 1998).

Although many Americans regularly embark on a diet, few are successful in keeping weight off long-term. Some critics argue that all diets fail (Wooley & Garner, 1991). However, studies show that some individuals do lose weight and maintain the loss (Brownell & Cohen, 1995). How often this occurs and whether some diet programs work better than others are still open questions.

The current hot diet trend is a low-carbohydrate diet promoted by Robert Atkins (1997) in his book, *Dr. Atkins' NEW Diet Revolution.* The diet restricts carbohydrates to less than 10 percent of total calories eaten, whereas people in the United States typically get more than 50 percent of their total calories from carbohydrates such as bread, processed foods, starch in vegetables, and sugar in fruits. On the Atkins diet, individuals eat as much protein and fat as they want. Short-term studies show that individuals who follow the Atkins diet do lose weight (Noakes & Clifton, 2004; Stern & others, 2004). However, critics argue that long-term studies have yet to be carried out and that the Atkins diet may pose health risks, especially for the heart, over the long term (Mayo Clinic, 2004). It is well-documented that foods promoted in the low-carbohydrate diets—for example, foods high in saturated fats such as meat, butter, or cream—increase the risk of heart disease and some types of cancer. And foods restricted on these diets—such as whole grains, vegetables, and fruits—have vitamins, minerals, and other nutrients that reduce the risk of heart disease, cancer, and other diseases.

What we do know about losing weight is that the most effective programs include exercise (Bray & Champagne, 2004; Kemper, Stasse-Wolthuis, & Bosman, 2004). Exercise not only burns up calories, but continues to elevate the person's metabolic rate for several hours *after* exercising (Janssen & others, 2004). Also, exercise lowers a person's set point for weight, which makes it easier to maintain a lower weight (Bennett & Gurin, 1982).

Even when diets do produce weight loss, they can place the dieter at risk for other health problems. One main concern focuses on weight cycling—yo-yo dieting—in which the person is in a recurring cycle of dieting and weight gain (Wadden & others, 1996). Researchers have found a link between frequent changes in weight and chronic disease (Brownell & Rodin, 1994). Also, liquid diets and other very low calorie strategies are linked with gallbladder damage.

With these problems in mind, when overweight people diet and maintain their weight loss, they do become less depressed and reduce their risk for a number of health-impairing disorders (Christensen, 1996; Wadden & others, 2004).

Regular Exercise

In 1961, President John F. Kennedy offered this message: "We are under-exercised as a nation. We look instead of play. We ride instead of walk. Our existence deprives us of the minimum of physical activity essential for healthy living." Without question, people are jogging, cycling, and aerobically exercising more today than in 1961, but far too many of us are still couch potatoes, spending most of our leisure time in front of the TV or a computer screen.

One of the main reasons that health experts want people to exercise is that it helps to prevent heart disease, diabetes, and other diseases (Church & others, 2004; Lane & others, 2004). Although exercise designed to strengthen muscles and bones or to improve flexibility is important to fitness, many health experts have stressed aerobic exercise. **Aerobic exercise** is sustained exercise—jogging, swimming, or cycling, for example—that stimulates heart and lung activity.

restrained eaters Individuals who chronically restrict their food intake to control their weight. Restrained eaters are often on diets, are very conscious of what they eat, and tend to feel guilty after splurging on sweets.

aerobic exercise Sustained exercise (such as jogging, swimming, or cycling) that stimulates heart and lung activity.

People in some occupations get more vigorous exercise than those in others (Howley, 2001). For example, longshoremen, who are on their feet all day and lift, push, and carry heavy cargo, have about half the risk of fatal heart attacks as coworkers like crane drivers and clerks, who have physically less demanding jobs. Elaborate studies of 17,000 male alumni of Harvard University found that those who exercised strenuously on a regular basis had a lower risk of heart disease and were more likely to still be alive in their middle adulthood years than their more sedentary counterparts (Lee, Hsieh, & Paffenbarger, 1995; Paffenbarger & others, 1986).

Some experts conclude that, regardless of other risk factors (smoking, high blood pressure, overweight, heredity), if you exercise enough to burn more than 2,000 calories a week, you can cut your risk of heart attack by an impressive two-thirds (Sherwood, Light, & Blumenthal, 1989). Burning up 2,000 calories a week through exercise requires considerable effort, far more than most individuals are willing to expend. To burn 300 calories a day, through exercise, you would have to do one of the following: swim or run for about 25 minutes, walk for 45 minutes at about 4 miles an hour, or participate in aerobic dancing for 30 minutes.

As a more realistic goal, health experts recommend that adults engage in 30 minutes or more of moderate-intensity physical activity on most, preferably all, days of the week. Most recommend that you should try to raise your heart rate to at least 60 percent of your maximum heart rate. However, only about one-fifth of adults are active at these recommended levels of physical activity. Examples of the physical activities that qualify as moderate or vigorous are listed in figure 14.5.

Researchers have found that exercise benefits not only physical health, but mental health as well (Faulkner & Biddle, 2002; King, 2000; Phillips, Kiernan, & King, 2001). In particular, exercise improves self-concept and reduces anxiety and depression (Moses & others, 1989).

Research on the benefits of exercise suggests that both moderate and intense activities produce important physical and psychological gains (Thayer & others, 1996). Some people enjoy rigorous, intense exercise. Others enjoy more moderate exercise routines. The enjoyment and pleasure we derive from exercise added to its aerobic benefits make exercise one of life's most important activities (Corbin & others, 2005; Fahey, Insel, & Roth, 2005).

Here are some helpful strategies for building exercise into your life:

- *Reduce TV time.* Heavy TV viewing by college students is linked to poor health (Astin, 1983). Replace some of your TV time with exercise.
- *Chart your progress.* Systematically recording your exercise workouts will help you to chart your progress. This strategy is especially helpful over the long term.
- *Get rid of excuses.* People make up all kinds of excuses for not exercising. A typical excuse is, "I don't have enough time." You likely do have enough time.
- *Imagine the alternative.* Ask yourself whether you are too busy to take care of your own health. What will your life be like if you lose your health?
- *Learn more about exercise.* The more you know about exercise, the more you are likely to start an exercise program and continue it.

Substance Abuse

In chapter 12, "Physical and Cognitive Development in Adolescence," we explored the nature of substance abuse in adolescence. Let's now examine the extent of substance abuse in college students and young adults.

Alcohol   Heavy, binge drinking often increases in college, and it can take its toll on students (Eisenberg & Wechsler, 2003; Glassman, 2003). Chronic binge drinking is more common among college men than women and students living away from home, especially in fraternity houses (Schulenberg & others, 2000). In a national

Aerobic Institute
Women and Exercise

Moderate

Walking, briskly (3 to 4 mph)

Cycling, for pleasure or transportation (≤10 mph)

Swimming, moderate effort

Conditioning exercise, general calisthenics

Racket sports, table tennis

Golf, pulling cart or carrying clubs

Canoeing, leisurely (2.0 to 3.9 mph)

Home care, general cleaning

Mowing lawn, with power mower

Home repair, painting

Vigorous

Walking, briskly uphill or with a load

Cycling, fast or racing (>10 mph)

Swimming, fast-treading crawl

Conditioning exercise, stair ergometer or ski machine

Racket sports, singles tennis or racketball

Golf, practice at driving range

Canoeing, rapidly (≥4 mph)

Moving furniture

Mowing lawn, with hand mower

Home repair, fix-up projects

FIGURE 14.5 Moderate and Vigorous Physical Activities

survey of drinking patterns on 140 campuses, almost half of the binge drinkers reported problems that included (Wechsler & others, 1994):

- missing classes,
- physical injuries,
- troubles with police, and
- having unprotected sex.

For example, binge-drinking college students were 11 times more likely to fall behind in school, 10 times more likely to drive after drinking, and twice as likely to have unprotected sex than college students who did not binge drink. Also, one recent study found that after an evening of binge drinking memory retrieval was significantly impaired during the alcohol hangover the next morning (Verster & others, 2003).

More than 40,000 full-time U.S. college students were asked about their drinking habits in 1993, 1997, 1999, and 2001 (Wechsler & others, 2002). Binge-drinking rates (men who drank five or more drinks in a row and women who drank four or more drinks at least once in the two weeks prior to the questionnaire) remained remarkably consistent—at about 44 percent—over the eight years. Further, almost 75 percent of underage students living in fraternities or sororities were binge drinkers, and 70 percent of traditional-age college students who lived away from home were binge drinkers. The lowest rate of binge drinking—25 percent—occurred for students living at home with their parents.

A special concern is the increase in binge drinking by females during emerging adulthood. One study found a 125 percent increase in binge drinking at all-women colleges from 1993 through 2001 (Wechsler & others, 2002).

Fortunately, by the time individuals reach their mid-twenties, many have reduced their use of alcohol and drugs. That is the conclusion reached by Jerald Bachman and his colleagues (1996, 2002) in a longitudinal analysis of more than 38,000 individuals (see figure 14.6). They were evaluated from the time they were high school seniors through their twenties. Here are some of the main findings in the study:

- College students drink more than youth who end their education after high school.
- Those who don't go to college smoke more.
- Singles use marijuana more than married individuals.

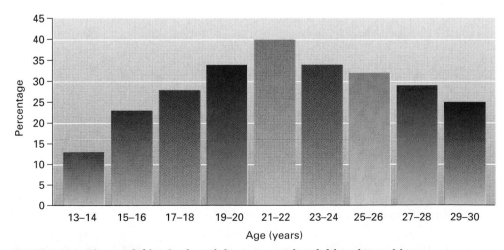

FIGURE 14.6 Binge Drinking in the Adolescence–Early Adulthood Transition
Note that the percentage of individuals engaging in binge drinking peaked at 21 to 22 years of age and then began to gradually decline through the remainder of the twenties. Binge drinking was defined as having five or more alcoholic drinks in a row in the past two weeks.

- Drinking is heaviest among singles and divorced individuals. Becoming engaged, married, or even remarried quickly brings down alcohol use. Thus, living arrangements and marital status are key factors in alcohol and drug use rates during the twenties.

- Individuals who consider religion to be very important in their lives and who frequently attend religious services are less likely to take drugs than their less religious counterparts.

Cultural Variations   Around the world, there are differences in alcohol use by religion and gender (Bjarnason & others, 2003; Weijers & others, 2003). Catholics, Reform Jews, and liberal Protestants all consume alcohol at a fairly high level. Males drink alcohol more than females.

Europeans, especially the French, drink alcohol at high rates. Estimates are that about 30 percent of French adults have impaired health related to alcohol consumption. Alcohol use is also high in Russia but its use in China is low. In some religions, such as the Muslim religion, use of alcohol is forbidden.

Alcoholism   *Alcoholism* is a disorder that involves long-term, repeated, uncontrolled, compulsive, and excessive use of alcoholic beverages and that impairs the drinker's health and social relationships. One in nine individuals who drink continues the path to alcoholism. Those who do are disproportionately related to alcoholics (Jang, 2005). Family studies consistently find a high frequency of alcoholism in the first-degree relatives of alcoholics (Conway, Swendsen, & Merikangas, 2003; Pastor & Evans, 2003). Indeed, researchers found that heredity likely plays a role in alcoholism, although the precise hereditary mechanism has not been found (Crabbe, 2002; Wall & others, 2001). An estimated 50 to 60 percent of individuals who become alcoholics are believed to have a genetic predisposition for it.

Although studies reveal a genetic influence on alcoholism, they also show that environmental factors play a role (Hahn, Payne, & Maver, 2005; Heath & Nelson, 2002). For example, family studies indicate that many alcoholics do not have close relatives who are alcoholics (Martin & Sher, 1994). The large cultural variations in alcohol use mentioned earlier also underscore the environment's role in alcoholism.

About one-third of alcoholics recover whether or not they are in a treatment program. This figure was found in a long-term study of 700 individuals over 50 years and has consistently been found by other researchers as well (Vaillant, 1992). There is a "one-third rule" for alcoholism: by age 65, one-third are dead or in terrible shape, one-third are abstinent or drinking socially, and one-third are still trying to beat their addiction. A positive outcome and recovery from alcoholism are predicted by certain factors: (1) a strong negative experience related to drinking, such as a serious medical emergency or condition; (2) finding a substitute dependency to compete with alcohol abuse, such as meditation, exercise, or overeating (which of course has its own negative health consequences); (3) having new social supports (such as a concerned, helpful employer or a new marriage); and (4) joining an inspirational group, such as a religious organization or Alcoholics Anonymous (Vaillant, 1992).

Cigarette Smoking   Converging evidence from a number of studies underscores the dangers of smoking or being around those who do (Naess & others, 2004). For example, smoking is linked to 30 percent of cancer deaths, 21 percent of heart disease deaths, and 82 percent of chronic pulmonary disease deaths. Secondhand smoke is implicated in as many as 9,000 lung cancer deaths a year. Children of smokers are at special risk for respiratory and middle-ear diseases (Wallace-Bell, 2003).

Fewer people smoke today than in the past, and almost half of all living adults who ever smoked have quit. The prevalence of smoking in men has dropped from over 50 percent in 1965 to about 28 percent today (National Center for Health

Clearinghouse for Drug
Information
Alcoholism
Smoking/Tobacco Control
Smoking Cessation

Statistics, 2004). However, more than 50 million Americans still smoke cigarettes today. And cigar smoking and tobacco chewing, with risks similar to those of cigarette smoking, have increased.

Most adult smokers would like to quit, but their addiction to nicotine often makes quitting a challenge (Thompson & others, 2003). Nicotine, the active drug in cigarettes, is a stimulant that increases the smoker's energy and alertness, a pleasurable and reinforcing experience. Nicotine also stimulates neurotransmitters that have a calming or pain-reducing effect.

How can smokers quit? Four main methods are used to help smokers quit:

- *Using a substitute source of nicotine.* Nicotine gum, the nicotine patch, the nicotine inhaler, and nicotine spray work on the principle of supplying small amounts of nicotine to diminish the intensity of withdrawal. Recent research shows that the percentage of individuals who are still not smoking after five months ranges from 18 percent for the nicotine patch to 30 percent for the nicotine spray (Centers for Disease Control and Prevention, 2001).
- *Taking an antidepressant.* Bupropion, an antidepressant sold as Zyban, helps smokers control their cravings while they ease off nicotine. Recent research indicates that smokers using Zyban to quit have had a 30 percent average success rate for five months after they started taking the drug (Centers for Disease Control and Prevention, 2001).
- *Controlling stimuli associated with smoking.* This behavior modification technique sensitizes the smoker to social cues associated with smoking. For example, the smoker might associate a morning cup of coffee or a social drink with smoking. Stimulus control strategies help the smoker to avoid these cues or learn to substitute other behaviors for smoking.
- *Going "cold turkey."* Some people succeed by simply stopping smoking without making any major changes in their lifestyle. They decide they are going to quit and they do. Lighter smokers usually have more success with this approach than heavier smokers.

Studies indicate that when people do stop smoking their risk of cancer is reduced (Centers for Disease Control and Prevention, 2001; Hughes, 2003). Five years after people stop smoking their health risk is noticeably lower than people who continue to smoke (U.S. Surgeon General's Report, 1990).

Addiction   **Addiction** is a pattern of behavior characterized by an overwhelming involvement with using a drug and securing its supply. This can occur despite adverse consequences associated with the use of the drug. There is a strong tendency to relapse after quitting or withdrawal. Withdrawal symptoms consist of significant changes in physical functioning and behavior. Depending on the drug, these symptoms might include insomnia, tremors, nausea, vomiting, cramps, elevation of heart rate and blood pressure, convulsions, anxiety, and depression when a physically dependent person stops taking the drug. Experts on drug abuse use the term *addiction* to describe either a physical or psychological dependence on the drug or both (Fields, 2005; Ray & Ksir, 2004).

Controversy continues about whether addictions are diseases (Campbell, 2003; Heather, 2004). The **disease model of addiction** describes addictions as biologically based, lifelong diseases that involve a loss of control over behavior and require medical and/or spiritual treatment for recovery. In the disease model, addiction is either inherited or developed early in life. Current or recent problems or relationships are not believed to be causes of the disease. Once involved in the disease, you can never completely rid yourself of it, according to this model. The disease model has been strongly promoted and supported by the medical profession and Alcoholics Anonymous (AA) (Humphreys, 2000). Recent research studies have found that AA is often successful in reducing substance abuse (Humphreys, 2003; McKellar, Stewart, & Humphreys, 2003). Reasons given for the success of AA include

addiction A pattern of behavior characterized by an overwhelming involvement with using a drug and securing its supply.

disease model of addiction The view that addictions are biologically based, lifelong diseases that involve a loss of control over behavior and require medical and/or spiritual treatment for recovery.

the spiritual aspects of the treatment and the social network and support provided by the AA group (Bond, Kaskutas, & Weisner, 2003).

In contrast to the disease model of addiction, which focuses on biological mechanisms, some psychologists believe that understanding addiction requires that it be placed in context as part of people's lives, their personalities, their relationships, their environments, and their perspectives. In this **life-process model of addiction,** addiction is not a disease but rather a habitual response and a source of gratification or security that can be understood best in the context of social relationships and experiences.

Each of these views of addiction—the disease model and the nondisease, life-process model—has its supporters.

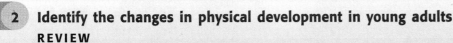

Review and Reflect: Learning Goal 2

2 **Identify the changes in physical development in young adults**

REVIEW

- How does physical performance peak and then slow down in early adulthood?
- What are some important things to know about eating and weight?
- What are the benefits of exercise?
- How extensive is substance abuse in young adults? What effects does it have on their lives?

REFLECT

- To discourage smoking, many governments now levy heavy taxes on cigarettes because of their negative health effects. Would you recommend that the U.S. government levy similar heavy taxes on fatty foods because of their negative health effects? Explain.

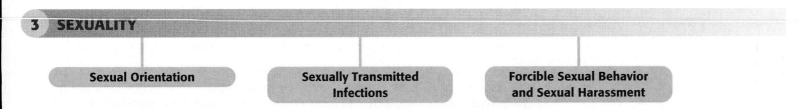

3 SEXUALITY

| Sexual Orientation | Sexually Transmitted Infections | Forcible Sexual Behavior and Sexual Harassment |

We do not need sex for everyday survival the way we need food and water, but we do need it for the survival of the species. What is the nature of sexuality in the human species?

Sexual Orientation

Let's explore sexual orientation and various aspects of heterosexual and homosexual attitudes and behaviors.

Heterosexual Attitudes and Behavior   In a well-designed, comprehensive study of Americans' sexual patterns, Robert Michael and his colleagues (1994) interviewed more than 3,000 people from 18 to 59 years of age who were randomly selected, a sharp contrast from earlier samples that were based on unrepresentative groups of volunteers.

Here are some of the key findings from the 1994 Sex in America survey:

- Americans tend to fall into three categories: One-third have sex twice a week or more, one-third a few times a month, and one-third a few times a year or not at all.

life-process model of addiction The view that addiction is not a disease but rather a habitual response and a source of gratification and security that can be understood only in the context of social relationships and experiences.

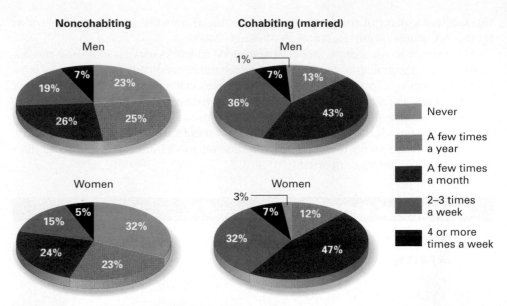

FIGURE 14.7 The Sex in America Survey
Percentages show noncohabiting and cohabiting (married) males' and females' responses to the question "How often have you had sex in the past year?"

- Married (and cohabiting) couples have sex more often than noncohabiting couples (see figure 14.7).
- Most Americans do not engage in kinky sexual acts. When asked about their favorite sexual acts, the vast majority (96 percent) said that vaginal sex was "very" or "somewhat" appealing. Oral sex was in third place, after an activity that many have not labeled a sexual act—watching a partner undress.
- Adultery is clearly the exception rather than the rule. Nearly 75 percent of the married men and 85 percent of the married women indicated that they have never been unfaithful.
- Men think about sex far more than women do—54 percent of the men said they think about it every day or several times a day, whereas 67 percent of the women said they think about it only a few times a week or a few times a month.

In sum, one of the most powerful messages in the 1994 survey was that Americans' sexual lives are more conservative than previously believed. Although 17 percent of the men and 3 percent of the women said they have had sex with at least 21 partners, the overall impression from the survey was that sexual behavior is ruled by marriage and monogamy for most Americans.

Attitudes and Behavior of Lesbians and Gay Males Until the end of the nineteenth century, it was generally believed that people were either heterosexual or homosexual. Today, it is more accepted to view sexual orientation along a continuum from exclusive male-female relations to exclusive same-sex relations rather than an either/or proposition (King, 2005). Some individuals are also *bisexual,* being sexually attracted to people of both sexes. In the Sex in America survey, 2.7 percent of the men and 1.3 percent of the women reported that they had had same-sex relations in the past year (Michael & others, 1994).

Why are some individuals lesbian, gay, or bisexual (LGB) and others heterosexual? Speculation about this question has been extensive (Herek, 2000; King, 2005). All people, regardless of their sexual orientation, have similar physiological responses during sexual arousal and seem to be aroused by the same types of tactile stimulation. Investigators typically find no differences between LGBs and heterosexuals in a wide range of attitudes, behaviors, and adjustments (Hyde & De Lamater, 2005). One recent review did find a higher prevalence of mental disorders in lesbians, gay men,

Human Sexuality
American Sexual Behavior
Lesbian and Gay Issues

and bisexuals than in heterosexuals and concluded that the difference was due to the stress associated with minority status involving stigma, prejudice, and discrimination (Meyer, 2003). Homosexuality once was classified as a mental disorder, but both the American Psychiatric Association and the American Psychological Association discontinued this classification as a mental disorder in the 1970s.

Recently, researchers have explored the possible biological basis of same-sex relations (D'Auqelli, 2000; Quinsey, 2003). The results of hormone studies have been inconsistent. If gay males are given male sex hormones (androgens), their sexual orientation doesn't change. Their sexual desire merely increases. A very early prenatal critical period might influence sexual orientation (Swaab & others, 2002). In the second to fifth months after conception, exposure of the fetus to hormone levels characteristic of females might cause the individual (male or female) to become attracted to males (Ellis & Ames, 1987). If this critical-period hypothesis turns out to be correct, it would explain why clinicians have found that sexual orientation is difficult, if not impossible, to modify.

With regard to anatomical structures, neuroscientist Simon LeVay (1991) found that an area of the hypothalamus that governs sexual behavior is twice as large (about the size of a grain of sand) in heterosexual males as in gay males. This area was found to be about the same size in gay males and heterosexual females. Critics of this research point out that many of the gay males in the study had AIDS and suggest that their brains could have been altered by the disease.

What likely determines an individual's sexual preference?

An individual's sexual orientation—same-sex, heterosexual, or bisexual—is most likely determined by a combination of genetic, hormonal, cognitive, and environmental factors (Baldwin & Baldwin, 1998). Most experts on same-sex relations believe that no one factor alone causes sexual orientation and that the relative weight of each factor can vary from one individual to the next. In effect, no one knows exactly why some individuals are lesbian, gay, or bisexual. Nevertheless, scientists have a clearer picture of what does not cause individuals to be lesbian or gay. For example, as we saw in chapter 9, "Socioemotional Development in Early Childhood," children raised by gay or lesbian parents or couples are no more likely to be LGB than are children raised by heterosexual parents (Patterson, 2002). There also is no evidence that being a gay male is caused by a dominant mother or a weak father, or that being a lesbian is caused by girls choosing male role models. Researchers have found that having an older brother increases the odds of being a gay male but the route by which this occurs has not been determined (Mustanski, Chivers, & Bailey, 2002).

Many gender differences that appear in heterosexual relationships occur in same-sex relationships (Savin-Williams & Diamond, 2004). For example, like heterosexual women, lesbians have fewer sexual partners than gay men and lesbians have less permissive attitudes about casual sex outside a primary relationship than gay men (Peplau, 2002, 2003; Peplau, Fingerhut, & Beals, 2004).

How can lesbians and gay males adapt to a world in which they are a minority? According to psychologist Laura Brown (1989), lesbians and gay males experience life as a minority in a dominant, majority culture. For lesbians and gay men, developing a *bicultural identity* creates new ways of defining themselves. Brown believes that lesbians and gay males adapt best when they don't define themselves in polarities, such as trying to live in an encapsulated lesbian or gay male world completely divorced from the majority culture or completely accepting the dictates and bias of the majority culture. Balancing the demands of the two cultures—the minority lesbian/gay male culture and the majority heterosexual culture—can often lead to more effective coping for lesbians and gay males, says Brown.

Sexually Transmitted Infections

Sexually transmitted infections (STIs)
Diseases that are contracted primarily through sex.

Sexually transmitted infections (STIs) are diseases that are primarily contracted through sex—intercourse as well as oral-genital and anal-genital sex. STIs affect about

STI	Description/cause	Incidence	Treatment
Gonorrhea	Commonly called the "drip" or "clap." Caused by the bacterium *Neisseria gonorrhoeae*. Spread by contact between infected moist membranes (genital, oral-genital, or anal-genital) of two individuals. Characterized by discharge from penis or vagina and painful urination. Can lead to infertility.	500,000 cases annually in U.S.	Penicillin, other antibiotics
Syphilis	Caused by the bacterium *Treponema pallidum*. Characterized by the appearance of a sore where syphilis entered the body. The sore can be on the external genitals, vagina, or anus. Later, a skin rash breaks out on palms of hands and bottom of feet. If not treated, can eventually lead to paralysis or even death.	100,000 cases annually in U.S.	Penicillin
Chlamydia	A common STI named for the bacterium *Chlamydia trachomatis*, an organism that spreads by sexual contact and infects the genital organs of both sexes. A special concern is that females with chlamydia may become infertile. It is recommended that adolescent and young adult females have an annual screening for this STI.	About 3 million people in U.S. annually; estimates are that 10 percent of adolescent girls have this STI.	Antibiotics
Genital herpes	Caused by a family of viruses with different strains. Involves an eruption of sores and blisters. Spread by sexual contact.	One of five U.S. adolescents and adults	No known cure but antiviral medications can shorten outbreaks
AIDS	Caused by a virus, the human immunodeficiency virus (HIV), which destroys the body's immune system. Semen and blood are the main vehicles of transmission. Common symptoms include fevers, night sweats, weight loss, chronic fatigue, and swollen lymph nodes.	4,000 13- to 19-year-olds in the U.S.; epidemic incidence in sub-Saharan adolescent girls	New treatments have slowed the progression from HIV to AIDS; no cure
Genital warts	Caused by the human papillomavirus, which does not always produce symptoms. Usually appear as small, hard painless bumps in the vaginal area, or around the anus. Very contagious. Certain high-risk types of this virus cause cervical cancer and other genital cancers. May recur despite treatment.	About 5.5 million new cases annually; considered the most common STI in the U.S.	A topical drug, freezing, or surgery

FIGURE 14.8 Sexually Transmitted Infections

Center for AIDS Prevention Studies
HIV/STD Education
Signs of HIV Infection in Females

acquired immune deficiency syndrome (AIDS) A sexually transmitted infection caused by the HIV virus, which destroys the body's immune system.

one of every six U.S. adults (National Center for Health Statistics, 2004). Among the most prevalent STIs are bacterial infections (such as gonorrhea, syphilis, and chlamydia), and STIs caused by viruses—genital herpes, genital warts, and AIDS. Figure 14.8 describes these sexually transmitted infections.

No single STI has had a greater impact on sexual behavior, or created more public fear in the last several decades than AIDS (Kelly, 2001; Strong & others, 2005). **Acquired immune deficiency syndrome (AIDS)** is a sexually transmitted infection that is caused by the human immunodeficiency virus (HIV), which destroys the body's immune system. Following exposure to HIV, an individual's body is vulnerable to germs that a normal immune system could destroy.

As of January 1, 2003, more than 300,000 cases of AIDS in 25- to 34-year-olds had been reported in the United States with about 80 percent of these being males and almost half intravenous (IV) drug users (National Center for HIV, STD, and TB Prevention, 2003). Because of education and the development of more effective drug treatments, deaths due to AIDS have begun to decline in the United States (Donnerer & others, 2003; National Center for Health Statistics, 2004). The greatest concern about AIDS is in sub-Saharan Africa, where it has reached epidemic proportions (Ford, Odallo, & Chorlton, 2003; Obregon, 2003).

Just asking a date about his or her sexual behavior does not guarantee protection from AIDS and other sexually transmitted infections (Emmers-Sommer & Allen, 2005). For example, in one investigation, 655 college students were asked to answer questions about lying and sexual behavior (Cochran & Mays, 1990). Of the 422 respondents who said they were sexually active, 34 percent of the men and 10 percent of the women said they had lied so their partner would have sex with them. Much higher percentages—47 percent of the men and 60 percent of the women—said they had been lied to by a potential sexual partner. When asked what aspects of their past they would be most likely to lie about, more than 40 percent of the men and women said they would understate the number of their sexual partners. Twenty percent of the men, but only 4 percent of the women, said they would lie about their results from an AIDS blood test. What are some good strategies for protecting against AIDS and other sexually transmitted infections? They include:

- *Knowing your and your partner's risk status.* Anyone who has had previous sexual activity with another person might have contracted an STI without being aware of it. Spend time getting to know a prospective partner before you have sex. Use this time to inform the other person of your STI status and inquire about your partner's. Remember that many people lie about their STI status.
- *Obtaining medical examinations.* Many experts recommend that couples who want to begin a sexual relationship should have a medical checkup to rule out STIs before they engage in sex. If cost is an issue, contact your campus health service or a public health clinic.
- *Having protected, not unprotected, sex.* When correctly used, latex condoms help to prevent many STIs from being transmitted. Condoms are most effective in preventing gonorrhea, syphilis, chlamydia, and AIDS. They are less effective against the spread of herpes.
- *Not having sex with multiple partners.* One of the best predictors of getting an STI is having sex with multiple partners. Having more than one sex partner elevates the likelihood that you will encounter an infected partner.

What are some good strategies for protecting against AIDS and other sexually transmitted infections? How effectively have you practiced these strategies?

Forcible Sexual Behavior and Sexual Harassment

Too often, sex involves the exercise of power. Here we will briefly look at two of the problems that may result: rape and sexual harassment.

Rape   **Rape** is forcible sexual intercourse with a person who does not give consent. Legal definitions of rape differ from state to state. For example, in some states, husbands are not prohibited from forcing their wives to have intercourse, although this has been challenged in several states (Kilpatrick, 2004). Because victims may be reluctant to suffer the consequences of reporting rape, the actual incidence is not easily determined. Rape occurs most often in large cities, where it has been reported that 8 of every 10,000 women 12 years and older are raped each year. Nearly 200,000 rapes are reported each year in the United States.

Although most victims of rape are women, rape of males does occur (Ellis, 2002). Men in prisons are especially vulnerable to rape, usually by heterosexual males who use rape as a means of establishing their dominance and power (Robertson, 2003). Though it might seem impossible for a man to be raped by a woman, a man's erection is not completely under his voluntary control, and some cases of men being raped by women have been reported (Sarrel & Masters, 1982). Male victims account for fewer than 5 percent of all rapes.

Why does rape of women occur so often in the United States? Among the causes given are that males are socialized to be sexually aggressive, to regard women as inferior beings, and to view their own pleasure as the most important objective in sexual relations (Adams-Curtis & Forbes, 2004; Kalmuss, 2004). Researchers have found that male rapists share the following characteristics: aggression enhances their sense of power or masculinity; they are angry at women in general; and they want to hurt and humiliate their victims (Chiroro & others, 2004; Giotakos & others, 2003).

Rape is a traumatic experience for the victims and those close to them (Christopher & Sprecher, 2000; Robinson, 2003). Victims initially feel shock and

www.mhhe.com/santrockld10

Sexual Assault

rape Forcible sexual intercourse with a person who does not consent to it.

numbness and often are acutely disorganized. Some show their distress through words and tears, others internalize their suffering. As victims strive to get their lives back to normal, they may experience depression, fear, and anxiety for months or years (Frazier, 2003; Thompson & others, 2003). Sexual dysfunctions, such as reduced sexual desire and an inability to reach orgasm, occur in 50 percent of female rape victims (Sprei & Courtois, 1988). Many victims make changes in their lives—such as moving to a new apartment or refusing to go out at night. Recovery depends on the victim's coping abilities, psychological adjustments prior to the assault, and social support (Frazier & others, 2004). Parents, partner, and others close to the victim can provide important support for recovery, as can mental health professionals (Farevo & others, 2004; Mein & others, 2003; Robinson, 2003).

An increasing concern is **date or acquaintance rape,** which is coercive sexual activity directed at someone with whom the victim is at least casually acquainted (Adams-Curtis & Forbes, 2004; Danielson & Holmes, 2004). By some estimates, one in three adolescent girls will be involved in a controlling, abusive relationship before she graduates from high school, and two-thirds of college freshman women report having been date-raped or having experienced an attempted date rape at least once (Watts & Zimmerman, 2002). About two-thirds of college men admit that they fondle women against their will, and half admit to forcing sexual activity. To read further about rape on college campuses, see the Research in Life-Span Development interlude.

Research in Life-Span Development

Campus Sexual Assault

A major study that focused on campus sexual assault involved a phone survey of 4,446 women attending two- or four-year colleges (Fisher, Cullen, & Turner, 2001). Sexual victimization was measured in a two-stage process. First, a series of screening questions were asked to determine if the respondent had experienced an act that might possibly be a victimization. Second, if the respondent answered "yes," the respondent was asked detailed questions about the incident, such as the type of unwanted contact and the means of coercion. In addition, respondents were asked about other aspects of their lives, including their lifestyles, routine activities, living arrangements, and prior sexual victimization.

Slightly less than 3 percent said that they either had experienced a rape or an attempted rape during the academic year. About 1 of 10 college women said that they had experienced rape in their lifetime. Unwanted or uninvited sexual contacts were widespread with more than one-third of the college women reporting these incidents. As shown in figure 14.9, in this study, most women (about 9 of 10) knew the person who sexually victimized them. Most of the women attempted to take protective actions against their assailants but were then reluctant to report the victimization to the police for a number of reasons (such as embarrassment, not clearly understanding the legal definition of rape, or not wanting to define someone they knew who victimized them as a rapist). Several factors were associated with sexual victimization: living on campus, being unmarried, getting drunk frequently, and experiencing prior sexual victimization. The majority of rapes occurred in living quarters.

date or acquaintance rape Coercive sexual activity directed at someone with whom the perpetrator is at least casually acquainted.

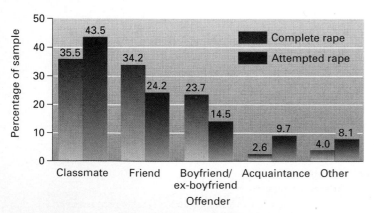

FIGURE 14.9 Completed Rape and Attempted Rape of College Women According to Victim-Offender Relationship

In addition, this research examined a form of sexual victimization that has been studied infrequently: stalking. Thirteen percent of the female students said they had been stalked since the school year began. As with other sexual victimizations, 80 percent knew their stalkers, who most often were boyfriends (42 percent) or classmates (24 percent). Stalking incidents lasted an average of 60 days.

Sexual Harassment   Sexual harassment takes many forms—from inappropriate sexual remarks and physical contact (patting, brushing against one's body) to blatant propositions and sexual assaults (Bronner, Peretz, & Ehrenfeld, 2003; Cortina, 2004; Gregg, 2004; Kern & Alessi, 2003). Millions of women experience sexual harassment each year in work and educational settings (Kovera, 2004; Rospenda, 2004; Shrier, 2003). Sexual harassment of men by women also occurs but to a far lesser extent than sexual harassment of women by men.

Sexual harassment can result in serious psychological consequences for the victim (Erlick Robinson, 2003; Hoffman, 2004). Sexual harassment is a manifestation of power of one person over another. The elimination of such exploitation requires the development of work and academic environments that provide equal opportunities to develop a career and obtain education in a climate free of sexual harassment (Hyde & DeLamater, 2005; Strong & others, 2005).

Review and Reflect: Learning Goal 3

3   **Discuss sexuality in young adults**

REVIEW

- What is the nature of heterosexuality and same-sex sexual orientation?
- What are sexually transmitted infections? What are some important things to know about AIDS?
- What are the effects of forcible sexual behavior and sexual harassment?

REFLECT

- What can be done to reduce forcible sexual behavior and sexual harassment?

4   COGNITIVE DEVELOPMENT

Cognitive Stages   **Creativity**

To explore the nature of cognition in early adulthood, we will focus on issues related to cognitive stages and creative thinking.

Cognitive Stages

Are young adults more advanced in their thinking than adolescents are? Let's explore what Piaget and others have said about this intriguing question.

Piaget's View   Piaget believed that an adolescent and an adult think qualitatively in the same way. That is, Piaget argued that formal operational thought (more logical, abstract, and idealistic than the concrete operational thinking of 7- to 11-year-olds) is entered in early adolescence at approximately 11 to 15 years of age. Piaget did believe that young adults are more *quantitatively* advanced in their thinking in the sense that they have more knowledge than adolescents. He also believed, as do information-processing psychologists, that adults especially increase their knowledge in a specific area, such as a physicist's understanding of physics or a financial analyst's knowledge about finance.

Some developmentalists believe it is not until adulthood that many individuals consolidate their formal operational thinking. That is, they may begin to plan and hypothesize about intellectual problems in adolescence, but they become more systematic and sophisticated at this as young adults. Nonetheless, many adults do not think in formal operational ways at all (Keating, 1990).

Realistic and Pragmatic Thinking   Other developmentalists believe that the idealism Piaget described as part of formal operational thinking decreases in early adulthood. This especially occurs as young adults move into the world of work and face the constraints of reality (Labouvie-Vief, 1986).

A related perspective on adult cognitive change was proposed by K. Warner Schaie and Sherry Willis (2000). They concluded that it is unlikely that adults go beyond the powerful methods of scientific thinking characteristic of the formal operational stage. However, Schaie argued that adults do progress beyond adolescents in their *use* of intellect. For example, he said that in early adulthood individuals often switch from acquiring knowledge to applying knowledge. This especially occurs as individuals pursue long-term career goals and attempt to achieve success in their work.

Reflective and Relativistic Thinking   William Perry (1970, 1999) also described some changes in cognition that take place in early adulthood. He said that adolescents often view the world in terms of polarities—right/wrong, we/they, good/bad. As youth move into adulthood, they gradually move away from this type of absolute thinking as they become aware of the diverse opinions and multiple perspectives of others. Thus, in Perry's view, the *absolute, dualistic thinking* (either/or) of adolescence gives way to the *reflective, relativistic thinking* of adulthood.

As we see next, some theorists have pieced together some of these different aspects of thinking and proposed a new qualitative stage of cognitive development.

Is There a Fifth, Postformal Stage?   Some theorists have pieced together cognitive changes in young adults and proposed a new stage of cognitive development. **Postformal thought** is qualitatively different from Piaget's formal operational thought. Postformal thought involves understanding that the correct answer to a problem requires reflective thinking and can vary from one situation to another, and that the search for truth is often an ongoing, neverending process. Postformal thought also includes the belief that solutions to problems need to be realistic and that emotion and subjective factors can influence thinking (Kramer, Kahlbaugh, & Goldston, 1992). Researchers have found that young adults are more likely to engage in this postformal thinking than adolescents are (Commons & others, 1989).

As young adults engage in more reflective judgment when solving problems, they might think deeply about many aspects of politics, their career and work, relationships, and other areas of life (Labouvie-Vief & Diehl, 1999). They might understand that what might be the best solution to a problem at work (with a co-worker or boss) might not be the best solution at home (with a romantic partner). Many young adults also become more skeptical about there being a single truth and often are not willing to accept an answer as final. They also often recognize that thinking can't just be abstract but rather has to be realistic and pragmatic. And many

postformal thought   A form of thought that is qualitatively different from Piaget's formal operational thought. It involves understanding that the correct answer to a problem can require reflective thinking, that the correct answer can vary from one situation to another, and that the search for truth is often an ongoing, neverending process. It also involves the belief that solutions to problems need to be realistic and that emotion and subjective factors can influence thinking.

young adults understand that emotions can play a role in thinking—for example, that one likely thinks more clearly in a calm, collected state than in an angry, highly aroused state.

How strong is the research evidence for a fifth, postformal stage of cognitive development? The fifth stage is controversial, and some critics argue that the research evidence has yet to be provided to document it as clearly a qualitatively more advanced stage than formal operational thought.

Creativity

In chapter 10, "Physical and Cognitive Development in Middle and Late Childhood," we studied creative thinking in children. The strategies for being creative in adulthood are essentially the same as in childhood. Here we focus on the issue of whether creativity might decline at some point in adulthood and explore Mihaly Csikszentmihalyi's ideas about how to lead a more creative life.

Adult Developmental Changes   At the age of 30, Thomas Edison invented the phonograph, Hans Christian Andersen wrote his first volume of fairy tales, and Mozart composed *The Marriage of Figaro.* One early study of creativity found that individuals' most creative products were generated in their thirties and that 80 percent of the most important creative contributions were completed by age 50 (Lehman, 1960). More recently, researchers have found that creativity does peak in adulthood and then decline, but that the peak often occurs in the forties. However, qualifying any conclusion about age and creative accomplishments are (1) the magnitude of the decline in productivity, (2) contrasts across creative domains, and (3) individual differences in lifetime output (Simonton, 1996).

Even though a decline in creative contributions is often found in the fifties and later, the decline is not as great as commonly thought. An impressive array of creative accomplishments occur in late adulthood. Benjamin Franklin invented the bifocal lens when he was 78 years old; Harriet Doerr wrote her first novel—*Stones from Ibarra,* which won the National Book Award in 1984—at the age of 73. And one of the most remarkable examples of creative accomplishment in late adulthood can be found in the life of Henri Chevreul. After a distinguished career as a physicist, Chevreul switched fields in his nineties to become a pioneer in gerontological research. He published his last research paper just a year prior to his death at the age of 103!

Any consideration of decline in creativity with age requires consideration of the domain involved. In such fields as philosophy and history, older adults often show as much creativity as when they were in their thirties and forties. By contrast, in such fields as lyric poetry, abstract math, and theoretical physics, the peak of creativity is often reached in the twenties or thirties.

There also is extensive individual variation in the lifetime output of creative individuals. Typically, the most productive creators in any field are far more prolific than their least productive counterparts. The contrast is so extreme that the top 10 percent of creative producers frequently account for 50 percent of the creative output in a particular domain. For instance, only sixteen composers account for half of the music regularly performed in the classical repertoire.

Csikszentmihalyi's Ideas   Mihaly Csikszentmihalyi (pronounced ME-high CHICK-sent-me-high-ee) (1995) interviewed 90 leading figures in art, business, government, education, and science to learn how creativity works. He discovered that creative people regularly experience a state he calls *flow,* a heightened state of pleasure we experience when we are engaged in mental and physical challenges that absorb us. Csikszentmihalyi (1997, 2000; Nakamura & Csikszentmihalyi, 2002) believes everyone is capable of achieving flow. Based on his interviews with some

Careers in Life-Span Development

Mihaly Csikszentmihalyi, University Professor and Researcher

Mihaly Csikszentmihalyi, born in Hungary and a professor at the University of Chicago for many years, currently is a professor at Claremont Graduate School in California. Mihaly has had a special interest in adolescents, initially conducting a number of research studies on what they do in their lives, the contexts in which they spend their time, and the people with whom they interact, and how they are feeling.

Currently he is one of the main architects of changing psychology's focus from the negative to the positive, believing that for too long the field has studied the dark side of life and that it is high time psychologists started focusing more on the good aspects of people—things like optimistic thinking, being altruistic, having good relationships, and being creative.

Mihaly has conducted a study of highly creative people in different walks of life—business, the arts, science—to discover what they are thinking, feeling, and doing when they come up with their most creative insights (Csikszentmihalyi, 1995). One thing he found was that certain settings are more likely to stimulate creativity than others. *When and where do you get your most creative thoughts?*

Mihaly Csikszentmihalyi, in the setting where he gets his most creative ideas.

of the most creative people in the world, the first step toward a more creative life is cultivating your curiosity and interest. How can you do this?

- *Try to be surprised by something every day.* Maybe it is something you see, hear, or read about. Become absorbed in a lecture or a book. Be open to what the world is telling you. Life is a stream of experiences. Swim widely and deeply in it, and your life will be richer.
- *Try to surprise at least one person every day.* In a lot of things you do, you have to be predictable and patterned. Do something different for a change. Ask a question you normally would not ask. Invite someone to go to a show or a museum you never have visited.
- *Write down each day what surprised you and how you surprised others.* Most creative people keep a diary, notes, or lab records to ensure that their experience is not fleeting or forgotten. Start with a specific task. Each evening record the most surprising event that occurred that day and your most surprising action. After a few days, reread your notes and reflect on your past experiences. After a few weeks, you might see a pattern of interest emerging in your notes, one that might suggest an area you can explore in greater depth.
- *When something sparks your interest, follow it.* Usually when something captures your attention, it is short-lived—an idea, a song, a flower. Too often we are too busy to explore the idea, song, or flower further. Or we think these areas are none of our business because we are not experts about them. Yet the world is our business. We can't know which part of it is best suited to our interests until we make a serious effort to learn as much about as many aspects of it as possible.
- *Wake up in the morning with a specific goal to look forward to.* Creative people wake up eager to start the day. Why? Not necessarily because they are cheerful, enthusiastic types but because they know that there is something meaningful to accomplish each day, and they can't wait to get started.
- *Spend time in settings that stimulate your creativity.* In Csikszentmihalyi's (1995) research, he gave people an electronic pager and beeped them randomly at different times of the day. When he asked them how they felt, they reported the highest levels of creativity when walking, driving, or swimming. I (your author) do my most creative thinking when I'm jogging. These activities are semiautomatic in that they take a certain amount of attention while leaving some time free to make connections among ideas. Another setting in which highly creative people report coming up with novel ideas is the sort of half-asleep, half-awake state we are in when we are deeply relaxed or barely awake.

To read further about Mihaly Csikszentmihalyi's work, see the Careers in Life-Span Development insert. You will find out about the setting in which he gets his most creative ideas.

Review and Reflect: Learning Goal 4

4 **Characterize cognitive changes in early adulthood**

REVIEW

- What changes in cognitive development in young adults have been proposed?
- Does creativity decline in adulthood? How can people lead more creative lives?

REFLECT

- What do you think are the most important cognitive changes that take place in young adults?

---

5 CAREERS AND WORK

- Developmental Changes
- Personality Types
- Values and Careers
- Monitoring the Occupational Outlook
- The Impact of Work

At age 21, Thomas Smith graduated from college and accepted a job as a science teacher at a high school in Boston. At age 26, Mary Lou Hernandez graduated from medical school and took a job as an intern at a hospital in Los Angeles. At age 20, Barbara Breck finished her training at a vocational school and went to work as a computer programmer for an engineering firm in Chicago. Earning a living, choosing an occupation, establishing a career, and developing in a career—these are important themes of early adulthood.

Developmental Changes

Many children have idealistic fantasies about what they want to be when they grow up. For example, many young children want to be superheros, sports stars, or movie stars. In the high school years, they often have begun to think about careers on a somewhat less idealistic basis. In their late teens and early twenties, their career decision making has usually turned more serious as they explore different career possibilities and zero in on the career they want to enter. In college, this often means choosing a major or specialization that is designed to lead to work in a particular field. By their early and mid-twenties, many individuals have completed their education or training and started to enter a full-time occupation. From the mid-twenties through the remainder of early adulthood, individuals often seek to establish their emerging career in a particular field. They may work hard to move up the career ladder and improve their financial standing.

"Your son has made a career choice, Mildred. He's going to win the lottery and travel a lot."

Copyright © 1985. Reprinted courtesy of Bunny Hoest and *Parade Magazine*.

Personality Types

Personality type theory is John Holland's view that it is important to match an individual's personality with a particular career. Holland believes that when individuals find

personality type theory John Holland's view that it is important for individuals to select a career that matches up well with their personality type.

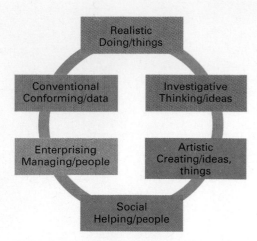

FIGURE 14.10 Holland's Model of Personality Types and Career Choices

Holland's Personality Types
Steps to Successful
Career Planning
Journal of Vocational Behavior
Career Development Quarterly
Journal of Counseling Psychology

careers that fit their personality, they are more likely to enjoy the work and stay in the job longer than if they'd taken a job not suited to their personality. Holland proposed six basic career-related personality types: realistic, investigative, artistic, social, enterprising, and conventional (see figure 14.10):

- *Realistic.* They like the outdoors and working in manual activities. They often are less social, have difficulty in demanding situations, and prefer to work alone. This personality type matches up best with such jobs as laborer, farmer, truck driver, construction worker, engineer, and pilot.
- *Investigative.* They are interested in ideas more than people, are rather indifferent to social relationships, are troubled by emotional situations, and are often aloof and intelligent. This personality type matches up well with scientific, intellectually oriented professions.
- *Artistic.* They are creative and enjoy working with ideas and materials that allow them to express themselves in innovative ways. They value nonconformity. Sometimes they have difficulties in social relationships. Not many jobs match up with the artistic personality type. Consequently, some artistic individuals work in jobs that are their second or third choices and express their artistic interests through hobbies and leisure.
- *Social.* They like to work with people and tend to have a helping orientation. They like doing social things considerably more than engaging in intellectual tasks. This personality type matches up with jobs in teaching, social work, and counseling.
- *Enterprising.* They also are more oriented toward people than things or ideas. They may try to dominate others to reach their goals. They are often good at persuading others to do things. The enterprising type matches up with careers in sales, management, and politics.
- *Conventional.* They function best in well-structured situations and are skilled at working with details. They often like to work with numbers and perform clerical tasks rather than working with ideas or people. The conventional type matches up with such jobs as accountant, bank teller, secretary, or file clerk.

If all individuals (and careers) fell conveniently into Holland's personality types, career counselors would have an easy job. However, individuals are typically more varied and complex than Holland's theory suggests. Even Holland (1987) states that individuals rarely are pure types, and most persons are a combination of two or three types. Still, the basic idea of matching personality traits to particular careers is an important contribution to the career development field. Holland's personality types are incorporated into the Strong-Campbell Interest Inventory, a widely used measure in career guidance.

Values and Careers

An important aspect of choosing a career is that it also match up with your values. When people know what they value most—what is important to them in life—they can refine their career choice more effectively. Some values are reflected in Holland's personality types, such as whether a person values working in a career that involves helping others or in a career in which creativity is valued. Among the values that some individuals think are important in choosing a career are working with people they like, working in a career with prestige, making a lot of money, being happy, not having to work long hours, being mentally challenged, having plenty of time for leisure pursuits, working in the right geographical location, and working where physical and mental health are important.

Monitoring the Occupational Outlook

As you explore the type of work you are likely to enjoy and in which you can succeed, it is important to be knowledgeable about different fields and companies.

Occupations may have many job openings one year but few in another year as economic conditions change. Thus, it is critical to keep up with the occupational outlook in various fields. An excellent source for doing this is the *Occupational Outlook Handbook*, which is revised every two years. Based on the 2004–2005 handbook, service industries are expected to provide the most new jobs with professional and related occupations projected to increase the most. Approximately three-fourths of the job growth will come from three groups of professional occupations: computer and mathematical occupations; health practitioners and technical occupations; and education, training, and library occupations (*Occupational Outlook Handbook*, 2004–2005).

Projected job growth varies widely by education requirements. Jobs that require a college degree are expected to grow the fastest. Education is essential to getting a high-paying job. All but one of the 50 highest-paying occupations require a college degree (*Occupational Outlook Handbook*, 2004–2005).

The Impact of Work

Do you work to live or live to work? Most individuals spend about one-third of their lives at work. In one survey, 35 percent of Americans worked 40 hours a week, but 18 percent worked 51 hours or more per week (Center for Survey Research at the University of Connecticut, 2000). Only 10 percent worked less than 30 hours a week.

Work defines people in fundamental ways (Osipow, 2000). It is an important influence on their financial standing, housing, the way they spend their time, where they live, their friendships, and their health (Warr, 2004). Some people define their identity through their work. Work also creates a structure and rhythm to life that is often missed when individuals do not work for an extended period. When unable to work, many individuals experience emotional distress and low self-esteem.

Of course, work also creates stress (Barling, Kelloway, & Frone, 2004; Boswell, Olson-Buchanan, & LePine, 2004). Four characteristics of work settings are linked with employee stress and health problems (Moos, 1986): (1) high job demands such as having a heavy workload and time pressure, (2) inadequate opportunities to participate in decision making, (3) a high level of supervisor control, and (4) a lack of clarity about the criteria for competent performance.

Work During College   Eighty percent of U.S. undergraduate students worked during the 1999–2000 academic year (National Center for Education Statistics, 2002). Forty-eight percent of undergraduates identified themselves mainly as students working to meet school expenses and 32 percent as employees who decided to enroll in school. Undergraduate students who identified themselves as working to meet expenses worked an average of 26 hours per week; those who considered themselves to be employees worked an average of 40 hours per week.

Working can pay or help offset some costs of schooling, but working also can restrict students' opportunities to learn. For those who identified themselves primarily as students, one recent national study found that as the number of hours worked per week increased, their grades suffered (National Center for Education Statistics, 2002) (see figure 14.11). Other research has found that as the number of hours college students work increases, the more likely they are to drop out of college (National Center for Education Statistics, 2002). Thus, college students need to carefully examine whether the number of hours they work is having a negative impact on their college success.

Of course, jobs also can contribute to your education. More than 1,000 colleges in the United States offer *cooperative (co-op) programs*, which are paid apprenticeships in a field that you are interested in pursuing. (You may not be permitted to participate in a co-op program until your junior year.) Other useful opportunities for working while going to college include internships and part-time or summer jobs

Occupational Outlook
Career and Job-Hunting Resources
What Color Is Your Parachute?
Job Interviewing
Work and Family Issues

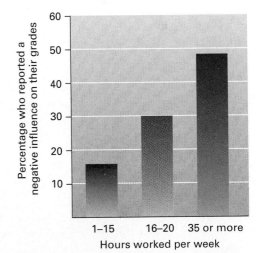

FIGURE 14.11 The Relation of Hours Worked Per Week in College to Grades
Among students working to pay for school expenses, 16 percent of those working 1 to 15 hours per week reported that working negatively influenced their grades. Thirty percent of college students who worked 16 to 20 hours a week said the same, as did 48 percent who worked 35 hours or more per week.

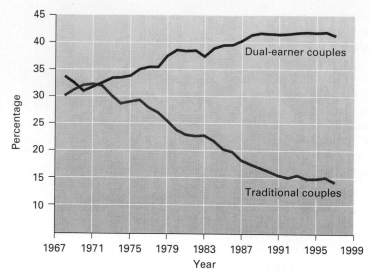

FIGURE 14.12 Changes in the Percentage of U.S. Traditional and Dual-Career Couples
Notice the dramatic increase in dual-earner couples in the last three decades. Traditional couples are those in which the husband is the sole breadwinner.

relevant to your field of study. In a national survey of employers, almost 60 percent said their entry-level college hires had co-op or internship experience (Collins, 1996). Participating in these work experiences can be a key factor in whether you land the job you want when you graduate.

Unemployment Unemployment produces stress regardless of whether the job loss is temporary, cyclical, or permanent (Hoyer & Roodin, 2003; Probst, 2004). Researchers have found that unemployment is related to physical problems (such as heart attack and stroke), mental problems (such as depression and anxiety), marital difficulties, and homicide (Papalia & others, 2002). A recent 15-year longitudinal study of more than 24,000 adults found that life satisfaction dropped considerably following unemployment and increased after becoming re-employed but did not completely return to the life satisfaction level previous to being unemployed (Lucas & others, 2004).

Stress comes not only from a loss of income and the resulting financial hardships but also from decreased self-esteem (Voydanoff, 1990). Individuals who cope best with unemployment have financial resources to rely on, often savings or the earnings of other family members. The support of understanding, adaptable family members also helps individuals cope with unemployment. Job counseling and self-help groups can provide practical advice on job searching, resumes, and interviewing skills, and also give emotional support.

Dual-Career Couples Dual-career couples may have particular problems finding a balance between work and the rest of life (Bellevia & Frone, 2004; Desmarais & Alksnis, 2004; Greenhaus, Collins, & Shaw, 2003). If both partners are working, who cleans up the house or calls the repairman or takes care of the other endless details involved in maintaining a home? If the couple has children, who is responsible for being sure that the children get to school or to piano practice, who writes the notes to approve field trips or meets the teacher or makes the dental appointments?

Although single-earner married families still make up a sizeable minority of families, the two-earner couple has increased considerably in the last three decades (Barnett, 2001) (see figure 14.12). As more U.S. women worked outside the home, the division of responsibility for work and family changed. Recent research suggests that (Barnett, 2001; Barnett & others, 2001):

- *U.S. husbands are taking increased responsibility for maintaining the home.* Men in dual-career families do about 45 percent of the housework.
- *U.S. women are taking increased responsibility for breadwinning.* In about one-third of two-earner couples, wives earn as much as or more than their husbands.
- *U.S. men are showing greater interest in their families and parenting.* Young adult men are reporting that family is at least as important to them as work. Among men with egalitarian attitudes toward gender roles, fatherhood is linked with a decrease of 9 hours per week at work; among men with more traditional views about gender roles, fatherhood is associated with an increase of almost 11 hours per week.

In the Diversity in Life-Span Development interlude, we further explore gender and work by examining gender in the workplace. Ethnic diversity in the workplace also is discussed in the interlude.

View the video "On Being a Working Mom" to gain the perspectives of working parents struggling to maintain a balance between work and the rest of life.

Diversity in Life-Span Development

Diversity in the Workplace

The workplace is becoming increasingly diverse (Desmaris & Alksnis, 2004). Whereas at one time few women were employed outside the home, in developed countries women have increasingly entered the labor force (Helgeson, 2005; Lakes & Carter, 2004). In 2001, 74 percent of U.S. men were in the labor force compared with 60 percent of U.S. women (U.S. Bureau of Labor Statistics, 2003). Only in Scandanavian countries such as Sweden did women participate in the labor force at the same rate as American women. In the United States, more than one-fourth of all lawyers, physicians, computer scientists, and chemists today are females.

Ethnic diversity also is increasing in the workplace in every developed country except France. In the United States, between 1980 and 2002, the percentage of Latinos and Asian Americans more than doubled, a trend that is expected to continue (U.S. Bureau of Labor Statistics, 2003). Latinos are projected to constitute a larger percentage of the labor force than African Americans by 2012, growing from 12 percent to 15 percent (*Occupational Outlook Handbook,* 2004–2005). Asian Americans will continue to be the fastest growing of the labor force groups. The increasing diversity in the workplace requires a sensitivity to cultural differences, and the cultural values that workers bring to a job need to be recognized and appreciated (Powell, 2004).

Despite the increasing diversity in the workplace, women and ethnic minorities experience difficulty in breaking through the *glass ceiling*. This invisible barrier to career advancement prevents women and ethnic minorities from holding managerial or executive jobs regardless of their accomplishments and merits (Dipboye & Colella, 2005). Females' share of executive management positions dropped from 32 percent in 1990 to 19 percent in 2000 (U.S. Bureau of Labor Statistics, 2003). However, over the same period, the percentage of ethnic minorities in management jobs increased from 13 percent in 1990 to 17 percent in 2000.

Review and Reflect: Learning Goal 5

5 **Explain the key dimensions of careers and work in early adulthood**

REVIEW

- What are some developmental changes in careers and work?
- How might personality types be linked to career choice?
- Why is it important to examine your values when thinking about a career?
- In which areas are there likely to be the greatest increase in jobs through 2010?
- What are some important things to know about work?

REFLECT

- What careers do you want to pursue? How much education will they take? What are some changes in men's roles in home and family matters in the last 40 years?

Reach Your Learning Goals

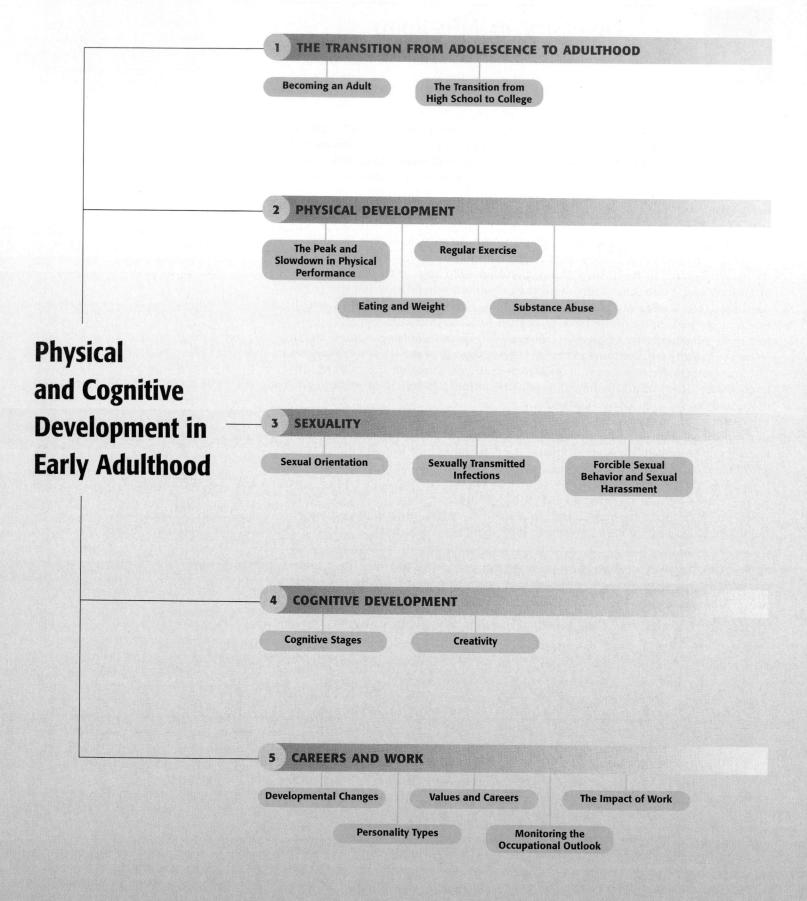

Physical and Cognitive Development in Early Adulthood

1 THE TRANSITION FROM ADOLESCENCE TO ADULTHOOD

Becoming an Adult

The Transition from High School to College

2 PHYSICAL DEVELOPMENT

The Peak and Slowdown in Physical Performance

Regular Exercise

Eating and Weight

Substance Abuse

3 SEXUALITY

Sexual Orientation

Sexually Transmitted Infections

Forcible Sexual Behavior and Sexual Harassment

4 COGNITIVE DEVELOPMENT

Cognitive Stages

Creativity

5 CAREERS AND WORK

Developmental Changes

Values and Careers

The Impact of Work

Personality Types

Monitoring the Occupational Outlook

Summary

1 ***Learning Goal 1: Describe the transition from adolescence to adulthood***

- During the transition to adulthood, there is often personal and economic temporariness. Two criteria for adult status are economic independence and independent decision making. Emerging adulthood is the term now given to the transition from adolescence to adulthood. Its age range is about 18 to 25 years of age, and it is characterized by experimentation and exploration.
- There is both continuity and change in the transition to adulthood, and the transition can involve both positive and negative features. An increasing number of college students are returning students.

2 ***Learning Goal 2: Identify the changes in physical development in young adults***

- Peak physical performance is often reached between 19 and 26 years of age. There is a hidden hazard in this time period—bad health habits are often formed then. Toward the latter part of early adulthood, a detectable slowdown in physical performance is apparent for most individuals.
- Obesity is a serious problem, with about one-third of Americans overweight enough to be at increased health risk. Heredity and set point are biological factors involved in obesity. Environmental factors and culture influence obesity. Ethnicity-gender factors are linked to obesity. Most diets don't work long term. For those that do, exercise is usually an important component. Dieting can be harmful; however, when overweight people diet and maintain their weight loss, it can have positive effects.
- Both moderate and intense exercise produce important physical and psychological gains, such as lowered risk of heart disease and lowered anxiety.
- Although some reduction in alcohol use has occurred among college freshmen, binge drinking is still a major concern. By the mid-twenties a reduction in drug use often takes place. Around the world, there are differences in alcohol use by religion and gender. Alcoholism is a disorder that involves long-term, repeated, uncontrolled, compulsive, and excessive use of alcoholic beverages and that impairs the drinker's health and social relationships. A number of strategies, such as nicotine substitutes, have shown some success in getting smokers to quit, but quitting is difficult because of the addictive properties of nicotine. Two strategies for intervening in addictions are the disease model and the life-process model, each of which has supporters.

3 ***Learning Goal 3: Discuss sexuality in young adults***

- Describing sexual practices in America always has been challenging. The 1994 Sex in America survey was a major improvement over the earlier Kinsey survey. In the 1994 survey, Americans' sexual lives were portrayed as more conservative than in the earlier surveys. It generally is

accepted to view sexual orientation along a continuum from exclusively heterosexual to exclusively homosexual. An individual's sexual preference likely is the result of a combination of genetic, hormonal, cognitive, and environmental factors.

- Also called STIs, sexually transmitted infections are contracted primarily through sexual contact. Gonorrhea, syphilis, chlamydia, and genital herpes are among the most common STIs. The STI that has received the most attention in the last several decades is AIDS (acquired immune deficiency syndrome), which is caused by HIV, a virus that destroys the body's immune system. Some good strategies for protecting against AIDS and other STIs are to (1) know your and your partner's risk status; (2) obtain medical examinations; (3) have protected, not unprotected, sex; and (4) not have sex with multiple partners.
- Rape is forcible sexual intercourse with a person who does not give consent. Rape usually produces traumatic reactions in its victims. Date or acquaintance rape involves coercive sexual activity directed at someone with whom the victim is at least casually acquainted. Sexual harassment occurs when one person uses his or her power over another individual in a sexual manner and can result in serious psychological consequences for the victim.

4 ***Learning Goal 4: Characterize cognitive changes in early adulthood***

- Formal operational thought, entered at age 11 to 15, is Piaget's final cognitive stage. Piaget did say that adults are quantitatively more knowledgeable than adolescents but that adults do not enter a new, qualitatively different stage. Some experts argue that the idealism of Piaget's formal operational stage declines in young adults, replaced by more realistic, pragmatic thinking. Perry said that adolescents often engage in dualistic, absolute thinking, whereas young adults are more likely to engage in reflective, relativistic thinking. Postformal thought is qualitatively different from Piaget's formal operational thought. It involves understanding that the correct answer might require reflective thinking and might vary from one situation to another, and that the search for truth is often neverending. Also, the postformal stage includes the understanding that solutions to problems often need to be realistic and that emotion and subjective factors can be involved in thinking.
- Creativity peaks in adulthood, often in the forties, and then declines. However, (1) the magnitude of the decline is often slight; (2) the creativity-age link varies by domain; and (3) there is extensive individual variation in lifetime creative output. Based on interviews with leading experts in different domains, Csikszentmihalyi charted the way creative people go about living a creative life, such as waking up every morning with a mission and spending time in settings that stimulate their creativity.

5 *Learning Goal 5: Explain the key dimensions of careers and work in early adulthood*

- Many young children have idealistic fantasies about a career. In the late teens and early twenties, their career thinking has usually turned more serious. By their early to mid-twenties, many individuals have completed their education or training and started in a career. In the remainder of early adulthood, they seek to establish their emerging career and start moving up the career ladder.

- John Holland proposed that it is important for individuals to choose a career that is compatible with their personality type. He proposed six personality types: realistic, conventional, artistic, enterprising, investigative and social.

- It is important to match up a career to your values. There are many different values, ranging from the importance of money to working in a preferred geographical location.

- Service-producing industries will account for the most jobs in America in the next decade. Employment in the computer industry is especially projected to grow rapidly. Jobs that require a college education will be the fastest growing and highest paying. Labor force participation of women will increase and so will that of Latinos and African Americans.

- Work defines people in fundamental ways and is a key aspect of their identity. Most individuals spend about one-third of their adult life at work. People often become stressed if they are unable to work but work also can produce stress, as when there is a heavy workload and time pressure. Eighty percent of U.S. college students work while going to college. Working during college can have negative outcomes, especially when students work long hours, or positive outcomes, especially when students participate in co-op programs, internships, or part-time or summer work relevant to their field of study. Unemployment produces stress regardless of whether the job loss is temporary, cyclical, or permanent. Unemployment is related to physical problems, mental problems, and other difficulties. The increasing number of women who work in careers outside the home has led to new work-related issues. There has been a considerable increase in the time men spend in household work and child care.

Key Terms

emerging adulthood 433
restrained eaters 440
aerobic exercise 440
addiction 444

disease model of
   addiction 444
life-process model of
   addiction 445

sexually transmitted infections
   (STIs) 447
acquired immune deficiency
   syndrome (AIDS) 448

rape 449
date or acquaintance rape 450
postformal thought 452
personality type theory 455

Key People

Robert Michael 445
Simon LeVay 447
Laura Brown 447

Jean Piaget 451
K. Warner Schaie and Sherry
   Willis 452

William Perry 452
Mihaly Csikszentmihalyi 453

John Holland 455

E-Learning Tools

To help you master the material in this chapter, you'll find a number of valuable study tools on the LifeMap CD-ROM that accompanies this book and on the Online Learning Center for *Life-Span Development,* tenth edition, at www.mhhe.com/santrockld10.

Video Clips

In the margins of this book there are icons directing you to the LifeMap CD-ROM that accompanies the book. There you'll find a video for chapter 14 called "On Being a Working Mom." The working parents profiled in this segment offer two perspectives on the problem of maintaining the proper balance between work and the rest of life.

Self-Assessment

Connect to www.mhhe.com/santrockld10 to examine some topics that are important to young adults by completing the self-assessments, *How Much Do I Know About STDs?, Matching My Personality Type to Careers,* and *My Career Goals.*

Taking It to the Net

Connect to www.mhhe.com/santrockld10 to research the answers to these questions.

1. Brian is a college senior who just turned 21. Brian's mother and grandfather both suffered from alcoholism; he has painful memories of his mother's out-of-control drinking when he was a child. Now that he is of legal drinking age, Brian would like to drink recreationally and sensibly, but he is concerned that he may have a psychological or genetic tendency toward alcohol abuse. What are some warning signs of a predisposition toward alcoholism? What precautions should Brian take to ensure that he remains a responsible drinker?

2. Nanette is working part-time in her college human resources office. She has been asked to start gathering information for a sexual harassment information booklet. What are the essential

characteristics of sexual harassment and how should she communicate how the signs are identified?

3. Lisa is a 28-year-old graphic designer who lost her job in the dot-com industry after working only two years at a design agency. She has been forced to work as a freelance designer for the past three years, without health benefits or job security, and she is beginning to despair of finding a full-time job in her field. How is unemployment and lack of job security linked to depression? How might Lisa's experience have been different if she had found herself unemployed at the age of 50?

Health and Well-Being, Parenting, and Education Exercises

Build your decision-making skills by trying your hand at the health and well-being, parenting, and education exercises.

Connect to www.mhhe.com/santrockld10 to research the answers and complete the exercises.

*Love is a canvas
furnished by nature and
embroidered
by imagination.*
—Voltaire
French Essayist, 18th Century

Socioemotional Development in Early Adulthood

Chapter Outline

CONTINUITY AND DISCONTINUITY FROM CHILDHOOD TO ADULTHOOD **1**

Temperament

Attachment

ATTRACTION, LOVE, AND CLOSE RELATIONSHIPS **2**

Attraction

The Faces of Love

Falling Out of Love

Loneliness

MARRIAGE AND THE FAMILY **3**

The Family Life Cycle

Marriage

Parental Roles

THE DIVERSITY OF ADULT LIFESTYLES **4**

Single Adults

Cohabiting Adults

Divorced Adults

Remarried Adults

Gay and Lesbian Adults

GENDER, RELATIONSHIPS, AND SELF-DEVELOPMENT **5**

Women's Development

Men's Development

Learning Goals

1 Describe continuity and discontinuity in temperament and attachment from childhood to adulthood

2 Identify some key aspects of attraction, love, and close relationships

3 Discuss marriage and the family

4 Explain the diversity of lifestyles

5 Characterize the role of gender in relationships

Images of Life-Span Development

Gwenna and Greg: Her Pursuit and His Lack of Commitment

Commitment is an important issue in a romantic relationship for most individuals. Consider the following circumstance in which Gwenna decides that it is time to have a talk with Greg about his commitment to their relationship (Lerner, 1989, pp. 44–45):

> She shared her perspective on both the strengths and weaknesses of their relationship and what her hopes were for the future. She asked Greg to do the same. Unlike earlier conversations, this one was conducted without her pursuing him, pressuring him, or diagnosing his problems with women. At the same time, she asked Greg some clear questions, which exposed his vagueness.
>
> "How will you know when you *are* ready to make a commitment? What specifically would you need to change or be different than it is today?"
>
> "I don't know," was Greg's response. When questioned further, the best he could come up with was that he'd just feel it.
>
> "How much more time do you need to make a decision one way or another?"
>
> "I'm not sure," Greg replied. "Maybe a couple of years, but I really can't answer a question like that. I can't predict my feelings."
>
> And so it went.
>
> Gwenna really loved this man, but two years (and maybe longer) was longer than she could comfortably wait. So, after much thought, she told Greg that she would wait till fall (about ten months), but that she would move on if he couldn't commit himself to marriage by then. She was open about her wish to marry and have a family with him, but she was equally clear that her first priority was a mutually committed relationship. If Greg was not at that point by fall, then she would end the relationship—painful though it would be.
>
> During the waiting period, Gwenna was able to *not* pursue him and *not* get distant or otherwise reactive to his expressions of ambivalence and doubt. *In this way she gave Greg emotional space to struggle with his dilemma and the relationship had its best chance of succeeding.* Her bottom-line position ("a decision by fall") was not a threat or an attempt to rope Greg in, but rather, a clear statement of what was acceptable to her.
>
> When fall arrived, Greg told Gwenna he needed another six months to make up his mind. Gwenna deliberated a while and decided she could live with that. But when the six months were up, Greg was uncertain and asked for more time. It was then that Gwenna took the painful but ultimately empowering step of ending their relationship.

PREVIEW

Love is of central importance in each of our lives, as it is in Gwenna and Greg's lives. Shortly, we will discuss the many faces of love, as well as marriage and the family, the diversity of adult lifestyles, and the role of gender in relationships. To begin, though, we will return to an issue we initially raised in chapter 1: continuity and discontinuity.

1 CONTINUITY AND DISCONTINUITY FROM CHILDHOOD TO ADULTHOOD

| Temperament | Attachment |

We no longer believe in the infant determinism of Freud's psychosexual theory, which argued that our personality as adults is virtually cast in stone by the time we are 5 years of age. But the first 20 years of life are not meaningless in predicting an adult's personality. And there is every reason to believe that later experiences in the early adult years are important in determining what the individual is like as an adult. In trying to understand the young adult's personality, it would be misleading to look only at the adult's life in present tense, ignoring the developmental unfolding of personality. So, too, would it be far off target to only search through a 30-year-old's first 5 to 10 years of life in trying to predict why he or she is having difficulty in a close relationship. The truth about adult personality development, then, lies somewhere between the infant determinism of Freud and a contextual approach that ignores the antecedents of the adult years altogether.

Temperament

A common finding is that the smaller the time intervals over which we measure personality characteristics, the more similar an individual will look from one measurement to the next. Thus, if we measure an individual's self-concept at the age of 20 and then again at the age of 30, we will probably find more stability than if we measured the individual's self-concept at the age of 10 and then again at the age of 30. Let's now explore some research findings that reflect these ideas about continuity and discontinuity.

In chapter 7, we described *temperament* as an individual's behavioral style and characteristic emotional responses. How stable is temperament? Do young adults show the same behavioral style and characteristic emotional responses as when they were infants or young children?

Activity level is an important dimension of temperament. Is a child's activity level linked to her or his personality in early adulthood? In one longitudinal study, children who were highly active at age 4 were likely to be very outgoing at age 23, which reflects continuity (Franz, 1996). From adolescence into early adulthood, most individuals show fewer emotional mood swings, become more responsible, and engage in less risk-taking behavior, which reflects discontinuity (Caspi, 1998).

Is temperament in childhood linked with adjustment in adulthood? Here is what we know based on the few longitudinal studies that have been conducted on this topic (Caspi, 1998). Recall from chapter 7 the distinction between an easy and a difficult temperament. In one longitudinal study, children who had an easy temperament at 3 to 5 years of age were likely to be well-adjusted as young adults (Chess & Thomas, 1987). In contrast, many children who had a difficult temperament at 3 to 5 years of age were not well-adjusted as young adults. Also, other researchers have found that boys with a difficult temperament in childhood are less likely as adults to continue their formal education, whereas girls with a difficult temperament in childhood are more likely to experience marital conflict as adults (Wachs, 2000).

Inhibition is another temperament characteristic that has been studied extensively (Kagan, 2000, 2002, 2003). Researchers have found that individuals with an inhibited temperament in childhood are less likely as adults to be assertive or experience social support, and more likely to delay entering a stable job track (Wachs, 2000).

Yet another aspect of temperament involves emotionality and the ability to control one's emotions. In one longitudinal study, when 3-year-old children showed

Initial Temperament Trait: Inhibition

	Child A	Child B
Intervening Context		
Caregivers	Caregivers (parents) who are sensitive and accepting, and let child set his or her own pace.	Caregivers who use inappropriate "low-level control" and attempt to force the child into new situations.
Physical Environment	Presence of "stimulus shelters" or "defensible spaces" that the children can retreat to when there is too much stimulation.	Child continually encounters noisy, chaotic environments that allow no escape from stimulation.
Peers	Peer groups with other inhibited children with common interests, so the child feels accepted.	Peer groups consist of athletic extroverts, so the child feels rejected.
Schools	School is "undermanned" so inhibited children are more likely to be tolerated and feel they can make a contribution.	School is "overmanned" so inhibited children are less likely to be tolerated and more likely to feel undervalued.
Personality Outcomes		
	As an adult, individual is closer to extroversion (outgoing, sociable) and is emotionally stable.	As an adult, individual is closer to introversion and has more emotional problems.

FIGURE 15.1 Temperament in Childhood, Personality in Adulthood, and Intervening Contexts

Varying experiences with caregivers, the physical environment, peers, and schools can modify links between temperament in childhood and personality in adulthood. The example given here is for inhibition.

good control of their emotions and were resilient in the face of stress, they were likely to continue to handle emotions effectively as adults (Block, 1993). By contrast, when 3-year-olds had low emotional control and were not very resilient, they were likely to show problems in these areas as young adults.

In sum, these studies reveal some continuity between certain aspects of temperament in childhood and adjustment in early adulthood. However, keep in mind that these connections between childhood temperament and adult adjustment are based on only a small number of studies and more research is needed to verify these linkages. Indeed, Theodore Wachs (1994, 2000) proposed ways that linkages between temperament in childhood and personality in adulthood might vary depending on the intervening contexts in individuals' experience (see figure 15.1).

Attachment

Attachment is another topic we highlighted in chapter 7, "Socioemotional Development in Infancy." We also described attachment in chapter 13, "Socioemotional Development in Adolescence." Let's examine attachment in young adults and the extent to which it is linked to attachment earlier in development.

The concepts of secure and insecure attachment continue to be used to describe attachment relationships in adulthood (Collins & Feeney, 2004; Crowell & others, 2002; Edelstein & Shaver, 2004; Shaver & Mikulincer, 2003; Treboux, Crowell, & Waters, 2004). About 50 to 60 percent of adults in nonclinical samples are *securely attached*. These individuals provide realistic, coherent descriptions of their childhood and appear to understand how past experiences affect their current lives as adults. Approximately 25 to 30 percent of adults fall into the *insecure-dismissing* category of attachment. These adults don't want to discuss their relationships with their parents or do not seem invested in them. Their memories often focus on negative experiences such as being rejected or neglected by a parent. *Insecure-preoccupied* individuals make up about 15 percent of adults. In contrast to dismissing adults, preoccupied adults readily talk about their relationships but they tend to be incoherent and disorganized.

They appear unable to move beyond their childhood issues with parents and often express anger toward them or ongoing efforts to please them.

Although relationships with romantic partners differ from those with parents in important ways (such as sexuality and reciprocal caregiving), romantic partners fulfill for adults some of the same needs as parents do for their children. Adults count on their romantic partners to be a secure base to which they can return and obtain comfort and security in stressful times.

Adult Attachment

Cindy Hazan and Phillip Shaver (1987; Shaver & Hazan, 1993) have examined the continuity between childhood attachment relationships and romantic relationships in a number of studies. They interview adults about their relationships with their parents as they were growing up and about their current romantic relationship. They find that the quality of childhood attachment relationships is linked with the quality of adult romantic relationships. For example, adults who report that they were securely attached to their parents are more likely to say that they have a secure attachment to their romantic partner than are adults who report having had an insecure attachment to their parents when they were growing up. In one longitudinal study, individuals who were securely attached to caregivers at 1 year of age also were likely to have secure attachments to parents and romantic partners 20 years later (Waters & others, 2000).

Researchers have found other links between attachment in childhood and relationship patterns in adulthood (Atkinson & Goldberg, 2003; Bartholomew & Horowitz, 1991; Edelstein & Shaver, 2004; Egeland & Carlson, 2004; Feeney, 1996; Fraley, 2002):

- As adults, individuals who were securely attached to a caregiver in childhood find it easy to get close to others and don't worry much about becoming too dependent on someone or being abandoned.
- As adults, individuals who had an avoidant attachment style in childhood find it difficult to develop intimate relationships. Compared with securely attached adults, once in a relationship, they are more likely to quickly end it and more likely to engage in one-night stands without love. Gwenna, the woman described in the chapter-opening story, had a father who was rarely involved in her upbringing. The distant relationship with her father was likely related to her pattern of choosing distant males with poor track records in relationships (Lerner, 1989).
- As adults, individuals who had an ambivalent attachment style in childhood are less trusting, which makes them more possessive and jealous, than securely attached adults. They may break up with the same individuals several times and when discussing conflicts they often become emotionally intense and angry.

Nonetheless, attachment styles are not cast in stone (Lewis, Feiring, & Rosenthal, 2000). For example, research indicates that links between earlier and later attachment styles are lessened by stressful and disruptive life experiences (such as the death of a parent and instability of caregiving) (Collins & Laursen, 2000). Also, some individuals revise their attachment styles as they experience relationships in their adult years (Baldwin & Fehr, 1995). For example, in one study, approximately 30 percent of young adults changed their attachment style over a four-year period (Kirkpatrick & Hazan, 1994).

Review and Reflect: Learning Goal 1

 1 Describe continuity and discontinuity in temperament and attachment from childhood to adulthood

REVIEW

- How stable is temperament from childhood to adulthood?
- How much does attachment change from childhood to adulthood?

REFLECT

- What was your temperament like as a child? What is it like now?

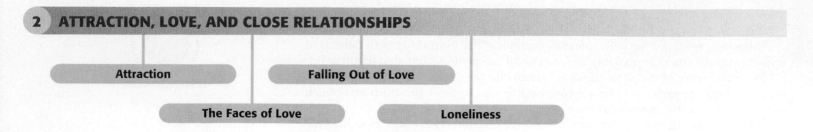

ATTRACTION, LOVE, AND CLOSE RELATIONSHIPS

What attracts us to others and motivates us to spend more time with them? This and another question has intrigued philosophers, poets, and songwriters for centuries: What is love? Is it lustful and passionate? Or should we be more cautious in our pursuit of love, as a Czech proverb advises, "Do not choose your wife at a dance, but in the fields among the harvesters."

Another important question is why relationships dissolve. Many of us know all too well that an individual we thought was a marvelous human being with whom we wanted to spend the rest of our life may not turn out to be so marvelous after all. But often it is said that it is better to have loved and lost than never to have loved at all. Loneliness is a dark cloud over many individuals' lives, something few human beings want to feel. These are the themes of our exploration of close relationships: how they get started in the first place, the faces of love, falling out of love, and loneliness.

Attraction

What attracts people like Gwenna and Greg to each other and motivates them to spend more time with each other? Does just being around someone increase the likelihood a relationship will develop? Or are we likely to seek out and associate with those who are similar to us? How important is physical attraction in the initial stages of a relationship? How much do the individuals' personality traits matter in forming a relationship?

Familiarity and Similarity   Familiarity breeds contempt, as the old saying goes, but social psychologists have found that familiarity is a necessary condition for a close relationship to develop. For the most part, friends and lovers are people who have been around each other for a long time; they may have grown up together, gone to high school or college together, worked together, or gone to the same social events (Brehm, 2002).

Another old saying, "Birds of a feather flock together," also helps to explain attraction. One of the most powerful lessons generated by the study of close relationships is that we like to associate with people who are similar to us (Berscheid, 2000). Our friends and lovers are much more like us than unlike us. We have similar attitudes, behavior patterns, and personal characteristics, as well as similar taste in clothes, intelligence, personality, other friends, values, lifestyle, physical attractiveness, and so on. In some limited cases and on some isolated characteristics, opposites may attract. An introvert may wish to be with an extravert, or someone with little money may wish to associate with someone who has a lot of money, for example. But overall we are attracted to individuals with similar rather than opposite characteristics. One study, for example, found that depressed college students preferred to meet unhappy others, whereas nondepressed college students preferred to meet happy others (Wenzlaff & Prohaska, 1989).

Why are people attracted to others who are similar to them? **Consensual validation** is one reason. Our own attitudes and behavior are supported when someone else's attitudes and behavior are similar to ours—their attitudes and behavior validate ours. Another reason that similarity matters is that people tend to shy away

consensual validation An explanation of why individuals are attracted to people who are similar to them. Our own attitudes and behavior are supported and validated when someone else's attitudes and behavior are similar to our own.

DILBERT reprinted by permission of United Feature Syndicate, Inc.

from the unknown. We often prefer to be around people whose attitudes and behavior we can predict. And similarity implies that we will enjoy doing things with another person who likes the same things and has similar attitudes. In one study, this sort of similarity was shown to be especially important in successful marriages (Swann, De La Ronde, & Hixon, 1994).

Physical Attractiveness You may be thinking at this point that something is missing from our discussion of attraction. As important as familiarity and similarity may be, they do not explain the spark that often ignites a romantic relationship: physical attractiveness. How important is physical attractiveness in relationships?

Many advertising agencies would have us believe that physical attractiveness is the most important factor in establishing and maintaining a relationship. Psychologists do not consider the link between physical beauty and attraction to be so clear-cut. For example, they have determined that heterosexual men and women differ on the importance of good looks when they seek an intimate partner. Women tend to rate as most important such traits as considerateness, honesty, dependability, kindness, and understanding; men prefer good looks, cooking skills, and frugality (Buss & Barnes, 1986).

Complicating research about the role of physical attraction is changing standards of what is deemed attractive. The criteria for beauty can differ, not just *across* cultures, but over time *within* cultures as well (Lamb & others, 1993). In the 1940s, the ideal of female beauty in the United States was typified by the well-rounded figure of Marilyn Monroe. Today, Monroe's 135-pound, 5-foot, 5-inch physique might be regarded as a bit overweight. The current ideal physique for both men and women is neither pleasingly plump nor extremely slender.

Social psychologists have found that the force of similarity also operates at a physical level. We usually seek out someone at our own level of attractiveness in both physical characteristics and social attributes. Research validates the **matching hypothesis**—which states that, although we may prefer a more attractive person in the abstract, in the real world we end up choosing someone who is close to our own level (Kalick & Hamilton, 1986).

Much of the research on physical attraction has focused on initial or short-term encounters; researchers have not often evaluated attraction over the course of months and years.

The Faces of Love

Once attraction initiates a relationship, other opportunities exist to deepen the relationship to love. *Love* refers to a vast and complex territory of human behavior. As you read about love, you will see that there are different types of love, such as

matching hypothesis States that although we prefer a more attractive person in the abstract, in the real world we end up choosing someone who is close to our own level.

friendship, romantic love, and affectionate love. Altruism, discussed in chapter 11, "Socioemotional Development in Middle and Late Childhood," also is classified as a type of love by some experts (Berscheid, 1988). To begin, though, we will focus on a very important theme in the lives of young adults—intimacy, which is especially important in friendship and affectionate love.

Intimacy   Let's explore Erik Erikson's view of intimacy, the role of intimacy in relationship maturity, and how people juggle the motivation for intimacy and the motivation for independence.

We are what we love.

—ERIK ERIKSON

Danish-Born American Psychoanalyst and Author, 20th Century

Erikson's Stage: Intimacy Versus Isolation   As we go through our adult lives, most of us are motivated to successfully juggle the development of identity and intimacy. Recall from our discussion in chapter 13 that Erik Erikson (1968) believes that identity versus identity confusion—pursuing who we are, what we are all about, and where we are going in life—is the most important issue to be negotiated in adolescence. Erikson thinks that intimacy should come after individuals are well on their way to establishing stable and successful identities. Intimacy is another life crisis in Erikson's scheme. If intimacy is not developed in early adulthood, the individual may be left with what Erikson calls "isolation." Intimacy versus isolation is Erikson's sixth developmental stage, which individuals experience in early adulthood. At this time, individuals face the task of forming intimate relationships with others. Erikson describes intimacy as finding oneself yet losing oneself in another person. If young adults form healthy friendships and an intimate relationship with another individual, intimacy will be achieved. If not, isolation will result.

An inability to develop meaningful relationships with others can harm an individual's personality. It may lead individuals to repudiate, ignore, or attack those who frustrate them. Such circumstances account for the shallow, almost pathetic attempts of youth to merge themselves with a leader. Many youth want to be apprentices or disciples of leaders and adults who will shelter them from the harm of the "out-group" world. If this fails, and Erikson believes that it must, sooner or later the individuals recoil into a self-search to discover where they went wrong. This introspection sometimes leads to painful depression and isolation. It also may contribute to a mistrust of others.

Intimacy and Independence   The early adult years are a time when individuals usually develop an intimate relationship with another individual. An important aspect of this relationship is the commitment of the individuals to each other. At the same time, individuals show a strong interest in independence and freedom. Development in early adulthood often involves an intricate balance of intimacy and commitment on the one hand, and independence and freedom on the other.

Recall that intimacy is the aspect of development that follows identity in Erikson's eight stages of development. A related aspect of developing an identity in adolescence and early adulthood is independence. At the same time as individuals are trying to establish an identity, they face the difficulty of having to cope with increasing their independence from their parents, developing an intimate relationship with another individual, and increasing their friendship commitments. They also face the task of being able to think for themselves and do things without always relying on what others say or do.

The extent to which the young adult has begun to develop autonomy has important implications for early adulthood maturity. The young adult who has not sufficiently moved away from parental ties may have difficulty in both interpersonal relationships and a career. Consider the mother who overprotects her daughter, continues to support her financially, and does not want to let go of her. In early adulthood, the daughter may have difficulty developing mature intimate relationships and she may have career difficulties. When a promotion comes up that involves more responsibility and possibly more stress, she may turn it down. When things do not go well in her relationship with a young man, she may go crying to her mother.

The balance between intimacy and commitment, on the one hand, and independence and freedom, on the other, is delicate. Keep in mind that these important dimensions of adult development are not necessarily opposite ends of a continuum. Some individuals are able to experience a healthy independence and freedom along with an intimate relationship. These dimensions also may fluctuate with social and historical change. And keep in mind that intimacy and commitment, and independence and freedom, are not just concerns of early adulthood. They are important themes of development that are worked and reworked throughout the adult years. Next, we will explore an important aspect of adults' close relationships in which intimacy plays a key role: friendship.

Friendship   Increasingly researchers are finding that friendship plays an important role in development throughout the human life span (Hartup, 2000; Pruchno & Rosenbaum, 2003). In the words of American historian Henry Adams, "One friend in life is much, two are many, and three hardly possible." **Friendship** is a form of close relationship that involves enjoyment (we like to spend time with our friends), acceptance (we accept our friends without trying to change them), trust (we assume our friends will act in our best interest), respect (we think our friends make good judgments), mutual assistance (we help and support our friends and they us), confiding (we share experiences and confidential matters with a friend), understanding (we feel that a friend knows us well and understands what we like), and spontaneity (we feel free to be ourselves around a friend). In an inquiry of more than 40,000 individuals, many of these characteristics were given when people were asked what a best friend should be like (Parlee, 1979).

Intimate Relationships
Ellen Berscheid's Research
Friendship

As we saw in chapter 11, friendship can serve many functions—such as companionship, intimacy/affection, support, and a source of self-esteem. In some cases, friends can provide a better buffer from stress and be a better source of emotional support than family members. This might be because friends choose each other, whereas family ties are obligatory. Individuals often select a friend in terms of such criteria as loyalty, trustworthiness, and support. Thus, it is not surprising that in times of stress individuals turn to their friends for emotional support (Fehr, 2000).

Zick Rubin (1970) argues that liking involves our sense that someone else is similar to us; it includes a positive evaluation of the individual. Loving, he believes, involves being close to someone; it includes dependency, a more selfless orientation toward the individual, and qualities of absorption and exclusiveness.

But friends and lovers are similar in some ways. In one study, friends and romantic partners shared the characteristics of acceptance, trust, respect, confiding, understanding, spontaneity, mutual assistance, and happiness (Davis, 1985). However, relationships with spouses or lovers were more likely to also involve fascination and exclusiveness.

As with children, adult friends usually come from the same age group. For many individuals, friendships formed in the twenties often continue through the twenties and into the thirties, although some new friends may be made in the thirties and some lost because of moving or other circumstances.

As in the childhood years, there are sex differences in adult friendship (Winstead & Griffin, 2001). We first will focus on friendships between women and, second, friendships between men, and then examine friendships between women and men.

Friendships Between Women   Compared with men, women have more close friends and their friendships involve more self-disclosure and exchange of mutual support (Wood, 2001). Women are more likely to listen at length to what a friend has to say and be sympathetic, and women have been labeled as "talking companions" because talk is so central to their relationship (Gouldner & Strong, 1987). Women's friendships tend to be characterized not only by depth but also by breadth: Women share many aspects of their experiences, thoughts, and feelings (Wood, 2001).

friendship A form of close relationship that involves enjoyment, acceptance, trust, respect, mutual assistance, confiding, understanding, and spontaneity.

How is adult friendship different among female friends, male friends, and cross-sex friends?

Friendships Between Men When female friends get together, they like to talk, but male friends are more likely to engage in activities, especially outdoors. Thus, the adult male pattern of friendship often involves keeping one's distance while sharing useful information. Men are less likely than women to talk about their weaknesses with their friends, and men want practical solutions to their problems rather than sympathy (Tannen, 1990). Also, adult male friendships are more competitive than those of women (Wood, 2001). For example, male friends disagree with each other more.

Friendships Between Women and Men What about female-male friendship? Cross-gender friendships are more common among adults than among elementary school children, but not as common as same-gender friendships in adulthood (Fehr, 2000). Cross-gender friendships can provide both opportunities and problems. The opportunities involve learning more about common feelings and interests and shared characteristics, as well as acquiring knowledge and understanding of beliefs and activities that historically have been typical of one gender.

Problems can arise in cross-gender friendships because of different expectations. For example, a woman might expect sympathy from a male friend but might receive a proposed solution rather than a shoulder to cry on (Tannen, 1990). Another problem that can plague an adult cross-gender friendship is unclear sexual boundaries, which can produce tension and confusion (Swain, 1992).

Romantic Love Some friendships evolve into **romantic love,** which is also called passionate love, or eros. Poets, playwrights, and musicians through the ages have lauded the fiery passion of romantic love—and lamented the searing pain when it fails. Think for a moment about songs and books that hit the top of the charts. Chances are they are about love.

Romantic love has strong components of sexuality and infatuation, and it often predominates in the early part of a love relationship (Hendrick & Hendrick, 2000, 2004; Metts, 2004). Well-known love researcher Ellen Berscheid (1988) says that it is romantic love we mean when we say that we are "in love" with someone. It is romantic love she believes we need to understand if we are to learn what love is all about. Berscheid believes that sexual desire is the most important ingredient of romantic love.

In our culture, romantic love is the main reason we get married. In 1967, a famous study showed that most men maintained that they would not get married if they were not "in love." Women either were undecided or said that they would get married even if they did not love their prospective husband (Kephart, 1967). In the 1980s, both women and men tended to agree that they would not get married unless they were "in love." More than half of today's men and women say that not being "in love" is sufficient reason to dissolve a marriage (Berscheid, Snyder, & Omoto, 1989). Romantic love is especially important among college students. One study of unattached college men and women found that more than half identified a romantic partner, rather than a parent, sibling, or friend, as their closest relationship (Berscheid, Snyder, & Omoto, 1989).

Romantic love includes a complex intermingling of different emotions—fear, anger, sexual desire, joy, and jealousy, for example (Harris, 2002). Obviously, some of these emotions are a source of anguish (Daley & Hammen, 2002). One study found that romantic lovers were more likely than friends to be the cause of depression (Berscheid & Fei, 1977).

Affectionate Love Love is more than just passion. **Affectionate love,** also called companionate love, is the type of love that occurs when someone desires to have the other person near and has a deep, caring affection for the person.

There is a growing belief that the early stages of love have more romantic ingredients, but as love matures, passion tends to give way to affection (Berscheid &

Reis, 1998; Harvey & Weber, 2002). Phillip Shaver (1986) proposed a developmental model of love in which the initial phase of romantic love is fueled by a mixture of sexual attraction and gratification, a reduced sense of loneliness, uncertainty about the security of developing another attachment, and excitement from exploring the novelty of another human being. With time, he says, sexual attraction wanes, attachment anxieties either lessen or produce conflict and withdrawal, novelty is replaced with familiarity, and lovers either find themselves securely attached in a deeply caring relationship or distressed—feeling bored, disappointed, lonely, or hostile, for example. In the latter case, one or both partners may eventually end the relationship as Gwenna did with Greg in the chapter-opening story, and then move on to another relationship.

Consummate Love So far we have discussed two forms of love: romantic (or passionate) and affectionate (or companionate). Robert J. Sternberg (1988) described a third form of love, *consummate love*, which he said is the strongest, fullest type of love. Sternberg's triarchic theory of love can be thought of as a triangle with three main dimensions—passion, intimacy, and commitment. Passion, as described earlier, is physical and sexual attraction to another. Intimacy is emotional feelings of warmth, closeness, and sharing in a relationship. Commitment is our cognitive appraisal of the relationship and our intent to maintain the relationship even in the face of problems (Rusbult & others, 2001). Passion and intimacy were present in Gwenna and Greg's relationship, but commitment was absent on Greg's part.

Sternberg's theory states that the ideal form of love involves all three dimensions (see figure 15.2). If passion is the only ingredient in a relationship (with intimacy and commitment low or absent), we are merely *infatuated*. An affair or a fling in which there is little intimacy and even less commitment would be an example. A relationship marked by intimacy and commitment but low or lacking in passion is called *affectionate love,* a pattern often found among couples who have been married for many years. If passion and commitment are present but intimacy is not, Sternberg calls the relationship *fatuous love,* as when one person worships another from a distance. But if couples share all three dimensions—passion, intimacy, and commitment—they will experience *consummate love.*

Falling Out of Love

For Gwenna, as with most people, falling out of love was painful and highly emotional. The collapse of a close relationship may feel tragic. In the long run, however, as was the case for Gwenna, our happiness and personal development may benefit from getting over being in love and ending a close relationship.

In particular, falling out of love may be wise if you are obsessed with a person who repeatedly betrays your trust; if you are involved with someone who is draining you emotionally or financially; or if you are desperately in love with someone who does not return your feelings, which was occurring in Gwenna's relationship with Greg.

Being in love when love is not returned can lead to depression, obsessive thoughts, sexual dysfunction, inability to work effectively, difficulty in making new friends, and self-condemnation. Thinking clearly in such relationships is often difficult, because they are so colored by arousing emotions.

Some people get taken advantage of in relationships. For example, without either person realizing it, a relationship can evolve in a way that creates dominant

Types of Love	Passion	Intimacy	Commitment
Infatuation	Present	Absent or low	Absent or low
Affectionate love	Absent or low	Present	Present
Fatuous love	Present	Absent or low	Present
Consummate love	Present	Present	Present

Present   Absent or low

FIGURE 15.2 Sternberg's Triangle of Love
Sternberg identified three types of love: passion, intimacy, and commitment. Various combinations of these types of love result in these patterns of love: infatuation, affectionate love, fatuous love, and consummate love.

 Examine the video "Falling in Love" for a case study of some developmental patterns experienced by couples falling in love.

romantic love Also called passionate love, or eros, romantic love has strong sexual and infatuation components and often predominates in the early period of a love relationship.

affectionate love In this type of love, also called companionate love, an individual desires to have the other person near and has a deep, caring affection for the other person.

and submissive roles. Detecting this pattern is an important step toward learning either to reconstruct the relationship or to end it if the problems cannot be worked out. To read further about romantic relationship breakups, see the Research in Life-Span Development interlude.

Research in Life-Span Development

Personal Growth Following a Romantic Relationship Breakup

Studies of romantic breakups have mainly focused on their negative aspects (Frazier & Cooke, 1993; Kurdek, 1997). Few studies have examined the possibility that a romantic breakup might lead to positive changes.

One recent study assessed the personal growth that can follow the breakup of a romantic relationship (Tahsiro & Frazier, 2003). The participants were 92 undergraduate students who had experienced a relationship breakup in the past nine months. They were asked to describe "what positive changes, if any, have happened as a result of your breakup that might serve to improve your future romantic relationships" (p. 118).

Self-reported positive growth was common following a romantic breakup. Changes were categorized in terms of person, relational, and environmental changes. The most commonly reported types of growth were person changes, which included feeling stronger and more self-confident, more independent, and better off emotionally. Relational positive changes included gaining relational wisdom, and environmental positive changes included having better friendships because of the breakup. Figure 15.3 provides examples of these positive changes. Women reported more positive growth than did men.

Change category	Exemplars of frequently mentioned responses
Person positives	1. "I am more self-confident." 2. "Through breaking up I found I could handle more on my own." 3. "I didn't always have to be the strong one, it's okay to cry or be upset without having to take care of him."
Relational positives	1. "Better communication." 2. "I learned many relationship skills that I can apply in the future (for example, the importance of saying you're sorry)." 3. "I know not to jump into a relationship too quickly."
Environmental positives	1. "I rely on my friends more. I forgot how important friends are when I was with him." 2. "Concentrate on school more: I can put so much more time and effort toward school." 3. "I believe friends' and family's opinions count—will seek them out in future relationships."

FIGURE 15.3 Examples of Positive Changes in the Aftermath of a Romantic Breakup

Loneliness

In some cases, loneliness can set in when individuals leave a close relationship, and individuals who don't have friends are vulnerable to loneliness. Let's now explore what it is like to be lonely.

Recall that Erik Erikson (1968) believes that intimacy versus isolation is the key developmental issue for young adults to resolve. Social isolation can result in loneliness.

Each of us has times in our lives when we feel lonely, but for some people loneliness is a chronic condition. More than just an unwelcome social situation, chronic loneliness is linked with impaired physical and mental health (Cacioppo & Hawkley, 2003). Chronic loneliness even can lead to an early death (Cuijpers, 2001).

Our society's emphasis on self-fulfillment and achievement, the importance we attach to commitment in relationships, and a decline in stable close relationships are among the reasons loneliness is common today (de Jong-Gierveld, 1987). Researchers have found that married individuals are less lonely than their nonmarried counterparts (never married, divorced, or widowed) in studies conducted in more than 20 countries (Perlman & Peplau, 1998).

How do you determine if you are lonely? Scales of loneliness ask you to respond to items like "I don't feel in tune with the people around me" and "I can find companionship when I want it." If you consistently respond that you never or rarely feel in tune with people around you and rarely or never can find companionship when you want it, you are likely to fall into the category of people who are described as moderately or intensely lonely (Russell, 1996).

Loneliness and Life's Transitions   Loneliness is interwoven with how people pass through life transitions, such as a move to a different part of the country, a divorce, or the death of a close friend or family member (Valeri, 2003). Another situation that often creates loneliness is the first year of college. When students leave the familiar world of their hometown and family to enter college, they especially can feel lonely. Many college freshmen feel anxious about meeting new people and developing a new social life can create considerable anxiety. As one student commented:

> My first year here at the university has been pretty lonely. I wasn't lonely at all in high school. I lived in a fairly small town—I knew everybody and everyone knew me. I was a member of several clubs and played on the basketball team. It's not that way at the university. It is a big place and I've felt like a stranger on so many occasions. I'm starting to get used to my life here and the last few months I've been making myself meet people and get to know them, but it has not been easy.

As this comment illustrates, freshmen rarely bring their popularity and social standing from high school into the college environment. There may be a dozen high school basketball stars, National Merit scholars, and former student council presidents in a single dormitory wing. Especially if students attend college away from home, they face the task of forming completely new social relationships.

One study found that two weeks after the school year began, 75 percent of 354 college freshmen felt lonely at least part of the time (Cutrona, 1982). More than 40 percent said their loneliness was moderate to severe. Students who were the most optimistic and had the highest self-esteem were more likely to overcome their loneliness by the end of their freshman year. Loneliness is not reserved for college freshmen, though. Upperclassmen are often lonely as well. In one recent study of more than 2,600 undergraduates, lonely individuals were less likely to actively cope with stress than individuals who were able to make friends (Cacioppo & others, 2000). Also in this study, lonely college students had higher levels of stress-related hormones and poorer sleep patterns than students who had positive relationships with others.

Loneliness
Shyness

"What I'm trying to say, Mary, is that I want your site to be linked to my site."

It is important to distinguish chronic loneliness from the desire of some people to have some time to themselves. Some individuals, especially those who are involved in intense careers that involve extensive interactions with people, value solitary time.

Loneliness and Technology   One of the factors that may be contributing to loneliness in contemporary society is technology. Although invention of the telephone more than a century ago seems to have decreased social isolation for many individuals and families, psychologists have found a link between TV viewing and loneliness. Correlation does not equal causation, but it does seem plausible that television can contribute to social disengagement.

Because most people isolate themselves at their computers when they use the Internet, the Internet also may increase disengagement. One study focused on 169 individuals during their first several years online (Kraut & others, 1998). In this study, greater use of the Internet was associated with declines in participants' communication with family members in the household and increases in depression and loneliness. At the same time, however, some people use the Internet to form potentially strong new ties (Clay, 2000). Especially for socially anxious and lonely individuals, the Internet may provide a safe way to begin contacts that eventually lead to face-to-face meetings and possibly even intimate relationships.

Strategies for Reducing Loneliness   If you are lonely, how can you become better connected with others? Here are some strategies:

- *Participate in activities that you can do with others.* Join organizations or volunteer your time for a cause you believe in. You likely will get to know others whose views are similar to yours. Going to just one social gathering can help you develop social contacts. When you go, introduce yourself to others and start a conversation. Another strategy is to sit next to new people in your classes or find someone to study with.
- *Engage in positive behaviors when you meet new people.* You will improve your chances of developing enduring relationships if, when you meet new people, you are nice, considerate, honest, trustworthy, and cooperative. Have a positive attitude, be supportive of the other person, and make positive comments about him or her.
- *See a counselor or read a book on loneliness.* If you can't get rid of your loneliness on your own, you might want to contact the counseling services at your college. The counselor can talk with you about strategies for reducing your loneliness. You also might want to read a good book on loneliness such as *Intimate Connections* by David Burns (1985).

Review and Reflect: Learning Goal 2

2 **Identify some key aspects of attraction, love, and close relationships**

REVIEW

- What attracts someone to another person?
- What are some different types of love?
- What characterizes falling out of love?
- What is the nature of loneliness and how does it affect people?

REFLECT

- If you were to give someone advice about love, what would it be?

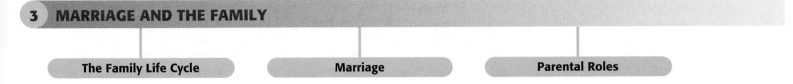

3 **MARRIAGE AND THE FAMILY**

The Family Life Cycle   Marriage   Parental Roles

Should I get married? If I wait any longer, will it be too late? Will I get left out? Should I stay single or is it too lonely a life? Do I want to have children? How will it affect my marriage? These are questions that many young adults pose to themselves as they consider their lifestyle options. But before we explore these lifestyle options, let's examine the nature of the family life cycle.

The Family Life Cycle

As we go through life, we are at different points in the family life cycle. Here are the six stages of the family life cycle (Carter & McGoldrick, 1988) (see figure 15.4):

- **Leaving home and becoming a single adult** is the first stage in the family life cycle, and it involves **launching,** the process in which youth move into adulthood and exit their family of origin. Adequate completion of launching requires that the young adult separate from the family of origin without cutting off ties completely or fleeing in a reactive way to find some form of substitute emotional refuge. The launching period is a time for the youth and young adult to formulate personal life goals, to develop an identity, and to become more independent before joining with another person to form a new family. This is a time for young people to sort out emotionally what they will take along from the family of origin, who they will leave behind, and what they will do to develop into themselves.

    Complete cutoffs from parents rarely resolve emotional problems. The shift to adult-to-adult status between parents and children requires a mutually respectful and personal form of relating, in which young adults can appreciate parents as they are, needing neither to make them into what they are not nor to blame them for what they could not be. Neither do young adults need to comply with parental expectations and wishes at their own expense.

- The **new couple** is the second stage in the family life cycle, in which two individuals from separate families unite to form a new family system. This stage involves not only the development of a new marital system, but also a realignment with extended families and friends to include the spouse. Women's changing roles, the increasingly frequent marriage of partners from divergent cultural backgrounds, and the increasing physical distances between family members are placing a much stronger burden on couples to define their relationships for themselves than was true in the past. Marriage is usually described as the union of two individuals, but in reality it is the union of two entire family systems and the development of a new, third system.

- **Becoming parents and a family with children** is the third stage in the family life cycle. Entering this stage requires that adults now move up a generation and become caregivers to the younger generation. Moving through this lengthy stage successfully requires a commitment of time as a parent, understanding the roles of parents, and adapting to developmental changes in children. Problems that emerge when a couple first assumes the parental role are struggles with each other about taking responsibility, as well as refusal or inability to function as competent parents to children. We extensively discussed this stage of the family life cycle in chapters 7, 9, and 11.

- The **family with adolescents** represents the fourth stage of the family life cycle. Adolescence is a period of development in which individuals push for autonomy and seek to develop their own identity. The development of mature autonomy and identity is a lengthy process, transpiring over at least

Family Life-Cycle Stages	Emotional Process of Transition: Key Principles
1. Leaving home: single young adults	Accepting emotional and financial responsibility for self
2. The joining of families through marriage: the new couple	Commitment to new system
3. Becoming parents and families with children	Accepting new members into the system
4. The family with adolescents	Increasing flexibility of family boundaries to include children's independence and grandparents' frailties
5. The family at midlife	Accepting a multitude of exits and entries into the family system
6. The family in later life	Accepting the shifting of generational roles

FIGURE 15.4 The Family Life Cycle

10 to 15 years. Compliant children become noncompliant adolescents. Parents tend to adopt one of two strategies to handle noncompliance. They either clamp down and put more pressure on the adolescent to conform to parental values, or they become more permissive and let the adolescent have extensive freedom. Neither is a wise overall strategy. A more flexible, adaptive approach is best. We discussed the family with adolescents in chapter 13.

- The **family at midlife** is the fifth stage in the family life cycle. It is a time of launching children, playing an important role in linking generations, and adapting to midlife changes in development. Until about a generation ago, most families were involved in raising their children for much of their adult lives until old age. Because of the lower birth rate and longer life of most adults, parents now launch their children about 20 years before retirement, which frees many midlife parents to pursue other activities. We will discuss midlife families in greater detail in chapter 17.
- The **family in later life** is the sixth and final stage in the family life cycle. Retirement alters a couple's lifestyle, requiring adaptation. Grandparenting also characterizes many families in this stage. We will discuss the family in later life in chapter 20.

Some critics argue that the stage concept of the family life cycle is misleading. They argue that clearly defined stages often do not develop and the stages do not always occur in an orderly, sequential fashion (Elder, 1998). Further, they state that it is the variability associated with the stages which should be emphasized. For example, some women have children early (adolescence), or late (thirties, forties), some women have children outside of marriage, and some women have a career before parenthood or experience both simultaneously. Age and entry into these roles are increasingly independent. Further, many individuals have multiple families (such as children from a first marriage and children from a remarriage), and these may develop at different points in the life course.

Marriage

Our exploration of marriage focuses on some marital trends, expectations and myths about marriage, what makes marriages work, and the benefits of a good marriage.

Marital Trends   Until about 1930, stable marriage was widely accepted as the endpoint in adult development. Since then, however, personal fulfillment has emerged as a competing goal. More adults are remaining single longer today, but eventually they are likely to marry at least once and for a little while. However, approximately 50 percent of marriages end in divorce. Let's examine some further statistics on marriage:

- *The United States is still a marrying society.* In 2002, 95 percent of U.S. adults had eventually married at least once and for a little while by the time they were 55 years of age, although this figure is likely to decline in the future as more young adults today choose not to marry (U.S. Bureau of the Census, 2003). In 2002, almost 60 percent of all U.S. adults were currently married. By age 30, 65 percent of men and 71 percent of women have married.
- *Despite being a marrying society, marriages occur later, the percentage of adults married at any one point in time has declined, and divorce is commonplace.* On average, brides and grooms in the United States are older than they used to be. In 2002, the average age for a first marriage climbed to almost 27 years for men and just over 25 years for women, up from 26 years for men and 24 years for women in 1990, and 23 years for men and 21 years for women in 1970 (U.S. Bureau of the Census, 2004) (see figure 15.5). Further, the percentage of adults who are married at any one point when surveyed has steadily declined. And once married, approximately one-third of the couples become divorced before their tenth wedding anniversary. On average, a first marriage lasts for approximately eight years, a second marriage about seven years, before a divorce.

---

leaving home and becoming a single adult The first stage in the family life cycle. It involves launching.

launching The process in which youth move into adulthood and exit their family of origin.

new couple Forming the new couple is the second stage in the family life cycle. Two individuals from separate families of origin unite to form a new family system.

becoming parents and a family with children The third stage in the family life cycle. Adults who enter this stage move up a generation and become caregivers to the younger generation.

family with adolescents The fourth stage of the family life cycle, in which adolescent children push for autonomy and seek to develop their own identities.

family at midlife The fifth stage in the family life cycle, a time of launching children, linking generations, and adapting to midlife developmental changes.

family in later life The sixth and final stage in the family life cycle, involving retirement and, in many families, grandparenting.

What do young adults want from a marriage? In a recent national survey, young adults portrayed how they believe it is important for a marriage to be emotionally deep and communicative (Whitehead & Popenoe, 2001):

- A large majority (94 percent) of never-married singles said that when you marry, the most important consideration is that your spouse is your soul mate.
- Most young adults said that it is not a good strategy for a woman to rely on marriage for financial security.
- More than 80 percent of women reported that it is more important for them to have a husband who can communicate his deepest feelings than to have a husband who makes a good living.
- A high percentage (86 percent) indicated that marriage is hard work and a full-time job.

The sociocultural context is a powerful influence on marriage. The age at which individuals marry, expectations about what the marriage will be like, and the developmental course of the marriage vary not only across historical time within a given culture, but also across cultures. For example, a new marriage law took effect in China in 1981. The law sets a minimum age for marriage—22 years for males, 20 years for females. Late marriage and late childbirth are critical efforts in China's attempt to control population growth. More information about the nature of marriage in different cultures appears in the Diversity in Life-Span Development interlude.

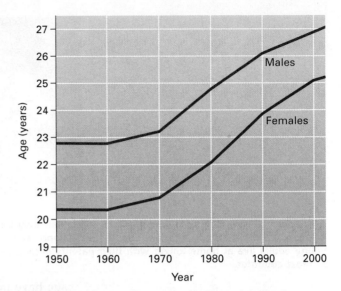

FIGURE 15.5 Increase in Age at First Marriage in the United States

Shown here are average ages at first marriage in the United States. Notice that since the 1960s, the age at which this important life event occurs has steadily increased.

Diversity in Life-Span Development
Marriage Around the World

The traits that people look for in a marriage partner vary around the world. In one large-scale study of 9,474 adults from 37 cultures on six continents and five islands, people varied the most on how much they valued chastity—desiring a marital partner with no previous experience in sexual intercourse (Buss & others, 1990). Chastity was the most important factor in marital selection in China, India, Indonesia, Iran, Taiwan, and the Palestinian Arab culture. Adults from Ireland and Japan placed moderate importance on chastity. In contrast, adults in Sweden, Finland, Norway, the Netherlands, and Germany generally said that chastity was not important in selecting a marital partner.

In this study, domesticity was also valued in some cultures and not in others. Adults from the Zulu culture in South Africa, Estonia, and Colombia placed a high value on housekeeping skills in their marital preference. By contrast, adults in the United States, Canada, and all Western European countries except Spain said that housekeeping was not an important trait in their partner.

Religion plays an important role in marital preferences in many cultures (Sherif-Trask, 2003). For example, Islam stresses the honor of the male and the purity of the female. It also emphasizes the woman's role in childbearing, child rearing, educating children, and instilling the Islamic faith in their children.

International comparisons of marriage also reveal that individuals in Scandinavian countries marry late, whereas their counterparts in Eastern Europe marry early (Blanchi & Spani, 1986). In Denmark, for example, almost 80 percent of the women and 90 percent of the men aged 20 to 24 have never been married. In Hungary less than 40 percent of the women and 70 percent of the men the same

(a)

(b)

(c)

(a) **In Scandinavian countries, cohabitation is popular; only a small percentage of 20- to 24-year-olds are married.** *(b)* **Islam stresses male honor and female purity.** *(c)* **Japanese young adults live at home longer with their parents before marrying than young adults in most countries.**

age have never been married. In Scandinavian countries, cohabitation is popular among young adults; however, most Scandinavians eventually marry. Only 5 percent of the women and 11 percent of the men in their early forties have never been married. Some countries such as Hungary encourage early marriage and childbearing to offset current and future population losses. Like Scandinavian countries, Japan has a high proportion of unmarried young people. However, rather than cohabitating as the Scandinavians do, unmarried Japanese young adults live at home longer with their parents before marrying.

Marital Expectations and Myths Among the explanations of our nation's high divorce rate and high degree of dissatisfaction in many marriages is that we have such strong expectations of marriage. We expect our spouse to simultaneously be a lover, a friend, a confidant, a counselor, a career person, and a parent, for example. In one study, unhappily married couples expressed unrealistic expectations about marriage (Epstein & Eidelson, 1981).

Marriage therapists believe it is important to have realistic expectations about a marriage (Sharp & Ganong, 2000). Researchers have found that unrealistic expectations are linked with lower levels of marital satisfaction (Larson & Holman, 1994). Similarly, individuals who have highly romantic beliefs about marriage are likely to encounter disappointment as they realize that sustaining their romantic ideal is not possible (Huston, Neihuis, & Smith, 1997).

Underlying unrealistic expectations about marriage are numerous myths about marriage (Flanagan & others, 2001; Markman, 2000). A myth is a widely held belief unsupported by facts. To study college students' beliefs in the myths of marriage, Jeffry Larson (1988) constructed a marriage quiz to measure college students' information about marriage and compared their responses with what is known about marriage in the research literature. The college students responded incorrectly to almost half of the items. Female students missed fewer items than male students, and students with a less romantic perception of marriage missed fewer items than more romantically inclined students.

What are some of the myths about marriage? They include these (Gottman & Silver, 1999):

- *Avoiding conflict will ruin your marriage.* Couples have different styles of conflict. Some avoid fights at all costs, some fight a lot, and some choose to "talk out" their differences and find solutions to problems without ever raising their voices. As long as the style works for both partners, no one style is necessarily better than the others. Couples can get into trouble if one partner wants to talk out a conflict while the other just wants to watch a favorite TV show that night.

W hen two people are under the influence of the most violent, most insane, most delusive, and most transient of passions, they are required to swear that they will remain in that excited, abnormal, and exhausting condition continuously until death do them part.

—George Bernard Shaw
Irish Playwright, 20th Century

- *Affairs are the main cause of divorce.* In most instances, it is the other way around. Marital problems send the couple on a downward trajectory, and one or both partners seek an intimate relationship outside of the marriage. In many instances, these affairs are not about sex but rather are about seeking to find friendship, support, understanding, respect, and caring.
- *Men are not biologically made for marriage.* This myth holds that men are philanderers by nature and thus ill-suited for monogamy. This is sometimes called "the law of the jungle": The male of the species seeks to create as many offspring as possible and his allegiance to one mate restricts him from attaining this goal. Also involved is the view that the female's main task is to tend to her young, so she seeks a single mate who will provide for her and her children. However, as more women have sought employment outside the home, the rate at which women have extramarital affairs has increased dramatically; women's rate of extramarital affairs now slightly exceeds that of men.
- *Men and women are from different planets.* According to a best-selling book by John Gray (1992), men and women have serious relationship problems because he is from Mars and she is from Venus. Gender differences can contribute to marital problems, but they usually don't cause them. For example, the key factor in whether wives or husbands feel satisfied with the sex, romance, and passion in their marriage is the quality of the couple's friendship.

Marriage Support
Journal of Family Psychology

What Makes Marriages Work   John Gottman (1994; Gottman & Notarius, 2000; Gottman & Silver, 1999; Gottman & others, 1998) has been studying married couples' lives since the early 1970s. He uses extensive methods to study what makes marriages work. Gottman interviews couples about the history of their marriage, their philosophy about marriage, and how they view their parents' marriages. He videotapes them talking to each other about how their day went and evaluates what they say about the good and bad times of their marriages. Gottman also uses physiological measures to measure their heart rate, blood flow, blood pressure, and immune functioning moment by moment. He also checks back in with the couples every year to see how their marriage is faring. Gottman's research represents the most extensive assessment of marital relationships available. Currently he and his colleagues are following 700 couples in seven different studies.

In his research, Gottman has found that seven main principles determine whether a marriage will work or not:

- *Establishing love maps.* Individuals in successful marriages have personal insights and detailed maps of each other's life and world. They aren't psychological strangers. In good marriages, partners are willing to share their feelings with each other. They use these "love maps" to express not only their understanding of each other but also their fondness and admiration.
- *Nurturing fondness and admiration.* In successful marriages, partners sing each other's praises. More than 90 percent of the time, when couples put a positive spin on their marriage's history, the marriage is likely to have a positive future.
- *Turning toward each other instead of away.* In good marriages, spouses are adept at turning toward each other regularly. They see each other as friends and this friendship acts as a powerful shield against conflict. The friendship doesn't keep arguments from occurring, but it can prevent differences of opinion from overwhelming a relationship. In these good marriages, spouses respect each other and appreciate each other's point of view even though they might not agree with it.
- *Letting your partner influence you.* Bad marriages often involve one spouse who is unwilling to share power with the other. Although power-mongering is more common in husbands, some wives also show this problem. A willingness to share power and to respect the other person's view is a prerequisite to compromising.

*U*nlike most approaches to helping couples, mine is based on knowing what makes marriages succeed rather than fail.

—**JOHN GOTTMAN**
Contemporary Psychologist,
University of Washington

What makes marriages work? What are the benefits of having a good marriage?

• *Solving solvable conflicts.* Gottman has found two types of problems that occur in marriage: (1) perpetual and (2) solvable. Perpetual problems include spouses differing on whether to have children and one spouse wanting sex far more frequently than the other. Solvable problems include not helping each other reduce daily stresses and not being verbally affectionate. Unfortunately, more than two-thirds of marital problems fall into the perpetual category—those that won't go away. Fortunately, marital therapists have found that couples often don't have to solve their perpetual problems for the marriage to work. In his research, Gottman has found that resolving conflicts works best when couples start out solving the problem with a soft rather than a harsh approach, make an effort to make and receive repair attempts, regulate their emotions, compromise, and are tolerant of each other's faults. Conflict resolution is not about one person making changes, it is about negotiating and accommodating each other.

Work, stress, in-laws, money, sex, housework, a new baby: These are among the typical areas of marital conflict. Even in happy marriages, these areas are often hot buttons in a relationship. When there is conflict in these areas, it usually means that a husband and wife have different ideas about the tasks involved, their importance, or how they should be accomplished. If the conflict is perpetual, no amount of problem-solving expertise will fix it. The tension will decrease only when both partners feel comfortable living with the ongoing difference. However, when the issue is solvable, the challenge is to find the right strategy for dealing with it. Strategies include:

• Scheduling formal griping sessions about stressful issues
• Learning to talk about sex in a way that both partners feel comfortable with
• Creating lists of who does what to see how household labor is divided up

• *Overcoming gridlock.* One partner wants the other to attend church, the other is an atheist. One partner is a homebody, the other wants to go out and socialize a lot. Such problems often produce gridlock. Gottman believes the key to ending gridlock is not to solve the problem, but to move from gridlock to dialogue and be patient.

• *Creating shared meaning.* The more partners can speak candidly and respectfully with each other, the more likely it is that they will create shared meaning in their marriage. This also includes sharing goals with one's spouse and working together to achieve each other's goals.

The Benefits of a Good Marriage   Now that you know what makes a marriage work, are there any benefits to having a good marriage? There are. An unhappy marriage increases an individual's risk of getting sick by approximately one-third and can even shorten a person's life by an average of four years (Gove, Style, & Hughes, 1990). On the other hand, individuals who are happily married live longer, healthier lives than divorced individuals or those who are unhappily married (Cotten, 1999). One recent study of 493 women 42 to 50 years of age found that women in happy marriages had lower levels of biological and cardiovascular risk factors—such as blood pressure, cholesterol levels, and body mass index—and lower levels of depression, anxiety, and anger than did women in unhappy marriages (Gallo & others, 2003).

What are the reasons for these benefits of a happy marriage? People in happy marriages likely feel less physically and emotionally stressed, which puts less wear and tear on a person's body. Such wear and tear can lead to numerous physical ailments, such as high blood pressure and heart disease, as well as psychological problems such as anxiety, depression, and substance abuse. Further, marriage may offer a health advantage by providing social support and protecting against the risks associated with social isolation.

Gender and Emotion in Marriage Wives consistently disclose more to their partners than husbands do (Hendrick, 2001). And women tend to express more tenderness, fear, and sadness than their partners. A common complaint expressed by women in a marriage is that their husbands do not care about their emotional lives and do not express their own feelings and thoughts. Women often point out that they have to literally pull things out of their husbands and push them to open up. Men frequently respond either that they are open or that they do not understand what their wives want from them. It is not unusual for men to protest that no matter how much they talk it is not enough for their wives. Women also say they want more warmth as well as openness from their husbands. For example, women are more likely than men to give their partners a spontaneous kiss or hug when something positive happens. Overall, women are more expressive and affectionate than men in marriage, and this difference bothers many women (Fox & Murry, 2000; Streil, 2001).

Parental Roles

For many adults, parental roles are well planned and coordinated with other roles in life and developed with the individual's economic situation in mind. For others, the discovery that they are about to become parents is a startling surprise. In either event, the prospective parents may have mixed emotions and romantic illusions about having a child. Parenting consists of a number of interpersonal skills and emotional demands, yet there is little in the way of formal education for this task. Most parents learn parenting practices from their own parents—some they accept, some they discard. Husbands and wives may bring different viewpoints of parenting practices to the marriage (Huston & Holmes, 2004). Unfortunately, when methods of parents are passed on from one generation to the next, both desirable and undesirable practices are perpetuated.

The needs and expectations of parents have stimulated many myths about parenting:

- The birth of a child will save a failing marriage.
- As a possession or extension of the parent, the child will think, feel, and behave like the parents did in their childhood.
- Children will take care of parents in their old age.
- Having a child gives the parents a "second chance" to achieve what they should have achieved.
- If parents learn the right techniques, they can mold their children into what they want.
- It's the parents' fault when children fail.
- Mothers are naturally better parents than fathers.
- Parenting is an instinct and requires no training.

In earlier times, women considered motherhood a full-time occupation. Currently, women have fewer children, and, as birth control has become common practice, many individuals consciously choose when they will have children and how many children they will rear. The number of one-child families is increasing, for example. By giving birth to fewer children and reducing the demands of child care, women free up a significant portion of their life spans for other endeavors. As women's childbearing trends change, so do other factors: (1) as working women increase in number, they invest less actual time in the child's development; (2) men are apt to invest a greater amount of time in fathering; and (3) parental care in the home is often supplemented by institutional care (child care, for example).

As more women show an increased interest in developing a career, they are not only marrying later, but also having children later (Azar, 2003; Grolnick & Gurland, 2001). What are some of the advantages of having children early or late? Some of the advantages of having children early (in the twenties) are that the parents are likely to have more physical energy (for example, they can cope better with such matters as getting up in the middle of the night with infants and waiting up until adolescents

> *We never know the love of our parents until we have become parents.*
> —HENRY WARD BEECHER
> *American Clergyman, 19th Century*

Careers in Life-Span Development

Janis Keyser, Parent Educator

Janis Keyser is a parent educator and teaches in the Department of Early Childhood Education at Cabrillo College in California. In addition to teaching college classes and conducting parenting workshops, she also has coauthored a book with Laura Davis (1997), *Becoming the Parent You Want to Be: A Source-Book of Strategies for the First Five Years.*

Janis also writes as an expert on the iVillage website (www.parentsplace.com). And she also co-authors a nationally syndicated parenting column, "Growing Up, Growing Together." She is the mother of three, stepmother of five, grandmother of twelve, and great grandmother of six.

Janis Keyser *(right),* conducting a parenting workshop.

come home at night); the mother is likely to have fewer medical problems with pregnancy and childbirth; and the parents may be less likely to build up expectations for their children, as do many couples who have waited many years to have children. By contrast, there are also advantages to having children later (in the thirties): The parents will have had more time to consider their goals in life, such as what they want from their family and career roles; the parents will be more mature and will be able to benefit from their life experiences to engage in more competent parenting; and the parents will be better established in their careers and have more income for child-rearing expenses.

Parent educators seek to help individuals to become better parents. To read about the work of one parent educator, see the Careers in Life-Span Development insert.

A special concern that has recently surfaced involves many successful women feeling anxiety about being childless. A recent book, *Creating a Life: Professional Women and the Quest for Children* (Hewlett, 2002), described the results of interviews with 1,186 high-achieving career women (income in the top 10 percent of their age group) from 28 to 55 years of age. Among the findings were:

- Thirty-three percent were childless at age 40.
- Forty-two percent who worked in corporations were childless.
- Forty-nine percent of "ultraachievers" (earning more than $100,000 a year) were childless.
- Twenty-five percent of childless high achievers from 41 to 55 years of age would still like to have a child and 31 percent of "ultraachievers" would still like to have one.
- No high achiever from 41 to 55 years of age had a first child after age 39 and no "ultraachiever" had one after age 36.

Many of the study's childless women in their forties and fifties recommended that younger women spend more time envisioning what their life will be like when they become middle-aged and whether they want their life to include a child. They argue that many high-achieving women will ultimately be happier if they have a child in their twenties or thirties. Critics argue that the optimal age for motherhood depends on the individual and that many women become mothers after they are 35 years of age.

Review and Reflect: Learning Goal 3

3 Discuss marriage and the family

REVIEW

- What are the six stages of the family life cycle?
- What characterizes marriage and marital relationships?
- What are some parental roles?

REFLECT

- Are there more pressures on marriage today than in the past? Explain.

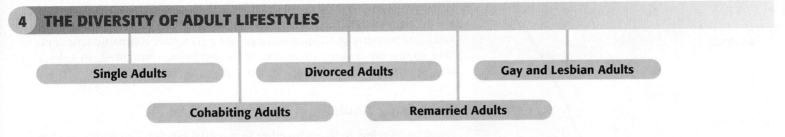

4 THE DIVERSITY OF ADULT LIFESTYLES

- Single Adults
- Divorced Adults
- Gay and Lesbian Adults
- Cohabiting Adults
- Remarried Adults

Today's adult lifestyles are diverse. We have single-career families; dual-career families; single-parent families, including mother custody, father custody, and joint custody; the remarried or stepfamily; the kin family (made up of bilateral or intergenerationally linked members); and even the experimental family (individuals in multiadult households—communes—or cohabiting adults). And, of course, there are many single adults.

Single Adults

There is no rehearsal. One day you don't live alone, the next day you do. College ends. Your wife walks out. Your husband dies. Suddenly, you live in this increasingly modern condition, living alone. Maybe you like it, maybe you don't. Maybe you thrive on the solitude, maybe you ache as if in exile. Either way, chances are you are only half prepared, if at all, to be sole proprietor of your bed, your toaster, and your time. Most of us were raised in the din and clutter of family life, jockeying for a place in the bathroom in the morning, fighting over the last piece of cake, and obliged to compromise on the simplest of choices—the volume of the stereo, the channel on the TV, for example. Few of us grew up thinking that home would be a way station in our life course.

There has been a dramatic rise in the percentage of single adults, who now number 86 million in the United States; homes headed by singles (either living alone or with dependents) make up almost 50 percent of U.S. households. Figure 15.6 shows the increase in the percentage of single adults in the age period of the early thirties.

A history of myths and stereotypes is associated with being single, ranging from the "swinging single" to the "desperately lonely, suicidal single." Of course, most single adults are somewhere between these extremes.

What are some of the advantages of being single? They include time to make decisions about one's life course, time to develop personal resources to meet goals, freedom to make autonomous decisions and pursue one's own schedule and interests, opportunity to explore new places and try out new things, and availability of privacy.

Many single adults cite personal freedom as one of the major advantages of being a single adult. One woman who never married commented, "I enjoy knowing that I can satisfy my own whims without someone else's interferences. If I want to wash my hair at two o'clock in the morning, no one complains. I can eat when I'm hungry and watch my favorite television shows without contradictions from anyone. I enjoy these freedoms. I would feel very confined if I had to adjust to another person's schedule." Common problems of single adults focus on intimate relationships with other adults, confronting loneliness, and finding a niche in a marriage-oriented society.

Some adults never marry. Initially, they are perceived as living glamorous, exciting lives, but once they reach the age of 30, singles can feel pressure to settle down and get married. If a woman wants to bear children, she might feel a sense of urgency when she reaches 30. This is when many single adults make a conscious decision either to marry or to remain single. As one 30-year-old male recently commented, "It's real. You are supposed to get married by 30—that is a standard. It is part of getting on with your life that you are supposed to do. You have career and who-am-I concerns in your twenties. In your thirties, you have to get on with

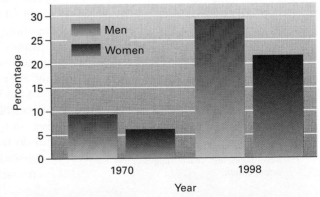

FIGURE 15.6 Percentage of Single Adults 30 to 34 Years of Age in 1970 and 1998

In less than three decades, the percentage of single adults 30 to 34 years of age more than tripled.

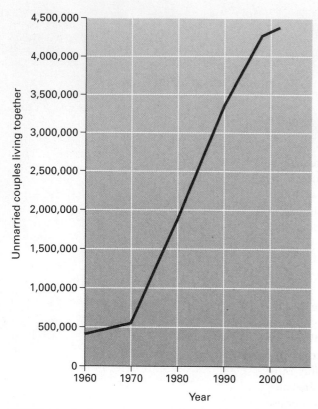

FIGURE 15.7 The Increase in Cohabitation in the United States

Since 1970, there has been a dramatic increase in the number of unmarried adults living together in the United States.

Look at the video "Choosing Not to Cohabitate" and consider the motives, advantages, and disadvantages of this living arrangement.

it, keep on track, make headway, financially and family-wise." But, to another 30-year-old, getting married is less important than buying a house and some property. A training manager for a computer company, Jane says, "I'm competent in forming relationships and being committed, so I don't feel a big rush to get married. When it happens, it happens."

Cohabiting Adults

Cohabitation refers to living together in a sexual relationship without being married. Cohabitation has undergone considerable changes in recent years (Jamieson & others, 2003; Means & others, 2003; Oppenheimer, 2003; Seltzer, 2004) (see figure 15.7). The percentage of U.S. couples who cohabit before marriage has increased from approximately 11 percent in 1970 to almost 60 percent at the beginning of the twenty-first century (Bumpass & Lu, 2000). Cohabiting rates are even higher in some countries—in Sweden, cohabitation before marriage is virtually universal. In the United States, cohabiting arrangements tend to be short-lived, with one-third lasting less than a year (Hyde & DeLamater, 2005). Less than 1 out of 10 lasts five years. Of course, it is easier to dissolve a cohabitation relationship than to divorce. A number of couples view their cohabitation not as a precursor to marriage but as an ongoing lifestyle. These couples do not want the official aspects of marriage.

Do cohabiting relationships differ from marriage in other ways? Relationships between cohabiting men and women tend to be more equal than those between husbands and wives (Wineberg, 1994).

Although cohabitation offers some advantages, it also can produce some problems (Seltzer, 2004; Solot & Miller, 2002). Disapproval by parents and other family members can place emotional strain on the cohabiting couple. Some cohabiting couples have difficulty owning property jointly. Legal rights on the dissolution of the relationship are less certain than in a divorce.

Does cohabiting help or harm the chances that a couple will have a stable and happy marriage? Some researchers have found no differences in marital quality between individuals who earlier cohabited and those who did not (Watson & DeMeo, 1987). Other researchers have found lower rates of marital satisfaction in couples who lived together before getting married (Whitehead & Popenoe, 2003). For example, in one study of 13,000 individuals, married couples who cohabited prior to their marriage reported lower levels of happiness with and commitment to their marital relationship than their counterparts who had not previously cohabited (Nock, 1995). And in a recent study, after 10 years of marriage, 40 percent of couples who lived together before marriage had divorced, whereas 31 percent of those who had not cohabited first had divorced (Centers for Disease Control and Prevention, 2002). A longitudinal study found that the timing of cohabitation is a key factor in marital outcomes (Kline & others, 2004). Couples who cohabitated before they became engaged were at greater risk for poor marital outcomes than those who cohabited only after becoming engaged.

What might explain the finding that cohabiting is linked with divorce more than not cohabiting? Researchers have found that couples who cohabit before marrying have more negative interaction patterns prior to marriage than their counterparts who do not cohabit (Kline & others, 2004). Also, the more nontraditional lifestyle of cohabitation may attract less conventional individuals who are not great believers in marriage in the first place (Manning & Smock, 2002).

Divorced Adults

Divorce has become epidemic in our culture. The number of divorced adults rose from 2 percent of the adult population in 1950 to 3 percent in 1970 to 10 percent in 2002. Figure 15.8 shows the percentage of divorced men and women in the United States in 1950 and 2002 (U.S. Bureau of the Census, 2003). The divorce rate was increasing annually by 10 percent, but has been declining since the 1980s. While divorce has increased for all socioeconomic groups, those in disadvantaged groups have a higher incidence of divorce. Youthful marriage, low educational level, and low income are associated with increases in divorce. So too is premarital pregnancy. One study revealed that half of the women who were pregnant before marriage did not live with the husband for more than five years (Sauber & Corrigan, 1970).

If a divorce is going to occur, it usually takes place early in a marriage, peaking in the fifth to tenth years of marriage (National Center for Health Statistics, 2000) (see figure 15.9). Some partners in a troubled marriage might stay in it and try to work things out. If after several years these efforts don't improve the relationship, they might seek a divorce.

Many adults, even those who initiated the divorce, experience changes and challenges in their lives following marital dissolution (Amato, 2000, 2004; Hetherington, 2000; Martin, Emery, & Peris, 2004). Both divorced women and divorced men complain of loneliness, diminished self-esteem, anxiety about the unknowns in their lives, and difficulty in forming satisfactory new intimate relationships.

The stress of separation and divorce places both men and women at risk for psychological and physical difficulties (Hetherington & Stanley-Hagan, 2002; Kitzman & Gaylord, 2002). Separated and divorced women and men have higher rates of psychiatric disorders, admission to psychiatric hospitals, clinical depression, alcoholism, and psychosomatic problems, such as sleep disorders, than do married adults. There is increasing evidence that stressful events of many types—including marital separation—reduce the immune system's capabilities, rendering separated and divorced individuals vulnerable to disease and infection. In one study, the most recently separated women (one year or less) were more likely to show impaired immunological functioning than women whose separations had occurred several years earlier (one to six years) (Kiecolt-Glaser & Glaser, 1988). Also in this study, unhappily married individuals had immune systems that were not functioning as effectively as those of happily married individuals.

Custodial parents have concerns about child rearing and overload in their lives. Noncustodial parents register complaints about alienation from, or lack of time with, their children. Men show only modest declines in income following a divorce but women reveal a significant decline in income following a divorce, with estimates of the decline ranging from 20 to 35 percent. For divorced women, the financial decline means living in a less desirable neighborhood with fewer resources, less effective schools, and more deviant peer groups for their children. Nonetheless, the economic decline for women following a divorce has diminished as increasing numbers of women have a better education and job.

Psychologically, one of the most common characteristics of divorced adults is the difficulty they have in trusting someone else in a romantic relationship. Following a divorce, though, people's lives can take diverse turns. In E. Mavis Hetherington's research, men and women took six common pathways out of divorce (Hetherington and Kelly, 2002, pp. 98–108):

- *The enhancers.* Accounting for 20 percent of the divorced group, most were females who "grew more competent, well adjusted, and self-fulfilled" following their divorce. They were competent in multiple areas of life, showed a remarkable ability to bounce back from stressful circumstances, and created something meaningful out of the problems.
- *The good enoughs.* The largest group of divorced individuals, they were described as average people coping with divorce. They

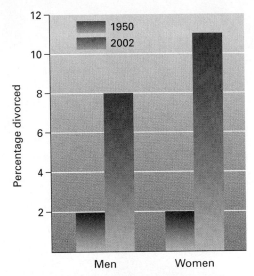

FIGURE 15.8 Percentage of Divorced U.S. Men and Women: 1950 and 2002

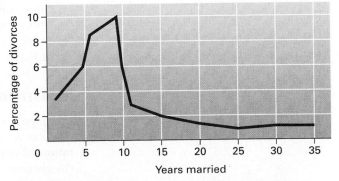

FIGURE 15.9 The Divorce Rate in Relation to Number of Years Married

Shown here is the percentage of divorces as a function of how long couples have been married. Notice that most divorces occur in the early years of marriage, peaking in the fifth to tenth years of marriage.

Psychological Aspects of Divorce
Divorced and Remarried Parents
Remarried Adults' Resources
Stepfamily Interventions

showed some strengths and some weaknesses, some successes and some failures. When they experienced a problem, they tried to solve it. Many attended night classes, found new friends, developed active social lives, and were motivated to get higher-paying jobs. However, they were not as good at planning and were less persistent than the enhancers. Good enough women typically married men who educationally and economically were similar to their first husbands, often going into a new marriage that was not much of an improvement over the first one.

- *The seekers.* These individuals were motivated to find new mates as soon as possible. "At one year postdivorce, 40 percent of the men and 38 percent of women had been classified as seekers. But as people found new partners or remarried, or became more secure or satisfied in their single life, this category shrunk and came to be predominated by men" (p. 102).
- *The libertines.* They often spent more time in singles bars and had more casual sex than their counterparts in the other divorce categories. However, by the end of the first year postdivorce, they often grew disillusioned with their sensation-seeking lifestyle and wanted a stable relationship.
- *The competent loners.* These individuals, which made up only about 10 percent of the divorced group, were "well adjusted, self-sufficient, and socially skilled." They had a successful career, an active social life, and a wide range of interests. However, "unlike enhancers, competent loners had little interest in sharing their lives with anyone" (p. 105).
- *The defeated.* Some of these individuals had problems prior to their divorce, and these problems increased after the divorce when "the added stress of a failed marriage was more than they could handle. Others had difficulty coping because divorce cost them a spouse who had supported them, or in the case of a drinking problem, restricted them" (p. 106).

Hetherington recommends these strategies for divorced adults (Hetherington & Kelly, 2002):

- Think of divorce as a chance to grow personally and to develop more positive relationships.
- Make decisions carefully. The consequences of your decision making regarding work, lovers, and children may last a lifetime.
- Focus more on the future than the past. Think about what is most important to you going forward in your life, set some challenging goals, and plan how to reach them.
- Use your strengths and resources to cope with difficulties.
- Don't expect to be successful and happy in everything you do. "The road to a more satisfying life is bumpy and it will have many detours" (p. 109).
- Remember that "you are never trapped by one pathway. Most of those who were categorized as defeated immediately after divorce gradually moved on to a better life, but moving onward usually requires some effort" (p. 109).

Remarried Adults

In chapter 11, we discussed stepfamilies with a special emphasis on the effects of living in a stepfamily on children's development. Here we will continue our exploration of stepfamilies with a stronger focus on the relationships of remarried adults. On average, divorced adults remarry within four years after their divorce, with men doing this sooner than women.

Stepfamilies come in many sizes and forms. The custodial and noncustodial parents and stepparent all might have been married and divorced, in some cases more than once. These parents might have residential children from prior marriages and a large network of grandparents and other relatives. Regardless of their form and size, the newly reconstituted families face some unique tasks. The couple must define and strengthen their marriage and at the same time renegotiate the biological parent-child relationships and establish stepparent-stepchild and stepsibling relationships (Coleman, Ganong, & Fine, 2000, 2004; Hetherington & Stanley-Hagan, 2002).

The complex histories and multiple relationships make adjustment difficult in a stepfamily (Coleman, Ganong, & Weaver, 2001; Pasley & Moorefield, 2004; Thomson & others, 2001). The difficulty of adjusting to life in a stepfamily is borne out by the data—only one-third of stepfamily couples stay remarried (Gerlach, 1998).

Why do remarried adults find it so difficult to stay remarried? For one thing, many remarry not for love but for financial reasons, for help in rearing children, and to reduce loneliness. They also might carry into the stepfamily negative relationship patterns that resulted in the failure of an earlier marriage. Remarried couples also experience more stress in rearing children than parents in never-divorced families (Ganong & Coleman, 1994).

Among the strategies that help remarried couples cope with the stress of living in a stepfamily are these (Visher & Visher, 1989):

- *Have realistic expectations.* Allow time for loving relationships to develop, and look at the complexity of the stepfamily as a challenge to overcome.
- *Develop new positive relationships within the family.* Create new traditions and ways of dealing with difficult circumstances that work. Allocation of time is especially important with all of the people involved. In this regard, the remarried couple needs to allot time alone for each other.
- *Learn from the first marriage.* Face your own shortcomings and don't make the same mistakes the second time around.
- *Don't expect instant love from stepchildren.* Relationships in stepfamilies are built over time.

Gay and Lesbian Adults

Researchers have found that gay and lesbian relationships are similar to heterosexual relationships in their satisfactions, loves, joys, and conflicts (Hyde & DeLamater, 2005; Julian & others, 2003; Peplau & Beals, 2002, 2004). For example, like heterosexual couples, gay and lesbian couples need to find a balance in their relationships that is acceptable to both partners in terms of romantic love, affection, how much autonomy is acceptable, and how equal the relationship will be. Lesbian couples especially place a high priority on equality in their relationships (Kurdek, 2003, 2004). In one study, gay and lesbian couples listed the areas of conflict in order of frequency: finances, driving style, affection and sex, being overly critical, and household tasks (Kurdek, 1995). The components of this list are likely to be familiar to heterosexual couples as well.

There are a number of misconceptions about gay and lesbian couples (Kurdek, 2004). For example, many people think that one partner is masculine and the other feminine in these relationships. This appears to be true only in a small percentage of cases. Indeed, some researchers have found that gay and lesbian couples are more flexible in their gender roles than heterosexual individuals are (Marecek, Finn, & Cardell, 1988). Another misconception is that gay and lesbian couples have a huge amount of sex. Again, this is true only of a small segment of the gay male population, and it is uncommon among lesbians. Yet another misconception about gay and lesbian couples is that they don't get involved in long-term relationships. Researchers have found that gay and lesbian couples prefer long-term, committed relationships (Peplau & Beals, 2002). About half of committed gay male couples do have an open relationship that allows the possibility of sex (but not affectionate love) outside of the relationship. Lesbian couples usually do not have this open relationship.

One aspect of relationships in which heterosexual and same-sex couples differ involves the obstacles that make it difficult to end a relationship (Peplau &

www.mhhe.com/santrockld10

Gay and Lesbian Relationships

What are the research findings regarding the development and psychological well-being of children raised by gay and lesbian couples?

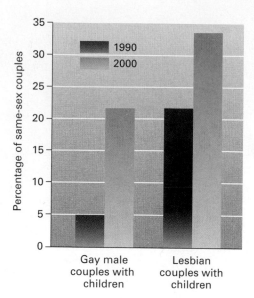

FIGURE 15.10 Percentage of Gay Male and Lesbian Couples with Children: 1990 and 2000

Beals, 2002, 2004). In this regard, the legal and social context of marriage creates barriers to breaking up that do not usually exist for same-sex partners (Peplau & Beals, 2002, 2004). However, this situation is changing in some states; for example, Vermont allows same-sex civil unions. Massachusetts recently legalized same-sex marriage and many other states, municipalities, and corporations, allow domestic partnership registration, which provides some of the benefits (and obstacles to separation) of marriage (Patterson, 2004). Increasingly, gay and lesbian couples are creating families that include children (see figure 15.10). This is controversial to many heterosexual individuals who view a gay or lesbian family as damaging to the development of a child. However, researchers have found that children growing up in gay or lesbian families are just as popular with their peers, and there are no differences in the adjustment and mental health of children living in these families when they are compared with children in heterosexual families (Hyde & DeLamater, 2005). Also, as we indicated in chapter 9, the overwhelming majority of children growing up in a gay or lesbian family have a heterosexual orientation (Patterson, 2002).

Review and Reflect: Learning Goal 4

4 Explain the diversity of lifestyles

REVIEW

- What characterizes single adults?
- What are the lives of cohabiting adults like?
- How does divorce affect adults?
- What are the lives of remarried parents like?
- What characterizes the lifestyles of gay and lesbian adults?

REFLECT

- Which type of lifestyle are you living today? What do you think are the advantages and disadvantages of this lifestyle for you? If you could have a different lifestyle, which one would it be? Why?

5 GENDER, RELATIONSHIPS, AND SELF-DEVELOPMENT

Women's Development   **Men's Development**

Gender and Communication
Women's Issues
Gender and Society

In chapters 9 and 11, we discussed a number of ideas about gender development in children. Also, earlier in this chapter we explored gender in friendship, gender and family, work, and the mother's and the father's roles. Here we will further examine gender by focusing on some issues involving relationships and self-development.

Women's Development

Jean Baker Miller (1986) has been an important voice in stimulating the examination of psychological issues from a female perspective. She argues that the study of women's psychological development opens up paths to a better understanding of all psychological development, male or female. She also concludes that when researchers examine what women have been doing in life, a large part of it is active participation in the development of others. In Miller's view, women often try to interact with others in ways that will foster the other person's development along many dimensions—emotionally, intellectually, and socially.

Most experts believe it is important for women to not only maintain their competency in relationships but to be self-motivated, too (Bannon, 2005; Denmark, Rabinowitz, & Sechzer, 2005; Donelson, 1998). Miller stresses that through increased self-determination, coupled with already developed relationship skills, many women will gain greater power in the American culture. And as Harriet Lerner (1989) concludes in her book *The Dance of Intimacy,* it is important for women to bring to their relationships nothing less than a strong, assertive, independent, and authentic self. She emphasizes that competent relationships are those in which the separate "I-ness" of both persons can be appreciated and enhanced while still staying emotionally connected to each other.

Deborah Tannen (1990) analyzed the talk of women and men. She reported that a common complaint that wives have about their husbands is, "He doesn't listen to me anymore." Another is, "He doesn't talk to me anymore." Lack of communication, while high on women's lists of reasons for divorce, is much less often mentioned by men.

Tannen distinguishes between rapport talk and report talk. *Rapport talk* is the language of conversation and a way of establishing connections and negotiating relationships. *Report talk* is public speaking, which men feel more comfortable doing. Men hold center stage through such verbal performances as storytelling, joking, or imparting information. Men learn to use talking as a way of getting and keeping attention. By contrast, women enjoy private speaking more, talk that involves discussing similarities and matching experiences. It is men's lack of interest in rapport talk that bothers many women.

Women's dissatisfaction with men's silence at home is captured in a typical cartoon depicting a husband and wife sitting at a breakfast table; he's reading the newspaper; she's glaring at the back of the newspaper. Another cartoon shows a husband opening a newspaper and asking his wife, "Is there anything you want to say to me before I begin reading the newspaper?" He knows there isn't, but that as soon as he starts reading the paper, she will think of something. *To him, talk is for information.* So when his wife interrupts his reading, it must be to inform him of something he needs to know. So, since this is the case, she might as well tell him what she thinks he needs to know before he starts reading. *But for her, talk is for interaction.* She believes saying things is a way to show involvement; listening is a way to show caring and interest.

The problem, then, may not be an individual man, or even men's styles alone, but the difference between women's and men's styles. If so, both men and women can make adjustments. A woman can push herself to speak up without being invited, or begin to speak even at the slightest pause in talk. The adjustment should not be just one-sided. Men can learn that women who are not accustomed to speaking up in groups are not as free as they are to do so. By understanding this reluctance on the part of women, men can make them feel more comfortable by warmly encouraging and allowing them to speak rather than hogging public talk.

Critics of Tannen's view on gender differences in women's and men's relationships point out that they are too stereotypical (Edwards & Hamilton, 2004; Hyde & DeLamater, 2005). They argue that greater individual variation in women's and men's relationship styles exist than Tannen acknowledges. Further, some researchers have found similarities in males' and females' relationship communication strategies. In one recent study, in their talk men and women described and responded to relationship problems in ways that were more similar than different (MacGeorge & others, 2004).

"You have no idea how nice it is to have someone to talk to."

Understanding the other's ways of talking is a giant leap across the communication gap between women and men, and a giant step toward opening lines of communication.

—**DEBORAH TANNEN**
Contemporary Sociologist, Georgetown University

How might men be able to reconstruct their masculinity in positive ways?

The Men's Bibliography
Psychological Study of
Men and Masculinity
Male Issues

Men's Development

The male of the species—what is he really like? What are his concerns? According to Joseph Pleck's (1995) *role-strain* view, male roles are contradictory and inconsistent. Men not only experience stress when they violate men's roles, they also are harmed when they *do* act in accord with men's roles. Here are some of the areas where men's roles can cause considerable strain (Levant, 2002; Levant & Brooks, 1997):

- *Health.* Men live 8 to 10 years less than women do. They have higher rates of stress-related disorders, alcoholism, car accidents, and suicide. Men are more likely than women to be the victims of homicide. In sum, the male role is hazardous to men's health.
- *Male-female relationships.* Too often, the male's role involves images that men should be dominant, powerful, and aggressive and should control women. Also, the male role has involved looking at women in terms of their bodies rather than their minds and feelings. Earlier, we described Deborah Tannen's (1990) concept that men show too little interest in rapport talk and relationships. And the male role has included the view that women should not be considered equal to men in work, earnings, and many other aspects of life. Too often these dimensions of the male role have produced men who have disparaged women, been violent toward women, and been unwilling to have equal relationships with women.
- *Male-male relationships.* Too many men have had too little interaction with their fathers, especially fathers who are positive role models. Nurturing and being sensitive to others have been considered aspects of the female role, not the male role. And the male role emphasizes competition rather than cooperation. All of these aspects of the male role have left men with inadequate positive, emotional connections with other males.

To reconstruct their masculinity in more positive ways, Ron Levant (2002) suggests that every man should (1) reexamine his beliefs about manhood, (2) separate out the valuable aspects of the male role, and (3) get rid of those parts of the masculine role that are destructive. All of this involves becoming more "emotionally intelligent"—that is, becoming more emotionally self-aware, managing emotions more effectively, reading emotions better (one's own emotions and others'), and being motivated to improve close relationships.

Review and Reflect: Learning Goal 5

5 **Characterize the role of gender in relationships**

REVIEW

- What are some important aspects of the woman's role in relationships?
- What are some important aspects of the man's role in relationships?

REFLECT

- If you are female, what would you change about the way men function in relationships? If you are male, what would you change about the way women function in relationships?

Reach Your Learning Goals

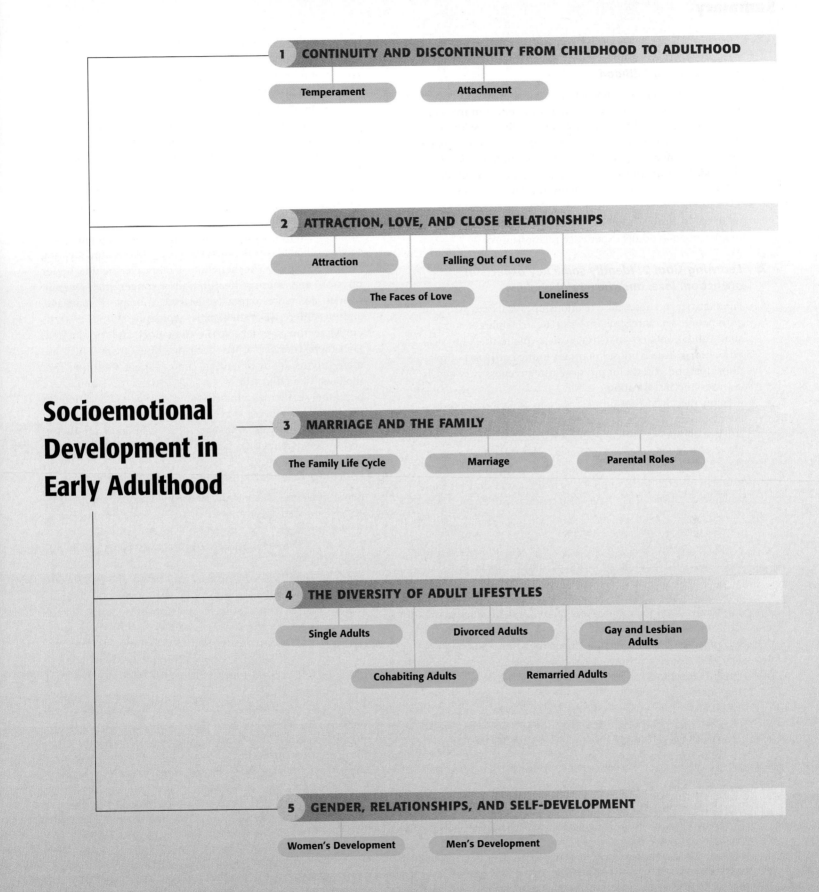

Socioemotional Development in Early Adulthood

1 CONTINUITY AND DISCONTINUITY FROM CHILDHOOD TO ADULTHOOD

Temperament

Attachment

2 ATTRACTION, LOVE, AND CLOSE RELATIONSHIPS

Attraction

The Faces of Love

Falling Out of Love

Loneliness

3 MARRIAGE AND THE FAMILY

The Family Life Cycle

Marriage

Parental Roles

4 THE DIVERSITY OF ADULT LIFESTYLES

Single Adults

Cohabiting Adults

Divorced Adults

Remarried Adults

Gay and Lesbian Adults

5 GENDER, RELATIONSHIPS, AND SELF-DEVELOPMENT

Women's Development

Men's Development

Summary

Learning Goal 1: Describe continuity and discontinuity in temperament and attachment from childhood to adulthood

- The first 20 years are important in predicting an adult's personality, but so, too, are continuing experiences in the adult years. Activity level in early childhood is linked with being an outgoing young adult. Young adults show fewer mood swings, are more responsible, and engage in less risk taking than adolescents. In some cases, temperament in childhood is linked with adjustment problems in early adulthood.
- Attachment styles in young adults are linked with their attachment history, although attachment styles can change in adulthood as adults experience relationships.

Learning Goal 2: Identify some key aspects of attraction, love, and close relationships

- Familiarity precedes a close relationship. We like to associate with people who are similar to us. The principles of consensual validation and matching can explain this. Physical attraction is usually most important in the early part of relationships, and criteria for physical attractiveness vary across cultures and historical time.
- Erikson theorized that intimacy versus isolation is the key developmental issue in early adulthood. There is a delicate balance between intimacy and commitment, on the one hand, and independence and freedom on the other. Friendship plays an important role in adult development, especially in terms of emotional support. Female, male, and female-male friendships often have different characteristics. For example, self-disclosure is more common in female friendships. Romantic love, also called passionate love, is involved when we say we are "in love." It includes passion, sexuality, and a mixture of emotions, not all of which are positive. Affectionate love, also called companionate love, usually becomes more important as relationships mature. Shaver proposed a developmental model of love and Sternberg a triarchic model of love (passion, intimacy, and commitment).
- The collapse of a close relationship can be traumatic, but for some individuals it results in happiness and personal development. For most individuals, falling out of love is painful and emotionally intense.
- Loneliness often emerges when people make life transitions, so it is not surprising that loneliness is common among college freshmen. Changes in dealing with loneliness are emerging as technology changes.

Learning Goal 3: Discuss marriage and the family

- There are six stages in the family life cycle: leaving home and becoming a single adult; the new couple; becoming parents and a family with children; the family with adolescents; the midlife family; and the family in later life.
- Even though adults are remaining single longer and the divorce rate is high, we still show a strong predilection for marriage. The age at which individuals marry, expectations about what the marriage will be like, and the developmental course of marriage may vary not only across historical time within a culture, but also across cultures. Unrealistic expectations and myths about marriage contribute to marital dissatisfaction and divorce. Among the marital myths are that avoiding conflict will ruin a marriage, men are not biologically made for marriage, and men and women are "from different planets." Gottman has conducted extensive research on what makes marriages work. In his research, these principles characterize good marriages: establishing love maps, nurturing fondness and admiration, turning toward each other instead of away, letting your partner influence you, solving solvable conflicts, overcoming gridlock, and creating shared meaning. The benefits of marriage include better physical and mental health and a longer life. Overall, women are more expressive and affectionate in marriage, and this difference bothers many women.
- For some, the parental role is well planned and coordinated. For others, there is surprise and sometimes chaos. There are many myths about parenting, among them the myth that the birth of a child will save a failing marriage. Families are becoming smaller, and many women are delaying childbirth until they have become well established in a career. There are some advantages to having children earlier in adulthood, and some advantages to having them later.

Learning Goal 4: Explain the diversity of lifestyles

- Being single has become an increasingly prominent lifestyle. Myths and stereotypes about singles abound, ranging from "swinging single" to "desperately lonely, suicidal single." There are advantages and disadvantages to being single, autonomy being one of the advantages. Intimacy, loneliness, and finding a positive identity in a marriage-oriented society are concerns of single adults.
- Cohabitation is an increasing lifestyle for many adults. Cohabitation offers some advantages as well as problems. Cohabitation does not lead to greater marital happiness but rather to no differences or differences suggesting that cohabitation is not good for a marriage unless the cohabitation occurs after becoming engaged.
- Divorce has increased dramatically, although its rate of increase has begun to slow. Divorce is complex and emotional. In the first year following divorce, a disequilibrium in the divorced adult's behavior occurs, but by several years after the divorce, more stability has been achieved. The divorced displaced homemaker may encounter excessive stress. Men do not go through a divorce unscathed either.
- Stepfamilies are complex and adjustment is difficult. Only about one-third of remarried adults stay remarried.
- One of the most striking findings about gay and lesbian couples is how similar they are to heterosexual couples. There are a number of misconceptions about same-sex couples.

Researchers have found that the children of gay and lesbian parents are as well adjusted as those of heterosexual couples. The overwhelming majority of children in gay and lesbian families grow up to be heterosexual.

 5 *Learning Goal 5: Characterize the role of gender in relationships*

- Many experts believe that it is important for females to retain their competence and interest in relationships, but also to direct more effort into self-development. Tannen distinguishes between rapport talk, which many women prefer, and report talk, which many men prefer. Critics of Tannen's view argue that there is more individual variation in women's and men's relationship styles than she acknowledges.
- Men have been successful at achieving but the male role involves considerable strain. There is diversity among males, just as there is diversity among females.

Key Terms

consensual validation 470
matching hypothesis 471
friendship 473
romantic love 474

affectionate love 474
leaving home and becoming a
    single adult 479
launching 479

new couple 479
becoming parents and a family
    with children 479
family with adolescents 479

family at midlife 480
family in later life 480

Key People

Theodore Wachs 468
Cindy Hazan and Phillip
    Shaver 469

Erik Erikson 472
Zick Rubin 473
Ellen Berscheid 474

Robert J. Sternberg 475
John Gottman 483
Jean Baker Miller 492

Harriet Lerner 493
Deborah Tannen 493
Joseph Pleck 494

 ## E-Learning Tools

To help you master the material in this chapter, you'll find a number of valuable study tools on the LifeMap CD-ROM that accompanies this book and on the Online Learning Center for *Life-Span Development,* tenth edition, at www.mhhe.com/santrockld10.

Video Clips

In the margins of this book there are icons directing you to the LifeMap CD-ROM that accompanies the book. There you'll find two videos for chapter 15. The first is called "Falling in Love." Are there patterns in the process of falling in love that apply generally? When does romantic love lead to companionate love? One couple offer themselves as a case study. The second video is called "Choosing Not to Cohabitate." This segment explores some of the motives for cohabitation (i.e., living together out of wedlock), as well as some of the advantages and disadvantages of this life choice.

Self-Assessment

Connect to www.mhhe.com/santrockld10 to learn more about falling in love and finding a mate by completing the self-assessments, *What Is My Love Like?, The Characteristics I Desire in a Potential Mate,* and *My Attitudes Towards Women.*

Taking It to the Net

Connect to www.mhhe.com/santrockld10 to research the answers to these questions.

1. Yolanda, who is divorced with two young children, is contemplating a marriage proposal from her boyfriend Dana, also divorced with one young child. She is concerned about the potential issues that may arise from this union. What should Yolanda consider before making this decision about her future?
2. Kelly, at 29 years old, is surprised to hear about two close friends from college, both of whom are getting divorced after only a few years of marriage. One of these friends, April, tells her that "starter marriages" are happening more and more frequently. Is April correct about a growing trend of divorces before the age of 30 and, if so, what might some of the factors behind this trend be?
3. Rochelle and her boyfriend Mark are both 18 years old and are attending college. Rochelle would like to drop out of school to get married and have children, arguing that she can finish college and pursue a career later on. What are some of the advantages and disadvantages of this plan, as compared with waiting to have children until she and her husband-to-be have finished college and established themselves in careers?

Health and Well-Being, Parenting, and Education Exercises

Build your decision-making skills by trying your hand at the health and well-being, parenting, and education exercises.

Connect to www.mhhe.com/santrockld10 to research the answers and complete the exercises.

CHAPTER

16

When more time stretches before one, some assessments,
however reluctantly and incompletely, begin to be made.
—JAMES BALDWIN
American Novelist, 20th Century

Physical and Cognitive Development in Middle Adulthood

Chapter Outline

Learning Goals

Images of Life-Span Development
Time Perspectives

Our perception of time depends on where we are in the life span. We are more concerned about time at some points in life than others (Schroots, 1996). Jim Croce's song "Time in a Bottle" reflects a time perspective that develops in the adult years:

> *If I could save Time in a bottle*
> *The first thing that I'd like to do*
> *Is to save every day*
> *Til Eternity passes away*
> *Just to spend them with you . . .*
> *But there never seems to be enough time*
> *To do the things you want to do*
> *Once you find them*
> *I've looked around enough to know*
> *That you're the one I want to go*
> *Through time with*

—JIM CROCE, "TIME IN A BOTTLE"

Jim Croce's song connects time with love and the hope of going through time with someone we love. Love and intimacy are important themes of adult development. So is time. Middle-aged adults begin to look back to where they have been, reflecting on what they have done with the time they have had. They look toward the future more in terms of how much time remains to accomplish what they hope to do with their lives.

Interest in middle age is essentially a phenomenon of the late twentieth century and early twenty-first century. As you read in chapter 1, in 1900 the average life expectancy was 47 years of age; today it is 77 years of age (U.S. Bureau of the Census, 2004). It only has been since a much larger percentage of people began living to older ages that it made any sense to label, describe, and investigate a period in the human life span called "middle adulthood."

PREVIEW

When young adults look forward in time to what their lives might be like as middle-aged adults, too often they anticipate that things will go downhill. However, like all periods of the human life span, for most individuals there usually are positive and negative features of middle age. In this first chapter on middle adulthood, we will discuss physical changes; cognitive changes; changes in careers, work, and leisure; as well as the importance of religion and meaning in life during middle adulthood. To begin, though, we will explore how middle age is changing.

1 CHANGING MIDDLE AGE

Each year, for $8, about 2.5 to 3 million Americans who have turned 50 become members of the American Association for Retired Persons, now called simply, AARP. There is something incongruous about so many 50-year-olds joining a retirement group when hardly any of them are retired. Indeed, many of today's 50-year-olds are in better shape, more alert, and more productive than their 40-year-old counterparts from a generation or two earlier. As more people lead healthier lifestyles and medical discoveries help to stave off the aging process, the boundaries of middle age are being pushed upward. It looks like middle age is starting later and lasting longer for increasing numbers of active, healthy, and productive people. One study found that almost half of the individuals 65 to 69 years of age considered themselves middle-aged (National Council on Aging, 2000) and another study found a similar pattern: Half of the 60- to 75-year-olds viewed themselves as in middle age (Lachman, Maier, & Budner, 2000). Also, some individuals consider the upper boundary of midlife as the age at which they make the transition from work to retirement.

Sigmund Freud and Carl Jung studied midlife transitions around the turn of the twentieth century. Jung (1933) referred to midlife as the afternoon of life. Midlife serves as an important preparation for late adulthood, "the evening of life" (Lachman, 2004, p. 306). But "midlife" came much earlier in Jung's time. As we just mentioned, in 1900 the average life expectancy was only 47 years of age; only 3 percent of the population lived past 65. Today, the average life expectancy is 77; 12 percent of the U.S. population is older than 65. As a much greater percentage of the population lives to an older age, the midpoint of life and what constitutes middle age or middle adulthood are getting harder to pin down (Staudinger & Bluck, 2001). In only one century, we have added 30 years to the average life expectancy. Statistically, the middle of life today is about 38 years of age—hardly any 38-year-olds, though, wish to be called "middle-aged"! What we think of as middle age comes later—anywhere from 40 to about 60 or 65 years of age. And as more people live longer, the 60 to 65 years upper boundary will likely be nudged upward. When the American Board of Family Practice asked a random sample of 1,200 Americans when middle age begins, 41 percent said it was when you worry about having enough money for health-care concerns, 42 percent said it was when your last child moves out, and 46 percent said it was when you don't recognize the names of music groups on the radio anymore (Beck, 1992).

Although middle adulthood has been a relatively neglected period of the human life span (except for pop psychology portrayals of the midlife crisis), this age period is beginning to be given more attention by life-span developmentalists (Brim, Ryff, & Kessler, 2004; Lachman, 2001, 2004; Willis & Reid, 1999). One reason for the increased attention is that the largest cohort in U.S. history is currently moving through the middle-age years. From 1990 to 2015, the middle-aged U.S. population is projected to increase from 47 million to 80 million, a 72 percent increase. Because of the size of the baby-boom cohort (recall from chapter 2 that a *cohort* is a group of people born in a particular year or time period), the median age of the U.S. population will increase from 33 years in 1990 to 42 years in 2050. The baby boomers, born from 1946 to 1964, are of interest to developmentalists not only because of their increased numbers but also because they are the best-educated and most affluent cohorts in history to pass through middle age.

Though the age boundaries are not set in stone, we will consider **middle adulthood** as the developmental period that begins at approximately 40 years of age and extends to about 60 years of age. However, as we just pointed out, for many increasingly healthy adults, middle age is starting later and lasting longer. Remember from our discussion in chapter 1 that we have not only a chronological age, but biological, psychological, and social ages.

> *M*iddle age is a mix of new opportunities and expanding resources accompanied by declines in physical abilities.
>
> —Lois Verbrugge
> *University of Michigan*

Network on Successful
Midlife Development
Exploring Middle Age

middle adulthood The developmental period beginning at approximately 40 years of age and extending to about 60.

For many people, middle adulthood is a time of declining physical skills and expanding responsibility; a period in which people become more conscious of the young-old polarity and the shrinking amount of time left in life; a point when individuals seek to transmit something meaningful to the next generation; and a time when people reach and maintain satisfaction in their careers. In sum, middle adulthood involves "balancing work and relationship responsibilities in the midst of the physical and psychological changes associated with aging" (Lachman, 2004, p. 305).

In midlife, as in other age periods, individuals make choices, selecting what to do, how to invest time and resources, and evaluating what aspects of their lives they need to change. In midlife, "a serious accident, loss, or illness" may be a "wake-up call" and produce "a major restructuring of time and a reassessment" of life's priorities (Lachman, 2004, p. 310).

But these characteristics don't describe everybody in middle age (Brim, Ryff, Kessler, 2004). As life-span expert Gilbert Brim (1992) commented, middle adulthood is full of changes, twists, and turns; the path is not fixed. People move in and out of states of success and failure.

Review and Reflect: Learning Goal 1

1 Explain how middle age is changing

REVIEW

- How is middle age today different than in past generations?

REFLECT

- How do you think you will experience (are experiencing or have experienced) middle age differently from your parents or grandparents?

2 PHYSICAL DEVELOPMENT

Physical Changes

Health and Disease

Mortality Rates

Sexuality

When I was a college student and my father was 45 years old, I thought he was really old. I could not conceive of myself ever being that old! But it happened, and now I have a few gray hairs. I'm wearing reading glasses while I'm typing this sentence. I can't run as fast as I could, although I still run 15 to 20 miles every week to keep my body from falling apart. What physical changes accompany this change to middle adulthood?

Physical Changes

Unlike the rather dramatic physical changes that occur in early adolescence and the sometimes abrupt decline in old age, midlife physical changes are usually gradual (Ebersole, Hess, & Luggen, 2004; Merrill & Verbrugge, 1999). Although everyone experiences some physical change due to aging in the middle adulthood years, the rates of this aging vary considerably from one individual to another. Genetic makeup and lifestyle factors play important roles in whether chronic disease will appear and when. Middle age is a window through which we can glimpse later life while there is still time to engage in prevention and to influence some of the course of aging (Lachman, 2004).

As mentioned earlier, the baby-boom generation is moving through middle adulthood in record numbers. "The Baby Boomers at Midlife, a national survey by the American Association of Retired Persons (2002), tracks baby boomers annually and compares them to those who are younger and older" (Lachman, 2004, p. 314). In this survey, baby boomers said that in terms of their health they were worse off than they expected but that they had a good deal of control over their health outcomes. Let's now explore some of these changes that baby boomers and others go through in middle age.

Visible Signs   One of the most visible signs of physical changes in middle adulthood is physical appearance. The first outwardly noticeable signs of aging usually are apparent by the forties or fifties. The skin begins to wrinkle and sag because of a loss of fat and collagen in underlying tissues (Giacomoni & Rein, 2004). Small, localized areas of pigmentation in the skin produce aging spots, especially in areas that are exposed to sunlight, such as the hands and face. Hair becomes thinner and grayer due to a lower replacement rate and a decline in melanin production. Fingernails and toenails develop ridges and become thicker and more brittle.

Since a youthful appearance is stressed in our culture, many individuals whose hair is graying, whose skin is wrinkling, whose bodies are sagging, and whose teeth are yellowing strive to make themselves look younger. Undergoing cosmetic surgery, dyeing hair, purchasing wigs, enrolling in weight reduction programs, participating in exercise regimens, and taking heavy doses of vitamins are common in middle age. One study found that middle-aged women focus more attention on facial attractiveness than do older or younger women (Nowak, 1977). In this same study, middle-aged women were more likely to perceive the signs of aging as having a negative effect on their physical appearance. In our culture, some aspects of aging in middle adulthood are taken as signs of attractiveness in men. Facial wrinkles and gray hair symbolize strength and maturity in men but may be perceived as unattractive in women.

The cultural emphasis on youthful appearance and avoiding or minimizing the physical changes associated with aging characterizes the baby-boom generation (Lachman, 2004). For example, baby boomers have a strong interest in plastic surgery and Botox, which may reflect their desire to take control of the aging process (Lachman & Firth, 2004).

Height and Weight   Individuals lose height in middle age, and many gain weight. Adults lose about a half inch of height per decade beginning in their forties (Memmler & others, 1995). On the average, body fat accounts for about 10 percent of body weight in adolescence; it makes up 20 percent or more in middle age.

Being overweight is a critical health problem in middle adulthood. For individuals who are 30 percent or more overweight, the probability of dying in middle adulthood increases by about 40 percent. Obesity increases the probability that an individual will suffer a number of other ailments, among them hypertension and digestive disorders (Daviglus & others, 2003).

In a large-scale study of middle-aged individuals, 7 of 10 said that they are overweight (Brim, 1999). Nearly half of the individuals over the age of 45 said they are less fit than they were five years ago.

Strength, Joints, and Bones   As we saw in chapter 14, maximum physical strength often is attained in the twenties. Peak functioning of the body's joints also usually occurs in the twenties. The term *sarcopenia* is given to age-related loss of muscle mass and strength. The rate of muscle loss with age occurs at a rate of approximately 1 to 2 percent per year past the age of 50 (Marcell, 2003). A loss of strength especially occurs in the back and legs. Exercise can reduce the

Famous actor Sean Connery as a young adult in his twenties (*top*) and as a middle-aged adult in his fifties (*bottom*). *What are some of the most outwardly noticeable signs of aging in the middle adulthood years?*

Middle age is when your age starts to show around your middle.

—Bob Hope
American Comedian, 20th Century

Women's Health in Middle Age
Midlife Baby-Boomer
Characteristics

decline involved in sarcopenia (Hawkins, Wiswell, & Marcell, 2003; Kamel, 2003; Yarasheski, 2003).

The cushions for the movement of bones (such as tendons and ligaments) become less efficient in the middle-adult years, a time when many individuals experience joint stiffness and more difficulty in movement. Maximum bone density occurs by the mid to late thirties, from which point there is a progressive loss of bone. The rate of this bone loss begins slowly but accelerates in the fifties (Whitbourne, 2001). Women experience about twice the rate of bone loss as men. By the end of midlife, bones break more easily and heal more slowly.

Vision   Accommodation of the eye—the ability to focus and maintain an image on the retina—experiences its sharpest decline between 40 and 59 years of age. In particular, middle-aged individuals begin to have difficulty viewing close objects, which means that many individuals have to wear glasses with bifocal lenses (Fozard & Gordon-Salant, 2001). The eye's blood supply also diminishes, although usually not until the fifties or sixties. The reduced blood supply may decrease the visual field's size and account for an increase in the eye's blind spot. Also, there is some evidence that the retina becomes less sensitive to low levels of illumination.

Hearing   Hearing also can start to decline by the age of 40. Sensitivity to high pitches usually declines first. The ability to hear low-pitched sounds does not seem to decline much in middle adulthood, though. Men usually lose their sensitivity to high-pitched sounds sooner than women do. However, this sex difference might be due to men's greater exposure to noise in occupations such as mining, automobile work, and so on (Kline & Scialfa, 1996).

Researchers are identifying new possibilities for improving the vision and hearing of people as they age (Fozard & Gordon-Salant, 2001). One way this is being carried out is through better control of glare or background noise. Further, recent advances in hearing aids dramatically improve hearing for many individuals (Birren, 2002).

Cardiovascular System   Midlife is the time when high blood pressure and high cholesterol "often take adults by surprise" (Lachman, 2004, p. 307). Indeed, the cardiovascular system changes in middle adulthood and, as indicated in figure 16.1, cardiovascular disease increases considerably in middle age (Hankinson & others, 2001; Safar & Smulyan, 2004). Fatty deposits and scar tissue slowly accumulate in the linings of blood vessels, gradually reducing blood flow to various organs, including the heart and brain (Ferrari, Radaelli, & Centola, 2003). Fatty deposits can begin in adolescence. Thus, eating food high in fat content and being overweight in adolescence may have later life consequences (Birren, 2002).

Blood pressure, too, usually rises in the forties and fifties (Siegler & others, 1999). At menopause, a woman's blood pressure rises sharply and usually remains

FIGURE 16.1 The Relation of Age and Gender to Cardiovascular Disease
Notice the sharp increase in cardiovascular disease in middle age.

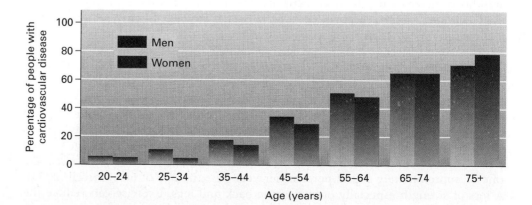

above that of a man through life's later years. Exercise, weight control, and a diet rich in fruits, vegetables, and whole grains can often help to stave off many cardio-vascular problems in middle age (Sleight, 2003). To read further about the link between exercise and cardiovascular disease, see the Research in Life-Span Development interlude.

Research in Life-Span Development
Fitness in Young Adults and Heart Health in Middle Age

A recent longitudinal study was the first large-scale observational study to examine the role of fitness on healthy young adults' development of risk factors for heart disease (Carnethon & others, 2003). Previous studies had focused on the relation between fitness and death from heart disease and stroke.

The study involved 4,487 men and women in four cities (Birmingham, Alabama; Chicago, Illinois; Minneapolis, Minnesota; and Oakland, California). Initial assessments were made when the participants were 18 to 30 years of age with follow-up assessments conducted 2, 5, 7, 10, and 15 years later. Cardiorespiratory fitness was measured with an exercise treadmill test, which consisted of up to nine 2-minute stages of progressive difficulty.

Poor cardiorespiratory fitness in young men and women, determined by the duration of their treadmill exercise test, was associated with the risk of developing hypertension, diabetes, and metabolic syndrome (a constellation of factors that includes excess abdominal fat, elevated blood pressure and triglycerides, and low levels of the high-density lipoprotein, the "good" cholesterol) in middle age. Improved fitness over seven years was related to a reduced risk of developing diabetes and metabolic syndrome.

Lungs There is little change in lung capacity through most of middle adulthood. However, at about the age of 55, the proteins in lung tissue become less elastic. This change, combined with a gradual stiffening of the chest wall, decreases the lungs' capacity to shuttle oxygen from the air people breathe to the blood in their veins. As shown in figure 16.2, the lung capacity of individuals who are smokers drops precipitously in middle age, but if the individuals quit smoking their lung capacity improves, although not to the level of individuals who have never smoked (Williams, 1995).

Sleep Some aspects of sleep become more problematic in middle age (Feinsliver, 2003; Vitiello, Larsen, & Moe, 2004). The total number of hours slept usually remains the same as in early adulthood, but beginning in the forties, wakeful periods are more frequent and there is less of the deepest type of sleep (stage 4). The amount of time spent lying awake in bed at night begins to increase in middle age, and this can produce a feeling of being less rested in the morning (Abbot, 2003). Sleep problems in middle-aged adults are more common in individuals who use a higher number of prescription and nonprescription drugs, are obese, have cardiovascular disease, or are depressed (Foley & others, 2004; Giron & others, 2002; Hoffman, 2003).

Health and Disease

In middle adulthood, the frequency of accidents declines and individuals are less susceptible to colds and allergies than in childhood, adolescence, or early adulthood.

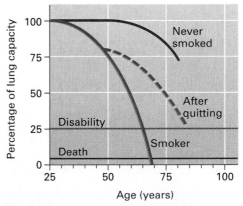

FIGURE 16.2 The Relation of Lung Capacity to Age and Cigarette Smoking
Lung capacity shows little change through middle age for individuals who have not smoked. However, smoking is linked with reduced lung capacity in middle-aged and older adults. When individuals stop smoking, their lung capacity becomes greater than those who continue to smoke, but not as great as the lung capacity of individuals who have never smoked.

Indeed, many individuals live through middle adulthood without having a disease or persistent health problem. However, disease and persistent health problems become more common in middle adulthood for other individuals (Spiro, 2001).

Only 7 percent of individuals in their early forties report having a disability but that number more than doubles by the early fifties (16 percent), and by the early sixties, 30 percent report having a disability (Bumpess & Acquino, 1995; Lachman, 2004). When individuals were asked to rate their health in early, middle, and late adulthood, they indicated that their health was not as good as in early adulthood but better than in late adulthood (National Center for Health Statistics, 1999). Men rated their health as somewhat better than women in midlife but in late adulthood the gender differences virtually disappeared.

Chronic disorders are characterized by a slow onset and a long duration. Chronic disorders are rare in early adulthood, increase in middle adulthood, and become common in late adulthood. Arthritis is the leading chronic disorder in middle age, followed by hypertension.

The most common chronic disorders in middle age vary for females and males. Men have a higher incidence of fatal chronic conditions (such as coronary heart disease, cancer, and stroke); women have a higher incidence of nonfatal ones (such as arthritis, varicose veins, and bursitis).

Stress and Disease Stress is increasingly being found to be a factor in disease, and the cumulative effect of stress often has a toll on the health of individuals by the time they reach middle age. Links of stress to disease involve the immune system and cardiovascular disease.

The Immune System and Stress The immune system keeps us healthy by recognizing foreign materials such as bacteria, viruses, and tumors and then destroying them. Its machinery consists of billions of white blood cells located in the circulatory system. The number of white blood cells and their effectiveness in killing foreign viruses or bacteria are related to stress levels. When a person is under stress, viruses and bacteria are more likely to multiply and cause disease. Immune system functioning decreases with normal aging (Hawkley & Cacioppo, 2004).

Stress and the Cardiovascular System You may have heard someone say something like "It's no wonder she died of a heart attack with all of the stress he put her through." But is it true that emotional stress can cause a person to have a heart attack? A clear link has not been found, but there is evidence that chronic emotional stress is associated with high blood pressure, heart disease, and early death (Kiecolt-Glaser & others, 2003). Apparently, the surge in adrenaline caused by severe emotional stress causes the blood to clot more rapidly, and blood clotting is a major factor in heart attacks (Fogoros, 2001). Researchers have found that stress and negative emotions can affect the development and course of cardiovascular disease by altering underlying physiological processes (Claar & Blumenthal, 2003). People who live in a chronically stressed condition are more likely to take up smoking, start overeating, and avoid exercising. All of these stress-related behaviors are linked with the development of cardiovascular disease (Schneiderman & others, 2001).

Emotional stress can contribute to cardiovascular disease in several other ways (Fogoros, 2001). For instance, people who have had major life changes (loss of a spouse or other close relative, loss of a job) have a higher incidence of cardiovascular disease and early death (Taylor, 2003). And, as we will see shortly, people who are quick to anger or who display frequent hostility have an increased risk of cardiovascular disease (Williams, 2001).

Culture, Personality, Relationships, and Health Emotional stability and personality are related to health in middle adulthood. In the Berkeley Longitudinal Study, as individuals aged from 34 to 50, those who were the most healthy were

chronic disorders Disorders that are characterized by slow onset and long duration. They are rare in early adulthood, they increase during middle adulthood, and they become common in late adulthood.

also the most calm, the most self-controlled, and the most responsible (Livson & Peskin, 1981). Let's now explore the role of culture in cardiovascular disease and two personality profiles that are associated with health and illness.

Culture and Cardiovascular Disease   Culture plays an important role in coronary disease. Cross-cultural psychologists believe that studies of migrant ethnic groups help shed light on the role culture plays in health. As ethnic groups migrate, the health practices dictated by their cultures change while their genetic predispositions to certain disorders remain constant (Ilola, 1990). The Ni-Hon-San Study (Nipon–Honolulu–San Francisco), part of the Honolulu Heart Study, is an ongoing study of approximately 12,000 Japanese men in Hiroshima and Nagasaki (Japan), Honolulu, and San Francisco. In the study, the Japanese men living in Japan have had the lowest rate of coronary heart disease, those living in Honolulu have had an intermediate rate, and those living in San Francisco have had the highest rate. Acculturation provides a valuable framework for understanding why the Japanese men's cholesterol level, glucose level, and weight all increased as they migrated and acculturated. As the Japanese men migrated farther away from Japan, their health practices, such as diet, changed. The Japanese men in California, for example, ate 40 percent more fat than the men in Japan.

Conversely, Japanese men in California have much lower rates of cerebrovascular disease (stroke) than Japanese men living in Japan. Businessmen in Japan tend to consume vast quantities of alcohol and to chain-smoke, both of which are high-risk factors for stroke. As a result, stroke was the leading cause of death in Japan until it was surpassed by cancer in 1981. However, death rates from stroke for Japanese American men are at the same level as those of White American men. Researchers suspect that this level is related to a change in behavior. That is, Japanese American men consume less alcohol and smoke less than their counterparts in Japan. To read more about cultural factors in health, see the Diversity in Life-Span Development interlude.

Diversity in Life-Span Development
Health Promotion in African Americans, Latinos, Asian Americans, and Native Americans

There are differences within ethnic groups as well as among them. This is just as true of health among ethnic groups as it is of, say, family structure. The spectrum of living conditions and lifestyles within an ethnic group is influenced by socioeconomic status, immigrant status, social and language skills, occupational opportunities, and such social resources as the availability of meaningful support networks—all of which can play a role in the health of ethnic minority individuals (Dreachslin, Weech-Maldonado, & Dansky, 2004; Gwyn & others, 2004; Low, 2004).

Prejudice and racial segregation are the historical underpinnings for the chronic stress of discrimination and poverty that adversely affects the health of many African Americans (Wolinsky & others, 2004). Support systems, such as an extended family network, may be especially important resources to improve the health of African Americans and help them cope with stress (Boyd-Franklin, 1989).

Some of the same stressors mentioned for African Americans are associated with migration to the United States by Puerto Ricans, Mexicans, and Latin Americans. Language is often a barrier for unacculturated Latinos in doctor-patient communications. In addition, there is increasing evidence that diabetes occurs at an above-average rate in Latinos, making this disease a major health problem that parallels the above-average rate of high blood pressure among African Americans (Banister & others, 2004).

Asian Americans are characterized by their broad diversity in national backgrounds and lifestyles. They range from highly acculturated Japanese Americans, who may be better educated than many White Americans and have excellent access to health care, to the many Indochinese refugees who have few economic resources and may be in poor health.

Cultural barriers to adequate health care include a lack of financial resources and poor language skills. In addition, members of ethnic minority groups often are unfamiliar with how the medical system operates, confused about the need to see numerous people, and uncertain about why they have to wait so long for service (Snowden & Cheung, 1990).

Health-care professionals can increase their effectiveness with ethnic minority patients by improving their knowledge of patients' attitudes, beliefs, and folk practices regarding health and disease. Such information should be integrated into Western treatment rather than ignored at the risk of alienating patients.

Type A/Type B Behavioral Patterns In the middle of the twentieth century, a secretary for two California cardiologists, Meyer Friedman and Ray Rosenman, observed that the chairs in their waiting rooms were tattered and worn, but only on the front edges. The cardiologists had noticed the impatience of their cardiac patients, who often arrived exactly on time for an appointment and were in a great hurry to leave. Subsequently they conducted a study of 3,000 healthy men between the ages of 35 and 59 over a period of eight years (Friedman & Rosenman, 1974). During the eight years, one group of men had twice as many heart attacks or other forms of heart disease as anyone else. And autopsies of the men who died revealed that this same group had coronary arteries that were more obstructed than those of other men. Friedman and Rosenman described the coronary disease group as characterized by **Type A behavior pattern,** a cluster of characteristics—being excessively competitive, hard-driven, impatient, and hostile—thought to be related to the incidence of heart disease. Rosenman and Friedman labeled the behavior of the other group, who were relaxed and easygoing, **Type B behavior pattern.**

However, further research on the link between Type A behavior and coronary disease indicates that the association is not as strong as Friedman and Rosenman believed (Suls & Swain, 1998; Williams, 1995, 2001). Researchers have examined the components of Type A behavior, such as hostility, competitiveness, a strong drive to accomplish goals, and impatience, to determine a more precise link with coronary risk. The Type A behavior component most consistently associated with coronary problems is hostility (Williams, 2001). People who are hostile outwardly or turn anger inward are more likely to develop heart disease than their less angry counterparts (Allan & Scheidt, 1996). Such people have been called "hot reactors" because of their intense physiological reactions to stress. Their hearts race, their breathing quickens, and their muscles tense up. Redford Williams (1995), a leading behavioral medicine researcher, believes that such people can develop the ability to control their anger and develop more trust in others, which he thinks can reduce their risk for heart disease.

The role of personality factors, including hostility, in health were examined in one longitudinal study of more than 1,500 men from 28 to 80 years of age with an average age of 47 at the initial assessment (Aldwin & others, 2001). Men who had high, increasing symptoms of poor health were characterized by hostility and anxiety, were overweight, and smoked. Those with few symptoms of poor health were emotionally stable, educated, thin nonsmokers.

Hardiness **Hardiness** is a personality style characterized by a sense of commitment (rather than alienation), control (rather than powerlessness), and a perception of

Type Z behavior

www.mhhe.com/santrockld10

Behavioral Medicine
Controlling Anger and Developing Life Skills

Type A behavior pattern A cluster of characteristics—being excessively competitive, hard-driven, impatient, and hostile—thought to be related to the incidence of heart disease.

Type B behavior pattern Being primarily calm and easygoing.

hardiness A personality style characterized by a sense of commitment (rather than alienation), control (rather than powerlessness), and a perception of problems as challenges (rather than threats).

problems as challenges (rather than threats). In the Chicago Stress Project, male business managers 32 to 65 years of age were studied over a five-year period. During the five years, most of the managers experienced stressful events, such as divorce, job transfers, the death of a close friend, inferior performance evaluations at work, and working at a job with an unpleasant boss. In one study, managers who developed an illness (ranging from the flu to a heart attack) were compared with those who did not (Kobasa, Maddi, & Kahn, 1982). The latter group was more likely to have a hardy personality. In another study, whether or not hardiness along with exercise and social support buffered stress and reduced illness in executives' lives was investigated (Kobasa & others, 1986). When all three factors were present in an executive's life the level of illness dropped dramatically (see figure 16.3). This suggests the power of multiple buffers of stress, rather than a single buffer, in maintaining health (Harris, 2004; Maddi, 1998; Ouellette & DiPlacido, 2001).

Health and Social Relationships In chapter 15, "Socioemotional Development in Early Adulthood," we saw that being in a happy marriage is linked with getting sick less, having less physical and emotional stress, and living longer than being in an unhappy marriage. These results hold for middle-aged as well as young adults.

Researchers also have revealed links between health in middle age and earlier pathways of relationships (Ryff & Singer, 2000). In one recent longitudinal study, individuals who were on a positive relationship pathway from childhood to middle age had significantly fewer biological problems (cardiovascular disease, physical decline) than their counterparts who were on a negative relationship pathway (Ryff & others, 2001). In another longitudinal study, adults who experienced more warmth and closeness with their parents during childhood had fewer diagnosed diseases (coronary artery disease, hypertension, ulcer, alcoholism) than those who did not experience warmth and closeness with their parents in childhood (Russek & Schwartz, 1997). These studies reflect continuity in development over many years in the human life span. Thus, health in middle age is related to the current quality of social relationships and to the pathways of those relationships earlier in development.

Mortality Rates

Infectious disease was the main cause of death until the middle of the twentieth century. As infectious disease rates declined and more individuals lived through middle age, chronic disorders increased.

Chronic diseases are now the main causes of death for individuals in middle adulthood (Merrill & Verbrugge, 1999). Heart disease is the leading cause of death in middle age, followed by cancer and cerebrovascular disease (National Center for Health Statistics, 2004). In the first half of middle age, cancer claims more lives than heart disease; this is reversed in the second half.

Figure 16.4 shows the leading causes of death in middle age. In middle age, many deaths are caused by a single, readily identifiable condition, while in old age, death is more likely to result from the combined effects of several chronic conditions (Gessert, Elliott, & Haller, 2003). Men have higher mortality rates than women for all of the leading causes of death.

Sexuality

What kinds of changes characterize the sexuality of women and men as they go through middle age? **Climacteric** is a term that is used to describe the midlife transition in which fertility declines. Let's explore the substantial differences in the climacteric of women and men.

Menopause Most of us know something about menopause. But is what we know accurate? Stop for a moment and think about your knowledge of menopause. What

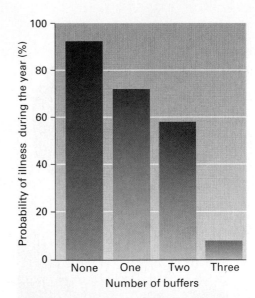

FIGURE 16.3 Illness in High-Stress Business Executives

In one study of high-stress business executives (all of whom were selected for this analysis because they were above the stress mean for the entire one year of the study), three buffers (hardiness, exercise, and social support) were examined (Kobasa & others, 1986). Having one buffer reduced the probability of illness, two buffers reduced the illness risk further, but high-stress business executives with all three buffers had by far the lowest probability of illness.

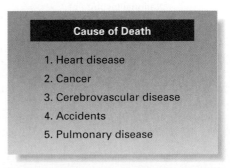

Cause of Death

1. Heart disease
2. Cancer
3. Cerebrovascular disease
4. Accidents
5. Pulmonary disease

FIGURE 16.4 Leading Causes of Death in Middle Adulthood

climacteric The midlife transition in which fertility declines.

Researchers have found that almost 50 percent of Canadian and American women have occasional hot flashes, but only 1 in 7 Japanese women do (Lock, 1998). *What factors might account for these variations?*

www.mhhe.com/santrockld10

Menopause: Information and Resources
National Institute of Aging: Menopause
Medline: Menopause

menopause The complete cessation of a woman's menstruation, which usually occurs in the late forties or early fifties.

is menopause? When does it occur? Can it be treated? Most of us share some assumptions about menopause—we might think that it is a disease, that it involves numerous complaints, that women who are undergoing menopause deeply regret losing their reproductive capacity, their sexuality, and their femininity, and that they become deeply depressed. Are these assumptions accurate?

Menopause is the time in middle age, usually in the late forties or early fifties, when a woman's menstrual periods completely cease. The average age at which women have their last period is 51. However, there is a large variation in the age at which menopause occurs—from 39 to 59 years of age. *Perimenopause* is the transitional period from normal menstrual periods to no menstrual periods at all, which often takes up to 10 years. Perimenopause is most common in the forties but can occur in the thirties (Landgren & others, 2004). One recent study of 30- to 50-year-old women found that depressed feelings, headaches, moodiness, and palpitations were the symptoms that these women most frequently discussed with health-care providers (Lyndaker & Hulton, 2004).

In menopause, there is a dramatic decline in the production of estrogen by the ovaries. Estrogen decline produces some uncomfortable symptoms in some menopausal women—"hot flashes," nausea, fatigue, and rapid heartbeat, for example (Fitzpatrick, 2004; Joffe, Soares, & Cohen, 2003). Some menopausal women report depression and irritability, but in some instances these feelings are related to other circumstances in the woman's life, such as becoming divorced, losing a job, caring for a sick parent, and so on (Gannon, 1998). In sum, there is variation in women's experience of menopause (Rossi, 2004; Symons & Symons, 2004).

In a large-scale study of Americans in midlife, almost two-thirds of postmenopausal women said they felt relief that their periods had stopped (Brim, 1999). Only 1 percent said they felt "only regret" that they no longer had their period. Just over 50 percent of middle-aged women reported having no hot flashes at all. Why, then, do so many individuals have the idea that menopause is such a big deal? Why do we have so many erroneous assumptions—that menopausal women will lose their sexuality and femininity, and that they will become deeply depressed? Much of the research on menopause is based on small, selective samples of women who go to physicians or therapists because they are having problems associated with menopause. These women are unrepresentative of the large population of women in the United States. Further, women have been influenced by misinformation and myths about menopause (Short, 2003).

Cross-cultural studies reveal wide variations in the menopause experience (Avis, 1999). For example, hot flashes are uncommon in Mayan women (Beyene, 1986). Asian women report fewer hot flashes than women in Western societies (Payer, 1991). It is difficult to determine the extent to which these cross-cultural variations in the menopause experience are due to genetic, dietary, reproductive, or cultural factors.

Our portrayal of menopause has been much more positive than its usual portrayals in the past. Although menopause overall is not the negative experience for most women it was once thought to be, the loss of fertility is an important marker for women—it means that they have to make final decisions about having children. Women in their thirties who have never had children sometimes speak about being "up against the biological clock" because they cannot postpone questions about having children much longer.

Hormone replacement therapy (HRT) augments the declining levels of reproductive hormone production by the ovaries (Quilliam, 2004). HRT can consist of various forms of estrogen, and usually a progestin. Concerns about an increased risk of stroke have led the National Institutes of Health (2004) to end part of a major hormone replacement therapy study a year early, telling the women to stop taking the estrogen supplements. Estrogen alone increased the risk of stroke by about the same amount as estrogen combined with progestin. Preliminary data also indicated a trend toward increased risk of dementia (a brain disorder involving deterioration of mental functioning). On the positive side, the study found that estrogen lowered the risk of hip fractures and did not increase the risk of heart attacks or breast cancer. One study found that after learning about the growing risks of hormone therapy, about 50 percent of hormone users stopped taking hormones (Ettinger & others, 2003). However, approximately one-fourth of women who quit taking hormones later resumed taking them to relieve hot flashes, fatigue, depression, and other menopausal symptoms (Ettinger & others, 2003).

The National Institutes of Health recommends that women with a uterus who are currently taking hormones should consult with their doctor to determine whether they should continue the hormone therapy. If they are taking the hormone treatment for short-term relief of symptoms, the benefits may outweigh the risks. However, the recent negative hormone therapy results suggest that long-term hormone therapy should be seriously reevaluated (Rosano & others, 2003; Turgeon & others, 2004; Warren & Valente, 2004).

Hormonal Changes in Middle-Aged Men Do men go through anything like the menopause that women experience? That is, is there a male menopause? During middle adulthood, most men do not lose their capacity to father children, although there usually is a modest decline in their sexual hormone level and activity. Men experience hormonal changes in their fifties and sixties, but nothing like the dramatic drop in estrogen that women experience (Leonard, 2004; Sommer, 2001). Testosterone production begins to decline about 1 percent a year during middle adulthood, and sperm count usually shows a slow decline, but men do not lose their fertility in middle age. What has been referred to as "male menopause," then, probably has less to do with hormonal change than with the psychological adjustment men must make when they are faced with declining physical energy and family and work pressures. Testosterone therapy has not been found to relieve such symptoms, suggesting that they are not induced by hormonal change.

In middle age, men's testosterone levels gradually drop, which can reduce their sexual drive (Gooren, 2003). Their erections are less full and less frequent, and require more stimulation to achieve them. Researchers once attributed these changes to psychological factors, but increasingly they find that as many as 75 percent of the erectile dysfunctions in middle-aged men stem from physiological problems. Smoking, diabetes, hypertension, and elevated cholesterol levels are at fault in many erectile problems in middle-aged men (Shiri & others, 2003).

Recently, the most attention in helping individuals with a sexual dysfunction has focused on Viagra, a drug designed to conquer impotence. Viagra works by allowing increased blood flow into the penis, which produces an erection. Its success rate is in the range of 60 to 80 percent, and its prescription rate has outpaced such popular drugs as Prozac (antidepressant) and Rogaine (baldness remedy) in first-year comparisons (Carson, 2003; Morales, 2003). The possible side effects of Viagra are headaches in 1 of 10 men, blackouts (Viagra can trigger a sudden drop in blood pressure), and seeing blue (because the eyes contain an enzyme similar to the one on which Viagra works in the penis, about 3 percent of users develop temporary vision problems ranging from blurred vision to a blue or green halo effect). Viagra should not be taken by men using nitroglycerin for the treatment of cardiovascular disease because the combination can significantly lower blood pressure and lead to fainting or even death in some men (Cheitlin, 2003). Also, scientists do not know the long-term effects of taking the drug, although in short-term trials it appears to be a relatively safe drug (Briganti & others, 2004; Burnett, 2004). Recently, two alternatives to Viagra (Levitra and Cialis) for improving erectile dysfunction have been approved and early studies indicate they are as successful as Viagra in treating erectile dysfunction, and also

www.mhhe.com/santrockld10

Medline: Middle-Age Sexuality
Midlife Male Hormone Changes

		Percentage engaging in sex			
Age groups	Not at all	A few times per year	A few times per month	2–3 times a week	4 or more times a week
Men					
18–24	15	21	24	28	12
25–29	7	15	31	36	11
30–39	8	15	37	23	6
40–49	9	18	40	27	6
50–59	11	22	43	20	3
Women					
18–24	11	16	2	9	12
25–29	5	10	38	37	10
30–39	9	16	6	33	6
40–49	15	16	44	20	5
50–59	30	22	35	12	2

FIGURE 16.5 The Sex in America Survey: Frequency of Sex at Different Points in Adult Development

have few side effects (Govier & others, 2003; Keating & Scott, 2003; Stroberg, Murphy, & Costigan, 2003).

Sexual Attitudes and Behavior Although the ability of men and women to function sexually shows little biological decline in middle adulthood, sexual activity usually occurs on a less frequent basis than in early adulthood (Burgess, 2004). Career interests, family matters, energy level, and routine may contribute to this decline. In the Sex in America survey, frequency of having sex was greatest for individuals aged 25 to 29 years old (47 percent had sex twice a week or more) and dropped off for individuals in their fifties (23 percent of 50- to 59-year-old males said they had sex twice a week or more, while only 14 percent of the females in this age group reported this frequency) (Michael & others, 1994). Figure 16.5 shows the age trends in frequency of sex from the Sex in America survey.

Living with a spouse or partner makes all the difference in whether people engage in sexual activity, especially for women over 40 years of age. In one study conducted by the MacArthur Foundation, 95 percent of women in their forties with partners said that they have been sexually active in the last six months, compared with only 53 percent of those without partners (Brim, 1999). By their fifties, 88 percent of women living with a partner have been sexually active in the last six months, but only 37 percent of those who are neither married nor living with someone say they have had sex in the last six months.

Review and Reflect: Learning Goal 2

 Discuss physical changes in middle adulthood

REVIEW

- What are some key physical changes in middle adulthood?
- How would you characterize health and disease in middle adulthood?
- What are the main causes of death in middle age?
- What are the sexual lives of middle-aged adults like?

REFLECT

- Were you surprised by any of the characteristics of the sexual lives of middle-aged adults? If so, which ones?

3 COGNITIVE DEVELOPMENT

| Intelligence | | Information Processing |

We have seen that the decline in many physical characteristics in middle adulthood is not just imagined. Middle-aged adults may not see as well, run as fast, or be as healthy as they were in their twenties and thirties. But what about their cognitive skills? In chapter 14, "Physical and Cognitive Development in Early Adulthood," we saw that cognitive abilities are very strong in early adulthood. Do they decline as we enter and move through middle adulthood? To answer this question we will explore the possibility of cognitive changes in intelligence and information processing.

Intelligence

Our exploration of possible changes in intelligence in middle adulthood focuses on the concepts of fluid and crystallized intelligence, the Seattle Longitudinal Study, and cohort effects.

Fluid and Crystallized Intelligence   John Horn believes that some abilities begin to decline in middle age while others increase (Horn & Donaldson, 1980). Horn argues that **crystallized intelligence,** an individual's accumulated information and verbal skills, continues to increase in middle adulthood, while **fluid intelligence,** one's ability to reason abstractly, begins to decline in the middle adulthood years (see figure 16.6).

Horn's data were collected in a cross-sectional manner. Remember from chapter 2, "The Science of Life-Span Development," that this involves assessing individuals of different ages at the same point in time. For example, a cross-sectional study might assess the intelligence of different groups of 40-, 50-, and 60-year-olds in a single evaluation, such as 1980. The average 40-year-old and the average 60-year-old were born in different eras, which produced different economic and educational opportunities. For example, as the 60-year-olds grew up they likely had fewer educational opportunities, which probably influenced their scores on intelligence tests. Thus, if we find differences between 40- and 60-year-olds on intelligence tests when they are assessed cross-sectionally, these differences might be due to cohort effects related to educational differences rather than to age.

By contrast, remember from chapter 2 that in a longitudinal study, the same individuals are studied over a period of time. Thus, a longitudinal study of intelligence in middle adulthood might consist of giving the same intelligence test to the same individuals when they are 40, 50, and 60 years of age. As we see next, whether data on intelligence are collected cross-sectionally or longitudinally can make a difference in what is found about intellectual decline.

The Seattle Longitudinal Study   K. Warner Schaie (1996) is conducting an extensive study of intellectual abilities in the adulthood years. Five hundred individuals initially were tested in 1956. New waves of participants are added periodically. The main focus in the Seattle Longitudinal Study has been on individual change and stability in intelligence. A psychometric, measurement-based approach, described in chapter 10, "Physical and Cognitive Development in Middle and Late Childhood," is used.

The main mental abilities tested were:

- *Vocabulary* (ability to understand ideas expressed in words)
- *Verbal memory* (ability to encode and recall meaningful language units, such as a list of words)

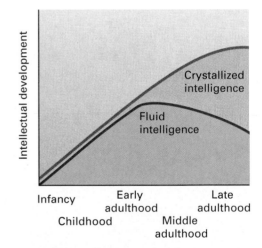

FIGURE 16.6 Fluid and Crystallized Intellectual Development Across the Life Span
According to Horn, crystallized intelligence (based on cumulative learning experiences) increases throughout the life span, but fluid intelligence (the ability to perceive and manipulate information) steadily declines from middle adulthood.

crystallized intelligence Accumulated information and verbal skills, which increase with age, according to Horn.

fluid intelligence The ability to reason abstractly, which steadily declines from middle adulthood on, according to Horn.

FIGURE 16.7 Longitudinal Changes in Six Intellectual Abilities from Age 25 to Age 67

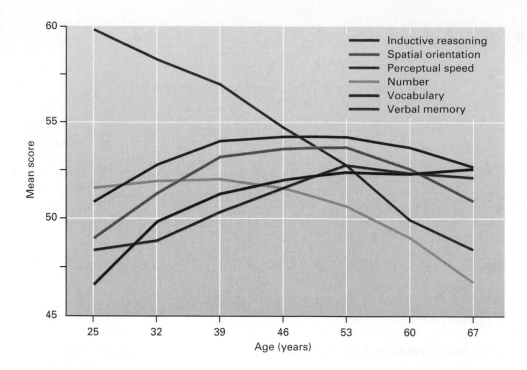

K. Warner Schaie

- *Number* (ability to perform simple mathematical computations such as addition, subtraction, and multiplication)
- *Spatial orientation* (ability to visualize and mentally rotate stimuli in two- and three-dimensional space)
- *Inductive reasoning* (ability to recognize and understand patterns and relationships in a problem and use this understanding to solve other instances of the problem)
- *Perceptual speed* (ability to quickly and accurately make simple discriminations in visual stimuli)

As shown in figure 16.7, the highest level of functioning for four of the six intellectual abilities occurred in the middle adulthood years (Willis & Schaie, 1999). For both women and men, peak performance on vocabulary, verbal memory, inductive reasoning, and spatial orientation was attained in middle age. For only two of the six abilities—numerical ability and perceptual speed—were there declines in middle age. Perceptual speed showed the earliest decline, actually beginning in early adulthood.

When Schaie (1994) assessed intellectual abilities both cross-sectionally and longitudinally, he found decline more likely in the cross-sectional than in the longitudinal assessments. For example, as shown in figure 16.8, when assessed longitudinally, inductive reasoning increased until toward the end of middle adulthood, when it began to show a slight decline. By contrast, when assessed cross-sectionally, inductive reasoning showed a consistent decline in the middle adulthood years.

Interestingly, in terms of John Horn's ideas that were discussed earlier, middle age was a time of peak performance for both some aspects of crystallized intelligence (vocabulary) and fluid intelligence (spatial orientation and inductive reasoning) for the participants in the Seattle Longitudinal Study.

Thus, in Schaie's view, it is in middle adulthood, not early adulthood, that people reach a peak in their cognitive functioning for many intellectual skills.

Information Processing

Recall from our discussion of theories of development in chapter 2 and in a number of child development and adolescence chapters (8, 10, and 12), we also examined

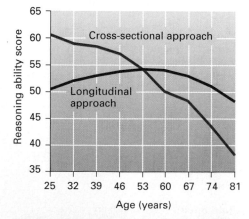

FIGURE 16.8 Cross-Sectional and Longitudinal Comparisons of Intellectual Change in Middle Adulthood

the information-processing approach to cognition. Among the information-processing changes that take place in middle adulthood are those involved in speed of processing information, memory, expertise, and practical problem-solving skills.

Speed of Information Processing   As we saw in Schaie's (1994, 1996) Seattle Longitudinal Study, perceptual speed begins declining in early adulthood and continues to decline in middle adulthood. A common way to assess speed of information is through a reaction-time task, in which individuals simply press a button as soon as they see a light appear (Madden, 2001). Middle-aged adults are slower to push the button when the light appears than young adults are. However, keep in mind that the decline is not dramatic—under 1 second in most investigations. Also, for unknown reasons, the decline in reaction time is stronger for women than for men (Salthouse, 1994).

Memory   In Schaie's (1994, 1996) Seattle Longitudinal Study, verbal memory peaked in the fifties. However, in some other studies, verbal memory has shown a decline in middle age, especially when assessed in cross-sectional studies. For example, in several studies, when asked to remember lists of words, numbers, or meaningful prose, younger adults outperformed middle-aged adults (Salthouse, 1991; Salthouse & Skovronek, 1992). Although there still is some controversy about whether memory declines in the middle adulthood years, most experts conclude that it does decline (Salthouse, 2000). However, some experts argue that studies that have concluded there is a decline in memory during middle age often have compared young adults in their twenties with older middle-aged adults in their late fifties and even have included some individuals in their sixties (Schaie, 2000). In this latter view, memory decline in the early part of middle age either is nonexistent or minimal, not occurring until the latter part of middle age or late adulthood (Backman, Small, & Wahlin, 2001).

Aging and cognition expert Denise Park (2001) argues that starting in late middle age, more time is needed to learn new information. **Working memory** is closely linked to short-term memory but places more emphasis on memory as a place for mental work. Working memory is like a "workbench" where individuals can manipulate and assemble information when making decisions, solving problems, and comprehending written and spoken language (Baddeley, 2000). Linked to the slowdown in learning new information in late middle age, working memory capacity—the amount of information that can be immediately retrieved and used—becomes more limited (Leonards, Ibanez, & Giannakopoulous, 2002). Think of this situation as an overcrowded desk with many items in disarray. As a result of the overcrowding and disarray, long-term memory becomes less reliable, more time is needed to enter new information into long-term storage, and more time is required to retrieve the information. Thus, Park believes that much of the blame for declining memory in late middle age is a result of information overload that continues to build up as we go through the adult years.

Memory decline is more likely to occur when individuals don't use effective memory strategies, such as organization and imagery. By organizing lists of phone numbers into different categories or imagining the phone numbers as representing different objects around the house, many people can improve their memory in middle adulthood.

Expertise   As we learned in chapter 10, *expertise* involves having an extensive, highly organized knowledge and understanding of a particular domain. Individuals can have expertise in areas as diverse as physics, art, or knowledge of wine. Developing expertise and becoming an "expert" in a field usually is the result of many years of experience, learning, and effort. Because it takes so long to attain, expertise often shows up more in the middle adulthood than in the early adulthood years (Clancy & Hoyer, 1994; Hoyer & Roodin, 2003).

working memory   Closely related to short-term memory but places more emphasis on mental work. Working memory is like a "workbench" where individuals can manipulate and assemble information when making decisions, solving problems, and comprehending written and spoken language.

Stephen J. Hawking is a world-renowned expert in physics. Hawking authored the best-selling book, *A Brief History of Time*. Hawking has a neurological disorder that prevents him from walking or talking. He communicates with the aid of a voice-equipped computer. *What distinguishes experts from novices?*

Strategies that distinguish experts from novices include these:

- Experts are more likely to rely on their accumulated experience to solve problems.
- Experts often process information automatically and analyze it more efficiently when solving a problem in their domain than novices do.
- Experts have better strategies and shortcuts to solving problems in their domain than novices do.
- Experts are more creative and flexible in solving problems in their domain than novices are (Csikszentmihalyi, 1997).

Practical Problem Solving   A final difference in the information processing of middle-aged and young adults involves solving practical problems. Nancy Denney (1986, 1990) assessed practical problem-solving abilities in adults by observing such circumstances as how they handled a landlord who would not fix their stove and what they did if a bank mistakenly did not deposit a check in their account. She found that the ability to solve such practical problems increased through the forties and fifties as individuals accumulated practical experience.

Review and Reflect: Learning Goal 3

3 **Identify cognitive changes in middle adulthood**

REVIEW

- How does intelligence develop in middle adulthood?
- What changes take place in processing information during middle age?

REFLECT

- What do you think are the most important cohort effects that can influence the development of intelligence in middle age? How are these likely to change in the future?

4 CAREERS, WORK, AND LEISURE

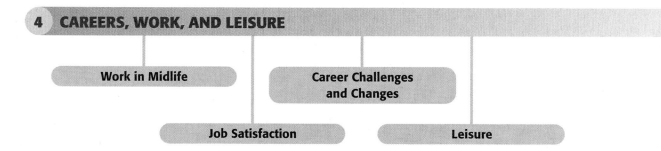

Work in Midlife

Career Challenges and Changes

Job Satisfaction

Leisure

What are some issues that workers face in midlife? Are middle-aged workers as satisfied with their jobs as young adult workers?

Work in Midlife

The role of work, whether one works in a full-time career, a part-time job, as a volunteer, or a homemaker, is central during the middle years. Middle-aged adults may reach their peak in position and earnings. They may also be saddled with multiple financial burdens from rent or mortgage, child care, medical bills, home repairs, college tuition, loans to family members, or bills from nursing homes.

The progression of career trajectories in middle age is diverse. Some individuals have stable careers, with little mobility, while others move in and out of the labor force, experiencing layoffs and unemployment. Middle-aged adults may experience age discrimination in some job situations, and finding a job in midlife may be difficult because pay demands of older workers are higher than those of younger workers, or technological advances may render the midlife worker's skills outdated or obsolete. (Lachman, 2004, p. 323)

In the United States, approximately 80 percent of individuals 40 to 59 years of age are employed. In the 51-to-59 age group, slightly less than 25 percent do not work. More than half of this age group say that a health condition or an impairment limits the type of paid work that they do (Sterns & Huyck, 2001). Further, U.S. labor force participation is projected to grow to 37 percent for the 55-and-older age group, a 6.5 percent increase over the participation rate for 1996 with the 55-to-64 age group to add 7.3 million workers (Schwerha & McMullin, 2002). The majority of these increases are expected to be in the service industry.

An important issue in midlife is whether individuals will continue to do the type of work that they want to do. Mental and physical capabilities will not be a major impediment for many middle-aged adults if they want to continue working.

For many people, midlife is a time of evaluation, assessment, and reflection in terms of the work they do and want to do in the future. Among the work issues that some people face in midlife are recognizing limitations in career progress, deciding whether to change jobs or careers, deciding whether to rebalance family and work, and planning for retirement (Sterns & Huyck, 2001).

 Watch the video "Interview with Stay-Home Dad" to hear a father's reflections on his decision to be the primary child-care parent.

Job Satisfaction

Work satisfaction increases steadily throughout the work life—from age 20 to at least age 60, for both college-educated and non-college-educated adults (Rhodes, 1983) (see figure 16.9). This same pattern has been found for both women and men. Satisfaction probably increases because as we get older we get paid more, we are in higher positions, and we have more job security. There is also a greater commitment to the job as we get older. We take our jobs more seriously, have lower rates of avoidable absenteeism, and are more involved with our work in middle adulthood than in early adulthood. Younger adults are still experimenting with their work and still searching for the right occupation. They may be inclined to seek out what is wrong with their current job rather than focusing on what is right about it. For the most part, researchers have found the highest levels of physical and psychological well-being in people who are doing as much paid work as they would like to do.

Career Challenges and Changes

The current middle-aged worker faces several important challenges in the twenty-first century (Avolio & Sosik, 1999). These include the globalization of work, rapid developments in information technologies, downsizing of organizations, and early retirement.

Globalization has replaced the traditional White male workforce with employees of different ethnic and national backgrounds. The proliferation of computer technology compels middle-aged adults to become increasingly computer literate to maintain their work competence (Csaja, 2001). To improve profits, many companies are restructuring and downsizing. One of the outcomes of this is to offer incentives to middle-aged employees to retire early—in their fifties, or in some cases even forties, rather than their sixties.

Some midlife career changes are self-motivated, others are the consequence of losing one's job (Moen, 1998; Moen &

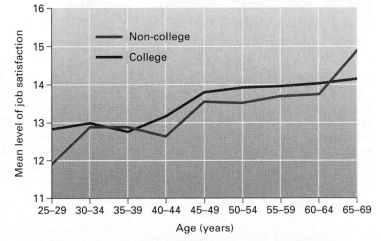

FIGURE 16.9 Age and Job Satisfaction
Job satisfaction increases with age, for both college- and non-college-educated adults. Among the reasons for increased satisfaction are more income, higher-status jobs, greater job security, and stronger job commitment.

Women and Work in Midcareer

Wethington, 1999). Some individuals in middle age decide that they don't want to do the same work they have been doing for the rest of their lives (Hoyer & Roodin, 2003). One aspect of middle adulthood involves adjusting idealistic hopes to realistic possibilities in light of how much time individuals have before they retire and how fast they are reaching their occupational goals (Levinson, 1978). If individuals perceive that they are behind schedule, if their goals are unrealistic, they don't like the work they are doing, or their job has become too stressful, they could become motivated to change jobs.

Leisure

As adults, not only must we learn how to work well, but we also need to learn how to relax and enjoy leisure (Strain & others, 2002). With the kind of work ethic on which America is based, it is not surprising to find that many adults view leisure as boring and unnecessary. But even Aristotle recognized leisure's importance in life, stressing that we should not only work well but use leisure well. He described leisure as better because it was the end of work. How can we define leisure? **Leisure** refers to the pleasant times after work when individuals are free to pursue activities and interests of their own choosing—hobbies, sports, or reading, for example.

Sigmund Freud once commented that the two things adults need to do well to adapt to society's demands are to work and to love. To his list we add "to play." In our fast-paced society, it is all too easy to get caught up in the frenzied, hectic pace of our achievement-oriented work world and ignore leisure and play. *Imagine your life as a middle-aged adult. What would be the ideal mix of work and leisure? What leisure activities do you want to enjoy as a middle-aged adult?*

Leisure can be an especially important aspect of middle adulthood because of the changes many individuals experience at this point in the adult life span (Mannell, 2000; McGuire, 2000). The changes include physical changes, relationship changes with spouse and children, and career changes. By middle adulthood, more money is available to many individuals, and there may be more free time and paid vacations. These midlife changes may produce expanded opportunities for leisure. For many individuals, middle adulthood is the first time in their lives when they have the opportunity to diversify their interests.

In one study, 12,338 men 35 to 57 years of age were assessed each year for five years regarding whether they took vacations or not (Gump & Matthews, 2000). Then, the researchers examined the medical and death records over nine years for men who lived for at least a year after the last vacation survey. Compared with those who never took vacations, men who went on annual vacations were 21 percent less likely to die over the nine years and 32 percent less likely to die of coronary heart disease. The qualities that lead men to pass on a vacation tend to promote heart disease, such as not trusting anyone to fill in while you are gone or fearing that you will get behind in your work and someone will replace you. These are behaviors that sometimes have been described as part of the Type A behavioral pattern.

leisure The pleasant times after work when individuals are free to pursue activities and interests of their own choosing.

Adults at midlife need to begin preparing psychologically for retirement. Constructive and fulfilling leisure activities in middle adulthood are an important part of this preparation (Kelly, 1996). If an adult develops leisure activities that can be continued into retirement, the transition from work to retirement can be less stressful.

Review and Reflect: Learning Goal 4

 4 Characterize career development, work, and leisure in middle adulthood

REVIEW

- What are some issues that workers face in midlife?
- What is job satisfaction like in middle age?
- What career challenges and changes might people experience in middle adulthood?
- What characterizes leisure in middle age?

REFLECT

- What do you want your work life and leisure to be like in middle age? If you are middle aged, what is your work life and leisure like? If you are an older adult, what were they like in middle age?

5 RELIGION AND MEANING IN LIFE

Religion and Adult Lives   **Religion and Health**   **Meaning in Life**

What role does religion play in our development as adults? Is meaning of life an important theme for many middle-aged adults?

Religion and Adult Lives

In the MacArthur Study of Midlife Development, more than 70 percent of the individuals said they are religious and consider spirituality a major part of their lives (Brim, 1999). However, that does not mean they are committed to a single religion or house of worship. About half said they attend religious services less than once a month or never. In another study, about three-fourths of Americans said that they pray (*Religion in America*, 1993).

In a recent longitudinal study of individuals from their early thirties through their late sixties/early seventies, a significant increase in spirituality occurred between late middle (mid-fifties/early sixties) and late adulthood (Wink & Dillon, 2002) (see figure 16.10). Religion also is an important aspect of people's lives around the world—98 percent of respondents in India, 88 percent in Italy, 72 percent in France, and 63 percent in Scandinavia say that they believe in God (Gallup, 1987).

Females have consistently shown a stronger interest in religion than males have (Bijur & others, 1993). Compared with men, they participate more in both organized and personal forms of religion, are more likely to believe in a higher power or presence, and are more likely to feel that religion is an important dimension of their lives. In the recent longitudinal study just described, the spirituality of women increased more than men in the second half of life (Wink & Dillon, 2002).

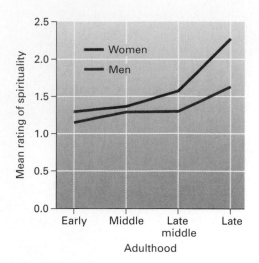

FIGURE 16.10 Level of Spirituality in Four Adult Age Periods

In a longitudinal study, the spirituality of individuals in four different adult age periods—early (30s), middle (40s), late middle (mid-50s/early 60s), and late (late 60s/early 70s) adulthood—was assessed (Wink & Dillon, 2002). Based on responses to open-ended questions in interviews, the spirituality of the individuals was coded on a 5-point scale with 5 being the highest level of spirituality and 1 the lowest.

Exploring the Psychology of Religion
Psychology of Religion Journals
Mental Health, Religion, and Culture

What roles do religion and spirituality play in the lives of middle-aged adults?

A series of recent studies have found that Americans are becoming less committed to particular religious denominations (such as Baptist or Catholic). They are more tolerant of other faiths and more focused on their own spiritual journeys (Paloutzian, 2000). This change may be partly generational, a consequence of postwar baby boomers' emphasis on experimentation and independent thinking that is reflected in a fluid religious orientation.

At the same time that many Americans show a strong interest in religion and believe in God, they also reveal a declining faith in mainstream religious institutions, in religious leaders, and in the spiritual and moral stature of the nation (*Religion in America*, 1993; Sollod, 2000).

In thinking about religion and adult development, it is important to consider the role of individual differences. Religion is a powerful influence in some adults' lives, whereas it plays little or no role in others' lives (Myers, 2000). Further, the influence of religion in people's lives may change as they develop. In John Clausen's (1993) longitudinal investigation, some individuals who had been strongly religious in their early adult years became less so in middle age; others became more religious in middle age.

Religion and Health

How might religion be related to physical health? To coping and happiness?

Religion and Physical Health   What might be some of the effects of religion on physical health? One example is cults or religious sects that encourage behaviors that are damaging to health. For example, some religious sects ignore sound medical advice or refuse pain-relieving medication. For individuals in the religious mainstream, there is generally either no link between religion and physical health or a positive effect. For example, in one review, five studies documented that religious commitment had a protective influence on blood pressure or hypertension rates (Levin & Vanderpool, 1989). Also, a number of studies have confirmed a positive association of religious participation and longevity (Hummer & others, 1999; Thoresen & Harris, 2002).

Why might religion promote physical health? There are several possible answers (Hill & Butter, 1995):

- *Lifestyle issues.* For example, religious individuals have lower drug use than their nonreligious counterparts (Gartner, Larson, & Allen, 1991).
- *Social networks.* The degree to which individuals are connected to others affects their health. Well-connected individuals have fewer health problems. Religious groups, meetings, and activities provide social connectedness for individuals.
- *Coping with stress.* Religion offers a source of comfort and support when individuals are confronted with stressful events. Although research has not clearly demonstrated prayer's positive effect on physical health, some investigators argue that prayer might be associated with such positive health-related changes as a decrease in the perception of pain and reduced muscle tension (McCullough, 1995).

It also has been stressed that religious organizations might have a stronger influence on physical health by providing more health-related services. For example, they could sponsor community-based health education and health-testing programs.

Coping   What is the relation between religion and the ability to cope with stress? Some psychologists have categorized prayer and religious commitment as defensive coping strategies, arguing that they are less effective in helping individuals cope than are life-skill, problem-solving strategies. However, recently researchers have found that some styles of religious coping are associated with high levels of personal initiative and competence, and that even when defensive religious strategies are initially adopted, they sometimes set the stage for the later appearance of more-active religious coping (Dunn & Horgas, 2004; Pargament & Park, 1995; Seifert, 2002). In one study, depression decreased during times of high stress when there was an increase in collaborative coping (in which people see themselves as active partners with God in solving problems) (Brickel & others, 1998). Also, in general, an intrinsic religious orientation tends to be associated with a sense of competence and control, freedom from worry and guilt, and an absence of illness, whereas an extrinsic orientation tends to be associated with the opposite characteristics (Ventis, 1995).

Instead of disintegrating during times of high stress, religious coping behaviors appear to function quite well in these periods (Koenig, 1998, 2001). In one study, individuals were divided into those who were experiencing high stress and those with low stress (Manton, 1989). In the high-stress group, spiritual support was significantly related to personal adjustment (indicated by low depression and high self-esteem). No such links were found in the low-stress group. In a study of 850 medically ill patients admitted to an acute-care hospital, religious coping was related to low depression (Koenig & others, 1992). In John Clausen's (1993) analysis of individuals in the Berkeley Longitudinal Studies, the more-competent women and men in middle age were more likely than their less-competent counterparts to have a religious affiliation and involvement.

In sum, various dimensions of religiousness can help some individuals cope more effectively with their lives (Paloutzian, 2000; Thoresen & Harris, 2002; Thrasher, Campbell, & Oates, 2004). Religious beliefs can shape a person's psychological perception of pain or disability. Religious cognitions can play an important role in maintaining hope and stimulating motivation toward recovery. Because of its effectiveness in reducing distress, religious coping can help prevent denial of the problem and thus facilitate early recognition and more appropriate health-seeking behavior. Religion also can forestall the development of anxiety and depression disorders by promoting communal or social interaction. Houses of religious worship are a readily available, acceptable, and inexpensive source of support for many individuals, especially the elderly. The socialization provided by religious organizations can help prevent isolation and loneliness (Koenig & Larson, 1998).

Religious counselors often advise people about mental health and coping. To read about the work of one religious counselor, see the Careers in Life-Span Development insert.

Happiness Are people who have a meaningful faith happier than those who do not? Reviews of the happiness literature suggest that happy people do tend to have a meaningful religious faith (Diener, Lucas, & Oishi, 2002). Remember, though, that knowing that two factors correlate does not mean that one causes the other (just as in the case of religion and mental disorder co-occurring in a few individuals). A number of researchers have found that religiously active individuals report greater happiness than do those who are religiously inactive (Diener, Lucas, & Oishi, 2002). However, we don't know whether this connection means that faith enhances happiness or whether happiness induces faith.

Careers in Life-Span Development

Alice McNair, Pastoral Counselor

Alice McNair is a pastoral counselor in Mocksville, North Carolina. She has a doctorate in pastoral counseling from Northwestern University. Prior to her present position, McNair was director of the Pastoral Ministries Institute near Washington, D.C. She also is an ordained Baptist minister. She works with adolescents and adults, providing individual, marital, and family counseling.

Meaning in Life

Austrian psychiatrist Viktor Frankl's mother, father, brother, and wife died in the concentration camps and gas chambers in Auschwitz, Poland. Frankl survived the concentration camp and went on to write about meaning in life. In his book, *Man's Search for Meaning*, Frankl (1984) emphasized each person's uniqueness and the finiteness of life. He believed that examining the finiteness of our existence and the certainty of death adds meaning to life. If life were not finite, said Frankl, we could spend our life doing just about whatever we please because time would continue forever.

Frankl said that the three most distinct human qualities are spirituality, freedom, and responsibility. Spirituality, in his view, does not have a religious underpinning. Rather, it refers to a human being's uniqueness—to spirit, philosophy, and mind. Frankl proposed that people need to ask themselves such questions as why they exist, what they want from life, and what the meaning of their life is.

It is in middle adulthood that individuals begin to be faced with death more often, especially the deaths of parents and other older relatives. Also faced with less time in their life, many individuals in middle age begin to ask and evaluate the questions that Frankl proposed.

Roy Baumeister and Kathleen Vohs (2002, pp. 610–611) argue that the quest for a meaningful life can be understood in terms of four main needs for meaning that guide how people try to make sense of their lives:

- *Need for purpose.* "Present events draw meaning from their connection with future events." Purposes can be divided into (1) goals and (2) fulfillments. Life can be oriented toward a future anticipated state, such as living happily ever after or being in love.
- *Need for values.* This "can lend a sense of goodness or positive characterization of life and justify certain courses of action. Values enable people to decide whether certain acts are right or wrong." Frankl's (1984) view of meaning in life emphasized value as the main form of meaning that people need.
- *Need for a sense of efficacy.* This involves the "belief that one can make a difference. A life that had purposes and values but no efficacy would be tragic. The person might know what is desirable but could not do anything with that knowledge." With a sense of efficacy, people believe that they can control their environment, which has positive physical and mental health benefits (Bandura, 2001).
- *Need for self-worth.* Most individuals want to be "good, worthy persons. Self-worth can be pursued individually, such as" finding out that one is very good at doing something, or collectively, as when people find self-esteem from belonging to a group or category of people.

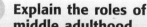

Review and Reflect: Learning Goal 5

5 **Explain the roles of religion and meaning in life during middle adulthood**

REVIEW

- What are some characteristics of religion in middle-aged individuals?
- How is religion linked to physical and mental health?
- What roles does meaning in life play in middle adulthood?

REFLECT

- What are the most important aspects of meaning in life? Might the components of meaning in life vary depending on how old someone is? Explain.

Reach Your Learning Goals

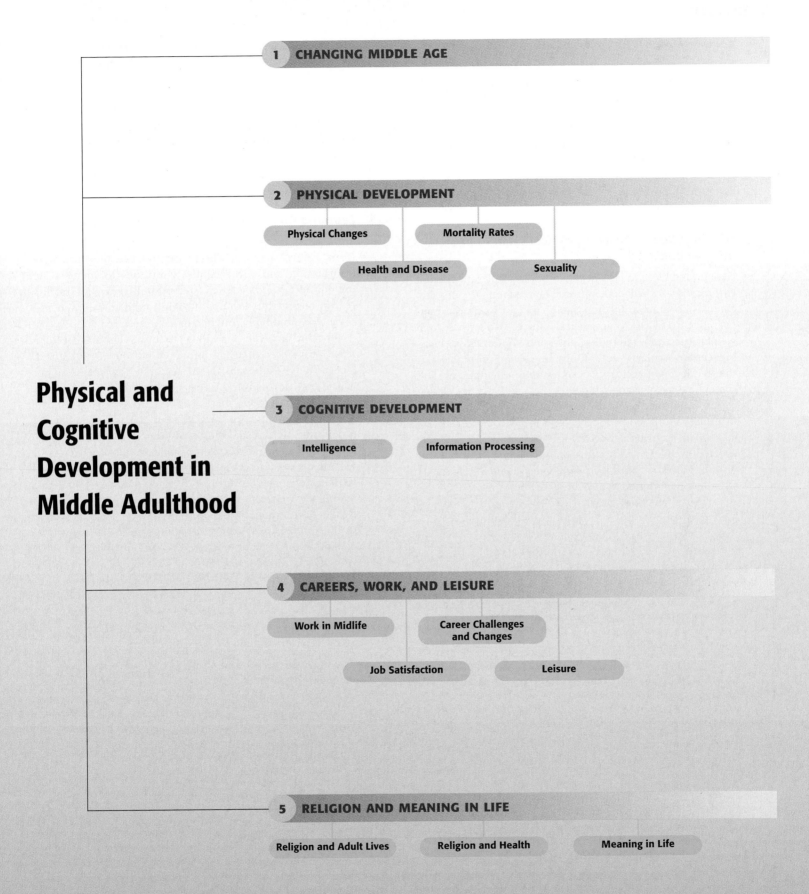

Physical and Cognitive Development in Middle Adulthood

1 **CHANGING MIDDLE AGE**

2 **PHYSICAL DEVELOPMENT**

Physical Changes

Mortality Rates

Health and Disease

Sexuality

3 **COGNITIVE DEVELOPMENT**

Intelligence

Information Processing

4 **CAREERS, WORK, AND LEISURE**

Work in Midlife

Career Challenges and Changes

Job Satisfaction

Leisure

5 **RELIGION AND MEANING IN LIFE**

Religion and Adult Lives

Religion and Health

Meaning in Life

Summary

 Learning Goal 1: Explain how middle age is changing

- The age boundaries of middle age are not set in stone. As more people live to an older age, what we think of as middle age seems to be occurring later. Developmentalists are beginning to study middle age more probably because of the dramatic increase in the number of individuals entering this period of the life span. Middle age involves extensive individual variation. With this variation in mind, we will consider middle adulthood to be entered at about 40 and exited at approximately 60 years of age. Midlife changes are often gradual.

 Learning Goal 2: Discuss physical changes in middle adulthood

- Genetic and lifestyle factors play important roles in whether chronic diseases will appear and when. Among the physical changes are outwardly noticeable changes in physical appearance (wrinkles, aging spots); height (decrease) and weight (increase); strength, joints, and bones; vision; hearing; cardiovascular system; lungs; and sleep. In middle age, the frequency of accidents declines and individuals are less susceptible to colds and allergies.
- Chronic disorders rarely appear in early adulthood, increase in middle adulthood, and become more common in late adulthood. Arthritis is the leading chronic disorder in middle age, followed by hypertension. Men have more fatal chronic disorders, women more nonfatal ones in middle age. Researchers have found that acute stressors can produce immunological changes and that chronic stressors are associated with a downturn in immune system functioning. Research with cancer patients shows that a good quality of life is associated with a healthier immune system. Emotional stress likely is an important factor contributing to cardiovascular disease. People who live in a chronically stressed condition are likelier to smoke, overeat, and not exercise. All of these stress-related behaviors are linked with cardiovascular disease. Culture plays an important role in coronary disease. The Type A behavior pattern has been proposed as having a link with heart disease, but it primarily is the hostility dimension of the pattern that is consistently associated with heart disease. Hardiness is a buffer of stress and is related to reduced illness. Health in middle age is linked to the current quality of social relationships and to developmental pathways of relationships.
- In middle age, the leading causes of death, in order, are heart disease, cancer, and cerebrovascular disease.
- Climacteric is the midlife transition in which fertility declines. Menopause is a marker that signals the end of childbearing capability, usually arriving in the late forties and early fifties. The vast majority of women do not have serious physical or psychological problems related to menopause. Hormone replacement therapy (HRT) augments the declining levels of reproductive hormone production by the ovaries. HRT consists of various forms of estrogen, and usually progestin. Recent negative hormone therapy results suggest that long-term hormone therapy should be seriously evaluated. Men do not experience an inability to father children in middle age, although their testosterone levels decline. A male menopause, like the dramatic decline in estrogen in women, does not occur. Sexual behavior occurs less frequently in middle adulthood than in early adulthood. Nonetheless, a majority of middle-aged adults show a moderate or strong interest in sex.

 Learning Goal 3: Identify cognitive changes in middle adulthood

- Horn argued that crystallized intelligence (accumulated information and verbal skills) continues to increase in middle adulthood, whereas fluid intelligence (ability to reason abstractly) declines. Schaie found that, when assessed longitudinally, intellectual abilities are less likely to decline and are even more likely to improve than when assessed cross-sectionally in middle adulthood. The highest level of four intellectual abilities (vocabulary, verbal memory, inductive reasoning, and spatial orientation) occurred in middle age.
- Speed of information processing, often assessed through reaction time, declines in middle adulthood. Although Schaie found that verbal memory increased in middle age, some researchers have found that memory declines in middle age. Working memory declines in late middle age. Memory is more likely to decline in middle age when individuals don't use effective strategies. Expertise involves having an extensive, highly organized knowledge and an understanding of a domain. Expertise often increases in the middle adulthood years. Practical problem solving often increases through the forties and fifties as individuals accumulate practical experience.

4 **Learning Goal 4: Characterize career development, work, and leisure in middle adulthood**

- Midlife workers face a number of issues and for many people midlife is a time of reflection, assessment, and evaluation of their current work and what they plan to do in the future. One important issue is whether individuals will continue to do the type of work they want to do.
- Work satisfaction increases steadily throughout life—from age 20 to at least age 60—for both college-educated and non-college-educated adults.
- The current middle-aged worker faces such challenges as the globalization of work, rapid developments in information technologies, downsizing of organizations, and early retirement. Midlife job or career changes can be self-motivated or forced on individuals.
- We not only need to learn to work well, but we also need to learn to enjoy leisure. Midlife may be an especially important

time for leisure because of the physical changes that occur and because of preparation for an active retirement.

5 *Learning Goal 5: Explain the roles of religion and meaning in life during middle adulthood*

- Religion is an important dimension of many Americans' lives, as well as the lives of people around the world. Females show a stronger interest in religion than males do. It is important to consider individual differences in religious interest.
- In some cases, religion can be negatively linked to physical health, as when cults or religious sects restrict individuals from obtaining medical care. In mainstream religions, reli-

gion usually shows either a positive association or no association with physical health. Religion can play an important role in coping, for some individuals. Happy people tend to have a meaningful religious faith, but it is important to remember that the link is correlational, not causal.
- Frankl believes that examining the finiteness of our existence leads to exploration of meaning in life. Faced with the death of older relatives and less time to live themselves, many middle-aged individuals increasingly examine life's meaning. Baumeister argues that a quest for a meaningful life involves four main needs: purpose, values, efficacy, and self-worth.

Key Terms

middle adulthood 501
chronic disorders 506
Type A behavior pattern 508

Type B behavior pattern 508
hardiness 508
climacteric 509

menopause 510
crystallized intelligence 513
fluid intelligence 513

working memory 515
leisure 518

Key People

Gilbert Brim 502
Meyer Friedman and Ray
  Rosenman 508

John Horn 513
K. Warner Schaie 513
Denise Park 515

Nancy Denney 516
John Clausen 520
Victor Frankl 522

Roy Baumeister and Kathleen
  Vohs 522

E-Learning Tools

To help you master the material in this chapter, you'll find a number of valuable study tools on the LifeMap CD-ROM that accompanies this book and on the Online Learning Center for *Life-Span Development*, tenth edition, at www.mhhe.com/santrockld10.

Video Clips

In the margins of this book there are icons directing you to the LifeMap CD-ROM that accompanies the book. There you'll find a video for chapter 16 called "Interview with Stay-Home Dad." An increasing number of fathers in developed countries have the choice of staying home to raise their children. In this segment, a father reflects on the choice he made to stay home.

Self-Assessment

Connect to www.mhhe.com/santrockld10 to reflect on philosophical issues by completing the self-assessments, *My Spiritual Well-Being* and *What Is My Purpose in Life?*

Taking It to the Net

Connect to www.mhhe.com/santrockld10 to research the answers to these questions.

1. In their book, *Midlife Crisis at 30: How the Stakes Have Changed for a New Generation and What to Do About It* (Rodale Press, 2004),

Lia Macko and Kerry Rubin describe how young professional women face a "midlife crisis." They claim that a woman's experience at age 30 today is analogous to what men have traditionally experienced at age 50. What changing factors would account for this alleged shift? Do you think Macko and Rubin overstate their case or oversimplify it at any point?

2. Advances in health and hygiene mean that Americans tend to live longer. What do we need to know about how to cultivate physical health and productivity in America's aging population?

3. Harry can't decide whether to go to theological seminary to study for the ministry or go to medical school. Recent polls indicate that his interests are not necessarily incompatible. What are people reporting about the role of religion in mental and physical health?

Health and Well-Being, Parenting, and Education Exercises

Build your decision-making skills by trying your hand at the health and well-being, parenting, and education exercises.

Connect to www.mhhe.com/santrockld10 to research the answers and complete the exercises.

CHAPTER

The generations of living things pass in a short time, and like runners, hand on the torch of life.
—LUCRETIUS
Roman Poet, 1st Century B.C.

Socioemotional Development in Middle Adulthood

Chapter Outline

PERSONALITY THEORIES AND DEVELOPMENT

Adult Stage Theories

The Life-Events Approach

Stress in Midlife

Contexts of Midlife Development

STABILITY AND CHANGE

Longitudinal Studies

Conclusions

CLOSE RELATIONSHIPS

Love and Marriage at Midlife

The Empty Nest and Its Refilling

Sibling Relationships and Friendships

Grandparenting

Intergenerational Relationships

Learning Goals

1 Describe personality theories and development in middle adulthood

2 Discuss stability and change in development during middle adulthood, including longitudinal studies

3 Identify some important aspects of close relationships in middle adulthood

Images of Life-Span Development
Middle-Age Variations

Forty-five-year-old Sarah feels tired, depressed, and angry when she looks back on the way her life has gone. She became pregnant when she was 17 and married Ben, the baby's father. They stayed together for three years after their son was born, and then Ben left her for another woman. Sarah went to work as a salesclerk to make ends meet. Eight years later, she married Alan, who had two children of his own from a previous marriage. Sarah stopped working for several years to care for the children. Then, like Ben, Alan started going out on her. She found out about it from a friend. Nevertheless, Sarah stayed with Alan for another year. Finally he was gone so much that she could not take it anymore and decided to divorce him. Sarah went back to work again as a salesclerk; she has been in the same position for 16 years now. During those 16 years, she has dated a number of men, but the relationships never seemed to work out. Her son never finished high school and has drug problems. Her father just died last year, and Sarah is trying to help her mother financially, although she can barely pay her own bills. Sarah looks in the mirror and does not like what she sees. She sees her past as a shambles, and the future does not look rosy, either.

Forty-five-year-old Wanda feels energetic, happy, and satisfied. As a young woman, she graduated from college and worked for three years as a high school math teacher. She married Andy, who had just finished law school. One year later, they had their first child, Josh. Wanda stayed home with Josh for two years, and then returned to her job as a math teacher. Even during her pregnancy, Wanda stayed active and exercised regularly, playing tennis almost every day. After her pregnancy, she kept up her exercise habits. Wanda and Andy had another child, Wendy. Now, as they move into their middle-age years, their children are both off to college, and Wanda and Andy are enjoying spending more time with each other. Last weekend they visited Josh at his college, and the weekend before they visited Wendy at her college. Wanda continued working as a high school math teacher until six years ago. She had developed computer skills as part of her job and taken some computer courses at a nearby college, doubling up during the summer months. She resigned her math teaching job and took a job with a computer company, where she has already worked her way into management. Wanda looks in the mirror and likes what she sees. She sees her past as enjoyable, although not without hills and valleys, and she looks to the future with zest and enthusiasm.

PREVIEW

As with Sarah and Wanda, there are individual variations in the way people experience middle age. To begin the chapter we will examine personality theories and development in middle age, including further ideas about individual variation. Then we will turn our attention to how much individuals change or stay the same as they go through the adult years and finally explore a number of aspects of close relationships during the middle adulthood years.

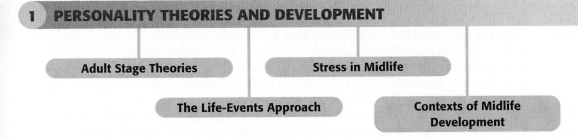

1 PERSONALITY THEORIES AND DEVELOPMENT

- Adult Stage Theories
- The Life-Events Approach
- Stress in Midlife
- Contexts of Midlife Development

What is the best way to conceptualize middle age? Is it a stage or a crisis? How pervasive are midlife crises? How extensively is middle age influenced by life events? Do middle-aged adults experience stress differently than young and older adults? Is personality linked with the contexts, such as the point in history in which individuals go through midlife, their culture, and their gender?

Adult Stage Theories

Adult stage theories have been plentiful, and they have contributed to the view that midlife is a crisis in development. Two prominent adult stage theories are Erik Erikson's life-span view and Daniel Levinson's seasons of a man's life.

Erikson's Stage of Generativity Versus Stagnation Erikson (1968) proposed that middle-aged adults face a significant issue in life—generativity versus stagnation, which is the name Erikson gave to the seventh stage in his life-span theory. Generativity encompasses adults' desire to leave legacies of themselves to the next generation (Petersen, 2002). Through generativity, adults achieve a kind of immortality by leaving these legacies. By contrast, stagnation (sometimes called "self-absorption") develops when individuals sense that they have done nothing for the next generation.

In George Vaillant's (2002) longitudinal studies of aging, in middle age, generativity (defined in this study as "taking care of the next generation") was more strongly related than intimacy to whether individuals would have an enduring and happy marriage at 75 to 80 years of age. One of the participants in Vaillant's studies said: "From twenty to thirty I learned how to get along with my wife. From thirty to forty I learned how to be a success at my job, and at forty to fifty I worried less about myself and more about the children" (p. 114).

In a longitudinal study of Smith College women, generativity increased from the thirties through the fifties (Cole & Stewart, 1996; Roberts & Helson, 1997; Stewart, Ostrove, & Helson, 2001; Zucker, Ostrove, & Stewart, 2002) (see figure 17.1). Also in this study, another aspect of Erikson's theory—identity—was assessed in terms of "identity certainty" and this increased from the thirties through the fifties. Figure 17.2 describes the items that were used to assess generativity and identity certainty in the Smith College study.

Middle-aged adults can develop generativity in a number of different ways (Kotre, 1984). Through biological generativity, adults conceive and give birth to an infant. Through parental generativity, adults provide nurturance and guidance to children. Through work generativity, adults develop skills that are passed down to others. And through cultural generativity, adults create, renovate, or conserve some aspect of culture that ultimately survives.

Through generativity, adults promote and guide the next generation by parenting, teaching, leading, and doing things that benefit the community (Pratt & others, 2001). Generative adults commit themselves to the continuation and improvement of society as a whole through their connection to the next generation. Generative adults develop a positive legacy of the self and then offer it as a gift to the next generation.

Does research support Erikson's theory that generativity is an important dimension of middle age? Yes, it does. In one study, Carol Ryff (1984) examined the views

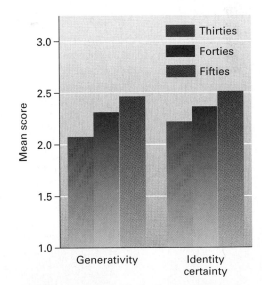

FIGURE 17.1 Changes in Generativity and Identity Certainty from the Thirties Through the Fifties

Both generativity and identity certainty increased in Smith College women as they aged from their thirties through their fifties (Stewart, Ostrove, & Helson, 2001). The women rated themselves on a 3-point scale indicating the extent to which they thought the statements about generativity and identity certainty were descriptive of their lives.

Generativity

Feeling needed by people

Effort to ensure that young people get their chance to develop

Influence in my community or area of interest

A new level of productivity or effectiveness

Appreciation and awareness of older people

Having a wider perspective

Interest in things beyond my family

Identity certainty

A sense of being my own person

Excitement, turmoil, confusion about my impulses and potential (reversed)

Coming near the end of one road and not yet finding another (reversed)

Feeling my life is moving well

Searching for a sense of who I am (reversed)

Wishing I had a wider scope to my life (reversed)

Anxiety that I won't live up to opportunities (reversed)

Feeling secure and committed

FIGURE 17.2 Items Used to Assess Generativity and Identity Certainty
These items were used to assess generativity and identity certainty in the longitudinal study of Smith College women (Stewart, Ostrove, & Helson, 2001). In the assessment of identity certainty, five of the items involved reversed scoring (for example, if an individual scored high on the item "Searching for a sense of who I am," it was an indication of identity uncertainty rather than identity certainty).

www.mhhe.com/santrockld10

Midlife Crisis
The MacArthur Foundation
Study of Midlife Development

of women and men at different ages across adulthood. The middle-aged adults especially were concerned about generativity and guiding younger adults. In another study, having a positive identity was linked with generativity in middle age (Vandewater, Ostrove, & Stewart, 1997). In another study, women developed generativity through different aspects of their lives (Peterson & Stewart, 1996). Generative women with careers found gratification through work; generative women who had not worked in a career experienced gratification through parenting.

In one modification of Erikson's theory, it was proposed that Erikson's three adult stages—involving intimacy (early adulthood), generativity (middle adulthood), and integrity (late adulthood)—are best viewed as developmental phases within identity. In this view, identity remains the central core of the self's development across all of the adult years (Whitbourne & Connolly, 1999).

Levinson's *Seasons of a Man's Life* In *The Seasons of a Man's Life* (1978), clinical psychologist Daniel Levinson reported the results of extensive interviews with forty middle-aged men. The interviews were conducted with hourly workers, business executives, academic biologists, and novelists. Levinson bolstered his conclusions with information from the biographies of famous men and the development of memorable characters in literature. Although Levinson's major interest focused on midlife change, he described a number of stages and transitions in the life span, ranging from 17 to 65 years of age, which are shown in figure 17.3.

Levinson emphasizes that developmental tasks must be mastered at each of these stages. In early adulthood, the two major tasks to be mastered are exploring the possibilities for adult living and developing a stable life structure. Levinson sees the twenties as a *novice phase* of adult development. At the end of one's teens, a transition from dependence to independence should occur. This transition is marked by the formation of a dream—an image of the kind of life the youth wants to have, especially in terms of a career and marriage. The novice phase is a time of reasonably free experimentation and of testing the dream in the real world.

From about the ages of 28 to 33, the man goes through a transition period in which he must face the more serious question of determining his goals. During the thirties, he usually focuses on family and career development. In the later years of this period, he enters a phase of *Becoming One's Own Man* (or BOOM, as Levinson calls it). By age 40, he has reached a stable location in his career, has outgrown his earlier, more tenuous attempts at learning to become an adult, and now must look forward to the kind of life he will lead as a middle-aged adult.

According to Levinson, the change to middle adulthood lasts about five years (ages 40 to 45) and requires the adult male to come to grips with four major conflicts that have existed in his life since adolescence: (1) being young versus being old, (2) being destructive versus being constructive, (3) being masculine versus being feminine, and (4) being attached to others versus being separated from them. Seventy to 80 percent of the men Levinson interviewed found the midlife transition tumultuous and psychologically painful, as many aspects of their lives came into question. According to Levinson, the success of the midlife transition rests on how effectively the individual reduces the polarities and accepts each of them as an integral part of his being.

Because Levinson interviewed middle-aged males, we can consider the data about middle adulthood more valid than the data about early adulthood. When individuals are asked to remember information about earlier parts of their lives, they may distort and forget things. The original Levinson data included no females, although Levinson (1996) reported that his stages, transitions, and the crisis of middle age hold for females as well as males. Levinson's work included no statistical analysis. However, the quality and quantity of the Levinson biographies are outstanding in the clinical tradition.

How Pervasive Are Midlife Crises? Levinson (1978) views midlife as a crisis, believing that the middle-aged adult is suspended between the past and the future, trying to cope with this gap that threatens life's continuity. George Vaillant (1977) concludes that just as adolescence is a time for detecting parental flaws and discovering the truth about childhood, the forties are a decade of reassessing and recording the truth about the adolescent and adulthood years. However, while Levinson sees midlife as a crisis, Vaillant believes that only a minority of adults experience a midlife crisis:

> Just as pop psychologists have reveled in the not-so-common high drama of adolescent turmoil, also the popular press, sensing good copy, had made all too much of the mid-life crisis. The term mid-life crisis brings to mind some variation of the renegade minister who leaves behind four children and the congregation that loved him in order to drive off in a magenta Porsche with a 25-year-old striptease artiste. As with adolescent turmoil, mid-life crises are much rarer in community samples. (pp. 222–223)

Vaillant's study—called the "Grant Study"—involved a follow-up of Harvard University men in their early thirties and in their late forties who initially had been interviewed as undergraduates. In Vaillant's words, "The high drama in Gail Sheehy's best-selling *Passages* was rarely observed in the lives of the Grant Study men" (p. 223).

The research studies listed here all document that midlife is not characterized by pervasive crises:

- One study assessed 3,032 Americans from 25 to 72 years of age (Brim, 1999). In this study, the individuals from 40 to 60 years of age were less nervous and worried than those under 40. The middle-aged adults reported a growing sense of control in their work and more financial security. The middle-aged adults also indicated a greater sense of environmental mastery—the ability to handle daily responsibilities—and autonomy than their younger counterparts.
- A longitudinal study of 2,247 individuals found few midlife crises (McCrae & Costa, 1990; Siegler & Costa, 1999). In this study, the emotional instability of individuals did not significantly increase through their middle-aged years (see figure 17.4).
- A study found that adults experienced a peak of personal control and power in middle age (Clark-Plaskie & Lachman, 1999).
- A study of individuals described as young (average age 19), middle-aged (average age 46), and older (average age 73) adults found that their ability to manage their environmental surroundings (environmental mastery) and self-determination (autonomy) increased in middle age (Keyes & Ryff, 1999) (see figure 17.5). Their investment in living (purpose in life) and desire for continued self-realization (personal growth) dropped slightly from early to middle adulthood but still remained high before declining in late adulthood.

Adult development experts are virtually unanimous in their belief that midlife crises have been exaggerated (Brim, Ryff, & Kessler, 2004; Etaugh & Bridges, 2001; Lachman, 2004; Reid & Willis, 1999; Wethington, Kessler, & Pixley, 2004). In sum:

- The stage theories place too much emphasis on crises in development, especially midlife crises.
- There often is considerable individual variation in the way people experience the stages, a topic that we will turn to next.

Era of late adulthood: 60 to ?

Late adult transition: Age 60 to 65

Culminating life structure for middle adulthood: 55 to 60

Age 50 transition: 50 to 55

Entry life structure for middle adulthood: 45 to 50

Middle adult transition: Age 40 to 45

Culminating life structure for early adulthood: 33 to 40

Age 30 transition: 28 to 33

Entry life structure for early adulthood: 22 to 28

Early adult transition: Age 17 to 22

FIGURE 17.3 Levinson's Periods of Adult Development

Summary

 Learning Goal 1: Describe personality theories and development in middle adulthood

- Erikson says that the seventh stage of the human life span, generativity versus stagnation, occurs in middle adulthood. Four types of generativity are biological, parental, work, and cultural. In Levinson's theory, developmental tasks should be mastered at different points in development and changes in middle age focus on four conflicts: being young versus being old, being destructive versus being constructive, being masculine versus being feminine, and being attached to others versus being separated from them. Levinson proposed that a majority of Americans, especially men, experience a midlife crisis. For the most part, though, midlife crises have been exaggerated. There is considerable individual variation in development during the middle adulthood years.

- In the early version of the life-events approach, life events produce taxing circumstances that create stress in people's lives. In the contemporary version of the life-events approach, how life events influence the individual's development depends not only on the life event, but also on mediating factors, adaptation to the event, the life-stage context, and the sociohistorical context.

- Researchers have found that young and middle-aged adults experience more stressful days, more multiple stressors, and more overload stressors than do older adults. Midlife adults report fewer stressors over which they have no control than young and older adults.

- Neugarten believes that the social environment of a particular cohort can alter its social clock—the timetable according to which individuals are expected to accomplish life's tasks, such as getting married, having children, and establishing a career. Critics say that the adult stage theories are male biased because they place too much emphasis on achievement and careers. The stage theories do not adequately address women's concerns about relationships. Midlife is a heterogeneous period for women, as it is for men. For some women, midlife is the prime of their lives. In many nonindustrialized societies, a woman's status often improves in middle age. In many cultures, the concept of middle age is not clear. Most cultures distinguish between young adults and old adults.

 Learning Goal 2: Discuss stability and change in development during middle adulthood, including longitudinal studies

- In Neugarten's Kansas City Study, both stability and change were found. Styles of coping, life satisfaction, and being goal-directed were the most stable. Individuals became more passive and feared the environment more as they aged through middle adulthood. In Costa and McCrae's Baltimore Study, the big five personality factors—emotional stability, extraversion, openness to experience, agreeableness, and conscientiousness—showed considerable stability. In the

Berkeley Longitudinal Studies, the extremes in the stability-change argument were not supported. The most stable characteristics were intellectual orientation, self-confidence, and openness to new experiences. The characteristics that changed the most were nurturance, hostility, and self-control. George Vaillant's research revealed links between a number of characteristics at age 50 and health and well-being at 75 to 80 years of age. In Helson's Mills College Study of women, there was a shift toward less traditional feminine characteristics from age 27 to the early forties, but this might have been due to societal changes. In their early forties, women experienced many of the concerns that Levinson described for men. However, rather than a midlife crisis, this is best called midlife consciousness.

- The issue of whether personality is stable or changes in adulthood continues to be debated. Some researchers believe that stability peaks in the fifties and sixties (Caspi & Roberts, 2001), others that it begins to stabilize at about 30 (Costa & McRae, 2000), and yet others argue for more change (Lewis, 2001). Some people change more than others.

3 **Learning Goal 3: Identify some important aspects of close relationships in middle adulthood**

- Affectionate love increases in midlife, especially in marriages that have endured many years. A majority of middle-aged adults who are married say that their marriage is good or excellent. Researchers recently have found that couples who divorce in midlife are more likely to have a cool, distant, emotionally suppressed relationship, whereas divorcing young adults are more likely to have an emotionally volatile and expressive relationship. Divorce is a special concern.

- Rather than decreasing marital satisfaction as once thought, the empty nest increases it for most parents. An increasing number of young adults are returning home to live with their parents.

- Sibling relationships continue throughout life. Some are close, others are distant. Friendships continue to be important in middle age.

- Most grandparents are satisfied with their role. There are different grandparent roles and styles. Grandmothers spend more time with grandchildren than grandfathers and the grandmother role involves greater expectations for maintaining ties across generations than the grandfather role. The profile of grandparents is changing, due to such factors as divorce and remarriage.

- Continuing contact across generations in families usually occurs. Mothers and daughters have the closest relationships. The middle-aged generation has been called the "sandwich" or "squeezed" generation because it is caught between obligations to children and obligations to parents. The middle-aged generation plays an important role in linking generations.

Key Terms

contemporary life-events
  approach 532

social clock 534

big five factors of
  personality 538

empty nest syndrome 542

Key People

Erik Erikson 529
George Vaillant 529, 531
Carol Ryff 529
Daniel Levinson 530

Bernice Neugarten 534, 537
Paul Costa and Robert
  McCrae 537
John Clausen 539

Ravenna Helson 539
Avshalom Caspi and Brent
  Roberts 540

Karen Fingerman 546

 E-Learning Tools

To help you master the material in this chapter, you'll find a number of valuable study tools on the LifeMap CD-ROM that accompanies this book and on the Online Learning Center for *Life-Span Development,* tenth edition, at www.mhhe.com/santrockld10.

Video Clips

In the margins of this book there are icons directing you to the LifeMap CD-ROM that accompanies the book. There you'll find a video for chapter 17 called "Balancing Work and Family." In this segment, a working mother describes her strategies for dealing with this challenge.

Self-Assessment

Connect to www.mhhe.com/santrockld10 to learn more about the stress-illness relationship, how extraverted or introverted you are, and how generative you are by completing the self-assessments, *Life Events and My Chance of Significant Illness in the Coming Year, Extraversion,* and *How Generative Am I?*

Taking It to the Net

Connect to www.mhhe.com/santrockld10 to research the answers to these questions.

1. Strether is experiencing what his friends have labeled a stereotypical "midlife crisis"—a desire to abandon his career for a more Bohemian lifestyle, a sexual attraction to younger women, deepening anxiety about death. How do these stereotypical symptoms fit in with the concept of "midlife crisis" as described in a popular psychology magazine?

2. Mona and Richard anticipate the onset of "empty nest syndrome" soon after their only daughter leaves home for college in August. What can they do ahead of time to make the transition a smooth one?

3. Larissa has been divorced for 10 years and has custody of her children. She has just learned that her 18-year-old daughter, Monica, is pregnant. The baby's father is unwilling to marry Monica or support the child, and frankly Larissa would not want her daughter marrying him anyway. Monica has three more years of school left to finish her training as a nurse. She has asked Larissa to help raise the child more than half of the time during the child's preschool years. What are some of the possible long-term effects of this scenario for both Larissa and the child?

Health and Well-Being, Parenting, and Education Exercises

Build your decision-making skills by trying your hand at the health and well-being, parenting, and education exercises.

Connect to www.mhhe.com/santrockld10 to research the answers and complete the exercises.

CHAPTER

*Each of us stands alone
at the heart of the earth,
pierced through by a ray
of sunshine: And
suddenly it is evening.*

—Salvatore Quasimodo
Italian Poet, 20th Century

Physical Development in Late Adulthood

Chapter Outline

Learning Goals

1 Characterize longevity and the biological aspects of aging

2 Describe how a person's brain and body change in late adulthood

3 Identify health problems in older adults and how they can be treated

Images of Life-Span Development
Learning to Age Successfully

Jonathan Swift said, "No wise man ever wished to be younger." Without a doubt, a 70-year-old body does not work as well as it once did. It is also true that an individual's fear of aging is often greater than need be. As more individuals live to a ripe *and* active old age, our image of aging is changing. While on the average a 75-year-old's joints should be stiffening, people can practice not to be average. For example, a 75-year-old man might *choose* to train for and run a marathon; an 80-year-old woman whose capacity for work is undiminished might *choose* to make and sell children's toys.

Consider 85-year-old Sadie Halperin, who has been working out for 11 months at a rehabilitation center for the aged in Boston. She lifts weights and rides a stationary bike. She says that before she started working out, about everything she did—shopping, cooking, walking—was a major struggle. Sadie says she always felt wobbly and held on to a wall when she walked. Now she walks down the center of the hallways and reports that she feels wonderful. Initially she could lift only 15 pounds with both legs; now she lifts 30 pounds. At first she could bench-press only 20 pounds; now she bench-presses 50 pounds. Sadie's exercise routine has increased her muscle strength and helps her to battle osteoporosis by slowing the calcium loss from her bones, which can lead to deadly fractures (Ubell, 1992).

Eighty-five-year-old Sadie Halperin doubled her strength in exercise after just 11 months. Before developing an exercise routine, she felt wobbly and often had to hold on to a wall when she walked. Now she walks down the middle of hallways and says she feels wonderful.

PREVIEW

The story of Sadie Halperin's physical development and well-being raises some truly fascinating questions about life-span development, which we will explore in this chapter. They include: Why do we age, and what, if anything, can we do to slow down the process? How long can we live? What chance do you have of living to be 100? Do older adults have sex? Can certain eating habits and exercise help us live longer?

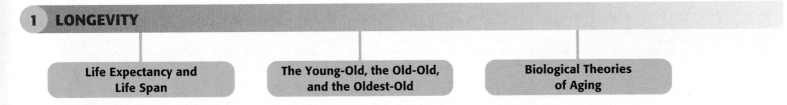

1 LONGEVITY

| Life Expectancy and Life Span | The Young-Old, the Old-Old, and the Oldest-Old | Biological Theories of Aging |

In his eighties, Linus Pauling argued that vitamin C slows the aging process. Aging researcher Roy Walford fasts two days a week because he believes undernutrition (not malnutrition) also slows the aging process. What do we really know about longevity?

Life Expectancy and Life Span

We are no longer a youthful society. As more individuals live to older ages, the proportion of individuals at different ages has become increasingly similar. Indeed, the concept of a period called "late adulthood" is a recent one—before the twentieth century most individuals died before they reached 65.

Recall from chapter 1 that although a much greater percentage of persons live to an older age, the life span has remained virtually unchanged since the beginning of recorded history. **Life span** is the upper boundary of life, the maximum number of years an individual can live. The maximum life span of human beings is approximately 120 to 125 years of age. **Life expectancy** is the number of years that will probably be lived by the average person born in a particular year. Improvements in medicine, nutrition, exercise, and lifestyle have increased our life expectancy an average of 30 additional years since 1900.

The average life expectancy of individuals born today in the United States is 77 years (80 for women, 74 for men). There is still a gap (7 years) between the life expectancy of non-Latino Whites (77) and African Americans (70) in the United States but the gap is narrowing. In 1970 the gap was 8 years (National Center for Health Statistics, 2004).

How does the United States fare in life expectancy, compared with other countries around the world? We do considerably better than some, a little worse than some others. For example, Japan has the highest life expectancy at birth today (81 years) (UNICEF, 2004). Differences in life expectancies across countries are due to such factors as health conditions and medical care throughout the life span.

Remember that the life expectancy figures we have cited indicate the years that a person born in a particular year can expect to live. How much longer can 65-year-olds in the United States expect to live? Today, they can expect to live an average of 18 more years (20 for females, 16 for males) (National Center for Health Statistics, 2004).

What about yourself? What is the likelihood that you will live to be 100? To evaluate this possibility, see figure 18.1.

Is there a sex difference in how long people live? Today, the life expectancy for females is 80 years of age, while for males it is 74. Beginning in the mid-thirties, females outnumber males; this gap widens during the remainder of the adult years. By the time adults are 75 years of age, more than 61 percent of the population is female; for those 85 and over, the figure is almost 70 percent female. Why? Social factors such as health attitudes, habits, lifestyles, and occupation are probably important. For example, men are more likely than women to die from the leading causes of death in the United States, such as cancer of the respiratory system, motor vehicle accidents, cirrhosis of the liver, emphysema, and coronary heart disease (Goldman & others, 2004). These causes of death are associated with lifestyle. For example, the sex difference in deaths due to lung cancer and emphysema occurs because men are heavier smokers than women.

Aging Research Center

life span The upper boundary of life, the maximum number of years an individual can live. The maximum life span of human beings is about 120 to 125 years of age.

life expectancy The number of years that will probably be lived by the average person born in a particular year.

This test gives you a rough guide for predicting your longevity. The basic life expectancy for males is age 73, and for females it is 80. Write down your basic life expectancy. If you are in your fifties or sixties, you should add ten years to the basic figure because you have already proved yourself to be a durable individual. If you are over age 60 and active, you can even add another two years.

Life Expectancy

Decide how each item applies to you and add or subtract the appropriate number of years from your basic life expectancy.

1. Family history
___ Add five years if two or more of your grandparents lived to 80 or beyond.
___ Subtract four years if any parent, grandparent, sister, or brother died of a heart attack or stroke before 50.
___ Subtract two years if anyone died from these diseases before 60.
___ Subtract three years for each case of diabetes, thyroid disorder, breast cancer, cancer of the digestive system, asthma, or chronic bronchitis among parents or grandparents.

2. Marital status
___ If you are married, add four years.
___ If you are over 25 and not married, subtract one year for every unmarried decade.

3. Economic status
___ Add two years if your family income is over $60,000 per year.
___ Subtract three years if you have been poor for the greater part of your life.

4. Physique
___ Subtract one year for every 10 pounds you are overweight.
___ For each inch your girth measurement exceeds your chest measurement deduct two years.
___ Add three years if you are over 40 and not overweight.

5. Exercise
___ Add three years if you exercise regularly and moderately (jogging three times a week).
___ Add five years if you exercise regularly and vigorously (long-distance running three times a week).
___ Subtract three years if your job is sedentary.
___ Add three years if your job is active.

6. Alcohol
___ Add two years if you are a light drinker (one to three drinks a day).
___ Subtract five to ten years if you are a heavy drinker (more than four drinks per day).
___ Subtract one year if you are a teetotaler.

7. Smoking
___ Subtract eight years if you smoke two or more packs of cigarettes per day.
___ Subtract two years if you smoke one to two packs per day.
___ Subtract two years if you smoke less than one pack.
___ Subtract two years if you regularly smoke a pipe or cigars.

8. Disposition
___ Add two years if you are a reasoned, practical person.
___ Subtract two years if you are aggressive, intense, and competitive.
___ Add one to five years if you are basically happy and content with life.
___ Subtract one to five years if you are often unhappy, worried, and often feel guilty.

9. Education
___ Subtract two years if you have less than a high school education.
___ Add one year if you attended four years of school beyond high school.
___ Add three years if you attended five or more years beyond high school.

10. Environment
___ Add four years if you have lived most of your life in a rural environment.
___ Subtract two years if you have lived most of your life in an urban environment.

11. Sleep
___ Subtract five years if you sleep more than nine hours a day.

12. Temperature
___ Add two years if your home's thermostat is set at no more than 68° F.

13. Health care
___ Add three years if you have regular medical checkups and regular dental care.
___ Subtract two years if you are frequently ill.
___ **Your Life Expectancy Total**

FIGURE 18.1 Can You Live to Be 100?

If life expectancy is influenced strongly by stress in the workplace, the sex difference should be narrowing, because so many more women have entered the labor force. Yet in the last 40 years, just the opposite has occurred: the gap is widening. Perhaps working outside the home brings women benefits such as improved self-esteem and work satisfaction that outweigh whatever additional stress might come from being in the workforce.

The sex difference in longevity also is influenced by biological factors. In virtually all species, females outlive males. Women have more resistance to infections and degenerative diseases. For example, the female's estrogen production helps to protect her from arteriosclerosis (hardening of the arteries). And the additional X chromosome that women carry in comparison to men may be associated with the production of more antibodies to fight off disease.

Centenarians   In 1980, there were only 15,000 centenarians (individuals 100 years and older) in the United States. In 2000, there were 77,000, and it is projected that this number will be 834,000 in 2050. Many people expect that "the older you get, the sicker you get." However, researchers are finding that is not true for some centenarians (Terry & others, 2004). One recent study found that 32 percent of the male and 15 percent of more than 400 centenarians had never been diagnosed with common age-associated diseases such as heart disease, cancer, and stroke (Evert & others, 2003).

Genes play an important role in surviving to an extreme old age (Martin & Buckwalter, 2001; Perls, Lauerman, & Silver, 1999). But there are also other factors at work. A disproportionate number of centenarians are women who have never been married. In the ongoing New England Centenarian Study, a majority of the centenarians have had difficult lives, such as surviving the Holocaust and living in extreme poverty as an immigrant to the United States (Perls, Lauerman, & Silver, 1999). What has contributed to their survival is their ability to cope successfully with stress.

In one study, 1,200 centenarians were interviewed about many aspects of their lives (Segerberg, 1982). Through their eyes, life looks like this:

- Mary Butler said that finding something to laugh about every day is important. She believes a good laugh is better than a dose of medicine anytime.
- Elza Wynn concluded that he has been able to live so long because he made up his mind to live. He was thinking about dying when he was 77, but decided he would wait a while.
- Anna Marie Robertson ("Grandma") Moses commented that she felt older at 16 than at any time since then. Even when she became very old, she said that she never thought about being old.
- Billy Red Fox believes that being active and not worrying are important keys to living to be 100. At 95, he switched jobs to become a public relations representative. Even at 100, Billy travels 11 months of the year, making public appearances and talking to civic clubs.

What chance do you have of living to be 100? According to the items in figure 18.1, among the most important factors in longevity are heredity and family history, health (weight, diet, smoking, and exercise), education, personality, and lifestyle. To further examine the factors that are involved in living to a very old age, read the following Diversity in Life-Span Development interlude.

Diversity in Life-Span Development

Living Longer in Okinawa

Individuals live longer on the Japanese island of Okinawa in the East China Sea than anywhere else in the world. In Okinawa, there are 34.7 centenarians for every 100,000 inhabitants, the highest ratio in the world. In comparison, the United States has about 10 centenarians for every 100,000 residents. The life expectancy in Okinawa is 81.2 years (86 for women, 78 for men), also highest in the world.

What is responsible for such longevity in Okinawa? Some possible explanations include (Willcox, Willcox, & Suzuki, 2002):

- *Diet.* Okinawans eat very healthy food, heavy on grains, fish, and vegetables, light on meat, eggs, and dairy products. The risk of dying of cancer is far lower among Okinawans than among Japanese and Americans (see figure 18.2). About 100,000 Okinawans moved to Brazil and quickly adopted the eating regimen of their new home, one heavy on red meat. The result: The life expectancy of the Brazilian Okinawans is now 17 years lower than Okinawa's 81 years!

To me old age is always fifteen years older than I am.

—**Bernard Baruch**
American Statesman, 20th Century

New England Centenarian Study
Life Expectancy Calculator

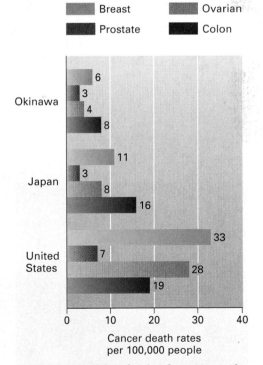

FIGURE 18.2 Risks of Dying from Cancer in Okinawa, Japan, and the United States
The risk of dying from different forms of cancer is lower in Okinawa than in the United States and Japan (Willcox, Willcox, & Suzuki, 2002). Okinawans eat lots of tofu and soy products, which are rich in flavonoids (believed to lower the risk of breast and prostate cancer). They also consume large amounts of fish, especially tuna, mackerel, and salmon, which reduce the risk of breast cancer.

Toskiko Taira, 80, weaves cloth from the fibers of banana trees on a loom in Okinawa. She, like many Okinawans, believes that such sense of purpose helps people to live longer.

- *Low-stress lifestyle.* The easygoing lifestyle in Okinawa more closely resembles that of a laid-back South Sea island than that of the high-stress world on the Japanese mainland.
- *Caring community.* Okinawans look out for each other and do not isolate or ignore their older adults. If older adults need help, they don't hesitate to ask a neighbor. Such support and caring is likely responsible for Okinawa having the lowest suicide rate among older women in East Asia, an area noted for its high suicide rate among older women.
- *Activity.* Many older adults in Okinawa are active, engaging in such activities as taking walks and working in their gardens. Many older Okinawans also continue working at their jobs.
- *Spirituality.* Many older adults in Okinawa find a sense of purpose in spiritual matters. Prayer is commonplace and believed to ease the mind of stress and problems.

The Young-Old, the Old-Old, and the Oldest-Old

Do you want to live to be 100, or 90? As we discussed in chapter 1, these ages are part of late adulthood, which begins in the sixties and extends to approximately 120 to 125 years of age. This is the longest span of any period of human development—50 to 60 years. Some developmentalists distinguish between the *young-old* (65 to 74 years of age) and the *old-old*, or *old age* (75 years and older) (Charness & Bosman, 1992). Yet others distinguish the *oldest-old* (85 years and older) from younger older adults (Baltes & Smith, 2003).

As we discussed in chapter 1, Paul Baltes (Baltes, 2000; Baltes & Smith, 2003) argues that the oldest-old (85 and over) face a number of problems, including sizeable losses in cognitive potential and ability to learn; an increase in chronic stress; a sizeable prevalence of physical and mental disabilities; high levels of frailty; increased loneliness; and the difficulty of dying at older ages with dignity. He contrasts the problems of the oldest-old with the increase in successful aging of adults in their sixties and seventies. Compared with the oldest-old, the young-old have a substantial potential for physical and cognitive fitness, higher levels of emotional well-being, and more effective strategies for mastering the gains and losses of old age.

The oldest-old today are mostly female and the majority of these women are widowed and live alone, if not institutionalized. The majority also are hospitalized at some time in the last years of life, and the majority die alone in a hospital or institution (Baltes & Smith, 2003). Their needs, capacities, and resources are often different from those of older adults in their sixties and seventies.

But even the oldest-old are a heterogeneous, diversified group (Roberts, Dunkle, & Haug, 1994). Many of the oldest-old have outlived their social and financial supports and depend on society for their daily living, but this is not true of all. A significant number have cognitive impairments, but many do not. Almost one-fourth of the oldest-old are institutionalized, and many report some limitation of activity or difficulties in caring for themselves. However, more than three-fourths are not institutionalized. The majority of older adults aged 80 and over continue to live in the community. More than one-third of older adults 80 and over who live in the community report that their health is excellent or good; 40 percent say that they have no activity limitation (Suzman & others, 1992).

Many experts on aging prefer to talk about such categories as the young-old, old-old, and oldest-old in terms of *function* rather than age. Remember from chapter 1 that we described age not only in terms of chronological age, but also in terms of biological age, psychological age, and social age. Thus, in terms of *functional age*—the person's actual ability to function—an 85-year-old might well be more biologically and psychologically fit than a 65-year-old. With this concept of functional age

One-hundred-year-old Iva Blake is among the oldest-old in America. Adapting to her changing circumstances, she still tends to her garden from a wheelchair. *What are some characteristics of the oldest-old?*

(a)   (b)

(*a*) **Frenchwoman Jeanne Louise Calment, who recently died at the age of 122. Greater ages have been claimed, but scientists say the maximum human life span is about 120 to 125. (*b*) Heredity is an important component of how long we will live. For example, in figure 18.1, you were able to add five years to your life expectancy if two or more of your grandparents lived to 80 or beyond. And if you were born a female, you start out with a basic life expectancy that is seven years more than if you were born a male. The three sisters shown here are all in their eighties.**

and its implication for individual differences in aging in mind, there still are, as we have just seen, some significant differences when the old age group segment still in their sixties or seventies is compared with the 85-and-older age group (Baltes & Smith, 2003; Suzman & others, 1992).

Biological Theories of Aging

Even if we stay remarkably healthy through our adult lives, we begin to age at some point. Life-span experts even argue that biological aging begins at birth (Schaie, 2000). What are the biological explanations of aging? Intriguing explanations of why we age are provided by four biological theories: cellular clock theory, free-radical theory, mitochondrial theory, and hormonal stress theory.

Cellular Clock Theory   **Cellular clock theory** is Leonard Hayflick's (1977) theory that cells can divide a maximum of about 75 to 80 times and that, as we age, our cells become less capable of dividing. Hayflick found that cells extracted from older adults, in their fifties to seventies, divided fewer than 75 to 80 times. Based on the ways cells divide, Hayflick places the upper limit of the human life-span potential at about 120 to 125 years of age.

In the last decade, scientists have tried to fill in a gap in cellular clock theory (Cherif & others, 2003; Riethman & others, 2004; Sharpless & DePaulo, 2004). Hayflick did not know why cells die. Recently, scientists have found that the answer may lie at the tips of chromosomes (Shay & Wright, 1999, 2000, 2002, 2004).

Telomeres are DNA sequences that cap chromosomes. Each time a cell divides, the telomeres become shorter and shorter (see figure 18.3). After about 70 or 80 replications, the telomeres are dramatically reduced and the cell no longer can reproduce.

www.mhhe.com/santrockld10

What Causes Aging?
Telomeres Research
Research on Telomeres and Telomerase
Genetic Studies of Aging

cellular clock theory Leonard Hayflick's theory that the maximum number of times that human cells can divide is about 75 to 80. As we age, our cells have less capability to divide.

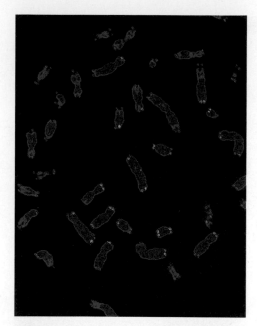

FIGURE 18.3 Telomeres and Aging
The photograph shows actual telomeres lighting up the tips of chromosomes.

Researchers also have found that injecting the enzyme *telomerase* into human cells grown in the laboratory can substantially extend the life of the cells beyond the approximately 70 to 80 normal cell divisions (Shay & Wright, 1999). In one study, age-related telomere erosion was linked with an impaired ability to recover from stress and an increased rate of cancer (Rudolf & others, 1999).

Free-Radical Theory   A second microbiological theory of aging is **free-radical theory,** which states that people age because inside their cells normal metabolism produces unstable oxygen molecules known as *free radicals*. These molecules ricochet around the cells, damaging DNA and other cellular structures (Berr, 2002; Poon & others, 2004). Like all organisms, cells generate waste when they metabolize energy. The problematic by-products of this process include these free-radical oxygen molecules. As the free radicals bounce around inside of cells, their damage can lead to a range of disorders, including cancer and arthritis (Hauck & Bartke, 2001; Troen, 2003). Overeating is linked with an increase in free radicals and researchers recently have found that calorie restriction—a diet restricted in calories although adequate in proteins, vitamins, and minerals—reduces the oxidative damage created by free radicals (Yu, Lim, & Sugano, 2002).

Mitochondrial Theory   **Mitochondrial theory** states that aging is due to the decay of mitochondria within cells. There is increasing interest in the role that *mitochondria*—tiny cellular bodies that supply energy for function, growth, and repair—might play in aging (Ames, 2004; Bertoni-Freddari & others, 2004; Kang & Hamasaki, 2003). It appears that the decay of mitochondria is primarily due to oxidative damage and loss of critical micronutrients supplied by the cell (Driver, Georgiou, & Georgiou, 2004; Genova & others, 2004; Merry, 2004; Pierson, 2003).

Among the by-products of mitochondrial energy production are the free radicals we just described. According to the mitochondrial theory, the damage caused by free radicals initiates a self-perpetuating cycle in which oxidative damage impairs mitochondrial function, which results in the generation of even greater amounts of free radicals. The result is that over time, the affected mitochondria become so inefficient that they cannot generate enough energy to meet cellular needs (Barja, 2004). Defects in mitochondria are linked with cardiovascular disease, neurodegenerative diseases such as dementia, and decline in liver functioning (Anantharaju, Feller, & Chedid, 2002; Floyd & Hensley, 2002). However, it is not known whether these defects in mitochondria cause aging or are merely accompaniments of the aging process (DiMauro & others, 2002).

Hormonal Stress Theory   The three theories—cellular clock, free radical, and mitochondrial—of aging that we have discussed so far attempt to explain aging at the cellular level. In contrast, **hormonal stress theory** argues that aging in the body's hormonal system can lower resistance to stress and increase the likelihood of disease (Finch & Seeman, 1999; Parsons, 2003). The hypothalamic-pituitary-adrenal (HPA) axis is one of the body's main regulatory systems for responding to external stress and maintaining the body's internal equilibrium. (Note that *hypothalamic* refers to the hypothalamus of the brain, *pituitary* to the body's master gland located near the hypothalamus, and *adrenal* to the two adrenal glands that sit just above the kidneys.)

As people age, the hormones stimulated by stress remain elevated longer than when people were younger. These prolonged, elevated levels of stress-related hormones are associated with increased risks for many diseases, including cardiovascular disease, cancer, diabetes, and hypertension. Recently, a variation of hormonal stress theory has emphasized the contribution of a decline in immune system functioning with aging (Hawkley & Cacioppo, 2004). Aging contributes to immune system deficits that give rise to infectious diseases in older adults. The extended duration

free-radical theory A microbiological theory of aging that states that people age because inside their cells normal metabolism produces unstable oxygen molecules known as free radicals. These molecules ricochet around inside cells, damaging DNA and other cellular structures.

mitochondrial theory The theory that aging is caused by the decay of mitochondria, tiny cellular bodies that supply energy for function, growth, and repair.

hormonal stress theory The theory that aging in the body's hormonal system can lower resilience to stress and increase the likelihood of disease.

of stress and diminished restorative processes in older adults may accelerate the effects of aging on immunity.

Which of these biological theories best explains aging? That question has not yet been answered. It might turn out that all of these biological processes are involved in aging.

Review and Reflect: Learning Goal 1

 1 **Characterize longevity and the biological aspects of aging**

REVIEW

- How can the concepts of life span and life expectancy be distinguished? What characterizes centenarians? What sex differences exist in longevity?
- How can the differences between the young-old, old-old, and oldest-old be summarized?
- What are the four main biological theories of aging?

REFLECT

- If we could increase the maximum human life span, would this be beneficial? If so, to whom?

---

2 **THE COURSE OF PHYSICAL DEVELOPMENT IN LATE ADULTHOOD**

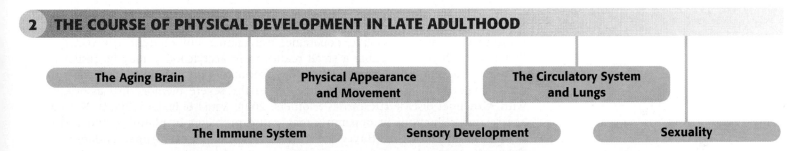

| The Aging Brain | Physical Appearance and Movement | The Circulatory System and Lungs |
| The Immune System | Sensory Development | Sexuality |

Although there are inevitable age-associated increases in the risks of physical disability, the actual onset of such problems is not uniform. Acknowledgment of considerable variability in rates of decline in functioning has generated increased attention to factors involved in the successful maintenance of functional abilities with age (Birren, 1996; Whitbourne, 2000). One analysis involved the MacArthur Research Network on Successful Aging Study, a three-site longitudinal study of successful aging in women and men aged 70 to 79 years of age. In this study, physical performance (such as walking efficiency, maintaining balance, and repeatedly standing up and sitting down) did decline with age, but there was considerable individual variation (Seeman & others, 1994). The physical performance of older adults in poor health from low-income backgrounds was inferior to that of their higher-income, healthy counterparts. A majority of the older adults also maintained their physical performance over a three-year period in their seventies, and some even improved their performance in this time frame.

As we discuss the nature of physical development, we will chronicle age-related changes in physical decline, but we will also stress new developments in aging research that underscore how bodily powers decline slowly and that sometimes even lost function can be restored. In one survey, disabilities among older adults had declined almost 15 percent from 1982 to 1994 (Manton, Corder, & Stallard, 1997). Exercise, fewer smokers, and improvements in medical care account for much of the decline in disability (Suzman, 1997).

The Aging Brain

Most research on the brains of adults focuses on the aging brain of older adults. What are some of the general findings about the aging brain? How much plasticity and adaptiveness does it retain?

The Shrinking, Slowing Brain On average, the brain loses 5 to 10 percent of its weight between the ages of 20 and 90. Brain volume also decreases. Scientists are not sure why these changes occur but believe these might result from the decrease in dendrites, damage to the myelin sheath that covers axons, or simply the death of brain cells.

Some areas shrink more than others. The prefrontal cortex is one area that shrinks with aging and recent research has found that this shrinkage is linked with a decrease in working memory in older adults (Salat, Kaye, & Janowski, 2002).

A general slowing of function in the brain and spinal cord begins in middle adulthood and accelerates in late adulthood (Birren, 2002). Both physical coordination and intellectual performance are affected. For example, after age 70, many adults no longer show a knee jerk and by age 90 most reflexes are much slower (Spence, 1989). The slowing of brain can impair the performance of older adults on intelligence tests, especially timed tests (Birren, Woods, & Williams, 1980).

If the brain were a computer, this description of the aging brain might lead you to think that it could not do much of anything. However, unlike a computer, the brain has remarkable repair capability. Even in late adulthood, the brain loses only a portion of its ability to function (Anderton, 2002).

Neurotransmitters Among the neurotransmitters that have been studied in the aging process are acetylcholine, dopamine, and gamma-aminobutyric acid (GABA). Some researchers believe that a small reduction in acetylcholine may be responsible for the decline of memory functioning associated with normal functioning and that a major reduction in acetylcholine causes the severe memory loss associated with Alzheimer disease (Descarries & others, 2004; Small & Fodero, 2002). Normal age-related reductions in dopamine may cause problems in planning and carrying out motor activities (Haycock & others, 2003; Salvatore, Apparsundaram, & Gerhardt, 2003). Age-related diseases characterized by a loss of motor control, such as Parkinson disease, are linked with a severe reduction in the production of dopamine (DeKosky & Marck, 2003; Piccini, Pavese, & Brooks, 2003). GABA inhibits neural signals in the brain and its production decreases with aging (Mhatre, Fernandez, & Ticku, 1991). GABA helps to control the preciseness of the signal being carried from one neuron to the next. One recent study found that injecting GABA in the brains of aging monkeys helped them to focus their vision and thinking by silencing interfering static from other neurons in their brains (Leventhal & others, 2003).

The Adapting Brain As the adult brain ages, it also adapts in several ways. First, humans can grow new brain cells throughout their lives (Gould & others, 1999; Kempermann, Wiskott, & Gage, 2004; Luque, Giminez, & Ribotta, 2004; Manev & Manev, 2005; Shi & others, 2004). The extent to which we do so, however, may depend in part on environmental stimulation through such activities as physical activity and learning (Churchill & others, 2002; Prickaerts & others, 2004; Schaffer & Gage, 2004; Zitnik & Martin, 2002). Figure 18.4 shows the results of one study in which adult mice that ran and adult mice that were placed in an enriched environment generated new brain cells.

A second type of adaptation was demonstrated in a study that compared the brains of adults at various ages (Coleman, 1986). From the forties through the seventies, the growth of dendrites increased. However, in people in their nineties, dendritic growth no longer occurred. This dendritic growth might compensate for the

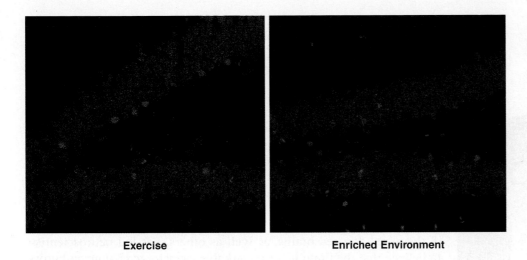

Exercise   Enriched Environment

FIGURE 18.4 Generating New Nerve Cells in Adult Mice
Researchers have found that exercise (running) and an enriched environment (a larger cage and many toys) can cause brain cells to divide and form new brain cells (Kempermann, van Praag, & Gage, 2000). Cells were labeled with a chemical marker that becomes integrated into the DNA of dividing cells (red). Four weeks later, they were also labeled to mark neurons (nerve cells). As shown here, both the running mice and the mice in an enriched environment had many cells that were still dividing (red) and others that had differentiated into new nerve cells (orange).

possible loss of neurons through the seventies but not in the nineties. Lack of dendritic growth in older adults could be due to a lack of environmental stimulation and activity.

Stanley Rapaport (1994), chief of the neurosciences laboratory at the National Institute on Aging, demonstrated another way in which the aging brain can adapt. He compared the brains of younger and older people engaged in the same tasks. The older brains had rewired themselves to compensate for losses. If one neuron was not up to the job, neighboring neurons helped to pick up the slack. Rapaport concluded that as brains age, they can shift responsibilities for a given task from one region to another.

Another way the brain adapts as people grow older is that myelination connecting the prefrontal cortex to the limbic system increases in the forties and fifties (Fischer & Pruyne, 2003). This type of myelination likely increases the integration of the emotional responses of the limbic system with the reasoning skills of the prefrontal cortex. This integration of cognition and emotion likely facilitates reflection, which characterizes many middle-aged adults.

Changes in lateralization may provide another type of adaptation in aging adults. Recall that lateralization is the specialization of function in one hemisphere of the brain or the other. Using neuroimaging techniques, researchers recently found that brain activity in the prefrontal cortex is lateralized less in older adults than in younger adults when they are engaging in cognitive tasks (Cabeza, 2002; Dixit & others, 2000). For example, figure 18.5 shows that when younger adults are given the task of recognizing words they have previously seen, they process the information primarily in the right hemisphere; older adults are more likely to use both hemispheres (Madden & others, 1999).

The decrease in lateralization in older adults might play a compensatory role in the aging brain. That is, using both hemispheres may improve the cognitive functioning of older adults. Support for this view comes from another study in which older adults who used both brain hemispheres were faster at completing a working memory task than their counterparts who primarily used only one hemisphere (Reuter-Lorenz & others, 2000). However, the decrease in lateralization may be a mere by-product of aging; it may reflect an age-related decline in the brain's ability to specialize functions. In this view, during childhood the brain becomes increasingly differentiated in terms of its functions; as adults become older, this process may reverse. Support for the dedifferentiation view is found in the higher intercorrelations of performance on cognitive tasks in older adults than in younger adults (Baltes & Lindenberger, 1997). To read further about aging and the brain, see the Research in Life-Span Development interlude.

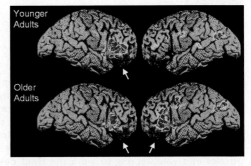

FIGURE 18.5 The Decrease in Brain Lateralization in Older Adults
Younger adults primarily used the right prefrontal region of the brain (*top left photo*) during a recall memory task, while older adults used both the left and right prefrontal regions (*bottom two photos*).

Research in Life-Span Development
The Nun Study

The Nun Study, directed by David Snowdon, is an intriguing ongoing investigation of aging in 678 nuns, many of whom are from a convent in Mankato, Minnesota (Danner, Snowdon, & Friesen, 2001; Kemper & others, 2001; Riley, Snowdon & Markesbery, 2002; Snowdon, 1995, 1997, 2002, 2003). Each of the 678 nuns agreed to participate in annual assessments of their cognitive and physical functioning. They also agreed to donate their brains for scientific research when they die and they are the largest group of brain donors in the world. Examination of the nuns' donated brains, as well as others, has led neuroscientists to believe that the brain has a remarkable capacity to change and grow, even in old age. The Sisters of Notre Dame in Mankato lead an intellectually challenging life, and brain researchers believe this contributes to their quality of life as older adults and possibly to their longevity.

Findings from the Nun Study so far include:

- Positive emotions early in adulthood were linked to their longevity (Danner, Snowdon, & Friesen, 2001). Handwritten autobiographies from 180 nuns, composed when they were 22 years of age, were scored for emotional content. The nuns whose early writings had higher scores for positive emotional content were more likely to still be alive at 75 to 95 years of age than their counterparts whose early writings were characterized by negative emotional content.
- Sisters who had taught for most of their lives showed more moderate declines in intellectual skills than those who had spent most of their lives in service-based tasks, which supports the notion that stimulating the brain with intellectual activity keeps neurons healthy and alive (Snowdon, 2002).
- Sisters with high levels of folic acid showed little evidence of Alzheimer-like damage to their brain after death (Snowdon & others, 2000). Possibly the substantial folic acid in the blood means less chance of having a stroke and possibly helps to protect the brain from decline.

This and other research provides hope that scientists will discover ways to tap into the brain's capacity to adapt in order to prevent and treat brain diseases. For example, scientists might learn more effective ways to help older adults recover from strokes. Even when areas of the brain are permanently damaged by stroke, new message routes can be created to get around the blockage or to resume the function of that area.

Top: **Sister Marcella Zachman (*left*) finally stopped teaching at age 97. Now, at 99, she helps ailing nuns exercise their brains by quizzing them on vocabulary or playing a card game called Skip-Bo, at which she deliberately loses. Sister Mary Esther Boor (*right*), also 99 years of age, is a former teacher who stays alert by doing puzzles and volunteering to work the front desk.** *Below:* **A technician holds the brain of a deceased Mankato nun. The nuns donate their brains for research that explores the effects of stimulation on brain growth.**

The Immune System

Decline in the functioning of the body's immune system with aging is well documented (Breitbart & others, 2002; Li & others, 2002; Morley, 2004). As we indicated earlier in our discussion of hormonal stress theory, the extended duration of stress and diminished restorative processes in older adults may accelerate the effects of aging on immunity (Hawkley & Cacioppo, 2004). Malnutrition involving low levels of protein is linked to further deterioration in the immune system, resulting in a decrease in T cells that destroy infected cells (Kaiser & Morley, 1994). Researchers have found that exercise can improve immune system functioning (Kohut & others, 2002; McElhaney, 2002). Because of the decline in immune system functioning in older adults, vaccination against influenza is especially important in older adults (Menec, MacWilliam, & Aoki, 2002).

Physical Appearance and Movement

In chapter 16, "Physical and Cognitive Development in Middle Adulthood," we pointed out some changes in physical appearance that take place. In late adulthood, these changes become more pronounced (Gilhar & others, 2004). The changes are most noticeable in the form of facial wrinkles and age spots.

We also get shorter when we get older. From 30 to 50 years of age, men lose about $\frac{1}{2}$ inch in height, then may lose another $\frac{3}{4}$ inch from 50 to 70 years of age. The height loss for women can be as much as 2 inches from 25 to 75 years of age (Hoyer & Roodin, 2003). Note that there are large variations in the extent to which individuals become shorter in middle and late adulthood. The decrease in height is due to bone loss in the vertebrae.

Our weight usually drops after we reach 60 years of age. This likely occurs because we lose muscle, which also gives our bodies a more "sagging" look. Figure 18.6 shows the decline in percentage of muscle and bone from age 25 to age 75, and the corresponding increase in the percentage of fat. The good news is that exercise and appropriate weight lifting can help to reduce the decrease in muscle mass and improve the older person's body appearance. We will have more to say about this later in this chapter.

Older adults move slower than young adults and this difference occurs across a wide range of movement difficulty (see figure 18.7). General slowing of movement in older adults has been found in everyday tasks such as reaching and grasping, moving from one place to another, and continuous movement (Lan & others, 2003). The ability to walk rapidly over a distance requires not only muscle strength but also the integration of cardiovascular fitness, vision, and postural stability (Morley, 2004). Regular walking has been shown to decrease the onset of physical disability in older adults (Wong & others, 2003).

Sensory Development

Sensory changes in late adulthood involve vision, hearing, taste, smell, touch, and pain.

Vision With aging, declines in visual acuity, color vision, and depth perception occur. Several diseases of the eye also may emerge in aging adults.

Visual Acuity In late adulthood, the decline in vision that began for most adults in early or middle adulthood becomes more pronounced (Crews & Campbell, 2004; Fozard, 2000). Night driving is especially difficult, to some extent because tolerance for glare diminishes. *Dark adaptation* is slower, meaning that older individuals take longer to recover their vision when going from a well-lighted room to semidarkness. The area of the visual field becomes smaller, suggesting that the intensity of a stimulus in the peripheral area of the visual field needs to be increased if the stimulus is to be seen. Events taking place away from the center of the visual field might not be detected (Fozard & Gordon-Salant, 2001).

This visual decline often can be traced to a reduction in the quality or intensity of light reaching the retina. In extreme old age, these

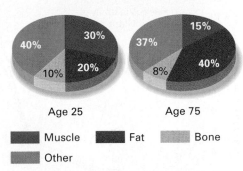

Percentage of total weight

Age 25

Age 75

■ Muscle ■ Fat ■ Bone
■ Other

FIGURE 18.6 Changes in Body Composition of Bone, Muscle, and Fat from 25 to 75 Years of Age
Notice the decrease in bone and muscle and the increase in fat from 25 to 75 years of age.

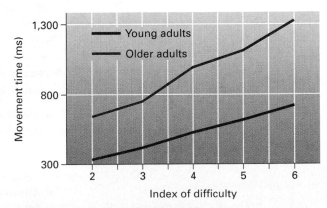

FIGURE 18.7 Movement and Aging
Older adults take longer to move than young adults and this occurs across a range of movement difficulty (Ketcham & Stelmach, 2001).

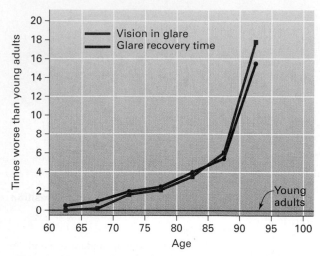

FIGURE 18.8 Rates of Decline in Visual Functioning Related to Glare in Adults of Different Ages
Older adults, especially those 85 and older, fare much worse than younger adults in being able to see clearly when glare is present, and their recovery from glare is much slower. These data were collected from a random sample of community-dwelling older adults living in Marin County, California. For each age, the factor by which the group's median performance was worse than normative values for young adults is shown.

changes might be accompanied by degenerative changes in the retina, causing severe difficulty in seeing. Large print books and magnifiers might be needed in such cases.

In one study of more than 500 adults 70 to 102 years of age, sensory functioning was linked with competence in everyday activities (Marsiske, Klumb, & Baltes, 1997). Sensory acuity, especially in vision, was related to whether and how well older adults bathed and groomed themselves, completed household chores, engaged in intellectual activities, and watched TV.

One recent extensive study of visual changes in adults found that the age of older adults was a significant factor in how extensively they differed in visual functioning from younger adults (Brabyn & others, 2001). Beyond 75, and more so beyond age 85, older adults showed significantly worse performance on a number of visual tasks when compared with young adults and older adults in their sixties and early seventies. The greatest decline in visual perception beyond 75, and especially beyond 85, involved glare. The older adults, especially those 85 and older, fared much worse in being able to see clearly when glare was present and their recovery from glare was much greater than for younger adults (see figure 18.8). For example, whereas young adults recover vision following glare in less than 10 seconds, 50 percent of 90-year-olds have not recovered vision after 1.5 minutes. Another aspect of visual functioning that declined in older adults in this study was the ability to see the periphery in a visual field.

Color Vision Color vision also may decline with age in older adults as a result of the yellowing of the lens of the eye (Weale, 1992). This change in color vision is most likely to occur in the green-blue-violet part of the color spectrum. As a result, it may be more difficult to accurately match up closely related colors such as navy socks and black socks.

Aging and Sensory Changes
Aging and Vision Problems

Depth Perception As with many other areas of perception, there are few changes in depth perception following infancy until adults become older. Depth perception typically declines in late adulthood, which can make it difficult for the older adult to determine how close or far away or how high or low something is (Brabyn & others, 2001; Zarof & others, 2003). A decline in depth perception can make steps or street curbs difficult to manage. A decrease in contrast sensitivity is one factor that diminishes the older adult's ability to perceive depth. Light-dark contrast is produced by the amount of light reflected by surfaces (a light object is brighter than a dark object). The difference in contrast makes objects that contrast with the background easier to see. Older adults need sharper contrasts and sharper edges around the object to differentiate the object from its background than younger adults.

Diseases of the Eye Three diseases that can impair the vision of older adults are cataracts, glaucoma, and macular degeneration:

- **Cataracts** involve a thickening of the lens of the eye that causes vision to become cloudy, opaque, and distorted (Fujikado & others, 2004). By age 70, approximately 30 percent of individuals experience a partial loss of vision due to cataracts. Initially, cataracts can be treated by glasses; if they worsen, a simple surgical procedure can remove them (Hylton & others, 2003; Stifer & others, 2004).
- **Glaucoma** involves damage to the optic nerve because of the pressure created by a buildup of fluid in the eye (Babaloa & others, 2003; Mok, Lee, & So, 2004). Approximately 1 percent of individuals in their seventies and 10 percent of those in their nineties have glaucoma, which can be treated with eyedrops, but if left untreated can ultimately destroy a person's vision.

cataracts Involve a thickening of the lens of the eye that causes vision to become cloudy, opaque, and distorted.

glaucoma Damage to the optic nerve because of the pressure created by a buildup of fluid in the eye.

Perceptual System	Young-Old (65 to 74 years)	Old-Old (75 years and older)
Vision	There is a loss of acuity even with corrective lenses. Less transmission of light occurs through the retina (half as much as in young adults). Greater susceptibility to glare occurs. Color discrimination ability decreases.	There is a significant loss of visual acuity and color discrimination, and a decrease in the size of the perceived visual field. In late old age, people are at significant risk for visual dysfunction from cataracts and glaucoma.
Hearing	There is a significant loss of hearing at high frequencies and some loss at middle frequencies. These losses can be helped by a hearing aid. There is greater susceptibility to masking of what is heard by noise.	There is a significant loss at high and middle frequencies. A hearing aid is more likely to be needed than in young-old age.

FIGURE 18.9 Vision and Hearing Decline in the Young-Old and the Old-Old

- **Macular degeneration** is a disease that involves deterioration of the *macula* of the retina, which corresponds to the focal center of the visual field. Individuals with macular degeneration may have relatively normal peripheral vision but be unable to see clearly what is right in front of them. It affects 1 in 25 individuals from 66 to 74 years of age and 1 in 6 of those 75 years old and older. If the disease is detected early, it can be treated with laser surgery (Howe, 2003). However, macular degeneration is difficult to treat and thus a leading cause of blindness in older adults (Chopdar, Chakravarthy, & Verma, 2003; Sarks, 2002).

Hearing Hearing impairment usually does not become much of an impediment until late adulthood (Crews & Campbell, 2004; Fozard, 2000; Fozard & Gordon-Salant, 2001). Even then, some, but not all, hearing problems can be corrected by hearing aids. Only 19 percent of individuals from 45 to 54 years of age experience some type of hearing problem, but for those 75 to 79, the figure reaches 75 percent (Harris, 1975). It has been estimated that 15 percent of the population over the age of 65 is legally deaf, usually due to degeneration of the *cochlea*, the primary neural receptor for hearing in the inner ear (Olsho, Harkins, & Lenhardt, 1985). Wearing two hearing aids that are balanced to correct each ear separately can sometimes help hearing-impaired adults.

Earlier, in our discussion of vision, we described research on the importance of the age of older adults in determining the degree of their visual decline. Age also is a factor in the degree of hearing decline in older adults (Stenkley, Vik, & Laukli, 2004). As indicated in figure 18.9, the decline in vision and hearing is much greater in individuals 75 years and older than in individuals 65 to 74 years of age (Charness & Bosman, 1992).

Smell and Taste Most older adults lose some of their sense of smell or taste, or both (Schiffman, 1996). These decrements can reduce their enjoyment of food and their life satisfaction. One negative outcome for a decline in the sense of smell is less ability to detect smoke from a fire. Smell and taste losses often begin around 60 years of age. Compounds that stimulate the olfactory nerve have been added to foods to increase intake by elderly individuals. Also, there is less decline in smell and taste in healthy older adults than in their less healthy counterparts.

Many older adults often prefer highly seasoned foods (sweeter, spicier, saltier) to compensate for their diminished taste and smell (Hoyer & Roodin, 2003). This can lead to eating more low-nutrient, highly seasoned "junk food."

Touch and Pain Changes in touch are associated with aging (Gescheider, 1997). One study found that, with aging, individuals could detect touch less in the lower extremities (ankles, knees, and so on) than in the upper extremities (wrists, shoulders, and so on) (Corso, 1977). For most older adults, a decline in touch sensitivity is not problematic (Hoyer & Roodin, 2003).

macular degeneration A disease that involves deterioration of the macula of the retina, which corresponds to the focal center of the visual field.

Older adults are less sensitive to pain and suffer from it less than younger adults (Harkins, Price, & Martinelli, 1986). Although decreased sensitivity to pain can help older adults cope with disease and injury, it can be harmful if it masks injury and illness that need to be treated.

The Circulatory System and Lungs

Not long ago it was believed that cardiac output—the amount of blood the heart pumps—declines with age even in healthy adults. However, we now know that when heart disease is absent, the amount of blood pumped is the same regardless of an adult's age.

In the past, a 60-year-old with a blood pressure reading of 160/90 would have been told, "For your age, that is normal." Now medication, exercise, and/or a healthier diet might be prescribed to lower blood pressure. Today, most experts on aging even recommend that consistent blood pressures above 120/80 should be treated to reduce the risk of heart attack, stroke, or kidney disease (Safer & Smulyan, 2004; Sleight, 2003). A rise in blood pressure with age can be linked with illness, obesity, anxiety, stiffening of blood vessels, or lack of exercise. The longer any of these factors persist, the worse the individual's blood pressure gets (Antelmi & others, 2004). A recent longitudinal study found that older adults with cardiovascular disease had a lower probability of subsequent successful aging (defined as remaining free of cardiovascular disease, cancer, and obstructive pulmonary disease, and with intact physical and cognitive functioning) than their counterparts without cardiovascular disease (Newman & others, 2003).

Lung capacity drops 40 percent between the ages of 20 and 80, even without disease (Fozard, 1992). Lungs lose elasticity, the chest shrinks, and the diaphragm weakens. The good news, though, is that older adults can improve lung functioning with diaphragm-strengthening exercises. Severe impairments in lung functioning and death can result from smoking.

Sexuality

Aging does induce some changes in human sexual performance, more so in the male than in the female. Orgasm becomes less frequent in males, occurring in every second to third attempt rather than every time. More direct stimulation usually is needed to produce an erection. From 65 to 80 years of age, approximately one out of four men have serious problems getting and/or keeping erections, and at over 80 years of age the percentage rises to one out of two men (Butler & Lewis, 2002).

In the absence of two circumstances—actual disease and the belief that old people are or should be asexual—sexuality can be lifelong. Even when actual intercourse is impaired by infirmity, other relationship needs persist, among them closeness, sensuality, and being valued as a man or a woman (Johnson, 1996).

Such a view, of course, is contrary to folklore, to the beliefs of many individuals in society, and even to many physicians and health-care personnel. Fortunately, many older adults have gone on having sex without talking about it, unabashed by the accepted and destructive social image of the dirty old man and the asexual, undesirable older woman.

In one study of older adults in their sixties, many were still having sex (Wiley & Bortz, 1996). The women rated kissing as one of the most satisfying sexual activities, while the men rated oral sex as the most satisfying. In another study of more than 1,200 older adults (mean age = 77), almost 30 percent had participated in sexual activity in the past month (Matthias & others, 1997). Two-thirds of the older adults were satisfied with their current level of sexual activity.

Various therapies for older adults who report sexual difficulties have been effective (Burgess, 2004; Carbone & Seftel, 2002). In one study, sex education—which consisted largely of simply giving sexual information—led to increased sexual interest, knowledge, and activity in older adults (White & Catania, 1981).

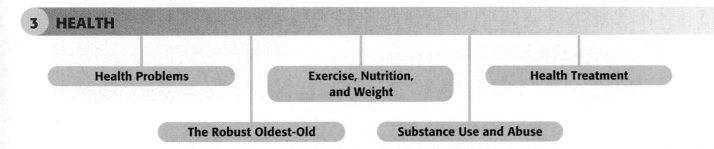

 Review and Reflect: Learning Goal 2

2 **Describe how a person's brain and body change in late adulthood**

REVIEW

- How much plasticity and adaptability does the aging brain have?
- How does the immune system change with aging?
- What changes in physical appearance and movement characterize late adulthood?
- How do vision, hearing, smell and taste, touch, and sensitivity to pain change in older adults?
- How does the circulatory system change in older adults? How do the lungs change in older adults?
- What is the nature of sexuality in late adulthood?

REFLECT

- If you could interview the Mankato nuns, what questions would you want to ask them?

3 HEALTH

Health Problems

The Robust Oldest-Old

Exercise, Nutrition, and Weight

Substance Use and Abuse

Health Treatment

How healthy are older adults? What types of health problems do they have? As we discuss the health of older adults, you will see that there are more healthy older adults than we used to envision.

Health Problems

As we age, the probability increases that we will have some disease or illness. For example, though many are still quite healthy overall, the majority of adults still alive at 80 years of age or older are likely to have some type of impairment. In chapter 16, "Physical and Cognitive Development in Middle Adulthood," we defined *chronic disorders* as disorders with a slow onset and a long duration. Chronic diseases are rare in early adulthood, increase in middle adulthood, and become more common in late adulthood. As shown in figure 18.10, arthritis is the most common chronic disorder in late adulthood, followed by hypertension. Older women have a higher incidence of arthritis and hypertension, and are more likely to have visual problems, but are less likely to have hearing problems than older men are.

Although adults over the age of 65 often have a physical impairment, many of them can still carry on their everyday activities or work. Chronic conditions associated with the greatest limitation on work are heart conditions (52 percent), diabetes (34 percent), asthma (27 percent), and arthritis (27 percent).

Lifestyle, social, and psychological factors are linked with health in older adults (Siegler, Bosworth, & Poon, 2003). In the McArthur Studies of Successful Aging, engaging in physical activity had a protective effect on health in virtually every group of older adults assessed (Seeman & Chen, 2002). Also, emotional support was linked with better functioning in individuals with cardiovascular disease and self-efficacy

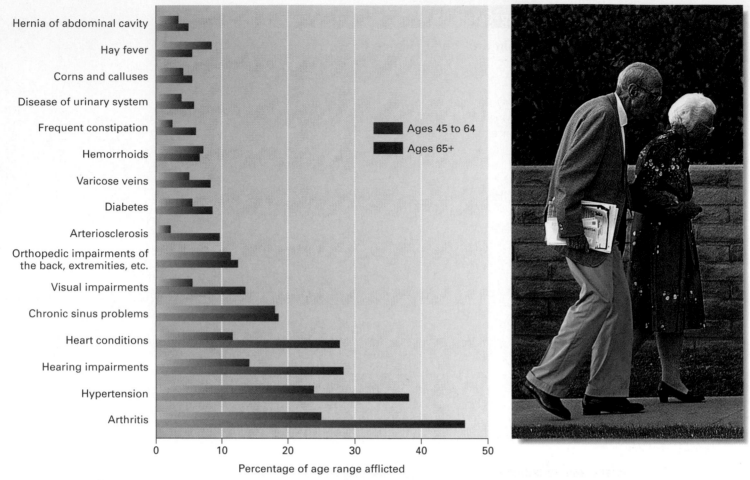

FIGURE 18.10 **The Most Prevalent Chronic Conditions in Middle and Late Adulthood**

was a protective factor for individuals with a history of cancer. Conflict in relationships was linked with greater decline in older adults with diabetes or hypertension. Low income is also strongly related to health problems in late adulthood. Approximately three times as many poor as nonpoor older adults report that their activities are limited by chronic disorders.

Causes of Death in Older Adults Nearly three-fourths of all older adults die of heart disease, cancer, or cerebrovascular disease (stroke). Chronic lung diseases, pneumonia and influenza, and diabetes round out the six leading causes of death among older adults. If cancer, the second leading cause of death in older adults, were completely eliminated, the average life expectancy would rise by only 1 to 2 years. However, if all cardiovascular and kidney diseases were eradicated, the average life expectancy of older adults would increase by approximately 10 years. This increase in longevity is already under way as the number of strokes among older adults has declined considerably in the last several decades. The decline in strokes is due to improved treatment of high blood pressure, a decrease in smoking, better diet, and an increase in exercise.

Ethnicity is linked with the death rates of older adults (Centers for Disease Control and Prevention, 2002). Among ethnic groups in the United States, African Americans have high death rates for stroke, heart disease, lung cancer, and female breast cancer. Asian Americans and Latinos have low death rates for these diseases. In the last decade, death rates for most diseases in African Americans, Latinos, and Asian Americans have decreased. However, death rates for most diseases still remain high for African Americans (Centers for Disease Control and Prevention, 2002).

Arthritis **Arthritis** is an inflammation of the joints accompanied by pain, stiffness, and movement problems. Arthritis is especially common in older adults. This disorder can affect hips, knees, ankles, fingers, and vertebrae. Individuals with arthritis often experience pain and stiffness, as well as problems in moving about and performing routine daily activities. There is no known cure for arthritis. However, the symptoms of arthritis can be reduced by drugs, such as aspirin, range-of-motion exercises for the afflicted joints, weight reduction, and, in extreme cases, replacement of the crippled joint with a prosthesis (Burke & others, 2003; Davenport, 2004; Kralik & others, 2004).

Osteoporosis Normal aging involves some loss of bone tissue from the skeleton. However, in some instances loss of bone tissue can become severe. **Osteoporosis** involves an extensive loss of bone tissue. Osteoporosis is the main reason many older adults walk with a marked stoop. Women are especially vulnerable to osteoporosis, the leading cause of broken bones in women (Tornetta & others, 2004). Approximately 80 percent of osteoporosis cases in the United States occur in females, 20 percent in males. Almost two-thirds of all women over the age of 60 are affected by osteoporosis. This aging disorder is more common in non-Latina White, thin, and small-framed women.

Osteoporosis is related to deficiencies in calcium, vitamin D, estrogen, and lack of exercise (Hauselmann & Rizzoli, 2003; Melton & others, 2004). To prevent osteoporosis, young and middle-aged women should eat foods rich in calcium, get more exercise, and avoid smoking (Whitehead & others, 2004). Calcium-rich foods include dairy products (low-fat milk and low-fat yogurt, for example) and certain vegetables (such as broccoli, turnip greens, and kale). Drugs such as Fosimax can be used to reduce the risk of osteoporosis. Aging women should also get bone density checks (Burke & others, 2003; Dolan & others, 2004).

A program of regular exercise has the potential to reduce osteoporosis (Fitzpatrick, 2003; Nies & others, 2003). In one study, women aged 50 to 70 lifted weights twice a week (Nelson & others, 1994). Their risk of osteoporosis (and resulting broken bones) was sharply reduced, while their balance and muscular strength improved. The weight-lifting program included three sets of eight repetitions on machines to strengthen muscles in the abdomen, back, thighs, and buttocks.

Accidents Accidents are the seventh leading cause of death among older adults. Injuries resulting from a fall at home or during a traffic accident in which an older adult is a driver or an older pedestrian is hit by a vehicle are common. Each year, approximately 200,000 adults over the age of 65 (most of them women) fracture a hip in a fall. Half of these older adults die within 12 months, frequently from pneumonia. Because healing and recuperation are slower in older adults, an accident that is only a temporary setback for a younger person may result in long-term hospital or home care for an older adult. In one study, an exercise program reduced the risk of falls in elderly adults (Province & others, 1995). In another study, Tai Chi, a form of balance training, improved the coordination of older adults in challenging conditions (Wong & others, 2001).

The Robust Oldest-Old

Our image of the oldest-old (85 years and older) is predominantly of being disabled and frail, an image that is fueled by the media. The implications of the projected rapid growth of the oldest-old population have often been pessimistic—an expensive burden in which the oldest-old often require the everyday help of other persons. However, as we discussed earlier in the chapter, the oldest-old are a heterogeneous group. For example, less than 50 percent of U.S. 85- to 89-year-olds have a disability (Siegler, Bosworth, & Poon, 2003).

Because so much attention has been given to chronic disabilities of the oldest-old, those who have aged successfully have gone virtually unnoticed and unstudied. An increased interest in successful aging is producing a more optimistic portrayal of the oldest-old than in the past (Freund & Riedeger, 2003). For example, cataract surgery and a variety of rehabilitation strategies can improve the functioning of the oldest-old. In one study, eight weeks of leg-strength training markedly improved the walking

How many of us older persons have really been prepared for the second half of life, for old age, and eternity?

—CARL JUNG
Swiss Psychoanalyst, 20th Century

www.mhhe.com/santrockld1o

Arthritis
Osteoporosis

View the video "Human Development: Cognitive Functioning in Centenarians" to assess a doctor's claim that the brain needs regular exercise.

arthritis Inflammation of the joints that is accompanied by pain, stiffness, and movement problems; especially common in older adults.

osteoporosis A chronic condition that involves an extensive loss of bone tissue and is the main reason many older adults walk with a marked stoop. Women are especially vulnerable to osteoporosis.

All we know about older adults indicates that they are healthier and happier the more active they are. Several decades ago, it was believed that older adults should be more passive and inactive to be well adjusted and satisfied with life. In today's world, we believe that while older adults may be in the evening of their life span, they are not meant to live out their remaining years passively.

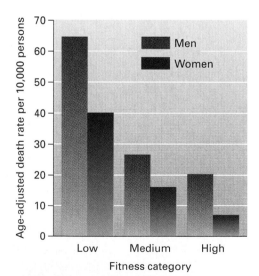

FIGURE 18.11 Physical Fitness and Mortality

In this study of middle-aged and older adults, being moderately fit or highly fit meant that individuals were less likely to die over a period of eight years than their low-fitness (sedentary) counterparts (Blair & others, 1989).

ability of nursing home residents who averaged 90 years of age (Fiatarone & others, 1990). Promising approaches for preventing or intervening in osteoporosis include calcium supplementation, estrogen replacement, and other hormone therapies.

In sum, earlier portraits of the oldest-old have been stereotypes. A substantial subgroup of the oldest-old are robust and active. And there is cause for optimism in the development of new regimens of prevention and intervention.

Exercise, Nutrition, and Weight

An important aspect of preventing health problems in older adults and improving their health is to encourage individuals to exercise more and to develop better nutritional habits.

Exercise   Although we may be in the evening of our lives in late adulthood, we are not meant to live out our remaining years passively. Everything we know about older adults suggests they are healthier and happier the more active they are. The possibility that regular exercise can lead to a healthier late adulthood and increase longevity has been raised. Let's examine several research studies on exercise and aging.

In one study, the cardiovascular fitness of 101 older men and women (average age = 67 years) was examined (Blumenthal & others, 1989). The older adults were randomly assigned to an aerobic exercise group, a yoga and flexibility control group, and a waiting list control group. The program lasted four months. Prior to and following the four-month program, the older adults underwent comprehensive physiological examinations. In the aerobics group, the older adults participated in three supervised exercise sessions per week for 16 weeks. Each session consisted of a 10-minute warm-up, 30 minutes of continuous exercise on a stationary bicycle, 15 minutes of brisk walking/jogging, and a 5-minute cool-down. In the yoga and flexibility control group, the older adults participated in 60 minutes of supervised yoga exercises at least twice a week for 16 weeks. Over the four-month period, the cardiovascular fitness—such as peak oxygen consumption, cholesterol level, and blood pressure—of the aerobic exercise group significantly improved. In contrast, the cardiovascular fitness of the yoga and waiting list groups did not improve.

In another study, exercise literally meant a difference in life or death for middle-aged and older adults (Blair, 1990). More than 10,000 men and women were divided into categories of low fitness, medium fitness, and high fitness (Blair & others, 1989). Then they were studied over a period of eight years. As shown in figure 18.11, sedentary participants (low fitness) were more than twice as likely to die during the eight-year time span of the study than those who were moderately fit and more than three times as likely to die as those who were highly fit. The positive effects of being physically fit occurred for both men and women in this study.

Gerontologists increasingly recommend strength training in addition to aerobic activity and stretching for older adults (Hunter, McCarthy, & Bamman, 2004; Pennix & others, 2002; Seynnes & others, 2004). The average person's lean body mass declines with age—about 6.6 pounds of lean muscle are lost each decade during the adult years. The rate of loss accelerates after age 45. Weight lifting can preserve and possibly increase muscle mass in older adults (Sequin & Nelson, 2003). In one study, it also reduced depression in the elderly (Singh, Clements, & Fiatarone, 1997). A recent review of 62 research studies concluded that strength training can improve muscle strength and some aspects of functional limitation, such as gait speed, in older adults (Latham & others, 2004).

Exercise is an excellent way to maintain health. Researchers continue to document its positive effects in older adults (Dejong & Franklin, 2004; Hawkins, Wiswell, & Marcell, 2003; McAuley, Kramer, & Colcombe, 2004). Exercise helps people to live independent lives with dignity in late adulthood. At 80, 90, and even 100 years of age, exercise can help prevent older adults from falling down or even being institutionalized. Being physically fit means being able to do the things you want to do, whether you are young or old. More about research on exercise's positive benefits for health is shown in figure 18.12.

Recent reviews of research on exercise and aging reached these conclusions (Singh, 2002, 2004):

- *Exercise can minimize the physiological changes associated with aging and contribute to health and well-being.* Changes that can be modified by exercise include motor coordination, cardiovascular function, metabolism (cholesterol, for example), and attention span (Brach & others, 2004; Ferrera, 2004).
- *Exercise can optimize body composition as aging occurs.* Exercise can increase muscle mass and bone mass, as well as decrease bone fragility (Karlsson, 2004).
- *Exercise is related to prevention of common chronic diseases.* Exercise can reduce the risk of cardiovascular disease, Type II diabetes, osteoporosis, stroke, and breast cancer (MaGavock & others, 2004).
- *Exercise is associated with improvement in the treatment of many diseases.* When exercise is used as part of the treatment, individuals with these diseases show improvement in symptoms: arthritis, pulmonary disease, congestive heart failure, coronary artery disease, hypertension, Type II diabetes, and obesity (Jadelis & others, 2001; Nazarian, 2004).
- *Exercise is linked to increased longevity.* Energy expenditure during exercise of at least 1,000 kcal/week reduces mortality by about 30 percent, while 2,000 kcal/week reduces mortality by about 50 percent (Lee & Skerrett, 2001).

Nutrition and Weight   Two aspects of undernutrition in older adults especially interest researchers: (1) vitamin and mineral deficiency, and (2) the role of calorie restriction in improving health and extending life.

Some older adults engage in dietary restriction that is harmful to their health, especially when they do not get adequate vitamins and minerals (Higgins & Barkley, 2004; Stokstad, 2003). One change in eating behavior in older adults is decreased snacking between meals, which may contribute to harmful weight loss, especially in women (Morley, 2003). Among the strategies for increasing weight gain in these women are the use of taste enhancers and providing calorie supplements between meals (Morley, 2003; Thomas, 2003).

Seventeenth-century English philosopher and essayist Francis Bacon was the first author to recommend scientific evaluation of diet and longevity. He advocated a frugal diet. Does a restricted intake of food increase longevity or could it possibly even extend the human life span?

Scientists have accumulated considerable evidence that calorie restriction (CR) in laboratory animals (in most cases rats) can increase the animals' life span (Goto & others, 2002; Heilbronn & Ravussin, 2003; Magwere, Chapman, & Partridge, 2004; Payne, Dodd, & Leewenburgh, 2003). Animals fed diets restricted in calories, although adequate in protein, vitamins, and minerals, live as much as 40 percent longer than animals given unlimited access to food. And chronic problems such as kidney disease appear at a later age. CR also delays biochemical alterations such as the age-related rise in cholesterol and triglycerides observed in both humans and animals (see figure 18.13).

Whether similar very-low-calorie diets (in some instances the animals eat 40 percent less than normal) can stretch the human life span is not known (Heilbronn & Ravussin, 2003; Lane & others, 2004; Roth & others, 2002). Most nutritional experts do not recommend very-low-calorie diets for older adults; rather, they recommend a well-balanced, low-fat diet that includes the nutritional factors needed to maintain good health.

No one knows for certain how CR works to increase the life span of animals. Some scientists believe it might lower the level of free radicals or potentially toxic particles created by the breakdown of food. Others believe calorie restriction might trigger a state of emergency called "survival mode" in which the body eliminates all unnecessary functions to focus only on staying alive. Encouraged by the research on animals, the National Institutes of Health is planning calorie restriction studies on humans (Johannes, 2002). Calorie restriction of 30 percent in humans would translate into about 1,120 calories a day for the average woman and 1,540 for the average man.

FIGURE 18.12 The Jogging Hog Experiment
Jogging hogs reveal the dramatic effects of exercise on health. In one investigation, a group of hogs was trained to run approximately 100 miles per week (Bloor & White, 1983). Then, the researchers narrowed the arteries that supplied blood to the hogs' hearts. The hearts of the jogging hogs developed extensive alternate pathways for blood supply, and 42 percent of the threatened heart tissue was salvaged compared with only 17 percent in a control group of nonjogging hogs.

Exercise and Aging
Roy Walford's Views

FIGURE 18.13 Calorie Restriction in Monkeys

Shown here are two monkeys at the Wisconsin Primate Research Center. Both are 24 years old. The monkey in the top photograph was raised on a calorie-restricted diet, while the monkey in the bottom photograph was raised on a normal diet. Notice that the monkey on the calorie-restricted diet looks younger; he also has lower glucose and insulin levels. The monkey raised on a normal diet has higher triglycerides and more oxidative damage to his cells.

Leaner men do live longer, healthier lives. In one study of 19,297 Harvard alumni, those weighing the least were less likely to die over the past three decades (Lee & others, 1993). The men were divided into five categories according to body mass index (a complex formula that takes into account weight and height). As body mass increased, so did risk of death. The most overweight men had a 67 percent higher risk of dying than the thinnest men. For example, the heaviest men (such as 181 pounds or more for a 5-foot-10-inch man) also had 2½ times the risk of death from cardiovascular disease. Currently, these researchers are studying the relation of body mass index to longevity in women and predict similar results to the study with men.

The Growing Controversy Over Vitamins and Aging For years, most experts on aging and health argued that a balanced diet was all that was needed for successful aging; vitamin supplements were not recommended. However, an increasing number of research studies raise questions about the practice of not recommending vitamin supplements for middle-aged and older adults. The new research suggests the possibility that some vitamin supplements—mainly a group called "antioxidants," which includes vitamin C, vitamin E, and beta-carotene—help to slow the aging process and improve the health of older adults.

The theory is that antioxidants counteract the cell damage caused by free radicals, which are produced both by the body's own metabolism and by environmental factors such as smoking, pollution, and bad chemicals in the diet. When free radicals cause damage (oxidation) in one cell, a chain reaction of damage follows. Antioxidants act much like a fire extinguisher, helping to neutralize free-radical activity.

Some research studies find links between the antioxidant vitamins and health. One recent study revealed that low blood vitamin C concentration in older adults was linked with an earlier incidence of death (Fletcher, Breeze, & Shetty, 2003). Another study found that people who took vitamin E supplements for two years significantly reduced their risk of heart disease—by up to 40 percent (Rimm & others, 1993). However, a recent analysis of 19 studies of vitamin E revealed that middle-aged and older adults who took 200 IU of vitamin E or more a day were more likely to die than their counterparts who did not take vitamin E (Miller & others, 2005, in press). The researchers concluded that most individuals get enough vitamin E in their diet and should not take vitamin E supplements. They argue that vitamin E in low doses may be a powerful antioxidant but in higher doses may increase oxidative damage.

There is no evidence that antioxidants can increase the human life span, but some aging and health experts believe that vitamin C and beta-carotene can reduce a person's risk of becoming frail and sick in the later adult years. However, there are still a lot of blanks and uncertainties in what we know (Stern, 1993). That is, we don't know which vitamins should be taken, how large a dose should be taken, what the restraints are, and so on. Critics also argue that the key experimental studies documenting the effectiveness of the vitamins in slowing the aging process have not been conducted. The studies in this area thus far have been so-called population studies that are correlational rather than experimental in nature. Other factors—such as exercise, better health practices, and good nutritional habits—might be responsible for the positive findings about vitamins and aging rather than vitamins per se. Also, the free-radical theory is a theory and not a fact, and is only one of a number of theories about why we age.

With these uncertainties in mind, some aging experts still recommend vitamin supplements in the following range (Blumberg, 1993): 250 to 1,000 milligrams of vitamin C and 15 to 30 milligrams of beta-carotene.

Possible links between vitamins and cognitive performance in older adults also have been the focus of increased research attention. A recent review of cross-sectional and longitudinal research studies concluded that taking B vitamins, especially folate, B_6, and B_{12}, is positively related to cognitive performance in older adults (Calvaresi & Bryan, 2001). This review also presented some evidence that supplementation with B vitamins can improve cognitive performance in older adults.

Now that we have considered older adults' health problems and the roles of exercise and nutrition, let's turn our attention to the health treatment available to older adults.

Substance Use and Abuse

How extensive is substance abuse in older adults? A recent national survey found that binge drinking (having five or more drinks in one day) peaks in the 18-to-24 age range and then declines through the late adulthood years (National Center for Health Statistics, 2002) (see figure 18.14). Indeed, a majority (58 percent) of U.S. adults 65 years and older completely abstain from alcohol, an increase from 38 percent of 45- to 64-year-olds. The reasons for these declines are usually attributed to an increase in illness and disease.

Despite these declines in alcohol use, the Substance Abuse and Mental Health Services Administration (2002) has identified substance abuse among older adults as the "invisible epidemic" in the United States. The belief is that substance abuse often goes undetected in older adults and there is concern about older adults who not only abuse illicit drugs but prescription drugs as well (Scott & Popovich, 2001). Too often, screening questionnaires are not appropriate for older adults and the consequences of alcohol abuse, such as depression, inadequate nutrition, congestive heart failure, and frequent falls, may erroneously be attributed to other medical or psychological conditions (Hoyer & Roodin, 2003). Because of the dramatic increase in the number of older adults anticipated over the twenty-first century, substance abuse is likely to characterize an increasing number of older adults (Atkinson, Ryan, & Turner, 2001).

Older adults have either a history of excessive consumption of alcohol over 40 to 50 years or a moderate consumption that increases in times of stress. *Late-onset alcoholism* is the label used to describe the onset of alcoholism after the age of 65. Late-onset alcoholism is often related to loneliness, loss of a spouse, or a disabling condition.

In many cases, older adults are taking multiple medications, which can present an increased risk. For example, when combined with taking tranquilizers or sedatives, alcohol use can impair breathing, produce excessive sedation, and be fatal.

Health Treatment

What is the quality of health treatment that older adults in the United States receive? A recent study of older adults with health problems revealed that they get the recommended medical care they need only half the time (Wenger & others, 2003). The researchers examined the medical records of 372 frail older adults who had been treated by two managed-care organizations over the course of one year. Then they documented the medical care each patient received and judged it using standard indicators of quality. For example, many older adults with an unsteady gait don't get the help they need, such as physical therapy to improve their walking ability. Clearly, the quality of health treatment older adults receive needs to be significantly improved (Rantz & others, 2004).

About 3 percent of adults 65 years of age and older in the United States reside in a nursing home at any point in time. However, as older adults age, their probability of being in a nursing home or other extended-care facility increases. Twenty-three percent of adults 85 years of age and older live in nursing homes or other extended-care facilities. What is the quality of nursing homes and extended-care facilities for older adults? What is the relationship between older adults and health-care providers?

The quality of nursing homes and other extended-care facilities for older adults varies enormously and is a source of continuing national concern. More than one-third are seriously deficient. They fail federally mandated inspections because they do not meet the minimum standards for physicians, pharmacists, and various rehabilitation specialists (occupational and physical therapists). Further concerns focus on the patient's right to privacy, access to medical information, safety, and lifestyle freedom within the individual's range of mental and physical capabilities.

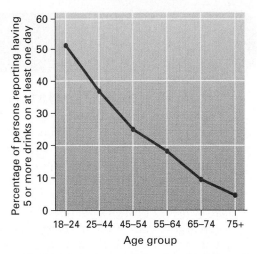

FIGURE 18.14 Age and the Consumption of Five or More Drinks on at Least One Day in the United States
The graph shows the considerable decline in having five or more drinks on at least one day as people get older (National Center for Health Statistics, 2002).

Trends in Health and Aging
Health and Aging:
Cross-Cultural Comparisons

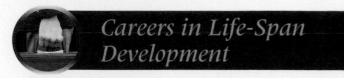

Careers in Life-Span Development

Sarah Kagan, Geriatric Nurse

Sarah Kagan is a professor of nursing at the University of Pennsylvania School of Nursing. She provides nursing consultation to patients, their families, nurses, and physicians on the complex needs of older adults related to their hospitalization for acute or chronic illness. She also consults on research and the management of patients who have head and neck cancers. Sarah also teaches in the undergraduate nursing program where she directs the required course, Nursing Care in the Older Adult. In 2003, she was awarded a $500,000 MacArthur Fellowship for her work in the field of nursing.

In Sarah's own words,

> I'm lucky to be doing what I love—caring for older adults and families—and learning from them so that I can share this knowledge and develop or investigate better ways of caring. My special interests in the care of older adults who have cancer allow me the intimate privilege of being with patients at the best and worst times of their lives. That intimacy acts as a beacon—it reminds me of the value I and nursing as a profession contribute to society and the rewards offered in return. (Kagan, 2004, p. 1)

Because of the inadequate quality of many nursing homes and the escalating costs for nursing home care, many specialists in the health problems of the aged believe that home health care, day-care centers, and preventive medicine clinics are good alternatives (Castle, 2001). They are potentially less expensive than hospitals and nursing homes. They also are less likely to engender the feelings of depersonalization and dependency that occur so often in residents of institutions (Greene & others, 1995).

In a classic study, Judith Rodin and Ellen Langer (1977) found that an important factor related to health, and even survival, in a nursing home is the patient's feelings of control and self-determination. A group of elderly nursing home residents were encouraged to make more day-to-day choices and thus feel they had more responsibility for control over their lives. They began to decide such matters as what they ate, when their visitors could come, what movies they saw, and who could come to their rooms. A similar group in the same nursing home was told by the administrator how caring the nursing home was and how much the staff wanted to help, but these elderly nursing home residents were given no opportunities to take more control over their lives. Eighteen months later, the residents given responsibility and control were more alert and active, and said they were happier, than the residents who were only encouraged to feel that the staff would try to satisfy their needs. And the "responsible" or "self-control" group had significantly better improvement in their health than did the "dependent" group. Even more important was the finding that after 18 months only half as many nursing home residents in the "responsibility" group had died as in the "dependent" group (see figure 18.15). Perceived control over one's environment, then, can literally be a matter of life or death.

In another research study, Rodin (1983) measured stress-related hormones in several groups of nursing home residents. Then she taught the residents coping skills to help them deal better with day-to-day problems. They were taught how to say no when they did not want something, without worrying whether they would offend someone. They were given assertiveness training and learned time-management skills. After the training, the nursing home residents had greatly reduced levels of cortisol (a hormone closely related to stress that has been implicated in a number of diseases). The cortisol levels of the assertiveness-training residents remained lower, even after 18 months. Further, these nursing home residents were healthier and had a reduced need for medication, compared with residents who had not been taught the coping skills. Rodin's research shows that simply giving nursing home residents options for control and teaching them coping skills can change their behavior and improve their health.

The attitudes of both the health-care provider and the older adult are important aspects of the older adult's health care (Akhter & Levinson, 2003; Hatcliff, 2003). Unfortunately, health-care providers too often share society's stereotypes and negative attitudes toward older adults. In a health-care setting, these attitudes can take the form of avoidance, dislike, and begrudged tolerance rather than positive, hopeful treatment. Health-care personnel are more likely to be interested in treating younger persons, who more often have acute problems with a higher prognosis for successful recovery. They often are less motivated to treat older persons, who are more likely to have chronic problems with a lower prognosis for successful recovery.

Not only are physicians less responsive to older patients, but older patients often take a less active role in medical encounters with health-care personnel than do

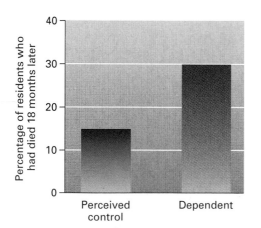

FIGURE 18.15 Perceived Control and Mortality

In the study by Rodin and Langer (1977), nursing home residents who were encouraged to feel more in control of their lives were more likely to be alive 18 months later than those who were treated to feel more dependent on the nursing home staff.

younger patients (Woodward & Wallston, 1987). Older adults should be encouraged to take a more active role in their own health care.

Geriatric nurses specialize in treating the health-care problems of older adults. To read about the work of one geriatric nurse, see the Careers in Life-Span Development insert.

Review and Reflect: Learning Goal 3

3 Identify health problems in older adults and how they can be treated

REVIEW

- What are some common health problems in older adults? What are the main causes of death in older adults?
- How can the robust oldest-old be described?
- How do exercise, nutrition, and weight influence development in late adulthood?
- What is substance use and abuse like in late adulthood?
- What are some options and issues in the health treatment of older adults?

REFLECT

- What changes in your lifestyle now might help you age more successfully when you become an older adult?

Reach Your Learning Goals

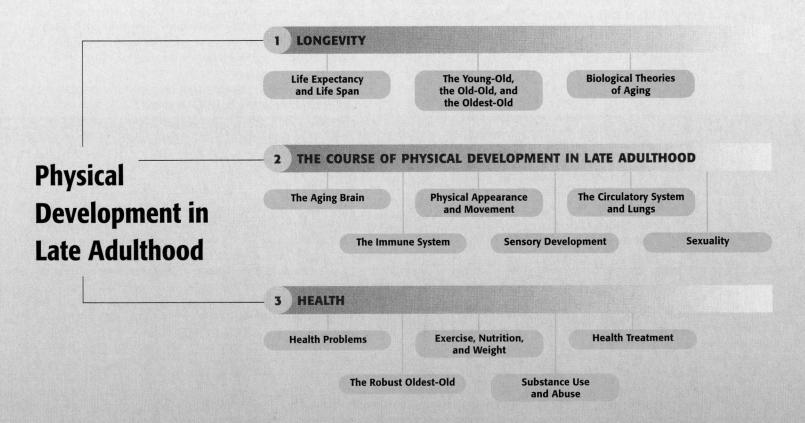

Physical Development in Late Adulthood

1 LONGEVITY
- Life Expectancy and Life Span
- The Young-Old, the Old-Old, and the Oldest-Old
- Biological Theories of Aging

2 THE COURSE OF PHYSICAL DEVELOPMENT IN LATE ADULTHOOD
- The Aging Brain
- Physical Appearance and Movement
- The Circulatory System and Lungs
- The Immune System
- Sensory Development
- Sexuality

3 HEALTH
- Health Problems
- Exercise, Nutrition, and Weight
- Health Treatment
- The Robust Oldest-Old
- Substance Use and Abuse

Summary

 Learning Goal 1: Characterize longevity and the biological aspects of aging

- Life expectancy refers to the number of years that will probably be lived by an average person born in a particular year. Life span is the maximum number of years any member of a species has been known to live. Life expectancy has dramatically increased; life span has not. An increasing number of individuals live to be 100 or older. On the average, females live about six years longer than males do. The sex difference is likely due to biological and social factors.

- In terms of chronological age, the young-old have been described as being 65 to 74 years of age, the old-old as 75 years and older, and the oldest-old as 85 years and older. Many experts on aging prefer to describe the young-old, old-old, and oldest-old in terms of functional age rather than chronological age. This view accounts for the fact that some 85-year-olds are more biologically and psychologically fit than some 65-year-olds. However, those 85 and older face significant problems, whereas those in their sixties and seventies are experiencing an increase in successful aging.

- Four biological theories are cellular clock theory, free-radical theory, mitochondrial theory, and hormonal stress theory. Hayflick proposed the cellular clock theory, which states that cells can divide a maximum of about 75 to 80 times and that as we age, our cells become less capable of dividing. In the last decade, scientists have found that telomeres are likely involved in explaining why cells lose their capacity to divide. According to free-radical theory, people age because unstable oxygen molecules called free radicals are produced in the cells. According to mitochondrial theory, aging is due to the decay of mitochondria, tiny cellular bodies that supply energy for function, growth, and repair. According to hormonal stress theory, aging in the body's hormonal system can lower resilience to stress and increase the likelihood of disease.

2 **Learning Goal 2: Describe how a person's brain and body change in late adulthood**

- There is a general slowing of function in the central nervous system that begins in middle adulthood and increases in late adulthood. The brain becomes less lateralized in older adults. Researchers have recently found that older adults can generate new neurons. We lose some neurons as we age, but how many is debated. The aging brain retains considerable plasticity and adaptiveness. Growth of dendrites can take place in older adults. The brain has the capacity to virtually rewire itself to compensate for loss in older adults.

- Decline in immune system functioning with aging is well documented. Exercise can improve immune system functioning.

- The most obvious signs of aging are wrinkled skin and age spots on the skin. People get shorter as they age, and their weight often decreases after age 60 because of loss of muscle.

The movement of older adults slows across a wide range of movement tasks.

- The visual system declines, but the vast majority of older adults can have their vision corrected so they can continue to work and function in the world. In aging, the yellowing of the eye's lens reduces color differentiation and the ability to see the periphery of a visual field declines in older adults. Significant declines in visual functioning related to glare characterize adults 75 years and older and even more so those 85 and older. Three diseases that can impair the vision of older adults are cataracts, glaucoma, and macular degeneration. Hearing decline can begin in middle age but usually does not become much of an impediment until late adulthood. Hearing aids can diminish hearing problems for many older adults. Smell and taste can decline, although the decline is minimal in healthy older adults. Changes in touch sensitivity are associated with aging, although this does not present a problem for most older adults. Sensitivity to pain decreases in late adulthood.

- When heart disease is absent, the amount of blood pumped is the same regardless of an adult's age. High blood pressure no longer is just accepted but rather is treated with medication, exercise, and/or a healthy diet. Blood pressure can rise in older adults due to a number of factors, which can be modified. Lung capacity does drop, but older adults can improve lung functioning with diaphragm-strengthening exercises.

- Aging in late adulthood does include some changes in sexual performance, more for males than females. Nonetheless, there are no known age limits to sexual activity.

 Learning Goal 3: Identify health problems in older adults and how they can be treated

- As we age, our probability of disease or illness increases. Chronic disorders are rare in early adulthood, increase in middle adulthood, and become more common in late adulthood. The most common chronic disorder in late adulthood is arthritis. Nearly three-fourths of older adults die of heart disease, cancer, or stroke. Osteoporosis is the main reason many older adults walk with a stoop; women are especially vulnerable. Accidents are usually more debilitating to older than to younger adults.

- Early portraits of the oldest-old were too negative; there is cause for optimism in the development of new regimens and interventions.

- The physical benefits of exercise have clearly been demonstrated in older adults. Aerobic exercise and weight lifting are both recommended if the adults are physically capable of them. There is concern about older adults who do not get adequate vitamins and minerals, especially women. Calorie restriction in animals can increase the animals' life span, but whether this works with humans is not known. In humans, being overweight is associated with an increased mortality rate. Most nutritional experts recommend a well-balanced, low-fat diet for older adults, but do not recommend an extremely low-calorie diet. The vitamin and aging controversy focuses on whether vitamin supplements—especially the antioxidants vitamin C, vitamin E, and beta-carotene—can slow the aging process and improve older adults' health. Recent research has found a link between taking B vitamins and positive cognitive performance in older adults.

- Alcohol use and abuse declines in older adults, although this is more difficult to detect in older adults than in younger adults.

- Although only 3 percent of adults over 65 reside in nursing homes, 23 percent of adults 85 and over do. The quality of nursing homes varies enormously. Alternatives to nursing homes are being proposed. Simply giving nursing home residents options for control and teaching coping skills can change their behavior and improve their health. The attitudes of both the health-care provider and the older adult patient are important aspects of the older adult's health care. Too often health-care personnel share society's negative view of older adults.

Key Terms

life span 555	free-radical theory 560	cataracts 566	arthritis 571
life expectancy 555	mitochondrial theory 560	glaucoma 566	osteoporosis 571
cellular clock theory 559	hormonal stress theory 560	macular degeneration 567	

Key People

Stanley Rapaport 563	Ellen Langer 576	Judith Rodin 576

E-Learning Tools

To help you master the material in this chapter, you'll find a number of valuable study tools on the LifeMap CD-ROM that accompanies this book and on the Online Learning Center for *Life-Span Development*, tenth edition, at www.mhhe.com/santrockld10.

Video Clips

● In the margins of this book there are icons directing you to the LifeMap CD-ROM that accompanies the book. There you'll find a video for chapter 18 called "Human Development: Cognitive Functioning in Centenarians." Do mental faculties invariably diminish as one gets older? Or is the brain, as Dr. Marjorie Silver claims in this segment, a muscle that requires regular exercise?

Self-Assessment

Connect to www.mhhe.com/santrockld10 to reflect on what aging means to you by completing the self-assessment, *My Beliefs About Aging*.

Taking It to the Net

Connect to www.mhhe.com/santrockld10 to research the answers to these questions.

1. Do you think you will live to be 100? Investigate your chances of being a centenarian by reading the results from an ongoing Harvard University Medical School study.
2. Seventy-year-old Jack knows that regular exercise is important to maintain a healthy heart. But what are the other benefits to staying active, and how much exercising should Jack do?
3. Patty's 85-year-old mother, who lives with her and her family, has begun eating less and less. She tells Patty, "Eating is no fun anymore. I can't taste anything." What can Patty do to make meals more appealing for her mother?

Health and Well-Being, Parenting, and Education Exercises

Build your decision-making skills by trying your hand at the health and well-being, parenting, and education exercises.

Connect to www.mhhe.com/santrockld10 to research the answers and complete the exercises.

The night hath not yet come: We are not quite cut off from labor by the failing of light; some work remains for us to do and dare.

—HENRY WADSWORTH LONGFELLOW
American Poet, 19th Century

Cognitive Development in Late Adulthood

Chapter Outline

Learning Goals

1 Describe the cognitive functioning of older adults

2 Discuss aging and adaptations to work and retirement

3 Characterize mental health problems and their treatment in older adults

4 Explain the role of religion in the lives of older adults

Images of Life-Span Development
Lily Hearst and Sister Mary, Active Minds

Throughout her life, Lily Hearst has pursued a range of interests

including the arts, music, science, and politics. She has a degree in music and reads and speaks three languages. Now, at 101 years old, she lives independently and exercises every day. She reads *The Wall Street Journal* daily, teaches piano, and plays in a classical trio at the North Berkeley Senior Center [in Berkeley, California].

Lily keeps a strict daily routine that begins at seven o'clock, when she gets out of bed, exercises, and fixes her own breakfast. At nine she goes to the pool and swims eight laps. A friend drives her to the senior center where she attends classes, reads, watches movies, and plays piano. Lily keeps track of her life with a date book, writing down engagements and other things she needs to remember. She takes pride in the fact that she is never late for an appointment. (Exploratorium, 2004, pp. 1–2)

Another centenarian, Sister Mary, was a participant in the Nun Study, which we described in chapter 18. She died in 1993 at 101 years of age. Even at 100, Sister Mary continued to score high on measures of cognitive skills (Snowdon, 1997). She loved to read and late in her life was often observed looking through a magnifying glass as she read books, magazines, and newspapers.

PREVIEW

Lily Hearst and Sister Mary led very active cognitive lives as older adults. Just how well older adults can and do function cognitively is an important question we will explore in this chapter. We also will examine the important topics of work and retirement, mental health, and religion.

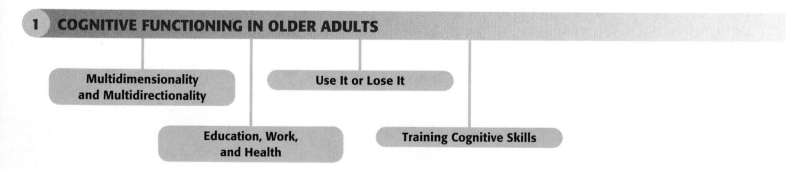

1   COGNITIVE FUNCTIONING IN OLDER ADULTS

Multidimensionality and Multidirectionality

Education, Work, and Health

Use It or Lose It

Training Cognitive Skills

At the age of 70, John Rock invented the birth control pill. At age 76, Anna Mary Robertson Moses, better known as Grandma Moses, took up painting and became internationally famous, staging fifteen one-woman shows throughout Europe. At age 89, Arthur Rubinstein gave one of his best performances at New York's Carnegie Hall. When Pablo Casals was 95, a reporter asked him, "Mr. Casals, you are the greatest cellist who ever lived. Why do you still practice six hours a day?" Mr. Casals replied, "Because I feel like I am making progress" (Canfield & Hansen, 1995).

Multidimensionality and Multidirectionality

In thinking about the nature of cognitive change in adulthood, it is important to consider that cognition is a multidimensional concept (Dixon & Cohen, 2003). It is also important to consider that although some dimensions of cognition might decline as we age, others might remain stable or even improve.

Cognitive Mechanics and Cognitive Pragmatics Paul Baltes (2000) clarified the distinction between those aspects of the aging mind that show decline and those that remain stable or even improve. He makes a distinction between "cognitive mechanics" and "cognitive pragmatics."

Grandma Moses, known in her time as the "grand old lady of American art," took up painting at the age of 76 and continued to paint past her hundredth birthday.

- **Cognitive mechanics** are the "hardware" of the mind and reflect the neurophysiological architecture of the brain developed through evolution. Cognitive mechanics consist of the speed and accuracy of the processes involved in sensory input, attention, visual and motor memory, discrimination, comparison, and categorization. Because of the strong influence of biology, heredity, and health on cognitive mechanics, their decline with aging is likely.
- **Cognitive pragmatics** are the culture-based "software programs" of the mind. Cognitive pragmatics include reading and writing skills, language comprehension, educational qualifications, professional skills, and also the type of knowledge about the self and life skills that help us to master or cope with life. Because of the strong influence of culture on cognitive pragmatics, their improvement into old age is possible. Thus, although cognitive mechanics may decline in old age, cognitive pragmatics may actually improve (see figure 19.1).

One recent study focused on older adults (age range: 70 to 100 years of age with a mean age of 85) over a six-year period (Singer & others, 2003). In support of the cognitive mechanics/pragmatics distinction, they found that perceptual speed, memory, and categorization declined with age but that knowledge remained stable up to age 90 before it began to decline.

Now that we have examined the distinction between cognitive mechanics and cognitive pragmatics, let's explore some of the more specific cognitive processes that reflect these two general domains. We begin with these aspects of cognitive mechanics: sensory/motor and speed of processing.

Sensory/Motor and Speed-of-Processing Dimensions In the Berlin Study of Aging, the key factors that accounted for age differences in intelligence were visual and auditory acuity (Lindenberger & Baltes, 1994). Thus, sensory functioning was a strong late-life predictor of individual differences in intelligence. It is also now well accepted that the speed of processing information declines in late adulthood (Hoyer & others, 2004; Salthouse, 1996, 2000; Salthouse & Miles, 2002) (see figure 19.2).

Although speed of processing information slows down in late adulthood, there is considerable individual variation in this ability. And it is not clear that this slowdown affects our lives in substantial ways. For example, in one experiment, the reaction time and typing skills of typists of varying ages were studied (Salthouse, 1994). The older typists usually had slower reactions, but they actually typed just as fast as the younger typists. Possibly the older typists were faster when they were younger and had slowed down, but the results in another experimental condition suggested that something else was involved. When the number of characters that the typists could look ahead at was limited, the older typists slowed considerably; the younger typists were affected much less by this restriction. Thus, the older typists had learned to look farther ahead, allowing them to type as fast as their younger counterparts.

cognitive mechanics The "hardware" of the mind, reflecting the neurophysiological architecture of the brain as developed through evolution. Cognitive mechanics involve the speed and accuracy of the processes involving sensory input, visual and motor memory, discrimination, comparison, and categorization.

cognitive pragmatics The culture-based "software programs" of the mind. Cognitive pragmatics include reading and writing skills, language comprehension, educational qualifications, professional skills, and also the type of knowledge about the self and life skills that help us to master or cope with life.

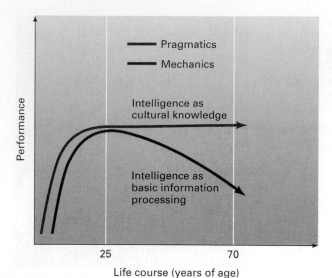

FIGURE 19.1 Theorized Age Changes in Cognitive Mechanics and Cognitive Pragmatics

Baltes argues that cognitive mechanics decline during aging, whereas cognitive pragmatics do not. Cognitive mechanics have a biological/genetic foundation; cognitive pragmatics have an experiential/cultural foundation.

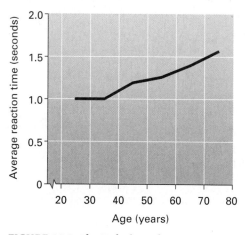

FIGURE 19.2 The Relation of Age to Reaction Time

In one study, the average reaction time began to slow in the forties and this decline accelerated in the sixties and seventies (Salthouse, 1994). The task used to assess reaction time required individuals to match numbers with symbols on a computer screen.

selective attention Focusing on a specific aspect of experience that is relevant while ignoring others that are irrelevant.

divided attention Concentrating on more than one activity at the same time.

sustained attention The state of readiness to detect and respond to small changes occurring at random times in the environment.

The decline in processing speed in older adults is likely due to a decline in functioning of the brain and central nervous system (Groth, Gilmore, & Thomas, 2003; Madden, 2001). Health and exercise may influence how much decline in processing speed occurs (Gerrotsen & others, 2003). One study found that following six months of aerobic exercise showed improvement on reaction time tasks (Kramer & others, 1999).

Attention Three aspects of attention that have been investigated in older adults are selective attention, divided attention, and sustained attention:

- **Selective attention** is focusing on a specific aspect of experience that is relevant while ignoring others that are irrelevant. An example of selective attention is the ability to focus on one voice among many in a crowded room or a noisy restaurant. Another is making a decision about which stimuli to attend to when making a left turn at an intersection. Generally, older adults are less adept at selective attention than younger adults are (Hogan, 2003; McDowd & others, 2003). However, on simple tasks involving a search for a feature, such as determining whether a target item is present on a computer screen, age differences are minimal when individuals are given sufficient practice.
- **Divided attention** involves concentrating on more than one activity at the same time. When the two competing tasks are reasonably easy, age differences among adults are minimal or nonexistent. However, the more difficult the competing tasks are, the less effectively older adults divide attention than younger adults (Maciokas & Corgnale, 2003; Wood, 2002). In one study, the ability to engage in a conversation while simultaneously driving a simulator through highway traffic (in an experimental laboratory) was examined in 17- to 25-year-olds, 26- to 49-year-olds, and 50- to 80-year-olds (McKnight & McKnight, 1993). A nondistraction control condition also was included. Overall, the participants performed more poorly in the divided attention condition than in the nondistraction control condition. Also, the older adults (50 to 80 years old) performed worse in the divided attention condition than the younger two groups but not in the control condition. Thus, placing more demands on the attention of the older adults led them to perform more poorly on the driving task.
- **Sustained attention** is the state of readiness to detect and respond to small changes occurring at random times in the environment. Sometimes sustained attention is referred to as *vigilance*. Researchers have found that older adults perform as well as middle-aged and younger adults on measures of sustained attention (Berardi, Parasuraman, & Haxby, 2001).

Memory Let's examine a research study that addresses how we remember as we age. Non-Latino adults of various ages in the United States were studied to determine how much Spanish they remembered from classes they had taken in high school or college (Bahrick, 1984). The individuals chosen for the study had used Spanish very little since they initially learned it in high school or college. Not surprisingly, the young adults who had taken Spanish within the last three years remembered Spanish best. After that, the deterioration in memory was gradual (see figure 19.3). For example, older adults who had studied Spanish 50 years earlier remembered about 80 percent of what young adults did who had studied it in the last three years! The most important factor in the adults' memory of Spanish was not how long ago they studied it but how well they initially learned it—those who got an A in Spanish 50 years earlier remembered more Spanish than adults who got a C when taking Spanish only one year earlier.

Memory does change during aging, but not all memory changes with age in the same way (Balota, Dolan, & Duchek, 2000). The main dimensions of memory and aging that have been studied include episodic memory, semantic memory, cognitive resources (such as working memory and perceptual speed), memory beliefs, and noncognitive factors such as health, education, and socioeconomic factors (Smith, 1996).

Episodic Memory **Episodic memory** is the retention of information about the where and when of life's happenings (Tulving, 2000). For example, what was it like when your younger sister or brother was born, what happened to you on your first date, what were you doing when you heard that the Persian Gulf War had begun, and what did you eat for breakfast this morning?

Younger adults have better episodic memory than older adults have (Parker & others, 2004; Piolino & others, 2002; Wingfield & Kahana, 2002). Older adults think that they can remember older events better than more recent events, typically reporting that they can remember what happened to them years ago but can't remember what they did yesterday. However, researchers consistently have found that, contrary to such self-reports, in older adults the older the memory, the less accurate it is. This has been documented in studies of memory for high school classmates, foreign language learned in school over the life span, names of grade school teachers, and autobiographical facts kept in diaries (Smith, 1996).

Semantic Memory **Semantic memory** is a person's knowledge about the world. It includes a person's fields of expertise, such as knowledge of chess for a skilled chess player; general academic knowledge of the sort learned in school, such as knowledge of geometry; and "everyday knowledge" about the meanings of words, famous individuals, important places, and common things, such as what day is Valentine's Day. Semantic memory appears to be independent of an individual's personal identity with the past. For example, you can access a fact—such as "Lima is the capital of Peru"—and not have the foggiest idea of when and where you learned it.

Does semantic memory decline during aging? Older adults do often take longer to retrieve semantic information, but usually they can ultimately retrieve it. For the most part, episodic memory declines more in older adults than semantic memory (Parkin & Walter, 1992).

Cognitive Resources: Working Memory and Perceptual Speed One view of memory suggests that a limited number of cognitive resources can be devoted to any cognitive task. Two important cognitive resource mechanisms are working memory and perceptual speed. Recall from chapter 16 that *working memory* is closely linked to short-term memory but places more emphasis on memory as a place for mental work. Working memory is like a mental "workbench" that allows individuals to manipulate and assemble information when making decisions, solving problems, and comprehending written and spoken language (Baddeley, 2000). Researchers have found declines in working memory during the late adulthood years (Chaytor & Schmitter-Edgecombe, 2004; Leonards, Ibanez, & Giannakopoulos, 2002; Missonnier & others, 2004; Park & others, 2002; Salthouse, 1994, 2000).

Perceptual speed is another cognitive resource that has been studied by researchers on aging. Perceptual speed is the ability to perform simple perceptual-motor tasks such as deciding whether pairs of two-digit or two-letter strings are the same or different or determining the time required to step on the brakes when the car directly ahead stops. Perceptual speed shows considerable decline in late adulthood, and it is strongly linked with decline in working memory (Hoyer & others, 2004; Salthouse, 2000).

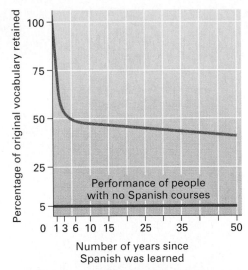

FIGURE 19.3 Memory for Spanish as a Function of Age Since Spanish Was Learned An initial steep drop over about a three-year period in remembering the vocabulary learned in Spanish classes occurred. However, there was little dropoff in memory for Spanish vocabulary from 3 years after taking Spanish classes to 50 years after taking them. Even 50 years after taking Spanish classes, individuals still remembered almost 50 percent of the vocabulary.

episodic memory The retention of information about the where and when of life's happenings.

semantic memory A person's knowledge about the world—including a person's fields of expertise, general academic knowledge of the sort learned in school, and "everyday knowledge."

Cognitive Psychology Laboratory
Timothy Salthouse's Research
Fredda Blanchard-Field's Research

Explicit and Implicit Memory   Researchers also have found that aging is linked with changes in explicit memory (Tulving, 2000). **Explicit memory** is memory of facts and experiences that individuals consciously know and can state. Explicit memory also is sometimes called *declarative memory*. Examples of explicit memory include being at a grocery store and remembering what you wanted to buy, being able to name the capital of Illinois, or recounting the events of a movie you have seen. **Implicit memory** is memory without conscious recollection; it involves skills and routine procedures that are automatically performed. Examples of implicit memory include driving a car, swinging a golf club, or typing on a computer keyboard, without having to consciously think about it.

Implicit memory is less likely to be adversely affected by aging than explicit memory (Schugens & others, 1997; Tulving, 2000). Thus, older adults are more likely to forget what items they wanted to buy at a grocery store (unless they write them down on a list and take it with them) than they are to forget how to drive a car. Their perceptual speed might be slower in driving the car, but they remember how to do it.

Source Memory   **Source memory** is the ability to remember where one learned something. Failures of source memory increase with age in the adult years and they can create awkward situations as when an older adult forgets who told a joke and retells it to the source (Hedden & Park, 2003; Hellmuth, 2003; Simons & others, 2004).

One recent study found that awareness of character can compensate for the age declines in source memory (Rahhal, May, & Hasher, 2002). In a typical memory source study, before playing a tape, participants listen to a series of statements spoken by either a male or a female voice. At the end, participants read the statements and say which voice spoke to them. The researchers added this twist to their study. Before playing the tape, some of the older adults were told that one voice belonged to a saintly person who never told a lie and that the other person was a dishonest cad. As in past studies, the older adults had difficulty in remembering which voice spoke which given line. However, those who were told about the trustworthiness of the speakers more accurately judged whether a given statement was likely to be true or false, suggesting that older adults can remember information about a source when it is important to them.

Lynn Hasher (2003, p. 1301), one of the researchers who conducted the memory source study just described, argues that age differences are substantial when individuals are asked "for a piece of information that just doesn't matter much. But if you ask for information that is important, old people do every bit as well as young adults . . . young people have mental resources to burn. As people get older, they get more selective in how they use their resources."

Prospective Memory   **Prospective memory** involves remembering to do something in the future, such as remembering to take your medicine or remembering to do an errand. Although some researchers have found a decline in prospective memory with age, a number of studies show that whether there is a decline is complex and depends on such factors as the nature of the task and what is being assessed (Einstein & others, 2000; Henry & others, 2004; McDaniel & others, 2003; Vogels & others, 2002; West & Craik, 2001). For example, age-related deficits occur more often in time-based (such as remembering to call someone next Friday) than in event-based (remembering to tell your friend to read a particular book the next time you see her) prospective memory tasks.

Beliefs, Expectations, and Feelings   An increasing number of studies are finding that people's beliefs and expectancies about memory play a role in their actual memory (Cavanaugh, 2000; McDougall, 2004). It matters what people tell themselves about their ability to remember. Positive or negative beliefs or expectancies about

explicit memory Memory of facts and experiences that individuals consciously know and can state.

implicit memory Memory without conscious recollection; involves skills and routine procedures that are automatically performed.

source memory The ability to remember where one learned something.

prospective memory Involves remembering to do something in the future.

one's memory skills are related to actual memory performance (Hess, Hinson, & Statham, 2004; Kwon, 1999). Recall from the Research in Life-Span Development interlude in chapter 1 our description of a recent study in which older adults were randomly assigned to read one of two mock newspaper articles at the beginning of a testing situation (Hess & others, 2003). One described the declines in memory that characterize aging; the other emphasized research on the preservation of memory skills in older adults. The older adults who read the pessimistic account of memory and aging remembered 20 to 30 percent fewer words than people who read about the ability to maintain memory in old age.

Attitudes and feelings also matter. One study found that individuals with low anxiety about their memory skills and high self-efficacy regarding their use of memory in everyday contexts had better memory performance than their high-anxiety/low-self-efficacy counterparts (McDougall & others, 1999).

Noncognitive Factors Health, education, and socioeconomic status can influence an older adult's performance on memory tasks (Roman & others, 2004). Although such noncognitive factors as good health are associated with less memory decline in older adults, they do not eliminate memory decline.

One criticism of research on memory and aging is that it has relied primarily on laboratory tests of memory. The argument is that such tasks are contrived and do not represent the everyday cognitive tasks performed by older adults. If researchers used more everyday life memory tasks, would memory decline be found in older adults? A number of researchers have found that using more familiar tasks reduces age decrements in memory but does not eliminate them. Younger adults are better than older adults at remembering faces, routes through town, grocery items, and performed activities. In one study, young adults (20 to 40 years old) remembered news content in print, audio, and TV format better than old adults did (60 to 80 years old) (Frieske & Park, 1999).

Conclusions About Memory and Aging Some, but not all, aspects of memory decline in older adults. The decline occurs primarily in episodic and working memory, not in semantic memory or implicit memory. A decline in perceptual speed is associated with memory decline. Successful aging does not mean eliminating memory decline, but reducing it and adapting to it. As we will see later in this chapter, older adults can use certain strategies to reduce memory decline.

Wisdom Does wisdom, like good wine, improve with age? What is this thing we call "wisdom"? **Wisdom** is expert knowledge about the practical aspects of life that permits excellent judgment about important matters. This practical knowledge involves exceptional insight into human development and life matters, good judgment, and an understanding of how to cope with difficult life problems. Thus, wisdom, more than standard conceptions of intelligence, focuses on life's pragmatic concerns and human conditions (Baltes & Staudinger, 1998, 2000; Bluck & Gluck, 2004). This practical knowledge system can take many years to acquire, accumulating through intentional, planned experiences and accidental experiences. However, recent research has found no age differences in wisdom, with young adults showing as much wisdom as older adults (Baltes & Staudinger, 2000).

Wisdom involves solving practical problems. Fredda Blanchard-Fields (1996) reviewed the research on everyday problem solving in older adults. She concluded that, in contrast to research demonstrating a decline in older adults' ability to solve abstract problems, older adults' competency in problem solving is most evident in everyday types of situations.

Of course, not all older adults solve practical problems in competent ways. In one study, only 5 percent of adults' responses to life-planning problems were classified as wise, and the wise responses were equally distributed across the early, middle, and late adulthood years (Smith & Baltes, 1990).

Older adults might not be as quick with their thoughts or behavior as younger people, but wisdom may be an entirely different matter. This older woman shares the wisdom of her experience with a classroom of children. *How is wisdom described by life-span developmentalists?*

wisdom Expert knowledge about the practical aspects of life that permits excellent judgment about important matters.

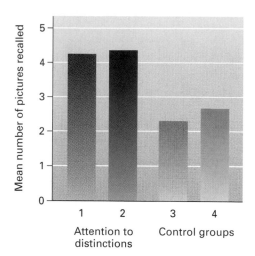

FIGURE 19.4 Improving Attention and Memory in Older Adults

In one study, older adult participants were randomly assigned to one of four attention interventions (Levy, Jennings, & Langer, 2001). In two of the groups, participants studying a set of pictures were told to notice either 3 (group 1) or 5 (group 2) distinctions. In two control groups, participants either were not given any directions related to attention (group 3) or just told to "pay attention." The older adults who viewed the pictures in terms of distinctions remembered more pictures than did the control groups.

many older adults, but (2) there is some loss in plasticity in late adulthood, especially in the oldest-old 85 years and older (Baltes & Smith, 2003).

Evidence of plasticity and the effectiveness of cognitive training comes from the research of Sherry Willis and K. Warner Schaie (1986), who studied approximately 400 adults, most of whom were older adults. Using individualized training, they improved the spatial orientation and reasoning skills of two-thirds of the adults. Nearly 40 percent of those whose abilities had declined returned to a level they had reached 14 years earlier. Further, the effects of training on reasoning lasted up to seven years after training (Saczynski & Willis, 2001). In another study, instructing older adults to notice distinctions in pictures improved their memory of the pictures (Levy, Jennings, & Langer, 2001) (see figure 19.4).

What activities are part of successful cognitive training? A seven-year longitudinal study by Sherry Willis and Carolyn Nesselroade (1990) used cognitive training to help adults maintain fluid intelligence (the ability to reason abstractly) with advancing age. The older adults were taught strategies for identifying the rule or pattern required to solve problems. After this cognitive training, adults in their seventies and eighties performed at a higher level than they had in their late sixties. The trainer modeled correct strategies for solving problems. Individuals practiced on training items, received feedback about the correct solutions to practice problems, and participated in group discussion. Other research supports the finding that cognitive training interventions can improve the mental functioning and daily functioning of older adults (Ball & others, 2003; Dunlosky, Kubat-Silman, & Hertzog, 2003).

As we discussed earlier in the chapter, researchers are also finding that improving the physical fitness of older adults can improve their cognitive functioning (Kramer & Willis, 2002). A recent review of studies revealed that aerobic fitness training improved the planning, scheduling, working memory, resistance to distraction, and processing involving multiple tasks in older adults (Colcombe & Kramer, 2003).

In sum, the cognitive vitality of older adults can be improved through cognitive and fitness training (Colcombe & others, 2004; Kramer & Willis, 2002; Noice, Noice, & Staines, 2004). However, benefits have not been observed in all studies (Salthouse, 1991). Further research is needed to determine more precisely which cognitive improvements occur in older adults (Dixon & Cohen, 2003).

Review and Reflect: Learning Goal 1

1 Describe the cognitive functioning of older adults

REVIEW

- How is cognition multidimensional and multidirectional in older adults? What changes in cognitive processes take place in aging adults?
- How do education, work, and health affect cognition in aging adults?
- What is the concept of "use it or lose it"?
- To what extent can older adults' cognitive skills be trained?

REFLECT

- Can you think of older adults who have made significant contributions in late adulthood other than those we mentioned in the chapter? Spend some time reading about these individuals and evaluate how their intellectual interests contributed to their life satisfaction as older adults.

2 WORK AND RETIREMENT

- **Work**
- **Retirement in the United States and Other Countries**
- **Adjustment to Retirement**

What percentage of older adults continue to work? How productive are they? Who adjusts best to retirement? What is the changing pattern of retirement in the United States and around the world? These are some of the questions we now examine.

Work

In the beginning of the twenty-first century, the percentage of men over the age of 65 who continue to work full-time is less than at the beginning of the twentieth century. The decline from 1900 to 2000 has been as much as 70 percent. An important change in older adults' work patterns is the increase in part-time work (Elder & Pavalko, 1993). The percentage of older adults who work part-time has steadily increased since the 1960s. Aging and work expert James House (1998) believes that many middle-aged workers would like to do less paid work, whereas many older adults would like to do more.

Some individuals maintain their productivity throughout their lives. Some of these older workers work as many or more hours than younger workers. In the National Longitudinal Survey of Older Men, good health, a strong psychological commitment to work, and a distaste for retirement were the most important characteristics related to continued employment into old age (seventies and eighties) (Parnes & Sommers, 1994). The probability of employment also was positively correlated with educational attainment and being married to a working wife.

Especially important to think about is the large cohort of baby boomers—78 million people who will begin to reach traditional retirement age in 2010. Because this cohort is so large, we are likely to see increasing numbers of older adults continue to work (Yeats, Folts, & Knapp, 1999).

Cognitive ability is one of the best predictors of job performance in older adults. And older workers have lower rates of absenteeism, fewer accidents, and increased job satisfaction, compared with their younger counterparts (Warr, 1994). This means that the older worker can be of considerable value to a company, above and beyond the older worker's cognitive competence. Changes in federal law now allow individuals over the age of 65 to continue working. Also, remember from our discussion earlier in the chapter that substantively complex work is linked with a higher level of intellectual functioning (Schooler, Mulatu, & Oates, 1999). This likely is a reciprocal relation—that is, individuals with higher cognitive ability likely continue to work as older adults, and when they work in substantively complex jobs, this likely enhances their intellectual functioning (Schooler, 2001).

An increasing number of middle-aged and older adults are embarking on a second or a third career (Moen & Wethington, 1999). In some cases, this is an entirely different type of work or a continuation of previous work but at a reduced level. Many older adults also participate in unpaid work—as a volunteer or as an active participant in a voluntary

Ninety-two-year-old Russell "Bob" Harrell (*right*) puts in 12-hour days at Sieco Consulting Engineers in Columbus, Indiana. A highway and bridge engineer, he designs and plans roads. James Rice (age 48), a vice president of client services at Sieco, says that "Bob" wants to learn something new every day and that he has learned many life lessons from being around him. Harrell says he is not planning on retiring. *What are some variations in work and retirement in older adults?*

association. These options afford older adults opportunities for productive activity, social interaction, and a positive identity.

Significant numbers of retirees only partially retire, moving to part-time employment by either reducing the number of hours they work on their career jobs or by taking on new (and frequently lower-paying) jobs (Dychtwald, Erickson, & Morison, 2004; Han & Moen, 1998). Self-employed men are especially likely to continue paid employment, either on the same job or on a new job. Nearly one-third of the men who take on a part-time job do not do so until two years after their retirement (Burkhauser & Quinn, 1989).

In a recent survey, 80 percent of baby boomers said that they expect to work during the retirement years (Roper Starch Worldwide, 2000). The main reason they plan to work when they get older is to engage in part-time work for interest or enjoyment (35 percent), followed by income (23 percent), desire to start a business (17 percent), and the desire to try a different field of work (5 percent). In another recent survey, nearly 70 percent of current employees said that they expect to work for pay once they retire, mainly because they enjoy working and want to stay active and involved (Anthony Greenwald & Associates, 2000).

In summary, age affects many aspects of work (Cleveland & Shore, 1996; Cowell & others, 2003). Nonetheless, many studies of work and aging—such as evaluation of hiring and performance—reveal inconsistent results. Important contextual factors, such as age composition of departments or applicant pools, occupations, and jobs, all affect decisions about older workers. It also is important to recognize that agist stereotypes of workers and of tasks can limit older workers' career opportunities and can encourage early retirement or other forms of downsizing that adversely affect older workers.

Retirement in the United States and Other Countries

A retirement option for older workers is a late-twentieth-century phenomenon in America. Recall from our earlier discussion that a much higher percentage of older Americans worked full-time in the early 1900s than today. The Social Security system, which establishes benefits for older workers when they retire, was implemented in 1935. On the average, today's workers will spend 10 to 15 percent of their lives in retirement.

In 1967, the Age Discrimination Act made it a federal policy to prohibit the firing of employees because of their age before they reach the mandatory retirement age. In 1978, Congress extended the mandatory retirement age from 65 to 70 in business, industry, and the federal government. In 1986, Congress voted to ban mandatory retirement for all but a few occupations, such as police officer, firefighter, and airline pilot, where safety is an issue. Federal law now prohibits employers from firing older workers, who have seniority and higher salaries, just to save money. As mandatory retirement continues to lessen, older workers will face the decision of when to retire rather than be forced into retirement.

Although the United States has extended the retirement age upward, early retirement continues to be followed in large numbers. In many European countries, officials have experimented with various financial inducements designed to reduce or control unemployment by encouraging the retirement of older workers (Elovaino & others, 2003). Germany, Sweden, Great Britain, Italy, France, Czechoslovakia, Hungary, and Russia are among the nations that are moving toward earlier retirement. Nonetheless, currently in the Netherlands, there is an effort to recruit retired persons to reenter the workforce because of low unemployment in the country. More information about cultural variations in retirement appears in the following Diversity in Life-Span Development interlude.

Diversity in Life-Span Development

*Work and Retirement in Japan, the
United States, and Europe*

Are a larger percentage of older adults in Japan in the labor force than in the United States and other industrialized countries? What are the attitudes of older Japanese adults toward work and retirement compared with their counterparts in other industrialized countries? To answer these questions, the Japanese Prime Minister's Office conducted national surveys of adults 60 years of age and older in four industrialized nations—Japan, the United States, England, and France. A much larger percentage of the men over 60 in Japan were in the labor force (57 percent) than in the United States (33 percent), England (13 percent), and France (8 percent).

When asked, "What do you think is the best age to retire?" a majority of the older men in England and France said 60 years of age. In sharp contrast, only 14 percent of the older men in Japan and 16 percent of the older men in the United States chose such an early age to retire. Another question the older men in the four countries were asked was, "Where should an older person's income come from?" In Japan and the United States, the proportion of older men who favored saving while working was at least twice that advising reliance on Social Security. In contrast, older adult men in France and England favored reliance on Social Security.

The marked differences in the rate of employment among those over 60 in Japan and the United States, compared with England and France, are mainly due to attitudes and values about work, and about reliance on oneself (and on relatives, in the case of Japan) rather than on the government and its Social Security system (Raymo & others, 2004).

Adjustment to Retirement

In thinking about adjustment to retirement, it is important to conceptualize retirement as a process rather than an event (Kim & Moen, 2002; Schlossberg, 2004). Much of the research on retirement has been cross-sectional rather than longitudinal and has focused on men rather than women. One recent study found that men had higher morale when they had retired within the last two years compared with men who had been retired for longer periods of time (Kim & Moen, 2002). Let's examine some other factors that may be linked to well-being in retirement.

Older adults who adjust best to retirement are healthy, have adequate income, are active, are better educated, have an extended social network including both friends and family, and usually were satisfied with their lives before they retired (Gall, Evans, & Howard, 1997; Moen & Quick, 1998; Palmore & others, 1985). Older adults with inadequate income and poor health, and who must adjust to other stress that occurs at the same time as retirement, such as the death of a spouse, have the most difficult time adjusting to retirement (Dunlop & others, 2004; Gallo & others, 2004; Silva, 2004).

Flexibility is also a key factor in whether individuals adjust well to retirement (Nusbaum, 2003; Schlossberg, 2004). When people retire, they no longer have the structured environment they had when they were working, so they need to be flexible and discover and pursue their own interests (Eisdorfer, 1996). Cultivating

AARP
Exploring Retirement
Baby Boomers and Retirement
Health and Retirement

interests and friends unrelated to work improves adaptation to retirement (Zarit & Knight, 1996).

Individuals who view retirement planning only in terms of finances don't adapt as well to retirement as those who have a more balanced retirement plan (Nuttman-Shwartz, 2004; Schlossberg, 2004). It is important not only to plan financially for retirement, but to consider other areas of your life as well (Choi, 2001; Lee, 2003). What are you going to do with your leisure time? What are you going to do to stay active? What are you going to do socially? What are you going to do to keep your mind active? Individuals who retire involuntarily are more unhealthy, depressed, and poorly adjusted than those who retire voluntarily (Swan, 1996). Options for control and self-determination are important aspects of older adults' mental health, the topic of our next section.

 Watch the "Retirement" video to examine the psychological factors in the decision to retire or continue working.

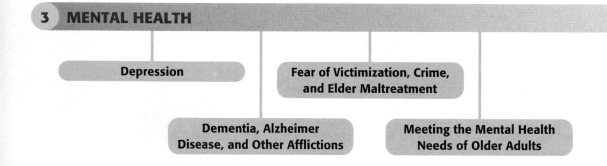

Review and Reflect: Learning Goal 2

2 **Discuss aging and adaptations to work and retirement**

REVIEW

- What characterizes the work of older adults?
- Compare retirement in the United States with other countries.
- How can individuals adjust effectively to retirement?

REFLECT

- At what age would you like to retire? Or would you prefer to continue working as an older adult as long as you are healthy? At what age did your father and/or mother retire? How well did they adjust to retirement? Explain.

3 **MENTAL HEALTH**

Depression

Dementia, Alzheimer Disease, and Other Afflictions

Fear of Victimization, Crime, and Elder Maltreatment

Meeting the Mental Health Needs of Older Adults

Although a substantial portion of the population can now look forward to a longer life, that life may unfortunately be hampered by a mental disorder in old age. This prospect is both troubling to the individual and costly to society. Mental disorders make individuals increasingly dependent on the help and care of others. The cost of mental health disorders in older adults is estimated at more than $40 billion per year in the United States. More important than the loss in dollars, though, is the loss of human potential and the suffering (Burns, Roth, & Christie, 1996). Although mental disorders in older adults are a major concern, older adults do not have a higher incidence of mental disorders than younger adults do (Busse & Blazer, 1996).

major depression A mood disorder in which the individual is deeply unhappy, demoralized, self-derogatory, and bored. The person does not feel well, loses stamina easily, has a poor appetite, and is listless and unmotivated. Major depression is so widespread that it has been called the "common cold" of mental disorders.

Depression

Major depression is a mood disorder in which the individual is deeply unhappy, demoralized, self-derogatory, and bored. The person does not feel well, loses stamina easily, has a poor appetite, and is listless and unmotivated. Major depression has been called the "common cold" of mental disorders. Researchers have found that depressive symptoms vary from less frequent to no more frequent in late adulthood than in middle adulthood (Blazer, 2003; Hybels & Blazer, 2004). One recent study found that the lower frequency of depressive symptoms in older adults compared with middle-aged adults was linked to fewer economic hardships, fewer negative social interchanges, and increased religiosity (Schieman, van Gundy, & Taylor, 2002). Depressive symptoms increase in the oldest-old (85 years and older) and this increase is associated with a higher percentage of women in the group, more physical disability, more cognitive impairment, and lower socioeconomic status (Blazer, 2002; Hybels & Blazer, 2004).

In the child, adolescent, and early adulthood years, females show greater depression than males do (Nolen-Hoeksema & Ahrens, 2002). Does this gender difference hold for middle-aged and older adults? One recent longitudinal study found greater depression in women than men at 50 and 60 years of age, but not at 80 years of age (Barefoot & others, 2001). Men showed increases in depressive symptoms from 60 to 80 but women did not. In this cohort, men may have undergone more profound role shifts after 60 years of age because they were more likely than women to have retired from active involvement in the work world. Thus, the absence of a gender difference in depression in older adults may be cohort-specific and may not hold as women who have entered the workforce in greater numbers are assessed in late adulthood.

Among the most common predictors of depression in older adults are earlier depressive symptoms, poor health, loss events such as the death of a spouse, and low social support (Kraehenbuhl & others, 2004; Loughlin, 2004; Nolen-Hoeksema & Ahrens, 2002; Steck & others, 2004; Wetterling & Junghanns, 2004). In one longitudinal study, widows showed elevated depressive symptoms up to two years following the death of a spouse (Turvey & others, 1999). In another study, depressive symptoms were higher in U.S. older adults who lived alone, especially immigrants (Wilmoth & Chen, 2003). However, good social support and being socially integrated in the community helped to buffer the effects of declining health on depression in these individuals (Blazer, 2002; Hybels & Blazer, 2004).

One recent study of older adults (average age = 72.5 years) compared those with chronic mild depression and those who were not depressed (McGuire, Kiecolt-Glaser, & Glaser, 2002). The older adults who had chronic mild depression had worse immune system functioning, which resulted in less ability to fight off an infectious agent than their nondepressed counterparts.

Depression is a treatable condition, not only in young adults but in older adults as well (Crossett, 2004; Rabheru, 2004). Unfortunately, as many as 80 percent of older adults with depressive symptoms receive no treatment at all. Combinations of medications and psychotherapy produce significant improvement in almost four out of five older adults with depression (Koenig & Blazer, 1996).

Major depression can result not only in sadness, but also in suicidal tendencies. Nearly 25 percent of individuals who commit suicide in the United States are 65 years of age or older (Church, Siegel, & Fowler, 1988). The older adult most likely to commit suicide is a male who lives alone, has lost his spouse, and is experiencing failing health (Juurlink & others, 2004; Mosciecki & Caine, 2004; Ono, 2004).

Dementia, Alzheimer Disease, and Other Afflictions

Among the most debilitating of mental disorders in older adults are the dementias (Cole, 2004; Peng, 2003). In recent years, extensive attention has been focused on the most common dementia, Alzheimer disease. Other afflictions common in older adults are multi-infarct dementia and Parkinson disease.

www.mhhe.com/santrockld10

Dementia Web
Exploring Dementia
Dementia Research and Treatment
Dementia Caregivers
Alzheimer Disease
Alzheimer Resources

Former president Ronald Reagan was diagnosed with Alzheimer disease at age 83.

Memory loss is a common characteristic of Alzheimer disease. Written reminders, like those shown here, can help individuals with Alzheimer remember daily tasks.

dementia A global term for any neurological disorder in which the primary symptoms involve a deterioration of mental functioning.

Alzheimer disease A progressive, irreversible brain disorder characterized by a gradual deterioration of memory, reasoning, language, and eventually physical function.

Dementia **Dementia** is a global term for any neurological disorder in which the primary symptoms involve a deterioration of mental functioning. Individuals with dementia often lose the ability to care for themselves and can lose the ability to recognize familiar surroundings and people (including family members) (Carpenter & Dave, 2004; Langa, Foster, & Larson, 2004; Snow & others, 2004).

It is estimated that 20 percent of individuals over the age of 80 have dementia. More than 70 types or causes of dementia have been identified (Skoog, Blennow, & Marcusson, 1996).

The most common form of dementia is **Alzheimer disease,** a progressive, irreversible disorder that is characterized by gradual deterioration of memory, reasoning, language, and eventually physical functioning. More than 50 percent of dementias involve Alzheimer disease. Approximately 10 to 20 percent of dementias stem from vascular disease (Epstein & Connor, 1999).

Alzheimer Disease Approximately 4 million adults in the United States have Alzheimer disease. It has been predicted that Alzheimer disease could triple in the next 50 years, as increasing numbers of people live to older ages. Because of the increasing prevalence of Alzheimer disease, researchers have stepped up their efforts to discover the causes of the disease and find more effective ways to treat it (Haan & Wallace, 2004).

Because of differences in onset, Alzheimer also is now described as *early-onset* (initially occurring in individuals younger than 65 years of age) or *late-onset* (which has its initial onset in individuals 65 years of age and older). Early-onset Alzheimer disease is rare (about 10 percent of all cases) and generally affects people 30 to 60 years of age.

Alzheimer disease was first diagnosed in 1906 by the German doctor Alois Alzheimer, but significant research on the disease did not begin until the 1950s, as Alzheimer disease became more clearly distinguished from other types of dementia. In the 1970s, it was discovered that Alzheimer disease involves a deficiency in the important brain messenger chemical acetylcholine, which plays an important role in memory (Sayer & others, 2004). Also, as Alzheimer disease progresses, the brain shrinks and deteriorates (see figure 19.5). The deterioration of the brain in Alzheimer disease is characterized by the formation of *amyloid plaques* (dense deposits of protein that accumulate in blood vessels) and *neurofibrillary tangles* (twisted fibers that build up in neurons) (Blumenthal, 2004; Leuba & others, 2004). Researchers are especially seeking ways to interrupt the progress of amyloid plaques in Alzheimer patients (Frenkel, Dori, & Solomon, 2004; Lopez-Toledano, & Shelanksi, 2004).

Although scientists are not certain what causes Alzheimer disease, age is an important risk factor and genes also likely play an important role (Huang & others, 2004; Josephs & others, 2004; Qu & others, 2004). The number of individuals with Alzheimer disease doubles every five years after the age of 65. A protein called *apolipoprotein E (apoE)*, which is linked to an increasing presence of plaques and tangles in the brain, could play a role in as many as one-third of the cases of Alzheimer disease.

For many years, scientists have known that a healthy diet, exercise, and weight control can lower the risk of cardiovascular disease. Now, they are finding that these healthy lifestyle factors may also lower the risk of Alzheimer disease. Researchers have revealed older adults with Alzheimer disease are more likely to also have cardiovascular disease than individuals who do not have Alzheimer disease (Fitzpatrick & others, 2004). Autopsies show that brains with the telltale signs of tangles and plaques of Alzheimer patients are three times more common in individuals with cardiovascular disease. In the Honolulu-Asia Aging Study, the higher individuals' blood pressure, the more tangles and plaques they had on autopsy (Petrovich & others, 2000). Recently, more cardiac risk factors have been implicated in Alzheimer disease—obesity, smoking, atherosclerosis, and high cholesterol (Gustafson & others, 2003).

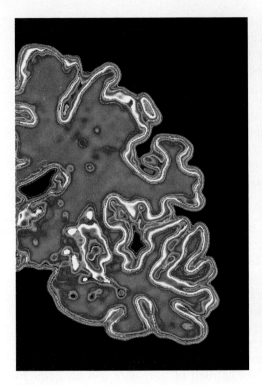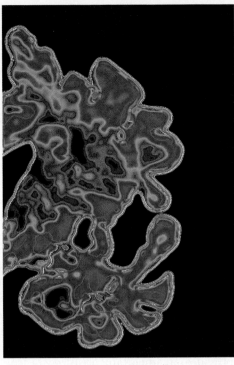

FIGURE 19.5 Two Brains: Normal Aging and Alzheimer Disease
The left computer graphic shows a slice of a normal aging brain, the right photograph a slice of a brain ravaged by Alzheimer disease. Notice the deterioration and shrinking in the Alzheimer disease brain.

Scientists also have recently found that antioxidant vitamins may help protect brain cells from Alzheimer disease (Serra & others, 2004; Zandi & others, 2004). In a study of 4,740 U.S. individuals 65 years and older taking vitamins C and E, almost 80 percent were less likely to have been diagnosed with Alzheimer disease at the beginning of the study and approximately 60 percent less likely to have developed the disease four years after the study began (Zandi & others, 2004). The researchers concluded that the most effective doses were vitamins E in liquid capsules of 400 to 1,000 International Units and vitamin C in pill form of 500 to 1,500 milligrams. Still, note that this study does not prove that these vitamins prevent Alzheimer disease. To do that, researchers would have to randomly assign participants to an experimental group (who took the vitamins) and a control group who did not.

As with many problems associated with aging, exercise also may reduce the risk of Alzheimer disease. One recent study of more than 2,000 men 71 to 93 years of age revealed that those who walked less than one-fourth of a mile a day were almost twice as likely to develop Alzheimer disease as their male counterparts who walked more than two miles a day (Abbott & others, 2004).

No treatment currently available can stop the downward spiral of physical decline that results from Alzheimer disease. However, some drugs such as tacrine can often prevent symptoms, such as memory loss, from becoming worse for a limited period of time.

Early Detection and Alzheimer Disease *Mild cognitive impairment (MCI)* represents a transitional state between the cognitive changes of normal aging and very early Alzheimer disease and other dementias (Grundman & others, 2004). MCI is increasingly recognized as a risk factor for Alzheimer disease, although it is difficult to distinguish between normal memory decline in aging and the mild cognitive impairment that may be a precursor to Alzheimer disease (Caselli, 2003; Meguro & others, 2004).

Special brain scans, such as MRI (magnetic resonance imaging), can detect changes in the brain that are fairly typical of early Alzheimer disease even before symptoms develop (Li & others, 2002). In addition, certain spinal fluids give early signals of Alzheimer disease. Recently a sophisticated urine test called the neural thread protein test has predicted the occurrence of Alzheimer in some individuals two years before symptoms (such as memory loss) appeared. When positive, the urine test allows preventive measures to be initiated that delay the cognitive decline of Alzheimer disease.

Progressive Decline There is a predictable, progressive decline in physical, cognitive, and social functioning when individuals have Alzheimer disease (Morris & others, 2001). Most Alzheimer patients, once diagnosed, live approximately eight years and progress from early problems of memory loss and declining intellectual function to later stages in which hospitalization in a near-vegetative state ensues (Weatherford, 1999).

Caring for Individuals with Alzheimer Disease A special concern is caring for Alzheimer patients (Bordaty & others, 2003; Vitaliano, Young, & Zhang, 2004). Health-care professionals believe that the family can be an important support system for the Alzheimer patient, but this support can have costs for the family, who can become emotionally and physically drained by the extensive care required for a person with Alzheimer (Gaugler, Zarit, & Perlin, 2003). For example, depression has been reported in 50 percent of family caregivers for Alzheimer patients (Redinbaugh, MacCallum, & Kiecolt-Glaser, 1995). Respite care has been developed to help people who have to meet the day-to-day needs of Alzheimer patients. This type of care provides an important break away from the burden of providing chronic care. To read further about individuals who care for Alzheimer patients, see the Research in Life-Span Development interlude.

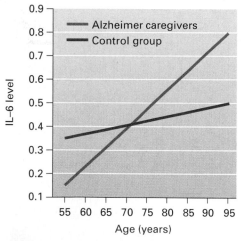

FIGURE 19.6 Comparison of IL-6 Levels in Alzheimer Caregivers and a Control Group of Noncaregivers

Notice that IL-6 (an immune chemical that places individuals at risk for a number of diseases) increased for both the Alzheimer caregivers and the control group of noncaregivers. However, also note that IL-6 increased significantly more in the Alzheimer caregivers. A higher score for IL-6 reflects a higher level of the immune chemical.

Research in Life-Span Development

The Stress of Caring for an Alzheimer Patient at Home

Researchers have recently found that the stress of caring for an Alzheimer patient at home can prematurely age the immune system, putting caregivers at risk for developing age-related diseases (Kiecolt-Glazer & others, 2003). They studied 119 older adults who were caring for a spouse with Alzheimer disease or another form of dementia (which can require up to 100 hours a week of time) and compared them with 106 older adults who did not have to care for a chronically ill spouse. The age of the older adults upon entry into the study ranged from 55 to 89 with an average of 70.

Periodically during the six-year study, blood samples were taken and the levels of a naturally produced immune chemical called interleukin-6, or IL-6, were measured. IL-6 increases with age and can place people at risk for a number of illnesses, including cardiovascular disease, Type II diabetes, frailty, and certain cancers. The researchers found that the levels of IL-6 increased four times as fast in the Alzheimer caregivers as in the older adults who did not have to care for a critically ill spouse (see figure 19.6). "There were no systematic differences in chronic health problems, medications, or health-relevant behaviors that might have accounted for" (Kiecolt-Glazer & others, 2003, p. 9090) the steeper increase in IL-6 levels for the Alzheimer caregivers.

Each time IL-6 was assessed by drawing blood, the participants also completed a 10-item perceived stress scale to assess the extent they perceived their

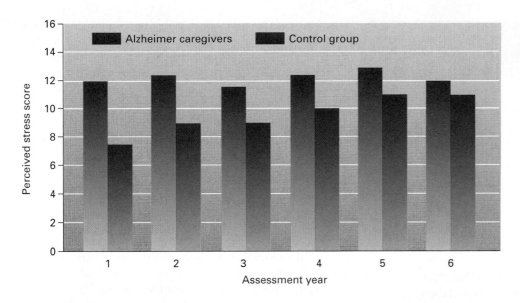

FIGURE 19.7 Comparison of Perceived Stress Levels of Alzheimer Caregivers and a Control Group of Noncaregivers
Note that Alzheimer caregivers perceived that they had more stress than the control group of noncaregivers in each of the six years it was assessed. Higher scores on the stress test reflect higher levels of perceived stress.

daily life during the prior week as "unpredictable, uncontrollable, and overloading" (Kiecolt-Glazer & others, 2003, p. 9091). Participants rated each item from 0 (never) to 4 (very often). Alzheimer caregivers reported greater stress than the noncaregivers controls across each of the six annual assessments (see figure 19.7).

There are many career opportunities for working with individuals who have Alzheimer disease. To read about the work of a director of an Alzheimer association, see the Careers in Life-Span Development insert.

Multi-Infarct Dementia **Multi-infarct dementia** involves a sporadic and progressive loss of intellectual functioning caused by repeated temporary obstruction of blood flow in cerebral arteries. The result is a series of mini-strokes. The term *infarct* refers to the temporary obstruction of blood vessels. It is estimated that 15 to 25 percent of dementias involve the vascular impairment of multi-infarct dementia.

Multi-infarct dementia is more common among men with a history of high blood pressure. The clinical picture of multi-infarct dementia is different than for Alzheimer disease—many patients recover from multi-infarct dementia, whereas Alzheimer disease shows a progressive deterioration. The symptoms of multi-infarct dementia include confusion, slurring of speech, writing impairment, and numbness on one side of the face, arm, or leg (Hoyer & Roodin, 2003). However, after each occurrence, there usually is a rather quick recovery, although each succeeding occurrence is usually more damaging. Approximately 35 to 50 percent of individuals who have these transient attacks will have a major stroke within five years unless the underlying problems are treated. Especially recommended for these individuals are exercise, improved diet, and appropriate drugs, which can slow or stop the progression of the underlying vascular disease.

Parkinson Disease Another type of dementia is **Parkinson disease,** a chronic, progressive disease characterized by muscle tremors, slowing of movement, and partial facial paralysis. Parkinson disease is triggered by degeneration of dopamine-producing neurons in the brain (Husiman, Uylings, & Hoogland, 2004; Monge & others, 2004; Silverdale & others, 2004). Dopamine is a neurotransmitter that is necessary for normal brain functioning. Why these neurons

Muhammad Ali, one of the world's leading sports figures, has Parkinson disease.

multi-infarct dementia Sporadic and progressive loss of intellectual functioning caused by repeated temporary obstruction of blood flow in cerebral arteries.

Parkinson disease A chronic, progressive disease characterized by muscle tremors, slowing of movement, and partial facial paralysis.

Careers in Life-Span Development

Jan Weaver, Director of the Alzheimer's Association of Dallas

Dr. Jan Weaver joined the Alzheimer's Associations, Greater Dallas Chapter, as director of services and education in 1999. Prior to that time, she served as associate director of education for the Texas Institute for Research and Education on Aging and director of the National Academy for Teaching and Learning About Aging at the University of North Texas. As a gerontologist, Jan plans and develops services and educational programs that address patterns of human development related to aging. Among the services of the Alzheimer's Association that Jan supervises are a resource center and helpline, a family assistance program, a care program, support groups, referral and information, educational conferences, and community seminars.

Jan recognizes that people of all ages should have an informed and balanced view of older adults that helps them perceive aging as a process of growth and fulfillment rather than a process of decline and dependency. Her recent publications include editing a special issue of *Educational Gerontology*, published in 1999, that addresses the importance of aging education throughout the life span. Jan earned her Ph.D. in sociology, with an emphasis in gerontology, from the University of North Texas in 1996.

Jan Weaver, giving a lecture on Alzheimer disease.

degenerate is not known. The main treatment for Parkinson disease involves administering drugs that enhance the effect of dopamine (dopamine agonists) in the disease's earlier stages and later administering the drug L-dopa, which is converted by the brain into dopamine. However, it is difficult to determine the correct level of dosage of L-dopa; it loses its efficacy over time and too much of it can produce schizophrenic symptoms (Sammi, Nutt, & Ransom, 2004).

Fear of Victimization, Crime, and Elder Maltreatment

Some of the physical decline and limitations that characterize development in late adulthood contribute to a sense of vulnerability and fear among older adults (Gray & Acierno, 2002). For some older adults, the fear of crime may become a deterrent to travel, attendance at social events, and the pursuit of an active lifestyle. Almost one-fourth of older adults say they have a basic fear of being the victim of a crime. However, in reality, possibly because of the precautions they take, older adults are less likely than younger adults to be the victim of a crime. However, the crimes committed against older adults are likely to be serious offenses, such as armed robbery (Cohn & Harlow, 1993). Older adults are also victims of nonviolent crimes such as fraud, vandalism, purse snatching, and harassment (Fulmer, Guadagno, & Bolton, 2004). Estimates of the incidence of crimes against older adults may be low because older adults may not report crimes, fearing retribution from criminals or believing the criminal justice system cannot help them.

Elder maltreatment can be perpetrated by anyone, but it is primarily carried out by family members. As with child maltreatment, elder maltreatment can involve neglect or physical abuse. Older adults are most often abused by their spouses. A special concern is the burden older women carry in facing possible physical violence. In one study of 614 cases of abuse in Hillsborough County, Florida, 37 percent involved physical assault, most of the abused were women, they were most likely to be living with their spouse, and they were most likely to be over 60 years of age (VandeWeerd & Paveza, 1999). The perpetrators were most likely to be male spouses. Older women also were more likely than elderly men to suffer property damage and robbery, but in these cases the perpetrator was most likely to be a young male (18 to 29 years of age) who was not related to the victim.

Meeting the Mental Health Needs of Older Adults

Older adults receive disproportionately fewer mental health services (Bartels, Miles, & Dums, 2004; Sadavoy & others, 1996). One estimate is that only 2.7 percent of all clinical services provided by psychologists go to older adults, although individuals aged 65 and over make up more than 11 percent of the population. Psychotherapy can be expensive. Although reduced fees and sometimes no fee can be arranged in public hospitals for older adults from low-income backgrounds, many older adults who need psychotherapy do not get it (Knight & others, 1996). It has been said that psychotherapists like to work with young, attractive, verbal, intelligent, and successful clients (called YAVISes) rather than those who are quiet, ugly, old, institutionalized, and different (called QUOIDs). Psychotherapists have been accused of failing to see older adults because they perceive that older adults have a poor prognosis for therapy success, they do not feel they have adequate training to treat older adults, who may have special problems requiring special treatment, and they may have stereotypes that label older adults as low-status and unworthy recipients of treatment (Knight, Nordhus, & Satre, 2003; Virnig & others, 2004).

How can we better meet the mental health needs of older adults? First, psychologists must be encouraged to include more older adults in their client lists, and older adults must be convinced that they can benefit from therapy. Second, we must make mental health care affordable: Medicare currently pays lower percentages for mental health care than for physical health care, for example.

Margaret Gatz (*right*) has been a crusader for better mental health treatment of the elderly. She believes that mental health professionals need to be encouraged to include more older adults in their client lists and that we need to better educate the elderly about how they can benefit from therapy. *What are some common mechanisms of change that can be used to improve the mental health of older adults?*

Review and Reflect: Learning Goal 3

 3 **Characterize mental health problems and their treatment in older adults**

REVIEW

- What is the nature of depression in older adults?
- What are dementia, Alzheimer disease, and other afflictions like in older adults?
- How extensive is fear of victimization, crime, and maltreatment in older adults?
- How can the mental health needs of older adults be met?

REFLECT

- Older adults do not have more mental health problems than younger adults do, although many people perceive that older adults have more mental problems. What might account for this misperception?

Multi-Infarct Dementia
National Parkinson Foundation
World Parkinson Disease Foundation
Resources for Parkinson Disease
Stages in Parkinson Disease

4 RELIGION

In chapter 16, we described religion and meaning in life with a special focus on middle age, including links between religion and health. Here we will continue our exploration of religion by describing its importance in the lives of many older adults.

In many societies around the world, older adults are the spiritual leaders in their churches and communities. For example, in the Catholic Church, more popes have been elected in their eighties than in any other 10-year period of the human life span.

During late adulthood, many individuals increasingly engage in prayer. *How might this be linked with longevity?*

Spirituality and Health in Older Adults

The religious patterns of older adults have increasingly been studied (Consedine, Magai, & Conway, 2004; Krause, 2004; Levin, Taylor, & Chatters, 1994). In one analysis, both older African Americans and older Whites attended religious services several times a month, said religion was important in their lives, read religious materials, listened to religious programming, and prayed frequently (Levin, Taylor, & Chatters, 1994). Also, in this analysis, older women had a stronger interest in religion than did older men.

Is religion related to a sense of well-being and life satisfaction in old age? In one recent study it was. Interviews were conducted with 1,500 U.S. White and African American individuals 66 years of age and older (Krause, 2003). Older adults who derived a sense of meaning in life from religion had higher levels of life satisfaction, self-esteem, and optimism. Also, older African American adults were more likely to find meaning in religion than their White counterparts. In another study, religious practices—such as prayer and scripture reading—and religious feelings were associated with a sense of well-being, especially for women and individuals over 75 years of age (Koenig, Smiley, & Gonzales, 1988). And in one study of low-income Latinos in San Diego, a strong religious orientation was associated with better health (Cupertino & Haan, 1999).

Religion can provide some important psychological needs in older adults, helping them face impending death, find and maintain a sense of meaningfulness and significance in life, and accept the inevitable losses of old age (Daaleman, Perera, & Studenski, 2004; Fry, 1999; Koenig & Larson, 1998). In one recent study, although church attendance decreased in older adults in their last year of life, their feelings of religiousness and the strength or comfort they received from religion were either stable or increased (Idler, Kasl, & Hays, 2001). Socially, the religious community can provide a number of functions for older adults, such as social activities, social support, and the opportunity to assume teaching and leadership roles. Older adults can become deacons, elders, or religion teachers, assuming leadership roles they might have been unable to take on before they retired (Cox & Hammonds, 1988).

Might praying or meditating actually be associated with longevity? In one recent study, they were (McCullough & others, 2000). Nearly 4,000 women and men 65 years and older, mostly Christians, were asked about their health and whether they prayed or meditated. Those who said they rarely or never prayed had about a 50 percent greater risk of dying during the six-year study compared with those who prayed or meditated at least once a month. In this study, the researchers controlled for many factors known to place people at risk for dying, such as smoking, drinking, and social isolation. It is possible that prayer and meditation lower the incidence of death in older adults because they reduce stress and dampen the body's production of stress hormones such as adrenaline. A decrease in stress hormones is linked with a number of health benefits, including a stronger immune system (McCullough & others, 2000).

Review and Reflect: Learning Goal 4

4 **Explain the role of religion in the lives of older adults**

REVIEW

- What are some characteristics of religion in older adults?

REFLECT

- Do you think you will become more or less religious as an older adult? Explain.

Reach Your Learning Goals

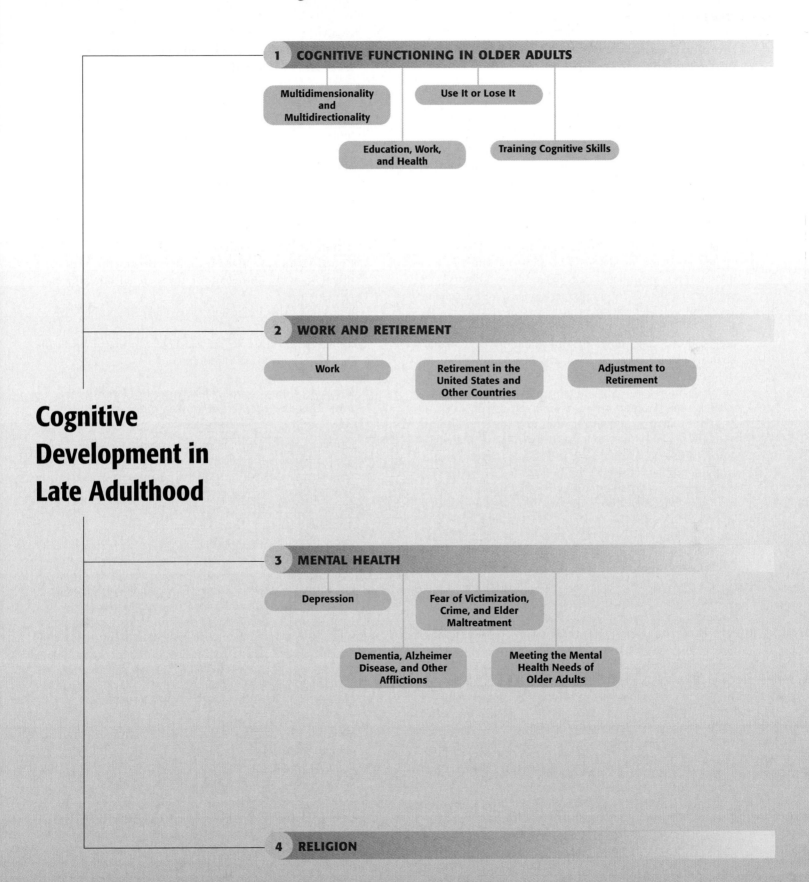

Cognitive Development in Late Adulthood

1 COGNITIVE FUNCTIONING IN OLDER ADULTS

- Multidimensionality and Multidirectionality
- Education, Work, and Health
- Use It or Lose It
- Training Cognitive Skills

2 WORK AND RETIREMENT

- Work
- Retirement in the United States and Other Countries
- Adjustment to Retirement

3 MENTAL HEALTH

- Depression
- Dementia, Alzheimer Disease, and Other Afflictions
- Fear of Victimization, Crime, and Elder Maltreatment
- Meeting the Mental Health Needs of Older Adults

4 RELIGION

Summary

 Learning Goal 1: Describe the cognitive functioning of older adults

- Baltes emphasizes a distinction between cognitive mechanics (the neurophysiological architecture, including the brain) and cognitive pragmatics (the culture-based software of the mind). Cognitive mechanics are more likely to decline in older adults than are cognitive pragmatics. Researchers have found that sensory/motor and speed-of-processing dimensions decline in older adults. Some changes in attention take place in adulthood. In selective attention, older adults fare more poorly than younger adults in general, but when tasks are simple and sufficient practice is given, age differences are minimal. Likewise, for divided attention, on simple tasks, adult age differences are minimal, but on difficult tasks older adults do worse than younger adults. Older adults perform as well as middle-aged and younger adults on measures of sustained attention. Younger adults have better episodic memory than older adults. Regarding semantic memory, older adults have more difficulty retrieving semantic information, but they usually can eventually retrieve it. Researchers have found declines in working memory and perceptual speed in older adults. Older adults are more likely to show declines in explicit than in implicit memory. Prospective memory involves remembering what to do in the future, and the relation of prospective memory to aging is complex. An increasing number of studies are finding that people's beliefs about memory play an important role in their memory performance. Noncognitive factors such as health, education, and socioeconomic status are linked with memory in older adults. Wisdom is expert knowledge about the practical aspects of life that permits excellent judgments about important matters. Although theorists propose that older adults have more wisdom, researchers usually find that younger adults show as much wisdom as older adults.
- Successive generations of Americans have been better educated. Education is positively correlated with scores on intelligence tests. Older adults may return to education for a number of reasons. Successive generations have had work experiences that include a stronger emphasis on cognitively oriented labor. The increased emphasis on information processing in jobs likely enhances an individual's intellectual abilities. Poor health is related to decreased performance on intelligence tests in older adults. Exercise is linked to higher cognitive functioning in older adults.
- Researchers are finding that older adults who engage in cognitive activities, especially challenging ones, have higher cognitive functioning that those who don't use their cognitive skills.
- There are two main conclusions that can be derived from research on training cognitive skills in older adults: (1) Training can improve the cognitive skills of many older adults, and (2) there is some loss in plasticity in late adulthood.

 Learning Goal 2: Discuss aging and adaptations to work and retirement

- Today, the percentage of men over 65 who continue to work full-time is less than at the beginning of the twentieth century. An important change in older adults' work patterns is the increase in part-time work. Some individuals continue a life of strong work productivity throughout late adulthood.
- A retirement option for older workers is a late-twentieth-century phenomenon in the United States. The United States has extended the mandatory retirement age upward, and efforts have been made to reduce age discrimination in work-related circumstances. Although the United States has moved toward increasing the age for retirement, many European countries are encouraging early retirement.
- Individuals who are healthy, have adequate income, are active, are better educated, have an extended social network of friends and family, and are satisfied with their lives before they retire adjust best to retirement.

3 **Learning Goal 3: Characterize mental health problems and their treatment in older adults**

- Depression has been called the "common cold" of mental disorders. However, a majority of older adults with depressive symptoms never receive mental health treatment.
- Dementia is a global term for any neurological disorder in which the primary symptoms involve a deterioration of mental functioning. Alzheimer disease is by far the most common dementia. This progressive, irreversible disorder is characterized by gradual deterioration of memory, reasoning, language, and eventually physical functioning. Special efforts are being made to discover the causes of Alzheimer disease and effective treatments for it. The increase in amyloid plaques and neurofibrillary tangles in Alzheimer patients may hold important keys to improving our understanding of the disease. Alzheimer disease involves a predictable, progressive decline, characterized by a deficiency in acetylcholine that affects memory. Also, in Alzheimer disease, the brain shrinks and deteriorates as plaques and tangles form. An important concern is caring for Alzheimer patients and the burdens this places on caregivers. In addition to Alzheimer disease, other types of dementia are multi-infarct dementia and Parkinson disease.
- Some of the physical decline and limitations that characterize development in late adulthood contribute to a sense of vulnerability and fear among older adults. Almost one-fourth of older adults say they have a basic fear of being the victim of a crime. Older women are more likely than older men to be victimized or abused.

• A number of barriers to mental health treatment in older adults exist; older adults receive disproportionately less mental health treatment. There are many different ways to treat the mental health problems of the elderly.

4 **_Learning Goal 4: Explain the role of religion in the lives of older adults_**

• Many older adults are spiritual leaders in their church and community. Religious interest increases in old age and is related to a sense of well-being in the elderly.

Key Terms

cognitive mechanics 583
cognitive pragmatics 583
selective attention 584
divided attention 584
sustained attention 584

episodic memory 585
semantic memory 585
explicit memory 586
implicit memory 586
source memory 586

prospective memory 586
wisdom 587
major depression 594
dementia 596

Alzheimer disease 596
multi-infarct dementia 599
Parkinson disease 599

Key People

Paul Baltes 583
Lynn Hasher 586

Fredda Blanchard-Fields 587
K. Warner Schaie 590

Sherry Willis 590

E-Learning Tools

To help you master the material in this chapter, you'll find a number of valuable study tools on the LifeMap CD-ROM that accompanies this book and on the Online Learning Center for _Life-Span Development,_ tenth edition, at www.mhhe.com/santrockld10.

Video Clips

⬤ In the margins of this book there are icons directing you to the LifeMap CD-ROM that accompanies the book. There you'll find a video for chapter 19 called "Retirement." Today's adults are among the first generation able to conceive of retirement as an _option._ This segment considers the psychological factors, rather than the purely economic motives, involved in the decision to retire or continue working.

Self-Assessment

Connect to www.mhhe.com/santrockld10 to reflect on aging and the workplace by completing the self-assessment, _My Perception of Older Workers._

Taking It to the Net

Connect to www.mhhe.com/santrockld10 to research the answers to these questions.

1. In past centuries, "senility" and "dementia"—like the concept of "hysteria"—often served as convenient terms for symptoms whose origins have not been understood. (Alzheimer disease was first identified in the early twentieth century.) Jonathan Swift and Ralph Waldo Emerson, for example, experienced a decline in their mental faculties late in life that their biographers routinely described as a descent into madness (in Swift's

case) or the onset of senility (in Emerson's case). Can we come up with more nuanced diagnoses today, based on our current knowledge of the diseases of late adulthood? How would such a diagnosis alter the biographical account of a famous person's later years?

2. Angela is interested in finding out more about how causes, nature, and treatment of depression change over the life span. Her Aunt Sadie has become very depressed as she has gotten older, and Angela worries her aunt might harm herself. What can Angela find out about the extent of depression in the elderly population and why it often goes undiagnosed, the causes, and the best treatment regimens?

3. Antonio was raised by "lapsed Catholic" parents whose outlook on life is best described as secular humanist. His father, now 67 years old and retired, recently revived his Catholic faith. Antonio has accused his father of "going soft" in his old age, of being motivated by a fear of death and a feeble desire for comfortable truths. How do the different perspectives of father and son reflect a more general shift in perspective with respect to religious faith that often occurs late in life?

Health and Well-Being, Parenting, and Education Exercises

Build your decision-making skills by trying your hand at the health and well-being, parenting, and education exercises.

Connect to www.mhhe.com/santrockld10 to research the answers and complete the exercises.

CHAPTER

20

I am the family face;
Flesh perishes, I live on,
Projecting trait and trace
Through time to times
anon,
And leaping from place to
place
Over oblivion.
—THOMAS HARDY
English Novelist and Poet,
19th Century

Socioemotional Development in Late Adulthood

Chapter Outline

THEORIES OF SOCIOEMOTIONAL DEVELOPMENT

Erikson's Theory

Disengagement Theory

Activity Theory

Socioemotional Selectivity Theory

Selective Optimization with Compensation Theory

THE SELF AND SOCIETY

The Self

Older Adults in Society

FAMILIES AND SOCIAL RELATIONSHIPS

Lifestyle Diversity

Older Adult Parents and Their Adult Children

Great-Grandparenting

Friendship

Social Support and Social Integration

Altruism and Volunteerism

ETHNICITY, GENDER, AND CULTURE

Ethnicity

Gender

Culture

SUCCESSFUL AGING

Learning Goals

1 Discuss five theories of socioemotional development and aging

2 Identify changes in the self and society in late adulthood

3 Characterize the families and social relationships of aging adults

4 Summarize how ethnicity, gender, and culture are linked with aging

5 Explain how to age successfully

Images of Life-Span Development
Bob Cousy

Bob Cousy was a star player on Boston Celtics teams that won numerous National Basketball Association championships. In recognition of his athletic accomplishments, Cousy was honored by ESPN as one of the top 100 athletes of the twentieth century. After he retired from professional basketball, he became a college basketball coach and then into his seventies was a broadcaster of Boston Celtics basketball games. Now in his eighties, Cousy has retired from broadcasting but continues to play golf and tennis on a regular basis. He has a number of positive social relationships, including a marriage of more than 50 years, children and grandchildren, and many friends.

As is the case with many famous people, their awards usually reveal little about their personal lives and contributions. Two situations exemplify his humanitarian efforts to help others (McClellan, 2004). When Cousy played for the Boston Celtics, his African American teammate, Chuck Cooper, was refused a room on a road trip because of his race. Cousy expressed his anger to his coach about the situation and then accompanied an appreciative Cooper on a train back to Boston. In a second

Bob Cousy, as a Boston Celtics star when he was a young adult (*left*) and as an older adult (*right*). *What are some changes he has made in his life as an older adult?*

situation: "Today the Bob Cousy Humanitarian Fund honors individuals who have given their lives to using the game of basketball as a medium to help others" (p. 4). The Humanitarian Fund reflects his motivation to care for others, be appreciative and give something back, and make the world less self-centered.

PREVIEW

Bob Cousy's life as an older adult reflects some of the themes of socioemotional development in older adults that we will discuss in this chapter. These include the important role that being active plays in life satisfaction, adapting to changing skills, caring, and the positive role of close relationships with friends and family in an emotionally fulfilling life.

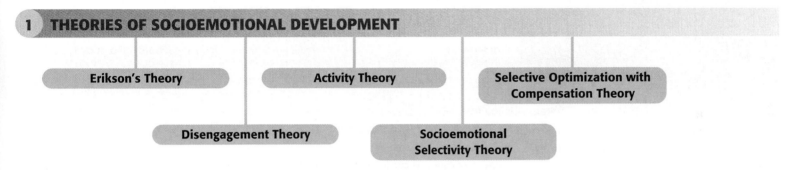

We will explore five main theories of socioemotional development that focus on late adulthood: Erikson's theory, disengagement theory, activity theory, socioemotional selectivity theory, and selective optimization with compensation theory.

Erikson's Theory

We initially described Erik Erikson's (1968) eight stages of the human life span in chapter 2, and as we explored different periods of development in this book we examined the stages in more detail. Here we will discuss his final stage.

Integrity versus despair is Erikson's eighth and final stage of development, which individuals experience during late adulthood. This stage involves reflecting on the past and either piecing together a positive review or concluding that one's life has not been well spent. Through many different routes, the older adult may have developed a positive outlook in each of the preceding periods. If so, retrospective glances and reminiscences will reveal a picture of a life well spent, and the older adult will be satisfied (integrity). But if the older adult resolved one or more of the earlier stages in a negative way (being socially isolated in early adulthood or stagnated in middle adulthood, for example), retrospective glances about the total worth of his or her life might be negative (despair). Figure 20.1 portrays how positive resolutions of Erikson's eight stages can culminate in wisdom and integrity for older adults.

Robert Peck's Reworking of Erikson's Final Stage Robert Peck (1968) reworked Erikson's final stage of development, integrity versus despair, by describing three developmental tasks, or issues, that men and women face when they become old:

- **Differentiation versus role preoccupation** involves redefining one's worth in terms of something other than work roles. Peck believes older adults need to pursue a set of valued activities so that time previously spent in an occupation and with children can be filled.

integrity versus despair Erikson's eighth and final stage of development, which individuals experience in late adulthood. This involves reflecting on the past and either piecing together a positive review or concluding that one's life has not been well spent.

differentiation versus role preoccupation One of the three developmental tasks of aging described by Peck, in which older adults must redefine their worth in terms of something other than work roles.

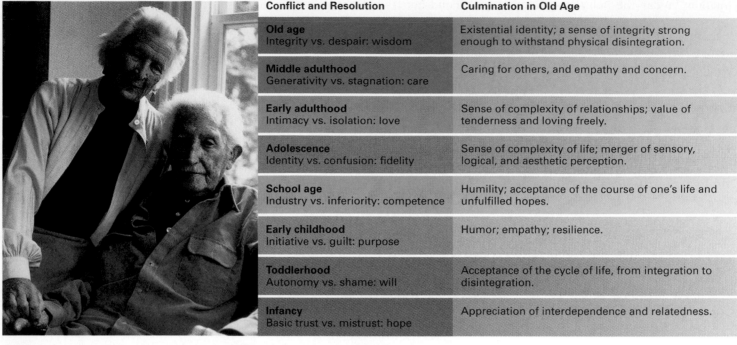

Conflict and Resolution	Culmination in Old Age
Old age Integrity vs. despair: wisdom	Existential identity; a sense of integrity strong enough to withstand physical disintegration.
Middle adulthood Generativity vs. stagnation: care	Caring for others, and empathy and concern.
Early adulthood Intimacy vs. isolation: love	Sense of complexity of relationships; value of tenderness and loving freely.
Adolescence Identity vs. confusion: fidelity	Sense of complexity of life; merger of sensory, logical, and aesthetic perception.
School age Industry vs. inferiority: competence	Humility; acceptance of the course of one's life and unfulfilled hopes.
Early childhood Initiative vs. guilt: purpose	Humor; empathy; resilience.
Toddlerhood Autonomy vs. shame: will	Acceptance of the cycle of life, from integration to disintegration.
Infancy Basic trust vs. mistrust: hope	Appreciation of interdependence and relatedness.

FIGURE 20.1 Erikson's View of How Positive Resolution of the Eight Stages of the Human Life Span Can Culminate in Wisdom and Integrity in Old Age
In Erikson's view, each stage of life is associated with a particular psychosocial conflict and a particular resolution. In this chart Erikson describes how the issue from each of the earlier stages can mature into the many facets of integrity and wisdom in old age. At left, Erikson is shown with his wife Joan, an artist.

- **Body transcendence versus body preoccupation** involves coping with declining physical well-being. As older adults age, they may experience a chronic illness and considerable deterioration in their physical capabilities. For men and women whose identity has revolved around their physical well-being, the decrease in health and deterioration of physical capabilities may present a severe threat to their identity and feelings of life satisfaction. However, while most older adults experience illnesses, many enjoy life through human relationships that allow them to go beyond a preoccupation with their aging body.
- **Ego transcendence versus ego preoccupation** involves recognizing that while death is inevitable and likely not very far away, it is adaptive to be at ease with oneself by realizing one's contributions to the future through rearing of children or through vocations or hobbies.

Life Review Life review is prominent in Erikson's final stage of integrity versus despair. Life review involves looking back at one's life experiences, evaluating them, interpreting them, and often reinterpreting them. Distinguished aging researcher Robert Butler (1975, 1996) believes the life review is set in motion by looking forward to death. Sometimes the life review proceeds quietly, at other times it is intense, requiring considerable work to achieve some sense of personality integration. The life review may be observed initially in stray and insignificant thoughts about oneself and one's life history. These thoughts may continue to emerge in brief intermittent spurts or become essentially continuous. One 76-year-old man commented, "My life is in the back of my mind. It can't be any other way. Thoughts of the past play on me. Sometimes I play with them, encouraging and savoring them; at other times I dismiss them."

body transcendence versus body preoccupation A developmental task of aging described by Peck, in which older adults must cope with declining physical well-being.

ego transcendence versus ego preoccupation A developmental task of aging described by Peck, in which older adults must come to feel at ease with themselves by recognizing that although death is inevitable and probably not too far away, they have contributed to the future through raising their children or through their vocations and ideas.

Life reviews can include sociocultural dimensions, such as culture, ethnicity, and gender. Life reviews also can include interpersonal, relationship dimensions, including sharing and intimacy with family members or a friend. And life reviews can include personal dimensions, which might involve the creation and discovery of meaning and coherence. These personal dimensions might unfold in such a way that the pieces do or don't make sense to the older adult. In the final analysis, each person's life review is to some degree unique.

As the past marches in review, the older adult surveys it, observes it, and reflects on it (Cully, LaVoie, & Gfeller, 2001). Reconsideration of previous experiences and their meaning occurs, often with revision or expanded understanding taking place. This reorganization of the past may provide a more valid picture for the individual, providing new and significant meaning to one's life (Hanaoka & Okamura, 2004). It may also help prepare the individual for death, in the process reducing fear.

Disengagement Theory

Disengagement theory states that to cope effectively, older adults should gradually withdraw from society. This theory was proposed almost half a century ago (Cumming & Henry, 1961). In this view, older adults develop increasing self-preoccupation, decrease their emotional ties with others, and show less interest in society's affairs. By following these strategies of disengagement, it was believed, older adults would enjoy enhanced life satisfaction. Some researchers have observed that society, in turn, may contribute to this phenomenon by becoming disengaged from older adults (Antonucci, 2004).

The theory generated a storm of protest and met with a quick death. We mention it because of its historical relevance. Although not formally proposed until 1961, it summarized the prevailing beliefs about older adults in the first half of the twentieth century.

Activities Resources for Older Adults

Activity Theory

Activity theory states that the more active and involved older adults are, the more likely they are to be satisfied with their lives. Thus, activity theory is the exact opposite of disengagement theory. Researchers have found strong support for activity theory, beginning in the 1960s and continuing into the twenty-first century (Haber & Rhodes, 2004; Neugarten, Havighurst, & Tobin, 1968; Riebe & others, 2004; Rook, 2000; Warr, Butcher, & Robertson, 2004). These researchers have found that when older adults are active, energetic, and productive, they age more successfully and are happier than if they disengage from society.

One recent large-scale longitudinal study of older adults in Manitoba, Canada, examined the relation between everyday activities and indicators of successful aging, namely well-being, functioning, and mortality, over a six-year period (Menec, 2003). Participants were asked to fill out a 21-item activities checklist to indicate their participation in each of the activities within the past week. The activities were grouped into three categories: social activities (visiting family or relatives, for example), productive activities (volunteer work, doing light house-work/gardening, for example), and solitary activities (collecting hobbies, for example). Well-being was assessed by asking participants how happy they were on a 5-point scale ranging from 1 = happy and interested in life to 5 = so unhappy that life is not worthwhile. Function was evaluated in terms of whether cognitive impairment or physical difficulties were present. Mortality (whether participants were dead or alive) was determined by examining data from the Office of Vital Statistics. The results indicated that greater overall activity (but especially social and productive activity) was related to happiness, better functioning, and a lower mortality rate.

disengagement theory The theory that to cope effectively, older adults should gradually withdraw from society.

activity theory The theory that the more active and involved older adults are, the more likely they are to be satisfied with their lives.

Activity theory suggests that many individuals will achieve greater life satisfaction if they continue their middle-adulthood roles into late adulthood. If these roles are stripped from them (as in early retirement), it is important for them to find substitute roles that keep them active and involved.

Socioemotional Selectivity Theory

Socioemotional selectivity theory states that older adults become more selective about their social networks. Because they place a high value on emotional satisfaction, older adults spend more time with familiar individuals with whom they have had rewarding relationships. Developed by Laura Carstensen (1995, 1998), this theory argues that older adults deliberately withdraw from social contact with individuals peripheral to their lives while they maintain or increase contact with close friends and family members with whom they have had enjoyable relationships. This selective narrowing of social interaction maximizes positive emotional experiences and minimizes emotional risks as individuals become older.

Socioemotional selectivity theory challenges the stereotype that the majority of older adults are in emotional despair because of their social isolation (Carstensen & Löckenhoff, 2004; Löckenhoff & Carstensen, 2004). Rather, older adults consciously choose to decrease the total number of their social contacts in favor of spending increasing time in emotionally rewarding moments with friends and family. That is, they systematically hone their social networks so that available social partners satisfy their emotional needs.

Is there research evidence to support life-span differences in the composition of social networks? Longitudinal studies reveal far smaller social networks for older adults than for younger adults (Lee & Markides, 1990; Palmore, 1981). In one study of individuals 69 to 104 years of age, the oldest participants had fewer peripheral social contacts than the relatively younger participants but about the same number of close emotional relationships (Lang & Carstensen, 1994).

Socioemotional selectivity theory also focuses on the types of goals that individuals are motivated to achieve (Charles & Carstensen, 2004; Carstensen, Isaacowitz, & Charles, 1999; Fung & Carstensen, 2004; Kennedy, Mather, & Carstensen, 2004). It states that two important classes of goals are (1) knowledge-related and (2) emotional. This theory emphasizes that the trajectory of motivation for knowledge-related goals starts relatively high in the early years of life, peaking in adolescence and early adulthood and then declining in middle and late adulthood (see figure 20.2). The emotion trajectory is high during infancy and early childhood, declines from middle childhood through early adulthood, and increases in middle and late adulthood.

One of the main reasons given for these changing trajectories in knowledge-related and emotion-related goals involves the perception of time. As older adults perceive that they have less time left in their lives, they spend more time seeking emotion-related goals rather than knowledge-related goals, perhaps because they find greater reward in emotion-related pursuits, such as improving relationships with family. Because striving for knowledge brings greater reward—for example, in terms of job performance—from late adolescence to middle age, it is pursued relentlessly even at the cost of emotional satisfaction.

Researchers have found that across diverse samples (Norwegians, Catholic nuns, African Americans, Chinese Americans, and European Americans) older adults report better control of their emotions and fewer negative emotions than younger adults (Lawton & others, 1992; Mroczek, 2001). Compared with younger adults, the

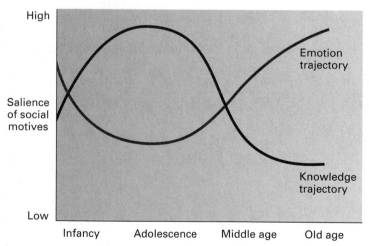

FIGURE 20.2 Idealized Model of Socioemotional Selectivity Through the Life Span

In Carstensen's theory of socioemotional selectivity, the motivation to reach knowledge-related and emotion-related goals changes across the life span.

socioemotional selectivity theory The theory that older adults become more selective about their social networks. Because they place a high value on emotional satisfaction, older adults often spend more time with familiar individuals with whom they have had rewarding relationships.

feelings of older adults mellow. Emotional life is on a more even keel with fewer highs and lows. It may be that although older adults have less extreme joy, they have more contentment, especially when they are connected in positive ways with friends and family. To read further about how emotion changes across the life span, see the Research in Life-Span Development interlude.

Research in Life-Span Development
Changes in Emotion Across Adulthood

One study examined how emotion changes across the adulthood years in 2,727 persons from 25 to 74 years of age in the United States (Mroczek & Kolarz, 1998). Participants completed a survey that assessed the frequency of their positive and negative emotions over a 30-day time frame. Two six-item scales were created, one for positive emotion, the other for negative emotion. Participants rated each of the following items from 1 = none of the time to 5 = all of the time:

Positive Affect	Negative Affect
1. Cheerful	1. So sad nothing could cheer you up
2. In good spirits	2. Nervous
3. Extremely happy	3. Restless or fidgety
4. Calm or peaceful	4. Hopeless
5. Satisfied	5. That everything was an effort
6. Full of life	6. Worthless

Thus, scores could range from 6 to 30 for positive affect and for negative affect.

The results were that older adults reported experiencing more positive emotion and less negative emotion than younger adults and the increase in positive emotion with age in adults increased at an accelerating rate (see figure 20.3). In sum, researchers have found that the emotional life of older adults is more positive than once believed (Carstensen, 1998; Mroczek, 2001).

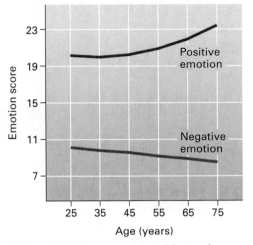

FIGURE 20.3 Changes in Positive and Negative Emotion Across the Adult Years Positive and negative scores had a possible range of 6 to 30 with higher scores reflecting positive emotion and lower scores negative emotion. Positive emotion increased in the middle adulthood and late adulthood years while negative emotion declined.

Selective Optimization with Compensation Theory

Selective optimization with compensation theory states that successful aging is linked with three main factors: selection, optimization, and compensation.

Selection is based on the concept that older adults have a reduced capacity and loss of functioning, which require a reduction in performance in most life domains. *Optimization* suggests that it is possible to maintain performance in some areas through continued practice and the use of new technologies. *Compensation* becomes relevant when life tasks require a level of capacity beyond the current level of the older adult's performance potential. Older adults especially need to compensate in circumstances with high mental or physical demands, such as when thinking about and memorizing new material very fast, reacting quickly when driving a car, or running fast. When older adults develop an illness, the need for compensation is obvious.

Selective optimization with compensation theory was proposed by Paul Baltes and his colleagues (Baltes, 2003; Baltes & Baltes, 1990; Baltes & Smith, 2003; Freund & Baltes, 2002; Marsiske & others, 1995). They describe the life of the late Arthur Rubinstein to illustrate their theory. When he was interviewed at 80 years of age, Rubinstein said that three factors were responsible for his ability to maintain his status as an admired concert pianist into old age. First, he mastered the weakness of old age by reducing the scope of his performances and playing fewer pieces (which reflects selection). Second, he spent more time at practice than earlier in

selective optimization with compensation theory The theory that successful aging is related to three main factors: selection, optimization, and compensation.

25 to 34 Years	35 to 54 Years	55 to 65 Years	70 to 84 Years	85 to105 Years
Work	**Family**	**Family**	**Family**	**Health**
Friends	Work	Health	Health	Family
Family	Friends	Friends	Cognitive fitness	Thinking about life
Independence	Cognitive fitness	Cognitive fitness	Friends	Cognitive fitness

FIGURE 20.4 Degree of Personal Life Investment at Different Points in Life

Shown here are the top four domains of personal life investment at different points in life. The highest degree of investment is listed at the top (for example, work was the highest personal investment from 25 to 34 years of age, family from 35 to 84, and health from 85 to 105).

his life (which reflects optimization). Third, he used special strategies, such as slowing down before fast segments, thus creating the image of faster playing (which reflects compensation).

The process of selective optimization with compensation is likely to be effective whenever loss is prominent in a person's life. Loss is a common dimension of old age, although there are wide variations in the nature of the losses involved. Because of this individual variation, the specific form of selection, optimization, and compensation will likely vary depending on the person's life history, pattern of interests, values, health, skills, and resources.

In Baltes' view (2000, 2003; Baltes & Smith, 2003; Krampe & Baltes, 2002), the selection of domains and life priorities is an important aspect of development. Life goals and priorities likely vary across the life course for most people. For many individuals, it is not just the sheer attainment of goals, but rather the attainment of *meaningful* goals, that makes life satisfying. In one study, younger adults were more likely to assess their well-being in terms of accomplishments and careers, whereas older adults were more likely to link well-being with good health and the ability to accept change. And as you read earlier in our discussion of socioemotional selectivity theory, emotion-related goals become increasingly important for older adults (Carstensen, 1998).

In one cross-sectional study, the personal life investments of 25- to 105-year-olds were assessed (Staudinger, 1996) (see figure 20.4). From 25 to 34 years of age, participants said that they personally invested more time in work, friends, family, and independence, in that order. From 35 to 54 and 55 to 65 years of age, family became more important than friends to them in terms of their personal investment. Little changed in the rank ordering of persons 70 to 84 years old, but for participants 85 to 105 years old, health became the most important personal investment. Thinking about life showed up for the first time on the most important list for those who were 85 to 105 years old.

One point to note about the study just described is the demarcation of late adulthood into the subcategories of 70 to 84 and 85 to 105 years of age. This fits with our comments on several occasions that researchers increasingly do not study late adulthood as a homogeneous category, an important point in Paul Baltes' view of aging.

Recall from chapter 1 that Baltes (2003) believes optimization is more difficult for the oldest-old (85 years and older) than the young-old (65 to 84 years of age). He argues that the oldest-old often experience losses in cognitive potential and ability to learn; an increase in chronic stress; the presence of dementia; high levels of frailty; and dying with decreased dignity. However, Baltes trumpets the following good news about aging: The young-old are experiencing an increase in life expectancy; substantial potential for better physical and mental fitness, including gains in these areas for successive cohorts; cognitive and emotional reserves in an aging mind; successful aging; high levels of emotional and personal well-being; and effective strategies for mastering the gains and losses of late life.

Review and Reflect: Learning Goal 1

 Discuss five theories of socioemotional development and aging

REVIEW

- What is Erikson's theory of late adulthood?
- What is disengagement theory?
- What is activity theory?
- What is socioemotional selectivity theory and how does research support it?
- What is selective optimization with compensation theory?

REFLECT

- Which of the five theories best describes the lives of older adults you know? Explain.

2 THE SELF AND SOCIETY

The Self   **Older Adults in Society**

Do self-perceptions change in late adulthood? How are older adults perceived and treated by society?

The Self

Our exploration of the self focuses on changes in self-esteem and self-acceptance. In chapter 13, we described how self-esteem drops in adolescence, especially for girls. How does self-esteem change in the adult years?

Self-Esteem In the cross-sectional study of self-esteem described in chapter 13, a very large, diverse sample of 326,641 individuals from 9 to 90 were assessed (Robins & others, 2002). About two-thirds of the participants were from the United States. The individuals were asked to respond to the item "I have high self-esteem" on the following 5-point scale:

1	2	3	4	5
Strongly Disagree				Strongly Agree

One cross-sectional study found that self-esteem was high in childhood, dropped in adolescence, increased through early and middle adulthood, then dropped in the seventies and eighties (Robins & others, 2002). More than 300,000 individuals were asked the extent to which they have high self-esteem on a 5-point scale with 5 being "Strongly Agree" and 1 being "Strongly Disagree."

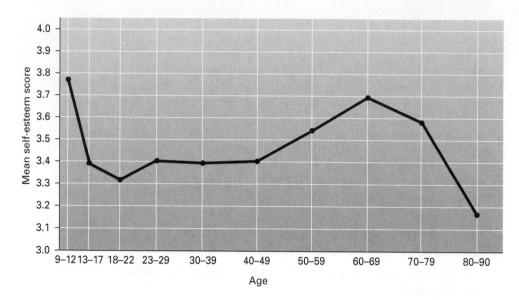

Self-esteem increased in the twenties, leveled off in the thirties and forties, rose considerably in the fifties and sixties, and then dropped significantly in the seventies and eighties (see figure 20.5). Through most of the adult years, the self-esteem of males was higher than the self-esteem of females. However, in the seventies and eighties, the self-esteem of males and females converged.

Why might self-esteem decline in older adults? Explanations include deteriorating physical health and negative societal attitudes toward older adults, although these factors were not examined in the large-scale study just described. Further research is needed to verify these developmental changes in self-esteem.

Self-Acceptance Another aspect of the self that changes across the adult years is self-acceptance. In one study, the self-acceptance of individuals at different points in adult development depended on whether they were describing their past, present, future, or ideal selves (Ryff, 1991). As shown in figure 20.6, young and middle-aged adults showed greater acceptance of their ideal and future selves than their present and past selves. However, in older adults there was little difference in acceptance of various selves because of decreased acceptance of ideal and future selves and increased acceptance of past selves.

Older Adults in Society

Does society negatively stereotype older adults? What are some social policy issues in an aging society? How do income and living arrangements affect older adults?

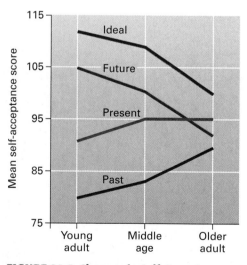

FIGURE 20.6 Changes in Self-Acceptance Across the Adult Years
Acceptance of ideal and future selves decreases with age, acceptance of past selves increases with age, and acceptance of present selves increases slightly in middle age and then levels off.

ageism Prejudice against other people because of their age, especially prejudice against older adults.

Stereotyping Older Adults **Ageism** is prejudice against others because of their age, especially prejudice against older adults. Like sexism, it is one of society's uglier words. Many older adults face painful discrimination and might be too polite and timid to attack it (McMullin & Marshall, 2001; Perdue, 2000). Older adults might not be hired for new jobs or might be eased out of old ones because they are perceived as rigid or feebleminded, or because employing older adults is considered not cost-effective (May, 2004). They could be shunned socially, possibly because they are perceived as senile or boring. At other times, they might be perceived as children and described with adjectives such as "cute" and "adorable." Older adults might be edged out of their family life by children who see them as sick, ugly, and parasitic. In sum, older adults might be perceived as incapable of thinking clearly, learning new things, enjoying sex, contributing to the community, and holding responsible jobs—inhumane perceptions to be sure, but often painfully real.

The personal consequences of negative stereotyping about aging can be serious. A physician (60 years old himself) recently told an 80-year-old: "Well, of course, you are tired. You just need to slow down. Don't try to do so much. After all you are very old." Many older adults accept this type of advice even though it is rooted in age stereotyping rather than medical records. One recent study found that ageism was widespread with the most frequent type occurring when people showed disrespect for older adults followed by assumptions about ailments or frailty caused by age (Palmore, 2001).

The increased number of adults living to an older age has led to active efforts to improve society's image of the older adults, obtain better living conditions for older adults, and gain political clout. The American Association of Retired Persons (AARP), with more than 30 million members, is bigger than most countries. The Gray Panthers, with 80,000 members, pressures Congress on everything from health insurance to housing costs for older adults. These groups have developed a formidable gray lobbying effort in state and national politics.

Policy Issues in an Aging Society The aging society and older persons' status in this society raise policy issues about the well-being of older adults. These include the status of the economy and the viability of the Social Security system, the provision of health care, supports for families who care for older adults, and generational inequity, each of which we consider in turn (Neugarten, 1988).

An important issue involving the economy and aging is the concern that our economy cannot bear the burden of so many older persons, who by reason of their age alone are usually consumers rather than producers. However, not all persons 65 and over are nonworkers and not all persons 18 to 64 are workers. And considerably more individuals in the 55-to-64 age group are in the workforce—three out of five men—than a decade ago. Thus, it is incorrect to simply describe older adults as consumers and younger adults as producers.

An aging society also brings with it various problems involving health care (Alemayehu & Warner, 2004; Barzilai & Rimm, 2004). Escalating health-care costs are currently causing considerable concern. One factor that contributes to the surge in health costs is the increasing number of older adults (Rice & Fineman, 2004). Older adults have more illnesses than younger adults, despite the fact that many older adults report their health as good. Older adults see doctors more often, are hospitalized more often, and have longer hospital stays. Approximately one-third of the total health bill of the United States is for the care of adults 65 and over, who comprise only 12 percent of the population. The health-care needs of older adults are reflected in Medicare, the program that provides health-care insurance to adults over 65 under the Social Security system. Of interest is the fact that the United States is the only industrialized nation that provides health insurance specifically for older adults rather than to the population at large, and the only industrialized nation currently without a national health-care system. Older adults themselves still pay about one-third of their total health-care costs. Thus, older adults as well as younger adults are adversely affected by rising medical costs (Alemayehu & Warner, 2004).

A special concern is that while many of the health problems of older adults are chronic rather than acute, the medical system is still based on a "cure" rather than a "care" model. Chronic illness is long-term, often lifelong, and requires long-term, if not life-term, management (Flesner, 2004). Chronic illness often follows a pattern of an acute period that may require hospitalization, followed by a longer period of remission, and then repetitions of this pattern. The patient's home, rather than the hospital, often becomes the center of managing the patient's chronic illness. In a home-based system, a new type of cooperative relationship between doctors, nurses, patients, family members, and other service

The Gray Panthers are actively involved in pressuring Congress on everything from health insurance to housing costs. Along with the American Association for Retired Persons, they have developed a formidable gray lobbying effort in state and national politics. *What are some of the policy issues in an aging society?*

providers needs to be developed (May & others, 2004). Health-care personnel need to be trained and be available to provide home services, sharing authority with the patient and perhaps yielding to it over the long term.

Eldercare is the physical and emotional caretaking of older members of the family, whether that care is day-to-day physical assistance or responsibility for arranging and overseeing such care. An important issue involving eldercare is how it can best be provided (Monahan & Hopkins, 2002; Tuch, Parrish, & Romer, 2003). With so many women in the labor market, who will replace them as caregivers? An added problem is that many caregivers are in their sixties, and many of them are ill themselves. They may find it especially stressful to be responsible for the care of relatives who are in their eighties or nineties.

In one study, two distinct systems of eldercare were found: individualistic and collectivistic (Pyke & Bengtson, 1996). Individualists approached parental caregiving reluctantly and considered it a burden. They often reported that they did not have adequate time for it and they relied on formal supports. In contrast, in collectivistic families, parental caregiving was assumed by family members, who emphasized family ties.

Some gerontologists advocate that the government should provide financial support to families to help with home services or substitute for the loss of income if a worker reduces outside employment to care for an aging relative (England & others, 1991). Some large corporations are helping workers with parent-caring by providing flexible work schedules and creating more part-time or at-home jobs. Government supports have been slow to develop. One reason for their slow development is that some persons believe such government interventions will weaken the family's responsibility and thus have a negative effect on the well-being of older, as well as younger, adults.

Yet another policy issue involving aging is **generational inequity** (discussed initially in chapter 1): The view that our aging society is being unfair to its younger members because older adults pile up advantages by receiving an inequitably large allocation of resources. Some authors have argued that generational inequity produces intergenerational conflict and divisiveness in the society at large (Longman, 1987). The generational equity issue raises questions about whether the young should be required to pay for the old. One claim is that today's baby boomers, now in their forties and fifties, will receive lower Social Security payments than are presently being paid out, or none at all, when they reach retirement age if the economy takes a downturn.

Income Also of special concern are older adults who are poor (Angel & others, 2004; Chen & Escarce, 2004; Yali & Revenson, 2004). One recent analysis found that lower health-related quality of life in U.S. older adults was linked with income of $15,000 or less (Centers for Disease Control and Prevention, 2003).

Recent census data suggest that although the overall number of older people living in poverty has declined since the 1960s, the percentage of older persons living in poverty has consistently remained in the 10 to 12 percent range since the early 1980s (U.S. Bureau of the Census, 2004). More than 25 percent of older women who live alone live in poverty. Also, the number of older single women just above the poverty line remains substantial. Poverty rates among ethnic minorities are two to three times higher than the rate for Whites. Combining sex and ethnicity, 60 percent of older African American women and 50 percent of older Latino women who live alone live in poverty. Also, the oldest-old are the age subgroup of older adults most likely to be living in poverty.

Many older adults are understandably concerned about their income (Chernichovsky & Markowitz, 2004). The average income of retired Americans is only about half of what they earned when they were fully employed. Although retired individuals need less income for job-related and social activities, adults 65 and over spend a greater proportion of their income for food, utilities, and health care. They spend a smaller

Social Aging Resources
Social Psychology of Aging
Ageism Resources

eldercare Physical and emotional caretaking for older members of the family, whether by giving day-to-day physical assistance or by being responsible for overseeing such care.

generational inequity The view that our aging society is being unfair to its younger members because older adults pile up advantages by receiving inequitably large allocations of resources.

proportion for transportation, clothing, pension and life insurance, and entertainment than do adults under the age of 65. Social Security is the largest contributor to the income of older Americans (38 percent), followed by assets, earnings, and pensions. There is a special concern about poverty in older women and the role of Social Security in providing a broad economic safety net for them (Rupp, Strand, & Davies, 2003).

Living Arrangements One stereotype of older adults is that they are often residents in institutions—hospitals, mental hospitals, nursing homes, and so on. However, nearly 95 percent of older adults live in the community. Almost two-thirds of older adults live with family members—spouse, a child, a sibling, for example—while almost one-third live alone. The older people become, the greater are their odds for living alone. Half of older women 75 years and older live alone. The majority of older adults living alone are widowed with three times as many of these individuals being women than men (U.S. Bureau of the Census, 2004). As with younger adults, living alone as an older adult does not mean being lonely (Kasper, 1988). Older adults who can sustain themselves while living alone often have good health and few disabilities, and they may have regular social exchanges with relatives, friends, and neighbors.

For many years researchers who studied the living arrangements of older adults focused on special situations such as nursing homes, public housing, mobile-home parks, welfare hotels, or retirement communities. However, less than 10 percent of older adults live in these types of housing arrangements. Nonetheless, the quality of housing for older adults is far from perfect. The vast majority of older adults prefer to live independently—either alone or with a spouse—rather than with a child, with a relative, or in an institution. However, too many older adults have inadequate housing. One study examined the relation between older adults' physical living environment and their self-rated health (Krause, 1996). Older adults who had the most dilapidated housing gave themselves worse health ratings than their counterparts who had better housing.

Only 5 percent of adults 65 years of age and older live in institutions, but the older adults become, the more likely they are to live in an institution. For example, 23 percent of adults 85 years and over live in institutions. The majority of the older adults in institutions are widows, many of whom cannot physically navigate their environment, are mentally impaired, or are incontinent (cannot control their excretory functions). Because the population is aging and because wives' life expectancies are increasing more rapidly than husbands', even greater numbers of widows are likely to be in institutions in the future.

Our coverage of older adults' housing arrangements so far has focused on the United States. One recent study examined living arrangements of older adults in 43 developing countries (Bongaarts & Zimmer, 2002). Older adult females were more likely to live alone than older adult males. Co-residence of older adults with their adult children was most prevalent in Asia and least prevalent in Africa.

Review and Reflect: Learning Goal 2

 2 **Identify changes in the self and society in late adulthood**

REVIEW
- How do self-esteem and self-acceptance change in late adulthood?
- How are older adults perceived and treated by society?

REFLECT
- What do you envision your life will be like as an older adult?

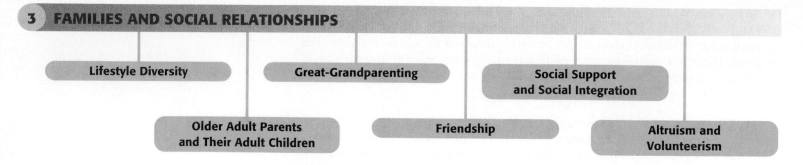

3 FAMILIES AND SOCIAL RELATIONSHIPS

Lifestyle Diversity

Older Adult Parents and Their Adult Children

Great-Grandparenting

Friendship

Social Support and Social Integration

Altruism and Volunteerism

Are the close relationships of older adults different from those of younger adults? What are the lifestyles of older adults like? What characterizes the relationships of older adult parents and their adult children? Is the role of great-grandparents different from the role of grandparents? What do friendships and social networks contribute to the lives of older adults? How might older adults' altruism and volunteerism contribute to positive outcomes?

Lifestyle Diversity

The lifestyles of older adults are changing. Formerly, the later years of life were likely to consist of marriage for men and widowhood for women (Allen, Blieszner, & Roberto, 2000). With demographic shifts toward marital dissolution characterized by divorce, one-third of adults can now expect to marry, divorce, and remarry during their lifetime. Let's now explore some of the diverse lifestyles of older adults, beginning with those who are married or partnered.

Married Older Adults   In 2000, older adult men were more likely to be married than older adult women—74 percent of men, 43 percent of women (U.S. Bureau of the Census, 2002). Almost half of all older adult women were widows (45 percent). There were more than four times as many widows as widowers.

The time from retirement until death is sometimes referred to as the "final stage in the marriage process." Retirement alters a couple's lifestyle, requiring adaptation (Dickson, Christian, & Remmo, 2004; Pruchno & Rosenbaum, 2003). The greatest changes occur in the traditional family, in which the husband works and the wife is a homemaker. The husband may not know what to do with his time, and the wife may feel uneasy having him around the house all of the time. In traditional families, both partners may need to move toward more expressive roles. The husband must adjust from being the provider outside of the home to being a helper around the house; the wife must change from being the only homemaker to being a partner who shares and delegates household duties. Marital happiness as an older adult is also affected by each partner's ability to deal with personal conflicts, including aging, illness, and eventual death (Field, 1996).

Individuals who are married or partnered in late adulthood are usually happier than those who are single (Lee, 1978). One recent study found that older adults were more satisfied with their marriages than were young and middle-aged adults (Bookwala & Jacobs, 2004). Indeed, the majority of older adults evaluate their marriages as happy or very happy (Huyck, 1995). Marital satisfaction is often greater for women than for men, possibly because women place more emphasis on attaining satisfaction through marriage than men do. However, as more women develop careers, this sex difference may not continue.

Divorced and Remarried Older Adults   Divorced and separated older adults represented only 8 percent of older adults in 2000 (U.S. Bureau of the Census, 2002). However, their numbers (2.6 million) have increased considerably since 1990 (1.5 million). Many of these individuals were divorced or separated before they entered late adulthood.

*G*row old with me!
The best is yet to be,
The last of life,
For which the first
was made.

—ROBERT BROWNING
English Poet, 19th Century

There are social, financial, and physical consequences of divorce for older adults (Jenkins, 2003; Pasley, 1996). Divorce can weaken kinship ties when it occurs in later life, especially in the case of older men (Cooney, 1994). Divorced older women are less likely to have adequate financial resources than married older women, and as earlier in adulthood, divorce is linked to more health problems in older adults (Lillard & Waite, 1995).

Rising divorce rates, increased longevity, and better health have led to an increase in remarriage by older adults (Coleman, Ganong, & Fine, 2000). What happens when an older adult wants to remarry or does remarry? Researchers have found that some older adults perceive negative social pressure about their decision to remarry (McKain, 1972). These negative sanctions range from raised eyebrows to rejection by adult children. However, the majority of adult children support the decision of their older adult parents to remarry. Researchers have found that remarried parents and stepparents provide less support to adult stepchildren than parents in first marriages (White, 1994).

Never Married Older Adults Not all older adults have been married. Approximately 8 percent of all individuals who reach the age of 65 have never been married. Contrary to the popular stereotype, older adults who have never been married seem to have the least difficulty coping with loneliness in old age. Many of them discovered long ago how to live autonomously and how to become self-reliant.

An increasing number of older adults cohabit. In 1960, hardly any older adults cohabited (Chevan, 1996). Today, approximately 3 percent of older adults cohabit (U.S. Bureau of the Census, 2004). In many cases, the cohabiting is more for companionship than for love. In other cases, for example, when one partner faces the potential for expensive care, a couple may decide to maintain their assets separately and thus not marry. It is expected that the number of cohabiting older adults will increase even further when baby boomers begin to turn 65 in 2010 and bring their historically more nontraditional values about love, sex, and relationships to late adulthood.

Romance and Sex in Older Adults' Relationships Few of us imagine older couples taking an interest in sex or romantic relationships. We might think of them as being interested in a game of bridge or a conversation on the porch, but not much else. In fact, a number of older adults date. The increased health and longevity of older adults have resulted in a much larger pool of active older adults. And the increased divorce rate has added more older adults to the adult dating pool.

Regarding their sexuality, older adults may express their sexuality differently than younger adults, especially when engaging in sexual intercourse becomes difficult. Older adults especially enjoy touching and caressing as part of their sexual relationship. When older adults are healthy, they still may engage in sexual activities. And with the increased use of drugs to treat erectile dysfunction, older adults can be expected to increase their sexual activity. However, companionship often becomes more important than sexual activity in older adults. Older couples often emphasize intimacy over sexual prowess.

View the video "Being in Love in Late Adulthood" to appreciate the sexual and emotional needs of older adults in relationships.

Older Adults and Their Families

Older Adult Parents and Their Adult Children

Approximately 80 percent of older adults have living children, many of whom are middle-aged. About 10 percent of older adults have children who are 65 years or older. Adult children are an important part of the aging parent's social network. Researchers have found that older adults with children have more contacts with relatives than those without children (Johnson & Troll, 1992).

Increasingly, diversity characterizes older adult parents and their adult children. Divorce, cohabitation, and nonmarital childbearing are more common in the history of older adults today than in the past (Allen, Blieszner, & Roberto, 2000). Also, one study found that only 10 of 45 older adults had adult children who were characterized as conventional in terms of marriage and parenting (Allen & others, 1999).

Gender plays an important role in relationships involving older adult parents and their children. Adult daughters rather than adult sons are more likely to be involved in the lives of aging parents. For example, adult daughters are three times more likely than are adult sons to give parents assistance with daily living activities (Dwyer & Coward, 1991).

An extremely valuable task that adult children can perform is to coordinate and monitor services for an aging parent who becomes disabled. This might involve locating a nursing home and monitoring its quality, procuring medical services, arranging public service assistance, and handling finances. In some cases, adult children provide direct assistance with daily living, including such activities as eating, bathing, and dressing. Even less severely impaired older adults may need help with shopping, housework, transportation, home maintenance, and bill paying.

Researchers have found that ambivalence characterized by both positive and negative perceptions is often present in relationships between adult children and their aging parents. These perceptions include love, reciprocal help, and shared values on the positive side and isolation, family conflicts and problems, abuse, neglect, and caregiver stress on the negative side (Fowler, 1999). One recent study of 1,599 adult children's relationships with their older adult parents found that ambivalence was likely to be present when relationships involved in-laws, those in poor health, and adult children with poor parental relationships in early life (Wilson, Shuey, & Elder, 2003).

Great-Grandparenting

Because of increased longevity more grandparents today than in the past are also great-grandparents. At the turn of the twentieth century, the three-generation family was common, but now the four-generation family is common. One contribution of great-grandparents is to transmit family history by telling their children, grandchildren, and great-grandchildren where the family came from, what their members achieved, what they endured, and how their lives changed over the years (Harris, 2002).

There has been little research on great-grandparenting. One study examined the relationship between young adults and their grandparents and great-grandparents (Roberto & Skoglund, 1996). The young adults interacted with and participated in more activities with their grandparents than great-grandparents. They also perceived their grandparents to have a more defined role and as more influential in their lives than great-grandparents.

Lillian Troll (1994, 2000) has found that older adults who are embedded in family relationships have much less distress than those who are family deprived. Next, we will consider these other aspects of social relationships in late adulthood: friendship, social support, and social integration.

At the beginning of the twentieth century, the three-generation family was common, but now the four-generation family is common as well. Thus, an increasing number of grandparents are also great-grandparents. The four-generation family shown here is the Jordans—author John Santrock's mother-in-law, daughter, granddaughter, and wife.

Friendship

Aging expert Laura Carstensen (1998) concluded that people choose close friends over new friends as they grow older. And as long as they have several close people in their network, they seem content, says Carstensen.

In one recent study of 128 married older adults, women were more depressed than men if they did not have a best friend, and women who did have a friend reported lower levels of depression (Antonucci, Lansford, & Akiyama, 2001). Similarly, women who did not have a best friend were less satisfied with life than women who did have a best friend.

In one study of young-old and old-old adult friendships, there was more continuity than change in amount of contact with friends (Field, 1999). There were, however, more changes in older adult male than older adult female friendships. Older men declined in number of new friends, in their desire for close friendships, and in involvement beyond family activities, whereas older women did not change in these areas.

What happens when older adults' friends die? One study found that one way older adults dealt with this loss was to loosen up their requirements for what they considered a friend (Johnson & Troll, 1994). Once "friends" probably meant intimate companions to them. Now they include the woman passed in the hall or the deliverer of Meals on Wheels.

What role does social support play in the health of the elderly?

Social Support and Social Integration

In the *social convoy* model of social relations, individuals go through life embedded in a personal network of individuals from whom they give and receive social support (Antonucci & Akiyama, 2002; Antonucci, Lansford, & Akiyama, 2001; Antonucci, Vandewater, & Lansford, 2000). Social support can help individuals of all ages cope more effectively.

Social support can improve the physical and mental health of older adults (Bisschop & others, 2004; Erber, 2005; Pruchno & Rosenbaum, 2003). Social support is linked with a reduction in symptoms of disease and with the ability to meet one's own health-care needs (Cohen, Teresi, & Holmes, 1985). Social support also decreases the probability that an older adult will be institutionalized (Antonucci, 1990). Social support is associated with a lower incidence of depression in older adults (Joiner, 2000).

The social support of older adults may depend on the gender of the older adult. One recent study showed that among married older adults, men primarily received emotional support from their spouses, whereas women were more likely to draw heavily on friends, relatives, and children for emotional support (Gurung, Taylor, & Seeman, 2003).

Social integration plays an important role in the lives of many older adults (Antonucci, Vandewater, & Lansford, 2000; Holtzman & others, 2004; Kelley-Moore & Ferraro, 2004; Luszcz & Giles, 2002). Being lonely and socially isolated is a significant health risk factor in older adults (Rowe & Kahn, 1997). In one study, being part of a social network was related to longevity, especially for men (House, Landis, & Umberson, 1988). And in a longitudinal study, both women and men with more organizational memberships lived longer than their counterparts with low organizational participation (Tucker & others, 1999).

Remember from our earlier discussion of socioemotional selectivity theory that many older adults choose to have fewer peripheral social contacts and more emotionally positive contacts with friends and family. Thus, although the overall social activity of many older adults decreases, this does not mean that they are emotionally distraught about this. Rather, it could reflect their greater interest in spending more time in the small circle of their friends and families where they are less likely to encounter negative emotional experiences.

Altruism and Volunteerism

A common perception is that older adults need to be given help rather than give help themselves. However, researchers recently have found that when older adults engage in altruistic behavior and volunteering they benefit from these activities. One recent study followed 423 older adult couples for five years (Brown & others, 2003). At the beginning of the study, the couples were asked about the extent to which they had given or received emotional or practical help in the past year. Five years later, those who said they had helped others were half as likely to have died. One possible reason for this finding is that helping others may reduce the output of stress hormones, which improves cardiovascular health and strengthens the immune system.

Researchers also have found that volunteering as an older adult is associated with a number of positive outcomes. An early study of individuals 65 years and older found that volunteer workers compared with nonvolunteers were more satisfied with their lives and were less depressed and anxious (Hunter & Linn, 1980). A study of 2,000 older adults in Japan revealed that those who gave more assistance to others had better physical health than their elderly counterparts who gave less assistance (Krause & others, 1999). And in a recent study, being a volunteer as an older adult was associated with more positive affect and less negative affect (Greenfield & Marks, 2004). Among the reasons for the positive outcomes of volunteering are its provision of constructive activities and productive roles, social integration, and enhanced meaningfulness.

Review and Reflect: Learning Goal 3

3 **Characterize the families and social relationships of aging adults**

REVIEW

- How would you profile the diversity of adult lifestyles?
- What characterizes the relationships of older adult parents and their adult children?
- Is the role of great-grandparents different than for grandparents?
- What is the friendship of older adults like?
- What roles do social support and social integration play in late adulthood?
- How are altruism and volunteerism linked to positive outcomes in older adults?

REFLECT

- If you were going to create a research study on close relationships in older adults, what topic would you want to study? Describe a study that you think would be interesting to conduct. Is it a correlational study or an experimental study? What type of measure (observation, interview, survey, for example) would you use?

4 ETHNICITY, GENDER, AND CULTURE

Ethnicity	Gender	Culture

How is ethnicity linked to aging? Do gender roles change in late adulthood? What are the social aspects of aging in different cultures?

Ethnicity

Of special concern are ethnic minority older adults, especially African Americans and Latinos, who are overrepresented in poverty statistics (Angel & others, 2004; Erber, 2005; Yali & Revenson, 2004). Consider Harry, a 72-year-old African American who lives in a run-down hotel in Los Angeles. He suffers from arthritis and uses a walker. He has not been able to work for years, and government payments are barely enough to meet his needs.

Comparative information about African Americans, Latinos, and Whites indicates a possible double jeopardy for elderly ethnic minority individuals. They face problems related to *both* ageism and racism (Barnes & others, 2004; Jackson, Chatters, & Taylor, 1993). Both the wealth and the health of ethnic minority older adults decrease more rapidly than for elderly Whites (Edmonds, 1993). Older ethnic minority individuals are more likely to become ill but less likely to receive treatment. They also are more likely to have a history of less education, unemployment, worse housing conditions, and shorter life expectancies than their older White counterparts (Himes, Hogan, & Eggebeen, 1996). And many ethnic minority workers never enjoy the Social Security and Medicare benefits to which their earnings contribute, because they die before reaching the age of eligibility for benefits.

Despite the stress and discrimination older ethnic minority individuals face, many of these older adults have developed coping mechanisms that allow them to survive in the dominant White world (Markides & Rudkin, 1996). Extension of family networks helps older minority-group individuals cope with the bare essentials of living and gives them a sense of being loved (Antonucci, Vandewater, & Lansford, 1998). Churches in African American and Latino communities provide avenues for meaningful social participation, feelings of power, and a sense of internal satisfaction. And residential concentrations of ethnic minority groups give their older members a sense of belonging. Thus, it always is important to consider individual variations in the lives of aging minorities (Whitfield & Baker-Thomas, 1999). To read about one individual who is providing help for aging minorities, see the Careers in Life-Span Development insert.

Gender

Do our gender roles change when we become older adults? Some developmentalists believe there is decreasing femininity in women and decreasing masculinity in men when they reach the late adulthood years (Gutmann, 1975). The evidence suggests that older men do become more feminine—nurturant, sensitive, and so on—but it

Careers in Life-Span Development

Norma Thomas, Social Work Professor and Administrator

Dr. Norma Thomas has worked for more than three decades in the field of aging. She obtained her undergraduate degree in social work from Pennsylvania State University and her doctoral degree in social work from the University of Pennsylvania. Norma's activities are varied. Earlier in her career, as a social work practitioner, she provided services to older adults of color in an effort to improve their lives. She currently is a professor and academic administrator at Widener University in Chester, Pennsylvania, a fellow of the Institute of Aging at the University of Pennsylvania, and the chief executive officer and cofounder of the Center on Ethnic and Minority Aging (CEMA). CEMA was formed to provide research, consultation, training, and services to benefit aging individuals of color, their families, and their communities. Norma has created numerous community service events that benefit older adults of color, especially African Americans and Latinos. She has also been a consultant to various national, regional, and state agencies in her effort to improve the lives of aging adults of color.

Norma Thomas, social work professor and administrator.

appears that older women do not necessarily become more masculine—assertive, dominant, and so on (Turner, 1982). Keep in mind that cohort effects are especially important to consider in areas such as gender roles. As sociohistorical changes take place and are assessed more frequently in life-span investigations, what were once perceived to be age effects may turn out to be cohort effects (Jacobs, 1994).

One study found that time spent in committed activities by older adults had shifted in opposite ways for women and men (Verbrugge, Gruber-Baldini, & Fozard, 1996). Between 1958 and 1992, older men decreased their time in paid work and spent more time doing housework, home repairs, yardwork, shopping, and child care. By contrast, older women engaged in more paid work and decreased their time in housework.

A possible double jeopardy also faces many women—the burden of *both* ageism and sexism (Lopata, 1994). The poverty rate for older adult females is almost double that of older adult males. According to Congresswoman Mary Rose Oakar, the number one priority for middle-aged and older women should be economic security. She predicts that 25 percent of all women working today can expect to be poor in old age. Yet only recently has scientific and political interest in the aging woman developed. For many years, the aging woman was virtually invisible in aging research and in protests involving rights for older adults (Markson, 1995). An important research and political agenda for the twenty-first century is increased interest in the aging and the rights of older adult women.

Not only is it important to be concerned about older women's double jeopardy of ageism and sexism, but special attention also needs to be devoted to female ethnic minority older adults (Locher & others, 2005). They face what could be described as triple jeopardy—ageism, sexism, and racism (Burton, 1996; Markides, 1995). More information about being female, ethnic, and old appears in the Diversity in Life-Span Development interlude.

Diversity in Life-Span Development
Being Female, Ethnic, and Old

Part of the unfortunate history of ethnic minority groups in the United States has been the negative stereotypes against members of their groups (Fernandez & Goldstein, 2004; Mureno-John & others, 2004). Many also have been hampered by their immigrant origins in that they are not fluent or literate in English, may not be aware of the values and norms involved in American social interaction, and may have lifestyles that differ from those of mainstream America (Organista, 1994). Often included in these cultural differences is the role of women in the family and in society. Many, but not all, immigrant ethnic groups traditionally have relegated the woman's role to family maintenance. Many important decisions may be made by a woman's husband or parents, and she is often not expected to seek an independent career or enter the workforce except in the case of dire financial need.

Some ethnic minority groups may define an older woman's role as unimportant, especially if she is unable to contribute financially. However, in some ethnic minority groups, an older woman's social status improves. For example, older

African American women can express their own needs and can be given status and power in the community. Despite their positive status in the African American family and the African American culture, African American women over the age of 70 are the poorest population group in the United States. Three of five older African American women live alone; most of them are widowed. The low incomes of older African American women translate into less than adequate access to health care. Substantially lower incomes for African American older women are related to the kinds of jobs they hold, which either are not covered by Social Security or, in the case of domestic service, are not reported even when reporting is legally required.

A portrayal of older African American women in cities reveals some of their survival strategies. They highly value the family as a system of mutual support and aid, adhere to the American work ethic, and view religion as a source of strength (Perry & Johnson, 1994). The use of religion as a way of coping with stress has a long history in the African American culture, with roots in the slave experience. The African American church came to fulfill needs and functions once met by religion-based tribal and community organizations that African Americans brought from Africa. In one study, the older African American women valued church organizations more than their male counterparts did, especially valuing the church's group activities (Taylor, 1982).

In sum, older African American women have faced considerable stress in their lives (Edmonds, 1993; Locher & others, 2005). In the face of this stress, they have shown remarkable adaptiveness, resilience, responsibility, and coping skills.

A special concern is the stress faced by older African American women, many of whom view religion as a source of strength to help them cope. *What are some other characteristics of being female, ethnic, and old?*

Culture

What factors are associated with whether older adults are accorded a position of high status in a culture? Seven factors are most likely to predict high status for older adults in a culture (Sangree, 1989):

- Older persons have valuable knowledge.
- Older persons control key family/community resources.
- Older persons are permitted to engage in useful and valued functions as long as possible.
- There is role continuity throughout the life span.
- Age-related role changes involve greater responsibility, authority, and advisory capacity.
- The extended family is a common family arrangement in the culture, and the older person is integrated into the extended family.
- In general, respect for older adults is greater in collectivistic cultures (such as China and Japan), than in individualistic cultures (such as the United States). However, some researchers are finding that this collectivistic/individualistic difference in respect for older adults is not as strong as it used to be and that in some cases older adults in individualistic cultures receive considerable respect (Antonucci, Vandewater, & Lansford, 2000).

Cultures vary in the prestige they give to older adults. In the Navajo culture, older adults are especially treated with respect because of their wisdom and extensive life experiences. *What are some other factors that are linked with respect for older adults in a culture?*

Review and Reflect: Learning Goal 4

4 **Summarize how ethnicity, gender, and culture are linked with aging**

REVIEW

- How does ethnicity modify the experience of aging?
- Do gender roles change in late adulthood? Explain.
- How is aging experienced in different cultures?

REFLECT

- What can America do to make being an older adult a more positive experience?

5 **SUCCESSFUL AGING**

John Glenn's space mission is emblematic of our rethinking of older adults in terms of successful aging.

Old Age Across
Cultures and Time
Culture and Aging

For too long, older adults were perceived as always being in decline, and the positive dimensions of aging were ignored (Holstein & Minkler, 2003; Phelan & others, 2004; Rowe & Kahn, 1997). Throughout our coverage of late adulthood, we have called attention to successful aging and how earlier stereotypes of aging are being overturned as researchers discover that being an older adult has many positive aspects. We indicated that once developmentalists began focusing on the positive aspects of aging rather than primarily focusing on its negative aspects, they realized there are far more robust, healthy older adults than they previously believed. In our discussion of aging, we have found that with a proper diet, an active lifestyle, mental stimulation and flexibility, positive coping skills, good social relationships and support, and the absence of disease, many of our abilities can be maintained, or in some cases even improved, as we get older. Improvements in medicine mean that increasing numbers of older adults with diseases can still lead active, constructive lives. Being active is especially important in successful aging (Freund & Riediger, 2003). Thus, older adults who get out and go to meetings, participate in church activities, go on trips, and exercise regularly are more satisfied with their lives than their counterparts who disengage from society and passively live out the last part of their lives (Mannell & Dupuis, 1996). In this chapter, we have seen that older adults who are emotionally selective, optimize their choices, and compensate effectively for any losses they might encounter increase their chances of aging successfully.

Successful aging also involves perceived control over the environment and a sense of self-efficacy (Bertrand & Lachman, 2003). In chapter 18, "Physical Development in Late Adulthood," we described how perceived control over the environment had a positive effect on nursing home residents' health and longevity. In recent years, the term *self-efficacy* has often been used to describe perceived control over the environment and the ability to produce positive outcomes (Bandura, 2002). Researchers have found that many older adults are quite effective in maintaining a sense of control and have a positive view of themselves (Brandstadter, Wentura, & Greve, 1993).

Review and Reflect: Learning Goal 5

5 **Explain how to age successfully**

REVIEW

- What factors are linked with aging successfully?

REFLECT

- How might aging successfully in late adulthood be related to what people have done earlier in their lives?

Reach Your Learning Goals

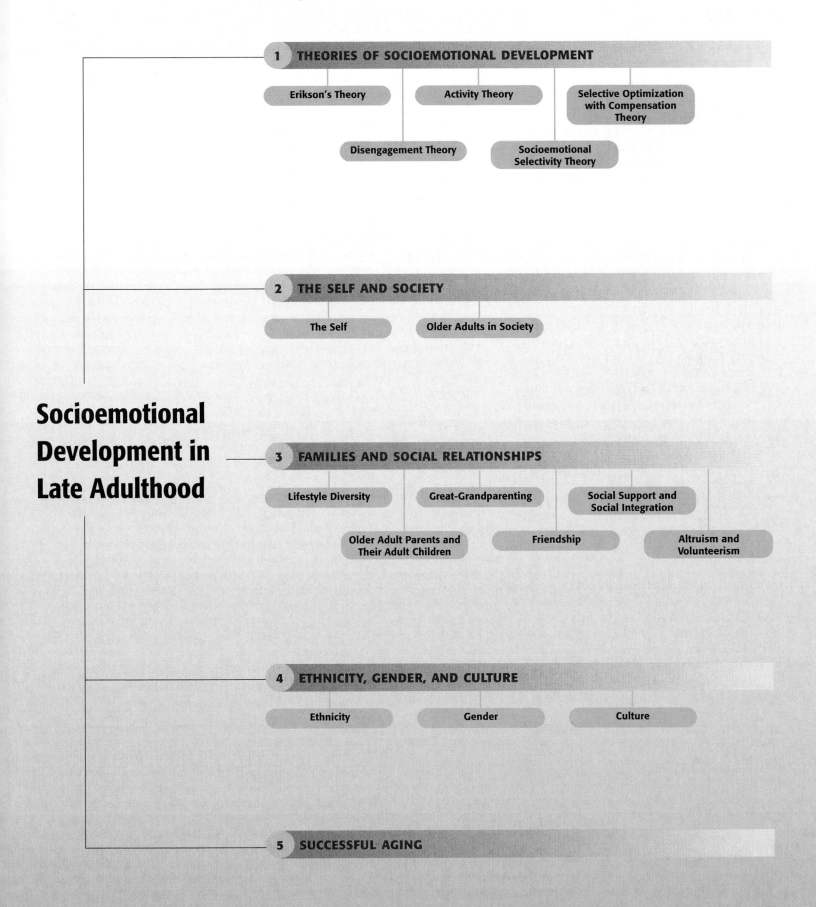

Socioemotional Development in Late Adulthood

1 THEORIES OF SOCIOEMOTIONAL DEVELOPMENT

- Erikson's Theory
- Disengagement Theory
- Activity Theory
- Socioemotional Selectivity Theory
- Selective Optimization with Compensation Theory

2 THE SELF AND SOCIETY

- The Self
- Older Adults in Society

3 FAMILIES AND SOCIAL RELATIONSHIPS

- Lifestyle Diversity
- Older Adult Parents and Their Adult Children
- Great-Grandparenting
- Friendship
- Social Support and Social Integration
- Altruism and Volunteerism

4 ETHNICITY, GENDER, AND CULTURE

- Ethnicity
- Gender
- Culture

5 SUCCESSFUL AGING

Summary

Learning Goal 1: Discuss five theories of socioemotional development and aging

- Erikson's eighth and final stage of development, which individuals experience in late adulthood, involves reflecting on the past and either integrating it positively or concluding that one's life has not been well spent. Peck described three developmental tasks that older adults face: (1) differentiation versus role preoccupation, (2) body transcendence versus preoccupation, and (3) ego transcendence versus ego preoccupation. Life review is an important theme in Erikson's stage of integrity versus despair.

- Disengagement theory is no longer a viable view. It stated that to be satisfied with their lives older adults need to withdraw from society.

- Activity theory states that the more active and involved older adults are, the more likely they are to be satisfied with their lives. This theory has been strongly supported.

- Socioemotional selectivity theory states that older adults become more selective about their social networks. Because they place a high value on emotional satisfaction, they are motivated to spend more time with familiar individuals with whom they have had rewarding relationships. Knowledge-related and emotion-related goals change across the life span, with emotion-related goals being more important when individuals get older.

- Selective optimization with compensation theory states that successful aging is linked with three main factors: (1) selection, (2) optimization, and (3) compensation. These are especially likely to be relevant when loss occurs.

Learning Goal 2: Identify changes in the self and society in late adulthood

- In one large-scale study, self-esteem increased through most of adulthood but declined in the seventies and eighties. Further research is needed to verify these developmental changes in self-esteem. Changes in types of self-acceptance occur through the adult years as acceptance of ideal and future selves decreases with age and acceptance of past selves increases.

- Ageism is prejudice against others because of their age. Too many negative stereotypes of older adults continue to exist. Social policy issues in an aging society include the status of the economy and the viability of the Social Security system, the provision of health care, eldercare, and generational inequity. Of special concern are older adults who are in poverty. Poverty rates are especially high among older women who live alone and ethnic minority older adults. Most older adults live in the community, not in institutions. Almost two-thirds of older adults live with family members.

Learning Goal 3: Characterize the families and social relationships of aging adults

- Older adult men are more likely to be married than older adult women. Almost half of older adult women are widowed.

Retirement alters a couple's lifestyle and requires adaptation. Married older adults are often happier than single older adults. There are social, financial, and physical consequences of divorce for older adults. More divorced older adults, increased longevity, and better health have led to an increase in remarriage by older adults. Some older adults perceive negative pressure about their decision to remarry, although the majority of adult children support the decision of their older adult parents to remarry. Approximately 8 percent of older adults have never been married. An increasing number of older adults cohabit. Older adults especially enjoy touching and caressing as part of their sexual relationship.

- Approximately 80 percent of older adults have living children, many of whom are middle-aged. Increasingly, diversity characterizes older parents and their adult children. Adult daughters are more likely than adult sons to be involved in the lives of aging parents. An important task that adult children can perform is to coordinate and monitor services for an aging parent who becomes disabled. Ambivalence can characterize the relationships of adult children with their aging parents.

- Because of increased longevity more grandparents today are also great-grandparents. One contribution of great-grandparents is family history. One research study found that young adults have a more involved relationship with grandparents than great-grandparents.

- There is more continuity than change in friendship for older adults, although there is more change for males than for females.

- Social support is linked with improved physical and mental health in older adults. Older adults who participate in more organizations live longer than their counterparts who have low participation rates. Older adults often have fewer peripheral social ties but a strong motivation to spend time in relationships with close friends and family members that are rewarding.

- Altruism is linked to having a longer life. Volunteering is associated with higher life satisfaction, less depression and anxiety, better physical health, and more positive affect and less negative affect.

Learning Goal 4: Summarize how ethnicity, gender, and culture are linked with aging

- Aging minorities face special burdens, having to cope with the double burden of ageism and racism. Nonetheless, there is considerable variation in aging minorities.

- There is stronger evidence that men become more feminine (nurturant, sensitive) as older adults than there is that women become more masculine (assertive). Older women face a double jeopardy of ageism and sexism.

- Historically, respect for older adults in China and Japan was high, but today their status is more variable. Factors that predict high status for the elderly across cultures range from their valuable knowledge to integration into the extended family.

5 *Learning Goal 5: Explain how to age successfully*

- Increasingly, the positive aspects of older adults are being studied. Factors that are linked with successful aging include

an active lifestyle, positive coping skills, good social relationships and support, and the absence of disease.

Key Terms

integrity versus despair 609
differentiation versus role preoccupation 609
body transcendence versus body preoccupation 610

ego transcendence versus ego preoccupation 610
disengagement theory 611
activity theory 611

socioemotional selectivity theory 612
selective optimization with compensation theory 613

ageism 616
eldercare 618
generational inequity 618

Key People

Erik Erikson 609
Robert Peck 609

Robert Butler 610
Laura Carstensen 612

Paul Baltes 613

E-Learning Tools

To help you master the material in this chapter, you'll find a number of valuable study tools on the LifeMap CD-ROM that accompanies this book and on the Online Learning Center for *Life-Span Development*, tenth edition, at www.mhhe.com/santrockld10.

Video Clips

In the margins of this book there are icons directing you to the LifeMap CD-ROM that accompanies the book. In chapter 20 you'll find a video called "Being in Love in Late Adulthood." This segment inquires into the sexual and emotional needs of older adults in various relationships. An older couple describes how the nature of their affection for each other has changed over the years.

Self-Assessment

Connect to www.mhhe.com/santrockld10 to reflect on your life satisfaction by completing the self-assessment, *How Satisfied Am I with My Life?*

Taking It to the Net

Connect to www.mhhe.com/santrockld10 to research the answers to these questions.

1. The viability of our Social Security program continues to be a hotly debated issue in our country, as evidenced in debates of

the last presidential election. What are some of the reforms being suggested for this program, and how much Social Security might you receive?

2. Ted is the activities director at an adult retirement community. A social worker at the community suggested that Ted might want to develop a program in which the residents engage in the process of reminiscence and life review. What benefits might the residents gain from such an activity?

3. Jessica, a 33-year-old single mother of three, has been diagnosed with breast cancer. As a precaution, Jessica has made arrangements for her parents to raise the children if something happens to her. What types of services and financial assistance would be available to Jessica's grandparents if they need to take on this responsibility?

Health and Well-Being, Parenting, and Education Exercises

Build your decision-making skills by trying your hand at the health and well-being, parenting, and education exercises.

Connect to www.mhhe.com/santrockld10 to research the answers and complete the exercises.

CHAPTER

*Sustained and soothed
by an unfaltering trust,
approach thy grave,
Like one who wraps the
Drapery of his couch
About him, and lies down
to pleasant dreams.*

—William Cullen Bryant
American Poet, 19th Century

Death and Grieving

Learning Goals

1 Evaluate issues in determining death and decisions regarding death

2 Describe the roles of cultural contexts in understanding death

3 Discuss death and attitudes about it at different points in development

4 Explain the psychological aspects involved in facing one's own death and the contexts in which people die

5 Identify ways to cope with the death of another person

Images of Life-Span Development
Paige Farley-Hackel and Ruth McCourt

Paige Farley-Hackel and her best friend, Ruth McCourt, teamed up to take McCourt's 4-year-old daughter, Juliana, to Disneyland. They were originally booked on the same flight from Boston to Los Angeles, but McCourt decided to use her frequent flyer miles and go on a different airplane. Both their flights exploded 17 minutes apart after terrorists hijacked them, then rammed them into the Twin Towers of the World Trade Center in New York City on 9/11/2001.

Forty-six-year-old Farley-Hackel was a writer, motivational speaker, and spiritual counselor who lived in Newton, Massachusetts. She was looking forward to the airing of the first few episodes of her new radio program, *Spiritually Speaking,* and wanted to eventually be on *The Oprah Winfrey Show.* Following 9/11, Oprah included a memorial tribute to Farley-Hackel, McCourt, and Juliana.

Forty-five-year-old Ruth McCourt was a homemaker from New London, Connecticut, who met Farley-Hackel at a day spa she used to own in Boston. McCourt gave up the business when she became married but the friendship between the two women lasted. They often traveled together and shared their passion for reading, cooking, and learning.

(Source: DallasNews.com, 2004)

PREVIEW

Death comes in many forms. For the three people just described, it was highly unexpected. For many people, it occurs in old age and can be expected after a long illness. In this chapter, we will explore many aspects of death and grieving, including issues in determining death, sociocultural/historical contexts of death, death and dying across the life span, how people face their own death, and how they cope with the death of someone else.

1 DEFINING DEATH AND LIFE/DEATH ISSUES

Issues in Determining Death	Decisions Regarding Life, Death, and Health Care

Is there one point in the process of dying that is *the* point at which death takes place, or is death a more gradual process? What are some decisions individuals can make about life, death, and health care?

Issues in Determining Death

Twenty-five years ago, determining whether someone was dead was simpler than it is today. The cessation of certain biological functions, such as breathing and blood pressure, and the rigidity of the body (rigor mortis) were considered to be clear signs of death. In the past several decades, defining death has become more complex (Corr,

Nabe, & Corr, 2003; Kyba, 2002). Consider the circumstance of Philadelphia Flyers hockey star Pelle Lindbergh, who slammed his Porsche into a cement wall on November 10, 1985. The newspaper headline the next day read, "Flyers' Goalie Declared Brain Dead." In spite of the claim that he was brain dead, the story reported that Lindbergh was listed in "critical condition" in the intensive care unit of a hospital.

Brain death is a neurological definition of death, which states that a person is brain dead when all electrical activity of the brain has ceased for a specified amount of time (Henneman & Karris, 2004; Shemie, 2004). A flat electroencephalogram (EEG) recording for a specified period of time is one criterion of brain death.

The higher portions of the brain often die sooner than the lower portions. Because the brain's lower portions monitor heartbeat and respiration, individuals whose higher brain areas have died may continue breathing and have a heartbeat. The definition of brain death currently followed by most physicians includes the death of both the higher cortical functions and the lower brain stem functions.

Brain death can be distinguished from being in a *coma,* a condition from which a person may emerge. A person in a coma—whether a deep coma that requires hospital care or a persistent vegetative state (allowing possible home care)—will show *some* sign of brain activity, but a brain dead patient will not.

Some medical experts argue that the criteria for death should include only higher cortical functioning. If the cortical death definition were adopted, then physicians could claim a person is dead who has no cortical functioning even though the lower brain stem is functioning. Supporters of the cortical death policy argue that the functions we associate with being human, such as intelligence and personality, are located in the higher cortical part of the brain. They believe that when these functions are lost, the "human being" is no longer alive.

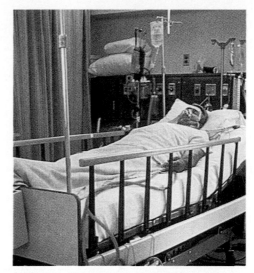

Advances in medical technology have complicated the definition of death. *What is the nature of the controversy about the criteria that should be used for determining when death occurs?*

Decisions Regarding Life, Death, and Health Care

In cases of catastrophic illness or accidents, patients might not be able to respond adequately to participate in decisions about their medical care. To prepare for this situation, some individuals make choices earlier.

Natural Death Act and Advanced Directive For many patients in a coma, it has not been clear what their wishes regarding termination of treatment might be if they still were conscious (Aiken, 2000). Recognizing that terminally ill patients might prefer to die rather than linger in a painful or vegetative state, the organization Choice in Dying created the living will. This document is designed to be filled in while the individual can still think clearly; it expresses the person's desires regarding extraordinary medical procedures that might be used to sustain life when the medical situation becomes hopeless.

Physicians' concerns over malpractice suits and the efforts of people who support the living will concept have produced natural death legislation in many states. For example, California's Natural Death Act permits individuals who have been diagnosed by two physicians as terminally ill to sign an *advanced directive,* which states that life-sustaining procedures shall not be used to prolong their lives when death is imminent (Chan, 2004; Kessler & McClellan, 2004). An advanced directive must be signed while the individual still is able to think clearly. Laws in all 50 states now accept advanced directives as reflecting an individual's wishes.

Euthanasia Euthanasia ("easy death") is the act of painlessly ending the lives of individuals who are suffering from an incurable disease or severe disability. Sometimes euthanasia is called *mercy killing.* Distinctions are made between two types of euthanasia, passive and active:

- **Passive euthanasia** occurs when a person is allowed to die by withholding available treatment, such as withdrawing a life-sustaining device. For example, this might involve turning off a respirator or a heart-lung machine.

brain death A neurological definition of death. A person is brain dead when all electrical activity of the brain has ceased for a specified period of time. A flat EEG recording is one criterion of brain death.

euthanasia The act of painlessly ending the lives of persons who are suffering from incurable diseases or severe disabilities; sometimes called *mercy killing.*

passive euthanasia The withholding of available treatments, such as life-sustaining devices, allowing the person to die.

Choice in Dying
Assisted Suicide
Exploring Euthanasia

- **Active euthanasia** occurs when death is deliberately induced, as when a lethal dose of a drug is injected.

Technological advances in life-support devices raise the issue of quality of life (Levy, 2004; Treece & others, 2004). Should individuals be kept alive in undignified and hopeless states? The trend is toward acceptance of passive euthanasia in the case of terminally ill patients. The inflammatory argument that once equated this practice with suicide rarely is heard today. However, experts do not yet entirely agree on the precise boundaries or the exact mechanisms by which treatment decisions should be implemented (Angus & others, 2004; Jennekens & Kater, 2002; Leeman, 2002; Zawistowski & DeVita, 2004). Can a comatose patient's life-support systems be disconnected when the patient has left no written instructions to that effect? Does the family of a comatose patient have the right to overrule the attending physician's decision to continue life-support systems? These questions have no simple or universally agreed-upon answers (Ardelt, 2003; Sharma, 2004). In one study of Canadian health-care workers, there was considerable variability in their decisions about whether to withdraw life support from critically ill patients (Cook & others, 1995).

A recent study in the Netherlands examined the effects of passive euthanasia on the bereaved family (Swarte & others, 2003). The grief of 189 bereaved family members and friends of terminally ill cancer patients who died by passive euthanasia was compared with the grief of 316 bereaved family members and friends of cancer patients who died a natural death. The bereaved family members and friends of cancer patients who died by passive euthanasia had less traumatic grief symptoms, less current feeling of grief, and less post-traumatic stress symptoms than the family members and friends of patients who died a natural death. The authors concluded that the results should not be interpreted as a plea for passive euthanasia but as a plea for the same level of care and openness in all patients who are terminally ill.

The most widely publicized cases of active euthanasia involve "assisted suicide" (Haider-Markely & Joslyn, 2004; Howard, 2004; Huxtable, 2004; Nelson, 2004; Rosenfeld, 2004; Volker, 2004). Jack Kevorkian, a Michigan physician, has assisted a number of terminally ill patients to end their lives. After a series of trials, Kevorkian was convicted of second-degree murder and given a long prison sentence. One reason for his conviction may have been that some of the patients were not considered to be terminally ill medically but were simply depressed and suicidal. In addition, Kevorkian went beyond providing patients with the means to commit suicide and, in at least one videotaped case, administered the lethal injection himself.

Active euthanasia is a crime in most countries (with the exception of the Netherlands and Uruguay) and in all states in the United States except one—Oregon (Hedberg, Hopkins, & Kohn, 2003). In 1994, the state of Oregon passed the Death with Dignity Act, which allows active euthanasia of individuals diagnosed with a terminal illness who are not expected to live for more than six months. Legal battles delayed implementation of the law until 1997, but since then more than 170 individuals have died by active euthanasia in Oregon. In May 2004, the Ninth Circuit Court of Appeals struck down an attempt by the U.S. Attorney General to hold physicians who distribute lethal medications in violation of the Controlled Substances Act.

A survey of more than 900 physicians assessed their attitudes about active euthanasia (Walker, Gruman, & Blank, 1999). Most opposed active euthanasia, said that adequate pain control often eliminates the need for it, and commented that the primary role of the physician is to preserve life. They also reported that the potential for abuse in active euthanasia is substantial, and many believed that it is morally wrong.

Dr. Jack Kevorkian assisted a number of people in Michigan to end their lives through active euthanasia. *Where do you stand on the use of active euthanasia?*

active euthanasia Death induced deliberately, as by injecting a lethal dose of a drug.

Needed: Better Care for Dying Individuals

Death in America is often lonely, prolonged, and painful (Institute of Medicine, 1997). Dying individuals often get too little or too much care. Scientific advances sometimes have made dying harder by delaying the inevitable (Muth, 2000). Also, even though painkillers are available, too many people experience severe pain during the last days and months of life (Fine & Peterson,

2002). Many health-care professionals have not been trained to provide adequate end-of-life care or to understand its importance (Hallberg, 2004; Robinson, 2004). In 1997, a panel of experts recommended that regulations be changed to make it easier for physicians to prescribe painkillers for dying patients who need them (Institute of Medicine, 1997).

End-of-life care should include respect for the goals, preferences, and choices of the patient and his or her family (Kirchhoff, 2002; Matzo & others, 2004). Many patients who are nearing death want companionship (Sheehan & Schirm, 2003).

There are few fail-safe measures for avoiding pain at the end of life. Still, you can do the following (Cowley & Hager, 1995):

- Make a living will, and be sure there is someone who will draw your doctor's attention to it.
- Give someone the power of attorney and make sure this person knows your wishes regarding medical care.
- Give your doctors specific instructions—from "Do not resuscitate" to "Do everything possible"—for specific circumstances.
- If you want to die at home, talk it over with your family and doctor.
- Check to see whether your insurance plan covers home care and hospice care.

Hospice is a humanitarian program committed to making the end of life as free from pain, anxiety, and depression as possible. Whereas a hospital's goals are to cure illness and prolong life, hospice care emphasizes **palliative care,** which involves reducing pain and suffering and helping individuals die with dignity (Claxton-Oldfield, Claxton-Oldfield, & Rishchynski, 2004; Horne & Payne, 2004). Health-care professionals work together to treat the dying person's symptoms, make the individual as comfortable as possible, show interest in the person and the person's family, and help them cope with death (Bakitas & others, 2004; Brenner & Krenzer, 2003; Meghani, 2004).

The hospice movement began toward the end of the 1960s in London, when a new kind of medical institution, St. Christopher's Hospice, opened. Little effort is made to prolong life at St. Christopher's—there are no heart-lung machines and there is no intensive care unit, for example. Only patients who are expected to live less than one year are admitted to St. Christopher's, although the criteria for hospice admission may vary. A primary goal is to bring pain under control and to help dying patients face death in a psychologically healthy way. The hospice also makes every effort to include the dying individual's family; it is believed that this strategy benefits not only the dying individual but family members as well, probably diminishing their guilt after the death (Mulholland, 2002; Reb, 2003).

The hospice movement has grown rapidly in the United States. More than 1,500 community groups are involved nationally in establishing hospice programs. Hospices are more likely to serve people with terminal cancer than those with other life-threatening conditions (Kastenbaum, 2004). Hospice advocates underscore that it is possible to control pain for almost any dying individual and that it is possible to create an environment for the patient that is superior to that found in most hospitals (Hayslip, 1996; Lyke & Colon, 2004).

Careers in Life-Span Development

Kathy McLaughlin, Home Hospice Nurse

Kathy McLaughlin is a home hospice nurse in Alexandria, Virginia. She provides care for individuals with terminal cancer, Alzheimer disease, and other diseases. There currently is a shortage of home hospice nurses in the United States.

Kathy says that she has seen too many people dying in pain, away from home, hooked up to needless machines. In her work as a home hospice nurse, she comments, "I know I'm making a difference. I just feel privileged to get the chance to meet this person who is not going to be around much longer. I want to enjoy the moment with this person. And I want them to enjoy the moment. They have great stories. They are better than novels" (McLaughlin, 2003, p. 1).

Kathy McLaughlin checks the vital signs of Kathryn Francis, 86, who is in an advanced stage of Alzheimer disease.

hospice A humanized program committed to making the end of life as free from pain, anxiety, and depression as possible. The goals of hospice contrast with those of a hospital, which are to cure disease and prolong life.

palliative care Emphasized in hospice care, involves reducing pain and suffering and helping individuals die with dignity.

Hospice Net
Hospice Foundation of America
Better Care for the Dying

Today more hospice programs are home-based, a blend of institutional and home care designed to humanize the end-of-life experience for the dying person. Whether the hospice program is carried out in the dying person's home, through a blend of home and institutional care, or in an institution often depends on medical needs and the availability of caregivers, including family and friends. To read about the work of a home hospice nurse, see the Careers in Life-Span Development insert.

Review and Reflect: Learning Goal 1

 Evaluate issues in determining death and decisions regarding death

REVIEW

• What are some issues regarding the determination of death?
• What are some decisions to be made regarding life, death, and health care?

REFLECT

• Do you think assisted suicide should be legal? Explain your answer.

2 DEATH AND CULTURAL CONTEXTS

Changing Historical Circumstances

Death in Different Cultures

When, where, and how people die have changed historically in the United States. Also, attitudes toward death vary across cultures.

Changing Historical Circumstances

We have already described one of the historical changes involving death—the increasing complexity of determining when someone is truly dead. Another historical change in death focuses on the age group in which death most often strikes. Two hundred years ago, almost one of every two children died before the age of 10, and one parent usually died before children grew up. Today, death occurs most often among the elderly. Life expectancy has increased from 47 years for a person born in 1900 to 77 years for someone born today (U.S. Bureau of the Census, 2004). In 1900, most people died at home, cared for by their family. As our population has aged and become more mobile, more older adults die apart from their families. In the United States today, more than 80 percent of all deaths occur in institutions or hospitals. The care of a dying older person has shifted away from the family and minimized our exposure to death and its painful surroundings.

Death in Different Cultures

To live a full life and die with glory was the prevailing goal of the ancient Greeks. Individuals are more conscious of death in times of war, famine, and plague. Whereas Americans are conditioned from early in life to live as though they were immortal, in much of the world this fiction cannot be maintained. Death crowds the streets of Calcutta in daily overdisplay, as it does the scrubby villages of

Africa's Sahel. Children live with the ultimate toll of malnutrition and disease, mothers lose as many babies as survive into adulthood, and it is rare that a family remains intact for many years. Even in peasant areas where life is better, and health and maturity may be reasonable expectations, the presence of dying people in the house, the large attendance at funerals, and the daily contact with aging adults prepare the young for death and provide them with guidelines on how to die. By contrast, in the United States it is not uncommon to reach adulthood without having seen someone die.

Most societies throughout history have had philosophical or religious beliefs about death, and most societies have a ritual that deals with death (see figure 21.1). Death may be seen as a punishment for one's sins, an act of atonement, or a judgment of a just God. For some, death means loneliness; for others, death is a quest for happiness. For still others, death represents redemption, a relief from the trials and tribulations of the earthly world. Some embrace death and welcome it; others abhor and fear it. For those who welcome it, death may be seen as the fitting end to a fulfilled life. From this perspective, how we depart from Earth is influenced by how we have lived.

FIGURE 21.1 A Ritual Associated with Death
Family memorial day at the national cemetery in Seoul, Korea.

In most societies, death is not viewed as the end of existence—though the biological body has died, the spiritual body is believed to live on. This religious perspective is favored by most Americans as well (Gowan, 2003). Cultural variations in attitudes toward death include belief in reincarnation, which is an important aspect of the Hindu and Buddhist religions (Dillon, 2003; Truitner & Truitner, 1993). In the Gond culture of India, death is believed to be caused by magic and demons. The members of the Gond culture react angrily to death. In the Tanala culture of Madagascar, death is believed to be caused by natural forces. The members of the Tanala culture show a much more peaceful reaction to death than their counterparts in the Gond culture.

Dying and Medicine in America

In many ways, we in the United States are death avoiders and death deniers (Neimeyer, Wittkowski, & Moser, 2004). This denial can take many forms:

- The tendency of the funeral industry to gloss over death and fashion lifelike qualities in the dead
- The adoption of euphemistic language for death—for example, *exiting, passing on, never say die*, and *good for life*, which implies forever
- The persistent search for a fountain of youth
- The rejection and isolation of the aged, who may remind us of death
- The adoption of the concept of a pleasant and rewarding afterlife, suggesting that we are immortal
- The medical community's emphasis on prolonging biological life rather than on diminishing human suffering

Review and Reflect: Learning Goal 2

2 Describe the roles of cultural contexts in understanding death

REVIEW
- What are some changing historical circumstances regarding death?
- What are some variations in death across cultures?

REFLECT
- Why is the United States such a death-denying culture? How could this be changed?

3 A DEVELOPMENTAL PERSPECTIVE ON DEATH

| Causes of Death and Expectations About Death | Attitudes Toward Death at Different Points in the Life Span |

Do the causes of death vary across the human life span? Do we have different expectations about death as we develop through the life span? What are our attitudes toward death at different points in our development?

Causes of Death and Expectations About Death

Death can occur at any point in the human life span. Death can occur during prenatal development through miscarriages or stillborn births. Death can also occur during the birth process or in the first few days after birth, which usually happens because of a birth defect or because infants have not developed adequately to sustain life outside the uterus. In chapter 5, "Physical Development in Infancy," we described *sudden infant death syndrome (SIDS),* in which infants stop breathing, usually during the night, and die without apparent cause (Corr & Corr, 2003). SIDS currently is the highest cause of infant death in the United States, with the risk highest at 4 to 6 weeks of age (American Academy of Pediatrics Task Force on Infant Sleep Position and SIDS, 2000).

In childhood, death occurs most often because of accidents or illness. Accidental death in childhood can be the consequence of such things as an automobile accident, drowning, poisoning, fire, or a fall from a high place. Major illnesses that cause death in children are heart disease, cancer, and birth defects. It is not unusual for terminally ill children to distance themselves from their parents as they approach the final phase of their illness. The distancing may be due to the depression that many dying patients experience, or it may be a child's way of protecting parents from the overwhelming grief they will experience at the death. Most dying children know they have a terminal illness. Their developmental level, social support, and coping skills influence how well they cope with knowing they will die.

Compared with childhood, death in adolescence is more likely to occur because of motor vehicle accidents, suicide, and homicide. Many motor vehicle accidents that cause death in adolescence are alcohol-related.

Like in adolescence, when young adults die it usually is not expected (Hayslip & Hansson, 2003). When a young adult dies, it is more likely due to an accident or violence rather than disease, although the increase in AIDS has led to an increased number of deaths in young adults (Lamb, 2003). Young adults who are dying often feel cheated more than do older adults who are dying (Hayslip & Hansson, 2003). Young adults are more likely to feel they have not had the opportunity to do what they want to with their lives. Young adults perceive they are losing what they might achieve; older adults perceive they are losing what they have.

An especially difficult circumstance involving death in early adulthood occurs for parents when their child dies (Hayslip & Hansson, 2003). Researchers have found that they may experience significant personal distress for as long as five years (Murphy & others, 1999). "When a child dies, the parents may assume that they are responsible, that they should have done something to prevent their child's death," and experience a range of intense negative emotions, including anger, resentment, and disappointment (Hayslip & Hansson, 2003, p. 442). The death of a young child can lead to adverse outcomes in parents, including divorce, physical illness, and mental illness. Professional and community help are especially important for parents when they experience the death of a child.

Middle-aged and older adults are more likely to die from chronic diseases, such as heart disease and cancer. Older adults' diseases often incapacitate before they kill, which produces a course of dying that slowly leads to death.

Attitudes Toward Death at Different Points in the Life Span

The ages of children and adults influence the way they experience and think about death. A mature, adultlike conception of death includes an understanding that death is final and irreversible, that death represents the end of life, and that all living things die. Most researchers have found that, as children grow, they develop a more mature approach to death (Wass & Stillion, 1988).

Childhood Most researchers believe that infants do not have even a rudimentary concept of death. However, as infants develop an attachment to a caregiver, they can experience loss or separation and an accompanying anxiety. But young children do not perceive time the way adults do. Even brief separations may be experienced as total losses. For most infants, the reappearance of the caregiver provides a continuity of existence and a reduction of anxiety. We know very little about the infant's actual experiences with bereavement, although the loss of a parent, especially if the caregiver is not replaced, can negatively affect the infant's health.

Even children 3 to 5 years of age have little or no idea of what death really means. They may confuse death with sleep or ask in a puzzled way, "Why doesn't it move?" Preschool-aged children rarely get upset by the sight of a dead animal or by being told that a person has died. They believe that the dead can be brought back to life spontaneously by magic or by giving them food or medical treatment. Young children often believe that only people who want to die, or who are bad or careless, actually die. They also may blame themselves for the death of someone they know well, illogically reasoning that the event may have happened because they disobeyed the person who died.

Sometime in the middle and late childhood years more realistic perceptions of death develop. In one early investigation of children's perception of death, children 3 to 5 years of age denied that death exists, children 6 to 9 years of age believed that death exists but only happens to some people, and children 9 years of age and older recognized death's finality and universality (Nagy, 1948). In a review of research on children's conception of death, it was concluded that children probably do not view death as universal and irreversible until about 9 years of age (Cuddy-Casey & Orvaschel, 1997). Most children under 7 do not see death as likely. Those who do, perceive it as reversible.

An expert on death and dying, Robert Kastenbaum (2004) takes a different view on developmental dimensions of death and dying. He believes that even very young children are acutely aware of and concerned about *separation* and *loss,* just as attachment theorist John Bowlby (1980) does. Kastenbaum also says that many children work hard at trying to understand death. Thus, instead of viewing young children as having illogical perceptions of death, Kastenbaum thinks a more accurate stance is to view them as having concerns about death and striving to understand it.

The deaths of parents, grandparents, friends, heros (such as sports figures and rock stars), and pets are powerful influences on children's awareness of death, as are widely publicized deaths in the media such as the deaths of Princess Diana, John F. Kennedy, the Columbine shootings in 1999, and the terrorist attacks on the World Trade Center and the Pentagon on September 11, 2001. Children also may reexperience grief, especially in response to the death of a parent, as they grow older. When children and adolescents experience the death of a parent, their school performance often suffers and their relationships with peers suffer (Worden, 2002).

"For some children, adolescents, and even adults, the impact of a parental death can be far-reaching and result in a hypersensitivity about death, including a fear of losing others close to the individual (Balk & Carr, 2001)." Similar negative outcomes

Grieving Children
Association for Death Education
and Counseling

have been observed in children who have lost siblings to death (Oltjenbruns, 2001). Nevertheless, it should be noted that the impacts on children of either a parent's or a sibling's death covary with a number of factors, such as the quality of the relationship and nature of the death (such as, through cancer, AIDS, suicide, murder) (Hayslip & Hansson, 2003, pp. 440–441).

Most psychologists believe that honesty is the best strategy in discussing death with children. Treating the concept as unmentionable is thought to be an inappropriate strategy, yet most of us have grown up in a society in which death is rarely discussed (Wass, 2004). In one study, the attitudes of 30,000 young adults toward death were evaluated (Shneidman, 1973). More than 30 percent said they could not recall any discussion of death during their childhood. An equal number said that, although death was discussed, the discussion took place in an uncomfortable atmosphere. Almost one of every two respondents said that the death of a grandparent was their first personal encounter with death.

In addition to honesty, what other strategies can be adopted in discussing death with children? The best response to the child's query about death might depend on the child's maturity level. For example, the preschool child requires a less elaborate explanation than an older child. Death can be explained to preschool children in simple physical and biological terms. Actually, what young children need more than elaborate explanations of death is reassurance that they are loved and will not be abandoned. Regardless of children's age, adults should be sensitive and sympathetic, encouraging them to express their own feelings and ideas.

Adolescence In adolescence, the prospect of death, like the prospect of aging, is regarded as a notion that is so remote that it does not have much relevance. The subject of death may be avoided, glossed over, kidded about, neutralized, and controlled by a cool, spectator-like orientation. This perspective is typical of the adolescent's self-conscious thought; however, some adolescents do show a concern for death, both in trying to fathom its meaning and in confronting the prospect of their own demise (Baxter, Stuart, & Stewart, 1998; Mearns, 2000).

Deaths of friends, siblings, parents, or grandparents bring death to the forefront of adolescents' lives. Deaths of peers who commit suicide "may be especially difficult for adolescents who feel guilty for having failed to prevent the suicide or feel that they should have died, or feel they are being rejected by their friends who hold them responsible for the death" (Hayslip & Hansson, 2003, p. 441).

Adolescents develop more abstract conceptions of death than children do. For example, adolescents describe death in terms of darkness, light, transition, or nothingness (Wenestam & Wass, 1987). They also develop religious and philosophical views about the nature of death and whether there is life after death.

You may recall the concepts of adolescent egocentrism and personal fable from chapter 12, "Physical and Cognitive Development in Adolescence"—adolescents' preoccupation with themselves and their belief that they are invincible and unique. Thus, it is not unusual for adolescents to think that they are somehow immune to death and that death is something that happens to other people but not to them.

Adulthood There is no evidence that a special orientation toward death develops in early adulthood. An increase in consciousness about death accompanies individuals' awareness that they are aging, which usually intensifies in middle adulthood. In our discussion of middle adulthood, we indicated that midlife is a time when adults begin to think more about how much time is left in their lives. Researchers have found that middle-aged adults actually fear death more than do young adults or older adults (Kalish & Reynolds, 1976). Older adults, though, think about death more and talk about it more in conversation with others than do middle-aged and young adults. They also have more direct experience with death as their friends and relatives become ill and die (Hayslip & Hansson, 2003). Older adults are forced to examine the meanings of life and death more frequently than are younger adults.

In old age, one's own death may take on an appropriateness it lacked in earlier years. Some of the increased thinking and conversing about death, and an increased sense of integrity developed through a positive life review, may help older adults accept death. Older adults are less likely to have unfinished business than are younger adults. They usually do not have children who need to be guided to maturity, their spouses are more likely to be dead, and they are less likely to have work-related projects that require completion. Lacking such anticipations, death may be less emotionally painful to them. Even among older adults, however, attitudes toward death vary. One 82-year-old woman declared that she had lived her life and was ready to see it come to an end. Another 82-year-old woman declared that death would be a regrettable interruption of her participation in activities and relationships.

We keep on thinking and rethinking death after we have passed through childhood's hour.

—**ROBERT KASTENBAUM**
Contemporary Gerontologist, Arizona State University

The video "On Dying at Age 72" presents the insights of a man pondering his own death.

Review and Reflect: Learning Goal 3

3 Discuss death and attitudes about it at different points in development

REVIEW

- What are some developmental changes in the cause of death and expectations for death?
- What are some attitudes about death at different points in development?

REFLECT

- What is your current attitude about death? Has it changed since you were an adolescent? If so, how?

4   FACING ONE'S OWN DEATH

Kübler-Ross' Stages of Dying	Perceived Control and Denial	The Contexts in Which People Die

Knowledge of death's inevitability permits us to establish priorities and structure our time accordingly. As we age, these priorities and structurings change in recognition of diminishing future time. Values concerning the most important uses of time also change. For example, when asked how they would spend six remaining months of life, younger adults described such activities as traveling and accomplishing things they previously had not done; older adults described more inner-focused activities—contemplation and meditation, for example (Kalish & Reynolds, 1976).

Most dying individuals want an opportunity to make some decisions regarding their own life and death (Kastenbaum, 2004). Some individuals want to complete unfinished business; they want time to resolve problems and conflicts and to put their affairs in order. Might there be a sequence of stages we go through as we face death?

Kübler-Ross' Stages of Dying

Elisabeth Kübler-Ross (1969) divided the behavior and thinking of dying persons into five stages: denial and isolation, anger, bargaining, depression, and acceptance.

Denial and isolation is Kübler-Ross' first stage of dying, in which the person denies that death is really going to take place. The person may say, "No, it

denial and isolation Kübler-Ross' first stage of dying, in which the dying person denies that she or he is really going to die.

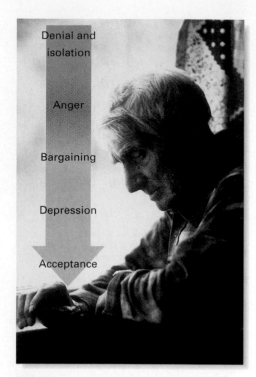

FIGURE 21.2 Kübler-Ross' Stages of Dying
According to Elisabeth Kübler-Ross, we go through five stages of dying: denial and isolation, anger, bargaining, depression, and acceptance. *Does everyone go through these stages, or go through them in the same order? Explain.*

Kübler-Ross on Dying

anger Kübler-Ross' second stage of dying, in which the dying person's denial often gives way to anger, resentment, rage, and envy.

bargaining Kübler-Ross' third stage of dying, in which the dying person develops the hope that death can somehow be postponed.

depression Kübler-Ross' fourth stage of dying, in which the dying person comes to accept the certainty of her or his death. A period of depression or preparatory grief may appear.

acceptance Kübler-Ross' fifth stage of dying, in which the dying person develops a sense of peace, an acceptance of her or his fate, and, in many cases, a desire to be left alone.

can't be me. It's not possible." This is a common reaction to terminal illness. However, denial is usually only a temporary defense and is eventually replaced with increased awareness when the person is confronted with such matters as financial considerations, unfinished business, and worry about surviving family members.

Anger is Kübler-Ross' second stage of dying, in which the dying person recognizes that denial can no longer be maintained. Denial often gives way to anger, resentment, rage, and envy. The dying person's question is, "Why me?" At this point, the person becomes increasingly difficult to care for as anger may become displaced and projected onto physicians, nurses, family members, and even God. The realization of loss is great, and those who symbolize life, energy, and competent functioning are especially salient targets of the dying person's resentment and jealousy.

Bargaining is Kübler-Ross' third stage of dying, in which the person develops the hope that death can somehow be postponed or delayed. Some persons enter into a bargaining or negotiation—often with God—as they try to delay their death. Psychologically, the person is saying, "Yes, me, but . . ." In exchange for a few more days, weeks, or months of life, the person promises to lead a reformed life dedicated to God or to the service of others.

Depression is Kübler-Ross' fourth stage of dying, in which the dying person comes to accept the certainty of death. At this point, a period of depression or preparatory grief may appear. The dying person may become silent, refuse visitors, and spend much of the time crying or grieving. This behavior is normal and is an effort to disconnect the self from love objects. Attempts to cheer up the dying person at this stage should be discouraged, says Kübler-Ross, because the dying person has a need to contemplate impending death.

Acceptance is Kübler-Ross' fifth stage of dying, in which the person develops a sense of peace, an acceptance of one's fate, and in many cases, a desire to be left alone. In this stage, feelings and physical pain may be virtually absent. Kübler-Ross describes this fifth stage as the end of the dying struggle, the final resting stage before death. A summary of Kübler-Ross' dying stages is presented in figure 21.2.

What is the current evaluation of Kübler-Ross' approach? According to psychology of death expert Robert Kastenbaum (2004), there are some problems with Kübler-Ross' approach:

- The existence of the five-stage sequence has not been demonstrated by either Kübler-Ross or independent research.
- The stage interpretation neglected the patients' situations, including relationship support, specific effects of illness, family obligations, and institutional climate in which they were interviewed.

However, Kübler-Ross' pioneering efforts were important in calling attention to those who are attempting to cope with life-threatening illnesses. She did much to encourage attention to the quality of life for dying persons and their families.

Because of the criticisms of Kübler-Ross' stages of dying, some psychologists prefer to describe them not as stages but as potential reactions to dying. At any one moment, a number of emotions may wax and wane. Hope, disbelief, bewilderment, anger, and acceptance may come and go as individuals try to make sense of what is happening to them.

In facing their own death, some individuals struggle until the end, desperately trying to hang on to their lives. Acceptance of death never comes for them. Some psychologists believe that the harder individuals fight to avoid the inevitable death they face and the more they deny it, the more difficulty they will have in dying peacefully and in a dignified way; other psychologists argue that not confronting death until the end may be adaptive for some individuals (Lifton, 1977).

The extent to which people have found meaning and purpose in their lives is linked with how they approach death. A recent study of 160 individuals with less than three months to live revealed that those who had found purpose and meaning in their lives felt the least despair in the final weeks, while dying individuals who saw no reason for living were the most distressed and wanted to hasten death (McClain, Rosenfeld, & Breitbart, 2003). In this and other studies, spirituality also helped to buffer dying individuals from severe depression (Smith, McCullough, & Poll, 2003).

Perceived Control and Denial

Perceived control and denial may work as an adaptive strategy for some older adults who face death. When individuals are led to believe they can influence and control events—such as prolonging their lives—they may become more alert and cheerful. Remember from chapter 18 that giving nursing home residents options for control improved their attitudes and increased their longevity (Rodin & Langer, 1977).

Denial also may be a fruitful way for some individuals to approach death. It can be adaptive or maladaptive. Denial can be used to avoid the destructive impact of shock by delaying the necessity of dealing with one's death. Denial can insulate the individual from having to cope with intense feelings of anger and hurt; however, if denial keeps us from having a life-saving operation, it clearly is maladaptive. Denial is neither good nor bad; its adaptive qualities need to be evaluated on an individual basis.

The Contexts in Which People Die

For dying individuals, the context in which they die is important. More than 50 percent of Americans die in hospitals, and nearly 20 percent die in nursing homes. Some people spend their final days in isolation and fear (Clay, 1997). An increasing number of people choose to die in the humane atmosphere of a hospice (Leming, 2003).

Hospitals offer several important advantages to the dying individual—for example, professional staff members are readily available, and the medical technology present may prolong life. But a hospital may not be the best place for many people to die. Most individuals say they would rather die at home (Kalish & Reynolds, 1976). Many feel, however, that they will be a burden at home, that there is limited space there, and that dying at home may alter relationships. Individuals who are facing death also worry about the competency and availability of emergency medical treatment if they remain at home.

> *M*an is the only animal that finds his own existence a problem he has to solve and from which he cannot escape. In the same sense man is the only animal who knows he must die.
>
> —ERICH FROMM
> *American Psychotherapist, 20th Century*

Review and Reflect: Learning Goal 4

4 **Explain the psychological aspects involved in facing one's own death and the contexts in which people die**

REVIEW

- What are Kübler-Ross' five stages of dying? What conclusion can be reached about them?
- What roles do perceived control and denial play in facing one's own death?
- What are the contexts in which people die?

REFLECT

- How do you think you will psychologically handle facing your own death?

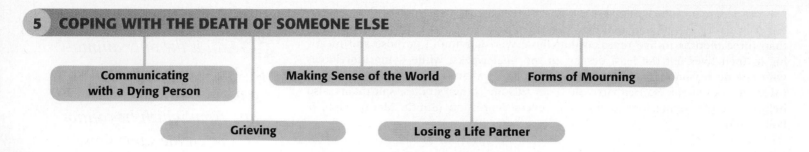

5 **COPING WITH THE DEATH OF SOMEONE ELSE**

Communicating with a Dying Person

Making Sense of the World

Forms of Mourning

Grieving

Losing a Life Partner

www.mhhe.com/santrockld10

Exploring Death and Dying
Death and Dying Resources

Loss can come in many forms in our lives—divorce, a pet's death, loss of a job—but no loss is greater than that which comes through the death of someone we love and care for—a parent, sibling, spouse, relative, or friend. In the ratings of life's stresses that require the most adjustment, death of a spouse is given the highest number. How should we communicate with a dying individual? How do we cope with the death of someone we love?

Communicating with a Dying Person

Most psychologists believe that it is best for dying individuals to know that they are dying and that significant others know they are dying so they can interact and communicate with each other on the basis of this mutual knowledge. What are some of the advantages of this open awareness for the dying individual? There are at least four advantages. First, dying individuals can close their lives in accord with their own ideas about proper dying. Second, they may be able to complete some plans and projects, can make arrangements for survivors, and can participate in decisions about a funeral and burial. Third, dying individuals have the opportunity to reminisce, to converse with others who have been important individuals in their life, and to end life conscious of what life has been like. And fourth, dying individuals have more understanding of what is happening within their bodies and what the medical staff is doing to them (Kalish, 1981).

In addition to keeping communication open, what are some suggestions for conversing with a dying individual? Some experts believe that conversation should not focus on mental pathology or preparation for death but should focus on strengths of the individual and preparation for the remainder of life. Since external accomplishments are not possible, communication should be directed more at internal growth. Keep in mind also that important support for a dying individual may come not only from mental health professionals, but also from nurses, physicians, a spouse, or intimate friends (De-Spelder & Strickland, 2005).

Effective strategies for communicating with a dying person include these:

- Establish your presence, be at the same eye level; don't be afraid to touch the dying person—dying individuals are often starved for human touch.
- Don't insist that the dying person feel acceptance about death if the dying person wants to deny the reality of the situation; on the other hand, don't insist on denial if the dying individual indicates acceptance.
- Allow the dying person to express guilt or anger; encourage the expression of feelings.
- Don't be afraid to ask the person what the expected outcome for their illness is. Discuss alternatives, unfinished business.
- Encourage the dying individual to reminisce, especially if you have memories in common.
- Express your regard for the dying individual. Don't be afraid to express love, and don't be afraid to say good-bye.

Grieving

Our exploration of grief focuses on dimensions of grieving, as well as cultural diversity in healthy grieving.

Dimensions of Grieving Grief is the emotional numbness, disbelief, separation anxiety, despair, sadness, and loneliness that accompany the loss of someone we love. Grief is not a simple emotional state but rather a complex, evolving process with multiple dimensions (Ott, 2003; Reed, 2003). In this view, pining for the lost person is one important dimension. Pining or yearning reflects an intermittent, recurrent wish or need to recover the lost person. Another important dimension of grief is separation anxiety, which not only includes pining and preoccupation with thoughts of the deceased person but also focuses on places and things associated with the deceased, as well as crying or sighing. Grief also may involve despair and sadness, which include a sense of hopelessness and defeat, depressive symptoms, apathy, loss of meaning for activities that used to involve the person who is gone, and growing desolation (Felden, 2003; Ringdal & others, 2001; Scannell-Desch, 2003).

These feelings do not represent a clear-cut stage but occur repeatedly shortly after a loss. Nonetheless, as time passes, pining and protest over the loss tend to diminish, although episodes of depression and apathy may remain or increase. The sense of separation anxiety and loss may continue to the end of one's life, but most of us emerge from grief's tears, turning our attention once again to productive tasks and regaining a more positive view of life (Bonanno, 2004; Powers & Wampold, 1994).

The grieving process is more like a roller-coaster ride than an orderly progression of stages with clear-cut time frames (Lund, 1996). The ups and downs of grief often involve rapidly changing emotions, meeting the challenges of learning new skills, detecting personal weaknesses and limitations, creating new patterns of behavior, and forming new friendships and relationships (Bruce, 2002; Carrington & Bogetz, 2004; Mitchell & Catron, 2002). For most individuals, grief becomes more manageable over time, with fewer abrupt highs and lows (Moules & others, 2004). But many grieving spouses report that even though time has brought some healing, they have never gotten over their loss. They have just learned to live with it (Davies, 2004; Levin, 2004).

Cognitive factors are involved in the severity of grief after a loved one has died. One recent study focused on 329 adults who had suffered the loss of a first-degree relative (Boelen, van den Bout, & van den Hout, 2003). The more negative beliefs and self-blame the adults had, the more severe were their symptoms of traumatic grief, depression, and anxiety.

Long-term grief is sometimes masked and can predispose individuals to become depressed and even suicidal (Davis, 2001; Kastenbaum, 2004; Macias & others, 2004). Good family communication can help reduce the incidence of depression and suicidal thoughts. For example, in one study, family members who communicated poorly with each other had more negative grief reactions six months later than those who communicated effectively with each other just after the loss of a family member (Schoka & Hayslip, 1999).

Grief counselors help individuals cope with their feelings of losing someone close to them (Mitchell & Catron, 2002; Worden, 2002).

Cultural Diversity in Healthy Grieving Some approaches to grieving emphasize the importance of breaking bonds with the deceased and returning to autonomous lifestyles. People who persist in holding on to the deceased are believed to be in need of therapy. Recent analyses, however, have cast doubt on whether this recommendation is always the best therapeutic advice (Reisman, 2001; Stroebe & others, 1992).

Analyses of non-Western cultures suggest that beliefs about continuing bonds with the deceased vary extensively. Maintenance of ties with the deceased is accepted and sustained in the religious rituals of Japan. In the Hopi of Arizona, the deceased are forgotten as quickly as possible and life is carried on as usual. Their funeral ritual concludes with a breakoff between mortals and spirits. The diversity of grieving is nowhere more clear than in two Muslim societies—one in Egypt, the other in Bali. In Egypt, the bereaved are encouraged to dwell at length on their grief, surrounded by others who relate similarly tragic accounts and express their own sorrow. By contrast, in Bali, the bereaved are encouraged to laugh and be joyful.

It is sweet to mingle tears with tears; griefs, where they wound in solitude, wound more deeply.

—SENECA
Roman Poet, 1st Century

grief The emotional numbness, disbelief, separation anxiety, despair, sadness, and loneliness that accompany the loss of someone we love.

In a longitudinal study of bereavement in the Netherlands, many people tended to maintain contact with the deceased, despite the contemporary emphasis on breaking such bonds (Stroebe & Stroebe, 1991). Many of the widowed persons were not planning a major break with their pasts, but rather were integrating the loss experience into their lifestyles and trying to carry on much as before the death of a loved one. Well over half "consulted" the deceased when having to make a decision. One widow said that she gained considerable comfort from knowing that her decision was exactly what her deceased husband would have wanted her to do.

In summary, people grieve in a variety of ways (Clements & others, 2003; Matzo & others, 2003). The diverse grieving patterns are culturally embedded practices (Haas, 2003). Thus, there is no one right, ideal way to grieve. There are many different ways to feel about a deceased person and no set series of stages that the bereaved must pass through to become well adjusted. The stoic widower may need to cry out over his loss at times. The weeping widow may need to put her husband's wishes aside as she becomes the financial manager of her estate. What is needed is an understanding that healthy coping with the death of a loved one involves growth, flexibility, and appropriateness within a cultural context.

Making Sense of the World

One beneficial aspect of grieving is that it stimulates many individuals to try to make sense of their world (Attig, 2004; Balk, 2004; Gamino & Sewell, 2004; Kalish, 1981, 1987). A common occurrence is to go over again and again all of the events that led up to the death. In the days and weeks after the death, the closest family members share experiences with each other, sometimes reminiscing over family experiences. In one recent study, women who became widowed in midlife were challenged by the crisis of their husband's death to examine meaningful directions for their lives (Danfroth & Glass, 2001). Another recent study found that mourners who expressed positive themes of hope for a positive future showed better adjustment than those who focused on negative themes of pain and suffering (Gamino & Sewell, 2004).

Mary Assanful (*front right* with other former restaurant workers) worked at Windows on the World restaurant located in the World Trade Center and lost her job when terrorist attacks came. She says that she still is not herself and regularly has nightmares. A Ghana native, Mary is still unemployed. She has joined several other workers who are now planning to return by opening a restaurant near Ground Zero. They hope the new restaurant will honor their co-workers who died and provide a focus and meaning for their still-unsettled lives. Mary says that since they have been working on this new project, her mind has calmed somewhat.

Each individual may offer a piece of death's puzzle. "When I saw him last Saturday, he looked as though he were rallying," says one family member. "Do you think it might have had something to do with his sister's illness?" remarks another. "I doubt it, but I heard from an aide that he fell going to the bathroom that morning," comments yet another. "That explains the bruise on his elbow," says the first individual. "No wonder he told me that he was angry because he could not seem to do anything right," chimes in a fourth family member. So it goes in the attempt to understand why someone who was rallying on Saturday was dead on Wednesday.

When a death is caused by an accident or a disaster, the effort to make sense of it is pursued more vigorously. As added pieces of news come trickling in, they are integrated into the puzzle. The bereaved want to put the death into a perspective that they can understand—divine intervention, a curse from a neighboring tribe, a logical sequence of cause and effect, or whatever it may be.

Losing a Life Partner

Widows outnumber widowers by the ratio of 5 to 1, because women live longer than men, because women tend to marry men older than themselves, and because a widowed man is more likely to remarry. Widowed women are probably the poorest group in America. One recent study found that most widows in the United States and Germany experienced a decline in living standards in the year following their husband's death, and many fell into poverty when they became widows (Hungerford, 2001). A study of Mexican Americans revealed that widows were more likely than widowers to report financial strain, welfare dependency, and use of Medicaid than widowers (Angel, Douglas, & Angel, 2003). In this study, widows received more emotional support than widowers. Another recent study of African American widows found that storytelling was at the heart of widows' description of their bereavement experience (Rodgers, 2004). Six themes were identified in their stories: awareness of death, caregiving, getting through, moving on, changing feelings, and financial security.

Those left behind after the death of an intimate partner suffer profound grief and often endure financial loss, loneliness, increased physical illness, and psychological disorders, including depression (Hungerford, 2001; Manor & Eisenbach, 2003; Valdimarsdottir & others, 2003). The Research in Life-Span Development interlude examines the relation of widowhood to health.

Grief and Bereavement
WidowNet

Research in Life-Span Development
The Women's Health Initiative Study of Widowhood and Health

One recent three-year longitudinal study of more than 120,000 women aged 50 to 79 years of age in the United States as part of the Women's Health Initiative examined the relationship of widowhood to physical and mental health, health behaviors, and health outcomes (Wilcox & others, 2003). Women were categorized as (1) remaining married, (2) transitioning from married to widowed, (3) remaining widowed, and (4) transitioning from widowed to married. Widows were further subdivided into the recently widowed (widowed for less than one year) and longer-term widowed (widowed for more than one year).

The measures used to assess the older women's health were (Wilcox & others, 2003, p. 515):

- *Physical health.* Blood pressure was assessed after five minutes of quiet rest using the average of two readings with 30 seconds between the readings. Hypertension was defined as more than 140/90. Body mass index (BMI) was calculated and used to determine whether a woman was obese. A health survey assessed physical function and health status.
- *Mental health.* Depressive symptoms were assessed by a six-item depression scale with participants rating "the frequency of their depressed thoughts during the past week." The participant's self-report of antidepressant medicine use was also obtained. Information about social functioning and mental health was based on participants' responses on the Social Functioning Scale (Ware, Kosinsky, & Dewey, 2000).
- *Health behaviors.* Dietary behaviors were assessed with a modified version of the National Cancer Institute Health Habits and History Questionnaire. Participants also were asked if they smoked tobacco, and if so, how much. "To assess physical activity, participants were asked how often each week they usually walked outside the home" and the extent to which they engaged in exercise of varying intensity. To assess health care use, they were asked whether they had been to a doctor in the past year.
- *Health outcomes.* Incidence of cardiovascular disease and cancer was assessed annually and any overnight hospitalizations were noted.

At the beginning of the three-year study,

married women reported better physical and mental health and generally better health behaviors than widowed women. Whereas women who remained married over the 3-year period showed stability in mental health, recent widows experienced marked impairments and longer-term widows showed stability or slight improvements (in mental health). Both groups of widows (recent and longer-term) reported more unintentional weight loss over the 3-year period. Findings underscore the resilience of older women and their capacity to reestablish connections, but point to the need for services that strengthen social support among women who have difficulty during the transition (from marriage to widowhood). (Wilcox & others, 2003, p. 513)

Optimal adjustment after a death depends on several factors (Attig, 2004; Gamino & Sewell, 2004; Leming & Dickinson, 2002). Women do better than men largely because, in our society, women are responsible for the emotional life of a couple, whereas men usually manage the finances and material goods (Fry, 2001). Thus, women have better networks of friends, closer relationships with relatives, and experience in taking care of themselves psychologically (Antonucci & others, 2001; Van Den Brink & others, 2004). Older widows do better than younger widows, perhaps because the death of a partner is more expected for older women. For their part, widowers usually have more money than widows do, and they are much more likely to remarry (DiGiulio, 1989).

One recent study found that psychological and religious factors—such as personal meaning, optimism, the importance of religion, and access to religious support—were related to the psychological well-being of older adults following the loss of a spouse (Fry, 2001). Other studies have indicated that religiosity and coping skills are related to well-being following the loss of a spouse in late adulthood (Michael, Crowther, & Allen, 2003).

Grieving is an important aspect of coping with the death of a spouse (Adams, 2003). The marital relationship before the death of a spouse is linked to the nature of grief after the spouse's death. One longitudinal investigation studied 1,532 married individuals aged 65 and older (Carr & others, 2000). Information was obtained about marital quality before the spouse's death and the widowed person's grief, anxiety, and depression were assessed 6, 18, and 48 months after the spouse's death. Widowhood was associated with increased anxiety among those who were highly dependent on their spouses; lower anxiety was more characteristic of those who did not depend on their spouse very much. Widowed persons whose relationship with their spouse was conflicted prior to the spouse's death reported lower yearning than their counterparts whose relationship was not conflicted. Women who depended a lot on their husbands for support reported more yearning than men who depended a lot on their wives. The findings of this study contradict the widespread belief that grief is more severe if the marriage was conflicted.

For either widows or widowers, social support helps them adjust to the death of a spouse (Boerner & Wortman, 1998; Kastenbaum, 2004). The Widow-to-Widow program, begun in the 1960s, provides support for newly widowed women. Volunteer widows reach out to other widows, introducing them to others who may have similar problems, leading group discussions, and organizing social activities. The program has been adopted by the American Association of Retired Persons and disseminated throughout the United States as the Widowed Person's Service. The model has since been adopted by numerous community organizations to provide support for those going through a difficult transition.

Forms of Mourning

One decision facing the bereaved is what to do with the body. Approximately 80 percent of corpses are disposed of by burial, the remaining 20 percent by cremation

A widow leading a funeral procession in the United States.

A crowd gathered at a cremation ceremony in Bali, Indonesia, balancing decorative containers on their heads.

(Cremation Association of America, 2000). Cremation is more popular in the Pacific region of the United States, less popular in the South. Cremation also is more popular in Canada than in the United States and most popular of all in Japan and many other Asian countries.

The funeral is an important aspect of mourning in many cultures. In one study, bereaved individuals who were personally religious derived more psychological benefits from a funeral, participated more actively in the rituals, and adjusted more positively to the loss (Hayslip, Edmondson, & Guarnaccia, 1999).

The funeral industry has been the source of controversy in recent years. Funeral directors and their supporters argue that the funeral provides a form of closure to the relationship with the deceased, especially when there is an open casket. Their critics claim that funeral directors are just trying to make money, and that embalming is grotesque. One way to avoid being exploited during bereavement is to purchase funeral arrangements in advance. However, in one survey, only 24 percent of individuals 60 and over had made any funeral arrangements (Kalish & Reynolds, 1976).

In some cultures, a ceremonial meal is held after death; in others, a black armband is worn for one year following a death. Cultures vary in how they practice mourning (Adamolekun, 2001; Clements & others, 2003; Morgan & Laungani, 2003; Shepard, 2002). To learn about two cultures with extensive mourning systems, see the Diversity in Life-Span Development interlude.

Buddhist Funeral Rites

Diversity in Life-Span Development

The Amish, Traditional Judaism, and Mourning

The family and the community have important roles in mourning in some cultures. Two of those cultures are the Amish and traditional Judaism (Worthington, 1989).

The Amish are a conservative group with approximately 80,000 members in the United States, Ontario, and several small settlements in South and Central America. The Amish live in a family-oriented society in which family and community support are essential for survival. Today, they live at the same unhurried

An Amish funeral procession in Pennsylvania. The funeral service is held in the barn in the warmer months and in the house during the colder months. Following the funeral, a high level of support is given to the bereaved family for at least a year.

pace as that of their ancestors, using horses instead of cars and facing death with the same steadfast faith as their forebears. At the time of death, close neighbors assume the responsibility of notifying others of the death. The Amish community handles virtually all aspects of the funeral.

The funeral service is held in a barn in warmer months and in a house during colder months. Calm acceptance of death, influenced by a deep religious faith, is an integral part of the Amish culture. Following the funeral, a high level of support is given to the bereaved family for at least a year. Visits to the family, special scrapbooks and handmade items for the family, new work projects started for the widow, and quilting days that combine fellowship and productivity are among the supports given to the bereaved family.

The family and community also have specific and important roles in mourning in traditional Judaism. The program of mourning is divided into graduated time periods, each with its appropriate practices. The observance of these practices is required of the spouse and the immediate blood relatives of the deceased. The first period is *aninut*, the period between death and burial. The next two periods make up *avelut*, or mourning proper. The first of these is *shivah*, a period of 7 days, which commences with the burial. It is followed by *sheloshim*, the 30-day period following the burial, including shivah. At the end of sheloshim, the mourning process is considered over for all but one's parents. For parents, mourning continues for 11 months, although observances are minimal.

The seven-day period of the shivah is especially important in traditional Judaism. The mourners, sitting together as a group through an extended period, have an opportunity to project their feelings to the group as a whole. Visits from others during shivah may help the mourner deal with feelings of guilt. After shivah, the mourner is encouraged to resume normal social interaction. In fact, it is customary for the mourners to walk together a short distance as a symbol of their return to society. In its entirety, the elaborate mourning system of traditional Judaism is designed to promote personal growth and to reintegrate the individual into the community.

Review and Reflect: Learning Goal 5

5 Identify ways to cope with the death of another person

REVIEW

- What are some strategies for communicating with a dying person?
- What is the nature of grieving?
- How is making sense of the world a beneficial outcome of grieving?
- What are some characteristics and outcomes of losing a life partner?
- What are some forms of mourning? What is the nature of the funeral?

REFLECT

- Is there a best or worst way to grieve? Explain.

We have arrived at the end of this book. I hope this book and course have been a window to the life span of the human species and a window to your own personal journey in life.

Our study of the human life span has been long and complex. You have read about many physical, cognitive, and socioemotional changes that take place from conception through death. This is a good time to reflect on what you have learned. Which theories, studies, and ideas were especially interesting to you? What did you learn about your own development?

Reach Your Learning Goals

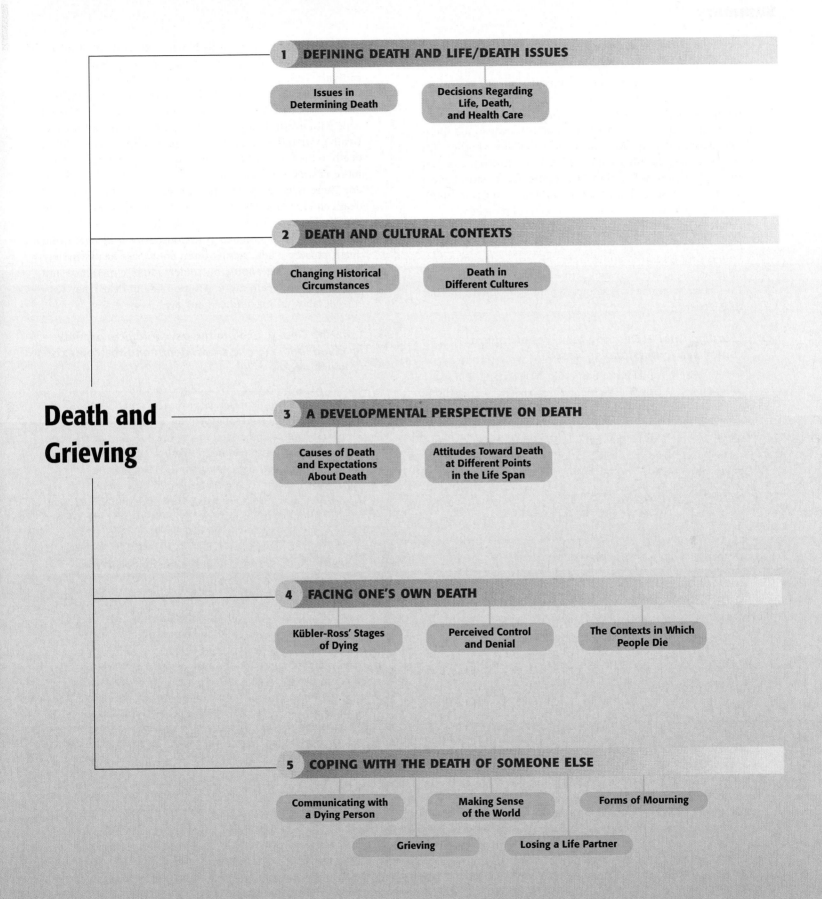

Death and Grieving

1 DEFINING DEATH AND LIFE/DEATH ISSUES

- Issues in Determining Death
- Decisions Regarding Life, Death, and Health Care

2 DEATH AND CULTURAL CONTEXTS

- Changing Historical Circumstances
- Death in Different Cultures

3 A DEVELOPMENTAL PERSPECTIVE ON DEATH

- Causes of Death and Expectations About Death
- Attitudes Toward Death at Different Points in the Life Span

4 FACING ONE'S OWN DEATH

- Kübler-Ross' Stages of Dying
- Perceived Control and Denial
- The Contexts in Which People Die

5 COPING WITH THE DEATH OF SOMEONE ELSE

- Communicating with a Dying Person
- Making Sense of the World
- Forms of Mourning
- Grieving
- Losing a Life Partner

Summary

 Learning Goal 1: Evaluate issues in determining death and decisions regarding death

- Twenty-five years ago, determining if someone was dead was simpler than it is today. Brain death is a neurological definition of death, which states that a person is brain dead when all electrical activity of the brain has ceased for a specified period of time. Medical experts debate whether this should mean the higher and lower brain functions or just the higher cortical functions. Currently, most states have a statute endorsing the cessation of brain function (both higher and lower) as a standard for determining death.

- Living wills and advanced directives are increasingly used. Euthanasia is the act of painlessly ending the life of a person who is suffering from an incurable disease or disability. Distinctions are made between active and passive euthanasia. Hospice care emphasizes reducing pain and suffering rather than prolonging life.

 Learning Goal 2: Describe the roles of cultural contexts in understanding death

- When, where, and why people die have changed historically. Today, death occurs most often among older adults. More than 80 percent of all deaths in the United States now occur in a hospital or other institution. Our exposure to death in the family has been minimized. Most societies throughout history have had philosophical or religious beliefs about death, and most societies have rituals that deal with death.

- Most cultures do not view death as the end of existence—spiritual life is thought to continue. The United States has been described as a death-denying and death-avoiding culture.

 Learning Goal 3: Discuss death and attitudes about it at different points in development

- Although death is more likely to occur in late adulthood, death can come at any point in development. The deaths of some persons, especially children and younger adults, are often perceived to be more tragic than those of others, such as very old adults, who have had an opportunity to live a long life. In children and younger adults, death is more likely to occur because of accidents; in older adults, death is more likely to occur because of chronic diseases. An especially difficult circumstance in early adulthood occurs for parents when their child dies.

- Infants do not have a concept of death. Preschool children also have little concept of death. Preschool children sometimes blame themselves for a person's death. In the elementary school years, children develop a more realistic orientation toward death. The deaths of parents, grandparents, and others can be powerful influences on children's awareness of death. For some children, the impact of a parent's death can be far-reaching and result in hypersensitivity about death. Nonetheless, the influence of a parent's or a sibling's death can vary with a number of factors including the quality of the relationship and the nature of the death. Most psychologists believe honesty is the best strategy for helping children cope with death. Death may be glossed over in adolescence. Death of friends, siblings, parents, or grandparents can bring death to the forefront of adolescents' lives. Adolescents have more abstract, philosophical views of death than children do. There is no evidence that a special orientation toward death emerges in early adulthood. When young adults die, it usually is unexpected. Middle adulthood is a time when adults show a heightened consciousness about death and death anxiety. Older adults often show less death anxiety than middle-aged adults, but older adults experience and converse about death more. Attitudes about death may vary considerably among adults of any age.

 Learning Goal 4: Explain the psychological aspects involved in facing one's own death and the contexts in which people die

- Kübler-Ross proposed five stages: denial and isolation, anger, bargaining, depression, and acceptance. Not all individuals go through the same sequence.

- Perceived control and denial may work together as an adaptive orientation for the dying individual. Denial can be adaptive or maladaptive, depending on the circumstance.

- Most deaths in the United States occur in hospitals; this has advantages and disadvantages. Most individuals say they would rather die at home, but they worry that they will be a burden and they worry about the lack of medical care.

 Learning Goal 5: Identify ways to cope with the death of another person

- Most psychologists recommend an open communication system with the dying. Communication should not dwell on pathology or preparation for death but should emphasize the dying person's strengths.

- Grief is the emotional numbness, disbelief, separation, anxiety, despair, sadness, and loneliness that accompany the loss of someone we love. Grief is multidimensional and in some cases may last for years. There are cultural variations in grieving.

- The grieving process may stimulate individuals to strive to make sense out of their world; each individual may contribute a piece to death's puzzle.

- Usually the most difficult loss is the death of a spouse. The bereaved are at risk for many health problems. Social support benefits widows and widowers.

- Forms of mourning vary across cultures. An important aspect of mourning in many cultures is the funeral. In recent years, the funeral industry has been the focus of controversy.

Key Terms

brain death 635
euthanasia 635
passive euthanasia 635

active euthanasia 636
hospice 637
palliative care 637

denial and isolation 643
anger 644
bargaining 644

depression 644
acceptance 644
grief 647

Key People

Elisabeth Kübler-Ross 643   Robert Kastenbaum 644

E-Learning Tools

To help you master the material in this chapter, you'll find a number of valuable study tools on the LifeMap CD-ROM that accompanies this book and on the Online Learning Center for *Life-Span Development,* tenth edition, at www.mhhe.com/santrockld10.

Video Clips

In the margins of this book there are icons directing you to the LifeMap CD-ROM that accompanies the book. In chapter 21 you'll find a video segment called "On Dying at Age 72." Our attitude toward death changes as we get older. This segment features an interview with an elderly man who has begun to think differently about death.

Self-Assessment

Connect to www.mhhe.com/santrockld10 to reflect on your feelings about the end of life by completing the self-assessments, *How Much Anxiety Do I Have About Death?* and *The Living Will.*

Taking It to the Net

Connect to www.mhhe.com/santrockld10 to research the answers to these questions.

1. Herman's mother has Parkinson disease. He wants her to make some difficult end-of-life decisions while she still can. He and his mother discuss the options of a health-care power of attorney, a living will, and/or a DNR. What purposes do these various documents serve, and what is the family's role in these decisions?

2. Letitia, a recent widow, is interested in starting a program for widowed women in her community. She is exploring some of the resources available from foundation grants. As part of this process, she will need to investigate the available data on those who have lost a spouse in the United States, including the age, sex, and socioeconomic status of widowers. What type of information is available to her and her group?

3. Ellen has taken care of her mother throughout her long, lingering illness that has just been diagnosed as terminal. Ellen does not think she alone can provide the type of care necessary to take care of her mother in her final weeks. Her neighbor suggested she contact the local hospice. What services does a hospice offer to families in this situation, and how do those services distinguish a hospice from a nursing home?

Health and Well-Being, Parenting, and Education Exercises

Build your decision-making skills by trying your hand at the health and well-being, parenting, and education exercises.

Connect to www.mhhe.com/santrockld10 to research the answers and complete the exercises.

Glossary

A̅B̅ error Occurs when infants make the mistake of selecting the familiar hiding place (A) rather than the new hiding place (B̅) as they progress into substage 4 in Piaget's sensorimotor stage. 179

acceptance Kübler-Ross' fifth stage of dying, in which the dying person develops a sense of peace, an acceptance of her or his fate, and, in many cases, a desire to be left alone. 644

accommodation Occurs when individuals adjust to new information. 46

acquired immune deficiency syndrome (AIDS) A sexually transmitted disease caused by the HIV virus, which destroys the body's immune system. 448

active euthanasia Death induced deliberately, as by injecting a lethal dose of a drug. 636

active (niche-picking) genotype-environment correlations Correlations that exist when children seek out environments they find compatible and stimulating. 96

activity theory The theory that the more active and involved older adults are, the more likely they are to be satisfied with their lives. 611

addiction A pattern of behavior characterized by an overwhelming involvement with using a drug and securing its supply. 444

adolescent egocentrism The heightened self-consciousness of adolescents. 384

adoption study A study in which investigators seek to discover whether the behavior and psychological characteristics of adopted children are more like their adoptive parents, who have provided a home environment, or more like their biological parents, who have contributed their heredity. Another form of the adoption study is to compare adopted and biological siblings. 95

aerobic exercise Sustained exercise (such as jogging, swimming, or cycling) that stimulates heart and lung activity. 440

affectionate love In this type of love, also called "companionate love," an individual desires to have the other person near and has a deep, caring affection for the other person. 474

affordances Opportunities for interaction offered by objects that are necessary to perform functional activities. 158

ageism Prejudice against other people because of their age, especially prejudice against older adults. 616

altruism Unselfish interest in helping another person. 337

Alzheimer disease A progressive, irreversible brain disorder characterized by a gradual deterioration of memory, reasoning, language, and eventually physical function. 596

amnion The life-support system that is a bag or envelope containing a clear fluid in which the developing embryo floats. 106

androgyny The presence of positive masculine and feminine characteristics in the same individual. 341

anger Kübler-Ross' second stage of dying, in which the dying person's denial often gives way to anger, resentment, rage, and envy. 644

anger cry A cry similar to the basic cry, with more excess air forced through the vocal cords. 203

animism The belief that inanimate objects have "lifelike" qualities and are capable of action. 235

anorexia nervosa An eating disorder that involves the relentless pursuit of thinness through starvation. 379

Apgar Scale A widely used method to assess the health of newborns at one and five minutes after birth. The Apgar Scale evaluates infants' heart rate, respiratory effort, muscle tone, body color, and reflex irritability. 126

aphasia A loss or impairment of language ability caused by brain damage. 191

arthritis Inflammation of the joints that is accompanied by pain, stiffness, and movement problems; especially common in older adults. 571

assimilation (Piaget) Occurs when individuals incorporate new information into their existing knowledge. 45

assimilation (Culture) The absorption of ethnic minority groups into the dominant group, which often involves the loss of some or virtually all of the behavior and values of the ethnic minority group. 418

associative play Play that involves social interaction with little or no organization. 282

attachment A close emotional bond between an infant and a caregiver. 210

attention The focusing of mental resources. 180

attention deficit hyperactivity disorder (ADHD) A disability in which children consistently show one or more of the following characteristics: (1) inattention, (2) hyperactivity, and (3) impulsivity. 299

authoritarian parenting A restrictive punitive style in which parents exhort the child to follow their directions and to respect work and effort. The authoritarian parent places firm limits and controls on the child and allows little verbal exchange. Authoritarian parenting is associated with children's social incompetence. 268

authoritative parenting A parenting style in which parents encourage their children to be independent but still place limits and controls on their actions. Extensive verbal give-and-take is allowed, and parents are warm and nurturant toward the child. Authoritative parenting is associated with children's social competence. 268

autonomous morality The second stage of moral development in Piaget's theory, displayed by older children (about 10 years of age and older). The child becomes aware that rules and laws are created by people and that, in judging an action, one should consider the actor's intentions as well as the consequences. 259

average children Children who receive an average number of both positive and negative nominations from peers. 347

Bargaining Kübler-Ross' third stage of dying, in which the dying person develops the hope that death can somehow be postponed. 644

basal metabolism rate (BMR) The minimum amount of energy a person uses in a resting state. 231

basic cry A rhythmic pattern usually consisting of a cry, a briefer silence, a shorter inspiratory whistle that is higher pitched than the main cry, and then a brief rest before the next cry. 203

basic-skills-and-phonics approach The idea that reading instruction should teach both phonics and the basic rules for translating written symbols into sounds. 320

Bayley Scales of Infant Development Scales developed by Nancy Bayley that are widely used in the assessment of infant development. The current version has three components: a mental scale, a motor scale, and an infant behavior profile. 183

becoming parents and a family with children The third stage in the family life cycle. Adults who enter this stage move up a generation and become caregivers to the younger generation. 479

behavior genetics The field that seeks to discover the influence of heredity and environment on individual differences in human traits and development. 94

big five factors of personality Emotional stability (neuroticism), extraversion, openness to experience, agreeableness, and conscientiousness. 538

biological age A person's age in terms of biological health. 21

biological processes Changes in an individual's physical nature. 17

blastocyst The inner mass of cells that develops during the germinal period. These cells later develop into the embryo. 105

body transcendence versus body preoccupation A developmental task of aging described by Peck, in which older adults must cope with declining physical well-being. 610

bonding The formation of a close connection, especially a physical bond between parents and their newborn in the period shortly after birth. 130

brain death A neurological definition of death. A person is brain dead when all electrical activity of the brain has ceased for a specified period of time. A flat EEG recording is one criterion of brain death. 635

brainstorming A technique in which individuals are encouraged to come up with creative ideas in a group, play off each other's ideas, and say practically whatever comes to mind. 306

Brazelton Neonatal Behavioral Assessment Scale A test performed within 24 to 36 hours after birth to assess newborns' neurological development, reflexes, and reactions to people. 126

breech position The baby's position in the uterus that causes the buttocks to be the first part to emerge from the vagina. 122

Broca's area An area in the brain's left frontal lobe next to the part that directs the muscle movements involved in speech production. 191

bulimia nervosa An eating disorder in which the individual consistently follows a binge-and-purge pattern. 379

Care perspective The moral perspective of Carol Gilligan, which views people in terms of their connectedness with others and emphasizes interpersonal communication, relationships with others, and concern for others. 336

case study An in-depth look at a single individual. 58

cataracts Involve a thickening of the lens of the eye that causes vision to become cloudy, opaque, and distorted. 566

cellular clock theory Leonard Hayflick's theory that the maximum number of times that human cells can divide is about 75 to 80. As we age, our cells have less capability to divide. 559

centration The focusing of attention on one characteristic to the exclusion of all others. 236

cephalocaudal pattern The sequence in which the earliest growth always occurs at the top—the head—with physical growth in size, weight, and feature differentiation gradually working from top to bottom. 137

child-centered kindergarten Education that involves the whole child by considering both the child's physical, cognitive, and social development and the child's needs, interests, and learning styles. 246

child-directed speech Language spoken in a higher pitch than normal with simple words and sentences. 193

chromosomes Threadlike structures that contain the remarkable substance DNA; there are 23 pairs of chromosomes. 80

chronic disorders Disorders that are characterized by slow onset and long duration. They are rare in early adulthood, they increase during middle adulthood, and they become common in late adulthood. 506

chronological age The number of years that have elapsed since birth. 21

climacteric The midlife transition in which fertility declines. 509

clique A small group that ranges from 2 to about 12 individuals, averaging about 5 to 6 individuals, and can form because adolescents engage in similar activities. 409

cognitive developmental theory of gender The theory that children's gender typing occurs after they have developed a concept of gender. Once they consistently conceive of themselves as male or female, children often organize their world on the basis of gender. 265

cognitive mechanics The "hardware" of the mind, reflecting the neurophysiological architecture of the brain as developed through evolution. Cognitive mechanics involve the speed and accuracy of the processes involving sensory input, visual and motor memory, discrimination, comparison, and categorization. 583

cognitive pragmatics The culture-based "software" programs of the mind. Cognitive pragmatics include reading and writing skills, language comprehension, educational qualifications, professional skills, and also the type of knowledge about the self and life skills that help us to master or cope with life. 583

cognitive processes Changes in an individual's thought, intelligence, and language. 17

cohort effects Effects due to a person's time of birth, era, or generation but not to actual age. 62

commitment Marcia's term for the part of identity development in which adolescents show a personal investment in what they are going to do. 399

connectedness Connectedness consists of two dimensions: mutuality (sensitivity to and respect for others' views) and permeability (openness to others' views). 400

consensual validation An explanation of why individuals are attracted to people who are similar to them. Our own attitudes and behavior are supported and validated when someone else's attitudes and behavior are similar to our own. 470

conservation In Piaget's theory, awareness that altering an object's or a substance's appearance does not change its quantitative properties. 236

constructive play Play that combines sensorimotor and repetitive activity with symbolic representation of ideas. Constructive play occurs when children engage in self-regulated creation or construction of a product or a problem solution.   283

contemporary life-events approach Emphasizes that how a life event influences the individual's development depends not only on the life event, but also on mediating factors, the individual's adaptation to the life event, the life-stage context, and the sociohistorical context.   533

context The setting in which development occurs, which is influenced by historical, economic, social, and cultural factors.   11

continuity-discontinuity issue Focuses on the extent to which development involves gradual, cumulative change (continuity) or distinct stages (discontinuity).   23

controversial children Children who are frequently nominated both as someone's best friend and as being disliked.   347

conventional reasoning The second, or intermediate, level in Kohlberg's theory of moral development. At this level, individuals abide by certain standards but they are the standards of others such as parents or the laws of society.   334

convergent thinking Thinking that produces one correct answer and is characteristic of the kind of thinking tested by standardized intelligence tests.   306

cooperative play Play that involves social interaction in a group with a sense of group identity and organized activity.   282

coordination of secondary circular reactions Piaget's fourth sensorimotor substage, which develops between 8 and 12 months of age. In this substage, several significant changes take place involving the coordination of schemes and intentionality.   176

correlational research The goal is to describe the strength of the relationship between two or more events or characteristics.   59

creative thinking The ability to think in novel and unusual ways and to come up with unique solutions to problems.   306

crisis Marcia's term for a period of identity development during which the adolescent is choosing among meaningful alternatives.   399

critical thinking Thinking reflectively and productively, as well as evaluating the evidence.   306

cross-cultural studies Comparisons of one culture with one or more other cultures. These provide information about the degree

to which development is similar, or universal, across cultures, and to the degree to which it is culture-specific.   12

cross-sectional approach A research strategy in which individuals of different ages are compared at one time.   60

crowd A larger group structure than a clique, a crowd is usually formed based on reputation and members may or may not spend much time together.   409

crystallized intelligence Accumulated information and verbal skills, which increase with age, according to Horn.   513

cultural-familial retardation Retardation that is characterized by no evidence of organic brain damage, but the individual's IQ is between 50 and 70.   318

culture The behavior patterns, beliefs, and all other products of a group that are passed on from generation to generation.   12

culture-fair tests Tests of intelligence that are designed to be free of cultural bias.   316

Date or acquaintance rape Coercive sexual activity directed at someone with whom the perpetrator is at least casually acquainted.   450

dating scripts The cognitive models that individuals use to guide and evaluate dating interactions.   411

deferred imitation Imitation that occurs after a time delay of hours or days. 181

dementia A global term for any neurological disorder in which the primary symptoms involve a deterioration of mental functioning.   596

denial and isolation Kübler-Ross' first stage of dying, in which the dying person denies that she or he is really going to die.   643

depression Kübler-Ross' fourth stage of dying, in which the dying person comes to accept the certainty of her or his death. A period of depression or preparatory grief may appear.   644

descriptive research Has the purpose of observing and recording behavior.   55

development The pattern of change that begins at conception and continues through the life span. Most development involves growth, although it also includes decline brought on by aging and dying.   5

developmental quotient (DQ) An overall developmental score that combines subscores in motor, language, adaptive, and personal/social domains in the Gesell assessment of infants.   183

developmentally appropriate practice Education that focuses on the typical developmental patterns of children (age-appropriateness) and the uniqueness of each child (individual-appropriateness).   247

differentiation versus role preoccupation One of the three developmental tasks of aging described by Peck, in which older adults must redefine their worth in terms of something other than work roles.   609

difficult child A child who tends to react negatively and cry frequently, who engages in irregular daily routines, and who is slow to accept new experiences.   205

direct instruction approach A teacher-centered approach characterized by teacher direction and control, mastery of academic skills, high expectations for students, and maximum time spent on learning tasks.   350

disease model of addiction The view that addictions are biologically based, life-long diseases that involve a loss of control over behavior and require medical and/or spiritual treatment for recovery.   444

disengagement theory The theory that to cope effectively, older adults should gradually withdraw from society.   611

dishabituation Recovery of an habituated response after a change in stimulation.   159

divergent thinking Thinking that produces many answers to the same question and is characteristic of creativity.   306

divided attention Concentrating on more than one activity at the same time.   584

DNA A complex molecule that contains genetic information.   80

doula A caregiver who provides continuous physical, emotional, and educational support for the mother before, during, and after childbirth.   120

Down syndrome A chromosomally transmitted form of mental retardation, caused by the presence of an extra copy of chromosome 21.   85

dynamic systems theory The perspective on motor development that seeks to explain how motor behaviors are assembled for perceiving and acting.   150

dyslexia A category of learning disabilities involving a severe impairment in the ability to read and spell.   298

Easy child A child who is generally in a positive mood, who quickly establishes regular routines in infancy, and who adapts easily to new experiences.   205

eclectic theoretical orientation An orientation that does not follow any one theoretical approach, but rather selects from each theory whatever is considered the best in it.   53

ecological theory Bronfenbrenner's environmental systems theory that focuses on five environmental systems: microsystem, mesosystem, exosystem, macrosystem, and chronosystem.   51

ecological view The view that perception functions to bring organisms in contact with the environment and to increase adaptation.   158

egocentrism The inability to distinguish between one's own perspective and someone else's (salient feature of the first substage of preoperational thought).   235

ego transcendence versus ego preoccupation A developmental task of aging described by Peck, in which older adults must come to feel at ease with themselves by recognizing that although death is inevitable and probably not too far away, they have contributed to the future through raising their children or through their vocations and ideas.   610

elaboration An important strategy that involves engaging in more extensive processing of information.   305

eldercare Physical and emotional caretaking for older members of the family, whether by giving day-to-day physical assistance or by being responsible for overseeing such care.   618

embryonic period The period of prenatal development that occurs from two to eight weeks after conception. During the embryonic period, the rate of cell differentiation intensifies, support systems for the cells form, and organs appear.   105

emerging adulthood The transition from adolescence to adulthood (approximately 18 to 25 years of age) that involves experimentation and exploration.   433

emotion Feeling, or affect, that occurs when a person is in a state or interaction that is important to them. Emotion is characterized by behavior that reflects (expresses) the pleasantness or unpleasantness of the state a person is in or the transactions being experienced.   201

emotional intelligence A form of social intelligence that involves the ability to monitor one's own and others' feelings and emotions, to discriminate among them, and to use this information to guide one's thinking and action.   331

empty nest syndrome A decrease in marital satisfaction after children leave home, because parents derive considerable satisfaction from their children.   542

epigenetic view Emphasizes that development is the result of an ongoing, bidirectional interchange between heredity and environment.   97

episodic memory The retention of information about the where and when of life's happenings.   585

equilibration A mechanism that Piaget proposed to explain how children shift from one stage of thought to the next. The shift occurs as children experience cognitive conflict, or disequilibrium, in trying to understand the world. Eventually, they resolve the conflict and reach a balance, or equilibrium, of thought.   174

Erikson's theory Includes eight stages of human development. Each stage consists of a unique developmental task that confronts individuals with a crisis that must be resolved.   43

ethnic gloss Using an ethnic label such as African American or Latino in a superficial way that portrays an ethnic group as being more homogeneous than it really is.   67

ethnic identity An enduring, basic aspect of the self that includes a sense of membership in an ethnic group and the attitudes and feelings related to that membership.   401

ethnicity A characteristic based on cultural heritage, nationality characteristics, race, religion, and language.   12

ethology Stresses that behavior is strongly influenced by biology, is tied to evolution, and is characterized by critical or sensitive periods.   50

euthanasia The act of painlessly ending the lives of persons who are suffering from incurable diseases or severe disabilities; sometimes called *mercy killing*.   635

evocative genotype-environment correlations Correlations that exist when the child's characteristics elicit certain types of environments.   96

evolutionary psychology Emphasizes the importance of adaptation, reproduction, and "survival of the fittest" in shaping behavior.   78

experiment A carefully regulated procedure in which one or more of the factors believed to influence the behavior being studied are manipulated while all other factors are held constant.   59

explicit memory Memory of facts and experiences that individuals consciously know and can state.   182, 586

Family at midlife The fifth stage in the family life cycle, a time of launching children, linking generations, and adapting to midlife developmental changes.   480

family in later life The sixth and final stage in the family life cycle, involving retirement and, in many families, grandparenting.   480

family with adolescents The fourth stage of the family life cycle, in which adolescent children push for autonomy and seek to develop their own identities.   479

fertilization A stage in the reproduction process whereby an egg and a sperm fuse to create a single cell, called a zygote.   82

fetal alcohol syndrome (FAS) A cluster of abnormalities that appears in the offspring of mothers who drink alcohol heavily during pregnancy.   111

fetal period The prenatal period of development that begins two months after conception and lasts for seven months, on average.   106

fine motor skills Motor skills that involve more finely tuned movements, such as finger dexterity.   156

first habits and primary circular reactions Piaget's second sensorimotor substage, which develops between 1 and 4 months of age. In this substage, infants' reflexes evolve into adaptive schemes that are more refined and coordinated.   175

fluid intelligence The ability to reason abstractly, which steadily declines from middle adulthood on, according to Horn.   513

fragile X syndrome A chromosome disorder involving an abnormality in the X chromosome, which becomes constricted and often breaks.   85

free-radical theory A microbiological theory of aging that states that people age because inside their cells normal metabolism produces unstable oxygen molecules known as free radicals. These molecules ricochet around inside cells, damaging DNA and other cellular structures.   560

friendship A form of close relationship that involves enjoyment, acceptance, trust, respect, mutual assistance, confiding, understanding, and spontaneity.   473

fuzzy trace theory States that memory is best understood by considering two types of memory representations: (1) verbatim memory trace and (2) gist. In this theory, older children's better memory is attributed to the fuzzy traces created by extracting the gist of information.   305

Games Activities engaged in for pleasure that include rules and often competition with one or more individuals. 283

gender The psychological and sociocultural dimensions of being female or male. 13, 261

gender identity The sense of being male or female, which most children acquire by the time they are 3 years old. 261

gender role A set of expectations that prescribes how females or males should think, act, and feel. 261

gender schema theory The theory that an individual's attention and behavior are guided by an internal motivation to conform to gender-based sociocultural standards and stereotypes. 265

gender stereotypes Broad categories that reflect our impressions and beliefs about females and males. 339

generational inequity The view that our aging society is being unfair to its younger members because older adults pile up advantages by receiving inequitably large allocations of resources. 15, 618

genes Units of hereditary information composed of DNA. Genes direct cells to reproduce themselves and to assemble proteins. 80

genotype A person's genetic heritage; the actual genetic material. 82

germinal period The period of prenatal development that takes place in the first two weeks after conception. It includes the creation of the zygote, continued cell division, and the attachment of the zygote to the uterine wall. 105

gifted Having above-average intelligence (an IQ of 130 or higher) and/or superior talent for something. 318

glaucoma Damage to the optic nerve because of the pressure created by a buildup of fluid in the eye. 566

gonads The sex glands—the testes in males and the ovaries in females. 366

goodness of fit Refers to the match between a child's temperament and the environmental demands with which the child must cope. 207

grasping reflex A neonatal reflex that occurs when something touches the infant's palms. The infant responds by grasping tightly. 151

grief The emotional numbness, disbelief, separation anxiety, despair, sadness, and loneliness that accompany the loss of someone we love. 647

gross motor skills Motor skills that involve large-muscle activities, such as walking. 152

Habituation Decreased responsiveness to a stimulus after repeated presentation of the stimulus. 159

hardiness A personality style characterized by a sense of commitment (rather than alienation), control (rather than powerlessness), and a perception of problems as challenges (rather than threats). 508

heritability The fraction of variance in a population that is attributed to genetics and is computed using correlational techniques. 312

heteronomous morality The first stage of moral development in Piaget's theory, occurring from approximately 4 to 7 years of age. Justice and rules are conceived of as unchangeable properties of the world, removed from the control of people. 259

heteronomous morality (Kohlberg's theory) Kohlberg's first stage in preconventional reasoning in which moral thinking is tied to punishment. 334

hormonal stress theory The theory that aging in the body's hormonal system can lower resilience to stress and increase the likelihood of disease. 560

hormones Powerful chemical substances secreted by the endocrine glands and carried through the body by the bloodstream. 366

hospice A humanized program committed to making the end of life as free from pain, anxiety, and depression as possible. The goals of hospice contrast with those of a hospital, which are to cure disease and prolong life. 637

hypothalamus A structure in the higher portion of the brain that monitors eating, drinking, and sex. 366

hypotheses Specific assumptions and predictions that can be tested to determine their accuracy. 41

hypothetical-deductive reasoning Piaget's formal operational concept that adolescents have the cognitive ability to develop hypotheses, or best guesses, about ways to solve problems, such as an algebraic equation. 383

Identity achievement Marcia's term for adolescents who have undergone a crisis and have made a commitment. 399

identity diffusion Marcia's term for adolescents who have not yet experienced a crisis (explored meaningful alternatives) or made any commitments. 399

identity foreclosure Marcia's term for adolescents who have made a commitment but have not experienced a crisis. 399

identity moratorium Marcia's term for adolescents who are in the midst of a crisis, but their commitments are either absent or vaguely defined. 399

imaginary audience Involves adolescents' belief that others are as interested in them as they themselves are; attention-getting behavior motivated by a desire to be noticed, visible, and "on stage." 384

immanent justice The concept that, if a rule is broken, punishment will be meted out immediately. 260

implicit memory Memory without conscious recollection; involves skills and routine procedures that are automatically performed. 182, 586

inclusion Educating a child with special education needs full-time in the regular classroom. 300

individual differences The stable, consistent ways in which people are different from each other. 308

individualism, instrumental purpose, and exchange The second Kohlberg stage of moral development. At this stage, individuals pursue their own interests but also let others do the same. 334

individuality Individuality consists of two dimensions: self-assertion (the ability to have and communicate a point of view) and separateness (the use of communication patterns to express how one is different from others). 400

individualized education plan (IEP) A written statement that spells out a program tailored to a child with a disability. The plan should be (1) related to the child's learning capacity, (2) specially constructed to meet the child's individual needs and not merely a copy of what is offered to other children, and (3) designed to provide educational benefits. 300

indulgent parenting A style of parenting in which parents are highly involved with their children but place few demands or controls on them. Indulgent parenting is associated with children's social incompetence, especially a lack of self-control. 268

infinite generativity The ability to produce an endless number of meaningful sentences using a finite set of words and rules. 185

information-processing theory Emphasizes that individuals manipulate information, monitor it, and strategize about it. Central to this theory are the processes of memory and thinking.   47

innate goodness The idea, presented by Swiss-born philosopher Jean-Jacques Rousseau, that children are inherently good.   6

insecure avoidant babies Babies that show insecurity by avoiding the caregiver.   212

insecure disorganized babies Babies that show insecurity by being disorganized and disoriented.   213

insecure resistant babies Babies that often cling to the caregiver, then resist her by fighting against the closeness, perhaps by kicking or pushing away.   212

integrity versus despair Erikson's eighth and final stage of development, which individuals experience in late adulthood. This involves reflecting on the past and either piecing together a positive review or concluding that one's life has not been well spent.   609

intelligence Problem-solving skills and the ability to learn from and adapt to the experiences of everyday life.   308

intelligence quotient (IQ) A person's mental age divided by chronological age, multiplied by 100.   308

intermodal perception The ability to relate and integrate information from two or more sensory modalities, such as vision and hearing.   165

internalization of schemes Piaget's sixth and final sensorimotor substage, which develops between 18 and 24 months of age. In this substage, the infant's mental functioning shifts from a purely sensorimotor plane to a symbolic plane, and the infant develops the ability to use primitive symbols and form enduring mental representations.   176

intimacy in friendships Self-disclosure and the sharing of private thoughts.   346

intuitive thought substage Piaget's second substage of preoperational thought, in which children begin to use primitive reasoning and want to know the answers to all sorts of questions (between 4 and 7 years of age).   235

Justice perspective A moral perspective that focuses on the rights of the individual; individuals independently make moral decisions.   336

juvenile delinquent An adolescent who breaks the law or engages in behavior that is considered illegal.   420

Kangaroo care A way of holding a preterm infant so that there is skin-to-skin contact.   125

Klinefelter syndrome A chromosome disorder in which males have an extra X chromosome, making them XXY instead of XY.   85

kwashiorkor A condition caused by a deficiency in protein in which the child's abdomen and feet become swollen with water; usually appears between 1 to 3 years of age.   148

Laboratory A controlled setting in which many of the complex factors of the "real world" are removed.   56

language A form of communication, whether spoken, written, or signed, that is based on a system of symbols.   185

language acquisition device (LAD) Chomsky's term that describes a biological endowment that enables the child to detect the features and rules of language, including phonology, syntax, and semantics.   191

lateralization Specialization of function in one hemisphere of the cerebral cortex or the other.   141

launching The process in which youth move into adulthood and exit their family of origin.   479

learning disability Includes three components: (1) a minimum IQ level; (2) a significant difficulty in a school-related area (especially reading and/or mathematics); and (3) exclusion of only severe emotional disorders, second-language background, sensory disabilities, and/or specific neurological deficits.   289

least restrictive environment (LRE) The concept that a child with a disability must be educated in a setting that is as similar as possible to the one in which children who do not have a disability are educated.   300

leaving home and becoming a single adult The first stage in the family life cycle. It involves launching.   479

leisure The pleasant times after work when individuals are free to pursue activities and interests of their own choosing.   518

life expectancy The number of years that will probably be lived by the average person born in a particular year.   555

life-history record A record of information about a lifetime chronology of events and activities that often involve a combination of data records on education, work, family, and residence.   58

life-process model of addiction The view that addiction is not a disease but rather a habitual response and a source of gratification and security that can be understood only in the context of social relationships and experiences.   445

life span The upper boundary of life, the maximum number of years an individual can live. The maximum life span of human beings is about 120 to 125 years of age.   555

life-span perspective The perspective that development is lifelong, multidimensional, multidirectional, plastic, multidisciplinary, and contextual, and involves growth, maintenance, and regulation.   7

longitudinal approach A research strategy in which the same individuals are studied over a period of time, usually several years or more.   60

long-term memory A relatively permanent type of memory that holds huge amounts of information for a long period of time.   304

low birth weight infants Infants that weigh less than 5½ pounds at birth.   123

Macular degeneration A disease that involves deterioration of the macula of the retina, which corresponds to the focal center of the visual field.   567

major depression A mood disorder in which the individual is deeply unhappy, demoralized, self-derogatory, and bored. The person does not feel well, loses stamina easily, has poor appetite, and is listless and unmotivated. Major depression is so widespread that it has been called the "common cold" of mental disorders.   594

marasmus A wasting away of body tissues in the infant's first year, caused by severe protein-calorie deficiency.   148

matching hypothesis States that although we prefer a more attractive person in the abstract, in the real world we end up choosing someone who is close to our own level.   471

meiosis A specialized form of cell division that produces cells with only one copy of each chromosome. Meiosis forms eggs and sperm (or gametes).   82

memory A central feature of cognitive development, pertaining to all situations in which an individual retains information over time.   182

menarche A girl's first menstruation.   365

menopause The complete cessation of a woman's menstruation, which usually occurs in the late forties or early fifties. 510

mental age (MA) Binet's measure of an individual's level of mental development, compared with that of others. 308

mental retardation A condition of limited mental ability in which an individual has a low IQ, usually below 70 on a traditional test of intelligence, and has difficulty adapting to everyday life. 317

metacognition Cognition about cognition, or knowing about knowing. 307

middle adulthood The developmental period beginning at approximately 40 years of age and extending to about 60. 501

mitochondrial theory The theory that aging is caused by the decay of mitochondria, tiny cellular bodies that supply energy for function, growth, and repair. 560

mitosis Cellular reproduction in which the cell's nucleus duplicates itself with two new cells being formed, each containing the same DNA as the parent cell, arranged in the same 23 pairs of chromosomes. 82

Montessori approach An educational philosophy in which children are given considerable freedom and spontaneity in choosing activities and are allowed to move from one activity to another as they desire. 247

moral development Development that involves thoughts, feelings, and actions regarding rules and conventions about what people should do in their interactions with other people. 259

Moro reflex A neonatal startle response that occurs in reaction to a sudden, intense noise or movement. When startled, the newborn arches its back, throws its head back, and flings out its arms and legs. Then the newborn rapidly closes its arms and legs to the center of the body. 151

morphology Units of meaning involved in word formation. 186

multi-infarct dementia Sporadic and progressive loss of intellectual functioning caused by repeated temporary obstruction of blood flow in cerebral arteries. 599

mutual interpersonal expectations, relationships, and interpersonal conformity Kohlberg's third stage of moral development. At this stage, individuals value trust, caring, and loyalty to others as a basis of moral judgments. 334

myelination The process by which the nerve cells are covered and insulated with a layer of fat cells, which increases the speed at which information travels through the nervous system. 228

Natural childbirth Developed in 1914 by Dick-Read, this method attempts to reduce the mother's pain by decreasing her fear through education about childbirth and relaxation techniques during delivery. 122

naturalistic observation Observing behavior in real-world settings. 57

nature-nurture issue Refers to the debate about whether development is primarily influenced by nature or nurture. Nature refers to an organism's biological inheritance, nurture to its environmental experiences. The "nature proponents" claim biological inheritance is the most important influence on development; the "nurture proponents" claim that environmental experiences are the most important. 22

neglected children Children who are infrequently nominated as a best friend but are not disliked by their peers. 347

neglectful parenting A style of parenting in which the parent is very uninvolved in the child's life; it is associated with children's social incompetence, especially a lack of self-control. 268

neo-Piagetians Developmentalists who have elaborated on Piaget's theory, giving more emphasis to information-processing, strategies, and precise cognitive steps. 304

neuron Nerve cell that handles information processing at the cellular level. 138

new couple Forming the new couple is the second stage in the family life cycle. Two individuals from separate families of origin unite to form a new family system. 479

nonshared environmental experiences The child's own unique experiences, both within the family and outside the family, that are not shared by another sibling. Thus, experiences occurring within the family can be part of the "nonshared environment." 97

normal distribution A symmetrical distribution with most scores falling in the middle of the possible range of scores and a few scores appearing toward the extremes of the range. 308

Object permanence The Piagetian term for one of an infant's most important accomplishments: understanding that objects and events continue to exist, even when they cannot directly be seen, heard, or touched. 176

onlooker play Play in which the child watches other children play. 282

operations In Piaget's theory, internalized sets of actions that allow children to do mentally what they formerly did physically. 234

organic retardation Mental retardation that involves some physical damage and is caused by a genetic disorder or brain damage. 317

organization Piaget's concept of grouping isolated behaviors into a higher-order, more smoothly functioning cognitive system; the grouping or arranging of items into categories. 174

organogenesis Organ formation that takes place during the first two months of prenatal development. 106

original sin The view that children were basically bad and born into the world as evil beings. 6

osteoporosis A chronic condition that involves an extensive loss of bone tissue and is the main reason many older adults walk with a marked stoop. Women are especially vulnerable to osteoporosis. 571

Pain cry A sudden appearance of loud crying without preliminary moaning, followed by breath holding. 203

palliative care Emphasized in hospice care, involves reducing pain and suffering and helping individuals die with dignity. 637

parallel play Play in which the child plays separately from others, but with toys like those the others are using or in a manner that mimics their play. 282

Parkinson disease A chronic, progressive disease characterized by muscle tremors, slowing of movement, and partial facial paralysis. 599

passive euthanasia The withholding of available treatments, such as life-sustaining devices, allowing the person to die. 635

passive genotype-environment correlations Correlations that exist when the natural parents, who are genetically related to the child, provide a rearing environment for the child. 96

perception The interpretation of what is sensed. 157

personal fable The part of adolescent egocentrism that involves an adolescent's sense of uniqueness and invincibility. 384

personality type theory John Holland's view that it is important for individuals to select a career that matches up well with their personality type.   455

phenotype The way an individual's genotype is expressed in observed and measurable characteristics.   82

phenylketonuria (PKU) A genetic disorder in which an individual cannot properly metabolize phenylalanine, an amino acid. PKU is now easily detected but, if left untreated, results in mental retardation and hyperactivity.   86

phonology The sound system of the language, including the sounds that are used and how they may be combined.   186

Piaget's theory States that children actively construct their understanding of the world and go through four stages of cognitive development.   45

pituitary gland An important endocrine gland that controls growth and regulates other glands.   366

placenta A disk-shaped group of tissues in which small blood vessels from the mother and offspring intertwine but do not join.   105

pluralism The coexistence of distinct ethnic and cultural groups in the same society. Individuals with a pluralistic stance usually advocate that cultural differences be maintained and appreciated.   418

popular children Children who are frequently nominated as a best friend and are rarely disliked by their peers.   347

postconventional reasoning The highest level in Kohlberg's theory of moral development. At this level, the individual recognizes alternative moral courses, explores the options, and then decides on a personal moral code.   334

postformal thought A form of thought that is qualitatively different from Piaget's formal operational thought. It involves understanding that the correct answer to a problem can require reflective thinking, that the correct answer can vary from one situation to another, and that the search for truth is often an ongoing, neverending process. It also involves the belief that solutions to problems need to be realistic and that emotion and subjective factors can influence thinking.   452

postpartum depression Characteristic of women who have such strong feelings of sadness, anxiety, or despair that they have trouble coping with daily tasks in the postpartum period.   129

postpartum period The period after childbirth when the mother adjusts, both physically and psychologically, to the

process of childbirth. This period lasts for about six weeks or until her body has completed its adjustment and returned to a near prepregnant state.   128

practice play Play that involves repetition of behavior when new skills are being learned or when physical or mental mastery and coordination of skills are required for games or sports.   283

pragmatics The appropriate use of language in different contexts.   187

preconventional reasoning The lowest level in Kohlberg's theory of moral development. The individual's moral reasoning is controlled primarily by external rewards and punishment.   334

prepared childbirth Developed by French obstetrician Ferdinand Lamaze, this childbirth strategy is similar to natural childbirth but includes a special breathing technique to control pushing in the final stages of labor and a more detailed anatomy and physiology course.   122

pretense/symbolic play Play in which the child transforms the physical environment into a symbol.   283

preterm infants Infants born three weeks or more before the pregnancy has reached its full term.   123

primary emotions Emotions that are present in humans and other animals, including surprise, joy, anger, sadness, fear, and disgust; appear in first six to eight months of life.   202

Project Head Start A government-funded program that is designed to provide children from low-income families the opportunity to acquire the skills and experiences important for school success.   248

prospective memory Involves remembering to do something in the future.   586

proximodistal pattern The sequence in which growth starts at the center of the body and moves toward the extremities.   138

psychoanalytic theory Describes development as primarily unconscious and heavily colored by emotion. Behavior is merely a surface characteristic and the symbolic workings of the mind have to be analyzed to understand behavior. Early experiences with parents are emphasized.   42

psychoanalytic theory of gender A theory deriving from Freud's view that the preschool child develops a sexual attraction to the opposite-sex parent, by approximately 5 or 6 years of age renounces this attraction because of anxious feelings, and subsequently identifies with the same-sex parent, uncon-

sciously adopting the same-sex parent's characteristics.   263

psychological age An individual's adaptive capacities compared with those of other individuals of the same chronological age.   21

puberty A period of rapid physical and sexual maturation that occurs mainly during early adolescence.   365

Rape Forcible sexual intercourse with a person who does not consent to it.   449

reciprocal socialization Socialization that is bidirectional; children socialize parents, just as parents socialize children.   216

reflexive smile A smile that does not occur in response to external stimuli. It happens during the month after birth, usually during sleep.   203

rejected children Children who are infrequently nominated as a best friend and are actively disliked by their peers.   347

restrained eaters Individuals who chronically restrict their food intake to control their weight. Restrained eaters are often on diets, are very conscious of what they eat, and tend to feel guilty after splurging on sweets.   440

rite of passage A ceremony or ritual that marks an individual's transition from one status to another. Most rites of passage focus on the transition to adult status.   415

romantic love Also called passionate love, or eros, romantic love has strong sexual and infatuation components and often predominates in the early period of a love relationship.   474

rooting reflex A newborn's built-in reaction that occurs when the infant's cheek is stroked or the side of the mouth is touched. In response, the infant turns his or her head toward the side that was touched, in an apparent effort to find something to suck.   151

Scaffolding Parents time interactions so that infants experience turn-taking with the parents.   216

schemes In Piaget's theory, actions or mental representations that organize knowledge.   173

secondary circular reactions Piaget's third sensorimotor substage, which develops between 4 and 8 months of age. In this substage, the infant becomes more object-oriented, or focused on the world, moving beyond preoccupation with the self in sensorimotor interactions.   176

securely attached babies Babies that use the caregiver as a secure base from which to explore the environment. 212

selective attention Focusing on a specific aspect of experience that is relevant while ignoring others that are irrelevant. 584

selective optimization with compensation theory The theory that successful aging is related to three main factors: selection, optimization, and compensation. 613

self-concept Domain-specific evaluations of the self. 329

self-conscious emotions Emotions that require cognition, especially consciousness; include empathy, jealousy, embarrassment, pride, shame, and guilt; appear for the first time from the middle of the second year through the middle of the third year of life. 202

self-esteem The global evaluative dimension of the self. Self-esteem is also referred to as self-worth or self-image. 329

self-understanding The child's cognitive representation of self, the substance and content of the child's self-conceptions. 257

semantic memory A person's knowledge about the world—including a person's fields of expertise, general academic knowledge of the sort learned in school, and "everyday knowledge." 585

semantics The meaning of words and sentences. 187

sensation The product of the interaction between information and the sensory receptors—the eyes, ears, tongue, nostrils, and skin. 157

sensorimotor play Behavior engaged in by infants to derive pleasure from exercising their existing sensorimotor schemas. 282

sensorimotor stage The first of Piaget's stages, which lasts from birth to about 2 years of age; infants construct an understanding of the world by coordinating sensory experiences (such as seeing and hearing) with motoric actions. 174

separation anxiety An infant's distressed reaction when the caregiver leaves. 204

sequential approach A combined cross-sectional, longitudinal design. 61

seriation The concrete operation that involves ordering stimuli along a quantitative dimension (such as length). 302

service learning A form of education that promotes social responsibility and service to the community. 390

sexually transmitted infections (STIs) Infections that are contracted primarily through sexual contact, which is not limited to sexual intercourse. Oral-genital and anal-genital contact also can transmit STIs. 372, 447

shape constancy The recognition that an object's shape remains the same even though its orientation to us changes. 162

shared environmental experiences Siblings' common environmental experiences, such as their parents' personalities and intellectual orientation, the family's socioeconomic status, and the neighborhood in which they live. 97

short-term memory The memory component in which individuals retain information for up to 30 seconds, assuming there is no rehearsal of the information. 241

sickle-cell anemia A genetic disorder that affects the red blood cells and occurs most often in people of African descent. 87

simple reflexes Piaget's first sensorimotor substage, which corresponds to the first month after birth. In this substage, the basic means of coordinating sensation and action is through reflexive behaviors, such as rooting and sucking, which the infant has at birth. 175

size constancy The recognition that an object remains the same even though the retinal image of the object changes. 162

slow-to-warm-up child A child who has a low activity level, is somewhat negative, and displays a low intensity of mood. 205

small for date infants Also called small for gestational age infants, these infants' birth weights are below normal when the length of pregnancy is considered. Small for date infants may be preterm or full term. 123

social age Social roles and expectations related to a person's age. 21

social clock The timetable according to which individuals are expected to accomplish life's tasks, such as getting married, having children, or establishing themselves in a career. 534

social cognitive theory The view of psychologists who emphasize behavior, environment, and cognition as the key factors in development. 49

social cognitive theory of gender A theory that emphasizes that children's gender development occurs through the observation and imitation of gender behavior and through the rewards and punishments children experience for gender-appropriate and gender-inappropriate behavior. 263

social constructivist approach An approach that emphasizes the social contexts of learning and that knowledge is mutually built and constructed. Vygotsky's theory reflects this approach. 239

social contract or utility and individual rights The fifth Kohlberg stage. At this stage, individuals reason that values, rights, and principles undergird or transcend the law. 334

social conventional reasoning Thoughts about social consensus and convention, as opposed to moral reasoning that stresses ethical issues. 337

social play Play that involves social interactions with peers. 283

social policy A national government's course of action designed to promote the welfare of its citizens. 14

social referencing "Reading" emotional cues in others to help determine how to act in a particular situation. 204

social role theory A theory that gender differences result from the contrasting roles of men and women. 263

social smile A smile in response to an external stimulus, which, early in development, typically is a face. 203

social systems morality The fourth stage in Kohlberg's theory of moral development. Moral judgments are based on understanding the social order, law, justice, and duty. 334

socioeconomic status (SES) Refers to the grouping of people with similar occupational, educational, and economic characteristics. 12

socioemotional processes Changes in an individual's relationships with other people, emotions, and personality. 17

socioemotional selectivity theory The theory that older adults become more selective about their social networks. Because they place a high value on emotional satisfaction, older adults often spend more time with familiar individuals with whom they have had rewarding relationships. 612

solitary play Play in which the child plays alone and independently of others. 281

source memory The ability to remember where one learned something. 586

stability-change issue Involves the degree to which we become older renditions of our early experience (stability) or whether we develop into someone different from who we were at an earlier point in development (change). 23

standardized test A test with uniform procedures for administration and scoring. Many standardized tests allow a person's performance to be compared with the performance of other individuals. 57

stereotype threat The anxiety that one's behavior might confirm a negative stereotype about one's group. 315

Strange Situation An observational measure of infant attachment that requires the infant to move through a series of introductions, separations, and reunions with the caregiver and an adult stranger in a prescribed order. 211

stranger anxiety An infant's fear and wariness of strangers; it tends to appear in the second half of the first year of life. 203

strategies Cognitive processes that do not occur automatically but require work and effort. These processes are under the learner's conscious control and can be used to improve memory. They are also called *control processes.* 305

sucking reflex A newborn's built-in reaction to automatically suck an object placed in its mouth. The sucking reflex enables the infant to get nourishment before he or she has associated a nipple with food. 151

sudden infant death syndrome (SIDS) A condition that occurs when an infant stops breathing, usually during the night, and suddenly dies without an apparent cause. 144

sustained attention The state of readiness to detect and respond to small changes occurring at random times in the environment. 584

symbolic function substage Piaget's first substage of preoperational thought, in which the child gains the ability to mentally represent an object that is not present (between 2 and 4 years of age). 234

syntax The ways words are combined to form acceptable phrases and sentences. 186

Tabula rasa The idea, proposed by John Locke, that children are like a "blank tablet." 6

telegraphic speech The use of short and precise words without grammatical markers such as articles, auxiliary verbs, and other connectives. 190

temperament An individual's behavioral style and characteristic way of emotionally responding. 205

teratogen From the Greek word *tera,* meaning "monster." Any agent that causes a birth defect. The field of study that investigates the causes of birth defects is called teratology. 109

tertiary circular reactions, novelty, and curiosity Piaget's fifth sensorimotor substage, which develops between 12 and 18 months of age. In this substage, infants become intrigued by the variety of properties that objects possess and by the multiplicity of things they can make happen to objects. 176

theory An interrelated, coherent set of ideas that helps to explain and make predictions. 41

theory of mind Refers to the awareness of one's own mental processes and the mental processes of others. 244

top-dog phenomenon The circumstance of moving from the top position in elementary school to the lowest position in middle or junior high school. 387

transitivity The ability to logically combine relations to understand certain conclusions. 302

triarchic theory of intelligence Sternberg's theory that intelligence consists of analytical intelligence, creative intelligence, and practical intelligence. 310

trophoblast An outer layer of cells that develops in the germinal period. These cells will become part of the placenta. 105

Turner syndrome A chromosome disorder in females in which either an X chromosome is missing, making the person XO instead of XX, or the second X chromosome is partially deleted. 86

twin study A study in which the behavioral similarity of identical twins is compared with the behavioral similarity of fraternal twins. 94

Type A behavior pattern A cluster of characteristics—being excessively competitive, hard-driven, impatient, and hostile—thought to be related to the incidence of heart disease. 508

Type B behavior pattern Being primarily calm and easygoing. 508

Umbilical cord Contains two arteries and one vein; connects the baby to the placenta. 106

universal ethical principles The sixth and highest stage in Kohlberg's theory of moral development. Individuals develop a moral standard based on universal human rights. 334

unoccupied play Play in which the child is not engaging in play as it is commonly understood and might stand in one spot, or perform random movements that do not seem to have a goal. 281

Visual preference method A method used to determine whether infants can distinguish one stimulus from another by measuring the length of time they attend to different stimuli. 159

Vygotsky's theory A sociocultural cognitive theory that emphasizes how culture and social interaction guide cognitive development. 47

Wernicke's area An area of the brain's left hemisphere that is involved in language comprehension. 191

whole-language approach An approach to reading instruction based on the idea that instruction should parallel children's natural language learning. Reading materials should be whole and meaningful. 320

wisdom Expert knowledge about the practical aspects of life that permits excellent judgment about important matters. 587

working memory Closely related to short-term memory but places more emphasis on mental work. Working memory is like a "workbench" where individuals can manipulate and assemble information when making decisions, solving problems, and comprehending written and spoken language. 515

XYY syndrome A chromosome disorder in which males have an extra Y chromosome. 86

Zone of proximal development (ZPD) Vygotsky's term for tasks too difficult for children to master alone but that can be mastered with assistance. 237

zygote A single cell formed through fertilization. 82

References

AARP (2004). *The divorce experience: A study of divorce at midlife and beyond.* Washington, DC: Author.

Abbassi, V. (1998). Growth and normal puberty. *Pediatrics (Suppl.), 102,* 507–511.

Abbott, A. (2003). Restless nights, listless days. *Nature, 425,* 896–898.

Abbott, R. D., White, L. R., Ross, G. W., Masaki, K. M., Cub, J. D., & Petrovitch, H. (2004). Walking and dementia in physically capable elderly men. *Journal of the American Medical Association, 292,* 1147–1453.

Abel, E. L., Kruger, M., & Burd, L. (2002). Effects of maternal and paternal age on Caucasian and Native American preterm births and birth weights. *American Journal of Perinatology, 19,* 49–54.

Aboud, F., & Skerry, S. (1983). Self and ethnic concepts in relation to ethnic constancy. *Canadian Journal of Behavioral Science, 15,* 3–34.

Acebo, C., & Carskadon, M. A. (2002). Influence of irregular sleep patterns on waking behavior. In M. A. Carskadon (Ed.), *Adolescent sleep patterns.* New York: Cambridge University Press.

Acredolo, I. P., & Hake, J. L. (1982). Infant perception. In B. B. Wolman (Ed.), *Handbook of developmental psychology.* Englewood Cliffs, NJ: Prentice Hall.

Adamolekun, K. (2001). Survivors' motives for extravagant funerals among the Yorubas of western Nigeria. *Death Studies, 25,* 609–619.

Adams, C. A. (2003). *ABCs of grief: A handbook for survivors.* Amityville, NY: Baywood.

Adams, R. J. (1989). Newborns' discrimination among mid- and long-wavelength stimuli. *Journal of Experimental Child Psychology, 47,* 130–141.

Adams, R., & Laursen, B. (2001). The organization of adolescent conflict with parents and friends. *Journal of Marriage and the Family, 63,* 97–110.

Adams-Curtis, L. E., & Forbes, G. B. (2004). College women's experiences of sexual coercion: A review of cultural, perpetrator, victim, and situational variables. *Trauma, Violence, and Abuse, 5,* 91–122.

Adamson, H. D. (2004). *Language minority students in American schools.* Mahwah, NJ: Erlbaum.

Addis, A., Magrini, N., & Mastroiacovo, P. (2001). Drug use during pregnancy. *Lancet, 357,* 800.

Adler, S. A., & Haith, M. M. (2003). The nature of infants' visual expectations for event content. *Infancy, 4,* 389–411.

Adler, T. (1991, January). Seeing double? Controversial twins study is widely reported, debated. *APA Monitor, 22,* 1, 8.

Adolph, K. E. (1997). Learning in the development of infant locomotion. *Monographs of the Society for Research in Child Development, 62* (3, Serial No. 251).

Adolph, K. E. (2002). Babies' steps make giant strides toward a science of development. *Infant Behavior and Development, 25,* 86–90.

Adolph, K. E. (2005). Learning to learn in the development of action. In J. J. Reiser, J. J. Lockman, & C. E. Nelson (Eds.), *The role of action in learning and development.* Mahwah, NJ: Erlbaum.

Adolph, K. E., & Avolio, A. M. (2000). Walking infants adapt locomotion to changing body dimensions. *Journal of Experimental Psychology: Human Perception and Performance, 26,* 1148–1166.

Adolph, K. E., Vereijken, B., & Shrout, P. E. (2003). What changes in infant walking and why. *Child Development, 74,* 475–497.

Adolph, K. E., Weise, I., & Marin, L. (2003). Motor development. In L. Nadel (Ed.), *The encyclopedia of cognitive science.* London: Macmillan Reference Ltd.

Agras, W. S., & others. (2004). Report of the National Institutes of Health workshop on overcoming barriers to treatment research in anorexia nervosa. *International Journal of Eating Disorders, 35,* 509–521.

Agviar, A., & Baillargeon, R. (2002). Developments in young infants' reasoning about occluded objects. *Cognitive Psychology, 45,* 263–336.

Ahluwalia, I. B., Tessaro, I., Grumer-Strawn, L. M., MacGowan, C., & Benton-Davis, S. (2000). Georgia's breastfeeding promotion program for low-income women. *Pediatrics, 105,* E85–E87.

Ahn, N. (1994). Teenage childbearing and high school completion: Accounting for individual heterogeneity. *Family Planning Perspectives, 26,* 17–21.

Ahrons, C. (2004). *We're still family.* New York: Harper Collins.

Aiken, L. (2000). *Dying, death, and bereavement* (4th ed.). Mahwah, NJ: Erlbaum.

Aiken, L. R. (2003). *Psychological testing and assessment* (11th ed.). Boston: Allyn & Bacon.

Ainsworth, M. D. S. (1979). Infant-mother attachment. *American Psychologist, 34,* 932–937.

Aitken, M. E., Graham, C. J., Killingsworth, J. B., Mullins, S. H., Parnell, D. N., & Dick, R. M. (2004). All-terrain injury in children: Strategies for prevention. *Injury Prevention, 10,* 180–185.

Akhter, M. N., & Levinson, R. A. (2003). Eliminating health disparities associated with long-term care to promote graceful aging in place. *Care Management Journal, 4,* 88–93.

Akiyama, H., & Antonucci, T. C. (1999, November). *Mother-daughter dynamics over the life course.* Paper presented at the meeting of the Gerontological Association of America, San Francisco.

Alan Guttmacher Institute (1998). *Teen sex and pregnancy.* New York: Alan Guttmacher Institute.

Aldwin, C. M., & Levenson, M. R. (2001). Stress, coping, and health at midlife: A developmental perspective. In M. E. Lachman (Ed.), *Handbook of midlife development.* New York: John Wiley.

Aldwin, C. M., Spiro, A., Levenson, M. R., & Cupertino, A. P. (2001). Longitudinal findings from the Normative Aging Study: III. Personality, individual health trajectories, and mortality. *Psychology and Aging, 16,* 450–465.

Alemayehu, B., & Warner, K. E. (2004). The lifetime distribution of health care costs. *Health Services Resources, 39,* 627–642.

Alexander, G. R., Kogan, M. D., & Nabukera, S. (2002). Racial differences in prenatal care use in the United States: Are disparities increasing? *American Journal of Public Health, 92,* 1970–1975.

Allan, R., & Scheidt, S. (Eds.). (1996). *Heart and mind.* Washington, DC: American Psychological Association.

Allen, J. P., & others. (2002). Attachment and autonomy as predictors of the development of social skills and deviance during mid-adolescence. *Journal of Consulting & Clinical Psychology, 70,* 56–66.

Allen, J. P., Hauser, S. T., & Borman-Spurrell, E. (1996). Attachment security and related sequelae of severe adolescent psychopathology: An eleven-year follow-up study. *Journal of Consulting and Clinical Psychology, 64,* 254–263.

Allen, J. P., McElhaney, K. B., Land, D. J., Kuperminc, G. P., Moore, C. W., O-Beirne-Kelly, H., & Kilmer, S. L. (2003). A secure base in adolescence: Markers of attachment security in the mother-adolescent relationship. *Child Development, 74,* 292–307.

Allen, J. P., Moore, C., Kuperminc, G., & Bell, K. (1998). Attachment and adolescent psychosocial functioning. *Child Development, 69,* 1406–1419.

Allen, K. R., Blieszner, R., & Roberto, K. A. (2000). Families in the middle and later years: A review and critique of research in the 1990s. *Journal of Marriage and the Family, 62,* 911–926.

Allen, K. R., Blieszner, R., Roberto, K. A., Farnsworth, E., & Wilcox, K. L. (1999). Older adults and their children: Family patterns of structural diversity. *Family Relations, 48,* 151–157.

Allen, M., Brown, P., & Finlay, B. (1992). *Helping children by strengthening families.* Washington, DC: Children's Defense Fund.

Almeida, D., & Horn, M. (2004). Is daily life more stressful during middle adulthood? In G. Brim, C. D. Ryff, & R. Kessler (Eds.), *How healthy we are: A national study of well-being in midlife.* Chicago: University of Chicago Press.

Alpha-Tocopherol, Beta-Carotene Cancer Prevention Study Group (1994). The effect of Vitamin E and beta-carotene on the incidence of lung cancer and other cancers in non-smokers. *New England Journal of Medicine, 330,* 1029–1035.

Al-Sendi, A. M., Sherry, P., Musaiger, A. O., & Myatt, M. (2003). Relationship between body composition and blood pressure in Bahaini adolescents. *British Journal of Nursing, 90,* 837–844.

Alvarez, M. (2004). Caregiving and early infant crying in a Danish community. *Journal of Developmental and Behavioral Pediatrics, 25,* 91–98.

Amabile, T. M. (1993). Commentary. In D. Goleman, P. Kaufman, & M. Ray, *The creative spirit.* New York: Plume.

Amabile, T. M., & Hennesey, B. A. (1992). The motivation for creativity in children. In A. K. Boggiano & T. S. Pittman (Eds.), *Achievement and motivation.* New York: Cambridge.

Amato, P. (2004). Divorce in social and historical context. In M. Coleman & L. Ganong (Eds.), *Handbook of contemporary families.* Thousand Oaks, CA: Sage.

Amato, P. (2004). To have and have not: Marriage and divorce in the United States. In M. Coleman & L. Ganong (Eds.), *Handbook of contemporary families.* Thousand Oaks, CA: Sage.

Amato, P. R. (2000). The consequences of divorce for adults and children. *Journal of Marriage and the Family, 62,* 1269–1287.

Amato, P. R., & Booth, A. (1996). A prospective study of divorce and parent-child relationships. *Journal of Marriage and the Family, 58,* 356–365.

Ambrosio, J. (2004). No child left behind. *Phi Delta Kappan, 85,* 709–711.

American Academy of Pediatrics Task Force on Infant Positioning and SIDS (AAPTFIPS) (2000). Changing concepts of sudden infant death syndrome. *Pediatrics, 105,* 650–656.

American Academy of Pediatrics Work Group on Breastfeeding (AAPWGB) (1997). Breastfeeding and the use of human milk. *Pediatrics, 100,* 1035–1039.

American Academy of Pediatrics (2001). *Toilet training.* Available on the Internet at: www.aap.org/family./toil.htm.

American Association of Retired Persons (2002). *Tracking Study of the Baby Boomers in Midlife.* Washington, DC: Author.

American Psychological Association (2003). *Psychology: Scientific problem solvers.* Washington, DC: Author.

Ames, B. N. (2004). Mitochondrial decay, a major cause of aging can be delayed. *Journal of Alzheimer's Disease, 6,* 117–121.

Amsterdam, B. K. (1968). *Mirror behavior in children under two years of age.* Unpublished doctoral dissertation, University of North Carolina, Chapel Hill.

Anantharaju, A., Feller, A., & Chedid, A. (2002). Aging liver: A review. *Gerontology, 48,* 343–348.

Anastasi, A., & Urbina, S. (1996). *Psychological testing* (7th ed.). Upper Saddle River, NJ: Prentice Hall.

Anderson, C. A., Berkowitz, L., Donnerstein, E., Huesmann, L. R., Johnson, J. D., Linz, D., Malamuth, N. M., & Wartella, A. (2003). The influence of media violence on youth. *Psychological Science in the Public Interest, 4,* 81–110.

Anderson, C. A., & Bushman, B. J. (2001). Effects of violent video games on aggressive behavior, aggressive cognition, aggressive affect, physiological arousal, and prosocial behavior: A meta-analytic review of the scientific literature. *Psychological Science, 12,* 353–359.

Anderson, C. A., & Dill, K. E. (2000). Video games and aggressive thoughts, feelings, and behavior in the laboratory and in life. *Journal of Personality and Social Psychology, 78,* 772–790.

Anderson, D. R., Huston, A. C., Schmitt, K., Linebarger, D. L., & Wright, J. C. (2001). Early childhood viewing and adolescent behavior: The recontact study. *Monographs of the Society for Research in Child Development, 66* (1, Serial No. 264).

Anderson, D. R., Lorch, E. P., Field, D. E., Collins, P. A., & Nathan, J. G. (1985, April). *Television viewing at home: Age trends in visual attention and time with TV.* Paper presented at the biennial meeting of the Society for Research in Child Development, Toronto.

Anderson, E., Greene, S. M., Hetherington, E. M., & Clingempeel, W. G. (1999). The dynamics of parental remarriage. In E. M. Hetherington (Ed.), *Coping with divorce, single parenting, and remarriage.* Mahwah, NJ: Erlbaum.

Anderton, B. H. (2002). Aging of the brain. *Mechanisms of Aging and Development, 123,* 811–817.

Andrade, S. E., Gurwitz, J. H., Davis, R. L., Chan, K. A., Finkelstein, J. A., Fortman, K., McPhillips, H., Raebel, M. A., Roblin, D., Smith, D. H., Yood, M. U., Morse, A. N., & Platt, R. (2004). Prescription drug use in pregnancy. *American Journal of Obstetrics and Gynecology, 191,* 398–407.

Angel, J. L., Douglas, N., & Angel, R. J. (2003). Gender, widowhood, and long-term care in the older Mexican population. *Journal of Women and Aging, 15,* 89–105.

Angel, R. J., Frisco, M., Angel, J. L., & Chiriboga, D. A. (2004). Financial strain and health among elderly Mexican-origin individuals. *Journal of Health and Social Behavior, 44,* 536–551.

Angus, D. C., & others. (2004). Use of intensive care at the end of life in the United States: An epidemiologic study. *Critical Care Medicine, 32,* 638–643.

Anstey, K. J., & Smith, G. A. (1999). Interrelationships among biological markers of aging, health, activity, acculturation, and cognitive performance in late adulthood. *Psychology and Aging, 14,* 605–618.

Antelmi, I., de Paula, R. S., Shinzato, A. R., Peres, C. A., Mansur, A. J., & Grupi, C. J. (2004). Influence of age, gender, body mass index, and functional capacity heart rate variability in a cohort of subjects without heart disease. *American Journal of Cardiology, 93,* 381–385.

Anthony Greenwald & Associates (2000). *Current views toward retirement: A poll.* New York: Author.

Antonucci, T. C. (1989). Understanding adult social relationships. In K. Kreppner & R. M. Lerner (Eds.), *Family systems and life-span development.* Hillsdale, NJ: Erlbaum.

Antonucci, T. C. (1990). Social supports and relationships. In R. H. Binstock & L. K. George (Eds.), *Handbook of aging and the social sciences.* San Diego: Academic Press.

Antonucci, T. C. (2004). Unpublished review of J. W. Santrock's *Life-span development* (10th ed.). New York: McGraw-Hill.

Antonucci, T. C., & Akiyama, H. (2002). Aging and close relationships over the life span. *International Society for the Study of Behavioural Development Newsletter* (1, Serial No. 41), 2–5.

Antonucci, T. C., Lansford, J. E., & Akiyama, H. (2001). The impact of positive and negative aspects of marital relationships and friendships on the well-being of older adults. In J. P. Reinhardt (Ed.), *Negative and positive support.* Mahwah, NJ: Erlbaum.

Antonucci, T. C., Lansford, J. E., Schaabeg, L., Smith, J., Baltes, M., Akiyama, H., Takahashi, K., & Fuhrer, R. (2001). Widowhood and illness: A comparison of social network characteristics in France, Germany, Japan, and the United States. *Psychology and Aging, 16,* 655–665.

Antonucci, T. C., Vandewater, E. A., & Lansford, J. E. (1998). Extended family relationships. In H. S. Friedman (Ed.), *Encyclopedia of mental health* (Vol. 2). San Diego: Academic Press.

Antonucci, T. C., Vandewater, E. A., & Lansford, J. E. (2000). Adulthood and aging: Social processes and development. In A. Kazdin (Ed.), *Encyclopedia of psychology.* Washington, DC, & New York: American Psychological Association and Oxford University Press.

Arai, M. (2004). Japan. In K. Malley-Morrison (Ed.), *International perspectives on family violence and abuse.* Mahwah, NJ: Erlbaum.

Arbuckle, T. Y., Maag, U., Pushkar, D., & Chalkelsen, J. S. (1998). Individual differences in trajectory of intellectual development over 45 years of adulthood. *Psychology and Aging, 13,* 663–675.

Archer, S. L. (Ed.). (1994). *Intervention for adolescent identity development.* Newbury Park, CA: Sage.

Archibald, A. B., Graber, J. A., & Brooks-Gunn, J. (1999). Associations among parent-adolescent relationships, pubertal growth, dieting, and body image in young adolescent girls: A short-term longitudinal study. *Journal of Research on Adolescence, 9,* 395–415.

Archibald, A. B., Graber, J. A., & Brooks-Gunn, J. (2003). Pubertal processes and physical growth in adolescence. In G. R. Adams & M. Berzonsky (Eds.), *Handbook on adolescence.* Malden, MA: Blackwell.

Ardelt, M. (2003). Physician-assisted suicide. In C. D. Bryant (Ed.), *Handbook of death and dying.* Thousand Oaks, CA: Sage.

Arendt, R., Angelopoulos, J., Salvator, A., & Singer, L. (1999). Motor development of cocaine-exposed children at age two years. *Pediatrics, 103,* 86–92.

Arias, I. (2004). The legacy of child maltreatment: Long-term health consequences for women. *Journal of Women's Health, 13,* 468–473.

Arima, A. N. (2003). Gender stereotypes in Japanese television advertisements. *Sex Roles, 49,* 81–90.

Ariza, A. J., Greenberg, R. S., & Unger, R. (2004). Childhood overweight. *Pediatric Annals, 33,* 33–38.

Arnett, J. J. (1995, March). *Are college students adults?* Paper presented at the meeting of the Society for Research in Child Development, Indianapolis.

Arnett, J. J. (2000). Emerging adulthood. *American Psychologist, 55,* 469–480.

Arnett, J. J. (2004). *Emerging adulthood.* New York: Oxford U. Press.

Aronson, E. (1986, August). *Teaching students things they think they already know about: The case of prejudice and desegregation.* Paper presented at the meeting of the American Psychological Association, Washington, DC.

Aronson, J. (2002). Stereotype threat: Contending and coping with unnerving expectations. In J. Aronson (Ed.), *Improving academic achievement.* San Diego: Academic Press.

Aronson, J., Fried, C. B., & Good, C. (2002). Reducing the effects of stereotype threat on African American college students by shaping theories of intelligence. *Journal of Experimental Social Psychology, 38,* 113–125.

Aronson, J. M., Lustina, M. J., Good, C., Keough, K., Steele, C. M., & Brown, J. (1999). When white men can't do math: Necessary and sufficient factors in stereotype threat. *Journal of Experimental Social Psychology, 35,* 29–46.

Arpanantikul, M. (2004). Midlife experiences of Thai women. *Journal of Advanced Nursing, 47,* 49–56.

Arshad, S. H. (2001). Food allergen avoidance in primary prevention of food allergy. *Allergy, 56,* 113–116.

Asher, J., & Garcia, R. (1969). The optimal age to learn a foreign language. *Modern Language Journal, 53,* 334–341.

Ashmead, G. G. (2003). Smoking and pregnancy. *Journal of Maternal, Fetal, and Neonatal Medicine, 14,* 297–304.

Ashy, M. A. (2004). Saudi Arabia. In K. Malley-Morrison (Ed.), *International perspectives on family violence and abuse.* Mahwah, NJ: Erlbaum.

Aslin, R. N., Jusczyk, P. W., & Pisoni, D. B. (1998). Speech and auditory processing during infancy: Constraints on and precursors to language. In W. Damon (Ed.), *Handbook of child psychology* (5th ed., Vol. 2). New York: Wiley.

Astin, A. W. (1993). *What matters in college.* San Francisco: Jossey-Bass.

Atinmo, T., & Oyewole, D. (2004). Finding solutions to the nutritional dilemmas in Africa for child health: HIV/AIDS orphans, poverty, and hunger. *Asian Pacific Journal of Clinical Nutrition, 13* (Supplement), S6.

Atkins, R. C. (1997). *Dr. Atkins' NEW diet revolution.* New York: Avon.

Atkinson, L., & Goldberg, S. (2003). Clinical application of attachment. In L. Atkinson & S. Goldberg (Eds.), *Attachment issues in psychopathology and intervention.* Mahwah, NJ: Erlbaum.

Atkinson, L., & Goldberg, S. (Eds.) (2004). *Attachment issues in psychopathology and intervention.* Mahwah, NJ: Erlbaum.

Atkinson, R. (1988). *The teenage world: Adolescent self-image in ten countries.* New York: Plenum Press.

Atkinson, R. M., Ryan, S. C., & Turner, J. A. (2001). Variation among aging alcoholic patients in treatment. *American Journal of Geriatric Psychiatry, 9,* 275–282.

Attie, I., & Brooks-Gunn, J. (1989). Development of eating problems in adolescent girls: A longitudinal study. *Developmental Psychology, 25,* 70–79.

Attig, T. (2004). Meaning of death seen through the lens of grieving. *Death Studies, 28,* 341–360.

Auchus, R. J., & Rainey, W. E. (2004). Adrenarche—physiology, biochemistry, and human disease. *Clinical Endocrinology, 60,* 288–296.

Austin, A. A., & Chorpita, B. F. (2004). Temperament, anxiety, and depression: Comparisons across five ethnic groups of children. *Journal of Clinical Child and Adolescent Psychology, 33,* 216–226.

Avis, N. E. (1999). Women's health at midlife. In S. L. Willis & J. D. Reid (Eds.), *Life in the middle: Psychological and social development in middle age.* San Diego: Academic Press.

Avolio, B. J., & Sosik, J. J. (1999). A lifespan framework for assessing the impact of work on white-collar workers. In S. L. Willis & J. D. Reid (Eds.), *Life in the middle: Psychological and social development in middle age.* San Diego: Academic Press.

Azar, S. T. (2002). Parenting and child maltreatment. In M. H. Bornstein (Ed.), *Handbook of parenting* (2nd ed., Vol. 4). Mahwah, NJ: Erlbaum.

Azar, S. T. (2003). Adult development and parenting. In J. Demick & C. Andreoletti:

(Eds.), *Handbook of adult development.* New York: Kluwer.

Babalola, O. E., Murdoch, I. E., Cousens, S., Abiose, A., & Jones, B. (2003). Blindness: How to assess numbers and causes. *British Journal of Ophthalmology, 87,* 282–284.

Bacchini, D., & Magliulo, F. (2003). Self-image and perceived self-efficacy during adolescence. *Journal of Youth and Adolescence, 32,* 337–350.

Bachman, J. G., Johnston, L. D., O'Malley, P., & Schulenberg, J. (1996). Transitions in drug use during late adolescence and young adulthood. In J. A. Graber, J. Brooks-Gunn, & A. C. Petersen (Eds.), *Transitions through adolescence.* Mahwah, NJ: Erlbaum.

Bachman, J. G., O'Malley, P. M., Schulenberg, J., Johnston, L. D., Bryant, A. L., & Merline, A. C. (2002). *The decline of substance abuse in young adulthood.* Mahwah, NJ: Erlbaum.

Backman, L., Small, B. J., & Wahlin, A. (2001). Aging and memory: Cognitive and behavioral processes. In J. E. Birren & K. W. Schaie (Eds.), *Handbook of the psychology of aging* (5th ed.). San Diego: Academic Press.

Baddeley, A. (2000). Short-term and working memory. In E. Tulving & F. I. M. Craik (Eds.), *The Oxford handbook of memory.* New York: Oxford University Press.

Bagwell, C. L. (2004). Friendships, peer networks, and antisocial behavior. In J. B. Kupersmidt & K. A. Dodge (Eds.), *Children's peer relations.* Washington, DC: American Psychological Association.

Bahado-Singh, R. O., Choic, S. J., Oz, U., Mendilcioglu, I., Rowther, M., & Persutte, W. (2003). Early second-trimester individualized estimation of trisomy 18 risk by ultrasound. *Obstetrics and Gynecology, 101,* 463–468.

Bahrick, H. P. (1984). Semantic memory content in permastore: Fifty years of memory for Spanish learned in school. *Journal of Experimental Psychology: General, 113,* 1–35.

Bailey, B., Forget, S., & Koren, G. (2002). Pregnancy outcome of women who failed appointments at a teratogen information service clinic. *Reproductive Toxicology, 16,* 77–80.

Baillargeon, R. (1995). The object concept revisited: New directions in the investigation of infants' physical knowledge. In C. E. Granrud (Ed.), *Visual perception and cognition in infancy.* Hillsdale, NJ: Erlbaum.

Baillargeon, R. (2004). The acquisition of physical knowledge in infancy: A summary in eight lessons. In U. Goswami (Ed.), *Blackwell handbook of childhood cognitive development.* Malden, MA: Blackwell.

Baillargeon, R., & Devos, J. (1991). Object permanence in young children: Further evidence. *Child Development, 62,* 1227–1246.

Baird, A. A., Gruber, S. A., Cohen, B. M., Renshaw, R. J., & Yureglun-Todd, D. A. (1999). MRI of the amygdala in children and adolescents. *American Academy of Child and Adolescent Psychiatry, 38,* 195–199.

Bakeman, R., & Brown, J. V. (1980). Early interaction: Consequences for social and mental development at three years. *Child Development, 51,* 437–447.

Bakermans-Kranenburg, M. J., van Uzendoorn, M. H., Bokhorst, C. L., & Schuengel, C. (2004). The importance of shared environment in infant-father attachment: A behavioral genetic study of the attachment q-sort. *Journal of Family Psychology, 18,* 545–549.

Bakitas, M., Stevens, M., Ahles, T., Kirn, M., Skalla, K., Kane, N., Greenberg, E. R., & the Project Enable Co-Investigators. (2004). Project ENABLE: A palliative care demonstration project for advanced cancer patients in three settings. *Journal of Palliative Medicine, 7,* 363–372.

Baldry, A. C., & Farrington, D. P. (2004). Evaluation of an intervention program for the reduction of bullying and victimization in schools. *Aggressive Behavior, 30,* 1–15.

Baldwin, J. D., & Baldwin, J. I. (1998). Sexual behavior. In H. S. Friedman (Ed.), *Encyclopedia of mental health* (Vol. 3). San Diego: Academic Press.

Baldwin, M., & Fehr, B. (1995). On the instability of attachment ratings. *Personal Relationships, 2,* 247–261.

Baldwin, S., & Hoffman, J. P. (2002). The dynamics of self-esteem: A growth curve analysis. *Journal of Youth and Adolescence, 31,* 101–113.

Balk, D. E. (2004). Recovery following bereavement: An examination of the concept. *Death Studies, 28,* 361–373.

Balk, D., & Corr, C. (2001). Bereavement during adolescence: A review of research. In M. Stroebe, R. O. Hansson, W. Stroebe, & H. Schut (Eds.), *Handbook of bereavement research: Consequences, coping, and care.* Washington, DC: American Psychological Association.

Ball, K., & others. (2003). Effects of cognitive training interventions with older adults. *Journal of the American Medical Association, 288,* 2271–2281.

Balota, D. A., Dolan, P. O., & Ducheck, J. M. (2000). Memory changes in healthy older adults. In E. Tulving & F. I. M. Craik (Eds.), *The Oxford handbook of memory.* New York: Oxford University Press.

Baltes, P. B. (1987). Theoretical propositions of life-span developmental psychology: On the dynamics between growth and decline. *Developmental Psychology, 23,* 611–626.

Baltes, P. B. (2000). Life-span developmental theory. In A. Kazdin (Ed.), *Encyclopedia of psychology.* Washington, DC, & New York: American Psychological Association and Oxford University Press.

Baltes, P. B. (2003). On the incomplete architecture of human ontogeny: Selection, optimization, and compensation as foundation for developmental theory. In U. M. Staudinger & U. Lindenberger (Eds.), *Understanding human development.* Boston: Kluwer.

Baltes, P. B., & Baltes, M. M. (1990). Psychological perspectives on successful aging: The model of selective optimization with compensation. In P. B. Baltes & M. M. Baltes (Eds.), *Successful aging: Perspectives from the behavioral sciences.* New York: Cambridge University Press.

Baltes, P. B., & Kunzmann, U. (2003). Wisdom. *The Psychologist, 16,* 131–132.

Baltes, P. B., & Lindenberger, U. (1997). Emergence of a powerful connection between sensory and cognitive functions across the adult life span: A new window to the study of cognitive aging? *Psychology and Aging, 12,* 12–21.

Baltes, P. B., & Smith, J. (2003). New frontiers in the future of aging: From successful aging of the young old to the dilemmas of the fourth age. *Gerontology, 49,* 123–135.

Baltes, P. B., & Staudinger, U. M. (1998). Wisdom. In H. S. Friedman (Ed.), *Encyclopedia of mental health* (Vol. 3). San Diego: Academic Press.

Baltes, P. B., & Staudinger, U. M. (2000). Wisdom. *American Psychologist, 55,* 122–136.

Baltes, P. B., Staudinger, U. M., & Lindenberger, U. (1999). Lifespan psychology: Theory and application to intellectual functioning. *Annual Review of Psychology, 50,* 471–507.

Bandstra, E. S., Morrow, C. E., Anthony, J. C., Haynes, V. L., Johnson, A. L., Xue, L., & Audrey, Y. (2000, May). *Effects of prenatal cocaine exposure on attentional processing in children through five years of age.* Paper presented at the joint meetings of the Pediatric Academic Societies and the American Academy of Pediatrics, Boston.

Bandstra, E. S., Vogel, A. L., Morrow, C. E., Xue, L., & Anthony, J. C. (2004). Severity of prenatal cocaine exposure and child language functioning through age seven years: A longitudinal latent growth curve analysis. *Substance Use and Misuse, 39,* 25–39.

Bandura, A. (1965). Influence of models' reinforcement of contingencies on the acquisition of imitative responses. *Journal of Personality and Social Psychology, 1,* 589–595.

Bandura, A. (1986). *Social foundations of thought and action: A social cognitive theory.* Englewood Cliffs, NJ: Prentice Hall.

Bandura, A. (1998, August). *Swimming against the mainstream: Accentuating the positive aspects of humanity.* Paper presented at the meeting of the American Psychological Association, San Francisco.

Bandura, A. (1999). Moral disengagement in the perpetuation of inhumanities. *Personality and Social Psychology Review, 3,* 193–209.

Bandura, A. (2001). Social cognitive theory. *Annual Review of Psychology* (Vol. 52). Palo Alto, CA: Annual Reviews.

Bandura, A. (2002). Selective moral disengagement in the exercise of moral agency. *Journal of Moral Education, 31,* 101–119.

Bandura, A. (2002). Social cognitive theory. *Annual Review of Psychology* (Vol. 52). Palo Alto, CA: Annual Reviews.

Bandura, A. (2004). *Toward a psychology of human agency.* Paper presented at the meeting of the American Psychological Society, Chicago.

Banister, N. A., Jastrow, S. T., Hodges, V., Loop, R., & Gillham, M. B. (2004). Diabetes self-management training program in a community clinic improves patient outcomes at modest cost. *Journal of the American Diet Association, 104,* 807–810.

Bank, L., Burraston, B., & Snyder, J. (2004). Sibling conflict and ineffective parenting as predictors of adolescent boys' antisocial behavior and peer difficulties: Additive and interactional effects. *Journal of Research on Adolescence, 14,* 99–125.

Banks, E. C. (1993, March). *Moral education curriculum in a multicultural context: The Malaysian primary curriculum.* Paper presented at the biennial meeting of the Society for Research in Child Development, New Orleans.

Banks, J. A. (2002). *Introduction to multicultural education* (3rd ed.). Boston: Allyn & Bacon.

Banks, M. S. (2005). The benefits and costs of combining information between and within the senses. In J. J. Reiser, J. J. Lockman, & C. A. Nelson (Eds.), *The role of action in learning and development.* Mahwah, NJ: Erlbaum.

Banks, M. S., & Salapatek, P. (1983). Infant visual perception. In P. H. Mussen (Ed.), *Handbook of child psychology* (4th ed., Vol. 2). New York: Wiley.

Bannon, L. (2005). *Gender: psychological perspectives* (4th ed.). Boston: Allyn & Bacon.

Barefoot, J. C., Mortensen, E. L., Helms, J., Avlund, K., & Schroll, M. (2001). A longitudinal study of gender differences in depressive symptoms from age 50 to 80. *Psychology and Aging, 16,* 342–345.

Barja, G. (2004). Aging in vertebrates, and the effect of caloric restriction: A mitochondrial free radical production DNA-damage mechanism. *Biological Reviews for the Cambridge Philosophical Society, 79,* 235–251.

Barling, J., Kelloway, E. K., & Frone, M. R. (Eds.). (2004). *Handbook of work and stress.* Thousand Oaks, CA: Sage.

Barnes, D. L. (2002). What midwives need to know about postpartum depression. *Midwifery Today, 61,* 18–19.

Barnes, L. L., Mendes de Leon, C. F., Bienias, J. L., & Evans, D. A. (2004). A longitudinal study of black-white differences in social resources. *Journals of Gerontology B: Psychological Sciences and Social Sciences, 59,* S146–S153.

Barnet, B., Arroyo, C., Devoe, M., & Duggan, A. K. (2004). Reduced school dropout rates among adolescent mothers receiving school-based prenatal care. *Archives of Pediatric and Adolescent Medicine, 158,* 262–268.

Barnett, D., Ganiban, J., & Cicchetti, D. (1999). Maltreatment, negative expressivity, and the development of type D attachments from 12 to 24 months of age. In J. I. Vondra & D. Barnett (Eds.), *Monograph of the Society for Research in Child Development, 64* (3, Serial No. 258), 97–118.

Barnett, R. C. (2001). Work-family balance. In J. Worell (Ed.), *Encyclopedia of women and gender.* San Diego: Academic Press.

Barnett, R. C., Gareis, K. C., James, J. B., & Steele, J. (2001, August). *Planning ahead: College seniors' concerns about work-family conflict.* Paper presented at the meeting of the American Psychological Association, San Francisco.

Barnett, S. B., & Maulik, D. (2001). Guidelines and recommendations for safe use of Doppler ultrasound in perinatal applications. *Journal of Maternal and Fetal Medicine, 10,* 75–84.

Bar-Oz, B., Levicheck, Z., Moretti, M. E., Mah, C., Andreou, S., & Koren, G. (2004). Pregnancy outcome following rubella vaccination: A prospective study. *American Journal of Medical Genetics, 130A,* 52–54.

Barr, H. M., & Streissguth, A. P. (2001). Identifying maternal self-reported alcohol use associated with fetal alcohol disorders. *Alcoholism: Clinical and Experimental Research, 25,* 283–287.

Barrett, D. E., Radke-Yarrow, M., & Klein, R. E. (1982). Chronic malnutrition and child behavior: Effects of calorie supplementation on social and emotional functioning at school age. *Developmental Psychology, 18,* 541–556.

Bartels, S. J., Miles, K. M., & Dums, A. R. (2002). Improving the quality of care for older adults with mental disorders. *Center for Home Care Policy Research: Policy Briefs, 9,* 1–6.

Bartholomew, K., & Horowitz, L. (1991). Attachment styles among young adults: A test of a four-category model. *Journal of Personality and Social Psychology, 61,* 226–244.

Barton, W. H. (2004). Bridging juvenile justice and positive youth development. In S. F. & M. A. Hamilton (Eds.), *The youth development handbook.* Thousand Oaks, CA: Sage.

Barzilai, K., & Rimm, A. (2004). Longevity and health care expenditures: The real reasons older people spend more. *Journals of Gerontology B: Psychological Sciences and Social Sciences, 59,* S197.

Bass, S., Shields, M. K., & Behrman, R. E. (2004). Children, families, and foster care. *Future Child, 14,* 4–29.

Bates, A. S., Fitzgerald, J. F., Dittus, R. S., & Wollinsky, F. D. (1994). Risk factors for underimmunization in poor urban infants. *Journal of the American Medical Association, 272,* 1105–1109.

Bauer, P. J. (2004). Early memory development. In U. Goswami (Ed.), *Blackwell handbook of childhood cognitive development.* Malden, MA: Blackwell.

Bauer, P. J., Wenner, J. A., Dropik, P. L., & Wewerka, S. S. (2000). Parameters of remembering and forgetting in the transition from infancy to early childhood. *Monographs of the Society for Research in Child Development, 65* (4, Serial No. 263).

Bauer, P. J., Wiebe, S. A., Carver, L. J., Waters, J. M., & Nelson, C. A. (2003). Developments in long-term explicit memory late in the first year of life: Behavioral and electrophysiological indices. *Psychological Science, 14,* 629–635.

Bauman, K. E., Ennett, S. T., Foshee, V. A., Pemberton, M., King, T. S., & Koch, G. G. (2002). Influence of a family program on adolescent smoking and drinking prevalence. *Prevention Science, 3,* 35–42.

Baumeister, R. F. (1991). *Meaning of life.* New York: Guilford.

Baumeister, R. F., Campbell, J. D., Krueger, J. I., & Vohs, K. D. (2003). Does high self-esteem cause better performance, interpersonal success, happiness, or healthier lifestyles? *Psychological Science in the Public Interest, 4* (No. 1), 1–44.

Baumeister, R. F., & Vohs, K. D. (2002). The pursuit of meaningfulness in life. In C. R. Snyder & S. J. Lopez (Eds.), *Handbook of positive psychology.* New York: Oxford University Press.

Baumrind, D. (1971). Current patterns of parental authority. *Developmental Psychology Monographs, 4* (1, Pt. 2).

Baumrind, D. (1999, November). Unpublished review of J. W. Santrock's *Child development* (9th ed.). New York: McGraw-Hill.

Baumrind, D., Larzelere, R. E., & Cowan, P. A. (2002). Ordinary physical punishment: Is it harmful? Comment on Gershoff (2002). *Psychological Bulletin, 128,* 590–595.

Bauserman, R. (2002). Child adjustment in joint-custody versus sole-custody arrangements: A meta-analytic review. *Journal of Family Psychology, 16,* 91–102.

Baxter, G. W., Stuart, W. J., & Stewart, W. J. (1998). *Death and the adolescent.* Toronto: University of Toronto Press.

Bayley, N. (1969). *Manual for the Bayley Scales of Infant Development.* New York: Psychological Corporation.

Bayley, N. (1970). Development of mental abilities. In P. H. Mussen (Ed.), *Manual of child psychology* (3rd ed., Vol. 1). New York: Wiley.

Beachy, J. M. (2003). Premature infant massage in the NICU. *Neonatal Network, 22,* 39–45.

Beal, C. R. (1994). *Boys and girls: The development of gender roles.* Boston: McGraw-Hill.

Bearison, D. J., & Dorval, B. (2002). *Collaborative cognition.* Westport, CT: Ablex.

Bearman, P. S., & Moody, J. (2004). Suicide and friendships among American adolescents. *American Journal of Public Health, 94,* 89–95.

Bechtold, A. G., Busnell, E. W., & Salapatek, P. (1979, April). *Infants' visual localization of visual and auditory targets.* Paper presented at the meeting of the Society for Research in Child Development, San Francisco.

Beck, C. T. (2002). Theoretical perspectives of postpartum depression and their treatment implications. *American Journal of Maternal/Child Nursing, 27,* 282–287.

Beck, M. (1992, December 7). Middle Age. *Newsweek,* pp. 50–56.

Bednar, R. L., Wells, M. G., & Peterson, S. R. (1995). *Self-esteem* (2nd ed.). Washington, DC: American Psychological Association.

Bell, M. A., & Fox, N. A. (1992). The relations between frontal brain electrical activity and cognitive development during infancy. *Child Development, 63,* 1142–1163.

Bell, S. M., & Ainsworth, M. D. S. (1972). Infant crying and maternal responsiveness. *Child Development, 43,* 1171–1190.

Belle, D. (1999). *The after school lives of children.* Mahwah, NJ: Erlbaum.

Bellevia, G., & Frone, M. R. (2004). Work-family conflict. In J. Baring, E. K. Kelloway, & M. R. Frone (Eds.), *Handbook of work stress.* Thousand Oaks, CA: Sage.

Bellinger, D., Leviton, A., Waternaux, C., Needleman, H., & Rabinowitz, M. (1987). Longitudinal analysis of prenatal and postnatal lead exposure and early cognitive development. *New England Journal of Medicine, 316,* 1037–1043.

Belloc, N. B., & Breslow, L. (1972). Relationships of physical health status and health practices. *Preventive Medicine, 1,* 409–421.

Belsky, J. (1981). Early human experience: A family perspective. *Developmental Psychology, 17,* 3–23.

Belsky, J., & Eggebeen, D. (1991). Early and extensive maternal employment/child care and 4–6-year-olds socioemotional development: Children of the National Longitudinal Survey of Youth. *Journal of Marriage and the Family, 53,* 1083–1099.

Belsky, J., Jaffe, S., Hsieh, K., & Silva, P. (2001). Child-rearing antecedents of intergenerational relations in young adulthood: A prospective study. *Developmental Psychology, 37,* 801–813.

Belson, W. (1978). *Television violence and the adolescent boy.* London: Saxon House.

Bem, S. L. (1977). On the utility of alternative procedures for assessing psychological androgyny. *Journal of Consulting and Clinical Psychology, 45,* 196–205.

Bendelius, J. (2004). Obesity: Possible solutions. *School Nurse News, 21,* 29–30.

Bendersky, M., & Sullivan, M. W. (2002). Basic methods in infant research. In A. Slater & M. Lewis (Eds.), *Infant development.* New York: Oxford University Press.

Benenson, J. F., Apostolaris, N. H., & Parnass, J. (1997). Age and sex differences in dyadic and group interaction. *Developmental Psychology, 33,* 538–543.

Benfey, P. (2005). *Essentials of genomics.* Upper Saddle River, NJ: Prentice Hall.

Bengtson, V. L. (1985). Diversity and symbolism in grandparental roles. In V. L. Bengtson & J. Robertson (Eds.), *Grandparenthood.* Newbury Park, CA: Sage.

Bengtson, V. L. (2001). Beyond the nuclear family: The increasing importance of multi-generational bonds. *Journal of Marriage and the Family, 63,* 1–16.

Benini, A. L., Camilloni, M. A., Scordato, C., Lezzi, G., Savia, G., Oriani, G., Bertoli, S., Balzola, F., Liuzzi, A., & Petroni, M. L. (2001). Contribution of weight cycling to serum leptin in human obesity. *International Journal of Obesity and Related Metabolic Disorders, 25,* 721–726.

Bennett, C. I. (2003). *Comprehensive multicultural education* (5th ed.). Boston: Allyn & Bacon.

Bennett, K. M. (2004). Why did he die? The attributions of cause of death among women widowed in later life. *Journal of Health Psychology, 9,* 345–353.

Bennett, W. I., & Gurin, J. (1982). *The dieter's dilemma: Eating less and weighing more.* New York: Basic Books.

Benson, E. (2003, February). Intelligence across cultures. *Monitor on Psychology, 34* (No. 2), 56–58.

Benson, P. (1993). *The troubled journey.* Minneapolis: The Search Institute.

Berado, F. M. (2003). Widowhood and its social implications. In C. D. Bryant (Ed.), *Handbook of death and dying.* Thousand Oaks, CA: Sage.

Berardi, A., Parasuraman, R., & Haxby, J. V. (2001). Overall vigilance and sustained attention decrements in healthy aging. *Experimental Aging Research, 27,* 19–39.

Berenbaum, S. A., & Bailey, J. M. (2003). Effects on gender identity of prenatal androgens and genital appearance: Evidence from girls with congenital adrenal hyperplasia. *Journal of Endocrinology and Metabolism, 88,* 1102–1106.

Bergen, D. (1988). Stages of play development. In D. Bergen (Ed.), *Play as medium for learning and development.* Portsmouth, NH: Heinemann.

Berger, S. E., & Adolph, K. E. (2003). Infants use handrails as tools in a locomotor task. *Developmental Psychology, 39,* 594–605.

Berghout, A., & others (2004). Childhood growth hormone deficiency (GHD) and idiopathic short stature (ISS): How far can a consensus go? *Journal of Pediatric Endocrinology and Metabolism, 17 (Suppl. 2),* 251–256.

Bergmann, K. E., Bergmann, R. L., Von Kries, R., Bohm, R., Richter, R., Dudenhausen, J. W., & Wahn, U. (2003). Early determinants of childhood overweight and adiposity in a birth cohort study: Role of breastfeeding. *International Journal of Obesity and Related Metabolic Disorders, 27,* 162–172.

Berk, L. E. (1994). Why children talk to themselves. *Scientific American, 271* (5), 78–83.

Berk, L. E., & Spuhl, S. T. (1995). Maternal interaction, private speech, and task performance in preschool children. *Early Childhood Research Quarterly, 10,* 145–169.

Berko Gleason, J. (2000). Language: An overview. In A. Kazdin (Ed.), *Encyclopedia of psychology.* Washington, DC, & New York: American Psychological Association and Oxford University Press.

Berko Gleason, J. (2001). *The development of language* (5th ed.). Boston: Allyn & Bacon.

Berko Gleason, J. (2002). Review of J. W. Santrock's *Life-span development,* 4th ed. (New York: McGraw-Hill).

Berko Gleason, J. (2003). Unpublished review of J. W. Santrock's *Life-span development,* 9th ed. (New York: McGraw-Hill).

Berko Gleason, J. (2005). *The development of language* (6th ed.). Boston: Allyn & Bacon.

Berko, J. (1958). The child's learning of English morphology. *Word, 14,* 150–177.

Berkowitz, C. D. (2004). Cosleeping: Benefits, risks, and cautions. *Advances Pediatrics, 51,* 329–349.

Berlin, L., & Cassidy, J. (2000). Understanding parenting: Contributions of attachment theory and research. In J. D. Osofsky & H. E. Fitzgerald (Eds.), *WAIMH handbook of infant mental health* (Vol. 3). New York: Wiley.

Berlyne, D. E. (1960). *Conflict, arousal, and curiosity.* New York: McGraw-Hill.

Berman, B. A., Wong, G. C., Bastani, R., Hoang, T., Jones, C., Goldstein, D. R., Bernert, J. T., Hammond, K. S., Tashkin, D., & Lewis, M. A. (2003). Household smoking behavior and ETS exposure among children with asthma in low-income, minority households. *Addictive Behaviors, 28,* 111–128.

Berndt, T. J. (2002). Friendship quality and social development. *Current Directions in Psychological Science, 11,* 7–10.

Berndt, T. J., & Perry, T. B. (1990). Distinctive features and effects of early adolescent friendships. In R. Montemayor (Ed.), *Advances in adolescent research.* Greenwich, CT: JAI Press.

Bernier, M. O., Plu-Bureau, G., Bossard, N., Ayzac, L., Thalabard, J. C. (2000). Breastfeeding and risk of breast cancer: A meta-analysis of published studies. *Human Reproduction Update, 6,* 374–386.

Berninger, V. W., Dunn, A., Shin-Ju, C. L., & Shimada, S. (2004). School evolution: Scientist-practitioner educators creating optimal learning environments for all students. *Journal of Learning Disabilities, 37,* 500–508.

Bernstein, J. (2004). The low-wage labor market: Trends and policy implications. In A. C. Crouter & A. Booth (Eds.), *Work-family challenges for low-income families and their children.* Mahwah, NJ: Erlbaum.

Berr, C. (2002). Oxidative stress and cognitive impairment in the elderly. *Journal of Nutrition, Health, and Aging, 6,* 261–266.

Berscheid, E. (1988). Some comments on love's anatomy: Or, whatever happened to old-fashioned lust? In R. J. Sternberg (Ed.), *Anatomy of love.* New Haven, CT: Yale University Press.

Berscheid, E. (2000). Attraction. In A. Kazdin (Ed.), *Encyclopedia of psychology.* Washington, DC, & New York: American Psychological Association and Oxford University Press.

Berscheid, E., & Fei, J. (1977). Sexual jealousy and romantic love. In G. Clinton & G. Smith (Eds.), *Sexual jealousy.* Englewood Cliffs, NJ: Prentice-Hall.

Berscheid, E., & Reis, H. T. (1998). Attraction and close relationships. In D. T. Gilbert, S. T. Fiske, & G. Lindzey (Eds.), *Handbook of social psychology* (4th ed., Vol. 2). New York: McGraw-Hill.

Berscheid, E., Snyder, M., & Omoto, A. M. (1989). Issues in studying close relationships: Conceptualizing and measuring closeness. In C. Hendrick (Ed.), *Close relationships*. Newbury Park, CA: Sage.

Bertelsen, A. (2004). Contributions of Danish registers to understanding psychopathology (A lifetime of 30 years' collaboration with Irving I. Gottesman). In L. F. DiLalla (Ed.), *Behavior genetics principles*. Washington, DC: American Psychological Association.

Bertenthal, B. (2005). Theories, methods, and models: Discussion of the chapters by Newcombe, Thelen, and Whitmeyer. In J. J. Reiser, J. J. Lockman, & C. A. Nelson (Eds.), *The role of action in learning and development*. Mahwah, NJ: Erlbaum.

Bertoni-Freddari, C., Fattoretti, P., Giorgetti, B., Solazzi, M., Balietti, M., & Meier-Ruge, W. (2004). Role of mitochondrial deterioration in physiological and pathological brain aging. *Gerontology, 50,* 187–192.

Bertrand, R. M., & Lachman, M. E. (2003). Personality development in adulthood and old age. In I. B. Weiner (Ed.), *Handbook of psychology* (Vol. VI). New York: Wiley.

Best, D. (2001). Cross-cultural gender roles. In J. Worell (Ed.), *Encyclopedia of women and gender*. San Diego: Academic Press.

Best, J. W., & Kahn, J. V. (2003). *Research in education* (9th ed.). Boston: Allyn & Bacon.

Beyene, Y. (1986). Cultural significance and physiological manifestations of menopause: A biocultural analysis. *Culture, Medicine and Psychiatry, 10,* 47–71.

Bialystok, E. (1993). Metalinguistic awareness: The development of children's representations in language. In C. Pratt & A. Garton (Eds.), *Systems of representation in children*. London: Wiley.

Bialystok, E. (1997). Effects of bilingualism and biliteracy on children's emerging concepts of print. *Developmental Psychology, 33,* 429–440.

Bialystok, E. (1999). Cognitive complexity and attentional control in the bilingual mind. *Child Development, 70,* 537–804.

Bialystok, E. (2001). *Bilingualism in development: Language, literacy, and cognition*. New York: Cambridge University Press.

Bianchi, S. M., & Spani, D. (1986). *American women in transition*. New York: Russell Sage Foundation.

Biderman, J., & Faraone, S. V. (2003). Current concepts on the neurobiology of attention-deficit/hyperactivity disorder. *Journal of Attention Disorders, 6 (Suppl. 1),* S7–S16.

Bierman, K. L. (2004). *Peer rejection*. New York: Guilford.

Bigler, R. S., Averhart, C. J., & Liben, L. S. (2003). Race and the workforce: Occupational status, aspirations, and stereotyping among African American children. *Developmental Psychology, 19,* 572–580.

Bijur, P. E., Wallston, K. A., Smith, C. A., Lifrak, S., & Friedman, S. B. (1993, August). *Gender differences in turning to religion for coping*. Paper presented at the meeting of the American Psychological Association, Toronto.

Billman, J. (2003). *Observation and participation in early childhood settings: A practicum guide* (2nd ed.). Boston: Allyn & Bacon.

Billy, J. O. G., Rodgers, J. L., & Udry, J. R. (1984). Adolescent sexual behavior and friendship choice. *Social Forces, 62,* 653–678.

Bingham, C. R., & Crockett, L. J. (1996). Longitudinal adjustment patterns of boys and girls experiencing early, middle, and late sexual intercourse. *Developmental Psychology, 32,* 647–658.

Birney, D. P., Citron-Pusty, J. H., Lutz, D. J., & Sternberg, R. J. (2005). The development of cognitive and intellectual abilities. In M. H. Bornstein & M. E. Lamb (Eds.), *Developmental science* (5th ed.). Mahwah, NJ: Erlbaum.

Birren, J. E. (Ed.). (1996). *Encyclopedia of gerontology*. San Diego: Academic Press.

Birren, J. E. (2002). Unpublished review of J. W. Santrock's *Life-span development* (9th ed.). New York: McGraw-Hill.

Birren, J. E., & Schaie, K. W. (Eds.). (2001). *Handbook of the psychology of aging* (5th ed.). San Diego: Academic Press.

Birren, J. E., Woods, A. M., & Williams, M. V. (1980). Behavioral slowing with age: Causes, organization, & consequences. In L. W. Poon (Ed.), *Aging in the 1980s: Psychological issues*. Washington, DC: American Psychological Association.

Bissada, A., & Briere, J. (2001). Child abuse: Physical and sexual. In J. Worell (Ed.), *Encyclopedia of women and gender*. San Diego: Academic Press.

Bisschop, M. I., Kriegsman, D. M., Beekman, A. T., & Deeg, D. J. (2004). Chronic diseases and depression. *Social Science Medicine, 59,* 721–733.

Bjarnason, T., Andersson, B., Choquet, M., Elekes, Z., Morgan, M., & Rapinett, G. (2003). Alcohol culture, family structure, and adolescent alcohol use: Multilevel modeling of frequency of heavy drinking among 15–16 year old students in 11 European countries. *Journal of Studies on Alcohol, 64,* 200–208.

Bjorklund, D. F. (2005). *Children's thinking* (4th ed.). Belmont, CA: Wadsworth.

Bjorklund, D. F., & Pellegrini, A. D. (2002). *The origins of human nature*. New York: Oxford University Press.

Blaasaas, K. G., Tynes, T., & Lie, R. T. (2004). Risk of selected birth defects by maternal residence close to power lines during pregnancy. *Occupational and Environmental Medicine, 61,* 174–176.

Black, J. E. (2001, April). *Complex and interactive effects of enriched experiences on brain development*. Paper presented at the meeting of the Society for Research in Child Development, Minneapolis.

Blair, C., & Ramey, C. (1996). Early intervention with low birth weight infants: The path to second generation research. In M. J. Guralnick (Ed.), *The effectiveness of early intervention*. Baltimore: Paul H. Brookes.

Blair, J. M., Hanson, D. L., Jones, H., & Dworkin, M. S. (2004). Trends in pregnancy rates among women with human immunodeficiency virus. *Obstetrics and Gynecology, 103,* 663–668.

Blair, S. N. (1990, January). *Personal communication*. Aerobics Institute, Dallas.

Blair, S. N., Kohl, H. W., Paffenbarger, R. S., Clark, D. G., Cooper, K. H., & Gibbons, L. W. (1989). Physical fitness and all-cause mortality: A prospective study of healthy men and women. *Journal of the American Medical Association, 262,* 2395–2401.

Blanchard-Fields, F. (1996). Decision making and everyday problem solving. In J. E. Birren (Ed.), *Encyclopedia of gerontology* (Vol. 1). San Diego: Academic Press.

Blazer, D. (2002). *Depression in late life* (3rd ed.). New York: Springer.

Blazer, D. G. (2003). Depression in late life: Review and commentary. *Journals of Gerontology A: Biological Sciences and Medical Sciences, 58,* M240–M265.

Block, J. (1993). Studying personality the long way. In D. Funder, R. D. Parke, C. Tomlinson-Keasey, & K. Widaman (Ed.), *Studying lives through time*. Washington, DC: American Psychological Association.

Block, J. H., & Block, J. (1980). The role of ego-control and ego-resiliency in the organization of behavior. In W. A. Collins (Ed.), *Minnesota symposium on child psychology* (Vol. 13). Minneapolis: University of Minnesota Press.

Blonna, R. (2005). *Coping with stress in a changing world* (3rd ed.). New York: McGraw-Hill.

Bloom, B. (1985). *Developing talent in young people.* New York: Ballentine.

Bloom, L. (1998). Language acquisition in developmental context. In W. Damon (Ed.), *Handbook of child psychology* (5th ed., Vol. 5). New York: Wiley.

Bloom, L., Lifter, K., & Broughton, J. (1985). The convergence of early cognition and language in the second year of life: Problems in conceptualization and measurement. In M. Barrett (Ed.), *Single word speech.* London: Wiley.

Bloor, C., & White, F. (1983). *Unpublished manuscript.* University of California at San Diego, LaJolla, CA.

Bluck, S., & Gluck, J. (2004). Making things better and learning a lesson: Experiencing wisdom across the lifespan. *Journal of Personality, 72,* 543–572.

Blum, L. M. (2000). *At the breast: Ideologies of breastfeeding and motherhood in the contemporary United States.* Boston: Beacon Press.

Blum, N. J., Taubman, B., & Nemeth, N. (2003). Relationship between age at initiation of toilet training and duration of training: A prospective study. *Pediatrics, 111,* 810–814.

Blum, N. J., Taubman, B., & Nemeth, N. (2004). Why is toilet training occurring at older ages? A study of factors associated with later training. *Journal of Pediatrics, 145,* 107–111.

Blum, R., & Nelson-Mmari, K. (2004). Adolescent health from an international perspective. In R. Lerner & L. Steinberg (Eds.), *Handbook of adolescent psychology.* New York: Wiley.

Blumberg, J. (1993, June 2). Commentary in "Lowly vitamin supplements pack a big health punch." *USA Today,* p. 3D.

Blumenfeld, P. C., Modell, J., Bartko, T., Secade, J., Fredricks, J., Friedel, J., & Paris, A. (2005). School engagement of inner city students during middle childhood. In C. R. Cooper, C. T. G. Coll, W. T. Bartko, H. M. Davis, & C. Chatman (Eds.), *Developmental pathways through middle childhood.* Mahwah, NJ: Erlbaum.

Blumenfeld, P. C., Pintrich, P. R., Wessles, K., & Meece, J. (1981, April). *Age and sex differences in the impact of classroom experiences on self-perceptions.* Paper presented at the biennial meeting of the Society of Research in Child Development, Boston.

Blumenthal, H. T. (2004). Amyloidosis: A universal disease of aging? *Journals of Gerontology A: Biological Sciences and Medical Sciences, 59,* M361–M369.

Blumenthal, J. A., Emery, C. F., Madden, D. J., George, L. K., Coleman, R. E., Riddle, M. W., McKee, D. C., Reasoner, J., & Williams, R. S. (1989). Cardiovascular and behavioral effects of aerobic exercise training in healthy older men and women. *Journals of Gerontology A: Biological Sciences and Medical Sciences, 44,* M147–M157.

Blumenthal, J., Jeffries, N. O., Castellanos, F. X., Liu, H., Zidjdenbos, A., Paus, T., Evans, A. C., Rapoport, J. L., & Giedd, J. N. (1999). Brain development during childhood and adolescence: A longitudinal MRI study. *Nature Neuroscience, 10,* 861–863.

Blundell, J. E. (1984). Systems and interactions: An approach to the pharmacology of feeding. In A. J. Stunkdard & E. Stellar (Eds.), *Eating and its disorders.* New York: Raven Press.

Bodrova, E., & Leong, D. J. (2003). Learning and development of preschool children from the Vygotskian perspective. In A. Kozulin, B. Gindis, V. S. Ageyev, & S. M. Miller (Eds.), *Vygotsky's educational theory in cultural context.* New York: Cambridge University Press.

Boelen, P. A., van den Bout, J., & van den Hout, M. A. (2003). The role of cognitive variables in psychological functioning after the death of a first degree relative. *Behavior Research and Therapy, 41,* 1123–1136.

Boerner, K., & Wortman, C. B. (1998). Grief and loss. In H. S. Freeman (Ed.), *Encyclopedia of mental health* (Vol. 2). San Diego: Academic Press.

Bogenschneider, K. (2002). *Family policy matters.* Mahwah, NJ: Erlbaum.

Bohlin, G., & Hagekull, B. (1993). Stranger wariness and sociability in the early years. *Infant Behavior and Development, 16,* 53–67.

Bohnhorst, B., Heyne, T., Peter, C. S., & Poets, C. F. (2002). Skin-to-skin (kangaroo) care, respiratory control, and thermoregulation. *Journal of Pediatrics, 138,* 193–197.

Bolen, J. C., Bland, S. D., & Sacks, J. J. (1999, April). *Injury prevention behaviors: Children's use of occupant restraints and bicycle helmets.* Paper presented at the meeting of the Society for Research in Child Development, Albuquerque.

Bolger, K. E., & Patterson, C. J. (2001). Developmental pathways from child maltreatment to peer rejection. *Child Development, 72,* 549–568.

Bonanno, G. A. (2004). Loss, trauma, and human resilience: Have we underestimated the human capacity to thrive after extremely aversive events? *American Psychologist, 59,* 20–28.

Bonanno, G. A., Noll, J. G., Putnam, F. W., O'Neil, M., & Trickett, P. K. (2003). Predicting the willingness to disclose information about sexual abuse from measures of repressive coping and dissociative tendencies. *Child Maltreatment, 8,* 302–318.

Bonanno, G. A., Wortman, C. B., & Nesse, R. M. (2004). Prospective patterns of resilience and maladjustment during widowhood. *Psychology and Aging, 19,* 260–271.

Bonari, L., Bennett, H., Einarson, A., & Koren, G. (2004). Risk of untreated depression during pregnancy. *Journal of Family Health Care, 13,* 144–145.

Bond, J., Kaskutas, L. A., & Weisner, C. (2003). The persistent influence of social networks and Alcoholics Anonymous on abstinence. *Journal of Studies on Alcohol, 64,* 579–588.

Bongaarts, J., & Zimmer, Z. (2002). Living arrangements of older adults in the developing world: An analysis of demographic and health survey household surveys. *Journals of Gerontology B: Psychological Sciences and Social Sciences, 57,* S145–S157.

Books, S. (2004). *Poverty and schooling in the U.S.* Mahwah, NJ: Erlbaum.

Bookstein, F. L., Streissguth, A. P., Sampson, P. D., Connor, P. D., & Barr, H. M. (2002). Corpus callosum shape and neuropsychological deficits in adult males with heavy fetal alcohol exposure. *Neuroimage, 15,* 233–251.

Bookwala, J., & Jacobs, J. (2004). Age, marital processes, and depressed affect. *The Gerontologist, 44,* 328–338.

Booth, M. (2002). Arab adolescents facing the future: Enduring ideals and pressures to change. In B. B. Brown, R. W. Larson, & T. S. Saraswathi (Eds.), *The world's youth.* New York: Cambridge University Press.

Bor, W., McGee, T. R., & Fagan, A. A. (2004). Early risk factors for adolescent antisocial behavior: An Australian longitudinal study. *Australian and New Zealand Journal of Psychiatry, 38,* 365–372.

Borawski, E. A., Ievers-Landis, C. E., Lovegreen, L. D., & Trapl, B. A. (2003).

Parental monitoring, negotiated unsupervised time, and parental trust: The role of perceived parenting practices in adolescent health risk behaviors. *Journal of Adolescent Health, 33,* 60–70.

Bordaty, H., Draper, B. M., Millar, J., Low, L. F., Lie, D., Sharah, S., & Paton, H. (2003). Randomized controlled trial of different models of care for nursing home residents with dementia complicated by depression or psychosis. *Journal of Clinical Psychiatry, 64,* 63–72.

Bornstein, M. H., Arterberry, M. E., & Mash, C. (2005). Perceptual development. In M. H. Bornstein & M. E. Lamb (Eds.), *Developmental psychology* (5th ed.). Mahwah, NJ: Erlbaum.

Bornstein, M. H., & Bradley, R. H. (Eds.). (2003). *Socioeconomic status, parenting, and child development.* Mahwah, NJ: Erlbaum.

Bornstein, M. H., & Sigman, M. D. (1986). Continuity in mental development from infancy. *Child Development, 57,* 251–274.

Borowsky, I. W., Ireland, M., & Resnick, M. D. (2001). Adolescent suicide attempts: Risks and protectors. *Pediatrics, 107,* 485–493.

Borra, S. T., Kelly, L., Shirreffs, M. B., Neville, K., & Geiger, C. J. (2003). Developing health messages. *Journal of the American Dietary Association, 103,* 721–728.

Bosma, H. A., & Kunnen, E. S. (Eds.). (2001). *Identity and emotion.* New York: Cambridge University Press.

Boswell, W. R., Olson-Buchanan, J. B., & LePine, M. A. (2004). Relations between stress and work outcomes. *Journal of Vocational Behavior, 64,* 165–181.

Botwinick, J. (1978). *Aging and behavior* (2nd ed.). New York: Springer.

Bouchard, T. J. (1995, August). *Henuibility of intelligence.* Paper presented at the meeting of the American Psychological Association, New York, NY.

Bouchard, T. J., Lykken, D. T., McGue, M., Segal, N. L., & Tellegen, A. (1990). Source of human psychological differences. The Minnesota Study of Twins Reared Apart. *Science, 250,* 223–228.

Bouchard, T. J., Segal, N. L., Tellegen, A., McGue, M., Keyes, M., & Krueger, R. (2004). Genetic influences on social attitudes: Another challenge to psychologists from behavior genetics. In L. F. DiLalla (Ed.), *Behavior genetics principles.* Washington, DC: American Psychological Association.

Bouchey, H. A., & Furman, W. (2003). Dating and romantic relationships in adolescence. In G. Adams & M. Berzonsky (Eds.), *Blackwell handbook of adolescence.* Malden, MA: Blackwell.

Bower, B. (1985). The left hand of math and verbal talent. *Science News, 127,* 263.

Bower, B. (1999, March 20). Minds on the move. *Science News,* 1–5.

Bower, T. G. R. (1966). Slant perception and shape constancy in infants. *Science, 151,* 832–834.

Bower, T. G. R. (2002). Space and objects. In A. Slater & M. Lewis (Eds.), *Introduction to infant development.* New York: Oxford University Press.

Bowlby, J. (1969). *Attachment and loss* (Vol. 1). London: Hogarth Press.

Bowlby, J. (1980). *Attachment and loss: Vol. 3. Loss, sadness, and depression.* New York: Basic Books.

Bowlby, J. (1989). *Secure and insecure attachment.* New York: Basic Books.

Bowles, T. (1999). Focusing on time orientation to explain adolescent self concept and academic achievement: Part II. Testing a model. *Journal of Applied Health Behaviour, 1,* 1–8.

Boyd-Franklin, N. (1989). *Black families in therapy. A multisystems approach.* New York: Guilford Press.

Boyer, K., & Diamond, A. (1992). Development of memory for temporal order in infants and young children. In A. Diamond (Ed.), *Development and neural bases of higher cognitive function.* New York: New York Academy of Sciences.

Brabeck, M. M. (2000). Kohlberg, Lawrence. In A. Kazdin (Ed.), *Encyclopedia of psychology.* Washington, DC, and New York: American Psychological Association and Oxford University Press.

Brabyn, J. A., Schneck, M. E., Haegerstrom-Portnoy, G., & Lott, L. (2001). The Smith-Kettlewell Institute (SKI) Longitudinal Study of Vision Function and Its Impact Among the Elderly: An overview. *Ophthalmology and Vision Science, 78,* 2464–2469.

Bracey, J. R., Bamaca, M. Y., & Umana-Taylor, A. J. (2004). Examining ethnic identity among biracial and monoracial adolescents. *Journal of Youth and Adolescence, 33,* 123–132.

Brach, J. S., Simonsick, E. M., Kritchevsky, S., Yaffe, K., Newman, A. B., & the Health, Aging, and Body Composition Study Research Group. (2004). The association between physical function and lifestyle activity in the Health, Aging, and Body Composition Study. *Journal of the American Geriatrics Society, 52,* 502–509.

Bracken, M. B., Eskenazi, B., Sachse, K., McSharry, J., Hellenbrand, K., & Leo-Summers, L. (1990). Association of cocaine use with sperm concentration, motility, and morphology. *Fertility and Sterility, 53,* 315–322.

Bradley, R. H., & Corwyn, R. F. (2002). Socioeconomic status and child development. *Annual Review of Psychology* (Vol. 53). Palo Alto, CA: Annual Reviews.

Bradshaw, C. P., & Garbarino, J. (2004). Using and building family strengths to promote youth development. In S. F. Hamilton & M. A. Hamilton (Eds.), *The youth development handbook.* Thousand Oaks, CA: Sage.

Brainerd, C. J., & Reyna, V. E. (1993). Domains of fuzzy-trace theory. In M. L. Howe & R. Pasnak (Eds.), *Emerging themes in cognitive development.* New York: Springer.

Brandstadter, J., Wentura, D., & Greve, W. (1993). Adaptive resources of the aging self: Outlines of an emergent perspective. *Journal of Behavioral Development, 16,* 323–349.

Bray, G. A., & Champagne, C. M. (2004). Obesity and the metabolic syndrome. *Journal of the American Dietetic Association, 104,* 86–89.

Brazelton, T. B. (1956). Sucking in infancy. *Pediatrics, 17,* 400–404.

Brazelton, T. B., Nugent, J. K., & Lester, B. M. (1987). Neonatal behavioral assessment scale. In J. D. Osofsky (Ed.), *Handbook of infant development* (2nd ed.). New York: Wiley.

Bredekamp, S. (1987). *Developmentally appropriate practice in early childhood programs serving children from birth through age 8.* Washington, DC: National Association for the Education of Young Children.

Bredekamp, S. (1997). NAEYC issues revised position statement on developmentally appropriate practice in early childhood programs. *Young Children, 52,* 34–40.

Breheny, M., & Stephens, C. (2004). Barriers to effective contraception and strategies for overcoming them among adolescent mothers. *Public Health Nursing, 21,* 220–227.

Brehm, S. S. (2002). *Intimate relationships* (3rd ed.). New York: McGraw-Hill.

Breitbart, E., Wang, X., Leka, L. S., Dallal, G. E., Meydani, S. N., & Stollar, B. D. (2002). Altered memory B-cell homeostasis in human aging. *Journals of Gerontology A:*

Biological Sciences and Medical Sciences, 57, B304–B311.

Bremner, G. (2004). Cognitive development: Knowledge of the physical world. In A. Fogel & G. Bremner (Eds.), *Blackwell handbook of infant development.* London: Blackwell.

Brenner, Z. R., & Krenzer, M. E. (2003). Using complementary and alternative therapies to promote comfort at end of life. *Critical Care Nursing Clinics of North America, 15,* 355–362.

Brent, R. L. (2004). Environmental causes of human congenital malformations. *Pediatrics (4 Suppl.), 113,* 957–968.

Brent, R. L., & Fawcett, L. B. (2000, May). *Environmental causes of human birth defects: What have we learned about the mechanism, nature, and etiology of congenital malformations in the past 50 years?* Paper presented at the joint meetings of the Pediatric Academic Societies and the American Academy of Pediatrics, Boston.

Bretherton, I., Stolberg, U., & Kreye, M. (1981). Engaging strangers in proximal interaction: Infants' social initiative. *Developmental Psychology, 17,* 746–755.

Brewer, J. A. (2004). *Introduction to early childhood education* (5th ed.). Boston: Allyn & Bacon.

Breysse, P., Farr, N., Galke, W., Lanphear, B., Morely, R., & Bergofsky, L. (2004). The relationship between housing and health: Children at risk. *Environmental Health Perspectives, 112,* 1583–1588.

Brickel, C. O., Ciarrocchi, J. W., Sheers, N. J., Estadt, B. K., Powell, D. A., & Pargament, K. I. (1998). Perceived stress, religious coping styles, and depressive affect. *Journal of Psychology and Christianity, 17,* 33–42.

Briem, V., Radeborg, K., Salo, I., & Bengtsson, H. (2004). Developmental aspects of children's behavior and safety while cycling. *Journal of Pediatric Psychology, 29,* 369–377.

Briganti, A., Salonia, A., Gallina, A., Suardi, N., Rigatti, P., & Montorsi, F. (2004). Emerging oral drugs for erectile dysfunction. *Expert Opinions on Emerging Drugs, 9,* 179–189.

Bril, B. (1999). Dires sur l'enfant selon les cultures. Etat des lieux et perspectives. In B. Bril, P. R. Dasen, C. Sabatier, & B. Krewer (Eds.), *Propos sur l'enfant et l'adolescent. Quels enfants pour quelles cultures?* Paris: L'Harmattan.

Brim, G. (1992, December 7). Commentary, *Newsweek,* p. 52.

Brim, G., Ryff, C. D., & Kessler, R. (Eds.). (2004). *How healthy we are: A national study of well-being in midlife.* Chicago: University of Chicago Press.

Brim, O. (1999). *The MacArthur Foundation study of midlife development.* Vero Beach, FL: MacArthur Foundation.

Brim, O. G., Ryff, C. D., & Kessler, R. (Eds.). (2004). *How healthy are we: A national study of well-being in midlife.* Chicago: University of Chicago Press.

Brisk, M. E. (2005). *Bilingual education.* Mahwah, NJ: Erlbaum.

Brissette, I., Scheier, M. F., & Carver, C. S. (2002). The role of optimism and social network development, coping, and psychological adjustment during a life transition. *Journal of Personality and Social Psychology, 82,* 102–111.

Brittle, C., & Zint, M. (2003). Do newspapers lead with lead? A content analysis of how lead health risks to children are covered. *Journal of Environmental Health, 65,* 17–22, 30, 34.

Brody, G. (2004). Siblings' direct and indirect contributions to child development. *Current Directions in Psychological Science, 13,* 124–126.

Brody, G. H., & Ge, X. (2001). Linking parenting processes and self-regulation to psychological functioning and alcohol use during early adolescence. *Journal of Family Psychology, 15,* 82–94.

Brody, J. E. (1994, April 6). The value of breast milk. *New York Times,* p. C11.

Brody, N. (2000). Intelligence. In A. Kazdin (Ed.), *Encyclopedia of psychology.* Washington, DC, & New York: American Psychological Association and Oxford University Press.

Brodzinsky, D. M., Lang, R., & Smith, D. W. (1995). Parenting adopted children. In M. H. Bornstein (Ed.), *Handbook of parenting* (Vol. 3). Hillsdale, NJ: Erlbaum.

Brodzinsky, D. M., & Pinderhughes, E. (2002). Parenting and child development in adoptive families. In M. H. Bornstein (Ed.), *Handbook of parenting* (Vol. 1). Mahwah, NJ: Erlbaum.

Bronfenbrenner, U. (1986). Ecology of the family as a context for human development: Research perspectives. *Developmental Psychology, 22,* 723–742.

Bronfenbrenner, U. (2000). Ecological theory. In A. Kazdin (Ed.), *Encyclopedia of psychology.* Washington, DC, & New York: American Psychological Association and Oxford University Press.

Bronfenbrenner, U. (2004). *Making human beings human.* Thousand Oaks, CA: Sage.

Bronfenbrenner, U., & Morris, P. (1998). The ecology of developmental processes. In W. Damon (Ed.), *Handbook of child psychology* (5th ed., Vol. 1). New York: Wiley.

Bronner, G., Peretz, C., & Ehrenfeld, M. (2003). Sexual harassment of nurses and nursing students. *Journal of Advanced Nursing, 42,* 637–644.

Brook, J. S., Brook, D. W., Gordon, A. S., Whiteman, M., & Cohen, P. (1990). The psychological etiology of adolescent drug use: A family interactional approach. *Genetic Psychology Monographs, 116,* no. 2.

Brook, J. S., Whiteman, M., Balka, E. B., Win, P. T., & Gursen, M. D. (1998). Drug use among Puerto Ricans: Ethnic identity as a protective factor. *Hispanic Journal of Behavioral Sciences, 20,* 241–254.

Brooker, R. (2005). *Genetics* (2nd ed.). New York: McGraw-Hill.

Brooks, J. G., & Brooks, M. G. (2001). *The case for constructivist classrooms* (2nd ed.). Upper Saddle River, NJ: Erlbaum.

Brooks-Gunn, J. (2003). Do you believe in magic?: What we can expect from early childhood programs. *Social Policy Report, Society for Research in Child Development, XVII* (No. 1), 1–13.

Brooks-Gunn, J., Currie, J., Emde, R. E., & Zigler, E. (2003). Do you believe in magic? What we can expect from early childhood intervention programs. *SRCD Social Policy Report, 17* (1), 3–15.

Brooks-Gunn, J., Graber, J. A., & Paikoff, R. L. (1994). Studying links between hormones and negative affect: Models and measures. *Journal of Research on Adolescence, 4,* 469–486.

Brooks-Gunn, J., Han, W. J., & Waldfogel, J. (2002). Maternal employment and child cognitive outcomes in the first three years of life: The NICHD Study of Early Child Care. *Child Development, 73,* 1052–1072.

Brooks-Gunn, J., & Paikoff, R. (1993). "Sex is a gamble, kissing is a game": Adolescent sexuality, contraception, and sexuality. In S. P. Millstein, A. C. Petersen, & E. O. Nightingale (Eds.), *Promoting the health behavior of adolescents.* New York: Oxford University Press.

Brooks-Gunn, J., & Warren, M. P. (1989). The psychological significance of secondary sexual characteristics in 9- to 11-year-old girls. *Child Development, 59,* 161–169.

Brown, B. B. (1999). "You're going with whom?!": Peer group influences on adolescent romantic relationships. In W. Furman,

B. B. Brown, & C. Feiring (Eds.), *The development of romantic relationships in adolescence*. Cambridge: Cambridge University Press.

Brown, B. B. (2003). Crowds, cliques, and friendships. In G. Adams & M. Berzonsky (Eds.), *Blackwell handbook of adolescence*. Malden, MA: Blackwell.

Brown, B. B. (2004). Adolescents' relationships with peers. In R. Lerner & L. Steinberg (Eds.), *Handbook of adolescent psychology*. New York: Wiley.

Brown, B. B., & Larson, R. W. (2002). The kaleidoscope of adolescence: Experiences of the world's youth at the beginning of the 21st century. In B. B. Brown, R. W. Larson, & T. S. Saraswathi (Eds.), *The world's youth*. New York: Cambridge University Press.

Brown, B. B., & Lohr, M. J. (1987). Peer-group affiliation and adolescent self-esteem: An integration of ego-identity and symbolic-interaction theories. *Journal of Personality and Social Psychology, 52,* 47–55.

Brown, E. (2003). When breast just isn't best. *Practicing Midwife, 6,* 42.

Brown, J., Cohen, P., Chen, I. I., Smailes, E., & Johnson, J. G. (2004). Sexual trajectories of abused and neglected youth. *Journal of Developmental and Behavioral Pediatrics, 25,* 77–82.

Brown, L. S. (1989). New voices, new visions: Toward a lesbian/gay paradigm for psychology. *Psychology of Women Quarterly, 13,* 445–458.

Brown, R. (1958). *Words and things*. Glencoe, IL: Free Press.

Brown, R. (1973). *A first language: The early stages*. Cambridge, MA: Harvard University Press.

Brown, R. (1986). *Social psychology* (2nd ed.). New York: Free Press.

Brown, S. L., Nesse, R. M., Vinokur, A. D., & Smith, D. M. (2003). Providing social support may be more beneficial than receiving it: Results from a prospective study of mortality. *Psychological Science, 14,* 320–327.

Brownell, K. (2000). Dieting. In A. Kazdin (Ed.), *Encyclopedia of psychology*. Washington, DC, & New York: American Psychological Association and Oxford University Press.

Brownell, K. D. (2002, June 18). Commentary. *USA Today,* p. 8D.

Brownell, K. D., & Cohen, L. R. (1995). Adherence to dietary regimens. *Behavioral Medicine, 20,* 226–242.

Brownell, K. D., & Rodin, J. (1994). The dieting maelstrom: Is it possible to lose weight? *American Psychologist, 9,* 781–791.

Brownlee, S. (1998, June 15). Baby talk. *U.S. News & World Report,* pp. 48–54.

Bruce, C. A. (2002). The grief process for patient, family, and physician. *Journal of the American Osteopathic Association, 102 (9, Suppl. 3),* S28–S32.

Bruce, J. M., Olen, K., & Jensen, S. J. (1999, April). *The role of emotion and regulation in social competence*. Paper presented at the meeting of the Society for Research in Child Development, Albuquerque.

Bruck, M., & Ceci, S. J. (1999). The suggestibility of children's memory. *Annual Review of Psychology, 50,* 419–439.

Bryant, J. B. (2005). Language in social contexts: The development of communicative competence. In J. Berko Gleason, *The development of language* (6th ed.). Boston: Allyn & Bacon.

Bugental, D. B., & Happaney, K. (2004). Predicting infant maltreatment in low-income families: The interactive effects of maternal attributions and child status at birth. *Developmental Psychology, 40,* 234–243.

Buhrmester, D. (1998). Need fulfillment, interpersonal competence, and the developmental contexts of early adolescent friendship. In W. M. Bukowski & A. F. Newcomb (Eds.), *The company they keep: Friendship in childhood and adolescence*. New York: Cambridge University Press.

Buhrmester, D. (2001, April). *Romantic development: Does age at which romantic involvement starts matter?* Paper presented at the meeting of the Society for Research in Child Development, Minneapolis.

Buhrmester, D. (2003). Unpublished review of J. W. Santrock's *Adolescence* (10th ed.). New York: McGraw-Hill.

Buhs, E. S., & Ladd, G. W. (2002). Peer rejection as antecedent of young children's school adjustment: An examination of mediating processes. *Developmental Psychology, 37,* 550–560.

Bumpas, M. F., Crouter, A. C., & McHale, M. (2001). Parental autonomy granting during adolescence: Exploring gender differences in context. *Developmental Psychology, 37,* 163–173.

Bumpass, L. L., & Aquilino, W. S. (Eds.). (1995). *A social map of midlife: Family and work over the middle life course*. Vero Beach, FL: MacArthur Foundation Research Network: Successful Midlife Development.

Bumpass, L. L., & Lu, H. H. (2000). Trends in cohabitation and implications for children's family contexts in the United States. *Population Studies, 54,* 29–41.

Bumpass, L., & Aquilino, W. (1994). *A social map of midlife: Family and work over the middle life course*. Center for Demography & Ecology, University of Wisconsin, Madison, WI.

Burchinal, M. R., Roberts, J. E., Nabors, L. A., & Bryant, D. M. (1996). Quality of center child care and infant cognitive and language development. *Child Development, 67,* 606–620.

Burgess, E. O. (2004). Sexuality in midlife and later life couples. In J. H. Harvey & A. Wetzel (Eds.), *The handbook of sexuality in close relationships*. Mahwah, NJ: Erlbaum.

Burke, H. M., Zautra, A. J., Davis, M. C., Schultz, A. S., & Reich, J. W. (2003). Arthritis and musculoskeletal conditions. In I. B. Weiner (Ed.), *Handbook of psychology* (Vol. IX). New York: Wiley.

Burkhauser, R. V., & Quinn, J. F. (1989). American patterns of work and retirement. In W. Schmall (Ed.), *Redefining the process of retirement*. Berlin: Springer.

Burnett, A. L. (2004). The impact of sildenafil on molecular science and sexual health. *European Urology, 46,* 9–14.

Burns, A., Roth, M., & Christie, S. (1996). The natural history of mental disorder in old age. *International Journal of Geriatric Psychiatry, 11,* 7–14.

Burns, D. (1985). *Intimate connections*. New York: Morrow.

Burton, L. M. (1996). The timing of child-bearing, family structure, and the role of responsibilities of aging Black women. In E. M. Hetherington & E. A. Blechman (Eds.), *Stress, coping, and resilience in children and families*. Hillsdale, NJ: Erlbaum.

Buss, D. (2000). Evolutionary psychology. In A. Kazdin (Ed.), *Encyclopedia of psychology*. Washington, DC, & New York: American Psychological Association and Oxford University Press.

Buss, D. M. (1995). Psychological sex differences: Origins through sexual selection. *American Psychologist, 50,* 164–168.

Buss, D. M. (2000). Evolutionary psychology. In A. Kazdin (Ed.), *Encyclopedia of psychology*. Washington, DC, & New York: American Psychological Association and Oxford University Press.

Buss, D. M. (2004). *Evolutionary psychology: The new science of the mind* (2nd ed.). Boston: Allyn & Bacon.

Buss, D. M., & Barnes, M. (1986). Preferences in human mate selection. *Journal of Personality and Social Psychology, 50,* 559–570.

Buss, D. M., & others. (1990). International preferences in selecting mates: A study of 37 cultures. *Journal of Cross-Cultural Psychology, 21,* 5–47.

Buss, D. M., & Schmitt, D. P. (1993). Sexual strategies theory: An evolutionary perspective on human mating. *Psychological Review, 100,* 204–232.

Busse, E. W., & Blazer, D. G. (1996). *The American Psychiatric Press textbook of geriatric psychiatry* (2nd ed.). Washington, DC: American Psychiatric Press.

Bussey, K., & Bandura A. (1999). Social cognitive theory of gender development and differentiation. *Psychological Review, 106,* 676–713.

Butler, R. N. (1975). *Why survive? Being old in America.* New York: Harper & Row.

Butler, R. N. (1996). Global aging: Challenges and opportunities of the next century. *Ageing International, 21,* 12–32.

Butler, R. N., & Lewis, M. (2002). *The new love and sex after 60.* New York: Ballentine.

Buzwell, S., & Rosenthal, D. (1996). Constructing a sexual self: Adolescents' sexual self-perceptions and sexual risk-taking. *Journal of Research on Adolescence, 6,* 489–513.

Bybee, J. (Ed.). (1999). *Guilt and children.* San Diego: Academic Press.

Byrnes, J. P. (1997). *The nature and development of decision making.* Mahwah, NJ: Erlbaum.

Byrnes, J. P. (2001). *Minds, brains, and learning.* New York: Guilford Press.

Byrnes, J. P. (2003). Cognitive development during adolescence. In G. Adams & M. Berzonsky (Eds.), *Blackwell handbook of adolescence.* Malden, MA: Blackwell.

Cabeza, R. (2002). Hemispheric asymmetry reduction in older adults: The HAROLD model. *Psychology and Aging, 17,* 85–100.

Cacioppo, J. T., Ernst, J. M., Burleson, M. H., McClintock, M. K., Malarkey, W. B., Hawkley, L. C., Kowalewski, R. B., Paulsen, A., Hobson, J. A., Hugdahl, K., Spiegel, D., Berntson, G. G. (2000). Lonely traits and concomitant physiological processes: The MacArthur Social Neuroscience Studies. *International Journal of Psychophysiology, 35,* 143–154.

Cacioppo, J. T., & Hawkley, L. C. (2003). Social isolation and health, with an emphasis on underlying mechanisms. *Perspectives on Biology and Medicine, 46 (3 Suppl.),* 539–552.

Calabrese, R. L., & Schumer, H. (1986). The effects of service activities on adolescent alienation. *Adolescence, 21,* 675–687.

Calkins, S. D. (2004). Early attachment processes and the development of emotional self-regulation. In R. F. Baumeister & K. D. Vohs (Eds.), *Handbook of self-regulation.* New York: Guilford.

Call, K. A., Riedel, A., Hein, K., McLoyd, V., Kipke, M., & Petersen, P. (2002). Adolescent health and well-being in the 21st century: A global perspective. *Journal of Research on Adolescence, 12,* 69–98.

Call, K., Riedel, A., Hein, K., McLoyd, V., Kipke, M., & Petersen, A. (2003). Adolescent health and well-being in the 21st century: A global perspective. In R. Larson, B. Brown, & J. Mortimer (Eds.), *Adolescents' preparation for the future: Perils and promises.* Malden, MA: Blackwell.

Callan, J. E. (2001). Gender development: Psychoanalytic perspectives. In J. Worrel (Ed.), *Encyclopedia of women and gender.* San Diego: Academic Press.

Calvaresi, E., & Bryan, J. (2001). B vitamins, cognition, and aging: A review. *Journals of Gerontology B: Psychological Sciences and Social Sciences, 56,* 327–339.

Camaioni, L. (2004). The transition from communication to language. In A. Fogel & G. Bremner (Eds.), *Blackwell handbook of infant development.* Malden, MA: Blackwell.

Cameron, J. L. (2004). Interrelationships between hormones, behavior, and affect during adolescence: understanding hormonal, physical, and brain changes occurring in association with pubertal activation of the reproductive axis: Introduction to Part III. *Annals of the New York Academy of Sciences, 1021,* 110–123.

Cameron, J., Cowan, L., Holmes, B., Hurst, P., & McLean, M. (Eds.). (1983). *International handbook of educational systems.* New York: Wiley.

Camilli, G., & Monfils, L. (2004). Test scores and equity. In W. A. Firestone, L. F. Monfils, & R. Y. Schoor (Eds.), *The ambiguity of teaching to the test.* Mahwah, NJ: Erlbaum.

Campbell, F. A., Pungello, E. P., Miller-Johnson, S., Burchinal, M., & Ramey, C. T. (2001). The development of cognitive and academic abilities: Growth curves from an early childhood educational experiment. *Developmental Psychology, 37,* 231–243.

Campbell, L., Campbell, B., & Dickinson, D. (2004). *Teaching and learning through multiple intelligences* (3rd ed.). Boston: Allyn & Bacon.

Campbell, W. G. (2003). Addiction: A disease of volition caused by cognitive impairment. *Canadian Journal of Psychiatry, 48,* 669–674.

Campos, J. J. (2001, April). *Emotion in emotional development: Problems and prospects.* Paper presented at the meeting of the Society for Research in Child Development, Minneapolis.

Campos, J. J. (2004). Unpublished review of J. W. Santrock's *Life-span development* (10th ed.). New York: McGraw-Hill.

Campos, J. J., Frankel, C. B., & Camras, L. (2004). On the nature of emotion regulation. *Child Development, 75,* 377–394.

Campos, J. J., Langer, A., & Krowitz, A. (1970). Cardiac responses on the visual cliff in prelocomotor human infants. *Science, 170,* 196–197.

Canfield, J., & Hansen, M. V. (1995). *A second helping of chicken soup for the soul.* Deerfield Beach, FL: Health Communications.

Canfield, R. L., & Haith, M. M. (1991). Young infants' visual expectations for symmetric and asymmetric stimulus sequences. *Developmental Psychology, 27,* 198–208.

Canfield, R. L., Henderson, C. R., Cory-Slechta, D. A., Cox, C., Jusko, T. A., & Lamphear, B. P. (2003). Intellectual impairment in children with blood lead concentrations below 10 μg per deciliter. *New England Journal of Medicine, 348,* 1517–1526.

Carbone, D. J., & Seftel, A. D. (2002). Erectile dysfunctions: Diagnosis and treatment in older men. *Geriatrics, 57(9),* 18–24.

Carbonell, O. A., Alzte, G., Bustamante, M. R., & Quiceno, J. (2002). Maternal caregiving and infant security in two cultures. *Developmental Psychology, 38,* 67–78.

Carbonne, B., Tsatsaris, V., & Goffinet, F. (2001). The new tocolytics. *Gynecology, Obstetrics, and Fertility, 29,* 316–319.

Carlisle, J. F. (2004). Morphological processes that influence learning to read. In C. A. Stone, E. R. Silliman, B. J. Ehren, & K. Apel (Eds.), *Handbook of language and literacy.* New York: Guilford.

Carlson, E. A., Sroufe, L. A., & Egeland, B. (2004). The construction of experience: A longitudinal study of representation and behavior. *Child Development, 75,* 66–83.

Carly, A. (2003). Anemia: When is it iron deficiency? *Pediatric Nursing 29,* 127–133.

Carmichael, S. L., Shaw, G. M., & Nelson, V. (2002). Timing of prenatal care initiation and risk of congenital malformations. *Teratology, 66,* 326–330.

Carnegie Corporation (1989). *Turning points: Preparing youth for the 21st century.* New York: Author.

Carnegie Council on Adolescent Development (1995). *Great transitions.* New York: The Carnegie Corporation.

Carnethon, M. R., Gidding, S. S., Nehgme, R., Sidney, S., Jacobs, D. R., & Liu, K. (2003). Cardiorespiratory fitness in young adulthood and the development of cardiovascular disease risk factors. *Journal of the American Medical Association, 290,* 3092–3100.

Carolo, G. (2005). Care and altruism. In M. Killen & J. Smetana (Eds.), *Handbook of moral development.* Mahwah, NJ: Erlbaum.

Carpendale, J. I., & Chandler, M. J. (1996). On the distinction between false belief understanding and subscribing to an interpretive theory of mind. *Child Development, 67,* 1686–1706.

Carpenter, B., & Dave, J. (2004). Disclosing a dementia diagnosis. *The Gerontologist, 44,* 149–158.

Carr, D., House, J. S., Kessler, R. C., Nesse, R. M., Sonnege, J., & Wortman, C. (2000). Marital quality and psychological adjustment to widowhood among older adults: A longitudinal analysis. *Journals of Gerontology B: Psychological Sciences and Social Sciences, 55,* S197–S207.

Carrington, N. A., & Bogetz, J. F. (2004). Normal grief and bereavement. *Journal of Palliative Medicine, 7,* 309–323.

Carroll, W. L., Bhojwani, D., Min, D. J., Raetz, E., Relling, M., Davies, S., Downing, J. R., Wilman, C. L., & Reed, J. C. (2003). Pediatric acute lymphoblastic leukemia. *Hematology, 21,* 102–131.

Carskadon, M. A. (Ed.). (2002). *Adolescent sleep patterns.* New York: Cambridge University Press.

Carskadon, M. A. (2004). Sleep difficulties in young people. *Archives of Pediatric and Adolescent Medicine, 158,* 597–598.

Carskadon, M. A., Acebo, C., & Jenni, O. G. (2004). Regulation of adolescent sleep: Implications for behavior. *Annals of the New York Academy of Sciences, 102,* 276–291.

Carskadon, M. A., Wolfson, A. R., Acebo, C., Tzischinsky, O., & Seifer, R. (1998). Adolescent sleep patterns, circadian timing, and sleepiness at a transition to early school days. *Sleep, 21,* 873–884.

Carson, C. C. (2003). Sildenafil: A 4-year update in the treatment of 20 million erectile dysfunction patients. *Current Urology Reports, 4,* 488–496.

Carstensen, L. L. (1995). Evidence for a life-span theory of socioemotional selectivity. *Current Directions in Psychological Science, 4,* 151–156.

Carstensen, L. L. (1998). A life-span approach to social motivation. In J. Heckhausen & C. Dweck (Eds.), *Motivation and self-regulation across the life span.* New York: Cambridge University Press.

Carstensen, L. L., Isaacowitz, D. M., & Charles, S. T. (1999). Taking time seriously: A theory of socioemotional selectivity. *American Psychologist, 54,* 165–181.

Carstensen, L. L., & Löckenhoff, C. E. (2004). Aging, emotion, and evolution: The bigger picture. In P. Ekman, J. J. Campos, R. J. Davidson, & F. B. M. de Waal (Eds.), *Emotions inside out: 130 years after Darwin's* The Expression of the Emotions in Man and Animals. New York: Annals of the New York Academy of Sciences.

Carter, B., & McGoldrick, M. (1988). Overview: The changing family life cycle—A framework for family therapy. In B. Carter & M. McGoldrick (Eds.), *The changing family life cycle* (2nd ed.). Boston: Allyn & Bacon.

Carter, P. A. (2004). Education and work as human rights for women. In R. D. Lakes & P. A. Carter (Eds.), *Globalizing education for work.* Mahwah, NJ: Erlbaum.

Carter-Saltzman, L. (1980). Biological and sociocultural effects on handedness: Comparison between biological and adoptive families. *Science, 209,* 1263–1265.

Carver, K., Joyner, K., & Udry, J. R. (2003). National estimates of romantic relationships. In P. Florsheim (Ed.), *Adolescent romantic relations and sexual behavior.* Mahwah, NJ: Erlbaum.

Carver, L. J., & Bauer, P. J. (2001). The dawning of a past: The emergence of long-term explicit memory in infancy. *Journal of Experimental Psychology: General, 130,* 726–745.

Case, R. (1999). Conceptual development in the child and the field: A personal view of the Piagetian legacy. In E. K. Skolnick, K. Nelson, S. A. Gelman, & P. H. Miller (Eds.), *Conceptual development.* Mahwah, NJ: Erlbaum.

Case, R., Kurland, D. M., & Goldberg, J. (1982). Operational efficiency and the growth of short-term memory span. *Journal of Experimental Child Psychology, 33,* 386–404.

Case, R., & Mueller, M. P. (2001). Differentiation, integration, and covariance mapping as fundamental processes in cognitive and neurological growth. In J. L. McClelland & R. S. Siegler (Eds.), *Mechanisms of cognitive development.* Mahwah, NJ: Erlbaum.

Caselli, R. J. (2003). Current issues in the diagnosis and management of dementia. *Seminars in Neurology, 23,* 231–240.

Casey, B. J., Durston, S., & Fossella, J. A. (2001). Evidence for a mechanistic model of cognitive control. *Clinical Neuroscience Research, 1,* 267–282.

Casey, B., Giedd, J., & Thomas, K. (2000). Structural and functional brain development and its relation to cognitive development. *Biological Psychology, 54,* 241–257.

Casey, B. M., McIntire, D. D., & Leveno, K. J. (2001). The continuing value of the Apgar score for the assessment of newborn infants. *New England Journal of Medicine, 344,* 467–471.

Caspi, A. (1998). Personality development across the life course. In W. Damon (Ed.), *Handbook of child psychology* (Vol. 3). New York: Wiley.

Caspi, A., & Roberts, B. W. (2001). Personality development across the life course: The argument for change and continuity. *Psychological Inquiry, 12,* 49–66.

Castle, N. G. (2001). Innovation in nursing homes. *The Gerontologist, 41* (No. 2), 161–172.

Cauce, A. M., Domenech-Rodriquez, M., Paradise, M., Cochran, B. N., Shea, J. M., Srebnik, D., & Baydar, N. (2002). Cultural and contextual influences in mental health help seeking: A focus on ethnic minority youth. *Journal of Consulting and Clinical Psychology, 70,* 44–55.

Cauffman, B. E. (1994, February). *The effects of puberty, dating, and sexual involvement on dieting and disordered eating in young adolescent girls.* Paper presented at the meeting of the Society for Research on Adolescence, San Diego.

Caulfield, R. A. (2001). *Infants and toddlers.* Upper Saddle River, NJ: Prentice Hall.

Cavanaugh, J. (2000, January). Commentary. *American Psychologist, 31,* p. 25.

Cavanaugh, S. E. (2004). The sexual debut of girls in adolescence: The intersection of race, pubertal timing, and friendship group characteristics. *Journal of Research on Adolescence, 14,* 285–312.

Ceci, S. J. (2000). Bronfenbrenner, Urie. In A. Kazdin (Ed.), *Encyclopedia of psychology.* Washington, DC, & New York: American Psychological Association and Oxford University Press.

Ceci, S. J. (2003). Cast in six ponds and you'll reel in something: Looking back on 25 years of research. *American Psychologist, 58*, 855–864.

Ceci, S. J., Fitneva, S. A., & Gilstrap, L. L. (2003). Memory development and eyewitness testimony. In A. Slater & G. Bremner (Eds.), *An introduction to developmental psychology.* Malden, MA: Blackwell.

Ceci, S. J., & Gilstrap, L. L. (2000). Determinants of intelligence: Schooling and intelligence. In A. Kazdin (Ed.), *Encyclopedia of psychology.* Washington, DC, & New York: American Psychological Association and Oxford University Press.

Center for Survey Research at the University of Connecticut (2000). *Hours on the job.* Storrs: University of Connecticut, Center for Survey Research.

Centers for Disease Control and Prevention (2000). *Reproductive health.* Atlanta: Author.

Centers for Disease Control and Prevention (2001). *Strategies for stopping smoking.* Atlanta, GA: Author.

Centers for Disease Control and Prevention (2002). *Cohabitation.* Atlanta, GA: Author.

Centers for Disease Control and Prevention (2002). *Sexually transmitted diseases.* Atlanta: Author.

Centers for Disease Control and Prevention (2002). Trends in racial and ethnic-specific rates for health status indicators: United States, 1990–1998. *Healthy People 2000: Statistical Notes, 23*, 1–16.

Centers for Disease Control and Prevention (2003). Physical activity levels among children aged 9–13—United States, 2002. *Morbidity and Mortality Weekly Report, 52*, 785–788.

Centers for Disease Control and Prevention (2003). Public health and aging: Health-related quality of life among low-income persons aged 45–64 years—United States. *Morbity and Mortality Weekly Reports, 21*, 1120–1124.

Centers for Disease Control and Prevention (2004). *Sexually transmitted diseases.* Atlanta: Author.

Centers for Disease Control and Prevention (2005). *Lifestyle and weight.* Atlanta: Centers for Disease Control and Prevention.

Chama, C. M., Audu, B. M., & Kyari, O. (2004). Prevention of mother-to-child transmission of HIV at Maiduguri, Nigeria. *Journal of Obstetrics and Gynecology, 24*, 266–269.

Chan, H. M. (2004). Sharing death and dying: Advanced directives, autonomy, and the family. *Bioethics, 18*, 87–103.

Chang, S. C., O'Brien, K. O., Nathanson, M. S., Mancini, J., & Witter, F. R. (2003). Characteristics and risk factors for adverse birth outcomes in pregnant black adolescents. *Journal of Obstetrics and Gynecology Canada, 25*, 751–759.

Chan-Yeung, M., & Dimich-Ward, H. (2003). Respiratory health effects of exposure to environmental tobacco smoke. *Respirology, 8*, 131–139.

Chao, R. (2001). Extending research on the consequences of parenting style for Chinese Americans and European Americans. *Child Development, 72*, 1832–1843.

Chao, R., & Tseng, V. (2002). Parenting of Asians. In M. H. Bornstein (Series Ed.), *Handbook of parenting: Vol. 4. Social conditions and applied parenting* (2nd ed.). Mahwah, NJ: Erlbaum.

Charles, S. T., & Carstensen, L. L. (2004). A life-span view of emotional functioning in adulthood and old age. In P. Costa (Ed.), *Advances in cell aging and gerontology series.* New York: Elsevier.

Charness, N., & Bosman, E. A. (1992). Human factors and aging. In F. I. M. Craik & T. A. Salthouse (Eds.), *The handbook of aging and cognition.* Hillsdale, NJ: Erlbaum.

Charness, N., Krampe, R. T., & Mayr, U. (1996). The role of practice and coaching in entrepreneurial skill domains: An international comparison of life-span chess skill acquisition. In K. A. Ericsson (Ed.), *The road to excellence: The acquisition of expert performance in the arts, sciences, sports, and games.* Mahwah, NJ: Erlbaum.

Chase-Lansdale, P. L., Coley, R. L., & Grining, C. P. L. (2001, April). *Low-income families and child care.* Paper presented at the meeting of the Society for Research in Child Development, Minneapolis.

Chaudhari, S., Otiv, M., Chitale, A., Pandit, A., & Hoge, M. (2004). Pune low birth weight study–cognitive abilities and educational performance at twelve years. *Indian Pediatrics, 41*, 121–128.

Chauhuri, J. H., & Williams, P. H. (1999, April). *The contribution of infant temperament and parent emotional availability to toddler attachment.* Paper presented at the meeting of the Society for Research in Child Development, Albuquerque.

Chavkin, W. (2001). Cocaine and pregnancy—time to look at the evidence. *Journal of the American Medical Association, 285*, 1626–1628.

Chaytor, N., & Scmitter-Edgecombe, M. (2004). Working memory and aging: A cross-sectional and longitudinal analysis using a self-ordered pointing task. *Journal of the International Neuropsychological Society, 10*, 489–503.

Cheitlin, M. D. (2003). Sexual activity and cardiovascular disease. *American Journal of Cardiology, 92*, 3M–9M.

Chemaitilly, W., Trivin, C., Suberbielle, J. C., & Brauner, R. (2003). Assessing short-statured children for growth deficiency. *Hormone Research, 60*, 34–42.

Chen, A. Y., & Escarce, J. J. (2004). Quantifying income-related inequality in healthcare delivery in the United States. *Medical Care, 42*, 38–47.

Chen, C., & Stevenson, H. W. (1989). Homework: A cross-cultural comparison. *Child Development, 60*, 551–561.

Chen, X., Hastings, P. D., Rubin, K. H., Chen, H., Cen, G., & Stewart, S. L. (1998). Childrearing attitudes and behavioral inhibition in Chinese and Canadian toddlers: A cross-cultural study. *Developmental Psychology, 34*, 677–686.

Chen, Z., & Siegler, R. S. (2000). Across the great divide: Bridging the gap between understanding of toddlers' and older children's thinking. *Monograph of the Society for Research in Child Development, 65* (No. 2).

Cherif, H., Tarry, J. L., Ozanne, S. E., & Hales, C. N. (2003). Aging and telomeres: A study into organ- and gender-specific telomere shortening. *Nucleic Acids Research, 31*, 1576–1583.

Cherlin, A. J., & Furstenberg, F. F. (1994). Stepfamilies in the United States: A reconsideration. In J. Blake & J. Hagen (Eds.), *Annual review of sociology.* Palo Alto, CA: Annual Reviews.

Chernausek, S. D. (2004). Growth hormone treatment of short children born small for gestational age: A U.S. perspective. *Hormone Research, 62, Supplement 3,* S124–S127.

Chernichovsky, D., & Markowitz, S. (2004). Aging and aggregate costs of medical care: Conceptual and policy issues. *Health Economics, 13*, 543–562.

Chess, S., & Thomas, A. (1977). Temperamental individuality from childhood to adolescence. *Journal of Child Psychiatry, 16*, 218–226.

Chess, S., & Thomas, A. (1987). *Origins and evolution of behavior disorders.* Cambridge, MA: Harvard University Press.

Chevan, A. (1996). As cheaply as one: Cohabitation in the older population. *Journal of Marriage and the Family, 58,* 656–667.

Chi, M. T. (1978). Knowledge structures and memory development. In R. S. Siegler (Ed.), *Children's thinking: What develops?* Hillsdale, NJ: Erlbaum.

Child Trends (2001). *Trends among Hispanic children, youth, and families.* Washington, DC: Author.

Children's Defense Fund (2004). *State of America's children.* Washington, DC: Author.

Chiriboga, D. (1997). Crisis, challenge, and stability in the middle years. In M. E. Lachman & J. B. James (Eds.), *Multiple paths of midlife development.* Chicago: University of Chicago Press.

Chiriboga, D. A. (1982). Adaptation to marital separation in later and earlier life. *Journal of Gerontology, 37,* 109–114.

Chiriboga, D. A. (1989). Mental health at the midpoint: Crisis, challenge, or relief? In S. Hunter & M. Sundel (Eds.), *Midlife myths.* Newbury Park, CA: Sage.

Chiroro, P., Bohner, G., Viki, G. T., & Jarvis, C. I. (2004). Rape myth acceptance and rape proclivity: Expected dominance versus expected arousal as mediators in acquaintance rape situations. *Journal of Interpersonal Violence, 19,* 427–442.

Chisholm, K. (1998). A three-year follow-up of attachment and indiscriminate friendliness in children adopted from Romanian orphanages. *Child Development, 69,* 1092–1106.

Choi, N. G. (2001). Relationship between life satisfaction and postretirement employment among older women. *International Journal of Aging and Human Development, 52,* 45–70.

Chomsky, N. (1957). *Syntactic structures.* The Hague: Mouton.

Chong, D. S., Yip, P. S., & Karlberg, J. (2004). Maternal smoking: An increasing risk factor for sudden infant death syndrome in Sweden. *Acta Pediatrics, 93,* 471–478.

Chopdar, A., Chakravarthy, U., & Verma, D. (2003). Age related macular degeneration. *British Journal of Medicine, 326,* 485–488.

Chopra, M. (2003). Risk factors for under-nutrition of young children in a rural area

of South Africa. *Public Health Nursing, 6,* 645–652.

Christensen, H., Korten, A., Jorm, A. F., Henderson, A. S., Scott, R., & MacKinnon, A. J. (1996). Activity levels and cognitive functioning in an elderly community sample. *Age and Aging, 25,* 72–80.

Christensen, L. (1996). *Diet-behavior relationships.* Washington, DC: American Psychological Association.

Christensen, S. L., & Thurlow, M. L. (2004). School dropouts: Prevention, considerations, interventions, and challenges. *Current Directions in Psychological Science, 13,* 36–39.

Christian, K., Bachnan, H. J., & Morrison, F. J. (2001). Schooling and cognitive development. In R. J. Sternberg & E. L. Grigorenko (Eds.), *Environmental effects on cognitive development.* Mahwah, NJ: Erlbaum.

Christopher, F. S., & Sprecher, S. (2000). Sexuality in marriage, dating, and other relationships: Decade review. *Journal of Marriage and Family, 62,* 999–1017.

Chronis, A. M., Chacko, A., Fabiano, G. A., Wymbs, B. T., & Pelham, W. E. (2004). Enhancements to the behavioral parent training paradigm for families of children with ADHD: Review and future directions. *Clinical Child and Family Psychology Review, 7,* 1–27.

Chuang, M. E., Lamb, C. P., & Hwang, C. P. (2004). Internal reliability, temporal stability, and correlates of individual differences in paternal involvement: A 15-year longitudinal study in Sweden. In R. D. Day & M. E. Lamb (Eds.), *Conceptualizing and measuring father involvement.* Mahwah, NJ: Erlbaum.

Chun, K. M., & Akutsu, P. D. (2003). Acculturation among ethnic minority families. In K. M. Chun, P. B. Organista, & G. Marin (Eds.), *Acculturation.* Washington, DC: American Psychological Association.

Church, D. K., Siegel, M. A., & Fowler, C. D. (1988). *Growing old in America.* Wylie, TX: Information Aids.

Church, T. S., Cheng, Y. J., Earnest, C. P., Barlow, C. E., Gibbons, L. W., Priest, E. L., & Blair, S. N. (2004). Exercise capacity and body composition as predictors of mortality among men with diabetes. *Diabetes Care, 27,* 83–88.

Churchill, J. D., Galvez, R., Colcombe, S., Swain, R. A., Kramer, A. F., & Greenough, W. T. (2002). Exercise, experience, and the aging brain. *Neurobiology of Aging, 23,* 941–955.

Chwo, M. J., Anderson, G. C., Good, M., Dowling, D. A., Shaiau, S. H., & Chu, D. M. (2002). A randomized controlled trial of early kangaroo care for preterm infants: Effects on temperature, weight, behavior, and acuity. *Journal of Nursing Research, 10,* 129–142.

Cicchetti, D. (2001). How a child builds a brain. In W. W. Hartup & R. A. Weinberg (Eds.), *Child psychology in retrospect and prospect.* Mahwah, NJ: Erlbaum.

Cicchetti, D., & Toth, S. L. (1998). Perspectives on research and practice in developmental psychology. In W. Damon (Ed.), *Handbook of child psychology* (Vol. 4). New York: Wiley.

Cicirelli, V. G. (1991). Sibling relationships in adulthood. *Marriage and Family Review, 16,* 291–310.

Cillessen, A. H. N., & Mayeux, L. (2004). Sociometric status and peer group behavior: Previous findings and current directions. In J. B. Kupersmidt & K. A. Dodge (Eds.), *Children's peer relations: From development to intervention.* Washington, DC: American Psychological Association.

Claar, R. L., & Blumenthal, J. A. (2003). The value of stress-management interventions in life-threatening medical conditions. *Current Directions in Psychological Science, 12,* 133–137.

Clampet-Lundquist, S., Edin, K., London, A., Scott, E., & Hunter, V. (2004). "Making a way out of no way": How mothers meet the basic family needs while moving from welfare to work. In A. C. Crouter & A. Booth (Eds.), *Work-family challenges for low-income families and their children.* Mahwah, NJ: Erlbaum.

Clancy, S. M., & Hoyer, W. J. (1994). Age and skill in visual search. *Developmental Psychology, 30,* 545–552.

Clark, R. D., & Hatfield, E. (1989). Gender differences in receptivity to sexual offers. *Journal of Psychology and Human Sexuality, 2,* 39–55.

Clark, S. D., Zabin, L. S., & Hardy, J. B. (1984). Sex, contraception, and parenthood: Experience and attitudes among urban black young men. *Family Planning Perspectives, 16,* 77–82.

Clarke, J., Preston, M., Raksin, J., & Bengtson, V. L. (1999). Types of conflicts and tensions between older adults and adult children. *Gerontologist, 39,* 261–270.

Clark-Plaskie, M., & Lachman, M. E. (1999). The sense of control in midlife. In

S. L. Willis & J. D. Reid (Eds.), *Life in the middle.* San Diego: Academic Press.

Clarkson-Smith, L., & Hartley, A. A. (1989). Relationships between physical exercise and cognitive abilities in older adults. *Psychology and Aging, 4,* 183–189.

Clausen, J. A. (1993). *American lives.* New York: Free Press.

Claxton-Oldfield, S., Claxton-Oldfield, J., & Rishchynski, G. (2004). Understanding the term "palliative care": A Canadian survey. *American Journal of Hospice and Palliative Care, 21,* 105–110.

Clay, E. C., & Seehusen, D. A. (2004). A review of postpartum depression for the primary care physician. *Southern Medical Journal, 97,* 157–162.

Clay, R. A. (1997, April). Helping dying patients let go of life in peace. *APA Monitor,* p. 42.

Clay, R. A. (2000, April). Linking up online: Is the Internet enhancing interpersonal connections or leading to greater isolation? *Monitor on Psychology,* 20–23.

Clements, P. T., Vigil, G. J., Manno, M. S., Henry, G. C., Wilks, B., Das, S., Kellywood, R., & Foster, W. (2003). Cultural perspectives on death, grief, and bereavement. *Journal of Psychosocial Nursing and Mental Health Services, 41,* 18–26.

Cleveland, J. N., & Shore, L. M. (1996). Work and employment. In J. E. Birren (Ed.), *Encyclopedia of aging* (Vol. 2). San Diego: Academic Press.

Cleves, M. A., Hobbs, C. A., Collins, H. B., Andrews, N., Smith, L. N., & Robbins, J. N. (2004). Folic acid use by women receiving gynecologic care. *Obstetrics and Gynecology, 103,* 746–753.

Clifford, B. R., Gunter, B., & McAleer, J. L. (1995). *Television and children.* Hillsdale, NJ: Erlbaum.

Clifton, R. K., Morrongiello, B. A., Kulig, J. W., & Dowd, J. M. (1981). Developmental changes in auditory localization in infancy. In R. N. Aslin, J. R. Alberts, & M. R. Petersen (Eds.), *Development of perception* (Vol. 1). Orlando, FL: Academic Press.

Clifton, R. K., Muir, D. W., Ashmead, D. H., & Clarkson, M. G. (1993). Is visually guided reaching in early infancy a myth? *Child Development, 64,* 1099–1110.

Clingempeel, W. G., & Brand-Clingempeel, E. (2004). Pathogenic conflict: Families and children. In M. Coleman & L. Ganong (Eds.), *Handbook of contemporary families.* Thousand Oaks, CA: Sage.

Clinton Smith, J. (2004). The current epidemic of childhood obesity and its implications for future coronary heart disease. *Pediatric Clinics of North America, 51,* 1679–1695.

Cnattingius, S., Bergstrom, R., Lipworth, L., & Kramer, M. S. (1998). Prepregnancy weight and the risk of adverse pregnancy outcomes. *New England Journal of Medicine, 338,* 147–152.

Cnattingius, S., Signorello, L. B., Anneren, G., Classon, B., Ekbom, A., Ljunger, E., Blot, W. J., McLaughlin, J. K., Petersson, G., Rane, A., & Granath, F. (2000). Caffeine intake and the risk of first-trimester spontaneous abortion. *New England Journal of Medicine, 343,* 1839–1845.

Cochran, S. D., & Mays, V. M. (1990). Sex, lies, and HIV. *New England Journal of Medicine, 322*(11), 774–775.

Cohen, C. I., Teresi, J., & Holmes, D. (1985). Social networks, stress, adaptation, and health. *Research on Aging, 7,* 409–431.

Cohen, L. B. (1995). Violent video games: Aggression, arousal, and desensitization in young adolescent boys. Doctoral dissertation, University of Southern California, 1995. *Dissertation Abstracts International, 57* (2-B), 1463. University Microfilms No. 9616947.

Cohen, P., Kasen, S., Chen, H., Hartmark, C., & Gordon, K. (2003). Variations in patterns of developmental transitions in the emerging adulthood period. *Developmental Psychology, 39,* 657–669.

Cohen, S. S. (2004). Child care: A crucial legislative issue. *Journal of Pediatric Health Care, 18,* 312–314.

Cohn, E., & Harlow, K. (1993, October). *Elders as victims: Randomized studies in two states.* Paper presented at the meeting of the Gerontological Association of America, New Orleans.

Coie, J. (2004). The impact of negative social experiences on the development of antisocial behavior. In J. B. Kupersmidt & K. A. Dodge (Eds.), Children's peer relations: From development to intervention. Washington, DC: American Psychological Association.

Colby, A., Kohlberg, L., Gibbs, J., & Lieberman, M. (1983). A longitudinal study of moral judgment. *Monographs of the Society for Research in Child Development* (Serial No. 201).

Colcombe, S. J., Erickson, K. I., Raz, N., Webb, A. G., Cohen, N. J., McAuley, E., & Kramer, A. F. (2003). Aerobic fitness reduces brain tissue loss in aging humans. *Journals of Gerontology: Biological Sciences and Medical Sciences, 58,* 176–180.

Colcombe, S. J., & Kramer, A. F. (2003). Fitness effects on the cognitive function of older adults: A meta-analytic study. *Psychological Science, 14,* 125–130.

Colcombe, S. J., Kramer, A. F., Rickson, K. I., Scalf, P., McAuley, E., Cohen, N. J., Webb, A., Jerome, G. J., Marquez, D. X., & Elavsky, S. (2004). Cardiovascular fitness, cortical plasticity, and aging. *Proceedings of the National Academy of Science, 101,* 3316–3321.

Cole, C. M., Waldron, N., & Majd, M. (2004). Academic progress of students across inclusive and traditional settings. *Mental Retardation, 42,* 136–144.

Cole, E. R., & Stewart, A. J. (1996). Black and White women's political activism: Personality development, political identity and social responsibility. *Journal of Personality and Social Psychology, 71,* 130–140.

Cole, M. G. (2004). Delirium in elderly patients. *American Journal of Geriatric Psychiatry, 12,* 7–21.

Cole, M. (2005). Culture in development. In M. H. Bornstein & M. E. Lamb (Eds.), *Developmental science* (5th ed.). Mahwah, NJ: Erlbaum.

Cole, P. M., Martin, S. E., & Dennis, T. A. (2004). Emotion regulation as a scientific construct: Methodological challenges and directions for child development research. *Child Development, 75,* 317–333.

Coleman, M., Ganong, L., & Fine, M. (2000). Reinvestigating remarriage: Another decade of progress. *Journal of Marriage and the Family, 62,* 1288–1307.

Coleman, M., Ganong, L., & Fine, M. (2004). Communication in stepfamilies. In A. L. Vangelisti (Ed.), *Handbook of family communication.* Mahwah, NJ: Erlbaum.

Coleman, M., Ganong, L., & Weaver, S. E. (2001). Relationship maintenance and enhancement in remarried families. In J. H. Harvey & A. Wenzel (Eds.), *Close romantic relationships.* Mahwah, NJ: Erlbaum.

Coleman, P. D. (1986, August). *Regulation of dendritic extent: Human aging brain and Alzheimer's disease.* Paper presented at the meeting of the American Psychological Association, Washington, DC.

Coles, R. (1970). *Erik H. Erikson: The growth of his work.* Boston: Little, Brown.

Coley, R. (2001). *Differences in the gender gap: Comparisons across racial/ethnic groups in education and work.* Princeton: Educational Testing Service.

Coley, R. L., Morris, J. E., & Hernandez, D. (2004). Out-of-school care and problem behavior trajectories among low-income adolescents: Individual, family, and neighborhood characteristics and added risks. *Child Development, 75,* 948–965.

Coll, C. T. G., Meyer, E. C., & Brillion, L. (1995). Ethnic and minority parenting. In M. H. Bornstein (Ed.), *Children and parenting* (Vol. 2). Hillsdale, NJ: Erlbaum.

Coll, C. T. G., & Pachter, L. M. (2002). Ethnic and minority parenting. In M. H. Bornstein (Ed.), *Handbook of parenting* (2nd ed., Vol. 4). Mahwah, NJ: Erlbaum.

Collaku, A., Rankinen, T., Rice, T., Leon, A. S., Rao, D. C., Skinner, J. S., Wilmore, J. H., & Bouchard, C. (2004). A genome-wide linkage scan for dietary energy and nutrient intakes. *American Journal of Clinical Nutrition, 79,* 881–886.

Collins, N. L., & Feeney, B. C. (2004). An attachment theory perspective on closeness and intimacy. In D. J. Mashek & A. P. Aron (Eds.), *Handbook of closeness and intimacy.* Mahwah, NJ: Erlbaum.

Collins, R. L., Elliott, M. N., Berry, S. H., Kanocouse, D. E., Kunkel, D., Hunter, S. B., & Miu, A. (2004). Watching sex on television predicts adolescent initiation of sexual behavior. *Pediatrics, 114,* e280–e289.

Collins, W. A., & Laursen, B. (2000). Adolescent relationships: The art of fugue. In C. Hendrick & S. S. Hendrick (Eds.), *Close relationships: A sourcebook.* Thousand Oaks, CA: Sage.

Collins, W. A., & Laursen, B. (2004). Parent-adolescent relationships and influences. In R. Lerner & L. Steinberg (Eds.), *Handbook of adolescent psychology.* New York: Wiley.

Collins, W. A., Maccoby, E. E., Steinberg, L., Hetherington, E. M., & Bornstein, M. H. (2000). Contemporary research on parenting: The case for nature and nurture. *American Psychologist, 55,* 218–232.

Collins, W. A., Maccoby, E. E., Steinberg, L., Hetherington, E. M., & Bornstein, M. H. (2001). Toward nature WITH nurture. *American Psychologist, 56,* 171–173.

Collins, W. A., Madsen, S. D., & Susman-Stillman, A. (2002). Parenting during middle childhood. In M. Bornstein (Ed.), *Handbook of parenting* (2nd ed.). Mahwah, NJ: Erlbaum.

Comas-Díaz, L. (2001). Hispanics, Latinos, or Americanos: The evolution of identity. *Cultural Diversity and Ethnic Minority Psychology, 7,* 115–120.

Comer, J. P. (1988). Educating poor minority children. *Scientific American, 259,* 42–48.

Comer, J. P., Haynes, N. M., Joyner, E. T., & Ben-Avie, M. (1996). *Rallying the whole village: The Comer process for reforming urban education.* New York: Teachers College Press.

Comijs, H., Deeg, D., Dik, M., Twisk, J., & Jonker, C. (2002). *Memory complaints.* Unpublished manuscript, Department of Psychiatry, Vrije University, Amsterdam, The Netherlands.

Committee on Fetus and Newborn (2000). Prevention and management of pain and stress in the newborn. *Pediatrics, 105,* 454–461.

Commoner, B. (2002). Unraveling the DNA myth: The spurious foundation of genetic engineering. *Harper's Magazine, 304,* 39–47.

Commons, M. L., Sinnott, J. D., Richards, F. A., & Armon, C. (1989). *Adult development: Vol. 1. Comparisons and applications of developmental models.* New York: Praeger.

Compas, B. (2004). Processes of risk and resilience during adolescence: Linking contexts and individuals. In R. Lerner & L. Steinberg (Eds.), *Handbook of adolescent psychology.* New York: Wiley.

Compas, B. E., Connor-Smith, J. K., Saltzman, H., Thomsen, A. H., & Wadsworth, M. E. (2001). Coping with stress during childhood and adolescence: Problems, progress, and potential in theory and research. *Psychological Bulletin, 127,* 87–127.

Compas, B. E., & Grant, K. E. (1993, March). *Stress and adolescent depressive symptoms: Underlying mechanisms and processes.* Paper presented at the biennial meeting of the Society for Research in Child Development, New Orleans.

Condry, K. F., Smith, W. C., & Spelke, E. S. (2001). Development of perceptual organization. In F. Lacerda, C. von Hofsten, & M. Heimann (Eds.), *Emerging cognitive abilities in infancy.* Mahwah, NJ: Erlbaum.

Conduct Problems Prevention Research Group (2002). Evaluation of the first 3 years of the Fast Track prevention trial with children at high risk for adolescent conduct problems. *Journal of Abnormal Child Psychology, 30,* 19–35.

Conduct Problems Prevention Research Group (2004). The Fast Track experiment: Translating the developmental model into a preventive design. In J. B. Kupersmidt & K. A. Dodge (Eds.), *Children's peer relations: From development to intervention.* Washington, DC: American Psychological Association.

Conger, K. J., & Bryant, C. M. (2004). The changing nature of adolescent sibling relationships. In R. D. Conger, F. O. Lorenz, & K. A. S. Wickrama (Eds.), *Continuity and change in family relations.* Mahwah, NJ: Erlbaum.

Conger, R. D., & Chao, W. (1996). Adolescent depressed mood. In R. L. Simons (Ed.), *Understanding differences between divorced and intact families: Stress, interaction, and child outcome.* Thousand Oaks, CA: Sage.

Conger, R. D., & Ge, X. (1999). Conflict and cohesion in parent-adolescent relations: Changes in emotional expression. In M. J. Cox & J. Brooks-Gunn (Eds.), *Conflict and cohesion in families.* Mahwah, NJ: Erlbaum.

Conger, R., & Reuter, M. (1996). Siblings, parents, and peers: A longitudinal study of social influences in adolescent risk for alcohol use and abuse. In G. H. Brody (Ed.), *Sibling relationships: Their causes and consequences.* Norwood, NJ: Ablex.

Consedine, N. S., Magai, C., & Conway, F. (2004). Predicting ethnic variation in adaptation to later life: Styles of socioemotional functioning and contrained heterotypy. *Journal of Cross Cultural Gerontology, 19,* 97–131.

Contemporary Research Press (1993). *American working women: A statistical handbook.* Dallas: Author.

Conway, K. P., Swendsen, J. D., & Merikangas, K. R. (2003). Alcohol expectancies, alcohol consumption, and problem drinking: The moderating role of family history. *Addictive Behavior, 28,* 823–836.

Cook, D. J., Guyatt, G. H., Jaeschke, R., Reeve, J., Spanier, A., King, D., Molloy, D., Willan, A., & Streiner, D. (1995). Determinants in Canadian health care workers of the decision to withdraw life support from the critically ill. *Journal of the American Medical Association, 273,* 703–708.

Cook, M., & Birch, R. (1984). Infant perception of the shapes of tilted plane forms. *Infant Behavior and Development, 7,* 389–402.

Cooney, T. M. (1994). Young adults' relations with parents: The influence of recent parental divorce. *Journal of Marriage and the Family, 56,* 45–56.

Cooper, C. R., & Grotevant, H. D. (1989, April). *Individuality and connectedness in the family and adolescent's self and relational competence.* Paper presented at the meeting of the Society for Research in Child Development, Kansas City.

Cooper, C. R., Grotevant, H. D., Moore, M. S., & Condon, S. M. (1982, August). *Family support and conflict: Both foster adolescent identity and role taking.* Paper presented at the meeting of the American Psychological Association, Washington, DC.

Cooper, D. M., Nemet, D., & Galassetti, P. (2004). Exercise, stress, and inflammation in the growing child. *Current Opinions in Pediatrics, 16,* 286–292.

Cooter, R. B. (Ed.). (2004). *Perspectives on rescuing urban literacy education.* Mahwah, NJ: Erlbaum.

Corbin, C. B., Welk, G. J., Corbin, W. R., & Welk, K. A. (2005). *Concepts of physical fitness* (12th ed.). New York: McGraw-Hill.

Corbin, C. B., Welk, G. J., Lindsey, R., & Corbin, W. R. (2004). *Concepts of fitness and wellness* (5th ed.). New York: McGraw-Hill.

Cornish, K. (2004). The role of cognitive neuroscience in understanding atypical developmental pathways. *Journal of Cognitive Neuroscience, 16,* 4–5.

Corr, C. A., & Corr, D. M. (2003). Sudden infant death syndrome. In C. D. Bryant (Ed.), *Handbook of death and dying.* Thousand Oaks, CA: Sage.

Corr, C. A., Nabe, C. M., & Corr, D. M. (2003). *Death and dying, life and living* (4th ed.). Belmont, CA: Wadsworth.

Corrigan, R. (1981). The effects of task and practice on search for invisibly displaced objects. *Developmental Review, 1,* 1–17.

Corsica, J. A., & Perri, M. G. (2003). Obesity. In I. B. Weiner (Ed.), *Handbook of psychology* (Vol. IX). New York: Wiley.

Corsini, R. J. (1999). *The dictionary of psychology.* Philadelphia: Brunner/Mazel.

Corso, J. F. (1977). Auditory perception and communication. In J. E. Birren & K. W. Schaie (Eds.), *Handbook of the psychology of aging* (2nd ed.). New York: Van Nostrand Reinhold.

Cortesi, F., Giannotti, F., Sebastiani, T., & Vagnoni, C. (2004). Cosleeping and sleep behavior in Italian school-aged children. *Journal of Developmental and Behavioral Pediatrics, 25,* 28–33.

Cortina, L. M. (2004). Hispanic perspectives on sexual harassment and social support. *Personality and Social Psychology Bulletin, 30,* 574–584.

Cosey, E. J., & Bechtel, G. A. (2001). Family support and prenatal care among unmarried African American teenage primiparas. *Journal of Community Health and Nursing, 18,* 107–114.

Cosmides, L., Tooby, J., Cronin, H., & Curry, O. (Eds.). (2003). *What is evolutionary psychology? Explaining the new science of the mind.* New Haven, CT: Yale University Press.

Costa, P. T., & McCrae, R. R. (1995). Solid ground on the wetlands of personality: A reply to Black. *Psychological Bulletin, 117,* 216–220.

Costa, P. T., & McCrae, R. R. (1998). Personality assessment. In H. S. Friedman (Ed.), *Encyclopedia of mental health* (Vol. 3). San Diego: Academic Press.

Costa, P. T., & McCrae, R. R. (1999). Contemporary personality psychology: Implications for geriatric neuropsychiatry. In C. E. Coffey and J. L. Cummings (Eds.), *Textbook of geriatric neuropsychiatry* (2nd ed.). Washington, DC: American Psychiatric Press.

Costa, P. T., & McCrae, R. R. (2000). Contemporary personality psychology. In C. E. Coffey and J. L. Cummings (Eds.), *Textbook of geriatric neuropsychiatry.* Washington, DC: American Psychiatric Press.

Cotten, S. R. (1999). Marital status and mental health revisited: Examining the importance of risk factors and resources. *Family Relations, 48,* 225–233.

Council of Economic Advisors (2000). *Teens and their parents in the 21st century: An examination of trends in teen behavior and the role of parent involvement.* Washington, DC: Author.

Courage, M. L., Howe, M. L., & Squires, S. E. (2004). Individual differences in 3.5 month olds' visual attention: What do they predict at 1 year? *Infant Behavior and Development, 127,* 19–30.

Courtenay, W. H., McCreary, D. R., & Merighi, J. R. (2002). Gender and ethnic differences in health beliefs and behaviors. *Journal of Health Psychology, 7,* 219–231.

Cowan, C. P., & Cowan, P. A. (2000). *When partners become parents.* Mahwah, NJ: Erlbaum.

Cowell, R., Weeks, S., Humm, C., & John, M. (2003). Work until you drop. *Nursing Standards, 17,* 23.

Cowley, G. (1998, April 6). Why children turn violent. *Newsweek,* 24–25.

Cowley, G., & Hager, M. (1995, December 4). Terminal care: Too painful, too prolonged. *Newsweek,* pp. 74–75.

Cox, H., & Hammonds, A. (1998). Religiosity, aging, and life satisfaction. *Journal of Religion and Aging, 5,* 1–21.

Crabbe, J. C. (2002). Alcohol and genetics: New models. *American Journal of Genetics, 114,* 969–974.

Crandall, C., Crosby, R. D., & Carlson, G. A. (2004). Does pregnancy affect outcome of methadone maintenance treatment?

Journal of Substance Abuse Treatment, 26, 295–303.

Cremation Association of America (2000). *Fact sheet.* Milwaukee, WI: Author.

Crews, J. E., & Campbell, V. A. (2004). Vision impairment and hearing loss among community-dwelling older Americans: Implications for health and functioning. *American Journal of Public Health, 94,* 823–829.

Crick, N. R., Ostrov, J. M., Appleyard, K., Jansen, E. A., & Casas, J. F. (2004). Relational aggression in early childhood. In M. Putallaz & K. L. Bierman (Eds.), *Aggression, antisocial behavior, and violence among girls.* New York: Guilford.

Crockenberg, S. B. (1986). Are temperamental differences in babies associated with predictable differences in caregiving? In J. V. Lerner & R. M. Lerner (Eds.), *Temperament and social interaction during infancy and childhood.* San Francisco: Jossey-Bass.

Crockett, L. J., Raffaelli, M., & Moilanen, K. (2003). Adolescent sexuality: Behavior and meaning. In G. Adams & M. Berzonsky (Eds.), *Blackwell handbook of adolescence.* Malden, MA: Blackwell.

Crossett, J. H. (2004). The best is yet to be: Preventing, detecting, and treating depression in older women. *Journal of the American Medical Women's Association, 59,* 210–215.

Crouter, A. C., & Booth, A. (Eds.). (2004). *Work-family challenges for low-income families and their children.* Mahwah, NJ: Erlbaum.

Crowell, J. A., Treboux, D., Gao, Y., Fyffe, C., Pan, H., & Waters, E. (2002). Assessing secure base behavior in adulthood: Development of a measure, links to adult attachment representations, and relations to couples' communication and reports of relationships. *Developmental Psychology, 38,* 679–693.

Crowley, K., Callahan, M. A., Tenenbaum, H. R., & Allen, E. (2001). Parents explain more to boys than to girls during shared scientific thinking. *Psychological Science, 12,* 258–261.

Csaja, S. J. (2001). Technological change and the older worker. In J. E. Birren & K. W. Schaie (Eds.), *Handbook of the psychology of aging* (5th ed.). San Diego: Academic Press.

Csikszentmihalyi, M. (1995). *Creativity.* New York: HarperCollins.

Csikszentmihalyi, M. (1997). *Finding flow.* New York: Basic Books.

Csikszentmihalyi, M. (2000). Creativity: An overview. In A. Kazdin (Ed.), *Encyclopedia of psychology.* Washington, DC, & New York:

American Psychological Association and Oxford University Press.

Csikszentmihalyi, M., & Rathunde, K. (1998). The development of the person: An experiential perspective on the ontogenesis of psychological complexity. In W. Damon (Ed.), *Handbook of child psychology* (5th ed., Vol. 1). New York: Wiley.

Cuddy-Casey, M., & Orvaschel, H. (1997). Children's understanding of death in relation to child suicidality and homicidality. *Death Studies, 17,* 33–45.

Cuéllar, I., Siles, R. I., & Bracamontes, E. (2004). Acculturation: A psychological construct of continued relevance for Chicana/o psychology. In R. J. Velasquez, B. W. McNeil, & L. M. Arellano (Eds.), *The handbook of Chicano psychology and mental health.* Mahwah, NJ: Erlbaum.

Cui, X., & Vaillant, G. E. (1996). Antecedents and consequents of negative life events in adulthood: A longitudinal study. *American Journal of Psychiatry, 153,* 123–126.

Cuijpers, P. (2001). Mortality and depressive symptoms in inhabitants of residential homes. *International Journal of Geriatric Psychiatry, 16,* 131–138.

Cullen, K. (2001). *Context and eating behavior in children.* Unpublished research, Children's Nutrition Research Center, Baylor School of Medicine, Houston.

Cully, J. A., LaVoie, D., & Gfeller, J. D. (2001). Reminiscence, personality, and psychological functioning in older adults. *The Gerontologist, 41* (No. 1), 89–95.

Cumming, E., & Henry, W. (1961). *Growing old.* New York: Basic Books.

Cummings, E. M. (1987). Coping with background anger in early childhood. *Child Development, 58,* 976–984.

Cummings, E. M., Braungart-Rieker, J. M., & Du Rocher-Schudlich, T. (2003). Emotion and personality development in childhood. In I. B. Weiner (Ed.), *Handbook of psychology* (Vol. 6). New York: Wiley.

Cupertino, A. P., & Haan, M. N. (1999, November). *Religiosity and health among elderly Latinos.* Paper presented at the meeting of the Gerontological Society of America, San Francisco.

Curran, K., DuCette, J., Eisenstein, J., & Hyman, I. A. (2001, August). *Statistical analysis of the cross-cultural data: The third year.* Paper presented at the meeting of the American Psychological Association, San Francisco.

Cushner, K. H. (2003). *Human diversity in action* (2nd ed.). New York: McGraw-Hill.

Cutrona, C. E. (1982). Transition to college: Loneliness and the process of social adjustment. In L. A. Peplau & D. Perlman (Eds.), *Loneliness.* New York: Wiley.

D'**Augelli, A. R.** (1991). Gay men in college: Identity processes and adaptations. *Journal of College Student Development, 32,* 140–146.

D'Augelli, A. (2000). Sexual orientation. In A. Kazdin (Ed.), *Encyclopedia of psychology,* Washington, DC, & New York: American Psychological Association and Oxford University Press.

Daaleman, T. P., Perera, S., & Studenski, S. A. (2004). Religion, spirituality, and health status in geriatric outpatients. *Annals of Family Medicine, 2,* 49–53.

Dabis, F., Newell, M. L., Fowler, M. G., Read, J. S., Ghent, I. A. S., and the Working Group on HIV in Women and Children (2004). Prevention of HIV transmission through breast feeding: Strengthening of the research agenda. *Journal of Acquired Immune Deficiency Syndrome, 35,* 167–168.

Dahl, R. E. (2004). Adolescent brain development: A period of vulnerabilities and opportunities. *Annals of the New York Academy of Sciences, 1021,* 1–22.

Dahl, R. E., & Lewin, D. S. (2002). Pathways to adolescent health sleep regulation and behavior. *Journal of Adolescent Health, 31* (6 Suppl.), 175–184.

Dale, P., & Goodman, J. (2004). Commonality and differences in vocabulary growth. In M. Tomasello & D. I. Slobin (Eds.), *Beyond nature-nurture.* Mahwah, NJ: Erlbaum.

Daley, S. E., & Hammen, C. (2002). Depressive symptoms and close relationships during the transition to adulthood: Perspectives from dysphoric women, their best friends, and their romantic partners. *Journal of Consulting and Clinical Psychology, 70,* 129–141.

Daley, T. C., Whaley, S. E., Sigman, M. D., Espinosa, M. P., & Neumann, C. (2003). IQ on the rise: The Flynn effect in rural Kenyan children. *Psychological Science, 14,* 215–219.

DallasNews.com (2004). Obituaries. Available on the Internet at: www.legacy.com/dallasmorningnews/Sept11.asp?Page=Tribute FullText&PageNo=2&Memorial=AAII.

Damico, J. S., Tetenowski, J. A., & Nettleton, S. K. (2004). Emerging issues and trends in attention deficit hyperactivity disorder: An update for the speech-language pathologist. *Seminars and Speech and Language, 25,* 207–213.

Damon, W. (1988). *The moral child.* New York: Free Press.

Damon, W., & Hart, D. (1992). Self-understanding and its role in social and moral development. In M. H. Bornstein & M. E. Lamb (Eds.), *Developmental psychology: An advanced textbook* (3rd ed.). Hillsdale, NJ: Erlbaum.

Danforth, M. M., & Glass, J. C. (2001). Listen to my words, give meaning to my sorrow: A study in cognitive constructs in middle-aged bereaved widows. *Death Studies, 25,* 513–548.

Danielson, C. K., & Holmes, M. M. (2004). Adolescent sexual assault: An update of the literature. *Current Opinions in Obstetrics and Gynecology, 16,* 383–388.

Danner, D., Snowdon, D., & Friesen, W. (2001). Positive emotions in early life and longevity: Findings from the Nun Study. *Journal of Personality and Social Psychology, 80,* 814–823.

Darwin, C. (1859). *On the origin of species.* London: John Murray.

Darwin, C. (1965). *The expression of emotions in man and animals.* Chicago: University of Chicago Press. (Original work published 1872.)

Datar, A., & Sturm, R. (2004). Childhood overweight and parent- and teacher-reported behavior problems: Evidence from a prospective study of kindergartners. *Archives of Pediatric and Adolescent Medicine, 158,* 804–810.

Dattilio, F. M. (Ed.). (2001). *Case studies in couple and family therapy.* New York: Guilford.

Davenport, G. (2004). Rheumatology and musculoskeletal medicine. *British Journal of General Practice, 54,* 457–464.

Davidson, J. (2000). Giftedness. In A. Kazdin (Ed.), *Encyclopedia of psychology.* Washington, DC, & New York: American Psychological Association and Oxford University Press.

Davies, J., & Brember, I. (1999). Reading and mathematics attainments and self-esteem in years 2 and 6—an eight-year cross-sectional study. *Educational Studies, 25,* 145–157.

Davies, R. (2004). New understandings of parental grief. *Journal of Advanced Nursing, 46,* 506–513.

Daviglus, M. L., Liu, K., Yan, L. L., Pirzada, A., Garside, D. B., Schiffer, L.,

Dyer, A. R., Greenland, P., & Stamler, J. (2003). Body mass index in middle age and health-related quality of life in older age: The Chicago Heart Association Detection Project in Industry Study. *Archives of Internal Medicine, 163,* 2448–2455.

Davis, C. G., Nolen-Hoeksema, S., & Larson, J. (1998). Making sense of loss and benefiting from the experience: Two construals of meaning. *Journal of Personality & Social Psychology, 75,* 561–574.

Davis, E. K. (2004). Sports and recreational injuries in children and adolescents. *Journal of the Oklahoma State Medical Association, 97,* 18–21.

Davis, G. F. (2001). Loss and duration of grief. *Journal of the American Medical Association, 285,* 1152–1153.

Davis, K. E. (1985, February). Near and dear: Friendship and love compared. *Psychology Today,* pp. 22–29.

Davis, L., & Keyser, J. (1997). *Becoming the parent you want to be: A sourcebook of strategies for the first five years.* New York: Broadway.

Davison, G. C., & Neale, J. M. (2004). *Abnormal psychology* (9th ed.). New York: Wiley.

Davison, K. K., & Birth, L. L. (2001). Weight status, parent reaction, and self-concept in five-year-old girls. *Pediatrics, 107,* 46–53.

Davisson, M. T., Gardiner, K., & Costa, A. C. (2001). Report of the ninth international workshop on the molecular biology of human chromosome 21 and Down syndrome. *Cytogenetic Cell Genetics, 92,* 1–22.

Daws, D. (2000). *Through the night.* San Francisco: Free Association Books.

Day, N. L., Leech, S. L., Richardson, G. A., Cornelius, M. D., Robles, N., & Larkby, C. (2002). Prenatal alcohol exposure predicts continued deficits in offspring size at 14 years of age. *Alcohol: Clinical and Experimental Research, 26,* 1584–1591.

Day, R. D., & Lamb, M. E. (Eds.) (2004). *Conceptualizing and measuring father involvement.* Mahwah, NJ: Erlbaum.

Day, R. H., & McKenzie, B. E. (1973). Perceptual shape constancy in early infancy. *Perception, 2,* 315–320.

De Graaf, C., Blom, W. A., Smeets, P. A., Stafleu, A., & Hendriks, H. F. (2004). Biomarkers of satiation and satiety. *American Journal of Clinical Nutrition, 79,* 946–961.

de Jong, J. (2004). Grammatical impairment. In L. Verhoeven & H. Van Balkom (Eds.), *The classification of language disorders.* Mahwah, NJ: Erlbaum.

de Jong-Gierveld, J. (1987). Developing and testing a model of loneliness. *Journal of Personality and Social Psychology, 53,* 119–128.

de la Rocheborchard, E., & Thonneau, P. (2002). Paternal age and maternal age are risk factors for miscarriage: Results of a multicentre European study. *Human Reproduction, 17,* 1649–1656.

Deater-Deckard, K., & Dodge, K. (1997). Externalizing behavior problems and discipline revisited: Non-linear effects and variation by culture, context and gender. *Psychological Inquiry, 8,* 161–175.

DeCasper, A. J., & Spence, M. J. (1986). Prenatal maternal speech influences newborn's perception of speech sounds. *Infant Behavior and Development, 9,* 133–150.

Dejong, A., & Franklin, B. A. (2004). Prescribing exercise for the elderly: Current research and recommendations. *Current Sports Medicine Reports, 3,* 337–343.

DeKosky, S. T., & Marck, K. (2003). Looking backward to move forward: Early detection of neurodegenerative disorders. *Science, 302,* 830–834.

DeLamater, J., & MacCorquodale, P. (1979). *Premarital sexuality.* Madison: University of Wisconsin Press.

DeLoache, J. S. (2004). Early development of the understanding and use of symbolic artifacts. In U. Goswami (Ed.), *Blackwell handbook of childhood cognitive development.* Malden, MA: Blackwell.

DeMarie, D., Abshier, D. W., & Ferron, J. (2001, April). *Longitudinal study of predictors of memory improvement over the elementary school years: Capacity, strategies, and metamemory revisited.* Paper presented at the meeting of the Society for Research in Child Development, Minneapolis.

Demorest, R. A., & Landry, A. G. (2003). Prevention of pediatric sports injuries. *Current Sports Medicine Reports, 2,* 337–343.

Demorest, R. A., & Landry, G. L. (2004). Training issues in elite young athletes. *Current Sports Medicine Reports, 3,* 167–172.

Dempster, F. N. (1981). Memory span: Sources of individual and developmental differences. *Psychological Bulletin, 80,* 63–100.

Denham, S. A. (1998). *Emotional development in young children.* New York: Guilford.

Denmark, F. L., Rabinowitz, V. C., & Sechzer, J. A. (2005). *Engendering psychology: Women and gender revisited* (2nd ed.). Boston: Allyn & Bacon.

Denmark, F. L., Russo, N. F., Frieze, I. H., & Eschuzur, J. (1988). Guidelines for avoiding sexism in psychological research: A report of the ad hoc committee on nonsexist research. *American Psychologist, 43,* 582–585.

Denney, N. W. (1986, August). *Practical problem solving.* Paper presented at the meeting of the American Psychological Association, Washington, DC.

Denney, N. W. (1990). Adult age differences in traditional and practical problem solving. *Advances in Psychology, 72,* 329–349.

Dennis, C. L. (2004). Can we identify mothers at risk for postpartum depression in the immediate postpartum period using the Edinburgh Postnatal Depression Scale? *Journal of Affective Disorders, 78,* 163–169.

Dennis, C. L., & Stewart, D. E. (2004). Treatment of postpartum depression, part I: A critical review of biological interventions. *Journal of Clinical Psychiatry, 65,* 1242–1251.

Denny, C. B. (2001). Stimulant effects in attention deficit hyperactivity disorder. *Journal of Clinical Child Psychology, 30,* 98–109.

DeRosier, M. E. (2004). Building relationships and combating bullying. *Journal of Clinical Child and Adolescent Psychology, 33,* 196–201.

Descarries, L., Mechawar, N., Anavour, N., & Watkins, K. C. (2004). Structural determinants of the roles of acetylcholine in the cerebral cortex. *Progress in Brain Research, 145,* 45–58.

Desmarais, S., & Alksnis, C. (2004). Gender issues. In J. Barling, E. K. Kelloway, & M. R. Frone (Eds.), *Handbook of work and stress.* Thousand Oaks, CA: Sage.

DeSpelder, L. A., & Strickland, A. L. (2005). *The last dance: Encountering death and dying* (6th ed., rev. update). Mountain View, CA: Mayfield.

Dettmer, P., Dyck, N., & Thurston, L. (2002). *Consultation, collaboration, and teamwork for students with special needs* (4th ed.). Boston: Allyn & Bacon.

Deutsch, F. M. (1991). Women's lives: The story not told by theories of development. *Contemporary Psychology, 36,* 237–238.

Dewey, J. (1993). *How we think.* Lexington, MA: D. C. Heath.

Dewey, K. G. (2003). Is breastfeeding protective against childhood obesity? *Journal of Human Lactation, 19,* 9–18.

Diamond, A. (2001). A model system for studying the role of dopamine in the prefrontal cortex during early development in humans: Early and continuously treated phenylketonuria. In C. Nelson & M. Luciana (Eds.), *Handbook of developmental cognitive neuroscience*. Cambridge, MA: MIT Press.

Diamond, A. D. (1985). Development of the ability to use recall to guide action, as indicated by infants' performance on A$\overline{B}$. *Child Development, 56,* 868–883.

Diamond, L. M. (2003). Love matters: Romantic relationships among sexual-minority adolescents. In P. Florsheim (Ed.), *Adolescent romantic relationships and sexual behavior.* Mahwah, NJ: Erlbaum.

Diamond, L. M., & Lucas, S. (2004). Sexual-minority and heterosexual youths' peer relationships: Experiences, expectations, and implications for well-being. *Journal of Research on Adolescence, 14,* 313–340.

Diamond, L. M., & Savin-Williams, R. C. (2003). The intimate relationships of sexual-minority youths. In G. Adams & M. Berzonsky (Eds.), *Blackwell handbook of adolescence.* Malden, MA: Blackwell.

Diaz-Rico, L. (2004). *Teaching English learners.* Boston: Allyn & Bacon.

Dickson, F. C., Christian, A., & Remmo, C. J. (2004). Exploration of marital and family issues of the later-life adult. In C. Segrin & J. Flora (Eds.), *Family Communication.* Mahwah, NJ: Erlbaum.

Diener, E. (2004). *Frequently asked questions (FAQs) about subjective well-being (happiness and life-satisfaction).* Champaign: University of Illinois, Department of Psychology.

Diener, E., Lucas, R. E., & Oishi, S. (2002). Subjective well-being: The science of happiness and satisfaction. In C. R. Snyder & S. J. Lopez (Eds.), *Handbook of positive psychology.* New York: Oxford University Press.

Diener, E., & Seligman, M. E. P. (2002). Very happy people. *Psychological Science, 13,* 81–84.

Dietz, W. H. (2004). Overweight in childhood and adolescence. *New England Journal of Medicine, 350,* 855–857.

Diggs, R. C., & Socha, T. (2004). Communication, families, and exploring the boundaries of cultural diversity. In A. Vangelisti (Ed.), *Handbook of family communication.* Mahwah, NJ: Erlbaum.

DiGiulio, R. C. (1989). *Beyond widowhood.* New York: Free Press.

DiLalla, L. F. (Ed.). (2004). *Behavior genetics principles.* Washington, DC: American Psychological Association.

Dill, E. J., Vernberg, E. M., & Fonagy, P. (2004). Negative affect in victimized children. *Journal of Abnormal Psychology, 32,* 159–173.

Dillon, J. (2003). Reincarnation: The technology of death. In C. D. Bryant (Ed.), *Handbook of death and dying.* Thousand Oaks, CA: Sage.

DiMauro, S., Tanji, K., Bonilla, E., Palloti, F., & Schon, E. A. (2002). Mitochondrial abnormalities in muscle and other aging cells: Classification, causes, and effects. *Muscle and Nerve, 26,* 597–607.

Dipboye, R., & Colella, A. (Eds.) (2005). *Discrimination at work.* Mahwah, NJ: Erlbaum.

Dixit, N. K., Gerton, B. K., Dohn, P., Meyer-Lindenberg, A., & Berman, K. F. (2000, June). *Age-related changes in rCBF activation during an N-Back working memory paradigm occur prior to age 50.* Paper presented at the Human Brain Mapping meeting, San Antonio, TX.

Dixon, R., & Cohen, A. (2003). Cognitive development in adulthood. In I. B. Weiner (Ed.), *Handbook of psychology* (Vol. VI). New York: Wiley.

Dodge, K. A. (1983). Behavioral antecedents of peer social status. *Child Development, 54,* 1386–1399.

Dodge, K. A. (2000). Developmental psychology. In M. H. Ebert, P. T. Loosen, & B. Nurcombe (Eds.), *Current diagnosis and treatment in psychiatry.* East Norwalk, CT: Appleton & Lange.

Dodge, K. A. (2001). The science of youth violence prevention: Progressing from developmental psychopathology to efficacy to effectiveness in public policy. *American Journal of Preventive Medicine, 20,* 63–70.

Doherty, W. J., & Beaton, J. M. (2004). Mothers and fathers parenting together. In A. Vangelisti (Ed.), *Handbook of family communication.* Mahwah, NJ: Erlbaum.

Dohrenwend, B. S., & Dohrenwend, B. P. (1978). Some issues in research on stressful life events. *Journal of Nervous and Mental Disease, 166,* 7–15.

Dohrenwend, B. S., & Shrout, P. E. (1985). "Hassles" in the conceptualization and measurement of life stress variables. *American Psychologist, 40,* 780–785.

Dolan, A. L., Koshy, E., Waker, M., & Goble, C. M. (2004). Access to bone densitometry increases general practitioners' prescribing for osteoporosis in steroid treated patients. *Annals of Rheumatoid Diseases, 63,* 183–186.

Donelson, F. E. (1998). *Women's experiences.* Mountain View, CA: Mayfield.

Donnerer, J., Kronawetter, M., Kapper, A., Haas, I., & Kessler, H. H. (2003).

Therapeutic drug monitoring of the HIV/AIDS drugs abacavir, zidovudine, efavirenz, nevirapine, indinavir, lopinavir, and nelfinavir. *Pharmacology, 69,* 197–204.

Donovan, P. (1993). *Testing positive: Sexually transmitted disease and the public health response.* New York: Alan Guttmacher Institute.

Dorn, L. D., Williamson, D. E., & Ryan, N. D. (2002, April). *Maturational hormone differences in adolescents with depression and risk for depression.* Paper presented at the meeting of the Society for Research on Adolescence, New Orleans.

Dorr, A., Rabin, B. E., & Irlen, S. (2002). Parents, children, and the media. In M. H. Bornstein (Ed.), *Handbook of parenting* (2nd ed., Vol. 5). Mahwah, NJ: Erlbaum.

Dowda, M., Ainsworth, B. E., Addy, C. L., Saunders, R., & Riner, W. (2001). Environmental influences, physical activity, and weight status in 8- to 16-year-olds. *Archives of Pediatric and Adolescent Medicine, 155,* 711–717.

Doyle, L. W., Faber, B., Callanan, C., Ford, G. W., & Davis, N. M. (2004). Extremely low birth weight and body size in early adulthood. *Archives of Disorders in Childhood, 89,* 347–350.

Dreachslin, J. L., Weech-Maldonado, R., & Dansky, K. H. (2004). Racial and ethnic diversity and organizational behavior. *Social Science Medicine, 59,* 961–971.

Drew, C., & Hardman, M. L. (2000). *Mental retardation* (7th ed.). Columbus, OH: Merrill.

Drewes, A. A., Carey, L. J., & Schaefer, C. E. (Eds.). (2003). *School-based play therapy.* New York: Wiley.

Driscoll, A., & Nagel, N. G. (2005). *Early childhood education* (3rd ed.). Boston: Allyn & Bacon.

Driver, C., Georgiou, A., & Georgiou, G. (2004). The contribution of mitochondrially induced oxidative damage to aging *Drosophila melanogaster. Biogerontology, 5,* 185–192.

Droege, K. L. (2004). Turning accountability on its head. *Phi Delta Kappan, 85,* 610–612.

Drongowski, R. A., Lee, D., Reynolds, P. I., Malviya, S., Harmon, C. S., Geiger, J., Lelli, J. L., & Coran, A. G. (2003). Increased respiratory symptoms following surgery in children exposed to environmental tobacco smoke. *Pediatric Anesthesiology, 13,* 304–310.

Dryfoos, J. G. (1990). *Adolescents at risk: Prevalence or prevention.* New York: Oxford University Press.

Dubay, L., Joyce, T., Kaestner, R., & Kenney, G. M. (2001). Changes in prenatal care timing and low birth weight by race and socioeconomic status: Implications for the Medicaid expansions for pregnant women. *Health Services Research, 36,* 373–398.

Dubowitz, H., Pitts, S. C., & Black, M. M. (2004). Measurement of three subtypes of child neglect. *Child Maltreatment, 9,* 344–356.

Duffy, T. M., & Kirkley, J. R. (Eds.) (2004). *Learner-centered theory and practice in distance education.* Mahwah, NJ: Erlbaum.

Dunkel-Schetter, C. (1998). Maternal stress and preterm delivery. *Prenatal and Neonatal Medicine, 3,* 39–42.

Dunkel-Schetter, C., Gurung, R. A. R., Lobel, M., & Wadhwa, P. D. (2001). Stress processes in pregnancy and birth. In A. Baum, T. A. Revenson, & J. E. Singer (Eds.), *Handbook of health psychology.* Mahwah, NJ: Erlbaum.

Dunlop, D. D., Lyons, J. S., Manheim, L. M., Song, J., & Chang, R. W. (2004). Arthritis and heart disease as risk factors for major depression. *Medical Care, 42,* 502–511.

Dunlosky, J., Kubat-Silman, A. K., & Hertzog, C. (2003). Training monitoring skills improves older adults' self-paced associative learning. *Psychology and Aging, 18,* 340–345.

Dunn, J. (1984). Sibling studies and the developmental impact of critical incidents. In P. B. Baltes & O. G. Brim (Eds.), *Life-span development and behavior* (Vol. 6). Orlando, FL: Academic Press.

Dunn, J. (2004). Sibling relationships. In P. Smith & C. Hart (Eds.), *Blackwell handbook of childhood social development.* Malden, MA: Blackwell.

Dunn, K. S., & Horgas, A. L. (2004). Religious and nonreligious coping in older adults experiencing chronic pain. *Pain Management Nursing, 5,* 19–28.

Durrant, J. E. (2002). Trends in youth crime and well-being since the abolition of corporal punishment in Sweden. *Youth and Society, 3,* 437–455.

Dusek, J. B., & McIntyre, J. G. (2003). Self-concept and self-esteem development. In G. Adams & M. Berzonsky (Eds.), *Blackwell handbook of adolescence.* Malden, MA: Blackwell.

Dwyer, J. W., & Coward, R. T. (1991). A multivariate comparison of the involvement of adult sons versus daughters in the care of impaired parents. *Journals of Gerontology B: Psychological Sciences and Social Sciences, 46,* S259–S269.

Dychtwald, K., Erickson, T., & Morison, B. (2004). It's time to retire. *Harvard Business Review, 82,* 48–57, 126.

Dynek, J. N., & Smith, S. (2004). Resolution of sister telomere association is required for progression through mitosis. *Science, 304,* 97–100.

Eagle, M. (2000). Psychoanalytic theory: History of the field. In A. Kazdin (Ed.), *Encyclopedia of psychology.* Washington, DC, & New York: American Psychological Association and Oxford University Press.

Eagly, A. H. (2000). Gender roles. In A. Kazdin (Ed.), *Encyclopedia of psychology.* Washington, DC, & New York: American Psychological Association and Oxford University Press.

Eagly, A. H. (2001). Social role theory of sex differences and similarities. In J. Worrell (Ed.), *Encyclopedia of women and gender.* San Diego: Academic Press.

Eagly, A. H., & Crowley, M. (1986). Gender and helping: A meta-analytic review of the social psychological literature. *Psychological Bulletin, 108,* 233–256.

Eagly, A. H., & Diekman, A. B. (2003). The malleability of sex differences in response to social roles. In L. G. Aspinwall & V. M. Staudinger (Eds.), *A psychology of human strengths.* Washington, DC: American Psychological Association.

Eagly, A. H., & Steffen, V. J. (1986). Gender and aggressive behavior: A meta-analytic review of the social psychological literature. *Psychological Bulletin, 100,* 309–330.

Ebersole, P., Hess, P., & Luggen, A. S. (2004). *Toward healthy aging* (6th ed.). St. Louis: Mosby.

Eccles, J. (2000). Adolescence: Social patterns, achievements, and problems. In A. Kazdin (Ed.), *Encyclopedia of psychology.* Washington, DC, & New York: American Psychological Association and Oxford University Press.

Eccles, J. (2003). Education: Junior and high school. In G. Adams & M. Berzonsky (Eds.), *Blackwell handbook of adolescence.* Malden, MA: Blackwell.

Eccles, J. S., & Roeser, R. W. (2005). School and community influences on human development. In M. H. Bornstein & M. E. Lamb (Eds.), *Developmental psychology* (5th ed.). Mahwah, NJ: Erlbaum.

Eccles, J., Wigfield, A., & Byrnes, J. (2003). Cognitive development in adolescence. In I. B. Weiner (Ed.), *Handbook of psychology* (Vol. VI). New York: Wiley.

Edelman, M. W. (1995). *The state of America's children.* Washington, DC: The Children's Defense Fund.

Edelman, M. W. (1997, April). *Children, families and social policy.* Paper presented at the meeting of the Society for Research in Child Development, Washington, DC.

Edelstein, R. S., & Shaver, P. R. (2004). Avoidant attachment: Exploration of an oxymoron. In D. Mashek & A. Aron (Eds.), *Handbook of closeness and intimacy.* Mahwah, NJ: Erlbaum.

Edmonds, M. M. (1993). Physical health. In J. S. Jackson, L. M. Chatters, & R. J. Taylor (Eds.), *Aging in Black America.* Newbury Park, CA: Sage.

Educational Testing Service (1992, February). *Cross-national comparison of 9–13 year olds' science and math achievement.* Princeton, NJ: Author.

Edwards, C. P. (2002). Three approaches from Europe: Waldorf, Montessori, and Reggio Emilia. *Early Childhood Practice and Research, 4,* 36–40.

Edwards, R., & Hamilton, M. A. (2004). You need to understand my gender role: An empirical test of Tannen's model of gender and communication. *Sex Roles, 50,* 491–504.

Egeland, B., & Carlson, B. (2004). Attachment and psychopathology. In L. Atkinson & S. Goldberg (Eds.), *Attachment issues in psychopathology and intervention.* Mahwah, NJ: Erlbaum.

Egeland, B., Jacobvitz, D., & Sroufe, L. A. (1988). Breaking the cycle of abuse. *New Directions for Child Development, 11,* 77–92.

Eichorn, D. H., Clausen, J. A., Haan, N., Honzik, M. P., & Mussen, P. H. (Eds.). (1981). *Present and past in middle life.* New York: Academic Press.

Eiferman, R. R. (1971). Social play in childhood. In R. Herron & B. Sutton-Smith (Eds.), *Child's play.* New York: Wiley.

Einstein, G. O., McDaniel, M. A., Manzi, M., Cochran, B., & Baker, M. (2000). Prospective memory and aging: Forgetting intentions over short delays. *Psychology and Aging, 15,* 671–683.

Eisdorfer, C. (1996, December). Interview. *APA Monitor,* p. 35.

Eisenberg, M., & Wechsler, H. (2003). Substance use behaviors among college students with same-sex and opposite-sex experience: Results from a national study. *Addictive Behaviors, 28,* 899–913.

Eisenberg, N. (Ed.) (1982). *The development of prosocial behavior.* New York: Wiley.

Eisenberg, N. (2001). Emotion-regulated regulation and its relation to quality of social functioning. In W. W. Hartup & R. A. Weinberg (Eds.), *Child psychology in retrospect and prospect.* Mahwah, NJ: Erlbaum.

Eisenberg, N. (2005). Empathy-related responding in children. In M. Killen & J. G. Smetana (Eds.), *Handbook of moral development.* Mahwah, NJ: Erlbaum.

Eisenberg, N., & Fabes, R. A. (1998). Prosocial development. In N. Eisenberg (Ed.), *Handbook of child psychology* (5th ed., Vol. 3). New York: Wiley.

Eisenberg, N., Fabes, R. A., Guthrie, I. K., & Reiser, M. (2002). The role of emotionality and regulation in children's social competence and adjustment. In L. Pulkkinen & A. Caspi (Eds.), *Paths to successful development.* New York: Cambridge University Press.

Eisenberg, N., Gutherie, I. K., Murphy, B. C., Shepard, S. A., Cumberland, A., & Carlo, G. (1999). Consistency and development of prosocial dispositions: A longitudinal study. *Child Development, 70,* 1360–1372.

Eisenberg, N., & Morris, A. (2004). Moral cognitions and prosocial responding in adolescence. In R. Lerner & L. Steinberg (Eds.), *Handbook of adolescent psychology.* New York: Wiley.

Eisenberg, N., & Morris, A. S. (2004). Moral cognitions and social responding in adolescence. In R. Lerner & L. Steinberg (Eds.), *Handbook of adolescent psychology.* New York: Wiley.

Eisenberg, N., & Spinrad, T. L. (2004). Emotion-related regulation: Sharpening the definition. *Child Development, 75,* 334–339.

Eisenberg, N., Spinrad, T. L., & Smith, C. L. (2004). Emotion-related regulation: Its conceptualization, relations to social functioning, and socialization. In P. Philippot & R. S. Feldman (Eds.), *The regulation of emotion.* Mahwah, NJ: Erlbaum.

Eisinger, F., & Burke, W. (2003). Breast cancer and breastfeeding. *Lancet, 361,* 176–177.

Ekwo, E. E., & Moawad, A. (2000). Maternal age and preterm births in a black population. *Pediatric Perinatal Epidemiology, 2,* 145–151.

Elder, G. H. (1998). The life course and human development. In W. Damon (Ed.), *Handbook of child development* (5th ed.). New York: Wiley.

Elder, G. H., & Pavalko, E. K. (1993). Work careers in men's later years: Transitions, trajectories, and historical change. *Journals of Gerontology B: Psychological Sciences and Social Sciences, 48,* S180–S191.

Eley, T. C., Liang, H., Plomin, R., Sham, P., Sterne, A., Williamson, R., & Purcell, S. (2004). Parental family vulnerability, family environment, and their interactions as predictors of depressive symptoms in adolescents. *Journal of the American Academy of Child and Adolescent Psychiatry, 43,* 298–306.

Elias, M. (1998, June 23). For 50 years pediatrics has taken giant steps. *USA Today,* pp. 1, 2D.

Elkind, D. (1970, April 5). Erik Erikson's eight ages of man. *New York Times Magazine.*

Elkind, D. (1976). *Child development and education: A Piagetian perspective.* New York: Oxford University Press.

Elkind, D. (1988, January). Educating the very young: A call for clear thinking. *NEA Today,* pp. 22–27.

Ellis, C. D. (2002). Male rape. *Collegian, 9,* 34–39.

Ellis, L., & Ames, M. A. (1987). Neurohormonal functioning and sexual orientation. *Psychological Bulletin, 101,* 233–258.

Elmes, D. G., Kantowitz, B. H., & Roedinger, H. L. (2005). *Research methods in psychology* (8th ed.). Belmont, CA: Wadsworth.

Elovainio, M., Kivimaki, M., Vahtera, J., Ojanlatva, A., Korkeila, K., Suominen, S., Helenius, H., & Koskenvuo, M. (2003). Social support, early retirement, and a retirement preference: A study of 10,489 Finnish adults. *Journal of Occupational and Environmental Medicine, 45,* 433–439.

Emde, R. N., Gaensbauer, T. G., & Harmon, R. J. (1976). Emotional expression in infancy: A biobehavioral study. *Psychological Issues: Monograph Series, 10* (37).

Emmers-Sommer, T. M., & Allen, M. (2005). *Safer sex in personal relationships: The role of sexual scripts in HIV infection and prevention.* Mahwah, NJ: Erlbaum.

Enger, E., Ross, F., & Bailey, D. (2005). *Concepts in biology* (11th ed.). New York: McGraw-Hill.

England, S. E., Linsk, N. L., Simon-Rusinowitz, L., & Keigher, S. M. (1991). Paying kin for care: Agency barriers to formalizing informal care. *Journal of Aging and Social Policy, 2,* 63–86.

Engler, A. J., Ludington-Hoe, S. M., Cusson, R. M., Adams, R., Bahnsen, M., Brumbaugh, E., Coates, P., Grief, J., McHargue, L., Ryan, D. L., Settle, M., & Williams, D. (2002). Kangaroo care: National survey of practice, knowledge, barriers, and perceptions. *American Journal of Maternal/Child Nursing, 27,* 146–153.

Enright, R. D., Lapsley, D. K., Dricas, A. S., & Fehr, L. A. (1980). Parental influence on the development of adolescent autonomy and identity. *Journal of Youth and Adolescence, 9,* 529–546.

Epstein, D. K., & Connor, J. R. (1999, Fall). Dementia in the elderly: An overview. *Generations,* pp. 9–16.

Epstein, J. A., Botvin, G. J., & Díaz, T. (1998). Linguistic acculturation and gender effects on smoking among Hispanic youth. *Preventive Medicine, 27,* 538–589.

Epstein, N., & Eidelson, R. J. (1981). Unrealistic beliefs of clinical couples: Their relationship to expectations, goals, and satisfaction. *American Journal of Family Therapy, 9,* 13–21.

Erber, J. T. (2005). *Aging & older adulthood.* Belmont, CA: Wadsworth.

Erdem, A., Erdem, M., Arslan, M., Yazici, G., Eskandari, R., & Himmetogulu, O. (2002). The effects of maternal anemia and iron deficiency on fetal erythropoiesis: Comparison between serum erythropoietin, hemoglobin and ferritin levels in mothers and newborns. *Journal of Maternal, Fetal, and Neonatal Medicine, 11,* 329–332.

Ericsson, K. A., Krampe, R., & Tesch-Romer, C. (1993). The role of deliberate practice in the acquisition of expert performance. *Psychological Review, 100,* 363–406.

Erikson, E. H. (1950). *Childhood and society.* New York: W. W. Norton.

Erikson, E. H. (1968). *Identity: Youth and crisis.* New York: W. W. Norton.

Erikson, E. H. (1969). *Ghandi's truth.* New York: Norton.

Erlick Robinson, G. (2003). Violence against women in North America. *Archives of Women's Mental Health, 6,* 185–191.

Eskenazi, B., Stapleton, A. L., Kharrazi, M., & Chee, W. Y. (1999). Associations between maternal decaffeinated and caffeinated coffee consumption and fetal growth and gestational duration. *Epidemiology, 10,* 242–249.

Eslea, M., Menesini, E., Monta, Y., O'Moor, M., More-Merchen, J. A., Pereira, B., & Smith, P. K. (2004). Friendship and loneliness among bullies and victims: Data from seven countries. *Aggressive Behavior, 30,* 71–83.

Espelage, D. L., & Swearer, S. M. (Eds.) (2004). *Bullying in American schools.* Mahwah, NJ: Erlbaum.

Estes, L. S. (2004). *Essentials of child care and early education.* Boston: Allyn & Bacon.

Etaugh, C. A., & Bridges, J. S. (2001). Midlife transitions. In J. Worell (Ed.), *Encyclopedia of women and gender.* San Diego: Academic Press.

Etaugh, C., & Bridges, J. S. (2004). *The psychology of women* (2nd ed.). Boston: Allyn & Bacon.

Etelson, D., Brand, D. A., Patrick, P. A., & Shirali, A. (2003). Childhood obesity: Do parents recognize the risk? *Obesity Research, 11,* 1362–1368.

Ettinger, D., Grady, D., Tosteson, N. A., Pressman, A., & Macer, J. L. (2003). Effect of the Women's Health Initiative on women's decisions to discontinue postmenopausal hormone therapy. *Obstetrics & Gynecology, 102,* 1225–1232.

Etzel, R. (1988, October). *Children of smokers.* Paper presented at the American Academy of Pediatrics meeting, New Orleans.

Evans, G. W. (2004). The environment of childhood poverty. *American Psychologist, 59,* 77–92.

Evans, G. W., & English, G. W. (2002). The environment of poverty. *Child Development, 73,* 1238–1248.

Evans, M. I., Lluba, E., Landsberger, E. J., O'Brien, J. E., & Harrison, H. H. (2004). Impact of folic acid fortification in the United States: Markedly diminished high maternal serum alpha-fetoprotein values. *Obstetrics and Gynecology, 103,* 474–479.

Evert, J., Lawler, E., Bogan, H., & Perls, T. (2003). Morbidity profiles of centenarians: Survivors, delayers, and escapers. *Journals of Gerontology A: Biological Sciences and Medical Sciences, 58,* 232–237.

Exploratorium (2004). *Young in mind.* Available on the Internet at: www.exploratorium.edu/exploring/exploring_memory/ memory_2.html.

Faber, L., Karim, I. A., Jawdat, A. M., Fausi, M., & Merlob, P. (2004). Awareness of folic acid for prevention of neural tube defects in a community with high prevalence of consanguineous marriages. *Annals of Genetics, 47,* 69–75.

Fabes, R. A., Hanish, L. D., & Martin, C. L. (2003). Children at play: The role of peers in understanding the effects of child care. *Child Development, 74,* 1039–1043.

Fagan, J. F. (1992). Intelligence: A theoretical viewpoint. *Current Directions in Psychological Science, 1,* 82–86.

Fagot, B. I. (1995). Parenting boys and girls. In M. H. Bornstein (Ed.), *Handbook of parenting* (Vol. 1). Hillsdale, NJ: Erlbaum.

Fagot, B. I., Rodgers, C. S., & Leinbach, M. D. (2000). Theories of gender socialization. In T. Eckes & H. M. Trautner (Eds.), *The developmental social psychology of gender.* Mahwah, NJ: Erlbaum.

Fahey, T. D., Insel, P. M., & Roth, W. T. (2005). *Fit & well* (6th ed.). New York: McGraw-Hill.

FairTest (2004). "No child left behind" after two years: A track record of failure. Available on the Internet at: www.fairtest.org.

Falbo, T., & Poston, D. L. (1993). The academic, personality, and physical outcomes of only children in China. *Child Development, 64,* 18–35.

Falicov, C., & Karrer, B. (1980). Cultural variations in the family life cycle: The Mexican American family. In E. Carter & M. McGoldrick (Eds.), *The family life cycle: A framework for family therapy.* New York: Gardner Press.

Fang, J., Madhaven, S., & Alderman, M. H. (1999). Low birth weight: Race and maternal nativity—Impact of community income. *Pediatrics, 103,* e5.

Fantz, R. I. (1963). Pattern vision in newborn infants. *Science, 140,* 296–297.

Faraveo, C., Giugni, A., Salvarori, S., & Ricca, V. (2004). Psychopathology after rape. *American Journal of Psychiatry, 161,* 1483–1485.

Farone, S. V., & Doyle, A. E. (2001). The nature and heritability of attention deficit hyperactivity disorder. *Psychiatric Clinics of North America, 10,* 299–316.

Farr, M. (Ed.). (2005). *Latino language and literacy in ethnolinguistic Chicago.* Mahwah, NJ: Erlbaum.

Farrell, M. P., & Rosenberg, S. D. (1981). *Men at mid-life.* Boston: Auburn House.

Farrington, D. (2004). Conduct disorder, aggression, and delinquency. In R. Lerner & L. Steinberg (Eds.), *Handbook of adolescent psychology.* New York: Wiley.

Faulkner, G., & Biddle, S. (2002). Mental health nursing and the promotion of physical activity. *Journal of Psychiatric and Mental Health Nursing, 9,* 659–665.

Federal Interagency Forum on Child and Family Statistics (2002). *Key national indicators of well-being.* Washington, DC: U.S. Government Printing Office.

Federenko, I. S., & Wadhwa, P. D. (2004). Women's mental health during pregnancy influences fetal and infant developmental and health outcomes. *CNS Spectrum, 9,* 198–206.

Feeney, J. A. (1996). Attachment, caregiving, and marital satisfaction. *Personal Relationships, 3,* 401–416.

Feenstra, J. S., Banyard, V. L., Rines, E. N., & Hopkins, K. R. (2001). First-year students' adaptation to college: The role of family variables and individual coping. *Journal of College Student Development, 42,* 106–113.

Fehr, B. (2000). The life cycle of friendships. In C. Hendrick, & S. S. Hendrick (Eds.), *Close relationships.* Thousand Oaks, CA: Sage.

Feinberg, M., & Hetherington, E. M. (2001). Differential parenting as a within-family variable. *Journal of Family Psychology, 15,* 22–37.

Feinsilver, S. H. (2003). Sleep in the elderly. *Clinical Geriatric Medicine, 19,* 177–188.

Feiring, C. (1996). Concepts of romance in 15-year-old adolescents. *Journal of Research on Adolescence, 6,* 181–200.

Fekkes, M., Pijpers, F. I., & Verloove-Vanhorick, S. P. (2004). Bullying behavior and associations with psychosomatic complaints and depression in victims. *Journal of Pediatrics, 144,* 17–22.

Feldman, H. D. (2001, April). *Contemporary developmental theories and the concept of talent.* Paper presented at the meeting of the Society for Research in Child Development, Minneapolis.

Feldman, R., Greenbaum, C. W., & Yirmiya, N. (1999). Mother-infant affect synchrony as an antecedent of the emergence of self-control. *Developmental Psychology, 35,* 223–231.

Feldman, R., Sussman, A. L., & Zigler, E. (2004). Parental leave and work adaptation at the transition to parenthood: Individual, marital, and social correlates. *Journal of*

Applied Developmental Psychology, 25, 459–479.

Feldman, R., Weller, A., Sirota, L., & Eidelman, A. I. (2002). Skin-to-skin contact (kangaroo care) promotes self-regulation in premature infants: Sleep-wake cyclicity, arousal modulation, and sustained exploration. *Developmental Psychology, 38,* 194–207.

Feldman, R., Weller, A., Sirota, L., & Eidelman, A. I. (2003). Testing a family intervention hypothesis: The contribution of mother-infant skin-to-skin (kangaroo care) to family interaction, proximity, and touch. *Journal of Family Psychology, 17,* 94–107.

Feldman, S. S. (1999). Unpublished review of J. W. Santrock's *Adolescence* (8th ed.). New York: McGraw-Hill.

Feldman, S. S., & Elliott, G. R. (1990). Progress and promise of research on normal adolescent development. In S. S. Feldman & G. Elliott (Eds.), *At the threshold: The developing adolescent.* Cambridge, MA: Harvard University Press.

Feldman, S. S., Turner, R., & Aruajo, K. (1999). Interpersonal context as an influence on sexual timetables of youths: Gender and ethnic effects. *Journal of Research on Adolescence, 9,* 25–52.

Feldman, S. S., & Weinberger, D. A. (1994). Self-restraint as a mediator of family influences on boys' delinquent behavior: A longitudinal study. *Child Development, 65,* 195–211.

Feldon, J. M. (2003). Grief as a transformative experience: Weaving through different lifeworlds after a loved one has committed suicide. *International Journal of Mental Health Nursing, 12,* 74–85.

Ferber, S. G., & Makhoul, J. R. (2004). The effect of skin-to-skin contact (kangaroo care) shortly after birth on the neurobehavioral responses of the term newborn. *Pediatrics, 113,* 858–865.

Ferguson, D. M., Harwood, L. J., & Shannon, F. T. (1987). Breastfeeding and subsequent social adjustment in 6- to 8-year-old children. *Journal of Child Psychology and Psychiatry, 28,* 378–386.

Fernald, A. (2001). Two hundred years of research on the early development of language comprehension. In W. W. Hartup & R. A. Weinberg (Eds.), *Child psychology in retrospect and prospect.* Mahwah, NJ: Erlbaum.

Fernandes, O., Sabharwal, M., Smiley, T., Pastuszak, A., Koren, G., & Einarson, T. (1998). Moderate to heavy caffeine consumption during pregnancy and relationship to spontaneous abortion and abnormal fetal growth: A meta-analysis. *Reproductive Toxicology, 12,* 435–444.

Fernandez, A., & Goldstein, L. (2004). Primary care physicians who treat blacks and whites. *New England Journal of Medicine, 351,* 2126–2127.

Ferrara, N. (2004). The aging heart and exercise training. *Archives of Gerontology and Geriatrics, 35 (Suppl.),* 145–156.

Ferrari, A. U., Radaelli, A., & Centola, M. (2003). Invited review: Aging and the cardiovascular system. *Journal of Applied Physiology, 95,* 2591–2597.

Ferrer-Wreder, L., Lorene, C. C., Kurtines, W., Briones, E., Bussell, J., Berman, S., & Arrufat, O. (2002). Promoting identity development in marginalized youth. *Journal of Adolescent Research, 17,* 168–187.

Fiatarone, M. A., Marks, E. C., Meredith, C. N., Lipsitz, L. A., & Evans, W. J. (1990). High intensity strength training in nonagenarians: Effects on skeletal muscle. *Journal of the American Medical Association, 263,* 3029–3034.

Field, A. E., Cambargo, C. A., Taylor, C. B., Berkey, C. S., Roberts, S. B., & Colditz, G. A. (2001). Peer, parent, and media influences on the development of weight concerns and frequent dieting among preadolescent and adolescent girls and boys. *Pediatrics, 107,* 54–60.

Field, D. (1996). Review of relationships in old age by Hansson & Carpenter. *Contemporary Psychology, 41,* 44–45.

Field, D. (1999). A cross-cultural perspective on continuity and change in social relations in old age: Introduction to a special issue. *International Journal of Aging and Human Development, 48,* 257–262.

Field, T. M. (1992, September). Stroking babies helps growth, reduces stress. *Brown University Child and Adolescent Behavior Letter,* pp. 1, 6.

Field, T. M. (1998). Massage therapy effects. *American Psychologist, 53,* 1270–1281.

Field, T. M. (2000). Child abuse. In A. Kazdin (Ed.), *Encyclopedia of psychology.* Washington, DC, & New York: American Psychological Association and Oxford University Press.

Field, T. M. (2001). Massage therapy facilitates weight gain in preterm infants. *Current Directions in Psychological Science, 10,* 51–55.

Field, T. M. (2002). Massage therapy. *Medical Clinics of North America, 86,* 163–171.

Field, T. M. (2003). Stimulation of preterm infants. *Pediatric Review, 24,* 4–11.

Field, T. M., Diego, M., Hernandez-Reif, M., Schanberg, S., Kuhn, C., Ynado, R., & Bendell, D. (2003). Pregnancy anxiety and comormid depression and anger: Effects on the fetus and neonate. *Depression and Anxiety, 17,* 140–151.

Field, T. M., Grizzle, N., Scafidi, F., & Schanberg, S. (1996). Massage and relaxation therapies' effects on depressed adolescent mothers. *Adolescence, 31,* 903–911.

Field, T. M., Hernandez-Reif, M., & Freedman, J. (2004). Stimulation programs for preterm infants. *Social Policy Report, Society for Research in Child Development,* XVIII (No. 1), 1–19.

Field, T. M., Hernandez-Reif, M., Seligman, S., Krasnegor, J., & Sunshine, W. (1997). Juvenile rheumatoid arthritis: Benefits from massage therapy. *Journal of Pediatric Psychology, 22,* 607–617.

Field, T. M., Hernandez-Reif, M., Taylor, S., Quintino, O., & Burman, I. (1997). Labor pain is reduced by massage therapy. *Journal of Psychosomatic Obstetrics and Gynecology, 18,* 286–291.

Field, T. M., Lasko, D., Mundy, P., Henteleff, T., Kabat, S., Talpins, S., & Dowling, M. (1997). Brief report: Autistic children's attentiveness and responsivity improve after touch therapy. *Journal of Autism and Developmental Disorders, 27,* 333–338.

Field, T. M., Quintino, O., Hernandez-Reif, M., & Koslosky, G. (1998). Adolescents with attention deficit hyperactivity disorder benefit from massage therapy. *Adolescence, 33,* 103–108.

Field, T. M., Schanberg, S. M., Scafidi, F., Bauer, C. R., Vega-Lahr, N., Garcia, R., Nystrom, J., & Kuhn, C. M. (1986). Tactile/kinesthetic stimulation effects on preterm neonates. *Pediatrics, 77,* 654–658.

Fields, R. (2005). *Drugs in perspective* (5th ed.). New York: McGraw-Hill.

Finch, C. E., & Seeman, T. E. (1999). Stress theories of aging. In V. L. Bengtson & K. W. Schaie (Eds.), *Handbook of theories of aging.* New York: Springer.

Fine, P. G., & Peterson, D. (2002). Caring what dying patients care about caring. *Journal of Pain Symptom Management, 23,* 267–268.

Fingerman, K. L. (2000). Age and generational differences in mothers' and daughters' descriptions of enjoyable visits. *Journals of Gerontology B: Psychological Sciences and Social Sciences, 55,* P95–P106.

Fingerman, K. L. (2003, April). Commentary in "Researchers replace midlife myths with facts." *Monitor on Psychology, 34,* 40.

Fingerman, K. L., & Lang, F. R. (2004). Coming together: A perspective on relationships across the life span. In F. R. Lang & K. L. Fingerman (Eds.), *Growing together.* New York: Cambridge University Press.

Firlik, R. (1996). Can we adapt the philosophies and practices of Reggio Emilia, Italy, for use in American schools? *Young Children, 51,* 217–220.

Fisch, S. M. (2004). *Children's learning from educational television.* Mahwah, NJ: Erlbaum.

Fischer, K. W., & Bidell, T. R. (1998). Dynamic development of psychological structures in action and thought. In W. Damon (Ed.), *Handbook of child psychology* (Vol. 1). New York: Wiley.

Fischer, K. W., & Pruyne, E. (2003). Reflective thinking in adulthood. In J. Demick & C. Andreoletti (Eds.), *Handbook of adult development.* New York: Kluwer.

Fischer, K. W., & Rose, S. P. (1995, Fall). Concurrent cycles in the dynamic development of brain and behavior. *SRCD Newsletter,* pp. 3–4, 15–16.

Fisher, B. S., Cullen, F. T., & Turner, M. G. (2001). *The sexual victimization of college women.* Washington, DC: National Institute of Justice.

Fitzgerald, E. F., Hwang, S. A., Lannguth, K., Cayo, M., Yang, B. Z., Bush, S., Worswick, P., & Lauzon, T. (2004). Fish consumption and other environmental exposures and their associations with serum PCB concentrations among Mohawk women at Akwesasne. *Environmental Research, 94,* 160–170.

Fitzgerald, H., Mann, T., Cabrera, N., & Wong, M. M. (2003). Diversity in caregiving contexts. In I. B. Weiner (Ed.), *Handbook of psychology* (Vol. VI). New York: Wiley.

Fitzpatrick, A. L., Kuller, L. H., Ives, D. G., Lopez, O. L., Jagust, W., Breitner, J. C., Jones, B., Lyketsos, C., & Dulberg, C. (2004). Incidence and prevalence of dementia in the cardiovascular health study. *Journal of the American Geriatric Society, 52,* 195–204.

Fitzpatrick, L. A. (2003). Phytoestrogens—mechanism of action and effect on bone mineral density. *Endocronology and Metabolism Clinics of North America, 32,* 233–252.

Fitzpatrick, L. A. (2004). Menopause and hotflashes: No easy answers to a complex problem. *Mayo Clinic Proceedings, 79,* 735–737.

Flanagan, C. (2002, April). *Inclusion and reciprocity: Developmental sources of social trust and civic hope.* Paper presented at the meeting of the Society for Research on Adolescence, New Orleans.

Flanagan, C. (2004). Volunteerism, leadership, political socialization, and civic engagement. In R. Lerner & L. Steinberg (Eds.), *Handbook of adolescent psychology* (2nd ed.). New York: Wiley.

Flanagan, C., & Faison, N. (2001). Youth civic development: Implications of research for social policy and programs. *Social Policy Report, XV* (No. 1), 1–14.

Flanagan, C., Gill, S., & Gallay, L. (1998, November). *Intergroup understanding, social justice, and the "social contract" in diverse communities of youth: Foundations for civic understanding.* Project report prepared for the workshop on research to improve intergroup relations among youth, Forum on Adolescence, Board on Children, Youth, and Families, National Research Council, Washington, DC.

Flanagan, K. M., Clements, M. L., Whitton, S. W., Portney, M. J., Randall, D. W., & Markman, H. J. (2001). Retrospect and prospect in the psychological study of marital and couple relationships. In J. P. McHale & W. S. Grolnick (Eds.), *Retrospect and prospect in the psychological study of families.* Mahwah, NJ: Erlbaum.

Flannery, D. J., Hussey, D., Biebelhausen, L., & Wester, K. (2003). Crime, delinquency, and youth gangs. In G. Adams & M. Berzonsky (Eds.), *Blackwell handbook of adolescence.* Malden, MA: Blackwell.

Flavell, J. H. (1999). Cognitive development: Children's knowledge about the mind. *Annual Review of Psychology* (Vol. 50). Palo Alto, CA: Annual Reviews.

Flavell, J. H. (2004). Theory-of-mind development: Retrospect and prospect. *Merrill-Palmer Quarterly, 50,* 274–290.

Flavell, J. H., Friedrichs, A., & Hoyt, J. (1970). Developmental changes in memorization processes. *Cognitive Psychology, 1,* 324–340.

Flavell, J. H., Green, F. L., & Flavell, E. R. (1998). The mind has a mind of its own: Developing knowledge about mental uncontrollability. *Cognitive Development, 13,* 127–138.

Flavell, J. H., Miller, P. H., & Miller, S. (2002). *Cognitive development* (4th ed.). Upper Saddle River, NJ: Prentice Hall.

Flesner, M. K. (2004). Care of the elderly as a global nursing issue. *Nursing Administration Quarterly, 28,* 67–72.

Fletcher, A. C., Steinberg, L., & Williams-Wheeler, M. (2004). Parental influences on adolescent problem behavior: Revisiting Stattin and Kerr. *Child Development, 75,* 781–796.

Fletcher, A. E., Breeze, E., & Shetty, P. S. (2003). Antioxidant vitamins and mortality in older persons. *American Journal of Nutrition, 78,* 999–1010.

Flick, L., White, D. K., Vemulapalli, C., Stulac, B. B., & Kemp, J. S. (2001). Sleep position and the use of soft bedding during bed sharing among African American infants at increased risk for sudden infant death syndrome. *Journal of Pediatrics, 138,* 338–343.

Flohr, J. W., Atkins, D. H., Bower, T. G. R., & Aldridge, M. A. (2001, April). *Infant music preferences.* Paper presented at the meeting of the Society for Research in Child Development, Minneapolis.

Flores, D. L., & Hendrick, V. C. (2002). Etiology and treatment of postpartum depression. *Current Psychiatry Reports, 4,* 461–466.

Florsheim, P., Moore, D., & Edgington, C. (2003). Romantic relationships among pregnant and parenting adolescents. In P. Florsheim (Ed.), *Adolescent romantic relations and sexual behavior.* Mahwah, NJ: Erlbaum.

Florsheim, P., Sumida, E., McCann, C., Winstanley, M., Fukui, R., Seefeldt, T., & Moore, D. (2003). The transition to parenthood among young African American and Latino couples: Relational predictors of risk for parental dysfunction. *Journal of Family Psychology, 17,* 65–79.

Floyd, R. A., & Hensley, K. (2002). Oxidative stress in brain aging. Implications for therapeutics of neurogenerative diseases. *Neurobiology of Aging, 23,* 795–807.

Flynn, J. R. (1999). Searching for justice: The discovery of IQ gains over time. *American Psychologist, 54,* 5–20.

Fodor, I. G., & Franks, V. (1990). Women in midlife and beyond. The new prime of life? *Psychology of Women Quarterly, 14,* 445–449.

Fogel, A. (2001). *Infancy* (4th ed.). Belmont, CA: Wadsworth.

Fogoros, R. N. (2001). *Does stress really cause heart disease?* Retrieved October 10, 2001, from www.about.com.

Foley, D., Ancoli-Israel, S., Britz, P., & Walsh, J. (2004). Sleep disturbances and chronic diseases in older adults: Results of the 2003 National Sleep Foundation Sleep in America survey. *Journal of Psychosomatic Research, 56,* 497–502.

Folkman, S., & Moskowitz, J. T. (2004). Coping: Pitfalls and promises. *Annual Review* *of Psychology* (Vol. 55). Palo Alto, CA: Annual Reviews.

Ford, K., Sohn, W., & Lepkowski, J. (2001). Characteristics of adolescents' sexual partners and their association with use of condoms and other contraceptive methods. *Family Planning Perspectives, 33*, 100–105, 132.

Ford, N., Odallo, D., & Chorlton, R. (2003). Communication from a human rights perspective: Responding to the HIV/AIDS pandemic in eastern and southern Africa. *Journal of Health Communication, 8*, 599–602.

Forrest, J. D., & Singh, S. (1990). The sexual and reproductive behavior of American women, 1982–1988. *Family Planning Perspectives, 22*, 206–214.

Fowler, G. (1999). *As we grow old: How adult children and their parents can face aging with candor and grace.* Valley Forge, PA: Judson Press.

Fox, B., & Hull, M. (2002). *Phonics for the teacher of reading* (8th ed.). Upper Saddle River, NJ: Merrill.

Fox, G. L., & Murry, V. M. (2000). Gender and families: Feminist perspectives and family research. *Journal of Marriage and the Family, 62*, 1160–1172.

Fox, K. R. (2004). Childhood obesity and the role of physical activity. *Journal of Research in Social Health, 124*, 34–39.

Fox, M. K., Pac, S., Devaney, B., & Jankowski, L. (2004). Feeding infants and toddlers study: What foods are infants and toddlers eating? *American Dietetic Association Journal (Suppl.), 104*, S22–S30.

Fox, N. A., Henderson, H. A., Marshall, P. J., Nichols, K. E., & Ghera, M. M. (2004). Behavioral inhibition: Linking biology and behavior within a developmental framework. *Annual Review of Psychology, 55*. Palo Alto, CA: Annual Reviews.

Fox, N. C., & Schott, J. M. (2004). Imaging cerebral atrophy: Normal aging to Alzheimer disease. *Lancet, 363*, 392–394.

Fox, P. G., Burns, K. R., Popovich, J. M., Belknap, R. A., & Frank-Stromberg, M. (2004). Southeast Asia refugee children: Self-esteem as a predictor of depression and scholastic achievement in the U.S. *International Journal of Nursing Research, 9*, 1063–1072.

Fozard, J. L. (1992, December 6). Commentary in "We can age successfully." *Parade Magazine*, pp. 14–15.

Fozard, J. L. (2000). Sensory and cognitive changes with age. In K. W. Schaie &

M. Pietrucha (Eds.), *Mobility and transportation in the elderly.* New York: Springer.

Fozard, J. L., & Gordon-Salant, S. (2001). Changes in vision and hearing with aging. In J. E. Birren & K. W. Schaie (Eds.), *Handbook of the psychology of aging* (5th ed.). San Diego: Academic Press.

Fraga, C. G., Motchnik, P. A., Shigenaga, M. K., Helbock, H. J., Jacob, R. A., & Ames, B. N. (1991). Ascorbic acid protects against endogenous oxidative DNA damage in human sperm. *Proceedings of the National Academy of Sciences of the United States, 88*, 11003–11006.

Fraiberg, S. (1959). *The magic years.* New York: Scribner's.

Fraley, R. C. (2002). Attachment stability from infancy to adulthood: Meta-analysis and dynamic modeling of developmental mechanisms. *Personality and Social Psychology Review, 6*, 123–151.

Frank, D. A., Augustyn, M., Knight, W. G., Pell, T., & Zuckerman, B. (2001). Growth, development, and behavior in early childhood following prenatal cocaine exposure: A systematic review. *Journal of the American Medical Association, 285*, 1613–1625.

Franke, T. M. (2000, Winter). The role of attachment as a protective factor in adolescent violent behavior. *Adolescent & Family Health, 1*, 29–39.

Frankl, V. (1984). *Man's search for meaning.* New York: Basic Books.

Franz, C. E. (1996). The implications of preschool tempo and motoric activity level for personality decades later. Reported in A. Caspi, Personality development across the life course, in W. Damon (Ed.), *Handbook of child psychology*, Vol. 3 (New York: Wiley), p. 337.

Fraser, S. (Ed.). (1995). *The bell curve wars.* New York: Basic Books.

Frazier, P. A. (2003). Perceived control and distress following sexual assault: A longitudinal test of a new model. *Journal of Personality and Social Psychology, 84*, 1257–1269.

Frazier, P. A., & Cook, S. W. (1993). Correlates of distress following heterosexual relationship dissolution. *Journal of Social and Personal Relationships, 10*, 55–67.

Frazier, P., Tashiro, T., Berman, M., Steger, M., & Long, J. (2004). Correlates of levels and patterns of positive life changes following sexual assault. *Journal of Consulting and Clinical Psychology, 72*, 19–30.

Frede, E. C. (1995). The role of program quality in producing early childhood

program benefits. *The Future of Children* (Vol. 5, No. 3), 115–132.

Frederikse, M., Lu, A., Aylward, E., Barta, P., Sharma, T., & Pearlson, G. (2000). Sex differences in inferior lobule volume in schizophrenia. *American Journal of Psychiatry, 157*, 422–427.

Fredrickson, D. D. (1993). Breastfeeding research priorities, opportunities, and study criteria: What we learned from the smoking trail. *Journal of Human Lactation, 3*, 147–150.

Fredriksen, K., Rhodes, J., Reddy, R., & Way, N. (2004). Sleepless in Chicago: Tracking the effects of adolescent sleep loss during the middle school years. *Child Development, 75*, 84–95.

Freeman, S., & Herron, J. (2004). *Evolutionary analysis* (3rd ed.). Upper Saddle River, NJ: Prentice Hall.

Freeman-Fobbs, P. (2003). Feeding our children to death. *Journal of the National Medical Association, 95*, 119.

Frenkel, D., Dori, M., & Solomon, B. (2004). Generation of anti-beta-amyloid antibodies via phage display technology. *Vaccine, 22*, 2505–2508.

Frenn, M., Malin, S., Bansal, N., Delgado, M., Greer, Y., Havice, M., Ho, M., & Schweizer, H. (2003). Addressing health disparities in middle school students' nutrition and exercise. *Journal of Community Health and Nursing, 20*, 1–14.

Freud, A., & Dann, S. (1951). Instinctual anxiety during puberty. In A. Freud (Ed.), *The ego and its mechanisms of defense.* New York: International Universities Press.

Freud, S. (1917). *A general introduction to psychoanalysis.* New York: Washington Square Press.

Freund, A. M., & Baltes, P. B. (2002). Life-management strategies of selection, optimization, and compensation: Measurement by self-report and construct validity. *Journal of Personality and Social Psychology, 82*, 642–662.

Freund, A. M., & Riediger, M. (2003). Successful aging. In I. B. Weiner (Ed.), *Handbook of psychology* (Vol. VI). New York: Wiley.

Fridrich, A. H., & Flannery, D. J. (1995). The effects of ethnicity and acculturation on early adolescent delinquency. *Journal of Child & Family Studies, 4*, 69–87.

Fried, P. A. (2002). Conceptual issues in behavioral teratology and their application in determining long-term sequelae of prenatal marijuana exposure. *Journal of Child Psychology and Psychiatry, 43*, 81–102.

Fried, P. A., & Watkinson, B. (1990). 36- and 48-month neurobehavioral follow-up of children prenatally exposed to marijuana, cigarettes, and alcohol. *Developmental and Behavioral Pediatrics, 11,* 49–58.

Friedman, M., & Rosenman, R. (1974). *Type A behavior and your heart.* New York: Knopf.

Friedman, S. L., Randolph, S., & Kochanoff, A. (2004). Child care research. In J. G. Bremner & A. Fogel (Eds.), *Blackwell handbook of infant development.* Malden, MA: Blackwell.

Friend, M. (2005). *Special education.* Boston: Allyn & Bacon.

Frieske, D. A., & Park, D. C. (1999). Memory for news in young and old adults. *Psychology and aging, 14,* 90–98.

Fry, P. S. (1999, November). *Significance of religiosity and spirituality to psychological well-being of older adults.* Paper presented at the meeting of the Gerontological Society of America, San Francisco.

Fry, P. S. (2001). The unique contribution of key existential factors to the prediction of psychological well-being of older adults following spousal loss. *The Gerontologist, 41,* 69–81.

Frye, D. (1999). Development of intention: The relation of executive function to theory of mind. In P. D. Zelazo, J. W. Astington, & D. R. Olson (Eds.), *Developing theories of intention: Social understanding and self-control.* Mahwah, NJ: Erlbaum.

Fujikado, T., Kuroa, T., Maeda, N., Ninomiya, S., Goto, H., Tano, Y., Oshika, T., Hiroshara, Y., & Mihashi, T. (2004). Light scattering and optical aberrations as objective parameters to predict visual deterioration in eyes with cataracts. *Journal of Cataract and Refractive Surgery, 30,* 1198–1208.

Fuligni, A. J., Alvarez, J., Bachman, M., & Ruble, D. N. (2005). Family obligation and the motivation of young children from immigrant families. In C. R. Cooper, C. T. Garcia Coll, W. T. Bartko, H. M. Davis, & C. Chatman (Eds.), *Developmental pathways through middle childhood.* Mahwah, NJ: Erlbaum.

Fuligni, A. J., & Yoshikawa, H. (2003). Socioeconomic resources, poverty, and child development among immigrant families. In M. H. Bornstein & R. H. Bradley (Eds.), *Socioeconomic status, parenting, and child development.* Mahwah, NJ: Erlbaum.

Fuligni, A., & Yoshikawa, H. (2004). Investments in children among immigrant families. In A. Kalil & T. DeLeire (Eds.), *Family investments in children's potential.* Mahwah, NJ: Erlbaum.

Fuller-Thomson, E., & Minkler, M. (2001). American grandparents providing extensive care to their grandchildren: Prevalence and profile. *The Gerontologist, 41* (No. 2), 201–209.

Fulmer, T., Guadagno, L., & Bolton, M. M. (2004). Elder mistreatment in women. *Journal of Obstetrics, Gynecological, and Neonatal Nursing, 33,* 657–663.

Fung, H., & Carstensen, L. L. (2004). Motivational changes in response to blocked goals and foreshortened time: Testing alternatives to socioemotional selectivity theory. *Psychology and Aging, 19,* 68–78.

Furman, W., & Shaffer, L. (2003). The role of romantic relationships in adolescent development. In P. Florsheim (Ed.), *Adolescent romantic relations and sexual behavior.* Mahwah, NJ: Erlbaum.

Furth, H. G., & Wachs, H. (1975). *Thinking goes to school.* New York: Oxford University Press.

Galambos, N. L. (2004). Gender and gender role development in adolescence. In R. Lerner & L. Steinberg (Eds.), *Handbook of adolescence.* New York: Wiley.

Galambos, N. L., & Maggs, J. L. (1989, April). *The afterschool ecology of young adolescents and self-reported behavior.* Paper presented at the biennial meeting of the Society for Research in Child Development, Kansas City.

Gale, C. R., & Martin, C. N. (2004). Birth weight and later risk of depression in a national cohort. *British Journal of Psychiatry, 184,* 28–33.

Galician, M-L. (2004). *Sex, love, and romance in the mass media.* Mahwah, NJ: Erlbaum.

Gall, M. D., Borg, W. R., & Gall, J. P. (2003). *Educational research* (7th ed.). Boston: Allyn & Bacon.

Gall, T. L., Evans, D. R., & Howard, J. (1997). The retirement adjustment process: Changes in well-being of male retirees across time. *Journals of Gerontology B: Psychological Sciences and Social Sciences, 52,* P110–P117.

Gallagher, C. (2000). A seat at the table: Teachers reclaiming assessment through rethinking accountability. *Phi Delta Kappan, 81,* 502–507.

Gallo, L. C., Troxel, W. M., Matthews, K. A., & Kuller, L. W. (2003). Marital status and quality in middle-aged women: Associations with levels and trajectories of cardiovascular risk factors. *Health Psychology, 22,* 453–463.

Gallo, W. T., Bradley, E. H., Falba, T. A., Dubin, J. A., Cramer, L. D., Bogardus, S. T., & Kasl, S. V. (2004). Involuntary job loss as a risk factor for subsequent myocardial infarction and stroke: Findings from the Health and Retirement Survey. *American Journal of Industrial Medicine, 45,* 408–416.

Galloway, J. C., & Thelen, E. (2004). Feet first: Object exploration in young infants. *Infant Behavior and Development, 27,* 107–112.

Gallup, G. H. (1987). *The Gallup poll: Public opinion 1986.* Wilmington, DE: Scholarly Resources.

Galotti, K. M., & Kozberg, S. F. (1996). Adolescents' experience of a life-framing decision. *Journal of Youth and Adolescence, 25,* 3–16.

Gamino, L. A., & Sewell, K. W. (2004). Meaning constructs as predictors of bereavement adjustment: A report from the Scott & White grief study. *Death Studies, 28,* 397–421.

Gandour, J., Wong, D., Dzemidzic, M., Lowe, M., Tong, Y., & Li, X. (2003). A cross-linguistic fMRI study of perception of intonation and emotion in Chinese. *Human Brain Mapping, 18,* 149–157.

Gannon, L. (1998). Menopause. In H. S. Friedman (Ed.), *Encyclopedia of mental health* (Vol. 2). San Diego: Academic Press.

Ganong, L. H., & Coleman, M. (1994). *Remarried family relationships.* Thousand Oaks, CA: Sage.

Gao, Y., Elliott, M. E., & Waters, E. (1999, April). *Maternal attachment representations and support for three-year-olds' secure base behavior.* Paper presented at the meeting of the Society for Research in Child Development, Albuquerque.

Garbarino, J. (1999). *Lost boys: Why our sons turn violent and how we can save them.* New York: Free Press.

Garbarino, J. (2001). Violent children. *Archives of Pediatrics & Adolescent Medicine, 155,* 1–2.

Garbarino, J., Bradshaw, C. P., & Kostelny, K. (2005). Neighborhood and community influences on parenting. In T. Luster & L. Okaghi (Eds.), *Parenting: An ecological perspective.* Mahwah, NJ: Erlbaum.

Garbarino, J., Dubrow, N., Kostelny, K., & Pardo, C. (1992). *Children in danger.* San Francisco: Jossey-Bass.

Garcia-Alba, C. (2004). Anorexia and depression. *Spanish Journal of Psychology,* 7, 40–52.

Gard, J. W., Alexander, J. M., Bawdon, R. E., & Albrecht, J. T. (2002). Oxytocin preparation stability in several common intravenous solutions. *American Journal of Obstetrics and Gynecology, 186,* 496–498.

Gardner, H. (1983). *Frames of mind.* New York: Basic Books.

Gardner, H. (1993). *Multiple intelligences.* New York: Basic Books.

Gardner, H. (2002). The pursuit of excellence through education. In M. Ferrari (Ed.), *Learning from extraordinary minds.* Mahwah, NJ: Erlbaum.

Garofalo, R., Wolf, R. C., Wissow, L. S., Woods, E. R., & Goodman, E. (1999). Sexual orientation and risk of suicide attempts among a representative sample of youth. *Archives of Pediatrics and Adolescent Medicine, 153,* 487–493.

Gartner, J., Larson, D. B., & Allen, G. D. (1991). Religious commitment and mental health: A review of the empirical literature. *Journal of Psychology and Theology, 19,* 6–25.

Garton, A. F. (2004). *Exploring cognitive development: The child as a problem solver.* Malden, MA: Blackwell.

Gaugler, J. E., Zarit, S. H., & Perlin, L. (2003). The onset of dementia caregiving and its longitudinal implications. *Psychology and Aging, 18,* 171–180.

Gaulin, J. C., & McBurney, D. H. (2004). *Evolutionary psychology* (2nd ed.). Upper Saddle River, NJ: Prentice Hall.

Gavrilov, L. A., & Gavrilova, N. S. (2002). Evolutionary theories of aging and longevity. *The Scientific World Journal, 2,* 339–356.

Gehrman, C., & Hovell, M. (2003). Protecting children from environmental tobacco smoke (ETS) exposure: A critical review. *Nicotine and Tobacco Research, 5,* 289–301.

Gelman, R. (1969). Conservation acquisition: A problem of learning to attend to relevant attributes. *Journal of Experimental Child Psychology, 7,* 67–87.

Gelman, R., & Brenneman, K. (1994). Domain specificity and cultural variation are not inconsistent. In L. A. Hirschfeld & S. Gelman (Eds.), *Mapping the mind: Domain specificity in cognition and culture.* New York: Cambridge University Press.

Gelman, R., & Williams, E. M. (1998). Enabling constraints for cognitive development and learning. In W. Damon (Ed.), *Handbook of child psychology* (5th ed., Vol. 4). New York: Wiley.

Gelman, S. A., & Opfer, J. E. (2004). Development of the animate-inanimate distinction. In U. Goswami (Ed.), *Blackwell handbook of childhood cognitive development.* Malden, MA: Blackwell.

Gelman, S. A., Taylor, M. G., & Nguyen, S. P. (2004). Mother-child conversations about gender. *Monographs of the Society for Research in Child Development, Vol. 69 (No. 1), Serial No. 275.*

Genova, M. L., Pich, M. M., Bernacchia, A., Bianchi, C., Biondi, A., Bovina, C., Falasca, A. I., Formiggini, G., Castelli, G. P., & Lenaz, G. (2004). The mitochondrial production of reactive oxygen species in relation to aging and pathology. *Annals of the New York Academy of Science, 1011,* 86–100.

Gerlach, P. (1998). *Stepfamily in formation.* Chicago: Stepfamily Association of Illinois.

Gerrard, J. A., & Chudasama, G. (2003). Screening to reduce HIV transmission from mother to baby. *Nursing Times, 99,* 44–45.

Gerrotsen, M., Berg, I., Deelman, B., Visser-Keizer, A., & Jong, B. (2003). Speed of information processing after unilateral stroke. *Journal of Clinical and Experimental Neuropsychology, 25,* 1–13.

Gershoff, E. T. (2002). Corporal punishment by parents and associated child behaviors and experiences: A meta-analysis and theoretical review. *Psychological Bulletin, 128,* 539–579.

Gescheider, G. A. (1997). *Psychophysics: The fundamentals.* Mahwah, NJ: Erlbaum.

Gesell, A. (1934). *An atlas of infant behavior.* New Haven, CT: Yale University Press.

Gesell, A. L. (1934). *Infancy and human growth.* New York: Macmillan.

Gessert, C. E., Elliott, B. A., & Haller, I. V. (2003). Mortality patterns in middle and old age. *Journals of Gerontology A: Biological and Medical Sciences, 58,* B967.

Gewirtz, J. (1977). Maternal responding and the conditioning of infant crying: Directions of influence within the attachment-acquisition process. In B. C. Etzel, J. M. LeBlanc, & D. M. Baer (Eds.), *New developments in behavioral research.* Hillsdale, NJ: Erlbaum.

Giacomoni, P. U., & Rein, G. (2004). A mechanistic model for the aging of human skin. *Micron, 35,* 179–184.

Giammattei, J., Blix, G., Marshak, H. H., Wollitzer, A. O., & Pettitt, D. J. (2003). Television watching and soft drink consumption: Associations with obesity in 11- to 13-year-old schoolchildren. *Archives of Pediatric and Adolescent Medicine, 157,* 882–886.

Gibbons, J. L. (2000). Gender development in cross-cultural perspective. In T. Eckes & H. M. Trautner (Eds.), *The developmental social psychology of gender.* Mahwah, NJ: Erlbaum.

Gibbons, J., & Ng, S. H. (2004). Acting bilingual and thinking bilingual. *Journal of Language and Social Psychology, 23,* 4–6.

Gibbs, J. C. (1993, March). *Inductive discipline's contribution to moral motivation.* Paper presented at the biennial meeting of the Society for Research in Child Development, New Orleans.

Gibbs, J. C. (2003). *Moral development & reality.* Thousand Oaks, CA: Sage.

Gibson, E. J. (1969). *Principles of perceptual learning and development.* New York: Appleton-Century-Crofts.

Gibson, E. J. (1989). Exploratory behavior in the development of perceiving, acting, and the acquiring of knowledge. *Annual Review of Psychology* (Vol. 39). Palo Alto, CA: Annual Reviews.

Gibson, E. J. (2001). *Perceiving the affordances.* Mahwah, NJ: Erlbaum.

Gibson, E. J., Riccio, G., Schmuckler, M. A., Stoffregen, T. A., Rosenberg, D., & Taormina, J. (1987). Detection of the traversability of surfaces by crawling and walking infants. *Journal of Experimental Psychology: Human Perception and Performance, 13,* 533–544.

Gibson, E. J., & Walk, R. D. (1960). The "visual cliff." *Scientific American, 202,* 64–71.

Gibson, J. H., Harries, M., Mitchell, A., Godfrey, R., Lunt, M., & Reeve, J. (2000). Determinants of bone density and prevalence of osteopenia among female runners in their second to seventh decades of age. *Bone, 26,* 591–598.

Gibson, J. J. (1966). *The senses considered as perceptual systems.* Boston: Houghton Mifflin.

Gibson, J. J. (1979). *The ecological approach to visual perception.* Boston: Houghton Mifflin.

Giedd, J. N. (2004). Structural magnetic resonance imaging of the adolescent brain. *Annals of the New York Academy of Sciences, 1021,* 77–85.

Giedd, J., Jeffries, N., Blumenthal, J., Castellanos, F., Vaituzis, A., Fernandez, T., Hamburger, S., Liu, H., Nelson, J., Bedwell, J., Tran, L., Lenane, M., Nicolson, R., & Rapoport, J. (1999). Childhood-onset schizophrenia: Progressive brain changes during adolescence. *Biological Psychiatry, 46,* 892–898.

Gifford-Smith, M. E., & Rabiner, D. L. (2004). Children's understanding and regulation of emotion in the context of their peer relations. In J. B. Kupersmidt & K. A. Dodge (Eds.), *Children's peer relations.* Washington, DC: American Psychological Association.

Gilhar, A., Ullman, Y., Karry, R., Shalaginov, R., Assy, B., Serafimovich, S., & Kalish, R. S. (2004). Aging of human epidermis. *Journals of Gerontology A: Biological Sciences and Medical Sciences, 59,* B411–B415.

Gilligan, C. (1982). *In a different voice.* Cambridge, MA: Harvard University Press.

Gilligan, C. (1992, May). *Joining the resistance: Girls' development in adolescence.* Paper presented at the symposium on development and vulnerability in close relationships, Montreal, Quebec.

Gilligan, C. (1996). The centrality of relationships in psychological development: A puzzle, some evidence, and a theory. In G. G. Noam & K. W. Fischer (Eds.), *Development and vulnerability in close relationships.* Hillsdale, NJ: Erlbaum.

Giotakos, O., Markianos, M., Vaidakis, N., & Christodoulou, G. N. (2003). Aggression, impulsivity, plasma sex hormones, and biogenic amine turnover in a forensic population of rapists. *Journal of Sex and Marital Therapy, 29,* 215–225.

Giron, M. S. T., Forsell, Y., Bernsten, C., Thorslund, M., Winblad, B., & Fastborn, J. (2002). Sleep problems in a very old population: Drug use and clinical correlates. *Journal of Gerontology: Medical Sciences, 57A,* M236–M240.

Glassman, T. (2002). The failure of higher education to reduce the binge drinking rate. *Journal of American College Health, 51,* 143–144.

Glei, D. A. (1999). Measuring contraceptive use patterns among teenage and adult women. *Family Planning Perspectives, 31,* 73–80.

Godding, V., Bonnier, C., Fiasse, L., Michel, M., Longueville, E., Lebecque, P., Robert, A., & Galanti, L. (2004). Does in utero exposure to heavy maternal smoking induce nicotine withdrawal symptoms in neonates? *Pediatric Research, 55,* 645–651.

Golan, M., & Crow, S. (2004). Parents are key players in the prevention and treatment of weight-related problems. *Nutrition Review, 62,* 39–50.

Goldman, N., Weinstein, M., Cornman, J., Singer, B., Seeman, T., Goldman, N., & Chang, M. C. (2004). Sex differentials in biological risk factors for chronic disease. *Journal of Women's Health, 13,* 393–403.

Goldsmith, H. H. (2002). Genetics of emotional development. In R. J. Davidson, K. R. Scherer, & H. H. Goldsmith (Eds.), *Handbook of affective sciences.* New York: Oxford University Press.

Goldsmith, H. H., & Davidson, R. J. (2004). Disambiguating the components of emotion regulation. *Child Development, 75,* 361–365.

Goldsmith, H. H., & Gottesman, I. I. (1981). Origins of variation in behavioral style: A longitudinal study of temperament in young twins. *Child Development, 52,* 91–103.

Goldsmith, H. H., Lemery, K. S., & Essex, M. J. (2004). Temperament as a liability factor for behavioral disorders of childhood. In L. F. DiLalla (Ed.), *Behavior genetics principles.* Washington, DC: American Psychological Association.

Goldstein, J. M., Seidman, L. J., Horton, N. J., Makris, N., Kennedy, D. N., Caviness, V. S., Faraone, S. V., & Tsuang, M. T. (2001). Normal sexual dimorphism of the adult human brain assessed by in vivo magnetic resonance imaging. *Cerebral Cortex, 11,* 490–497.

Goleman, D. (1995). *Emotional intelligence.* New York: Basic Books.

Goleman, D., Kaufman, P., & Ray, M. (1993). *The creative spirit.* New York: Plume.

Golombok, S., MacCallum, F., & Goodman, E. (2001). The "test-tube" generation: Parent-child relationships and the psychological well-being of in vitro fertilization children at adolescence. *Child Development, 72,* 599–608.

Gonzales, N. A., Knight, G. P., Birman, D., & Sirolli, A. A. (2004). Acculturation and enculturation among Latino youths. In K. L. Maton, C. J. Schellenbach, B. J. Leadbetter, & A. L. Solarz (Eds.), *Investing in children, youth, families, and communities.* Mahwah, NJ: Erlbaum.

Gonzales, N. A., Knight, G. P., Morgan Lopez, A., Saenz, D., & Sirolli, A. (2002). Acculturation and the mental health of Latino youths: An integration and critique of the literature. In J. M. Contreras, K. A. Kerns, & A. M. Neal-Barnett (Eds.), *Latino children and families in the United States.* Westport, CT: Greenwood.

Gonzalez-del Angel, A. A., Vidal, S., Saldan, Y., del Castillo, V., Angel, M., Macias, M., Luna, P., & Orozco, L. (2000). Molecular diagnosis of the fragile X and FRAXE syndromes in patients with mental retardation of unknown cause in Mexico. *Annals of Genetics, 43,* 29–34.

Goodman, C. C. (2003). Intergenerational triads in grandparent-headed families. *Journals of Gerontology B: Psychological Sciences and Social Sciences, 58,* S281–S289.

Goodman, J. H. (2004). Paternal postpartum depression: Its relationship to maternal postpartum depression, and implications for family health. *Journal of Advanced Nursing, 45,* 26–35.

Gooren, L. J. (2002). Psychological consequences. *Seminars in Reproductive Medicine, 20,* 285–296.

Gooren, L. J. (2003). Androgen deficiency in the aging male: Benefits and risks of androgen supplementation. *Journal of Steroid Biochemistry and Molecular Biology, 85,* 349–355.

Goorhuis-Brouwer, S., Coster, H., Nakken, H., & Spelberg, H. L. (2004). Environmental factors in developmental language disorders. In L. Verhoeven & H. Van Balkom (Eds.), *The classification of language disorders.* Mahwah, NJ: Erlbaum.

Goos, M. (2004). Learning mathematics in a classroom community of inquiry. *Journal for Research in Mathematics Education, 35,* 258–291.

Gotesdam, K. G., & Agras, W. S. (1995). General population-based epidemiological survey of eating disorders in Norway. *International Journal of Eating Disorders, 18,* 119–126.

Goto, S., Takashasi, R., Araki, S., & Nakamoto, H. (2002). Dietary restriction initiated in late adulthood can reverse age-related alterations of protein and protein metabolism. *Annals of the New York Academy of Science, 959,* 50–60.

Gottesman, I. I. (2004). Postscript: Eyewitness to maturation. In L. F. DiLalla (Ed.), *Behavior genetics principles.* Washington, DC: American Psychological Association.

Gottfried, A. E., Gottfried, A. W., & Bathurst, K. (2002). Maternal and dual-earner employment status and parenting. In M. H. Bornstein (Ed.), *Handbook of parenting* (2nd ed., Vol. 2). Mahwah, NJ: Erlbaum.

Gottlieb, G. (1998). Normally occurring environmental and behavioral influences on gene activity: From central dogma to probabilistic epigenesis. *Psychological Review, 105,* 792–802.

Gottlieb, G. (2002). Origin of species: The potential significance of early experience for evolution. In W. W. Hartup & R. A. Weinberg (Eds.), *Child psychology in retrospect and prospect.* Mahwah, NJ: Erlbaum.

Gottlieb, G. (2003). *Developmental behavioral genetics and the statistical concept of interaction.* Unpublished manuscript, Department of Psychology, University of North Carolina, Chapel Hill.

Gottlieb, G. (2004). Normally occurring environmental and behavioral influences on gene activity. In C. G. Coll, E. L. Bearer, & R. M. Lerner (Eds.), *Nature and nurture.* Mahwah, NJ: Erlbaum.

Gottlieb, G., Wahlsten, D., & Lickliter, R. (1998). The significance of biology for human development: A developmental psychobiological systems view. In W. Damon (Ed.), *Handbook of child psychology* (5th ed., Vol. 1). New York: Wiley.

Gottman, J. M. (1994). *Why marriages succeed or fail.* New York: Simon & Schuster.

Gottman, J. M., Coan, J., Carrere, S., & Swanson, C. (1998). Predicting marital happiness and stability from newlywed interactions. *Journal of Marriage and the Family, 60,* 5–22.

Gottman, J. M., & DeClaire, J. (1997). *The heart of parenting: Raising an emotionally intelligent child.* New York: Simon & Schuster.

Gottman, J. M., & Levenson, R. W. (2000). The timing of divorce: Predicting when a couple will divorce over a 14-year period. *Journal of Marriage and the Family, 62,* 737–745.

Gottman, J. M., & Notarius, C. I. (2000). Decade review: Observing marital interaction. *Journal of Marriage and the Family, 62,* 927–947.

Gottman, J. M., & Parker, J. G. (Eds.) (1987). *Conversations of friends.* New York: Cambridge University Press.

Gottman, J. M., Ryan, K. D., Carrere, S., & Erley, A. M. (2002). Toward a scientifically based marital therapy. In H. A. Liddle & D. A. Santisteban (Eds.), *Family psychology.* Washington, DC: American Psychological Association.

Gottman, J. M., & Silver, N. (1999). *The seven principles for making marriages work.* New York: Crown.

Gould, E., Reeves, A. J., Graziano, M. S., & Gross, C. G. (1999). Neurogenesis in the neocortex of adult primates. *Science, 286* (1), 548–552.

Gould, M. (2001, December 5). *Science for all: Just growing pains? The mental health of our children.* Washington, DC: National Institute of Mental Health.

Gould, S. J. (1981). *The mismeasure of man.* New York: W. W. Norton.

Gouldner, H., & Strong, M. M. (1987). *Speaking of friendship.* New York: Greenwood Press.

Gounin-Decarie, T. (1996). Revisiting Piaget, or the vulnerability of Piaget's infancy theory in the nineties. In G. G. Noam & K. W. Fischer (Eds.), *Development and vulnerability in close relationships.* Hillsdale, NJ: Erlbaum.

Gove, W. R., Style, C. B., & Hughes, M. (1990). The effect of marriage on the well-being of adults: A theoretical analysis. *Journal of Health and Social Behavior, 24,* 122–131.

Govier, F., Potempa, A. J., Kaufman, J., Denne, J., Kovalenko, P., & Ahuja, S. (2003). A multicenter, randomized, double-blind, crossover study of patient preference for tadalafil 20 mg or sildenafil citrate 50 mg during initiation of treatment for erectile dysfunction. *Clinical Therapeutics, 25,* 2709–2723.

Gowan, D. E. (2003). Christian beliefs concerning death and life after death. In C. D. Bryant (Ed.), *Handbook of death and dying.* Thousand Oaks, CA: Sage.

Gowers, S., & Bryant-Waugh, R. (2004). Management of child and adolescent eating disorders. *Journal of Child Psychology and Psychiatry and Allied Disciplines, 45,* 68–83.

Graber, J. A. (2003). *Early puberty and drug use.* Unpublished data, Department of Psychology, University of Florida, Gainsville.

Graber, J. A. (2004). Internalizing problems during adolescence. In R. Lerner & L. Steinberg (Eds.), *Handbook of adolescent psychology* (2nd ed.). New York: Wiley.

Graber, J. A., & Brooks-Gunn, J. (2001). Body image. In R. M. Lerner & J. V. Lerner (Eds.), *Adolescence in America.* Santa Barbara, CA: ABC-CLIO.

Graber, J. A., & Brooks-Gunn, J. (2002). Adolescent girls' sexual development. In G. M. Wingood & R. J. DiClemente (Eds.), *Handbook of sexual and reproductive health.* New York: Plenum.

Graber, J. A., Seeley, J. R., Brooks-Gunn, J., & Lewinsohn, P. M. (2004). Is pubertal timing associated with psychopathology in young adulthood? *Journal of the American Academy of Child and Adolescent Psychiatry, 43,* 718–726.

Graham, S. (1992). Most of the subjects were white and middle class. *American Psychologist, 47,* 629–637.

Grambs, J. D. (1989). *Women over forty* (rev. ed.). New York: Springer.

Grandjean, P., White, R. F., Weihe, P., & Jorgensen, P. J. (2003). Neurotoxic risk caused by stable and variable exposure to methylmercury from seafood. *Ambulatory Pediatrics, 1,* 18–23.

Grant, J. P. (1997). *The state of the world's children.* New York: UNICEF and Oxford University Press.

Grantham-McGregor, S., Ani, C., & Fernald, L. (2001). The role of nutrition in cognitive development. In R. J. Sternberg & E. I. Grigorenko (Eds.), *Environmental effects on cognitive abilities.* Mahwah, NJ: Erlbaum.

Gray, J. (1992). *Men are from Mars, women are from Venus.* New York: HarperCollins.

Gray, M. J., & Acierno, R. (2002). Symptom presentation of older adult crime victim description of a clinical sample. *Journal of Anxiety Disorders, 16,* 299–309.

Green, L. A., Fryer, G. E., Yawn, B. P., Lanier, D., & Dovey, S. M. (2001). The ecology of medical care revisited. *New England Journal of Medicine, 344,* 2021–2025.

Greenberger, E., & Steinberg, L. (1986). *When teenagers work: The psychological social costs of adolescent employment.* New York: Basic Books.

Greene, V. L., Lovely, M. E., Miller, M. D., & Ondrich, J. I. (1995). Reducing nursing home use through community long-term care: An optimization analysis. *Journals of Gerontology B: Psychological Sciences and Social Sciences, 50,* S259–S268.

Greenfield, E. A., & Marks, N. F. (2004). Formal volunteering as a protective factor for older adults' psychological well-being. *Journals of Gerontology B: Psychological Sciences and Social Sciences, 59,* S258–S264.

Greenfield, P. M., Keller, H., Fuligni, A., & Maynard, A. (2003). Cultural pathways through universal development. *Annual Review of Psychology, 54,* 461–490.

Greenhaus, J. H., Collins, K. M., & Shaw, J. D. (2003). The relation between work-family balance and quality of life. *Journal of Vocational Behavior, 63,* 510–531.

Greenough, W. T. (1997, April 21). Commentary in article, "Politics of biology." *U.S. News & World Report,* p. 79.

Greenough, W. T. (1999, April). *Experience, brain development, and links to mental retardation.* Paper presented at the meeting of the Society for Research in Child Development, Albuquerque.

Greenough, W. T. (2001, April). *Nature and nurture in the brain development process.* Paper presented at the meeting of the Society for Research in Child Development, Minneapolis.

Greenough, W. T., Klintsova, A. Y., Irvan, S. A., Galvez, R., Bates, K. E., & Weiler, I. J. (2001). Synaptic regulation of protein synthesis and the fragile X protein. *Proceedings of the National Academy of Science USA, 98,* 7101–7106.

Gregg, R. E. (2004). Restrictions on workplace romance and consensual relationship policies. *Journal of Medical Practice Management, 19,* 314–316.

Gregory, R. J. (2004). *Psychological testing* (4th ed.). Boston: Allyn & Bacon.

Greven, P. (1991). *Spare the child: The religious roots of punishment and the psychological impact of physical abuse.* New York: Knopf.

Griffith Joyner, F., & Hanc, J. (1999). *Running for dummies.* Foster City, CA: IDG Books.

Grigorenko, E. (2000). Heritability and intelligence. In R. J. Sternberg (Ed.), *Handbook of intelligence.* New York: Cambridge University Press.

Grigorenko, E. L. (2001). The invisible danger: The impact of ionizing radiation on cognitive development and functioning. In R. J. Sternberg & E. L. Grigorenko (Eds.), *Environmental effects on cognitive abilities.* Mahwah, NJ: Erlbaum.

Grigorenko, E. L., Geissler, P., Prince, R., Okatcha, F., Nokes, C., Kenney, D. A., Bundy, D. A., & Sternberg, R. J. (2001). The organization of Luo conceptions of intelligence: A study of implicit theories in a Kenyan village. *International Journal of Behavioral Development, 25,* 367–378.

Grigoriadis, S., & Kennedy, S. H. (2002). Role of estrogen in the treatment of depression. *American Journal of Therapy, 9,* 503–509.

Grogan-Kaylor, A. (2003). The effect of childhood maltreatment on adult criminality: A tobit regression analysis. *Child Maltreatment, 8,* 129–137.

Grolnick, W. S., Bridges, L. J., & Connell, J. P. (1996). Emotion regulation in two-year-olds: Strategies and emotional expression in four contexts. *Child Development, 67,* 928–941.

Grolnick, W. S., & Gurland, S. T. (2001). Mothering: Retrospect and prospect. In J. P. McHale & W. S. Grolnick (Eds.), *Retrospect and prospect in the psychological study of families.* Mahwah, NJ: Erlbaum.

Gross, R. T. (1984). Patterns of maturation: Their effects on behavior and development. In M. D. Levine & P. Satz (Eds.), *Middle childhood: Development and dysfunction.* Baltimore: University Park Press.

Grossmann, K., Grossmann, K. E., Spangler, G., Suess, G., & Unzner, L. (1985). Maternal sensitivity and newborns' orientation responses as related to quality of attachment in Northern Germany. In I. Bretherton & E. Waters (Eds.), Growing points of attachment theory and research. *Monographs of the Society for Research in Child Development, 50* (1–2, Serial No. 209).

Grotevant, H. D., & McRoy, R. G. (1990). Adopted adolescents in residential treatment: The role of the family. In D. M. Brodzinsky & M. D. Schechter (Eds.), *The psychology of adoption.* New York: Oxford University Press.

Groth, K. E., Gilmore, G. C., & Thomas, C. W. (2003). Impact of stimulus integrity on age differences in letter matching. *Experimental Aging Research, 29,* 155–172.

Gruber, E., & Gruber, J. W. (2000). Adolescent sexuality and the media: A review of current knowledge and implications. *Western Journal of Medicine, 172,* 210–214.

Grundman, M., & others. (2004). Mild cognitive impairment can be distinguished from Alzheimer disease and normal aging for clinical trials. *Archives of Neurology, 61,* 59–66.

Grusec, J. (2005). Development of moral behavior and conscience. In M. Killen & J. G. Smetana (Eds.), *Handbook of moral development.* Mahwah, NJ: Erlbaum.

Grusec, J., Davidov, M., & Lundell, L. (2002). Prosocial and helping behavior. In P. K. Smith & C. H. Hart (Eds.), *Blackwell handbook of childhood social development.* Malden, MA: Blackwell.

Guastello, D. D., & Guastello, S. J. (2003). Androgyny, gender role behavior, and emotional intelligence among college students and their parents. *Sex Roles, 49,* 663–673.

Gudykunst, W. B. (2004). *Bridging differences* (4th ed.). Thousand Oaks, CA: Sage.

Guilford, J. P. (1967). *The structure of intellect.* New York: McGraw-Hill.

Gump, B., & Matthews, K. (2000, March). *Annual vacations, health, and death.* Paper presented at the meeting of American Psychosomatic Society, Savannah, GA.

Gunnar, M. R. (2000). Early adversity and the development of stress reactivity and regulation. In C. A. Nelson (Ed.), *The effects of early adversity on neurobehavioral development. The Minnesota Symposia on Child Psychology* (Vol. 31). Mahwah, NJ: Erlbaum.

Gunnar, M. R., & Davis, E. P. (2003). Stress and emotion in early childhood. In I. B. Weiner (Ed.), *Handbook of psychology* (Vol. 6). New York: Wiley.

Gunnar, M. R., Malone, S., & Fisch, R. O. (1987). The psychobiology of stress and coping in the human neonate: Studies of the adrenocortical activity in response to stress in the first week of life. In T. Field, P. McCabe, & N. Scheiderman (Eds.), *Stress and coping.* Hillsdale, NJ: Erlbaum.

Guo, Y. L., Lambert, G. H., Hsu, C. C., & Hsu, M. M. (2004). Yucheng: Health effects of prenatal exposure to polychlorinated biphenyls and dibenzofurans. *International Archives of Occupational and Environmental Health, 77,* 153–158.

Gur, R. C., Mozley, L. H., Mozley, P. D., Resnick, S. M., Karp, J. S., Alavi, A., Arnold, S. E., & Gur, R. E. (1995). Sex differences in regional cerebral glucose metabolism during a resting state. *Science, 267,* 528–531.

Gurung, R. A., Taylor, S. E., & Seeman, T. E. (2003). Accounting for changes in social support among older adults: Insights from the MacArthur Studies of Successful Aging. *Psychology and Aging, 18,* 487–496.

Gurwitch, R. H., Silovsky, J. F., Schultz, S., Kees, M., & Burlingame, B. A. (2001). Reactions and guidelines for children following trauma/disaster. *APA Online.* Washington, DC: American Psychological Association.

Gustafson, D., Rothenberg, E., Blennow, K., Steen, B., & Skoog, I. (2003). An 18-year follow-up of overweight and risk of Alzheimer disease. *Archives of Internal Medicine, 163,* 1524–1528.

Gutman, L. M. (2002, April). *The role of stage-environment fit from early adolescence to young adulthood.* Paper presented at the meeting of the Society for Research on Adolescence, New Orleans.

Gutmann, D. L. (1975). Parenthood: A key to the comparative study of the life cycle. In N. Datan & L. Ginsberg (Eds.), *Life-span developmental psychology: Normative life crises.* New York: Academic Press.

Gwyn, K., Bondy, M. L., Cohen, D. S., Lund, M. J., Liff, J. M., Flagg, E. W., Brinton, L. A., Eley, J. W., & Coates, R. J. (2004). Racial differences in diagnosis, treatment, and clinical delays in a population-based study of patients with newly diagnosed breast carcinoma. *Cancer, 100,* 1595–1604.

Gyamfi, P., Brooks-Gunn, J., & Jackson, A. P. (2001). Associations between employment and financial and parental stress in low-income single Black mothers. In M. C. Lennon (Ed.), *Welfare, work, and well-being.* New York: Haworth Press.

Haager, D., & Klingner, J. K. (2005). *Differentiating instruction in inclusive classrooms.* Boston: Allyn & Bacon.

Haan, M. N., & Wallace, R. (2004). Can dementia be prevented? Brain aging in a population-based context. *Annual Review of Public Health, 25,* 1–24.

Haas, F. (2003). Bereavement care: Seeing the body. *Nursing Standards, 17,* 33–37.

Haber, D., & Rhodes, D. (2004). Health contract with sedentary older adults. *Gerontologist, 44,* 827–835.

Hagestad, G. O. (1985). Continuity and connectedness. In V. L. Bengtson (Ed.), *Grandparenthood.* Beverly Hills, CA: Sage.

Hahn, C. S., & DiPietro, J. A. (2001). In vitro fertilization and the family: Quality of parenting, family functioning, and child psychosocial adjustment. *Developmental Psychology, 37,* 37–48.

Hahn, D. B., Payne, W. A., & Mauer, E. B. (2005). *Focus on health* (7th ed.). New York: McGraw-Hill.

Hahn, W. K. (1987). Cerebral lateralization of function: From infancy through childhood. *Psychological Bulletin, 101,* 376–392.

Haider-Markely, D. P., & Joslyn, M. R. (2004). Just how important is the messenger versus the message? The case of framing physician-assisted suicide. *Death Studies, 28,* 243–262.

Haith, M. M., & Benson, J. B. (1998). Infant cognition. In W. Damon (Ed.), *Handbook of child psychology* (5th ed., Vol. 2). New York: Wiley.

Haith, M. M., Hazen, C., & Goodman, G. S. (1988). Expectation and anticipation of dynamic visual events by 3.5 month old babies. *Child Development, 59,* 467–479.

Hakuta, K. (2000). Bilingualism. In A. Kazdin (Ed.), *Encyclopedia of psychology.* Washington, DC, & New York: American Psychological Association and Oxford University Press.

Hakuta, K. (2001, April). *Key policy milestones and directions in the education of English language learners.* Paper prepared for the Rockefeller Foundation Symposium, Leveraging change: An emerging framework for educational equity, Washington, DC.

Hakuta, K., Butler, Y. G., & Witt, D. (2000). *How long does it take English learners to attain proficiency?* Berkeley, CA: The University of California Linguistic Minority Research Institute Policy Report 2000–1.

Halford, G. S. (2004). Information processing models of cognitive development. In U. Goswami (Ed.), *Blackwell handbook of cognitive development.* Malden, MA: Blackwell.

Hall, G. S. (1904). *Adolescence* (Vols. 1 & 2). Englewood Cliffs, NJ: Prentice Hall.

Hallahan, D. P., & Kaufmann, J. M. (2003). *Exceptional learners* (9th ed.). Boston: Allyn & Bacon.

Hallahan, D. P., Lloyd, J. W., Kauffman, J. M., Weiss, M. P., & Martinez, E. A. (2005). *Learning disabilities* (3rd ed.). Boston: Allyn & Bacon.

Hallberg, I. R. (2004). Death and dying from old people's point of view. *Aging: Clinical and Experimental Research, 16,* 87–103.

Hallfors, D. D., Waller, M. W., Ford, C. A., Halpern, C. T., Brodish, P. H., & Iritani, B. (2004). Adolescent depression and suicide risk: Association with sex and drug behavior. *American Journal of Preventive Medicine, 27,* 224–231.

Halliburton, R. (2004). *Introduction to population genetics.* Upper Saddle River, NJ: Prentice Hall.

Halonen, J., & Santrock, J. W. (1999). *Psychology: Contexts and applications.* Boston: McGraw-Hill.

Halpern, D. (2001). Sex difference research: Cognitive abilities. In J. Worell (Ed.), *Handbook of women and gender.* San Diego: Academic Press.

Hambleton, R. K. (2002). How can we make NAEP and state test score reporting scales and reports more understandable? In R. W. Lissitz & W. D. Schafer (Eds.), *Assessment in educational reform: Both means and ends.* Boston: Allyn & Bacon.

Hamburg, B., & Hamburg, D. (2004). On the future of adolescent psychology. In R. Lerner & L. Steinberg (Eds.), *Handbook of adolescent psychology.* New York: Wiley.

Hamburg, D. A. (1997). Meeting the essential requirements for healthy adolescent development in a transforming world. In R. Takanishi & D. Hamburg (Eds.), *Preparing adolescents for the 21st century.* New York: Cambridge University Press.

Hamet, P., & Tremblay, J. (2003). Genes of aging. *Metabolism (Suppl.), 52,* 5–9.

Hamilton, M. A., & Hamilton, S. F. (2004). Designing work and service for learning. In S. F. Hamilton & M. A. Hamilton (Eds.), *The youth development handbook.* Thousand Oaks, CA: Sage.

Hammen, C. (2003). Mood disorders. In I. B. Weiner (Ed.), *Handbook of psychology* (Vol. VIII). New York: Wiley, p. 15.

Han, S. K., & Moen, P. (1998). *Clocking out: Multiplex time use in retirement.* Bronfenbrenner Life Course Center Working Paper Series #98-03m. Ithaca, NY: Cornell University.

Hanaoka, H., & Okamura, H. (2004). Study on the effects of life review activities on the quality of life of the elderly: A randomized controlled trial. *Psychotherapy and Psychosomatics, 73,* 302–311.

Hanevold, C., Waller, J., Daniels, S., Portman, R., & Sorol, J. (2004). The effects of obesity, gender, and ethnic group on left ventricular hypertrophy and geometry in hypertensive children: A collaborative study of the International Pediatric Hypertension Association. *Pediatrics, 113,* 328–333.

Hankinson, S. E., Colditz, G. A., Manson, J. E., & Speizer, F. E. (2001). *Healthy women, healthy lives.* Dallas: American Heart Association.

Hannish, L. D., & Guerra, N. G. (2004). Aggressive victims, passive victims, and bullies: Developmental continuity or developmental change? *Merrill-Palmer Quarterly, 50,* 17–38.

Hansford, B. C., & Hattie, J. A. (1982). The relationship between self and achievement/performance measures. *Review of Educational Research, 52,* 123–142.

Harding, B., Risdon, R. A., & Krous, H. F. (2004). Shaken baby syndrome. *British Medical Journal, 328,* 719–720.

Hardman, M. L., Drew, C. J., & Egan, M. W. (2005). *Human exceptionality* (8th ed.). Boston: Allyn & Bacon.

Hariri, A. R., Mahay, V. S., Tessitore, A., Kolachana, B., Fera, F., Goldman, D., Egan, M. F., & Weinberger, D. R. (2002). Serotonin transporter genetic variation and the response of the human amygdala. *Science, 297,* 400–403.

Harkins, S. W., Price, D. D., & Martinelli, M. (1986). Effects of age on pain perception. *Journal of Gerontology, 41,* 58–63.

Harkness, S., & Super, C. M. (1995). Culture and parenting. In M. H. Bornstein (Ed.), *Handbook of parenting* (Vol. 3). Hillsdale, NJ: Erlbaum.

Harkness, S., & Super, C. M. (2002). Culture and parenting. In M. H. Bornstein (Ed.), *Handbook of parenting* (2nd ed., Vol. 2). Mahwah, NJ: Erlbaum.

Harlow, H. F. (1958). The nature of love. *American Psychologist, 13,* 673–685.

Harris, C. R. (2002). Sexual and romantic jealousy in heterosexual and homosexual adults. *Psychological Science, 13,* 7–12.

Harris, G. (2002). *Grandparenting: How to meet its responsibilities.* Los Angeles: The Americas Group.

Harris, G., Thomas, A., & Booth, D. A. (1990). Development of salt taste in infancy. *Developmental Psychology, 26,* 534–538.

Harris, J. R. (1998). *The nurture assumption: Why children turn out the way they do: Parents matter less than you think and peers matter more.* New York: Free Press.

Harris, L. (1975). *The myth and reality of aging in America.* Washington, DC: National Council on Aging.

Harris, L. (1987, September 3). The latchkey child phenomena. *Dallas Morning News,* pp. 1A, 10A.

Harris, L. (1997). *A national poll of children and exercise.* Washington, DC: Lou Harris & Associates.

Harris, S. M. (2004). The effect of health value and ethnicity on the relationship between hardiness and health behaviors. *Journal of Personality, 72,* 379–412.

Harrison-Hale, A. O., McLoyd, V. C., & Smedley, B. (2004). Racial and ethnic status: Risk and protective processes among African-American families. In K. L. Maton, C. J. Schellenbach, B. J. Leadbetter, & A. L. Solarz (Eds.), *Investing in children, youth, families, and communities.* Washington, DC: American Psychological Association.

Hart, B., & Risley, T. R. (1995). *Meaningful differences in the everyday experience of young Americans.* Baltimore: Paul H. Brookes.

Hart, C. H., Burts, D. C., Durland, M. A., Charlesworth, R., DeWolf, M., & Fleege, P. O. (1998). Stress behaviors and activity type participation of preschoolers in more and less developmentally appropriate classrooms: SES and sex differences. *Journal Research in Childhood Education, 12,* 176–196.

Hart, C. H., Charlesworth, R., Burts, D. C., & DeWolf, M. (1993, March). *The relationship of attendance in developmentally appropriate or inappropriate kindergarten classrooms to first-grade behavior.* Paper presented at the biennial meeting of the Society for Research in Child Development, New Orleans.

Hart, C. H., Yang, C., Charlesworth, R., & Burts, D. C. (2003, April). *Early childhood teachers' curriculum beliefs, classroom practices, and children's outcomes: What are the connections?* Paper presented at the biennial meeting of the Society for Research in Child Development, Tampa, FL.

Hart, D. (2005). Service commitment and care exemplars. In M. Killen & J. G. Smetana (Eds.), *Handbook of moral development.* Mahwah, NJ: Erlbaum.

Harter, S. (1990). Processes underlying adolescent self-concept formation. In R. Montemayor, G. R. Adams, & R. P. Gulotta (Eds.), *From childhood to adolescence: A transitional period?* Newbury Park, CA: Sage.

Harter, S. (1999). *The construction of the self.* New York: Guilford.

Harter, S. (2002). Unpublished review of J. W. Santrock's *Child development* (10th ed.). New York: McGraw-Hill.

Harter, S., & Whitesell, N. (2001, April). *What we have learned from Columbine: The impact of self-esteem on suicidal and violent ideation among adolescents.* Paper presented at the meeting of the Society for Research in Child Development, Minneapolis.

Hartshorne, H., & May, M. S. (1928–1930). *Moral studies in the nature of character: Studies in the nature of character.* New York: Macmillan.

Hartup, W. W. (1983). The peer system. In P. H. Mussen (Ed.), *Handbook of child psychology* (4th ed., Vol. 4). New York: Wiley.

Hartup, W. W. (1996). The company they keep: Friendships and their development significance. *Child Development, 67,* 1–13.

Hartup, W. W. (1999, April). *Peer relations and the growth of the individual child.* Paper presented at the meeting of the Society for Research in Child Development. Albuquerque.

Hartup, W. W. (2000). Middle childhood: Socialization and social context. In A. Kazdin (Ed.), *Encyclopedia of psychology.* Washington, DC, & New York: American Psychological Association and Oxford University Press.

Hartup, W. W., & Abecassis, M. (2004). Friends and enemies. In P. K. Smith & C. H. Hart (Eds.), *Blackwell handbook of childhood social development.* Malden, MA: Blackwell.

Harvey, J. H., & Weber, A. L. (2002). *The odyssey of the heart* (2nd ed.). Mahwah, NJ: Erlbaum.

Harwood, R., Leyendecker, B., Carlson, V., Asencio, M., & Miller, A. (2002). Parenting among Latino families in the U.S. In M. H. Bornstein (Ed.), *Handbook of parenting* (2nd ed.). Mahwah, NJ: Erlbaum.

Haselager, G. J. T., Cilessen, A. H. N., Van Lieshout, C. F. M., Riksen-Walraen, J. M. A., & Hartup, W. W. (2002). Heterogeneity among peer-rejected boys across middle childhood: Developmental pathways of social behavior. *Developmental Psychology, 38,* 446–456.

Hasher, L. (2003, February 28). Commentary in "The wisdom of the wizened." *Science, 299,* 1300–1302.

Hasher, L., Chung, C., May, C. P., & Foong, N. (2001). Age, time of testing, and proactive interference. *Canadian Journal of Experimental Psychology, 56,* 200–207.

Hatcliffe, S. (2003). Standing in their shoes: An experiential learning experience in promoting age sensitivity. *Journal of Nurses and Staff Development, 19,* 183–186.

Hauck, S. J., & Bartke, A. (2001). Free radical defenses in the liver and kidney of human growth hormone transgenic mice. *Journals of Gerontology A: Biological Sciences and Medical Sciences, 56,* B153–B162.

Haugaard, J. J., & Hazan, C. (2004). Recognizing and treating uncommon behavioral and emotional disorders in children and adolescents who have been severely maltreated: Reactive attachment disorder. *Child Maltreatment, 9,* 154–160.

Hauselmann, H. J., & Rizzoli, R. (2003). A comprehensive review of treatments for postmenopausal osteoporosis. *Osteoporosis International, 14,* 2–12.

Havighurst, S. S., Harley, A., & Prior, M. (2004). Building preschool children's emotional competence. *Early Education and Development, 15,* 423–447.

Hawkins, D. N., & Whiteman, S. D. (2004). Balancing work and family: Problems and solutions with low-income families. In A. C. Crouter & A. Booth (Eds.), *Work-family challenges for low-income parents and their children.* Mahwah, NJ: Erlbaum.

Hawkins, J. A., & Berndt, T. J. (1985, April). *Adjustment following the transition to junior high school.* Paper presented at the biennial meeting of the Society for Research in Child Development, Toronto.

Hawkins, S. A., Wiswell, R. A., & Marcell, T. J. (2003). Exercise and the master athlete—a model of successful aging? *Journals of Gerontology A: Biological and Medical Sciences, 58,* M1009–M1011.

Hawkley, L. C., & Cacioppo, J. T. (2004). Stress and the aging immune system. *Brain, Behavior, and Immunity, 18,* 114–119.

Hay, D. F., Payne, A., & Chadwick, A. (2004). Peer relations in childhood. *Journal of Child Psychology and Psychiatry, 45,* 84–108.

Haycock, J. W., Becker, L., Ang, L., Furukawa, Y., Hornykiewicz, O., & Kish, S. J. (2003). Marked disparity between age-related changes in dopamine and other presynaptic dopaminergic markers in human striatum. *Journal of Neurochemistry, 87,* 574–585.

Hayflick, L. (1977). The cellular basis for biological aging. In C. E. Finch & L. Hayflick (Eds.), *Handbook of the biology of aging.* New York: Van Nostrand.

Haynie, D. L., Nansel, T., Eitel, P., Crump, A. D., Saylor, K., Yu, K., & Simons-Morton, B. (2001). Bullies, victims, and bully/victims: Distinct groups of at-risk youth. *Journal of Early Adolescence, 21,* 29–49.

Hayslip, B. (1996). Hospice. In J. E. Birren (Ed.), *Encyclopedia of gerontology* (Vol. 1). San Diego Academic Press.

Hayslip, B., Edmondson, R., & Guarnaccia, C. (1999, November). *Religiousness, perceptions of funerals, and bereavement adjustment in adulthood.* Paper presented at the meeting of the Gerontological Society of America, San Francisco.

Hayslip, B., & Hansson, R. (2003). Death awareness and adjustment across the life span. In C. D. Bryant (Ed.), *Handbook of death and dying.* Thousand Oaks, CA: Sage.

Hazan, C., & Shaver, P. R. (1987). Romantic love conceptualized as an attachment process. *Journal of Personality and Social Psychology, 52,* 522–524.

Health Management Resources. (2001). *Child health and fitness.* Boston: Author.

Heath, A. C., & Nelson, E. C. (2002). Effects of the interaction between genotype and environment. *Alcohol Research and Health, 26,* 193–206.

Heather, N. (2004). Addiction treatment: A strengths perspective. *Alcohol and Alcoholism, 39,* 70–71.

Hedberg, K., Hopkins, D., & Kohn, M. (2003). Five years of legal physician-assisted suicide in Oregon. *New England Journal of Medicine, 348,* 961–964.

Hedden, T., & Park, D. C. (2003). Contributions of source and inhibitory mechanisms to age-related retroactive interference in verbal working memory. *Journal of Experimental Psychology: General, 132,* 93–112.

Heilbronn, L. K., & Ravussin, E. (2003). Calorie restriction and aging: Review of the literature and implications for studies in humans. *American Journal of Clinical Nutrition, 78,* 361–369.

Heilman, A. W., Blair, T. R., & Rupley, W. H. (2002). *Principles and practices of teaching reading* (10th ed.). Upper Saddle River, NJ: Merrill.

Heinicke, C. M. (2002). The transition to parenting. In M. H. Bornstein (Ed.), *Handbook of parenting* (2nd ed.). Mahwah, NJ: Erlbaum.

Helgeson, V. S. (2005). *Psychology of gender* (2nd ed.). Upper Saddle River, NJ: Prentice Hall.

Helmuth, L. (2003, February 28). The wisdom of the wizened. *Science, 299,* 1300–1302.

Helson, R. (1997, August). *Personality change: When is it adult development?* Paper presented at the meeting of the American Psychological Association, Chicago.

Helson, R., Mitchell, V., & Moane, G. (1984). Personality change in women from college to midlife. *Journal of Personality and Social Psychology, 53,* 176–186.

Helson, R., & Wink, P. (1992). Personality change in women from the early 40s to early 50s. *Psychology and Aging, 7,* 46–55.

Helwig, C., & Turiel, E. (2004). Moral reasoning and social development. In P. Smith & C. Hart (Eds.), *Blackwell handbook of social development.* Malden, MA: Blackwell.

Henderson, P., Martines, J., & de Zoysa, I. (2004). Mortality associated with reasons for not breastfeeding. *AIDS, 18,* 361–362.

Hendrick, C., & Hendrick, S. S. (Eds.). (2000). *Close relationships.* Thousand Oaks, CA: Sage.

Hendrick, C., & Hendrick, S. S. (2004). Sex and romantic love. In J. H. Harvey, A. Wenzel, & S. Sprecher (Eds.), *The handbook of sexuality in close relationships.* Mahwah, NJ: Erlbaum.

Hendrick, S. (2001). Intimacy and love. In J. Worell (Ed.), *Encyclopedia of women and gender.* San Diego: Academic Press.

Hendry, J. (1995). *Understanding Japanese society.* London: Routledge.

Hendry, J. (1999). *Social anthropology.* New York: Macmillan.

Hennemen, E. A., & Karris, G. E. (2004). Determining brain death in adults. *Critical Care Nurse, 50,* 54–56.

Henry, D. B., Tolan, P. H., & Gorman-Smith, D. (2001). Longitudinal family and peer group effects on violence and nonviolent delinquency. *Journal of Clinical Child Psychology, 30,* 172–186.

Henry, J. D., MacLeod, M. S., Philips, L. H., & Crawford, J. R. (2004). A meta-analytic review of prospective memory and aging. *Psychology and Aging, 19,* 27–39.

Hepper, P. G., Shahidullah, S., & White, R. (1990). Origins of fetal handedness. *Nature, 347,* 431.

Herbst, M. A., Mercer, B. M., Beasley, D., Meyer, N., & Carr, T. (2003). Relationship of prenatal care and perinatal morbidity in low-birth-weight infants. *American Journal of Obstetrics and Gynecology, 189,* 930–933.

Herek, G. (2000). Homosexuality. In A. Kazdin (Ed.), *Encyclopedia of psychology.* Washington, DC, & New York: American Psychological Association and Oxford University Press.

Herman-Giddens, M. E. (2004). What we can learn from the spectrum of infant physical abuse in Alaska. *Child Abuse & Neglect, 28,* 7–8.

Herrnstein, R. J., & Murray, C. (1994). *The bell curve: Intelligence and class structure in American life.* New York: Macmillan.

Hertenstein, M. J., & Campos, J. J. (2004). The retention effects of an adult's emotional displays on infant behavior. *Child Development, 75,* 595–613.

Hess, T. M., Auman, C., Colcombe, S. J., & Rahhal, T. A. (2003). The impact of stereotype threat on age differences in memory performance. *Journals of Gerontology B: Psychological Sciences and Social Sciences, 58,* P3–P11.

Hess, T. M., Hinson, J. T., & Statham, J. A. (2004). Explicit and implicit stereotype activation effects on memory: Do age and awareness moderate the impact of priming? *Psychology and Aging, 19,* 495–505.

Hetherington, E. M. (1989). Coping with family transitions: Winners, losers, and survivors. *Child Development, 60,* 1–14.

Hetherington, E. M. (1993). An overview of the Virginia Longitudinal Study of Divorce and Remarriage with a focus on early adolescence. *Journal of Family Psychology, 7,* 39–56.

Hetherington, E. M. (1999). Social capital and the development of youth from nondivorced, divorced, and remarried families. In W. A. Collins & B. Laursen (Eds.), *Relationships as developmental contexts.* Mahwah, NJ: Erlbaum.

Hetherington, E. M. (2000). Divorce. In A. Kazdin (Ed.), *Encyclopedia of psychology.*

Washington, DC, & New York: American Psychological Association and Oxford University Press.

Hetherington, E. M., Bridges, M., & Insabella, G. M. (1998). What matters? What does not? Five perspectives on the association between marital transitions and children's adjustment. *American Psychologist, 53,* 167–184.

Hetherington, E. M., & Kelly, J. (2002). *For better or for worse: Divorce reconsidered.* New York: W. W. Norton.

Hetherington, E. M., Reiss, D., & Plomin, R. (Eds.). (1994). *Separate social worlds of siblings: The impact of nonshared environment on development.* Hillsdale, NJ: Erlbaum.

Hetherington, E. M., & Stanley-Hagan, M. (2002). Parenting in divorced and remarried families. In M. H. Bornstein (Ed.), *Handbook of parenting.* Mahwah, NJ: Erlbaum.

Hewlett, S. A. (2002). *Creating a life: Professional women and the quest for children.* New York: Talk Miramax Books.

Hicks, J., Martinez, M. C., Schoor, R. Y., & Camilli, G. (2004). Teaching to the test. In W. A. Firestone, L. F. Monfils, & R. Y. Schoor (Eds.), *The ambiguity of teaching to the test.* Mahwah, NJ: Erlbaum.

Higgins, M. M., & Barkley, M. C. (2004). Barriers to nutrition education for older adults, and nutrition and aging training opportunities for educators, healthcare providers, volunteers, and caregivers. *Journal of Nutrition for the Elderly, 23,* 99–121.

Hill, C. R., & Stafford, F. P. (1980). Parental care of children: Time diary estimate of quantity, predictability, and variety. *Journal of Human Resources, 15,* 219–239.

Hill, J., Waldfogel, J., Brooks-Gunn, J., & Han, W. (2001, November). *Towards a better estimate of causal links in child policy: The case of maternal employment and child outcomes.* Paper presented at the Association for Public Policy Analysis and Management Fall Research Conference, Washington, DC.

Hill, L. T., Stremmel, A. J., & Fu, V. R. (2005). *Teaching as inquiry.* Boston: Allyn & Bacon.

Hill, R. D., Thorn, B. L., Bowling, J., & Morrison, A. (Eds.). (2002). *Geriatric residential care.* Mahwah, NJ: Erlbaum.

Hillis, S. D., Anda, R. F., Dube, S. R., Felitti, V. J., Marchbanks, P. A., & Marks, J. S. (2004). The association between adverse childhood experiences and adolescent pregnancy, long-term psychologi-cal consequences, and fetal death. *Pediatrics, 113,* 320–327.

Himes, C. L., Hogan, D. P., & Eggebeen, D. J. (1996). Living arrangements of minority elders. *Journals of Gerontology A: Biological Sciences and Medical Sciences, 51,* S42–S48.

Hintz, R. L. (2003). Confirming the diagnosis of growth hormone deficiency (GHD) and transitioning the care of patients with childhood-onset GHD. *Journal of Pediatric Endocrinology and Metabolism, 16 (Suppl. 3),* 637–643.

Hirsch, B. J., & Rapkin, B. D. (1987). The transition to junior high school: A longitudinal study of self-esteem, psychological symptomatology, school life, and social support. *Child Development, 58,* 1235–1243.

Hiscock, H., & Jordan, B. (2004). Problem crying in infancy. *Medical Journal of Australia, 181,* 507–512.

Hitch, G. J., Towse, J. N., & Hutton, U. (2001). What limits children's working memory span? Theoretical accounts and applications for scholastic development. *Journal of Experimental Psychology: General, 130,* 184–198.

Hjern, A., Vinnerljung, B., & Lindblad, F. (2004). Avoidable mortality among child welfare recipients and intercountry adoptees: A national cohort study. *Journal of Epidemiology and Community Health, 58,* 2–7.

Hobbins, D. (2004). Survivors of childhood sexual abuse: Implications for perinatal nursing care. *Journal of Obstetric, Gynecologic, and Neonatal Nursing, 33,* 485–497.

Hobel, C. J., Dunkel-Schetter, C., Roesch, S. C., Castro, L. C., & Arora, C. P. (1999). Maternal plasma corticotrophin-releasing hormone associated with stress at 20 weeks' gestation in pregnancies ending in preterm delivery. *American Journal of Obstetrics and Gynecology, 180,* S257–S263.

Hockenberry, M. (2005). *Wong's essentials of pediatric nursing* (7th ed.). St. Louis: Mosby.

Hoff, E. (2003). Language development in childhood. In I. B. Weiner (Ed.), *Handbook of psychology* (Vol. VI). New York: Wiley.

Hoff, E., Laursen, B., & Tardiff, T. (2002). Socioeconomic status and parenting. In M. H. Bornstein (Ed.), *Handbook of parenting* (2nd ed., Vol. 2). Mahwah, NJ: Erlbaum.

Hofferth, S. L., & Reid, L. (2002). Early childbearing and children's achievement behavior over time. *Perspectives on Sexual and Reproductive Health, 34,* 41–49.

Hoffman, L. W. (1989). Effects of maternal employment in two-parent families. *American Psychologist, 44,* 283–293.

Hoffman, L. W., & Youngblade, L. M. (1999). *Mothers at work: Effects on children's well-being.* New York: Cambridge.

Hoffman, M. L. (1970). Moral development. In P. H. Mussen (Ed.), *Manual of child psychology* (3rd ed., Vol. 2). New York: Wiley.

Hoffman, M. L. (2002). *Empathy and moral development.* New York: Cambridge University Press.

Hoffman, S. (2003). Sleep in the older adult. *Geriatric Nursing, 24,* 210–214.

Hoffman, S., Foster, E., & Furstenberg, F. (1993). Reevaluating the costs of teenage childbearing. *Demography, 30,* 1–13.

Hoffmann, E. A. (2004). Selective sexual harassment: Differential treatment of similar groups of women. *Law and Human Behavior, 28,* 29–45.

Hogan, M. J. (2003). Divided attention in older but not younger adults is impaired by anxiety. *Experimental Aging Research, 29,* 111–136.

Holding, S. (2002). Current state of screening for Down syndrome. *Annals of Clinical Biochemistry, 39,* 1–11.

Holland, J. L. (1987). Current status of Holland's theory of careers: Another perspective. *Career Development Quarterly, 36,* 24–30.

Hollier, L. M., Harstad, T. W., Sanchez, P. J., Twickler, D. M., & Wendel, G. D. (2001). Fetal syphilis: Clinical and laboratory characteristics. *Obstetrics and Gynecology, 97,* 947–953.

Holmbeck, G. N. (1996). A model of family relational transformations during the transition to adolescence: Parent-adolescent conflict and adaptation. In J. A. Graber, J. Brooks-Gunn, & A. C. Petersen (Eds.), *Transitions through adolescence.* Hillsdale, NJ: Erlbaum.

Holmes, T. H., & Rahe, R. H. (1967). The social readjustment rating scale. *Journal of Psychosomatic Research, 11,* 213–218.

Holstein, M. B., & Minkler, M. (2003). Self, society, and the "new gerontology." *Gerontologist, 43,* 787–796.

Holtzen, D. W. (2000). Handedness and professional tennis. *International Journal of Neuroscience, 105,* 101–119.

Holtzman, R. E., Rebok, G. W., Saczynski, J. S., Kouzis, A. C., Wilcox, D. K., &

Eaton, W. W. (2004). Social network characteristics and cognition in middle-aged and older adults. *Journals of Gerontology B: Psychological Sciences and Social Sciences, 59,* P278–P284.

Hopkins, B. (1991). Facilitating early motor development: An intracultural study of West Indian mothers and their infants living in Britain. In J. K. Nugent, B. M. Lester, & T. B. Brazelton (Eds.), *The cultural context of infancy: Vol. 2. Multicultural and interdisciplinary approaches to parent-infant relations.* Norwood, NJ: Ablex.

Hopkins, B., & Westra, T. (1988). Maternal handling and motor development: An intracultural study. *Genetic Psychology Monographs, 14,* 377–420.

Hopkins, B., & Westra, T. (1990). Motor development, maternal expectations, and the role of handling. *Infant Behavior and Development, 13,* 117–122.

Hopkins, J. R. (2000). Erikson, Erik H. In A. Kazdin (Ed.), *Encyclopedia of psychology.* Washington, DC, & New York: American Psychological Association and Oxford University Press.

Horn, I. B., Joseph, J. G., & Cheng, T. L. (2004). Nonabusive physical punishment and child behavior among African American children: A systematic review. *Journal of the National Medical Association, 96,* 1162–1168.

Horn, J. L., & Donaldson, G. (1980). Cognitive development II: Adulthood development of human abilities. In O. G. Brim & J. Kagan (Eds.), *Constancy and change in human development.* Cambridge, MA: Harvard University Press.

Horne, G., & Payne, S. (2004). Removing boundaries: Palliative care for patients with heart failure. *Palliative Medicine, 18,* 291–296.

Horne, R. S., Franco, P., Adamson, T. M., Groswasser, J., & Kahn, A. (2002). Effects of body position on sleep and arousal characteristics in infants. *Early Human Development, 69,* 25–33.

Horne, R. S., Franco, P., Adamson, T. M., Groswasser, J., & Kahn, A. (2004). Influences of maternal cigarette smoking on infant arousability. *Early Human Development, 79,* 49–58.

Horne, R. S., Parslow, P. M., & Harding, R. (2004). Respiratory control and arousal in sleeping infants. *Pediatric Respiratory Reviews, 5,* 190–198.

Horton, D. M. (2001). The disappearing bell curve. *Journal of Secondary Gifted Education, 12,* 185–188.

Hosa, B., Pelham, W. E., Waschbusch, D. A., Kipp, H., & Owens, J. S. (2001). Academic task persistence of normal achieving ADHD and control boys. *Journal of Consulting and Clinical Psychology, 69,* 271–283.

Hotton, T., & Haans, D. (2004). Alcohol and drug use in early adolescence. *Health Reports, 15,* 9–19.

House, J. S. (1998). Commentary: Age, work, and well-being. In K. W. Schaie & C. Schooler (Eds.), *The impact of work on older adults.* New York: Springer.

House, J. S., Landis, K. R., & Umberson, D. (1988). Social relationships and health. *Science, 241,* 540–545.

Howard, L. R. (2004). Speak out against physician assisted suicide and physician assisted death. *Hawaii Medical Journal, 63,* 68, 97.

Howard, R. W. (2001). Searching the real world for signs of rising population intelligence. *Personality & Individual Differences, 30,* 1039–1058.

Howe, L. J. (2003). Management of age related macular degeneration: Still room for improvement. *British Journal of Ophthalmology, 87,* 375.

Howe, M. J. A., Davidson, J. W., Moore, D. G., & Sloboda, J. A. (1995). Are there early childhood signs of musical ability? *Psychology of Music, 23,* 162–176.

Howe, M. L. (1997). Children's memory for traumatic experiences. *Learning and Individual Differences, 9,* 153–174 (p. 349).

Howell, E. M. (2001). The impact of Medicaid expansions for pregnant women: A synthesis of the evidence. *Medical Care Research Review, 58,* 3–30.

Howley, E. T. (2001). Type of activity: Resistance, aerobic and leisure versus occupational physical activity. *Medical Science and Sports Exercise, 33 (Suppl.),* S364–369.

Hoyer, W. J., & Roodin, P. A. (2003). *Adult development and aging* (5th ed.). New York: McGraw-Hill.

Hoyer, W. J., Stawski, R., Wasylyshyn, C., & Verhaeghen, P. (2004). Adult age and digit-symbol performance: A meta-analysis. *Psychology and Aging, 19,* 211–214.

Hsu, H-C. (2004). Antecedents and consequences of separation anxiety in first-time mothers: Infant, mother, and social-contextual characteristics. *Infant Behavior & Development, 27,* 113–133.

Hsu, L. K. (2004). Eating disorders: Practical interventions. *Journal of the American Medical Women's Association, 59,* 113–124.

Huang, W., Qui, C., von Strauss, E., Winblad, B., & Fratiglioni, L. (2004). APOE genotype, family history of dementia, and Alzheimer disease risk: A 6-year follow-up study. *Archives of Neurology, 61,* 1930–1934.

Huebner, A. J., & Howell, L. W. (2003). Examining the relationship between adolescent sexual risk-taking and perceptions of monitoring, communication, and parenting styles. *Journal of Adolescent Health, 33,* 71–78.

Huebner, A. M., & Garrod, A. C. (1993). Moral reasoning among Tibetan monks: A study of Buddhist adolescents and young adults in Nepal. *Journal of Cross-Cultural Psychology, 24,* 167–185.

Huesmann, L. R. (1986). Psychological processes promoting the relation between exposure to media violence and aggressive behavior by the viewer. *Journal of Social Issues, 42,* 125–139.

Huesmann, L. R., Moise-Titus, J., Podolski, C., & Eron, L. D. (2003). Longitudinal relations between exposure to TV violence and their aggressive and violent behavior in young adulthood: 1977–1992. *Developmental Psychology, 39,* 201–221.

Huffman, L. R., & Speer, P. W. (2000). Academic performance among at-risk children: The role of developmentally appropriate practices. *Early Childhood Research Quarterly, 15,* 167–184.

Hughes, J. R. (2003). Motivating and helping smokers to stop smoking. *Journal of General Internal Medicine, 18,* 1053–1057.

Huisman, E., Uylings, H. B., & Hoogland, P. V. (2004). A 100% increase of dopaminergic cells in the olfactory bulb may explain hyposmia in Parkinson's disease. *Movement Disorders, 19,* 687–692.

Hulme, P. A., & Agrawal, S. (2004). Patterns of sexual abuse characteristics and their relationships to other childhood abuse and adult health. *Journal of Interpersonal Violence, 19,* 389–405.

Hulse, G. K., O'Neill, G., Pereira, C., & Brewer, C. (2002). Obstetric and neonatal outcomes associated with maternal naltrexone exposure. *Australian and New Zealand Journal of Obstetrics and Gynecology, 41,* 424–428.

Hultsch, D. F., Hammer, M., & Small, B. J. (1993). Age differences in cognitive performance in later life: Relationships to self-reported health and activity life style. *Journal of Gerontology, 48,* P1–P11.

Hultsch, D. F., Hertzog, C., Small, B. J., & Dixon, R. A. (1999). Use it or lose it:

Engaged lifestyle as a buffer of cognitive decline in aging? *Psychology and Aging, 14,* 245–263.

Hultsch, D. F., & Plemons, J. K. (1979). Life events and life-span development. In P. B. Baltes & O. G. Brim (Eds.), *Life-span development and behavior.* New York: Academic Press.

Hummer, R. A., Rogers, R. G., Nam, C. B., & Ellison, C. G. (1999). Religious involvement and U.S. adult mortality. *Demography, 36,* 272–285.

Humphreys, K. (2000). Alcoholics Anonymous. In A. Kazdin (Ed.), *Encyclopedia of psychology.* Washington, DC, & New York: American Psychological Association and Oxford University Press.

Humphreys, K. (2003). Alcoholics Anonymous and 12-step alcoholism treatment programs. *Recent Developments in Alcoholism, 16,* 149–164.

Hungerford, T. L. (2001). The economic consequences of widowhood on elderly women in the United States and Germany. *The Gerontologist, 41,* 103–110.

Hunsley, M., & Thoman, E. B. (2002). The sleep of co-sleeping infants when they are not co-sleeping: Evidence that co-sleeping is stressful. *Developmental Psychobiology, 40,* 14–22.

Hunt, C. E., Lesko, S. M., Vezina, R. M., McCoy, R., Corwin, J. J., Mandell, F., Willinger, M., Hoffman, H. J., & Mitchell, A. A. (2003). Infant sleep position and associated health outcomes. *Archives of Pediatric and Adolescent Medicine, 157,* 469–474.

Hunter, G. R., McCarthy, J. P., & Bamman, M. M. (2004). Effects of resistance training on older adults. *Sports Medicine, 34,* 329–348.

Hunter, K. I., & Linn, M. W. (1980). Psychosocial differences between elderly volunteers and non-volunteers. *International Journal of Aging and Human Development, 12,* 205–213.

Huston, A. C. (1983). Sex-typing. In P. H. Mussen (Ed.), *Handbook of child psychology* (4th ed., Vol. 4). New York: Wiley.

Huston, A. C. (1999, August). *Employment interventions for parents in poverty: How do children fare?* Paper presented at the meeting of the Society for Research in Child Development, Albuquerque.

Huston, A. C., McLoyd, V. C., & Coll, C. G. (1994). Children and poverty: Issues in contemporary research. *Child Development, 65,* 275–282.

Huston, T. L., & Holmes, E. K. (2004). Becoming parents. In A. L. Vangelisti (Ed.), *Handbook of family communication.* Mahwah, NJ: Erlbaum.

Huston, T. L., Neihuis, S., & Smith, S. (1997, November). *Divergent experiential and behavioral pathways leading to marital distress and divorce.* Paper presented at the meeting of the National Council on Family Relations, Washington, DC.

Huttenlocher, J., Haight, W., Bruk, A., Seltzer, M., & Lyons, T. (1991). Early vocabulary growth: Relation to language input and gender. *Developmental Psychology, 27,* 236–248.

Huttenlocher, J., Levine, S., & Vevea, J. (1998). Environmental input and cognitive growth: A study using time-period comparisons. *Child Development, 69,* 1012–1029.

Huttenlocher, P. R., & Dabholkar, A. S. (1997). Regional differences in synaptogenesis in human cerebral cortex. *Journal of Comparative Neurology, 37,* 167–178.

Huxtable, R. (2004). Assisted suicide. *British Medical Journal, 328,* 1088–1089.

Huyck, M. H. (1995). Marriage and close relationships of the marital kind. In R. Blieszner & V. H. Bedford (Eds.), *Handbook of aging and the family.* Westport, CT: Greenwood Press.

Huyck, M. H. (1999). Gender roles and gender identity in midlife. In S. L. Willis & J. D. Reid (Eds.), *Life in the middle.* San Diego: Academic Press.

Huyck, M. H., & Hoyer, W. J. (1982). *Adult development and aging.* Belmont, CA: Wadsworth.

Hybels, C. F., & Blazer, D. G. (2004). Epidemiology of the late-life mental disorders. *Clinical Geriatric Medicine, 19,* 663–696.

Hyde, A., & Roche-Reid, B. (2004). Midwifery practice and the crisis of modernity. *Social Science Medicine, 58,* 2613–2623.

Hyde, J. S. (2004). *Half the human experience* (5th ed.). Boston: Houghton Mifflin.

Hyde, J. S., & DeLamater, J. D. (2005). *Understanding human sexuality* (8th ed., Rev. update). Boston: McGraw-Hill.

Hyde, J. S., & Mezulis, A. H. (2001). Gender difference research: Issues and critique. In J. Worrell (Ed.), *Encyclopedia of women and gender.* San Diego: Academic Press.

Hylton, C., Congdon, N., Friedman, D., Kempen, J., Quigley, H., Bass, E., & Jampel, H. (2003). Cataract after glaucoma filtration surgery. *American Journal of Ophthalmology, 135,* 231–232.

Hyman, I. E., & Loftus, E. F. (2001). False childhood memories and eye-witness errors. In M. L. Eisen, J. A. Quas, & G. S. Goodman (Eds.), *Memory and suggestibility in the forensic interview.* Mahwah, NJ: Erlbaum.

Hymel, S., McDougall, P., & Renshaw, P. (2004). Peer acceptance/rejection. In P. K. Smith & C. H. Hart (Eds.), *Blackwell handbook of childhood social development.* Malden, MA: Blackwell.

Iannucci, L. (2000). *Birth defects.* New York: Enslow.

Idler, E. L., Stanislav, V. K., & Hays, J. C. (2001). Patterns of religious practice and belief in the last year of life. *Journals of Gerontology B: Psychological Sciences and Social Sciences, 56,* S326–S334.

Ige, F., & Shelton, D. (2004). Reducing the risk of sudden infant death syndrome (SIDS) in African-American communities. *Journal of Pediatric Nursing, 19,* 290–292.

Ilola, L. M. (1990). Culture and health. In R. W. Brislin (Ed.), *Applied cross-cultural psychology.* Newbury Park, CA: Sage.

Inglehart, R. (1990). *Culture shift in advanced industrial society.* Princeton, NJ: Princeton University Press.

Inoff-Germain, G., Arnold, G. S., Nottelmann, E. D., Susman, E. J., Cutler, G. B., & Chrousos, G. P. (1988). Relations between hormone levels and observational measures of aggressive behavior of young adolescents in family interactions. *Developmental Psychology, 24,* 124–139.

Institute of Medicine (1997, June). *Approaching death: Improving care at the end of life.* Washington, DC: National Academy of Sciences.

International Human Genome Sequencing Consortium (2004). Finishing the euchromatic sequence of the human genome. *Nature, 431,* 931–945.

International Obesity Task Force (2004). The obesity epidemic, metabolic syndrome, and future prevention strategies. *European Journal of Cardiovascular Prevention and Rehabilitation, 11,* 3–8.

Irwin, C. E. (2004). Eating and physical activity during adolescence: Does it make a difference in adult health status? *Journal of Adolescent Health, 34,* 459–460.

Ishii-Kuntz, M. (2004). Asian American families. In M. Coleman & L. Ganong

(Eds.), *Handbook of contemporary families.* Thousand Oaks, CA: Sage.

Iverson, P., & Kuhl, P. K. (1996). Influences of phonetic identification and category goodness on American listeners' perception of /r/ and /l/. *Journal of the Acoustical Society of America, 99,* 1130–1140.

Iverson, P., Kuhl, P. K., Akahane-Yamada, R., Diesch, E., Tohkura, Y., Kettermann, A., & Siebert, C. (2003). A perceptual interference account of acquisition difficulties in non-native phonemes. *Cognition, 87,* B47–57.

Jackson, J. S., Chatters, L. M., & Taylor, R. J. (Eds.). (1993). *Aging in Black America.* Newbury Park, CA: Sage.

Jackson, R. (2004). Evolutionary psychology. In W. E. Craighead & C. B. Nemeroff (Eds.), *The concise Corsini encyclopedia of psychology and behavioral science.* New York: Wiley.

Jacob, N., Van Gestel, S., Derom, C., Theiry, E., Vernon, P., Derom, R., & Vlietinck, R. (2001). Heritability estimates of intelligence in twins: Effect of chorion type. *Behavior Genetics, 31,* 209–217.

Jacobs, J. E., & Klaczynski, P. A. (2002). The development of judgment and decision making during childhood and adolescence. *Current Directions in Psychological Science, 11,* 145–149.

Jacobs, J. E., & Potenza, M. (1990, March). *The use of decision-making strategies in late adolescence.* Paper presented at the meeting of the Society for Research in Adolescence, Atlanta.

Jacobs, J. E., & Tanner, J. L. (1999, August). *Stability and change in perceptions of parent-child relationships.* Paper presented at the meeting of the Gerontological Association of America, San Francisco.

Jacobs, R. H. (1994). His and her aging: Differences, difficulties, dilemmas, delights. *Journal of Geriatric Psychiatry, 27,* 113–128.

Jacobson, J. L., & Jacobson, S. W. (2003). Prenatal exposure to polychlorinated biphenyls and attention at school age. *Journal of Pediatrics, 143,* 780–788.

Jacobson, J. L., Jacobson, S. W., Fein, G. G., Schwartz, P. M., & Dowler, J. (1984). Prenatal exposure to an environmental toxin: A test of the multiple-effects model. *Developmental Psychology, 20,* 523–532.

Jacobson, J. L., Jacobson, S. W., Padgett, R. J., Brumitt, G. A., & Billings, R. L. (1992). Effects of prenatal PCB exposure on cognitive processing efficiency and sustained attention. *Developmental Psychology, 28,* 297–306.

Jadelis, K., Miller, M., Ettinger, W., & Messier, S. (2001). Strength, balance, and the modifying effects of obesity and knee pain: Results from the Observational Arthritis Study in Seniors (OASIS). *Journal of the American Geriatric Society, 49,* 884–891.

Jaffe, S. R. (2002). Pathways to adversity in young adulthood among early childbearers. *Journal of Family Psychology, 16,* 38–49.

Jaffee, S., & Hyde, J. S. (2000). Gender differences in moral orientation: A meta-analysis. *Psychological Bulletin, 126,* 703–726.

Jain, T., Missmer, S. A., & Hornstein, M. D. (2004). Trends in embryo-transfer practice and in outcomes of the use of assisted reproductive technology in the United States. *New England Journal of Medicine, 350,* 1639–1645.

James, W. (1890/1950). *The principles of psychology.* New York: Dover.

Jamieson, L., Anderson, M., McCrone, D., Bechhofer, F., Stewart, R., & Li, Y. (2003). Cohabitation and commitment: Partnership plans of young men and young women. *Sociological Review, 50,* 356–377.

Jamner, M. S., Spruijt-Metz, D., Bassin, S., & Cooper, D. M. (2004). A controlled evaluation of a school-based intervention to promote physical activity among sedentary adolescent females: Project FAB. *Journal of Adolescent Health, 34,* 279–289.

Jang, K. L. (2005). *Genetics of psychopathology.* Mahwah, NJ: Erlbaum.

Janssen, I., Craig, W. M., Boyce, W. F., & Pickett, W. (2004). Associations between overweight and obesity with bullying behaviors in school-aged children. *Pediatrics, 113,* 1187–1194.

Janssen, I., Katzmarzyk, P. T., Ross, R., Leon, A. S., Skinner, J. S., Rao, D. C., Wilmore, J. H., Rankinen, T., & Bouchard, C. (2004). Fitness alters the associations of BMI and waist circumference with total and abdominal fat. *Obesity Research, 12,* 525–537.

Jenkins, A. M., Albee, G. W., Paster, V. S., Sue, S., Baker, D., Comaz-Diaz, L., Puente, A., Suinn, R. M., Caldwell-Colbert, A. T., Williams, V. J., & Root, M. P. P. (2003). Ethnic minorities. In I. B. Weiner (Ed.), *Handbook of psychology* (Vol. I). New York: Wiley.

Jenkins, C. L. (2003). Introduction: Widows and divorcees in later life. *Journal of Women and Aging, 15,* 1–6.

Jenkins, J. M., & Astington, J. W. (1996). Cognitive factors and family structure associated with theory of mind development in young children. *Developmental Psychology, 32,* 70–78.

Jennekens, F. G., & Kater, L. (2002). Physician-assisted death. *New England Journal of Medicine, 347,* 1043.

Jensen, A. R. (1969). How much can we boost IQ and scholastic achievement? *Harvard Educational Review, 39,* 1–123.

Jessor, R., Turbin, M. S., & Costa, F. (1998). Protective factors in adolescent health behavior. *Journal of Personality and Social Psychology, 75,* 788–800.

Ji, B. T., Shu, X. O., Linet, M. S., Zheng, W., Wacholde, S., Gao, Y. T., Ying, D. M., & Jin, F. (1997). Paternal cigarette smoking and the risk of childhood cancer among offspring of nonsmoking mothers. *Journal of the National Cancer Institute, 89,* 238–244.

Jiao, S., Ji, G., & Jing, Q. (1996). Cognitive development of Chinese urban only children and children with siblings. *Child Development, 67,* 387–395.

Jimenez, V., Herniquez, M., Llanos, P., & Riquelme, G. (2004). Isolation and purification of human placental plasma membranes from normal and pre-eclamptic pregnancies: A comparative study. *Placenta, 25,* 422–437.

Jirtle, R. L., Sander, M., & Barrett, J. C. (2000). Genomic imprinting and environmental disease susceptibility. *Environmental Health Perspectives, 108,* 271–278.

Joffe, H., Soares, C. N., & Cohen, L. S. (2003). Assessment and treatment of hot flashes and menopausal mood disturbance. *Psychiatric Clinics of North America, 26,* 563–580.

Johannes, L. (2002, June 3). The surprising rise of a radical diet: "Calorie restriction." *The Wall Street Journal,* pp. A1, A10.

Johansson, A., Hermannsson, G., & Ludvigsson, J. (2004). How should parents protect their children from environmental tobacco-smoke exposure in the home? *Pediatrics, 113,* e291–e295.

Johnson, B. K. (1996). Older adults and sexuality: A multidimensional perspective. *Journal of Gerontological Nursing, 22,* 6–15.

Johnson, C. (1990, May). The new woman's ethics report. *New Woman,* p. 6.

Johnson, C. L., & Troll, L. E. (1992). Family functioning in late late life. *Journals of Gerontology B: Psychological Sciences and Social Sciences, 47,* S66–S72.

Johnson, C. L., & Troll, L. E. (1994). Constraints and facilitators to friendships in late late life. *Gerontologist, 34,* 79–87.

Johnson, D. J., Jaeger, E., Randolph, S. M., Cauce, A., Ward, J., & National Institute of Child Health and Human Development Early Child Care Research Network (2003). Studying the effects of early child care experiences on the development of children of color in the United States. *Child Development, 74,* 1227–1244.

Johnson, J. A., Musial, D. L., Hall, G. E., Gollnick, D. M., & Dupuis, V. L. (2005). *Introduction to the foundations of American education* (11th ed.). Boston: Allyn & Bacon.

Johnson, J. S., & Newport, E. L. (1991). Critical period effects on universal properties of language: The status of subjacency in the acquisition of a second language. *Cognition, 39,* 215–258.

Johnson, M. H. (2000). Infancy: Biological processes. In A. Kazdin (Ed.), *Encyclopedia of psychology.* Washington, DC, & New York: American Psychological Association and Oxford University Press.

Johnson, M. H. (2001). Functional brain development during infancy. In A. Fogel & G. Bremner (Eds.), *Blackwell handbook of infant development.* London: Blackwell.

Johnson, M. H. (2005). Developmental neuroscience. In M. H. Bornstein & M. E. Lamb (Eds.), *Developmental psychology* (5th ed.). Mahwah, NJ: Erlbaum.

Johnson, M. K., Beebe, T., Mortimer, J. T., & Snyder, M. (1998). Volunteerism in adolescence: A process perspective. *Journal of Research on Adolescence, 8,* 309–332.

Johnson, W., Bouchard, T. J., Krueger, R. F., McGue, M., & Gottesman, I. I. (2004). Just one *g*: Consistent results from three test batteries. *Intelligence, 32,* 95–107.

John-Steiner, V., & Mahn, H. (2003). Sociocultural contexts for teaching and learning. In I. B. Weiner (Ed.), *Handbook of psychology* (Vol. VII). New York: Wiley.

Johnston, L. D., O'Malley, P. M., & Bachman, J. G. (1992, January 25). *Most forms of drug use decline among American high school and college students.* News release, Institute of Social Research, University of Michigan, Ann Arbor.

Johnston, L. D., O'Malley, P. M., & Bachman, J. G. (2004). *Monitoring the future national results on adolescent drug use: Overview of key findings, 2003.* Bethesda, MD: National Institute of Drug Abuse.

Joiner, T. E. (2000). Depression: Current developments and controversies. In S. H.

Qualls & N. Abeles (Eds.), *Psychology and the aging revolution.* Washington, DC: American Psychological Association.

Jones, M. C. (1965). Psychological correlates of somatic development. *Child Development, 36,* 899–911.

Jones, T. G., & Fuller, M. L. (2003). *Teaching Hispanic children.* Boston: Allyn & Bacon.

Joseph, C. L. M. (1989). Identification of factors associated with delayed antenatal care. *Journal of the American Medical Association, 81,* 57–63.

Joseph, J. (2001). Separated twins and the genetics of personality differences: A critique. *American Journal of Psychology, 114,* 1–30.

Josephs, K. A., Tsuboi, Y., Cookson, N., Watt, H., & Dickson, D. W. (2004). Apolipoprotein E epsilon 4 is a determinant for Alzheimer-type pathologic features in taupathies, synucleinopathies, and frontotemporal degeneration. *Archives of Neurology, 61,* 1579–1584.

Judge, B., & Billick, S. B. (2004). Suicidality in adolescence: Review and legal considerations. *Behavioral Science and the Law, 22,* 681.

Julien, D., Chartrand, E., Simard, M., Bouthillier, D., & Begin, J. (2003). Conflict, social support, and relationship quality: An observational study of heterosexual, gay male, and lesbian couples. *Journal of Family Psychology, 17,* 419–428.

Jung, C. (1933). *Modern man in search of a soul.* New York: Harcourt Brace.

Jusczyk, P. W. (2000). *The discovery of spoken language.* Cambridge, MA: MIT Press.

Jusczyk, P. W., & Hohne, E. A. (1997). Infants' memory for spoken words. *Science, 277,* 1984–1986.

Juurlink, D. N., Herrmann, N., Szalai, J. P., Kopp, A., & Redelmeier, D. A. (2004). Medical illness and the risk of suicide in the elderly. *Archives of Internal Medicine, 164,* 1179–1184.

Kagan, J. (1987). Perspectives on infancy. In J. D. Osofsky (Ed.), *Handbook on infant development* (2nd ed.). New York: Wiley.

Kagan, J. (1992). Yesterday's promises, tomorrow's promises. *Developmental Psychology, 28,* 990–997.

Kagan, J. (1997). Temperament and the reactions to unfamiliarity. *Child Development, 68,* 139–143.

Kagan, J. (1998). The biology of the child. In W. Damon (Ed.), *Handbook of child psychology* (5th ed., Vol. 3). New York: Wiley.

Kagan, J. (2000). Temperament. In A. Kazdin (Ed.), *Encyclopedia of psychology.* Washington, DC, & New York: American Psychological Association and Oxford University Press.

Kagan, J. (2002). Behavioral inhibition as a temperamental category. In R. J. Davidson, K. R. Scherer, & H. H. Goldsmith (Eds.), *Handbook of affective sciences.* New York: Oxford University Press.

Kagan, J. (2003). Biology, context, and developmental inquiry. *Annual Review of Psychology* (Vol. 53). Palo Alto, CA: Annual Reviews.

Kagan, J., & Herschkowitz, N. (2005). *A young mind in a growing brain.* Mahwah, NJ: Erlbaum.

Kagan, J., Kearsley, R. B., & Zelazo, P. R. (1978). *Infancy: Its place in human development.* Cambridge, MA: Harvard University Press.

Kagan, J., & Snidman, N. (1991). Infant predictors of inhibited and uninhibited behavioral profiles. *Psychological Science, 2,* 40–44.

Kagan, S. H. (2004). Faculty profile, University of Pennsylvania School of Nursing. Available on the Internet at: www.nursing. upenn.edu/faculty/profile.asp?pid=33.

Kahn, A., Swaguchi, T., Swaguchi, A., Groswasser, J., Franco, P., Scaillet, S., Kelmanson, I., & Dan, B. (2002). Sudden infant deaths: From epidemiology to physiology. *Forensic Science International, 130,* Supplement: 8.

Kahn, J. A., Rosenthal, S. L., Succop, P. A., Ho, P. A., Ho, G. Y., & Burk, R. D. (2002). The interval between menarche and age of first sexual intercourse as a risk factor for subsequent HPV infection in adolescent and young adult women. *Journal of Pediatrics, 141,* 718–723.

Kaiser, F. E., & Morley, J. E. (1994). Idiopathic CD4$^+$ T lymphopenia in older persons. *Journal of the American Geriatric Society, 42,* 1291–1294.

Kalick, S. M., & Hamilton, T. E. (1986). The matching hypothesis reexamined. *Journal of Personality and Social Psychology, 51,* 673–682.

Kalil, A., & DeLeire, T. (Eds.). (2004). *Family investments in children's potential.* Mahwah, NJ: Erlbaum.

Kalish, R. A. (1981). *Death, grief, and caring relationships.* Monterey, CA: Brooks/Cole.

Kalish, R. A. (1987). Death. In G. L. Maddox (Ed.), *Encyclopedia of aging.* New York: Springer.

Kalish, R. A., & Reynolds, D. K. (1976). *An overview of death and ethnicity.* Farmingdale, NY: Baywood.

Kallen, B. (2004). Neonate characteristics after maternal use of antidepressants in late pregnancy. *Archives of Pediatric and Adolescent Medicine, 158,* 312–316.

Kalmuss, D. (2004). Nonvolitional sex and sexual health. *Archives of Sexual Behavior, 33,* 197–209.

Kamel, H. K. (2003). Sarcopenia and aging. *Nutrition Review, 61,* 157–167.

Kamerman, S. B. (1989). Child care, women, work, and the family: An international overview of child-care services and related policies. In J. S. Lande, S. Scarr, & N. Gunzenhauser (Eds.), *Caring for children: Challenge to America.* Hillsdale, NJ: Erlbaum.

Kamerman, S. B. (2000a). Parental leave policies. *Social Policy Report of the Society for Research in Child Development, XIV* (No. 2), 1–15.

Kamerman, S. B. (2000b). From maternity to paternity child leave policies. *Journal of the Medical Women's Association, 55,* 98–99.

Kamii, C. (1985). *Young children reinvent arithmetic: Implications of Piaget's theory.* New York: Teachers College Press.

Kamii, C. (1989). *Young children continue to reinvent arithmetic.* New York: Teachers College Press.

Kang, D., & Hamasaki, N. (2003). Mitochondrial oxidative stress and mitochondrial DNA. *Clinical Chemistry and Biological Medicine, 41,* 1281–1288.

Kanner, A. D., Coyne, J. C., Schaefer, C., & Lazarus, R. S. (1981). Comparison of two modes of stress measurement: Daily hassles and uplifts versus major life events. *Journal of Behavioral Medicine, 4,* 1–39.

Kanoy, K., Ulku-Steiner, B., Cox, M., & Burchinal, M. (2003). Marital relationship and individual psychological characteristics that predict physical punishment of children. *Journal of Family Psychology, 17,* 20–28.

Kantrowitz, B. (1991, Summer). The good, the bad, and the difference. *Newsweek,* pp. 48–50.

Kaplow, J. B., Curran, P. J., Dodge, K. A., & the Conduct Problems Prevention Research Group. (2002). Child, parent, and peer predictors of early-onset substance use: A multisite longitudinal study. *Journal of Abnormal Child Psychology, 30,* 199–216.

Karlsson, M. (2004). Has exercise an antifracture efficacy in women? *Scandanavian Journal of Medical Science and Sports, 14,* 2–15.

Karniol, R., Grosz, E., & Schorr, I. (2003). Caring, gender-role orientation, and volunteering. *Sex Roles, 49,* 11–19.

Karns, J. T. (2001). Health, nutrition, and safety. In A. Fogel & G. Bremner (Eds.), *Blackwell handbook of infant development.* London: Blackwell.

Kaslow, N. J., & others. (2004). Person factors associated with suicidal behavior among African American women and men. *Cultural Diversity and Ethnic Minority Psychology, 10,* 5–22.

Kasper, J. D. (1988). *Aging alone: Profiles and projections.* Report of the Commonwealth Fund Commission: Elderly People Living Alone. Baltimore: Commonwealth Fund Commission.

Kastenbaum, R. (2004). *Death, society, and the human experience* (8th ed.). Boston: Allyn & Bacon.

Katz, L. (1999). Curriculum disputes in early childhood education. *ERIC Clearinghouse on Elementary and Early Childhood Education,* Document EDO-PS-99-13.

Katz, L., & Chard, S. (1989). *Engaging the minds of young children: The project approach.* Norwood, NJ: Ablex.

Katz, L. F. (1999, April). *Toward a family-based hypervigilance model of childhood aggression: The role of the mother's and the father's meta-emotion philosophy.* Paper presented at the meeting of the Society for Research in Child Development, Albuquerque.

Katz, P. A. (1987, August). *Children and social issues.* Paper presented at the meeting of the American Psychological Association, New York.

Kauffman, J. M., & Hallahan, D. P. (2005). *Special education: What it is and why we need it.* Boston: Allyn & Bacon.

Kauffman, J. M., McGee, K., & Brigham, M. (2004). Enabling or disabling? Observations on changes in special education. *Phi Delta Kappan, 85,* 613–620.

Kaugers, A. S., Russ, S. W., & Singer, L. T. (2000, May). *Self-regulation among cocaine-exposed four-year-old children.* Paper presented at the joint meetings of the Pediatric Academic Societies and the American Academy of Pediatrics, Boston.

Kavšek, M. (2004). Predicting later IQ from infant visual habituation and dishabituation: A meta-analysis. *Journal of Applied Developmental Psychology, 25,* 369–393.

Kazdin, A. E., & Benjet, C. (2003). Spanking children: Evidence and issues. *Current Directions in Psychological Science, 12,* 99–103.

Keating, D. P. (1990). Adolescent thinking. In S. S. Feldman & G. R. Elliott (Eds.), *At the threshold: The developing adolescent.* Cambridge, MA: Harvard University Press.

Keating, D. P. (2003, April). *Cognitive integration in adolescence: The next sensitive period.* Paper presented at the meeting of the Society for Research in Child Development, Tampa, FL.

Keating, D. P. (2004). Cognitive and brain development. In R. Lerner & L. Steinberg (Eds.), *Handbook of adolescent psychology* (2nd ed.). New York: Wiley.

Keating, G. M., & Scott, L. J. (2003). Vardenafil: A review of its use in erectile dysfunction. *Drugs, 63,* 2673–2703.

Keel, P. K., Mitchell, J. E., Miller, K. B., Davis, T. L., & Crowe, S. J. (1999). Long-term outcome of bulimia nervosa. *Archives of General Psychiatry, 56,* 63–69.

Keen, R. (2005). Using perceptual representations to guide reaching and grasping. In J. J. Reiser, J. J. Lockman, & C. A. Nelson (Eds.), *The role of action in learning and development.* Mahwah, NJ: Erlbaum.

Keller, A., Ford, L., & Meacham, J. (1978). Dimensions of self-concept in preschool children. *Developmental Psychology, 14,* 483–489.

Keller, H. (2002). Culture and development: Developmental pathways to individualism and interrelatedness. In W. J. Lonner, D. L. Dinnel, S. A. Hayes, & D. N. Sattler (Eds.), *Online readings in psychology and culture* (unit 11, chapter 1). Available on the Internet at: www.wwu.edu/~culture. Bellingham, WA: Center for Cross-Cultural Research, Western Washington University.

Kelley-Moore, J. A., & Ferraro, K. F. (2004). The black/white disability gap: Persistent inequality in later life? *Journals of Gerontology B: Psychological Sciences and Social Sciences, 59,* S34–S43.

Kellman, P. J., & Banks, M. S. (1998). Infant visual perception. In W. Damon (Ed.), *Handbook of child psychology* (5th ed., Vol. 2). New York: Wiley.

Kelly, G. F. (2004). *Sexuality today* (7th ed., Updated). New York: McGraw-Hill.

Kelly, J. A. (2001). Safer sex behaviors. In J. Worell (Ed.), *Encyclopedia of women and gender.* San Diego: Academic Press.

Kelly, J. R. (1996). Leisure. In J. E. Birren (Ed.), *Encyclopedia of gerontology* (Vol. 2). San Diego: Academic Press.

Kemper, H. C., Stasse-Walthuis, M., & Bosman, W. (2004). The prevention and treatment of overweight and obesity. *Netherlands Journal of Medicine, 62,* 10–17.

Kemper, S., Greiner, L. H., Marquis, J. G., Prenovost, K., & Mitzner, T. L. (2001). Language decline across the life span: Findings from the Nun Study. *Psychology and Aging, 16,* 227–239.

Kempermann, G., Kuhn, H. G., & Gage, F. H. (1997). More hippocampal neurons in adult mice living in an enriched environment. *Nature, 386,* 493–495.

Kempermann, G., Wiskott, L., & Gage, F. H. (2004). Functional significance of neurogenesis. *Current Opinions in Neurobiology, 14,* 186–191.

Kennedy, H. P., Beck, C. T., & Driscoll, J. W. (2002). A light in the fog: Caring for women with postpartum depression. *Journal of Midwifery & Women's Health, 47,* 318–330.

Kennedy, M. F. (2004). Moving our children to health: Active play every day. *Canadian Family Physician, 50,* 601.

Kennedy, Q., Mather, M., & Carstensen, L. L. (2004). The role of motivation in the age-related positive bias in autobiographical memory. *Psychological Science, 15,* 208–214.

Kennell, J. H., & McGrath, S. K. (1999). Commentary: Practical and humanistic lessons from the third world for perinatal caregivers everywhere. *Birth, 26,* 9–10.

Kephart, W. M. (1967). Some correlates of romantic love. *Journal of Marriage and the Family, 29,* 470–474.

Kern, S. I., & Alessi, D. J. (2003). Sexual harassment complaints: Mandate from the board of medical examiners. *New Jersey Medicine, 100,* 23–25.

Kerr, M. (2001). Culture as a context for temperament. In T. D. Wachs & G. A. Kohnstamm (Eds.), *Temperament in context.* Mahwah, NJ: Erlbaum.

Kessen, W., Haith, M. M., & Salapatek, P. (1970). Human infancy. In P. H. Mussen (Ed.), *Manual of child psychology* (3rd ed., Vol. 1). New York: Wiley.

Kessler, D. P., & McClellan, M. B. (2004). Advance directives and medical treatment at the end of life. *Journal of Health Economics, 23,* 111–127.

Ketcham, C. J., & Stelmach, G. E. (2001). Age-related declines in motor control. In J. E. Birren & K. W. Schaie (Eds.), *Handbook of the psychology of aging* (5th ed.). San Diego: Academic Press.

Keyes, C., & Ryff, C. (1999). Psychological well-being in midlife. In S. L. Willis & J. D. Reid (Eds.), *Life in the middle.* San Diego: Academic Press.

Kiecolt-Glaser, J. K., & Glaser, R. (1988). Behavioral influences on immune function. In T. Field, P. McCabe, & N. Schneiderman (Eds.), *Stress and coping across development.* Hillsdale, NJ: Erlbaum.

Kiecolt-Glaser, J. K., Preacher, K. J., MacCallum, R. C., Atkinson, C., Malarkey, W. B., & Glaser, R. (2003). Chronic stress and age-related increases in the proinflammatory cytokine IL-6. *Proceedings of the National Academy of Science USA, 100,* 9090–9095.

Kilbride, H. W., Thorstad, K. K., & Daily, D. K. (2000, May). *Preschool outcome for extremely low birth weight infants compared to their full term siblings.* Paper presented at the joint meeting of the Pediatric Academic Societies and American Academy of Pediatrics, Boston.

Kilbride, H. W., Thorstad, K., & Daily, D. K. (2004). Preschool outcome of less than 801-gram preterm infants compared with full-term siblings. *Pediatrics, 113,* 742–747.

Kilpatrick, D. G. (2004). What is violence against women: Defining and measuring the problem. *Journal of Interpersonal Violence, 19,* 1209–1234.

Kim, J., & Cicchetti, D. (2004). A longitudinal study of child maltreatment, mother-child relationship quality and maladjustment: The role of self-esteem and social competence. *Journal of Abnormal Child Psychology, 32,* 341–354.

Kim, J. E., & Moen, P. (2002). Retirement transitions, gender, and psychological well-being: A life-course, ecological model. *Journals of Gerontology B: Psychological Sciences and Social Sciences, 57,* P212–P222.

Kimm, S. Y., & Obarzanek, E. (2002). Childhood obesity: A new pandemic of the new millennium. *Pediatrics, 110,* 1003–1007.

Kimm, S. Y., Glynn, N. W., Kriska, A. M., Barton, B. A., Kronsberg, S. S., Daniels, S. R., Crawford, P. B., Sabry, Z. I., & Liu, K. (2002). Decline in physical activity in black girls and white girls during adolescence. *New England Journal of Medicine, 347,* 709–715.

Kimura, D. (2000). *Sex and cognition.* Cambridge, MA: MIT Press.

King, A. (2000). Exercise and physical activity. In A. Kazdin (Ed.), *Encyclopedia of psychology.* Washington, DC, & New York: American Psychological Association and Oxford University Press.

King, B. M. (2005). *Human sexuality today* (5th ed.). Upper Saddle River, NJ: Prentice Hall.

King, P. M., & Mayhew, M. J. (2002). Moral judgment in higher education: Insights from the Defining Issues Test. *Journal of Moral Education, 31,* 247–269.

Kirchhoff, K. T. (2002). Promoting a peaceful death in the ICU. *Critical Care Nursing Clinics of North America, 14,* 201–206.

Kirk, R. E. (2003). Experimental design. In I. B. Weiner (Ed.), *Handbook of psychology* (Vol. II). New York: Wiley.

Kirkpatrick, L. A., & Hazan, C. (1994). Attachment styles and close relationships: A four-year prospective study. *Personal Relationships, 1,* 123–142.

Kisilevsky, B. S. (1995). The influence stimulus and subject variables on human fetal responses to sound and vibration. In J-P Lecauet, W. P. Fifer, M. A. Krasnegor, & W. P. Smotherman (Eds.), *Fetal development.* Hillsdale, NJ: Erlbaum.

Kisilevsky, B. S., Hains, S. M., Lee, K., Xic, X., Huang, H., Ye, H. H., Zhang, K., & Wang, Z. (2003). Effects of experience on fetal voice recognition. *Psychological Science, 14,* 220–224.

Kitzman, K. M., & Gaylord, N. K. (2002). Divorce and child custody. In J. Worell (Ed.), *Encyclopedia of women and gender.* San Diego: Academic Press.

Kivnick, H. Q., & Sinclair, H. M. (1996). Grandparenthood. In J. E. Birren (Ed.), *Encyclopedia of gerontology* (Vol. 1). San Diego: Academic Press.

Klaczynski, P. A., & Narasimham, G. (1998). Development of scientific reasoning biases: Cognitive versus ego-protective explanations. *Developmental Psychology, 34,* 175–187.

Klaus, M. H., & Kennell, H. H. (1976). *Maternal-infant bonding.* St. Louis: Mosby.

Klaus, M. H., Kennell, J. H., & Klaus, P. H. (1993). *Mothering the mother.* Reading, MA: Addison-Wesley.

Klesges, L. M., Johnson, K. C., Ward, K. D., & Barnard, M. (2001). Smoking cessation in pregnant women. *Obstetrics and Gynecological Clinics of North America, 28,* 269–282.

Kline, D. W., & Scialfa, C. T. (1996). Visual and auditory aging. In J. E. Birren & K. W. Schaie (Eds.), *Handbook of the psychology of aging* (4th ed.). San Diego: Academic Press.

Kline, G. H., Stanley, S. M., Markman, H. J., Olmos-Gallo, P. A., Peters, S. M., Whitton, S. W., & Prado, L. M. (2004). Timing is everything: Pre-engagement cohabitation and increased risk for poor marital outcomes. *Journal of Family Psychology, 18,* 311–318.

Kling, K. C., Hyde, J. S., Showers, C. J., & Buswell, B. N. (1999). Gender differences in self-esteem: A meta-analysis. *Psychological Bulletin, 125,* 470–500.

Klug, W. S., & Cummings, M. R. (2005). *Essentials of genetics* (5th ed.). Upper Saddle River, NJ: Prentice Hall.

Knecht, S., Drager, B., Deppe, M., Bobe, L., Lohmann, H., Floel, A., Ringelstein, E. B., & Henningsen, H. (2000). Handedness and hemispheric language dominance in healthy humans. *Brain, 135,* 2512–2518.

Knect, S., Jansen, A., Frank, A., van Randenborgh, J., Sommer, J., Kanowski, M., & Heinze, H. J. (2003). How atypical is atypical language dominance? *Neuroimage, 18,* 917–927.

Knight, B. G., Nordus, I. H., & Satre, D. D. (2003). Psychotherapy with older adults. In I. B. Weiner (Ed.), *Handbook of psychology* (Vol. VIII). New York: Wiley.

Knight, B. G., Teri, L., Wohlford, P., & Santos, J. (Eds.). (1996). *Mental health services for older adults.* Washington, DC: American Psychological Association.

Knowles, R. (2004). *Alzheimer's disease.* Upper Saddle River, NJ: Prentice Hall.

Kobak, R. (1999). The emotional dynamics of disruptions in attachment relationships: Implications for theory, research, and clinical intervention. In J. Cassidy & P. Shaver (Eds.), *Handbook of attachment.* New York: Guilford.

Kobasa, S. C., Maddi, S. R., & Kahn, S. (1982). Hardiness and health: A prospective study. *Journal of Personality and Social Psychology, 42,* 168–177.

Kobasa, S. C., Maddi, S. R., Puccetti, M. C., & Zola, M. (1986). Relative effectiveness of hardiness, exercise, and social support as resources against illness. *Journal of Psychosomatic Research, 29,* 525–533.

Kochanska, G., Friesenborg, A. E., Lange, L. A., Martel, M. M., & Kochanska, G. (2004). Parents' personality and infants' temperament as contributors to their emerging relationship. *Journal of Personality and Social Psychology, 86,* 744–759.

Koenig, H. G. (Ed.). (1998). *Handbook of religion and mental health.* San Diego: Academic Press.

Koenig, H. G. (2001). Religion and medicine II: Religion, mental health, and related behaviors. *International Journal of Psychiatry, 31,* 97–109.

Koenig, H. G., & Blazer, D. G. (1996). Depression. In J. E. Birren (Ed.), *Encyclopedia of gerontology* (Vol. 1). San Diego: Academic Press.

Koenig, H. G., Cohen, H. J., Blazer, D. G., Pieper, C., Meador, K. G., Shelp, F., Goldi, V., & DiPasquale, R. (1992). Religious coping and depression in elderly hospitalized medically ill men. *American Journal of Psychiatry, 149,* 1693–1700.

Koenig, H. G., & Larson, D. B. (1998). Religion and mental health. In H. S. Friedman (Ed.), *Encyclopedia of mental health* (Vol. 3). San Diego: Academic Press.

Koenig, H. G., Smiley, M., & Gonzales, J. A. T. (1988). *Religion, health, and aging.* New York: Greenwood Press.

Kogan, S. M. (2004). Disclosing unwanted sexual experiences: Results from a national sample of adolescent women. *Child Abuse & Neglect, 28,* 147–165.

Kohlberg, L. (1958). *The development on modes of moral thinking and choice in the years 10 to 16.* Unpublished doctoral dissertation, University of Chicago.

Kohlberg, L. (1966). A cognitive-developmental analysis of children's sex-role concepts and attitudes. In E. E. Maccoby (Ed.), *The development of sex differences.* Palo Alto, CA: Stanford University Press.

Kohlberg, L. (1969). Stage and sequence: The cognitive-developmental approach to socialization. In D. A. Goslin (Ed.), *Handbook of socialization theory and research.* Chicago: Rand McNally.

Kohlberg, L. (1986). A current statement of some theoretical issues. In S. Modgil & C. Modgil (Eds.), *Lawrence Kohlberg.* Philadelphia: Falmer.

Kohlberg, L., & Ryncarz, R. A. (1990). Beyond justice reasoning: Moral development and consideration of a seventh stage. In C. N. Alexander & E. J. Langer (Eds.), *Higher stages of human development.* New York: Oxford University Press.

Kohut, M. L., Cooper, M. M., Nickolaus, M. S., Russell, D. R., & Cunnick, J. E. (2002). Exercise and psychosocial factors modulate immunity to influenza vaccine in elderly individuals. *Journals of Gerontology A: Biological Sciences and Medical Sciences, 57,* M557–M562.

Kopp, C. B., & Neufeld, S. J. (2002). Emotional development in infancy. In R. Davidson & K. Scherer (Eds.), *Handbook of affective sciences.* New York: Oxford University Press.

Koppelman, K., & Goodhart, L. (2005). *Understanding human differences.* Boston: Allyn & Bacon.

Koriat, A., Goldsmith, M., Pansky, A. (2000). Toward a psychology of memory accuracy. *Annual Review of Psychology* (Vol. 51). Palo Alto, CA: Annual Reviews.

Kornhaber, M., Fierros, E., & Veenema, S. (2004). *Multiple intelligences.* Boston: Allyn & Bacon.

Kotch, J. B. (2003). Psychological maltreatment. *Pediatrics, 111,* 444–445.

Kotler, J. A., Wright, J. C., & Huston, A. C. (2001). Television use in families with children. In J. Bryant & J. A. Bryant (Eds.), *Television and the American Family.* Mahwah, NJ: Erlbaum.

Kotovsky, L., & Baillargeon, R. (1994). Calibration-based reasoning about collision events in 11-month-old infants. *Cognition, 51,* 107–129.

Kotre, J. (1984). *Outliving the self: Generativity and the interpretation of lives.* Baltimore: Johns Hopkins University Press.

Kottak, C. P. (2004). *Cultural anthropology* (10th ed.). New York: McGraw-Hill.

Kovera, M. B. (2004). Psychology, law, and the workplace. *Law and Human Behavior, 28,* 1–7.

Kozol, J. (1991). *Savage inequalities.* New York: Crown.

Kozulin, A. (2000). Vygotsky. In A. Kazdin (Ed.), *Encyclopedia of psychology.* Washington, DC, & New York: American Psychological Association and Oxford University Press.

Kozulin, A., Gindis, B., Ageyev, V. S., & Miller, S. M. (Eds.). (2003). *Vygotsky's educational theory in cultural context.* New York: Cambridge University Press.

Kraebel, K. S., Fable, J., & Gerhardtein, P. (2004). New methodology in infant operant kicking procedures. *Infant Behavior and Development, 127,* 1–18.

Kraehenbuhl, H., Preisig, M., Bula, C. J., & Waeber, G. (2004). Geriatric depression and vascular disease: What are the links? *Journal of Affective Disorders, 81,* 1–16.

Kralik, D., Koch, T., Price, K., & Howard, N. (2004). Chronic illness self-management: Taking action to create order. *Journal of Clinical Nursing, 13,* 259–267.

Kramer, A. F., Hahn, S., Cohen, N. J., Banich, M. T., McAuley, F., Harrison, C. R., Chason, J., Vakil, F., Bardell, L., Boileau, R. A., & Colcombe, A. (1999). Aging, fitness, and neurocognitive function. *Nature, 400,* 418–419.

Kramer, A. F., Hahn, S., McAuley, E., Cohen, N. J., Banich, M. T., Harrison, C., Chason, J., Boileau, R. A., Bardell, L., Colcombe, A., & Vakil, E. (2002). Exercise, aging and cognition: Healthy body, healthy mind? In A. D. Fisk & W. Rogers (Eds.), *Human factors interventions for the health care of older adults.* Mahwah, NJ: Erlbaum.

Kramer, A. F., & Willis, S. L. (2002). Enhancing the cognitive vitality of older adults. *Current Directions in Psychological Research, 11,* 173–177.

Kramer, D. A., Kahlbaugh, P. E., & Goldston, R. B. (1992). A measure of paradigm beliefs about the social world. *Journal of Gerontology, 47,* 180–189.

Kramer, M. (2003). Commentary: Breast-feeding and child health, growth, and survival. *International Journal of Epidemiology, 32,* 96–98.

Krampe, R. T., & Baltes, P. B. (2002). Intelligence as adaptive resource development and resource allocation: A new look through the lens of SOC and expertise. In R. J. Sternberg & E. L. Grigorenko (Eds.), *Perspectives on the psychology of abilities, competencies, and expertise.* New York: Cambridge University Press.

Krampe, R. T., & Baltes, P. B. (2003). Intelligence as adaptive resource development and resource allocation: A new look through the lens of SOC and expertise. In R. J. Sternberg & E. L. Grigorenko (Eds.), *Perspectives on the psychology of abilities, competencies, and expertise.* New York: Cambridge University Press.

Krause, K. H., Dresel, S. H., Krause, J., la Fougere, C., & Ackenheil, M. (2003). The dopamine transporter and neuroimaging in attention deficit hyperactivity disorder. *Neuroscience and Biobehavior Review, 27,* 605–613.

Krause, N. (1996). Neighborhood deterioration and self-rated health in later life. *Psychology and Aging, 11,* 342–352.

Krause, N. (2003). Religious meaning and subjective well-being in late life. *Journals of Gerontology B: Psychological Sciences and Social Sciences, 58,* S160–S170.

Krause, N. (2004). Common facets of religion, unique facets of religion, and life satisfaction among older adults. *Journals of Gerontology B: Psychological Sciences and Social Sciences, 59,* S109–S117.

Krause, N., Ingersoll-Dayton, B., Liang, J., & Sugisawa, H. (1999). Religion, social behavior, and health among the Japanese elderly. *Journal of Health and Social Behavior, 40,* 405–421.

Kraut, R., Patterson, M., Lundmark, V., Kiesler, S., Mukopadhyay, T., & Scherlis, W. (1998). Internet paradox. *American Psychologist, 53,* 1017–1031.

Kreutzer, M., Leonard, C., & Flavell, J. H. (1975). An interview study of children's knowledge about memory. *Monographs of the Society for Research in Child Development, 40* (1, Serial No. 159).

Krimer, L. S., & Goldman-Rakic, P. S. (2001). Prefrontal microcircuits. *Journal of Neuroscience, 21,* 3788–3796.

Kroger, J. (2003). Identity development in adolescence. In G. Adams & M. Berzonsky (Eds.), *Blackwell handbook of adolescence.* Malden, MA: Blackwell.

Krogh, D. (2005). *Biology* (3rd ed.). Upper Saddle River, NJ: Prentice Hall.

Krystal, A. D. (2004). Depression and insomnia in women. *Clinical Cornerstone, 2004, 6 Supplement 1B,* S19–S28.

Kübler-Ross, E. (1969). *On death and dying.* New York: Macmillan.

Kuebli, J. (1994, March). Young children's understanding of everyday emotions. *Young Children,* pp. 36–48.

Kuhl, P. K. (1993). Infant speech perception: A window on psycholinguistic development. *International Journal of Psycholinguistics, 9,* 33–56.

Kuhl, P. K. (2000). A new view of language acquisition. *Proceedings of the National Academy of Science, 97,* 11850–11857.

Kuhl, P. K. (2002, January 5). Commentary in Samuel, E. "Hellooooo baaay-beee." *The New Scientist, 173,* 10.

Kuhn, D. (1998). Afterword to Volume 2: Cognition, perception, and language. In W. Damon (Ed.), *Handbook of child psychology* (5th ed., Vol. 2). New York: Wiley.

Kuhn, D. (1999). A developmental model of critical thinking. *Educational Researcher, 28,* 16–25.

Kuhn, D. (2000). Adolescent thought processes. In A. Kazdin (Ed.), *Encyclopedia of psychology.* Washington, DC, & New York: American Psychological Association and Oxford University Press.

Kumari, A. S. (2001). Pregnancy outcome in women with morbid obesity. *International Journal of Gynecology and Obstetrics, 73,* 101–107.

Kupersmidt, J. B., & Coie, J. D. (1990). Preadolescent peer status, aggression, and school adjustment as predictors of externalizing problems in adolescence. *Child Development, 61,* 1350–1363.

Kupersmidt, J. B., & DeRosier, M. E. (2004). How peer problems lead to negative outcomes: An integrative mediational model. In J. B. Kupersmidt & K. A. Dodge (Eds.), *Children's peer relations: From development to intervention.* Washington, DC: American Psychological Association.

Kurdek, L. (2004). Gay men and lesbian couples. In M. Coleman & L. Ganong (Eds.), *Handbook of contemporary families.* Thousand Oaks, CA: Sage.

Kurdek, L. A. (1995). Developmental changes in relationship quality in gay and lesbian cohabiting couples. *Developmental Psychology, 31,* 86–94.

Kurdek, L. A. (1997). Adjustment to relationship dissolution in gay, lesbian, and heterosexual partners. *Personal Relationships, 4,* 145–161.

Kurdek, L. A. (2003). Differences between gay and lesbian cohabiting couples. *Journal of Social and Personal Relationships, 20,* 411–436.

Kwak, H. K., Kim, M., Cho, B. H., & Ham, Y. M. (1999, April). *The relationship between children's temperament, maternal control strategies, and children's compliance.* Paper presented at the meeting of the Society for Research in Child Development, Albuquerque.

Kwon, S. (1999, November). *Control beliefs and cognitive intervention gains: Early-dementia identification by non-intellective factors.* Paper presented at the meeting of the Gerontological Society of America, San Francisco.

Kyba, F. C. (2002). Legal and ethical issues in end-of-life care. *Critical Care and Nursing Clinics of North America, 14,* 141–155.

La Greca, A. M., Silverman, W. K., Vernberg, E. M., & Roberts, M. C. (Eds.). (2002). *Helping children cope with disasters and terrorism.* Washington, DC: American Psychological Association.

Labouvie-Vief, G. (1986, August). *Modes of knowing and life-span cognition.* Paper presented at the meeting of the American Psychological Association, Washington, DC.

Labouvie-Vief, G., & Diehl, M. (1999). Self and personality development. In J. C. Kavanaugh & S. K. Whitbourne (Eds.), *Gerontology: An interdisciplinary perspective.* New York: Oxford University Press.

Labouvie-Vief, G., Diehl, M., Tarnowski, A., & Shen, J. (2000). Age differences in personality: Findings from the United States and China. *Journals of Gerontology B: Psychological Sciences and Social Sciences, 55*, P4–P17.

Lachlan, R. F., & Feldman, M. W. (2003). Evolution of cultural communication systems. *Journal of Evolutionary Biology, 16*, 1084–1095.

Lachman, M. E. (Ed.). (2001). *Handbook of midlife development.* New York: John Wiley.

Lachman, M. E. (2004). Development in midlife. *Annual Review of Psychology* (Vol. 55). Palo Alto, CA: Annual Reviews.

Lachman, M. E., & Bertrand, R. M. (2001). Personality and the self in midlife. In M. E. Lachman (Ed.), *Handbook of midlife development.* New York: Wiley.

Lachman, M. E., & Firth, K. (2004). The adaptive value of feeling in control during midlife. In G. Brim, C. D. Ryff, & R. Kessler (Eds.), How healthy we are: A national study of well-being in midlife. Chicago: University of Chicago Press.

Lachman, M. E., Maier, H., & Budner, R. (2000). *A portrait of midlife.* Unpublished manuscript, Brandeis University, Waltham, MA.

Lachman, M. E., & Weaver, S. L. (1998). Sociodemographic variations in the sense of control by domain: Findings from the MacArthur Study of midlife. *Psychology and Aging, 13*, 553–562.

Lackmann, G. M., Salzberger, U., Tollner, U., Chen, M., Carmella, S. G., & Hecht, S. S. (1999). Metabolites of a tobacco-specific carcinogen in urine from newborns. *Journal of the National Cancer Institute, 91*, 459–465.

Ladd, G. W., Buhs, E., & Troop, W. (2004). School adjustment and social skills training. In P. K. Smith & C. H. Hart (Eds.), *Blackwell handbook of childhood social development.* Malden, MA: Blackwell.

Ladd, G. W., & Kochenderfer-Ladd, B. (2002). Identifying victims of peer aggression from early to middle childhood: Analysis of cross-informant data for concordance, incidence of victimization, characteristics of identified victims, and estimation of relational adjustment. *Psychological Assessment, 14*, 74–96.

Laible, D. J., Carlo, G., & Raffaeli, M. (2000). The differential relations of parent and peer attachment to adolescent adjustment. *Journal of Youth and Adolescence, 29*, 45–53.

Lakes, R. D., & Carter, P. A. (2004). Globalization, vocational education, and gender equity: A review. In R. D. Lakes &

P. A. Carter (Eds.), *Globalizing education for work.* Mahwah, NJ: Erlbaum.

Lamb, C. S., Jackson, L. A., Cassiday, P. B., & Priest, D. J. (1993). Body figure preferences of men and women: A comparison of two generations. *Sex Roles, 28*, 345–358.

Lamb, M. E. (1977). The development of mother-infant and father-infant attachments in the second year of life. *Developmental Psychology, 13*, 637–648.

Lamb, M. E. (1986). *The father's role: Applied perspectives.* New York: Wiley.

Lamb, M. E. (1994). Infant care practices and the application of knowledge. In C. B. Fisher & R. M. Lerner (Eds.), *Applied developmental psychology.* New York: McGraw-Hill.

Lamb, M. E. (2000). The history of research on father involvement: An overview. *Marriage and Family Review, 29*, 23–42.

Lamb, M. E., Bornstein, M. H., & Teti, D. M. (2002). *Development in infancy* (4th ed.). Mahwah, NJ: Erlbaum.

Lamb, M. E., Frodi, A. M., Hwant, C. P., Frodi, M., & Steinberg, J. (1982). Mother and father-infant interaction involving play and holding in traditional and nontraditional Swedish families. *Developmental Psychology, 18*, 215–221.

Lamb, M. E., & Lewis, C. (2005). The role of parent-child relationships in child development. In M. H. Bornstein & M. E. Lamb (Eds.), *Developmental psychology* (5th ed.). Mahwah, NJ: Erlbaum.

Lamb, V. L. (2003). Historical and epidemiological trends in mortality in the United States. In C. D. Bryant (Ed.), *Handbook of death and dying.* Thousand Oaks, CA: Sage.

Lammers, W. J., & Badia, P. (2005). *Fundamentals of behavioral research.* Belmont, CA: Wadsworth.

Lan, T-Y., Deeg, D. J. H., Guralnik, J. M., & Melzer, D. (2003). Responsiveness of the index of mobility limitation: Comparison with gait speed alone in the longitudinal aging study Amsterdam. *Journals of Gerontology A: Biological Sciences and Medical Sciences, 58*, M721–M727.

Landgren, B. M., Collins, A., Csemiczky, G., Burger, H. G., Baksheev, L., & Robertson, D. M. (2004). Menopause transition. *Journal of Clinical and Endocrinological Metabolism, 89*, 2763–2769.

Lane, J. T., Ford, T. C., Larson, L. R., Chambers, W. A., & Lane, P. H. (2004). Acute effects of exercise in normoalbumin-

uric/normotensive patients with type 1 diabetes. *Diabetes Care, 27*, 28–32.

Lane, M. A., Mattison, J. A., Roth, G. S., Brant, L. J., & Ingram, D. K. (2004). Effects of long-term diet restriction on aging and longevity in primates remains uncertain. *Journals of Gerontology A: Biological Sciences and Medical Sciences, 59*, B405–B407.

Lang, F. R., & Carstensen, L. L. (1994). Close emotional relationships in late life: Further support for proactive aging in the social domain. *Psychology and Aging, 9*, 315–324.

Langa, K. M., Albasanz, J. L., Martin, M., & Ferrer, I. (2004). Abnormal metabotropic glutamate receptor expression and signaling in the cerebral cortex in diffuse Lewy body disease is associated with irregular alpha-synuclein/phospholipase C (PLCbeta1) interactions. *Brain Pathology, 14*, 388–398.

Langlois, J. H., & Liben, L. S. (2003). Child care research: An editorial perspective. *Child Development, 74*, 969–1226.

Langston, W. (2002). *Research methods manual for psychology.* Belmont, CA: Wadsworth.

Lapsley, D. K. (1996). *Moral psychology.* Boulder, CO: Westview Press.

Lapsley, D. K. (2005). Stage theories generated by Kohlberg. In M. Killen & J. Smetana (Eds.), *Handbook of moral development.* Mahwah, NJ: Erlbaum.

Larson, J. (1988). The marriage quiz: College students' beliefs in selected areas of marriage. *Family Relations, 37*, 3–11.

Larson, J. H., & Holman, T. B. (1994). Premarital predictors of marital quality and stability. *Family Relations, 43*, 228–237.

Larson, R., & Lampman-Petraitis, C. (1989). Daily emotional states as reported by children and adolescents. *Child Development, 60*, 1250–1260.

Larson, R., & Richards, M. H. (1994). *Divergent realities.* New York: Basic Books.

Larson, R. W. (1999, September). Unpublished review of J. W. Santrock's *Adolescence,* 8th ed. (New York: McGraw-Hill).

Larson, R. W. (2001). How U.S. children and adolescents spend their time: What it does (and doesn't) tell us about their development. *Current Directions in Psychological Science, 10*, 160–164.

Larson, R. W., & Varma, S. (1999). How children and adolescents spend time across the world: Work, play, and developmental opportunities. *Psychological Bulletin, 125,* 701–736.

Larson, R. W., & Wilson, S. (2004). Adolescence across place and time: Globalization and the changing pathways to adulthood. In R. Lerner & L. Steinberg (Eds.), *Handbook of adolescent psychology.* New York: Wiley.

Latham, N. K., Bennett, D. A., Stretton, C. M., & Anderson, C. S. (2004). Systematic review of resistance strength training in older adults. *Journals of Gerontology A: Biological Sciences and Medical Sciences, 59,* M48–M61.

Laursen, B., & Collins, W. A. (2004). Parent-child communication during adolescence. In C. Segrin & J. Flora (Eds.), *Family communication.* Mahwah, NJ: Erlbaum.

Lawton, M. P., Kleban, M. H., Rajagopal, D., & Dean, J. (1992). The dimensions of affective experience in three age groups. *Psychology and Aging, 7,* 171–184.

Lazarus, R. S., & Folkman, S. (1984). *Stress, appraisal, and coping.* New York: Springer.

Leadbeater, B. J. R., & Way, N. (2001). *Growing up fast.* Mahwah, NJ: Erlbaum.

Leaper, C. (2002). Parenting girls and boys. In M. H. Bornstein (Ed.), *Handbook of parenting* (2nd ed., Vol. 1). Mahwah, NJ: Erlbaum.

Leary, M. R. (2004). *Introduction to behavioral research methods* (4th ed.). Boston: Allyn & Bacon.

Leavitt, C. H., Tonniges, T. F., & Rogers, M. F. (2003). Good nutrition: The imperative for positive development. In M. H. Bornstein, L. Davidson, C. L. M. Keyes, & K. A. Moore (Eds.), *Well-being.* Mahwah, NJ: Erlbaum.

LeDoux, J. E. (2000). Emotion circuits in the brain. *Annual Review of Neuroscience, 23,* 155–184.

LeDoux, J. E. (2002). *The synaptic self.* New York: Viking.

Lee, D. J., & Markides, K. S. (1990). Activity and mortality among aged persons over an eight-year period. *Journals of Gerontology B: Psychological Sciences and Social Sciences, 45,* S39–S42.

Lee, G. R. (1978). Marriage and morale in late life. *Journal of Marriage and the Family, 40,* 131–139.

Lee, I. M., Hsieh, C., & Paffenbarger, O. (1995). Exercise intensity and longevity in men. *Journal of the American Medical Association, 273,* 1179–1184.

Lee, I. M., Manson, J. E., Hennekens, C. H., & Paffenbarger, R. S. (1993).

Body-weight and mortality: A 27-year follow-up. *Journal of the American Medical Association, 270,* 2823–2828.

Lee, I. M., & Skerrett, P. J. (2001). Physical activity and all-cause mortality: What is the dose-response relation? *Medical Science and Sports Exercise, 33* (Suppl. 6), S459–S471.

Lee, S. Y., Kim, M. T., Kim, S. W., Song, M. S., & Yoon, S. J. (2003). Effect of lifetime lactation on breast cancer risk: A Korean women's cohort study. *International Journal of Cancer, 105,* 390–393.

Lee, W. K. (2003). Women and retirement planning: Towards the "feminization of poverty" in an aging Hong Kong. *Journal of Women and Aging, 15,* 31–53.

Leeman, C. P. (2002). Physician-assisted death. *New England Journal of Medicine, 347,* 1041–1042.

Lehman, H. C. (1960). The age decrement in outstanding scientific creativity. *American Psychologist, 15,* 128–134.

Lehr, C. A., Hanson, A., Sinclair, M. F., & Christensen, S. L. (2003). Moving beyond dropout prevention towards school completion. *School Psychology Review, 32,* 342–364.

Lehtonen, L., & Martin, R. J. (2004). Ontogeny of sleep and awake states in relation to breathing in preterm infants. *Seminars in Neonatology, 9,* 229–238.

Leifer, A. D. (1973). *Television and the development of social behavior.* Paper presented at the meeting of the International Society for the Study of Behavioral Development, Ann Arbor, MI.

Leming, M. R. (2003). The history of the hospice approach. In C. D. Bryant (Ed.), *Handbook of death and dying.* Thousand Oaks, CA: Sage.

Leming, M. R., & Dickinson, G. E. (2002). *Understanding death, dying, and bereavement* (5th ed.). Belmont, CA: Wadsworth.

Lenders, C. M., McElrath, T. F., & Scholl, T. O. (2000). Nutrition in pregnancy. *Current Opinions in Pediatrics, 12,* 291–296.

Lenoir, C. P., Mallet, E., & Calenda, E. (2000). Siblings of sudden infant death syndrome and near miss in about 30 families: Is there a genetic link? *Medical Hypotheses, 54,* 408–411.

Lenton, A. P., & Blair, I. V. (2004). Gender roles. In W. E. Craighead & C. B. Nemeroff (Eds.), *The concise Corsini encyclopedia of psychology and behavioral science.* New York: Wiley.

Leonard, B. (2004). Women's conditions occurring in men: Breast cancer, osteoporosis, male menopause, and eating disorders. *Nursing Clinics of North America, 39,* 379–393.

Leonards, U., Ibanez, V., & Giannakopoulos, P. (2002). The role of stimulus type in age-related changes of visual working memory. *Experimental Brain Research, 146,* 172–183.

Leong, F. T. L. (2000). Cultural pluralism. In A. Kazdin (Ed.), *Encyclopedia of psychology.* Washington, DC, and New York: American Psychological Association and Oxford University Press.

Lerner, H. G. (1989). *The dance of intimacy.* New York: Harper & Row.

Lerner, R. M. (2002). *Concepts and theories of human development* (3rd ed.). Mahwah, NJ: Erlbaum.

Lesaux, N. K., & Siegel, L. S. (2003). The development of reading in children who speak English as a second language. *Developmental Psychology, 39,* 1005–1019.

Lessow-Hurley, J. (2005). *The foundations of dual language instruction* (4th ed.). Boston: Allyn & Bacon.

Lester, B. (2000). Unpublished review of J. W. Santrock's *Life-span development* (8th ed.). New York: McGraw-Hill.

Lester, B. M., Tronick, E. Z., LaGasse, L., Seifer, R., Bauer, C. R., Shankaran, S., Bada, H. S., Wright, L. L., Smeriglio, V. L., Lu, J., Finnegan, L. P., & Maza, P. L. (2002). The maternal lifestyle study: Effects of substance exposure during pregnancy on neurodevelopmental outcome in 1-month-old infants. *Pediatrics, 110,* 1182–1192.

Leuba, G., Vernay, A., Va, D., Waltzer, C., Belloir, B., Kraftsik, R., Bouras, C., & Savioz, A. (2004). Differential expression of LMO4 protein in Alzheimer's disease. *Neuropathology and Applied Neurobiology, 30,* 57–69.

Levant, R. F. (2002). Men and masculinity. In J. Worell (Ed.), *Encyclopedia of women and gender.* San Diego: Academic Press.

Levant, R. F., & Brooks, G. R. (1997). *Men and sex: New psychological perspectives.* New York: Wiley.

LeVay, S. (1991). A difference in the hypothalamic structure between heterosexual and homosexual men. *Science, 253,* 1034–1037.

Levelt, W. J. M. (1989). *Speaking: From intention to articulation.* Cambridge, MA: MIT Press.

Leventhal, A. (1994, February). *Peer conformity during adolescence: An integration of* *developmental, situational, and individual characteristics.* Paper presented at the meeting of the Society for Research on Adolescence, San Diego.

Leventhal, A. G., Wang, Y., Pu, M., Zhou, Y., & Ma, Y. (2003). GABA and its agonists improved visual cortical function in senescent monkeys. *Science, 300,* 812–815.

Leventhal, T., & Brooks-Gunn, J. (2004). Diversity in developmental trajectories across adolescence: Neighborhood influences. In R. Lerner & L. Steinberg (Eds.), *Handbook of adolescent psychology.* New York: Wiley.

Levin, B. G. (2004). Coping with traumatic loss. *International Journal of Emergency Mental Health, 6,* 25–31.

Levin, J. S., Taylor, R. J., & Chatters, L. M. (1994). Race and gender differences in religiosity among older adults: Findings from four national surveys. *Journals of Gerontology B: Psychological Sciences and Social Sciences, 49,* S137–S145.

Levin, J. S., & Vanderpool, H. Y. (1989). Is religion therapeutically significant for hypertension? *Social Science and Medicine, 29,* 69–78.

LeVine, S. (1979). *Mothers and wives: Gusii women of East Africa.* Chicago: University of Chicago Press.

Levinson, D. J. (1978). *The seasons of a man's life.* New York: Knopf.

Levinson, D. J. (1996). *Seasons of a woman's life.* New York: Alfred Knopf.

Levy, B. R., Jennings, P., & Langer, E. J. (2001). Improving attention in old age. *Journal of Adult Development, 8,* 189–192.

Levy, G. D., Sadovsky, A. L., & Troseth, G. L. (2000). Aspects of young children's perceptions of gender-typed occupations. *Sex Roles, 42,* 993–1006.

Levy, M. M. (2004). Dying in America. *Critical Care Medicine, 32,* 879–880.

Lewallen, L. P. (2004). Healthy behaviors and sources of health information among low-income pregnant women. *Public Health Nursing, 21,* 200–206.

Lewis, C., & Carpendale, J. (2004). Social cognition. In P. K. Smith & C. H. Hart (Eds.), *Blackwell handbook of childhood social development.* Malden, MA: Blackwell.

Lewis, M. (1997). *Altering fate: Why the past does not predict the future.* New York: Guilford Press.

Lewis, M. (2001). Issues in the study of personality development. *Psychological Inquiry, 12,* 67–83.

Lewis, M. (2002). Early emotional development. In A. Slater & M. Lewis (Eds.), *Introduction to infant development.* New York: Oxford University Press.

Lewis, M., & Brooks-Gunn, J. (1979). *Social cognition and the acquisition of the self.* New York: Plenum.

Lewis, M., Feiring, C., & Rosenthal, S. (2000). Attachment over time. *Child Development, 71,* 707–720.

Lewis, M., & Ramsay, D. S. (1999). Effect of maternal soothing and infant stress response. *Child Development, 70,* 11–20.

Lewis, M. D., & Stieben, J. (2004). Emotion regulation in the brain: Conceptual issues and directions for developmental research. *Child Development, 75,* 371–376.

Lewis, M. W., Misra, S., Johnson, H. L., & Rosen, T. S. (2004). Neurological and developmental outcomes of prenatally cocaine-exposed offspring from 12 to 36 months. *American Journal of Drug and Alcohol Abuse, 30,* 299–320.

Lewis, R. (2005). *Human genetics* (6th ed.). New York: McGraw-Hill.

Lewkowicz, D. J. (2003). Learning and discrimination of audiovisual events in human infants: The hierarchical relation between intersensory temporal synchrony and rhythmic pattern cues. *Developmental Psychology, 39,* 795–804.

Leyendecker, B., Harwood, R. L., Comparini, L., & Yalcinkaya, A. (2005). Socioeconomic status, ethnicity, and parenting. In T. Luster & L. Okaghi (Eds.), *Parenting: An ecological perspective* (2nd ed.). Mahwah, NJ: Erlbaum.

Li, M., & others (2002). Defect in ERK2 and p54^JNK activation in aging mouse splenocytes. *Journals of Gerontology A: Biological Sciences and Medical Sciences, 57,* B41–B47.

Li, S. J., Li, Z., Wu, G., Zhang, M. J., Franczak, M., & Antuono, P. G. (2002). Alzheimer disease: Evaluation of functional MR imaging index as a marker. *Radiology, 225,* 253–259.

Li, S-C., Hommel, B., Aschersleben, G., Prinz, W., & Baltes, P. B. (2004). Transformations in the couplings among intellectual abilities and constituent cognitive processes across the life span. *Psychological Science, 15,* 155–163.

Lickliter, R., & Bahrick, L. E. (2000). The development of infant intersensory perception: Advantages of a comparative convergent-operations approach. *Psychological Bulletin, 126,* 260–280.

Lie, E., & Newcombe, N. (1999). Elementary school children's explicit and implicit memory for faces of preschool classmates. *Developmental Psychology, 35,* 102–112.

Lifshitz, F., Pugliese, M. T., Moses, N., & Weyman-Daum, M. (1987). Parental health beliefs as a cause of nonorganic failure to thrive. *Pediatrics, 80,* 175–182.

Lifton, R. J. (1977). The sense of immortality: On death and the continuity of life. In H. Feifel (Ed.), *New meanings of death.* New York: McGraw-Hill.

Lillard, Lee A., & Waite, Linda J. (1995). Til death do us part: Marital disruption and mortality. *American Journal of Sociology, 100,* 1131–1156.

Limber, S. P. (1997). Preventing violence among school children. *Family Futures, 1,* 27–28.

Limber, S. P. (2004). Implementation of the Olweus Bullying Prevention Program in American schools: Lessons learned from the field. In D. L. Espelage & S. M. Swearer (Eds.), *Bullying in American schools.* Mahwah, NJ: Erlbaum.

Lindenberger, U., & Baltes, P. B. (1994). Sensory functioning and intelligence in old age: A strong connection. *Psychology and Aging, 9,* 339–355.

Linver, M. R., Fuligni, A. J., Hernandez, M., & Brooks-Gunn, J. (2004). Poverty and child development. In P. Allen-Meares & M. Fraser (Eds.), *Intervention with children and adolescents.* Boston: Allyn & Bacon.

Lippa, R. A. (2005). *Gender, nature, and nurture* (2nd ed.). Mahwah, NJ: Erlbaum.

Liprie, M. L. (1993). Adolescents' contributions to family decision making. In B. H. Settles, R. S. Hanks, & M. B. Sussman (Eds.), *American families and the future: Analyses of possible destinies.* New York: Haworth Press.

Lipsitt, L. P. (2003). Crib death: Behavioral phenomenon? *Current Directions in Psychological Science, 12,* 164–168.

Lipsitz, J. (1983, October). *Making it the hard way: Adolescents in the 1980s.* Testimony presented at the Crisis Intervention Task Force, House Select Committee on Children, Youth, and Families, Washington, DC.

Litovsky, R. Y., & Ashmead, D. H. (1997). Development of binaural and spatial hearing in infants and children. In R. H. Gilkey & T. R. Anderson (Eds.), *Binaural and spatial hearing in real and virtual environments.* Mahwah, NJ: Erlbaum.

Litt, I. F. (2003). Parents are "in" again. *Journal of Adolescent Health, 33,* 59.

Little, H. A., Rowe, C. L., Dakof, G. A., Ungaro, R. A., & Henderson, C. E. (2004). Early intervention for adolescent substance abuse: Pretreatment to posttreatment outcomes of a randomized clinical trial comparing multidimensional family therapy and peer group treatment. *Journal of Psychoactive Drugs, 36,* 49–63.

Liu, H. M., Kuhl, P. K., & Tsao, F. M. (2003). An association between mothers' speech clarity and infants' speech discrimination skills. *Developmental Science, 6,* F1–F10.

Lively, W., & Bromley, D. (1973). *Person perception in childhood and adolescence.* New York: Wiley.

Livson, N., & Peskin, H. (1981). Psychological health at age 40: Prediction from adolescent personality. In D. M. Eichorn, J. Clausen, N. Haan, M. Honzik, & P. Mussen (Eds.), *Present and past in middle life.* New York: Academic Press.

Lobel, M., Yali, A. M., Zhu, W., DeVincent, C. J., & Meyer, B. A. (2002). Beneficial associations between optimistic disposition and emotional distress in high-risk pregnancy. *Psychology and Health, 17,* 77–95.

Locher, J. L., Ritchie, C. S., Roth, D. L., Baker, P. S., Bodner, E. V., & Allman, R. M. (2005). Social isolation, support, and capital and nutritional risk in an older sample: Ethnic and gender differences. *Social Science Medicine, 60,* 747–761.

Lock, A. (2004). Preverbal communication. In U. Goswami (Ed.), *Blackwell handbook of childhood cognitive development.* Malden, MA: Blackwell.

Lock, M. (1998). Menopause: Lessons from anthropology. *Psychosomatic Medicine, 60,* 410–419.

Lockenhoff, C. E., & Carstensen, L. L. (2004). Socioemotional selectivity theory, aging, and health: The increasingly delicate balance between regulating emotions and making tough choices. *Journal of Personality, 72,* 1305–1424.

Loeb, S., Fuller, B., Kagan, S. L., & Carrol, B. (2004). Child care in poor communities: Early learning effects of type, quality, and stability. *Child Development, 75,* 47–65.

Loeber, R., & Farrington, D. P. (Eds.). (2001). *Child delinquents: Development, intervention and service needs.* Thousand Oaks, CA: Sage.

Loeber, R., Farrington, D. P., Stouthamer-Loeber, M., Moffitt, T., & Caspi, A. (1998). The development of male offending: Key findings from the first decade of the Pittsburgh Youth Study. *Studies in Crime and Crime Prevention, 7,* 141–172.

Logsdon, M. C. (2004). Depression in adolescent girls: Screening and treatment strategies for primary care providers. *Journal of the American Women's Medical Association, 59,* 101–106.

London, M. L., Ladewig, P. W., Olds, S. B., & Ladewig, P. W. (2000). *Maternal newborn nursing care* (4th ed.). Boston: Addison-Wesley.

Long, T., & Long, L. (1983). *Latchkey children.* New York: Penguin.

Longman, P. (1987). *Born to pay: The new politics of aging in America.* Boston: Houghton-Mifflin.

Lopata, H. Z. (1994). *Circles and settings: Role changes of American women.* Albany State University of New York Press.

Lopez-Toledano, M. A., & Shelanski, M. L. (2004). Neurogenic effect of beta-amyloid peptide in the development of neural stem cells. *Journal of Neuroscience, 24,* 5439–5444.

Lorensen, M., Wilson, M. E., & White, M. A. (2004). Norwegian families: Transition to parenthood. *Health Care for Women International, 25,* 334–348.

Lorenz, K. Z. (1965). *Evolution and the modification of behavior.* Chicago: University of Chicago Press.

Lott, B., & Maluso, D. (2001). Gender development: Social learning. In J. Worrell (Ed.), *Encyclopedia of women and gender.* San Diego: Academic Press.

Loughlin, A. (2004). Depression and social support: Effective treatments for homebound elderly adults. *Journal of Gerontological Nursing, 30,* 11–15.

Loveland Cook, C. A., Flick, L. H., Homan, S. M., Campbell, C., McSweeney, M., & Gallagher, M. E. (2004). Posttraumatic stress disorder in pregnancy: Prevalence, risk factors, and treatment. *Obstetrics and Gynecology, 103,* 710–717.

Low, A. (2004). Health inequities. *Health Services Journal, 114,* 26–27.

Lowe, M. R., & Timko, C. A. (2004). What a difference a diet makes: Towards an understanding of differences between restrained dieters and restrained nondieters. *Eating Behavior, 5,* 199–208.

Lowe, X., Eskenazi, B., Nelson, D. O., Kidd, S., Alme, A., & Wyrobek, A. J. (2001). Frequency of XY sperm increases with age in fathers of boys with Klinefelter syndrome. *American Journal of Human Genetics, 69,* 1046–1054.

Lucas, R. E., Clark, A. E., Yannis, G., & Diener, E. (2004). Unemployment alters the setpoint for life satisfaction. *Psychological Science, 15,* 8–13.

Luciana, M., Sullivan, J., & Nelson, C. A. (2001). Associations between phenylalanine-to-tyrosine ratios and performance on tests of neuropsychological function in adolescents treated early and continuously for phenylketonuria. *Child Development, 72,* 1637–1652.

Lucurto, C. (1990). The malleability of IQ as judged from adoption studies. *Intelligence, 14,* 275–292.

Ludington-Hoe, S. M., Anderson, G. C., Swinth, J. Y., Thompson, C., & Hadeed, A. J. (2004). Randomized controlled trial of kangaroo care: Cardiorespiratory and thermal effects on healthy preterm infants. *Neonatal Network, 23,* 39–48.

Ludington-Hoe, S. M., Cong, X., & Hashemi, F. (2002). Infant crying: Nature, physiologic consequences, and select interventions. *Neonatal Network, 21,* 29–36.

Lund, D. A. (1996). Bereavement and loss. In J. E. Birren (Ed.), *Encyclopedia of gerontology* (Vol. 1). San Diego: Academic Press.

Luque, J. M., Gimenez, Y., & Ribotta, M. (2004). Neural stem cells and the quest for restorative neurology. *Histology and Histopathology, 19,* 271–280.

Luria, A., & Herzog, E. (1985, April). *Gender segregation across and within settings.* Paper presented at the biennial meeting of the Society for Research in Child Development, Toronto.

Luster, T., & Okaghi, L. (Eds.) (2005). *Parenting: An ecological perspective* (2nd ed.). Mahwah, NJ: Erlbaum.

Luszcz, M., & Giles, L. (2002). Benefits of close social relationships for health and longevity of older adults. *International Society for the Study of Behavioural Development Newsletter* (1, Serial No. 41), 15–16.

Lyke, J., & Colon, M. (2004). Practical recommendations for ethnically and racially sensitive hospice services. *American Journal of Hospice and Palliative Care, 21,* 131–133.

Lyndaker, C., & Hulton, L. (2004). The influence of age on symptoms of perimenopause. *Journal of Obstetric, Gynecological, and Neonatal Nursing, 33,* 340–347.

Lynn, R. (1996). Racial and ethnic differences in intelligence in the U.S. on the

Differential Ability Scale. *Personality and Individual Differences, 26,* 271–273.

Lyon, T. D., & Flavell, J. H. (1993). Young children's understanding of forgetting over time. *Child Development, 64,* 789–800.

Lyons, G. R. (1995). Toward a definition of dyslexia. *Annals of Dyslexia, 45,* 3–27.

Maccoby, E. E. (1984). Middle childhood in the context of the family. In *Development during middle childhood.* Washington, DC: National Academy Press.

Maccoby, E. E. (1987, November). Interview with Elizabeth Hall: All in the family. *Psychology Today,* pp. 54–60.

Maccoby, E. E. (1992). The role of parents in the socialization of children: An historical overview. *Developmental Psychology, 28,* 1006–1018.

Maccoby, E. E. (1998). The two sexes: Growing up apart, coming together. Cambridge, MA: Harvard University Press.

Maccoby, E. E. (2002). Gender and group processes. *Current Directions in Psychological Science, 11,* 54–58.

Maccoby, E. E. (2002). Parenting effects. In J. G. Borkowski, S. L. Ramey, & M. Bristol-Power (Eds.), *Parenting and the child's world.* Mahwah, NJ: Erlbaum.

Maccoby, E. E. (2003). The gender of child and parent as factors in family dynamics. In A. C. Crouter & A. Booth (Eds.), *Children's influence on family dynamics.* Mahwah, NJ: Erlbaum.

Maccoby, E. E., & Jacklin, C. N. (1974). *The psychology of sex differences.* Palo Alto, CA: Stanford University Press.

Maccoby, E. E., & Lewis, C. C. (2003). Less daycare or better daycare? *Child Development, 74,* 1069–1075.

Maccoby, E. E., & Mnookin, R. H. (1992). *Dividing the child: Social and legal dilemmas of custody.* Cambridge, MA: Harvard University Press.

MacDorman, M. F., Minino, A. M., Strobino, D. M., & Guyer, B. (2002). Annual summary of vital statistics—2001. *Pediatrics, 110,* 1037–1052.

MacFarlane, J. A. (1975). Olfaction in the development of social preferences in the human neonate. In *Parent-infant interaction,* Ciba Foundation Symposium No. 33. Amsterdam: Elsevier.

MacGeorge, E. L. (2003). Gender differences in attributions and emotions in helping contexts. *Sex Roles, 48,* 175–182.

MacGeorge, E. L., Graves, A. R., Feng, B., Gillihan, S. J., & Burleson, B. R. (2004). The myth of gender cultures: Similarities outweigh differences in men's and women's provisions and responses to supportive communication. *Sex Roles, 50,* 143–175.

Macias, C., Jonees, D., Harvey, J., Barreira, P., Harding, C., & Rodican, C. (2004). Bereavement in the context of serious mental illness. *Psychiatric Services, 55,* 421–426.

Maciokas, J. B., & Crognale, M. A. (2003). Cognitive and attentional changes with age: Evidence from attentional blink deficits. *Experimental Aging Research, 29,* 137–153.

MacLean, W. E. (2000). Down syndrome. In A. Kazdin (Ed.), *Encyclopedia of psychology.* Washington, DC, & New York: American Psychological Association and Oxford University Press.

MacWhinney, B. (2005). Language development. In M. H. Bornstein & M. E. Lamb (Eds.), *Developmental psychology* (6th ed.). Mahwah, NJ: Erlbaum.

Madden, D. J. (2001). Speed and timing of behavioral processes. In J. E. Birren & K. W. Schaie (Eds.), *Handbook of the psychology of aging* (5th ed.). San Diego: Academic Press.

Madden, D. J., & others. (1999). Aging and recognition memory: Changes in regional cerebral blood flow associated with components of reaction time distributions. *Journal of Cognitive Neuroscience, 11,* 511–520.

Maddi, S. (1998). Hardiness. In H. S. Friedman (Ed.), *Encyclopedia of mental health* (Vol. 3). San Diego: Academic Press.

Magnuson, K. A., & Duncan, G. J. (2002). Parents in poverty. In M. H. Bornstein (Ed.), *Handbook of parenting* (2nd ed., Vol. 4). Mahwah, NJ: Erlbaum.

Magnuson, K., & Duncan, G. (2004). Parent- vs. child-based intervention strategies for promoting children's well-being. In A. Kalil & T. DeLeire (Eds.), *Family investments in children's potential.* Mahwah, NJ: Erlbaum.

Magwere, T., Chapman, T., & Partridge, L. (2004). Sex differences in the effect of dietary restriction on lifespan and mortality rates in female and male *Drosophila Melanogaster. Journals of Gerontology A: Biological Sciences and Medical Sciences, 59,* B3–B9.

Mahler, M. (1979). *Separation-individuation* (Vol. 2). London: Jason Aronson.

Maidment, I. D. (2003). Efficacy of stimulants in adult ADHD. *Annals of Pharmacotherapy, 37,* 1884–1890.

Main, M. (2000). Attachment theory. In A. Kazdin (Ed.), *Encyclopedia of psychology.* Washington, DC, & New York: American Psychological Association and Oxford University Press.

Majumdar, I., Paul, P., Talib, V. H., & Ranga, S. (2003). The effect of iron therapy on the growth of iron-replete and iron-deplete children. *Journal of Tropical Pediatrics, 49,* 84–88.

Makrides, M., Neumann, M., Simmer, K., Pater, J., & Gibson, R. (1995). Are long-chain polyunsaturated fatty acids essential nutrients in infancy? *Lancet, 345,* 1463–1468.

Malinosky-Rummell, R., & Hansen, D. J. (1993). Long-term consequences of childhood physical abuse. *Psychological Bulletin, 114,* 68–79.

Malley-Morrison, K. (Ed.). (2004). *International perspectives on family violence and abuse.* Mahwah, NJ: Erlbaum.

Malmgren, K. W., & Meisel, S. M. (2004). Examining the link between child maltreatment and delinquency for youth with emotional and behavioral disorders. *Child Welfare, 83,* 175–188.

Mandler, J. M. (2000). Perceptual and conceptual processes in infancy. *Journal of Cognition and Development, 1,* 3–36.

Mandler, J. M. (2003). Conceptual categorization. In D. Rakison & L. M. Oakes (Eds.), *Early category and concept development.* New York: Oxford University Press.

Mandler, J. M. (2004). *The origins of mind.* New York: Oxford University Press.

Mandler, J. M., & McDonough, L. (1995). Long-term recall in infancy. *Journal of Experimental Child Psychology, 59,* 457–474.

Manev, R., & Manvev, H. (2005). The meaning of mammalian adult neurogenesis and the function of newly added neurons: The "small-world" network. *Medical Hypotheses, 64,* 114–117.

Mannell, R. C. (2000). Older adults, leisure, and wellness. *Journal of Leisurability, 26,* 3–10.

Mannell, R. C., & Dupuis, S. (1996). Life satisfaction. In J. E. Birren (Ed.), *Encyclopedia of gerontology* (Vol. 2). San Diego: Academic Press.

Mannessier, L., Alie-Daram, S., Roubinet, F., & Brossard, Y. (2000). Prevention of fetal hemolytic disease: It is time to take action. Transfusions in *Clinical Biology, 7,* 527–532.

Manning, W. D., & Smock, P. J. (2002). First comes cohabitation and then comes marriage. *Journal of Family Issues, 23,* 1065–1087.

Manor, O., & Eisenbach, Z. (2003). Mortality after spousal loss: Are there sociodemographic differences? *Social Science and Medicine, 56,* 405–413.

Manton, K. G., Corder, L., & Stallard, E. (1997, March 18). Chronic disability in elderly United States populations, 1982–1994. *Proceedings of the National Academy of Sciences, 94,* 2593–2598.

Manton, K. I. (1989). The stress-buffering role of spiritual support: Cross-sectional and prospective investigations. *Journal for the Scientific Study of Religion, 28,* 310–323.

Maracek, J., Kimmel, E. B., Crawford, M. E., & Hare-Muston, R. (2003). Psychology of women and gender. In I. B. Weiner (Ed.), *Handbook of psychology* (Vol. I). New York: Wiley.

Marcell, J. J. (2003). Sarcopenia: Causes, consequences, and preventions. *Journals of Gerontology A: Biological and Medical Sciences,* M911–M916.

Marchman, V. (2003). Review of J. W. Santrock's *Child development* (10th ed.). New York: McGraw-Hill.

Marchman, V., & Thal, D. (2005). Words and grammar. In M. Tomasello & D. I. Slobin (Eds.), *Beyond nature-nurture.* Mahwah, NJ: Erlbaum.

Marcia, J. E. (1980). Ego identity development. In J. Adelson (Ed.), *Handbook of adolescent psychology.* New York: Wiley.

Marcia, J. E. (1994). The empirical study of ego identity. In H. A. Bosma, T. L. G. Graafsma, H. D. Grotevant, & D. J. De Levita (Eds.), *Identity and development.* Newbury Park, CA: Sage.

Marcia, J. E. (2002). Identity and psychosocial development in adulthood. *Identity, 2,* 7–28.

Marcovitch, H. (2004). Use of stimulants for attention deficit hyperactivity disorder: AGAINST. *British Medical Journal, 329,* 908–909.

Marcus, D. L., Mulrine, A., & Wong, K. (1999, September 13). How kids learn. *U.S. News & World Report,* pp. 44–50.

Marecek, J., Finn, S. E., & Cardell, M. (1988). Gender roles in the relationships of lesbians and gay men. In J. P. De Cecco (Ed.), *Gay relationships.* New York: Harrington Park Press.

Margolin, L. (1994). Child sexual abuse by uncles. *Child Abuse & Neglect, 18,* 215–224.

Marild, S., Hansson, S., Jodal, U., Oden, A., & Svedberg, K. (2004). Protective effect of breastfeeding against urinary tract infection. *Acta Pediatrics, 93,* 164–168.

Markides, K. S. (1995). Aging and ethnicity. *Gerontologist, 35,* 276–277.

Markides, K. S., & Rudkin, L. (1996). Race and ethnic diversity. In J. E. Birren (Ed.), *Encyclopedia of gerontology* (Vol. 2). San Diego: Academic Press.

Markman, H. J. (2000). Marriage. In A. Kazdin (Ed.), *Encyclopedia of psychology.* Washington, DC, & New York: American Psychological Association and Oxford University Press.

Markowitz, M. (2000). Lead poisoning. *Pediatrics in Review, 21,* 327–335.

Markson, E. W. (1995). Older women: The silent majority? *Gerontologist, 35,* 278–281.

Markus, H. R., Ryff, C. D., Curhan, K., & Palmersheim, K. (2004). In their own words: Well-being among high school and college-educated adults. In G. Brim, C. D. Ryff, & R. Kessler (Eds.), *How healthy we are: A national study of well-being in midlife.* Chicago: University of Chicago Press.

Marshall, N. L. (2004). The quality of early child care and children's development. *Current Directions in Psychological Science, 13,* 165–168.

Marsiglio, W. (2004). When stepfathers claim children: A conceptual analysis. *Journal of Marriage and the Family, 66,* 22–39.

Marsiske, M., Klumb, P. L., & Baltes, M. M. (1997). Everyday activity patterns and sensory functioning in old age. *Psychology and Aging, 12,* 444–457.

Marsiske, M., Lang, F. R., Baltes, M. M., & Baltes, P. B. (1995). Selective optimization with compensation: Life-span perspectives on successful human development. In R. A. Dixon & L. Bäckman (Eds.), *Compensating for psychological deficits and declines: Managing losses and promoting gains* (pp. 35–79). Hillsdale, NJ: Erlbaum.

Martin, C. L., & Dinella, L. (2001). Gender development: Gender schema theory. In J. Worrell (Ed.), *Encyclopedia of women and gender.* San Diego: Academic Press.

Martin, C. L., & Fabes, R. A. (2001). The stability and consequences of young children's same-sex peer interactions. *Developmental Psychology, 37,* 431–446.

Martin, C. L., & Halverson, C. F. (1981). A schematic processing model of sex typing and stereotyping in children. *Child Development, 52,* 1119–1134.

Martin, C. L., & Ruble, D. (2004). Children's search for gender cues. *Current Directions in Psychological Science, 13,* 67–70.

Martin, E. D., & Sher, K. J. (1994). Family history of alcoholism, alcohol use disorders, and the five-factor model of personality. *Journal of Studies in Alcohol, 55,* 81–90.

Martin, J. A., & Buckwalter, J. A. (2001). Biomarkers of aging. *Journal of Gerontology, 56A* (No. 4), B172–B179.

Martin, M. T., Emery, R., & Peris, T. S. (2004). Children and parents in single-parent families. In M. Coleman & L. Ganong (Eds.), *Handbook of contemporary families.* Thousand Oaks, CA: Sage.

Martinez, E., & Halgunseth, L. (2004). Hispanics/Latinos. In M. Coleman & L. Ganong (Eds.), *Handbook of contemporary families.* Thousand Oaks, CA: Sage.

Marzano, R. J., Pickering, D. J., & Pollock, J. E. (2005). *Classroom instruction that works.* Boston: Allyn & Bacon.

Mason, J. A., & Hermann, K. R. (1998). Universal infant hearing screening by automated auditory brainstem response measurement. *Pediatrics, 101,* 221–228.

Masten, A. S. (2004). Regulatory processes, risk, and resilience in adolescent development. *Annals of the New York Academy of Sciences, 1021,* 310–319.

Matheny, A. P., & Phillips, K. (2001). Temperament and context: Correlates of home environment with temperament continuity and change. In T. D. Wachs & G. A. Kohnstamm (Eds.), *Temperament in context.* Mahwah, NJ: Erlbaum.

Mathew, J. L. (2004). Effect of maternal antibiotics on breast feeding infants. *Postgraduate Medical Journal, 80,* 196–200.

Mathews, F., Youngman, L., & Neil, A. (2004). Maternal circulating nutrient concentrations in pregnancy: Implications for birth and placental weights of term infants. *American Journal of Clinical Nutrition, 79,* 103–110.

Mathews, T. J., Menacker, F., & Mac-Dorman, M. F. (2003). Infant mortality statistics from the 2001 period linked birth/infant death data set. *National Vital Statistics Reports, 52,* 1–28.

Matlin, M. W. (2004). *The psychology of women* (5th ed.). Belmont, CA: Wadsworth.

Matsumoto, D. (2004). *Culture and psychology* (3rd ed.). Belmont, CA: Wadsworth.

Matthias, R. F., Lubben, J. E., Atchison, K. A., & Schweitzer, S. O. (1997). Sexual activity and satisfaction among very old adults: Results from a community-dwelling Medicare population survey. *Gerontologist, 37,* 6–14.

Matusov, E., Bell, N., & Rogoff, B. (2001). *Schooling as cultural process: Working together and guidance by children from schools differing in collaborative practices.* Unpublished manuscript, University of Delaware.

Matzo, M. L., Sherman, D. W., Lo, K., Egan, K. A., Grant, M., & Rhome, A. (2003). Strategies for teaching loss, grief, and bereavement. *Nursing Education, 28,* 71–76.

Matzo, M. L., Sherman, D. W., Nelson-Marten, P., Rhome, A., & Grant, M. (2004). Ethical and legal issues in end-of-life care: End-of-life nursing education consortium curriculum and teaching strategies. *Journal for Nurses in Staff Development, 20,* 59–66.

Maughan, A., & Cicchetti, D. (2002). Impact of child maltreatment and interadult violence on children's emotion regulation difficulties and socioemotional adjustment. *Child Development, 73,* 1525–1542.

Maulik, D. (2003). New directions in prenatal care. *Journal of Maternal, Fetal, and Neonatal Medicine, 13,* 361.

Maurer, D. (2001, April). *Variations in plasticity in visual development.* Paper presented at the meeting of the Society for Research in Child Development, Minneapolis.

Maurer, D., & Salapatek, P. (1976). Developmental changes in the scanning of faces by young infants. *Child Development, 47,* 523–527.

Mauro, V. P., Wood, I. C., Krushel, L., Crossin, K. L., & Edelman, G. M. (1994). Cell adhesion alters gene transcription in chicken embryo brain cells and mouse embryonal carcinoma cells. *Proceedings of the National Academy of Sciences USA, 91,* 2868–2872.

Maxson, S. (2003). Behavioral genetics. In I. B. Weiner (Ed.), *Encyclopedia of psychology* (Vol. III). New York: Wiley.

May, E. L. (2004). Looking for work? How to use your age as an asset. *Healthcare Executive, 19,* 8–10, 12, 14–15.

May, V., Onarcan, M., Oleschowski, C., & Mayron, Z. (2004). International perspectives on the role of home care and hospice in aging and long-term care. *Caring, 23,* 14–17.

Mayer, R. E. (2003). Memory and information processes. In I. B. Weiner (Ed.), *Handbook of psychology* (Vol. VII). New York: Wiley.

Mayer, R. E. (2004). Teaching of subject matter. *Annual Review of Psychology* (Vol. 55). Palo Alto, CA: Annual Reviews.

Mayes, L. (2003). Unpublished review of J. W. Santrock's *Topical life-span development* (2nd ed.). New York: McGraw-Hill.

Mayo Clinic (2004). *Special diets.* Rochester, MN: Author.

McAdams, D. P. (2001). Generativity in midlife. In M. E. Lachman (Ed.), *Handbook of midlife development.* New York: Wiley.

McAdoo, H. P. (Ed.). (1999). *Family ethnicity* (2nd ed.). Newbury Park, CA: Sage.

McAdoo, H. P. (2002). African-American parenting. In M. H. Bornstein (Ed.), *Handbook of parenting* (2nd ed.). Mahwah, NJ: Erlbaum.

McAuley, E., Kramer, A. F., & Colcombe, S. J. (2004). Cardiovascular fitness and neurocognitive function in older adults: A brief review. *Brain, Behavior, and Immunity, 18,* 214–220.

McCall, R. B., & Carriger, M. S. (1993). A meta-analysis of infant habituation and recognition memory performance as predictors of later IQ. *Child Development, 64,* 57–79.

McCartney, K. (2003, July 16). Interview with Kathleen McCartney. In A. Bucuvalas, Child care and behavior. *HGSE News,* pp. 1–4. Cambridge, MA: Harvard Graduate School of Education.

McCarty, M. E., & Ashmead, D. H. (1999). Visual control of reaching and grasping in infants. *Developmental Psychology, 35,* 620–631.

McClain, C. S., Rosenfeld, B., & Breitbart, W. S. (2003, March). *The influence of spirituality on end-of-life despair in cancer patients close to death.* Paper presented at the meeting of American Psychosomatic Society, Phoenix.

McClearn, G. E. (2004). Nature and nurture: Interaction and coaction. *American Journal of Medical Genetics, 124B,* 124–130.

McClellan, M. D. (2004, February 9). Captain Fantastic: The interview. *Celtic Nation,* pp. 1–9.

McCombs, B. L. (2003). Research to policy for guiding educational reform. In I. B. Weiner (Ed.), *Handbook of psychology* (Vol. 7). New York: Wiley.

McCormick, C. B. (2003). Metacognition and learning. In I. B. Weiner (Ed.), *Handbook of psychology* (Vol. VII). New York: Wiley.

McCormick, M. C. (2001). Prenatal care—necessary, but not sufficient. *Health Services Research, 36,* 399–403.

McCoy, R. C., Hunt, C. E., Lesko, S. M., Vezina, R., Corwin, M. J., Willinger, M., Hoffman, H. J., & Mitchell, A. A. (2004). Frequency of bed sharing and its relationship to breastfeeding. *Journal of Developmental and Behavioral Pediatrics, 25,* 141–149.

McCoy, S. J., Beal, J. M., & Watson, G. H. (2003). Endocrine factors and postpartum depression: A selected review. *Journal of Reproductive Medicine, 48,* 402–408.

McCrae, R. R. (2001). Traits through time. *Psychological Inquiry, 12,* 85–87.

McCrae, R. R., & Costa, P. T. (1990). *Personality in adulthood.* New York: Guilford.

McCrae, R. R., & Costa, P. T. (2003). *Personality in adulthood* (2nd ed.). New York: Guilford.

McCrae, R. R., Costa, P. T., Lima, M. P., Simoes, A., Ostendorf, F., et al. (1999). Age differences in personality across the adult lifespan: Parallels in five cultures. *Developmental Psychology, 35,* 466–477.

McCullough, M. E. (1995). Prayer and health: Conceptual issues, research review, and research agenda. *Journal of Psychology and Theology, 23,* 15–29.

McCullough, M. E., Hoyt, W. T., Larson, D. B., Koenig, H. G., & Thoresen, C. (2000). Religious involvement and mortality: A meta-analytic review. *Health psychology, 19,* 211–222.

McDaniel, M. A., Einstein, G. O., Stout, A. C., & Morgan, Z. (2003). Aging and maintaining intentions over delays: Do it or lose it. *Psychology and Aging, 18,* 823–835.

McDougall, G. J. (2004). Memory's self-efficacy and memory performance among black and white elders. *Nursing Research, 53,* 323–331.

McDougall, G. J., Strauss, M. E., Holston, E. C., & Martin, M. (1999, November). *Memory self-efficacy and memory-anxiety as predictors of memory performance in at-risk elderly.* Paper presented at the meeting of the Gerontological Society of America, San Francisco.

McDowd, J. M., Filion, D. L., Pohl, P. S., Richards, L. G., & Stiers, W. (2003). Attentional abilities and functional outcomes following a stroke. *Journals of Gerontology B: Psychological Sciences and Social Sciences, 58,* P45–P53.

McElhaney, J. E. (2002). Nutrition, exercise, and influenza vaccination. *Journals of Gerontology A: Biological Sciences and Medical Sciences, 57,* M555–M556.

McFarlane, T., Polivy, J., & Herman, C. P. (1998). Dieting. In H. S. Friedman (Ed.),

Encyclopedia of mental health (Vol. 1). San Diego: Academic Press.

McGavock, J. M., Eves, N. D., Mandie, S., Glenn, N. M., Quinney, H. A., & Haykowsky, M. J. (2004). The role of exercise in the treatment of cardiovascular disease associated with type 2 diabetes mellitus. *Sports Medicine, 34,* 27–48.

McGrath, S., Kennell, J., Suresh, M., Moise, K., & Hinkley, C. (1999, May). *Doula support vs. epidural analgesia: Impact on cesarean rates.* Paper presented at the meeting of the Society for Pediatric Research, San Francisco.

McGregor, K. K. (2004). Developmental dependencies between lexical semantics and reading. In C. A. Stone, E. R. Silliman, B. J. Ehren, & K. Apel (Eds.), *Handbook of language and literacy.* New York: Guilford.

McGuire, F. (2000). What do we know? Not much. The state of leisure and aging research. *Journal of Leisurability, 26,* 97–100.

McGuire, L., Kiecolt-Glaser, J. K., & Glaser, R. (2002). Depressive symptoms and lymphocyte proliferation in older adults. *Journal of Abnormal Psychology, 111,* 192–197.

McGuire, S. (2001). Are behavioral genetic and socialization research compatible? *American Psychologist, 56,* 171.

McHale, J. P., Johnson, D., & Sinclair, R. (1999). Family dynamics, preschoolers' family representations, and preschool peer relationships. *Early Education and Development, 10,* 373–401.

McHale, J. P., Khazan, I., Erera, P., Rotman, T., DeCourcey, W., & McConnell, M. (2002). Coparenting in diverse family systems. In M. H. Bornstein (Ed.), *Handbook of parenting* (2nd ed., Vol. 3). Mahwah, NJ: Erlbaum.

McHale, J. P., Kuersten-Hogan, R., & Rao, N. (2004). Growing points for coparenting theory and research. *Journal of Adult Development, 11,* 221–234.

McHale, J. P., Luretti, A., Talbot, J., & Pouquette, C. (2001). Retrospect and prospect in the psychological study of marital and couple relationships. In J. P. McHale & W. S. Grolnick (Eds.), *Retrospect and prospect in the psychological study of families.* Mahwah, NJ: Erlbaum.

McHale, S. M., Crouter, A. C., & Whiteman, S. D. (2003). The family contexts of gender development in childhood and adolescence. *Social Development, 12,* 125–152.

McKain, W. C. (1972). A new look at older marriages. *The Family Coordinator, 21,* 61–69.

McKellar, J., Stewart, E., & Humphreys, K. (2003). Alcoholics Anonymous involvement and positive alcohol-related outcomes. *Journal of Consulting and Clinical Psychology, 71,* 302–308.

McKenna, J. J., Mosko, S. S., & Richard, C. A. (1997). Bedsharing promotes breastfeeding. *Pediatrics, 100,* 214–219.

McKnight, A. J., & McKnight, A. S. (1993). The effect of cellular phone use upon driver attention. *Accident Analysis and Prevention, 25,* 259–265.

McLaughlin, K. (2003, December 30). Commentary in "Nurse K. Painter, Nurse dispenses dignity for dying." *USA Today,* Section D, pp. 1–2.

McLearn, K. T. (2004). Narrowing the income gaps in preventive care for young children: Families in healthy steps. *Journal of Urban Health, 81,* 556–567.

McLeod, J. D. (1996). Life events. In J. E. Birren (Ed.), *Encyclopedia of gerontology* (Vol. 1). San Diego: Academic Press.

McLoyd, V. C. (1998). Children in poverty: Development, public policy, and practice. In W. Damon (Ed.), *Handbook of child psychology* (5th ed., Vol. 4). New York: Wiley.

McLoyd, V. C. (1999). Cultural influences in a multicultural society: Conceptual and methodological issues. In A. S. Masten (Ed.), *Cultural processes in child development.* Mahwah, NJ: Erlbaum.

McLoyd, V. C. (2000). Poverty. In A. Kazdin (Ed.), *Encyclopedia of psychology.* Washington, DC, & New York: American Psychological Association and Oxford University Press.

McLoyd, V. C. (2005). Pathways to academic achievement among children from immigrant families: A commentary. In C. R. Cooper, C. T. G. Coll, W. T. Bartko, H. M. Davis, & C. Chatman (Eds.), *Developmental pathways through middle childhood.* Mahwah, NJ: Erlbaum.

McLoyd, V. C., & Smith, J. (2002). Physical discipline and behavior problems in African American, European American, and Hispanic children: Emotional support as a moderator. *Journal of Marriage and Family, 64,* 40–53.

McMillan, J. H. (2004). *Educational research* (4th ed.). Boston: Allyn & Bacon.

McMullin, J. A., & Marshall, V. W. (2001). Ageism, age relations, and garment industry work in Montreal. *The Gerontologist, 41* (No. 1), 111–119.

McNamara, F., & Sullivan, C. E. (2000). Obstructive sleep apnea in infants. *Journal of Pediatrics, 136,* 318–323.

McTigue, K. M., Garrett, J. M., & Popkin, B. M. (2002). The natural history of the development of obesity in a cohort of young U.S. adults between 1981 and 1998. *Annals of Internal Medicine, 136,* 857–864.

McVeigh, C. A., Baafi, M., & Williamson, B. (2002). Functional status after fatherhood: An Australian study. *Journal of Obstetrics, Gynecology, and Neonatal Nursing, 31,* 165–171.

Means, C., Adrienne, J., Snyder, D. K., & Negy, C. (2003). Assessing nontraditional couples. *Journal of Marital and Family Therapy, 29,* 69–83.

Mearns, S. (2000). The impact of loss on adolescents: Developing appropriate support. *International Journal of Palliative Nursing, 6,* 12–17.

Mecocci, P., Olidori, M. C., Troiano, L., Cherubin, A., Cecchetti, R., Pini, G., Straatman, M., Monti, D., Stahl, W., Sies, W., Franceschi, C., & Senin, U. (2000). Plasma antioxidants and longevity: A study on healthy centenarians. *Free Radical Biology and Medicine, 28,* 1243–1248.

MedLine Plus (2004). *Medical encyclopedia.* Available on the Internet at: www.nim.nih.gov/medlineplus/ency/.

Meghani, S. H. (2004). A concept analysis of palliative care in the United States. *Journal of Advanced Nursing, 46,* 152–161.

Meguro, K., Shimada, M., Yamaguchi, S., Sano, I., Inagaki, H., Matsushita, M., Sekita, Y., & Mori, E. (2004). Neuropsychological features of mild Alzheimer's disease (CDR 0.5) and progression to dementia in a community: The Tajiri Project. *Journal of Geriatric Psychiatry, 17,* 183–189.

Mehra, S., & Agrawal, D. (2004). Adolescent health determinants for pregnancy and child health outcomes among the urban poor. *Indian Pediatrics, 41,* 137–145.

Meier, P. P., Engstrom, J. L., Mingolelli, S. S., Miracle, D. J., & Kiesling, S. (2004). The Rush Mother's Milk Club: Breastfeeding interventions for mothers with very low birth weight infants. *Journal of Obstetrical, Gynecologic, and Neonatal Nursing, 33,* 164–174.

Mein, J. K., Palmer, C. M., Shand, M. C., Templeton, D. J., Parekh, V., Mobbs, M., Haig, K., Huffam, S. E., & Young, L. (2003). Management of acute sexual assault. *Medical Journal of Australia, 178,* 226–230.

Meis, P. J., & Peaceman, A. M. (2003). Prevention of recurrent preterm delivery by 17-alpha-hydroxyprogesterone caproate. *New England Journal of Medicine, 348,* 2379–2385.

Melton, L. J., Johnell, O., Lau, E., Mautalen, C. A., & Seeman, E. (2004). Osteoporosis and the global competition for health care resources. *Journal of Bone and Mineral Resources, 19,* 1055–1058.

Meltzoff, A. N. (1988). Infant imitation and memory: Nine-month-old infants in immediate and deferred tests. *Child Development, 59,* 217–225.

Meltzoff, A. N. (2000). Learning and cognitive development. In A. Kazdin (Ed.), *Encyclopedia of psychology.* Washington, DC, & New York: American Psychological Association and Oxford University Press.

Meltzoff, A. N. (2002). Elements of a developmental theory of imitation. In A. N. Meltzoff & W. Prinz (Eds.), *The imitative mind: Development, evolution, and brain bases.* New York: Cambridge University Press.

Meltzoff, A. N. (2004). Imitation as a mechanism of social cognition: Origins of empathy, theory of mind, and the representation of action. In U. Goswami (Ed.), *Blackwell handbook of childhood cognitive development.* Malden, MA: Blackwell.

Meltzoff, A. N., & Gopnik, A. (1997). *Words, thoughts, and theories.* Cambridge, MA: MIT Press.

Meltzoff, A. N., & Moore, M. K. (1999). A new foundation for cognitive development in infancy: The birth of the representational infant. In E. K. Skolnick, K. Nelson, S. A. Gelman, & P. H. Miller (Eds.), *Conceptual development.* Mahwah, NJ: Erlbaum.

Memmler, R. L., Cohen, B. J., Wood, D. L., & Schweglr, J. (1995). *The human body in health and disease* (8th ed.). Philadelphia: Lippincott Williams & Wilkins.

Menec, V. H. (2003). The relation between everyday activities and successful aging: A six-year longitudinal study. *Journals of Gerontology B: Psychological Sciences and Social Sciences, 58,* S74–S82.

Menec, V. H., MacWilliam, L., & Aoki, F. Y. (2002). Hospitalizations and death due to respiratory illnesses during influenza seasons: A comparison of community residents, senior housing residents, and nursing home residents. *Journals of Gerontology A: Biological Sciences and Medical Sciences, 57,* M629–M635.

Ment, L. R., Vohr, B., Allan, W., Katz, K. H., Schneider, C., Westerveld, M., Duncan, C. C., & Makuch, R. W. (2003). Change in cognitive function over time in very low-birthweight infants. *Journal of the American Medical Association, 289,* 705–711.

Menyuk, P., Liebergott, J., & Schultz, M. (1995). *Early language development in full-term and premature infants.* Hillsdale, NJ: Erlbaum.

Meredith, N.V. (1978). Research between 1960 and 1970 on the standing height of young children in different parts of the world. In H. W. Reece & L. P. Lipsitt (Eds.), *Advances in child development and behavior* (Vol. 12). New York: Academic Press.

Merrick, J., Aspler, S., & Schwartz, G. (2001). Should adults with phenylketonuria have diet treatment? *Mental Retardation, 39,* 215–217.

Merrill, S. S., & Verbrugge, L. M. (1999). Health and disease in midlife. In S. L. Willis & J. D. Reid (Eds.), *Life in the middle: Psychological and social development in middle age.* San Diego: Academic Press.

Merry, B. J. (2004). Oxidative stress and mitochondrial function with aging—the effects of calorie restriction. *Aging Cell, 3,* 7–12.

Metts, S. (2004). First sexual involvement in romantic relationships. In J. H. Harvey, A. Wenzel, & S. Sprecher (Eds.), *The handbook of sexuality in close relationships.* Mahwah, NJ: Erlbaum.

Meyer, I. H. (2003). Prejudice, social stress, and mental health in gay, lesbian, and bisexual populations: Conceptual issues and research evidence. *Psychological Bulletin, 129,* 674–697.

Mhatre, M. C., Fernandes, G., & Ticku, M. K. (1991). Aging reduces the mRNA of alpha 1 GABAA receptor subunit in rat cerebral cortex. *European Journal of Pharmacology, 208,* 171–174.

Michael, R. (2004). Family influences on children's verbal ability. In A. Kalil & T. DeLeire (Eds.), *Family investments in children's potential.* Mahwah, NJ: Erlbaum.

Michael, R. T., Gagnon, J. H., Laumann, E. O., & Kolata, G. (1994). *Sex in America.* Boston: Little, Brown.

Michael, S. T., Crowther, M. R., & Allen, R. S. (2003). Widowhood and spirituality: Coping responses to bereavement. *Journal of Women and Aging, 15,* 145–165.

Michel, G. L. (1981). Right-handedness: A consequence of infant supine head-orientation preference? *Science, 212,* 685–687.

Michel, R. S. (2000). Toilet training. *Pediatric Review, 20,* 240–245.

Miller, B. C., Fan, X., Christensen, M., Grotevant, H. D., & von Dulmen, M. (2000). Comparisons of adopted and non-adopted adolescents in a large, nationally representative sample. *Child Development, 71,* 1458–1473.

Miller, E. R., Pastor-Barriuso, R., Dalal, D., Riemersma, R. A., Appel, L. J., & Guallar, E. (2005, in press). Meta-analysis: High-dosage vitamin E supplementation may increase all-cause mortality. *Annals of Internal Medicine.*

Miller, J. B. (1986). *Toward a new psychology of women* (2nd ed.). Boston: Beacon Press.

Miller, J. G. (1995, March). *Culture, context, and personal agency: The cultural grounding of self and morality.* Paper presented at the meeting of the Society for Research in Child Development, Indianapolis.

Miller, J. G. (2005). Insights into moral development from cultural psychology. In M. Killen & J. Smetana (Eds.), *Handbook of moral development.* Mahwah, NJ: Erlbaum.

Miller, P. H. (2001). *Theories of developmental psychology* (4th ed.). New York: Worth.

Miller, P. H., & Seier, W. L. (1994). Strategy utilization deficiencies in children: When, where, and why. In H. W. Reese (Ed.), *Advances in child development and behavior* (Vol. 24). New York: Academic Press.

Miller-Day, M. A. (2004). *Communication among grandmothers, mothers, and adult daughters.* Mahwah, NJ: Erlbaum.

Miller-Johnson, S., Coie, J., & Malone, P. S. (2003). *Do aggression and peer rejection in childhood predict early adult outcomes?* Paper presented at the meeting of the Society for Research in Child Development, Tampa, FL.

Miller-Jones, D. (1989). Culture and testing. *American Psychologist, 44,* 360–366.

Minns, R. A., & Busuttil, A. (2004). Patterns of presentation of the shaken baby syndrome: Four types of inflicted brain injury predominate. *British Medical Journal, 328,* 766.

Minuchin, P. (2001). Looking toward the horizon: Present and future in the study of family systems. In J. P. McHale & W. S. Grolnick (Eds.), *Retrospect and prospect in the psychological study of families.* Mahwah, NJ: Erlbaum.

Minuchin, P. O., & Shapiro, E. K. (1983). The school as a context for social development. In P. H. Mussen (Ed.), *Handbook of child psychology* (4th ed., Vol. 4). New York: Wiley.

Mischel, W. (2004). Toward an integrative science of the person. *Annual Review of Psychology* (Vol. 55). Palo Alto, CA: Annual Reviews.

Misra, A., Arora, N., Mondal, S., Pandey, R. M., Jailkhani, B., Peshin, S., Chaudhary, D., Saluja, T., Singh, P., Chandra, S., Luithra, K., & Vikram, N. K. (2001). Relation between plasma leptin and anthropometric and metabolic covarites in lean and obese diabetic and hyperlipdaemic Asian Northern Indian subjects. *Diabetes, Nutrition, and Metabolism, 14,* 18–26.

Missonnier, P., Gold, G., Leonards, U., Costa-Fazio, L., Michel, J. P., Ibanez, V., & Giannakiopoulos, P. (2004). Aging and working memory: Early deficits in EEG activation of posterior cortical areas. *Journal of Neural Transmission, 111,* 1141–1154.

Mitchell, E. A., Stewart, A. W., Crampton, P., & Salmond, C. (2000). Deprivation and sudden infant death syndrome. *Social Science and Medicine, 51,* 147–150.

Mitchell, K. S., & Mazzeo, S. E. (2004). Binge eating and psychological distress in ethnically diverse undergraduate men and women. *Eating Behavior, 5,* 157–169.

Mitchell, M., & Catron, G. (2002). Teaching grief and bereavement: Involving support groups in educating student midwives. *The Practicing Midwife, 5,* 26–27.

Mitchell, M. L., & Jolley, H. M. (2004). *Research design* (5th ed.). Belmont, CA: Wadsworth.

Mitchell, V., & Helson, R. (1990). Women's prime of life: Is it the 50s? *Psychology of Women Quarterly, 14,* 451–470.

Modell, J., & Elder, G. H. (2002). Child development in history: So what's new? In W. W. Hartup & R. A. Weinberg (Eds.), *Child psychology in retrospect and prospect.* Mahwah, NJ: Erlbaum.

Moen, P. (1998). Recasting careers: Changing reference groups, risks, and realities. *Generations, 22,* 40–45.

Moen, P., & Quick, H. E. (1998). Retirement. In H. S. Friedman (Ed.), *Encyclopedia of mental health* (Vol. 3). San Diego: Academic Press.

Moen, P., & Wethington, E. (1999). Midlife development in a life course context. In S. L. Willis & J. D. Reid (Eds.), *Life in the middle: Psychological and social development in middle age.* San Diego: Academic Press.

Mok, K. H., Lee, V. W., & So, K. F. (2004). Retinal nerve fiber loss in high- and normal-tension glaucoma by optical coher-

ence tomography. *Optometry and Vision Science, 81,* 369–372.

Monahan, D. J., & Hopkins, K. (2002). Nurses, long-term care, and eldercare: Impact on work and performance. *Nursing Economics, 20,* 266–272, 291.

Monge, A., & others. (2004). Variation in the dopaminergic response during the day in Parkinson disease. *Clinical Neuropharmacology, 27,* 116–118.

Monk, C., Sloan, R. P., Myers, M. M., Ellman, L., Werner, E., Jeon, J., Tager, F., & Fifer, W. P. (2004). Fetal heart rate reactivity differs by women's psychiatric status: An early marker for developmental risk? *Journal of the American Academy of Child and Adolescent Psychiatry, 43,* 283–290.

Montemayor, R. (1982). The relationship between parent-adolescent conflict and the amount of time adolescents spend with parents, peers, and alone. *Child Development, 53,* 1512–1519.

Montgomery, M. J., & Cote, J. E. (2003). College as a transition to adulthood. In G. Adams & M. Berzonsky (Eds.), *Blackwell handbook of adolescence.* Malden, MA: Blackwell.

Moody, R. (2001). Adoption: Women must be helped to consider all options. *British Medical Journal, 323,* 867.

Moon, R. Y., Oden, R. P., & Grady, K. C. (2004). Back to sleep: An educational intervention with women, infants, and children program clients. *Pediatrics, 113,* 542–547.

Moore, C., & Lemmon, K. (Eds.). (2001). *The self in time.* Mahwah, NJ: Erlbaum.

Moore, D. (2001). *The dependent gene.* New York: W. H. Freeman.

Moos, R. H. (1986). Work as a human context. In M. S. Pallack & R. Perloff (Eds.), *Psychology and work: Productivity, change, and employment.* Washington, DC: American Psychological Association.

Morales, A. (2003). Erectile dysfunction: An overview. *Clinical Geriatric Medicine, 19,* 529–538.

More, J. (2003). New guidelines on infant feeding in the first 12 months of life. *Journal of Family Health Care, 13,* 89–90.

Morelli, G. A., Rogoff, B., Oppenheim, D., & Goldsmith, D. (1992). Cultural variation in infants' sleeping arrangements: Questions of independence. *Developmental Psychology, 28,* 604–613.

Moreno-John, G., Gachie, A., Fleming, C. M., Napoles-Springer, A., Mutran, E., Manson, S. M., & Perez-Stable, E. J.

(2004). Ethnic minority older adults participating in clinical research: Developing trust. *Journal of Aging Health, 16, 5 Supplement, 3,* 93S–123S.

Morgan, J. D., & Laungani, P. (Eds.). (2003). *Death and bereavement around the world,* Vol. 4.: *Death and bereavement in Asia, Australia, and New Zealand.* Amityville, NY: Baywood.

Morley, J. E. (2003). Anorexia and weight loss in older persons. *Journals of Gerontology A: Biological Sciences and Medical Sciences, 58,* M131–M137.

Morley, J. E. (2004). The top 10 hot topics in aging. *Journals of Gerontology A: Biological Sciences and Medical Sciences, 59,* M24–M33.

Morris, J. C., Storandt, M., Miller, J. P., McKeel, D., Price, J., Rubin, E. H., & Berg, L. (2001). Mild cognitive impairment represents early-stage Alzheimer's disease. *Archives of Neurology, 58,* 397–405.

Morris, J. K., Wald, N. J., Mutton, D. E., & Alberman, E. (2003). Comparison of models of maternal age-specific risk for Down syndrome live births. *Prenatal Diagnostics, 23,* 252–258.

Morrongiello, B. A., Fenwick, K. D., & Chance, G. (1990). Sound localization acuity in very young infants: An observer-based testing procedure. *Developmental Psychology, 26,* 75–84.

Morrow, C. E., Bandstra, E. S., Anthony, J. C., Ofir, A. Y., Xue, L., & Reyes, M. B. (2003). Influence of prenatal cocaine exposure on early language development: Longitudinal findings from four months to three years of age. *Journal of Developmental and Behavioral Pediatrics, 24,* 39–50.

Morrow, L. (1988, August 8). Through the eyes of children. *Time,* pp. 32–33.

Mortimer, J. T., & Larson, R. W. (2002). Macrostructural trends and the reshaping of adolescence. In J. T. Mortimer & R. W. Larson (Eds.), *The changing adolescent experience.* New York: Cambridge University Press.

Moscicki, E. K., & Caine, E. D. (2004). Opportunities of life: Preventing suicide in elderly patients. *Archives of Internal Medicine, 164,* 1171–1172.

Moses, J., Steptoe, A., Mathews, A., & Edwards, S. (1989). The effects of exercise training on mental well-being in a normal population: A controlled trial. *Journal of Psychosomatic Research, 33,* 47–61.

Moshman, D. (1999). *Adolescent psychological development: Rationality, morality, and identity.* Mahwah, NJ: Erlbaum.

Moshman, D. (2005). *Adolescent psychological development* (2nd ed.). Mahwah, NJ: Erlbaum.

Moules, N. J., Simonson, K., Prins, M., Angus, P., & Bell, J. M. (2004). Making room for grief. *Nursing Inquiry, 11,* 99–107.

Mounts, N. S. (2002). Parental management of adolescent peer relationships in context: The role of parenting style. *Journal of Family Psychology, 16,* 58–69.

Moya, J., Bearer, C. F., & Etzel, R. A. (2004). Children's behavior and physiology and how it affects exposure to environmental contaminants. *Pediatrics, 113 (Suppl. 4),* 996–1006.

Mozingo, J. N., Davis, M. W., Droppleman, P. G., & Merideth, A. (2000). "It wasn't working." Women's experiences with short-term breast feeding. *American Maternal Journal of Nursing, 25,* 120–126.

Mroczek, D. K. (2001). Age and emotion in adulthood. *Current Directions in Psychological Science, 10,* 87–90.

Mroczek, D. K., & Kolarz, C. M. (1998). The effect of age on positive and negative affect: A developmental perspective on happiness. *Journal of Personality and Social Psychology, 75,* 1333–1349.

Mueller, N., & Silverman, N. (1989). Peer relations in maltreated children. In D. Cicchetti & V. Carlson (Eds.), *Child maltreatment.* New York: Cambridge University Press.

Mulholland, H. (2002). Hospice care: A few home truths. *Nursing Times, 98* (40), 11.

Mullis, I. V. S. (1999, April). *Using TIMSS to gain new perspectives about different school organizations and policies.* Paper presented at the meeting of the American Educational Research Association, Montreal.

Mumme, D. L., Fernald, A., & Herrera, C. (1996). Infant's responses to facial & emotional signals in a social referencing paradigm. *Child Development, 67,* 3219–3237.

Murnane, R. J., & Levy, F. (1996). *Teaching the new basic skills.* New York: Free Press.

Murphy, M. C. (1996). Stressors on the college campus: A comparison of 1985 and 1993. *Journal of College Student Development, 37,* 20–28.

Murphy, S., Das-Gupta, A., Cain, K., Johnson, L., Lohan, J., Wu, L., & Mekwa, J. (1999). Changes in parents' mental distress after the violent deaths of an adolescent or young adult child: A longitudinal prospective analysis. *Death Studies, 23,* 129–159.

Murray, C. S., Woodcock, A., Smillie, F. I., Cain, G., Kissen, P., & Castovie, A. (2004). Tobacco smoke exposure, wheeze, and atopy. *Pediatric Pulmonology, 37,* 492–498.

Murray, J. P. (2000). Media effects. In A. Kazdin (Ed.), *Encyclopedia of psychology.* Washington, DC, & New York: American Psychological Association and Oxford University Press.

Murray, M. J., Tang, T., Ryder, C., Mabin, D., & Nicholson, J. C. (2004). Childhood leukemia masquerading as juvenile idiopathic arthritis. *British Medical Journal, 329,* 959–961.

Mussen, P. H., Honzik, M., & Eichorn, D. (1982). Early adult antecedents of life satisfaction at age 70. *Journal of Gerontology, 37,* 316–322.

Mustanski, B. S., Chivers, M. L., & Bailey, J. M. (2002). A critical review of recent biological research on human sexual orientation. *Annual Review of Sex Research, 13,* 89–140.

Muth, A. S. (Ed.). (2000). *Death and dying sourcebook: Basic consumer health information for the layperson about end-of-life care and related ethical issues.* Detroit: Omnigraphics.

Myers, D. G. (2000). *The American paradox.* New Haven, CT: Yale University Press.

Myers, D. L. (1999). *Excluding violent youths from juvenile court: The effectiveness of legislative waiver.* Doctoral dissertation, University of Maryland, College Park, MD.

Myerson, J., Rank, M. R., Raines, F. Q., & Schnitzler, M. A. (1998). Race and general cognitive ability: The myth of diminishing returns in education. *Psychological Science, 9,* 139–142.

Nadeau, J. W. (1998). *Families making sense of death.* Thousand Oaks, CA: Sage.

Nadelman, L. (Ed.). (2004). *Research manual in child development.* Mahwah, NJ: Erlbaum.

Nader, K. (2001). Treatment methods for childhood trauma. In J. P. Wilson, M. J. Friedman, & J. Lindy (Eds.), *Treating psychological trauma and PTSD.* New York: Guilford Press.

Naess, H., Nyland, H. I., Thomassen, L., Aarseth, J., & Myher, K. M. (2004). Etiology of and risk factors for cerebral infarction in young adults in western Norway: A population-based case-control study. *European Journal of Neurology, 11,* 25–30.

Naglieri, J. (2000). Stanford-Binet Intelligence Scale. In A. Kazdin (Ed.), *Encyclopedia of psychology.* Washington, DC, & New York: American Psychological Association and Oxford University Press.

Nagy, M. (1948). The child's theories concerning death. *Journal of Genetic Psychology, 73,* 3–27.

Nagy, Z., Westerberg, H., & Klingberg, T. (2004). Maturation of white matter is associated with the development of cognitive functions during childhood. *Journal of Cognitive Neuroscience, 16,* 1227–1233.

Nakamura, J., & Csikszentmihalyi, M. (2002). The concept of flow. In C. R. Snyder & S. J. Lopez (Eds.), *Handbook of positive psychology.* New York: Oxford University Press.

Nakano, H., & Blumstein, S. E. (2004). Deficits in thematic processes in Broca's and Wernicke's aphasia. *Brain and Language, 88,* 96–107.

Nansel, T. R., Overpeck, M., Pilla, R., Ruan, W., Simons-Morton, B., & Scheidt, P. (2001). Bullying behaviors among U.S. youth. *Journal of the American Medical Association, 285,* 2094–2100.

Narang, A., & Jain, N. (2001). Haemolytic disease of newborn. *Indian Journal of Pediatrics, 68,* 167–172.

Nash, J. M. (1997, February 3). Fertile minds. *Time,* pp. 50–54.

Nash, S. (2003). Does exclusive breastfeeding reduce the risk of the coeliac disease in children? *British Journal of Community Nursing, 8,* 127–132.

National Assessment of Educational Progress (1998). *National report: 1998.* Washington, DC: National Center for Educational Statistics.

National Assessment of Educational Progress (2000). *The nation's report card.* Washington, DC: National Center for Education Statistics.

National Assessment of Educational Progress (2001). *The nation's report card.* Washington, DC: National Center for Education Statistics.

National Association for the Education of Young Children (1986). Position statement on developmentally appropriate practice in programs for 4- and 5-year-olds. *Young Children, 41,* 20–29.

National Association for the Education of Young Children (2002). *Early learning standards: Creating the conditions for success.* Washington, DC: Author.

National Center for Addiction and Substance Abuse (2001). *2000 teen survey.* New York: National Center for Addiction and Substance Abuse, Columbia University.

National Center for Children Exposed to Violence (2001). *Statistics.* New Haven, CT: Author.

National Center for Education Statistics (2001). *Dropout rates in the United States: 2000.* Washington, DC: U.S. Department of Education.

National Center for Education Statistics (2002). *Work during college.* Washington, DC: U.S. Office of Education.

National Center for Health Statistics (1999). Current estimates from the National Health Interview Survey, 1996. *Vital and Health Statistics, Series 10* (No. 200). Atlanta: Centers for Disease Control and Prevention.

National Center for Health Statistics (2000). *Health United States, 2000, with adolescent health chartbook.* Bethesda, MD: U.S. Department of Health and Human Services.

National Center for Health Statistics (2000). *Health United States, 1999.* Atlanta: Centers for Disease Control and Prevention.

National Center for Health Statistics (2002). *Health United States, 2002.* Hyattsville, MD: U.S. Department of Health and Human Services.

National Center for Health Statistics (2002). *New CDC report tracks trends in cesarean births and VCACs during the 1990s.* Atlanta: Centers for Disease Control and Prevention.

National Center for Health Statistics (2004). *Births.* Atlanta: Centers for Disease Control and Prevention.

National Center for Health Statistics (2004). *Health United States.* Atlanta: Centers for Disease Control and Prevention.

National Center for Health Statistics (2004). *Health United States, 2003.* Atlanta: Centers for Disease Control and Prevention.

National Center for HIV, STD, and TB Prevention (2003). *HIV/AIDS.* Atlanta: Centers for Disease Control and Prevention.

National Clearinghouse on Child Abuse and Neglect (2002). *What is child maltreatment?* Washington, DC: Administration for Children and Families.

National Clearinghouse on Child Abuse and Neglect (2004). *What is child abuse and neglect?* Washington, DC: Administration for Children and Families.

National Commission on the High School Year (2001). *Youth at the crossroads: Facing high school and beyond.* Washington, DC: The Education Trust.

National Community Service Coalition (1995). *Youth volunteerism.* Washington, DC: Author.

National Council on Aging (2000, March). *Myths and realities survey results.* Washington, DC: Author.

National Institute of Drug Abuse (2001). *Marijuana.* Washington, DC: National Institutes of Health.

National Institutes of Health (2004). *Women's Health Initiative Hormone Therapy Study.* Bethesda, MD: Author.

National Research Council (1999). *How people learn.* Washington, DC: National Academy Press.

National Research Council (2001). *Knowing what students know.* Washington, DC: National Academy Press.

National Vital Statistics Reports (2001). Deaths and death rates for the 10 leading causes of death in specified age groups. *National Vital Statistics Reports, 48* (No. 11), Table 8.

National Vital Statistics Reports (2003). *Death rates for suicide, Table 46.* Atlanta: Centers for Disease Control and Prevention.

Natsopoulos, D., Kiosseoglou, G., Xeroxmeritou, A., & Alevriadou, A. (1998). Do the hands talk on the mind's behalf? Differences in language between left- and right-handed children. *Brain and Language, 64,* 182–214.

Navarrete, C., Martinez, I., & Salamanca, F. (1994). Paternal line of transmission in chorea of Huntington with very early onset. *Genetic Counseling, 5,* 175–178.

Nazarian, J. (2004). Cardiopulmonary rehabilitation after treatment for lung cancer. *Current Treatment Options in Oncology, 5,* 75–82.

Needham, A., Barrett, T., & Peterman, K. (2002). A pick-me-up for infants' exploratory skills: Early simulated experiences reaching for objects using "sticky mittens" enhances young infants' object exploration skills. *Infant Behavior and Development, 25,* 279–295.

Neglia, J. P., Friedman, D. L., Yasui, Y., Mertens, A., Hammond, S., Stoval, S., & Donaldson, M. (2001). Second malignant neoplasms in five-year survivors of childhood cancer. *Journal of the National Cancer Institute, 93,* 618–629.

Neill, M. (2003). Leaving children behind. *Phi Delta Kappan, 84,* 225–228.

Neimeyer, R. A., Wittkowski, J., & Moser, R. P. (2004). Psychological research on death attitudes: An overview and evaluation. *Death Studies, 28,* 309–340.

Neisser, U. (2004). Memory development: New questions and old. *Developmental Review, 24,* 154–158.

Neisser, U., Boodoo, G., Bouchard, T. J., Boykin, A. W., Brody, N., Ceci, S. J., Halpern, D. F., Loehlin, J. C., Perloff, R. J., Sternberg, R., & Urbina, S. (1996). Intelligence: Knowns and unknowns. *American Psychologist, 51,* 77–101.

Nelson, C. (1999). Research description. *Institute of Child Development biennial report.* Minneapolis: University of Minnesota Institute of Child Development.

Nelson, C. (2003, April). *Gray matters: A neuroconstructivist approach to cognitive development.* Paper presented at the meeting of the Society for Research in Child Development, Tamsa.

Nelson, K. (1999). Levels and modes of representation: Issues for the theory of conceptual change and development. In E. K. Skolnick, K. Nelson, S. A. Gelman, & P. H. Miller (Eds.), *Conceptual development.* Mahwah, NJ: Erlbaum.

Nelson, L. J., Badger, S., & Wu, B. (2004). The influence of culture in emerging adulthood: Perspectives of Chinese college students. *International Journal of Behavioral Development, 28,* 26–36.

Nelson, M. E., Fiatarone, M. A., Moranti, C. M., Trice, I., Greenberg, R. A., & Evans, W. J. (1994). Effects of high-intensity strength training on multiple risk factors for osteoporotic fractures: A randomized controlled trial. *Journal of the American Medical Association, 272,* 1909–1914.

Nelson, R. (2004). Oregon upholds assisted-suicide law. *Lancet, 363,* 1877.

Nelson-LeGall, S., & Kelly, K. (2001, April). *Gender and ethnicity in the schoolroom.* Paper presented at the meeting of the Society for Research in Child Development, Minneapolis.

Neugarten, B. L. (1964). *Personality in middle and late life.* New York: Atherton.

Neugarten, B. L. (1986). The aging society. In A. Pifer & L. Bronte (Eds.), *Our aging society: Paradox and promise.* New York: W. W. Norton.

Neugarten, B. L. (1988, August). *Policy issues for an aging society.* Paper presented at the meeting of the American Psychological Association, Atlanta.

Neugarten, B. L., & Weinstein, K. K. (1964). The changing American grandparent. *Journal of Marriage and the Family, 26,* 199–204.

Neugarten, B. L., Havighurst, R. J., & Tobin, S. S. (1968). Personality and patterns of aging. In B. L. Neugarten (Ed.), *Middle age and aging.* Chicago: University of Chicago Press.

Neville, H., & Bavelier, D. (2002). Human brain plasticity: Evidence from sensory deprivation and altered language experience. *Progress in Brain Research, 138,* 177–188.

Newcomb, M. D., & Bentler, P. M. (1989). Substance use and abuse among children and teenagers. *American Psychologist, 44,* 242–248.

Newcombe, N. S., Drummey, A. B., Fox, N. A., Lile, E., & Ottinger-Alberts, W. (2000). Remembering early childhood: How much, how, and why (or why not). *Current Directions in Psychological Science, 9,* 55–58.

Newcombe, N., & Fox, N. (1994). Infantile amnesia: Through a glass darkly. *Child Development, 65,* 31–40.

Newell, K., Scully, D. M., McDonald, P. V., & Baillargeon, R. (1989). Task constraints and infant grip configurations. *Developmental Psychobiology, 22,* 817–832.

Newman, A. B., & others. (2003). Effects of subclinical cardiovascular disease. *Archives of Internal Medicine, 163,* 2315–2322.

NHANES (2001, March). *National Health and Nutrition Examination Surveys.* Washington, DC: U.S. Department of Health and Human Services.

NICHD Early Child Care Research Network (2000). Factors associated with fathers' caregiving activities and sensitivity with young children. *Developmental Psychology, 14,* 200–219.

NICHD Early Child Care Research Network (2001). Nonmaternal care and family factors in early development: An overview of the NICHD Study of Early Child Care. *Journal of Applied Developmental Psychology, 22,* 457–492.

NICHD Early Child Care Research Network (2002). Structure→Process→ Outcome: Direct and indirect effects of child care quality on young children's development. *Psychological Science, 13,* 199–206.

NICHD Early Child Care Research Network (2003). Does amount of time spent in child care predict socioemotional adjustment during the transition to kindergarten? *Child Development, 74,* 976–1005.

NICHD Early Child Care Research Network (2004). Are child developmental outcomes related to before- and after-school care arrangement? *Child Development, 75,* 280–295.

Nichols, S., & Good, T. L. (2004). *America's teenagers—myths and realities.* Mahwah, NJ: Erlbaum.

Niederhofer, H., & Reiter, A. (2004). Prenatal maternal stress, prenatal fetal movements, and perinatal temperament factors influence behavior and school marks at the age of 6 years. *Fetal Diagnosis and Therapy, 19,* 160–162.

Nielsen, S. J., Siega-Riz, A. M., & Popkin, B. M. (2002). Trends in energy intake between 1977 and 1986: Similar shifts seen across age groups. *Obesity Research, 10,* 370–378.

Nies, M. A., Reisenberg, C. L., Chruscial, H. L., & Artibee, K. (2003). Southern women's response to walking intervention. *Public Health Nursing, 20,* 146–152.

Nisbett, R. (2003). *The geography of thought.* New York: Free Press.

Noakes, M., & Clifton, P. (2004). Weight loss, diet composition, and cardiovascular risk. *Current Opinions in Lipidology, 15,* 31–35.

Nock, S. (1995). A comparison of marriages and cohabitating relationships. *Journal of Family Issues, 16,* 53–76.

Noguera-Obenza, M., Ochoa, T. J., Gomez, H. F., Guerrero, M. L., Herrera-Insua, I., Morrow, A. L., Ruiz-Palacios, G., Pickering, L. K., Guzman, C. A., & Cleary, T. G. (2003). Human milk secretory antibodies against attaching and effacing *Escherichia coli* antigens. *Emerging and Infectuous Diseases, 9,* 545–551.

Noice, H., Noice, T., & Staines, G. (2004). A short-term intervention to enhance cognitive and affective functioning in older adults. *Journal of Aging Health, 16,* 562–585.

Nolan, K., Schell, L. M., Stark, A. D., & Gomez, M. I. (2002). Longitudinal study of energy and nutrient intakes for infants from low-income, urban families. *Public Health Nutrition, 5,* 405–412.

Nolen-Hoeksema, S. (1990). *Sex differences in depression.* Stanford, CA: Stanford University Press.

Nolen-Hoeksema, S. (2004). *Abnormal psychology* (3rd ed.). New York: McGraw-Hill.

Nolen-Hoeksema, S., & Ahrens, C. (2002). Age differences and similarities in correlates of depressive symptoms. *Psychology and Aging, 17,* 116–124.

Nottelmann, E. D., Susman, E. J., Blue, J. H., Inoff-Germain, G., Dorn, L. D., Loriaux, D. L., Cutler, G. B., & Chrousos, G. P. (1987). Gonadal and adrenal hormone correlates of adjustment in early adolescence. In R. M. Lerner & T. T. Foch (Eds.), *Biological-psychological interactions in early adolescence.* Hillsdale, NJ: Erlbaum.

Nowak, C. A. (1977). Does youthfulness equal attractiveness? In L. E. Troll, J. Israel, & K. Israel (Eds.), *Looking ahead: A woman's guide to the problems and joys of growing older.* Englewood Cliffs, NJ: Prentice Hall.

Nsamenang, A. B. (2002). Adolescence in sub-Saharan Africa: An image constructed from Africa's triple heritage. In B. B. Brown, R. W. Larson, & T. S. Saraswathi (Eds.), *The world's youth.* New York: Cambridge University Press.

Nucci, L. P. (2004). The development of moral reasoning. In P. Smith & C. Hart (Eds.), *Blackwell handbook of cognitive development.* Malden, MA: Blackwell.

Nugent, K., & Brazelton, T. B. (2000). Preventive infant mental health: Uses of the Brazelton scale. In J. D. Osofsky & H. E. Fitzgerald (Eds.), *WAIMH Handbook of infant mental health* (Vol. 2). New York: Wiley.

Nusbaum, N. J. (2003). Preparation for healthy retirement. *Journal of the American Geriatric Association, 51,* 429.

Nussbaum, J. F., & Coupland, J. (Eds.). (2004). *Handbook of communication and aging research.* Mahwah, NJ: Erlbaum.

Nuttman-Shwartz, O. (2004). Like a high wave: Adjustment to retirement. *The Gerontologist, 44,* 229–236.

O'Donnell, L., O'Donnell, C., Wardlaw, D. M., & Stueve, A. (2004). Risk and resiliency factors influencing suicidality among urban African American and Latino youth. *American Journal of Community Psychology, 33,* 37–49.

O'Donnell, W. T., & Warren, S. T. (2003). A decade of molecular studies of fragile X syndrome. *Annual Review of Neuroscience, 25,* 315–338.

O'Dowd, A. (2004). Why are midwife numbers in crisis? *Nursing Times, 100,* 12–13.

O'Leary, C. (2004). Fetal alcohol syndrome. *Journal of Pediatric Child Health, 40,* 2–7.

Oakes, L. M., Kannass, K. N., & Shaddy, D. J. (2002). Developmental changes in endogenous control of attention: The role of target familiarity on infants' distraction latency. *Child Development, 73,* 1644–1655.

Oates, J., & Grayson, A. (Eds.). (2004). *Cognitive and language development in children.* Malden, MA: Blackwell.

Oberauer, K., Demmrich, A., Mayr, U., & Kliegl, R. (2001). Dissociating retention and access in working memory. *Memory and cognition, 29,* 18–33.

Obregon, R. (2003). Communication from a human rights perspective: Responding to the HIV/AIDS pandemic in eastern and southern Africa. *Journal of Health Communication, 8,* 613–614.

Occupational Outlook Handbook (2004–2005). Washington, DC: U.S. Department of Labor, Bureau of Labor Statistics.

Oddy, W. H., Sherriff, J. L., de Klerk, N. H., Kendall, G. E., Sly, P. D., Beilin, L. J., Blake, K. B., Landau, L. I., & Stanley, F. J. (2004). *American Journal of Public Health, 94,* 1531–1537.

Oehninger, S. (2001). Strategies for the infertile man. *Seminars in Reproductive Medicine, 19,* 231–238.

Offer, D., Ostrov, E., Howard, K. I., & Atkinson, R. (1988). *The teenage world: Adolescents' self-image in ten countries.* New York: Plenum.

Offer, D., Ostrov, E., Howard, K. I., & Dolan, S. (1989). *The Offer Self Image Questionnaire for a manual* (4th ed.). Chicago: Reece Hospital and Medical Center.

Ogbu, J. U. (1989, April). *Academic socialization of Black children: An inoculation against future failure?* Paper presented at the meeting of the Society for Research in Child Development, Kansas City.

Ogbu, J. U. (2003). *Thinking and doing: The significance of minority status.* Paper presented at the meeting of the American Psychological Association, Toronto.

Ogbu, J., & Stern, P. (2001). Caste status and intellectual ability. In R. J. Sternberg & E. L. Grigorenko (Eds.), *Environmental effects on cognitive abilities.* Mahwah, NJ: Erlbaum.

Ogbu, J., & Stern, P. (2001). Caste status and intellectual development. In R. J. Sternberg & E. L. Grigorenko (Eds.), *Environmental effects on cognitive abilities.* Mahwah, NJ: Erlbaum.

O'Grady, W. (2005). *Syntactic carpentry.* Mahwah, NJ: Erlbaum.

Ohgi, S., Arisawa, K., Takahashi, T., Kusumoto, T., Goto, Y., & Saito, A. T. (2003). Neonatal behavioral assessment scale as a predictor of later developmental disabilities of low birth-weight and/or premature infants. *Brain Development, 25,* 313–321.

Ohgi, S., Fukuda, M., Moriuchi, H., Kusumoto, T., Akiyama, T., Nugent, J. K., Brazelton, T. B., Arisawa, K., Takahashi, T., & Saitoh, H. (2002). Comparison of kangaroo care and standard care: Behavioral organization, development, and temperament in healthy, low birth weight infants through 1 year. *Journal of Perinatology, 22,* 374–379.

Okagaki, L. (2000). Determinants of intelligence: Socialization of intelligence. In A. Kazdin (Ed.), *Encyclopedia of psychology.* Washington, DC, & New York: American Psychological Association and Oxford University Press.

Olivardia, R., Pope, H. G., Mangweth, B., & Hudson, J. I. (1995). Eating disorders in college men. *American Journal of Psychiatry, 152,* 1279–1284.

Olsho, L. W., Harkins, S. W., & Lenhardt, M. L. (1985). Aging and the auditory system. In J. E. Birren & K. W. Schaie (Eds.), *Handbook of the psychology of aging* (2nd ed.). New York: Van Nostrand Reinhold.

Olszewski-Kubilius, P. (2003). Gifted education programs and procedures. In I. B. Weiner (Ed.), *Handbook of psychology* (Vol. VII). New York: Wiley.

Oltjenbruns, K. (2001). The developmental content of childhood grief. In M. Stroebe, R. O. Hansson, W. Stroebe, & H. Schut (Eds.), *Handbook of bereavement research: Consequences, coping, and care.* Washington, DC: American Psychological Association.

Olweus, D. (1980). Bullying among school-boys. In R. Barnen (Ed.), *Children and violence.* Stockholm: Adaemic Litteratur.

Olweus, D. (1993). *Bullying at school.* Cambridge, MA: Blackwell.

Ono, Y. (2004). Suicide prevention program for the elderly. *Keio Journal of Medicine, 53,* 1–6.

Ontal-Grzebik, L. L., & Raffaelli, M. (2004). Individual and social influences on ethnic identity among Latino young adults. *Journal of Adolescent Research, 19,* 559–575.

Onwuegbuzi, A. J., & Daley, C. E. (2001). Racial differences in IQ revisited: A synthesis of nearly a century of research. *Journal of Black Psychology, 27,* 209–220.

Oppenheimer, V. K. (2003). Cohabiting and marriage during young men's career development process. *Demography, 40,* 127–149.

Organista, K. C. (1994). Overdue overview of elderly Latino mental health. *Contemporary Psychology, 39,* 61–62.

Osipow, S. (2000). Work. In A. Kazdin (Ed.), *Encyclopedia of psychology.* Washington, DC, & New York: American Psychological Association and Oxford University Press.

Ostrov, J. M., Keating, C. F., & Ostrov, J. M. (2004). Gender differences in preschool aggression during free play and structured interactions: An observational study. *Social Development, 13,* 255–277.

Ott, C. H. (2003). The impact of complicated grief on mental and physical health at various points in the bereavement process. *Death Studies, 27,* 249–272.

Ottley, C. (2004). Health and nutrition series—1. What do we know about . . . childhood obesity? *Journal of Family Health Care, 14,* 8–10.

Ouellette, S. C., & DiPlacido, J. (2001). Personality's role in the protection and enhancement of health. In A. Baum, T. A. Revenson, & J. E. Singer (Eds.), *Handbook of health psychology.* Mahwah, NJ: Erlbaum.

Overton, W. F. (2003). Development across the life span. In I. B. Weiner (Ed.), *Handbook of psychology* (Vol. VI). New York: Wiley.

Overton, W. F. (2004). Embodied development: Biology, person, and culture in a relational context. In C. G. Coll, E. L. Bearer, & R. M. Lerner (Eds.), *Nature and nurture.* Mahwah, NJ: Erlbaum.

Owens, J. A. (2004). Cosleeping. *Journal of Developmental and Behavioral Pediatrics, 23,* 254–255.

Paffenbarger, O., Hyde, R. T., Wing, A. L., & Hsieh, C. (1986). Physical activity, all-cause mortality, and longevity of college alumni. *New England Journal of Medicine, 324,* 605–612.

Paikoff, R. L., Buchanan, C. M., & Brooks-Gunn, J. (1991). Hormone-behavior links at puberty, methodological links in the study of. In R. M. Lerner, A. C. Petersen, & J. Brooks-Gunn (Eds.), *Encyclopedia of adolescence.* New York: Garland.

Palmer, S. E. (2004). Custody and access issues with children whose parents are separated or divorced. *Canadian Journal of Community Mental Health, 4 (Suppl.)* 25–38.

Palmore, E. (1981). *Social patterns in normal aging: Findings from the Duke Longitudinal Study.* Durham, NC: Duke University Press.

Palmore, E. (2001). The ageism survey: First findings. *The Gerontologist, 41,* 572–575.

Palmore, E. B., Burchett, B. M., Fillenbaum, C. G., George, L. K., & Wallman, L. M. (1985). *Retirement: Causes and consequences.* New York: Springer.

Paloutzian, R. (2000). *Invitation to the psychology of religion* (3rd ed.). Boston: Allyn & Bacon.

Pan, B. A. (2005). Semantic development. In J. Berko Gleason, *The development of language* (6th ed.). Boston: Allyn & Bacon.

Panchaud, C., Singh, S., Feivelson, D., & Darroch, J. E. (2000). Sexually transmitted diseases among adolescents in developed countries. *Family Planning Perspectives, 32,* 24–32.

Pang, V. (2005). *Multicultural education* (2nd ed.). New York: McGraw-Hill.

Papalia, D. E., Sterns, H. L., Feldman, R. D., & Camp, C. J. (2002). *Adult development and aging* (2nd ed.). New York: McGraw-Hill.

Papp, C., & Papp, Z. (2003). Chorionic villus sampling and amniocentesis: What are the risks in current practice? *Current Opinions in Obstetrics and Gynecology, 15,* 159–165.

Papp, Z. (2003). Breech deliveries and cesarean section. *Journal of Perinatal Medicine, 31,* 395–398.

Parazzini, F., Chatenoud, L., Surace, M., Tozzi, L., Salerio, B., Bettoni, G., & Benzi, G. (2003). Moderate alcohol drinking and risk of preterm birth. *European Journal of Clinical Nutrition, 57,* 1345–1349.

Pardo-Crespo, R., Perez-Igelia, R., Llorca, J., Alvarez-Granada, L., Garcia-Fuentes, M., Martinez-Gonzales, M. A., & Delgado-Rodriquez, M. (2004). Breast-feeding and risk of hospitalization for all factors and fever of unknown origin. *European Journal of Public Health, 14,* 230–234.

Pargament, K. I., & Park, C. L. (1995). Merely a defense? The variety of religious means and ends. *Journal of Social Issues, 51,* 13–32.

Park, D. (2001). Commentary in Restak, R., *The secret life of the brain.* Washington, DC: Joseph Henry Press.

Park, D. C., Lautenschalger, G., Hedden, T., Davidson, N. S., Smith, A. D., & Smith, P. K. (2002). Models of visuospatial and verbal memory across the adult life span. *Psychology and Aging, 17,* 299–320.

Parke, R. D. (2000). Father involvement: A developmental psychology perspective. *Marriage and Family Review, 29,* 43–58.

Parke, R. D. (2002). Fathering. In M. H. Bornstein (Ed.), *Handbook of parenting* (2nd ed.). Mahwah, NJ: Erlbaum.

Parke, R. D. (2004). Development in the family. *Annual Review of Psychology* (Vol. 55). Palo Alto, CA: Annual Reviews.

Parke, R. D., & Clarke-Stewart, K. A. (2003). Developmental psychology. In I. B. Weiner (Ed.), *Handbook of psychology* (Vol. I). New York: Wiley.

Parke, R. D., Dennis, J., Flyr, M. L., Leidy, M. S., & Schofield, T. J. (2005). Fathers: Cultural and ecological perspectives. In T. Luster & L. Okaghi (Eds.), *Parenting: An ecological perspective* (2nd ed.). Mahwah, NJ: Erlbaum.

Parker, E. S., Landau, S. M., Whipple, S. C., & Schwartz, B. L. (2004). Aging, recall, and recognition: A study on the sensitivity of the University of Southern California Repeatable Episodic Memory Test (USC-REMT). *Journal of Clinical and Experimental Neuropsychology, 26,* 428–440.

Parker, J. G., & Asher, S. R. (1987). Peer relations and later personal adjustment: Are low accepted children at risk? *Psychological Bulletin, 102,* 357–389.

Parker, P. S. (2004). *Race, gender, and leadership.* Mahwah, NJ: Erlbaum.

Parkin, A. J., & Walter, B. M. (1992). Recollective experience, normal aging, and frontal dysfunction. *Psychology and Aging, 7,* 290–298.

Parlee, M. B. (1979, April). The friendship bond: PT's survey report on friendship in America. *Psychology Today,* pp. 43–54, 113.

Parmet, S., Lynn, C., & Glass, R. M. (2004). Prenatal care. *Journal of the American Medical Association, 291,* 146.

Parnes, H. S., & Sommers, D. G. (1994). Shunning retirement: Work experiences of men in their seventies and early eighties. *Journals of Gerontology B: Psychological Sciences and Social Sciences, 49,* S117–S124.

Parsons, P. A. (2003). From the stress theory of aging to energetic and evolutionary explanations for longevity. *Biogerontology, 4,* 63–73.

Parten, M. (1932). Social play among preschool children. *Journal of Abnormal Social Psychology, 27,* 243–269.

Pascali-Bonaro, D. (2002). Pregnant and widowed on September 11: The birth community reaches out. *Birth, 29,* 62–64.

Pasch, L. A. (2001). Confronting fertility problems. In A. Baum, T. A. Revenson, & J. E. Singer (Eds.), *Handbook of health psychology.* Mahwah, NJ: Erlbaum.

Pasley, K. (1996, December). *Impact of divorce: Current research.* Presentation to the "Children of Divorce" Training Program of Family Life Council of Greater Greensboro, Inc., Greensboro, NC.

Pasley, K., & Moorefield, B. S. (2004). Stepfamilies. In M. Coleman & L. Ganong (Eds.), *Handbook of contemporary families.* Thousand Oaks, CA: Sage.

Passuth, P. M., Maines, D. R., & Neugarten, B. L. (1984). *Age norms and age constraints twenty years later.* Paper presented at the annual meeting of the Midwest Sociological Society, Chicago.

Pastor, A. D., & Evans, S. M. (2003). Alcohol outcome expectancies for alcohol use problems in women with and without a family history of alcoholism. *Drug and Alcohol Dependency, 70,* 201–214.

Patterson, B., Ryan, J., & Dickey, J. H. (2004). The toxicology of mercury. *New England Journal of Medicine, 350,* 945–947.

Patterson, C. J. (2002). Lesbian and gay parenthood. In M. H. Bornstein (Ed.), *Handbook of parenting* (2nd ed., Vol. 3). Mahwah, NJ: Erlbaum.

Patterson, C. J. (2004). What differences does a civil union make? Changing public policies and the experiences of same-sex couples: Comment on Solomon, Rothblum, and Balsam (2004). *Journal of Family Psychology, 18,* 287–289.

Patterson, G. R., De Baryshe, B. D., & Ramsey, E. (1989). A developmental perspective on antisocial behavior. *American Psychologist, 44,* 329–355.

Pavlov, I. P. (1927). In G. V. Anrep (Trans.), *Conditioned reflexes.* London: Oxford University Press.

Payer, L. (1991). The menopause in various cultures. In H. Burger & M. Boulet (Eds.), *A portrait of the menopause.* Park Ridge, NJ: Parthenon.

Payne, A. M., Dodd, S. L., & Leewenburgh, C. (2003). Life-long calorie restriction in Fischer 344 rats attenuates age-related loss in skeletal muscle force and reduces extracellular space. *Journal of Applied Physiology, 95,* 2554–2562.

Peck, R. C. (1968). Psychological developments in the second half of life. In B. L. Neugarten (Ed.), *Middle age and aging.* Chicago: University of Chicago Press.

Pedersen, P. B. (2004). Multicultural counseling. In W. E. Craighead & C. B. Nemeroff (Eds.), *The concise Corsini encyclopedia of psychology and behavioral science.* New York: Wiley.

Pederson, D. R., & Moran, G. (1996). Expressions of the attachment relationship outside of the Strange Situation. *Child Development, 67,* 915–927.

Pellizzer, C., Adler, S., Corvi, R., Hartung, T., & Bremer, S. (2004). Monitoring of teratogenic effects in vitro by analyzing a selected gene expression pattern. *Toxicology In Vitro, 18,* 325–335.

Peng, F. C. (2003). Is dementia a disease? *Gerontology, 49,* 384–391.

Penninx, B. W., Rejeski, W. J., Pandya, J., Miller, M. E., Di Bari, M., Applegate, W. B., & Pahor, M. (2002). Exercise and depressive symptoms: A comparison of aerobic and resistance exercise effects on emotional and physical function in older persons with high and low depressive symptomatology. *Journals of Gerontology B: Psychological Sciences and Social Sciences, 57,* P124–P132.

Peplau, L. A. (2002). *Current research on gender and sexuality.* Paper presented at the meeting of the American Psychological Association, Chicago.

Peplau, L. A. (2003). Human sexuality: How do men and women differ? *Current Directions in Psychological Science, 12,* 37–40.

Peplau, L. A., & Beals, K. P. (2002). Lesbians, gays, and bisexuals in relationships. In J. Worell (Ed.), *Encyclopedia of women and gender.* San Diego: Academic Press.

Peplau, L. A., & Beals, K. P. (2004). Family lives of lesbians and gay men. In A. L. Vangelisti (Ed.), *Handbook of family communication.* Mahwah, NJ: Erlbaum.

Peplau, L. A., Fingerhut, A., & Beals, K. P. (2004). Sexuality in the relationships of lesbians and gay men. In J. H. Harvey & K. Wenzel (Eds.), *The handbook of sexuality in close relationships.* Mahwah, NJ: Erlbaum.

Perdue, C. W. (2000). Ageism. In A. Kazdin (Ed.), *Encyclopedia of psychology.* Washington, DC, & New York: American Psychological Association and Oxford University Press.

Perez-Febles, A. M. (1992). *Acculturation and interactional styles of Latina mothers and their infants.* Unpublished honors thesis, Brown University, Providence, RI.

Perez-Perdomo, R., Perez-Cardona, C., Disdier-Flores, O., & Cintron, Y. (2003). Prevalence and correlates of asthma in the Puerto Rican population: Behavioral risk factor surveillance system, 2000. *Journal of Asthma, 40,* 465–474.

Perlman, D., & Peplau, L. A. (1998). Loneliness. In H. S. Friedman (Ed.), *Encyclopedia of mental health* (Vol. 2). San Diego: Academic Press.

Perls, T. (2004). Centenarians avoid dementia. *Trends in Neuroscience, 27,* 633–636.

Perls, T., Lauerman, J. F., & Silver, M. H. (1999). *Living to 100.* New York: Basic Books.

Perls, T., Shea-Drinkwater, M., Bowen-Flynn, J., Ridge, S. B., Kang, S., Joyce, E., Daly, M., Brewster, S. J., Kunkel, L., & Puca, A. A. (2000). Exceptional family clustering for extreme longevity in humans. *Journal of the American Geriatric Society, 48,* 1483–1485.

Perls, T., & Terry, D. (2003). Genetics of exceptional longevity. *Experimental Gerontology, 38,* 725–730.

Perls, T., Wilmoth, J., Levenson, R., Drinkwater, M., Cohen, M., Boggs, H., Joyce, E., Brewster, S. J., Kunkel, L., & Puca, A. A. (2002). Life-long sustained mortality advantage of siblings of centenarians. *Proceedings of the National Academy of Science USA, 99,* 8442–8447.

Perner, J., Stummer, S., Sprung, M., & Doherty, M. (2002). Theory of mind finds its Piagetian perspective: Why alternative naming comes with understanding belief. *Cognitive Development, 17,* 1451–1472.

Perry, C. M., & Johnson, C. L. (1994). Families and support networks among African American oldest-old. *International Journal of Aging on Human Development, 38,* 41–50.

Perry, P. (2001). Sick kids. *American Way, 4,* 64–65.

Perry, W. G. (1970). *Forms of intellectual and ethical development in the college years.* New York: Holt, Rinehart & Winston.

Perry, W. G. (1999). *Forms of ethical and intellectual development in the college years: A scheme.* San Francisco: Jossey Bass.

Perry-Jenkins, M. (2004). The time and timing of work: Unique challenges facing low-income families. In A. C. Crouter & A. Booth (Eds.), *Work-family challenges for low-income families and their children.* Mahwah, NJ: Erlbaum.

Peskin, E. G., & Rein, G. M. (2002). A guest editorial: What is the correct cesarian rate and how do we get there? *Obstetrics and Gynecological Survey, 57,* 189–190.

Peskin, H. (1967). Pubertal onset and ego functioning. *Journal of Abnormal Psychology, 72,* 1–15.

Petersen, A. C. (1979, January). Can puberty come any faster? *Psychology Today,* pp. 45–56.

Petersen, A. C. (1993). Creating adolescents: The role of context and process in developmental trajectories. *Journal of Research on Adolescence, 3,* 1–18.

Peterson, B. E. (2002). Longitudinal analysis of midlife generativity, intergenerational roles, and caregiving. *Psychology and Aging, 17,* 161–168.

Peterson, B. E., & Stewart, A. J. (1996). Antecedents and contexts of generativity motivation at midlife. *Psychology and Aging, 11,* 21–33.

Peterson, C. C. (1996). The ticking of the social clock: Adults' beliefs about the timing of transition events. *International Journal of Aging and Human Development, 42,* 189–203.

Peterson, C. C. (1999). Grandfathers' and grandmothers' satisfaction with the grandparenting role: Seeking new answers to old questions. *International Journal of Aging and Human Development, 49,* 61–78.

Peterson, C., & Slaughter, V. (2003). Opening windows to the mind: Mothers' preferences for mental state explanations and children's theory of mind. *Cognitive Development, 18,* 399–429.

Peterson, K. S. (1997, September 3). In high school, dating is a world into itself. *USA Today,* pp. 1–2D.

Petrovitch, H., & others. (2000). Midlife blood pressure and neurotic plaques, neurofibrillary tangles, and brain weight at death: The HAAS Honolulu-Asia aging study. *Neurobiology of Aging, 21,* 57–62.

Pettito, L. A., Kovelman, I., & Harasymowycz, U. (2003, April). *Bilingual language development: Does learning the new damage the old.* Paper presented at the meeting of the Society for Research in Child Development, Tampa.

Pfeifer, M., Goldsmith, H. H., Davidson, R. J., & Rickman, M. (2002). Continuity and change in inhibited and uninhibited children. *Child Development, 73,* 1474–1485.

Phelan, E. A., Anderson, L. A., Lacroix, A. Z., & Larson, E. B. (2004). Older adults' views of "successful aging"—How do they compare with researchers' definitions? *Journal of the American Geriatric Association, 52,* 211–216.

Philippakis, A., Hemenway, D., Alexe, D. M., Dessypris, N., Spyridopoulos, T., & Petridou, E. (2004). A quantification of preventable unintentional childhood injury mortality in the United States. *Injury Prevention, 10,* 79–82.

Phillips, D. A., Voran, K., Kisker, E., Howes, C., & Whitebook, M. (1994). Child care for children in poverty: Opportunity or inequity? *Child Development, 65,* 472–492.

Phillips, D., Prince, S., & Schiebelhut, L. (2004). Elementary school children's responses 3 months after the September 11 terrorist attacks: A study in Washington, DC. *American Journal of Orthopsychiatry, 74,* 509–528.

Phillips, S. (2003). Adolescent health. In I. B. Weiner (Ed.), *Handbook of psychology* (Vol. IX). New York: Wiley.

Phillips, W. T., Kiernan, R. M., & King, A. C. (2001). The effects of physical activity on physical and psychological health. In A. Baum, T. A. Revenson, & J. E. Singer (Eds.), *Handbook of health psychology.* Mahwah, NJ: Erlbaum.

Phinney, J. S. (1989). Stages of ethnic identity development in minority group adolescents. *Journal of Early Adolescence, 9,* 34–49.

Phinney, J. S. (1996). When we talk about American ethnic groups, what do we mean? *American Psychologist, 51,* 918–927.

Phinney, J. S. (2000). Ethnic identity. In A. Kazdin (Ed.), *Encyclopedia of psychology.* Washington, DC, and New York: American Psychological Association and Oxford University Press.

Phinney, J. S. (2003). Identity and acculturation. In K. M. Chun, P. B. Organista, & G. Marín (Eds.), *Acculturation.* Washington, DC: American Psychological Association.

Phinney, J. S., & Alipura, L. L. (1990). Ethnic identity in college students from four ethnic groups. *Journal of Adolescence, 13,* 171–183.

Phinney, J. S., & Devich-Navarro, M. (1997). Variations in bicultural identification among African American and Mexican American adolescents. *Journal of Research on Adolescence, 7,* 3–32.

Phinney, J. S., Ferguson, D. L., & Tate, J. D. (1997). Intergroup attitudes among ethnic minority adolescents: A causal model. *Child Development, 68,* 955–969.

Phinney, J. S., Ong, A., & Madden, T. (2000). Cultural values and intergenerational discrepancies in immigrant and non-immigrant families. *Child Development, 71,* 528–539.

Piaget, J. (1932). *The moral judgment of the child.* New York: Harcourt Brace Jovanovich.

Piaget, J. (1952). Jean Piaget. In C. A. Murchison (Ed.), *A history of psychology in autobiography* (Vol. 4). Worcester, MA: Clark University Press.

Piaget, J. (1952). *The origins of intelligence in children.* (M. Cook, Trans.). New York: International Universities Press.

Piaget, J. (1952). *The origins of intelligence in children.* New York: International Universities Press.

Piaget, J. (1954). *The construction of reality in the child.* New York: Basic Books.

Piaget, J. (1962). *Play, dreams, and imitation.* New York: W. W. Norton.

Piaget, J., & Inhelder, B. (1969). *The child's conception of space* (F. J. Langdon & J. L. Lunger, Trans.). New York: W. W. Norton.

Piccini, P., Pavese, N., & Brooks, D. J. (2003). Endogenous dopamine release after pharmacological challenges in Parkinson's disease. *Annals of Neurology, 53,* 647–653.

Pierce, K. M., Hamm, J. V., & Vandell, D. L. (1997, April). *Experiences in after-school programs and children's adjustment at school and at home.* Paper presented at the meeting of the Society for Research in Child Development, Washington, DC.

Pierson, R. N. (2003). Body composition in aging: A biological perspective. *Current Opinions in Clinical Nutrition and Metabolic Care, 6,* 15–20.

Pillow, D. R., Zautra, A. J., & Sandler, I. (1996). Major life events and minor stressors: Identifying mediational links in the stress process. *Journal of Personality and Social Psychology, 70,* 381–394.

Pinette, M. G., Wax, J., Blackstone, J., Cartin, A., & McCrann, D. (2004). Timing of early amniocentesis as a function of membrane fusion. *Journal of Clinical Ultrasound, 32,* 8–11.

Pinker, S. (1994). *The language instinct.* New York: HarperCollins.

Pintrich, P. R., & Maehr, M. L. (2004). *Motivating students, improving schools.* Mahwah, NJ: Erlbaum.

Piolino, P., Desgranges, B., Benali, K., & Eustache, F. (2002). Episodic and semantic remote autobiographical memory in aging. *Memory, 10,* 239–357.

Pittman, K., & Diversi, M. (2003). Social policy for the 21st century. In R. Larson, B. Brown, & J. Mortimer (Eds.), *Adolescents' preparation for the future: Perils and promise.* Malden, MA: Blackwell.

Pizzamiglio, A. P., Saygin, S. L., Small, S., & Wilson, S. (2005). Language and the brain. In M. Tomasello & D. A. Slobin (Eds.), *Beyond nature-nurture.* Mahwah, NJ: Erlbaum.

Plackslin, S. (2000). *Mothering the new mother: Women's feelings and needs after childbirth—A support and resource guide.* New York: Newmarket Press.

Pleck, J. H. (1995). The gender-role strain paradigm. In R. F. Levant & W. S. Pollack (Eds.), *A new psychology of men.* New York: Basic Books.

Plomin, R. (1993, March). *Human behavioral genetics and development: An overview and update.* Paper presented at the biennial meeting of the Society for Research in Child Development, New Orleans.

Plomin, R. (1999). Genetics and general cognitive ability. *Nature, 402* (Suppl.), C25–C29.

Plomin, R., Asbury, K., & Dunn, J. (2001). Why are children in the same family so different? Nonshared environment a decade later. *Canadian Journal of Psychiatry, 46,* 225–233.

Plomin, R., DeFries, J. C., McClearn, G. E., & McGuffin, P. (2001). *Behavioral genetics* (4th ed.). New York: Worth.

Plomin, R., Reiss, D., Hetherington, E. M., & Howe, G. W. (1994). Nature and nurture: Contributions to measures of the family environment. *Developmental Psychology, 30,* 32–43.

Poelmans, S. A. Y. (Ed.). (2005). *Work and family.* Mahwah, NJ: Erlbaum.

Polaha, J., Warzak, W. J., & Dittmer-Memahon, K. (2002). Toilet training in primary care: Current practice and recommendations from behavioral pediatrics. *Journal of Developmental and Behavioral Pediatrics, 23,* 424–429.

Polivy, J., Herman, C. P., Mills, J., & Brock, H. (2003). Eating disorders in adolescence. In G. Adams & M. Berzonsky (Eds.), *Blackwell handbook of adolescence.* Malden, MA: Blackwell.

Pollack, W. (1999). *Real boys.* New York: Owl Books.

Pollitt, E. P., Gorman, K. S., Engle, P. L., Martorell, R., & Rivera, J. (1993). Early supplementary feeding and cognition.

Monographs of the Society for Research in Child Development, 58 (7, Serial No. 235).

Ponterotto, J. G., Casas, J. M., Suzuki, L. A., & Alexander, C. M. (Eds.). (2001). *Handbook of multicultural counseling.* Thousand Oaks, CA: Sage.

Poole, D. A., & Lindsay, D. S. (1995). Interviewing preschoolers: Effects of nonsuggestive techniques, parental coaching and leading questions on reports of non-experienced events. *Journal of Experimental Child Psychology, 60,* 129–154.

Poole, D. A., & Lindsay, D. S. (1996). *Effects of parents' suggestions, interviewing techniques, and age on young children's event reports.* Paper presented at the NATO Advanced Study Institute, Porte de Bourgenay, France.

Poole, D. A., & Lindsay, D. S. (2001). Children's eyewitness reports after exposure to misinformation from parents. *Journal of Experimental Psychology: Applied, 7,* 27–50.

Poon, H. F., Calabrese, V., Scapagnini, G., & Butterfield, D. A. (2004). Free radicals and brain aging. *Clinical Geriatric Medicine, 20,* 329–359.

Popp, M. S. (2005). *Teaching language and literacy in elementary classrooms.* Mahwah, NJ: Erlbaum.

Porges, S. W., Doussard-Roosevelt, J. A., & Maiti, A. K. (1994). Vagal tone and the physiological regulation of emotion. In N. A. Fox (Ed.), *Emotion regulation: Behavioral and biological considerations. Monographs of the Society for Research in Child Development, 59* (Serial No. 240), 167–196.

Posner, J. K., & Vandell, D. L. (1994). Low-income children's after-school care: Are there benefits of after-school programs? *Child Development, 65,* 440–456.

Potter, S. M., Zelazo, P. R., Stack, D. M., & Papageorgiou, A. N. (2000). Adverse effects of fetal cocaine exposure on neonatal auditory information processing. *Pediatrics, 105,* e40–e41.

Potvin, L., Champagne, F., & Laberge-Nadeau, C. (1988). Mandatory driver training and road safety: The Quebec experience. *American Journal of Public Health, 78,* 1206–1212.

Powell, D. R. (2005). Searching for what works in parenting interventions. In T. Luster & L. Okagaki (Eds.), *Parenting.* Mahwah, NJ: Erlbaum.

Powell, G. N. (2004). *Managing a diverse workforce* (2nd ed.). Thousand Oaks, CA: Sage.

Powell, R. G., & Caseau, D. (2004). *Classroom communication and diversity.* Mahwah, NJ: Erlbaum.

Powers, L. E., & Wampold, B. E. (1994). Cognitive-behavioral factors in adjustment to adult bereavement. *Death Studies, 18,* 1–24.

Pratt, H. D., Patel, D. R., & Greydanus, D. E. (2003). Behavioral aspects of children's sports. *Pediatric Clinics of North America, 50,* 879–899.

Pratt, M. W., Danso, H. A., Arnold, M. L., Norris, J. E., & Filyer, R. (2001). Adult generativity and the socialization of adolescents. *Journal of Personality, 69,* 89–120.

Prescott, L. M., Harley, J. P., & Klein, D. A. (2005). *Microbiology* (6th ed.). New York: McGraw-Hill.

Prescott, S. L. (2003). Early origins of allergic disease. *Current Opinions on Allergy and Clinical Immunology, 3,* 125–132.

Pressley, M. (2000). What should comprehension instruction be the instruction of? In M. Kamil (Ed.), *Handbook of reading research.* Mahwah, NJ: Erlbaum.

Pressley, M. (2003). Literacy and literacy instruction. In I. B. Weiner (Ed.), *Handbook of psychology* (Vol. VII). New York: Wiley.

Pressley, M. (2003). Psychology of literacy and literacy instruction. In I. B. Weiner (Ed.), *Handbook of psychology* (Vol. VII). New York: Wiley.

Pressley, M., Cariligia-Bull, T., Deane, S., & Schneider, W. (1987). Short-term memory, verbal competence, and age as predictors of imagery instructional effectiveness. *Journal of Experimental Child Psychology, 43,* 194–211.

Preston, A. M., Rodriguez, C., Rivera, C. E., & Sahai, H. (2003). Influence of environmental tobacco smoke on vitamin C status in children. *American Journal of Clinical Nutrition, 77,* 167–172.

Prickaerts, J., Koopmans, G., Blokland, A., & Scheepens, A. (2004). Learning and adult neurogenesis: Survival with or without proliferation? *Neurobiology of Learning and Memory, 81,* 1–11.

Prinstein, M. J., & Aikins, J. W. (2004). Cognitive moderators of the longitudinal association between peer rejection and adolescent depressive symptoms. *Journal of Abnormal Child Psychology, 32,* 147–158.

Probst, T. M. (2004). Economic stressors. In J. Baring, E. K. Kelloway, & M. R. Frone (Eds.), *Handbook of work stress.* Thousand Oaks, CA: Sage.

Province, M. A., Hadley, E. C., Hornbrook, M. C., Lipitz, L. A., Miller, J. P., Mulrow, C. D., Ory, M. G., Sattin, R. W., Tinetti, M. E., & Wolf, S. L. (1995). The effects of exercise on falls in elderly patients. *Journal of the American Medical Association, 273,* 1341–1347.

Pruchno, R., & Rosenbaum, J. (2003). Social relationships in adulthood and old age. In I. B. Weiner (Ed.), *Handbook of psychology* (Vol. VI). New York: Wiley.

Pujol, J., Lopez-Sala, A., Sebastian-Galles, N., Deus, J., Cardoner, N., Soriano-Mas, C., Moreno, A., & Sans, A. (2004). Delayed myelination in children with developmental delay detected by volumetric MRI. *Neuroimage, 22,* 897–903.

Putnam, S. P., Sanson, A. V., & Rothbart, M. K. (2002). Child temperament and parenting. In M. H. Bornstein (Ed.), *Handbook of parenting* (2nd ed.). Mahwah, NJ: Erlbaum.

Putney, N. M., & Bengtson, V. L. (2001). Families, intergenerational relationships, and kinkeeping in midlife. In M. E. Lachman (Ed.), *Handbook of midlife development.* New York: Wiley.

Pyke, K. D., & Bengtson, V. L. (1996). Caring more or less: Individualistic and collectivist systems of family eldercare. *Journal of Marriage and the Family, 58,* 379–392.

Qu, B., Rosenberg, R. N., Li, L., Boyer, P. J., & Johnston, S. A. (2004). Gene vaccination to bias the immune response to amyloid-beta peptidea as therapy for Alzheimer disease. *Archives of Neurology, 61,* 1859–1864.

Quadflieg, N., & Fichter, M. M. (2003). The course and outcome of bulimia nervosa. *European Child and Adolescent Psychiatry, 12* (Suppl. 1), I199–I209.

Quilliam, S. (2004). Hormone replacement therapy (HRT). *Journal of Family Planning and Health Care, 30,* 59–61.

Quinsey, V. L. (2003). The etiology of anamolous sexual preferences in men. *Annals of the New York Academy of Science, 989,* 105–117.

Quintana, S. M. (2004). Ethnic identity development in Chicana/o youth. In R. J. Velasquez, B. W. McNeil, & L. M. Arellano (Eds.), *The handbook of Chicano psychology and mental health.* Mahwah, NJ: Erlbaum.

Qutub, M., Klapper, P., Vallely, P., & Cleator, G. (2001). Genital herpes in pregnancy: Is screening cost effective? *International Journal of STD and AIDS, 12,* 14–16.

Rabheru, K. (2004). Special issues in the management of depression in older patients. *Canadian Journal of Psychiatry, 49* (Suppl. 1), S41–S50.

Rabin, B. E., & Dorr, A. (1995, March). *Children's understanding of emotional events on family television series.* Paper presented at the meeting of the Society for Research in Child Development, Indianapolis.

Rae, C., Joy, P., Harasty, J., Kemp, A., Kuan, S., Christodoulou, J., Cowell, C. T., & Coltheart, M. (2004). Enlarged temporal lobes in Turner syndrome: An X-chromosome effect? *Cerebral cortex, 14,* 156–164.

Rafaelli, M., & Crockett, L. J. (2003). Sexual risk taking in adolescence: The role of self-regulation and attraction to risk. *Developmental Psychology, 39,* 1036–1046.

Raffaelli, M., & Ontai, L. (2001). "She's sixteen years old and there's boys calling over to the house": An exploratory study of sexual socialization in Latino families. *Culture, Health, and Sexuality, 3,* 295–310.

Rahhal, T. A., May, C. P., & Hasher, L. (2002). Truth and character: Sources that older adults can remember. *Psychological Science, 13,* 101–105.

Ramakrishnan, U. (2004). Maternal circulating nutrient concentrations in pregnancy. *American Journal of Clinical Nutrition, 79,* 17–21.

Ramchandani, N. (2004). Type 2 diabetes children: A burgeoning health problem among overweight children. *American Journal of Nursing, 104,* 65–68.

Ramey, C. T., & Campbell, F. A. (1984). Preventive education for high-risk children: Cognitive consequences of the Carolina Abecedarian Project. *American Journal of Mental Deficiency, 88,* 515–523.

Ramey, C. T., & Ramey, S. L. (1998). Early prevention and early experience. *American Psychologist, 53,* 109–120.

Ramey, C. T., Ramey, S. L., & Lanzi, R. G. (2001). Intelligence and experience. In R. J. Sternberg & E. L. Grigorenko (Eds.), *Environment effects on cognitive development.* Mahwah, NJ: Erlbaum.

Ramirez, M. (2004). Mestiza/o and Chicana/o: General issues. In R. J. Velasquez, B. W. McNeil, & L. M. Arellano

(Eds.), *The handbook of Chicano psychology and mental health.* Mahwah, NJ: Erlbaum.

Rampage, C., Eovaldi, M., Ma, C., & Weigel-Foy, C. (2003). Adoptive families. In F. Walsh (Ed.), *Normal family processes: Growing diversity and complexity* (3rd ed.). New York: Guilford Press.

Ramphal, C. (1962). *A study of three current problems in education.* Unpublished doctoral dissertation, University of Natal, India.

Ransjo-Arvidson, A. B., Matthiesen, A. S., Nissen, L. G., Widstrom, A. M., & Uvnas-Moberg, K. (2001). Maternal analgesia during labor disturbs newborn behavior: Effects on breastfeeding, temperature, and crying. *Birth, 28,* 5–12.

Rantz, M. J., Hicks, L., Petroski, G. F., Madsen, R. W., Mehr, D. R., Conn, V., Zwygart-Staffacher, & Maas, M. (2004). Stability and sensitivity of nursing home quality indicators. *Journals of Gerontology A: Biological Sciences and Medical Sciences, 59,* M79–M82.

Rapaport, S. (1994, November 28). Interview. *U.S. News & World Report,* p. 94.

Raudenbush, S. (2001). Longitudinal data analysis. *Annual Review of Psychology* (Vol. 52). Palo Alto, CA: Annual Reviews.

Raven, P. H., Johnson, G. B., Losos, J., & Singer, S. (2005). *Biology* (7th ed.). New York: McGraw-Hill.

Raver, C. C. (2004). Placing emotional self-regulation in sociocultural and socioeconomic contexts. *Child Development, 75,* 346–353.

Ravid, D., Levie, R., & Ben-Zvi, G. A. (2004). Morphological disorders. In L. Verhoeven & H. Van Balkom (Eds.), *The classification of language disorders.* Mahwah, NJ: Erlbaum.

Ray, O. S., & Ksir, C. J. (2004). *Drugs, society, and human behavior* (10th ed.). New York: McGraw-Hill.

Raymo, J. M., Liang, J., Sugisawa, H., Kobayashi, E., & Sugihara, Y. (2004). Work at older ages in Japan: Variation by gender and employment status. *Journals of Gerontology B: Psychological Sciences and Social Sciences, 59,* S154–S163.

Reb, A. M. (2003). Palliative and end-of-life care: Policy analysis. *Oncology Nursing Forum, 30,* 35–50.

Redinbaugh, E. M., MacCallum, J., & Kiecolt-Glaser, J. K. (1995). Recurrent syndromal depression in caregivers. *Psychology and Aging, 10,* 358–368.

Reed, K. S. (2003). Grief is more than tears. *Nursing Science Quarterly, 16,* 77–81.

Reeves, G., & Schweitzer, J. (2004). Pharmacological management of attention deficit hyperactivity disorder. *Expert Opinions in Pharmacotherapy, 5,* 1313–1320.

Regev, R. H., Lusky, A., Dolfin, T., Litmanovitz, I., Arnon, S., Reichman, B., & the Israel Neonatal Network. (2003). Excess mortality and morbidity among small-for-gestational-age premature infants: A population-based study. *Journal of Pediatrics, 143,* 186–191.

Reid, C. (2004). Kangaroo care. *Neonatal Network, 23,* 53.

Reid, J. D., & Willis, S. L. (1999). Middle age: New thoughts, new directions. In S. L. Willis & J. D. Reid (Eds.), *Life in the middle.* San Diego: Academic Press.

Reid, P. T., & Zalk, S. R. (2001). Academic environments: Gender and ethnicity in U.S. higher education. In J. Worell (Ed.), *Encyclopedia of women and gender.* San Diego: Academic Press.

Reilly, R. (1988, August 15). Here no one is spared. *Sports Illustrated,* 70–77.

Reiner, W. G., & Gearhart, J. P. (2004). Discordant sexual identity in some genetic males with cloacal exstrophy assigned to female sex at birth. *New England Journal of Medicine, 350,* 333–341.

Reis, D., Neiderhiser, J. M., Hetherington, E. M., & Plomin, R. (2000). *The relationship code.* Cambridge, MA: Harvard University Press.

Reisman, A. S. (2001). Death of a spouse: Basic assumptions and continuation of bonds. *Death Studies, 25,* 445–460.

Reitzes, D. C., & Mutran, E. J. (2004). Grandparenthood: Factors influencing frequency of grandparent-grandchildren contact and grandparent role satisfaction. *Journals of Gerontology B: Psychological Sciences and Social Sciences, 59,* S9–S16.

Relier, J. P. (2001). Influence of maternal stress on fetal behavior and brain development. *Biology of the Neonate, 79,* 168–171.

Religion in America (1993). Princeton, NJ: Princeton Religious Research Center.

Rest, J. R. (1986). *Moral development: Advances in theory and research.* New York: Praeger.

Rest, J. R., Narvaez, D., Bebeau, M. J., & Thoma, S. J. (1999). *Postconventional moral thinking.* Mahwah, NJ: Erlbaum.

Reuter-Lorenz, P. A., & others. (2000). Age differences in the frontal lateralization of verbal and spatial working memory revealed by PET. *Journal of Cognitive Neuroscience, 12,* 174–187.

Revelle, S. P. (2004). High standards + high-stakes = high achievement in Massachusetts. *Phi Delta Kappan, 85,* 591–597.

Reyna, V. F. (2004). How people make decisions that involve risk: A dual-process approach. *Current Directions in Psychological Science, 13,* 60–66.

Reyna, V. F., & Brainerd, C. J. (1995). Fuzzy-trace theory: An interim analysis. *Learning and Individual Differences, 7,* 1–75.

Reynolds, A. J. (1999, April). *Pathways to long-term effects in the Chicago Child-Parent Center Program.* Paper presented at the meeting of the Society for Research in Child Development, Albuquerque.

Rhodes, J. E., Grossman, J. B., & Resch, N. L. (2000). Agents of change: Pathways through which mentoring relationships influence adolescents' academic adjustment. *Child Development, 71,* 1662–1671.

Rhodes, S. R. (1983). Age-related differences in work attitudes and behavior: A review and conceptual analysis. *Psychological Bulletin, 93,* 329–367.

Rice, D. P., & Fineman, N. (2004). Economic implications of increased longevity in the United States. *Annual Review of Public Health, 25,* 457–473.

Richardson, G. A., Ryan, C., Willford, J., Day, N. L., & Goldschmidt, L. (2002). Prenatal alcohol and marijuana exposure: Effects on neuropsychological outcomes at 10 years. *Neurotoxicology and Teratology, 24,* 309–320.

Richter, L. (2003). Poverty, underdevelopment, and infant mental health. *Journal of Pediatric and Child Health, 39,* 243–248.

Rickards, T., & deCock, C. (2003). Understanding organizational creativity: Toward a paradigmatic approach. In M. A. Runco (Ed.), *Creativity research handbook.* Cresskill, NJ: Hampton Press.

Ridgeway, D., Waters, E., & Kuczaj, S. A. (1985). Acquisition of emotion-descriptive language: Receptive and productive vocabulary norms for ages 18 months to 6 years. *Developmental Psychology, 21,* 901–908.

Riebe, D., Garber, C. E., Rossi, J. S., Greaney, M. L., Nigg, C. R., Lees, F. D., Burbank, P. M., & Clark, P. G. (2005). Physical activity, physical function, and stages of change in older adults. *American Journal of Health Behavior, 29,* 70–80.

Riethman, H., Ambrosini, A., Castaneda, C., Finklestein, J., Hu, X. L., Mudumri, U. Y., & Wei, P. S. (2004). Mapping and initial analysis of human subtelomeric sequence assemblies. *Genome Research, 14,* 18–28.

Rigby, K. (2004). Bullying in childhood. In P. K. Smith & C. H. Hart (Eds.), *Blackwell handbook of childhood social development.* Malden, MA: Blackwell.

Righetti-Veltema, M., Conne-Perreard, E., Bousquest, A., & Manzano, J. (2002). Postpartum depression and mother-infant relationship at 3 months old. *Journal of Affective Disorders, 70,* 291–306.

Riley, K. P., Snowdon, D. A., & Markesbery, W. R. (2002). Alzheimer's neurofibrillary pathology and the spectrum of cognitive function: Findings from the Nun Study. *Annals of Neurology, 5,* 567–577.

Rimberg, H. M., & Lewis, R. J. (1994). Older adolescents and AIDS: Correlates of self-reported safer sex practices. *Journal of Research on Adolescence, 4,* 453–464.

Rimm, E. B., Stampfer, M. J., Ascherio, A., Giovannucci, E., Colditz, G. A., & Willett, W. C. (1993). Vitamin E consumption and the risk of coronary heart disease in men. *New England Journal of Medicine, 328,* 1450–1456.

Ringdal, G. I., Jordhoy, M. S., Ringdal, K., & Kaasa, S. (2001). The first year of grief and bereavement in close family members to individuals who have died of cancer. *Palliative Medicine, 15,* 91–105.

Rittey, C. D. (2003). Learning difficulties: What the neurologist needs to know. *Journal of Neurology and Neurological Psychiatry, 74,* Supplement 1, 30–36.

Rizzo, M. S. (1999, May 8). Genetic counseling combines science with a human touch. *Kansas City Star,* p. 3.

Robbins, G., Powers, D., & Burgess, S. (2005). *A wellness way of life* (6th ed.). New York: McGraw-Hill.

Roberto, K. A., Allen, K. R., & Blieszner, R. (2001). Grandfathers' perceptions and expectations of relationships with their adult grandchildren. *Journal of Family Issues, 22,* 407–426.

Roberto, K. A., & Skoglund, R. R. (1996). Interactions with grandparents and great-grandparents: A comparison of activities, influences, and relationships. *International Journal of Aging and Human Development, 43,* 107–117.

Roberts, B. L., Dunkle, R., & Haug, M. (1994). Physical, psychological, and social resources as moderators of stress to mental health of the very old. *Journal of Gerontology, 49,* S35–S43.

Roberts, B. W., & Helson, R. (1997). Changes in culture, changes in personality: The influence of individualism in a longitudinal study of women. *Journal of Personality and Social Psychology, 72,* 641–651.

Roberts, D. F., Henriksen, L., & Foehr, V. G. (2004). Adolescents and the media. In R. Lerner & L. Steinberg (Eds.), *Handbook of adolescent psychology.* New York: Wiley.

Roberts, R., O'Connor, T., Dunn, J., Golding, J., & the ALSPAC Study Team. (2004). The effects of child sexual abuse in later family life. *Child Abuse & Neglect, 5,* 525–545.

Robertson, H. (2003). Rape among incarcerated men: Sex, coercion, and STDs. *AIDS Patient Care and STDs, 17,* 423–430.

Robins, R. W., Trzesniewski, K. H., Tracey, J. L., Potter, J., & Gosling, S. D. (2002). Age differences in self-esteem from age 9 to 90. *Psychology and Aging, 17,* 423–434.

Robinson, D. P., & Greene, J. W. (1988). The adolescent alcohol and drug problem: A practical approach. *Pediatric Nursing, 14,* 305–310.

Robinson, R. (2004). End-of-life education in undergraduate nursing curricula. *Dimensions of Critical Care Nursing, 23,* 89–92.

Rochat, P. (2002). Origins of self concept. In G. Bremner & A. Fogel (Eds.), *Blackwell handbook of infant development.* Malden, MA: Blackwell.

Rode, S. S., Chang, P., Fisch, R. O., & Sroufe, L. A. (1981). Attachment patterns of infants separated at birth. *Developmental Psychology, 17,* 188–191.

Rodgers, L. S. (2004). Meaning of bereavement among older African American widows. *Geriatric Nursing, 25,* 10–16.

Rodier, P. M. (2004). Environmental causes of central nervous system maldevelopment. *Pediatrics, 113 (4 Supplement),* 1076–1083.

Rodin, J. (1983). Behavioral medicine: Beneficial effects of self-control training in aging. *International Review of Applied Psychology, 32,* 153–181.

Rodin, J., & Langer, E. J. (1977). Long-term effects of a control-relevant intervention with the institutionalized aged. *Journal of Personality and Social Psychology, 35,* 397–402.

Rogers, A. (1987). *Questions of gender differences: Ego development and moral voice in adolescence.* Unpublished manuscript, Department of Education, Harvard University.

Rogoff, B. (1998). Cognition as a collaborative process. In W. Damon (Ed.), *Handbook of child psychology* (5th ed., Vol. 2). New York: Wiley.

Rogoff, B. (2003). *The cultural nature of human development.* New York: Oxford University Press.

Rohner, R. P., & Rohner, E. C. (1981). Parental acceptance-rejection and parental control: Cross-cultural codes. *Ethnology, 20,* 245–260.

Roman, G. C., Sachdev, P., Royall, D. R., Bullock, R. A., Orgogozo, J. M., Lopez-Pousa, S., Arizaga, R., & Wallin, A. (2004). Vascular cognitive disorder: A new diagnostic category updating vascular cognitive impairment and vascular dementia. *Journal of Neurological Science, 226,* 81–87.

Rook, K. S. (2000). The evolution of social relationships in later adulthood. In S. H. Qualls & N. Abeles (Eds.), *Psychology and the aging revolution.* Washington, DC: American Psychological Association.

Roosa, M. W., Dumka, L. E., Gonzales, N. A., & Knight, G. P. (2002). Cultural/ethnic issues and the prevention scientist in the 21st century. *Prevention & Treatment, 5,* 1–13.

Roper Starch Worldwide. (2000). *Attitudes toward retirement: A poll.* New York: Author.

Rosano, G. M., Vitale, C., Silvestri, A., & Fini, M. (2003). Hormone replacement therapy and cardioprotection: The end of the tale? *Annals of the New York Academy of Science, 997,* 351–357.

Rose, A. A., Feldman, J. F., McCarton, C. M., & Wolfson, J. (1988). Information processing in seven-month-old infants as a function of risk status. *Child Development, 59,* 489–603.

Rose, L. C., & Gallup, A. M. (2000). The 32nd annual Phi Delta Kappa/Gallup Poll of the public's attitudes toward the public schools. *Phi Delta Kappan, 82* (10), 41–58.

Rose, S., & Frieze, I. R. (1993). Young singles' contemporary dating scripts. *Sex Roles, 28,* 499–509.

Rosenberg, E. B. (1992). *The adoption life cycle: The children and their families through the years.* New York: Free Press.

Rosenblith, J. F. (1992). *In the beginning* (2nd ed.). Newbury Park, CA: Sage.

Rosenblum, G. D., & Lewis, M. (2003). Emotional development in adolescence. In G. Adams & M. Berzonsky (Eds.), *Blackwell handbook of adolescence.* Malden, MA: Blackwell.

Rosenfeld, A., & Stark, E. (1987, May). The prime of our lives. *Psychology Today,* pp. 62–72.

Rosenfeld, B. (2004). *Assisted suicide and the right to die.* Washington, DC: American Psychological Association.

Rosenstein, D., & Oster, H. (1988). Differential facial responses to four basic tastes in newborns. *Child Development, 59,* 1555–1568.

Rosenthal, C. J., Martin-Matthews, A., & Matthews, S. H. (1996). Caught in the middle? Occupancy in multiple roles and help to parents in a national probability sample of Canadian adults. *Journals of Gerontology B: Psychological Sciences and Social Sciences, 51,* S274–S283.

Rosenzweig, M. R. (1969). Effects of heredity and environment on brain chemistry, brain anatomy, and learning ability in the rat. In M. Monosevitz, G. Lindzey, & D. D. Thiessen (Eds.), *Behavioral genetics.* New York: Appleton-Century-Crofts.

Rosenzweig, M. R. (2000). Ethology. In A. Kazdin (Ed.), *Encyclopedia of psychology.* Washington, DC, & New York: American Psychological Association and Oxford University Press.

Rosnow, R. L., & Rosenthal, R. L. (2005). *Beginning behavioral research* (5th ed.). Upper Saddle River, NJ: Prentice Hall.

Rospenda, K. M. (2004). Harassment and discrimination. In J. Barling, E. K. Kelloway, & M. R. Frone (Eds.), *Handbook of work stress.* Thousand Oaks, CA: Sage.

Rossi, A. S. (1989). A life-course approach to gender, aging, and intergenerational relations. In K. W. Schaie & C. Schooler (Eds.), *Social structure and aging.* Hillsdale, NJ: Erlbaum.

Rossi, A. S. (2004). The menopausal transition and aging processes. In G. Brim, C. D. Ryff, & R. Kessler (Eds.), How healthy we are: A national study of well-being in midlife. Chicago: University of Chicago Press.

Roth, G. S., Lane, M. A., Ingram, D. K., Mattison, J. A., Elahi, D., Tobin, J. D., Muller, D., & Metter, E. J. (2002). Biomarkers of caloric restriction may predict longevity in humans. *Science, 297,* 811.

Roth, J., & Brooks-Gunn, J. (2000). What do adolescents need for healthy development? Implications for youth policy. *Social Policy Report, Society for Research in Child Development, XIV* (No. 1), 3–19.

Rothbart, M. K. (2004). Temperament and the pursuit of an integrated developmental psychology. *Merrill-Palmer Quarterly, 50,* 492–505.

Rothbart, M. K., & Bates, J. E. (1998). Temperament. In W. Damon (Ed.), *Handbook of child psychology* (5th ed., Vol. 3). New York: Wiley.

Rothbart, M. K., Ellis, L. K., & Posner, M. I. (2004). Temperament and self-regulation. In R. F. Baumeister & K. D. Vohs (Eds.), *Handbook of self-regulation.* New York: Guilford.

Rothbart, M. K., Ellis, L. K., Rueda, M. R., & Posner, M. I. (2003). Developing mechanisms of effortful control. *Journal of Personality, 71,* 1113–1143.

Rothbart, M. K., & Putnam, S. P. (2002). Temperament and socialization. In L. Pulkkinen & A. Caspi (Eds.), *Paths to successful development.* New York: Cambridge University Press.

Rothbart, M. L. K. (1971). Birth order and mother-child interaction. *Dissertation Abstracts, 27,* 45–57.

Rothbaum, F., Poll, M., Azuma, H., Miyake, K., & Weisz, J. (2000). The development of close relationships in Japan and the United States: Paths of symbiotic harmony and generative tension. *Child Development, 71,* 1121–1142.

Rothstein, D. (2001, January 7). Commentary. *Parade Magazine,* p. 12.

Rovee-Collier, C. (1987). Learning and memory in children. In J. D. Osofsky (Ed.), *Handbook of infant development* (2nd ed.). New York: Wiley.

Rovee-Collier, C. (2002). Infant learning and memory. In U. Goswami (Ed.), *Blackwell handbook of childhood cognitive development.* Malden, MA: Blackwell.

Rovee-Collier, C., & Barr, R. (2004). Infant learning and memory. In G. Bremner & A. Fogel (Eds.), *Blackwell handbook of infant development.* Malden, MA: Blackwell.

Rovira, M. T., Antorn, M. T., Paya, A., Castellanos, E., Mur, A., & Carreras, R. (2001). Human immunodeficiency virus infection in pregnant women, transmission, and zidovudine therapy. *European Journal of Obstetrics, Gynecology, and Reproductive Biology, 97,* 46–49.

Rowe, J. W., & Kahn, R. L. (1997). *Successful aging.* New York: Pantheon Books.

Rowe, R., Maughan, B., Worthman, C. M., Costello, E. J., & Angold, A. (2004). Testosterone, antisocial behavior, and social dominance in boys: Pubertal development and biosocial interaction. *Biological Psychiatry, 55,* 546–552.

Rowe, S. M., & Wertsch, J. V. (2004). Vygotsky's model of cognitive development. In U. Goswami (Ed.), *Blackwell handbook of childhood cognitive development.* Malden, MA: Blackwell.

Rubia, K., Overmeyer, S., Taylor, E., Brammer, M., Williams, S., Simmons, A., Andrew, C., & Bullmore, E. (2000). Functional frontalisation with age: Mapping neurodevelopmental trajectories with fMRI. *Neuroscience & Biobehavioral Reviews, 24,* 13–19.

Rubin, D. H., Krasilnikoff, P. A., Leventhal, J. M., Weile, B., & Berget, A. (1986, August 23). Effect of passive smoking on birthweight. *The Lancet,* 415–417.

Rubin, K. (2000). Middle childhood: Social and emotional development. In A. Kazdin (Ed.), *Encyclopedia of psychology.* Washington, DC, & New York: American Psychological Association and Oxford University Press.

Rubin, K. H., Bukowski, W., & Parker, J. G. (1998). Peer interactions, relationships, and groups. In N. Eisenberg (Ed.), *Handbook of child psychology* (5th ed., Vol. 3). New York: Wiley.

Rubin, K. H., Maioni, T. L., & Hornung, M. (1976). Free play behaviors in middle and lower social class preschoolers: Parten and Piaget revisited. *Child Development, 47,* 414–419.

Rubin, Z. (1970). Measurement of romantic love. *Journal of Personality and Social Psychology, 16,* 265–273.

Rubin, Z., & Mitchell, C. (1976). Couples research as couples counseling. *American Psychologist, 31,* 17–25.

Ruble, D. N. (2000). Gender constancy. In A. Kazdin (Ed.), *Encyclopedia of psychology.* Washington, DC, and New York: American Psychological Association and Oxford University Press.

Rudolph, K. L., Chang, S., Lee, H., Gottlieb, G. J., Greider, C., & DePinho, R. A. (1999). Longevity, stress response, and cancer in aging telomerase-deficient mice. *Cell, 96,* 701–712.

Ruff, H. A., & Capozzoli, M. C. (2003). Development of attention and distractibility in the first 4 years of life. *Developmental Psychology, 39,* 877–890.

Rumberger, R. W. (1995). Dropping out of middle school: A multilevel analysis of students and schools. *American Education Research Journal, 3,* 583–625.

Runco, M. (2000). Research on the processes of creativity. In A. Kazdin (Ed.), *Encyclopedia of psychology.* Washington, DC, & New York: American Psychological Association and Oxford University Press.

Runco, M. A. (2004). Creativity. *Annual Review of Psychology* (Vol. 55). Palo Alto, CA: Annual Reviews.

Rupp, K., Strand, A., & Davies, P. S. (2003). Poverty among elderly women: Assessing the SSI options to strengthen Social Security reform. *Journals of Gerontology B: Psychological Sciences and Social Sciences, 58,* S359–S368.

Rusbult, C. E., Olsen, N., Davis, J. L., & Hannon, P. A. (2001). Commitment and relationship maintenance mechanisms. In J. H. Harvey & A. Wenzel (Eds.), *Close romantic relationships.* Mahwah, NJ: Erlbaum.

Russek, L. G., & Schwartz, G. E. (1997). Feelings of parental caring predict health status in midlife: A 35-year follow-up of the Harvard Mastery Study of Stress. *Journal of Behavioral Medicine, 30,* 1–13.

Russell, D. W. (1996). UCLA Loneliness Scale (Version 3): Reliability, validity and factor structure. *Journal of Personality, Assessment, 66,* 20–43.

Russell, S. T., & Joyner, K. (2001). Adolescent sexual orientation and suicide risk: Evidence from a national study. *American Journal of Public Health, 91,* 1276–1281.

Ruxton, C. (2004). Obesity in children. *Nursing Standards, 18,* 47–52.

Ryan, A. S. (1997). The resurgence of breastfeeding in the United States. *Pediatrics, 99,* E12.

Ryan, A. S., Wenjun, Z., & Acosta, A. (2002). Breastfeeding continues to increase into the new millennium. *Pediatrics, 110,* 1103–1109.

Ryff, C. D. (1984). Personality development from the inside: The subjective experience of change in adulthood and aging. In P. B. Baltes & O. G. Brim (Eds.), *Life-span development and behavior.* New York: Academic Press.

Ryff, C. D. (1991). Possible selves in adulthood and old age: A tale of shifting horizons. *Psychology and Aging, 6,* 286–295.

Ryff, C. D., & Singer, B. (2000). Interpersonal flourishing: A positive health agenda for the new millennium. *Personality and Social Psychology Review, 4,* 30–44.

Ryff, C. D., Singer, B., Wing, E. H., & Love, G. D. (2001). Elective affinities and uninvited agonies: Mapping emotion with significant others onto health. In C. D. Ryff & B. Singer (Eds.), *Emotion, social relationships, and health.* New York: Oxford University Press.

Saarni, C. (1999). *The development of emotional competence.* New York: Guilford.

Saarni, C. (2000). Emotional competence: A developmental perspective. In R. Bar-On & J. D. Parker (Eds.), *The handbook of emotional intelligence.* San Francisco: Jossey-Bass.

Sabol, W. J., Coulton, C. J., & Korbin, J. E. (2004). Building community capacity for violence prevention. *Journal of Interpersonal Violence, 19,* 322–340.

Sackett, P. (2003, February). Commentary on stereotype threat. *Monitor on Psychology, 34,* p. 52.

Sackett, P. R., Hardison, C. M., & Cullen, M. J. (2004). On interpreting stereotype threat as accounting for African-American White differences in cognitive tests. *American Psychologist, 59,* 7–13.

Saczynski, J., & Willis, S. L. (2001). *Cognitive training and maintenance of intervention effects in the elderly.* Unpublished manuscript. University Park, PA: Pennsylvania State University.

Sadavoy, J., Lazarus, L. W., Jarvik, L. E., & Grossberg, G. T. (Eds.). (1996). *Comprehensive review of geriatric psychiatry* (2nd ed.). Washington, DC: American Psychiatric Press.

Sadker, M. P., & Sadker, D. M. (2005). *Teachers, schools, and society* (7th ed.). New York: McGraw-Hill.

Safar, M. E., & Smulyan, H. (2004). Hypertension in women. *American Journal of Hypertension, 17,* 82–87.

Sagan, C. (1977). *The dragons of Eden.* New York: Random House.

Saigal, S., den Ouden, L., Wolke, D., Hoult, L., Paneth, N., Streiner, D. L., Whitaker, A., & Pinto-Martin, J. (2003). School-age outcomes in children who were extremely low birth weight from four international population-based cohorts. *Pediatrics, 112,* 943–950.

Salat, D. H., Kaye, J. A., & Janowsky, J. S. (2002). Greater orbital prefrontal lobe selectively predicts worse working memory performance in older adults. *Cerebral Cortex, 12,* 494–505.

Salovey, P., & Mayer, J. D. (1990). Emotional intelligence. *Imagination, Cognition, and Personality, 9,* 185–211.

Salthouse, T. A. (1991). *Theoretical perspectives on cognitive aging.* Mahwah, NJ: Erlbaum.

Salthouse, T. A. (1994). The nature of influence of speed on adult age differences in cognition. *Developmental Psychology, 30,* 240–259.

Salthouse, T. A. (1996). General and specific speed mediation of adult age differences in memory. *Journals of Gerontology A: Biological Sciences and Medical Sciences, 51,* P30–P42.

Salthouse, T. A. (2000). Adulthood and aging: Cognitive processes and development. In A. Kazdin (Ed.), *Encyclopedia of psychology.* Washington, DC, & New York: American Psychological Association and Oxford University Press.

Salthouse, T. A., & Miles, J. D. (2002). Aging and time-sharing aspects of executive control. *Memory and Cognition, 30,* 572–582.

Salthouse, T. A., & Skovronek, E. (1992). Within-context assessment of working memory. *Journal of Gerontology, 47,* P110–P117.

Salvatore, M. E., Apparsundaram, S., & Gerhardt, G. A. (2003). Decreased plasma membrane expression of striatal dopamine transporter in aging. *Neurobiology of Aging, 24,* 1147–1154.

Samaniego, R. Y., & Gonzales, N. A. (1999). Multiple mediators of the effects of acculturation status on delinquency for Mexican American adolescents. *American Journal of Community Psychology, 27,* 189–210.

Samii, A., Nutt, J. G., & Ransom, B. R. (2004). Parkinson's disease. *Lancet, 363,* 1783–1793.

Samour, P. Q., Helm, K. K., & Lang, C. E. (Eds.). (2000). *Handbook of pediatric nutrition* (2nd ed.). Aspen, CO: Aspen.

Samuelsson, S., Lundberg, I., & Herkner, B. (2004). ADHD and reading disability in male adults. *Journal of Learning Disabilities, 37,* 155–168.

Sanchez-Johnsen, L. A., Fitzgibbon, M. L., Matinovich, Z., Stolley, M. R., Dyer, A. R., & Van Horn, L. (2004). Ethnic differences in correlates of obesity between Latin-American and Black women. *Obesity Research, 12,* 652–660.

Sands, R. G., & Goldberg-Glen, R. S. (2000). Factors associated with stress among grandparents raising their grandchildren. *Family Relations, 49,* 97–105.

Sandstrom, M. J., & Zakriski, A. L. (2004). Understanding the experience of peer rejection. In J. B. Kupersmidt & K. A. Dodge (Eds.), *Children's peer relations: From development to intervention.* Washington, DC: American Psychological Association.

Sangree, W. H. (1989). Age and power: Life-course trajectories and age structuring of power relations in East and West Africa. In D. I. Kertzer & K. W. Schaie (Eds.), *Age structuring in comparative perspective.* Hillsdale, NJ: Erlbaum.

Sanson, A., & Rothbart, M. K. (1995). Child temperament and parenting. In M. H. Bornstein (Ed.), *Handbook of parenting* (Vol. 4). Hillsdale, NJ: Erlbaum.

Sanson, A., Smart, D., & Hemphill, S. (2004). Temperament and social development. In P. Smith & C. Hart (Eds.), *Blackwell handbook of childhood social development.* Malden, MA: Blackwell.

Santiago-Delefosse, M. J., & Delefosse, J. M. O. (2002). Three positions on child thought and language. *Theory and Psychology, 12,* 723–747.

Santiseban, D. A., & Mitrani, V. B. (2003). The influence of acculturation processes on the family. In K. M. Chun, P. B. Organista, & G. Marin (Eds.), *Acculturation.* Washington, DC: American Psychological Association.

Santrock, J. W. (2004). *Educational psychology* (2nd ed.). New York: McGraw-Hill.

Santrock, J. W. (2006). *Educational psychology* (2nd ed., Rev. Update). New York: McGraw-Hill.

Santrock, J. W., & Halonen, J. A. (2004). *Your guide to college success* (3rd ed.). Belmont, CA: Wadsworth.

Santrock, J. W., & Halonen, J. A. (2006). *Your guide to college success* (4th ed.). Belmont, CA: Wadsworth.

Santrock, J. W., Sitterle, K. A., & Warshak, R. A. (1988). Parent-child relationships in stepfather families. In P. Bronstein & C. P. Cowan (Eds.), *Fatherhood today: Men's changing roles in the family.* New York: Wiley.

Santrock, J. W., & Warshak, R. A. (1979). Father custody and social development in boys and girls. *Journal of Social Issues, 35,* 112–125.

Saraswathi, T. S., & Mistry, J. (2003). The cultural context of child development. In I. B. Weiner (Ed.), *Handbook of psychology* (Vol. VI). New York: Wiley.

Sarigiani, P. A., & Petersen, A. C. (2000). Adolescence: Puberty and biological maturation. In A. Kazdin (Ed.), *Encyclopedia of psychology.* Washington, DC, & New York: American Psychological Association and Oxford University Press.

Sarks, A. J. (2002). Age related macular degeneration. *Clinical Evidence, 8,* 614–628.

Sarrel, P., & Masters, W. (1982). Sexual molestation of men by women. *Archives of Human Sexuality, 11,* 117–131.

Sauber, M., & Corrigan, E. M. (1970). *The six year experience of unwed mothers as parents.* New York: Community Council of Greater New York.

Savell, V. H., Hughes, S. M., Bower, C., & Parham, D. M. (2004). Lymphocytic infiltration in pediatric thyroid carcinomas. *Pediatric and Developmental Pathology, 7,* 487–492.

Savin-Williams, R. C. (2001). *Mom, dad, I'm gay.* Washington, DC: American Psychological Association.

Savin-Williams, R., & Diamond, L. (2004). Sex. In R. Lerner & L. Steinberg (Eds.), *Handbook of adolescent psychology* (2nd ed.). New York: Wiley.

Sawnani, H., Jackson, T., Murphy, T., Beckerman, R., & Simakajornboon, N. (2004). The effect of maternal smoking on respiratory and arousal patterns in preterm infants during sleep. *American Journal of Respiratory and Critical Care Medicine, 169,* 733–738.

Sax, L. J., Astin, A. W., Lindholm, J. A., Korn, W. S., Saenz, V. B., & Mahoney, K. M. (2003). *The American college freshman: National norms for fall 2003.* Los Angeles: Higher Education Research Institute, Los Angeles.

Saxena, R., Borzewski, D. L., & Rickert, V. I. (2002). Physical activity levels among urban adolescent females. *Journal of Pediatric and Adolescent Gynecology, 15,* 279–284.

Sayer, R., Law, E., Connelly, P. J., & Breen, K. C. (2004). Association of acetylcholinesterase with Alzheimer's disease and response to cholinesterase inhibitors. *Clinical Biochemistry, 36,* 98–104.

Scafidi, F., & Field, T. M. (1996). Massage therapy improves behavior in neonates born to HIV-positive mothers. *Journal of Pediatric Psychology, 21,* 889–897.

Scannell-Desch, E. (2003). Women's adjustment to widowhood: Theory, research, and methods. *Journal of Psychosocial Nursing and Mental Health Services, 41,* 28–36.

Scaramella, L. V., & Conger, R. D. (2004). Continuity versus discontinuity in parent and adolescent negative affect. In R. D. Conger, F. O. Lorenz, & K. A. S. Wickrama (Eds.), *Continuity and change in family relations.* Mahwah, NJ: Erlbaum.

Scarr, S. (1993). Biological and cultural diversity: The legacy of Darwin for development. *Child Development, 64,* 1333–1353.

Scarr, S. (2000). Day care. In A. Kazdin (Ed.), *Encyclopedia of psychology.* Washington, DC, & New York: American Psychological Association and Oxford University Press.

Scarr, S., & Weinberg, R. A. (1983). The Minnesota adoption studies: Genetic differences and malleability. *Child Development, 54,* 182–259.

Schaalma, H. P., Abraham, C., Gillmore, M. R., & Kok, G. (2004). Sex education as health promotion: What does it take? *Archives of Sexual Behavior, 33,* 259–269.

Schachman, K. A., Lee, R. K., & Lederma, R. P. (2004). Baby boot camp: Facilitating maternal role adaptation among military wives. *Nursing Research, 53,* 107–115.

Schachter, S. C., & Ransil, B. J. (1996). Handedness distributions in nine professional groups. *Perceptual and Motor Skills, 82,* 51–63.

Schaffer, D. V., & Gage, F. H. (2004). Neurogenesis and neuroadaptation. *Neuromolecular Medicine, 5,* 1–9.

Schaffer, H. R. (1996). *Social development.* Malden, MA: Blackwell.

Schaie, K. W. (1993). The Seattle longitudinal studies of adult intelligence. *Current Directions in Psychological Science, 2,* 171–175.

Schaie, K. W. (1994). The life course of adult intellectual abilities. *American Psychologist, 49,* 304–313.

Schaie, K. W. (1996). *Intellectual development in adulthood: The Seattle Longitudinal Study.* New York: Cambridge University Press.

Schaie, K. W. (2000). Unpublished review of J. W. Santrock's *Life-span development* (8th ed.). New York: McGraw-Hill.

Schaie, K. W., & Willis, S. L. (2000). A stage theory model of adult development revisited. In R. Rubinstein, M. Moss, & M. Kleban (Eds.), *The many dimensions of aging: Essays in honor of M. Powell Lawton.* New York: Springer.

Schaie, K. W., & Willis, S. (2002). *Adult development and aging* (5th ed.). Upper Saddle River, NJ: Prentice Hall.

Schalagar, B. L., Brown, T. T., Lugar, H. M., Visscher, K. M., Miezin, F. M., & Petersen, S. E. (2002). Functional neuroanatomical differences between adults and

school-age children in processing single words. *Science, 296,* 1476–1479.

Schank, R. C. (2004). *Making minds less well educated than our own.* Mahwah, NJ: Erlbaum.

Scheer, S. D. (1996, March). *Adolescent to adult transitions: Social status and cognitive factors.* Paper presented at the meeting of the Society for Research on Adolescence, Boston.

Schegel, A. (2000). The global spread of adolescent culture. In L. J. Crockett & R. K. Silbereisen (Eds.), *Negotiating adolescence in times of social change.* New York: Cambridge University Press.

Schellenbach, C., Leadbeater, B., & Moore, K. A. (2004). Enhancing the developmental outcomes of adolescent parents and their children. In K. I. Maton, C. J. Schellenbach, B. J. Leadbeater, & A. L. Solarz (Eds.), *Investing in children, youth, families, and communities.* Thousand Oaks, CA: Sage.

Schieman, S., Van Gundy, K., & Taylor, J. (2002). The relationship between age and depressive symptoms: A test of competing explanatory and suppression influences. *Journal of Aging and Health, 14,* 260–285.

Schiffman, S. S. (1996). Smell and taste. In J. E. Birren (Ed.), *Encyclopedia of gerontology.* San Diego: Academic Press.

Schlegel, M. (2000). All work and play. *Monitor on Psychology, 31* (11), 50–51.

Schlossberg, N. K. (2004). *Retire smart retire happy.* Washington, DC: American Psychological Association.

Schmidt, U. (2003). Aetiology of eating disorders in the 21st century: New answers to old questions. *European Child and Adolescent Psychiatry, 12* (Suppl. 1), I130–I137.

Schneider, B. H., Atkinson, L., & Tardif, C. (2001). Child-parent attachment and children's peer relations: A quantitative review. *Developmental Psychology, 37,* 86–100.

Schneider, W. (2004). Memory development in childhood. In P. Smith & C. Hart (Eds.), *Blackwell handbook of childhood cognitive development.* Malden, MA: Blackwell.

Schneider, W., & Pressley, M. (1997). *Memory development from 2 to 20* (2nd ed.). Mahwah, NJ: Erlbaum.

Schneiderman, N., Antoni, M. H., Saab, P. G., & Ironson, G. (2001). Health psychology: Psychological and biobehavioral aspects of chronic disease management. *Annual Review of Psychology* (Vol. 52). Palo Alto, CA: Annual Reviews.

Schoka, E., & Hayslip, B. (1999, November). *Grief and the family system: The roles of communication, affect, and cohesion.* Paper presented at the meeting of the Gerontological Society of America, San Francisco.

Schooler, C. (2001). The intellectual effects of the demands of the work environment. In R. J. Sternberg & E. L. Grigorenko (Eds.), *Environmental effects on cognitive abilities.* Mahwah, NJ: Erlbaum.

Schooler, C., Mulatu, S., & Oates, G. (1999). The continuing effects of substantively complex work on the intellectual functioning of older workers. *Psychology and Aging, 14,* 483–506.

Schrag, S. G., & Dixon, R. L. (1985). Occupational exposure associated with male reproductive dysfunction. *Annual Review of Pharmacology and Toxicology, 25,* 467–592.

Schugens, M. M., Daum, I., Spindler, M., & Birbaumer, N. (1997). Differential effects of aging on explicit and implicit memory. *Aging, Neuropsychology, and Cognition, 4,* 33–44.

Schulenberg, J., O'Malley, P. M., Bachman, J. G., & Johnson, L. D. (2000). "Spread your wings and fly": The course of health and well-being during the transition to young adulthood. In L. Crockett & R. Silbereisen (Eds.), *Negotiating adolescence in times of social change.* New York: Cambridge University Press.

Schultz, R., & Curnow, C. (1988). Peak performance and age among super athletes: Track and field, swimming, baseball, tennis, and golf. *Journal of Gerontology, 43,* P113–P120.

Schum, T. R., McAuliffe, T. L., Simms, M. D., Walter, J. A., Lewis, M., & Pupp, R. (2001). Factors associated with toilet training in the 1990s. *Ambulatory Pediatrics, 1,* 79–86.

Schwarzer, R., & Schultz, U. (2003). Stressful life events. In I. B. Weiner (Ed.), *Handbook of psychology* (Vol. IX). New York: Wiley.

Schwerha, D. J., & McMullin, D. L. (2002). Prioritizing ergonomic research in aging for the 21st century American workforce. *Experimental Aging Research, 28,* 99–110.

Schwimmer, J. B., Burwinkle, T. M., & Varni, J. W. (2003). Health-related quality of life of severely obese children and adolescents. *Journal of the American Medical Association, 289,* 1813–1819.

Scott, C. M. (2004). Syntactic contributions to literacy learning. In C. A. Stone, E. R. Silliman, B. J. Ehren, & K. Apel (Eds.),

Handbook of language and literacy. New York: Guilford.

Scott, C. M., & Popovich, D. J. (2001). Undiagnosed alcoholism and prescription drug misuse among the elderly. *Caring, 20,* 20–23.

Scott-Jones, D. (1995, March). *Incorporating ethnicity and socioeconomic status in research with children.* Paper presented at the meeting of the Society for Research in Child Development, Indianapolis.

Sears, R. R., & Feldman, S. S. (Eds.). (1973). *The seven ages of man.* Los Altos, CA: Kaufmann.

Sebre, S., Sprugevica, I., Novotni, A., Boneveski, D., Pakalniskiene, V., Popuescu, D., Turchina, T., Friedrich, W., & Lewis, O. (2004). Cross cultural comparisons of child-reported emotional and physical abuse: Rates, risk factors, and psychosocial symptoms. *Child Abuse & Neglect, 28,* 113–127.

Sedgh, G., Spiegelman, D., Larsen, C., Msamanga, G., & Pawzi, W. W. (2004). Breastfeeding and maternal HIV-1 disease progression and mortality. *AIDS, 18,* 1043–1049.

Seeman, T. E., Charpentier, P. A., Berkman, L. F., Tinetti, M. E., Guralnik, J. M., Albert, M., Blazer, D., & Rowe, J. W. (1994). Predicting changes in physical performance in a high-functioning elderly cohort: MacArthur Studies of Successful Aging. *Journal of Gerontology, 49,* M97–M108.

Seeman, T. E., & Chen, X. (2002). Risk and protective factors for physical functioning in older adults with and without chronic conditions: MacArthur Studies of Successful Aging. *Journals of Gerontology B: Psychological Sciences and Social Sciences, 57,* S135–S144.

Segerberg, O. (1982). *Living to be 100: 1200 who did and how they did it.* New York: Scribner's.

Segrin, C., & Flora, J. (2005). *Family communication.* Mahwah, NJ: Erlbaum.

Seguin, R., & Nelson, M. E. (2003). The benefits of strength training for older adults. *American Journal of Preventive Medicine, 25* (Suppl. 2), 141–149.

Seidenfeld, M. E., Sosin, E., & Rickert, V. I. (2004). Nutrition and eating disorders in adolescents. *Mt. Sinai Journal of Medicine, 71,* 155–161.

Seidman, E. (2000). School transitions. In A. Kazdin (Ed.), *Encyclopedia of psychology.* Washington, DC, & New York: American Psychological Association and Oxford University Press.

Seifert, L. S. (2002). Toward a psychology of religion, spirituality, meaning-search, and aging: Past research and practical application. *Journal of Adult Development, 9,* 61–78.

Seltzer, J. (2004). Cohabitation and family change. In M. Coleman & L. Ganong (Eds.), *Handbook of contemporary families.* Thousand Oaks, CA: Sage.

Seroczynski, A. D., Jacquez, F. M., & Cole, D. (2003). Depression and suicide during adolescence. In G. Adams & M. Berzonsky (Eds.), *Blackwell handbook of adolescence.* Malden, MA: Blackwell.

Serpell, R. (1974). Aspects of intelligence in a developing country. *African Social Research, 17,* 576–596.

Serpell, R. (1982). Measures of perception, skills, and intelligence. In W. W. Hartup (Ed.), *Review of child development research* (Vol. 6, pp. 392–440). Chicago: University of Chicago Press.

Serpell, R. (2000). Culture and intelligence. In A. Kazdin (Ed.), *Encyclopedia of psychology.* Washington, DC, & New York: American Psychological Association and Oxford University Press.

Serra, J. A., & others. (2004). Oxidative stress in Alzheimer's and vascular dementias. *Journal of Neurological Science, 218,* 17–24.

Seynnes, O., Singh, M. A. F., Hue, O., Pras, P., Legros, P., & Bernard, P. L. (2004). Physiological and functional responses to low-moderate versus high-intensity progressive resistance training in frail elders. *Journals of Gerontology A: Biological Sciences and Medical Sciences, 59,* M503–M509.

Shafii, T., Stovel, K., Davis, R., & Holmes, K. (2004). Is condom use habit forming? Condom use at sexual debut and subsequent condom use. *Sexually Transmitted Diseases, 31,* 366–372.

Shamir, A., & Tzuriel, D. (2004). Children's mediational teaching style as a function of intervention for cross-age peer interaction. *School Psychology International, 25,* 59–78.

Shapiro, K., & Caramazza, A. (2003). The representation of grammatical categories in the brain. *Trends in Cognitive Science, 7,* 201–206.

Sharma, A. R., McGue, M. K., & Benson, P. L. (1996). The emotional and behavioral adjustment of adopted adolescents: Part I: Age at adoption. *Children and Youth Services Review, 18,* 101–114.

Sharma, A. R., McGue, M. K., & Benson, P. L. (1998). The psychological adjustment of United States adopted adolescents and their nonadopted siblings. *Child Development, 69,* 791–802.

Sharma, B. R. (2004). Withholding and withdrawing of life support: A medicolegal dilemma. *American Journal of Forensic and Medical Pathology, 25,* 150–155.

Sharma, V. (2002). Pharmacotherapy of postpartum depression. *Expert Opinions on Pharmacotherapy, 3,* 1421–1431.

Sharp, E. A., & Ganong, L. H. (2000). Awareness about expectations: Are unrealistic beliefs changed by integrative teaching? *Family Relations, 49,* 71–76.

Sharp, L., Cardy, A. H., Cotton, S. C., & Little, J. (2004). CYP17 gene polymorphisms: Prevalence and associations with hormone levels and related factors, a HuGE review. *American Journal of Epidemiology, 160,* 729–740.

Sharpless, N. E., & DePinho, R. A. (2004). Telomeres, stem cells, senescence, and cancer. *Journal of Clinical Investigation, 113,* 160–168.

Shaver, P. R. (1986, August). *Being lonely, falling in love: Perspectives from attachment theory.* Paper presented at the meeting of the American Psychological Association, Washington, DC.

Shaver, P. R., & Hazan, C. (1993). Adult romantic attachment: Theory and evidence. In W. H. Jones & D. Perlman (Eds.), *Advances in personal relationships.* London: Jessica Kingsley.

Shaver, P. R., & Mikulincer, M. (2003). The psychodynamics of social judgments: An attachment theory perspective. In J. P. Forgas, K. D. Williams, & W. von Hippel (Eds.), *Social judgments: Implicit and explicit processes.* Philadelphia: Psychology Press.

Shay, J. W., & Wright, W. E. (1999). Telomeres and telomerase in the regulation of cellular aging. In V. A. Bohr, B. F. Clark, & T. Stevenser (Eds.), *Molecular biology of aging.* Copenhagen, Denmark: Munksgaard.

Shay, J. W., & Wright, W. E. (2000). The use of telomerized cells for tissue engineering. *Nature Biotechnology, 18,* 22–23.

Shay, J. W., & Wright, W. E. (2002). Telomerase: A target for cancer therapeutics. *Cancer Cell, 2,* 257–265.

Shay, J. W., & Wright, W. E. (2004). Telomeres are double-strand DNA breaks hidden from DNA damage responses. *Molecular Cell, 14,* 420–421.

Sheehan, D. K., & Schirm, V. (2003). End-of-life care of older adults. *American Journal of Nursing, 103,* 48–51.

Sheets, R. H. (2005). *Diversity pedagogy.* Boston: Allyn & Bacon.

Shemie, S. D. (2004). Variability of brain death practices. *Critical Care Medicine, 32,* 2564–2565.

Shepard, G. H. (2002). Three days for weeping: Dreams, emotions, and death in Peruvian Amazon. *Medical Anthropology Quarterly, 16,* 200–209.

Sheridan, L., & Ghrorayeb, G. (2004). Lebanon. In K. Malley-Morrison (Ed.), *International perspectives on family violence and abuse.* Mahwah, NJ: Erlbaum.

Sherif-Trask, B. (2003). Love, courtship, and marriage from a cross-cultural perspective. In R. R. Hamon & B. B. Ingoldsby (Eds.), *Mate selection across cultures.* Thousand Oaks, CA: Sage.

Sherwood, A., Light, K. C., & Blumenthal, J. A. (1989). Effects of aerobic exercise training on hemodynamic responses during psychosocial stress in normotensive and borderline hypertensive Type A men: A preliminary report. *Psychosomatic Medicine, 51,* 123–136.

Shi, Y., Chichung Lie, D., Taupin, P., Nakashima, K., Ray, J., Yu, R. T., Gage, F. H., & Evans, R. M. (2004). Expression and function of orphan nuclear receptor TLX in adult neural stem cells. *Nature, 427,* 78–83.

Shields, S. A. (1991). Gender in the psychology of emotion. In K. T. Strongman (Ed.), *International review of studies of emotion* (Vol. 1). New York: Wiley.

Shiri, R., Koskimaki, J., Hakam, M., Hakkinen, J., Tammela, T. L., Huhtala, H., & Auvinen, A. (2003). Effect of chronic diseases on incidence of erectile dysfunction. *Urology, 62,* 1097–1102.

Shneidman, E. S. (1973). *Deaths of man.* New York: Quadrangle/New York Times.

Shonk, S. M., & Cicchetti, D. (2001). Maltreatment, competency deficits, and risk for academic and behavioral maladjustment. *Developmental Psychology, 37,* 3–17.

Short, M. (2003). Menopause, mood, and management. *Climacteric, 6 (Suppl. 2),* 33–36.

Shrier, D. K. (2003). Psychosocial aspects of women's lives: Work, family, and life cycle issues. *Psychiatric Clinics of North America, 26,* 741–757.

Shulman, S., & Ben-Artzi, E. (2003). Age-related differences in the transition from adolescence to adulthood and links with family relationships. *Journal of Adult Development, 10,* 217–226.

Siegel, L. S. (1988). Evidence that IQ scores are irrelevant to the definition and analysis of reading disability. *Canadian Journal of Psychology, 42,* 202–215.

Siegel, L. S. (1989, April). *Perceptual-motor, cognitive, and language skills as predictors of cognitive abilities at school age.* Paper presented at the biennial meeting of the Society for Research in Children, Kansas City.

Siegel, L. S. (2003). Learning disabilities. In I. B. Weiner (Ed.), *Handbook of psychology* (Vol. VI). New York: Wiley.

Siegel, L. S., & Himel, N. (1998). Socioeconomic status, age and the classification of dyslexic and poor readers: Further evidence of the irrelevancy of IQ to reading disability. *Dyslexia, 4,* 90–104.

Siegfried, T. (2002, January 16). Explaining aging requires complicated brains. *Dallas Morning News,* p. 3F.

Siegler, I. C., Bosworth, H. B., & Poon, L. W. (2003). Disease, health, and aging. In I. B. Weiner (Ed.), *Handbook of psychology* (Vol. VI). New York: Wiley.

Siegler, I. C., & Costa, P. T. (1999, August). *Personality change and continuity in midlife: UNC Alumni Heart Study.* Paper presented at the meeting of the American Psychological Association, Boston.

Siegler, I. C., Kaplan, B. H., Von Dras, D. D., & Mark, D. B. (1999). Cardiovascular health: A challenge for midlife. In S. L. Willis & J. D. Reid (Eds.), *Life in the middle: Psychological and social development in middle age.* San Diego: Academic Press.

Siegler, R. S. (1998). *Children's thinking* (3rd ed.). Upper Saddle River, NJ: Prentice Hall.

Siegler, R. S. (2003). Relations between short-term and long-term cognitive development. *Psychological Science Agenda, 16,* 8–10.

Siegler, R. S., & Alibali, M. W. (2005). *Children's thinking* (4th ed.). Upper Saddle River, NJ: Prentice Hall.

Signore, C. (2001). Rubella. *Primary Care Update in Obstetrics and Gynecology, 8,* 133–137.

Silva, A. (2004). Convergence of long-term care planning and retirement planning at the work place. *Journal of Aging and Social Policy, 16,* 85–102.

Silva, C., & Martins, M. (2003). Relations between children's invented spelling and children's phonological awareness. *Educational Psychology, 23,* 3–16.

Silverdale, M. A., Nicholson, S. L., Ravenscroft, P., Crossman, A. R., Millan, M. J., & Brotchie, J. M. (2004). Selective blockade of D(3) dopamine receptors enhances the anti-parkinsonian properties of ropinirole and levodopa in the MPTP-lesioned primate. *Experimental Neurology, 188,* 128–138.

Silverstein, L. B. (2001). Father and families. In J. P. McHale & W. S. Grolnick (Eds.), *Retrospect and prospect in the psychological study of families.* Mahwah, NJ: Erlbaum.

Silverstein, M., Conroy, S. J., Wang, H., Giarrusso, R., & Bengston, V. L. (2002). Reciprocity in parent-child relation over the adult life course. *Journals of Gerontology B: Psychological Sciences and Social Sciences, 57,* S3–S13.

Simmons, R. G., & Blyth, D. A. (1987). *Moving into adolescence.* Hawthorne, NY: Aldine.

Simons, J. M., Finlay, B., & Yang, A. (1991). *The adolescent and young adult fact book.* Washington, DC: Children's Defense Fund.

Simons, J. S., Dodson, C. S., Bell, D., & Schacter, D. L. (2004). Specific- and partial-source memory: Effects on aging. *Psychology and Aging, 19,* 689–694.

Simons-Morton, B., Haynie, D. L., Crump, A. D., Eitel, P., & Saylor, K. E. (2001). Peer and parent influences on smoking and drinking among early adolescents. *Health Education and Behavior, 28,* 95–107.

Simonton, D. K. (1996). Creativity. In J. E. Birren (Ed.), *Encyclopedia of aging.* San Diego: Academic Press.

Singer, D. G. (1993). Creativity of children in a changing world. In G. L. Berry & J. K. Asamen (Eds.), *Children and television: Images in a changing sociocultural world.* Newbury Park, CA: Sage.

Singer, L. T., Arendt, R., Fagan, J., Minnes, S., Salvator, A., Bolek, T., & Becker, M. (1999). Neonatal visual information processing in cocaine-exposed and non-exposed infants. *Infant Behavior and Development, 22,* 1–15.

Singer, T., Lindenberger, U., & Baltes, P. B. (2003). Plasticity of memory for new learning in very old age: Six-year longitudinal findings in the Berlin Aging Study (BASE). *Psychology and Aging, 18,* 318–331.

Singer, T., Verhaeghen, P., Ghisletta, P., Lindenberger, U., & Baltes, P. B. (2003). The fate of cognition in very old age: Six-year longitudinal findings in the Berlin Aging Study (BASE). *Psychology and Aging, 18*, 318–331.

Singh, M. A. F. (2002). Exercise comes of age: Rationale and recommendations for a geriatric exercise prescription. *Journals of Gerontology A: Biological Sciences and Medical Sciences, 57*, M262–M282.

Singh, M. A. F. (2004). Exercise and aging. *Clinical Geriatric Medicine, 20*, 201–221.

Singh, N. A., Clements, K. M., & Fiatarone, M. A. (1997). A randomized controlled trial of progressive resistance training in depressed elders. *Journals of Gerontology A: Biological Sciences and Medical Sciences, 52*, M27–M35.

Singh, S., Darroch, J. E., Vlasoff, M., & Nadeau, J. (2004). *Adding it up: The benefits of investing in sexual and reproductive health care.* New York: The Alan Guttmacher Institute.

Singh, S., Wulf, D., Samara, R., & Cuca, Y. P. (2000). Gender differences in the timing of first intercourse: Data from 14 countries. *International Family Planning Perspectives, 26*, 21–28, 43.

Skinner, B. F. (1938). *The behavior of organisms: An experimental analysis.* New York: Appleton-Century-Crofts.

Skinner, B. F. (1957). *Verbal behavior.* New York: Appleton-Century-Crofts.

Skoog, I., Blennow, K., & Marcusson, J. (1996). Dementia. In J. E. Birren (Ed.), *Encyclopedia of gerontology* (Vol. 1). San Diego: Academic Press.

Slater, A. (2004). Visual perception. In A. Fogel & G. Bremner (Eds.), *Blackwell handbook of infant development.* London: Blackwell.

Slater, A., Field, T., & Hernandez-Reif, M. (2002). The development of the senses. In A. Slater & M. Lewis (Eds.), *Introduction to infant development.* New York: Oxford University Press.

Slater, A., Morison, V., & Somers, M. (1988). Orientation discrimination and cortical function in the human newborn. *Perception, 17*, 597–602.

Sleet, D. A., & Mercy, J. A. (2003). Promotion of safety, security, and well-being. In M. H. Bornstein, L. Davidson, C. L. M. Keyes, & K. A. Moore (Eds.), *Well-being.* Mahwah, NJ: Erlbaum.

Sleight, P. (2003). Current options in the management of coronary artery disease. *American Journal of Cardiology, 92*, 4N–8N.

Slijper, F. M., Drop, S. L., Molennar, J. C., & de Muinck Keizer-Schrama, S. M. (1998). Long-term psychological evaluation of intersex children. *Archives of Sexual Behavior, 27*, 125–144.

Slobin, D. (1972, July). Children and language: They learn the same way around the world. *Psychology Today*, 71–76.

Slomkowski, C., Rende, R., Conger, K. J., Simons, R. L., & Conger, R. D. (2001). Sisters, brothers, and delinquency: Social influence during early and middle adolescence. *Child Development, 72*, 271–283.

Small, D. H., & Fodero, L. R. (2002). Cholinergic regulation of synaptic plasticity as a therapeutic target in Alzheimer's disease. *Journal of Alzheimer's Disease, 4*, 349–355.

Small, S. A. (1990). *Preventive programs that support families with adolescents.* Washington, DC: Carnegie Council on Adolescent Development.

Smetana, J. (2005). Social domain theory. In M. Killen & J. Smetana (Eds.), *Handbook of moral development.* Mahwah, NJ: Erlbaum.

Smetana, J., & Turiel, E. (2003). Moral development during adolescence. In G. Adams & M. Berzonsky (Eds.), *Blackwell handbook of adolescence.* Malden, MA: Blackwell.

Smit, E. M. (2002). Adopted children. *Journal of Child and Adolescent Psychiatric Nursing, 15*, 143–150.

Smith, A. D. (1996). Memory. In J. E. Birren (Ed.), *Encyclopedia of gerontology* (Vol. 2). San Diego: Academic Press.

Smith, D. (2004a). *Introduction to special education* (5th ed.). Boston: Allyn & Bacon.

Smith, D. (2005). *Working with gifted and talented pupils in the secondary school.* Thousand Oaks, CA: Sage.

Smith, J., & Baltes, P. B. (1990). Wisdom-related knowledge: Age-cohort differences in responses to life-planning problems. *Developmental Psychology, 26*, 494–505.

Smith, K. (2002). *Who's minding the kids? Child care arrangements: Spring 1977.* Current Population Reports, P70–86. Washington, DC: U.S. Census Bureau.

Smith, L., Muir, D. W., & Kisilevsky, B. (2001, April). *Preterm infants' responses to auditory stimulation of varying intensity.* Paper presented at the meeting of the Society for Research in Child Development, Minneapolis.

Smith, L. B., & Samuelson, L. K. (2003). Different is good: Connectionism and dynamic systems theory are complementary emergentist approaches to development. *Developmental Science, 6*, 434–439.

Smith, L. M., Chang, L., Yonekura, M. L., Gilbride, K., Kuo, J., Poland, R. E., Walot, I., & Ernst, T. (2001). Brain proton magnetic resonance spectroscopy and imaging in children exposed to cocaine in utero. *Pediatrics, 107*, 227.

Smith, P. H., White, J. W., & Holland, L. J. (2003). A longitudinal perspective on dating violence among adolescent and college-age women. *American Journal of Public Health, 93*, 1104–1109.

Smith, R. A., & Davis, S. F. (2004). *The psychologist as detective* (3rd ed.). Upper Saddle River, NJ: Prentice Hall.

Smith, T. B., McCullough, M. E., & Poll, J. (2003). Religiousness and depression: Evidence for a main effect and the moderating influence of stressful life events. *Psychological Bulletin, 129*, 614–636.

Smulian, J. C., Ananth, C. V., Vintzileos, A. M., Scorza, W. E., & Knuppel, R. A. (2002). Parental age difference and adverse perinatal outcomes in the United States. *Pediatric and Perinatal Epidemiology, 16*, 320–327.

Snarey, J. (1987, June). A question of morality. *Psychology Today*, pp. 6–8.

Snow, A. L., Norris, M. P., Doody, R., Molinari, V. A., Orengo, C. A., & Kunik, M. E. (2004). Dementia deficits scale. *Alzheimer's Disorders and Associated Disorders, 18*, 22–31.

Snowden, L. R., & Cheung, F. K. (1990). Use of inpatient mental health services by members of ethnic minority groups. *American Psychologist, 45*, 347–355.

Snowdon, D. A. (1995). *An epidemiological study of aging in a select population and its relationship to Alzheimer's disease.* Unpublished manuscript, Sanders Brown Center on Aging, Lexington, KY.

Snowdon, D. A. (1997). Aging and Alzheimer's disease: Lessons from the Nun Study. *Gerontologist, 37*, 150–156.

Snowdon, D. A. (2002). *Aging with grace: What the Nun Study teaches us about leading longer, healthier, and more meaningful lives.* New York: Bantam.

Snowdon, D. A. (2003). Healthy aging and dementia: Findings from the Nun Study. *Annals of Internal Medicine, 139*, 450–454.

Snowdon, D. A., Tully, C. L., Smith, C. D., Riley, K. P., & Markesbery, W. R. (2000). Serum folate and the severity of atrophy of the neocortex in Alzheimer's disease: Findings from the Nun Study. *American Journal of Clinical Nutrition, 71,* 993–998.

Snowling, M. J. (2004). Reading development and dyslexia. In U. Goswami (Ed.), *Blackwell handbook of childhood cognitive development.* Malden, MA: Blackwell.

Snyder, H. N., & Sickmund, M. (1999, October). *Juvenile offenders and victims: 1999 national report.* Washington, DC: National Center for Juvenile Justice.

Sollod, R. N. (2000). Religious and spiritual practices. In A. Kazdin (Ed.), *Encyclopedia of psychology.* Washington, DC, & New York: American Psychological Association and Oxford University Press.

Solomon, D., Battistich, V., Watson, M., Schaps, E., & Lewis, C. (2000). A six-district study of educational change: Direct and mediated effects of the Child Development Project. *Social Psychology of Education, 4,* 3–51.

Solot, D., & Miller, M. (2002). *Unmarried to each other.* New York: Marlowe.

Soltero, S. W. (2004). *Dual language: Teaching and learning in two languages.* Boston: Allyn & Bacon.

Sommer, B. (2001). Menopause. In J. Worell (Ed.), *Encyclopedia of women and gender.* San Diego: Academic Press.

Soong, W. T., Chao, K. Y., Jang, C. S., & Wang, J. D. (1999). Long-term effect of increased lead absorption on intelligence of children. *Archives of Environmental Health, 54,* 297–301.

Sophian, C. (1985). Perseveration and infants' search: A comparison of two- and three-location tasks. *Developmental Psychology, 21,* 187–194.

Sorokin, P. (2002). New agents and future directions in biotherapy. *Clinical Journal of Oncological Nursing, 6,* 19–24.

Sowell, E., & Jernigan, T. (1998). Further MRI evidence of late brain maturation: Limbic volume increases and changing asymmetries during childhood and adolescence. *Developmental Neuropsychology, 14,* 599–617.

Spafford, C. S., & Grosser, G. S. (2005). *Dyslexia and reading difficulties* (2nd ed.). Boston: Allyn & Bacon.

Spear, H. J., & Kulbok, P. A. (2001). Adolescent health behaviors and related factors: A review. *Public Health Nursing, 18,* 82–93.

Spearman, C. E. (1927). *The abilities of man.* New York: Macmillan.

Spelke, E. S. (1979). Perceiving bimodally specified events in infancy. *Developmental Psychology, 5,* 626–636.

Spelke, E. S. (1991). Physical knowledge in infancy: Reflections on Piaget's theory. In S. Carey & R. Gelman (Eds.), *The epigenesis of mind: Essays on biology and cognition.* Hillsdale, NJ: Erlbaum.

Spelke, E. S. (2000). Core knowledge. *American Psychologist, 55,* 1233–1243.

Spelke, E. S., Breinlinger, K., Macomber, J., & Jacobson, K. (1992). Origins of knowledge. *Psychological Review, 99,* 605–632.

Spelke, E. S., & Hespos. S. J. (2001). Continuity, competence, and the object concept. In E. Dupoux (Ed.), *Language, brain, and behavior.* Cambridge, MA: Bradford/MIT Press.

Spelke, E. S., & Newport, E. L. (1998). Nativism, empiricism, and the development of knowledge. In W. Damon (Ed.), *Handbook of child psychology* (5th ed., Vol. 2). New York: Wiley.

Spelke, E. S., & Owsley, C. J. (1979). Intermodal exploration and knowledge in infancy. *Infant Behavior and Development, 2,* 13–28.

Spence, A. P. (1989). *Biology of human aging.* Englewood Cliffs, NJ: Prentice Hall.

Spence, J. T., & Buckner, C. E. (2000). Instrumental and expressive traits, trait stereotypes, and sexist attitudes: What do they signify? *Psychology of Women Quarterly, 24,* 44–62.

Spence, J. T., & Helmreich, R. (1978). *Masculinity and femininity: Their psychological dimensions.* Austin: University of Texas Press.

Spence, M. J., & DeCasper, A. J. (1987). Prenatal experience with low-frequency maternal voice sounds influences neonatal perception of maternal voice samples. *Infant Behavior and Development, 10,* 133–142.

Spencer, J. P., Vereijken, B., Diedrich, F. J., & Thelen, E. (2000). Posture and the emergence of manual skills. *Developmental Science, 3,* 216–233.

Spencer, M. B. (1990). Commentary in Spencer, M. B., & Dornbusch, S. Challenges in studying ethnic minority youth. In S. S. Feldman & G. R. Elliott (Eds.), *At the threshold: The developing adolescent.* Cambridge, MA: Harvard University Press.

Spencer, M. B. (1999). Social and cultural influences on school adjustment: The application of an identity-focused cultural ecological perspective. In K. Wentzel & T. Berndt (Eds.), *Social influences on school adjustment.* Mahwah, NJ: Erlbaum.

Spencer, M. B., & Dornbusch, S. M. (1990). Challenges in studying minority youth. In S. S. Feldman & G. R. Elliott (Eds.), *At the threshold: The developing adolescent.* Cambridge, MA: Harvard University Press.

Spencer, M. B., & Harpalani, V. (2004). Nature, nurture, and the question of "how?" In C. G. Coll, E. L. Bearer, & R. M. Lerner (Eds.), *Nature and nurture.* Mahwah, NJ: Erlbaum.

Spencer, M. B., Noll, E., Stoltzfuz, J., & Harpalani, V. (2001). Identity and school adjustment: Revisiting the "acting white" assumption. *Educational Psychologist, 36,* 21–30.

Spielberger, C. D., & Grier, K. (1983). Unpublished manuscript, University of South Florida, Tampa.

Spiro, A. (2001). Health in midlife: Toward a lifespan view. In M. E. Lachman (Ed.), *Handbook of midlife development.* New York: John Wiley.

Spodek, B., & Saracho, O. N. (2003). "On the shoulders of giants": Exploring the traditions of early childhood education. *Early Childhood Education Journal, 31,* 3–10.

Sprei, J. E., & Courtois, C. A. (1988). The treatment of women's sexual dysfunctions arising from sexual assault. In R. A. Brown & J. R. Fields (Eds.), *Treatment of sexual problems in individual and group therapy.* Great Neck, NY: PMA.

Spring, J. (2002). *American education* (10th ed.). New York: McGraw-Hill.

Springer, S. P., & Deutsch, G. (1985). *Left brain, right brain.* New York: W. H. Freeman.

Sroufe, L. A. (2000, Spring). The inside scoop on child development: Interview. *Cutting through the hype.* Minneapolis: College of Education and Human Development, University of Minnesota.

Sroufe, L. A. (2001). From infant attachment to adolescent autonomy: Longitudinal data on the role of parents in development. In J. Borkowski, S. Ramey, & M. Bristol-Power (Eds.), *Parenting and your child's world.* Mahwah, NJ: Erlbaum.

Sroufe, L. A., Egeland, B., Carlson, E., & Collins, W. A. (2005). The place of early attachment in developmental context. In K. E. Grossman, K. Krossman, & E. Waters (Eds.), *The power of longitudinal attachment research: From infancy and childhood to adulthood.* New York: Guilford Press.

Sroufe, L. A., & Waters, E. (1976). The ontogenesis of smiling and laughter: A perspective on the organization of development in infancy. *Psychological Review, 83,* 173–198.

Sroufe, L. A., Waters, E., & Matas, L. (1974). Contextual determinants of infant affectional response. In M. Lewis & L. Rosenblum (Eds.), *Origins of fear.* New York: Wiley.

St. Pierre, R., Layzer, J., & Barnes, H. (1996). *Regenerating two-generation programs.* Cambridge, MA: Abt Associates.

Stahl, S. (2002, January). *Effective reading instruction in the first grade.* Paper presented at the Michigan Reading Recovery conference, Dearborn, MI.

Stanford University Medical Center (2003). *Diabetes and other endocrine and metabolic disorders.* Palo Alto, CA: Author.

Stanhope, L., & Corter, C. (1993, March). *The mother's role in the transition to siblinghood.* Paper presented at the biennial meeting of the Society for Research in Child Development, New Orleans.

Stanovich, K. E. (1986). Cognitive processes and the reading problems of learning disabled children: Evaluating the assumption of specificity. In J. Torgesen & B. Wong (Eds.), *Psychological and educational perspectives on learning disabilities.* Orlando, FL: Academic Press.

Stanovich, K. E. (2004). *How to think straight about psychology* (7th ed.). Boston: Allyn & Bacon.

Stanwood, G. D., & Levitt, P. (2004). Drug exposure early in life: Functional repercussions of changing neuropharmacology during sensitive periods of brain development. *Current Opinions in Pharmacology, 4,* 65–71.

Stattin, H., & Magnusson, D. (1990). *Pubertal maturation in female development: Paths through life* (Vol. 2). Hillsdale, NJ: Erlbaum.

Staudinger, U. M. (1996). Psychologische Produktivitat und Selbstenfaltung im Alter. In M. M. Baltes & L. Montada (Eds.), *Produktives Leben im Alter.* Frankfurt: Campus.

Staudinger, U. M., & Bluck, S. (2001). A view on midlife development from lifespan theory. In M. E. Lachman (Ed.), *Handbook of midlife development.* New York: John Wiley.

Steele, C. M., & Aronson, J. (1995). Stereotype threat and the intellectual test performance of African-Americans. *Journal of Personality and Social Psychology, 69,* 797–811.

Steele, C. M., & Aronson, J. A. (2004). Stereotype threat does not live by Steele and Aronson (1995) alone. *American Psychologist, 59,* 47–48.

Stegelin, D. A. (2003). Application of Reggio Emilia approach to early childhood science curriculum. *Early Childhood Education Journal, 30,* 163–169.

Steiger, H., Bruce, K. R., & Israel, M. (2003). Eating disorders. In I. B. Weiner (Ed.), *Handbook of psychology* (Vol. VIII). New York: Wiley.

Stein, M. T., Kennell, J. H., & Fulcher, A. (2003). Benefits of a doula present at the birth of a child. *Journal of Developmental and Behavioral Pediatrics, 24,* 195–198.

Stein, M. T., & Perrin, J. M. (2003). Diagnosis and treatment of ADHD in school-age children in primary care settings: A synopsis of the AAP practice guidelines. *Pediatric Review, 24,* 92–98.

Steinberg, L. (2004). Risk taking in adolescence: What changes, and why? *Annals of the New York Academy of Sciences, 1021,* 51–58.

Steinberg, L. D. (1986). Latchkey children and susceptibility to peer pressure: An ecological analysis. *Developmental Psychology, 22,* 433–439.

Steinberg, L., & Cauffman, E. (2001). Adolescents as adults in court. *Social Policy Report, SRC D, XV* (No. 4), 1–13.

Steinberg, L. D., & Levine, A. (1997). *You and your adolescent* (2nd ed.). New York: Harper Perennial.

Steinberg, L. D., & Silk, J. S. (2002). Parenting adolescents. In M. H. Bornstein (Ed.), *Handbook of parenting* (2nd ed., Vol. 1). Mahwah, NJ: Erlbaum.

Steiner, J. E. (1979). Human facial expressions in response to taste and smell stimulation. In H. Reese & L. Lipsitt (Eds.), *Advances in child development and behavior* (Vol. 13). New York: Academic Press.

Stek, M. L., Gussekoo, J., Beekman, A. T. F., van Tilburg, W., & Westendorp, R. G. J. (2004). Prevalence, correlates, and recognition of depression in the oldest old: The Leiden 85-plus study. *Journal of Affective Disorders, 78,* 193–200.

Stenkley, N. C., Vik, O., & Laukli, E. (2004). The aging ear. *Acta Otolaryngology, 124,* 69–76.

Stephenson, J. (2004). FDA warns on mercury in tuna. *Journal of the American Medical Association, 291,* 171.

Steptoe, A., & Ayers, S. (2005). Stress, health, and illness. In S. Sutton, A. Baum, & M. Johnston (Eds.), *The SAGE handbook of health psychology.* Thousand Oaks, CA: Sage.

Stern, D. N., Beebe, B., Jaffe, J., & Bennett, S. L. (1977). The infant's stimulus world during social interaction: A study of caregiver behaviors with particular reference to repetition and timing. In H. R. Schaffer (Ed.), *Studies in mother-infant interaction.* London: Academic Press.

Stern, J. S. (1993, June 2). Commentary in "Lowly vitamin supplements pack a big health punch." *USA Today,* p. 3D.

Stern, L., Iqbal, N., Seshadri, P., Chicano, K. L., Daily, D. A., McGrory, J., Williams, M., Gracely, E. J., & Samantha, F. F. (2004). The effects of low-carbohydrate versus conventional weight loss diets in severely obese adults: One-year follow-up of a randomized trial. *Annals of Internal Medicine, 140,* 778–785.

Sternberg, R. J. (1986). *Intelligence applied.* San Diego: Harcourt Brace Jovanovich.

Sternberg, R. J. (1988). *The triangle of love.* New York: Basic Books.

Sternberg, R. J. (2001). Is there a heredity-environment paradox? In R. J. Sternberg & E. L. Grigorenko (Eds.), *Environmental effects on cognitive abilities.* Mahwah, NJ: Erlbaum.

Sternberg, R. J. (2002). Intelligence: The triarchic theory of intelligence. In J. W. Gutherie (Ed.), *Encyclopedia of education* (2nd ed.). New York: Macmillan.

Sternberg, R. J. (2003). Contemporary theories of intelligence. In I. B. Weiner (Ed.), *Handbook of psychology* (Vol. VII). New York: Wiley.

Sternberg, R. J. (2004). Individual differences in cognitive development. In U. Goswami (Ed.), *Blackwell handbook of childhood cognitive development.* Malden, MA: Blackwell.

Sternberg, R. J., & Grigorenko, E. L. (Eds.) (2001). *Environmental effects on cognitive abilities.* Mahwah, NJ: Erlbaum.

Sternberg, R. J., & Grigorenko, E. L. (Eds.). (2004). *Culture and competence.* Washington, DC: American Psychological Association.

Sternberg, R. J., Grigorenko, E. L., & Singer, J. L. (Eds.). (2004). *Creativity: From potential to realization.* Washington, DC: American Psychological Association.

Sternberg, R. J., Nokes, K., Geissler, P. W., Prince, R., Okatcha, F., Bundy, D. A., & Grigorenko, E. L. (2001). The relationship between academic and practical intelligence: A case study in Kenya. *Intelligence, 29,* 401–418.

Sternberg, R. J., & Preiss, D. D. (Eds.). (2005). *Intelligence and technology.* Mahwah, NJ: Erlbaum.

Sterns, H., & Huyck, M. H. (2001). The role of work in midlife. In M. Lachman (Ed.), *Handbook of midlife development.* New York: Wiley.

Stetsenko, A. (2002). Adolescents in Russia: Surviving the turmoil and creating a brighter future. In B. B. Brown, R. W. Larson, & T. S. Saraswathi (Eds.), *The world's youth.* New York: Cambridge University Press.

Steur, F. B., Applefield, J. M., & Smith, R. (1971). Televised aggression and interpersonal aggression of preschool children. *Journal of Experimental Child Psychology, 11,* 442–447.

Stevenson, H. W. (1995). Mathematics achievement of American students: First in the world by 2000? In C. A. Nelson (Ed.), *Basic and applied perspectives in learning, cognition, and development.* Minneapolis: University of Minnesota Press.

Stevenson, H. W. (2000). Middle childhood: Education and schooling. In A. Kazdin (Ed.), *Encyclopedia of psychology.* Washington, DC, & New York: American Psychological Association and Oxford University Press.

Stevenson, H. W., & Hofer, B. K. (1999). Education policy in the United States and abroad: What we can learn from each other. In G. J. Cizek (Ed.), *Handbook of educational policy.* San Diego: Academic Press.

Stevenson, H. W., Lee, S., & Stigler, J. W. (1986). Mathematics achievement of Chinese, Japanese, and American children. *Science, 231,* 693–699.

Stevenson, H. W., & Zusho, A. (2002). Adolescence in China and Japan: Adapting to a changing environment. In B. B. Brown, R. W. Larson, & T. S. Saraswathi (Eds.), *The world's youth.* New York: Cambridge University Press.

Stewart, A. J., Ostrove, J. M., & Helson, R. (2001). Middle aging in women: Patterns of personality change from the 30s to the 50s. *Journal of Adult Development, 8,* 23–37.

Stice, E., Presnell, K., & Spangler, D. (2002). Risk factors for binge eating onset in adolescent girls: A 2-year prospective investigation. *Health Psychology, 21,* 131–138.

Stifter, E., Sacu, S., Weghaupt, H., Konig, F., Richter-Muksch, S., Thaler, A., Velikay-Parel, M., & Radner, W. (2004). Reading performance depending on the type of cataract and its predictability on the visual outcome. *Journal of Cataract and Refractive Surgery, 30,* 1259–1267.

Stipek, D., Recchia, S., & McClintic, S. (1992). Self-evaluation in young children. *Monographs of the Society for Research in Child Development, 57* (1, Serial No. 226).

Stocks, J., & Dezateux, C. (2003). The effects of parental smoking on lung function and development during infancy. *Respirology, 8,* 266–285.

Stoel-Gammon, C. (2005). Phonological development. In J. Berko Gleason, *The development of language* (6th ed.). Boston: Allyn & Bacon.

Stokstad, E. (2003). Nutrition: The vitamin D deficit. *Science, 302,* 1886–1888.

Stolley, K. S. (1993). Statistics on adoption in the United States. *The Future of Children, 3,* 26–42.

Stouthamer-Loeber, M., Loeber, R., Wei, E., Farrington, D. P., & Wikstrom, P. H. (2002). Risk and promotive effects in the explanation of serious delinquency in boys. *Journal of Consulting and Clinical Psychology, 20,* 111–123.

Strain, L. A., Grabusie, C. C., Searle, M. S., & Dunn, N. J. (2002). Continuing and ceasing leisure activities in later life: A longitudinal study. *The Gerontologist, 42,* 217–223.

Strauss, M. A. (2001). *Beating the devil out of them* (2nd ed.). New Brunswick, NJ: Transaction Publications.

Strauss, M. A., Sugarman, D. B., Giles-Sims, J. (1997). Spanking by parents and subsequent anti-social behavior in children. *Archives of Pediatrics and Adolescent Medicine, 151,* 761–767.

Strauss, R. S. (2001). Environmental tobacco smoke and serum vitamin C levels in children. *Pediatrics, 107,* 540–542.

Streil, J. (2001). Marriage: Still "his" and "hers"? In J. Worell (Ed.), *Encyclopedia of women and gender.* San Diego: Academic Press.

Streissguth, A. P., Martin, D. C., Sandman, B. M., Kirchner, G. L., & Darby, B. L. (1984). Intrauterine alcohol and nicotine exposure: Attention and reaction time in four-year-old children. *Developmental Psychology, 20,* 533–543.

Striegel-Moore, R. H., Franko, D. L., Thompson, D., Barton, B., Schreiber, G. B., & Daniels, S. R. (2004). Changes in weight and body image over time in women with eating disorders. *International Journal of Eating Disorders, 36,* 315–327.

Striegel-Moore, R. H., Silberstein, L. R., & Rodin, J. (1993). The social self in bulimia nervosa: Public self-consciousness,

social anxiety, and perceived fraudulence. *Journal of Abnormal Psychology, 102,* 297–303.

Stroberg, P., Murphy, A., & Costigan, T. (2003). Switching patients with erectile dysfunction from sildenafil citrate to tadalafil: Results of a European multicenter, open-label study of patient preference. *Clinical Therapeutics, 25,* 2724–2737.

Stroebe, M., Gergen, M. H., Gergen, K. J., & Stroebe, W. (1992). Broken hearts or broken bonds: Love and death in historical perspective. *American Psychologist, 47,* 1205–1212.

Stroebe, M., & Stroebe, W. (1991). Does "grief work" work? *Journal of Consulting and Clinical Psychology, 59,* 57–65.

Strong, B., DeVault, C., Sayad, B., & Yarber, W. (2005). *Human sexuality* (5th ed.). New York: McGraw-Hill.

Stunkard, A. (2000). Obesity. In A. Kazdin (Ed.), *Encyclopedia of psychology.* Washington, DC, & New York: American Psychological Association and Oxford University Press.

Substance Abuse and Mental Health Services Administration (2002). *Older adults.* Bethesda, MD: U.S. Department of Health and Human Services.

Sue, S. (1990, August). *Ethnicity and culture in psychological research and practice.* Paper presented at the meeting of the American Psychological Association, Boston.

Sullivan, H. S. (1953). *The interpersonal theory of psychiatry.* New York: W. W. Norton.

Sullivan, J. L. (2003). Prevention to mother-to-child transmission of HIV—what next? *Journal of Acquired Immune Deficiency Syndrome (Suppl. 1), 34,* S67–S72.

Sullivan, K., & Sullivan, A. (1980). Adolescent-parent separation. *Developmental Psychology, 16,* 93–99.

Suls, J., & Swain, A. (1998). Type A–Type B personalities. In H. S. Friedman (Ed.), *Encyclopedia of mental health* (Vol. 3). San Diego: Academic Press.

Sun, M., & Rugolotto, S. (2004). Assisted infant toilet training in a Western family setting. *Journal of Developmental and Behavioral Pediatrics, 25,* 99–101.

Suomi, S. J., Harlow, H. F., & Domek, C. J. (1970). Effect of repetitive infant-infant separations of young monkeys. *Journal of Abnormal Psychology, 76,* 161–172.

Super, C., & Harkness, S. (1997). The cultural structuring of child development. In J. W. Berry, Y. H. Poortinga, & J. Pandey (Eds.), *Handbook of cross-cultural psychology:*

Theory and method. Vol. 2. Boston: Allyn & Bacon.

Susman, E. J., Dorn, L. D., & Schiefelbein, V. L. (2003). Puberty, sexuality, and health. In I. B. Weiner (Ed.), *Handbook of psychology* (Vol. VI). New York: Wiley.

Susman, E. J., Murowchick, E., Worrall, B. K., & Murray, D. A. (1995, March). *Emotionality, adrenal hormones, and context interactions during puberty and pregnancy.* Paper presented at the meeting of the Society for Research in Child Development, Indianapolis.

Susman, E. J., & Rogol, A. (2004). Puberty and psychological development. In R. Lerner & L. Steinberg (Eds.), *Handbook of adolescent psychology.* New York: Wiley.

Sutton-Smith, B. (2000). Play. In A. Kazdin (Ed.), *Encyclopedia of psychology.* Washington, D. C. & New York: American Psychological Association and Oxford University Press.

Suzman, R. (1997, March 18). Commentary, *USA Today*, p. 1A.

Suzman, R. M., Harris, T., Hadley, E. C., Kovar, M. G., & Weindruch, R. (1992). The robust oldest old: Optimistic perspectives for increasing healthy life expectancy. In R. M. Suzman, D. P. Willis, & K. G. Manton (Eds.), *The oldest old.* New York: Oxford University Press.

Swaab, D. F., Chung, W. C., Kruijver, F. P., Hofman, M. A., & Ishunina, T. A. (2001). Structural and functional sex differences in the human hypothalamus. *Hormones and Behavior, 40,* 93–98.

Swaab, D. F., Chung, W. C., Kruijver, F. P., Hofman, M. A., & Ishunina, T. A. (2002). Sexual differentiation of the human hypothalamus. *Advances in Experimental Medicine and Biology, 511,* 75–100.

Swain, S. O. (1992). Men's friendships with women. In P. Nardi (Ed.), *Gender in intimate relationships.* Belmont, CA: Wadsworth.

Swan, G. E. (1996). Interview. *APA Monitor,* p. 35.

Swann, W. B., De La Ronde, C., & Hixon, J. G. (1994). Authenticity and positive strivings in marriage and courtship. *Journal of Personality and Social Psychology, 66,* 857–869.

Swanson, J. M., & others (2001). Clinical relevance of the primary findings of MTA: Success rates based on severity of ADHD and ODD symptoms at the end of treatment. *Journal of the American Academy of Child and Adolescent Psychiatry, 40,* 168–179.

Swarte, N. B., van der Lee, M. L., van der Bom, J. G., van der Bout, J., & Heintz, A. P. (2003). Effects of euthanasia on the bereaved family and friends: A cross-sectional study. *British Medical Journal, 327,* 189.

Sylvia, S. N. (2004). Health behaviors and physical activity: Are they related? *Journal of Adolescent Health, 34,* 128.

Symonds, E. M., & Symonds, I. M. (2004). *Essential obstetrics and gynecology* (4th ed.). New York: Elsevier.

Tager-Flusberg, H. (2005). Morphology and syntax in the preschool years. In J. Berko Gleason, *The development of language* (6th ed.). Boston: Allyn & Bacon.

Takahashi, K. (1990). Are the key assumptions of the "Strange Situation" procedure universal? A view from Japanese research. *Human Development, 33,* 23–30.

Tamis-LeMonda, C. S., Bornstein, M. H., & Baumwell, L. (2001). Maternal responsiveness and children's achievement of language milestones. *Child Development, 72,* 748–767.

Tang, M. P., Chon, H. C., Tsao, K. I., & Hsich, W. S. (2004). Outcome of very low birth weight infants with sonographic enlarged occipital horn. *Pediatric Neurology, 30,* 42–45.

Tannen, D. (1990). *You just don't understand: Women and men in conversation.* New York: Ballantine.

Tappan, M. (2005). Sociocultural approaches to morality. In M. Killen & J. Smetana (Eds.), *Handbook of moral development.* Mahwah, NJ: Erlbaum.

Tashiro, T., & Frazier, P. (2003). "I'll never be in a relationship like that again": Personal growth following romantic relationship breakups. *Personal Relationships, 10,* 113–128.

Tasker, F. L., and Golombok, S. (1997). *Growing up in a lesbian family: Effects on child development.* New York: Guilford.

Tasker, F. L., and Golombok, S. (1998). The role of co-mothers in planned lesbian-led families. In G. A. Dunne (Ed.), *Living difference: Lesbian perspectives on work and family life.* New York: Harrington Park Press.

Taylor, H. G., Klein, N., & Hack, M. (1994). Academic functioning in <750 gm birthweight children who have normal cognitive abilities: Evidence for specific learning disabilities. *Pediatric Research, 35,* 289A.

Taylor, H. G., Klein, N., Minich, N. M., & Hack, M. (2000). Middle-school-age outcomes with very low birth weight. *Child Development, 71,* 1495–1511.

Taylor, L. S., & Whittaker, C. R. (2003). *Bridging multiple worlds.* Boston: Allyn & Bacon.

Taylor, S. E. (2003). *Health psychology* (5th ed.). New York: McGraw-Hill.

Taylor, S. P. (1982). Mental health and successful coping among Black women. In R. C. Manuel (Ed.), *Minority aging.* Westport, CT: Greenwood Press.

Teissedre, F., & Chabrol, H. (2004). Detecting women at risk for postnatal depression using the Edinburgh Postnatal Depression Scale at 2 to 3 days postpartum. *Canadian Journal of Psychiatry, 49,* 51–54.

Tenenbaum, H. R., Callahan, M., Alba-Speyer, C., & Sandoval, L. (2002). Parent-child science conversations in Mexican descent families: Educational background, activity, and past experience as moderators. *Hispanic Journal of Behavioral Sciences, 24,* 225–248.

Terman, D. L., Larner, M. B., Stevenson, C. S., & Behrman, R. E. (1996). Special education for students with disabilities: Analysis and recommendations. *The Future of Children 6* (1), 4–24.

Terman, L. (1925). *Genetic studies of genius, Vol. 1: Mental and physical traits of a thousand gifted children.* Stanford, CA: Stanford University Press.

Terry, D. F., Wilcox, M. A., McCormick, M. A., & Perls, T. T. (2004). Cardiovascular disease delay in centenarian offspring. *Journals of Gerontology A: Biological Sciences and Medical Sciences, 59,* M385–M389.

Terry, D. F., Wilcox, M., McCormick, M. A., Lawler, E., & Perls, T. T. (2003). Cardiovascular advantages among the offspring of centenarians. *Journals of Gerontology A: Biological Sciences and Medical Sciences, 58,* M425–M431.

Terry, W. S. (2003). Learning and memory (2nd ed.). Boston: Allyn & Bacon.

Teti, D. M. (2001). Retrospect and prospect in the study of sibling relationships. In J. P. McHale & W. S. Grolnick (Eds.), *Retrospect and prospect in the psychological study of families.* Mahwah, NJ: Erlbaum.

Teti, D. M., Sakin, J., Kucera, E., Caballeros, M., & Corns, K. M. (1993, March). *Transitions to siblinghood and security of firstborn attachment: Psychosocial and psychiatric correlates of changes over time.* Paper presented at the biennial meeting of the Society for Research in Child Development, New Orleans.

Tetreault, M. K. T. (1997). Classrooms for diversity: Rethinking curriculum and pedagogy. In J. A. Banks & C. A. Banks (Eds.), *Multicultural education* (3rd ed.). Boston: Allyn & Bacon.

Thapar, A., Fowler, T., Rice, F., Scourfield, J., Van Den Bree, M., Thomas, S., Harold, G., & Hay, D. (2003). Maternal smoking during pregnancy and attention deficit hyperactivity disorder symptoms in offspring. *American Journal of Psychiatry, 160,* 1985–1989.

Tharp, R. G. (1994). Intergroup differences among Native Americans in socialization and child cognition: An erthogenetic analysis. In P. M. Greenfield & R. Cocking (Eds.), *Cross-cultural roots of minority child development.* Mahwah, NJ: Erlbaum.

Tharp, R. G., & Gallimore, R. (1988). *Rousing minds to life: Teaching, learning, and schooling in social context.* New York: Cambridge University Press.

Thayer, J. F., Rossy, I., Sollers, J., Friedman, B. H., & Allen, M. T. (1996, March). *Relationships among heart period variability and cardiodynamic measures vary as a function of fitness.* Paper presented at the meeting of the American Psychosomatic Society, Williamsburg, VA.

Thelen, E. (1995). Motor development: A new synthesis. *American Psychologist, 50,* 79–95.

Thelen, E. (2000). Perception and motor development. In A. Kazdin (Ed.), *Encyclopedia of psychology.* Washington, DC, & New York: American Psychological Association and Oxford University Press.

Thelen, E. (2001). Dynamic mechanisms of change in early perceptual-motor development. In J. L. McClelland & R. S. Siegler (Eds.), *Mechanisms of cognitive development.* Mahwah, NJ: Erlbaum.

Thelen, E., Corbetta, D., Kamm, K., Spencer, J. P., Schneider, K., & Zernicke, R. F. (1993). The transition to reaching: Mapping intention and intrinsic dynamics. *Child Development, 64,* 1058–1098.

Thelen, E., & Smith, L. B. (1998). Dynamic systems theory. In W. Damon (Ed.), *Handbook of child psychology* (5th ed., Vol. 1). New York: Wiley.

Thelen, E., & Whitmeyer, V. (2005). Using dynamic systems theory to conceptualize the interface of perception, action, and cognition. In J. J. Reiser, J. J. Lockman, & C. A. Nelson (Eds.), *The role of action in learning and development.* Mahwah, NJ: Erlbaum.

Thoma, S. J. (2002). An overview of the Minnesota approach to moral development. *Journal of Moral Education, 31,* 225–245.

Thomas, A., & Chess, S. (1991). Temperament in adolescence and its functional significance. In R. M. Lerner, A. C. Petersen, & J. Brooks-Gunn (Eds.), *Encyclopedia of adolescence* (Vol. 2). New York: Garland.

Thomas, D. R. (2003). The relationship between functional status and inflammatory disease in older adults. *Journals of Gerontology A: Biological Sciences and Medical Sciences, 58,* M995–M998.

Thomas, K. (1998, November 4). Teen cyberdating is a new wrinkle for parents, too. *USA Today,* p. 9D.

Thompson, B., Thompson, A., Thompson, J., Fredickson, C., & Bishop, S. (2003). Heavy smokers: A quantitative analysis of attitudes and beliefs concerning cessation and continued smoking. *Nicotine and Tobacco Research, 5,* 923–933.

Thompson, J. W., Ryan, K. W., Pindiya, S. D., & Bost, J. E. (2003). Quality of care for children in commercial and Medicaid managed care. *Journal of the American Medical Association, 290,* 1486–1493.

Thompson, K. M., Crosby, R. D., Wonderlich, S. A., Mitchell, J. E., Redlin, J., Demuth, G., Smyth, J., & Haseltine, B. (2003). Psychopathology and sexual trauma in childhood and adulthood. *Journal of Traumatic Stress, 16,* 35–38.

Thompson, P. M., Giedd, J. N., Woods, R. P., MacDonald, D., Evans, A. C., & Toga, A. W. (2000). Growth patterns in the developing brain detected by using continuum mechanical tensor maps. *Nature, 404,* 190–193.

Thompson, R. A. (1994). Emotion regulation: A theme in search of a definition. *Monographs of the Society for Research in Child Development, 59* (Serial No. 240), 2–3.

Thompson, R. A. (1999). The individual child: Temperament, emotion, self, and personality. In M. H. Bornstein & M. E. Lamb (Eds.), *Developmental psychology: An advanced textbook* (4th ed.). Mahwah, NJ: Erlbaum.

Thompson, R. A. (2000). Early experience and socialization. In A. Kazdin (Ed.), *Encyclopedia of psychology.* Washington, DC, & New York: American Psychological Association and Oxford University Press.

Thompson, R. A., Easterbrooks, M. A., & Walker, L. (2003). Social and emotional development in infancy. In I. B. Weiner (Ed.), *Handbook of psychology* (Vol. 6). New York: Wiley.

Thompson, R. A., & Goodvin, R. (2005). The individual child: Temperament, emotion, self, and personality. In M. H. Bornstein &

M. E. Lamb (Eds.), *Developmental psychology* (5th ed.). Mahwah, NJ: Erlbaum.

Thompson, R. A., & Nelson, C. A. (2001). Developmental science and the media. *American Psychologist, 56,* 5–15.

Thompson, T. L., Robinson, J. D., & Beiseker, A. E. (2004). The elderly patient-physician interaction. In J. F. Nussbaum & J. Coupland (Eds.), *Handbook of communication and aging research.* Mahwah, NJ: Erlbaum.

Thomson, E., Mosley, J., Hanson, T. L., McLanahan, S. S. (2001). Remarriage, cohabitation, and changes in mothering behavior. *Journal of Marriage and the Family, 63,* 370–380.

Thomson, M. (2003). Monitoring dyslexics' intelligence and attainments: A follow-up study. *Dyslexia, 9,* 3–17.

Thoresen, C. E., & Harris, A. H. S. (2002). Spirituality and health: What's the evidence and what's needed? *Annals of Behavioral Medicine, 24,* 3–13.

Thorton, A., & Camburn, D. (1989). Religious participation and sexual behavior and attitudes. *Journal of Marriage and the Family, 49,* 117–128.

Thrasher, J. F., Campbell, M. K., & Oates, V. (2004). Behavior-specific social support for healthy behaviors among African American church members: Applying optimal matching theory. *Healthy Education and Behavior, 31,* 193–205.

Thurstone, L. L. (1938). *Primary mental abilities.* Chicago: University of Chicago Press.

Tinsley, B. J. (2003). *How children learn to be healthy.* New York: Cambridge University Press.

Tobin, J. J., Wu, D. Y. H., & Davidson, D. H. (1989). *Preschool in three cultures.* New Haven, CT: Yale University Press.

Tolan, P. H. (2001). Emerging themes and challenges in understanding youth violence. *Journal of Clinical Child Psychology, 30,* 233–239.

Tomasello, M., & Slobin, D. I. (Eds.). (2005). *Beyond nature & nurture.* Mahwah, NJ: Erlbaum.

Torff, B. (2000). Multiple intelligences. In A. Kazdin (Ed.), *Encyclopedia of psychology.* Washington, DC, & New York: American Psychological Association and Oxford University Press.

Toth, G., & Siegel, L. S. (1994). A critical evaluation of the IQ-achievement discrepancy based definition of dyslexia. In K. P. van den Bos, L. S. Siegel, D. J. Bakker, & D. L. Share

(Eds.), *Current directions in dyslexia research.* Lisse, The Netherlands: Swets & Zeitlinger.

Tough, S. C., Newburn-Cook, C., Johnston, D. W., Svenson, L. W., Rose, S., & Belik, J. (2002). Delayed childbearing and its impact on population rate changes in lower birth weight, multiple birth, and preterm delivery. *Pediatrics, 109,* 399–403.

Tournetta, P., Hirsch, E. F., Howard, R., McConnell, T., & Ross, E. (2004). Skeletal injury patterns in older females. *Clinical Orthopedics, 422,* 556–561.

Trasler, J. (2000). Paternal exposures: Altered sex ratios. *Teratology, 62,* 6–7.

Trasler, J. M., & Doerksen, T. (2000, May). *Teratogen update: Paternal exposure-reproductive risks.* Paper presented at the joint meeting of the Pediatric Academic Societies and American Academy of Pediatrics, Boston.

Treboux, D., Crowell, J. A., & Waters, E. (2004). When "new" meets "old": Configurations of adult attachment representations and their implications for marital functioning. *Developmental Psychology, 40,* 295–314.

Treece, P. D., Engelberg, R. A., Crowley, L., Chan, J. D., Rubenfeld, G. G., Steinberg, K. P., & Curtis, J. R. (2004). Evaluation of a standardized order form for the withdrawal of life support in the intensive care unit. *Critical Care Medicine, 32,* 1141–1148.

Treffers, P. E., Eskes, M., Kleiverda, G., & van Alten, D. (1990). Home births and minimal medical interventions. *Journal of the American Medical Association, 246,* 2207–2208.

Trehub, S. E., Schneider, B. A., Thorpe, L. A., & Judge, P. (1991). Observational measures of auditory sensitivity in early infancy. *Developmental Psychology, 27,* 40–49.

Tremblay, T., Monetta, L., & Joanette, Y. (2004). Phonological processing of words in right- and left-handers. *Brain and Cognition, 55,* 427–432.

Tresaco, B., Bueno, G., Moreno, L. A., Garagorri, J. M., & Bueno, M. (2004). Insulin resistance and impaired glucose intolerance in obese children and adolescents. *Journal of Physiology and Biochemistry, 59,* 217–223.

Triandis, H. C. (2001). Individualism and collectivism. In D. Matsumoto (Ed.), *The handbook of culture and psychology.* New York: Oxford University Press.

Trimble, J. E. (1989, August). *The enculturation of contemporary psychology.* Paper presented at the meeting of the American Psychological Association, New Orleans.

Tritten, J. (2004). Embracing midwives everywhere. *Practicing Midwife, 7,* 4–5.

Troen, B. R. (2003). The biology of aging. *Mt. Sinai Journal of Medicine, 70,* 3–22.

Troiano, R. P., & Flegal, K. M. (1998). Overweight children and adolescents: Description, epidemiology, and demographics. *Pediatrics, 101,* 497–504.

Troll, L. E. (1994). Family-embedded versus family-deprived oldest-old: A study of contrasts. *International Journal of Aging and Human Development, 38,* 51–64.

Troll, L. E. (2000). Transmission and transmutation. In J. E. Birren & J. J. F. Schroots (Eds.), *A history of geropsychology in autobiography.* Washington, DC: American Psychological Association.

Trommsdorff, G. (2002). An eco-cultural and interpersonal relations approach to development of the lifespan. In W. J. Lonner, D. L. Dinnel, S. A. Hayes, & D. N. Sattler (Eds.), *Online readings in psychology and culture* (unit 12, chapter 1). Available on the Internet at: www.wwu.edu/~culture. Bellingham, WA: Center for Cross-Cultural Research, Western Washington University.

Truitner, K., & Truitner, N. (1993). Death and dying in Buddhism. In D. P. Irish & K. F. Lundquist (Eds.), *Ethnic variations in dying, death, and grief: Diversity in universality.* Washington, DC: Taylor & Francis.

Tseng, V. (2004). Family interdependence and academic adjustment in college: Youth from immigrant and U.S.-born families. *Child Development, 75,* 966–983.

Tsigos, C., & Chrousos, G. P. (2002). Hypothalamic-pituitary-adrenal axis, neuroendocrine factors, and stress. *Journal of Psychosomatic Research, 53,* 865–871.

Tubman, J. G., & Windle, M. (1995). Continuity of difficult temperament in adolescence: Relations with depression, life events, family support, and substance abuse. *Journal of Youth and Adolescence, 24,* 133–152.

Tuch, H., Parrish, P., & Romer, A. L. (2003). Integrating palliative care into nursing homes. *Journal of Palliative Medicine, 6,* 297–309.

Tucker, B., Subramanian, S. K., & James, A. (2004). Diversity in African American families. In M. Coleman & L. Ganong (Eds.), *Handbook of contemporary families.* Thousand Oaks, CA: Sage.

Tucker, J. S., Ellickson, P. L., & Klein, M. S. (2003). Predictors of the transition to regular smoking during adolescence and young adulthood. *Journal of Adolescent Health, 32,* 314–324.

Tucker, J. S., Schwartz, J. E., Clark, K. M., & Friedman, H. S. (1999). Age-related changes in the associations of social network ties with mortality risk. *Psychology and Aging, 14,* 564–571.

Tudge, J. (2004). Practice and discourse as the intersection of individual and social in human development. In A. N. Perret-Clermont, L. Resnick, C. Pontecorvo, & B. Burge (Eds.), *Joining society: Social interactions and learning in adolescence and youth.* New York: Cambridge University Press.

Tudge, J., & Scrimsher, S. (2003). Lev S. Vygotsky on education: A cultural-historical, interpersonal, and individual approach to development. In B. J. Zimmerman & D. H. Schunk (Eds.), *Educational psychology: A century of contributions.* Mahwah, NJ: Erlbaum.

Tuladhar, R., Harding, R., Cranage, S. M., Adamson, T. M., & Horne, R. S. (2003). Effects of sleep position, sleep state and age on heart rate responses following provoked arousal in term infants. *Early Human Development, 71,* 157–169.

Tulving, E. (2000). Concepts of memory. In E. Tulving & F. I. M. Craik (Eds.), *The Oxford handbook of memory.* New York: Oxford University Press.

Turgeon, J. L., McDonnell, D. P., Martin, K. A., & Wise, P. M. (2004). Hormone therapy: Physiological complexity belies therapeutic simplicity. *Science, 304,* 1269–1273.

Turiel, E. (1998). The development of morality. In N. Eisenberg (Ed.), *Handbook of child psychology* (5th ed., Vol. 3). New York: Wiley.

Turiel, E. (2003). *The culture of morality.* New York: Cambridge University Press.

Turiel, E. (2005). Thought, emotions, and social international processes in moral development. In M. Killen & J. Smetana (Eds.), *Handbook of moral development.* Mahwah, NJ: Erlbaum.

Turk, D. C., Rudy, T. E., & Salovey, P. (1984). Health protection: Attitudes and behaviors of LPN's teachers, and college students. *Health Psychology, 3,* 189–210.

Turner, B. F. (1982). Sex-related differences in aging. In B. B. Wolman (Ed.), *Handbook of developmental psychology.* Englewood Cliffs, NJ: Prentice Hall.

Turvey, C. L., Carney, C., Arndt, S., & Wallace, R. B. (1999, November). *Conjugal loss and syndromal depression in a sample of elders ages 70 years and older.* Paper presented at the meeting of the Gerontological Society of America, San Francisco.

U.S. Bureau of the Census (2004). *People.* Washington, DC: Author.

U.S. Bureau of Labor Statistics (2003). *People.* Washington, DC: U.S. Department of Labor.

U.S. Bureau of the Census (2001). *Census data: 2000.* Washington, DC: Author.

U.S. Bureau of the Census (2002). *Statistical abstracts of the United States.* Washington, DC: U.S. Government Printing Office.

U.S. Bureau of the Census (2003). *Population statistics.* Washington, DC: Author.

U.S. Bureau of the Census (2004). *Death Statistics.* Washington, DC: Author.

U.S. Bureau of the Census (2004). *Family and living arrangements: Table MS-2.* Washington, DC: Author.

U.S. Bureau of the Census (2004). *Statistical abstracts of the United States.* Washington, DC: U.S. Government Printing Office.

U.S. Department of Education (1996). *Number and disabilities of children and youth served under IDEA.* Washington, DC: Office of Special Education Programs, Data Analysis System.

U.S. Department of Education (1999). *Digest of education statistics.* Washington. DC: Author.

U.S. Department of Education (2000). *To assure a free and appropriate public education of all children with disabilities.* Washington, DC: U.S. Office of Education.

U.S. Department of Education (2003, December 23). *The NCES fast facts: What are the trends in the educational level of the United States population?* Washington, DC: U.S. Office of Education.

U.S. Department of Energy (2001). *The Human Genome Project.* Washington, DC: Author.

U.S. Department of Health and Human Services (2001). *Youth violence.* Rockville, MD: Author.

U.S. Department of Health and Human Services (2003). *Child abuse and neglect statistics.* Washington, DC: Author.

U.S. Food and Drug Administration (2004). *Consumer advisory regarding the risks of mercury in fish.* Washington, DC: Author.

U.S. Surgeon General's Report (1990). *The health benefits of smoking cessation.* Bethesda, MD: U.S. Department of Health and Human Services.

Ubell, C. (1992, December 6). We can age successfully. *Parade,* pp. 14–15.

Umana-Taylor, A. J. (2004). Ethnic identity and self-esteem: Examining the role of social contexts. *Journal of Adolescence, 27,* 139–146.

Underwood, M. (2004). Sticks and stones and social exclusion: Aggression among boys and girls. In P. K. Smith & C. H. Hart (Eds.), *Blackwell handbook of childhood social development.* Malden, MA: Blackwell.

Underwood, M. K. (2003). *Social aggression among girls.* New York: Guilford.

Unger, B., Kemp, J. S., Wilins, D., Psara, R., Ledbetter, T., Graham, M., Case, M., & Thach, B. T. (2003). Racial disparity and modifiable risk factors among infants dying suddenly and unexpectedly. *Pediatrics, 111,* E127–E131.

UNICEF (2002). *The state of the world's children 2002.* Geneva: Author.

UNICEF (2003). *The state of the world's children 2003.* Geneva: Author.

UNICEF (2004). *The state of the world's children 2002.* Geneva: Author.

United Nations (2002). *Improving the quality of life of girls.* New York: Author.

Urbano, M. T., & Tait, D. M. (2004). Can the irradiated uterus sustain a pregnancy? *Clinical Oncology, 16,* 24–28.

Vaillant, G. E. (1977). *Adaptation to life.* Boston: Little, Brown.

Vaillant, G. E. (1992). Is there a natural history of addiction? In C. P. O'Brien & J. H. Jaffe (Eds.), *Addictive states.* Cambridge, MA: Harvard University Press.

Vaillant, G. E. (2002). *Aging well.* Boston: Little, Brown.

Valdimarsdottir, U., Helgason, A. R., Furst, C. J., Adolfsson, J., & Steineck, G. (2003). Long-term effects of widowhood after terminal cancer: A Swedish nationwide follow-up. *Scandinavian Journal of Public Health, 31,* 31–36.

Valencia, R. R., & Suzuki, L. A. (2001). *Intelligence testing and minority students.* Thousand Oaks, CA: Sage.

Valeri, S. M. (2003). Social factors: Isolation and loneliness versus social activity. In A. Spirito & J. C. Overholser (Eds.), *Evaluating and treating adolescent suicide attempters.* San Diego: Academic Press.

Van Beveren, T. T. (2002). *Prenatal development and the newborn.* Unpublished manuscript, University of Texas at Dallas, Richardson.

Van Buren, E., & Graham, S. (2003). *Redefining ethnic identity: Its relationship to positive and negative school adjustment outcomes for minority youth.* Paper presented at the meeting of the Society for Research in Child Development, Tampa.

van den Boom, D. C. (1989). Neonatal irritability and the development of attachment. In G. A. Kohnstamm, J. E. Bates, & M. K. Rothbart (Eds.), *Temperament in childhood.* New York: Wiley.

Van Den Brink, C. L., Tijhuis, M., Van Den Bos, G. A., Giampaoli, S., Kivinen, P., Nissinen, A., & Kromhout, D. (2004). Effect of widowhood on disability onset in elderly men from three European countries. *Journal of the American Geriatric Society, 52,* 353–358.

Van Egeren, L. A., & Hawkins, D. P. (2004). Coming to terms with coparenting: implications of definition and measurement. *Journal of Adult Development, 11,* 165–178.

Van Evra, J. (2004). *Television and child development.* Mahwah, NJ: Erlbaum.

van IJzendoorn, M. H., & Kroonenberg, P. M. (1988). Cross-cultural patterns of attachment: A meta-analysis of the Strange Situation. *Child Development, 59,* 147–156.

Van Mierlo, J., & Van den Buick, J. (2004). Benchmarking the cultivation approach to video game effects. *Journal of Adolescence, 27,* 97–111.

Vandell, D. L. (2004). Early child care: The known and unknown. *Merrill-Palmer Quarterly, 50,* 387–414.

Vandell, D. L., & Wilson, K. S. (1988). Infants' interactions with mother, sibling, and peer: Contrasts and relations between interaction systems. *Child Development, 48,* 176–186.

Vandewater, E. A., Ostrove, J. M., & Stewart, A. J. (1997). Predicting women's well-being in mid-life: The importance of personality development and social role involvements. *Journal of Personality and Social Development, 72,* 1147–1160.

VandeWeerd, C., & Paveza, G. (1999, November). *Physical violence in old age: A look at the burden of women.* Paper presented at the meeting of the Gerontological Society of America, San Francisco.

Vastag, B. (2004). Does video game violence sow aggression? *Journal of the American Medical Association, 291,* 1822–1824.

Ventis, W. L. (1995). The relationships between religion and mental health. *Journal of Social Issues, 51,* 33–48.

Ventura, S. J., Martin, J. A., Curtin, S. C., & Mathews, T. J. (1997, June 10). *Report of final natality statistics, 1995.* Washington, DC: National Center for Health Statistics.

Verbrugge, L. M., Gruber-Baldini, A. L., & Fozard, J. L. (1996). Age differences and age changes in activities: Baltimore Longitudinal Study of Aging. *Journals of Gerontology B: Psychological Sciences and Social Sciences, 51,* S30–S41.

Verhaeghen, P., Marcoen, A., & Goossens, L. (1995). Facts and fiction about memory aging: A quantitative integration of research findings. *Journal of Gerontology, 48,* P157–P171.

Verma, S., & Saraswathi, T. S. (2002). Adolescence in India: Street urchins or silicon valley millionaires? In B. B. Brown, R. W. Larson, & T. S. Saraswathi (Eds.), *The world's youth.* New York: Cambridge University Press.

Verster, J. C., van Duin, D., Volkerts, E. R., Schreueder, A. H., & Verbaten, M. N. (2003). Alcohol hangover effects on memory functioning and vigilance performance after an evening of binge drinking. *Neuropsychopharmacology, 28,* 740–746.

Vidaeff, A. C., & Mastrobattista, J. M. (2003). In utero cocaine exposure: A thorny mix of science and mythology. *American Journal of Perinatology, 20,* 165–172.

Vidal, F. (2000). Piaget's theory. In A. Kazdin (Ed.), *Encyclopedia of psychology.* Washington, DC, & New York: American Psychological Association and Oxford University Press.

Vidyasagar, T. R. (2004). Neural underpinnings of dyslexia as a disorder of visuospatial attention. *Clinical and Experimental Optometry, 87,* 4–10.

Vintzileos, A. M., Guzman, E. R., Smulian, J. C., Scorza, W. E., & Knuppel, R. A. (2002). Second-trimester genetic sonography in patients with advanced maternal age and normal triple screen. *Obstetrics and Gynecology, 99,* 993–995.

Virnig, B., Huang, Z., Lurie, N., Musgrave, D., McBean, A. M., & Dowd, B. (2004). Does Medicare managed care provide equal treatment for mental illness across race? *Archives of General Psychiatry, 61,* 201–205.

Visher, E., & Visher, J. (1989). Parenting coalitions after remarriage: Dynamics and therapeutic guidelines. *Family Relations, 38,* 65–70.

Vitaliano, P. P., Young, H. M., & Zhang, J. (2004). Is caregiving a risk factor for illness? *Current Directions in Psychological Science, 13,* 13–16.

Vitiello, M. V., Larsen, L. H., & Moe, K. E. (2004). Age-related sleep change: Gender and estrogen effects on the subjective-objective sleep quality relationships of healthy, noncomplaining older men and women. *Journal of Psychosomatic Research, 56,* 503–510.

Voelker, R. (2004). Stress, sleep loss, and substance abuse create potent recipe for college depression. *Journal of the American Medical Association, 291,* 2177–2179.

Voeller, K. K. (2004). Attention-deficit hyperactivity disorder. *Journal of Child Neurology, 19,* 798–814.

Vogels, W. W., Dekker, M. R., Brouwer, W. H., & de Jong, R. (2002). Age-related changes in event-related prospective memory performance: A comparison of four prospective memory tasks. *Brain and Cognition, 49,* 341–362.

Volker, D. L. (2004). Methodological issues associated with studying an illegal act: Assisted dying. *Advanced Nursing Science, 27,* 117–128.

Volterra, M. C., Caselli, O., Capirci, E., & Pizzuto, E. (2005). Gesture and the emergence and development of language. In M. Tomasello & D. I. Slobin (Eds.), *Beyond nature-nurture.* Mahwah, NJ: Erlbaum.

Votruba-Drzal, E., Coley, R. L., & Chase-Lansdale, P. L. (2004). Child care and low-income children's development: Direct and moderated effects. *Child Development, 75,* 296–312.

Voydanoff, P. (1990). Economic distress and family relations: A review of the eighties. *Journal of Marriage and the Family, 52,* 1099–1115.

Vreugdenhil, H. J., Mulder, P. G., Emmen, H. H., & Weisglas-Kuperus, N. (2004). Effects of perinatal exposure to PCBs on neuropsychological functions in the Rotterdam cohort at 9 years of age. *Neuropsychology, 18,* 185–193.

Vurpillot, E. (1968). The development of scanning strategies and their relation to visual differentiation. *Journal of Experimental Child Psychology, 6,* 632–650.

Vygotsky, L. S. (1962). *Thought and language.* Cambridge, MA: MIT Press.

Wachs, T. D. (1994). Fit, context and the transition between temperament and personality. In C. Halverson, G. Kohnstamm, & R. Martin (Eds.), *The developing structure of personality from infancy to adulthood.* Hillsdale, NJ: Erlbaum.

Wachs, T. D. (2000). *Necessary but not sufficient.* Washington, DC: American Psychological Association.

Wachs, T. D., & Kohnstamm, G. A. (Eds.). (2001). *Temperament in context.* Mahwah, NJ: Erlbaum.

Wadden, T. A., Foster, G. D., Sarwer, D. B., Anderson, D. A., Gladis, M., Sanderson, R. S., Letchak, R. V., Berkowitz, R. I., & Phelan, S. (2004). Dieting and the development of eating disorders in obese women: Results of a randomized trial. *American Journal of Clinical Nutrition, 80,* 560–568.

Wadden, T. A., Foser, G. D., Stunkard, A. J., & Conill, A. M. (1996). Effects of weight cycling on the resting energy expenditure and body composition of obese women. *Eating Disorders, 19,* 5–12.

Wagstaff, A., Bustreo, F., Bryce, J., Claeson, M., and the WHO-World Bank Child Health and Poverty Working Group (2004). Child health: Reaching the poor. *American Journal of Public Health, 94,* 726–736.

Wainryb, C. (2005). Culture and morality. In M. Killen & J. Smetana (Eds.), *Handbook of moral development.* Mahwah, NJ: Erlbaum.

Walden, T. (1991). Infant social referencing. In J. Garber & K. Dodge (Eds.), *The development of emotional regulation and dysregulation.* New York: Cambridge University Press.

Walker, C., Gruman, C., & Blank, K. (1999, November). *Physician-assisted suicide: Looking beyond the numbers.* Paper presented at the meeting of the Gerontological Society of America, San Francisco.

Walker, E. F. (2002). Adolescent neurodevelopment and psychopathology. *Current Directions in Psychological Science, 11,* 24–28.

Walker, H. (1998, May 31). Youth violence: Society's problem. *Eugene Register Guard,* p. 1C.

Walker, L. (2001). Battering in adult relationships. In J. Worell (Ed.), *Encyclopedia of women and gender.* San Diego: Academic Press.

Walker, L. (2005). Gender and morality. In M. Killen & J. Smetana (Eds.), *Handbook of moral development.* Mahwah, NJ: Erlbaum.

Wall, T. L., Shea, S. H., Chan, K. K., & Carr, L. G. (2001). A genetic association with the development of alcohol and other substance abuse behavior in Asian

Americans. *Journal of Abnormal Psychology, 110,* 173–178.

Wallace-Bell, M. (2003). The effects of passive smoking on adult and child health. *Professional Nurse, 19,* 217–219.

Wallerstein, J. S., & Johnson-Reitz, L. (2004). Communication in divorced and single parent families. In A. L. Vangelisti (Ed.), *Handbook of family communication.* Mahwah, NJ: Erlbaum.

Walsh, L. A. (2000, Spring). The inside scoop on child development: Interview. *Cutting through the hype.* Minneapolis: College of Education & Human Development, University of Minnesota.

Walters, E., & Kendler, K. S. (1994). Anorexia nervosa and anorexia-like symptoms in a population based twin sample. *American Journal of Psychiatry, 152,* 62–71.

Ward, B. M., Lambert, S. B., & Lester, R. A. (2001). Rubella vaccination in prenatal and postnatal women: Why not use MMR? *Medical Journal of Australia, 174,* 311–312.

Ward, L. M. (2003). Understanding the role of entertainment media in the sexual socialization of American youth: A review of empirical research. *Developmental Review, 23,* 347–388.

Ward, L. M., & Caruthers, A. (2001). Media influences. In J. Worell (Ed.), *Encyclopedia of women and gender.* San Diego: Academic Press.

Ward, R. A., & Spitze, G. D. (2004). Marital implications of parent-adult child coresidence: A longitudinal view. *Journals of Gerontology B: Psychological Sciences and Social Sciences, 59,* S2–S8.

Wardle, F. (2003). *Introduction to special education.* Boston: Allyn & Bacon.

Wardle, J., Cooke, E. J., Gibson, E. L., Sapochnik, M., Sheiham, A., & Lawson, M. (2003). Increasing children's acceptance of vegetables: A randomized trial of parent-led exposure. *Appetite, 40,* 155–162.

Ware, J. E., Kosinski, M., & Dewey, J. E. (2000). *How to score Version 2 of the SF-36 Health Survey.* Boston: QualityMetric.

Wark, G. R., & Krebs, D. L. (2000). The construction of moral dilemmas in everyday life. *Journal of Moral Education, 29,* 5–21.

Wark, M. J., Kruczek, T., & Boley, A. (2003). Emotional neglect and family structure. *Child Abuse & Neglect, 27,* 1033–1043.

Warner, L., & Sower, J. C. (2005). *Educating children from preschool through primary grades.* Boston: Allyn & Bacon.

Warr, P. (1994). Age and employment. In M. Dunnette, L. Hough, & H. Triandis (Eds.), *Handbook of industrial and organizational psychology* (Vol. 4). Palo Alto, CA: Consulting Psychologists Press.

Warr, P. (2004). Work, well-being, and mental health. In J. Baring, E. K. Kelloway, & M. R. Frone (Eds.), *Handbook of work stress.* Thousand Oaks, CA: Sage.

Warr, P., Butcher, V., & Roberts, I. (2004). Activity and psychological well-being in old people. *Aging and Mental Health, 8,* 172–183.

Warren, M. P., & Valente, J. S. (2004). Menopause and patient management. *Clinical Obstetrics and Gynecology, 47,* 450–470.

Warrick, P. (1992, March 1). The fantastic voyage of Tanner Roberts. *Los Angeles Times,* pp. E1, 12, 13.

Warshak, R. A. (2003, January). Personal communication, Department of Psychology, University of Texas at Dallas, Richardson.

Wass, H. (2004). A perspective on the current state of death education. *Death Studies, 28,* 289–308.

Wass, H., & Stillion, J. M. (1988). Death in the lives of children and adolescents. In H. Wass, F. M. Berardo, & R. A. Neimeyer (Eds.), *Dying: Facing the facts* (2nd ed.). Washington, DC: Hemisphere.

Watenberg, N., Silver, S., Harel, S., & Lerman-Sagie, T. (2002). Significance of microencephaly among children with developmental disabilities. *Journal of Child Neurology, 17,* 117–122.

Waterman, A. S. (1992). Identity as an aspect of optimal psychological functioning. In G. R. Adams, T. P. Gullotta, & R. Montemayor (Eds.), *Adolescent identity formation.* Newbury Park, CA: Sage.

Waters, E. (2001, April). *Perspectives on continuity and discontinuity in relationships.* Paper presented at the meeting of the Society for Research in Child Development, Minneapolis.

Waters, E., Merrick, S., Albersheim, L., Treboux, D., & Crowell, J. (2000). Attachment theory from infancy to adulthood: A 20-year-longitudinal study of relations between infant Strange Situation classification and attachment representations in adulthood. *Child Development, 71,* 684–689.

Watson, J. B. (1928). *Psychological care of infant and child.* New York: W. W. Norton.

Watson, J. B., & Rayner, R. (1920). Conditioned emotional reactions. *Journal of Experimental Psychology, 3,* 1–14.

Watson, R., & DeMeo, P. (1987). Premarital cohabitation vs. traditional courtship and subsequent marital adjustment: A replication and follow-up. *Family Relations, 36,* 193–197.

Watts, C., & Zimmerman, C. (2002). Violence against women: Global scope and magnitude. *Lancet, 359,* 1232–1237.

Watts, K., Beye, P., Siafarikas, A., O'Driscoll, G., Jones, T. W., Davis, E. A., & Green, D. J. (2004). Effects of exercise training on vascular function in obese children. *Journal of Pediatrics, 144,* 620–625.

Waxman, S. R. (2004). Early word-learning and conceptual development. In U. Goswami (Ed.), *Blackwell handbook of infant development.* Malden, MA: Blackwell.

Waylen, A., & Wolke, D. (2004). Sex 'n' rock 'n' roll: The meaning and consequences of pubertal timing. *European Journal of Endocrinology, 151, Supplement 3,* U15I–U159.

Weale, R. A. (1992). *The senescence of human vision.* New York: Oxford University Press.

Weatherford, W. (1999, October 31). Alzheimer's disease—What's new? *Dallas Morning News,* p. 4B.

Weaver, A., & Dobson, P. (2004). Home and dry—some toilet training tips to give parents. *Journal of Family Health Care, 14,* 64, 66.

Weaver, R. F. (2005). *Molecular biology* (3rd ed.). New York: McGraw-Hill.

Webster, W. S., & Freeman, J. A. (2003). Prescription drugs and pregnancy. *Expert Opinions in Pharmacotherapy, 4,* 949–961.

Wechsler, H., Davenport, A., Sowdall, G., Moetykens, B., & Castillo, S. (1994). Health and behavioral consequences of binge drinking in college. *Journal of the American Medical Association, 272,* 1672–1677.

Wechsler, H., Lee, J. E., Kuo, M., Seibring, M., Nelson, T. F., & Lee, H. (2002). Trends in college binge drinking during a period of increased prevention efforts: Findings from 4 Harvard School of Public Health college alcohol study surveys: 1993–2001. *Journal of American College Health, 50,* 203–217.

Wehrens, X. H., Offermans, J. P., Snijders, M., & Peeters, L. L. (2004). Fetal cardiovascular response to large placental chorionangiomas. *Journal of Perinatal Medicine, 32,* 107–112.

Weijers, H. G., Wiesbeck, G. A., Wodarz, N., Keller, H., Michel, T., & Boning, J. (2003). Gender and personality in alcoholism. *Archives of Women's Mental Health, 6,* 245–252.

Weikert, D. P. (1993). [Long-term positive effects in the Perry Preschool Head Start Program.] Unpublished data, High Scope Foundation, Ypsilanti, MI.

Weincke, J. K., Thurston, S. W., Kelsey, K. T., Varkonyi, A., Wain, J. C., Mark, E. J., & Christiani, D. C. (1999). Early age at smoking initiation and tobacco carcinogen DNA damage in the lung. *Journal of the National Cancer Institute, 91,* 614–619.

Weinraub, M., Horuath, D. L., & Gringlas, M. B. (2002). Single parenthood. In M. H. Bornstein (Ed.), *Handbook of parenting* (2nd ed., Vol. 3). Mahwah, NJ: Erlbaum.

Weinstein, N. D. (1984). Reducing unrealistic optimism about illness susceptibility. *Health Psychology, 3,* 431–457.

Weinstock, H., Berman, S., & Cates, W. (2004). Sexually transmitted diseases among American youth: Incidence and prevalence estimates, 2000. *Perspectives on Sexual and Reproductive Health, 36,* 6–10.

Weiss, R. E. (2001). *Pregnancy and birth: Rh factor in pregnancy.* Available on the Internet at: www.about.com.

Weisz, A. N., & Black, B. M. (2002). Gender and moral reasoning: African American youth respond to dating dilemmas. *Journal of Human Behavior in the Social Environment, 5,* 35–52.

Welch, R. A., Blessed, W. B., & Lacoste, H. (2003). Five-year experience with midsemester amniocentesis performed by a single group of obstetrician-gynecologists at a community hospital. *American Journal of Obstetrics and Gynecology, 188,* 600–601.

Wellman, H. M. (1997, April). *Ten years of theory of mind: Telling the story backwards.* Paper presented at the meeting of the Society for Research in Child Development, Washington, DC.

Wellman, H. M. (2000). Early childhood. In A. Kazdin (Ed.), *Encyclopedia of psychology.* Washington, DC, & New York: American Psychological Association and Oxford University Press.

Wellman, H. M. (2004). Understanding the psychological world: Developing a theory of mind. In U. Goswami (Ed.), *Blackwell handbook of childhood cognitive development.* Malden, MA: Blackwell.

Wellman, H. M., Cross, D., & Watson, J. (2001). Meta-analysis of theory-of-mind development: The truth about false belief. *Child Development, 72,* 655–684.

Welti, C. (2002). Adolescents in Latin America: Facing the future with skepticism. In B. B. Brown, R. W. Larson, & T. S. Saraswathi (Eds.), *The world's youth.* New York: Cambridge University Press.

Wenestam, C. G., & Wass, H. (1987). Swedish and U.S. children's thinking about death: A qualitative study and cross-cultural comparison. *Death Studies, 11,* 99–121.

Wenger, N. S., & others. (2003). The quality of medical care provided to vulnerable community-dwelling older patients. *Annals of Internal Medicine, 139,* 740–747.

Wentworth, R. A. L. (1999). *Montessori for the millennium.* Mahwah, NJ: Erlbaum.

Wentzel, K. R., & Asher, S. R. (1995). The academic lives of neglected, rejected, popular, and controversial children. *Child Development, 66,* 754–763.

Wentzel, K. R., Barry, C. M., & Caldwell, K. A. (2004). Friendships in middle school: Influences on motivation and school adjustment. *Journal of Educational Psychology, 96,* 195–203.

Wenze, G. T., & Wenze, N. (2004). Helping left-handed children adapt to school experiences. *Childhood Education, 81,* 25–31.

Wenzlaff, R. M., & Prohaska, M. L. (1989). When misery loves company: Depression, attributions, and responses to others' moods. *Journal of Experimental Social Psychology, 25,* 220–223.

Werth, J. L. (2004). The relationships among clinical depression, suicide, and other actions that may hasten death. *Behavioral Science and the Law, 22,* 627.

West, R., & Craik, F. I. M. (2001). Influences on the efficiency of prospective memory in younger and older adults. *Psychology and Aging, 16,* 682–696.

Wethington, E., Kessler, R., & Pixley, J. (2004). Turning points in adulthood. In G. Brim, C. D. Ryff, & R. Kessler (Eds.), *How healthy we are: A national study of well-being in midlife.* Chicago: University of Chicago Press.

Wetterling, T., & Junghanns, K. (2004). Affective disorders in older inpatients. *International Journal of Geriatric Psychiatry, 19,* 487–492.

Whiffen, V. (2001). Depression. In J. Worell (Ed.), *Encyclopedia of women and gender.* San Diego: Academic Press.

Whitbourne, S. K. (2000). Adult development and aging: Biological processes and physical development. In A. Kazdin (Ed.), *Encyclopedia of psychology.* Washington, DC, & New York: American Psychological Association and Oxford University Press.

Whitbourne, S. K. (2001). The physical aging process in midlife: Interactions with psychological and sociocultural factors. In M. E. Lachman (Ed.), *Handbook of midlife development.* New York: John Wiley.

Whitbourne, S. K., & Connolly, L. A. (1999). The developing self in midlife. In S. L. Willis & J. D. Reid (Eds.), *Life in the middle.* San Diego: Academic Press.

White, B., Castle, P., & Held, R. (1964). Observations on the development of visually directed reaching. *Child Development, 35,* 349–364.

White, C. B., & Catania, J. (1981). Psychoeducational intervention for sexuality with the aged, family members of the aged, and people who work with the aged. *International Journal of Aging and Human Development.*

White, C. W., & Coleman, M. (2000). *Early childhood education.* Columbus, OH: Merrill.

White, J. W. (2001). Aggression and gender. In J. Worell (Ed.), *Encyclopedia of gender and women.* San Diego: Academic Press.

White, L. (1994). Stepfamilies over the life course: Social support. In A. Booth and J. Dunne (Eds.), *Stepfamilies: Who benefits and who does not.* Hillsdale, NJ: Erlbaum.

White, L. (2001). Sibling relationships over the life course. *Journal of Marriage and the Family, 63,* 555–568.

Whitehead, B. D., & Popenoe, D. (2001). *The state of our unions: The social health of America in 2001.* New Brunswick, NJ: Rutgers University.

Whitehead, B. D., & Popenoe, D. (2003). *The state of our unions.* New Brunswick, NJ: Rutgers University.

Whitehead, D., Keast, J., Montgomery, V., & Hayman, S. (2004). A preventive health education program for osteoporosis. *Journal of Advanced Nursing, 47,* 15–24.

White-Traut, R. (2004). Providing a nurturing environment for infants in adverse situations: Multisensory strategies for newborn care. *Journal of Midwifery and Womens Health, 49* (4 Supplement 1), 36–41.

Whitfield, K. E., & Baker-Thomas, T. (1999). Individual differences in aging minorities. *International Journal of Aging and Human Development, 48,* 73–79.

Whiting, B. B., & Edwards, C. P. (1988). *Children of different worlds.* Cambridge, MA: Harvard University Press.

Whitman, T. L., Borkowski, J. G., Keogh, D. A., & Weed, K. (2001). *Interwoven lives.* Mahwah, NJ: Erlbaum.

Wickelgren, I. (1999). Nurture helps to mold able minds. *Science, 283,* 1832–1834.

Wiesner, M., & Ittel, A. (2002). Relations of pubertal timing and depressing symptoms to substance use in early adolescence. *Journal of Early Adolescence, 22,* 5–23.

Wilcox, S., Evenson, K. R., Aragaki, A., Wassertheil-Smoller, S., Mouton, C. P., & Loevinger, B. L. (2003). The effects of widowhood on physical and mental health, health behaviors, and health outcomes: The women's health initiative. *Health Psychology, 22,* 513–522.

Wilens, T. E. (2003). Drug therapy for adults with attention deficit hyperactivity disorder. *Drugs, 63,* 2395–2411.

Wiley, D., & Bortz, W. M. (1996). Sexuality and aging—usual and successful. *Journal of Gerontology, 51A,* M142–M146.

Wilkie, F., & Eisdorfer, C. (1971). Intelligence and blood pressure in the aged. *Science, 172,* 959–962.

Willcox, B. J., Willcox, M. D., & Suzuki, M. (2002). *The Okinawa Program.* New York: Crown.

Willford, J. A., Richardson, G. A., Leech, S. L., & Day, N. L. (2004). Verbal and visuopatial learning and memory function in children with moderate prenatal alcohol exposure. *Alcoholism: Clinical and Experimental Research, 28,* 497–507.

Williams, A., & Nussbaum, J. F. (2001). *Intergenerational communication across the life span.* Mahwah, NJ: Erlbaum.

Williams, C. R. (1986). *The impact of television: A natural experiment in three communities.* New York: Academic Press.

Williams, J. E., & Best, D. L. (1982). *Measuring sex stereotypes: A thirty-nation study.* Newbury Park, CA: Sage.

Williams, J. E., & Best, D. L. (1989). *Sex and psyche: Self-concept viewed cross-culturally.* Newbury Park, CA: Sage.

Williams, M. H. (2005). *Nutrition for health, fitness, & sport* (7th ed.). New York: McGraw-Hill.

Williams, R. B. (1995). Coronary prone behaviors, hostility, and cardiovascular health. In K. Orth-Gomer & N. Schneiderman (Eds.), *Behavioral medicine approaches to cardiovascular disease prevention.* Mahwah, NJ: Erlbaum.

Williams, R. B. (2001). Hostility (and other psychosocial risk factors): Effects on health and the potential for successful behavioral approaches to prevention and treatment. In A. Baum, T. A. Revenson, & J. E. Singer (Eds.), *Handbook of health psychology.* Mahwah, NJ: Erlbaum.

Willis, S. L., & Nesselroade, C. S. (1990). Long-term effects of fluid ability training in old age. *Developmental Psychology, 26,* 905–910.

Willis, S. L., & Reid, J. D. (Eds.). (1999). *Life in the middle: Psychological and social development in middle age.* San Diego: Academic Press.

Willis, S. L., & Schaie, K. W. (1986). Training the elderly on the ability factors of spatial orientation and inductive reasoning. *Psychology and Aging, 1,* 239–247.

Willis, S. L., & Schaie, K. W. (1994). Assessing everyday competence in the elderly. In C. Fisher & R. Lerner (Eds.), *Applied developmental psychology.* Hillsdale, NJ: Erlbaum.

Willis, S. L., & Schaie, K. W. (1999). Intellectual functioning in midlife. In S. L. Willis & J. D. Reid (Eds.), *Life in the middle: Psychological and social development in middle age.* San Diego: Academic Press.

Willis, W. O., Eder, C. H., Lindsay, S. P., Chavez, G., & Shelton, S. T. (2004). Lower rates of low birthweight and preterm births in the California Black Infant Health Program. *Journal of the National Medical Association, 96,* 315–324.

Wills, T. A., Resko, J. A., Ainette, M. G., & Mendoza, D. (2004). Role of parental support and peer support in adolescent substance use: A test of mediated effects. *Psychology of Addictive Behaviors, 18,* 122–134.

Wilmoth, J. M., & Chen, P-C. (2003). Immigrant status, living arrangements, and depressive symptoms among middle-aged and older adults. *Journals of Gerontology B: Psychological Sciences and Social Sciences, 58,* S305–S313.

Wilson, A. E., Shuey, K. M., & Elder, G. H. (2003). Ambivalence in relationships of adult children to aging parents and in-laws. *Journal of Marriage and the Family, 65,* 1055–1072.

Wilson, B. (2001, April). *The role of television in children's emotional development and socialization.* Paper presented at the meeting of the Society for Research in Child Development, Minneapolis.

Wilson, R. S., Mendes de Leon, C. F., Barnes, L. L., Schneider, J. A., Bienias, J., Evans, D. A., & Bennett, D. A. (2002). Participation in cognitively stimulating activities and risk of incident Alzheimer disease. *Journal of the American Medical Association, 287,* 742–748.

Windle, M., & Windle, R. C. (2003). Alcohol and other substance use and abuse. In G. Adams & M. Berzonsky (Eds.), *Blackwell handbook of adolescence.* Malden, MA: Blackwell.

Windle, W. F. (1940). *Physiology of the human fetus.* Philadelphia: W. B. Saunders.

Wineberg, H. (1994). Marital reconciliation in the United States: Which couples are successful? *Journal of Marriage and the Family, 56,* 80–88.

Wingfield, A., & Kahana, M. J. (2002). The dynamics of memory retrieval in older adulthood. *Canadian Journal of Experimental Psychology, 56,* 187–199.

Wink, P., & Dillon, M. (2002). Spiritual development across the adult life course: Findings from a longitudinal study. *Journal of Adult Development, 9,* 79–94.

Winner, E. (1986, August). Where pelicans kiss seals. *Psychology Today,* pp. 24–35.

Winner, E. (1996). *Gifted children: Myths and realities.* New York: Basic Books.

Winner, E. (2000). The origins and ends of giftedness. *American Psychologist, 55,* 159–169.

Winsler, A., Carlton, M. P., & Barry, M. J. (2000). Age-related changes in preschool children's systematic use of private speech in a natural setting. *Journal of Child Language, 27,* 665–687.

Winsler, A., Caverly, S. L., Willson-Quayle, A., Carlton, M. P., & Howell, C. (2002). The social and behavioral ecology of mixed-age and same-age preschool classrooms: A natural experiment. *Journal of Applied Developmental Psychology, 23,* 305–330.

Winstead, B., & Griffin, J. L. (2001). Friendship styles. In J. Worell (Ed.), *Encyclopedia of women and gender.* San Diego: Academic Press.

Wintre, M. G., & Vallance, D. D. (1994). A developmental sequence in the comprehension of emotions: Intensity, multiple emotions, and valence. *Developmental Psychology, 30,* 509–514.

Witkin, H. A., Mednick, S. A., Schulsinger, R., Bakkestrom, E., Christiansen, K. O., Goodenbough, D. R., Hirchhorn, K., Lunsteen, C., Owen, D. R., Philip, J., Ruben, D. B., & Stocking, M. (1976). Criminality in XYY and XXY men. *Science, 193,* 547–555.

Wolinsky, F. D., Miller, D. K., Andresen, E. M., Malmstrom, T. K., & Miller, J. P. (2004). Health-related quality of life in middle-aged African Americans. *Journals of Gerontology B: Psychological and Social Sciences, 59,* S118–S123.

Wong, A. M., Lin, Y. C., Chou, S. W., Tang, F. T., & Wong, P. Y. (2001). Coordination exercise and postural stability in elderly people: Effect of Tai Chi Chuan. *Archives of Physical Medicine & Rehabilitation, 82,* 608–612.

Wong, C. H., Wong, S. F., Pang, W. S., Azizah, M. Y., & Dass, M. J. (2003). Habitual walking and its correlation to better physical function: Implications for prevention of physical disability in older persons. *Journals of Gerontology A: Biological Sciences and Medical Sciences, 58,* M555–M560.

Wong, D. L., Perry, S. E., & Hockenberry, M. (2001). *Maternal child nursing care* (2nd ed.). St. Louis: Mosby.

Wood, A. G., Harvey, A. S., Wellard, R. M., Abbott, D. F., Anderson, V., Kean, M., Saling, M. M., & Jackson, G. D. (2004). Language cortex activation in normal children. *Neurology, 63,* 1035–1044.

Wood, J. M. (2002). Age and visual impairment decrease driving performance as measured on a closed-road circuit. *Human Factors, 44,* 482–494.

Wood, J. T. (2001). *Gendered lives* (4th ed.). Belmont, CA: Wadsworth.

Wood, M. D., Read, J. P., Mitchell, R. E., & Brand, N. H. (2004). Do parents still matter? Parent and peer influences on alcohol involvement among recent high school graduates. *Psychology of Addictive Behaviors, 18,* 19–30.

Woods, S., & Walker, D. (2004). Direct and relational bullying among primary school children and academic achievement. *Journal of School Psychology, 2,* 135–155.

Woodward, A. L., & Markman, E. M. (1998). Early word learning. In D. Kuhn & R. S. Siegler (Eds.), *Handbook of child psychology* (5th ed., Vol. 2). New York: Wiley.

Woodward, N. J., & Wallston, B. S. (1987). Age and health-care beliefs: Self-efficacy as a mediator of low desire for control. *Psychology and Aging, 2,* 3–8.

Wooley, S. C., & Garner, D. M. (1991). Obesity treatment: The high cost of false hope. *Journal of the American Dietetic Association, 91,* 1248–1251.

Worden, J. W. (2002). *Grief counseling and grief therapy* (3rd ed.). New York: Springer.

World Health Organization (2000, February 2). *Adolescent health behavior in 28 countries.* Geneva: Author.

World Health Organization (2002). *The world health report 2002.* Geneva: World Health Organization.

Worobey, J., & Belsky, J. (1982). Employing the Brazelton scale to influence mothering: An experimental comparison of three strategies. *Developmental Psychology, 18,* 736–743.

Worthington, E. L. (1989). Religious faith across the life span: Implications for counseling and research. *Counseling Psychologist, 17,* 555–612.

Wozniak, R. (2004). An introduction to scientific research. In L. N. Adelman (Ed.), *Research manual in child development* (2nd ed.). Mahwah, NJ: Erlbaum.

Wren, T., & Mendoza, C. (2004). Cultural identity and personal identity. In D. Lapsley & D. Narvaez (Eds.), *Moral development, self, and identity.* Mahwah, NJ: Erlbaum.

Wright, M. R. (1989). Body image satisfaction in adolescent girls and boys. *Journal of Youth and Adolescence, 18,* 71–84.

Wrosch, C., Schultz, R., & Heckhausen, J. (2004). Health stress and depressive symptomatology in the elderly: A control-process approach. *Current Directions in Psychological Science, 13,* 17–20.

Yaffe, K., Barnes, D., Nevitt, M., Lui, L., & Covinsky, K. (2001). A prospective study of physical activity and cognitive decline in elderly women. *Archives of Internal Medicine, 161,* 1703–1708.

Yali, A. M., & Revenson, T. A. (2004). How changes in population demographics will impact health psychology. *Health Psychology, 23,* 147–155.

Yang, J., McCrae, R. R., & Costa, P. T. (1998). Adult age differences in personality traits in the United States and the People's Republic of China. *Journals of Gerontology B: Psychological Sciences and Social Sciences, 53,* P375–P383.

Yang, N. (2005). Effects of individualism-collectivism on perceptions and outcomes of work-family interfaces: A Sino-U.S. comparison. In S. A. Y. Poelmans (Ed.), *Work and family.* Mahwah, NJ: Erlbaum.

Yang, S., & Sternberg, R. J. (1997). Taiwanese Chinese people's conceptions of intelligence. *Intelligence, 25,* 21–36.

Yarasheski, K. E. (2003). Exercise, aging, and muscle protein metabolism. *Journals of Gerontology A: Biological Sciences and Medical Sciences, 58,* M918–M922.

Yates, M. (1995, March). *Political socialization as a function of volunteerism.* Paper presented at the meeting of the Society for Research in Child Development, Indianapolis.

Yeats, D. E., Folts, W. E., & Knapp, J. (1999). Older workers' adaptation to a changing workplace: Employment issues for the 21st century. *Educational Gerontology, 25,* 331–347.

Young, D. (2001). The nature and management of pain: What is the evidence? *Birth, 28,* 149–151.

Young, K. T. (1990). American conceptions of infant development from 1955 to 1984: What the experts are telling parents. *Child Development, 61,* 17–28.

Young, S. K., & Shahinfar, A. (1995, March). *The contributions of maternal sensitivity and child temperament to attachment status at 14 months.* Paper presented at the meeting of the Society for Research in Child Development, Indianapolis.

Youniss, J., Silbereisen, R., Christmas-Best, V., Bales, S., Diversi, M., & McLaughlin, M. (2003). Civic and community engagement of adolescents in the 21st century. In R. Larson, B. Brown, & J. Mortimer (Eds.), *Adolescents' preparation for the future: Perils and promises.* Malden, MA: Blackwell.

Yu, B. P., Lim, B. O., & Sugano, M. (2002). Dietary restriction downregulates free radical and lipid peroxide production: Plausible mechanism for elongation of life span. *Journal of Nutritional Science, and Vitaminology, 48,* 257–284.

Yu, V. Y. (2000). Developmental outcome of extremely preterm infants. *American Journal of Perinatology, 17,* 57–61.

Zajonc, R. B. (2001). The family dynamics of intellectual development. *American Psychologist, 56,* 523–524.

Zald, D. H. (2003). The human amygdala and the emotional evaluation of sensory stimuli. *Brain Research Review, 41,* 88–123.

Zandi, P. P., & others. (2004). Reduced risk of Alzheimer disease in users of antioxidant vitamin supplements: The Cache County Study. *Archives of Neurology, 61,* 82–88.

Zarit, S. H., & Knight, B. G. (Eds.). (1996). *A guide to psychotherapy and aging.* Washington, DC: American Psychological Association.

Zarof, C. M., Knutelska, M., & Frumkes, T. E. (2003). Variation in stereoacuity: Normative description, fixation disparity, and the roles of aging and gender. *Investigative Ophthalmology and Vision Science, 44,* 891–900.

Zaslow, M. (2004). Childcare for low-income families. In A. C. Crouter & A. Booth (Eds.), *Work-family challenges for low-income parents and their children.* Mahwah, NJ: Erlbaum.

Zawistowski, C. A., & DeVita, M. A. (2004). A descriptive study of children dying in the pediatric intensive care unit after withdrawal of life-sustaining treatment. *Pediatric Critical Care Medicine, 5,* 216–223.

Zelazo, P. D., & Müller, U. (2004). Executive function in typical and atypical development. In U. Goswami (Ed.), *Blackwell handbook of cognitive development.* Malden, MA: Blackwell.

Zelazo, P. D., Müller, U., Frye, D., & Marcovitch, S. (2003). The development of executive function in early childhood. *Monographs of the Society for Research in Child Development, 68* (3, Serial No. 274).

Zeskind, P. S., Klein, L., & Marshall, T. R. (1992). Adults' perceptions of

experimental modifications of durations and expiratory sounds in infant crying. *Developmental Psychology, 28,* 1153–1162.

Zigler, E. F., & Styco, S. (2004). Moving Head Start to the states: One experiment too many. *Journal of Applied Developmental Science, 8,* 51–55.

Zimmer-Gemback, M. J., & Collins, W. A. (2003). Autonomy development during adolescence. In G. Adams & M. Berzonsky (Eds.), *Blackwell handbook of adolescence.* Malden, MA: Blackwell.

Zimmerman, R. S., Khoury, E., Vega, W. A., Gil, A. G., & Warheit, G. J. (1995). Teacher and student perceptions of behavior problems among a sample of African American, Hispanic, and non-Hispanic White students. *American Journal of Community Psychology, 23,* 181–197.

Zinn, M. B., & Wells, B. (2000). Diversity within Latino families: New lessons for family social science. In D. H. Demo, K. R. Allen, & M. A. Fine (Eds.), *Handbook of family diversity.* New York: Oxford University Press.

Zitnik, G., & Martin, G. M. (2002). Age-related decline in neurogenesis: Old cells or new environment? *Journal of Neuroscience Research, 70,* 258–263.

Zoppi, M. A., Ibba, R. M., Putzolu, M., Floris, M., & Monni, G. (2001). Nuchal translucency and the acceptance of invasive prenatal chromosomal diagnosis in women aged 35 and older. *Obstetrics and Gynecology, 97,* 916–920.

Zucker, A. N., Ostrove, J. M., & Stewart, A. J. (2002). College educated women's personality development in adulthood: Perceptions and age differences. *Psychology and Aging, 17,* 236–244.

Zuk, C. V., & Zuk, G. H. (2002). Origins of dreaming. *American Journal of Psychiatry, 159,* 495–496.

Zukow-Goldring, P. (2002). Sibling caregiving. In M. H. Bornstein (Ed.), *Handbook of parenting* (Vol. 3). Mahwah, NJ: Erlbaum.

Credits

Line Art and Text Credits

Chapter 1

Figure 1.4: From "Percentage of Children 7 to 18 Years of Age Around the World Who Have Never Been to School of Any Kind," 2004, *The State of the World's Children*, Geneva, Switzerland: UNICEF, Fig. 5, p. 27. **Figure 1.9:** From Inglehart, Robert, *Culture Shift in Advanced Industrial Society*, Copyright © 1990 by Princeton University Press. Reprinted by permission of Princeton University Press.

Chapter 2

Figure 2.5: From "Bronfenbrenner's Ecological Theory of Development," C. B. Kopp & J. B. Krakow, 1982, *Child Development in the Social Context*, p. 648. Addison-Wesley Longman, Inc. Reprinted by permission of Pearson Education, Inc.

Chapter 3

Pp. 78–79: From D. Bjorklund and A. Pellegrini, *The Origins of Human Nature*, American Psychological Association, 2002, pp. 336–340. Copyright © 2002 American Psychological Association. Reprinted with permission. **Figure 3.1:** From Santrock, *Topical Life-Span Development*, 2/e. Copyright © 2005 The McGraw-Hill Companies. Reproduced with permission of The McGraw-Hill Companies. **Figure 3.2:** From P. B. Baltes, U. M. Staudinger, & U. Lindenberger, 1999, "Lifespan Psychology," *Annual Review of Psychology*, 50, p. 474, Fig. 1. With permission, from the *Annual Review of Psychology*, Volume 50 © 1999 by Annual Reviews, www.annualreview.org, and by permission of Paul Baltes. **Figure 3.3:** From Santrock, *Psychology*, 7/e. Copyright © 2003 The McGraw-Hill Companies. Reproduced with permission of The McGraw-Hill Companies. **Figure 3.6:** From Santrock, *Children*, 5/e. Copyright © 1997 The McGraw-Hill Companies. Reproduced with permission of The McGraw-Hill Companies. **Figure 3.9:** From "Exploring Your Genetic Future," NOVA at www.pbs.org/wgbh/nova/genome/survey.html. Copyright © 2002 WGBH/Boston. **Pp. 92–93:** From D. Brodzinsky and E. Pinderhughes, "Parenting and Child Development in Adoptive Families" in M. Bornstein, ed., *Handbook of Parenting*, 2nd Ed., Vol. I, Lawrence Erlbaum Associates, pp. 288–292. Reprinted with permission. **P. 93:** From D. Brodzinsky and E. Pinderhughes, "Parenting and Child Development in Adoptive Families" in M. Bornstein, ed., *Handbook of Parenting*, 2nd Ed., Vol. I, Lawrence Erlbaum Associates, pp. 280–282. Reprinted with permission. **Figure 3.13:** From Santrock, *Children*, 7/e. Copyright © 2003 The McGraw-Hill Companies. Reproduced with permission of The McGraw-Hill Companies.

Chapter 4

P. 104: From P. Warrick, "The Fantastic Voyage of Tanner Roberts," *Los Angeles Times*, March 1, 1992, pp. E1, E12, E13. Copyright © 1992 Time, Inc. Reprinted with permission. **Figure 4.3:** From Santrock, *Children*, 5/e. Copyright © 1997 The McGraw-Hill Companies. Reproduced with permission of The McGraw-Hill Companies. **Figure 4.4:** Copyright © 1984 by the Childbirth Association of Seattle. Reprinted from *Pregnancy, Childbirth and the Newborn: The Complete Guide*, with permission of its publisher, Meadowbrook Press. **Figure 4.6:** From Santrock, *Children*, 8/e, Figure 4.6. Copyright © 2005 The McGraw-Hill Companies. Reproduced with permission of The McGraw-Hill Companies. **Figure 4.8:** From Santrock, *Child Development*, 10/e, Figure 4.8. Copyright © 2004 The McGraw-Hill Companies. Reproduced with permission of The McGraw-Hill Companies. **Figure 4.9:** From Santrock, *Child Development*, 10/e, Figure 4.9. Copyright © 2004 The McGraw-Hill Companies. Reproduced with permission of The McGraw-Hill Companies. **Figure 4.10:** From Virginia A. Apgar, 1975, "A Proposal for a New Method of Evaluation of a Newborn Infant," in *Anesthesia and Analgesia*, Vol. 32, pp. 260–267. Reprinted by permission. **Figure 4.11:** From Santrock, *Child Development*, 10/e, Figure 4.11. Copyright © 2004 The McGraw-Hill Companies. Reproduced with permission of The McGraw-Hill Companies.

Chapter 5

Figure 5.1: From Santrock, *Children*, 7/e. Copyright © 2003 The McGraw-Hill Companies. Reproduced with permission of The McGraw-Hill Companies. **Figure 5.2:** From Santrock, *Child Development*, 9/e. Copyright © 2001 The McGraw-Hill Companies. Reproduced with permission of The McGraw-Hill Companies. **Figure 5.3:** Reprinted by permission of the publisher from *The Postnatal Development of the Human Cerebral Cortex, Vol. I–VIII*, by Jesse LeRoy Conel. Cambridge, MA: Harvard University Press, Copyright © 1939, 1975 by the President and Fellows of Harvard College. **Figure 5.4:** From Santrock, *Topical Life-Span Development*. Copyright © 2002 The McGraw-Hill Companies. Reproduced with permission of The McGraw-Hill Companies. **Figure 5.9:** From H. P. Roffwarg, J. M. Muzio and W. C. Dement, 1966, "Ontogenetic Development of Human Dream Sleep Cycle," *Science*, Vol. 152, pp. 604–619. Reprinted with permission from American Association for the Advancement of Science. **Figure 5.10:** From Santrock, *Child Development*, 10/e, Figure 5.11. Copyright © 2004 The McGraw-Hill Companies. Reproduced with permission of The McGraw-Hill Companies. **Figure 5.11:** From Santrock, *Children*, 5/e. Copyright © 1997 The McGraw-Hill Companies. Reproduced with permission of The McGraw-Hill Companies. **Figure 5.16:** From A. Slater, V. Morison, & M. Somers, 1988, "Orientation Discrimination and Cortical Functions in the Human Newborn," *Perception*, Vol. 17, pp. 597–602, Fig. 1 and Table 1. Reprinted by permission of Pion, London. **Figure 5.18:** From Santrock, *Child Development*, 9/e, Fig. 5.15. Copyright © 2001 The McGraw-Hill Companies. Reproduced with permission of The McGraw-Hill Companies.

Chapter 6

P. 172: From J. Piaget, *The Origins of Intelligence*, W. W. Norton, 1952, pp. 27, 159, 225, 273, 339. Reprinted with permission. **Figure 6.3:** From R. Raillargeon & J. DeVoe, "Using the Violation of Expectations Method to Study Object Permanence in Infants," 1991, "Object Permanence in Young Children: Further Evidence," *Child Development*, 62, pp. 1227–1246. Reprinted with permission of the Society for Research in Child Development. **Figure 6.4:** From Santrock, *Children*, 7/e. Copyright © 2003 The McGraw-Hill Companies. Reproduced with permission of The McGraw-Hill Companies. **Figure 6.7:** From "The Rule Systems of Language," from S. L. Haight, *Language Overview*. Reprinted by permission. **Figure 6.9:** From Santrock, *Children*, 7/e. Copyright © 2003 The McGraw-Hill Companies. Reproduced with permission of The McGraw-Hill Companies. **Figure 6.10:** From Santrock, *Children*, 7/e. Copyright © 2003 The McGraw-Hill Companies. Reproduced with permission of The McGraw-Hill Companies. **Figure 6.11:** From Santrock, *Child Development*, 10/e, Figure 10.2. Copyright © 2004 The McGraw-Hill Companies. Reproduced with permission of The McGraw-Hill Companies. **Figure 6.12:** From Santrock, *Children*, 7/e. Copyright © 2003 The McGraw-Hill

Companies. Reproduced with permission of The McGraw-Hill Companies. **Figure 6.13:** From Hart & Risley, (1995), *Meaningful Differences in the Everyday Experiences of Young American Children*, Baltimore: Brookes Publishing. Reprinted by permission of Brookes Publishing.

Chapter 7

Figure 7.1: From J. Lewis, 2002, "Early Emotional Development," in A. Slater & M. Lewis (eds.), *Infant Development*. New York: Oxford University Press. **Figure 7.3:** Reprinted by permission of the publisher from *Infancy: Its Place in Human Development*, by Jerome Kagan, R. B. Kearsley and P. R. Zelazo, p. 107. Cambridge, MA: Harvard University Press, Copyright © 1978 by the President and Fellows of Harvard College. **Figure 7.4:** From Santrock, *Life-Span Development*, 4/e. Copyright © 1999 The McGraw-Hill Companies. Reproduced with permission of The McGraw-Hill Companies. **Figure 7.6:** From Ainsworth, M. D. S. & Bell, S. M., adapted from "Attachment, Exploration, and Separation: Illustrated by the Behavior of One-Year-Olds in a Strange Situation," 1971, *Child Development*, Vol. 41 (1), pp. 49–67. Reprinted by permission of the Society for Research in Child Development. **Figure 7.7:** From van Ijzendoorn & Kroonenberg, 1988, "Cross Cultural Patterns of Attachment," *Child Development*, 59, 147–156. Adapted by permission of the Society for Research in Child Development. **Figure 7.8:** From Jay Belsky, "Early Human Experiences: A Family Perspective," in *Developmental Psychology*, Vol. 17, pp. 3–23. Copyright © 1981 by the American Psychological Association. Reprinted by permission.

Chapter 8

Figure 8.1: From Santrock, *Children*, 7/e. Copyright © 2003 The McGraw-Hill Companies. Reproduced with permission of The McGraw-Hill Companies. **Figure 8.2:** From G. J. Schirmer (ed.) *Performance Objectives for Preschool Children*, Adapt Press, Sioux Falls, SD, 1974. **Figure 8.3:** From G. J. Schirmer (Ed.) *Performance Objectives for Preschool Children*, Adapt Press, Sioux Falls, SD, 1974. **Figure 8.4:** From Santrock, *Children*, 7/e. Copyright © 2003 The McGraw-Hill Companies. Reproduced with permission of The McGraw-Hill Companies. **Figure 8.5:** From Sleet & Mercy, 2003, "Promotion of Safety, Security, and Well-Being," in M. H. Bornstein, et al. (eds.), *Well-Being*, Mahwah, NJ, Erlbaum, Table 7.2. Reprinted by permission. **Figure 8.6:** From Santrock, *Psychology*, 7/e. Copyright © 2003 The McGraw-Hill Companies. Reproduced with permission of The McGraw-Hill Companies. **Figure 8.7:** From "The Symbolic Drawings of Young Children," reprinted courtesy of D. Wolf and J. Nove. Reprinted by permission of Dennie Palmer Wolf, Annenberg Institute, Brown University. **Figure 8.12:** From Santrock, *Children*, 7/e. Copyright © 2003 The McGraw-Hill Companies. Reproduced with permission of The McGraw-Hill Companies. **Pp. 242–243:** From M. Bruch and S. J. Ceci, "The Suggestibility of Children's Memory," *Annual Review of Psychology*, 50, 1999, pp. 429–430. Reprinted with permission. **Figure 8.16:** From Jean Berko, 1958, "The Child's Learning of English Morphology," in *Word*, Vol. 14, p. 154. From Young Children, Vol. 41, pp. 23–27, September 1986. Reprinted with permission from the National Association for the Education of Young Children. **Figure 8.17:** From Santrock, *Life-Span Development*, 9/e, Figure 8.18. Copyright © 2004 The McGraw-Hill Companies. Reproduced with permission of The McGraw-Hill Companies.

Chapter 9

Figure 9.1: From Santrock, *Children*, 7/e. Copyright © 2003 The McGraw-Hill Companies. Reproduced with permission of The McGraw-Hill Companies. **Figure 9.3:** From Santrock, *Child Development*, 10/e, Figure 13.3. Copyright © 2004 The McGraw-Hill Companies. Reproduced with permission of The McGraw-Hill Companies. **Figure 9.7:** From K. Curran, J. DuCette, J. Eisenstein, & I. Hyman, August 2001, "Statistical Analysis of the Cross-Cultural Data: The Third Year," Paper presented at the meeting of the American Psychological Association, San Francisco, CA. Reprinted by permission. **Pp. 278–279:** From C. G. Coll and L. Pachter, "Ethnic and Minority Parenting" in M. H. Bornstein, ed., *Handbook of Parenting*, Vol. 4, 2002, pp. 7–8, Lawrence Erlbaum Associates. Reprinted with permission.

Chapter 10

Figure 10.2: From Santrock, *Children*, 6/e. Copyright © 2000 The McGraw-Hill Companies. Reproduced with permission of The McGraw-Hill Companies. **Figure 10.5:** From "The Role of Expertise in Memory," from M. T. H. Chi, "Knowledge Structures and Memory Development," in R. S. Siegler (ed.) *Children's Thinking: What Develops?* Mahwah, NJ: Lawrence Erlbaum. Reprinted by permission. **Figure 10.9:** From "The Rise in IQ Scores from 1932 to 1997," from The Increase in IQ Scores from 1932 to 1997," by Dr. Ulric Neisser. Reprinted by permission. **Figure 10.10:** From "Sample Item from the Raven Progressive Matrices Test," from *Raven's Standard Progressive Matrices*, Item A5. Reprinted by permission of J. C. Raven Ltd. **Figure 10.12:** From Santrock, *Life-Span Development*, 9/e, Figure 10.11. Copyright © 2004 The McGraw-Hill Companies. Reproduced with permission of The McGraw-Hill Companies.

Chapter 11

Figure 11.2: From Colby, et al., 1983, "A Longitudinal Study of Moral Judgment," *Monographs of the Society for Research in Child Development*, Serial No. 201. Reprinted with permission of the Society for Research in Child Development. **Figure 11.4:** From Nansel, et al., 2001, "Bullying Behaviors Among U.S. Youth," *Journal of the American Medical Association*, Vol. 285, pp. 2094–2100. **Figure 11.5:** Reprinted with permission from Stevenson, Lee & Stigler, 1986, Figure 6, "Mathematics Achievement of Chinese, Japanese and American Children," *Science*, Vol. 231, pp. 693–699.

Chapter 12

P. 362: From L. Morrow, "Through the Eyes of Children," *Time*, August 8, 1988, pp. 32–33. Copyright © 1988 Time, Inc. Reprinted with permission. **Figure 12.1:** From Santrock, *Adolescence*, 8/e. Copyright © 2001 The McGraw-Hill Companies. Reproduced with permission of The McGraw-Hill Companies. **Figure 12.2:** From Santrock, *Adolescence*, 8/e. Copyright © 2001 The McGraw-Hill Companies. Reproduced with permission of The McGraw-Hill Companies. **Figure 12.3:** From Santrock, *Children*, 7/e. Copyright © 2003 The McGraw-Hill Companies. Reproduced with permission of The McGraw-Hill Companies. **Figure 12.4:** From Santrock, *Children*, 7/e. Copyright © 2003 The McGraw-Hill Companies. Reproduced with permission of The McGraw-Hill Companies. **Figure 12.5:** From Santrock, *Adolescence*, 8/e. Copyright © 2001 The McGraw-Hill Companies. Reproduced with permission of The McGraw-Hill Companies. **Figure 12.6:** From Santrock, *Child Development*, 10/e, Figure 6.14. Copyright © 2004 The McGraw-Hill Companies. Reproduced with permission of The McGraw-Hill Companies. **Figure 12.8:** From "Trends in Drug Use by U.S. Eighth-, Tenth- and Twelfth-Grade Students," by L. D. Johnston, P. M. O'Malley, & J. G. Bachman, 2001, *The Monitoring of the Future: National Results on Adolescent Drug Use*, Washington, DC: National Institute on Drug Abuse. **Pp. 377–378:** From K. E. Bauman, S. T. Ennett, V. A. Foshee, M. Pemberton, T. S. King, G. G. Koch, "Influence of a Family Program on Adolescent Smoking and Drinking Prevalence," *Prevention Science* 3, 2002, pp. 35–42. Reprinted with permission. **Figure 12.9:** From "Young Adolescents' Reports of Alcohol Use in the Family Matters Program," from K. E. Bauman, S. T. Ennett, et al., 2002, "Influence of a Family Program on Adolescent Smoking and Drinking Prevalence," *Prevention Science*, 3, pp. 35–42. With kind permission of Springer Science and Business Media. **Figure 12.10:** From "Young Adolescents' Reports of Cigarette Smoking in the Family Matters Program," from K. E. Bauman, S. T. Ennett, et al., 2002, "Influence of a Family Program on Adolescent Smoking and Drinking Prevalence," *Prevention Science*, 3, pp. 35–42. With kind permission of Springer Science and Business Media. **Figure 12.11:** From Santrock, *Children*, 7/e. Copyright © 2003 The McGraw-Hill Companies. Reproduced with permission of The McGraw-Hill Companies.

Chapter 13

P. 396: From S. Harter, "Self and Identity Development" in S. S. Feldman and G. R. Eliot, eds., *At the Threshold*, Harvard University Press, 1990, p. 352. Copyright © 1990 Fellows of Harvard College. Reprinted with permission from the publisher. **Figure 13.2:** From Reed Larson & Maryse Richards, "Self-Reported Extremes of Emotion by Adolescents, Mothers, and Fathers Using the Experience Sampling Method," 1994, *Divergent Realities*, Fig. 4.1, p. 82. Basic Books. Reprinted by permission of Perseus Books. **Figure 13.5:** "Age of Onset of Romantic Activity," from

Romantic Development: Does Age at Which Romantic Involvement Starts Matter? by Duane Buhrmester, April 2001, paper presented at the meeting of the Society for Research in Child Development, Minneapolis, MN. **Figure 13.6:** From "Average Daily Time Use of Adolescents in Different Regions of the World," from R. Larson, 2001, "How U.S. Children and Adolescents Spend Time," *Current Directions in Psychological Science*, 10, pp. 160–164. Reprinted with permission from Blackwell Publishing.

Chapter 14

Figure 14.1: "Self-Perceptions of Adult Status," from J. Arnett, "Emerging Adulthood," in *American Psychologist*, Vol. 55, pp. 469–480, Fig. 2. Copyright © 2000 by the American Psychological Association. Reprinted with permission. Copyright © 2000 by the American Psychological Association. Reprinted by permission. **Figure 14.2:** From "Characteristics of Very Happy College Students," from Diener & Seligman, 2002, "Very Happy People," *Psychological Science*, Vol. 13, pp. 81–84. Reprinted with permission from Blackwell Publishing. **Figure 14.5:** From Pate, et al., *Journal of the American Medical Association*, 273, 404. Copyright © 1995 American Medical Association. **Figure 14.7:** From *Sex in America*, by Robert T. Michael, et al. Copyright © 1994 by CSG Enterprises, Inc., Edward O. Laumann, Robert T. Michael, and Gina Kolata. By permission of Little, Brown & Company, Inc. **Figure 14.8:** From Santrock, *Children*, 7/e. Copyright © 2003 The McGraw-Hill Companies. Reproduced with permission of The McGraw-Hill Companies. **Figure 14.9:** From "Completed Rape and Attempted Rape of College Women According to Victim-Offender Relationship," from Fisher, Cullen & Turner, 2000, *The Sexual Victimization of College Women*, Exhibit 8, p. 19. Reprinted by permission of the National Institute of Justice. **Figure 14.10:** Reproduced by special permission of the publisher, Psychological Assessment Resources from *Making Vocational Choices: A Theory of Vocational Choices and Work Environments*. Copyright © 1973, 1985, 1992 by Psychological Assessment Resources, Inc. All rights reserved. **Figure 14.12:** From "Changes in the Percentage of U.S. Traditional and Dual-Career Couples," from "Work-Family Balance," by R. Barnett, in *Encyclopedia of Woman and Gender: Sex Similarities and Differences and the Impact of Society on Gender*, 2 Volume Set, by Judith Worell (Ed.). Reprinted with permission from Elsevier.

Chapter 15

P. 466: From M. Lerner, *The Dance of Intimacy*, HarperCollins, 1989, pp. 44–45. Reprinted with permission. **Figure 15.1:** From "Temperament in Childhood, Personality in Adulthood, and Intervening Contexts," from Wachs, T. D. "Fit, Context, and the Transition Between Temperament and Personality," in C. Halverson, G. Kohnstamm & R. Martin (Eds.) *The Developing Structure of Personality from Infancy to Adulthood*. NJ: Lawrence Erlbaum Associates, Inc. Reprinted by permission. **Figure 15.3:** From

"Examples of Positive Changes in the Aftermath of a Romantic Breakup," by T. Tashiro & P. Frazier, 2003, "I'll Never Be in a Relationship Like That Again: Personal Growth Following Romantic Relationship Breakups," *Personal Relationships*, 10, after Table 1, p. 120. Reprinted with permission from Blackwell Publishing. **Figure 15.4:** Reproduced by special permission of the publisher, Psychological Assessment Resources, Inc. from *The Changing Family Life Cycle*, 2/e. Copyright © 1989 by Psychological Assessment Resources, Inc. All rights reserved.

Chapter 16

P. 500: From Jim Croce, "Time in a Bottle." Copyright © 1972, 1985 Denjac Music Co. Reprinted with permission. **Figure 16.1:** Adapted from *Newsweek*, "Health for Life," Special Section, Fall/Winter 2001. Copyright © Newsweek, Inc. All rights reserved. Reprinted by permission. **Figure 16.2:** Adapted from *Newsweek*, "Health for Life," Special Section, Fall/Winter 2001. Copyright © Newsweek, Inc. All rights reserved. Reprinted by permission. **Figure 16.5:** From *Sex in America*, by Robert T. Michael, et al. Copyright © 1994 by CSG Enterprises, Inc., Edward O. Laumann, Robert T. Michael, and Gina Kolata. By permission of Little, Brown & Company, Inc. **Figure 16.10:** From *Men in Their Forties: The Transition to Middle Age*, by Lois M. Tamir, 1982. Copyright © 1982 by Springer Publishing Company. Adapted by permission of Springer Publishing Company, New York 10012.

Chapter 17

Figure 17.1: From "Changes in Generativity and Identity Certainty from the 30s through the 50s," from Stewart, Osgrove & Helson, 2002, "Middle Aging in Women: Patterns of Personality Change from the 30s to the 50s," Fig. 3, *Journal of Adult Development*, Vol. 8, pp. 23–37. With kind permission of Springer Science and Business Media. **Figure 17.2:** From "Items Used to Assess Generativity and Identify Certainty," from Stewart, Osgrove & Helson, 2002, "Middle Aging in Women: Patterns of Personality Change from the 30s to the 50s," Table II, *Journal of Adult Development*, Vol. 8, pp. 23–37. With kind permission of Springer Science and Business Media. **Figure 17.7:** From "The Ten Most Frequent Daily Hassles and Uplifts of Middle-Aged Adults over a 9-Month Period," from D. Kenner, et al., in *Journal of Behavioral Medicine*, Vol. 4, 1981. With kind permission of Springer Science and Business Media. **Figure 17.8:** From "Individuals' Conceptions of the Right Age for Major Life Events and Achievements: Late 1950s and Late 1970s," from D. F. Hultsch and J. K. Plemons, "Life Events and Life Span Development," *in Life Span Development and Behavior*, Vol. 2, by P. B. Baltes and O. G. Brun (eds.). Reprinted with permission from Elsevier. **Figure 17.9:** From Santrock, *Psychology*, 7/e, Fig. 12.11. Copyright © 2003 The McGraw-Hill Companies. Reproduced with permission of The McGraw-Hill Companies.

Chapter 18

Figure 18.1: From *The Psychology of Death, Dying and Bereavement*, by Richard Schulz, Copyright © 1978. Reproduced with permission of The McGraw-Hill Companies. **Figure 18.2:** From *The Okinawa Program*, by Bradley J. Willcox, D. Craig Willcox and Makoto Suzuki. Copyright © 2001 by Bradley J. Willcox, D. Craig Willcox and Makoto Suzuki. Used by permission of Clarkson Potter Publishers, a division of Random House, Inc. **Figure 18.6:** Adapted from *Newsweek*, "Health for Life," Special Section, Fall/Winter 2001. Copyright © Newsweek, Inc. All rights reserved. Reprinted by permission. **Figure 18.8:** From "Rates of Decline in Visual Functioning Related to Glare in Adults of Different Ages," after graph presented by Dr. John Brabyn. **Figure 18.14:** From "Age and the Consumption of Five or More Drinks on at Least One Day in the United States," from National Center for Health Statistics, 2002.

Chapter 19

Figure 19.6: From J. Kiecolt-Glaser, et al., 2003, "Comparison of IL-6 Levels in Alzheimer's Caregivers and a Control Group of Non-Caregivers," from "Chronic Stress and Age-Related Increases in the Proinflammatory Cytokine IL-g," *Proceedings of the National Academy of Science USA*, 100, after Figure 1. Copyright © 2003 National Academy of Sciences, U.S.A. Used with permission. **Figure 19.7:** From J. Kiecolt-Glaser, et al., 2003, "Comparison of IL-6 Levels in Alzheimer's Caregivers and a Control Group of Non-Caregivers," from "Chronic Stress and Age-Related Increases in the Proinflammatory Cytokine IL-g," *Proceedings of the National Academy of Science USA*, 100, after Figure 2. Copyright © 2003 National Academy of Sciences, U.S.A. Used with permission.

Chapter 20

Figure 20.1: From "Erikson's View . . . Conflict and Resolution: Culmination in Old Age." Copyright © 1988 by *The New York Times*. Reprinted by permission. **Figure 20.2:** From L. Carstensen, et al., "The Social Context of Emotion," in the *Annual Review of Geriatrics and Gerontology*, by Schaie/Lawton, 1997, Vol. 17, p. 331. Copyright © 1997 by Springer Publishing Company. Adapted by permission of Springer Publishing Company, New York 10012. **Figure 20.3:** From "Changes in Positive and Negative Emotion Across the Adult Years," from D. Mroczek and C. M. Kolarz, "The Effect of Age in Positive and Negative Affect," in *Journal of Personality and Social Psychology*, Vol. 75, pp. 1333–1349. Reprinted with permission. Copyright © 1998 by the American Psychological Association. Reprinted by permission. **Figure 20.5:** From "Self-Esteem Across the Life Span," from Robins, et al., "Age Differences in Self-Esteem from 9 to 90," in *Psychology and Aging*, Vol. 17, pp. 423–434. Copyright © 2002 by the American Psychological Association. Reprinted by permission.

Photo Credits

Chapter 1

Opener: © Bob Torrz/Stone/Getty Images; **p. 4 (top):** © Seana O'Sullivan/CORBIS/Sygma; **p. 4 (bottom):** © AP/Wide World Photos; **p. 8:** Courtesy K. Warner Schaie; **p. 9:** Courtesy of Paul Baltes, Margaret Baltes Foundation; **p. 10:** Courtesy of Luis Vargas; **p. 11:** © National Association for the Education of Young Children, Robert Maust/Photo Agora; **p. 12:** © Nancy Agostini; **p. 14:** © James Pozarik; **p. 15 (top):** Courtesy of Marian Wright Edelman, The Children's Defense Fund, photograph by Rick Reinhard; **p. 15 (bottom):** © Dennis Brack Ltd./Black Star/Stock Photo; **1.8 (left to right):** Courtesy of Landrum Shettles, MD; John Santrock; © Joe Sohm/The Image Works; © CORBIS website; © James L. Shaffer; © Vol. 155/CORBIS; © CORBIS website; © CORBIS website; **p. 24:** © Joel Gordon 1995

Chapter 2

Opener: © Michael Krasowitz/FPG/Getty Images; **p. 42:** © Bettmann/CORBIS; **p. 44:** © Bettmann/CORBIS; **p. 45:** © Yves de Braine/Black Star/Stock Photo; **p. 47:** A. R. Lauria/Dr. Michael Cole, Laboratory of Human Cognition, University of California, San Diego; **p. 49:** © Bettmann/CORBIS; **p. 50:** Courtesy of Stanford University News Service; **p. 51:** Photo by Nina Leen/Timepix/Getty Images; **p. 52:** Courtesy of Urie Bronfenbrenner; **p. 53:** © Julian Hirshowitz/CORBIS; **p. 54 (Freud):** © Bettmann Archives; **p. 54 (Pavlov):** © Bettmann Archives; **p. 54 (Piaget):** © Yves de Braine/Black Star/Stock Photo; **p. 54 (Vygotsky):** A. R. Lauria/Dr. Michael Cole, Laboratory of Human Cognition, University of California, San Diego; **p. 54 (Skinner):** © Harvard University News Office; **p. 54 (Erikson):** © UPI/Bettmann Newsphotos; **p. 54 (Bandura):** Courtesy of Stanford University News Service; **p. 54 (Bronfenbrenner):** Courtesy of Urie Bronfenbrenner; **p. 56:** © Richard T. Nowitz/Photo Researchers, Inc.; **p. 58:** © Bettmann/CORBIS; **p. 59:** © S. Fraser/Photo Researchers; **2.12a:** © Photo Researchers, Inc.; **2.12b:** © AP/Wide World Photos; **2.12c:** © AP/Wide World Photos; **2.12d:** © Bettmann/CORBIS; **2.12e:** © Sukie Hill Photography; **2.12f:** © Lawrence Migdale/Photo Researchers, Inc.; **p. 64:** © McGraw-Hill Higher Education, photographer John Thoeming; **p. 67 (left):** © AFP/Getty Images; **p. 67 (right):** © Stuart McClymont/Stone/Getty Images; **p. 68:** Courtesy of Pam Trotman Reid

Chapter 3

Opener: © Hua China Tourism Press, Shao/The Image Bank/Getty Images; **p. 76:** © Enrico Ferorelli Enterprises; **3.4:** © Sundstrom/Liaison Agency/Gamma; **3.5 (a&b):** © Custom Medical Stock Photo; **p. 85:** © Joel Gordon 1989; **p. 87:** Courtesy of Holly Ishmael; **p. 89:** © Jacques Pavlousky/Sygma/CORBIS; **p. 93:** © Randy Santos/SuperStock

Chapter 4

Opener: Photo Lennart Nilsson/Albert Bonniers Forlag AB, *A Child is Born*, Dell Publishing Company; **p. 107:** © David Young-Wolff/PhotoEdit; **4.3 (all):** Photo Lennart Nilsson/Albert Bonniers Forlag AB, *A Child is Born*, Dell Publishing Company; **4.5:** Courtesy of Ann Streissguth; **p. 112:** © John Chiasson; **p. 113:** © R.I.A./Liaison Agency/Gamma; **p. 115 (top):** © Betty Press/Woodfin Camp & Associates; **p. 116 (top):** © Alon Reininger/Contract Press Images; **p. 118:** © Vivian Moos/CORBIS; **p. 120 (top):** © SIU/Peter Arnold, Inc.; **p. 120 (bottom):** © Marjorie Shostak/Anthro-Photo; **p. 121:** Courtesy of Linda Pugh; **p. 122:** © Roger Tully/Stone/Getty; **p. 124:** © Charles Gupton/Stock Boston; **p. 125 (top):** Courtesy of Dr. Susan M. Ludington; **p. 125 (bottom):** Courtesy of Dr. Tiffany Field; **4.10:** © Stephen Marks, Inc./The Image Bank/Getty Images; **p. 130:** © Michael Newman/Photo Edit

Chapter 5

Opener: © Joe McNally; **5.2 (right):** Photo Lennart Nilsson/Albert Bonniers Forlag; **5.5:** © 1999 Kenneth Jarecke/Contact Press Images; **5.6:** © A. Glauberman/Photo Researchers, Inc.; **5.7 (a&b):** Courtesy of Dr. Harry T. Chugani, Children's Hospital of Michigan; **5.8a:** © David Grugin Productions, Inc. Reprinted by permission; **5.8b:** Image courtesy of Dana Boatman, Ph.D., Department of Neurology, John Hopkins University, reprinted with permission from *The Secret Life of the Brain*, Joseph Henry Press; **p. 145:** © SuperStock; **p. 146:** © Bruce McAllister/Image Works; **p. 147:** Hawaiian Family Support Healthy Start Program; **p. 148:** © Bob Dammrich/The Image Works; **p. 149:** Courtesy of T. Berry Brazelton; **p. 150:** Courtesy of Esther Thelen; **5.12 (left & right):** Courtesy Dr. Karen Adolph, New York University; **p. 155 (left):** © Michael Greenlar/The Image Works; **p. 155 (right):** © Frank Baily Studios; **p. 156:** Courtesy Amy Needham, Duke University; **5.15:** © David Linton; **5.16 (all):** Courtesy of Dr. Charles Nelson; **5.19:** © Enrico Ferorelli Enterprises; **5.22 (left):** © Michael Siluk; **5.20 (right):** © Dr. Melanie Spence, University of Texas; **5.21:** © Jean Guichard/Sygma/CORBIS; **5.22 (a–c):** From D. Rosenstein and H. Oster "Differential Facial Responses to Four Basic Tastes in Newborns," *Child Development*, Vol. 59, 1988. © Society for Research in Child Development, Inc.

Chapter 6

Opener: © Spencer Grant/Photo Edit; **6.2 (left & right):** © Doug Goodman/Photo Researchers; **6.5:** Courtesy of Dr. Carolyn Rovee-Collier; **6.6:** © Enrico Ferorelli Enterprises; **p. 184:** Courtesy of John Santrock; **6.8 (left & right):** Courtesy of Dr. Patricia K. Kuhl, Center for Mind, Brain & Learning, University of Washington; **p. 190:** © ABPL Image Library/Animals Animals/Earth Scenes; **p. 191:** © Tim Davis/CORBIS

Chapter 7

Opener: © Jamie Marcial/SuperStock; **p. 200:** © Andy Sacks/Stone/Getty Images; **7.2 (all):** © Michael Lewis, Institute for the Study of Child Development, Robert Wood Johnson Medical School; **p. 203:** © Andy Cox/Stone/Getty Images; **p. 206:** © Michael Tcherevkoff/The Image Bank/Getty Images; **p. 207:** © Judith Oddie/Photo Edit; **7.4:** © Myrleen Ferguson Cate/Photo Edit; **p. 209 (bottom):** © Vol. 63 PhotoDisc/Getty Images; **7.5:** © Martin Rogers/Stock Boston; **7.6:** © Daniel Grogan; **p. 213:** © David Young-Wolff/Photo Edit; **p. 216:** © BrandXPictures/Getty Images; **p. 219:** Courtesy of Rashmi Nakhre, The Hattie Daniels Day Care Center

Chapter 8

Opener: © Ariel Skelley/The Stock Market/CORBIS; **p. 226:** From "Open Window"; © 1994 Municipality of Reggio Emilia; Infant-Toddler Centers and Preschools; Published by Reggio Children; **p. 227:** © Bob Daemmrich/The Image Works; **p. 229:** © Joel Gordon 1993; **p. 231:** © Eyewire Vol. EP078/Getty Images; **8.8:** © Paul Fusco/Magnum Photos; **8.10:** © Elizabeth Crews/The Image Works; **8.11 (left):** A. R. Lauria/Dr. Michael Cole, Laboratory of Human Cognition, University of California, San Diego; **8.11 (right):** © Bettmann/CORBIS; **p. 242:** © 1999 James Kamp; **p. 246:** © Roseanne Olson/Stone/Getty Images; **p. 249:** Courtesy of Yolanda Garcia; **p. 250:** © Ronnie Kaufman/The Stock Market/CORBIS

Chapter 9

Opener: © Hermine Dreyfuss; **p. 262:** © Digital Stock; **9.6:** © Peter Correz/Stone/Getty Images; **p. 274:** Courtesy of Darla Botkin; **p. 275:** © Christopher Arnesen/Stone/Getty Images; **p. 278:** © Karen Kasmauski/Woodfin Camp; **p. 279:** © Spencer Grant/Photo Edit; **p. 282:** © Richard Hutchings/Photo Edit; **p. 283:** © Bryan Peterson

Chapter 10

Opener: © Michael Pole/CORBIS; **p. 292:** © Joe McNally; **p. 296:** Courtesy of Sharon McLeod; **p. 299:** © David Young-Wolff/Photo Edit; **p. 300:** © Will McIntyre/Photo Researchers, Inc.; **p. 303:** © Archives Jean Piaget, Universite De Geneve, Switzerland; **p. 304:** © Bernheim/Woodfin Camp; **p. 311:** © Joe McNally; **p. 315:** Reprinted with the permission of The Free Press, a Division of Simon & Schuster Adult Publishing Group. From *The Bell Curve* by Richard J. Hernstein and Charles Murray. Jacket, Copyright © 1994 by Simon & Schuster, Inc.; **p. 317:** © Jill Cannefax/EKM-Nepenthe/Coyote Crossings, Inc.; **p. 318:** Courtesy of Sterling C. Jones, Jr.; **p. 320:** © Richard Howard

Chapter 11

Opener: © Rob Lewine/The Stock Market/CORBIS; **p. 332:** © Reuters/NewMedia Inc./CORBIS; **p. 336:** © Raghu-Rai/Magnum

Photos; **p. 337:** © Keith Carter Photography; **p. 342:** © Catherine Gehm; **p. 344:** © Michael Newman/Photo Edit; **p. 346:** © PhotoDisc/Getty Images website; **p. 352:** © Lonnie Harp; **p. 354:** © John S. Abbott

Chapter 12

Opener: © Paul Barton/CORBIS; **p. 363:** © M. Regine/The Image Bank/Getty Images; **p. 369:** © Joel Gordon 1995; **p. 370:** © Lawrence Migdale/Stock Boston; **p. 373:** Courtesy of Lynn Blankinship; **p. 379:** © Tony Freeman/Photo Edit; **p. 381:** © Rob Lewine Photography/CORBIS/The Stock Market; **p. 383:** © David Young-Wolff/Photo Edit; **p. 384:** © Stewart Cohen/Stone/Getty Images; **p. 385:** © Susan Lapides 2002; **p. 387:** © Mark Antman/The Image Works; **p. 390 (top):** © H. Yamaguchi/Gamma Liaison/Gamma; **p. 390 (bottom):** © Tony Freeman/Photo Edit

Chapter 13

Opener: © Lisette Le Bon/SuperStock; **p. 401:** © USA Today Library, photo by Robert Deutsch; **13.3:** © Spencer Grant/Photo Edit; **p. 408:** © Tony Freeman/Photo Edit; **p. 409:** © Michael Siluk/The Image Works; **p. 411:** © Tessa Codrington/Stone/Getty Images; **p. 414 (left):** © AFP/Getty Images; **p. 414 (middle):** © Dain Gair Photographic/Index Stock; **p. 414 (right):** © AP/Wide World Photos; **p. 416:** © Daniel Laine; **p. 417:** © USA Today Library, photo by H. Darr Beiser; **p. 418:** Courtesy of Carola Suarez-Orozco and photographer Kris Snibble/Harvard News; Office, © 2003 President and Fellows of Harvard College; **p. 419:** Courtesy of El Puente Academy; **p. 421:** © Charlie Neuman/SDUT/Zuma; **p. 423:** Courtesy of Rodney Hammond

Chapter 14

Opener: © Ariel Skelley/CORBIS; **p. 432:** © Bettmann/CORBIS; **p. 434:** © David Young-Wolff/Stone/Getty Images; **p. 435:** Courtesy of Grace Leaf; **14.4:** © AP/Wide World Photos; **p. 447:** © 1996 Rob Lewine/The Stock Market/CORBIS; **p. 449:** © Barry O'Rourke/The Stock Market/CORBIS; **p. 454:** Courtesy Mihaly Csikszentmihaly

Chapter 15

Opener: © Ariel Skelley/CORBIS; **p. 474 (top):** © David Young-Wolff/Photo Edit; **p. 474 (middle):** © Tony Freeman/Photo Edit; **p. 474 (bottom):** © James McLoughlin; **p. 482 (left):** © Explorer/J. P. Nacivet/Photo Researchers; **p. 482 (middle):** © Dean Press Images/Image Works; **p. 482 (right):** © David Hanover/Stone/Getty Images; **p. 484:** © Ronald Mackechnie/Stone/Getty Images; **p. 486:** Courtesy of Janis Keyser; **p. 491:** © S. Gazin/The Image Works; **p. 494:** © EyeWire EP036/Getty Images

Chapter 16

Opener: © Tom Stewart/CORBIS; **p. 503 (left):** © Bettmann/CORBIS; **p. 503 (right):** © Matthew Mendelsohn/CORBIS; **p. 510:** © 1998 Tom & Dee McCarthy/The Stock Market/CORBIS; **p. 512:** © Vol. 155/CORBIS; **p. 516:** © Reuters Newmedia Inc./CORBIS; **p. 518:** © Chris Cheadle/Stone/Getty Images; **p. 520:** © Tony Freeman/Photo Edit

Chapter 17

Opener: © Savin Patrick/Sygma/CORBIS; **17.3 (top):** © CORBIS website; **17.3 (middle):** © Eyewire/Getty website; **17.3 (bottom):** © Vol. 67/PhotoDisc; **17.8 (top):** © Bettmann/CORBIS; **17.8 (bottom):** © EyeWire/Getty Images website; **p. 535 (bottom):** © Rhoda Sidney/Photo Edit; **p. 536:** © Betty Press/Woodfin Camp & Associates; **p. 540:** © Bettmann/CORBIS; **p. 541:** © Everett Collection; **p. 544:** © Jose Luis Pelaez, Inc./CORBIS; **p. 545:** © William Hubbell/Woodfin Camp & Associates; **p. 548:** Courtesy of Lillian Troll

Chapter 18

Opener: © Chuck Savage/CORBIS; **p. 554:** © John Goodman; **p. 558 (top):** © USA Today, Paul Wiseman, photographer; **p. 558 (bottom):** © Jim Richardson/Westlight/CORBIS; **p. 559a:** © Pascal Parrot/Sygma/CORBIS; **p. 559b:** © Thomas Del Brase; **p. 560:** Courtesy of Dr. Jerry Shay, Ph.D., UT Southwestern Medical Center; **18.4 (left & right):** Courtesy of Dr. Fred Gage; **18.5:** From R. Cabeza, et al., "Age-related; differences in neural activity during memory encoding and retrieval: A positron emission tomography study" in *Journal of Neuroscience*, 17, 391–400, 1997; **p. 564 (top & bottom):** © James Balog; **18.10:** © George Gardner/The Image Works; **p. 572:** © Bob Daemmrich/Stock Boston; **18.12:** Courtesy of Colin M. Bloor; **18.13 (top & bottom):** © Ethan Hill

Chapter 19

Opener: © Cleo Photography/Photo Edit; **p. 583:** © Cornell Capa/Magnum Photos; **p. 587:** © Elizabeth Crews; **p. 591:** © Greg Sailor; **p. 596 (top):** © Bettmann/CORBIS; **p. 596 (bottom):** © Ira Wyman/Sygma/CORBIS; **p. 597 (left & right):** © Alfred Pasieka/Science Photo Library/Photo Researchers, Inc; **p. 599:** © AP/Wide World Photos; **p. 600:** Courtesy of Jan W. Weaver; **p. 601:** Courtesy of Donna Polisar; **p. 602:** © Bryan Peterson/The Stock Market/CORBIS

Chapter 20

Opener: © Chuck Savage/CORBIS; **p. 608 (left):** © AP/Wide World Photos; **p. 608 (right):** Photo by Steve Lipofsky BasketballPhoto.com; **20.1:** © Sarah Putman/Picture Cube/Index Stock; **20.4 (left to right):** © Eyewire/Getty Images website; © PhotoDisc/Getty Images website; © Corbis website; © PhotoDisc website; © Vol. 34/CORBIS; **p. 617:** Photo by Mariou Ruiz/Timepix/Getty Images; **p. 622:** John Santrock; **p. 623:** © Frank Conaway/Index Stock; **p. 625:** Courtesy of Dr. Norma Thomas; **p. 627 (top):** © G. Wayne Floyd/Unicorn Stock Photos; **p. 627 (bottom):** © Suzi Moore-McGregor/Woodfin Camp & Associates; **p. 628:** © NASA/Liaison Agency/Getty Images News Service

Chapter 21

Opener: © Stan Honda/AP Wide World Photos; **p. 635:** © Herb Snitzer/Stock Boston; **p. 636:** Reprinted with permission from The Detroit News; **p. 637:** © USA Today, photographer Tim Dillon; **21.1:** © Patrick Ward/Stock Boston; **p. 644:** © Eastcott Momatinck/The Image Works; **p. 648:** © Jennifer S. Altman; **p. 651 (left):** © Russell Underwood/CORBIS; **p. 651 (right):** © Paul Almasy/CORBIS; **p. 652:** © Hermine Dreyfuss

Name Index

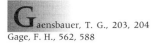

Subject Index